P9-DHK-963

Collins
German
Dictionary

HarperCollins Publishers
Westerhill Road
Bishopbriggs
Glasgow
G64 2QT
Great Britain

First Edition 2005

© HarperCollins Publishers 2005

ISBN 0-00-720321-7

Collins® and Bank of English® are
registered trademarks of
HarperCollins Publishers Limited

www.collins.co.uk

A catalogue record for this book is
available from the British Library

HarperCollins Publishers, Inc.
10 East 53rd Street, New York,
NY 10022

ISBN 0-06-074901-6

Library of Congress Cataloging-in-
Publication Data has been applied for

www.harpercollins.com

HarperCollins books may be
purchased for educational, business,
or sales promotional use. For
information, please write to:
Special Markets Department,
HarperCollins Publishers Inc., 10 East
53rd Street, New York, NY 10022

Typeset by Morton Word Processing
Ltd, Scarborough

Printed in Italy by Amadeus S.r.l.

Acknowledgements
We would like to thank those authors
and publishers who kindly gave
permission for copyright material to
be used in the Collins Word Web. We
would also like to thank Times
Newspapers Ltd for providing
valuable data.

All rights reserved. No part of this
publication may be reproduced,
stored in a retrieval system or
transmitted, in any form or by any
means, electronic, mechanical,
photocopying, recording or
otherwise, without the prior
permission of the publisher. This
book is sold subject to the conditions
that it shall not, by way of trade or
otherwise, be lent, re-sold, hired out
or otherwise circulated without the
publisher's prior consent in any form
of binding or cover other than that in
which it is published and without a
similar condition including this
condition being imposed on the
subsequent purchaser.

Entered words that we have reason to
believe constitute trademarks have
been designated as such. However,
neither the presence nor absence of
such designation should be regarded
as affecting the legal status of any
trademark.

ZUM GEBRAUCH IHRES COLLINS WÖRTERBUCHS

Das Wörterbuch enthält eine Fülle von Informationen, die mithilfe von unterschiedlichen Schriften und Schriftgrößen, Symbolen, Abkürzungen und Klammern vermittelt werden. Die dabei verwendeten Regeln und Symbole werden in den folgenden Abschnitten erklärt.

Stichwörter

Die Wörter, die Sie im Wörterbuch nachschlagen — "Stichwörter" — sind alphabetisch geordnet. Sie sind **in Farbe** gedruckt, damit man sie schnell erkennt. Die beiden Stichwörter oben links und rechts auf jeder Doppelseite geben das erste bzw. letzte Wort an, das auf den betreffenden Seiten behandelt wird.

Informationen zur Verwendung oder zur Form bestimmter Stichwörter stehen in Klammern hinter der Lautschrift. Sie erscheinen meist in abgekürzter Form und sind kursiv gedruckt (z. B. (*fam*), (*COMM*)).

Wo es angebracht ist, werden mit dem Stichwort verwandte Wörter im selben Artikel behandelt (z. B. **accept, acceptance**). Sie sind wie das Stichwort fett, aber etwas kleiner gedruckt.

Häufig verwendete Ausdrücke, in denen das Stichwort vorkommt (z. B. **to be cold**), sind in einer anderen Schrift halbfett gedruckt.

Lautschrift

Die Lautschrift für jedes Stichwort (zur Angabe seiner Aussprache) steht in eckigen Klammern direkt hinter dem Stichwort (z. B. **Quark** [kvark]; **knead** [ni:d]). Die Symbole der Lautschrift sind auf Seite xii erklärt.

Übersetzungen

Die Übersetzungen des Stichworts sind normal gedruckt. Wenn es mehr als eine Bedeutung oder Verwendung des Stichworts gibt, sind diese durch ein Semikolon voneinander getrennt. Vor den Übersetzungen stehen oft andere, kursiv gedruckte Wörter in Klammern. Sie geben an, in welchem Zusammenhang das Stichwort erscheinen könnte (z. B. **rough** (*voice*) oder (*weather*)), oder sie sind Synonyme (z. B. **rough** (*violent*)).

Schlüsselwörter

Besonders behandelt werden bestimmte deutsche und englische Wörter, die man als "Schlüsselwörter" der jeweiligen Sprache betrachten kann. Diese Wörter kommen beispielsweise sehr häufig vor oder werden unterschiedlich verwendet (z. B. **sein, auch; get, that**). Mithilfe von Rauten und Ziffern können Sie die verschiedenen Wortarten und Verwendungen unterscheiden. Weitere nützliche Hinweise finden Sie kursiv und in Klammern in der jeweiligen Sprache des Benutzers.

Grammatische Informationen

Wortarten stehen in abgekürzter Form kursiv gedruckt hinter der Aussprache des

INTRODUCTION

We are delighted you have decided to buy this Collins German Dictionary and hope you will enjoy and benefit from using it at home, at school, on holiday or at work.

The innovative use of colour guides you quickly and efficiently to the word you want, and the comprehensive wordlist provides a wealth of modern and idiomatic phrases not normally found in a dictionary this size.

In addition, the supplement provides you with guidance on using the dictionary, along with entertaining ways of improving your dictionary skills.

We hope that you will enjoy using it and that it will significantly enhance your language studies.

Zum Gebrauch Ihres Wörterbuchs	**vi**
Using your dictionary	**viii**
Abbreviations	**x**
Regular German noun endings	**xiii**
Phonetic symbols	**xiv**
Numbers	**xv**
Time	**xvii**
GERMAN-ENGLISH	**1-274**
VERB TABLES	**1-52**
ENGLISH-GERMAN	**327-608**
German verb forms	**609-613**
German spelling changes	**614**

editors/Redaktion
Veronika Schnorr • Ute Nicol • Peter Terrell
Bob Grossmith • Helga Holtkamp • Horst Kopleck
Beate Wengel • John Whitlam

editorial staff/Manuskriptbearbeitung
Joyce Littlejohn • Elspeth Anderson
Christine Bahr • John Podbielski

series editor/Gesamtleitung
Lorna Sinclair Knight

William Collins' dream of knowledge for all began with the publication of his first book in 1819. A self-educated mill worker, he not only enriched millions of lives, but also founded a flourishing publishing house. Today, staying true to this spirit, Collins books are packed with inspiration, innovation, and practical expertise. They place you at the centre of a world of possibility and give you exactly what you need to explore it.

Language is the key to this exploration, and at the heart of Collins Dictionaries, is language as it is really used. New words, phrases, and meanings spring up every day, and all of them are captured and analysed by the Collins Word Web. Constantly updated, and with over 2.5 billion entries, this living language resource is unique to our dictionaries.

Words are tools for life. And a Collins Dictionary makes them work for you.

Collins. Do more.

Stichworts (z. B. *vt, adv, conj*).

Die unregelmäßigen Formen englischer Substantive und Verben stehen in Klammern vor der Wortart (z. B. **man** (*pl* **men**) *n*, **give** (*pt* **gave**, *pp* **given**) *vt*).

Die deutsche Rechtschreibreform

Dieses Wörterbuch folgt durchweg der reformierten deutschen Rechtschreibung. Alle Stichwörter auf der deutsch-englischen Seite, die von der Rechtschreibreform betroffen sind, sind mit ▲ gekennzeichnet. Alte Schreibungen, die sich wesentlich von der neuen Schreibung unterscheiden und an einem anderen alphabetischen Ort erscheinen, sind jedoch weiterhin aufgeführt und werden zur neuen Schreibung verwiesen. Diese alten Schreibungen sind mit △ gekennzeichnet.

USING YOUR COLLINS DICTIONARY

A wealth of information is presented in the dictionary, using various typefaces, sizes of type, symbols, abbreviations and brackets. The conventions and symbols used are explained in the following sections.

Headwords

The words you look up in a dictionary — "headwords" — are listed alphabetically. They are printed in **colour** for rapid identification. The two headwords appearing at the top left and top right of each double page indicate the first and last word dealt with on the pages in question.

Information about the usage or form of certain headwords is given in brackets after the phonetic spelling. This usually appears in abbreviated form and in italics (e.g. (*umg*), (*COMM*)).

Where appropriate, words related to headwords are grouped in the same entry (**Glück, glücken**) in a slightly smaller bold type than the headword.

Common expressions in which the headword appears are shown in a different bold roman type (e.g. **Glück haben**).

Phonetic spellings

The phonetic spelling of each headword (indicating its pronunciation) is given in square brackets immediately after the headword (e.g. **Quark** [kvark]). A list of these symbols is given on page xii.

Meanings

Headword translations are given in ordinary type and, where more than one meaning or usage exists, these are separated by a semi-colon. You will often find other words in italics in brackets before the translations. These offer suggested contexts in which the headword might appear (e.g. **eng** (*Kleidung*) or (*Freundschaft*)) or provide synonyms (e.g. **eng** (*fig: Horizont*)).

"Key" words

Special status is given to certain German and English words which are considered as "key" words in each language. They may, for example, occur very frequently or have several types of usage (e.g. **sein, auch; get, that**). A combination of lozenges and numbers helps you to distinguish different parts of speech and different meanings. Further helpful information is provided in brackets and in italics in the relevant language for the user.

Grammatical information

Parts of speech are given in abbreviated form in italics after the phonetic spellings of headwords (e.g. *vt, adv, konj*).

Genders of German nouns are indicated as follows: *m* for a masculine and *f* for a feminine and *nt* for a neuter noun. The genitive and plural forms of regular nouns are shown on the table on page xi. Nouns which do not follow these rules have the genitive and plural in brackets immediately preceding the gender (e.g. **Spaß**, (**-es, ⁻e**), *m*).

Adjectives are normally shown in their basic form (e.g. **groß** *adj*), but where they are only used attributively (i.e. before a noun) feminine and neuter endings follow in brackets (**hohe (r, s)** *adj attrib*).

German spelling reform
The German spelling reform has been fully implemented in this dictionary. All headwords on the German-English side which are affected by the spelling changes are marked with ▲, but old spellings which are markedly different from the new ones and have a different alphabetical position are still listed and are cross-referenced to the new spellings. The old spellings are marked with △.

ABKÜRZUNGEN

ABBREVIATIONS

Abkürzung	abk, abbr	abbreviation
Akkusativ	acc	accusative
Adjektiv	adj	adjective
Adverb	adv	adverb
Landwirtschaft	AGR	agriculture
Akkusativ	akk	accusative
Anatomie	ANAT	anatomy
Architektur	ARCHIT	architecture
Astrologie	ASTROL	astrology
Astronomie	ASTRON	astronomy
attributiv	attrib	attributive
Kraftfahrzeuge	AUT	automobiles
Hilfsverb	aux	auxiliary
Luftfahrt	AVIAT	aviation
besonders	bes	especially
Biologie	BIOL	biology
Botanik	BOT	botany
britisch	BRIT	British
Chemie	CHEM	chemistry
Film	CINE	cinema
Handel	COMM	commerce
Komparativ	compar	comparative
Computer	COMPUT	computing
Konjunktion	conj	conjunction
Kochen und Backen	COOK	cooking
zusammengesetztes Wort	cpd	compound
Dativ	dat	dative
bestimmter Artikel	def art	definite article
Diminutiv	dimin	diminutive
kirchlich	ECCL	ecclesiastical
Eisenbahn	EISENB	railways
Elektrizität	ELEK, ELEC	electricity
besonders	esp	especially
und so weiter	etc	et cetera
etwas	etw	something
Euphemismus, Hüllwort	euph	euphemism
Interjektion, Ausruf	excl	exclamation
Femininum	f	feminine
übertragen	fig	figurative
Finanzwesen	FIN	finance
nicht getrennt gebraucht	fus	(phrasal verb) inseparable
Genitiv	gen	genitive
Geografie	GEOG	geography
Geologie	GEOL	geology
Grammatik	GRAM	grammar

Geschichte	HIST	history
unpersönlich	impers	impersonal
unbestimmter Artikel	indef art	indefinite article
umgangssprachlich (! vulgär)	inf(!)	informal (! particularly offensive)
Infinitiv, Grundform	infin	infinitive
nicht getrennt gebraucht	insep	inseparable
unveränderlich	inv	invariable
unregelmäßig	irreg	irregular
jemand	jd	somebody
jemandem	jdm	(to) somebody
jemanden	jdn	somebody
jemandes	jds	somebody's
Rechtswesen	JUR	law
Kochen und Backen	KOCH	cooking
Komparativ	kompar	comparative
Konjunktion	konj	conjunction
Sprachwissenschaft	LING	linguistics
Literatur	LITER	of literature
Maskulinum	m	masculine
Mathematik	MATH	mathematics
Medizin	MED	medicine
Meteorologie	MET	meteorology
Militär	MIL	military
Bergbau	MIN	mining
Musik	MUS	music
Substantiv, Hauptwort	n	noun
nautisch, Seefahrt	NAUT	nautical, naval
Nominativ	nom	nominative
Neutrum	nt	neuter
Zahlwort	num	numeral
Objekt	obj	object
oder	od	or
sich	o.s.	oneself
Parlament	PARL	parliament
abschätzig	pej	pejorative
Fotografie	PHOT	photography
Physik	PHYS	physics
Plural	pl	plural
Politik	POL	politics
Präfix, Vorsilbe	pp	prefix
Präposition	präp, prep	preposition
Typografie	PRINT	printing
Pronomen, Fürwort	pron	pronoun
Psychologie	PSYCH	psychology
1. Vergangenheit, Imperfekt	pt	past tense
Radio	RAD	radio
Eisenbahn	RAIL	railways
Religion	REL	religion

jemand(-en, -em)	**sb**	someone, somebody
Schulwesen	**SCH**	school
Naturwissenschaft	**SCI**	science
Singular, Einzahl	**sg**	singular
etwas	**sth**	something
Konjunktiv	**sub**	subjunctive
Subjekt	**subj**	(grammatical) subject
Superlativ	**superl**	superlative
Technik	**TECH**	technology
Nachrichtentechnik	**TEL**	telecommunications
Theater	**THEAT**	theatre
Fernsehen	**TV**	television
Typografie	**TYP**	printing
umgangssprachlich (! vulgär)	**umg(!)**	informal (! particularly offensive)
Hochschulwesen	**UNIV**	university
unpersönlich	**unpers**	impersonal
unregelmäßig	**unreg**	irregular
(nord)amerikanisch	**US**	(North) America
gewöhnlich	**usu**	usually
Verb	**vb**	verb
intransitives Verb	**vi**	intransitive verb
reflexives Verb	**vr**	reflexive verb
transitives Verb	**vt**	transitive verb
Zoologie	**ZOOL**	zoology
zusammengesetztes Wort	**zW**	compound
zwischen zwei Sprechern	—	change of speaker
ungefähre Entsprechung	≅	cultural equivalent
eingetragenes Warenzeichen	®	registered trademark

Warenzeichen

Note on trademarks

Wörter, die unseres Wissens eingetragene Warenzeichen darstellen, sind als solche gekennzeichnet. Es ist jedoch zu beachten, dass weder das Vorhandensein noch das Fehlen derartiger Kennzeichnungen die Rechtslage hinsichtlich eingetragener Warenzeichen berührt.

Words which we have reason to believe constitute trademarks have been designated as such. However, neither the presence nor the absence of such designation should be regarded as affecting the legal status of any trademark.

REGULAR GERMAN NOUN ENDINGS

nom		*gen*	*pl*
-ant	*m*	-anten	-anten
-anz	*f*	-anz	-anzen
-ar	*m*	-ar(e)s	-are
-chen	*nt*	-chens	-chen
-e	*f*	-	-n
-ei	*f*	-ei	-eien
-elle	*f*	-elle	-ellen
-ent	*m*	-enten	-enten
-enz	*f*	-enz	-enzen
-ette	*f*	-ette	-etten
-eur	*m*	-eurs	-eure
-euse	*f*	-euse	-eusen
-heit	*f*	-heit	-heiten
-ie	*f*	-ie	-ien
-ik	*f*	-ik	-iken
-in	*f*	-in	-innen
-ine	*f*	-ine	-inen
-ion	*f*	-ion	-ionen
-ist	*m*	-isten	-isten
-ium	*nt*	-iums	-ien
-ius	*m*	-ius	-iusse
-ive	*f*	-ive	-iven
-keit	*f*	-keit	-keiten
-lein	*nt*	-leins	-lein
-ling	*m*	-lings	-linge
-ment	*nt*	-ments	-mente
-mus	*m*	-mus	-men
-schaft	*f*	-schaft	-schaften
-tät	*f*	-tät	-täten
-tor	*m*	-tors	-toren
-ung	*f*	-ung	-ungen
-ur	*f*	-ur	-uren

PHONETIC SYMBOLS / LAUTSCHRIFT

[ː] *length mark/Längezeichen* ['] *stress mark/Betonung*
[|] *glottal stop/Knacklaut*

all vowel sounds are approximate only
alle Vokallaute sind nur ungefähre Entsprechungen

bet	[b]	**B**all		[e]	M**e**tall
dim	[d]	**d**ann		[eː]	g**e**ben
face	[f]	**F**ass	set	[ɛ]	h**ä**sslich
go	[g]	**G**ast	pity	[ɛ̃ː]	Co**u**sin
hit	[h]	**H**err		[ɪ]	B**i**schof
you	[j]	**j**a		[i]	v**i**tal
cat	[k]	**k**alt	green	[iː]	v**ie**l
lick	[l]	**L**ast	rot	[ɔ]	P**o**st
must	[m]	**M**ast	board	[ɔː]	
nut	[n]	**N**uss		[o]	M**o**ral
bang	[ŋ]	la**ng**		[oː]	**o**ben
pepper	[p]	**P**akt		[õ]	Champign**on**
red	[r]	**R**egen		[ø]	**ö**konomisch
sit	[s]	**R**asse		[œ]	g**ö**nnen
shame	[ʃ]	**Sch**al	full	[u]	k**u**lant
tell	[t]	**T**al	root	[uː]	H**u**t
chat	[tʃ]	**tsch**üs	come	[ʌ]	
vine	[v]	**w**as		[ʊ]	P**u**lt
wine	[w]			[y]	ph**y**sisch
loch	[x]	Ba**ch**		[yː]	f**ü**r
	[ç]	**ich**		[ʏ]	M**ü**ll
zero	[z]	Ha**s**e	above	[ə]	bitt**e**
leisure	[ʒ]	**G**enie	girl	[əː]	
join	[dʒ]				
thin	[θ]		lie	[aɪ]	w**ei**t
this	[ð]		now	[au]	
	[a]	Ha**s**t		[aʊ]	H**au**t
hat	[æ]		day	[eɪ]	
	[aː]	Ba**h**n	fair	[ɛə]	
farm	[ɑː]		beer	[ɪə]	
	[ã]	**En**semble	toy	[ɔɪ]	
fiancé	[ɑ̃ː]			[ɔʏ]	H**eu**
			pure	[uə]	

[ʳ] r can be pronounced before a vowel; Bindungs-R

ZAHLEN

NUMBERS

ein(s)	1	one	
zwei	2	two	
drei	3	three	
vier	4	four	
fünf	5	five	
sechs	6	six	
sieben	7	seven	
acht	8	eight	
neun	9	nine	
zehn	10	ten	
elf	11	eleven	
zwölf	12	twelve	
dreizehn	13	thirteen	
vierzehn	14	fourteen	
fünfzehn	15	fifteen	
sechzehn	16	sixteen	
siebzehn	17	seventeen	
achtzehn	18	eighteen	
neunzehn	19	nineteen	
zwanzig	20	twenty	
einundzwanzig	21	twenty-one	
zweiundzwanzig	22	twenty-two	
dreißig	30	thirty	
vierzig	40	forty	
fünfzig	50	fifty	
sechzig	60	sixty	
siebzig	70	seventy	
achtzig	80	eighty	
neunzig	90	ninety	
hundert	100	a hundred	
hunderteins	101	a hundred and one	
zweihundert	200	two hundred	
zweihunderteins	201	two hundred and one	
dreihundert	300	three hundred	
dreihunderteins	301	three hundred and one	
tausend	1000	a thousand	
tausend(und)eins	1001	a thousand and one	
fünftausend	5000	five thousand	
eine Million	1000000	a million	

erste(r, s)	1.	first	1st
zweite(r, s)	2.	second	2nd
dritte(r, s)	3.	third	3rd
vierte(r, s)	4.	fourth	4th
fünfte(r, s)	5.	fifth	5th
sechste(r, s)	6.	sixth	6th

siebte(r, s)	7.	seventh	7th
achte(r, s)	8.	eighth	8th
neunte(r, s)	9.	ninth	9th
zehnte(r, s)	10.	tenth	10th
elfte(r, s)	11.	eleventh	11th
zwölfte(r, s)	12.	twelfth	12th
dreizehnte(r, s)	13.	thirteenth	13th
vierzehnte(r, s)	14.	fourteenth	14th
fünfzehnte(r, s)	15.	fifteenth	15th
sechzehnte(r, s)	16.	sixteenth	16th
siebzehnte(r, s)	17.	seventeenth	17th
achtzehnte(r, s)	18.	eighteenth	18th
neunzehnte(r, s)	19.	nineteenth	19th
zwanzigste(r, s)	20.	twentieth	20th
einundzwanzigste(r, s)	21.	twenty-first	21st
dreißigste(r, s)	30.	thirtieth	30th
hundertste(r, s)	100.	hundredth	100th
hunderterste(r, s)	101.	hundred-and-first	101st
tausendste(r, s)	1000.	thousandth	1000th

Brüche usw.

Fractions etc.

ein Halb	$\frac{1}{2}$	a half	
ein Drittel	$\frac{1}{3}$	a third	
ein Viertel	$\frac{1}{4}$	a quarter	
ein Fünftel	$\frac{1}{5}$	a fifth	
null Komma fünf	0,5	(nought) point five	0.5
drei Komma vier	3,4	three point four	3.4
sechs Komma acht neun	6,89	six point eight nine	6.89
zehn Prozent	10%	ten per cent	
hundert Prozent	100%	a hundred per cent	

Beispiele

Examples

er wohnt in Nummer 10	he lives at number 10
es steht in Kapitel 7	it's in chapter 7
auf Seite 7	on page 7
er wohnt im 7. Stock	he lives on the 7th floor
er wurde 7.	he came in 7th
Maßstab eins zu zwanzigtausend	scale one to twenty thousand

UHRZEIT

THE TIME

wie viel Uhr ist es?, wie spät ist es?

what time is it?

es ist ...

it's ...

Mitternacht, zwölf Uhr nachts	midnight, twelve p.m.
ein Uhr (morgens *or* früh)	one o'clock (in the morning), one (a.m.)
fünf nach eins, ein Uhr fünf	five past one
zehn nach eins, ein Uhr zehn	ten past one
Viertel nach eins, ein Uhr fünfzehn	a quarter past one, one fifteen
fünf vor halb zwei, ein Uhr fünfundzwanzig	twenty-five past one, one twenty-five
halb zwei, ein Uhr dreißig	half past one, one thirty
fünf nach halb zwei, ein Uhr fünfunddreißig	twenty-five to two, one thirty-five
zwanzig vor zwei, ein Uhr vierzig	twenty to two, one forty
Viertel vor zwei, ein Uhr fünfundvierzig	a quarter to two, one forty-five
zehn vor zwei, ein Uhr fünfzig	ten to two, one fifty
zwölf Uhr (mittags), Mittag	twelve o'clock, midday, noon
halb eins (mittags *or* nachmittags), zwölf Uhr dreißig	half past twelve, twelve thirty (p.m.)
zwei Uhr (nachmittags)	two o'clock (in the afternoon), two (p.m.)
halb acht (abends)	half past seven (in the evening), seven thirty (p.m.)

um wie viel Uhr?

at what time?

um Mitternacht	at midnight
um sieben Uhr	at seven o'clock
in zwanzig Minuten	in twenty minutes
vor fünfzehn Minuten	fifteen minutes ago

DEUTSCH – ENGLISCH
GERMAN – ENGLISH

A, a

Aal [aːl] **(-(e)s, -e)** *m* eel

Aas [aːs] **(-es, -e** *od* **Äser)** *nt* carrion

SCHLÜSSELWORT
---

ab [ap] *präp +dat* from; **Kinder ab 12 Jahren** children from the age of 12; **ab morgen** from tomorrow; **ab sofort** as of now
♦ *adv* **1** off; **links ab** to the left; **der Knopf ist ab** the button has come off; **ab nach Hause!** off you go home
2 (*zeitlich*): **von da ab** from then on; **von heute ab** from today, as of today
3 (*auf Fahrplänen*): **München ab 12.20** leaving Munich 12.20
4 : **ab und zu** *od* **an** now and then *od* again

Abänderung [ˈap|ɛndərʊŋ] *f* alteration

Abbau [ˈapbaʊ] **(-(e)s)** *m* (+*gen*) dismantling; (*Verminderung*) reduction (in); (*Verfall*) decline (in); (*MIN*) mining; quarrying; (*CHEM*) decomposition;**a~en** *vt* to dismantle; (*MIN*) to mine; to quarry; (*verringern*) to reduce; (*CHEM*) to break down

abbeißen [ˈapbaɪsən] (*unreg*) *vt* to bite off

abbekommen [ˈapbəkɔmən] (*unreg*) *vt* (*Deckel, Schraube, Band*) to loosen; **etwas ~** (*beschädigt werden*) to get damaged; (: *Person*) to get injured

abbestellen [ˈapbəʃtɛlən] *vt* to cancel

abbezahlen [ˈapbətsaːlən] *vt* to pay off

abbiegen [ˈapbiːgən] (*unreg*) *vi* to turn off; (*Straße*) to bend ♦ *vt* to bend; (*verhindern*) to ward off

abbilden [ˈapbɪldən] *vt* to portray; **Abbildung** *f* illustration

abblenden [ˈapblɛndən] *vt, vi* (*AUT*) to dip (*BRIT*), to dim (*US*)

Abblendlicht [ˈapblɛntlɪçt] *nt* dipped (*BRIT*) *od* dimmed (*US*) headlights *pl*

abbrechen [ˈapbrɛçən] (*unreg*) *vt, vi* to break off; (*Gebäude*) to pull down; (*Zelt*) to take down; (*aufhören*) to stop; (*COMPUT*) to abort

abbrennen [ˈapbrɛnən] (*unreg*) *vt* to burn off; (*Feuerwerk*) to let off ♦ *vi* (*aux sein*) to burn down

abbringen [ˈapbrɪŋən] (*unreg*) *vt*: **jdn von etw ~** to dissuade sb from sth; **jdn vom Weg ~** to divert sb

abbröckeln [ˈapbrœkəln] *vt, vi* to crumble off *od* away

Abbruch [ˈapbrʊx] *m* (*von Verhandlungen etc*) breaking off; (*von Haus*) demolition; **jdm/ etw ~ tun** to harm sb/sth;**a~reif** *adj* only fit for demolition

abbrühen [ˈapbryːən] *vt* to scald; **abgebrüht** (*umg*) hard-boiled

abbuchen [ˈapbuːxən] *vt* to debit

abdanken [ˈapdaŋkən] *vi* to resign; (*König*) to abdicate;**Abdankung** *f* resignation; abdication

abdecken [ˈapdɛkən] *vt* (*Loch*) to cover; (*Tisch*) to clear; (*Plane*) to uncover

abdichten [ˈapdɪçtən] *vt* to seal; (*NAUT*) to caulk

abdrehen [ˈapdreːən] *vt* (*Gas*) to turn off; (*Licht*) to switch off; (*Film*) to shoot ♦ *vi* (*Schiff*) to change course

Abdruck [ˈapdrʊk] *m* (*Nachdrucken*) reprinting; (*Gedrucktes*) reprint; (*Gipsabdruck, Wachsabdruck*) impression; (*Fingerabdruck*) print;**a~en** *vt* to print, to publish

abdrücken [ˈapdrʏkən] *vt* (*Waffe*) to fire; (*Person*) to hug, to squeeze

Abend [ˈaːbənt] **(-s, -e)** *m* evening; **guten ~** good evening; **zu ~ essen** to have dinner *od* supper; **heute ~** this evening; **~brot** *nt* supper;**~essen** *nt* supper;**~garderobe** *f*

evening dress; **~kasse** *f* box office; **~kleid** *nt* evening dress; **~klasses** evening classes *pl*; **~land** *nt* (*Europa*) West; **a~lich** *adj* evening; **~mahl** *nt* Holy Communion; **~rot** *nt* sunset; **a~s** *adv* in the evening

Abenteuer ['a:bəntɔyər] (**-s, -**) *nt* adventure; **~film** *m* adventure film; **a~lich** *adj* adventurous; **~urlaub** *m* adventure holiday

Abenteurer (**-s, -**) *m* adventurer; **~in** *f* adventuress

aber ['a:bər] *konj* but; (*jedoch*) however
♦ *adv*: **das ist ~ schön** that's really nice; **nun ist ~ Schluss!** now that's enough!; **vielen Dank – ~ bitte!** thanks a lot – you're welcome; **A~glaube** *m* superstition; **~gläubisch** *adj* superstitious

aberkennen ['ap|ɛrkɛnən] (*unreg*) *vt* (*JUR*): **jdm etw ~** to deprive sb of sth, to take sth (away) from sb

abermals ['a:bəma:ls] *adv* once again

Abertausend, abertausend ['a:bətauzənt] *indef pron* **tausend** *od* **Tausend und ~** thousands upon thousands

Abf. *abk* (= *Abfahrt*) dep.

abfahren ['apfa:rən] (*unreg*) *vi* to leave, to depart ♦ *vt* to take *od* cart away; (*Strecke*) to drive; (*Reifen*) to wear; (*Fahrkarte*) to use

Abfahrt ['apfa:rt] *f* departure; (*SKI*) descent; (*Piste*) run; **~szeit** *f* departure time

Abfall ['apfal] *m* waste; (*von Speisen etc*) rubbish (*BRIT*), garbage (*US*); (*Neigung*) slope; (*Verschlechterung*) decline; **~eimer** *m* rubbish bin (*BRIT*), garbage can (*US*); **a~en** (*unreg*) *vi* (*auch fig*) to fall *od* drop off; (*sich neigen*) to fall *od* drop away

abfällig ['apfɛlɪç] *adj* disparaging, deprecatory

abfangen ['apfaŋən] (*unreg*) *vt* to intercept; (*Person*) to catch; (*unter Kontrolle bringen*) to check

abfärben ['apfɛrbən] *vi* to lose its colour; (*Wäsche*) to run; (*fig*) to rub off

abfassen ['apfasən] *vt* to write, to draft

abfertigen ['apfɛrtɪgən] *vt* to prepare for dispatch, to process; (*an der Grenze*) to clear; (*Kundschaft*) to attend to

Abfertigungsschalter *m* (*Flughafen*)
check-in desk

abfeuern ['apfɔyərn] *vt* to fire

abfinden ['apfɪndən] (*unreg*) *vt* to pay off ♦ *vr* to come to terms; **sich mit jdm ~/ nicht ~** to put up with/not get on with sb

Abfindung *f* (*von Gläubigern*) payment; (*Geld*) sum in settlement

abflauen ['apflauən] *vi* (*Wind, Erregung*) to die away, to subside; (*Nachfrage, Geschäft*) to fall *od* drop off

abfliegen ['apfli:gən] (*unreg*) *vi* (*Flugzeug*) to take off; (*Passagier auch*) to fly ♦ *vt* (*Gebiet*) to fly over

abfließen ['apfli:sən] (*unreg*) *vi* to drain away

Abflug ['apflu:k] *m* departure; (*Start*) take-off; **~halle** *f* departure lounge; **~zeit** *f* departure time

Abfluss ▲ ['apflus] *m* draining away; (*Öffnung*) outlet; **~rohr** *nt* drain pipe; (*von sanitären Anlagen auch*) waste pipe

abfragen ['apfra:gən] *vt* (*bes SCH*) to test orally (on)

Abfuhr ['apfu:r] (**-, -en**) *f* removal; (*fig*) snub, rebuff

abführen ['apfy:rən] *vt* to lead away; (*Gelder, Steuern*) to pay ♦ *vi* (*MED*) to have a laxative effect

Abführmittel ['apfy:rmɪtəl] *nt* laxative

abfüllen ['apfʏlən] *vt* to draw off; (*in Flaschen*) to bottle

Abgabe ['apga:bə] *f* handing in; (*von Ball*) pass; (*Steuer*) tax; (*eines Amtes*) giving up; (*einer Erklärung*) giving

Abgang ['apgaŋ] *m* (*von Schule*) leaving; (*THEAT*) exit; (*Abfahrt*) departure; (*der Post, von Waren*) dispatch

Abgas ['apga:s] *nt* waste gas; (*AUT*) exhaust

abgeben ['apge:bən] (*unreg*) *vt* (*Gegenstand*) to hand *od* give in; (*Ball*) to pass; (*Wärme*) to give off; (*Amt*) to hand over; (*Schuss*) to fire; (*Erklärung, Urteil*) to give; (*darstellen, sein*) to make ♦ *vr*: **sich mit jdm/etw ~** to associate with sb/bother with sth; **jdm etw ~** (*überlassen*) to let sb have sth

abgebrüht ['apgəbry:t] (*umg*) *adj* (*skrupellos*)

hard-boiled

abgehen ['apgeːən] (*unreg*) *vi* to go away, to leave; (*THEAT*) to exit; (*Knopf etc*) to come off; (*Straße*) to branch off ♦ *vt* (*Strecke*) to go *od* walk along; **etw geht jdm ab** (*fehlt*) sb lacks sth

abgelegen ['apgəleːgən] *adj* remote

abgemacht ['apgəmaxt] *adj* fixed; **~!** done!

abgeneigt ['apgənaɪkt] *adj* disinclined

abgenutzt ['apgənʊtst] *adj* worn

Abgeordnete(r) ['apgəɔrdnətə(r)] *f(m)* member of parliament; elected representative

abgeschlossen ['apgəʃlɔsən] *adj attrib* (*Wohnung*) self-contained

abgeschmackt ['apgəʃmakt] *adj* tasteless

abgesehen ['apgəzeːən] *adj*: **es auf jdn/ etw ~ haben** to be after sb/sth; **~ von ...** apart from ...

abgespannt ['apgəʃpant] *adj* tired out

abgestanden ['apgəʃtandən] *adj* stale; (*Bier auch*) flat

abgestorben ['apgəʃtɔrbən] *adj* numb; (*BIOL, MED*) dead

abgetragen ['apgətraːgən] *adj* shabby, worn out

abgewinnen ['apgəvɪnən] (*unreg*) *vt*: **einer Sache etw/Geschmack ~** to get sth/ pleasure from sth

abgewöhnen ['apgəvøːnən] *vt*: **jdm/sich etw ~** to cure sb of sth/give sth up

abgrenzen ['apgrɛntsən] *vt* (*auch fig*) to mark off; to fence off

Abgrund ['apgrʊnt] *m* (*auch fig*) abyss

abhacken ['aphakən] *vt* to chop off

abhaken ['aphaːkən] *vt* (*auf Papier*) to tick off

abhalten ['aphaltən] (*unreg*) *vt* (*Versammlung*) to hold; **jdn von etw ~** (*fern halten*) to keep sb away from sth; (*hindern*) to keep sb from sth

abhanden [ap'handən] *adj*: **~ kommen** to get lost

Abhandlung ['aphandlʊŋ] *f* treatise, discourse

Abhang ['aphaŋ] *m* slope

abhängen ['aphɛŋən] *vt* (*Bild*) to take down; (*Anhänger*) to uncouple; (*Verfolger*) to shake off ♦ *vi* (*unreg*: *Fleisch*) to hang; **von jdm/ etw ~** to depend on sb/sth

abhängig ['aphɛŋɪç] *adj*: **~ (von)** dependent (on); **A~keit** *f*: **A~keit (von)** dependence (on)

abhärten ['aphɛrtən] *vt, vr* to toughen (o.s.) up; **sich gegen etw ~** to inure o.s. to sth

abhauen ['aphavən] (*unreg*) *vt* to cut off; (*Baum*) to cut down ♦ *vi* (*umg*) to clear off *od* out

abheben ['apheːbən] (*unreg*) *vt* to lift (up); (*Karten*) to cut; (*Geld*) to withdraw, to take out ♦ *vi* (*Flugzeug*) to take off; (*Rakete*) to lift off ♦ *vr* to stand out

abheften ['apheftən] *vt* (*Rechnungen etc*) to file away

abhetzen ['aphɛtsən] *vr* to wear *od* tire o.s. out

Abhilfe ['aphɪlfə] *f* remedy; **~ schaffen** to put things right

abholen ['aphoːlən] *vt* (*Gegenstand*) to fetch, to collect; (*Person*) to call for; (*am Bahnhof etc*) to pick up, to meet

abholzen ['aphɔltsən] *vt* (*Wald*) to clear

abhorchen ['aphɔrçən] *vt* (*MED*) to listen to a patient's chest

abhören ['aphøːrən] *vt* (*Vokabeln*) to test; (*Telefongespräch*) to tap; (*Tonband etc*) to listen to

Abhörgerät *nt* bug

Abitur [abi'tuːr] (**-s, -e**) *nt* German school-leaving examination; **~i'ent(in)** *m(f)* candidate for school-leaving certificate

---
Abitur
---

i The **Abitur** is the German school-leaving examination taken in four subjects by pupils at a **Gymnasium** at the age of 18 or 19. It is necessary for entry to university.

Abk. *abk* (= *Abkürzung*) abbr.

abkapseln ['apkapsəln] *vr* to shut *od* cut o.s. off

abkaufen ['apkaʊfən] *vt*: **jdm etw ~** (*auch fig*) to buy sth from sb

abkehren ['apkeːrən] *vt* (*Blick*) to avert, to turn away ♦ *vr* to turn away

abklingen ['apklɪŋən] (*unreg*) *vi* to die away; (*Radio*) to fade out

abknöpfen ['apknœpfən] *vt* to unbutton; **jdm etw ~** (*umg*) to get sth off sb

abkochen ['apkɔxən] *vt* to boil

abkommen ['apkɔmən] (*unreg*) *vi* to get away; **von der Straße/von einem Plan ~** to leave the road/give up a plan; **A~ (-s, -)** *nt* agreement

abkömmlich ['apkœmlɪç] *adj* available, free

abkratzen ['apkratsən] *vt* to scrape off ♦ *vi* (*umg*) to kick the bucket

abkühlen ['apkyːlən] *vt* to cool down ♦ *vr* (*Mensch*) to cool down *od* off; (*Wetter*) to get cool; (*Zuneigung*) to cool

abkürzen ['apkʏrtsən] *vt* to shorten; (*Wort auch*) to abbreviate; **den Weg ~** to take a short cut

Abkürzung *f* (*Wort*) abbreviation; (*Weg*) short cut

abladen ['aplaːdən] (*unreg*) *vt* to unload

Ablage ['aplaːgə] *f* (*für Akten*) tray; (*für Kleider*) cloakroom

ablassen ['aplasən] (*unreg*) *vt* (*Wasser, Dampf*) to let off; (*vom Preis*) to knock off ♦ *vi*: **von etw ~** to give sth up, to abandon sth

Ablauf ['aplauf] *m* (*Abfluss*) drain; (*von Ereignissen*) course; (*einer Frist, Zeit*) expiry (*BRIT*), expiration (*US*); **a~en** (*unreg*) *vi* (*abfließen*) to drain away; (*Ereignisse*) to happen; (*Frist, Zeit, Pass*) to expire ♦ *vt* (*Sohlen*) to wear (down *od* out)

ablegen ['apleːgən] *vt* to put *od* lay down; (*Kleider*) to take off; (*Gewohnheit*) to get rid of; (*Prüfung*) to take, to sit; (*Zeugnis*) to give

Ableger (-s, -) *m* layer; (*fig*) branch, offshoot

ablehnen ['apleːnən] *vt* to reject; (*Einladung*) to decline, to refuse ♦ *vi* to decline, to refuse

ablehnend *adj* (*Haltung, Antwort*) negative; (*Geste*) disapproving; **ein ~er Bescheid** a rejection

Ablehnung *f* rejection; refusal

ableiten ['aplaɪtən] *vt* (*Wasser*) to divert; (*deduzieren*) to deduce; (*Wort*) to derive; **Ableitung** *f* diversion; deduction; derivation; (*Wort*) derivative

ablenken ['aplɛŋkən] *vt* to turn away, to deflect; (*zerstreuen*) to distract ♦ *vi* to change the subject; **Ablenkung** *f* distraction

ablesen ['apleːzən] (*unreg*) *vt* to read out; (*Messgeräte*) to read

ablichten ['aplɪçtən] *vt* to photocopy

abliefern ['apliːfərn] *vt* to deliver; **etw bei jdm ~** to hand sth over to sb

Ablieferung *f* delivery

ablösen ['apløːzən] *vt* (*abtrennen*) to take off, to remove; (*in Amt*) to take over from; (*Wache*) to relieve

Ablösung *f* removal; relieving

abmachen ['apmaxən] *vt* to take off; (*vereinbaren*) to agree; **Abmachung** *f* agreement

abmagern ['apmaːgərn] *vi* to get thinner

Abmagerungskur *f* diet; **eine ~ machen** to go on a diet

abmarschieren ['apmarʃiːrən] *vi* to march off

abmelden ['apmɛldən] *vt* (*Zeitungen*) to cancel; (*Auto*) to take off the road ♦ *vr* to give notice of one's departure; (*im Hotel*) to check out; **jdn bei der Polizei ~** to register sb's departure with the police

abmessen ['apmɛsən] (*unreg*) *vt* to measure; **Abmessung** *f* measurement

abmontieren ['apmɔntiːrən] *vt* to take off

abmühen ['apmyːən] *vr* to wear o.s. out

Abnahme ['apnaːmə] *f* (*+gen*) removal; (*COMM*) buying; (*Verringerung*) decrease (in)

abnehmen ['apneːmən] (*unreg*) *vt* to take off, to remove; (*Führerschein*) to take away; (*Prüfung*) to hold; (*Maschen*) to decrease ♦ *vi* to decrease; (*schlanker werden*) to lose weight; **(jdm) etw ~** (*Geld*) to get sth (out of sb); (*kaufen, umg: glauben*) to buy sth (from sb); **jdm Arbeit ~** to take work off sb's shoulders

Abnehmer (-s, -) *m* purchaser, customer

Abneigung ['apnaɪgʊŋ] *f* aversion, dislike

abnorm [ap'nɔrm] *adj* abnormal
abnutzen ['apnʊtsən] *vt* to wear out;
  Abnutzung *f* wear (and tear)
Abo ['abo] (*umg*) *nt abk* = **Abonnement**
Abonnement [abɔn(ə)'mã:] (**-s, -s**) *nt*
  subscription; **Abonnent(in)** [abɔ'nɛnt(ɪn)]
  m(f) subscriber; **abonnieren** *vt* to
  subscribe to
Abordnung ['ap|ɔrdnʊŋ] *f* delegation
abpacken ['appakən] *vt* to pack
abpassen ['appasən] *vt* (*Person, Gelegenheit*)
  to wait for
Abpfiff ['appfɪf] *m* final whistle
abplagen ['appla:gən] *vr* to wear o.s. out
abprallen ['appralən] *vi* to bounce off; to
  ricochet
abraten ['apra:tən] (*unreg*) *vi*: **jdm von etw**
  ~ to advise *or* warn sb against sth
abräumen ['aprɔymən] *vt* to clear up *od*
  away
abreagieren ['apreagi:rən] *vt*: **seinen Zorn**
  (an jdm/etw) ~ to work one's anger off
  (on sb/sth) ♦ *vr* to calm down
abrechnen ['aprɛçnən] *vt* to deduct, to take
  off ♦ *vi* to settle up; (*fig*) to get even
Abrechnung *f* settlement; (*Rechnung*) bill
Abrede ['apre:də] *f*: **etw in ~ stellen** to
  deny *od* dispute sth
Abreise ['apraɪzə] *f* departure; **a~n** *vi* to
  leave, to set off
abreißen ['apraɪsən] (*unreg*) *vt* (*Haus*) to tear
  down; (*Blatt*) to tear off
abrichten ['aprɪçtən] *vt* to train
abriegeln ['apri:gəln] *vt* (*Straße, Gebiet*) to
  seal off
Abruf ['apru:f] *m*: **auf ~** on call; **a~en**
  (*unreg*) *vt* (*Mensch*) to call away; (*COMM*:
  Ware) to request delivery of
abrunden ['aprʊndən] *vt* to round off
abrupt [a'brʊpt] *adj* abrupt
abrüsten ['aprʏstən] *vi* to disarm;
  Abrüstung *f* disarmament
abrutschen ['aprʊtʃən] *vi* to slip; (*AVIAT*) to
  sideslip
Abs. *abk* (= *Absender*) sender, from
Absage ['apza:gə] *f* refusal; **a~n** *vt* to
  cancel, to call off; (*Einladung*) to turn down

♦ *vi* to cry off; (*ablehnen*) to decline
absahnen ['apza:nən] *vt* to skim ♦ *vi* (*fig*) to
  rake in
Absatz ['apzats] *m* (*COMM*) sales *pl*;
  (*Bodensatz*) deposit; (*neuer Abschnitt*)
  paragraph; (*Treppenabsatz*) landing;
  (*Schuhabsatz*) heel; **~gebiet** *nt* (*COMM*)
  market
abschaffen ['apʃafən] *vt* to abolish, to do
  away with; **Abschaffung** *f* abolition
abschalten ['apʃaltən] *vt*, *vi* (*auch umg*) to
  switch off
abschätzen ['apʃɛtsən] *vt* to estimate;
  (*Lage*) to assess; (*Person*) to size up
abschätzig ['apʃɛtsɪç] *adj* disparaging,
  derogatory
Abschaum ['apʃaʊm] (**-(e)s**) *m* scum
Abscheu ['apʃɔy] (**-(e)s**) *m* loathing,
  repugnance; **~ erregend** repulsive,
  loathsome; **a~lich** [ap'ʃɔylɪç] *adj*
  abominable
abschicken ['apʃɪkən] *vt* to send off
abschieben ['apʃi:bən] (*unreg*) *vt* to push
  away; (*Person*) to pack off; (: *POL*) to deport
Abschied ['apʃi:t] (**-(e)s, -e**) *m* parting; (*von
  Armee*) discharge; (**von jdm**) **~ nehmen** to
  say goodbye (to sb), to take one's leave (of
  sb); **seinen ~ nehmen** (*MIL*) to apply for
  discharge; **~sbrief** *m* farewell letter;
  ~sfeier *f* farewell party
abschießen ['apʃi:sən] (*unreg*) *vt* (*Flugzeug*)
  to shoot down; (*Geschoss*) to fire
abschirmen ['apʃɪrmən] *vt* to screen
abschlagen ['apʃla:gən] (*unreg*) *vt*
  (*abhacken, COMM*) to knock off; (*ablehnen*)
  to refuse; (*MIL*) to repel
abschlägig ['apʃlɛ:gɪç] *adj* negative
Abschlagszahlung *f* interim payment
Abschlepp- ['apʃlɛp] *zW*: **~dienst** *m* (*AUT*)
  breakdown service (*BRIT*), towing company
  (*US*); **a~en** *vt* to (take in) tow; **~seil** *nt*
  towrope
abschließen ['apʃli:sən] (*unreg*) *vt* (*Tür*) to
  lock; (*beenden*) to conclude, to finish;
  (*Vertrag, Handel*) to conclude ♦ *vr* (*sich
  isolieren*) to cut o.s. off; **~d** *adj* concluding
Abschluss ▲ ['apʃlʊs] *m* (*Beendigung*) close,

conclusion; (COMM: *Bilanz*) balancing; (*von Vertrag, Handel*) conclusion; **zum ~ in** conclusion; **~feier** f (SCH) end of term party; **~prüfung** f final exam

abschneiden ['apʃnaɪdən] (*unreg*) vt to cut off ♦ vi to do, to come off

Abschnitt ['apʃnɪt] m section; (MIL) sector; (*Kontrollabschnitt*) counterfoil; (MATH) segment; (*Zeitabschnitt*) period

abschrauben ['apʃraʊbən] vt to unscrew

abschrecken ['apʃrɛkən] vt to deter, to put off; (*mit kaltem Wasser*) to plunge in cold water; **~d** adj deterrent; **~des Beispiel** warning

abschreiben ['apʃraɪbən] (*unreg*) vt to copy; (*verloren geben*) to write off; (COMM) to deduct

Abschrift ['apʃrɪft] f copy

Abschuss ▲ ['apʃʊs] m (*eines Geschützes*) firing; (*Herunterschießen*) shooting down; (*Tötung*) shooting

abschüssig ['apʃʏsɪç] adj steep

abschwächen ['apʃvɛçən] vt to lessen; (*Behauptung, Kritik*) to tone down ♦ vr to lessen

abschweifen ['apʃvaɪfən] vi to digress

abschwellen ['apʃvɛlən] (*unreg*) vi (*Geschwulst*) to go down; (*Lärm*) to die down

abschwören ['apʃvøːrən] vi (+*dat*) to renounce

absehbar ['apzeːbaːr] adj foreseeable; **in ~er Zeit** in the foreseeable future; **das Ende ist ~** the end is in sight

absehen ['apzeːən] (*unreg*) vt (*Ende, Folgen*) to foresee ♦ vi: **von etw ~** to refrain from sth; (*nicht berücksichtigen*) to leave sth out of consideration

abseilen ['apzaɪlən] vr (*Bergsteiger*) to abseil (down)

abseits ['apzaɪts] adv out of the way ♦ präp +*gen* away from; **A~** nt (SPORT) offside

absenden ['apzɛndən] (*unreg*) vt to send off, to dispatch

Absender (-s, -) m sender

absetzen ['apzɛtsən] vt (*niederstellen, aussteigen lassen*) to put down; (*abnehmen*)

to take off; (COMM: *verkaufen*) to sell; (FIN: *abziehen*) to deduct; (*entlassen*) to dismiss; (*König*) to depose; (*streichen*) to drop; (*hervorheben*) to pick out ♦ vr (*sich entfernen*) to clear off; (*sich ablagern*) to be deposited

Absetzung f (FIN: *Abzug*) deduction; (*Entlassung*) dismissal; (*von König*) deposing

absichern ['apzɪçərn] vt to make safe; (*schützen*) to safeguard ♦ vr to protect o.s.

Absicht ['apzɪçt] f intention; **mit ~** on purpose; **a~lich** adj intentional, deliberate

absinken ['apzɪŋkən] (*unreg*) vi to sink; (*Temperatur, Geschwindigkeit*) to decrease

absitzen ['apzɪtsən] (*unreg*) vi to dismount ♦ vt (*Strafe*) to serve

absolut [apzoˈluːt] adj absolute; **A~ismus** m absolutism

absolvieren [apzɔlˈviːrən] vt (SCH) to complete

absonder- ['apzɔndər] zW: **~lich** adj odd, strange; **~n** vt to separate; (*ausscheiden*) to give off, to secrete ♦ vr to cut o.s. off; **A~ung** f separation; (MED) secretion

abspalten ['apʃpaltən] vt to split off

abspannen ['apʃpanən] vt (*Pferde*) to unhitch; (*Wagen*) to uncouple

abspeisen ['apʃpaɪzən] vt (fig) to fob off

abspenstig ['apʃpɛnstɪç] adj: **(jdm) ~ machen** to lure away (from sb)

absperren ['apʃpɛrən] vt to block od close off; (*Tür*) to lock; **Absperrung** f (*Vorgang*) blocking od closing off; (*Sperre*) barricade

abspielen ['apʃpiːlən] vt (*Platte, Tonband*) to play; (SPORT: *Ball*) to pass ♦ vr to happen

Absprache ['apʃpraːxə] f arrangement

absprechen ['apʃprɛçən] (*unreg*) vt (*vereinbaren*) to arrange; **jdm etw ~** to deny sb sth

abspringen ['apʃprɪŋən] (*unreg*) vi to jump down/off; (*Farbe, Lack*) to flake off; (AVIAT) to bale out; (*sich distanzieren*) to back out

Absprung ['apʃprʊŋ] m jump

abspülen ['apʃpyːlən] vt to rinse; (*Geschirr*) to wash up

abstammen ['apʃtamən] vi to be descended; (*Wort*) to be derived; **Abstammung** f descent; derivation

Abstand ['apʃtant] *m* distance; *(zeitlich)* interval; **davon ~ nehmen, etw zu tun** to refrain from doing sth; **mit ~ der Beste** by far the best

abstatten ['apʃtatən] *vt (Dank)* to give; *(Besuch)* to pay

abstauben ['apʃtaubən] *vt, vi* to dust; *(umg: stehlen)* to pinch; *(: schnorren)* to scrounge

Abstecher ['apʃteçər] **(-s, -)** *m* detour

abstehen ['apʃte:ən] *(unreg) vi (Ohren, Haare)* to stick out; *(entfernt sein)* to stand away

absteigen ['apʃtaigən] *(unreg) vi (vom Rad etc)* to get off, to dismount; **(in die zweite Liga) ~** to be relegated (to the second division)

abstellen ['apʃtɛlən] *vt (niederstellen)* to put down; *(entfernt stellen)* to pull out; *(hinstellen: Auto)* to park; *(ausschalten)* to turn *od* switch off; *(Missstand, Unsitte)* to stop

Abstellraum *m* storage room

abstempeln ['apʃtɛmpəln] *vt* to stamp

absterben ['apʃtɛrbən] *(unreg) vi* to die; *(Körperteil)* to go numb

Abstieg ['apʃti:k] **(-(e)s, -e)** *m* descent; *(SPORT)* relegation; *(fig)* decline

abstimmen ['apʃtimən] *vi* to vote ♦ *vt:* **~ (auf +akk)** *(Instrument)* to tune (to); *(Interessen)* to match (with); *(Termine, Ziele)* to fit in (with) ♦ *vr* to agree

Abstimmung *f* vote

Abstinenz [apsti'nɛnts] *f* abstinence; teetotalism; **~ler(in)** **(-s, -)** *m(f)* teetotaller

abstoßen ['apʃto:sən] *(unreg) vt* to push off *od* away; *(verkaufen)* to unload; *(anekeln)* to repel, to repulse; **~d** *adj* repulsive

abstrakt [ap'strakt] *adj* abstract ♦ *adv* abstractly, in the abstract

abstreiten ['apʃtraitən] *(unreg) vt* to deny

Abstrich ['apʃtriç] *m (Abzug)* cut; *(MED)* smear; **~e machen** to lower one's sights

abstufen ['apʃtu:fən] *vt (Hang)* to terrace; *(Farben)* to shade; *(Gehälter)* to grade

Absturz ['apʃturts] *m* fall; *(AVIAT)* crash

abstürzen ['apʃtyrtsən] *vi* to fall; *(AVIAT)* to crash

absuchen ['apzu:xən] *vt* to scour, to search

absurd [ap'zurt] *adj* absurd

Abszess ▲ [aps'tsɛs] **(-es, -e)** *m* abscess

Abt [apt] **(-(e)s, ᵛe)** *m* abbot

Abt. *abk (= Abteilung)* dept.

abtasten ['aptastən] *vt* to feel, to probe

abtauen ['aptauən] *vt, vi* to thaw

Abtei [ap'tai] **(-, -en)** *f* abbey

Abteil [ap'tail] **(-(e)s, -e)** *nt* compartment; **'a~n** *vt* to divide up; *(abtrennen)* to divide off; **~ung** *f (in Firma, Kaufhaus)* department; *(in Krankenhaus)* section; *(MIL)* unit

abtippen ['aptipən] *vt (Text)* to type up

abtransportieren ['aptransporti:rən] *vt* to take away, to remove

abtreiben ['aptraibən] *(unreg) vt (Boot, Flugzeug)* to drive off course; *(Kind)* to abort ♦ *vi* to be driven off course; to abort

Abtreibung *f* abortion

abtrennen ['aptrɛnən] *vt (lostrennen)* to detach; *(entfernen)* to take off; *(abteilen)* to separate off

abtreten ['aptre:tən] *(unreg) vt* to wear out; *(überlassen)* to hand over, to cede ♦ *vi* to go off; *(zurücktreten)* to step down

Abtritt ['aptrit] *m* resignation

abtrocknen ['aptrɔknən] *vt, vi* to dry

abtun ['aptu:n] *(unreg) vt (fig)* to dismiss

abwägen ['apvɛ:gən] *(unreg) vt* to weigh up

abwälzen ['apvɛltsən] *vt (Schuld, Verantwortung):* **~ (auf +akk)** to shift (onto)

abwandeln ['apvandəln] *vt* to adapt

abwandern ['apvandərn] *vi* to move away; *(FIN)* to be transferred

abwarten ['apvartən] *vt* to wait for ♦ *vi* to wait

abwärts ['apvɛrts] *adv* down

Abwasch ['apvaʃ] **(-(e)s)** *m* washing-up; **a~en** *(unreg) vt (Schmutz)* to wash off; *(Geschirr)* to wash (up)

Abwasser ['apvasər] **(-s, -wässer)** *nt* sewage

abwechseln ['apvɛksəln] *vi, vr* to alternate; *(Personen)* to take turns; **~d** *adj* alternate; **Abwechslung** *f* change; **abwechslungsreich** *adj* varied

abwegig ['apve:gɪç] *adj* wrong

Abwehr ['apveːr] (-) *f* defence; (*Schutz*) protection; (*~dienst*) counterintelligence (service); **a~en** *vt* to ward off; (*Ball*) to stop

abweichen ['apvaiçən] (*unreg*) *vi* to deviate; (*Meinung*) to differ

abweisen ['apvaizən] (*unreg*) *vt* to turn away; (*Antrag*) to turn down; **~d** *adj* (*Haltung*) cold

abwenden ['apvɛndən] (*unreg*) *vt* to avert ♦ *vr* to turn away

abwerfen ['apvɛrfən] (*unreg*) *vt* to throw off; (*Profit*) to yield; (*aus Flugzeug*) to drop; (*Spielkarte*) to discard

abwerten ['apvɛrtən] *vt* (FIN) to devalue

abwertend *adj* (*Worte, Sinn*) pejorative

Abwertung *f* (*von Währung*) devaluation

abwesend ['apveːzənt] *adj* absent

Abwesenheit ['apveːzənhait] *f* absence

abwickeln ['apvikəln] *vt* to unwind; (*Geschäft*) to transact

abwimmeln ['apvimMəln] (*umg*) *vt* (*Menschen*) to get shot of

abwischen ['apvifən] *vt* to wipe *od* away; (*putzen*) to wipe

Abwurf ['apvurf] *m* throwing off; (*von Bomben etc*) dropping; (*von Reiter, SPORT*) throw

abwürgen ['apvyrgən] (*umg*) *vt* to scotch; (*Motor*) to stall

abzahlen ['aptsaːlən] *vt* to pay off

abzählen ['aptseːlən] *vt, vi* to count (up)

Abzahlung *f* repayment; **auf ~ kaufen** to buy on hire purchase

abzapfen ['aptsapfən] *vt* to draw off; **jdm Blut ~** to take blood from sb

abzäunen ['aptsɔynən] *vt* to fence off

Abzeichen ['aptsaiçən] *nt* badge; (*Orden*) decoration

abzeichnen ['aptsaiçnən] *vt* to draw, to copy; (*Dokument*) to initial ♦ *vr* to stand out; (*fig: bevorstehen*) to loom

abziehen ['aptsiːən] (*unreg*) *vt* to take off; (*Tier*) to skin; (*Bett*) to strip; (*Truppen*) to withdraw; (*subtrahieren*) to take away, to subtract; (*kopieren*) to run off ♦ *vi* to go away; (*Truppen*) to withdraw

abzielen ['aptsiːlən] *vi*: **~ auf** +*akk* to be aimed at

Abzug ['aptsuːk] *m* departure; (*von Truppen*) withdrawal; (*Kopie*) copy; (*Subtraktion*) subtraction; (*Betrag*) deduction; (*Rauchabzug*) flue; (*von Waffen*) trigger

abzüglich ['aptsyːkliç] *präp* +*gen* less

abzweigen ['aptsvaigən] *vi* to branch off ♦ *vt* to set aside

Abzweigung *f* junction

ach [ax] *excl* oh; **~ ja!** (oh) yes; **~ so!** I see; **mit A~ und Krach** by the skin of one's teeth

Achse ['aksə] *f* axis; (AUT) axle

Achsel ['aksəl] (-, -n) *f* shoulder; **~höhle** *f* armpit

acht [axt] *num* eight; **~ Tage** a week; **A~**[1] (-, -en) *f* eight; (*beim Eislaufen etc*) figure eight

Acht[2] (-, -en) *f*: **~ geben (auf** +*akk*) to pay attention (to); **sich in ~ nehmen (vor** +*dat*) to be careful (of), to watch out (for); **etw außer ~ lassen** to disregard sth; **a~bar** *adj* worthy

acht- *zW*: **~e(r, s)** *adj* eighth; **A~el** *num* eighth; **~en** *vt* to respect ♦ *vi*: **~en (auf** +*akk*) to pay attention (to); **~en, dass ...** to be careful that ...

ächten ['ɛçtən] *vt* to outlaw, to ban

Achterbahn ['axtər-] *f* roller coaster

acht- *zW*: **~fach** *adj* eightfold; **~geben** △ (*unreg*) *vi siehe* **Acht**[2]; **~hundert** *num* eight hundred; **~los** *adj* careless; **~mal** *adv* eight times; **~sam** *adj* attentive

Achtung ['axtuŋ] *f* attention; (*Ehrfurcht*) respect ♦ *excl* look out!; (MIL) attention!; **alle ~!** good for you/him *etc*

achtzehn *num* eighteen

achtzig *num* eighty

ächzen ['ɛçtsən] *vi* to groan

Acker ['akər] (-s, ") *m* field; **a~n** *vt, vi* to plough; (*umg*) to slog away

ADAC [aːdeːʔaːtseː] *abk* (= *Allgemeiner Deutscher Automobil-Club*) ≈ AA, RAC

Adapter [a'daptər] (-s, -) *m* adapter

addieren [a'diːrən] *vt* to add (up); **Addition** [aditsi'oːn] *f* addition

Adel ['aːdəl] (-s) *m* nobility; **a~ig** *adj* noble;

a~n vt to raise to the peerage
Ader ['a:dər] (-, -n) f vein
Adjektiv ['atjekti:f] (-s, -e) nt adjective
Adler ['a:dlər] (-s, -) m eagle
adlig adj noble
Adopt- zW: **a~ieren** [adɔp'ti:rən] vt to adopt; **~ion** [adɔptsi'o:n] f adoption; **~iveltern** pl adoptive parents; **~ivkind** nt adopted child
Adressbuch ▲ nt directory; (privat) address book
Adress- zW: **~e** [a'drɛsə] f address; **a~ieren** [adrɛ'si:rən] vt: **a~ieren (an** +akk) to address (to)
Adria ['a:dria] (-) f Adriatic
Advent [at'vɛnt] (-(e)s, -e) m Advent; **~skalender** m Advent calendar; **~skranz** m Advent wreath
Adverb [at'vɛrp] nt adverb
Aerobic [ae'ro:bik] nt aerobics sg
Affäre [a'fɛ:rə] f affair
Affe ['afə] (-n, -n) m monkey
Affekt [a'fɛkt] (-(e)s, -e) m: **im ~ handeln** to act in the heat of the moment; **a~iert** [afɛk'ti:rt] adj affected
Affen- zW: **a~artig** adj like a monkey; **mit a~artiger Geschwindigkeit** like a flash; **~hitze** (umg) f incredible heat
affig ['afɪç] adj affected
Afrika ['a:frika] (-s) nt Africa, **~ner(in)** [-'ka:nər(ɪn)] (-s, -) m(f) African; **a~nisch** adj African
AG [a:'ge:] abk (= Aktiengesellschaft) ≈ plc (BRIT); ≈ Inc. (US)
Agent [a'gɛnt] m agent; **~ur** f agency
Aggregat [agre'ga:t] (-(e)s, -e) nt aggregate; (TECH) unit
Aggress- zW: **~ion** [agrɛsi'o:n] f aggression; **a~iv** [agrɛ'si:f] adj aggressive; **~ivität** [agrɛsivi'tɛ:t] f aggressiveness
Agrarpolitik [a'gra:r-] f agricultural policy
Ägypten [e'gʏptən] (-s) nt Egypt; **ägyptisch** adj Egyptian
aha [a'ha:] excl aha
ähneln ['ɛ:nəln] vi +dat to be like, to resemble ♦ vr to be alike od similar
ahnen ['a:nən] vt to suspect; (Tod, Gefahr) to

have a presentiment of
ähnlich ['ɛ:nlɪç] adj (+dat) similar (to); **Ä~keit** f similarity
Ahnung ['a:nʊŋ] f idea, suspicion; presentiment; **a~slos** adj unsuspecting
Ahorn ['a:hɔrn] (-s, -e) m maple
Ähre ['ɛ:rə] f ear
Aids [e:dz] nt AIDS sg
Airbag ['ɛ:əbɛk] (-s, -s) m airbag
Akademie [akade'mi:] f academy; **Aka'demiker(in)** (-s, -) m(f) university graduate; **akademisch** adj academic
akklimatisieren [aklimati'zi:rən] vr to become acclimatized
Akkord [a'kɔrt] (-(e)s, -e) m (MUS) chord; **im ~ arbeiten** to do piecework
Akkordeon [a'kɔrdeɔn] (-s, -s) nt accordion
Akku ['aku] (-s, -s) m rechargeable battery
Akkusativ ['akuzati:f] (-s, -e) m accusative
Akne ['aknə] f acne
Akrobat(in) [akro'ba:t(ɪn)] (-en, -en) m(f) acrobat
Akt [akt] (-(e)s, -e) m act; (KUNST) nude
Akte ['aktə] f file
Akten- zW: **~koffer** m attaché case; **a~kundig** adj on the files; **~schrank** m filing cabinet; **~tasche** f briefcase
Aktie ['aktsiə] f share
Aktien- zW: **~gesellschaft** f public limited company; **~index** (-(es), -e od -indices) m share index; **~kurs** m share price
Aktion [aktsi'o:n] f campaign; (Polizeiaktion, Suchaktion) action
Aktionär [aktsio'nɛ:r] (-s, -e) m shareholder
aktiv [ak'ti:f] adj active; (MIL) regular; **~ieren** [-'vi:rən] vt to activate; **A~ität** f activity
Aktualität [aktuali'tɛ:t] f topicality; (einer Mode) up-to-dateness
aktuell [aktu'ɛl] adj topical; up-to-date
Akupunktur [akupʊŋk'tu:ər] f acupuncture
Akustik [a'kʊstɪk] f acoustics pl
akut [a'ku:t] adj acute
Akzent [ak'tsɛnt] m accent; (Betonung) stress
akzeptabel [aktsɛp'ta:bl] adj acceptable
akzeptieren [aktsɛp'ti:rən] vt to accept
Alarm [a'larm] (-(e)s, -e) m alarm; **a~bereit** adj standing by; **~bereitschaft** f stand-by;

a~ieren [-'mi:rən] *vt* to alarm
Albanien [al'ba:niən] **(-s)** *nt* Albania
albanisch *adj* Albanian
albern ['albərn] *adj* silly
Albtraum ▲ ['alptraom] *m* nightmare
Album ['albom] **(-s, Alben)** *nt* album
Alge ['algə] *f* algae
Algebra ['algebra] **(-)** *f* algebra
Algerier(in) [al'ge:riːr(ɪn)] **(-s, -)** *m(f)* Algerian
algerisch *adj* Algerian
alias ['a:lias] *adv* alias
Alibi ['a:libi] **(-s, -s)** *nt* alibi
Alimente [ali'mɛntə] *pl* alimony *sg*
Alkohol ['alkohɔl] **(-s, -e)** *m* alcohol; **a~frei** *adj* non-alcoholic; **~iker(in)** [alko'ho:likər(ɪn)] **(-s, -)** *m(f)* alcoholic; **a~isch** *adj* alcoholic; **~verbot** *nt* ban on alcohol
All [al] **(-s)** *nt* universe
all'abendlich *adj* every evening
'allbekannt *adj* universally known

SCHLÜSSELWORT

alle(r, s) ['alə(r,s)] *adj* **1** *(sämtliche)* all; **wir alle** all of us; **alle Kinder waren da** all the children were there; **alle Kinder mögen ...** all children like ...; **alle beide** both of us/them; **sie kamen alle** they all came; **alles Gute** all the best; **alles in allem** all in all
2 *(mit Zeit- oder Maßangaben)* every; **alle vier Jahre** every four years; **alle fünf Meter** every five metres
♦ *pron* everything; **alles was er sagt** everything he says, all that he says
♦ *adj (zu Ende, aufgebraucht)* finished; **die Milch ist alle** the milk's all gone, there's no milk left; **etw alle machen** to finish sth up

Allee [a'le:] *f* avenue
allein [a'laɪn] *adv* alone; *(ohne Hilfe)* on one's own, by oneself ♦ *konj* but, only; **nicht ~** *(nicht nur)* not only; **~ stehend** single; **A~erziehende(r)** *f(m)* single parent; **A~gang** *m*: **im A~gang** on one's own
allemal [alə'ma:l] *adv (jedes Mal)* always; *(ohne weiteres)* with no bother; *siehe* **Mal**

allenfalls [alən'fals] *adv* at all events; *(höchstens)* at most
aller- ['alər] *zW*: **~beste(r, s)** *adj* very best; **~dings** *adv (zwar)* admittedly; *(gewiss)* certainly
Allergie [aler'gi:] *f* allergy; **al'lergisch** *adj* allergic
aller- *zW*: **~hand** *(umg)* *adj inv* all sorts of; **das ist doch ~hand!** that's a bit much; **~hand!** *(lobend)* good show!; **A~'heiligen** *nt* All Saints' Day; **~höchstens** *adv* at the very most; **~lei** *adj inv* all sorts of; **~letzte(r, s)** *adj* very last; **A~seelen** **(-s)** *nt* All Souls' Day; **~seits** *adv* on all sides; **prost ~seits!** cheers everyone!

Allerheiligen

> *ⓘ* **Allerheiligen** *(All Saints' Day)* is celebrated on November 1st and is a public holiday in some parts of Germany and in Austria. **Allerseelen** *(All Souls' Day)* is celebrated on November 2nd in the Roman Catholic Church. It is customary to visit cemeteries and place lighted candles on the graves of relatives and friends.

Allerwelts- in *zW (Durchschnitts-)* common; *(nichts sagend)* commonplace
alles *pron* everything; **~ in allem** all in all; **~ Gute!** all the best!
Alleskleber **(-s, -)** *m* multi-purpose glue
allgemein ['algəmaɪn] *adj* general; **im A~en** in general; **~ gültig** generally accepted; **A~wissen** *nt* general knowledge
Alliierte(r) [ali'i:rtə(r)] *m(f)* ally
all- *zW*: **~jährlich** *adj* annual; **~mächtig** *adj* almighty; **~mählich** *adj* gradual; **A~tag** *m* everyday life; **~täglich** *adj, adv* daily; *(gewöhnlich)* commonplace; **~tags** *adv* on weekdays; **~'wissend** *adj* omniscient; **~zu** *adv* all too; **~ oft** all too often; **~ viel** too much
Allzweck- ['altsvɛk-] in *zW* multi-purpose
Alm [alm] **(-, -en)** *f* alpine pasture
Almosen ['almo:zən] **(-s, -)** *nt* alms *pl*
Alpen ['alpən] *pl* Alps; **~vorland** *nt* foothills *pl* of the Alps

Alphabet [alfaˈbeːt] (-(e)s, -e) *nt* alphabet;
a~isch *adj* alphabetical
Alptraum [ˈalptraʊm] = **Albtraum**

SCHLÜSSELWORT

als [als] *konj* **1** (*zeitlich*) when; (*gleichzeitig*)
as; **damals, als ...** (in the days) when ...;
gerade, als ... just as ...
2 (*in der Eigenschaft*) than; **als Antwort** as
an answer; **als Kind** as a child
3 (*bei Vergleichen*) than; **ich kam später als
er** I came later than he (did) *od* later than
him; **lieber ... als ...** rather ... than ...;
nichts als Ärger nothing but trouble
4 : als ob/wenn as if

also [ˈalzo:] *konj* so; (*folglich*) therefore; **~ gut**
od **schön!** okay then; **~, so was!** well
really!; **na ~!** there you are then!
Alsterwasser [ˈalstər-] *nt* shandy (*BRIT*),
beer and lemonade
Alt [alt] (-s, -e) *m* (*MUS*) alto
alt *adj* old; **alles beim A~en lassen** to leave
everything as it was
Altar [alˈtaːr] (-(e)s, -äre) *m* altar
Alt- *zW:* **~bau** *m* old building; **a~bekannt**
adj long-known; **~bier** *nt* top-fermented
German dark beer; **~eisen** *nt* scrap iron
Alten(wohn)heim *nt* old people's home
Alter [ˈaltər] (-s, -) *nt* age; (*hohes*) old age;
im ~ von at the age of; **a~n** *vi* to grow
old, to age
Alternativ- [alternaˈtiːf-] *in zW* alternative;
~e *f* alternative
Alters- *zW:* **~grenze** *f* age limit; **~heim** *nt*
old people's home; **~rente** *f* old age
pension; **a~schwach** *adj* (*Mensch*) frail;
~versorgung *f* old age pension
Altertum [ˈaltərtuːm] *nt* antiquity
alt- *zW:* **A~glas** *nt* glass for recycling;
A~glascontainer *m* bottle bank; **~klug**
adj precocious; **~modisch** *adj* old-
fashioned; **A~papier** *nt* waste paper;
A~stadt *f* old town
Alufolie [ˈaːlufoːlɪə] *f* aluminium foil
Aluminium [aluˈmiːnɪʊm] (-s) *nt* aluminium,
aluminum (*US*)

Alzheimerkrankheit [ˈaltshaɪmərˈkraŋkhaɪt]
f Alzheimer's (disease)
am [am] = **an dem**; **~ Schlafen**; (*umg*)
sleeping; **~ 15. März** on March 15th; **~
besten/schönsten** best/most beautiful
Amateur [amaˈtøːr] *m* amateur
Amboss ▲ [ˈambɔs] (-es, -e) *m* anvil
ambulant [ambuˈlant] *adj* outpatient;
Ambulanz *f* outpatients *sg*
Ameise [ˈaːmaɪzə] *f* ant
Ameisenhaufen *m* ant hill
Amerika [aˈmeːrika] (-s) *nt* America;
~ner(in) [-ˈkaːnər(ɪn)] (-s, -) *m(f)* American;
a~nisch [-ˈkaːnɪʃ] *adj* American
Amnestie [amnɛsˈtiː] *f* amnesty
Ampel [ˈampəl] (-, -n) *f* traffic lights *pl*
amputieren [ampuˈtiːrən] *vt* to amputate
Amsel [ˈamzəl] (-, -n) *f* blackbird
Amt [amt] (-(e)s, ⁀er) *nt* office; (*Pflicht*) duty;
(*TEL*) exchange; **a~ieren** [amˈtiːrən] *vi* to
hold office; **a~lich** *adj* official
Amts- *zW:* **~richter** *m* district judge;
~stunden *pl* office hours; **~zeichen** *nt*
dialling tone; **~zeit** *f* period of office
amüsant [amyˈzant] *adj* amusing
amüsieren [amyˈziːrən] *vt* to amuse ♦ *vr* to
enjoy o.s.
Amüsierviertel *nt* nightclub district

SCHLÜSSELWORT

an [an] *präp +dat* **1** (*räumlich: wo?*) at; (*auf,
bei*) on; (*nahe bei*) near; **an diesem Ort** at
this place; **an der Wand** on the wall; **zu
nahe an etw** too near to sth; **unten am
Fluss** down by the river; **Köln liegt am
Rhein** Cologne is on the Rhine
2 (*zeitlich: wann?*) on; **an diesem Tag** on
this day; **an Ostern** at Easter
3 : arm an Fett low in fat; **an etw sterben**
to die of sth; **an (und für) sich** actually
♦ *präp +akk* **1** (*räumlich: wohin?*) to; **er ging
ans Fenster** he went (over) to the
window; **etw an die Wand hängen/
schreiben** to hang/write sth on the wall
2 (*zeitlich: woran?*): **an etw denken** to think
of sth
3 (*gerichtet an*) to; **ein Gruß/eine Frage**

Spelling Reform: ▲ *new spelling* △ *old spelling (to be phased out)*

an dich greetings/a question to you
♦ *adv* **1** (*ungefähr*) about; **an die hundert** about a hundred
2 (*auf Fahrplänen*): **Frankfurt an 18.30** arriving Frankfurt 18.30
3 (*ab*): **von dort/heute an** from there/today onwards
4 (*angeschaltet, angezogen*) on; **das Licht ist an** the light is on; **ohne etwas an** with nothing on; *siehe auch* **am**

analog [ana'lo:k] *adj* analogous; **A~ie** [-'gi:] *f* analogy
Analphabet(in) [an|alfa'be:t(ɪn)] (**-en, -en**) *m(f)* illiterate (person)
Analyse [ana'ly:zə] *f* analysis
analysieren [analy'zi:rən] *vt* to analyse
Ananas ['ananas] (**-, -** *od* **-se**) *f* pineapple
Anarchie [anar'çi:] *f* anarchy
Anatomie [anato'mi:] *f* anatomy
anbahnen ['anba:nən] *vt, vr* to open up
Anbau ['anbau] *m* (AGR) cultivation; (*Gebäude*) extension; **a~en** *vt* (AGR) to cultivate; (*Gebäudeteil*) to build on
anbehalten ['anbəhaltən] (*unreg*) *vt* to keep on
anbei [an'bai] *adv* enclosed
anbeißen ['anbaisən] (*unreg*) *vt* to bite into
♦ *vi* to bite; (*fig*) to swallow the bait; **zum A~** (*umg*) good enough to eat
anbelangen ['anbəlaŋən] *vt* to concern; **was mich anbelangt** as far as I am concerned
anbeten ['anbe:tən] *vt* to worship
Anbetracht ['anbətraxt] *m*: **in ~** +*gen* in view of
anbieten ['anbi:tən] (*unreg*) *vt* to offer ♦ *vr* to volunteer
anbinden ['anbɪndən] (*unreg*) *vt* to tie up; **kurz angebunden** (*fig*) curt
Anblick ['anblɪk] *m* sight; **a~en** *vt* to look at
anbraten ['anbra:tən] *vt* to brown
anbrechen ['anbrɛçən] (*unreg*) *vt* to start; (*Vorräte*) to break into ♦ *vi* to start; (*Tag*) to break; (*Nacht*) to fall
anbrennen ['anbrɛnən] (*unreg*) *vi* to catch fire; (KOCH) to burn

anbringen ['anbrɪŋən] (*unreg*) *vt* to bring; (*Ware*) to sell; (*festmachen*) to fasten
Anbruch ['anbrʊx] *m* beginning; **~ des Tages/der Nacht** dawn/nightfall
anbrüllen ['anbrʏlən] *vt* to roar at
Andacht ['andaxt] (**-, -en**) *f* devotion; (*Gottesdienst*) prayers *pl*; **andächtig** *adj* ['andɛçtɪç] devout
andauern ['andauərn] *vi* to last, to go on; **~d** *adj* continual
Anden ['andən] *pl* Andes
Andenken ['andɛŋkən] (**-s, -**) *nt* memory; souvenir
andere(r, s) ['andərə(r, z)] *adj* other; (*verschieden*) different; **ein ~s Mal** another time; **kein ~r** nobody else; **von etw ~m sprechen** to talk about something else; **~rseits** *adv* on the other hand
andermal *adv*: **ein ~** some other time
ändern ['ɛndərn] *vt* to alter, to change ♦ *vr* to change
andernfalls ['andərnfals] *adv* otherwise
anders ['andərs] *adv*: **~ (als)** differently (from); **wer ~?** who else?; **jd/irgendwo ~** sb/somewhere else; **~ aussehen/klingen** to look/sound different; **~artig** *adj* different; **~herum** *adv* the other way round; **~wo** *adv* somewhere else; **~woher** *adv* from somewhere else
anderthalb ['andərt'halp] *adj* one and a half
Änderung ['ɛndərʊŋ] *f* alteration, change
Änderungsschneiderei *f* tailor (*who does alterations*)
anderweitig ['andər'vaitɪç] *adj* other ♦ *adv* otherwise; (*anderswo*) elsewhere
andeuten ['andɔytən] *vt* to indicate; (*Wink geben*) to hint at; **Andeutung** *f* indication; hint
Andrang ['andraŋ] *m* crush
andrehen ['andre:ən] *vt* to turn *od* switch on; **jdm etw ~** (*umg*) to unload sth onto sb
androhen ['andro:ən] *vt*: **jdm etw ~** to threaten sb with sth
aneignen ['an|aignən] *vt*: **sich** *dat* **etw ~** to acquire sth; (*widerrechtlich*) to appropriate sth

Rechtschreibreform: ▲ *neue Schreibung* △ *alte Schreibung (auslaufend)*

aneinander [an|ai'nandər] *adv* at/on/to *etc* one another *od* each other; **~ geraten** to clash

Anekdote [anɛk'do:tə] *f* anecdote

anekeln ['an|e:kəln] *vt* to disgust

anerkannt ['an|ɛrkant] *adj* recognized, acknowledged

anerkennen ['an|ɛrkɛnən] (*unreg*) *vt* to recognize, to acknowledge; (*würdigen*) to appreciate; **~d** *adj* appreciative

Anerkennung *f* recognition, acknowledgement; appreciation

anfachen ['anfaxən] *vt* to fan into flame; (*fig*) to kindle

anfahren ['anfa:rən] (*unreg*) *vt* to deliver; (*fahren gegen*) to hit; (*Hafen*) to put into; (*fig*) to bawl out ♦ *vi* to drive up; (*losfahren*) to drive off

Anfahrt ['anfa:rt] *f* (*~sweg*, *~szeit*) journey

Anfall ['anfal] *m* (*MED*) attack; **a~en** (*unreg*) *vt* to attack; (*fig*) to overcome ♦ *vi* (*Arbeit*) to come up; (*Produkt*) to be obtained

anfällig ['anfɛlıç] *adj* delicate; **~ für etw** prone to sth

Anfang ['anfaŋ] (**-(e)s, -fänge**) *m* beginning, start; **von ~ an** right from the beginning; **zu ~** at the beginning; **~ Mai** at the beginning of May; **a~en** (*unreg*) *vt, vi* to begin, to start; (*machen*) to do

Anfänger(in) ['anfɛŋər(ın)] (**-s, -**) *m(f)* beginner

anfänglich ['anfɛŋlıç] *adj* initial

anfangs *adv* at first; **A~buchstabe** *m* initial *od* first letter; **A~gehalt** *nt* starting salary

anfassen ['anfasən] *vt* to handle; (*berühren*) to touch ♦ *vi* to lend a hand ♦ *vr* to feel

anfechten ['anfɛçtən] (*unreg*) *vt* to dispute

anfertigen ['anfɛrtıgən] *vt* to make

anfeuern ['anfɔyərn] *vt* (*fig*) to spur on

anflehen ['anfle:ən] *vt* to implore

anfliegen ['anfli:gən] (*unreg*) *vt* to fly to

Anflug ['anflu:k] *m* (*AVIAT*) approach; (*Spur*) trace

anfordern ['anfɔrdərn] *vt* to demand; (*COMM*) to requisition

Anforderung *f* (*+gen*) demand (for)

Anfrage ['anfra:gə] *f* inquiry; **a~n** *vi* to inquire

anfreunden ['anfrɔyndən] *vr* to make friends

anfügen ['anfy:gən] *vt* to add; (*beifügen*) to enclose

anfühlen ['anfy:lən] *vt, vr* to feel

anführen ['anfy:rən] *vt* to lead; (*zitieren*) to quote; (*umg: betrügen*) to lead up the garden path

Anführer *m* leader

Anführungszeichen *pl* quotation marks, inverted commas

Angabe ['anga:bə] *f* statement; (*TECH*) specification; (*umg: Prahlerei*) boasting; (*SPORT*) service

angeben ['ange:bən] (*unreg*) *vt* to give; (*anzeigen*) to inform on; (*bestimmen*) to set ♦ *vi* (*umg*) to boast; (*SPORT*) to serve

Angeber (**-s, -**) (*umg*) *m* show-off; **Angebe'rei** (*umg*) *f* showing off

angeblich ['ange:plıç] *adj* alleged

angeboren ['angəbo:rən] *adj* inborn, innate

Angebot ['angəbo:t] *nt* offer; **~ (an +***dat*) (*COMM*) supply (of)

angebracht ['angəbraxt] *adj* appropriate, in order

angegriffen ['angəgrıfən] *adj* exhausted

angeheitert ['angəhaıtərt] *adj* tipsy

angehen ['ange:ən] (*unreg*) *vt* to concern; (*angreifen*) to attack; (*bitten*): **jdn ~ (um)** to approach sb (for) ♦ *vi* (*Feuer*) to light; (*umg: beginnen*) to begin; **~d** *adj* prospective

angehören ['angəhø:rən] *vi* (+ *dat*) to belong to; (*Partei*) to be a member of

Angehörige(r) *f(m)* relative

Angeklagte(r) ['angəkla:ktə(r)] *f(m)* accused

Angel ['aŋəl] (**-, -n**) *f* fishing rod; (*Türangel*) hinge

Angelegenheit ['angəle:gənhaıt] *f* affair, matter

Angel- *zW*: **~haken** *m* fish hook; **a~n** *vt* to catch ♦ *vi* to fish; **~n (-s)** *nt* angling, fishing; **~rute** *f* fishing rod; **~schein** *m* fishing permit

angemessen ['angəmɛsən] *adj* appropriate, suitable

angenehm ['angəne:m] *adj* pleasant; **~!** (*bei Vorstellung*) pleased to meet you

angeregt [angəre:kt] *adj* animated, lively

angesehen ['angəze:ən] *adj* respected

angesichts ['angəzɪçts] *präp +gen* in view of, considering

angespannt ['angəʃpant] *adj* (*Aufmerksamkeit*) close; (*Arbeit*) hard

Angestellte(r) ['angəʃtɛltə(r)] *f(m)* employee

angestrengt ['angəʃtrɛŋt] *adv* as hard as one can

angetan ['angəta:n] *adj*: **von jdm/etw ~ sein** to be impressed by sb/sth; **es jdm ~ haben** to appeal to sb

angetrunken ['angətrʊŋkən] *adj* tipsy

angewiesen ['angəvi:zən] *adj*: **auf jdn/etw ~ sein** to be dependent on sb/sth

angewöhnen ['angəvø:nən] *vt*: **jdm/sich etw ~** to get sb/become accustomed to sth

Angewohnheit ['angəvo:nhaɪt] *f* habit

angleichen ['anglaɪçən] (*unreg*) *vt, vr* to adjust

Angler ['anlər] (**-s, -**) *m* angler

angreifen ['angraɪfən] (*unreg*) *vt* to attack; (*beschädigen*) to damage

Angreifer (**-s, -**) *m* attacker

Angriff ['angrɪf] *m* attack; **etw in ~ nehmen** to make a start on sth

Angst (**-, ¨e**) *f* fear; **jdm ist a~** sb is afraid *od* scared; **~ haben (vor +***dat*) to be afraid *od* scared (of); **~ haben um jdn/etw** to be worried about sb/sth; **jdm ~ machen** to scare sb; **~hase** (*umg*) *m* chicken, scaredy-cat

ängst- ['ɛŋst] *zW*: **~igen** *vt* to frighten ♦ *vr*: **sich ~igen (vor +***dat od* **um)** to worry (o.s.) (about); **~lich** *adj* nervous; (*besorgt*) worried; **Ä~lichkeit** *f* nervousness

anhaben ['anha:bən] (*unreg*) *vt* to have on; **er kann mir nichts ~** he can't hurt me

anhalt- ['anhalt] *zW*: **~en** (*unreg*) *vt* to stop ♦ *vi* to stop; (*andauern*) to persist; **(jdm) etw ~en** to hold sth up (against sb); **jdn zur Arbeit/Höflichkeit ~en** to make sb work/be polite; **~end** *adj* persistent;

A~er(in) (**-s, -**) *m(f)* hitch-hiker; **per A~er fahren** to hitch-hike; **A~spunkt** *m* clue

anhand [an'hant] *präp +gen* with

Anhang ['anhaŋ] *m* appendix; (*Leute*) family; supporters *pl*

anhäng- ['anhɛŋ] *zW*: **~en** (*unreg*) *vt* to hang up; (*Wagen*) to couple up; (*Zusatz*) to add (on); **A~er** (**-s, -**) *m* supporter; (*AUT*) trailer; (*am Koffer*) tag; (*Schmuck*) pendant; **A~erschaft** *f* supporters *pl*; **~lich** *adj* devoted; **A~lichkeit** *f* devotion; **A~sel** (**-s, -**) *nt* appendage

Anhäufung ['anhɔyfʊŋ] *f* accumulation

anheben ['anhe:bən] (*unreg*) *vt* to lift up; (*Preise*) to raise

anheizen ['anhaɪtsən] *vt* (*Stimmung*) to lift; (*Moral*) to boost

Anhieb ['anhi:b] *m*: **auf ~** at the very first go; (*kurz entschlossen*) on the spur of the moment

Anhöhe ['anhø:ə] *f* hill

anhören ['anhø:rən] *vt* to listen to; (*anmerken*) to hear ♦ *vr* to sound

animieren [ani'mi:rən] *vt* to encourage, to urge on

Anis [a'ni:s] (**-es, -e**) *m* aniseed

Ank. *abk* (= *Ankunft*) arr.

Ankauf ['ankaʊf] *m* (*von Wertpapieren, Devisen, Waren*) purchase; **a~en** *vt* to purchase, to buy

Anker ['aŋkər] (**-s, -**) *m* anchor; **vor ~ gehen** to drop anchor

Anklage ['ankla:gə] *f* accusation; (*JUR*) charge; **~bank** *f* dock; **a~n** *vt* to accuse; **jdn (eines Verbrechens) a~n** (*JUR*) to charge sb (with a crime)

Ankläger ['ankle:gər] *m* accuser

Anklang ['anklaŋ] *m*: **bei jdm ~ finden** to meet with sb's approval

Ankleidekabine *f* changing cubicle

ankleiden ['anklaɪdən] *vt, vr* to dress

anklicken ['anklɪkən] *vt* (*COMPUT*) to click on

anklopfen ['anklɔpfən] *vt* to knock

anknüpfen ['anknʏpfən] *vt* to fasten *od* tie on; (*fig*) to start ♦ *vi* (*anschließen*): **~ an** *+akk* to refer to

ankommen ['ankɔmən] (*unreg*) *vi* to arrive;

(*näher kommen*) to approach; (*Anklang finden*): **bei jdm (gut) ~** to go down well with sb; **es kommt darauf an** it depends; (*wichtig sein*) that (is what) matters; **es darauf ~ lassen** to let things take their course; **gegen jdn/etw ~** to cope with sb/ sth; **bei jdm schlecht ~** to go down badly with sb

ankreuzen ['ankrɔytsən] *vt* to mark with a cross; (*hervorheben*) to highlight

ankündigen ['ankʏndɪgən] *vt* to announce; **Ankündigung** *f* announcement

Ankunft ['ankʊnft] (-, **-künfte**) *f* arrival; **~szeit** *f* time of arrival

ankurbeln ['ankʊrbəln] *vt* (*fig*) to boost

Anlage ['anlaːgə] *f* disposition; (*Begabung*) talent; (*Park*) gardens *pl*; (*Beilage*) enclosure; (*TECH*) plant; (*FIN*) investment; (*Entwurf*) layout

Anlass ▲ ['anlas] (**-es, -lässe**) *m*: **~ (zu)** cause (for); (*Ereignis*) occasion; **aus ~** +*gen* on the occasion of; **~ zu etw geben** to give rise to sth; **etw zum ~ nehmen** to take the opportunity of sth

anlassen (*unreg*) *vt* to leave on; (*Motor*) to start ♦ *vr* (*umg*) to start off

Anlasser (**-s, -**) *m* (*AUT*) starter

anlässlich ▲ ['anlɛslɪç] *präp* +*gen* on the occasion of

Anlauf ['anlaʊf] *m* run-up; **a~en** (*unreg*) *vi* to begin; (*neuer Film*) to show; (*SPORT*) to run up; (*Fenster*) to mist up; (*Metall*) to tarnish ♦ *vt* to call at; **rot a~en** to blush; **angelaufen kommen** to come running up

anlegen ['anleːgən] *vt* to put; (*anziehen*) to put on; (*gestalten*) to lay out; (*Geld*) to invest ♦ *vi* to dock; **etw an etw** *akk* **~** to put sth against *od* on sth; **ein Gewehr ~ (auf** +*akk*) to aim a weapon (at); **es auf etw** *akk* **~** to be out for sth/to do sth; **sich mit jdm ~** (*umg*) to quarrel with sb

Anlegestelle *f* landing place

anlehnen ['anleːnən] *vt* to lean; (*Tür*) to leave ajar; **(sich) an etw** *akk* **~** to lean on/ against sth

Anleihe ['anlaɪə] *f* (*FIN*) loan

anleiten ['anlaɪtən] *vt* to instruct;

Anleitung *f* instructions *pl*

anliegen ['anliːgən] (*unreg*) *vi* (*Kleidung*) to cling; **A~ (-s, -)** *nt* matter; (*Wunsch*) wish; **~d** *adj* adjacent; (*beigefügt*) enclosed

Anlieger (**-s, -**) *m* resident; **„~ frei"** "residents only"

anmachen ['anmaxən] *vt* to attach; (*ELEK*) to put on; (*Zigarette*) to light; (*Salat*) to dress

anmaßen ['anmaːsən] *vt*: **sich** *dat* **etw ~** (*Recht*) to lay claim to sth; **~d** *adj* arrogant

Anmaßung *f* presumption

anmelden ['anmɛldən] *vt* to announce ♦ *vr* (*sich ankündigen*) to make an appointment; (*polizeilich, für Kurs etc*) to register

Anmeldung *f* announcement; appointment; registration

anmerken ['anmɛrkən] *vt* to observe; (*anstreichen*) to mark; **sich** *dat* **nichts ~ lassen** to not give anything away

Anmerkung *f* note

anmieten ['anmiːtən] *vt* to rent; (*auch Auto*) to hire

Anmut ['anmuːt] (-) *f* grace; **a~en** *vt* to give a feeling; **a~ig** *adj* charming

annähen ['annɛːən] *vt* to sew on

annähern ['annɛːərn] *vr* to get closer; **~d** *adj* approximate

Annäherung *f* approach

Annäherungsversuch *m* advances *pl*

Annahme ['annaːmə] *f* acceptance; (*Vermutung*) assumption

annehm- ['anneːm] *zW*: **~bar** *adj* acceptable; **~en** (*unreg*) *vt* to accept; (*Namen*) to take; (*Kind*) to adopt; (*vermuten*) to suppose, to assume ♦ *vr* (+*gen*) to take care (of); **A~lichkeit** *f* comfort

Annonce [a'nõːsə] *f* advertisement

annoncieren [anõ'siːrən] *vt, vi* to advertise

annullieren [anʊ'liːrən] *vt* to annul

anonym [ano'nyːm] *adj* anonymous

Anorak ['anorak] (**-s, -s**) *m* anorak

anordnen ['anɔrdnən] *vt* to arrange; (*befehlen*) to order

Anordnung *f* arrangement; order

anorganisch ['anɔrgaːnɪʃ] *adj* inorganic

anpacken ['anpakən] *vt* to grasp; (*fig*) to tackle; **mit ~** to lend a hand

Spelling Reform: ▲ *new spelling* △ *old spelling (to be phased out)*

anpassen ['anpasən] vt: **(jdm)** ~ to fit (on sb); (*fig*) to adapt ♦ vr to adapt

anpassungsfähig adj adaptable

Anpfiff ['anpfɪf] m (*SPORT*) (starting) whistle; kick-off; (*umg*) rocket

anprallen ['anpralən] vi: ~ **(gegen** od **an** +*akk*) to collide (with)

anprangern ['anpraŋərn] vt to denounce

anpreisen ['anpraizən] (*unreg*) vt to extol

Anprobe ['anpro:bə] f trying on

anprobieren ['anprobi:rən] vt to try on

anrechnen ['anrɛçnən] vt to charge; (*fig*) to count; **jdm etw hoch** ~ to think highly of sb for sth

Anrecht ['anrɛçt] nt: ~ **(auf** +*akk*) right (to)

Anrede ['anre:də] f form of address; **a~n** vt to address; (*belästigen*) to accost

anregen ['anre:gən] vt to stimulate; **angeregte Unterhaltung** lively discussion; ~**d** adj stimulating

Anregung f stimulation; (*Vorschlag*) suggestion

anreichern ['anraiçərn] vt to enrich

Anreise ['anraizə] f journey; **a~n** vi to arrive

Anreiz ['anraits] m incentive

Anrichte ['anrɪçtə] f sideboard; **a~n** vt to serve up; **Unheil a~n** to make mischief

anrüchig ['anrʏçɪç] adj dubious

anrücken ['anrʏkən] vi to approach; (*MIL*) to advance

Anruf ['anru:f] m call; ~**beantworter** [-bə-'antvɔrtər] **(-s, -)** m answering machine; **a~en** (*unreg*) vt to call out to; (*bitten*) to call on; (*TEL*) to ring up, to phone, to call

ans [ans] = **an das**

Ansage ['anza:gə] f announcement; **a~n** vt to announce ♦ vr to say one will come; ~**r(in)** **(-s, -)** m(f) announcer

ansammeln ['anzaməln] vt (*Reichtümer*) to amass ♦ vr (*Menschen*) to gather, to assemble; (*Wasser*) to collect; **Ansammlung** f collection; (*Leute*) crowd

ansässig ['anzɛsɪç] adj resident

Ansatz ['anzats] m start; (*Haaransatz*) hairline; (*Halsansatz*) base; (*Verlängerungsstück*) extension; (*Veranschlagung*) estimate; ~**punkt** m starting point

anschaffen ['anʃafən] vt to buy, to purchase; **Anschaffung** f purchase

anschalten ['anʃaltən] vt to switch on

anschau- ['anʃau] zW: ~**en** vt to look at; ~**lich** adj illustrative; **A~ung** f (*Meinung*) view; **aus eigener A~ung** from one's own experience

Anschein ['anʃain] m appearance; **allem ~ nach** to all appearances; **den ~ haben** to seem, to appear; **a~end** adj apparent

anschieben ['anʃi:bən] vt to push

Anschlag ['anʃla:k] m notice; (*Attentat*) attack; (*COMM*) estimate; (*auf Klavier*) touch; (*Schreibmaschine*) character; **a~en** ['anʃla:gən] (*unreg*) vt to put up; (*beschädigen*) to chip; (*Akkord*) to strike; (*Kosten*) to estimate ♦ vi to hit; (*wirken*) to have an effect; (*Glocke*) to ring; **an etw** akk **a~en** to hit against sth

anschließen ['anʃli:sən] (*unreg*) vt to connect up; (*Sender*) to link up ♦ vi: **an etw** akk ~ to adjoin sth; (*zeitlich*) to follow sth ♦ vr: **sich jdm/etw** ~ to join sb/sth; (*beipflichten*) to agree with sb/sth; **sich an etw** akk ~ to adjoin sth; ~**d** adj adjacent; (*zeitlich*) subsequent ♦ adv afterwards

Anschluss ▲ ['anʃlʊs] m (*ELEK, EISENB*) connection; (*von Wasser etc*) supply; **im ~ an** +*akk* following; ~ **finden** to make friends; ~**flug** m connecting flight

anschmiegsam ['anʃmi:kza:m] adj affectionate

anschnallen ['anʃnalən] vt to buckle on ♦ vr to fasten one's seat belt

anschneiden ['anʃnaidən] (*unreg*) vt to cut into; (*Thema*) to introduce

anschreiben ['anʃraibən] (*unreg*) vt to write (up); (*COMM*) to charge up; (*benachrichtigen*) to write to

anschreien ['anʃraiən] (*unreg*) vt to shout at

Anschrift ['anʃrɪft] f address

Anschuldigung ['anʃʊldigʊŋ] f accusation

anschwellen ['anʃvɛlən] (*unreg*) vi to swell (up)

anschwindeln ['anʃvɪndəln] vt to lie to

ansehen ['anze:ən] (*unreg*) vt to look at;

jdm etw ~ to see sth (from sb's face); **jdn/etw als etw ~** to look on sb/sth as sth; **~ für** to consider; **A~ (-s)** nt respect; (*Ruf*) reputation

ansehnlich ['anze:nlɪç] adj fine-looking; (*beträchtlich*) considerable

ansetzen ['anzetsən] vt (*festlegen*) to fix; (*entwickeln*) to develop; (*Fett*) to put on; (*Blätter*) to grow; (*zubereiten*) to prepare ♦ vi (*anfangen*) to start, to begin; (*Entwicklung*) to set in; (*dick werden*) to put on weight ♦ vr (*Rost etc*) to start to develop; **~ an** +akk (*anfügen*) to fix on to; (*anlegen, an Mund etc*) to put to

Ansicht ['anzɪçt] f (*Anblick*) sight; (*Meinung*) view, opinion; **zur ~** on approval; **meiner ~ nach** in my opinion; **~skarte** f picture postcard; **~ssache** f matter of opinion

ansonsten [an'zɔnstən] adv otherwise

anspannen ['anʃpanən] vt to harness; (*Muskel*) to strain; **Anspannung** f strain

anspielen ['anʃpiːlən] vi (*SPORT*) to start play; **auf etw** akk **~** to refer od allude to sth

Anspielung f: **~ (auf** +akk) reference (to), allusion (to)

Anspitzer ['anʃpɪtsər] **(-s, -)** m pencil sharpener

Ansporn ['anʃpɔrn] **(-(e)s)** m incentive

Ansprache ['anʃpraːxə] f address

ansprechen ['anʃpreçən] (*unreg*) vt to speak to; (*bitten, gefallen*) to appeal to ♦ vi: **(auf etw** akk**) ~** to react (to sth); **jdn auf etw** akk **(hin) ~** to ask sb about sth; **~d** adj attractive

anspringen ['anʃprɪŋən] (*unreg*) vi (*AUT*) to start ♦ vt to jump at

Anspruch ['anʃprʊx] m (*Recht*): **~ (auf** +akk) claim (to); **hohe Ansprüche stellen/ haben** to demand/expect a lot; **jdn/etw in ~ nehmen** to occupy sb/take up sth; **a~slos** adj undemanding; **a~svoll** adj demanding

anstacheln ['anʃtaxəln] vt to spur on

Anstalt ['anʃtalt] **(-, -en)** f institution; **~en machen, etw zu tun** to prepare to do sth

Anstand ['anʃtant] m decency

anständig ['anʃtendɪç] adj decent; (*umg*) proper; (*groß*) considerable

anstandslos adv without any ado

anstarren ['anʃtarən] vt to stare at

anstatt [an'ʃtat] präp +gen instead of ♦ konj: **~ etw zu tun** instead of doing sth

Ansteck- ['anʃtek] zW: **a~en** vt to pin on; (*MED*) to infect; (*Pfeife*) to light; (*Haus*) to set fire to ♦ vr: **ich habe mich bei ihm angesteckt** I caught it from him ♦ vi (*fig*) to be infectious; **a~end** adj infectious; **~ung** f infection

anstehen ['anʃteːən] (*unreg*) vi to queue (up) (*BRIT*), to line up (*US*)

ansteigen ['anʃtaigən] vt (*Straße*) to climb; (*Gelände, Temperatur, Preise*) to rise

anstelle, an Stelle [an'ʃtelə] präp +gen in place of; **~n** [an-] vt (*einschalten*) to turn on; (*Arbeit geben*) to employ; (*machen*) to do ♦ vr to queue (up) (*BRIT*), to line up (*US*); (*umg*) to act

Anstellung f employment; (*Posten*) post, position

Anstieg ['anʃtiːk] **(-(e)s, -e)** m (+gen) climb; (*fig: von Preisen etc*) increase (in)

anstiften ['anʃtɪftən] vt (*Unglück*) to cause; **jdn zu etw ~** to put sb up to sth

anstimmen ['anʃtɪmən] vt (*Lied*) to strike up with; (*Geschrei*) to set up

Anstoß ['anʃtoːs] m impetus; (*Ärgernis*) offence; (*SPORT*) kick-off; **der erste ~** the initiative; **~ nehmen an** +dat to take offence at; **a~en** (*unreg*) vt to push; (*mit Fuß*) to kick ♦ vi to knock, to bump; (*mit der Zunge*) to lisp; (*mit Gläsern*): **a~en (auf** +akk) to drink (to), to drink a toast (to)

anstößig ['anʃtøːsɪç] adj offensive, indecent

anstreichen ['anʃtraiçən] (*unreg*) vt to paint

anstrengen ['anʃtrɛŋən] vt to strain; (*JUR*) to bring ♦ vr to make an effort; **~d** adj tiring

Anstrengung f effort

Anstrich ['anʃtrɪç] m coat of paint

Ansturm ['anʃtʊrm] m rush; (*MIL*) attack

Antarktis [ant'arktɪs] **(-)** f Antarctic

antasten ['antastən] vt to touch; (*Recht*) to infringe upon; (*Ehre*) to question

Anteil ['antail] **(-s, -e)** m share; (*Mitgefühl*)

sympathy; **~ nehmen (an** +*dat*) to share (in); (*sich interessieren*) to take an interest (in); **~nahme** (-) *f* sympathy

Antenne [an'tɛnə] *f* aerial

Anti- ['anti] *in zW* anti; **~alko'holiker** *m* teetotaller; **a~autori'tär** *adj* anti-authoritarian; **~babypille** *f* contraceptive pill; **~biotikum** [anti'bioːtikʊm] **(-s, -ka)** *nt* antibiotic

antik [an'tiːk] *adj* antique; **A~e** *f* (*Zeitalter*) ancient world

Antiquariat [antikvari'aːt] **(-(e)s, -e)** *nt* secondhand bookshop

Antiquitäten [antikvi'tɛːtən] *pl* antiques; **~händler** *m* antique dealer

Antrag ['antraːk] **(-(e)s, -träge)** *m* proposal; (*PARL*) motion; (*Gesuch*) application; **~steller(in) (-s, -)** *m(f)* claimant; (*für Kredit*) applicant

antreffen ['antrɛfən] (*unreg*) *vt* to meet

antreiben ['antraibən] (*unreg*) *vt* to drive on; (*Motor*) to drive

antreten ['antreːtən] (*unreg*) *vt* (*Amt*) to take up; (*Erbschaft*) to come into; (*Beweis*) to offer; (*Reise*) to start, to begin ♦ *vi* (*MIL*) to fall in; (*SPORT*) to line up; **gegen jdn ~** to play/fight (against) sth

Antrieb ['antriːp] *m* (*auch fig*) drive; **aus eigenem ~** of one's own accord

antrinken ['antrɪŋkən] (*unreg*) *vt* (*Flasche, Glas*) to start to drink from; **sich** *dat* **Mut/ einen Rausch ~** to give o.s. Dutch courage/get drunk; **angetrunken sein** to be tipsy

Antritt ['antrɪt] *m* beginning, commencement; (*eines Amts*) taking up

antun ['antuːn] (*unreg*) *vt*: **jdm etw ~** to do sth to sb; **sich** *dat* **Zwang ~** to force o.s.; **sich** *dat* **etwas ~** to (try to) take one's own life

Antwort ['antvɔrt] **(-, -en)** *f* answer, reply; **a~en** *vi* to answer, to reply

anvertrauen ['anfɛrtrauən] *vt*: **jdm etw ~** to entrust sb with sth; **sich jdm ~** to confide in sb

anwachsen ['anvaksən] (*unreg*) *vi* to grow; (*Pflanze*) to take root

Anwalt ['anvalt] **(-(e)s, -wälte)** *m* solicitor; lawyer; (*fig*) champion

Anwältin ['anvɛltɪn] *f siehe* **Anwalt**

Anwärter ['anvɛrtər] *m* candidate

anweisen ['anvaizən] (*unreg*) *vt* to instruct; (*zuteilen*) to assign

Anweisung *f* instruction; (*COMM*) remittance; (*Postanweisung, Zahlungsanweisung*) money order

anwend- ['anvɛnd] *zW*: **~bar** [anvɛnt-] *adj* practicable, applicable; **~en** (*unreg*) *vt* to use, to employ; (*Gesetz, Regel*) to apply; **A~ung** *f* use; application

anwesend ['anveːzənt] *adj* present; **die A~en** those present

Anwesenheit *f* presence

anwidern ['anviːdərn] *vt* to disgust

Anwohner(in) ['anvoːnər(ɪn)] **(-s, -)** *m(f)* neighbour

Anzahl ['antsaːl] *f*: **~ (an** +*dat*) number (of); **a~en** *vt* to pay on account; **~ung** *f* deposit, payment on account

Anzeichen ['antsaiçən] *nt* sign, indication

Anzeige ['antsaigə] *f* (*Zeitungsanzeige*) announcement; (*Werbung*) advertisement; (*bei Polizei*) report; **~ erstatten gegen jdn** to report sb (to the police); **a~n** *vt* (*zu erkennen geben*) to show; (*bekannt geben*) to announce; (*bei Polizei*) to report

anziehen ['antsiːən] (*unreg*) *vt* to attract; (*Kleidung*) to put on; (*Mensch*) to dress; (*Seil*) to pull tight; (*Schraube*) to tighten; (*Knie*) to draw up ♦ *vr* to get dressed; **~d** *adj* attractive

Anziehung *f* (*Reiz*) attraction; **~skraft** *f* power of attraction; (*PHYS*) force of gravitation

Anzug ['antsuːk] *m* suit; (*Herankommen*): **im ~ sein** to be approaching

anzüglich ['antsyːklɪç] *adj* personal; (*anstößig*) offensive; **A~keit** *f* offensiveness; (*Bemerkung*) personal remark

anzünden ['antsʏndən] *vt* to light

anzweifeln ['antsvaifəln] *vt* to doubt

apathisch [a'paːtɪʃ] *adj* apathetic

Apfel ['apfəl] **(-s, ⸚)** *m* apple; **~saft** *m* apple juice; **~sine** [-'ziːnə] *f* orange; **~wein** *m*

cider
Apostel [a'pɔstəl] **(-s, -)** m apostle
Apotheke [apo'te:kə] f chemist's (shop),
drugstore (US); **a~npflichtig** [-pflɪçtɪç] adj
available only at a chemist's shop (BRIT) or
pharmacy; **~r(in)** **(-s, -)** m(f) chemist,
druggist (US)

┌─────────────┐
│ **Apotheke** │
└─────────────┘

i *The* **Apotheke** *is a pharmacy selling*
medicines available only on prescription
and toiletries. The pharmacist is qualified to
give advice on medicines and treatments.

Apparat [apa'ra:t] **(-(e)s, -e)** m piece of
apparatus; camera; telephone; (RADIO, TV)
set; **am ~!** speaking!; **~ur** [-'tu:r] f
apparatus
Appartement [apart(ə)'mã:] **(-s, -s)** nt flat
appellieren [apɛ'li:rən] vi: **~ (an** +akk) to
appeal (to)
Appetit [ape'ti:t] **(-(e)s, -e)** m appetite;
guten ~! enjoy your meal; **a~lich** adj
appetizing; **~losigkeit** f lack of appetite
Applaus [ap'laʊs] **(-es, -e)** m applause
Aprikose [apri'ko:zə] f apricot
April [a'prɪl] **(-(s), -e)** m April
Aquarell [akva'rɛl] **(-s, -e)** nt watercolour
Äquator [ɛ'kva:tɔr] **(-s)** m equator
Arab- ['arab] zW: **~er(in)** **(-s, -)** m(f) Arab;
~ien [a'ra:biən] **(-s)** nt Arabia; **a~isch**
[a'ra:bɪʃ] adj Arabian
Arbeit ['arbaɪt] **(-, -en)** f work no art; (Stelle)
job; (Erzeugnis) piece of work;
(wissenschaftliche) dissertation; (Klassenarbeit)
test; **das war eine ~** that was a hard job;
a~en vi to work ♦ vt to work, to make;
~er(in) **(-s, -)** m(f) worker; (ungelernt)
labourer; **~erschaft** f workers pl, labour
force; **~geber** **(-s, -)** m employer;
~nehmer **(-s, -)** m employee
Arbeits- in zW labour; **a~am** adj
industrious; **~amt** nt employment
exchange; **~erlaubnis** f work permit;
a~fähig adj fit for work, able-bodied;
~gang m operation; **~kräfte** pl
(Mitarbeiter) workforce; **a~los** adj

unemployed, out-of-work; **~lose(r)** f(m)
unemployed person; **~losigkeit** f
unemployment; **~markt** m job market;
~platz m job; place of work; **a~scheu** adj
workshy; **~tag** m work(ing) day;
a~unfähig adj unfit for work; **~zeit** f
working hours pl; **~zimmer** nt study
Archäologe [arçeo'lo:gə] **(-n, -n)** m
archaeologist
Architekt(in) [arçi'tɛkt(ɪn)] **(-en, -en)** m(f)
architect; **~ur** [-'tu:r] f architecture
Archiv [ar'çi:f] **(-s, -e)** nt archive
arg [ark] adj bad, awful ♦ adv awfully, very
Argentinien [argɛn'ti:niən] **(-s)** nt
Argentina, the Argentine
argentinisch adj Argentinian
Ärger ['ɛrgər] **(-s)** m (Wut) anger;
(Unannehmlichkeit) trouble; **ä~lich** adj
(zornig) angry; (lästig) annoying,
aggravating; **ä~n** vt to annoy ♦ vr to get
annoyed
arg- zW: **~listig** adj cunning, insidious;
~los adj guileless, innocent
Argument [argu'mɛnt] nt argument
argwöhnisch adj suspicious
Arie ['a:riə] f aria
Aristokrat [aristo'kra:t] **(-en, -en)** m
aristocrat; **~ie** [-'ti:] f aristocracy
Arktis ['arktɪs] **(-)** f Arctic
Arm [arm] **(-(e)s, -e)** m arm; (Flussarm)
branch
arm adj poor
Armatur [arma'tu:r] f (ELEK) armature;
~enbrett nt instrument panel; (AUT)
dashboard
Armband nt bracelet; **~uhr** f (wrist) watch
Arme(r) f(m) poor man (woman); **die ~n**
the poor
Armee [ar'me:] f army
Ärmel ['ɛrməl] **(-s, -)** m sleeve; **etw aus**
dem ~ schütteln (fig) to produce sth just
like that; **~kanal** m English Channel
ärmlich ['ɛrmlɪç] adj poor
armselig adj wretched, miserable
Armut ['armu:t] **(-)** f poverty
Aroma [a'ro:ma] **(-s, Aromen)** nt aroma;
~therapie f aromatherapy; **a~tisch**

[aro'ma:tɪʃ] *adj* aromatic

arrangieren [arã'ʒi:rən] *vt* to arrange ♦ *vr* to come to an arrangement

Arrest [a'rɛst] (**-(e)s, -e**) *m* detention

arrogant [aro'gant] *adj* arrogant

Arsch [arʃ] (**-es, ꞈe**) (*umg!*) *m* arse (*BRIT!*), ass (*US!*)

Art [a:rt] (**-, -en**) *f* (*Weise*) way; (*Sorte*) kind, sort; (*BIOL*) species; **eine ~ (von) Frucht** a kind of fruit; **Häuser aller ~** houses of all kinds; **es ist nicht seine ~, das zu tun** it's not like him to do that; **ich mache das auf meine ~** I do that my (own) way

Arterie [ar'te:riə] *f* artery; **~nverkalkung** *f* arteriosclerosis

artig ['a:rtɪç] *adj* good, well-behaved

Artikel [ar'ti:kəl] (**-s, -**) *m* article

Artillerie [artɪlə'ri:] *f* artillery

Artischocke [artɪ'ʃɔkə] *f* artichoke

Artist(in) [ar'tɪst(ɪn)] (**-en, -en**) *m(f)* (circus/variety) artiste *od* performer

Arznei [a:rts'nai] *f* medicine; **~mittel** *nt* medicine, medicament

Arzt [a:rtst] (**-es, ꞈe**) *m* doctor; **~helferin** *f* (doctor's) receptionist

Ärztin ['ɛ:rtstɪn] *f* doctor

ärztlich ['ɛ:rtstlɪç] *adj* medical

As △ [as] (**-ses, -se**) *nt* = **Ass**

Asche ['aʃə] *f* (**-, -n**) ash, cinder

Aschen- *zW:* **~bahn** *f* cinder track; **~becher** *m* ashtray

Aschermittwoch *m* Ash Wednesday

Äser ['ɛ:zər] *pl von* **Aas**

Asiat(in) [azi'a:t(ɪn)] (**-en, -en**) *m(f)* Asian; **asiatisch** [-'a:tɪʃ] *adj* Asian

Asien ['a:ziən] (**-s**) *nt* Asia

asozial ['azotsia:l] *adj* antisocial; (*Familien*) asocial

Aspekt [as'pɛkt] (**-(e)s, -e**) *m* aspect

Asphalt [as'falt] (**-(e)s, -e**) *m* asphalt

Ass ▲ [as] (**-es, -e**) *nt* ace

aß *etc* [a:s] *vb siehe* **essen**

Assistent(in) [asɪs'tɛnt(ɪn)] *m(f)* assistant

Assoziation [asotsiatsi'o:n] *f* association

Ast [ast] (**-(e)s, ꞈe**) *m* bough, branch

ästhetisch [es'te:tɪʃ] *adj* aesthetic

Asthma ['astma] (**-s**) *nt* asthma; **~tiker(in)**

(**-s, -**) *m(f)* asthmatic

Astro- [astro] *zW:* **~'loge** (**-n, -n**) *m* astrologer; **~lo'gie** *f* astrology; **~'naut** (**-en, -en**) *m* astronaut; **~'nom** (**-en, -en**) *m* astronomer; **~no'mie** *f* astronomy

Asyl [a'zy:l] (**-s, -e**) *nt* asylum; (*Heim*) home; (*Obdachlosenasyl*) shelter; **~ant(in)** [azy'lant(ɪn)] (**-en, -en**) *m(f)* asylum-seeker; **~bewerber(in)** *m(f)* asylum-seeker

Atelier [atəli'e:] (**-s, -s**) *nt* studio

Atem ['a:təm] (**-s**) *m* breath; **den ~ anhalten** to hold one's breath; **außer ~** out of breath; **a~beraubend** *adj* breathtaking; **a~los** *adj* breathless; **~not** *f* difficulty in breathing; **~pause** *f* breather; **~zug** *m* breath

Atheismus [ate'ɪsmʊs] *m* atheism

Atheist *m* atheist; **a~isch** *adj* atheistic

Athen [a'te:n] (**-s**) *nt* Athens

Äthiopien [eti'o:piən] (**-s**) *nt* Ethiopia

Athlet [at'le:t] (**-en, -en**) *m* athlete

Atlantik [at'lantɪk] (**-s**) *m* Atlantic (Ocean)

Atlas ['atlas] (**- *od* -ses, -se *od* Atlanten**) *m* atlas

atmen ['a:tmən] *vt, vi* to breathe

Atmosphäre [atmo'sfɛ:rə] *f* atmosphere; **atmosphärisch** *adj* atmospheric

Atmung ['a:tmʊŋ] *f* respiration

Atom [a'to:m] (**-s, -e**) *nt* atom; **a~ar** *adj* atomic; **~bombe** *f* atom bomb; **~energie** *f* atomic *od* nuclear energy; **~kern** *m* atomic nucleus; **~kraftwerk** *nt* nuclear power station; **~krieg** *m* nuclear *od* atomic war; **~müll** *m* atomic waste; **~strom** *m* (electricity generated by) nuclear power; **~versuch** *m* atomic test; **~waffen** *pl* atomic weapons; **a~waffenfrei** *adj* nuclear-free; **~zeitalter** *nt* atomic age

Attentat [atɛn'ta:t] (**-(e)s, -e**) *nt:* **~ (auf** +*akk*) (attempted) assassination (of)

Attentäter [atɛn'tɛ:tər] *m* (would-be) assassin

Attest [a'tɛst] (**-(e)s, -e**) *nt* certificate

Attraktion [atraktsi'o:n] *f* (*Tourismus, Zirkus*) attraction

attraktiv [atrak'ti:f] *adj* attractive

Attrappe [a'trapə] *f* dummy

Rechtschreibreform: ▲ *neue Schreibung* △ *alte Schreibung (auslaufend)*

Attribut [atri'buːt] (**-(e)s, -e**) *nt* (*GRAM*) attribute

ätzen ['ɛtsən] *vi* to be caustic; **~d** *adj* (*Säure*) corrosive; (*fig: Spott*) cutting

au [au] *excl* ouch!; **~ ja!** oh yes!

Aubergine [obɛr'ʒiːnə] *f* aubergine, eggplant

SCHLÜSSELWORT

auch [aux] *adv* **1** (*ebenfalls*) also, too, as well; **das ist auch schön** that's nice too *od* as well; **er kommt - ich auch** he's coming - so am I, me too; **auch nicht** not ... either; **ich auch nicht** nor I, me neither; **oder auch** or; **auch das noch!** not that as well!

2 (*selbst, sogar*) even; **auch wenn das Wetter schlecht ist** even if the weather is bad; **ohne auch nur zu fragen** without even asking

3 (*wirklich*) really; **du siehst müde aus - bin ich auch** you look tired - (so) I am; **so sieht es auch aus** it looks like it too

4 (*auch immer*): **wer auch** whoever; **was auch** whatever; **wie dem auch sei** be that as it may; **wie sehr er sich auch bemühte** however much he tried

---

SCHLÜSSELWORT

auf [auf] *präp +dat* (*wo?*) on; **auf dem Tisch** on the table; **auf der Reise** on the way; **auf der Post/dem Fest** at the post office/party; **auf der Straße** on the road; **auf dem Land/der ganzen Welt** in the country/the whole world

♦ *präp +akk* **1** (*wohin?*) on(to); **auf den Tisch** on(to) the table; **auf die Post gehen** go to the post office; **auf das Land** into the country; **etw auf einen Zettel schreiben** to write sth on a piece of paper

2: **auf Deutsch** in German; **auf Lebenszeit** for my/his lifetime; **bis auf ihn** except for him; **auf einmal** at once; **auf seinen Vorschlag (hin)** at his suggestion

♦ *adv* **1** (*offen*) open; **auf sein** (*umg*) (*Tür, Geschäft*) to be open; **das Fenster ist auf** the window is open

2 (*hinauf*) up; **auf und ab** up and down; **auf und davon** up and away; **auf!** (*los!*) come on!

3 (*aufgestanden*) up; **auf sein** to be up; **ist er schon auf?** is he up yet?

♦ *konj*: **auf dass** (so) that

---

aufatmen ['aufʔaːtmən] *vi* to heave a sigh of relief

aufbahren ['aufbaːrən] *vt* to lay out

Aufbau ['aufbau] *m* (*Bauen*) building, construction; (*Struktur*) structure; (*aufgebautes Teil*) superstructure; **a~en** *vt* to erect, to build (up); (*Existenz*) to make; (*gestalten*) to construct; **a~en (auf +dat)** (*gründen*) to found *od* base (on)

aufbauschen ['aufbauʃən] *vt* to puff out; (*fig*) to exaggerate

aufbekommen ['aufbəkɔmən] (*unreg*) *vt* (*öffnen*) to get open; (*Hausaufgaben*) to be given

aufbessern ['aufbɛsərn] *vt* (*Gehalt*) to increase

aufbewahren ['aufbəvaːrən] *vt* to keep; (*Gepäck*) to put in the left-luggage office (*BRIT*) *od* baggage check (*US*)

Aufbewahrung *f* (safe)keeping; (*Gepäckaufbewahrung*) left-luggage office (*BRIT*), baggage check (*US*)

aufbieten ['aufbiːtən] (*unreg*) *vt* (*Kraft*) to summon (up); (*Armee, Polizei*) to mobilize

aufblasen ['aufblaːzən] (*unreg*) *vt* to blow up, to inflate ♦ *vr* (*umg*) to become bigheaded

aufbleiben ['aufblaibən] (*unreg*) *vi* (*Laden*) to remain open; (*Person*) to stay up

aufblenden ['aufblɛndən] *vt* (*Scheinwerfer*) to switch on full beam ♦ *vi* (*Fahrer*) to have the lights on full beam; (*AUT: Scheinwerfer*) to be on full beam

aufblicken ['aufblikən] *vi* to look up; **~ zu** to look up at; (*fig*) to look up to

aufblühen ['aufblyːən] *vi* to blossom, to flourish

aufbrauchen ['aufbrauxən] *vt* to use up

aufbrausen ['aufbrauzən] *vi* (*fig*) to flare up; **~d** *adj* hot-tempered

---

Spelling Reform: ▲ *new spelling* △ *old spelling (to be phased out)*

aufbrechen ['aʊfbrɛçən] (*unreg*) *vt* to break *od* prise (*BRIT*) open ♦ *vi* to burst open; (*gehen*) to start, to set off

aufbringen ['aʊfbrɪŋən] (*unreg*) *vt* (*öffnen*) to open; (*in Mode*) to bring into fashion; (*beschaffen*) to procure; (*FIN*) to raise; (*ärgern*) to irritate; **Verständnis für etw ~** to be able to understand sth

Aufbruch ['aʊfbrʊx] *m* departure

aufbrühen ['aʊfbryːən] *vt* (*Tee*) to make

aufbürden ['aʊfbʏrdən] *vt*: **jdm etw ~** to burden sb with sth

aufdecken ['aʊfdɛkən] *vt* to uncover

aufdrängen ['aʊfdrɛŋən] *vt*: **jdm etw ~** to force sth on sb ♦ *vr* (*Mensch*): **sich jdm ~** to intrude on sb

aufdrehen ['aʊfdreːən] *vt* (*Wasserhahn etc*) to turn on; (*Ventil*) to open up

aufdringlich ['aʊfdrɪŋlɪç] *adj* pushy

aufeinander [aʊfaɪ'nandər] *adv* on top of each other; (*schießen*) at each other; (*vertrauen*) each other; **~ folgen** to follow one another; **~ folgend** consecutive; **~ prallen** to hit one another

Aufenthalt ['aʊfɛnthalt] *m* stay; (*Verzögerung*) delay; (*EISENB: Halten*) stop; (*Ort*) haunt

Aufenthaltserlaubnis *f* residence permit

auferlegen ['aʊfɛrleːgən] *vt*: **(jdm) ~** impose (upon sb)

Auferstehung ['aʊfɛrʃteːʊŋ] *f* resurrection

aufessen ['aʊfɛsən] (*unreg*) *vt* to eat up

auffahr- ['aʊfaːr] *zW*: **~en** (*unreg*) *vi* (*herankommen*) to draw up; (*hochfahren*) to jump up; (*wütend werden*) to flare up; (*in den Himmel*) to ascend ♦ *vt* (*Kanonen, Geschütz*) to bring up; **~en auf** +*akk* (*Auto*) to run *od* crash into; **~end** *adj* hot-tempered; **A~t** *f* (*Hausauffahrt*) drive; (*Autobahnauffahrt*) slip road (*BRIT*), (freeway) entrance (*US*); **A~unfall** *m* pile-up

auffallen ['aʊffalən] (*unreg*) *vi* to be noticeable; **jdm ~** to strike sb

auffällig ['aʊffɛlɪç] *adj* conspicuous, striking

auffangen ['aʊffaŋən] (*unreg*) *vt* to catch; (*Funkspruch*) to intercept; (*Preise*) to peg

auffassen ['aʊffasən] *vt* to understand, to

comprehend; (*auslegen*) to see, to view

Auffassung *f* (*Meinung*) opinion; (*Auslegung*) view, concept; (*auch*: **~sgabe**) grasp

auffindbar ['aʊffɪntbaːr] *adj* to be found

auffordern ['aʊffɔrdərn] *vt* (*befehlen*) to call upon, to order; (*bitten*) to ask

Aufforderung *f* (*Befehl*) order; (*Einladung*) invitation

auffrischen ['aʊffrɪʃən] *vt* to freshen up; (*Kenntnisse*) to brush up; (*Erinnerungen*) to reawaken ♦ *vi* (*Wind*) to freshen

aufführen ['aʊffyːrən] *vt* (*THEAT*) to perform; (*in einem Verzeichnis*) to list, to specify ♦ *vr* (*sich benehmen*) to behave

Aufführung *f* (*THEAT*) performance; (*Liste*) specification

Aufgabe ['aʊfgaːbə] *f* task; (*SCH*) exercise; (*Hausaufgabe*) homework; (*Verzicht*) giving up; (*von Gepäck*) registration; (*von Post*) posting; (*von Inserat*) insertion

Aufgang ['aʊfgaŋ] *m* ascent; (*Sonnenaufgang*) rise; (*Treppe*) staircase

aufgeben ['aʊfgeːbən] (*unreg*) *vt* (*verzichten*) to give up; (*Paket*) to send, to post; (*Gepäck*) to register; (*Bestellung*) to give; (*Inserat*) to insert; (*Rätsel, Problem*) to set ♦ *vi* to give up

Aufgebot ['aʊfgeboːt] *nt* supply; (*Eheaufgebot*) banns *pl*

aufgedunsen ['aʊfgedʊnzən] *adj* swollen, puffed up

aufgehen ['aʊfgeːən] (*unreg*) *vi* (*Sonne, Teig*) to rise; (*sich öffnen*) to open; (*klar werden*) to become clear; (*MATH*) to come out exactly; **~ (in** +*dat*) (*sich widmen*) to be absorbed (in); **in Rauch / Flammen ~** to go up in smoke/flames

aufgelegt ['aʊfgeleːkt] *adj*: **gut / schlecht ~ sein** to be in a good/bad mood; **zu etw ~ sein** to be in the mood for sth

aufgeregt ['aʊfgəreːkt] *adj* excited

aufgeschlossen ['aʊfgəʃlɔsən] *adj* open, open-minded

aufgeweckt ['aʊfgəvɛkt] *adj* bright, intelligent

aufgießen ['aʊfgiːsən] (*unreg*) *vt* (*Wasser*) to

pour over; (*Tee*) to infuse

aufgreifen ['aʊfɡraɪfən] (*unreg*) *vt* (*Thema*) to take up; (*Verdächtige*) to pick up, to seize

aufgrund, auf Grund [aʊf'ɡrʊnt] *präp* +*gen* on the basis of; (*wegen*) because of

aufhaben ['aʊfha:bən] (*unreg*) *vt* to have on; (*Arbeit*) to have to do

aufhalsen ['aʊfhalzən] (*umg*) *vt*: **jdm etw ~** to saddle *od* lumber sb with sth

aufhalten ['aʊfhaltən] (*unreg*) *vt* (*Person*) to detain; (*Entwicklung*) to check; (*Tür, Hand*) to hold open; (*Augen*) to keep open ♦ *vr* (*wohnen*) to live; (*bleiben*) to stay; **sich mit etw ~** to waste time over sth

aufhängen ['aʊfhɛŋən] (*unreg*) *vt* (*Wäsche*) to hang up; (*Menschen*) to hang ♦ *vr* to hang o.s.

Aufhänger (*-s, -*) *m* (*am Mantel*) loop; (*fig*) peg

aufheben ['aʊfhe:bən] (*unreg*) *vt* (*hochheben*) to raise, to lift; (*Sitzung*) to wind up; (*Urteil*) to annul; (*Gesetz*) to repeal, to abolish; (*aufbewahren*) to keep ♦ *vr* to cancel itself out; **bei jdm gut aufgehoben sein** to be well looked after at sb's; **viel A~(s) machen (von)** to make a fuss (about)

aufheitern ['aʊfhaɪtərn] *vt, vr* (*Himmel, Miene*) to brighten; (*Mensch*) to cheer up

aufhellen ['aʊfhɛlən] *vt, vr* to clear up; (*Farbe, Haare*) to lighten

aufhetzen ['aʊfhɛtsən] *vt* to stir up

aufholen ['aʊfho:lən] *vt* to make up ♦ *vi* to catch up

aufhorchen ['aʊfhɔrçən] *vi* to prick up one's ears

aufhören ['aʊfhø:rən] *vi* to stop; **~, etw zu tun** to stop doing sth

aufklappen ['aʊfklapən] *vt* to open

aufklären ['aʊfklɛ:rən] *vt* (*Geheimnis etc*) to clear up; (*Person*) to enlighten; (*sexuell*) to tell the facts of life to; (*MIL*) to reconnoitre ♦ *vr* to clear up

Aufklärung *f* (*von Geheimnis*) clearing up; (*Unterrichtung, Zeitalter*) enlightenment; (*sexuell*) sex education; (*MIL, AVIAT*) reconnaissance

aufkleben ['aʊfkle:bən] *vt* to stick on;

Aufkleber (*-s, -*) *m* sticker

aufknöpfen ['aʊfknœpfən] *vt* to unbutton

aufkommen ['aʊfkɔmən] (*unreg*) *vi* (*Wind*) to come up; (*Zweifel, Gefühl*) to arise; (*Mode*) to start; **für jdn/etw ~** to be liable *od* responsible for sb/sth

aufladen ['aʊfla:dən] (*unreg*) *vt* to load

Auflage ['aʊfla:ɡə] *f* edition; (*Zeitung*) circulation; (*Bedingung*) condition

auflassen ['aʊflasən] (*unreg*) *vt* (*offen*) to leave open; (*aufgesetzt*) to leave on

auflauern ['aʊflaʊərn] *vi*: **jdm ~** to lie in wait for sb

Auflauf ['aʊflaʊf] *m* (*KOCH*) pudding; (*Menschenauflauf*) crowd

aufleben ['aʊfle:bən] *vi* (*Mensch, Gespräch*) to liven up; (*Interesse*) to revive

auflegen ['aʊfle:ɡən] *vt* to put on; (*Telefon*) to hang up; (*TYP*) to print

auflehnen ['aʊfle:nən] *vt* to lean on ♦ *vr* to rebel

Auflehnung *f* rebellion

auflesen ['aʊfle:zən] (*unreg*) *vt* to pick up

aufleuchten ['aʊflɔɪçtən] *vi* to light up

auflisten ['aʊflɪstən] *vt* to list

auflockern ['aʊflɔkərn] *vt* to loosen; (*fig: Eintönigkeit etc*) to liven up

auflösen ['aʊflø:zən] *vt* to dissolve; (*Haare etc*) to loosen; (*Missverständnis*) to sort out ♦ *vr* to dissolve; to come undone; to be resolved; **(in Tränen) aufgelöst sein** to be in tears

Auflösung *f* dissolving; (*fig*) solution

aufmachen ['aʊfmaxən] *vt* to open; (*Kleidung*) to undo; (*zurechtmachen*) to do up ♦ *vr* to set out

Aufmachung *f* (*Kleidung*) outfit, get-up; (*Gestaltung*) format

aufmerksam ['aʊfmɛrkza:m] *adj* attentive; **jdn auf etw** *akk* **~ machen** to point sth out to sb; **A~keit** *f* attention, attentiveness

aufmuntern ['aʊfmʊntərn] *vt* (*ermutigen*) to encourage; (*erheitern*) to cheer up

Aufnahme ['aʊfna:mə] *f* reception; (*Beginn*) beginning; (*in Verein etc*) admission; (*in Liste etc*) inclusion; (*Notieren*) taking down; (*PHOT*) shot; (*auf Tonband etc*) recording;

Spelling Reform: ▲ *new spelling* △ *old spelling (to be phased out)*

a~fähig *adj* receptive; **~prüfung** *f* entrance test

aufnehmen ['aʊfneːmən] (*unreg*) *vt* to receive; (*hochheben*) to pick up; (*beginnen*) to take up; (*in Verein etc*) to admit; (*in Liste etc*) to include; (*fassen*) to hold; (*notieren*) to take down; (*fotografieren*) to photograph; (*auf Tonband, Platte*) to record; (*FIN: leihen*) to take out; **es mit jdm ~ können** to be able to compete with sb

aufopfern ['aʊf|ɔpfərn] *vt*, *vr* to sacrifice; **~d** *adj* selfless

aufpassen ['aʊfpasən] *vi* (*aufmerksam sein*) to pay attention; **auf jdn/etw ~** to look after *od* watch sb/sth; **aufgepasst!** look out!

Aufprall ['aʊfpral] (**-s**, **-e**) *m* impact; **a~en** *vi* to hit, to strike

Aufpreis ['aʊfprais] *m* extra charge

aufpumpen ['aʊfpʊmpən] *vt* to pump up

aufräumen ['aʊfrɔymən] *vt*, *vi* (*Dinge*) to clear away; (*Zimmer*) to tidy up

aufrecht ['aʊfrɛçt] *adj* (*auch fig*) upright; **~erhalten** (*unreg*) *vt* to maintain

aufreg- ['aʊfreːg] *zW*: **~en** *vt* to excite ♦ *vr* to get excited; **~end** *adj* exciting; **A~ung** *f* excitement

aufreibend ['aʊfraibənt] *adj* strenuous

aufreißen ['aʊfraisən] (*unreg*) *vt* (*Umschlag*) to tear open; (*Augen*) to open wide; (*Tür*) to throw open; (*Straße*) to take up

aufreizen ['aʊfraitsən] *vt* to incite, to stir up; **~d** *adj* exciting, stimulating

aufrichten ['aʊfrɪçtən] *vt* to put up, to erect; (*moralisch*) to console ♦ *vr* to rise; (*moralisch*): **sich ~ (an** +*dat*) to take heart (from)

aufrichtig ['aʊfrɪçtɪç] *adj* sincere, honest; **A~keit** *f* sincerity

aufrücken ['aʊfrʏkən] *vi* to move up; (*beruflich*) to be promoted

Aufruf ['aʊfruːf] *m* summons; (*zur Hilfe*) call; (*des Namens*) calling out; **a~en** (*unreg*) *vt* (*Namen*) to call out; (*auffordern*): **jdn a~en (zu)** to call upon sb (for)

Aufruhr ['aʊfruːr] (**-(e)s**, **-e**) *m* uprising, revolt

aufrührerisch ['aʊfryːrərɪʃ] *adj* rebellious

aufrunden ['aʊfrʊndən] *vt* (*Summe*) to round up

Aufrüstung ['aʊfrʏstʊŋ] *f* rearmament

aufrütteln ['aʊfrʏtəln] *vt* (*auch fig*) to shake up

aufs [aʊfs] = **auf das**

aufsagen ['aʊfzaːgən] *vt* (*Gedicht*) to recite

aufsässig ['aʊfzɛsɪç] *adj* rebellious

Aufsatz ['aʊfzats] *m* (*Geschriebenes*) essay; (*auf Schrank etc*) top

aufsaugen ['aʊfzaʊgən] (*unreg*) *vt* to soak up

aufschauen ['aʊfʃaʊən] *vi* to look up

aufscheuchen ['aʊfʃɔyçən] *vt* to scare *od* frighten away

aufschieben ['aʊfʃiːbən] (*unreg*) *vt* to push open; (*verzögern*) to put off, to postpone

Aufschlag ['aʊfʃlaːk] *m* (*Ärmelaufschlag*) cuff; (*Jackenaufschlag*) lapel; (*Hosenaufschlag*) turn-up; (*Aufprall*) impact; (*Preisaufschlag*) surcharge; (*Tennis*) service; **a~en** [-gən] (*unreg*) *vt* (*öffnen*) to open; (*verwunden*) to cut; (*hochschlagen*) to turn up; (*aufbauen: Zelt, Lager*) to pitch, to erect; (*Wohnsitz*) to take up ♦ *vi* (*aufprallen*) to hit; (*teurer werden*) to go up; (*Tennis*) to serve

aufschließen ['aʊfʃliːsən] (*unreg*) *vt* to unlock ♦ *vi* (*aufrücken*) to close up

aufschlussreich ▲ *adj* informative, illuminating

aufschnappen ['aʊfʃnapən] *vt* (*umg*) to pick up ♦ *vi* to fly open

aufschneiden ['aʊfʃnaidən] (*unreg*) *vt* (*Brot*) to cut up; (*MED*) to lance ♦ *vi* to brag

Aufschneider (**-s**, **-**) *m* boaster, braggart

Aufschnitt ['aʊfʃnɪt] *m* (slices of) cold meat

aufschrauben ['aʊfʃraʊbən] *vt* (*festschrauben*) to screw on; (*lösen*) to unscrew

aufschrecken ['aʊfʃrɛkən] *vt* to startle ♦ *vi* (*unreg*) to start up

aufschreiben ['aʊfʃraibən] (*unreg*) *vt* to write down

aufschreien ['aʊfʃraiən] (*unreg*) *vi* to cry out

Aufschrift ['aʊfʃrɪft] *f* (*Inschrift*) inscription; (*auf Etikett*) label

Rechtschreibreform: ▲ *neue Schreibung* △ *alte Schreibung (auslaufend)*

Aufschub ['aʊfʃuːp] (**-(e)s, -schübe**) *m* delay, postponement

Aufschwung ['aʊfʃvʊŋ] *m* (*Elan*) boost; (*wirtschaftlich*) upturn, boom; (*SPORT*) circle

aufsehen ['aʊfzeːən] (*unreg*) *vi* to look up; **~ zu** to look up at; (*fig*) to look up to; **A~ (-s)** *nt* sensation, stir; **~ erregend** sensational

Aufseher(in) (**-s, -**) *m(f)* guard; (*im Betrieb*) supervisor; (*Museumsaufseher*) attendant; (*Parkaufseher*) keeper

auf sein ▲ *siehe* **auf**

aufsetzen ['aʊfzɛtsən] *vt* to put on; (*Dokument*) to draw up ♦ *vr* to sit up(right) ♦ *vi* (*Flugzeug*) to touch down

Aufsicht ['aʊfzɪçt] *f* supervision; **die ~ haben** to be in charge

Aufsichtsrat *m* (supervisory) board

aufsitzen ['aʊfzɪtsən] (*unreg*) *vi* (*aufrecht hinsitzen*) to sit up; (*aufs Pferd, Motorrad*) to mount, to get on; (*Schiff*) to run aground; **jdm ~** (*umg*) to be taken in by sb

aufsparen ['aʊfʃpaːrən] *vt* to save (up)

aufsperren ['aʊfʃpɛrən] *vt* to unlock; (*Mund*) to open wide

aufspielen ['aʊfʃpiːlən] *vr* to show off

aufspießen ['aʊfʃpiːsən] *vt* to spear

aufspringen ['aʊfʃprɪŋən] (*unreg*) *vi* (*hochspringen*) to jump up; (*sich öffnen*) to spring open; (*Hände, Lippen*) to become chapped; **auf etw** *akk* **~** to jump onto sth

aufspüren ['aʊfʃpyːrən] *vt* to track down, to trace

aufstacheln ['aʊfʃtaxəln] *vt* to incite

Aufstand ['aʊfʃtant] *m* insurrection, rebellion; **aufständisch** ['aʊfʃtɛndɪʃ] *adj* rebellious, mutinous

aufstehen ['aʊfʃteːən] (*unreg*) *vi* to get up; (*Tür*) to be open

aufsteigen ['aʊfʃtaɪgən] (*unreg*) *vi* (*hochsteigen*) to climb; (*Rauch*) to rise; **auf etw** *akk* **~** to get onto sth

aufstellen ['aʊfʃtɛlən] *vt* (*aufrecht stellen*) to put up; (*aufreihen*) to line up; (*nominieren*) to nominate; (*formulieren: Programm etc*) to draw up; (*leisten: Rekord*) to set up

Aufstellung *f* (*SPORT*) line-up; (*Liste*) list

Aufstieg ['aʊfʃtiːk] (**-(e)s, -e**) *m* (*auf Berg*) ascent; (*Fortschritt*) rise; (*beruflich, SPORT*) promotion

aufstocken ['aʊfʃtɔkən] *vt* (*Kapital*) to increase

aufstoßen ['aʊfʃtoːsən] (*unreg*) *vt* to push open ♦ *vi* to belch

aufstützen ['aʊfʃtʏtsən] *vt* (*Körperteil*) to prop, to lean; (*Person*) to prop up ♦ *vr*: **sich auf etw** *akk* **~** to lean on sth

aufsuchen ['aʊfzuːxən] *vt* (*besuchen*) to visit; (*konsultieren*) to consult

Auftakt ['aʊftakt] *m* (*MUS*) upbeat; (*fig*) prelude

auftanken ['aʊftaŋkən] *vi* to get petrol (*BRIT*) *od* gas (*US*) ♦ *vt* to refuel

auftauchen ['aʊftaʊxən] *vi* to appear; (*aus Wasser etc*) to emerge; (*U-Boot*) to surface; (*Zweifel*) to arise

auftauen ['aʊftaʊən] *vt* to thaw ♦ *vi* to thaw; (*fig*) to relax

aufteilen ['aʊftaɪlən] *vt* to divide up; (*Raum*) to partition; **Aufteilung** *f* division; partition

Auftrag ['aʊftraːk] (**-(e)s, -träge**) *m* order; (*Anweisung*) commission; (*Aufgabe*) mission; **im ~ von** on behalf of; **a~en** [-gən] (*unreg*) *vt* (*Essen*) to serve; (*Farbe*) to put on; (*Kleidung*) to wear out; **jdm etw a~en** to tell sb sth; **dick a~en** (*fig*) to exaggerate; **~geber(-s, -)** *m* (*COMM*) purchaser, customer

auftreiben ['aʊftraɪbən] (*unreg*) *vt* (*umg: beschaffen*) to raise

auftreten ['aʊftreːtən] (*unreg*) *vt* to kick open ♦ *vi* to appear; (*mit Füßen*) to tread; (*sich verhalten*) to behave; **A~ (-s)** *nt* (*Vorkommen*) appearance; (*Benehmen*) behaviour

Auftrieb ['aʊftriːp] *m* (*PHYS*) buoyancy, lift; (*fig*) impetus

Auftritt ['aʊftrɪt] *m* (*des Schauspielers*) entrance; (*Szene: auch fig*) scene

aufwachen ['aʊfvaxən] *vi* to wake up

aufwachsen ['aʊfvaksən] (*unreg*) *vi* to grow up

Aufwand ['aʊfvant] (**-(e)s**) *m* expenditure; (*Kosten auch*) expense; (*Luxus*) show

Spelling Reform: ▲ *new spelling* △ *old spelling (to be phased out)*

aufwändig ▲ ['aʊfvɛndɪç] *adj* costly

aufwärmen ['aʊfvɛrmən] *vt* to warm up; (*alte Geschichten*) to rake up

aufwärts ['aʊfvɛrts] *adv* upwards; **A~entwicklung** *f* upward trend

Aufwasch ['aʊfvaʃ] *m* washing-up

aufwecken ['aʊfvɛkən] *vt* to wake up, to waken up

aufweisen ['aʊfvaɪzən] (*unreg*) *vt* to show

aufwenden ['aʊfvɛndən] (*unreg*) *vt* to expend; (*Geld*) to spend; (*Sorgfalt*) to devote

aufwendig *adj siehe* **aufwändig**

aufwerfen ['aʊfvɛrfən] (*unreg*) *vt* (*Fenster etc*) to throw open; (*Probleme*) to throw up, to raise

aufwerten ['aʊfvɛrtən] *vt* (*FIN*) to revalue; (*fig*) to raise in value

aufwickeln ['aʊfvɪkəln] *vt* (*aufrollen*) to roll up; (*umg: Haar*) to put in curlers

aufwiegen ['aʊfviːgən] (*unreg*) *vt* to make up for

Aufwind ['aʊfvɪnt] *m* up-current

aufwirbeln ['aʊfvɪrbəln] *vt* to whirl up; **Staub ~** (*fig*) to create a stir

aufwischen ['aʊfvɪʃən] *vt* to wipe up

aufzählen ['aʊftsɛːlən] *vt* to list

aufzeichnen ['aʊftsaɪçnən] *vt* to sketch; (*schriftlich*) to jot down; (*auf Band*) to record

Aufzeichnung *f* (*schriftlich*) note; (*Tonbandaufzeichnung*) recording; (*Filmaufzeichnung*) record

aufzeigen ['aʊftsaɪgən] *vt* to show, to demonstrate

aufziehen ['aʊftsiːən] (*unreg*) *vt* (*hochziehen*) to raise, to draw up; (*öffnen*) to pull open; (*Uhr*) to wind; (*umg: necken*) to tease; (*großziehen: Kinder*) to raise, to bring up; (*Tiere*) to rear

Aufzug ['aʊftsuːk] *m* (*Fahrstuhl*) lift, elevator; (*Aufmarsch*) procession, parade; (*Kleidung*) get-up; (*THEAT*) act

aufzwingen ['aʊftsvɪŋən] (*unreg*) *vt*: **jdm etw ~** to force sth upon sb

Augapfel ['aʊkʔapfəl] *m* eyeball; (*fig*) apple of one's eye

Auge ['aʊgə] (**-s, -n**) *nt* eye; (*Fettauge*) globule of fat; **unter vier ~n** in private

Augen- *zW*: **~blick** *m* moment; **im ~blick** at the moment; **a~blicklich** *adj* (*sofort*) instantaneous; (*gegenwärtig*) present; **~braue** *f* eyebrow; **~optiker(in)** *m(f)* optician; **~weide** *f* sight for sore eyes; **~zeuge** *m* eye witness

August [aʊˈgʊst] (**-(e)s** *od* **-, -e**) *m* August

Auktion [aʊktsiˈoːn] *f* auction

Aula ['aʊla] (**-, Aulen** *od* **-s**) *f* assembly hall

SCHLÜSSELWORT

aus [aʊs] *präp +dat* **1** (*räumlich*) out of; (*von ... her*) from; **er ist aus Berlin** he's from Berlin; **aus dem Fenster** out of the window

2 (*gemacht/hergestellt aus*) made of; **ein Herz aus Stein** a heart of stone

3 (*auf Ursache deutend*) out of; **aus Mitleid** out of sympathy; **aus Erfahrung** from experience; **aus Spaß** for fun

4: **aus ihr wird nie etwas** she'll never get anywhere

♦ *adv* **1** (*zu Ende*) finished, over; **aus sein** to be over; **aus und vorbei** over and done with

2 (*ausgeschaltet, ausgezogen*) out; (*Aufschrift an Geräten*) off; **aus sein** (*nicht brennen*) to be out; (*abgeschaltet sein: Radio, Herd*) to be off; **Licht aus!** lights out!

3 (*nicht zu Hause*): **aus sein** to be out

4 (*in Verbindung mit von*): **von Rom aus** from Rome; **vom Fenster aus** from the window; **von sich aus** (*selbstständig*) of one's own accord; **von ihm aus** as far as he's concerned

---

ausarbeiten ['aʊsʔarbaɪtən] *vt* to work out

ausarten ['aʊsʔartən] *vi* to degenerate

ausatmen ['aʊsʔaːtmən] *vi* to breathe out

ausbaden ['aʊsbaːdən] (*umg*) *vt*: **etw ~ müssen** to carry the can for sth

Ausbau ['aʊsbaʊ] *m* extension, expansion; removal; **a~en** *vt* to extend, to expand; (*herausnehmen*) to take out, to remove; **a~fähig** *adj* (*fig*) worth developing

ausbessern ['aʊsbɛsərn] *vt* to mend, to

repair

ausbeulen ['aʊsbɔylən] *vt* to beat out

Ausbeute ['aʊsbɔytə] *f* yield; (*Fische*) catch; **a~n** *vt* to exploit; (*MIN*) to work

ausbild- ['aʊsbɪld] *zW:* **~en** *vt* to educate; (*Lehrling, Soldat*) to instruct, to train; (*Fähigkeiten*) to develop; (*Geschmack*) to cultivate; **A~er** **(-s, -)** *m* instructor; **A~ung** *f* education; training, instruction; development; cultivation

ausbleiben ['aʊsblaɪbən] (*unreg*) *vi* (*Personen*) to stay away, not to come; (*Ereignisse*) to fail to happen, not to happen

Ausblick ['aʊsblɪk] *m* (*auch fig*) prospect, outlook, view

ausbrechen ['aʊsbrɛçən] (*unreg*) *vi* to break out ♦ *vt* to break off; **in Tränen/Gelächter ~** to burst into tears/out laughing

ausbreiten ['aʊsbraɪtən] *vt* to spread (out); (*Arme*) to stretch out ♦ *vr* to spread; **sich über ein Thema ~** to expand *od* enlarge on a topic

ausbrennen ['aʊsbrɛnən] (*unreg*) *vt* to scorch; (*Wunde*) to cauterize ♦ *vi* to burn out

Ausbruch ['aʊsbrʊx] *m* outbreak; (*von Vulkan*) eruption; (*Gefühlsausbruch*) outburst; (*von Gefangenen*) escape

ausbrüten ['aʊsbryːtən] *vt* (*auch fig*) to hatch

Ausdauer ['aʊsdaʊər] *f* perseverance, stamina; **a~nd** *adj* persevering

ausdehnen ['aʊsdeːnən] *vt, vr* (*räumlich*) to expand; (*zeitlich, auch Gummi*) to stretch; (*Nebel, fig: Macht*) to extend

ausdenken ['aʊsdɛŋkən] (*unreg*) *vt:* **sich** *dat* **etw ~** to think sth up

Ausdruck ['aʊsdrʊk] *m* expression, phrase; (*Kundgabe, Gesichtsausdruck*) expression; (*COMPUT*) print-out, hard copy; **a~en** *vt* (*COMPUT*) to print out

ausdrücken ['aʊsdrykən] *vt* (*auch vr:* *formulieren, zeigen*) to express; (*Zigarette*) to put out; (*Zitrone*) to squeeze

ausdrücklich ['aʊsdryklɪç] *adj* express, explicit

ausdrucks- *zW:* **~los** *adj* expressionless, blank; **~voll** *adj* expressive; **A~weise** *f*

mode of expression

auseinander [aʊsaɪˈnandər] *adv* (*getrennt*) apart; **~ schreiben** to write as separate words; **~ bringen** to separate; **~ fallen** to fall apart; **~ gehen** (*Menschen*) to separate; (*Meinungen*) to differ; (*Gegenstand*) to fall apart; **~ halten** to tell apart; **~ nehmen** to take to pieces, to dismantle; **~ setzen** (*erklären*) to set forth, to explain; **sich ~ setzen** (*sich verständigen*) to come to terms, to settle; (*sich befassen*) to concern o.s.; **A~setzung** *f* argument

ausfahren ['aʊsfaːrən] (*unreg*) *vt* (*spazieren fahren: im Auto*) to take for a drive; (*: im Kinderwagen*) to take for a walk; (*liefern*) to deliver

Ausfahrt *f* (*des Zuges etc*) leaving, departure; (*Autobahnausfahrt*) exit; (*Garagenausfahrt etc*) exit, way out; (*Spazierfahrt*) drive, excursion

Ausfall ['aʊsfal] *m* loss; (*Nichtstattfinden*) cancellation; (*MIL*) sortie; (*radioaktiv*) fall-out; **a~en** (*unreg*) *vi* (*Zähne, Haare*) to fall out *od* come out; (*nicht stattfinden*) to be cancelled; (*wegbleiben*) to be omitted; (*Person*) to drop out; (*Lohn*) to be stopped; (*nicht funktionieren*) to break down; (*Resultat haben*) to turn out; **~straße** *f* arterial road

ausfertigen ['aʊsfɛrtɪgən] *vt* (*förmlich: Urkunde, Pass*) to draw up; (*Rechnung*) to make out

Ausfertigung ['aʊsfɛrtɪgʊŋ] *f* drawing up; making out; (*Exemplar*) copy

ausfindig ['aʊsfɪndɪç] *adj:* **~ machen** to discover

ausfließen ['aʊsfliːsən] (*unreg*) *vi* (*her~*): **~ (aus)** to flow out (of); (*auslaufen: Öl etc*): **~ (aus)** to leak (out of)

Ausflucht ['aʊsflʊxt] **(-, -flüchte)** *f* excuse

Ausflug ['aʊsfluːk] *m* excursion, outing; **Ausflügler** ['aʊsflyːklər] **(-s, -)** *m* tripper

Ausflugslokal ['aʊsfluːkslokaːl] *nt* tourist café

Ausfluss ▲ ['aʊsflʊs] *m* outlet; (*MED*) discharge

ausfragen ['aʊsfraːgən] *vt* to interrogate, to question

ausfressen ['aʊsfrɛsən] (*unreg*) *vt* to eat up;

Spelling Reform: ▲ *new spelling* △ *old spelling (to be phased out)*

(*aushöhlen*) to corrode; (*umg: anstellen*) to be up to

Ausfuhr ['aʊsfuːr] (**-**, **-en**) *f* export, exportation ♦ *in zW* export

ausführ- ['aʊsfyːr] *zW*: **~en** *vt* (*verwirklichen*) to carry out; (*Person*) to take out; (*Hund*) to take for a walk; (*COMM*) to export; (*erklären*) to give details of; **~lich** *adj* detailed ♦ *adv* in detail; **A~lichkeit** *f* detail; **A~ung** *f* execution, performance; (*Durchführung*) completion; (*Herstellungsart*) version; (*Erklärung*) explanation

ausfüllen ['aʊsfʏlən] *vt* to fill up; (*Fragebogen etc*) to fill in; (*Beruf*) to be fulfilling for

Ausgabe ['aʊsgaːbə] *f* (*Geld*) expenditure, outlay; (*Aushändigung*) giving out; (*Gepäckausgabe*) left-luggage office; (*Buch*) edition; (*Nummer*) issue; (*COMPUT*) output

Ausgang ['aʊsgaŋ] *m* way out, exit; (*Ende*) end; (*~spunkt*) starting point; (*Ergebnis*) result; (*Ausgehtag*) free time, time off; **kein ~** no exit

Ausgangs- *zW*: **~punkt** *m* starting point; **~sperre** *f* curfew

ausgeben ['aʊsgeːbən] (*unreg*) *vt* (*Geld*) to spend; (*austeilen*) to issue, to distribute ♦ *vr*: **sich für etw/jdn ~** to pass o.s. off as sth/ sb

ausgebucht ['aʊsgəbuːxt] *adj* (*Vorstellung, Flug, Maschine*) fully booked

ausgedient ['aʊsgədiːnt] *adj* (*Soldat*) discharged; (*verbraucht*) no longer in use; **~ haben** to have done good service

ausgefallen ['aʊsgəfalən] *adj* (*ungewöhnlich*) exceptional

ausgeglichen ['aʊsgəglɪçən] *adj* (well-) balanced; **A~heit** *f* balance; (*von Mensch*) even-temperedness

ausgehen ['aʊsgeːən] (*unreg*) *vi* to go out; (*zu Ende gehen*) to come to an end; (*Benzin*) to run out; (*Haare, Zähne*) to fall *od* come out; (*Feuer, Ofen, Licht*) to go out; (*Strom*) to go off; (*Resultat haben*) to turn out; **mir ging das Benzin aus** I ran out of petrol (*BRIT*) *od* gas (*US*); **von etw ~** (*wegführen*) to lead away from sth; (*herrühren*) to come

from sth; (*zugrunde legen*) to proceed from sth; **wir können davon ~, dass ...** we can take as our starting point that ...; **leer ~** to get nothing

ausgelassen ['aʊsgəlasən] *adj* boisterous, high-spirited

ausgelastet ['aʊsgəlastət] *adj* fully occupied

ausgelernt ['aʊsgəlɛrnt] *adj* trained, qualified

ausgemacht ['aʊsgəmaxt] *adj* settled; (*umg: Dummkopf etc*) out-and-out, downright; **es war eine ~e Sache, dass ...** it was a foregone conclusion that ...

ausgenommen ['aʊsgənɔmən] *präp +gen* except ♦ *konj* except; **Anwesende sind ~** present company excepted

ausgeprägt ['aʊsgəprɛːkt] *adj* distinct

ausgerechnet ['aʊsgəreçnət] *adv* just, precisely; **~ du/heute** you of all people/ today of all days

ausgeschlossen ['aʊsgəʃlɔsən] *adj* (*unmöglich*) impossible, out of the question

ausgeschnitten ['aʊsgəʃnɪtən] *adj* (*Kleid*) low-necked

ausgesprochen ['aʊsgəʃprɔxən] *adj* (*Faulheit, Lüge etc*) out-and-out; (*unverkennbar*) marked ♦ *adv* decidedly

ausgezeichnet ['aʊsgətsaɪçnət] *adj* excellent

ausgiebig ['aʊsgiːbɪç] *adj* (*Gebrauch*) thorough, good; (*Essen*) generous, lavish; **~ schlafen** to have a good sleep

ausgießen ['aʊsgiːsən] *vt* to pour out; (*Behälter*) to empty

Ausgleich ['aʊsglaɪç] (**-(e)s**, **-e**) *m* balance; (*Vermittlung*) reconciliation; (*SPORT*) equalization; **zum ~ einer Sache** *gen* in order to offset sth; **a~en** (*unreg*) *vt* to balance (out); to reconcile; (*Höhe*) to even up ♦ *vi* (*SPORT*) to equalize

ausgraben ['aʊsgraːbən] (*unreg*) *vt* to dig up; (*Leichen*) to exhume; (*fig*) to unearth

Ausgrabung *f* excavation; (*Ausgraben auch*) digging up

Ausguss ▲ ['aʊsgʊs] *m* (*Spüle*) sink; (*Abfluss*) outlet; (*Tülle*) spout

aushalten ['aʊshaltən] (*unreg*) *vt* to bear, to

stand; (*Geliebte*) to keep ♦ *vi* to hold out;
das ist nicht zum A~ that is unbearable
aushandeln ['aʊshandəln] *vt* to negotiate
aushändigen ['aʊshɛndɪgən] *vt*: **jdm etw ~**
to hand sth over to sb
Aushang ['aʊshaŋ] *m* notice
aushängen ['aʊshɛŋən] (*unreg*) *vt* (*Meldung*)
to put up; (*Fenster*) to take off its hinges
♦ *vi* to be displayed
ausharren ['aʊsharən] *vi* to hold out
ausheben ['aʊshe:bən] (*unreg*) *vt* (*Erde*) to
lift out; (*Grube*) to hollow out; (*Tür*) to take
off its hinges; (*Diebesnest*) to clear out; (*MIL*)
to enlist
aushecken ['aʊshɛkən] (*umg*) *vt* to cook up
aushelfen ['aʊshɛlfən] (*unreg*) *vi*: **jdm ~** to
help sb out
Aushilfe ['aʊshɪlfə] *f* help, assistance;
(*Person*) (temporary) worker
Aushilfs- *zW*: **~kraft** *f* temporary worker;
a~weise *adv* temporarily, as a stopgap
ausholen ['aʊsho:lən] *vi* to swing one's arm
back; (*zur Ohrfeige*) to raise one's hand;
(*beim Gehen*) to take long strides
aushorchen ['aʊshɔrçən] *vt* to sound out,
to pump
auskennen ['aʊskɛnən] (*unreg*) *vr* to know a
lot; (*an einem Ort*) to know one's way
about; (*in Fragen etc*) to be knowledgeable
Ausklang ['aʊsklaŋ] *m* end
auskleiden ['aʊsklaɪdən] *vr* to undress ♦ *vt*
(*Wand*) to line
ausklingen ['aʊsklɪŋən] (*unreg*) *vi* (*Ton, Lied*)
to die away; (*Fest*) to peter out
ausklopfen ['aʊsklɔpfən] *vt* (*Teppich*) to
beat; (*Pfeife*) to knock out
auskochen ['aʊskɔxən] *vt* to boil; (*MED*) to
sterilize; **ausgekocht** (*fig*) out-and-out
Auskommen (-s) *nt*: **sein A~ haben** to
have a regular income; **a~** (*unreg*) *vi*: **mit
jdm a~** to get on with sb; **mit etw a~** to
get by with sth
auskosten ['aʊskɔstən] *vt* to enjoy to the
full
auskundschaften ['aʊskʊntʃaftən] *vt* to
spy out; (*Gebiet*) to reconnoitre
Auskunft ['aʊskʊnft] (-, **-künfte**) *f*

information; (*nähere*) details *pl*, particulars
pl; (*Stelle*) information office; (*TEL*) directory
inquiries *sg*
auslachen ['aʊslaxən] *vt* to laugh at, to
mock
ausladen ['aʊsla:dən] (*unreg*) *vt* to unload;
(*umg: Gäste*) to cancel an invitation to
Auslage ['aʊsla:gə] *f* shop window (display);
~n *pl* (*Ausgabe*) outlay *sg*
Ausland ['aʊslant] *nt* foreign countries *pl*;
im ~ abroad; **ins ~** abroad
Ausländer(in) ['aʊslɛndər(ɪn)] (**-s, -**) *m(f)*
foreigner
ausländisch *adj* foreign
Auslands- *zW*: **~gespräch** *nt*
international call; **~reise** *f* trip abroad;
~schutzbrief *m* international travel cover
auslassen ['aʊslasən] (*unreg*) *vt* to leave
out; (*Wort etc auch*) to omit; (*Fett*) to melt;
(*Kleidungsstück*) to let out ♦ *vr*: **sich über
etw** *akk* **~** to speak one's mind about sth;
seine Wut *etc* **an jdm ~** to vent one's rage
etc on sb
Auslassung *f* omission
Auslauf ['aʊslaʊf] *m* (*für Tiere*) run; (*Ausfluss*)
outflow, outlet; **a~en** (*unreg*) *vi* to run out;
(*Behälter*) to leak; (*NAUT*) to put out (to
sea); (*langsam aufhören*) to run down
Ausläufer ['aʊslɔʏfər] *m* (*von Gebirge*) spur;
(*Pflanze*) runner; (*MET: von Hoch*) ridge;
(*: von Tief*) trough
ausleeren ['aʊsle:rən] *vt* to empty
auslegen ['aʊsle:gən] *vt* (*Waren*) to lay out;
(*Köder*) to put down; (*Geld*) to lend;
(*bedecken*) to cover; (*Text etc*) to interpret
Auslegung *f* interpretation
ausleiern ['aʊslaɪərn] *vi* (*Gummi*) to wear
out
Ausleihe ['aʊslaɪə] *f* issuing; (*Stelle*) issue
desk; **a~n** (*unreg*) *vt* (*verleihen*) to lend; **sich
dat etw a~n** to borrow sth
Auslese ['aʊsle:zə] *f* selection; (*Elite*) elite;
(*Wein*) choice wine; **a~n** (*unreg*) *vt* to
select; (*umg: zu Ende lesen*) to finish
ausliefern ['aʊsli:fərn] *vt* to deliver (up), to
hand over; (*COMM*) to deliver; **jdm/etw
ausgeliefert sein** to be at the mercy of

sb/sth

ausloggen [ˈaʊslɔgən] *vi* (COMPUT) to log off

auslöschen [ˈaʊslœʃən] *vt* to extinguish; (*fig*) to wipe out, to obliterate

auslosen [ˈaʊsloːzən] *vt* to draw lots for

auslösen [ˈaʊsløːzən] *vt* (*Explosion, Schuss*) to set off; (*hervorrufen*) to cause, to produce; (*Gefangene*) to ransom; (*Pfand*) to redeem

ausmachen [ˈaʊsmaxən] *vt* (*Licht, Radio*) to turn off; (*Feuer*) to put out; (*entdecken*) to make out; (*vereinbaren*) to agree; (*beilegen*) to settle; (*Anteil darstellen, betragen*) to represent; (*bedeuten*) to matter; **macht es Ihnen etwas aus, wenn ...?** would you mind if ...?

ausmalen [ˈaʊsmaːlən] *vt* to paint; (*fig*) to describe; **sich** *dat* **etw ~** to imagine sth

Ausmaß [ˈaʊsmaːs] *nt* dimension; (*fig auch*) scale

ausmessen [ˈaʊsmɛsən] (*unreg*) *vt* to measure

Ausnahme [ˈaʊsnaːmə] *f* exception; **~fall** *m* exceptional case; **~zustand** *m* state of emergency

ausnahms- *zW*: **~los** *adv* without exception; **~weise** *adv* by way of exception, for once

ausnehmen [ˈaʊsneːmən] (*unreg*) *vt* to take out, to remove; (*Tier*) to gut; (*Nest*) to rob; (*umg: Geld abnehmen*) to clean out; (*ausschließen*) to make an exception of ♦ *vr* to look, to appear; **~d** *adj* exceptional

ausnützen [ˈaʊsnʏtsən] *vt* (*Zeit, Gelegenheit*) to use, to turn to good account; (*Einfluss*) to use; (*Mensch, Gutmütigkeit*) to exploit

auspacken [ˈaʊspakən] *vt* to unpack

auspfeifen [ˈaʊspfaɪfən] (*unreg*) *vt* to hiss/boo at

ausplaudern [ˈaʊsplaʊdərn] *vt* to blab

ausprobieren [ˈaʊsprobiːrən] *vt* to try (out)

Auspuff [ˈaʊspʊf] (**-(e)s, -e**) *m* (TECH) exhaust; **~rohr** *nt* exhaust (pipe)

ausradieren [ˈaʊsradiːrən] *vt* to erase, to rub out; (*fig*) to annihilate

ausrangieren [ˈaʊsrãʒiːrən] (*umg*) *vt* to chuck out

ausrauben [ˈaʊsraʊbən] *vt* to rob

ausräumen [ˈaʊsrɔʏmən] *vt* (*Dinge*) to clear away; (*Schrank, Zimmer*) to empty; (*Bedenken*) to dispel

ausrechnen [ˈaʊsrɛçnən] *vt* to calculate, to reckon

Ausrede [ˈaʊsreːdə] *f* excuse; **a~n** *vi* to have one's say ♦ *vt*: **jdm etw a~n** to talk sb out of sth

ausreichen [ˈaʊsraɪçən] *vi* to suffice, to be enough; **~d** *adj* sufficient, adequate; (SCH) adequate

Ausreise [ˈaʊsraɪzə] *f* departure; **bei der ~** when leaving the country; **~erlaubnis** *f* exit visa; **a~n** *vi* to leave the country

ausreißen [ˈaʊsraɪsən] (*unreg*) *vt* to tear *od* pull out ♦ *vi* (*Riss bekommen*) to tear; (*umg*) to make off, to scram

ausrenken [ˈaʊsrɛŋkən] *vt* to dislocate

ausrichten [ˈaʊsrɪçtən] *vt* (*Botschaft*) to deliver; (*Gruß etc*) to pass on; (*Hochzeit etc*) to arrange; (*in gerade Linie bringen*) to get in a straight line; (*angleichen*) to bring into line; (TYP) to justify; **ich werde es ihm ~** I'll tell him; **etwas/nichts bei jdm ~** to get somewhere/nowhere with sb

ausrotten [ˈaʊsrɔtən] *vt* to stamp out, to exterminate

Ausruf [ˈaʊsruːf] *m* (*Schrei*) cry, exclamation; (*Bekanntmachung*) proclamation; **a~en** (*unreg*) *vt* to cry out, to exclaim; to call out; **~ezeichen** *nt* exclamation mark

ausruhen [ˈaʊsruːən] *vt, vr* to rest

ausrüsten [ˈaʊsrʏstən] *vt* to equip, to fit out

Ausrüstung *f* equipment

ausrutschen [ˈaʊsrʊtʃən] *vi* to slip

Aussage [ˈaʊszaːgə] *f* (JUR) statement; **a~n** *vt* to say, to state ♦ *vi* (JUR) to give evidence

ausschalten [ˈaʊsʃaltən] *vt* to switch off; (*fig*) to eliminate

Ausschank [ˈaʊsʃaŋk] (**-(e)s, -schänke**) *m* dispensing, giving out; (COMM) selling; (*Theke*) bar

Ausschau [ˈaʊsʃaʊ] *f*: **~ halten (nach)** to look out (for), to watch (for); **a~en** *vi*: **a~en (nach)** to look out (for), to be on the look-out (for)

ausscheiden [ˈaʊsʃaɪdən] (*unreg*) *vt* to take

out; (MED) to secrete ♦ vi: ~ **(aus)** to leave;
(SPORT) to be eliminated (from) od knocked
out (of)

Ausscheidung f separation; secretion;
elimination; (aus Amt) retirement

ausschenken ['ausʃɛŋkən] vt (Alkohol,
Kaffee) to pour out; (COMM) to sell

ausschildern ['ausʃɪldərn] vt to signpost

ausschimpfen ['ausʃɪmpfən] vt to scold, to
tell off

ausschlafen ['ausʃlaːfən] (unreg) vi, vr to
have a good sleep ♦ vt to sleep off; **ich bin
nicht ausgeschlafen** I didn't have od get
enough sleep

Ausschlag ['ausʃlaːk] m (MED) rash;
(Pendelausschlag) swing; (Nadelausschlag)
deflection; **den ~ geben** (fig) to tip the
balance; **a~en** [-gən] (unreg) vt to knock
out; (auskleiden) to deck out; (verweigern) to
decline ♦ vi (Pferd) to kick out; (BOT) to
sprout; **a~gebend** adj decisive

ausschließen ['ausʃliːsən] (unreg) vt to shut
od lock out; (fig) to exclude

ausschließlich adj exclusive ♦ adv
exclusively ♦ präp +gen exclusive of,
excluding

Ausschluss ▲ ['ausʃlʊs] m exclusion

ausschmücken ['ausʃmʏkən] vt to
decorate; (fig) to embellish

ausschneiden ['ausʃnaɪdən] (unreg) vt to
cut out; (Büsche) to trim

Ausschnitt ['ausʃnɪt] m (Teil) section; (von
Kleid) neckline; (Zeitungsausschnitt) cutting;
(aus Film etc) excerpt

ausschreiben ['ausʃraɪbən] (unreg) vt (ganz
schreiben) to write out (in full); (ausstellen)
to write (out); (Stelle, Wettbewerb etc) to
announce, to advertise

Ausschreitung ['ausʃraɪtʊŋ] f (usu pl) riot

Ausschuss ▲ ['ausʃʊs] m committee,
board; (Abfall) waste, scraps pl; (COMM:
auch: **~ware**) reject

ausschütten ['ausʃʏtən] vt to pour out;
(Eimer) to empty; (Geld) to pay ♦ vr to
shake (with laughter)

ausschweifend ['ausʃvaɪfənt] adj (Leben)
dissipated, debauched; (Fantasie)
extravagant

aussehen ['ausze:ən] (unreg) vi to look; **es
sieht nach Regen aus** it looks like rain; **es
sieht schlecht aus** things look bad; **A~** (-
s) nt appearance

aus sein ▲ siehe aus

außen ['ausən] adv outside; (nach ~)
outwards; ~ **ist es rot** it's red (on the)
outside

Außen- zW: **~dienst** m: **im ~dienst sein**
to work outside the office; **~handel** m
foreign trade; **~minister** m foreign
minister; **~ministerium** nt foreign office;
~politik f foreign policy; **a~politisch** adj
(Entwicklung, Lage) foreign; **~seite** f
outside; **~seiter** (-s, -) m outsider;
~stände pl outstanding debts;
~stehende(r) f(m) outsider; **~welt** f
outside world

außer ['ausər] präp +dat (räumlich) out of;
(abgesehen von) except ♦ konj
(ausgenommen) except; ~ **Gefahr** out of
danger; ~ **Zweifel** beyond any doubt; ~
Betrieb out of order; ~ **Dienst** retired; ~
Landes abroad; ~ **sich** dat **sein** to be
beside o.s.; ~ **sich** akk **geraten** to go wild;
~ **wenn** unless; ~ **dass** except; **~dem** konj
besides, in addition

äußere(r, s) ['ɔysərə(r, s)] adj outer, external

außergewöhnlich adj unusual

außerhalb präp +gen outside ♦ adv outside

äußerlich adj external

äußern vt to utter, to express; (zeigen) to
show ♦ vr to give one's opinion; (Krankheit
etc) to show itself

außerordentlich adj extraordinary

außerplanmäßig adj unscheduled

äußerst ['ɔysərst] adv extremely, most; **~e(r,
s)** adj utmost; (räumlich) farthest; (Termin)
last possible; (Preis) highest

Äußerung f remark, comment

aussetzen ['auszɛtsən] vt (Kind, Tier) to
abandon; (Boote) to lower; (Belohnung) to
offer; (Urteil, Verfahren) to postpone ♦ vi
(aufhören) to stop; (Pause machen) to have a
break; **jdm/etw ausgesetzt sein** to be
exposed to sb/sth; **an jdm/etw etwas ~** to

find fault with sb/sth

Aussicht ['aʊszɪçt] f view; (*in Zukunft*) prospect; **etw in ~ haben** to have sth in view

Aussichts- *zW*: **a~los** *adj* hopeless; **~punkt** *m* viewpoint; **a~reich** *adj* promising; **~turm** *m* observation tower

aussöhnen ['aʊszøːnən] *vt* to reconcile ♦ *vr* to reconcile o.s., to become reconciled

aussondern ['aʊszɔndərn] *vt* to separate, to select

aussortieren ['aʊszɔrtiːrən] *vt* to sort out

ausspannen ['aʊsʃpanən] *vt* to spread *od* stretch up; (*Pferd*) to unharness; (*umg*: *Mädchen*): **(jdm) jdn ~** to steal sb (from sb) ♦ *vi* to relax

aussperren ['aʊsʃpɛrən] *vt* to lock out

ausspielen ['aʊsʃpiːlən] *vt* (*Karte*) to lead; (*Geldprämie*) to offer as a prize ♦ *vi* (*KARTEN*) to lead; **jdn gegen jdn ~** to play sb off against sb; **ausgespielt haben** to be finished

Aussprache ['aʊsʃpraːxə] f pronunciation; (*Unterredung*) (frank) discussion

aussprechen ['aʊsʃprɛçən] (*unreg*) *vt* to pronounce; (*äußern*) to say, to express ♦ *vr* (*sich äußern*): **sich ~ (über** +*akk*) to speak (about); (*sich anvertrauen*) to unburden o.s. (about *od* on); (*diskutieren*) to discuss ♦ *vi* (*zu Ende sprechen*) to finish speaking

Ausspruch ['aʊsʃprʊx] *m* saying, remark

ausspülen ['aʊsʃpyːlən] *vt* to wash out; (*Mund*) to rinse

Ausstand ['aʊsʃtant] *m* strike; **in den ~ treten** to go on strike

ausstatten ['aʊsʃtatən] *vt* (*Zimmer etc*) to furnish; (*Person*) to equip, to kit out

Ausstattung f (*Ausstatten*) provision; (*Kleidung*) outfit; (*Aufmachung*) make-up; (*Einrichtung*) furnishing

ausstechen ['aʊsʃtɛçən] (*unreg*) *vt* (*Augen, Rasen, Graben*) to dig out; (*Kekse*) to cut out; (*übertreffen*) to outshine

ausstehen ['aʊsʃteːən] (*unreg*) *vt* to stand, to endure ♦ *vi* (*noch nicht da sein*) to be outstanding

aussteigen ['aʊsʃtaɪɡən] (*unreg*) *vi* to get

out, to alight

ausstellen ['aʊsʃtɛlən] *vt* to exhibit, to display; (*umg*: *ausschalten*) to switch off; (*Rechnung etc*) to make out; (*Pass, Zeugnis*) to issue

Ausstellung f exhibition; (*FIN*) drawing up; (*einer Rechnung*) making out; (*eines Passes etc*) issuing

aussterben ['aʊsʃtɛrbən] (*unreg*) *vi* to die out

Aussteuer ['aʊsʃtɔyər] f dowry

Ausstieg ['aʊsʃtiːk] **(-(e)s, -e)** *m* exit

ausstopfen ['aʊsʃtɔpfən] *vt* to stuff

ausstoßen ['aʊsʃtoːsən] (*unreg*) *vt* (*Luft, Rauch*) to give off, to emit; (*aus Verein etc*) to expel, to exclude; (*Auge*) to poke out

ausstrahlen ['aʊsʃtraːlən] *vt, vi* to radiate; (*RADIO*) to broadcast

Ausstrahlung f radiation; (*fig*) charisma

ausstrecken ['aʊsʃtrɛkən] *vt, vr* to stretch out

ausstreichen ['aʊsʃtraɪçən] (*unreg*) *vt* to cross out; (*glätten*) to smooth (out)

ausströmen ['aʊsʃtrøːmən] *vi* (*Gas*) to pour out, to escape ♦ *vt* to give off; (*fig*) to radiate

aussuchen ['aʊszuːxən] *vt* to select, to pick out

Austausch ['aʊstaʊʃ] *m* exchange; **a~bar** *adj* exchangeable; **a~en** *vt* to exchange, to swap

austeilen ['aʊstaɪlən] *vt* to distribute, to give out

Auster ['aʊstər] **(-, -n)** f oyster

austoben ['aʊstoːbən] *vr* (*Kind*) to run wild; (*Erwachsene*) to sow one's wild oats

austragen ['aʊstraːɡən] (*unreg*) *vt* (*Post*) to deliver; (*Streit etc*) to decide; (*Wettkämpfe*) to hold

Australien [aʊsˈtraːliən] **(-s)** *nt* Australia; **Australier(in) (-s, -)** *m(f)* Australian; **australisch** *adj* Australian

austreiben ['aʊstraɪbən] (*unreg*) *vt* to drive out, to expel; (*Geister*) to exorcize

austreten ['aʊstreːtən] (*unreg*) *vi* (*zur Toilette*) to be excused ♦ *vt* (*Feuer*) to tread out, to trample; (*Schuhe*) to wear out; (*Treppe*) to

wear down; **aus etw ~** to leave sth
austrinken [ˈaʊstrɪŋkən] (unreg) vt (Glas) to drain; (Getränk) to drink up ♦ vi to finish one's drink, to drink up
Austritt [ˈaʊstrɪt] m emission; (aus Verein, Partei etc) retirement, withdrawal
austrocknen [ˈaʊstrɔknən] vt, vi to dry up
ausüben [ˈaʊsˌyːbən] vt (Beruf) to practise, to carry out; (Funktion) to perform; (Einfluss) to exert; **einen Reiz auf jdn ~** to hold an attraction for sb; **eine Wirkung auf jdn ~** to have an effect on sb
Ausverkauf [ˈaʊsfɛrkaʊf] m sale; **a~en** vt to sell out; (Geschäft) to sell up; **a~t** adj (Karten, Artikel) sold out; (THEAT: Haus) full
Auswahl [ˈaʊsvaːl] f: **eine ~ (an** +dat) a selection (of), a choice (of)
auswählen [ˈaʊsvɛːlən] vt to select, to choose
Auswander- [ˈaʊsvandər] zW: **~er** m emigrant; **a~n** vi to emigrate; **~ung** f emigration
auswärtig [ˈaʊsvɛrtɪç] adj (nicht am/vom Ort) out-of-town; (ausländisch) foreign
auswärts [ˈaʊsvɛrts] adv outside; (nach außen) outwards; **~ essen** to eat out; **A~spiel** [ˈaʊsvɛrtsˌʃpiːl] nt away game
auswechseln [ˈaʊsvɛksəln] vt to change, to substitute
Ausweg [ˈaʊsveːk] m way out; **a~los** adj hopeless
ausweichen [ˈaʊsvaɪçən] (unreg) vi: **jdm/etw ~** to move aside od make way for sb/sth; (fig) to side-step sb/sth; **~d** adj evasive
ausweinen [ˈaʊsvaɪnən] vr to have a (good) cry
Ausweis [ˈaʊsvaɪs] (-es, -e) m identity card; passport; (Mitgliedsausweis, Bibliotheksausweis etc) card; **a~en** [-zən] (unreg) vt to expel, to banish ♦ vr to prove one's identity; **~kontrolle** f identity check; **~papiere** pl identity papers; **~ung** f expulsion
ausweiten [ˈaʊsvaɪtən] vt to stretch
auswendig [ˈaʊsvɛndɪç] adv by heart
auswerten [ˈaʊsveːrtən] vt to evaluate; **Auswertung** f evaluation, analysis; (Nutzung) utilization

auswirken [ˈaʊsvɪrkən] vr to have an effect; **Auswirkung** f effect
auswischen [ˈaʊsvɪʃən] vt to wipe out; **jdm eins ~** (umg) to put one over on sb
Auswuchs [ˈaʊsvuːks] m (out)growth; (fig) product
auszahlen [ˈaʊstsaːlən] vt (Lohn, Summe) to pay out; (Arbeiter) to pay off; (Miterbe) to buy out ♦ vr (sich lohnen) to pay
auszählen [ˈaʊstsɛːlən] vt (Stimmen) to count
auszeichnen [ˈaʊstsaɪçnən] vt to honour; (MIL) to decorate; (COMM) to price ♦ vr to distinguish o.s.
Auszeichnung f distinction; (COMM) pricing; (Ehrung) awarding of decoration; (Ehre) honour; (Orden) decoration; **mit ~** with distinction
ausziehen [ˈaʊstsiːən] (unreg) vt (Kleidung) to take off; (Haare, Zähne, Tisch etc) to pull out; (nachmalen) to trace ♦ vr to undress ♦ vi (aufbrechen) to leave; (aus Wohnung) to move out
Auszubildende(r) [ˈaʊstsubɪldəndə(r)] f(m) trainee
Auszug [ˈaʊstsuːk] m (aus Wohnung) removal; (aus Buch etc) extract; (Konto~) statement; (Ausmarsch) departure
Auto [ˈaʊto] (-s, -s) nt (motor)car; **~ fahren** to drive; **~atlas** m road atlas; **~bahn** f motorway; **~bahndreieck** nt motorway junction; **~bahngebühr** f toll; **~bahnkreuz** nt motorway intersection; **~bus** m bus; **~fähre** f car ferry; **~fahrer(in)** m(f) motorist, driver; **~fahrt** f drive; **a~gen** [-ˈgeːn] adj autogenous; **~'gramm** nt autograph

---
Autobahn
---

i An **Autobahn** is a motorway. In former West Germany there is a widespread motorway network but in the former **DDR** the motorways are somewhat less extensive. There is no overall speed limit but a limit of 130 km/hour is recommended and there are lower mandatory limits on certain stretches of road. As yet there are no tolls payable on

German Autobahnen. However, a yearly toll is payable in Switzerland and tolls have been introduced in Austria.

Auto- *zW:* **~'mat** (**-en, -en**) *m* machine; **~matik** [auto'maːtɪk] *f* (*AUT*) automatic; **a~'matisch** *adj* automatic; **a~nom** [-'noːm] *adj* autonomous

Autor(in) ['autor(ɪn)] (**-s, -en**) *m(f)* author

Auto- *zW:* **~radio** *nt* car radio; **~reifen** *m* car tyre; **~reisezug** *m* motorail train; **~rennen** *nt* motor racing

autoritär [autori'tɛːr] *adj* authoritarian

Autorität *f* authority

Auto- *zW:* **~telefon** *nt* car phone; **~unfall** *m* car *od* motor accident; **~vermietung** *m* car hire (*BRIT*) *od* rental (*US*); **~waschanlage** *f* car wash

Axt [akst] (**-, ⁺e**) *f* axe

B, b

Baby ['beːbi] (**-s, -s**) *nt* baby; **~nahrung** *f* baby food; **~sitter** (**-s, -**) *m* baby-sitter

Bach [bax] (**-(e)s, ⁺e**) *m* stream, brook

Backbord (**-(e)s, -e**) *nt* (*NAUT*) port

Backe ['bakə] *f* cheek

backen ['bakən] (*unreg*) *vt, vi* to bake

Backenzahn *m* molar

Bäcker ['bɛkər(ɪn)] (**-s, -**) *m* baker; **~ei** *f* bakery; (**~eiladen**) baker's (shop)

Back- *zW:* **~form** *f* baking tin; **~obst** *nt* dried fruit; **~ofen** *m* oven; **~pflaume** *f* prune; **~pulver** *nt* baking powder; **~stein** *m* brick

Bad [baːt] (**-(e)s, ⁺er**) *nt* bath; (*Schwimmen*) bathe; (*Ort*) spa

Bade- ['baːdə] *zW:* **~anstalt** *f* (swimming) baths *pl*; **~anzug** *m* bathing suit; **~hose** *f* bathing *od* swimming trunks *pl*; **~kappe** *f* bathing cap; **~mantel** *m* bath(ing) robe; **~meister** *m* baths attendant; **b~n** *vi* to bathe, to have a bath ♦ *vt* to bath; **~ort** *m* spa; **~tuch** *nt* bath towel; **~wanne** *f* bath (tub); **~zimmer** *nt* bathroom

Bagatelle [baga'tɛlə] *f* trifle

Bagger ['bagər] (**-s, -**) *m* excavator; (*NAUT*) dredger; **b~n** *vt, vi* to excavate; to dredge

Bahn [baːn] (**-, -en**) *f* railway, railroad (*US*); (*Weg*) road, way; (*Spur*) lane; (*Rennbahn*) track; (*ASTRON*) orbit; (*Stoffbahn*) length; **b~brechend** *adj* pioneering; **~Card** ['baːnkaːrd] (**-, -s**) ℝ *f* ≈ railcard; **~damm** *m* railway embankment; **b~en** *vt:* **sich/ jdm einen Weg b~en** to clear a way/a way for sb; **~fahrt** *f* railway journey; **~fracht** *f* rail freight; **~hof** (**-, -s**) *m* station; **auf dem ~hof** at the station; **~hofshalle** *f* station concourse; **~linie** *f* (railway) line; **~steig** *m* platform; **~übergang** *m* level crossing, grade crossing (*US*)

Bahre ['baːrə] *f* stretcher

Bakterien [bak'teːriən] *pl* bacteria *pl*

Balance [ba'lãːsə] *f* balance, equilibrium

balan'cieren *vt, vi* to balance

bald [balt] *adv* (*zeitlich*) soon; (*beinahe*) almost; **~ig** ['baldɪç] *adj* early, speedy

Baldrian ['baldriaːn] (**-s, -e**) *m* valerian

Balkan ['balkaːn] (**-s**) *m:* **der ~** the Balkans *pl*

Balken ['balkən] (**-s, -**) *m* beam; (*Tragbalken*) girder; (*Stützbalken*) prop

Balkon [bal'kõː] (**-s, -s** *od* **-e**) *m* balcony; (*THEAT*) (dress) circle

Ball [bal] (**-(e)s, ⁺e**) *m* ball; (*Tanz*) dance, ball

Ballast ['balast] (**-(e)s, -e**) *m* ballast; (*fig*) weight, burden

Ballen ['balən] (**-s, -**) *m* bale; (*ANAT*) ball; **b~** *vt* (*formen*) to make into a ball; (*Faust*) to clench ♦ *vr* (*Wolken etc*) to build up; (*Menschen*) to gather

Ballett [ba'lɛt] (**-(e)s, -e**) *nt* ballet

Ballkleid *nt* evening dress

Ballon [ba'lõː] (**-s, -s** *od* **-e**) *m* balloon

Ballspiel *nt* ball game

Ballungsgebiet ['balʊŋsgəbiːt] *nt* conurbation

Baltikum ['baltikʊm] (**-s**) *nt:* **das ~** the Baltic States

Banane [ba'naːnə] *f* banana

Band¹ [bant] (**-(e)s, ⁺e**) *m* (*Buchband*) volume

Rechtschreibreform: ▲ *neue Schreibung* △ *alte Schreibung (auslaufend)*

Band² (-(e)s, ⁻er) *nt* (*Stoffband*) ribbon, tape; (*Fließband*) production line; (*Tonband*) tape; (*ANAT*) ligament; **etw auf ~ aufnehmen** to tape sth; **am laufenden ~** (*umg*) non-stop

Band³ (-(e)s, -e) *nt* (*Freundschaftsband etc*) bond

Band⁴ [bɛnt] (-, -s) *f* band, group

band *etc vb siehe* **binden**

Bandage [ban'daːʒə] *f* bandage

banda'gieren *vt* to bandage

Bande ['bandə] *f* band; (*Straßenbande*) gang

bändigen ['bɛndɪɡən] *vt* (*Tier*) to tame; (*Trieb, Leidenschaft*) to control, to restrain

Bandit [ban'diːt] (-en, -en) *m* bandit

Band- *zW:* **~nudel** *f* (*KOCH: gew pl*) ribbon noodles *pl*; **~scheibe** *f* (*ANAT*) disc; **~wurm** *m* tapeworm

bange ['baŋə] *adj* scared; (*besorgt*) anxious; **jdm wird es ~** sb is becoming scared; **jdm B~ machen** to scare sb; **~n** *vi*: **um jdn/ etw ~n** to be anxious *od* worried about sb/sth

Bank¹ [baŋk] (-, ⁻e) *f* (*Sitz~*) bench; (*Sand~ etc*) (sand)bank, (sand)bar

Bank² [baŋk] (-, -en) *f* (*Geldbank*) bank; **~anweisung** *f* banker's order; **~einzug** *m* direct debit

Bankett [ban'kɛt] (-(e)s, -e) *nt* (*Essen*) banquet; (*Straßenrand*) verge (*BRIT*), shoulder (*US*)

Bankier [baŋki'eː] (-s, -s) *m* banker

Bank- *zW:* **~konto** *m* bank account; **~leitzahl** *f* bank sort code number; **~note** *f* banknote; **~raub** *m* bank robbery

Bankrott [baŋ'krɔt] (-(e)s, -e) *m* bankruptcy; **~ machen** to go bankrupt; **b~** *adj* bankrupt

Bankverbindung *f* banking arrangements *pl*; **geben Sie bitte Ihre ~ an** please give your account details

Bann [ban] (-(e)s, -e) *m* (*HIST*) ban; (*Kirchenbann*) excommunication; (*fig: Zauber*) spell; **b~en** *vt* (*Geister*) to exorcize; (*Gefahr*) to avert; (*bezaubern*) to enchant; (*HIST*) to banish

Banner (-s, -) *nt* banner, flag

Bar (-, -s) *f* bar

bar [baːr] *adj* (+*gen*) (*unbedeckt*) bare; (*frei von*) lacking (in); (*offenkundig*) utter, sheer; **~e(s) Geld** cash; **etw (in) ~ bezahlen** to pay sth (in) cash; **etw für ~e Münze nehmen** (*fig*) to take sth at its face value

Bär [bɛːr] (-en, -en) *m* bear

Baracke [ba'rakə] *f* hut

barbarisch [bar'baːrɪʃ] *adj* barbaric, barbarous

Bar- *zW:* **b~fuß** *adj* barefoot; **~geld** *nt* cash, ready money; **b~geldlos** *adj* non-cash

Barkauf *m* cash purchase

Barkeeper ['baːrkiːpər] (-s, -) *m* barman, bartender

barmherzig [barm'hɛrtsɪç] *adj* merciful, compassionate

Baron [ba'roːn] (-s, -e) *m* baron; **~in** *f* baroness

Barren ['barən] (-s, -) *m* parallel bars *pl*; (*Goldbarren*) ingot

Barriere [bari'ɛːrə] *f* barrier

Barrikade [bari'kaːdə] *f* barricade

Barsch [barʃ] (-(e)s, -e) *m* perch

barsch [barʃ] *adj* brusque, gruff

Bar- *zW:* **~schaft** *f* ready money; **~scheck** *m* open *od* uncrossed cheque (*BRIT*), open check (*US*)

Bart [baːrt] (-(e)s, ⁻e) *m* beard; (*Schlüsselbart*) bit; **bärtig** ['bɛːrtɪç] *adj* bearded

Barzahlung *f* cash payment

Base ['baːzə] *f* (*CHEM*) base; (*Kusine*) cousin

Basel ['baːzəl] *nt* Basle

Basen *pl von* **Base; Basis**

basieren [ba'ziːrən] *vt* to base ♦ *vi* to be based

Basis ['baːzɪs] (-, **Basen**) *f* basis

Bass ▲ [bas] (-es, ⁻e) *m* bass

Bassin [ba'sɛ̃ː] (-s, -s) *nt* pool

basteln ['bastəln] *vt* to make ♦ *vi* to do handicrafts

bat *etc* [baːt] *vb siehe* **bitten**

Bataillon [batal'joːn] (-s, -e) *nt* battalion

Batik ['baːtɪk] *f* (*Verfahren*) batik

Batterie [batə'riː] *f* battery

Bau [bau] (-(e)s) *m* (~en) building,

Spelling Reform: ▲ *new spelling* △ *old spelling (to be phased out)*

construction; (*Aufbau*) structure; (*Körperbau*) frame; (*~stelle*) building site; (*pl ~e: Tierbau*) hole, burrow; (: *MIN*) working(s); (*pl ~ten: Gebäude*) building; **sich im ~ befinden** to be under construction; **~arbeiten** *pl* building *od* construction work *sg*; **~arbeiter** *m* building worker

Bauch [baux] (*-(e)s, Bäuche*) *m* belly; (*ANAT auch*) stomach, abdomen; **~fell** *nt* peritoneum; **b~ig** *adj* bulbous; **~nabel** *m* navel; **~redner** *m* ventriloquist; **~schmerzen** *pl* stomachache; **~weh** *nt* stomachache

Baudenkmal *nt* historical monument

bauen ['bauǝn] *vt, vi* to build; (*TECH*) to construct; **auf jdn/etw ~** to depend *od* count upon sb/sth

Bauer[1] ['bauǝr] (*-n od -s, -n*) *m* farmer; (*Schach*) pawn

Bauer[2] ['bauǝr] (*-s, -*) *nt od m* (bird)cage

Bäuerin ['bɔyǝrɪn] *f* farmer; (*Frau des Bauers*) farmer's wife

bäuerlich *adj* rustic

Bauern- *zW*: **~haus** *nt* farmhouse; **~hof** *m* farm(yard)

Bau- *zW*: **b~fällig** *adj* dilapidated; **~gelände** *nt* building site; **~genehmigung** *f* building permit; **~gerüst** *nt* scaffolding; **~herr** *m* purchaser; **~kasten** *m* box of bricks; **~land** *nt* building land; **b~lich** *adj* structural

Baum [baum] (*-(e)s, Bäume*) *m* tree

baumeln ['baumǝln] *vi* to dangle

bäumen ['bɔymǝn] *vr* to rear (up)

Baum- *zW*: **~schule** *f* nursery; **~stamm** *m* tree trunk; **~stumpf** *m* tree stump; **~wolle** *f* cotton

Bau- *zW*: **~plan** *m* architect's plan; **~platz** *m* building site

bauspar- *zW*: **~en** *vi* to save with a building society; **B~kasse** *f* building society; **B~vertrag** *m* building society savings agreement

Bau- *zW*: **~stein** *m* building stone, freestone; **~stelle** *f* building site; **~teil** *nt* prefabricated part of **Bau**; **~ten** *pl von* **Bau**; **~unternehmer** *m* building

contractor; **~weise** *f* (method of) construction; **~werk** *nt* building; **~zaun** *m* hoarding

Bayern ['baiǝrn] *nt* Bavaria

bayrisch ['bairɪʃ] *adj* Bavarian

Bazillus [ba'tsɪlʊs] (*-, Bazillen*) *m* bacillus

beabsichtigen [bǝ'apzɪçtɪgǝn] *vt* to intend

beacht- [bǝ'axt] *zW*: **~en** *vt* to take note of; (*Vorschrift*) to obey; (*Vorfahrt*) to observe; **~lich** *adj* considerable; **B~ung** *f* notice, attention, observation

Beamte(r) [bǝ'amtǝ(r)] (*-n, -n*) *m* official; (*Staatsbeamte*) civil servant; (*Bankbeamte etc*) employee

Beamtin *f siehe* **Beamte(r)**

beängstigend [bǝ'ɛŋstɪgǝnt] *adj* alarming

beanspruchen [bǝ'anʃpruxǝn] *vt* to claim; (*Zeit, Platz*) to take up, to occupy; **jdn ~** to take up sb's time

beanstanden [bǝ'anʃtandǝn] *vt* to complain about, to object to

beantragen [bǝ'antra:gǝn] *vt* to apply for, to ask for

beantworten [bǝ'antvɔrtǝn] *vt* to answer; **Beantwortung** *f* (*+gen*) reply (to)

bearbeiten [bǝ'arbaitǝn] *vt* to work; (*Material*) to process; (*Thema*) to deal with; (*Land*) to cultivate; (*CHEM*) to treat; (*Buch*) to revise; (*umg: beeinflussen wollen*) to work on

Bearbeitung *f* processing; cultivation; treatment; revision

Bearbeitungsgebühr *f* handling charge

Beatmung [bǝ'a:tmʊŋ] *f* respiration

beaufsichtigen [bǝ'aufzɪçtɪgǝn] *vt* to supervise; **Beaufsichtigung** *f* supervision

beauftragen [bǝ'auftra:gǝn] *vt* to instruct; **jdn mit etw ~** to entrust sb with sth

Beauftragte(r) [f(m)] representative

bebauen [bǝ'bauǝn] *vt* to build on; (*AGR*) to cultivate

beben ['be:bǝn] *vi* to tremble, to shake; **B~** (*-s, -*) *nt* earthquake

Becher ['beçǝr] (*-s, -*) *m* mug; (*ohne Henkel*) tumbler

Becken ['bɛkǝn] (*-s, -*) *nt* basin; (*MUS*) cymbal; (*ANAT*) pelvis

bedacht [bəˈdaxt] *adj* thoughtful, careful; **auf etw** *akk* ~ **sein** to be concerned about sth

bedächtig [bəˈdɛçtɪç] *adj* (*umsichtig*) thoughtful, reflective; (*langsam*) slow, deliberate

bedanken [bəˈdaŋkən] *vr:* **sich (bei jdm) ~** to say thank you (to sb)

Bedarf [bəˈdarf] (**-(e)s**) *m* need, requirement; (*COMM*) demand; **je nach ~** according to demand; **bei ~** if necessary; **~ an etw** *dat* **haben** to be in need of sth

Bedarfs- *zW:* **~fall** *m* case of need; **~haltestelle** *f* request stop

bedauerlich [bəˈdaʊərlɪç] *adj* regrettable

bedauern [bəˈdaʊərn] *vt* to be sorry for; (*bemitleiden*) to pity; **B~ (-s)** *nt* regret; **~swert** *adj* (*Zustände*) regrettable; (*Mensch*) pitiable, unfortunate

bedecken [bəˈdɛkən] *vt* to cover

bedeckt *adj* covered; (*Himmel*) overcast

bedenken [bəˈdɛŋkən] (*unreg*) *vt* to think over, to consider

Bedenken (**-s, -**) *nt* (*Überlegen*) consideration; (*Zweifel*) doubt; (*Skrupel*) scruple

bedenklich *adj* doubtful; (*bedrohlich*) dangerous, risky

Bedenkzeit *f* time to think

bedeuten [bəˈdɔytən] *vt* to mean; to signify; (*wichtig sein*) to be of importance; **~d** *adj* important; (*beträchtlich*) considerable

bedeutsam *adj* (*wichtig*) significant

Bedeutung *f* meaning; significance; (*Wichtigkeit*) importance; **b~slos** *adj* insignificant, unimportant; **b~svoll** *adj* momentous, significant

bedienen [bəˈdiːnən] *vt* to serve; (*Maschine*) to work, to operate ♦ *vr* (*beim Essen*) to help o.s.; **sich jds/einer Sache ~** to make use of sb/sth

Bedienung *f* service; (*Kellnerin*) waitress; (*Verkäuferin*) shop assistant; (*Zuschlag*) service (charge)

Bedienungsanleitung *f* operating instructions *pl*

bedingen- [bəˈdɪŋən] *vt* (*verursachen*) to cause

bedingt *adj* (*Richtigkeit, Tauglichkeit*) limited; (*Zusage, Annahme*) conditional

Bedingung *f* condition; (*Voraussetzung*) stipulation; **b~slos** *adj* unconditional

bedrängen [bəˈdrɛŋən] *vt* to pester, to harass

bedrohen [bəˈdroːən] *vt* to threaten; **Bedrohung** *f* threat, menace

bedrücken [bəˈdrʏkən] *vt* to oppress, to trouble

bedürf- [bəˈdʏrf] *zW:* **~en** (*unreg*) *vi* +*gen* to need, to require; **B~nis** (**-ses, -se**) *nt* need; **~tig** *adj* in need, poor, needy

beeilen [bəˈʔaɪlən] *vr* to hurry

beeindrucken [bəˈʔaɪndrʊkən] *vt* to impress, to make an impression on

beeinflussen [bəˈʔaɪnflʊsən] *vt* to influence

beeinträchtigen [bəˈʔaɪntrɛçtɪgən] *vt* to affect adversely; (*Freiheit*) to infringe upon

beend(ig)en [bəˈʔɛnd(ɪg)ən] *vt* to end, to finish, to terminate

beengen [bəˈʔɛŋən] *vt* to cramp; (*fig*) to hamper, to oppress

beerben [bəˈʔɛrbən] *vt:* **jdn ~** to inherit from sb

beerdigen [bəˈʔeːrdɪgən] *vt* to bury; **Beerdigung** *f* funeral, burial

Beere [ˈbeːrə] *f* berry; (*Traubenbeere*) grape

Beet [beːt] (**-(e)s, -e**) *nt* bed

befähigen [bəˈfɛːɪgən] *vt* to enable

befähigt *adj* (*begabt*) talented; **~ (für)** (*fähig*) capable (of)

Befähigung *f* capability; (*Begabung*) talent, aptitude

befahrbar [bəˈfaːrbaːr] *adj* passable; (*NAUT*) navigable

befahren [bəˈfaːrən] (*unreg*) *vt* to use, to drive over; (*NAUT*) to navigate ♦ *adj* used

befallen [bəˈfalən] (*unreg*) *vt* to come over

befangen [bəˈfaŋən] *adj* (*schüchtern*) shy, self-conscious; (*voreingenommen*) biased

befassen [bəˈfasən] *vt* to concern o.s.

Befehl [bəˈfeːl] (**-(e)s, -e**) *m* command, order; **b~en** (*unreg*) *vt* to order ♦ *vi* to give orders; **jdm etw b~en** to order sb to do sth; **~sverweigerung** *f* insubordination

befestigen [bə'fɛstɪgən] vt to fasten; (*stärken*) to strengthen; (MIL) to fortify; **~ an** +*dat* to fasten to

Befestigung f fastening; strengthening; (MIL) fortification

befeuchten [bə'fɔyçtən] vt to damp(en), to moisten

befinden [bə'fɪndən] (*unreg*) vr to be; (*sich fühlen*) to feel ♦ vt: **jdn/etw für** *od* **als etw ~** to deem sb/sth to be sth ♦ vi: **~ (über** +*akk*) to decide (on), to adjudicate (on); **B~ (-s)** nt health, condition; (*Meinung*) view, opinion

befolgen [bə'fɔlgən] vt to comply with, to follow

befördern [bə'fœrdərn] vt (*senden*) to transport, to send; (*beruflich*) to promote; **Beförderung** f transport; promotion

befragen [bə'fra:gən] vt to question

befreien [bə'fraɪən] vt to set free; (*erlassen*) to exempt; **Befreiung** f liberation, release; (*Erlassen*) exemption

befreunden [bə'frɔyndən] vr to make friends; (*mit Idee etc*) to acquaint o.s.

befreundet adj friendly

befriedigen [bə'fri:dɪgən] vt to satisfy; **~d** adj satisfactory

Befriedigung f satisfaction, gratification

befristet [bə'frɪstət] adj limited

befruchten [bə'frʊxtən] vt to fertilize; (*fig*) to stimulate

Befruchtung f: **künstliche ~** artificial insemination

Befugnis [bə'fu:knɪs] **(-, -se)** f authorization, powers pl

befugt adj authorized, entitled

Befund [bə'fʊnt] **(-(e)s, -e)** m findings pl; (MED) diagnosis

befürchten [bə'fʏrçtən] vt to fear; **Befürchtung** f fear, apprehension

befürworten [bə'fy:rvɔrtən] vt to support, to speak in favour of; **Befürworter (-s, -)** m supporter, advocate

begabt [bə'ga:pt] adj gifted

Begabung [bə'ga:bʊŋ] f talent, gift

begann etc [bə'gan] vb siehe **beginnen**

begeben [bə'ge:bən] (*unreg*) vr (*gehen*) to

betake o.s.; (*geschehen*) to occur; **sich ~ nach** *od* **zu** to proceed to(wards); **B~heit** f occurrence

begegnen [bə'ge:gnən] vi: **jdm ~** to meet sb; (*behandeln*) to treat sb; **einer Sache** dat **~** to meet with sth

Begegnung f meeting

begehen [bə'ge:ən] (*unreg*) vt (*Straftat*) to commit; (*abschreiten*) to cover; (*Straße etc*) to use, to negotiate; (*Feier*) to celebrate

begehren [bə'ge:rən] vt to desire

begehrt adj in demand; (*Junggeselle*) eligible

begeistern [bə'gaɪstərn] vt to fill with enthusiasm, to inspire ♦ vr: **sich für etw ~** to get enthusiastic about sth

begeistert adj enthusiastic

Begierde [bə'gi:rdə] f desire, passion

begierig [bə'gi:rɪç] adj eager, keen

begießen [bə'gi:sən] (*unreg*) vt to water; (*mit Alkohol*) to drink to

Beginn [bə'gɪn] **(-(e)s)** m beginning; **zu ~** at the beginning; **b~en** (*unreg*) vt, vi to start, to begin

beglaubigen [bə'glaʊbɪgən] vt to countersign; **Beglaubigung** f countersignature

begleichen [bə'glaɪçən] (*unreg*) vt to settle, to pay

Begleit- [bə'glaɪt] zW: **b~en** vt to accompany; (MIL) to escort; **~er (-s, -)** m companion; (*Freund*) escort; (MUS) accompanist; **~schreiben** nt covering letter; **~umstände** pl concomitant circumstances; **~ung** f company; (MIL) escort; (MUS) accompaniment

beglücken [bə'glʏkən] vt to make happy, to delight

beglückwünschen [bə'glʏkvʏnʃən] vt: **~ (zu)** to congratulate on

begnadigen [bə'gna:dɪgən] vt to pardon; **Begnadigung** f pardon, amnesty

begnügen [bə'gny:gən] vr to be satisfied, to content o.s.

begonnen etc [bə'gɔnən] vb siehe **beginnen**

begraben [bə'gra:bən] (*unreg*) vt to bury; **Begräbnis (-ses, -se)** [bə'grɛ:pnɪs] nt burial, funeral

Rechtschreibreform: ▲ *neue Schreibung* △ *alte Schreibung (auslaufend)*

begreifen [bə'graɪfən] (*unreg*) vt to understand, to comprehend

begreiflich [bə'graɪflɪç] adj understandable

begrenzen [bə'grɛntsən] vt (*beschränken*) to limit

Begrenztheit [bə'grɛntsthaɪt] f limitation, restriction; (*fig*) narrowness

Begriff [bə'grɪf] (**-(e)s, -e**) m concept, idea; **im ~ sein, etw zu tun** to be about to do sth; **schwer von ~** (*umg*) slow, dense

begriffsstutzig adj slow, dense

begründ- [bə'grʏnd] zW: **~en** vt (*Gründe geben*) to justify; **~et** adj well-founded, justified; **B~ung** f justification, reason

begrüßen [bə'gry:sən] vt to greet, to welcome; **Begrüßung** f greeting, welcome

begünstigen [bə'gʏnstɪgən] vt (*Person*) to favour; (*Sache*) to further, to promote

begutachten [bə'gu:t|axtən] vt to assess

begütert [bə'gy:tərt] adj wealthy, well-to-do

behaart [bə'ha:rt] adj hairy

behagen [bə'ha:gən] vi: **das behagt ihm nicht** he does not like it

behaglich [bə'ha:klɪç] adj comfortable, cosy; **B~keit** f comfort, cosiness

behalten [bə'haltən] (*unreg*) vt to keep, to retain; (*im Gedächtnis*) to remember

Behälter [bə'hɛltər] (**-s, -**) m container, receptacle

behandeln [bə'handəln] vt to treat; (*Thema*) to deal with; (*Maschine*) to handle

Behandlung f treatment; (*von Maschine*) handling

beharren [bə'harən] vi: **auf etw** dat **~** to stick od keep to sth

beharrlich [bə'harlɪç] adj (*ausdauernd*) steadfast, unwavering; (*hartnäckig*) tenacious, dogged; **B~keit** f steadfastness; tenacity

behaupten [bə'haʊptən] vt to claim, to assert, to maintain; (*sein Recht*) to defend ♦ vr to assert o.s.

Behauptung f claim, assertion

beheben [bə'he:bən] (*unreg*) vt to remove

behelfen [bə'hɛlfən] (*unreg*) vr: **sich mit etw ~** to make do with sth

behelfsmäßig adj improvised, makeshift;

(*vorübergehend*) temporary

behelligen [bə'hɛlɪgən] vt to trouble, to bother

beherbergen [bə'hɛrbɛrgən] vt to put up, to house

beherrsch- [bə'hɛrʃ] zW: **~en** vt (*Volk*) to rule, to govern; (*Situation*) to control; (*Sprache, Gefühle*) to master ♦ vr to control o.s.; **~t** adj controlled; **B~ung** f rule; control; mastery

beherzigen [bə'hɛrtsɪgən] vt to take to heart

beherzt adj courageous, brave

behilflich [bə'hɪlflɪç] adj helpful; **jdm ~ sein (bei)** to help sb (with)

behindern [bə'hɪndərn] vt to hinder, to impede

Behinderte(r) f(m) disabled person

Behinderung f hindrance; (*Körperbehinderung*) handicap

Behörde [bə'hø:rdə] f (*auch pl*) authorities pl

behördlich [bə'hø:rtlɪç] adj official

behüten [bə'hy:tən] vt to guard; **jdn vor etw** dat **~** to preserve sb from sth

behutsam [bə'hu:tza:m] adj cautious, careful; **B~keit** f caution, carefulness

---

SCHLÜSSELWORT

---

bei [baɪ] präp +dat **1** (*nahe bei*) near; (*zum Aufenthalt*) at, with; (*unter, zwischen*) among; **bei München** near Munich; **bei uns** at our place; **beim Friseur** at the hairdresser's; **bei seinen Eltern wohnen** to live with one's parents; **bei einer Firma arbeiten** to work for a firm; **etw bei sich haben** to have sth on one; **jdn bei sich haben** to have sb with one; **bei Goethe** in Goethe; **beim Militär** in the army

2 (*zeitlich*) at, on; (*während*) during; (*Zustand, Umstand*) in; **bei Nacht** at night; **bei Nebel** in fog; **bei Regen** if it rains; **bei solcher Hitze** in such heat; **bei meiner Ankuft** on my arrival; **bei der Arbeit** when I'm *etc* working; **beim Fahren** while driving

---

beibehalten ['baɪbəhaltən] (*unreg*) vt to keep, to retain

Spelling Reform: ▲ *new spelling* △ *old spelling (to be phased out)*

beibringen ['baɪbrɪŋən] (*unreg*) *vt* (*Beweis, Zeugen*) to bring forward; (*Gründe*) to adduce; **jdm etw ~** (*lehren*) to teach sb sth; (*zu verstehen geben*) to make sb understand sth; (*zufügen*) to inflict sth on sb

Beichte ['baɪçtə] *f* confession; **b~n** *vt* to confess ♦ *vi* to go to confession

beide(s) ['baɪdə(s)] *pron, adj* both; **meine ~n Brüder** my two brothers, both my brothers; **die ersten ~n** the first two; **wir ~** we two; **einer von ~n** one of the two; **alles ~s** both (of them)

beider- ['baɪdər] *zW*: **~lei** *adj inv* of both; **~seitig** *adj* mutual, reciprocal; **~seits** *adv* mutually ♦ *präp +gen* on both sides of

beieinander [baɪaɪ'nandər] *adv* together

Beifahrer ['baɪfaːrər] *m* passenger

Beifall ['baɪfal] (**-(e)s**) *m* applause; (*Zustimmung*) approval

beifügen ['baɪfyːgən] *vt* to enclose

beige ['beːʒ] *adj* beige, fawn

beigeben ['baɪgeːbən] (*unreg*) *vt* (*zufügen*) to add; (*mitgeben*) to give ♦ *vi* (*nachgeben*) to give in

Beihilfe ['baɪhɪlfə] *f* aid, assistance; (*Studienbeihilfe*) grant; (*JUR*) aiding and abetting

beikommen ['baɪkɔmən] (*unreg*) *vi +dat* to get at; (*einem Problem*) to deal with

Beil [baɪl] (**-(e)s, -e**) *nt* axe, hatchet

Beilage ['baɪlaːgə] *f* (*Buchbeilage etc*) supplement; (*KOCH*) vegetables and potatoes *pl*

beiläufig ['baɪlɔyfɪç] *adj* casual, incidental ♦ *adv* casually, by the way

beilegen ['baɪleːgən] *vt* (*hinzufügen*) to enclose, to add; (*beimessen*) to attribute, to ascribe; (*Streit*) to settle

Beileid ['baɪlaɪt] *nt* condolence, sympathy; **herzliches ~** deepest sympathy

beiliegend ['baɪliːgənt] *adj* (*COMM*) enclosed

beim [baɪm] = **bei dem**

beimessen ['baɪmɛsən] (*unreg*) *vt* (*+dat*) to attribute (to), to ascribe (to)

Bein [baɪn] (**-(e)s, -e**) *nt* leg

beinah(e) ['baɪnaː(ə)] *adv* almost, nearly

Beinbruch *m* fracture of the leg

beinhalten [bə'ʔɪnhaltən] *vt* to contain

Beipackzettel ['baɪpaktsɛtəl] *m* instruction leaflet

beipflichten ['baɪpflɪçtən] *vi*: **jdm/etw ~** to agree with sb/sth

beisammen [baɪ'zamən] *adv* together; **B~sein** (**-s**) *nt* get-together

Beischlaf ['baɪʃlaːf] *m* sexual intercourse

Beisein ['baɪzaɪn] (**-s**) *nt* presence

beiseite [baɪ'zaɪtə] *adv* to one side, aside; (*stehen*) on one side, aside; **etw ~ legen** (*sparen*) to put sth by

beisetzen ['baɪzɛtsən] *vt* to bury; **Beisetzung** *f* funeral

Beisitzer ['baɪzɪtsər] (**-s, -**) *m* (*bei Prüfung*) assessor

Beispiel ['baɪʃpiːl] (**-(e)s, -e**) *nt* example; **sich +dat an jdm ein ~ nehmen** to take sb as an example; **zum ~** for example; **b~haft** *adj* exemplary; **b~los** *adj* unprecedented; **b~sweise** *adv* for instance *od* example

beißen ['baɪsən] (*unreg*) *vt, vi* to bite; (*stechen: Rauch, Säure*) to burn ♦ *vr* (*Farben*) to clash; **~d** *adj* biting, caustic; (*fig auch*) sarcastic

Beistand ['baɪʃtant] (**-(e)s, ⁻e**) *m* support, help; (*JUR*) adviser

beistehen ['baɪʃteːən] (*unreg*) *vi*: **jdm ~** to stand by sb

beisteuern ['baɪʃtɔyərn] *vt* to contribute

Beitrag ['baɪtraːk] (**-(e)s, ⁻e**) *m* contribution; (*Zahlung*) fee, subscription; (*Versicherungsbeitrag*) premium; **b~en** ['baɪtraːgən] (*unreg*) *vt, vi*: **b~en (zu)** to contribute (to); (*mithelfen*) to help (with)

beitreten ['baɪtreːtən] (*unreg*) *vi +dat* to join

Beitritt ['baɪtrɪt] *m* joining, membership

Beiwagen ['baɪvaːgən] *m* (*Motorradbeiwagen*) sidecar

beizeiten [baɪ'tsaɪtən] *adv* in time

bejahen [bə'jaːən] *vt* (*Frage*) to say yes to, to answer in the affirmative; (*gutheißen*) to agree with

bekämpfen [bə'kɛmpfən] *vt* (*Gegner*) to fight; (*Seuche*) to combat ♦ *vr* to fight;

Bekämpfung f fight, struggle

bekannt [bə'kant] adj (well-)known; (nicht fremd) familiar; **~ geben** to announce publicly; **mit jdm ~ sein** to know sb; **~ machen** to announce; **jdn mit jdm ~ machen** to introduce sb to sb; **das ist mir ~** I know that; **es/sie kommt mir ~ vor** it/she seems familiar; **B~e(r)** f(m) acquaintance; friend; **B~enkreis** m circle of friends; **~lich** adv as is well known, as you know; **B~machung** f publication; announcement; **B~schaft** f acquaintance

bekehren [bə'ke:rən] vt to convert ♦ vr to be od become converted

bekennen [bə'kɛnən] (unreg) vt to confess; (Glauben) to profess; **Farbe ~** (umg) to show where one stands

Bekenntnis [bə'kɛntnɪs] (**-ses, -se**) nt admission, confession; (Religion) confession, denomination

beklagen [bə'kla:gən] vt to deplore, to lament ♦ vr to complain

bekleiden [bə'klaɪdən] vt to clothe; (Amt) to occupy, to fill

Bekleidung f clothing

beklemmen [bə'klɛmən] vt to oppress

beklommen [bə'klɔmən] adj anxious, uneasy

bekommen [bə'kɔmən] (unreg) vt to get, to receive; (Kind) to have; (Zug) to catch, to get ♦ vi: **jdm ~** to agree with sb

bekömmlich [bə'kœmlɪç] adj easily digestible

bekräftigen [bə'krɛftɪgən] vt to confirm, to corroborate

bekreuzigen [bə'krɔytsɪgən] vr to cross o.s.

bekunden [bə'kʊndən] vt (sagen) to state; (zeigen) to show

belächeln [bə'lɛçəln] vt to laugh at

beladen [bə'la:dən] (unreg) vt to load

Belag [bə'la:k] (**-(e)s, ⁻e**) m covering, coating; (Brotbelag) spread; (Zahnbelag) tartar; (auf Zunge) fur; (Bremsbelag) lining

belagern [bə'la:gərn] vt to besiege;

Belagerung f siege

Belang [bə'laŋ] (**-(e)s**) m importance; **~e** pl (Interessen) interests, concerns; **b~los** adj trivial, unimportant

belassen [bə'lasən] (unreg) vt (in Zustand, Glauben) to leave; (in Stellung) to retain

belasten [bə'lastən] vt to burden; (fig: bedrücken) to trouble, to worry; (COMM: Konto) to debit; (JUR) to incriminate ♦ vr to weigh o.s. down; (JUR) to incriminate o.s.; **~d** adj (JUR) incriminating

belästigen [bə'lɛstɪgən] vt to annoy, to pester; **Belästigung** f annoyance, pestering

Belastung [bə'lastʊŋ] f load; (fig: Sorge etc) weight; (COMM) charge, debit(ing); (JUR) incriminatory evidence

belaufen [bə'laʊfən] (unreg) vr: **sich ~ auf** +akk to amount to

beleben [bə'le:bən] vt (anregen) to liven up; (Konjunktur, jds Hoffnungen) to stimulate ♦ vr (Augen) to light up; (Stadt) to come to life

belebt [bə'le:pt] adj (Straße) busy

Beleg [bə'le:k] (**-(e)s, -e**) m (COMM) receipt; (Beweis) documentary evidence, proof; (Beispiel) example; **b~en** vt to cover; (Kuchen, Brot) to spread; (Platz) to reserve, to book; (Kurs, Vorlesung) to register for; (beweisen) to verify, to prove; (MIL: mit Bomben) to bomb; **~schaft** f personnel, staff; **b~t** adj: **b~tes Brot** open sandwich

belehren [bə'le:rən] vt to instruct, to teach; **Belehrung** f instruction

beleibt [bə'laɪpt] adj stout, corpulent

beleidigen [bə'laɪdɪgən] vt to insult, to offend; **Beleidigung** f insult; (JUR) slander, libel

beleuchten [bə'lɔyçtən] vt to light, to illuminate; (fig) to throw light on

Beleuchtung f lighting, illumination

Belgien ['bɛlgiən] nt Belgium; **Belgier(in)** m(f) Belgian; **belgisch** adj Belgian

belichten [bə'lɪçtən] vt to expose

Belichtung f exposure; **~smesser** m exposure meter

Belieben [bə'li:bən] nt: **(ganz) nach ~** (just) as you wish

beliebig [bə'li:bɪç] adj any you like ♦ adv as you like; **ein ~es Thema** any subject you like od want; **~ viel/viele** as much/many as you like

beliebt [bə'li:pt] *adj* popular; **sich bei jdm ~ machen** to make o.s. popular with sb; **B~heit** *f* popularity

beliefern [bə'li:fərn] *vt* to supply

bellen ['bɛlən] *vi* to bark

belohnen [bə'lo:nən] *vt* to reward; **Belohnung** *f* reward

Belüftung [bə'lʏftʊŋ] *f* ventilation

belügen [bə'ly:gən] (*unreg*) *vt* to lie to, to deceive

belustigen [bə'lʊstɪgən] *vt* to amuse; **Belustigung** *f* amusement

bemalen [bə'ma:lən] *vt* to paint

bemängeln [bə'mɛŋəln] *vt* to criticize

bemerk- [bə'mɛrk] *zW:* **~bar** *adj* perceptible, noticeable; **sich ~bar machen** (*Person*) to make *od* get o.s. noticed; (*Unruhe*) to become noticeable; **~en** *vt* (*wahrnehmen*) to notice, to observe; (*sagen*) to say, to mention; **~enswert** *adj* remarkable, noteworthy; **B~ung** *f* remark; (*schriftlich auch*) note

bemitleiden [bə'mɪtlaɪdən] *vt* to pity

bemühen [bə'my:ən] *vr* to take trouble *od* pains; **Bemühung** *f* trouble, pains *pl*, effort

benachbart [bə'naxba:rt] *adj* neighbouring

benachrichtigen [bə'na:xrɪçtɪgən] *vt* to inform; **Benachrichtigung** *f* notification, information

benachteiligen [bə'na:xtaɪlɪgən] *vt* to put at a disadvantage; to victimize

benehmen [bə'ne:mən] (*unreg*) *vr* to behave; **B~** (**-s**) *nt* behaviour

beneiden [bə'naɪdən] *vt* to envy; **~swert** *adj* enviable

benennen [bə'nɛnən] (*unreg*) *vt* to name

Bengel ['bɛŋəl] (**-s, -**) *m* (little) rascal *od* rogue

benommen [bə'nɔmən] *adj* dazed

benoten [bə'no:tən] *vt* to mark

benötigen [bə'nø:tɪgən] *vt* to need

benutzen [bə'nʊtsən] *vt* to use

Benutzer (**-s, -**) *m* user

Benutzung *f* utilization, use

Benzin [bɛnt'si:n] (**-s, -e**) *nt* (*AUT*) petrol

(*BRIT*), gas(oline) (*US*); **~kanister** *m* petrol (*BRIT*) *od* gas (*US*) can; **~tank** *m* petrol tank (*BRIT*), gas tank (*US*); **~uhr** *f* petrol (*BRIT*) *od* gas (*US*) gauge

beobachten [bə'o:baxtən] *vt* to observe; **Beobachter** (**-s, -**) *m* observer; (*eines Unfalls*) witness; (*PRESSE, TV*) correspondent; **Beobachtung** *f* observation

bepacken [bə'pakən] *vt* to load, to pack

bequem [bə'kve:m] *adj* comfortable; (*Ausrede*) convenient; (*Person*) lazy, indolent; **~en** *vr*: **sich ~en(, etw zu tun)** to condescend (to do sth); **B~lichkeit** [-'lɪçkaɪt] *f* convenience, comfort; (*Faulheit*) laziness, indolence

beraten [bə'ra:tən] (*unreg*) *vt* to advise; (*besprechen*) to discuss, to debate ♦ *vr* to consult; **gut/schlecht ~ sein** to be well/ill advised; **sich ~ lassen** to get advice

Berater (**-s, -**) *m* adviser

Beratung *f* advice; (*Besprechung*) consultation; **~sstelle** *f* advice centre

berauben [bə'raubən] *vt* to rob

berechenbar [bə'rɛçənba:r] *adj* calculable

berechnen [bə'rɛçnən] *vt* to calculate; (*COMM: anrechnen*) to charge; **~d** *adj* (*Mensch*) calculating, scheming

Berechnung *f* calculation; (*COMM*) charge

berechtigen [bə'rɛçtɪgən] *vt* to entitle; to authorize; (*fig*) to justify

berechtigt [bə'rɛçtɪçt] *adj* justifiable, justified

Berechtigung *f* authorization; (*fig*) justification

bereden [bə're:dən] *vt* (*besprechen*) to discuss; (*überreden*) to persuade ♦ *vr* to discuss

Bereich [bə'raɪç] (**-(e)s, -e**) *m* (*Bezirk*) area; (*PHYS*) range; (*Ressort, Gebiet*) sphere

bereichern [bə'raɪçərn] *vt* to enrich ♦ *vr* to get rich

bereinigen [bə'raɪnɪgən] *vt* to settle

bereisen [bə'raɪzən] *vt* (*Land*) to travel through

bereit [bə'raɪt] *adj* ready, prepared; **zu etw ~ sein** to be ready for sth; **sich ~ erklären** to declare o.s. willing; **~en** *vt* to prepare, to make ready; (*Kummer, Freude*) to cause;

~halten (*unreg*) *vt* to keep in readiness; **~legen** *vt* to lay out; **~machen** *vt, vr* to prepare, to get ready; **~s** *adv* already; **B~schaft** *f* readiness; (*Polizei*) alert; **B~schaftsdienst** *m* emergency service; **~stehen** (*unreg*) *vi* (*Person*) to be prepared; (*Ding*) to be ready; **~stellen** *vt* (*Kisten, Pakete etc*) to put ready; (*Geld etc*) to make available; (*Truppen, Maschinen*) to put at the ready; **~willig** *adj* willing, ready; **B~willigkeit** *f* willingness, readiness

bereuen [bə'rɔyən] *vt* to regret

Berg [berk] **(-(e)s, -e)** *m* mountain; hill; **b~ab** *adv* downhill; **~arbeiter** *m* miner; **b~auf** *adv* uphill; **~bahn** *f* mountain railway; **b~an** *adv* uphill; **~bahn** *f* mountain railway

bergen ['bergən] (*unreg*) *vt* (*retten*) to rescue; (*Ladung*) to salvage; (*enthalten*) to contain

Berg- *zW*: **~führer** *m* mountain guide; **~gipfel** *m* peak, summit; **b~ig** ['bergɪç] *adj* mountainous; hilly; **~kette** *f* mountain range; **~mann** (*pl* **~leute**) *m* miner; **~rettungsdienst** *m* mountain rescue team; **~rutsch** *m* landslide; **~steigen** *nt* mountaineering; **~steiger(in) (-s, -)** *m(f)* mountaineer, climber; **~tour** *f* mountain climb

Bergung ['bergʊŋ] *f* (*von Menschen*) rescue; (*von Material*) recovery; (*NAUT*) salvage

Berg- *zW*: **~wacht** *f* mountain rescue service; **~wanderung** *f* hike in the mountains; **~werk** *nt* mine

Bericht [bə'rɪçt] **(-(e)s, -e)** *m* report, account; **b~en** *vt, vi* to report; **~erstatter (-s, -)** *m* reporter; (*newspaper*) correspondent

berichtigen [bə'rɪçtɪgən] *vt* to correct; **Berichtigung** *f* correction

Bernstein ['bernʃtaɪn] *m* amber

bersten ['berstən] (*unreg*) *vi* to burst, to split

berüchtigt [bə'rʏçtɪçt] *adj* notorious, infamous

berücksichtigen [bə'rʏkzɪçtɪgən] *vt* to consider, to bear in mind; **Berücksichtigung** *f* consideration

Beruf [bə'ruːf] **(-(e)s, -e)** *m* occupation, profession; (*Gewerbe*) trade; **b~en** (*unreg*)

vt: **b~en zu** to appoint to ♦ *vr*: **sich auf jdn/etw b~en** to refer *od* appeal to sb/sth ♦ *adj* competent, qualified; **b~lich** *adj* professional

Berufs- *zW*: **~ausbildung** *f* job training; **~berater** *m* careers adviser; **~beratung** *f* vocational guidance; **~geheimnis** *nt* professional secret; **~leben** *nt* professional life; **~schule** *f* vocational *od* trade school; **~sportler** [-ʃpɔrtlər] *m* professional (sportsman); **b~tätig** *adj* employed; **b~unfähig** *adj* unfit for work; **~verkehr** *m* rush-hour traffic

Berufung *f* vocation, calling; (*Ernennung*) appointment; (*JUR*) appeal; **~ einlegen** to appeal

beruhen [bə'ruːən] *vi*: **auf etw** *dat* **~** to be based on sth; **etw auf sich ~ lassen** to leave sth at that

beruhigen [bə'ruːɪgən] *vt* to calm, to pacify, to soothe ♦ *vr* (*Mensch*) to calm (o.s.) down; (*Situation*) to calm down

Beruhigung *f* soothing; (*der Nerven*) calming; **zu jds ~** (in order) to reassure sb; **~smittel** *nt* sedative

berühmt [bə'ryːmt] *adj* famous; **B~heit** *f* (*Ruf*) fame; (*Mensch*) celebrity

berühren [bə'ryːrən] *vt* to touch; (*gefühlsmäßig bewegen*) to affect; (*flüchtig erwähnen*) to mention, to touch on ♦ *vr* to meet, to touch

Berührung *f* contact

besagen [bə'zaːgən] *vt* to mean

besänftigen [bə'zɛnftɪgən] *vt* to soothe, to calm

Besatz [bə'zats] **(-es, ⸚e)** *m* trimming, edging

Besatzung *f* garrison; (*NAUT, AVIAT*) crew

Besatzungsmacht *f* occupying power

beschädigen [bə'ʃɛːdɪgən] *vt* to damage; **Beschädigung** *f* damage; (*Stelle*) damaged spot

beschaffen [bə'ʃafən] *vt* to get, to acquire ♦ *adj*: **das ist so ~, dass** that is such that; **B~heit** *f* (*von Mensch*) constitution, nature

Beschaffung *f* acquisition

beschäftigen [bə'ʃɛftɪgən] *vt* to occupy;

(*beruflich*) to employ ♦ *vr* to occupy *od* concern o.s.

beschäftigt *adj* busy, occupied

Beschäftigung *f* (*Beruf*) employment; (*Tätigkeit*) occupation; (*Befassen*) concern

beschämen [bə'ʃɛːmən] *vt* to put to shame; ~d *adj* shameful; (*Hilfsbereitschaft*) shaming

beschämt *adj* ashamed

Bescheid [bə'ʃaɪt] (-(e)s, -e) *m* information; (*Weisung*) directions *pl*; ~ **wissen (über** +*akk*) to be well-informed (about); **ich weiß** ~ I know; **jdm** ~ **geben** *od* **sagen** to let sb know

bescheiden [bə'ʃaɪdən] (*unreg*) *vr* to content o.s. ♦ *adj* modest; **B~heit** *f* modesty

bescheinen [bə'ʃaɪnən] (*unreg*) *vt* to shine on

bescheinigen [bə'ʃaɪnɪgən] *vt* to certify; (*bestätigen*) to acknowledge

Bescheinigung *f* certificate; (*Quittung*) receipt

beschenken [bə'ʃɛŋkən] *vt*: **jdn mit etw** ~ to give sb sth as a present

bescheren [bə'ʃeːrən] *vt*: **jdm etw** ~ to give sb sth as a Christmas present; **jdn** ~ to give Christmas presents to sb

Bescherung *f* giving of Christmas presents; (*umg*) mess

beschildern [bə'ʃɪldərn] *vt* to put signs/a sign on

beschimpfen [bə'ʃɪmpfən] *vt* to abuse; **Beschimpfung** *f* abuse; insult

Beschlag [bə'ʃlaːk] (-(e)s, ⁺e) *m* (*Metallband*) fitting; (*auf Fenster*) condensation; (*auf Metall*) tarnish; finish; (*Hufeisen*) horseshoe; **jdn/etw in** ~ **nehmen** *od* **mit** ~ **belegen** to monopolize sb/sth; **b~en** [bə'ʃlaːgən] (*unreg*) *vt* to cover; (*Pferd*) to shoe ♦ *vi*, *vr* (*Fenster etc*) to mist over; **b~en sein (in** *od* **auf** +*dat*) to be well versed (in); **b~nahmen** *vt* to seize, to confiscate; (*requisition*) to requisition; ~**nahmung** *f* confiscation, sequestration

beschleunigen [bə'ʃlɔʏnɪgən] *vt* to accelerate, to speed up ♦ *vi* (*AUT*) to accelerate; **Beschleunigung** *f* acceleration

beschließen [bə'ʃliːsən] (*unreg*) *vt* to decide on; (*beenden*) to end, to close

Beschluss ▲ [bə'ʃlʊs] (-es, ⁺e) *m* decision, conclusion; (*Ende*) conclusion, end

beschmutzen [bə'ʃmʊtsən] *vt* to dirty, to soil

beschönigen [bə'ʃøːnɪgən] *vt* to gloss over

beschränken [bə'ʃrɛŋkən] *vt*, *vr*: **(sich)** ~ **(auf** +*akk*) to limit *od* restrict (o.s.) (to)

beschränk- *zW*: ~**t** *adj* confined, restricted; (*Mensch*) limited, narrow-minded; **B~ung** *f* limitation

beschreiben [bə'ʃraɪbən] (*unreg*) *vt* to describe; (*Papier*) to write on

Beschreibung *f* description

beschriften [bə'ʃrɪftən] *vt* to mark, to label; **Beschriftung** *f* lettering

beschuldigen [bə'ʃʊldɪgən] *vt* to accuse; **Beschuldigung** *f* accusation

Beschuss ▲ [bə'ʃʊs] *m*: **jdn/etw unter** ~ **nehmen** (*MIL*) to open fire on sb/sth

beschützen [bə'ʃʏtsən] *vt*: ~ **(vor** +*dat*) to protect (from); **Beschützer (-s, -)** *m* protector

Beschwerde [bə'ʃveːrdə] *f* complaint; (*Mühe*) hardship; ~**n** *pl* (*Leiden*) trouble

beschweren [bə'ʃveːrən] *vt* to weight down; (*fig*) to burden ♦ *vr* to complain

beschwerlich *adj* tiring, exhausting

beschwichtigen [bə'ʃvɪçtɪgən] *vt* to soothe, to pacify

beschwindeln [bə'ʃvɪndəln] *vt* (*betrügen*) to cheat; (*belügen*) to fib to

beschwingt [bə'ʃvɪŋt] *adj* in high spirits

beschwipst [bə'ʃvɪpst] (*umg*) *adj* tipsy

beschwören [bə'ʃvøːrən] (*unreg*) *vt* (*Aussage*) to swear to; (*anflehen*) to implore; (*Geister*) to conjure up

beseitigen [bə'zaɪtɪgən] *vt* to remove; **Beseitigung** *f* removal

Besen ['beːzən] (-s, -) *m* broom; ~**stiel** *m* broomstick

besessen [bə'zɛsən] *adj* possessed

besetz- [bə'zɛts] *zW*: ~**en** *vt* (*Haus, Land*) to occupy; (*Platz*) to take, to fill; (*Posten*) to fill; (*Rolle*) to cast; (*mit Edelsteinen*) to set; ~**t** *adj* full; (*TEL*) engaged, busy; (*Platz*) taken;

(*WC*) engaged; **B~tzeichen** *nt* engaged tone; **B~ung** *f* occupation; filling; (*von Rolle*) casting; (*die Schauspieler*) cast

besichtigen [bə'zɪçtɪɡən] *vt* to visit, to have a look at; **Besichtigung** *f* visit

besiegen [bə'zi:ɡən] *vt* to defeat, to overcome

besinn- [bə'zɪn] *zW:* **~en** (*unreg*) *vr* (*nachdenken*) to think, to reflect; (*erinnern*) to remember; **sich anders ~en** to change one's mind; **B~ung** *f* consciousness; **zur B~ung kommen** to recover consciousness; (*fig*) to come to one's senses; **~ungslos** *adj* unconscious

Besitz [bə'zɪts] (**-es**) *m* possession; (*Eigentum*) property; **b~en** (*unreg*) *vt* to possess, to own; (*Eigenschaft*) to have; **~er(in)** (**-s, -**) *m(f)* owner, proprietor; **~ergreifung** *f* occupation, seizure

besoffen [bə'zɔfən] (*umg*) *adj* drunk, stoned

besohlen [bə'zo:lən] *vt* to sole

Besoldung [bə'zɔldʊŋ] *f* salary, pay

besondere(r, s) [bə'zɔndərə(r, s)] *adj* special; (*eigen*) particular; (*gesondert*) separate; (*eigentümlich*) peculiar

Besonderheit [bə'zɔndərhaɪt] *f* peculiarity

besonders [bə'zɔndərs] *adv* especially, particularly; (*getrennt*) separately

besonnen [bə'zɔnən] *adj* sensible, level-headed

besorg- [bə'zɔrg] *zW:* **~en** *vt* (*beschaffen*) to acquire; (*kaufen auch*) to purchase; (*erledigen: Geschäfte*) to deal with; (*sich kümmern um*) to take care of; **B~nis** (**-, -se**) *f* anxiety, concern; **~t** [bə'zɔrçt] *adj* anxious, worried; **B~ung** *f* acquisition; (*Kauf*) purchase

bespielen [bə'ʃpi:lən] *vt* to record

bespitzeln [bə'ʃpɪtsəln] *vt* to spy on

besprechen [bə'ʃprɛçən] (*unreg*) *vt* to discuss; (*Tonband etc*) to record, to speak onto; (*Buch*) to review ♦ *vr* to discuss, to consult; **Besprechung** *f* meeting, discussion; (*von Buch*) review

besser ['bɛsər] *adj* better; **es geht ihm ~** he is feeling better; **~n** *vt* to make better, to improve ♦ *vr* to improve; (*Menschen*) to

reform; **B~ung** *f* improvement; **gute B~ung!** get well soon!; **B~wisser** (**-s, -**) *m* know-all

Bestand [bə'ʃtant] (**-(e)s, �430e**) *m* (*Fortbestehen*) duration, stability; (*Kassenbestand*) amount, balance; (*Vorrat*) stock; **~ haben, von ~ sein** to last long, to endure

beständig [bə'ʃtɛndɪç] *adj* (*ausdauernd: auch fig*) constant; (*Wetter*) settled; (*Stoffe*) resistant; (*Klagen etc*) continual

Bestandsaufnahme [bə'ʃtantsaufna:mə] *f* stocktaking

Bestandteil *m* part, component; (*Zutat*) ingredient

bestärken [bə'ʃtɛrkən] *vt:* **jdn in etw** *dat* **~** to strengthen *od* confirm sb in sth

bestätigen [bə'ʃtɛ:tɪgən] *vt* to confirm; (*anerkennen, COMM*) to acknowledge; **Bestätigung** *f* confirmation; acknowledgement

bestatten [bə'ʃtatən] *vt* to bury

Bestattung *f* funeral

Bestattungsinstitut *nt* funeral director's

bestaunen [bə'ʃtaʊnən] *vt* to marvel at, gaze at in wonder

beste(r, s) ['bɛstə(r, s)] *adj* best; **so ist es am ~n** it's best that way; **am ~n gehst du gleich** you'd better go at once; **jdn zum B~n haben** to pull sb's leg; **einen Witz** *etc* **zum B~n geben** to tell a joke *etc*; **aufs B~** *od* **~** in the best possible way; **zu jds B~n** for the benefit of sb

bestechen [bə'ʃtɛçən] (*unreg*) *vt* to bribe; **bestechlich** *adj* corruptible; **Bestechung** *f* bribery, corruption

Besteck [bə'ʃtɛk] (**-(e)s, -e**) *nt* knife, fork and spoon, cutlery; (*MED*) set of instruments

bestehen [bə'ʃte:ən] (*unreg*) *vi* to be; to exist; (*andauern*) to last ♦ *vt* (*Kampf, Probe, Prüfung*) to pass; **~ auf** +*dat* to insist on; **~ aus** to consist of

bestehlen [bə'ʃte:lən] (*unreg*) *vt:* **jdn (um etw) ~** to rob sb (of sth)

besteigen [bə'ʃtaɪgən] (*unreg*) *vt* to climb, to ascend; (*Pferd*) to mount; (*Thron*) to ascend

Spelling Reform: ▲ *new spelling* △ *old spelling (to be phased out)*

Bestell- [bə'ʃtɛl] *zW:* **~buch** *nt* order book;
b~en *vt* to order; (*kommen lassen*) to
arrange to see; (*nominieren*) to name;
(*Acker*) to cultivate; (*Grüße, Auftrag*) to pass
on; **~formular** *nt* order form; **~nummer** *f*
order code; **~ung** *f* (*COMM*) order; (*~en*)
ordering

bestenfalls ['bɛstən'fals] *adv* at best

bestens ['bɛstəns] *adv* very well

besteuern [bə'ʃtɔyərn] *vt* (*jdn, Waren*) to tax

Bestie ['bɛstiə] *f* (*auch fig*) beast

bestimm- [bə'ʃtɪm] *zW:* **~en** *vt* (*Regeln*) to
lay down; (*Tag, Ort*) to fix; (*beherrschen*) to
characterize; (*vorsehen*) to mean; (*ernennen*)
to appoint; (*definieren*) to define;
(*veranlassen*) to induce; **~t** *adj* (*entschlossen*)
firm; (*gewiss*) certain, definite; (*Artikel*)
definite ♦ *adv* (*gewiss*) definitely, for sure;
suchen Sie etwas B~tes? are you looking
for something in particular?; **B~theit** *f*
firmness; certainty; **B~ung** *f* (*Verordnung*)
regulation; (*Festsetzen*) determining;
(*Verwendungszweck*) purpose; (*Schicksal*)
fate; (*Definition*) definition; **B~ungsland** *nt*
(country of) destination; **B~ungsort** *m*
(place of) destination

Bestleistung *f* best performance

bestmöglich *adj* best possible

bestrafen [bə'ʃtra:fən] *vt* to punish;
Bestrafung *f* punishment

bestrahlen [bə'ʃtra:lən] *vt* to shine on;
(*MED*) to treat with X-rays

Bestrahlung *f* (*MED*) X-ray treatment,
radiotherapy

Bestreben [bə'ʃtre:bən] (**-s**) *nt* endeavour,
effort

bestreiten [bə'ʃtraitən] (*unreg*) *vt* (*abstreiten*)
to dispute; (*finanzieren*) to pay for, to
finance

bestreuen [bə'ʃtrɔyən] *vt* to sprinkle, to
dust; (*Straße*) to grit

bestürmen [bə'ʃtyrmən] *vt* (*mit Fragen,
Bitten etc*) to overwhelm, to swamp

bestürzend [bə'ʃtyrtsənd] *adj* (*Nachrichten*)
disturbing

bestürzt [bə'ʃtyrtst] *adj* dismayed

Bestürzung *f* consternation

Besuch [bə'zu:x] (**-(e)s, -e**) *m* visit; (*Person*)
visitor; **einen ~ machen bei jdm** to pay sb
a visit *od* call; **~ haben** to have visitors; **bei
jdm auf** *od* **zu ~ sein** to be visiting sb;
b~en *vt* to visit; (*SCH etc*) to attend; **gut
b~t** well-attended; **~er(in)** (**-s, -**) *m(f)*
visitor, guest; **~szeit** *f* visiting hours *pl*

betätigen [bə'tɛ:tɪgən] *vt* (*bedienen*) to work,
to operate ♦ *vr* to involve o.s.; **sich als etw
~** to work as sth

Betätigung *f* activity; (*beruflich*)
occupation; (*TECH*) operation

betäuben [bə'tɔybən] *vt* to stun; (*fig:
Gewissen*) to still; (*MED*) to anaesthetize

Betäubung *f* (*Narkose*): **örtliche ~** local
anaesthetic

Betäubungsmittel *nt* anaesthetic

Bete ['be:tə] *f*: **Rote ~** beetroot (*BRIT*), beet
(*US*)

beteilig- [bə'tailɪg] *zW:* **~en** *vr:* **sich ~en
(an** +*dat*) to take part (in), to participate
(in), to share (in); (*an Geschäft: finanziell*) to
have a share (in) ♦ *vt:* **jdn ~en (an** +*dat*) to
give sb a share *od* interest (in); **B~te(r)**
f(m) (*Mitwirkender*) partner; (*finanziell*)
shareholder; **B~ung** *f* participation; (*Anteil*)
share, interest; (*Besucherzahl*) attendance

beten ['be:tən] *vt, vi* to pray

beteuern [bə'tɔyərn] *vt* to assert; (*Unschuld*)
to protest

Beton [be'tõ:] (**-s, -s**) *m* concrete

betonen [bə'to:nən] *vt* to stress

betonieren [beto'ni:rən] *vt* to concrete

Betonung *f* stress, emphasis

betr. *abk* (= *betrifft*)

Betracht [bə'traxt] *m*: **in ~ kommen** to be
considered *od* relevant; **etw in ~ ziehen** to
take sth into consideration; **außer ~
bleiben** not to be considered; **b~en** *vt* to
look at; (*fig*) to look at, to consider; **~er(in)**
(**-s, -**) *m(f)* observer

beträchtlich [bə'trɛçtlɪç] *adj* considerable

Betrachtung *f* (*Ansehen*) examination;
(*Erwägung*) consideration

Betrag [bə'tra:k] (**-(e)s, ⁻e**) *m* amount;
b~en (*unreg*) *vt* to amount to ♦ *vr* to
behave; **~en** (**-s**) *nt* behaviour

Rechtschreibreform: ▲ *neue Schreibung* △ *alte Schreibung (auslaufend)*

Betreff *m*: ~ **Ihr Schreiben vom ...** re your letter of ...

betreffen [bə'trɛfən] (*unreg*) *vt* to concern, to affect; **was mich betrifft** as for me; **~d** *adj* relevant, in question

betreffs [bə'trɛfs] *präp +gen* concerning, regarding; (*COMM*) re

betreiben [bə'traɪbən] (*unreg*) *vt* (*ausüben*) to practise; (*Politik*) to follow; (*Studien*) to pursue; (*vorantreiben*) to push ahead; (*TECH*: *antreiben*) to drive

betreten [bə'tre:tən] (*unreg*) *vt* to enter; (*Bühne etc*) to step onto ♦ *adj* embarrassed; **B~ verboten** keep off/out

Betreuer(in) [bə'trɔyər(ɪn)] (**-s, -**) *m(f)* (*einer Person*) minder; (*eines Gebäudes, Arbeitsgebiets*) caretaker; (*SPORT*) coach

Betreuung *f* care

Betrieb [bə'tri:p] (**-(e)s, -e**) *m* (*Firma*) firm, concern; (*Anlage*) plant; (*Tätigkeit*) operation; (*Treiben*) traffic; **außer ~ sein** to be out of order; **in ~ sein** to be in operation

Betriebs- *zW*: **~ausflug** *m* works outing; **b~bereit** *adj* operational; **b~fähig** *adj* in working order; **~ferien** *pl* company holidays (*BRIT*), company vacation *sg* (*US*); **~klima** *nt* (*working*) atmosphere; **~kosten** *pl* running costs; **~rat** *m* workers' council; **b~sicher** *adj* safe (to operate); **~störung** *f* breakdown; **~system** *nt* (*COMPUT*) operating system; **~unfall** *m* industrial accident; **~wirtschaft** *f* economics

betrinken [bə'trɪŋkən] (*unreg*) *vr* to get drunk

betroffen [bə'trɔfən] *adj* (*bestürzt*) full of consternation; **von etw ~ werden** *od* **sein** to be affected by sth

betrüben [bə'try:bən] *vt* to grieve

betrübt [bə'try:pt] *adj* sorrowful, grieved

Betrug [bə'tru:k] (**-(e)s**) *m* deception; (*JUR*) fraud

betrügen [bə'try:gən] (*unreg*) *vt* to cheat; (*JUR*) to defraud; (*Ehepartner*) to be unfaithful to ♦ *vr* to deceive o.s.

Betrüger (**-s, -**) *m* cheat, deceiver; **b~isch** *adj* deceitful; (*JUR*) fraudulent

betrunken [bə'trʊŋkən] *adj* drunk

Bett [bɛt] (**-(e)s, -en**) *nt* bed; **ins** *od* **zu ~ gehen** to go to bed; **~bezug** *m* duvet cover; **~decke** *f* blanket; (*Daunenbett*) quilt; (*Überwurf*) bedspread

Bettel- ['bɛtəl] *zW*: **b~arm** *adj* very poor, destitute; **~ei** [bɛtə'laɪ] *f* begging; **b~n** *vi* to beg

bettlägerig ['bɛtlɛːgərɪç] *adj* bedridden

Bettlaken *nt* sheet

Bettler(in) ['bɛtlər(ɪn)] (**-s, -**) *m(f)* beggar

Bett- *zW*: **~tuch** ▲ *nt* sheet; **~vorleger** *m* bedside rug; **~wäsche** *f* bed linen; **~zeug** *nt* bed linen *pl*

beugen ['bɔygən] *vt* to bend; (*GRAM*) to inflect ♦ *vr* (*sich fügen*) to bow

Beule ['bɔylə] *f* bump, swelling

beunruhigen [bə'ʊnruːɪgən] *vt* to disturb, to alarm ♦ *vr* to become worried

Beunruhigung *f* worry, alarm

beurlauben [bə'uːrlaʊbən] *vt* to give leave *od* a holiday to (*BRIT*), to grant vacation time to (*US*)

beurteilen [bə'ʊrtaɪlən] *vt* to judge; (*Buch etc*) to review

Beurteilung *f* judgement; review; (*Note*) mark

Beute ['bɔytə] (**-**) *f* booty, loot

Beutel (**-s, -**) *m* bag; (*Geldbeutel*) purse; (*Tabakbeutel*) pouch

Bevölkerung [bə'fœlkərʊŋ] *f* population

bevollmächtigen [bə'fɔlmɛçtɪgən] *vt* to authorize

Bevollmächtigte(r) *f(m)* authorized agent

bevor [bə'foːr] *konj* before; **~munden** *vt insep* to treat like a child; **~stehen** (*unreg*) *vi*: (*jdm*) **~stehen** to be in store (for sb); **~stehend** *adj* imminent, approaching; **~zugen** *vt insep* to prefer

bewachen [bə'vaxən] *vt* to watch, to guard

Bewachung *f* (*Bewachen*) guarding; (*Leute*) guard, watch

bewaffnen [bə'vafnən] *vt* to arm

Bewaffnung *f* (*Vorgang*) arming; (*Ausrüstung*) armament, arms *pl*

bewahren [bə'vaːrən] *vt* to keep; **jdn vor jdm/etw ~** to save sb from sb/sth

bewähren [bəˈvɛːrən] *vr* to prove o.s.; (*Maschine*) to prove its worth

bewahrheiten [bəˈvaːrhaɪtən] *vr* to come true

bewährt *adj* reliable

Bewährung *f* (*JUR*) probation

bewältigen [bəˈvɛltɪgən] *vt* to overcome; (*Arbeit*) to finish; (*Portion*) to manage

bewandert [bəˈvandərt] *adj* expert, knowledgeable

bewässern [bəˈvɛsərn] *vt* to irrigate

Bewässerung *f* irrigation

bewegen [bəˈveːgən] *vt, vr* to move; **jdn zu etw ~** to induce sb to do sth; **~d** *adj* touching, moving

Beweg- [bəˈveːk] *zW:* **~grund** *m* motive; **b~lich** *adj* movable, mobile; (*flink*) quick; **b~t** *adj* (*Leben*) eventful; (*Meer*) rough; (*ergriffen*) touched

Bewegung *f* movement, motion; (*innere*) emotion; (*körperlich*) exercise; **~sfreiheit** *f* freedom of movement; (*fig*) freedom of action; **b~ungslos** *adj* motionless

Beweis [bəˈvaɪs] (**-es, -e**) *m* proof; (*Zeichen*) sign; **b~en** [-zən] (*unreg*) *vt* to prove; (*zeigen*) to show; **~mittel** *nt* evidence

Bewerb- [bəˈvɛrb] *zW:* **b~en** (*unreg*) *vr* to apply (for); **~er(in)** (**-s, -**) *m(f)* applicant; **~ung** *f* application

bewerkstelligen [bəˈvɛrkʃtɛlɪgən] *vt* to manage, to accomplish

bewerten [bəˈveːrtən] *vt* to assess

bewilligen [bəˈvɪlɪgən] *vt* to grant, to allow

Bewilligung *f* granting

bewirken [bəˈvɪrkən] *vt* to cause, to bring about

bewirten [bəˈvɪrtən] *vt* to feed, to entertain (to a meal)

bewirtschaften [bəˈvɪrtʃaftən] *vt* to manage

Bewirtung *f* hospitality

bewog *etc* [bəˈvoːk] *vb siehe* **bewegen**

bewohn- [bəˈvoːn] *zW:* **~bar** *adj* habitable; **~en** *vt* to inhabit, to live in; **B~er(in)** (**-s, -**) *m(f)* inhabitant; (*von Haus*) resident

bewölkt [bəˈvœlkt] *adj* cloudy, overcast

Bewölkung *f* clouds *pl*

Bewunder- [bəˈvʊndər] *zW:* **~er** (**-s, -**) *m* admirer; **b~n** *vt* to admire; **b~nswert** *adj* admirable, wonderful; **~ung** *f* admiration

bewusst ▲ [bəˈvʊst] *adj* conscious; (*absichtlich*) deliberate; **sich** *dat* **einer Sache** *gen* **~ sein** to be aware of sth; **~los** *adj* unconscious; **B~losigkeit** *f* unconsciousness; **B~sein** *nt* consciousness; **bei B~sein** conscious

bezahlen [bəˈtsaːlən] *vt* to pay for

Bezahlung *f* payment

bezaubern [bəˈtsaʊbərn] *vt* to enchant, to charm

bezeichnen [bəˈtsaɪçnən] *vt* (*kennzeichnen*) to mark; (*nennen*) to call; (*beschreiben*) to describe; (*zeigen*) to show, to indicate; **~d** *adj*: **~d (für)** characteristic (of), typical (of)

Bezeichnung *f* (*Zeichen*) mark, sign; (*Beschreibung*) description

bezeugen [bəˈtsɔʏgən] *vt* to testify to

Bezichtigung [bəˈtsɪçtɪgʊŋ] *f* accusation

beziehen [bəˈtsiːən] (*unreg*) *vt* (*mit Überzug*) to cover; (*Bett*) to make; (*Haus, Position*) to move into; (*Standpunkt*) to take up; (*erhalten*) to receive; (*Zeitung*) to subscribe to, to take ♦ *vr* (*Himmel*) to cloud over; **etw auf jdn/etw ~** to relate sth to sb/sth; **sich ~ auf** +*akk* to refer to

Beziehung *f* (*Verbindung*) connection; (*Zusammenhang*) relation; (*Verhältnis*) relationship; (*Hinsicht*) respect; **~en haben** (*vorteilhaft*) to have connections *pl* of contacts; **b~sweise** *adv* or; (*genauer gesagt auch*) that is, or rather

Bezirk [bəˈtsɪrk] (**-(e)s, -e**) *m* district

Bezug [bəˈtsuːk] (**-(e)s, ⁴e**) *m* (*Hülle*) covering; (*COMM*) income, salary; (*Beziehung*): **~ (zu)** relation(ship) (to); **in ~ auf** +*akk* with reference to; **~ nehmen auf** +*akk* to refer to

bezüglich [bəˈtsyːklɪç] *präp* +*gen* concerning, referring to ♦ *adj* (*GRAM*) relative; **auf etw** *akk* **~** relating to sth

bezwecken [bəˈtsvɛkən] *vt* to aim at

bezweifeln [bəˈtsvaɪfəln] *vt* to doubt, to query

Rechtschreibreform: ▲ *neue Schreibung* △ *alte Schreibung (auslaufend)*

BH *m abk von* **Büstenhalter**

Bhf. *abk* (= *Bahnhof*) station

Bibel ['biːbəl] (-, -n) *f* Bible

Biber ['biːbər] (-s, -) *m* beaver

Biblio- [biːblio] *zW:* **~grafie** ▲ [-gra'fiː] *f* bibliography; **~thek** [-'teːk] (-, -en) *f* library; **~thekar(in)** [-te'kaːr(ɪn)] (-s, -e) *m(f)* librarian

biblisch ['biːblɪʃ] *adj* biblical

bieder ['biːdər] *adj* upright, worthy; (*Kleid etc*) plain

bieg- ['biːg] *zW:* **~en** (*unreg*) *vt, vr* to bend ♦ *vi* to turn; **~sam** ['biːk-] *adj* flexible; **B~ung** *f* bend, curve

Biene ['biːnə] *f* bee

Bienenhonig *m* honey

Bienenwachs *nt* beeswax

Bier [biːr] (-(e)s, -e) *nt* beer; **~deckel** *m* beer mat; **~garten** *m* beer garden; **~krug** *m* beer mug; **~zelt** *nt* beer tent

Biest [biːst] (-(e)s, -er) (*umg: pej*) *nt* (*Tier*) beast, creature; (*Mensch*) beast

bieten ['biːtən] (*unreg*) *vt* to offer; (*bei Versteigerung*) to bid ♦ *vr* (*Gelegenheit*): **sich jdm ~** to present itself to sb; **sich** *dat* **etw ~ lassen** to put up with sth

Bikini [bi'kiːni] (-s, -s) *m* bikini

Bilanz [bi'lants] *f* balance; (*fig*) outcome; **~ziehen (aus)** to take stock (of)

Bild [bɪlt] (-(e)s, -er) *nt* (*auch fig*) picture; photo; (*Spiegelbild*) reflection; **~bericht** *m* photographic report

bilden ['bɪldən] *vt* to form; (*erziehen*) to educate; (*ausmachen*) to constitute ♦ *vr* to arise; (*erziehen*) to educate o.s.

Bilderbuch *nt* picture book

Bilderrahmen *m* picture frame

Bild- *zW:* **~fläche** *f* screen; (*fig*) scene; **~hauer** (-s, -) *m* sculptor; **b~hübsch** *adj* lovely, pretty as a picture; **b~lich** *adj* figurative; pictorial; **~schirm** *m* television screen; (*COMPUT*) monitor; **~schirmschoner** *m* (*COMPUT*) screen saver; **b~schön** *adj* lovely

Bildung [bɪldʊŋ] *f* formation; (*Wissen, Benehmen*) education

Billard ['bɪljart] (-s, -e) *nt* billiards *sg*;

~kugel *f* billiard ball

billig ['bɪlɪç] *adj* cheap; (*gerecht*) fair, reasonable; **~en** ['bɪlɪgən] *vt* to approve of

Binde ['bɪndə] *f* bandage; (*Armbinde*) band; (*MED*) sanitary towel; **~gewebe** *nt* connective tissue; **~glied** *nt* connecting link; **~hautentzündung** *f* conjunctivitis; **b~n** (*unreg*) *vt* to bind, to tie; **~strich** *m* hyphen

Bindfaden ['bɪnt-] *m* string

Bindung *f* bond, tie; (*Skibindung*) binding

binnen ['bɪnən] *präp* (+*dat od gen*) within; **B~hafen** *m* river port; **B~handel** *m* internal trade

Bio- [bio-] *in zW* bio-; **~chemie** *f* biochemistry; **~grafie** ▲ [-gra'fiː] *f* biography; **~laden** *m* wholefood shop; **~loge** [-'loːgə] (-n, -n) *m* biologist; **~logie** [-lo'giː] *f* biology; **b~logisch** [-'loːgɪʃ] *adj* biological; **~top** *m od nt* biotope

---

Bioladen

i A **Bioladen** *is a shop specializing in environmentally-friendly products such as phosphate-free washing powders, recycled paper and organically-grown vegetables.*

Birke ['bɪrkə] *f* birch

Birne ['bɪrnə] *f* pear; (*ELEK*) (light) bulb

SCHLÜSSELWORT

bis [bɪs] *präp +akk, adv* **1** (*zeitlich*) till, until; (*bis spätestens*) by; **Sie haben bis Dienstag Zeit** you have until *od* till Tuesday; **bis Dienstag muss es fertig sein** it must be ready by Tuesday; **bis auf weiteres** until further notice; **bis in die Nacht** into the night; **bis bald/gleich** see you later/soon **2** (*räumlich*) (up) to; **ich fahre bis Köln** I'm going to *od* I'm going as far as Cologne; **bis an unser Grundstück** (right *od* up) to our plot; **bis hierher** this far **3** (*bei Zahlen*) up to; **bis zu** up to **4**: **bis auf etw** *akk* (*außer*) except sth; (*einschließlich*) including sth ♦ *konj* **1** (*mit Zahlen*) to; **10 bis 20** 10 to 20 **2** (*zeitlich*) till, until; **bis es dunkel wird** till

---

od until it gets dark; **von ... bis ...** from ... to ...

Bischof ['bɪʃɔf] **(-s, ⁻e)** *m* bishop; **bischöflich** ['bɪʃøːflɪç] *adj* episcopal
bisher [bɪs'heːr] *adv* till now, hitherto; **~ig** *adj* till now
Biskuit [bɪs'kviːt] **(-(e)s, -s** *od* **-e)** *m od nt* (fatless) sponge
Biss ▲ [bɪs] **(-es, -e)** *m* bite
biss ▲ *etc vb siehe* **beißen**
bisschen ▲ ['bɪsçən] *adj, adv* bit
Bissen ['bɪsən] **(-s, -)** *m* bite, morsel
bissig ['bɪsɪç] *adj* (*Hund*) snappy; (*Bemerkung*) cutting, biting
bist [bɪst] *vb siehe* **sein**
bisweilen [bɪs'vaɪlən] *adv* at times, occasionally
Bitte ['bɪtə] *f* request; **b~** *excl* please; (*wie b~?*) (I beg your) pardon? ♦ *interj* (*als Antwort auf Dank*) you're welcome; **darf ich? – aber b~!** may I? – please do; **b~ schön!** it was a pleasure; **b~n** (*unreg*) *vt, vi*: **b~n (um)** to ask (for); **b~nd** *adj* pleading, imploring
bitter ['bɪtər] *adj* bitter; **~böse** *adj* very angry; **B~keit** *f* bitterness; **~lich** *adj* bitter
Blähungen ['blɛːʊŋən] *pl* (*MED*) wind *sg*
blamabel [bla'maːbəl] *adj* disgraceful
Blamage [bla'maːʒə] *f* disgrace
blamieren [bla'miːrən] *vr* to make a fool of o.s., to disgrace o.s. ♦ *vt* to let down, to disgrace
blank [blaŋk] *adj* bright; (*unbedeckt*) bare; (*sauber*) clean, polished; (*umg: ohne Geld*) broke; (*offensichtlich*) blatant
blanko ['blaŋko] *adv* blank; **B~scheck** *m* blank cheque
Blase ['blaːzə] *f* bubble; (*MED*) blister; (*ANAT*) bladder; **~balg(-(e)s, -bälge)** *m* bellows *pl*; **b~n** (*unreg*) *vt, vi* to blow; **~nentzündung** *f* cystitis
Blas- ['blaːs] *zW*: **~instrument** *nt* wind instrument; **~kapelle** *f* brass band
blass ▲ [blas] *adj* pale
Blässe ['blɛsə] (*-*) *f* paleness, pallor
Blatt [blat] **(-(e)s, ⁻er)** *nt* leaf; (*von Papier*)

sheet; (*Zeitung*) newspaper; (*KARTEN*) hand
blättern ['blɛtərn] *vi*: **in etw** *dat* **~** to leaf through sth
Blätterteig *m* flaky *od* puff pastry
blau [blaʊ] *adj* blue; (*umg*) drunk, stoned; (*KOCH*) boiled; (*Auge*) black; **~er Fleck** bruise; **Fahrt ins B~e** mystery tour; **~äugig** *adj* blue-eyed
Blech [blɛç] **(-(e)s, -e)** *nt* tin, sheet metal; (*Backblech*) baking tray; **~büchse** *f* tin, can; **~dose** *f* tin, can; **b~en** (*umg*) *vt, vi* to fork out; **~schaden** *m* (*AUT*) damage to bodywork
Blei [blaɪ] **(-(e)s, -e)** *nt* lead
Bleibe ['blaɪbə] *f* roof over one's head; **b~n** (*unreg*) *vi* to stay, to remain; **~ lassen** to leave alone; **b~nd** *adj* (*Erinnerung*) lasting; (*Schaden*) permanent
bleich [blaɪç] *adj* faded, pale; **~en** *vt* to bleach
Blei- *zW*: **b~ern** *adj* leaden; **b~frei** *adj* (*Benzin*) lead-free; **~stift** *m* pencil
Blende ['blɛndə] *f* (*PHOT*) aperture; **b~n** *vt* to blind, to dazzle; (*fig*) to hoodwink; **b~nd** (*umg*) *adj* grand; **b~nd aussehen** to look smashing
Blick [blɪk] **(-(e)s, -e)** *m* (*kurz*) glance, glimpse; (*Anschauen*) look; (*Aussicht*) view; **b~en** *vi* to look; **sich b~en lassen** to put in an appearance; **~fang** *m* eye-catcher
blieb *etc* [bliːp] *vb siehe* **bleiben**
blind [blɪnt] *adj* blind; (*Glas etc*) dull; **~er Passagier** stowaway; **B~darm** *m* appendix; **B~darmentzündung** *f* appendicitis; **B~enschrift** ['blɪndən-] *f* Braille; **B~heit** *f* blindness; **~lings** *adv* blindly
blink- ['blɪŋk] *zW*: **~en** *vi* to twinkle, to sparkle; (*Licht*) to flash, to signal; (*AUT*) to indicate ♦ *vt* to flash, to signal; **B~er(-s, -)** *m* (*AUT*) indicator; **B~licht** *nt* (*AUT*) indicator; (*an Bahnübergängen usw*) flashing light
blinzeln ['blɪntsəln] *vi* to blink, to wink
Blitz [blɪts] **(-es, -e)** *m* (flash of) lightning; **~ableiter** *m* lightning conductor; **b~en** *vi* (*aufleuchten*) to flash, to sparkle; **es b~t**

Rechtschreibreform: ▲ *neue Schreibung* △ *alte Schreibung (auslaufend)*

(MET) there's a flash of lightning; **~licht** nt flashlight; **b~schnell** adj lightning ♦ adv (as) quick as a flash

Block [blɔk] (**-(e)s, ⁻e**) m block; (von Papier) pad; **~ade** [blɔ'kaːdə] f blockade; **~flöte** f recorder; **b~frei** adj (POL) unaligned; **~haus** nt log cabin; **b~ieren** [blɔ'kiːrən] vt to block ♦ vi (Räder) to jam; **~schrift** f block letters pl

blöd [bløːt] adj silly, stupid; **~eln** ['bløːdəln] (umg) vi to act the goat (fam), to fool around; **B~sinn** m nonsense; **~sinnig** adj silly, idiotic

blond [blɔnt] adj blond, fair-haired

SCHLÜSSELWORT

bloß [bloːs] adj **1** (unbedeckt) bare; (nackt) naked; **mit der bloßen Hand** with one's bare hand; **mit bloßem Auge** with the naked eye

2 (alleinig, nur) mere; **der bloße Gedanke** the very thought; **bloßer Neid** sheer envy ♦ adv only, merely; **lass das bloß!** just don't do that!; **wie ist das bloß passiert?** how on earth did that happen?

Blöße ['bløːsə] f bareness; nakedness; (fig) weakness

bloßstellen vt to show up

blühen ['blyːən] vi to bloom (lit), to be in bloom; (fig) to flourish; **~d** adj (Pflanze) blooming; (Aussehen) blooming, radiant; (Handel) thriving, booming

Blume ['bluːmə] f flower; (von Wein) bouquet

Blumen- zW: **~kohl** m cauliflower; **~topf** m flowerpot; **~zwiebel** f bulb

Bluse ['bluːzə] f blouse

Blut [bluːt] (**-(e)s**) nt blood; **b~arm** adj anaemic; (fig) penniless; **b~befleckt** adj bloodstained; **~bild** nt blood count; **~druck** m blood pressure

Blüte ['blyːtə] f blossom; (fig) prime

Blut- zW: **b~en** vi to bleed; **~er** m (MED) haemophiliac; **~erguss** ▲ m haemorrhage; (auf Haut) bruise

Blütezeit f flowering period; (fig) prime

Blut- zW: **~gruppe** f blood group; **b~ig** adj bloody; **b~jung** adj very young; **~probe** f blood test; **~spender** m blood donor; **~transfusion** f (MED) blood transfusion; **~ung** f bleeding, haemorrhage; **~vergiftung** f blood poisoning; **~wurst** f black pudding

Bö [bøː] (**-, -en**) f squall

Bock [bɔk] (**-(e)s, ⁻e**) m buck, ram; (Gestell) trestle, support; (SPORT) buck; **~wurst** f type of pork sausage

Boden ['boːdən] (**-s, ⁻**) m ground; (Fußboden) floor; (Meeresboden, Fassboden) bottom; (Speicher) attic; **b~los** adj bottomless; (umg) incredible; **~nebel** m ground mist; **~personal** nt (AVIAT) ground staff; **~schätze** pl mineral resources; **~see** m: **der ~see** Lake Constance; **~turnen** nt floor exercises pl

Böe ['bøːə] f squall

Bogen ['boːgən] (**-s, -**) m (Biegung) curve; (ARCHIT) arch; (Waffe, MUS) bow; (Papier) sheet

Bohne ['boːnə] f bean

bohnern vt to wax, to polish

Bohnerwachs nt floor polish

Bohr- ['boːr] zW: **b~en** vt to bore; (**-s, -**) m drill; **~insel** f oil rig; **~maschine** f drill; **~turm** m derrick

Boiler ['bɔylər] (**-s, -**) m (hot-water) tank

Boje ['boːjə] f buoy

Bolzen ['bɔltsən] (**-s, -**) m bolt

bombardieren [bɔmbar'diːrən] vt to bombard; (aus der Luft) to bomb

Bombe ['bɔmbə] f bomb

Bombenangriff m bombing raid

Bombenerfolg (umg) m smash hit

Bon [bɔŋ] (**-s, -s**) m voucher, chit

Bonbon [bõ'bõː] (**-s, -s**) m od nt sweet

Boot [boːt] (**-(e)s, -e**) nt boat

Bord [bɔrt] (**-(e)s, -e**) m (AVIAT, NAUT) board ♦ nt (Brett) shelf; **an ~** on board

Bordell [bɔr'dɛl] (**-s, -e**) nt brothel

Bordstein m kerb(stone)

borgen ['bɔrgən] vt to borrow; **jdm etw ~** to lend sb sth

borniert [bɔr'niːrt] adj narrow-minded

Börse ['bœːrzə] f stock exchange; (*Geldbörse*) purse; **~nmakler** m stockbroker

Borte ['bɔrtə] f edging; (*Band*) trimming

bös [bøːs] adj = **böse**

bösartig ['bøːz-] adj malicious

Böschung ['bœʃʊŋ] f slope; (*Uferböschung etc*) embankment

böse ['bøːzə] adj bad, evil; (*zornig*) angry

boshaft ['boːshaft] adj malicious, spiteful

Bosheit f malice, spite

Bosnien ['bɔsniən] (**-s**) nt Bosnia; ~ **und Herzegowina** [-hɛrtsə'goːvina] nt Bosnia (and) Herzegovina

böswillig ['bøːsvɪlɪç] adj malicious

bot etc [boːt] vb siehe **bieten**

Botanik [bo'taːnɪk] f botany; **botanisch** adj botanical

Bot- [boːt] zW: **~e** (**-n, -n**) m messenger; **~schaft** f message, news; (*POL*) embassy; **~schafter** (**-s, -**) m ambassador

Bottich ['bɔtɪç] (**-(e)s, -e**) m vat, tub

Bouillon [bu'ljõː] (**-, -s**) f consommé

Bowle ['boːlə] f punch

Box- [bɔks] zW: **b~en** vi to box; **~er** (**-s, -**) m boxer; **~kampf** m boxing match

boykottieren [bɔykɔ'tiːrən] vt to boycott

brach etc [braːx] vb siehe **brechen**

brachte etc ['braxtə] vb siehe **bringen**

Branche ['brãːʃə] f line of business

Branchenverzeichnis nt Yellow Pages® pl

Brand [brant] (**-(e)s, ⁻e**) m fire; (*MED*) gangrene; **b~en** ['brandən] vi to surge; (*Meer*) to break; **b~marken** vt to brand; (*fig*) to stigmatize; **~salbe** f ointment for burns; **~stifter** [-ʃtɪftər] m arsonist, fire raiser; **~stiftung** f arson; **~ung** f surf

Branntwein ['brantvaɪn] m brandy

Brasilien [bra'ziːliən] nt Brazil

Brat- ['braːt] zW: **~apfel** m baked apple; **b~en** (*unreg*) vt to roast; to fry; **~en** (**-s, -**) m roast, joint; **~hähnchen** nt roast chicken; **~huhn** nt roast chicken; **~kartoffeln** pl fried *od* roast potatoes; **~pfanne** f frying pan

Bratsche ['braːtʃə] f viola

Bratspieß m spit

Bratwurst f grilled/fried sausage

Brauch [braux] (**-(e)s, Bräuche**) m custom; **b~bar** adj usable, serviceable; (*Person*) capable; **b~en** vt (*bedürfen*) to need; (*müssen*) to have to; (*umg: verwenden*) to use

Braue ['brauə] f brow

brauen ['brauən] vt to brew

Braue'rei f brewery

braun [braun] adj brown; (*von Sonne auch*) tanned; ~ **gebrannt** tanned

Bräune ['brɔynə] (**-**) f brownness; (*Sonnenbräune*) tan; **b~n** vt to make brown; (*Sonne*) to tan

Brause ['brauzə] f shower bath; (*von Gießkanne*) rose; (*Getränk*) lemonade; **b~n** vi to roar; (*auch vr: duschen*) to take a shower

Braut [braut] (**-, Bräute**) f bride; (*Verlobte*) fiancée

Bräutigam ['brɔytɪgam] (**-s, -e**) m bridegroom; fiancé

Brautpaar nt bride and (bride)groom, bridal pair

brav [braːf] adj (*artig*) good; (*ehrenhaft*) worthy, honest

bravo ['braːvo] excl well done

BRD ['beːʔɛr'deː] (**-**) f abk = **Bundesrepublik Deutschland**

BRD

i The **BRD** (*Bundesrepublik Deutschland*) is the official name for the Federal Republic of Germany. It comprises 16 **Länder** (*see* **Land**). It was formerly the name given to West Germany as opposed to East Germany (the **DDR**). The two Germanies were reunited on 3rd October 1990.

Brech- [brɛç] zW: **~eisen** nt crowbar; **b~en** (*unreg*) vt, vi to break; (*Licht*) to refract; (*fig: Mensch*) to crush; (*speien*) to vomit; **~reiz** m nausea, retching

Brei [braɪ] (**-(e)s, -e**) m (*Masse*) pulp; (*KOCH*) gruel; (*Haferbrei*) porridge

breit [braɪt] adj wide, broad; **sich ~ machen** to spread o.s. out; **B~e** f width; (*bes bei*

Maßangaben) breadth; (GEOG) latitude; ~en
vt: etw über etw akk ~en to spread sth
over sth; B~engrad m degree of latitude;
~treten (unreg) (umg) vi to go on about

Brems- ['brɛms] zW: ~belag m brake
lining; ~e [-zə] f brake; (ZOOL) horsefly;
b~en [-zən] vi to brake ♦ vt (Auto) to brake;
(fig) to slow down; ~flüssigkeit f brake
fluid; ~licht nt brake light; ~pedal nt
brake pedal; ~spur f skid mark(s pl); ~weg
m braking distance

Brenn- ['brɛn] zW: b~bar adj inflammable;
b~en (unreg) vi to burn, to be on fire;
(Licht, Kerze etc) to burn ♦ vt (Holz etc) to
burn; (Ziegel, Ton) to fire; (Kaffee) to roast;
darauf b~en, etw zu tun to be dying to
do sth; ~nessel ▲ f stinging nettle;
~punkt m (PHYS) focal point; (Mittelpunkt)
focus; ~stoff m fuel

brenzlig ['brɛntslɪç] adj (fig) precarious

Bretagne [brə'tanjə] f: die ~ Brittany

Brett [brɛt] (-(e)s, -er) nt board, plank;
(Bord) shelf; (Spielbrett) board; ~er pl (SKI)
skis; (THEAT) boards; schwarzes ~ notice
board; ~erzaun m wooden fence; ~spiel
nt board game

Brezel ['bre:tsəl] (-, -n) f pretzel

brichst etc [brɪçst] vb siehe brechen

Brief [bri:f] (-(e)s, -e) m letter; ~freund m
penfriend; ~kasten m letterbox; b~lich
adj, adv by letter; ~marke f (postage)
stamp; ~papier nt notepaper; ~tasche f
wallet; ~träger m postman; ~umschlag
m envelope; ~waage f letter scales;
~wechsel m correspondence

briet etc [bri:t] vb siehe braten

Brikett [bri'kɛt] (-s, -s) nt briquette

brillant [brɪl'jant] adj (fig) brilliant; B~ (-en,
-en) m brilliant, diamond

Brille ['brɪlə] f spectacles pl; (Schutzbrille)
goggles pl; (Toilettenbrille) (toilet) seat;
~ngestell nt (spectacle) frames

bringen ['brɪŋən] (unreg) vt to bring;
(mitnehmen, begleiten) to take; (einbringen:
Profit) to bring in; (veröffentlichen) to
publish; (THEAT, CINE) to show; (RADIO, TV) to
broadcast; (in einen Zustand versetzen) to

get; (umg: tun können) to manage; jdn
dazu ~, etw zu tun to make sb do sth; jdn
nach Hause ~ to take sb home; jdn um
etw ~ to make sb lose sth; jdn auf eine
Idee ~ to give sb an idea

Brise ['bri:zə] f breeze

Brit- ['bri:t] zW: ~e m Briton; ~in f Briton;
b~isch adj British

bröckelig ['brœkəlɪç] adj crumbly

Brocken ['brɔkən] (-s, -) m piece, bit;
(Felsbrocken) lump of rock

brodeln ['bro:dəln] vi to bubble

Brokkoli ['brɔkoli] pl (BOT) broccoli

Brombeere ['brɔmbe:rə] f blackberry,
bramble (BRIT)

Bronchien ['brɔnçiən] pl bronchia(l tubes)
pl

Bronchitis [brɔn'çi:tis] (-) f bronchitis

Bronze ['brõ:sə] f bronze

Brosche ['brɔʃə] f brooch

Broschüre [brɔ'ʃy:rə] f pamphlet

Brot [bro:t] (-(e)s, -e) nt bread; (Laib) loaf

Brötchen ['brø:tçən] nt roll

Bruch [brʊx] (-(e)s, ⁺e) m breakage;
(zerbrochene Stelle) break; (fig) split, breach;
(MED: Eingeweidebruch) rupture, hernia;
(Beinbruch etc) fracture; (MATH) fraction

brüchig ['brʏçɪç] adj brittle, fragile; (Haus)
dilapidated

Bruch- zW: ~landung f crash landing;
~strich m (MATH) line; ~stück nt
fragment; ~teil m fraction; ~zahl [brʊxtsa:l]
f (MATH) fraction

Brücke ['brʏkə] f bridge; (Teppich) rug

Bruder ['bru:dər] (-s, ⁺) m brother;
brüderlich adj brotherly

Brühe ['bry:ə] f broth, stock; (pej) muck

brüllen ['brʏlən] vi to bellow, to roar

brummen ['brʊmən] vi (Bär, Mensch etc) to
growl; (Insekt) to buzz; (Motoren) to roar;
(murren) to grumble

brünett [brʏ'nɛt] adj brunette, dark-haired

Brunnen ['brʊnən] (-s, -) m fountain; (tief)
well; (natürlich) spring

Brust [brʊst] (-, ⁺e) f breast; (Männerbrust)
chest

brüsten ['brʏstən] vr to boast

Spelling Reform: ▲ *new spelling* △ *old spelling (to be phased out)*

Brust- *zW:* **~kasten** *m* chest;
~schwimmen *nt* breast-stroke
Brüstung ['brʏstʊŋ] *f* parapet
Brut [bruːt] (**-, -en**) *f* brood; (*Brüten*)
hatching
brutal [bru'taːl] *adj* brutal
Brutali'tät *f* brutality
brüten ['bryːtən] *vi* (*auch fig*) to brood
Brutkasten *m* incubator
brutto ['brʊto] *adv* gross; **B~einkommen** *nt*
gross salary; **B~gehalt** *nt* gross salary;
B~gewicht *nt* gross weight; **B~lohn** *m*
gross wages *pl*; **B~sozialprodukt** *nt* gross
national product
BSE *f abk* (= *Bovine Spongiforme*
Enzephalopathie) BSE
Bube ['buːbə] (**-n, -n**) *m* (*Schurke*) rogue;
(*KARTEN*) jack
Buch [buːx] (**-(e)s, ̈er**) *nt* book; (*COMM*)
account book; **~binder** *m* bookbinder;
~drucker *m* printer
Buche *f* beech tree
buchen *vt* to book; (*Betrag*) to enter
Bücher- ['byːçər] *zW:* **~brett** *nt* book-
helf; **~ei** [-'raɪ] *f* library; **~regal** *nt* book-
shelves *pl*, bookcase; **~schrank** *m* bookcase
Buch- *zW:* **~führung** *f* book-keeping,
accounting; **~halter(in)** (**-s, -**) *m(f)* book-
keeper; **~handel** *m* book trade;
~händler(in) *m(f)* bookseller; **~handlung**
f bookshop
Büchse ['bʏksə] *f* tin, can; (*Holzbüchse*) box;
(*Gewehr*) rifle; **~nfleisch** *nt* tinned meat;
~nmilch *f* (*KOCH*) evaporated milk, tinned
milk; **~nöffner** *m* tin *od* can opener
Buchstabe (**-ns, -n**) *m* letter (of the
alphabet)
buchstabieren [buːxʃta'biːrən] *vt* to spell
buchstäblich ['buːxʃtɛːplɪç] *adj* literal
Bucht ['bʊxt] (**-, -en**) *f* bay
Buchung ['buːxʊŋ] *f* booking; (*COMM*) entry
Buckel ['bʊkəl] (**-s, -**) *m* hump
bücken ['bʏkən] *vr* to bend
Bude ['buːdə] *f* booth, stall; (*umg*) digs *pl*
(*BRIT*)
Büfett [bʏ'fɛt] (**-s, -s**) *nt* (*Anrichte*) sideboard;

(*Geschirrschrank*) dresser; **kaltes ~** cold
buffet
Büffel ['bʏfəl] (**-s, -**) *m* buffalo
Bug [buːk] (**-(e)s, -e**) *m* (*NAUT*) bow; (*AVIAT*)
nose
Bügel ['byːgəl] (**-s, -**) *m* (*Kleider~*) hanger;
(*Steig~*) stirrup; (*Brillen~*) arm; **~brett** *nt*
ironing board; **~eisen** *nt* iron; **~falte** *f*
crease; **b~frei** *adj* crease-resistant, noniron;
b~n *vt, vi* to iron
Bühne ['byːnə] *f* stage; **~nbild** *nt* set,
scenery
Buhruf ['buːruːf] *m* boo
buk *etc* [buːk] *vb siehe* **backen**
Bulgarien [bʊl'gaːriən] *nt* Bulgaria
Bull- ['bʊl] *zW:* **~auge** *nt* (*NAUT*) porthole;
~dogge *f* bulldog; **~dozer** ['bʊldoːzər] (**-s,
-**) *m* bulldozer; **~e** (**-n, -n**) *m* bull
Bumerang ['buːməraŋ] (**-s, -e**) *m*
boomerang
Bummel ['bʊməl] (**-s, -**) *m* stroll;
(*Schaufensterbummel*) window-shopping;
~ant [-'lant] *m* slowcoach; **~ei** [-'laɪ] *f*
wandering; dawdling; skiving; **b~n** *vi* to
wander, to stroll; (*trödeln*) to dawdle;
(*faulenzen*) to skive, to loaf around; **~streik**
['bʊməlʃtraɪk] *m* go-slow
Bund[1] [bʊnt] (**-(e)s, ̈e**) *m*
(*Freundschaftsbund etc*) bond; (*Organisation*)
union; (*POL*) confederacy; (*Hosenbund,
Rockbund*) waistband
Bund[2] (**-(e)s, -e**) *nt* bunch; (*Strohbund*)
bundle
Bündel ['bʏndəl] (**-s, -**) *nt* bundle, bale; **b~n**
vt to bundle
Bundes- ['bʊndəs] *in zW* Federal; **~bürger**
m German citizen; **~hauptstadt** *f* Federal
capital; **~kanzler** *m* Federal Chancellor;
~land *nt* Land; **~liga** *f* football league;
~präsident *m* Federal President; **~rat** *m*
upper house of German Parliament;
~regierung *f* Federal government;
~republik *f* Federal Republic (of
Germany); **~staat** *m* Federal state;
~straße *f* Federal road; **~tag** *m* German
Parliament; **~wehr** *f* German Armed Forces
pl; **b~weit** *adj* nationwide

Bundespräsident

The Bundespräsident is the head of state of the Federal Republic of Germany. He is elected every 5 years - no-one can be elected more than twice - by the members of the Bundesversammlung, a body formed especially for this purpose. His role is to represent Germany at home and abroad. In Switzerland the Bundespräsident is the head of the government, known as the Bundesrat.

The Bundesrat is the Upper House of the German Parliament whose 68 members are nominated by the parliaments of the Länder. Its most important function is to approve federal laws concerned with the jurisdiction of the Länder; it can raise objections to other laws, but can be outvoted by the Bundestag. In Austria the Länder are also represented in the Bundesrat.

Bundestag

The Bundestag is the Lower House of the German Parliament and is elected by the people by proportional representation. There are 672 MPs, half of them elected directly from the first vote (Erststimme), and half from the regional list of parliamentary candidates resulting from the second vote (Zweitstimme). The Bundestag exercises parliamentary control over the government.

Bündnis ['byntnɪs] (-ses, -se) nt alliance
bunt [bʊnt] adj coloured; (gemischt) mixed; **jdm wird es zu ~** it's getting too much for sb; **B~stift** m coloured pencil, crayon
Burg [bʊrk] (-, -en) f castle, fort
Bürge ['byrgə] (-n, -n) m guarantor; **b~n für** to vouch for
Bürger(in) ['byrgər(ɪn)] (-s, -) m(f) citizen; member of the middle class; **~krieg** m civil war; **b~lich** adj (Rechte) civil; (Klasse) middle-class; (pej) bourgeois; **~meister** m

mayor; **~recht** nt civil rights pl; **~schaft** f (Vertretung) City Parliament; **~steig** m pavement
Bürgschaft f surety; **~ leisten** to give security
Büro [by'ro:] (-s, -s) nt office; **~angestellte(r)** f(m) office worker; **~klammer** f paper clip; **~kra tie** f bureaucracy; **b~'kratisch** adj bureaucratic; **~schluss** ▲ m office closing time
Bursche ['bʊrʃə] (-n, -n) m lad, fellow; (Diener) servant
Bürste ['byrstə] f brush; **b~n** vt to brush
Bus [bʊs] (-ses, -se) m bus; **~bahnhof** m bus/coach (BRIT) station
Busch [bʊʃ] (-(e)s, ⁺e) m bush, shrub
Büschel ['byʃəl] (-s, -) nt tuft
buschig adj bushy
Busen ['bu:zən] (-s, -) m bosom; (Meerbusen) inlet, bay
Bushaltestelle f bus stop
Buße ['bu:sə] f penance; (Geld) fine
büßen ['by:sən] vi to do penance, to atone ♦ vt to do penance for, to atone for
Bußgeld ['bu:sgelt] nt fine; **~bescheid** m notice of payment due (for traffic offence etc)
Büste ['bystə] f bust; **~nhalter** m bra
Butter ['bʊtər] (-) f butter; **~blume** f buttercup; **~brot** nt (piece of) bread and butter; (umg) sandwich; **~brotpapier** nt greaseproof paper; **~dose** f butter dish; **~milch** f buttermilk; **b~weich** ['bʊtərvaɪç] adj soft as butter; (fig, umg) soft
b. w. abk (= bitte wenden) p.t.o.
bzgl. abk (= bezüglich) re
bzw. abk = beziehungsweise

C, c

ca. [ka] abk (= circa) approx.
Cabin Crew [kebɪnkru:] f cabin crew
Café [ka'fe:] (-s, -s) nt café
Cafeteria [kafete'ri:a] (-, -s) f cafeteria
Camcorder (-s, -) m camcorder
Camp- ['kɛmp] zW: **c~en** vi to camp; **~er**

(**-s**, **-**) *m* camper; **~ing** (**-s**) *nt* camping;
~ingführer *m* camping guide (book);
~ingkocher *m* camping stove; **~ingplatz**
m camp(ing) site

CD-Spieler *m* CD (player)

Cello ['tʃɛlo] (**-s**, **-s** *od* **Celli**) *nt* cello

Celsius ['tsɛlzɪʊs] (**-**) *nt* centigrade

Cent [sɛnt] (**-s**, **-s**) *m* cent

Champagner [ʃam'panjər] (**-s**, **-**) *m*
champagne

Champignon ['ʃampɪnjõ] (**-s**, **-s**) *m* button
mushroom

Chance ['ʃãːs(ə)] *f* chance, opportunity

Chaos ['kaːɔs] (**-**, **-**) *nt* chaos; **chaotisch**
[ka'oːtɪʃ] *adj* chaotic

Charakter [ka'raktər, *pl* karak'teːrə] (**-s**, **-e**) *m*
character; **c~fest** *adj* of firm character,
strong; **c~i'sieren** *vt* to characterize;
c~istisch [karakte'rɪstɪʃ] *adj*: **c~istisch (für)**
characteristic (of), typical (of); **c~los** *adj*
unprincipled; **~losigkeit** *f* lack of principle;
~schwäche *f* weakness of character;
~stärke *f* strength of character; **~zug** *m*
characteristic, trait

charmant [ʃar'mant] *adj* charming

Charme [ʃarm] (**-s**) *m* charm

Charterflug ['tʃartərfluːk] *m* charter flight

Chauffeur [ʃɔ'føːr] *m* chauffeur

Chauvinist [ʃovi'nɪst] *m* chauvinist, jingoist

Chef [ʃɛf] (**-s**, **-s**) *m* head; (*umg*) boss; **~arzt**
m senior consultant; **~in** (*umg*) *f* boss

Chemie [çe'miː] (**-**) *f* chemistry; **~faser** *f*
man-made fibre

Chemikalie [çemi'kaːliə] *f* chemical

Chemiker ['çeːmikər] (**-s**, **-**) *m* (industrial)
chemist

chemisch ['çeːmɪʃ] *adj* chemical; **~e**
Reinigung dry cleaning

Chicorée ['ʃikoreː] (**-s**) *m* *od* *f* chicory

Chiffre ['ʃɪfrə] *f* (*Geheimzeichen*) cipher; (*in*
Zeitung) box number

Chile ['tʃiːle] *nt* Chile

Chin- ['çiːn] *zW*: **~a** *nt* China; **~akohl** *m*
Chinese leaves; **~ese** [-'neːza] *m* Chinese;
~esin *f* Chinese; **c~esisch** *adj* Chinese

Chip [tʃɪp] (**-s**, **-s**) *m* (*Kartoffelchips*) crisp
(*BRIT*), chip (*US*); (*COMPUT*) chip; **~karte** *f*
smart card

Chirurg [çi'rʊrg] (**-en**, **-en**) *m* surgeon; **~ie**
[-'giː] *f* surgery; **c~isch** *adj* surgical

Chlor [kloːr] (**-s**) *nt* chlorine; **~o'form** (**-s**)
nt chloroform

cholerisch [ko'leːrɪʃ] *adj* choleric

Chor [koːr] (**-(e)s**, **⁓e**) *m* choir; (*Musikstück*,
THEAT) chorus; **~al** [ko'raːl] (**-s**, **-äle**) *m*
chorale

Choreograf ▲ [koreo'graːf] (**-en**, **-en**) *m*
choreographer

Christ [krɪst] (**-en**, **-en**) *m* Christian; **~baum**
m Christmas tree; **~entum** *nt* Christianity;
~in *f* Christian; **~kind** *nt* ≈ Father
Christmas; (*Jesus*) baby Jesus; **c~lich** *adj*
Christian; **~us** (**-**) *m* Christ

Chrom [kroːm] (**-s**) *nt* chromium; chrome

Chron- ['kroːn] *zW*: **~ik** *f* chronicle; **c~isch**
adj chronic; **c~ologisch** [-o'loːgɪʃ] *adj*
chronological

circa ['tsɪrka] *adv* about, approximately

Clown [klaʊn] (**-s**, **-s**) *m* clown

Cocktail ['kɔkteːl] (**-s**, **-s**) *m* cocktail

Cola ['koːla] (**-**, **-s**) *f* Coke ®

Computer [kɔm'pjuːtər] (**-s**, **-**) *m* computer;
~spiel *nt* computer game

Cord [kɔrt] (**-s**) *m* cord, corduroy

Couch [kaʊtʃ] (**-**, **-es** *od* **-en**) *f* couch

Coupon [ku'põː] (**-s**, **-s**) *m* = **Kupon**

Cousin [ku'zɛ̃ː] (**-s**, **-s**) *m* cousin; **~e**
[ku'ziːnə] *f* cousin

Creme [kreːm] (**-**, **-s**) *f* cream; (*Schuhcreme*)
polish; (*Zahncreme*) paste; (*KOCH*) mousse;
c~farben *adj* cream(-coloured)

cremig ['kreːmɪç] *adj* creamy

Curry ['kari] (**-s**) *m* *od* *nt* curry powder;
~pulver *nt* curry powder; **~wurst** *f* curried
sausage

D, d

SCHLÜSSELWORT

da [daː] *adv* **1** (*örtlich*) there; (*hier*) here; **da**
draußen out there; **da sein** to be there; **da**

bin ich here I am; **da, wo** where; **ist noch Milch da?** is there any milk left?
2 (*zeitlich*) then; (*folglich*) so
3: da haben wir Glück gehabt we were lucky there; **da kann man nichts machen** nothing can be done about it
♦ *konj* (*weil*) as, since

dabehalten (*unreg*) *vt* to keep
dabei [da'baɪ] *adv* (*räumlich*) close to it; (*noch dazu*) besides; (*zusammen mit*) with them; (*zeitlich*) during this; (*obwohl doch*) but, however; **was ist schon ~?** what of it?; **es ist doch nichts ~, wenn ...** it doesn't matter if ...; **bleiben wir ~** let's leave it at that; **es bleibt ~** that's settled; **das Dumme/Schwierige ~** the stupid/difficult part of it; **er war gerade ~ zu gehen** he was just leaving; **~ sein** (*anwesend*) to be present; (*beteiligt*) to be involved; **~stehen** (*unreg*) *vi* to stand around
Dach [dax] (**-(e)s, ¨er**) *nt* roof; **~boden** *m* attic, loft; **~decker** (**-s, -**) *m* slater, tiler; **~fenster** *nt* skylight; **~gepäckträger** *m* roof rack; **~luke** *f* skylight; **~pappe** *f* roofing felt; **~rinne** *f* gutter
Dachs [daks] (**-es, -e**) *m* badger
dachte *etc* ['daxtə] *vb siehe* **denken**
Dackel ['dakəl] (**-s, -**) *m* dachshund
dadurch [da'dʊrç] *adv* (*räumlich*) through it; (*durch diesen Umstand*) thereby, in that way; (*deshalb*) because of that, for that reason
♦ *konj*: **~, dass** because
dafür [da'fy:r] *adv* for it; (*anstatt*) instead; **er kann nichts ~** he can't help it; **er ist bekannt ~** he is well-known for that; **was bekomme ich ~?** what will I get for it?
dagegen [da'ge:gən] *adv* against it; (*im Vergleich damit*) in comparison with it; (*bei Tausch*) for it/them ♦ *konj* however; **ich habe nichts ~** I don't mind; **ich war ~** I was against it; (*aber*) **~ kann man nichts tun** one can't do anything about it; **~halten** (*unreg*) *vt* (*vergleichen*) to compare with it; (*entgegnen*) to object to it; **~sprechen** (*unreg*) *vi*: **es spricht nichts ~** there's no reason why not

daheim [da'haɪm] *adv* at home; **D~** (**-s**) *nt* home
daher [da'he:r] *adv* (*räumlich*) from there; (*Ursache*) from that ♦ *konj* (*deshalb*) that's why
dahin [da'hɪn] *adv* (*räumlich*) there; (*zeitlich*) then; (*vergangen*) gone; **~ gehend** on this matter; **~'gegen** *konj* on the other hand; **~gestellt** *adv*: **~gestellt bleiben** to remain to be seen; **~gestellt sein lassen** to leave open *od* undecided
dahinten [da'hɪntən] *adv* over there
dahinter [da'hɪntər] *adv* behind it; **~ . kommen** to get to the bottom of it
dalli ['dali] (*umg*) *adv* chop chop
damalig ['da:ma:lɪç] *adj* of that time, then
damals ['da:ma:ls] *adv* at that time, then
Dame ['da:mə] *f* lady; (*SCHACH, KARTEN*) queen; (*Spiel*) draughts *sg*; **~nbinde** *f* sanitary towel *od* napkin (*US*); **d~nhaft** *adj* ladylike; **~ntoilette** *f* ladies' toilet *od* restroom (*US*); **~nwahl** *f* ladies' excuse-me
damit [da'mɪt] *adv* with it; (*begründend*) by that ♦ *konj* in order to, in order to; **was meint er ~?** what does he mean by that?; **genug ~!** that's enough!
dämlich ['dɛ:mlɪç] (*umg*) *adj* silly, stupid
Damm [dam] (**-(e)s, ¨e**) *m* dyke; (*Staudamm*) dam; (*Hafendamm*) mole; (*Bahndamm, Straßendamm*) embankment
dämmen ['dɛmən] *vt* (*Wasser*) to dam up; (*Schmerzen*) to keep back
dämmer- *zW*: **~ig** *adj* dim, faint; **~n** *vi* (*Tag*) to dawn; (*Abend*) to fall; **D~ung** *f* twilight; (*Morgendämmerung*) dawn; (*Abenddämmerung*) dusk
Dampf [dampf] (**-(e)s, ¨e**) *m* steam; (*Dunst*) vapour; **d~en** *vi* to steam
dämpfen ['dɛmpfən] *vt* (*KOCH*) to steam; (*bügeln*) to iron with a damp cloth; (*fig*) to dampen, to subdue
Dampf- *zW*: **~schiff** *nt* steamship; **~walze** *f* steamroller
danach [da'na:x] *adv* after that; (*zeitlich*) after that, afterwards; (*gemäß*) accordingly; according to which; according to that; **er sieht ~ aus** he looks it

Däne ['dɛːnə] **(-n, -n)** *m* Dane

daneben [da'neːbən] *adv* beside it; (*im Vergleich*) in comparison; **~benehmen** (*unreg*) *vr* to misbehave; **~gehen** (*unreg*) *vi* to miss; (*Plan*) to fail

Dänemark ['dɛːnəmark] *nt* Denmark; **Dänin** *f* Dane; **dänisch** *adj* Danish

Dank [daŋk] **(-(e)s)** *m* thanks *pl*; **vielen** *od* **schönen ~** many thanks; **jdm ~ sagen** to thank sb; **d~** *präp* (+*dat od gen*) thanks to; **d~bar** *adj* grateful; (*Aufgabe*) rewarding; **~barkeit** *f* gratitude; **d~e** *excl* thank you, thanks; **d~en** *vi* +*dat* to thank; **d~enswert** *adj* (*Arbeit*) worthwhile; rewarding; (*Bemühung*) kind; **d~sagen** *vi* to express one's thanks

dann [dan] *adv* then; **~ und wann** now and then

daran [da'ran] *adv* on it; (*stoßen*) against it; **es liegt ~, dass ...** the cause of it is that ...; **gut/schlecht ~ sein** to be well-/badly off; **das Beste/Dümmste ~** the best/ stupidest thing about it; **ich war nahe ~ zu ...** I was on the point of ...; **er ist ~ gestorben** he died from it *od* of it; **~gehen** (*unreg*) *vi* to start; **~setzen** *vt* to stake

darauf [da'rauf] *adv* (*räumlich*) on it; (*zielgerichtet*) towards it; (*danach*) afterwards; **es kommt ganz ~ an, ob ...** it depends whether ...; **die Tage ~** the days following *od* thereafter; **am Tag ~** the next day; **~ folgend** (*Tag, Jahr*) next, following; **~ legen** to lay *od* put on top

daraus [da'raus] *adv* from it; **was ist ~ geworden?** what became of it?; **~ geht hervor, dass ...** this means that ...

Darbietung ['daːrbiːtʊŋ] *f* performance

darf *etc* [darf] *vb siehe* **dürfen**

darin [da'rɪn] *adv* in (there), in it

darlegen ['daːrleːgən] *vt* to explain, to expound, to set forth; **Darlegung** *f* explanation

Darleh(e)n **(-s, -)** *nt* loan

Darm [darm] **(-(e)s, ⁼e)** *m* intestine; (*Wurstdarm*) skin; **~grippe** *f* (*MED*) gastric influenza *od* flu

darstell- ['daːrʃtɛl] *zW*: **~en** *vt* (*abbilden, bedeuten*) to represent; (*beschreiben*) to describe *od* to appear to be; (*THEAT*) to act; **D~er(in)** **(-s, -)** *m(f)* actor (actress); **D~ung** *f* portrayal, depiction

darüber [da'ryːbər] *adv* (*räumlich*) over it, above it; (*fahren*) over it; (*mehr*) more; (*währenddessen*) meanwhile; (*sprechen, streiten*) about it; **~ geht nichts** there's nothing like it

darum [da'rʊm] *adv* (*räumlich*) round it ♦ *konj* that's why; **er bittet ~** he is pleading for it; **es geht ~, dass ...** the thing is that ...; **er würde viel ~ geben, wenn ...** he would give a lot to ...; **ich tue es ~, weil ...** I am doing it because ...

darunter [da'rʊntər] *adv* (*räumlich*) under it; (*dazwischen*) among them; (*weniger*) less; **ein Stockwerk ~** one floor below (it); **was verstehen Sie ~?** what do you understand by that?

das [das] *def art* the ♦ *pron* that

Dasein ['daːzain] **(-s)** *nt* (*Leben*) life; (*Anwesenheit*) presence; (*Bestehen*) existence

da sein *△ siehe* **da**

dass ▲ [das] *konj* that

dasselbe [das'zɛlbə] *art, pron* the same

dastehen ['daːʃteːən] (*unreg*) *vi* to stand there

Datei [da'tai] *f* file

Daten- ['daːtən] *zW*: **~bank** *f* data base; **~schutz** *m* data protection; **~verarbeitung** *f* data processing

datieren [da'tiːrən] *vt* to date

Dativ ['daːtiːf] **(-s, -e)** *m* dative (case)

Dattel ['datəl] **(-, -n)** *f* date

Datum ['daːtʊm] **(-s, Daten)** *nt* date; **Daten** *pl* (*Angaben*) data *pl*

Dauer ['dauər] **(-, -n)** *f* duration; (*gewisse Zeitspanne*) length; (*Bestand, Fortbestehen*) permanence; **es war nur von kurzer ~** it didn't last long; **auf die ~** in the long run; (*auf längere Zeit*) indefinitely; **~auftrag** *m* standing order; **d~haft** *adj* lasting, durable; **~karte** *f* season ticket; **~lauf** *m* jog(ging); **d~n** *vi* to last; **es hat sehr lang gedauert, bis er ...** it took him a long time to ...;

d~nd adj constant; ~parkplatz m long-stay car park; ~welle f perm, permanent wave; ~wurst f German salami; ~zustand m permanent condition

Daumen ['daʊmən] (-s, -) m thumb

Daune ['daʊnə] f down; ~ndecke f down duvet, down quilt

davon [da'fɔn] adv of it; (räumlich) away; (weg von) from it; (Grund) because of it; **das kommt ~!** that's what you get; **~ abgesehen** apart from that; **~ sprechen/ wissen** to talk/know of od about it; **was habe ich ~?** what's the point?; ~kommen (unreg) vi to escape; ~laufen (unreg) vi to run away

davor [da'foːr] adv (räumlich) in front of it; (zeitlich) before (that); **~ warnen** to warn about it

dazu [da'tsuː] adv (legen, stellen) by it; (essen, singen) with it; **und ~ noch** and in addition; **ein Beispiel/seine Gedanken ~** one example for/his thoughts on this; **wie komme ich denn ~?** why should I?; **~ fähig sein** to be capable of it; **sich ~ äußern** to say something on it; ~gehören vi to belong to it; ~kommen (unreg) vi (Ereignisse) to happen too; (an einen Ort) to come along

dazwischen [da'tsvɪʃən] adv in between; (räumlich auch) between (them); (zusammen mit) among them; ~kommen (unreg) vi (hineingeraten) to get caught in it; **es ist etwas ~gekommen** something cropped up; ~reden vi (unterbrechen) to interrupt; (sich einmischen) to interfere; ~treten (unreg) vi to intervene

---

DDR

*The **DDR** (Deutsche Demokratische Republik) was the name by which the former Communist German Democratic Republic was known. It was founded in 1949 from the Soviet-occupied zone. After the Berlin Wall was built in 1961 it was virtually sealed off from the West. Mass demonstrations and demands for reform forced the opening of the borders in 1989*

*and the **DDR** merged in 1990 with the BRD.*

Debatte [de'batə] f debate

Deck [dɛk] (-(e)s, -s od -e) nt deck; **an ~ gehen** to go on deck

Decke f cover; (Bettdecke) blanket; (Tischdecke) tablecloth; (Zimmerdecke) ceiling; **unter einer ~ stecken** to be hand in glove; ~l (-s, -) m lid; d~n vt to cover ♦ vr to coincide

Deckung f (Schützen) covering; (Schutz) cover; (SPORT) defence; (Übereinstimmen) agreement

Defekt [de'fɛkt] (-(e)s, -e) m fault, defect; d~ adj faulty

defensiv [defɛn'siːf] adj defensive

definieren [defi'niːrən] vt to define; **Definition** [definitsi'oːn] f definition

Defizit ['deːfitsɪt] (-s, -e) nt deficit

deftig ['dɛftɪç] adj (Essen) large; (Witz) coarse

Degen ['deːgən] (-s, -) m sword

degenerieren [degene'riːrən] vi to degenerate

dehnbar ['deːnbaːr] adj elastic; (fig: Begriff) loose

dehnen vt, vr to stretch

Deich [daɪç] (-(e)s, -e) m dyke, dike

deichseln (umg) vt (fig) to wangle

dein(e) [daɪn(ə)] adj your; ~e(r, s) pron yours; ~er (gen von du) pron of you; ~erseits adv on your part; ~esgleichen pron people like you; ~etwegen adv (für dich) for your sake; (wegen dir) on your account; ~etwillen adv: **um ~etwillen** = **deinetwegen;** ~ige pron: **der/die/das ~ige** od **D~ige** yours

Deklination [deklinatsi'oːn] f declension

deklinieren [dekli'niːrən] vt to decline

Dekolleté, Dekolletee ▲ [dekɔl'teː] (-s, -s) nt low neckline

Deko- [deko] zW: ~rateur [-ra'tøːr] m window dresser; ~ration [-ratsi'oːn] f decoration; (in Laden) window dressing; d~rativ [-ra'tiːf] adj decorative; d~rieren [-'riːrən] vt to decorate; (Schaufenster) to dress

Delegation [delegatsi'o:n] *f* delegation
delegieren [dele'gi:rən] *vt*: ~ **an** +*akk* (*Aufgaben*) to delegate to
Delfin ▲ [dɛl'fi:n] (**-s, -e**) *m* dolphin
delikat [deli'ka:t] *adj* (*zart, heikel*) delicate; (*köstlich*) delicious
Delikatesse [delika'tɛsə] *f* delicacy; **~n** *pl* (*Feinkost*) delicatessen food; **~ngeschäft** *nt* delicatessen
Delikt [de'lɪkt] (**-(e)s, -e**) *nt* (*JUR*) offence
Delle ['dɛlə] (*umg*) *f* dent
Delphin △ [dɛl'fi:n] (**-s, -e**) *m* = **Delfin**
dem [de(:)m] *art dat von* **der**
Demagoge [dema'go:gə] (**-n, -n**) *m* demagogue
dementieren [demɛn'ti:rən] *vt* to deny
dem- *zW*: **~gemäß** *adv* accordingly; **~nach** *adv* accordingly; **~nächst** *adv* shortly
Demokrat [demo'kra:t] (**-en, -en**) *m* democrat; **~ie** [-'ti:] *f* democracy; **d~isch** *adj* democratic; **d~isieren** [-i'zi:rən] *vt* to democratize
demolieren [demo'li:rən] *vt* to demolish
Demon- [dɛmɔn] *zW*: **~strant(in)** [-'strant(ɪn)] *m(f)* demonstrator; **~stration** [-stratsi'o:n] *f* demonstration; **d~strativ** [-stra'ti:f] *adj* demonstrative; (*Protest*) pointed; **d~strieren** [-'stri:rən] *vt, vi* to demonstrate
Demoskopie [demosko'pi:] *f* public opinion research
Demut ['de:mu:t] (**-**) *f* humility
demütig ['de:my:tɪç] *adj* humble; **~en** ['de:my:tɪgən] *vt* to humiliate; **D~ung** *f* humiliation
demzufolge ['de:mtsu'fɔlgə] *adv* accordingly
den [de(:)n] *art akk von* **der**
denen ['de:nən] *pron dat pl von* **der**; **die**; **das**
Denk- [dɛŋk] *zW*: **d~bar** *adj* conceivable; **~en** (**-s**) *nt* thinking; **d~en** (*unreg*) *vt, vi* to think; **d~faul** *adj* lazy; **~fehler** *m* logical error; **~mal** (**-s, ⁺er**) *nt* monument; **~malschutz** *m* protection of historical monuments; **unter ~malschutz stehen** to be classified as a historical monument; **d~würdig** *adj* memorable; **~zettel** *m*: **jdm**

einen ~zettel verpassen to teach sb a lesson
denn [dɛn] *konj* for ♦ *adv* then; (*nach Komparativ*) than; **warum ~?** why?
dennoch ['dɛnɔx] *konj* nevertheless
Denunziant [denʊntsi'ant(ɪn)] *m* informer
Deodorant [de|odo'rant] (**-s, -s** *od* **-e**) *nt* deodorant
Deponie [depo'ni:] *f* dump
deponieren [depo'ni:rən] *vt* (*COMM*) to deposit
Depot [de'po:] (**-s, -s**) *nt* warehouse; (*Busdepot, EISENB*) depot; (*Bankdepot*) strongroom, safe (*US*)
Depression [depresi'o:n] *f* depression; **depres'siv** *adj* depressive
deprimieren [depri'mi:rən] *vt* to depress

┌─────────────────┐
│ *SCHLÜSSELWORT* │
└─────────────────┘

der [de(:)r] (*f* **die**, *nt* **das**, *gen* **des, der, des**, *dat* **dem, der, dem**, *akk* **den, die, das**, *pl* **die**) *def art* the; **der Rhein** the Rhine; **der Klaus** (*umg*) Klaus; **die Frau** (*im Allgemeinen*) women; **der Tod/das Leben** death/life; **der Fuß des Berges** the foot of the hill; **gib es der Frau** give it to the woman; **er hat sich die Hand verletzt** he has hurt his hand
♦ *relativ pron* (*bei Menschen*) who, that; (*bei Tieren, Sachen*) which, that; **der Mann, den ich gesehen habe** the man who *od* whom *od* that I saw
♦ *demonstrativ pron* he/she/it; (*jener, dieser*) that; (*pl*) those; **der/die war es** it was him/her; **der mit der Brille** the one with glasses; **ich will den (da)** I want that one

derart ['de:r|a:rt] *adv* so; (*solcher Art*) such; **~ig** *adj* such, this sort of
derb [dɛrp] *adj* sturdy; (*Kost*) solid; (*grob*) coarse
der- *zW*: '**~'gleichen** *pron* such; '**~jenige** *pron* he; she; it; the one (who); that (which); '**~'maßen** *adv* to such an extent, so; **~'selbe** *art, pron* the same; '**~'weil(en)** *adv* in the meantime; '**~'zeitig** *adj* present, current; (*damalig*) then

des [dɛs] *art gen von* **der**

desertieren [dezɛr'tiːrən] *vi* to desert

desgleichen ['dɛs'glaiçən] *adv* likewise, also

deshalb ['dɛs'halp] *adv* therefore, that's why

Desinfektion [dezɪnfɛktsi'oːn] *f* disinfection; **~smittel** *nt* disinfectant

desinfizieren [dezɪnfi'tsiːrən] *vt* to disinfect

dessen ['dɛsən] *pron gen von* **der**; **das**; **~ ungeachtet** nevertheless, regardless

Dessert [dɛ'sɛːr] (**-s, -s**) *nt* dessert

destillieren [dɛstɪ'liːrən] *vt* to distil

desto ['dɛsto] *adv* all the, so much the; **~ besser** all the better

deswegen ['dɛs've:gən] *konj* therefore, hence

Detail [de'tai] (**-s, -s**) *nt* detail

Detektiv [detɛk'tiːf] (**-s, -e**) *m* detective

deut- ['dɔyt] *zW:* **~en** *vt* to interpret, to explain ♦ *vi:* **~en (auf** +*akk*) to point (to *od* at); **~lich** *adj* clear; (*Unterschied*) distinct; **D~lichkeit** *f* clarity; distinctness

Deutsch [dɔytʃ] *nt* German

deutsch *adj* German; **auf D~** in German; **D~e Demokratische Republik** (*HIST*) German Democratic Republic, East Germany; **~es Beefsteak** ≃ hamburger; **D~e(r)** *mf* German; **ich bin D~er** I am German; **D~land** *nt* Germany

Devise [de'viːzə] *f* motto, device; **~n** *pl* (*FIN*) foreign currency, foreign exchange

Dezember [de'tsɛmbər] (**-s, -**) *m* December

dezent [de'tsɛnt] *adj* discreet

dezimal [detsi'maːl] *adj* decimal; **D~system** *nt* decimal system

d. h. *abk* (= *das heißt*) i.e.

Dia ['diːa] (**-s, -s**) *nt* (*PHOT*) slide, transparency

Diabetes [dia'beːtes] (**-, -**) *m* (*MED*) diabetes

Diagnose [dia'gnoːzə] *f* diagnosis

diagonal [diago'naːl] *adj* diagonal

Dialekt [dia'lɛkt] (**-(e)s, -e**) *m* dialect; **d~isch** *adj* dialectal; (*Logik*) dialectical

Dialog [dia'loːk] (**-(e)s, -e**) *m* dialogue

Diamant [dia'mant] *m* diamond

Diaprojektor ['diːaprojektor] *m* slide projector

Diät [di'ɛːt] (**-, -en**) *f* diet

dich [dɪç] (*akk von du*) *pron* you; yourself

dicht [dɪçt] *adj* dense; (*Nebel*) thick; (*Gewebe*) close; (*undurchlässig*) (water)tight; (*fig*) concise ♦ *adv:* **~ an/bei** close to; **~ bevölkert** densely *od* heavily populated; **D~e** *f* density; thickness; closeness; (water)tightness; (*fig*) conciseness

dichten *vt* (*dicht machen*) to make watertight, to seal; (*NAUT*) to caulk; (*LITER*) to compose, to write ♦ *vi* to compose, to write

Dichter(in) (**-s, -**) *m(f)* poet; (*Autor*) writer; **d~isch** *adj* poetical

dichthalten (*unreg*) (*umg*) *vi* to keep one's mouth shut

Dichtung *f* (*TECH*) washer; (*AUT*) gasket; (*Gedichte*) poetry; (*Prosa*) (piece of) writing

dick [dɪk] *adj* thick; (*fett*) fat; **durch ~ und dünn** through thick and thin; **D~darm** *m* (*ANAT*) colon; **D~e** *f* thickness; fatness; **~flüssig** *adj* viscous; **D~icht** (**-s, -e**) *nt* thicket; **D~kopf** *m* mule; **D~milch** *f* soured milk

die [diː] *def art siehe* **der**

Dieb(in) [diːp, 'diːbɪn] (**-(e)s, -e**) *m(f)* thief; **d~isch** *adj* thieving; (*umg*) immense; **~stahl** (**-(e)s, -e**) *m* theft; **~stahlversicherung** *f* insurance against theft

Diele ['diːlə] *f* (*Brett*) board; (*Flur*) hall, lobby

dienen ['diːnən] *vi:* (*jdm*) **~** to serve (sb)

Diener (**-s, -**) *m* servant; **~in** *f* (maid)servant; **~schaft** *f* servants *pl*

Dienst [diːnst] (**-(e)s, -e**) *m* service; **außer ~** retired; **~ haben** to be on duty; **~ habend** (*Arzt*) on duty

Dienstag ['diːnstaːk] *m* Tuesday; **d~s** *adv* on Tuesdays

Dienst- *zW:* **~bote** *m* servant; **~geheimnis** *nt* official secret; **~gespräch** *nt* business call; **~leistung** *f* service; **d~lich** *adj* official; **~mädchen** *nt* (house)maid; **~reise** *f* business trip; **~stelle** *f* office; **~vorschrift** *f* official regulations *pl*; **~weg** *m* official channels *pl*; **~zeit** *f* working hours *pl*; (*MIL*) period of service

dies [diːs] *pron* (*demonstrativ: sg*) this; (*: pl*) these; ~**bezüglich** *adj* (*Frage*) on this matter; ~**e(r, s)** [ˈdiːzə(r, s)] *pron* this (one)

Diesel [ˈdiːzəl] *m* (*Kraftstoff*) diesel

dieselbe [diːˈzɛlbə] *pron, art* the same

Dieselmotor *m* diesel engine

diesig [ˈdiːzɪç] *adj* drizzly

dies- *zW:* ~**jährig** *adj* this year's; ~**mal** *adv* this time; ~**seits** *präp +gen* on this side; **D~seits** (-) *nt* this life

Dietrich [ˈdiːtrɪç] (**-s, -e**) *m* picklock

diffamieren [dɪfaˈmiːrən] (*pej*) *vt* to defame

Differenz [dɪfaˈrɛnts] (-, **-en**) *f* (*Unterschied*) difference; ~**en** *pl* (*Meinungsverschiedenheit*) difference (of opinion); **d~ieren** *vt* to make distinctions in; **d~iert** *adj* (*Mensch etc*) complex

differenzial ▲ [dɪfaˈrɛntsiaːl] *adj* differential; **D~rechnung** *f* differential calculus

digital [digiˈtaːl] *adj* digital; **D~fernsehen** *f* digital TV

Dikt- [dɪkt] *zW:* ~**afon**, ~**aphon** [-aˈfoːn] *nt* dictaphone; ~**at** [-ˈtaːt] (**-(e)s, -e**) *nt* dictation; ~**ator** [-ˈtaːtɔr] *m* dictator; **d~atorisch** [-aˈtoːrɪʃ] *adj* dictatorial; ~**atur** [-aˈtuːr] *f* dictatorship; **d~ieren** [-ˈtiːrən] *vt* to dictate

Dilemma [diˈlɛma] (**-s, -s** *od* **-ta**) *nt* dilemma

Dilettant [dileˈtant] *m* dilettante, amateur; **d~isch** *adj* amateurish, dilettante

Dimension [dimɛnziˈoːn] *f* dimension

DIN *f abk* (= *Deutsche Industrie-Norm*) German Industrial Standard

Ding [dɪŋ] (**-(e)s, -e**) *nt* thing, object; **d~lich** *adj* real, concrete; ~**s(bums)** [ˈdɪŋks(bums)] (-) (*umg*) *nt* thingummybob

Diplom [diˈploːm] (**-(e)s, -e**) *nt* diploma, certificate; ~**at** [-ˈmaːt] (**-en, -en**) *m* diplomat; ~**atie** [-aˈtiː] *f* diplomacy; **d~atisch** [-ˈmaːtɪʃ] *adj* diplomatic; ~**ingenieur** *m* qualified engineer

dir [diːr] (*dat von* **du**) *pron* (to) you

direkt [diˈrɛkt] *adj* direct; **D~flug** *m* direct flight; **D~or** *m* director; (*SCH*) principal, headmaster; **D~übertragung** *f* live broadcast

Dirigent [diriˈgɛnt(ɪn)] *m* conductor

dirigieren [diriˈgiːrən] *vt* to direct; (*MUS*) to conduct

Diskette [dɪsˈkɛtə] *f* diskette, floppy disk

Diskont [dɪsˈkɔnt] (**-s, -e**) *m* discount; ~**satz** *m* rate of discount

Diskothek [dɪskoˈteːk] (-, **-en**) *f* disco(theque)

diskret [dɪsˈkreːt] *adj* discreet; **D~ion** *f* discretion

diskriminieren [dɪskrimiˈniːrən] *vt* to discriminate against

Diskussion [dɪskʊsiˈoːn] *f* discussion, debate; **zur ~ stehen** to be under discussion

diskutieren [dɪskuˈtiːrən] *vt, vi* to discuss; to debate

Distanz [dɪsˈtants] *f* distance; **distan'zieren** *vr*: **sich von jdm/etw d~ieren** to distance o.s. from sb/sth

Distel [ˈdɪstəl] (-, **-n**) *f* thistle

Disziplin [dɪstsiˈpliːn] *f* discipline

Dividende [diviˈdɛndə] *f* dividend

dividieren [diviˈdiːrən] *vt*: (**durch etw**) ~ to divide (by sth)

DM [deːˈʔɛm] *abk* (*HIST* = *Deutsche Mark*) German Mark

D-Mark [ˈdeːmark] *f* (*HIST*) D Mark, German Mark

SCHLÜSSELWORT

doch [dɔx] *adv* **1** (*dennoch*) after all; (*sowieso*) anyway; **er kam doch noch** he came after all; **du weißt es ja doch besser** you know better than I do anyway; **und doch ...** and yet ...

2 (*als bejahende Antwort*) yes I do/it does *etc*; **das ist nicht wahr - doch!** that's not true - yes it is!

3 (*auffordernd*): **komm doch** do come; **lass ihn doch** just leave him; **nicht doch!** oh no!

4: **sie ist doch noch so jung** but she's still so young; **Sie wissen doch, wie das ist** you know how it is (, don't you?); **wenn doch** if only

♦ *konj* (*aber*) but; (*trotzdem*) all the same;

und doch hat er es getan but still he did it

Docht [dɔxt] **(-(e)s, -e)** m wick

Dock [dɔk] **(-s, -s** od **-e)** nt dock

Dogge ['dɔgə] f bulldog

Dogma ['dɔgma] **(-s, -men)** nt dogma; **d~tisch** adj dogmatic

Doktor ['dɔktɔr, pl -'to:rən] **(-s, -en)** m doctor

Dokument [doku'mɛnt] nt document

Dokumentar- [dokumɛn'ta:r] zW: **~bericht** m documentary; **~film** m documentary (film); **d~isch** adj documentary

Dolch [dɔlç] **(-(e)s, -e)** m dagger

dolmetschen ['dɔlmɛtʃən] vt, vi to interpret; **Dolmetscher(in) (-s, -)** m(f) interpreter

Dom [do:m] **(-(e)s, -e)** m cathedral

dominieren [domi'ni:rən] vt to dominate ♦ vi to predominate

Donau ['do:nau] f Danube

Donner ['dɔnər] **(-s, -)** m thunder; **d~n** vi unpers to thunder

Donnerstag ['dɔnərsta:k] m Thursday

doof [do:f] (umg) adj daft, stupid

Doppel ['dɔpəl] **(-s, -)** nt duplicate; (SPORT) doubles; **~bett** nt double bed; **~deutig** adj ambiguous; **~fenster** nt double glazing; **~gänger (-s, -)** m double; **~punkt** m colon; **~stecker** m two-way adaptor; **d~t** adj double; **in d~ter Ausführung** in duplicate; **~verdiener** m person with two incomes; (pl: Paar) two-income family; **~zentner** m 100 kilograms; **~zimmer** nt double room

Dorf [dɔrf] **(-(e)s, ⁿer)** nt village; **~bewohner** m villager

Dorn [dɔrn] **(-(e)s, -en)** m (BOT) thorn; **d~ig** adj thorny

Dörrobst ['dœro:pst] nt dried fruit

Dorsch [dɔrʃ] **(-(e)s, -e)** m cod

dort [dɔrt] adv there; **~ drüben** over there; **~her** adv from there; **~hin** adv (to) there; **~ig** adj of that place; in that town

Dose ['do:zə] f box; (Blechdose) tin, can

Dosen pl von **Dose**; **Dosis**

Dosenöffner m tin od can opener

Dosis ['do:zɪs] **(-, Dosen)** f dose

Dotter ['dɔtər] **(-s, -)** m (egg) yolk

Drache ['draxə] **(-n, -n)** m (Tier) dragon

Drachen (-s, -) m kite; **~fliegen (-s)** nt hang-gliding

Draht [dra:t] **(-(e)s, ⁿe)** m wire; **auf ~ sein** to be on the ball; **d~ig** adj (Mann) wiry; **~seil** nt cable; **~seilbahn** f cable railway, funicular

Drama ['dra:ma] **(-s, Dramen)** nt drama, play; **~tiker** [-'ma:tikər] **(-s, -)** m dramatist; **d~tisch** [-'ma:tɪʃ] adj dramatic

dran [dran] (umg) adv: **jetzt bin ich ~!** it's my turn now; siehe **daran**

Drang [draŋ] **(-(e)s, ⁿe)** m (Trieb): **~ (nach)** impulse (for), urge (for), desire (for); (Druck) pressure

drängeln ['drɛŋəln] vt, vi to push, to jostle

drängen ['drɛŋən] vt (schieben) to push, to press; (antreiben) to urge ♦ vi (eilig sein) to be urgent; (Zeit) to press; **auf etw** akk **~** to press for sth

drastisch ['drastɪʃ] adj drastic

drauf [drauf] (umg) adv = **darauf**; **D~gänger (-s, -)** m daredevil

draußen ['drausən] adv outside

Dreck [drɛk] **(-(e)s)** m mud, dirt; **d~ig** adj dirty, filthy

Dreh- ['dre:] zW: **~arbeiten** pl (CINÉ) shooting sg; **~bank** f lathe; **~buch** nt (CINE) script; **d~en** vt to turn, to rotate; (Zigaretten) to roll; (Film) to shoot ♦ vi to turn, to rotate ♦ vr to turn; (handeln von): **es d~t sich um ...** it's about ...; **~orgel** f barrel organ; **~tür** f revolving door; **~ung** f (Rotation) rotation; (Umdrehung, Wendung) turn; **~zahl** f rate of revolutions; **~zahlmesser** m rev(olution) counter

drei [drai] num three; **~ viertel** three quarters; **D~eck** nt triangle; **~eckig** adj triangular; **~einhalb** num three and a half; **~erlei** adj inv of three kinds; **~fach** adj triple, treble ♦ adv three times; **~hundert** num three hundred; **D~königsfest** nt Epiphany; **~mal** adv three times; **~malig** adj three times

---

dreinreden ['draɪnre:dən] *vi*: **jdm ~** (*dazwischenreden*) to interrupt sb; (*sich einmischen*) to interfere with sb

Dreirad *nt* tricycle

dreißig ['draɪsɪç] *num* thirty

dreist [draɪst] *adj* bold, audacious

drei- *zW*: **~viertel** △ *num siehe* **drei**; **D~viertelstunde** *f* three-quarters of an hour; **~zehn** *num* thirteen

dreschen ['drɛʃən] (*unreg*) *vt* (*Getreide*) to thresh; (*umg: verprügeln*) to beat up

dressieren [drɛ'si:rən] *vt* to train

drillen ['drɪlən] *vt* (*bohren*) to drill, to bore; (*MIL*) to drill; (*fig*) to train

Drilling *m* triplet

drin [drɪn] (*umg*) *adv* = **darin**

dringen ['drɪŋən] (*unreg*) *vi* (*Wasser, Licht, Kälte*): **~ (durch/in** +*akk*) to penetrate (through/into); **auf etw** *akk* **~** to insist on sth

dringend ['drɪŋənt] *adj* urgent

Dringlichkeit *f* urgency

drinnen ['drɪnən] *adv* inside, indoors

dritte(r, s) [drɪtə(r, s)] *adj* third; **D~ Welt** Third World; **D~s Reich** Third Reich; **D~l** (**-s, -**) *nt* third; **~ns** *adv* thirdly

DRK [de:|ɛr'ka:] *nt abk* (= *Deutsches Rotes Kreuz*) German Red Cross

droben ['dro:bən] *adv* above, up there

Droge ['dro:gə] *f* drug

drogen *zW*: **~abhängig** *adj* addicted to drugs; **D~händler** *m* drug pedlar, pusher

Drogerie [dro:gə'ri:] *f* chemist's shop

Drogerie

ℹ️ The **Drogerie** as opposed to the **Apotheke** sells medicines not requiring a prescription. It tends to be cheaper and also sells cosmetics, perfume and toiletries.

Drogist [dro'gɪst] *m* pharmacist, chemist

drohen ['dro:ən] *vi*: **(jdm) ~** to threaten (sb)

dröhnen ['drø:nən] *vi* (*Motor*) to roar; (*Stimme, Musik*) to ring, to resound

Drohung ['dro:ʊŋ] *f* threat

drollig ['drɔlɪç] *adj* droll

Drossel ['drɔsəl] (**-, -n**) *f* thrush

drüben ['dry:bən] *adv* over there, on the other side

drüber ['dry:bər] (*umg*) *adv* = **darüber**

Druck [drʊk] (**-(e)s, -e**) *m* (*PHYS: Zwang*) pressure; (*TYP: Vorgang*) printing; (: *Produkt*) print; (*fig: Belastung*) burden, weight; **~buchstabe** *m* block letter

drücken ['drʏkən] *vt* (*Knopf, Hand*) to press; (*zu eng sein*) to pinch; (*fig: Preise*) to keep down; (: *belasten*) to oppress, to weigh down ♦ *vi* to press; to pinch ♦ *vr*: **sich vor etw** *dat* **~** to get out of (doing) sth; **~d** *adj* oppressive

Drucker (**-s, -**) *m* printer

Drücker (**-s, -**) *m* button; (*Türdrücker*) handle; (*Gewehrdrücker*) trigger

Druck- *zW*: **~e'rei** *f* printing works, press; **~erschwärze** *f* printer's ink; **~fehler** *m* misprint; **~knopf** *m* press stud, snap fastener; **~sache** *f* printed matter; **~schrift** *f* block *od* printed letters *pl*

drum [drʊm] (*umg*) *adv* = **darum**

drunten ['drʊntən] *adv* below, down there

Drüse ['dry:zə] *f* gland

Dschungel ['dʒʊŋəl] (**-s, -**) *m* jungle

du [du:] (*nom*) *pron* you; **~ sagen** = **duzen**

Dübel ['dy:bəl] (**-s, -**) *m* Rawlplug ®

ducken ['dʊkən] *vt* (*Kopf, Person*) to duck; (*fig*) to take down a peg or two ♦ *vr* to duck

Duckmäuser ['dʊkmɔyzər] (**-s, -**) *m* yes man

Dudelsack ['du:dəlzak] *m* bagpipes *pl*

Duell [du'ɛl] (**-s, -e**) *nt* duel

Duft [dʊft] (**-(e)s, -e**) *m* scent, odour; **d~en** *vi* to smell, to be fragrant; **d~ig** *adj* (*Stoff, Kleid*) delicate, diaphanous

dulden ['dʊldən] *vt* to suffer; (*zulassen*) to tolerate ♦ *vi* to suffer

dumm [dʊm] *adj* stupid; (*ärgerlich*) annoying; **der D~e sein** to be the loser; **~erweise** *adv* stupidly; **D~heit** *f* stupidity; (*Tat*) blunder, stupid mistake; **D~kopf** *m* blockhead

dumpf [dʊmpf] *adj* (*Ton*) hollow, dull; (*Luft*)

musty; (*Erinnerung, Schmerz*) vague

Düne ['dy:nə] *f* dune

düngen ['dyŋən] *vt* to manure

Dünger (**-s, -**) *m* dung, manure; (*künstlich*) fertilizer

dunkel ['dʊŋkəl] *adj* dark; (*Stimme*) deep; (*Ahnung*) vague; (*rätselhaft*) obscure; (*verdächtig*) dubious, shady; **im D~n tappen** (*fig*) to grope in the dark

Dunkel- *zW:* **~heit** *f* darkness; (*fig*) obscurity; **~kammer** *f* (*PHOT*) darkroom; **d~n** *vi unpers* to grow dark; **~ziffer** *f* estimated number of unreported cases

dünn [dʏn] *adj* thin; **~flüssig** *adj* watery, thin

Dunst [dʊnst] (**-es, ⁻e**) *m* vapour; (*Wetter*) haze

dünsten ['dʏnstən] *vt* to steam

dunstig ['dʊnstɪç] *adj* vaporous; (*Wetter*) hazy, misty

Duplikat [dupli'ka:t] (**-(e)s, -e**) *nt* duplicate

Dur [du:r] (**-, -**) *nt* (*MUS*) major

SCHLÜSSELWORT

durch [dʊrç] *präp +akk* **1** (*hindurch*) through; **durch den Urwald** through the jungle; **durch die ganze Welt reisen** to travel all over the world

2 (*mittels*) through, by (means of); (*aufgrund*) due to, owing to; **Tod durch Herzschlag/den Strang** death from a heart attack/by hanging; **durch die Post** by post; **durch seine Bemühungen** through his efforts

♦ *adv* **1** (*hindurch*) through; **die ganze Nacht durch** all through the night; **den Sommer durch** during the summer; **8 Uhr durch** past 8 o'clock; **durch und durch** completely

2 (*durchgebraten etc*): (**gut**) **durch** well-done

---

durch- *zW:* **~arbeiten** *vt, vi* to work through ♦ *vr* to work one's way through; **~'aus** *adv* completely; (*unbedingt*) definitely; **~aus nicht** absolutely not

Durchblick ['dʊrçblɪk] *m* view; (*fig*) comprehension; **d~en** *vi* to look through;

(*umg: verstehen*): (**bei etw**) **d~en** to understand (sth); **etw d~en lassen** (*fig*) to hint at sth

durchbrechen ['dʊrçbrɛçən] (*unreg*) *vt, vi* to break

durch'brechen ['dʊrçbrɛçən] (*unreg*) *vt insep* (*Schranken*) to break through; (*Schallmauer*) to break; (*Gewohnheit*) to break free from

durchbrennen ['dʊrçbrɛnən] (*unreg*) *vi* (*Draht, Sicherung*) to burn through; (*umg*) to run away

durchbringen (*unreg*) *vt* (*Kranken*) to pull through; (*umg: Familie*) to support; (*durchsetzen: Antrag, Kandidat*) to get through; (*vergeuden: Geld*) to get through, to squander

Durchbruch ['dʊrçbrʊx] *m* (*Öffnung*) opening; (*MIL*) breach; (*von Gefühlen etc*) eruption; (*der Zähne*) cutting; (*fig*) breakthrough; **zum ~ kommen** to break through

durch- *zW:* **~dacht** [-'daxt] *adj* well thought-out; **~'denken** (*unreg*) *vt* to think out; **~drehen** *vt* (*Fleisch*) to mince ♦ *vi* (*umg*) to crack up

durcheinander [dʊrçaɪ'nandər] *adv* in a mess, in confusion; (*umg: verwirrt*) confused; **~ bringen** to mess up; (*verwirren*) to confuse; **~ reden** to talk at the same time; **D~** (**-s**) *nt* (*Verwirrung*) confusion; (*Unordnung*) mess

durch- *zW:* **~fahren** (*unreg*) *vi* (*~ Tunnel usw*) to drive through; (*ohne Unterbrechung*) to drive straight through; (*ohne anzuhalten*): **der Zug fährt bis Hamburg ~** the train runs direct to Hamburg; (*ohne Umsteigen*): **können wir ~fahren?** can we go direct?, can we go non-stop?; **D~fahrt** *f* transit; (*Verkehr*) thoroughfare; **D~fall** *m* (*MED*) diarrhoea; **~fallen** (*unreg*) *vi* to fall through; (*in Prüfung*) to fail; **~finden** (*unreg*) *vr* to find one's way through; **~fragen** *vr* to find one's way by asking

durchführ- ['dʊrçfy:r] *zW:* **~bar** *adj* feasible, practicable; **~en** *vt* to carry out; **D~ung** *f* execution, performance

---

Spelling Reform: ▲ *new spelling* △ *old spelling (to be phased out)*

Durchgang ['dʊrçgaŋ] *m* passage(way); (*bei Produktion, Versuch*) run; (*SPORT*) round; (*bei Wahl*) ballot; „**~ verboten**" "no thoroughfare"

Durchgangsverkehr *m* through traffic

durchgefroren ['dʊrçgəfroːrən] *adj* (*Mensch*) frozen stiff

durchgehen ['dʊrçgeːən] (*unreg*) *vt* (*behandeln*) to go over ♦ *vi* to go through; (*ausreißen: Pferd*) to break loose; (*Mensch*) to run away; **mein Temperament ging mit mir durch** my temper got the better of me; **jdm etw ~ lassen** to let sb get away with sth; **~d** *adj* (*Zug*) through; (*Öffnungszeiten*) continuous

durch- *zW:* **~greifen** (*unreg*) *vi* to take strong action; **~halten** (*unreg*) *vi* to last out ♦ *vt* to keep up; **~kommen** (*unreg*) *vi* to get through; (*überleben*) to pull through; **~'kreuzen** *vt insep* to thwart, to frustrate; **~lassen** (*unreg*) *vt* (*Person*) to let through; (*Wasser*) to let in; **~lesen** (*unreg*) *vt* to read through; **~'leuchten** *vt insep* to X-ray; **~machen** *vt* to go through; **die Nacht ~machen** to make a night of it

Durchmesser (**-s, -**) *m* diameter

durch- *zW:* **~'nässen** *vt insep* to soak (through); **~nehmen** (*unreg*) *vt* to go over; **~nummerieren** ▲ *vt* to number consecutively; **~queren** [dʊrç'kveːrən] *vt insep* to cross; **D~reise** *f* transit; **auf der D~reise** passing through; (*Güter*) in transit; **~ringen** (*unreg*) *vr* to reach a decision after a long struggle

durchs [dʊrçs] = **durch das**

Durchsage ['dʊrçzaːgə] *f* intercom *od* radio announcement

durchschauen ['dʊrçʃauən] *vi* to look *od* see through; (*Person, Lüge*) to see through

durchscheinen ['dʊrçʃainən] (*unreg*) *vi* to shine through; **~d** *adj* translucent

Durchschlag ['dʊrçʃlaːk] *m* (*Doppel*) carbon copy; (*Sieb*) strainer; **d~en** [-gən] (*unreg*) *vt* (*entzweischlagen*) to split (in two); (*sieben*) to sieve ♦ *vi* (*zum Vorschein kommen*) to emerge, to come out ♦ *vr* to

get by

durchschlagend *adj* resounding

durchschneiden ['dʊrçʃnaidən] (*unreg*) *vt* to cut through

Durchschnitt ['dʊrçʃnit] *m* (*Mittelwert*) average; **über / unter dem ~** above/below average; **im ~** on average; **d~lich** *adj* average ♦ *adv* on average

Durchschnittswert *m* average

durch- *zW:* **D~schrift** *f* copy; **~sehen** (*unreg*) *vt* to look through; **~setzen** *vt* to enforce ♦ *vr* (*Erfolg haben*) to succeed; (*sich behaupten*) to get one's way; **seinen Kopf ~setzen** to get one's way; **~'setzen** *vt insep* to mix

Durchsicht ['dʊrçzict] *f* looking through, checking; **d~ig** *adj* transparent

durch- *zW:* **'~sprechen** (*unreg*) *vt* to talk over; **'~stehen** (*unreg*) *vt* to live through; **~stellen** *vt* (*an Telefon*) to put through; **~stöbern** (*auch untr*) *vt* (*Kisten*) to rummage through, to rifle through; (*Haus, Wohnung*) to ransack; **'~streichen** (*unreg*) *vt* to cross out; **'~suchen** *vt insep* to search; **D~'suchung** *f* search; **~'wachsen** *adj* (*Speck*) streaky; (*fig: mittelmäßig*) so-so; **D~wahl** *f* (*TEL*) direct dialling; **~weg** *adv* throughout, completely; **~ziehen** (*unreg*) *vt* (*Faden*) to draw through ♦ *vi* to pass through; **D~zug** *m* (*Luft*) draught; (*von Truppen, Vögeln*) passage

┌─── SCHLÜSSELWORT ───┐

dürfen ['dʏrfən] (*unreg*) *vi* **1** (*Erlaubnis haben*) to be allowed to; **ich darf das** I'm allowed to (do that); **darf ich?** may I?; **darf ich ins Kino?** can *od* may I go to the cinema?; **es darf geraucht werden** you may smoke

2 (*in Verneinungen*): **er darf das nicht** he's not allowed to (do that); **das darf nicht geschehen** that must not happen; **da darf sie sich nicht wundern** that shouldn't surprise her

3 (*in Höflichkeitsformeln*): **darf ich Sie bitten, das zu tun?** may *od* could I ask you to do that?; **was darf es sein?** what can I do for you?

Rechtschreibreform: ▲ *neue Schreibung* △ *alte Schreibung (auslaufend)*

4 (*können*): **das dürfen Sie mir glauben** you can believe me

5 (*Möglichkeit*): **das dürfte genug sein** that should be enough; **es dürfte Ihnen bekannt sein, dass ...** as you will probably know ...

dürftig ['dʏrftɪç] *adj* (*ärmlich*) needy, poor; (*unzulänglich*) inadequate

dürr [dʏr] *adj* dried-up; (*Land*) arid; (*mager*) skinny, gaunt; **D~e** *f* aridity; (*Zeit*) drought; (*Magerkeit*) skinniness

Durst [dʊrst] (**-(e)s**) *m* thirst; **~ haben** to be thirsty; **d~ig** *adj* thirsty

Dusche ['duʃə] *f* shower; **d~en** *vi*, *vr* to have a shower

Düse ['dyːzə] *f* nozzle; (*Flugzeugdüse*) jet

Düsen- *zW:* **~antrieb** *m* jet propulsion; **~flugzeug** *nt* jet (plane); **~jäger** *m* jet fighter

Dussel ['dʊsəl] (**-s, -**) (*umg*) *m* twit

düster ['dyːstər] *adj* dark; (*Gedanken, Zukunft*) gloomy

Dutzend ['dʊtsənt] (**-s, -e**) *nt* dozen; **~(e)** *od* **d~(e) Mal(e)** a dozen times

duzen ['duːtsən] *vt:* (**jdn**) **~** to use the familiar form of address "du" (to *od* with sb)

---
duzen

---

i There are two different forms of address in Germany: du and Sie. **Duzen** means addressing someone as 'du' - used with children, family and close friends - and **siezen** means addressing someone as 'Sie' - used for all grown-ups and older teenagers. Students almost always say 'du' to each other.

Dynamik [dy'naːmɪk] *f* (*PHYS*) dynamics *sg*; (*fig: Schwung*) momentum; (*von Mensch*) dynamism; **dynamisch** *adj* (*auch fig*) dynamic

Dynamit [dyna'miːt] (**-s**) *nt* dynamite

Dynamo [dy'naːmo] (**-s, -s**) *m* dynamo

DZ *nt abk* = **Doppelzimmer**

D-Zug ['deːtsuːk] *m* through train

E, e

Ebbe ['ɛbə] *f* low tide

eben ['eːbən] *adj* level, flat; (*glatt*) smooth ♦ *adv* just; (*bestätigend*) exactly; **~ deswegen** just because of that; **~bürtig** *adj:* **jdm ~bürtig sein** to be sb's equal; **E~e** *f* plain; (*fig*) level; **~falls** *adv* likewise; **~so** *adv* just as

Eber ['eːbər] (**-s, -**) *m* boar

ebnen ['eːbnən] *vt* to level

Echo ['ɛço] (**-s, -s**) *nt* echo

echt [ɛçt] *adj* genuine; (*typisch*) typical; **E~heit** *f* genuineness

Eck- ['ɛk] *zW:* **~ball** *m* corner (kick); **~e** *f* corner; (*MATH*) angle; **e~ig** *adj* angular; **~zahn** *m* eye tooth

ECU [e'kyː] (**-, -s**) *m* (*FIN*) ECU

edel ['eːdəl] *adj* noble; **E~metall** *nt* rare metal; **E~stahl** *m* high-grade steel; **E~stein** *m* precious stone

EDV [eːdeː'faʊ] (**-**) *f abk* (= *elektronische Datenverarbeitung*) electronic data processing

Efeu ['eːfɔy] (**-s**) *m* ivy

Effekt [ɛ'fɛkt] (**-s, -e**) *m* effect

Effekten [ɛ'fɛktən] *pl* stocks

effektiv [ɛfɛk'tiːf] *adj* effective, actual

EG ['eː'geː] *f abk* (= *Europäische Gemeinschaft*) EC

egal [e'gaːl] *adj* all the same

Ego- [e:go] *zW:* **~ismus** [-'ɪsmʊs] *m* selfishness, egoism; **~ist** [-'ɪst] *m* egoist; **e~istisch** *adj* selfish, egoistic

Ehe ['eːə] *f* marriage

ehe *konj* before

Ehe- *zW:* **~beratung** *f* marriage guidance (counselling); **~bruch** *m* adultery; **~frau** *f* married woman; wife; **~leute** *pl* married people; **e~lich** *adj* matrimonial; (*Kind*) legitimate

ehemalig *adj* former

ehemals *adv* formerly

Ehe- *zW:* **~mann** *m* married man; husband; **~paar** *nt* married couple

Spelling Reform: ▲ *new spelling* △ *old spelling (to be phased out)*

eher [ˈeːɐr] *adv (früher)* sooner; *(lieber)* rather, sooner; *(mehr)* more

Ehe- *zW:* **~ring** *m* wedding ring; **~schließung** *f* marriage ceremony

eheste(r, s) [ˈeːəstə(r, s)] *adj (früheste)* first, earliest; **am ~n** *(liebsten)* soonest; *(meist)* most; *(wahrscheinlichst)* most probably

Ehr- [ˈeːr] *zW:* **e~bar** *adj* honourable, respectable; **~e** *f* honour; **e~en** *vt* to honour

Ehren- [ˈeːrən] *zW:* **e~amtlich** *adj* honorary; **~gast** *m* guest of honour; **e~haft** *adj* honourable; **~platz** *m* place of honour *od (US)* honor; **~runde** *f* lap of honour; **~sache** *f* point of honour; **e~voll** *adj* honourable; **~wort** *nt* word of honour

Ehr- *zW:* **~furcht** *f* awe, deep respect; **e~fürchtig** *adj* reverent; **~gefühl** *nt* sense of honour; **~geiz** *m* ambition; **e~geizig** *adj* ambitious; **e~lich** *adj* honest; **~lichkeit** *f* honesty; **e~los** *adj* dishonourable; **~ung** *f* honour(ing); **e~würdig** *adj* venerable

Ei [aɪ] **(-(e)s, -er)** *nt* egg

Eich- *zW:* **~e** [ˈaɪçə] *f* oak (tree); **~l** **(-, -n)** *f* acorn; **~hörnchen** *nt* squirrel

Eichmaß *nt* standard

Eid [aɪt] **(-(e)s, -e)** *m* oath

Eidechse [ˈaɪdɛksə] *f* lizard

eidesstattlich *adj:* **~e Erklärung** affidavit

Eidgenosse *m* Swiss

Eier- *zW:* **~becher** *m* eggcup; **~kuchen** *m* omelette; pancake; **~likör** *m* advocaat; **~schale** *f* eggshell; **~stock** *m* ovary; **~uhr** *f* egg timer

Eifer [ˈaɪfər] **(-s)** *m* zeal, enthusiasm; **~sucht** *f* jealousy; **e~süchtig** *adj:* **e~süchtig (auf +akk)** jealous (of)

eifrig [ˈaɪfrɪç] *adj* zealous, enthusiastic

Eigelb [ˈaɪɡɛlp] **(-(e)s, -)** *nt* egg yolk

eigen [ˈaɪɡən] *adj* own; *(~artig)* peculiar; **mit der/dem ihm ~en ...** with that ... peculiar to him; **sich** *dat* **etw zu E~ machen** to make sth one's own; **E~art** *f* peculiarity; **e~artig** *adj* peculiar; characteristic; **E~bedarf** *m:* **zum E~bedarf** for (one's own) personal use/domestic requirements; **der Vermieter machte E~bedarf geltend**

the landlord showed he needed the house/flat for himself; **e~händig** *adj* with one's own hand; **E~heim** *nt* owner-occupied house; **E~heit** *f* peculiarity; **~mächtig** *adj* high-handed; **E~name** *m* proper name; **~s** *adv* expressly, on purpose; **E~schaft** *f* quality, property, attribute; **E~sinn** *m* obstinacy; **~sinnig** *adj* obstinate; **~tlich** *adj* actual, real ♦ *adv* actually, really; **E~tor** *nt* own goal; **E~tum** *nt* property; **E~tümer(in)** **(-s, -)** *m(f)* owner, proprietor; **~tümlich** *adj* peculiar; **E~tümlichkeit** *f* peculiarity; **E~tumswohnung** *f* freehold flat

eignen [ˈaɪɡnən] *vr* to be suited; **Eignung** *f* suitability

Eil- [ˈaɪl] *zW:* **~bote** *m* courier; **~brief** *m* express letter; **~e** *f* haste; **es hat keine ~e** there's no hurry; **e~en** *vi (Mensch)* to hurry; *(dringend sein)* to be urgent; **e~ends** *adv* hastily; **~gut** *nt* express goods *pl*, fast freight *(US)*; **e~ig** *adj* hasty, hurried; *(dringlich)* urgent; **es e~ig haben** to be in a hurry; **~zug** *m* semi-fast train, limited stop train

Eimer [ˈaɪmər] **(-s, -)** *m* bucket, pail

ein [aɪn] *adv:* **nicht ~ noch aus wissen** not to know what to do

ein(e) [ˈaɪn(ə)] *num* one ♦ *indef art* a, an

einander [aɪˈnandər] *pron* one another, each other

einarbeiten [ˈaɪnlarbaɪtən] *vt* to train ♦ *vr:* **sich in etw** *akk* **~** to familiarize o.s. with sth

einatmen [ˈaɪnlaːtmən] *vt, vi* to inhale, to breathe in

Einbahnstraße [ˈaɪnbaːnʃtrasə] *f* one-way street

Einband [ˈaɪnbant] *m* binding, cover

einbauen [ˈaɪnbaʊən] *vt* to build in; *(Motor)* to install, to fit

Einbaumöbel *pl* built-in furniture *sg*

einbegriffen [ˈaɪnbəɡrɪfən] *adj* included

einberufen [ˈaɪnbəruːfən] *(unreg) vt* to convene; *(MIL)* to call up

Einbettzimmer *nt* single room

einbeziehen [ˈaɪnbətsiːən] *(unreg) vt* to

include
einbiegen ['aɪnbiːgən] (*unreg*) *vi* to turn
einbilden ['aɪnbɪldən] *vt*: **sich** *dat* **etw ~** to imagine sth
Einbildung *f* imagination; (*Dünkel*) conceit; **~skraft** *f* imagination
Einblick ['aɪnblɪk] *m* insight
einbrechen ['aɪnbrɛçən] (*unreg*) *vi* (*in Haus*) to break in; (*Nacht*) to fall; (*Winter*) to set in; (*durchbrechen*) to break; **~ in** +*akk* (*MIL*) to invade
Einbrecher (**-s, -**) *m* burglar
einbringen ['aɪnbrɪŋən] (*unreg*) *vt* to bring in; (*Geld, Vorteil*) to yield; (*mitbringen*) to contribute
Einbruch ['aɪnbrʊx] *m* (*Hauseinbruch*) break-in, burglary; (*Eindringen*) invasion; (*des Winters*) onset; (*Durchbrechen*) break; (*MET*) approach; (*MIL*) penetration; (**bei/vor**) **~ der Nacht** at/before nightfall; **e~sicher** *adj* burglar-proof
einbürgern ['aɪnbʏrgərn] *vt* to naturalize ♦ *vr* to become adopted
einbüßen ['aɪnbyːsən] *vt* to lose, to forfeit
einchecken ['aɪntʃɛkən] *vt, vi* to check in
eincremen ['aɪnkreːmən] *vt* to put cream on
eindecken ['aɪndɛkən] *vr*: **sich (mit etw) ~** to lay in stocks (of sth); to stock up (with sth)
eindeutig ['aɪndɔytɪç] *adj* unequivocal
eindringen ['aɪndrɪŋən] (*unreg*) *vi*: **~ (in** +*akk*) to force one's way in(to); (*in Haus*) to break in(to); (*in Land*) to invade; (*Gas, Wasser*) to penetrate; (**auf jdn**) **~** (*mit Bitten*) to pester (sb)
eindringlich *adj* forcible, urgent
Eindringling *m* intruder
Eindruck ['aɪndrʊk] *m* impression
eindrücken ['aɪndrʏkən] *vt* to press in
eindrucksvoll *adj* impressive
eine(r, s) *pron* one; (*jemand*) someone
eineiig ['aɪn|aɪç] *adj* (*Zwillinge*) identical
eineinhalb ['aɪn|aɪn'halp] *num* one and a half
einengen ['aɪn|ɛŋən] *vt* to confine, to restrict

einer- ['aɪnər] *zW*: '**E~lei** (**-s**) *nt* sameness; '**~lei** *adj* (*gleichartig*) the same kind of; **es ist mir ~lei** it is all the same to me; **~seits** *adv* on the one hand
einfach ['aɪnfax] *adj* simple; (*nicht mehrfach*) single ♦ *adv* simply; **E~heit** *f* simplicity
einfädeln ['aɪnfɛːdəln] *vt* (*Nadel, Faden*) to thread; (*fig*) to contrive
einfahren ['aɪnfaːrən] (*unreg*) *vt* to bring in; (*Barriere*) to knock down; (*Auto*) to run in ♦ *vi* to drive in; (*Zug*) to pull in; (*MIN*) to go down
Einfahrt *f* (*Vorgang*) driving in; pulling in; (*MIN*) descent; (*Ort*) entrance
Einfall ['aɪnfal] *m* (*Idee*) idea, notion; (*Lichteinfall*) incidence; (*MIL*) raid; **e~en** (*unreg*) *vi* (*Licht*) to fall; (*MIL*) to raid; (*einstürzen*) to fall in, to collapse; (*einstimmen*): (**in etw** *akk*) **e~en** to join in (with sth); **etw fällt jdm ein** sth occurs to sb; **das fällt mir gar nicht ein** I wouldn't dream of it; **sich** *dat* **etw e~en lassen** to have a good idea
einfältig ['aɪnfɛltɪç] *adj* simple(-minded)
Einfamilienhaus ['aɪnfa'miːliənhaʊs] *nt* detached house
einfarbig ['aɪnfarbɪç] *adj* all one colour; (*Stoff etc*) self-coloured
einfetten ['aɪnfɛtən] *vt* to grease
einfließen ['aɪnfliːsən] (*unreg*) *vi* to flow in
einflößen ['aɪnfløːsən] *vt*: **jdm etw ~** to give sb sth; (*fig*) to instil sth in sb
Einfluss ▲ ['aɪnflʊs] *m* influence; **~bereich** *m* sphere of influence
einförmig ['aɪnfœrmɪç] *adj* uniform; **E~keit** *f* uniformity
einfrieren ['aɪnfriːrən] (*unreg*) *vi* to freeze (up) ♦ *vt* to freeze
einfügen ['aɪnfyːgən] *vt* to fit in; (*zusätzlich*) to add
Einfuhr ['aɪnfuːr] (**-**) *f* import; **~beschränkung** *f* import restrictions *pl*; **~bestimmungen** *pl* import regulations
einführen ['aɪnfyːrən] *vt* to bring in; (*Mensch, Sitten*) to introduce; (*Ware*) to import
Einführung *f* introduction

Spelling Reform: ▲ *new spelling* △ *old spelling (to be phased out)*

Eingabe ['aɪngaːbə] f petition; (COMPUT) input

Eingang ['aɪngaŋ] m entrance; (COMM: Ankunft) arrival; (Erhalt) receipt

eingeben ['aɪngeːbən] (unreg) vt (Arznei) to give; (Daten etc) to enter

eingebildet ['aɪngəbɪldət] adj imaginary; (eitel) conceited

Eingeborene(r) ['aɪngəboːrənə(r)] f(m) native

Eingebung f inspiration

eingefleischt ['aɪngəflaɪʃt] adj (Gewohnheit, Vorurteile) deep-rooted

eingehen ['aɪngeːən] (unreg) vi (Aufnahme finden) to come in; (Sendung, Geld) to be received; (Tier, Pflanze) to die; (Firma) to fold; (schrumpfen) to shrink ♦ vt to enter into; (Wette) to make; **auf etw** akk ~ to go into sth; **auf jdn** ~ to respond to sb; **jdm** ~ (verständlich sein) to be comprehensible to sb; ~**d** adj exhaustive, thorough

Eingemachte(s) ['aɪngəmaːxtə(s)] nt preserves pl

eingenommen ['aɪngənɔmən] adj: ~ **(von)** fond (of), partial (to); ~ **(gegen)** prejudiced (against)

eingeschrieben ['aɪngəfriːbən] adj registered

eingespielt ['aɪngəfpiːlt] adj: **aufeinander** ~ **sein** to be in tune with each other

Eingeständnis ['aɪngəftɛntnɪs] (-ses, -se) nt admission, confession

eingestehen ['aɪngəfteːən] (unreg) vt to confess

eingestellt ['aɪngəfte
lt] adj: **auf etw** ~ **sein** to be prepared for sth

eingetragen ['aɪngətraːgən] adj (COMM) registered

Eingeweide ['aɪngəvaɪdə] (-s, -) nt innards pl, intestines pl

Eingeweihte(r) ['aɪngəvaɪtə(r)] f(m) initiate

eingewöhnen ['aɪngəvøːnən] vr: **sich** ~ **in** +akk to settle (down) in

eingleisig ['aɪnglaɪzɪç] adj single-track

eingreifen ['aɪngraɪfən] (unreg) vi to intervene, to interfere; (Zahnrad) to mesh

Eingriff ['aɪngrɪf] m intervention,

interference; (Operation) operation

einhaken ['aɪnhaːkən] vt to hook in ♦ vr: **sich bei jdm** ~ to link arms with sb ♦ vi (sich einmischen) to intervene

Einhalt ['aɪnhalt] m: ~ **gebieten** +dat to put a stop to; **e~en** (unreg) vt (Regel) to keep ♦ vi to stop

einhändigen ['aɪnhɛndɪgən] vt to hand in

einhängen ['aɪnhɛŋən] vt to hang; (Telefon) to hang up ♦ vi (TEL) to hang up; **sich bei jdm** ~ to link arms with sb

einheimisch ['aɪnhaɪmɪʃ] adj native; **E~e(r)** f(m) local

Einheit ['aɪnhaɪt] f unity; (Maß, MIL) unit; **e~lich** adj uniform; ~**spreis** m standard price

einholen ['aɪnhoːlən] vt (Tau) to haul in; (Fahne, Segel) to lower; (Vorsprung aufholen) to catch up with; (Verspätung) to make up; (Rat, Erlaubnis) to ask ♦ vi (einkaufen) to shop

einhüllen ['aɪnhʏlən] vt to wrap up

einhundert ['aɪn'hʊndərt] num one hundred, a hundred

einig ['aɪnɪç] adj (vereint) united; ~ **gehen** to agree; **sich** dat ~ **sein** to be in agreement; ~ **werden** to agree

einige(r, s) ['aɪnɪgə(r, s)] adj, pron some ♦ pl some; (mehrere) several; ~ **Mal** a few times

einigen vt to unite ♦ vr: **sich** ~ **(auf** +akk) to agree (on)

einigermaßen adv somewhat; (leidlich) reasonably

einig- zW: **E~keit** f unity; (Übereinstimmung) agreement; **E~ung** f agreement; (Vereinigung) unification

einkalkulieren ['aɪnkalkuliːrən] vt to take into account, to allow for

Einkauf ['aɪnkaʊf] m purchase; **e~en** vt to buy ♦ vi to shop; **e~en gehen** to go shopping

Einkaufs- zW: ~**bummel** m shopping spree; ~**korb** m shopping basket; ~**wagen** m shopping trolley; ~**zentrum** nt shopping centre

einklammern ['aɪnklamərn] vt to put in brackets, to bracket

Einklang ['aɪnklaŋ] *m* harmony

einklemmen ['aɪnklɛmən] *vt* to jam

einkochen ['aɪnkɔxən] *vt* to boil down; (*Obst*) to preserve, to bottle

Einkommen ['aɪnkɔmən] (**-s, -**) *nt* income; **~(s)steuer** *f* income tax

Einkünfte ['aɪnkʏnftə] *pl* income *sg*, revenue *sg*

einladen ['aɪnlaːdən] (*unreg*) *vt* (*Person*) to invite; (*Gegenstände*) to load; **jdn ins Kino ~** to take sb to the cinema

Einladung *f* invitation

Einlage ['aɪnlaːgə] *f* (*Programm~*) interlude; (*Spar~*) deposit; (*Schuh~*) insole; (*Fußstütze*) support; (*Zahn~*) temporary filling; (*KOCH*) noodles *pl*, vegetables *pl etc* in soup

einlagern ['aɪnlaːgɐn] *vt* to store

Einlass ▲ ['aɪnlas] (**-es, ▀e**) *m* (*Zutritt*) admission

einlassen ['aɪnlasən] (*unreg*) *vt* to let in; (*einsetzen*) to set in ♦ *vr*: **sich mit jdm/auf etw** *akk* **~** to get involved with sb/sth

Einlauf ['aɪnlaʊf] *m* arrival; (*von Pferden*) finish; (*MED*) enema; **e~en** (*unreg*) *vi* to arrive, to come in; (*in Hafen*) to enter; (*SPORT*) to finish; (*Wasser*) to run in; (*Stoff*) to shrink ♦ *vt* (*Schuhe*) to break in ♦ *vr* (*SPORT*) to warm up; (*Motor, Maschine*) to run in; **jdm das Haus e~en** to invade sb's house

einleben ['aɪnleːbən] *vr* to settle down

einlegen ['aɪnleːgən] *vt* (*einfügen: Blatt, Sohle*) to insert; (*KOCH*) to pickle; (*Pause*) to have; (*Protest*) to make; (*Veto*) to use; (*Berufung*) to lodge; (*AUT: Gang*) to engage

einleiten ['aɪnlaɪtən] *vt* to introduce, to start; (*Geburt*) to induce; **Einleitung** *f* introduction; induction

einleuchten ['aɪnlɔʏçtən] *vi*: **(jdm) ~** to be clear *od* evident (to sb); **~d** *adj* clear

einliefern ['aɪnliːfɐn] *vt*: **~ (in** +*akk*) to take (into)

Einlieferungsschein *m* certificate of posting

Einliegerwohnung ['aɪnliːgɐvoːnʊŋ] *f* self-contained flat; (*für Eltern, Großeltern*) granny flat

einloggen ['aɪnlɔgən] *vi* (*COMPUT*) to log on

einlösen ['aɪnløːzən] *vt* (*Scheck*) to cash; (*Schuldschein, Pfand*) to redeem; (*Versprechen*) to keep

einmachen ['aɪnmaxən] *vt* to preserve

einmal ['aɪnmaːl] *adv* once; (*erstens*) first; (*zukünftig*) sometime; **nehmen wir ~ an** just let's suppose; **noch ~** once more; **nicht ~** not even; **auf ~** all at once; **es war ~** once upon a time there was/were; **E~'eins** *nt* multiplication tables *pl*; **~ig** *adj* unique; (*einmal erforderlich*) single; (*prima*) fantastic

Einmarsch ['aɪnmarʃ] *m* entry; (*MIL*) invasion; **e~ieren** *vi* to march in

einmischen ['aɪnmɪʃən] *vr*: **sich ~ (in** +*akk*) to interfere (with)

einmütig ['aɪnmyːtɪç] *adj* unanimous

Einnahme ['aɪnnaːmə] *f* (*von Medizin*) taking; (*MIL*) capture, taking; **~n** *pl* (*Geld*) takings, revenue *sg*; **~quelle** *f* source of income

einnehmen ['aɪnneːmən] (*unreg*) *vt* to take; (*Stellung, Raum*) to take up; **~ für/gegen** to persuade in favour of/against; **~d** *adj* charming

einordnen ['aɪnˌɔrdnən] *vt* to arrange, to fit in ♦ *vr* to adapt; (*AUT*) to get into lane

einpacken ['aɪnpakən] *vt* to pack (up)

einparken ['aɪnparkən] *vt* to park

einpendeln ['aɪnpɛndəln] *vr* to even out

einpflanzen ['aɪnpflantsən] *vt* to plant; (*MED*) to implant

einplanen ['aɪnplaːnən] *vt* to plan for

einprägen ['aɪnprɛːgən] *vt* to impress, to imprint; (*beibringen*): **(jdm) ~** to impress (on sb); **sich** *dat* **etw ~** to memorize sth

einrahmen ['aɪnraːmən] *vt* to frame

einräumen ['aɪnrɔʏmən] *vt* (*ordnend*) to put away; (*überlassen: Platz*) to give up; (*zugestehen*) to admit, to concede

einreden ['aɪnreːdən] *vt*: **jdm/sich etw ~** to talk sb/o.s. into believing sth

einreiben ['aɪnraɪbən] (*unreg*) *vt* to rub in

einreichen ['aɪnraɪçən] *vt* to hand in; (*Antrag*) to submit

Einreise ['aɪnraɪzə] *f* entry;

Spelling Reform: ▲ new spelling △ old spelling (to be phased out)

~**bestimmungen** *pl* entry regulations;
~**erlaubnis** *f* entry permit;
~**genehmigung** *f* entry permit; **e~n** *vi*:
(**in ein Land**) **e~n** to enter (a country)
einrichten ['aɪnrɪçtən] *vt* (*Haus*) to furnish;
(*schaffen*) to establish, to set up;
(*arrangieren*) to arrange; (*möglich machen*)
to manage ♦ *vr* (*in Haus*) to furnish one's
house; **sich ~ (auf** +*akk*) (*sich vorbereiten*)
to prepare o.s. (for); (*sich anpassen*) to adapt
(to)
Einrichtung *f* (*Wohnungseinrichtung*)
furnishings *pl*; (*öffentliche Anstalt*)
organization; (*Dienste*) service
einrosten ['aɪnrɔstən] *vi* to get rusty
einrücken ['aɪnrʏkən] *vi* (*MIL: in Land*) to
move in
Eins [aɪns] (-, -en) *f* one; **e~** *num* one; **es ist
mir alles e~** it's all one to me
einsam ['aɪnza:m] *adj* lonely, solitary;
E~keit *f* loneliness, solitude
einsammeln ['aɪnzaməln] *vt* to collect
Einsatz ['aɪnzats] *m* (*Teil*) inset; (*an Kleid*)
insertion; (*Verwendung*) use, employment;
(*Spieleinsatz*) stake; (*Risiko*) risk; (*MIL*)
operation; (*MUS*) entry; **im ~** in action;
e~bereit *adj* ready for action
einschalten ['aɪnʃaltən] *vt* (*einfügen*) to
insert; (*Pause*) to make; (*ELEK*) to switch on;
(*Anwalt*) to bring in ♦ *vr* (*dazwischentreten*)
to intervene
einschärfen ['aɪnʃɛrfən] *vt*: **jdm etw ~** to
impress sth (up)on sb
einschätzen ['aɪnʃɛtsən] *vt* to estimate, to
assess ♦ *vr* to rate o.s.
einschenken ['aɪnʃɛŋkən] *vt* to pour out
einschicken ['aɪnʃɪkən] *vt* to send in
einschl. *abk* (= *einschließlich*) incl.
einschlafen ['aɪnʃla:fən] (*unreg*) *vi* to fall
asleep, to go to sleep
einschläfernd ['aɪnʃlɛ:fərnt] *adj* (*MED*)
soporific; (*langweilig*) boring; (*Stimme*)
lulling
Einschlag ['aɪnʃla:k] *m* impact; (*fig:
Beimischung*) touch, hint; **e~en** [-gən]
(*unreg*) *vt* to knock in; (*Fenster*) to smash, to
break; (*Zähne, Schädel*) to smash in; (*AUT*:

Räder) to turn; (*kürzer machen*) to take up;
(*Ware*) to pack, to wrap up; (*Weg, Richtung*)
to take ♦ *vi* to hit; (*sich einigen*) to agree;
(*Anklang finden*) to work, to succeed; **in etw
akk/auf jdn e~en** to hit sth/sb
einschlägig ['aɪnʃlɛ:gɪç] *adj* relevant
einschließen ['aɪnʃli:sən] (*unreg*) *vt* (*Kind*) to
lock in; (*Häftling*) to lock up; (*Gegenstand*)
to lock away; (*Bergleute*) to cut off;
(*umgeben*) to surround; (*MIL*) to encircle;
(*fig*) to include, to comprise ♦ *vr* to lock
o.s. in
einschließlich *adv* inclusive ♦ *präp* +*gen*
inclusive of, including
einschmeicheln ['aɪnʃmaɪçəln] *vr*: **sich ~
(bei)** to ingratiate o.s. (with)
einschnappen ['aɪnʃnapən] *vi* (*Tür*) to click
to; (*fig*) to be touchy; **eingeschnappt sein**
to be in a huff
einschneidend ['aɪnʃnaɪdənt] *adj* drastic
Einschnitt ['aɪnʃnɪt] *m* cutting; (*MED*)
incision; (*Ereignis*) decisive point
einschränken ['aɪnʃrɛŋkən] *vt* to limit, to
restrict; (*Kosten*) to cut down, to reduce
♦ *vr* to cut down (on expenditure);
Einschränkung *f* restriction, limitation;
reduction; (*von Behauptung*) qualification
Einschreib- ['aɪnʃraɪb] *zW*: ~**(e)brief** *m*
recorded delivery letter; **e~en** (*unreg*) *vt* to
write in; (*Post*) to send recorded delivery
♦ *vr* to register; (*UNIV*) to enrol; ~**en** *nt*
recorded delivery letter
einschreiten ['aɪnʃraɪtən] (*unreg*) *vi* to step
in, to intervene; **~ gegen** to take action
against
einschüchtern ['aɪnʃʏçtərn] *vt* to intimidate
einschulen ['aɪnʃu:lən] *vt*: **eingeschult
werden** (*Kind*) to start school
einsehen ['aɪnze:ən] (*unreg*) *vt* (*hineinsehen
in*) to realize; (*Akten*) to have a look at;
(*verstehen*) to see; **E~** (**-s**) *nt*
understanding; **ein E~ haben** to show
understanding
einseitig ['aɪnzaɪtɪç] *adj* one-sided
Einsend- ['aɪnzɛnt] *zW*: **e~en** (*unreg*) *vt* to
send in; ~**er** (**-s, -**) *m* sender, contributor;
~**ung** *f* sending in

Rechtschreibreform: ▲ *neue Schreibung* △ *alte Schreibung (auslaufend)*

einsetzen ['aɪnzɛtsən] *vt* to put (in); (*in Amt*) to appoint, to install; (*Geld*) to stake; (*verwenden*) to use; (*MIL*) to employ ♦ *vi* (*beginnen*) to set in; (*MUS*) to enter, to come in ♦ *vr* to work hard; **sich für jdn/ etw ~** to support sb/sth

Einsicht ['aɪnzɪçt] *f* insight; (*in Akten*) look, inspection; **zu der ~ kommen, dass ...** to come to the conclusion that ...; **e~ig** *adj* (*Mensch*) judicious; **e~slos** *adj* unreasonable; **e~svoll** *adj* understanding

einsilbig ['aɪnzɪlbɪç] *adj* (*auch fig*) monosyllabic; (*Mensch*) uncommunicative

einspannen ['aɪnʃpanən] *vt* (*Papier*) to insert; (*Pferde*) to harness; (*umg*: *Person*) to rope in

Einsparung ['aɪnʃpaːrʊŋ] *f* economy, saving

einsperren ['aɪnʃpɛrən] *vt* to lock up

einspielen ['aɪnʃpiːlən] *vr* (*SPORT*) to warm up ♦ *vt* (*Film*: *Geld*) to bring in; (*Instrument*) to play in; **sich aufeinander ~** to become attuned to each other; **gut eingespielt** running smoothly

einsprachig ['aɪnʃpraːxɪç] *adj* monolingual

einspringen ['aɪnʃprɪŋən] (*unreg*) *vi* (*aushelfen*) to help out, to step into the breach

Einspruch ['aɪnʃprʊx] *m* protest, objection; **~srecht** *nt* veto

einspurig ['aɪnʃpuːrɪç] *adj* (*EISENB*) single-track; (*AUT*) single-lane

einst [aɪnst] *adv* once; (*zukünftig*) one day, some day

einstecken ['aɪnʃtɛkən] *vt* to stick in, to insert; (*Brief*) to post; (*ELEK*: *Stecker*) to plug in; (*Geld*) to pocket; (*mitnehmen*) to take; (*überlegen sein*) to put in the shade; (*hinnehmen*) to swallow

einstehen ['aɪnʃteːən] (*unreg*) *vi*: **für jdn/ etw ~** to guarantee sb/sth; (*verantworten*): **für etw ~** to answer for sth

einsteigen ['aɪnʃtaɪgən] (*unreg*) *vi* to get in *od* on; (*in Schiff*) to go on board; (*sich beteiligen*) to come in; (*hineinklettern*) to climb in

einstellen ['aɪnʃtɛlən] *vt* (*aufhören*) to stop; (*Geräte*) to adjust; (*Kamera etc*) to focus;

(*Sender, Radio*) to tune in; (*unterstellen*) to put; (*in Firma*) to employ, to take on ♦ *vi* (*Firma*) to take on staff/workers ♦ *vr* (*anfangen*) to set in; (*kommen*) to arrive; **sich auf jdn ~** to adapt to sb; **sich auf etw** *akk* **~** to prepare o.s. for sth

Einstellung *f* (*Aufhören*) suspension; adjustment; focusing; (*von Arbeiter etc*) appointment; (*Haltung*) attitude

Einstieg ['aɪnʃtiːk] (*-(e)s, -e*) *m* entry; (*fig*) approach

einstig ['aɪnstɪç] *adj* former

einstimmig ['aɪnʃtɪmɪç] *adj* unanimous; (*MUS*) for one voice

einstmals *adv* once, formerly

einstöckig ['aɪnʃtœkɪç] *adj* two-storeyed

Einsturz ['aɪnʃtʊrts] *m* collapse

einstürzen ['aɪnʃtʏrtsən] *vi* to fall in, to collapse

einst- *zW*: **~weilen** *adv* meanwhile; (*vorläufig*) temporarily, for the time being; **~weilig** *adj* temporary

eintägig ['aɪntɛːgɪç] *adj* one-day

eintauschen ['aɪntaʊʃən] *vt*: **~ (gegen** *od* **für)** to exchange (for)

eintausend ['aɪntaʊzənt] *num* one thousand

einteilen ['aɪntaɪlən] *vt* (*in Teile*) to divide (up); (*Menschen*) to assign

einteilig *adj* one-piece

eintönig ['aɪntøːnɪç] *adj* monotonous

Eintopf ['aɪntɔpf] *m* stew

Eintracht ['aɪntraxt] (*-*) *f* concord, harmony; **einträchtig** ['aɪntrɛçtɪç] *adj* harmonious

Eintrag ['aɪntraːk] (*-(e)s, -̈e*) *m* entry; **amtlicher ~** entry in the register; **e~en** [-gən] (*unreg*) *vt* (*in Buch*) to enter; (*Profit*) to yield ♦ *vr* to put one's name down

einträglich ['aɪntrɛːklɪç] *adj* profitable

eintreffen ['aɪntrɛfən] (*unreg*) *vi* to happen; (*ankommen*) to arrive

eintreten ['aɪntreːtən] (*unreg*) *vi* to occur; (*sich einsetzen*) to intercede ♦ *vt* (*Tür*) to kick open; **~ in** +*akk* to enter; (*in Klub, Partei*) to join

Eintritt ['aɪntrɪt] *m* (*Betreten*) entrance; (*Anfang*) commencement; (*in Klub etc*)

Spelling Reform: ▲ *new spelling* △ *old spelling (to be phased out)*

joining

Eintritts- *zW:* **~geld** *nt* admission charge; **~karte** *f* (admission) ticket; **~preis** *m* admission charge

einüben ['aɪn|yːbən] *vt* to practise

Einvernehmen ['aɪnfɛrneːmən] **(-s, -)** *nt* agreement, harmony

einverstanden ['aɪnfɛrʃtandən] *excl* agreed, okay ♦ *adj:* **~ sein** to agree, to be agreed

Einverständnis ['aɪnfɛrʃtɛntnɪs] *nt* understanding; (*gleiche Meinung*) agreement

Einwand ['aɪnvant] **(-(e)s, ⸚e)** *m* objection

Einwand- *zW:* **~erer** ['aɪnvandərər] *m* immigrant; **e~ern** *vi* to immigrate; **~erung** *f* immigration

einwandfrei *adj* perfect ♦ *adv* absolutely

Einweg- ['aɪnveːg-] *zW:* **~flasche** *f* no-deposit bottle; **~spritze** *f* disposable syringe

einweichen ['aɪnvaɪçən] *vt* to soak

einweihen ['aɪnvaɪən] *vt* (*Kirche*) to consecrate; (*Brücke*) to open; (*Gebäude*) to inaugurate; **~ (in** +*akk*) (*Person*) to initiate (in); **Einweihung** *f* consecration; opening; inauguration; initiation

einweisen ['aɪnvaɪzən] (*unreg*) *vt* (*in Amt*) to install; (*in Arbeit*) to introduce; (*in Anstalt*) to send

einwenden ['aɪnvɛndən] (*unreg*) *vt:* **etwas ~ gegen** to object to, to oppose

einwerfen ['aɪnvɛrfən] (*unreg*) *vt* to throw in; (*Brief*) to post; (*Geld*) to put in, to insert; (*Fenster*) to smash; (*äußern*) to interpose

einwickeln ['aɪnvɪkəln] *vt* to wrap up; (*fig: umg*) to outsmart

einwilligen ['aɪnvɪlɪgən] *vi:* **~ (in** +*akk*) to consent (to), to agree (to); **Einwilligung** *f* consent

einwirken ['aɪnvɪrkən] *vi:* **auf jdn/etw ~** to influence sb/sth

Einwohner ['aɪnvoːnər] **(-s, -)** *m* inhabitant; **~'meldeamt** *nt* registration office; **~schaft** *f* population, inhabitants *pl*

Einwurf ['aɪnvʊrf] *m* (*Öffnung*) slot; (*von Münze*) insertion; (*von Brief*) posting; (*Einwand*) objection; (*SPORT*) throw-in

Einzahl ['aɪntsaːl] *f* singular; **e~en** *vt* to pay

in; **~ung** *f* paying in; **~ungsschein** *m* paying-in slip, deposit slip

einzäunen ['aɪntsɔynən] *vt* to fence in

Einzel ['aɪntsəl] **(-s, -)** *nt* (*TENNIS*) singles; **~fahrschein** *m* one-way ticket; **~fall** *m* single instance, individual case; **~handel** *m* retail trade; **~handelspreis** *m* retail price; **~heit** *f* particular, detail; **~kind** *nt* only child; **e~n** *adj* single; (*vereinzelt*) the odd ♦ *adv* singly; **e~n angeben** to specify; **der/die E~ne** the individual; **das E~ne** the particular; **ins E~ne gehen** to go into detail(s); **~teil** *nt* component (part); **~zimmer** *nt* single room; **~zimmerzuschlag** *m* single room supplement

einziehen ['aɪntsiːən] (*unreg*) *vt* to draw in, to take in; (*Kopf*) to duck; (*Fühler, Antenne, Fahrgestell*) to retract; (*Steuern, Erkundigungen*) to collect; (*MIL*) to draft, to call up; (*aus dem Verkehr ziehen*) to withdraw; (*konfiszieren*) to confiscate ♦ *vi* to move in; (*Friede, Ruhe*) to come; (*Flüssigkeit*) to penetrate

einzig ['aɪntsɪç] *adj* only; (*ohnegleichen*) unique; **das E~e** the only thing; **der/die E~e** the only one; **~artig** *adj* unique

Einzug ['aɪntsuːk] *m* entry, moving in

Eis [aɪs] **(-es, -)** *nt* ice; (*Speiseeis*) ice cream; **~bahn** *f* ice *od* skating rink; **~bär** *m* polar bear; **~becher** *m* sundae; **~bein** *nt* pig's trotters *pl*; **~berg** *m* iceberg; **~café** *nt* ice-cream parlour (*BRIT*) *od* parlor (*US*); **~decke** *f* sheet of ice; **~diele** *f* ice-cream parlour

Eisen ['aɪzən] **(-s, -)** *nt* iron

Eisenbahn *f* railway, railroad (*US*); **~er (-s, -)** *m* railwayman, railway employee, railroader (*US*); **~schaffner** *m* railway guard; **~wagen** *m* railway carriage

Eisenerz *nt* iron ore

eisern ['aɪzərn] *adj* iron; (*Gesundheit*) robust; (*Energie*) unrelenting; (*Reserve*) emergency

Eis- *zW:* **e~frei** *adj* clear of ice; **~hockey** *nt* ice hockey; **e~ig** ['aɪzɪç] *adj* icy; **e~kalt** *adj* icy cold; **~kunstlauf** *m* figure skating; **~laufen** *nt* ice skating; **~pickel** *m* ice axe; **~schrank** *m* fridge, icebox (*US*); **~würfel**

m ice cube; **~zapfen** *m* icicle; **~zeit** *f* ice age

eitel ['aɪtəl] *adj* vain; **E~keit** *f* vanity

Eiter ['aɪtər] **(-s)** *m* pus; **e~ig** *adj* suppurating; **e~n** *vi* to suppurate

Eiweiß **(-es, -e)** *nt* white of an egg; (*CHEM*) protein

Ekel[1] ['e:kəl] **(-s, -)** *nt* (*umg*: *Mensch*) nauseating person

Ekel[2] ['e:kəl] **(-s)** *m* nausea, disgust; **~ erregend** nauseating, disgusting; **e~haft** *adj* nauseating, disgusting; **e~ig** *adj* nauseating, disgusting; **e~n** *vt* to disgust ♦ *vr*: **sich e~n (vor** +*dat*) to loathe, to be disgusted (at); **es e~t jdn** *od* **jdm** sb is disgusted; **e~nd** *adj* nauseating, disgusting

Ekstase [ɛk'staːzə] *f* ecstasy

Ekzem [ɛk'tseːm] **(-s, -e)** *nt* (*MED*) eczema

Elan [e'lãː] **(-s)** *m* elan

elastisch [e'lastɪʃ] *adj* elastic

Elastizität [elastitsi'tɛːt] *f* elasticity

Elch [ɛlç] **(-(e)s, -e)** *m* elk

Elefant [ele'fant] *m* elephant

elegant [ele'gant] *adj* elegant

Eleganz [ele'gants] *f* elegance

Elek- [e'lɛk] *zW*: **~triker** [-trikər] **(-s, -)** *m* electrician; **e~trisch** [-trɪʃ] *adj* electric; **e~trisieren** [-tri'ziːrən] *vt* (*auch fig*) to electrify; (*Mensch*) to give an electric shock to ♦ *vr* to get an electric shock; **~trizität** [tritsi'tɛːt] *f* electricity; **~trizitätswerk** *nt* power station; (*Gesellschaft*) electric power company

Elektro- [e'lɛktro] *zW*: **~de** [-'troːdə] *f* electrode; **~gerät** *nt* electrical appliance; **~herd** *m* electric cooker; **~n** **(-s, -en)** *nt* electron; **~nik** *f* electronics *sg*; **e~nisch** *adj* electronic; **~rasierer** *m* electric razor; **~technik** *f* electrical engineering

Element [ele'mɛnt] **(-s, -e)** *nt* element; (*ELEK*) cell, battery; **e~ar** [-'taːr] *adj* elementary; (*naturhaft*) elemental

Elend ['eːlɛnt] **(-(e)s)** *nt* misery; **e~** *adj* miserable; **~sviertel** *nt* slum

elf [ɛlf] *num* eleven; **E~ (-, -en)** *f* (*SPORT*) eleven

Elfe *f* elf

Elfenbein *nt* ivory

Elfmeter *m* (*SPORT*) penalty (kick)

Elite [e'liːtə] *f* elite

Ell- *zW*: **~bogen** *m* elbow; **~e** ['ɛlə] *f* ell; (*Maß*) yard; **~enbogen** *m* elbow; **~(en)bogenfreiheit** *f* (*fig*) elbow room

Elsass ▲ ['ɛlzas] **(- od -es)** *nt*: **das ~** Alsace

Elster ['ɛlstər] **(-, -n)** *f* magpie

Eltern ['ɛltərn] *pl* parents; **~beirat** *m* (*SCH*) ≈ PTA (*BRIT*), parents' council; **~haus** *nt* home; **e~los** *adj* parentless

E-Mail ['iːmeːl] **(-, -s)** *f* E-mail; **~-Adresse** *f* e-mail address

Emaille [e'maljə] **(-s, -s)** *nt* enamel

emaillieren [ema'jiːrən] *vt* to enamel

Emanzipation [emantsipatsi'oːn] *f* emancipation

emanzipieren *vt* to emancipate

Embryo ['ɛmbryo] **(-s, -s** *od* **Embryonen)** *m* embryo

Emi- *zW*: **~'grant(in)** *m(f)* emigrant; **~gration** *f* emigration; **e~grieren** *vi* to emigrate

Emissionen [emɪsi'oːnən] *fpl* emissions

Empfang [ɛm'pfaŋ] **(-(e)s, ⁺e)** *m* reception; (*Erhalten*) receipt; **in ~ nehmen** to receive; **e~en** (*unreg*) *vt* to receive ♦ *vi* (*schwanger werden*) to conceive

Empfäng- [ɛm'pfɛŋ] *zW*: **~er (-s, -)** *m* receiver; (*COMM*) addressee, consignee; **~erabschnitt** *m* receipt slip; **e~lich** *adj* receptive, susceptible; **~nis (-, -se)** *f* conception; **~nisverhütung** *f* contraception

Empfangs- *zW*: **~bestätigung** *f* acknowledgement; **~dame** *f* receptionist; **~schein** *m* receipt; **~zimmer** *nt* reception room

empfehlen [ɛm'pfeːlən] (*unreg*) *vt* to recommend ♦ *vr* to take one's leave; **~swert** *adj* recommendable

Empfehlung *f* recommendation

empfiehlst *etc* [ɛm'pfiːlst] *vb siehe* **empfehlen**

empfind- [ɛm'pfɪnt] *zW*: **~en** [-dən] (*unreg*) *vt* to feel; **~lich** *adj* sensitive; (*Stelle*) sore; (*reizbar*) touchy; **~sam** *adj* sentimental;

Spelling Reform: ▲ *new spelling* △ *old spelling (to be phased out)*

E~ung [-dʊŋ] *f* feeling, sentiment
empfohlen *etc* [ɛm'pfoːlən] *vb siehe* **empfehlen**
empor [ɛm'poːr] *adv* up, upwards
empören [ɛm'pøːrən] *vt* to make indignant; to shock ♦ *vr* to become indignant; **~d** *adj* outrageous
Emporkömmling [ɛm'poːrkœmlɪŋ] *m* upstart, parvenu
Empörung *f* indignation
emsig [ˈɛmzɪç] *adj* diligent, busy
End- [ˈɛnt] *in zW* final; **~e** (-s, -n) *nt* end; **am ~e** at the end; (*schließlich*) in the end; **am ~e sein** to be at the end of one's tether; **~e Dezember** at the end of December; **zu ~e sein** to be finished; **e~en** *vi* to end; **e~gültig** [ˈɛnt-] *adj* final, definite
Endivie [ɛnˈdiːviə] *f* endive
End- *zW:* **e~lich** *adj* final; (*MATH*) finite ♦ *adv* finally; **e~lich!** at last!; **komm e~lich!** come on!; **e~los** *adj* endless, infinite; **~spiel** *nt* final(s); **~spurt** *m* (*SPORT*) final spurt; **~station** *f* terminus; **~ung** *f* ending
Energie [enɛrˈgiː] *f* energy; **~bedarf** *m* energy requirement; **e~los** *adj* lacking in energy, weak; **~verbrauch** *m* energy consumption; **~versorgung** *f* supply of energy; **~wirtschaft** *f* energy industry
energisch [eˈnɛrgɪʃ] *adj* energetic
eng [ɛŋ] *adj* narrow; (*Kleidung*) tight; (*fig: Horizont*) narrow, limited; (*Freundschaft, Verhältnis*) close; **~ an etw** *dat* close to sth
Engagement [ãgaʒəˈmãː] (-s, -s) *nt* engagement; (*Verpflichtung*) commitment
engagieren [ãgaˈʒiːrən] *vt* to engage ♦ *vr* to commit o.s.
Enge [ˈɛŋə] *f* (*auch fig*) narrowness; (*Landenge*) defile; (*Meerenge*) straits *pl*; **jdn in die ~ treiben** to drive sb into a corner
Engel [ˈɛŋəl] (-s, -) *m* angel; **e~haft** *adj* angelic
England [ˈɛŋlant] *nt* England; **Engländer(in)** *m(f)* Englishman(-woman); **englisch** *adj* English
Engpass ▲ *m* defile, pass; (*fig, Verkehr*) bottleneck

en gros [ãˈgro] *adv* wholesale
engstirnig [ˈɛŋʃtɪrnɪç] *adj* narrow-minded
Enkel [ˈɛŋkəl] (-s, -) *m* grandson; **~in** *f* granddaughter; **~kind** *nt* grandchild
enorm [eˈnɔrm] *adj* enormous
Ensemble [ãˈsãbəl] (-s, -s) *nt* company, ensemble
entbehr- [ɛntˈbeːr-] *zW:* **~en** *vt* to do without, to dispense with; **~lich** *adj* superfluous; **E~ung** *f* deprivation
entbinden [ɛntˈbɪndən] (*unreg*) *vt* (+*gen*) to release (from); (*MED*) to deliver ♦ *vi* (*MED*) to give birth; **Entbindung** *f* release; (*MED*) confinement; **Entbindungsheim** *nt* maternity hospital
entdeck- [ɛntˈdɛk] *zW:* **~en** *vt* to discover; **E~er** (-s, -) *m* discoverer; **E~ung** *f* discovery
Ente [ˈɛntə] *f* duck; (*fig*) canard, false report
enteignen [ɛntˈaignən] *vt* to expropriate; (*Besitzer*) to dispossess
enterben [ɛntˈɛrbən] *vt* to disinherit
entfallen [ɛntˈfalən] (*unreg*) *vi* to drop, to fall; (*wegfallen*) to be dropped; **jdm ~** (*vergessen*) to slip sb's memory; **auf jdn ~** to be allotted to sb
entfalten [ɛntˈfaltən] *vt* to unfold; (*Talente*) to develop ♦ *vr* to open; (*Mensch*) to develop one's potential; **Entfaltung** *f* unfolding; (*von Talenten*) development
entfern- [ɛntˈfɛrn] *zW:* **~en** *vt* to remove; (*hinauswerfen*) to expel ♦ *vr* to go away, to withdraw; **~t** *adj* distant; **weit davon ~t sein, etw zu tun** to be far from doing sth; **E~ung** *f* distance; (*Wegschaffen*) removal
entfremden [ɛntˈfrɛmdən] *vt* to estrange, to alienate; **Entfremdung** *f* alienation, estrangement
entfrosten [ɛntˈfrɔstən] *vt* to defrost
Entfroster (-s, -) *m* (*AUT*) defroster
entführ- [ɛntˈfyːr] *zW:* **~en** *vt* to carry off, to abduct; to kidnap; **E~er** *m* kidnapper; **E~ung** *f* abduction; kidnapping
entgegen [ɛntˈgeːgən] *präp* +*dat* contrary to, against ♦ *adv* towards; **~bringen** (*unreg*) *vt* to bring; **jdm etw ~bringen** (*fig*) to show sb sth; **~gehen** (*unreg*) *vi* +*dat* to go to

meet, to go towards; **~gesetzt** adj opposite; (widersprechend) opposed; **~halten** (unreg) vt (fig) to object; **E~kommen** nt obligingness; **~kommen** (unreg) vi +dat to approach; to meet; (fig) to accommodate; **~kommend** adj obliging; **~nehmen** (unreg) vt to receive, to accept; **~sehen** (unreg) vi +dat to await; **~setzen** vt to oppose; **~treten** (unreg) vi +dat to step up to; (fig) to oppose, to counter; **~wirken** vi +dat to counteract

entgegnen [ɛnt'ge:gnən] vt to reply, to retort

entgehen [ɛnt'ge:ən] (unreg) vi (fig): **jdm ~** to escape sb's notice; **sich** dat **etw ~ lassen** to miss sth

Entgelt [ɛnt'gɛlt] (-(e)s, -e) nt compensation, remuneration

entgleisen [ɛnt'glaizən] vi (EISENB) to be derailed; (fig: Person) to misbehave; **~ lassen** to derail

entgräten [ɛnt'grɛ:tən] vt to fillet, to bone

Enthaarungscreme [ɛnt'ha:rʊŋs-] f hair-removing cream

enthalten [ɛnt'haltən] (unreg) vt to contain ♦ vr: **sich (von etw) ~** to abstain (from sth), to refrain (from sth)

enthaltsam [ɛnt'haltza:m] adj abstinent, abstemious

enthemmen [ɛnt'hɛmən] vt: **jdn ~** to free sb from his inhibitions

enthüllen [ɛnt'hʏlən] vt to reveal, to unveil

Enthusiasmus [ɛntuzi'asmʊs] m enthusiasm

entkommen [ɛnt'kɔmən] (unreg) vi: **~ (aus** od +dat**)** to get away (from), to escape (from)

entkräften [ɛnt'krɛftən] vt to weaken, to exhaust; (Argument) to refute

entladen [ɛnt'la:dən] (unreg) vt to unload; (ELEK) to discharge ♦ vr (ELEK: Gewehr) to discharge; (Ärger etc) to vent itself

entlang [ɛnt'laŋ] adv along; **~ dem Fluss, den Fluss ~** along the river; **~gehen** (unreg) vi to walk along

entlarven [ɛnt'larfən] vt to unmask, to expose

entlassen [ɛnt'lasən] (unreg) vt to discharge; (Arbeiter) to dismiss; **Entlassung** f discharge; dismissal

entlasten [ɛnt'lastən] vt to relieve; (Achse) to relieve the load on; (Angeklagten) to exonerate; (Konto) to clear

Entlastung f relief; (COMM) crediting

Entlastungszug m relief train

entlegen [ɛnt'le:gən] adj remote

entlocken [ɛnt'lɔkən] vt: **(jdm etw) ~** elicit (sth from sb)

entmutigen [ɛnt'mu:tɪgən] vt to discourage

entnehmen [ɛnt'ne:mən] (unreg) vt (+dat) to take out (of), to take (from); (folgern) to infer (from)

entreißen [ɛnt'raisən] (unreg) vt: **jdm etw ~** to snatch sth (away) from sb

entrichten [ɛnt'rɪçtən] vt to pay

entrosten [ɛnt'rɔstən] vt to remove rust from

entrümpeln [ɛnt'rʏmpəln] vt to clear out

entrüst- [ɛnt'rʏst] zW: **~en** vt to incense, to outrage ♦ vr to be filled with indignation; **~et** adj indignant, outraged; **E~ung** f indignation

entschädigen [ɛnt'ʃɛ:dɪgən] vt to compensate; **Entschädigung** f compensation

entschärfen [ɛnt'ʃɛrfən] vt to defuse; (Kritik) to tone down

Entscheid [ɛnt'ʃait] (-(e)s, -e) m decision; **e~en** [-dən] (unreg) vt, vi, vr to decide; **e~end** adj decisive; (Stimme) casting; **~ung** f decision

entschieden [ɛnt'ʃi:dən] adj decided; (entschlossen) resolute; **E~heit** f firmness, determination

entschließen [ɛnt'ʃli:sən] (unreg) vr to decide

entschlossen [ɛnt'ʃlɔsən] adj determined, resolute; **E~heit** f determination

Entschluss ▲ [ɛnt'ʃlʊs] m decision; **e~freudig** adj decisive; **~kraft** f determination, decisiveness

entschuldigen [ɛnt'ʃʊldɪgən] vt to excuse ♦ vr to apologize

Entschuldigung f apology; (Grund)

excuse; **jdn um ~ bitten** to apologize to sb; **~!** excuse me; (*Verzeihung*) sorry

entsetz- [ɛnt'zɛts] *zW:* **~en** *vt* to horrify; (*MIL*) to relieve ♦ *vr* to be horrified *od* appalled; **E~en (-s)** *nt* horror, dismay; **~lich** *adj* dreadful, appalling; **~t** *adj* horrified

Entsorgung [ɛnt'zɔrgʊŋ] *f* (*von Kraftwerken, Chemikalien*) (waste) disposal

entspannen [ɛnt'ʃpanən] *vt*, *vr* (*Körper*) to relax; (*POL: Lage*) to ease

Entspannung *f* relaxation, rest; (*POL*) détente; **~spolitik** *f* policy of détente

entsprechen [ɛnt'ʃprɛçən] (*unreg*) *vi* +*dat* to correspond to; (*Anforderungen, Wünschen*) to meet, to comply with; **~d** *adj* appropriate ♦ *adv* accordingly

entspringen [ɛnt'ʃprɪŋən] (*unreg*) *vi* (+*dat*) to spring (from)

entstehen [ɛnt'ʃteːən] (*unreg*) *vi*: **~ (aus** *od* **durch)** to arise (from), to result (from)

Entstehung *f* genesis, origin

entstellen [ɛnt'ʃtɛlən] *vt* to disfigure; (*Wahrheit*) to distort

entstören [ɛnt'ʃtøːrən] *vt* (*RADIO*) to eliminate interference from

enttäuschen [ɛnt'tɔyʃən] *vt* to disappoint; **Enttäuschung** *f* disappointment

entwaffnen [ɛnt'vafnən] *vt* (*lit, fig*) to disarm

entwässern [ɛnt'vɛsərn] *vt* to drain; **Entwässerung** *f* drainage

entweder [ɛnt'veːdər] *konj* either

entwenden [ɛnt'vɛndən] (*unreg*) *vt* to purloin, to steal

entwerfen [ɛnt'vɛrfən] (*unreg*) *vt* (*Zeichnung*) to sketch; (*Modell*) to design; (*Vortrag, Gesetz etc*) to draft

entwerten [ɛnt'veːrtən] *vt* to devalue; (*stempeln*) to cancel

Entwerter (-s, -) *m* ticket punching machine

entwickeln [ɛnt'vɪkəln] *vt*, *vr* (*auch PHOT*) to develop; (*Mut, Energie*) to show (o.s.), to display (o.s.)

Entwicklung [ɛnt'vɪklʊŋ] *f* development; (*PHOT*) developing

Entwicklungs- *zW:* **~hilfe** *f* aid for developing countries; **~land** *nt* developing country

entwöhnen [ɛnt'vøːnən] *vt* to wean; (*Süchtige*): **(einer Sache** *dat od* **von etw) ~** to cure (of sth)

Entwöhnung *f* weaning; cure, curing

entwürdigend [ɛnt'vyrdɪgənt] *adj* degrading

Entwurf [ɛnt'vʊrf] *m* outline, design; (*Vertragsentwurf, Konzept*) draft

entziehen [ɛnt'tsiːən] (*unreg*) *vt* (+*dat*) to withdraw (from), to take away (from); (*Flüssigkeit*) to draw (from), to extract (from) ♦ *vr* (+*dat*) to escape (from); (*jds Kenntnis*) to be outside *od* beyond; (*der Pflicht*) to shirk (from)

Entziehung *f* withdrawal; **~sanstalt** *f* drug addiction/alcoholism treatment centre; **~skur** *f* treatment for drug addiction/alcoholism

entziffern [ɛnt'tsɪfərn] *vt* to decipher; to decode

entzücken [ɛnt'tsykən] *vt* to delight; **E~ (-s)** *nt* delight; **~d** *adj* delightful, charming

entzünden [ɛnt'tsyndən] *vt* to light, to set light to; (*fig, MED*) to inflame; (*Streit*) to spark off ♦ *vr* (*auch fig*) to catch fire; (*Streit*) to start; (*MED*) to become inflamed

Entzündung *f* (*MED*) inflammation

entzwei [ɛnt'tsvaɪ] *adv* broken; in two; **~brechen** (*unreg*) *vt*, *vi* to break in two; **~en** *vt* to set at odds ♦ *vr* to fall out; **~gehen** (*unreg*) *vi* to break (in two)

Enzian ['ɛntsiaːn] **(-s, -e)** *m* gentian

Epidemie [epide'miː] *f* epidemic

Epilepsie [epilɛ'psiː] *f* epilepsy

Episode [epi'zoːdə] *f* episode

Epoche [e'pɔxə] *f* epoch; **~ machend** epoch-making

Epos ['eːpɔs] **(-s, Epen)** *nt* epic (poem)

er [eːr] (*nom*) *pron* he; it

erarbeiten [ɛr'|arbaɪtən] *vt* to work for, to acquire; (*Theorie*) to work out

erbarmen [ɛr'barmən] *vr* (+*gen*) to have pity *od* mercy (on); **E~ (-s)** *nt* pity

erbärmlich [ɛr'bɛrmlɪç] *adj* wretched,

Rechtschreibreform: ▲ *neue Schreibung* △ *alte Schreibung (auslaufend)*

pitiful; **E~keit** *f* wretchedness

erbarmungslos [ɛr'barmʊŋsloːs] *adj* pitiless, merciless

erbau- [ɛr'bau] *ZW:* **~en** *vt* to build, to erect; *(fig)* to edify; **E~er (-s, -)** *m* builder; **~lich** *adj* edifying

Erbe[1] ['ɛrbə] **(-n, -n)** *m* heir

Erbe[2] ['ɛrbə] *nt* inheritance; *(fig)* heritage

erben *vt* to inherit

erbeuten [ɛr'bɔytən] *vt* to carry off; *(MIL)* to capture

Erb- [ɛrb] *ZW:* **~faktor** *m* gene; **~folge** *f* (line of) succession; **~in** *f* heiress

erbittern [ɛr'bɪtərn] *vt* to embitter; *(erzürnen)* to incense

erbittert [ɛr'bɪtərt] *adj (Kampf)* fierce, bitter

erblassen [ɛr'blasən] *vi* to (turn) pale

erblich ['ɛrplɪç] *adj* hereditary

erblinden [ɛr'blɪndən] *vi* to go blind

erbrechen [ɛr'brɛçən] *(unreg) vt, vr* to vomit

Erbschaft *f* inheritance, legacy

Erbse ['ɛrpsə] *f* pea

Erbstück *nt* heirloom

Erd- [eːrd] *ZW:* **~achse** *f* earth's axis; **~atmosphäre** *f* earth's atmosphere; **~beben** *nt* earthquake; **~beere** *f* strawberry; **~boden** *m* ground; **~e** *f* earth; **zu ebener ~e** at ground level; **e~en** *vt (ELEK)* to earth

erdenklich [ɛr'dɛŋklɪç] *adj* conceivable

Erd- *ZW:* **~gas** *nt* natural gas; **~geschoss** ▲ *nt* ground floor; **~kunde** *f* geography; **~nuss** ▲ *f* peanut; **~öl** *nt* (mineral) oil

erdrosseln [ɛr'drɔsəln] *vt* to strangle, to throttle

erdrücken [ɛr'drʏkən] *vt* to crush

Erd- *ZW:* **~rutsch** *m* landslide; **~teil** *m* continent

erdulden [ɛr'dʊldən] *vt* to endure, to suffer

ereignen [ɛr'|aignən] *vr* to happen

Ereignis [ɛr'|aignɪs] **(-ses, -se)** *nt* event; **e~los** *adj* uneventful; **e~reich** *adj* eventful

ererbt [ɛr'ɛrpt] *adj (Haus)* inherited; *(Krankheit)* hereditary

erfahren [ɛr'faːrən] *(unreg) vt* to learn, to find out; *(erleben)* to experience ♦ *adj* experienced

Erfahrung *f* experience; **e~sgemäß** *adv* according to experience

erfassen [ɛr'fasən] *vt* to seize; *(fig: einbeziehen)* to include, to register; *(verstehen)* to grasp

erfind- [ɛr'fɪnd] *ZW:* **~en** *(unreg) vt* to invent; **E~er (-s, -)** *m* inventor; **~erisch** *adj* inventive; **E~ung** *f* invention

Erfolg [ɛr'fɔlk] **(-(e)s, -e)** *m* success; **~ versprechend** promising; **e~en** [-gən] *vi* to follow; *(sich ergeben)* to result; *(stattfinden)* to take place; *(Zahlung)* to be effected; **e~los** *adj* unsuccessful; **~losigkeit** *f* lack of success; **e~reich** *adj* successful

erforderlich *adj* requisite, necessary

erfordern [ɛr'fɔrdərn] *vt* to require, to demand

erforschen [ɛr'fɔrʃən] *vt (Land)* to explore; *(Problem)* to investigate; *(Gewissen)* to search; **Erforschung** *f* exploration; investigation; searching

erfreuen [ɛr'frɔyən] *vr:* **sich ~ an** +*dat* to enjoy ♦ *vt* to delight; **sich einer Sache** *gen* **~** to enjoy sth

erfreulich [ɛr'frɔylɪç] *adj* pleasing, gratifying; **~erweise** *adv* happily, luckily

erfrieren [ɛr'friːrən] *(unreg) vi* to freeze to death; *(Glieder)* to get frostbitten; *(Pflanzen)* to be killed by frost

erfrischen [ɛr'frɪʃən] *vt* to refresh; **Erfrischung** *f* refreshment

Erfrischungs- *ZW:* **~getränk** *nt* (liquid) refreshment; **~raum** *m* snack bar, cafeteria

erfüllen [ɛr'fʏlən] *vt (Raum etc)* to fill; *(fig: Bitte etc)* to fulfil ♦ *vr* to come true

ergänzen [ɛr'gɛntsən] *vt* to supplement, to complete ♦ *vr* to complement one another; **Ergänzung** *f* completion; *(Zusatz)* supplement

ergeben [ɛr'geːbən] *(unreg) vt* to yield, to produce ♦ *vr* to surrender; *(folgen)* to result ♦ *adj* devoted, humble

Ergebnis [ɛr'geːpnɪs] **(-ses, -se)** *nt* result; **e~los** *adj* without result, fruitless

ergehen [ɛr'geːən] *(unreg) vi* to be issued, to go out ♦ *vi unpers:* **es ergeht ihm gut/**

schlecht he's faring *od* getting on well/badly ♦ *vr*: **sich in etw** *dat* **~** to indulge in sth; **etw über sich ~ lassen** to put up with sth

ergiebig [ɛr'giːbɪç] *adj* productive

Ergonomie [ɛrɡono'miː] *f* ergonomics *sg*

Ergonomik [ɛrɡo'noːmɪk] *f* = **Ergonomie**

ergreifen [ɛr'ɡraɪfən] (*unreg*) *vt* (*auch fig*) to seize; (*Beruf*) to take up; (*Maßnahmen*) to resort to; (*rühren*) to move; **~d** *adj* moving, touching

ergriffen [ɛr'ɡrɪfən] *adj* deeply moved

Erguss ▲ [ɛr'ɡʊs] *m* discharge; (*fig*) outpouring, effusion

erhaben [ɛr'haːbən] *adj* raised, embossed; (*fig*) exalted, lofty; **über etw** *akk* **~ sein** to be above sth

erhalten [ɛr'haltən] (*unreg*) *vt* to receive; (*bewahren*) to preserve, to maintain; **gut ~** in good condition

erhältlich [ɛr'hɛltlɪç] *adj* obtainable, available

Erhaltung *f* maintenance, preservation

erhärten [ɛr'hɛrtən] *vt* to harden; (*These*) to substantiate, to corroborate

erheben [ɛr'heːbən] (*unreg*) *vt* to raise; (*Protest, Forderungen*) to make; (*Fakten*) to ascertain, to establish ♦ *vr* to rise (up)

erheblich [ɛr'heːplɪç] *adj* considerable

erheitern [ɛr'haɪtərn] *vt* to amuse, to cheer (up)

Erheiterung *f* exhilaration; **zur allgemeinen ~** to everybody's amusement

erhitzen [ɛr'hɪtsən] *vt* to heat ♦ *vr* to heat up; (*fig*) to become heated

erhoffen [ɛr'hɔfən] *vt* to hope for

erhöhen [ɛr'høːən] *vt* to raise; (*verstärken*) to increase

erhol- [ɛr'hoːl] *zW*: **~en** *vr* to recover; (*entspannen*) to have a rest; **~sam** *adj* restful; **E~ung** *f* recovery; relaxation, rest; **~ungsbedürftig** *adj* in need of a rest, run-down; **E~ungsgebiet** *nt* ≈ holiday area; **E~ungsheim** *nt* convalescent home

erhören [ɛr'høːrən] *vt* (*Gebet etc*) to hear; (*Bitte etc*) to yield to

erinnern [ɛr'|ɪnərn] *vt*: **~ (an** +*akk***)** to

remind (of) ♦ *vr*: **sich (an** *akk* **etw) ~** to remember (sth)

Erinnerung *f* memory; (*Andenken*) reminder

erkältet [ɛr'kɛltət] *adj* with a cold; **~ sein** to have a cold

Erkältung *f* cold

erkennbar *adj* recognizable

erkennen [ɛr'kɛnən] (*unreg*) *vt* to recognize; (*sehen, verstehen*) to see

erkennt- *zW*: **~lich** *adj*: **sich ~lich zeigen** to show one's appreciation; **E~lichkeit** *f* gratitude; (*Geschenk*) token of one's gratitude; **E~nis** (-, **-se**) *f* knowledge; (*das Erkennen*) recognition; (*Einsicht*) insight; **zur E~nis kommen** to realize

Erkennung *f* recognition

Erkennungszeichen *nt* identification

Erker ['ɛrkər] (**-s,** **-**) *m* bay

erklär- [ɛr'klɛːr] *zW*: **~bar** *adj* explicable; **~en** *vt* to explain; **~lich** *adj* explicable; (*verständlich*) understandable; **E~ung** *f* explanation; (*Aussage*) declaration

erkranken [ɛr'krankən] *vi* to fall ill; **Erkrankung** *f* illness

erkund- [ɛr'kʊnd] *zW*: **~en** *vt* to find out, to ascertain; (*bes MIL*) to reconnoitre, to scout; **~igen** *vr*: **sich ~igen (nach)** to inquire (about); **E~igung** *f* inquiry; **E~ung** *f* reconnaissance, scouting

erlahmen [ɛr'laːmən] *vi* to tire; (*nachlassen*) to flag, to wane

erlangen [ɛr'laŋən] *vt* to attain, to achieve

Erlass ▲ [ɛr'las] (**-es,** **ᵉe**) *m* decree; (*Aufhebung*) remission

erlassen (*unreg*) *vt* (*Verfügung*) to issue; (*Gesetz*) to enact; (*Strafe*) to remit; **jdm etw ~** to release sb from sth

erlauben [ɛr'laʊbən] *vt*: **(jdm etw) ~** to allow *od* permit (sb (to do) sth) ♦ *vr* to permit o.s., to venture

Erlaubnis [ɛr'laʊpnɪs] (-, **-se**) *f* permission; (*Schriftstück*) permit

erläutern [ɛr'lɔʏtərn] *vt* to explain; **Erläuterung** *f* explanation

erleben [ɛr'leːbən] *vt* to experience; (*Zeit*) to live through; (*miterleben*) to witness; (*noch* *miterleben*) to live to see

Erlebnis [ɛr'le:pnɪs] **(-ses, -se)** *nt* experience

erledigen [ɛr'le:dɪɡən] *vt* to take care of, to deal with; (*Antrag etc*) to process; (*umg: erschöpfen*) to wear out; (: *ruinieren*) to finish; (: *umbringen*) to do in

erleichtern [ɛr'laɪçtərn] *vt* to make easier; (*fig: Last*) to lighten; (*lindern, beruhigen*) to relieve; **Erleichterung** *f* facilitation; lightening; relief

erleiden [ɛr'laɪdən] (*unreg*) *vt* to suffer, to endure

erlernen [ɛr'lɛrnən] *vt* to learn, to acquire

erlesen [ɛr'le:zən] *adj* select, choice

erleuchten [ɛr'lɔʏçtən] *vt* to illuminate; (*fig*) to inspire

Erleuchtung *f* (*Einfall*) inspiration

Erlös [ɛr'lø:s] **(-es, -e)** *m* proceeds *pl*

erlösen [ɛr'lø:zən] *vt* to redeem, to save; **Erlösung** *f* release; (*REL*) redemption

ermächtigen [ɛr'mɛçtɪɡən] *vt* to authorize, to empower; **Ermächtigung** *f* authorization; authority

ermahnen [ɛr'ma:nən] *vt* to exhort, to admonish; **Ermahnung** *f* admonition, exhortation

ermäßigen [ɛr'mɛsɪɡən] *vt* to reduce; **Ermäßigung** *f* reduction

ermessen [ɛr'mɛsən] (*unreg*) *vt* to estimate, to gauge; **E~ (-s)** *nt* estimation; discretion; **in jds E~ liegen** to lie within sb's discretion

ermitteln [ɛr'mɪtəln] *vt* to determine; (*Täter*) to trace ♦ *vi*: **gegen jdn ~** to investigate sb

Ermittlung [ɛr'mɪtlʊŋ] *f* determination; (*Polizeiermittlung*) investigation

ermöglichen [ɛr'mø:klɪçən] *vt* (*+dat*) to make possible (for)

ermorden [ɛr'mɔrdən] *vt* to murder

ermüden [ɛr'my:dən] *vt, vi* to tire; (*TECH*) to fatigue; **~d** *adj* tiring; (*fig*) wearisome

Ermüdung *f* fatigue

ermutigen [ɛr'mu:tɪɡən] *vt* to encourage

ernähr- [ɛr'nɛ:r] *zW*: **~en** *vt* to feed, to nourish; (*Familie*) to support ♦ *vr* to support o.s., to earn a living; **sich ~en von** to live

on; **E~er (-s, -)** *m* breadwinner; **E~ung** *f* nourishment; nutrition; (*Unterhalt*) maintenance

ernennen [ɛr'nɛnən] (*unreg*) *vt* to appoint; **Ernennung** *f* appointment

erneu- [ɛr'nɔʏ] *zW*: **~ern** *vt* to renew; to restore; to renovate; **E~erung** *f* renewal; restoration; renovation; **~t** *adj* renewed, fresh ♦ *adv* once more

ernst [ɛrnst] *adj* serious; **~ gemeint** meant in earnest, serious; **E~ (-es)** *m* seriousness; **das ist mein E~** I'm quite serious; **im E~** in earnest; **E~ machen mit etw** to put sth into practice; **E~fall** *m* emergency; **~haft** *adj* serious; **E~haftigkeit** *f* seriousness; **~lich** *adj* serious

Ernte ['ɛrntə] *f* harvest; **e~n** *vt* to harvest; (*Lob etc*) to earn

ernüchtern [ɛr'nʏçtərn] *vt* to sober up; (*fig*) to bring down to earth

Erober- [ɛr'|o:bər] *zW*: **~er (-s, -)** *m* conqueror; **e~n** *vt* to conquer; **~ung** *f* conquest

eröffnen [ɛr'|œfnən] *vt* to open ♦ *vr* to present itself; **jdm etw ~** to disclose sth to sb

Eröffnung *f* opening

erörtern [ɛr'|œrtərn] *vt* to discuss

Erotik [e'ro:tɪk] *f* eroticism; **erotisch** *adj* erotic

erpress- [ɛr'prɛs] *zW*: **~en** *vt* (*Geld etc*) to extort; (*Mensch*) to blackmail; **E~er (-s, -)** *m* blackmailer; **E~ung** *f* extortion; blackmail

erprobt [ɛr'pro:pt] *adj* (*Gerät, Medikamente*) proven, tested

erraten [ɛr'ra:tən] (*unreg*) *vt* to guess

erreg- [ɛr're:g] *zW*: **~en** *vt* to excite; (*ärgern*) to infuriate; (*hervorrufen*) to arouse, to provoke ♦ *vr* to get excited *od* worked up; **E~er (-s, -)** *m* causative agent; **E~ung** *f* excitement

erreichbar *adj* accessible, within reach

erreichen [ɛr'raɪçən] *vt* to reach; (*Zweck*) to achieve; (*Zug*) to catch

errichten [ɛr'rɪçtən] *vt* to erect, to put up; (*gründen*) to establish, to set up

Spelling Reform: ▲ *new spelling* △ *old spelling (to be phased out)*

erringen [ɛrˈrɪŋən] (*unreg*) *vt* to gain, to win

erröten [ɛrˈrøːtən] *vi* to blush, to flush

Errungenschaft [ɛrˈrʊŋənʃaft] *f* achievement; (*umg*: *Anschaffung*) acquisition

Ersatz [ɛrˈzats] (**-es**) *m* substitute; replacement; (*Schadenersatz*) compensation; (*MIL*) reinforcements *pl*; **~dienst** *m* (*MIL*) alternative service; **~reifen** *m* (*AUT*) spare tyre; **~teil** *nt* spare (part)

erschaffen [ɛrˈʃafən] (*unreg*) *vt* to create

erscheinen [ɛrˈʃaɪnən] (*unreg*) *vi* to appear; **Erscheinung** *f* appearance; (*Geist*) apparition; (*Gegebenheit*) phenomenon; (*Gestalt*) figure

erschießen [ɛrˈʃiːsən] (*unreg*) *vt* to shoot (dead)

erschlagen [ɛrˈʃlaːɡən] (*unreg*) *vt* to strike dead

erschöpf- [ɛrˈʃœpf] *zW*: **~en** *vt* to exhaust; **~end** *adj* exhaustive, thorough; **E~ung** *f* exhaustion

erschrecken [ɛrˈʃrɛkən] *vt* to startle, to frighten ♦ *vi* to be frightened *od* startled; **~d** *adj* alarming, frightening

erschrocken [ɛrˈʃrɔkən] *adj* frightened, startled

erschüttern [ɛrˈʃʏtərn] *vt* to shake; (*fig*) to move deeply; **Erschütterung** *f* shaking; shock

erschweren [ɛrˈʃveːrən] *vt* to complicate

erschwinglich *adj* within one's means

ersetzen [ɛrˈzɛtsən] *vt* to replace; **jdm Unkosten** *etc* **~** to pay sb's expenses *etc*

ersichtlich [ɛrˈzɪçtlɪç] *adj* evident, obvious

ersparen [ɛrˈʃpaːrən] *vt* (*Ärger etc*) to spare; (*Geld*) to save

Ersparnis (**-**, **-se**) *f* saving

SCHLÜSSELWORT
---

erst [eːrst] *adv* **1** first; **mach erst mal die Arbeit fertig** finish your work first; **wenn du das erst mal hinter dir hast** once you've got that behind you

2 (*nicht früher als, nur*) only; (*nicht bis*) not till; **erst gestern** only yesterday; **erst morgen** not until tomorrow; **erst als** only when, not until; **wir fahren erst später**

we're not going until later; **er ist (gerade) erst angekommen** he's only just arrived

3: **wäre er doch erst zurück!** if only he were back!

---

erstatten [ɛrˈʃtatən] *vt* (*Kosten*) to (re)pay; **Anzeige** *etc* **gegen jdn ~** to report sb; **Bericht ~** to make a report

Erstattung *f* (*von Kosten*) refund

Erstaufführung [ˈeːrstʔaʊffyːrʊŋ] *f* first performance

erstaunen [ɛrˈʃtaʊnən] *vt* to astonish ♦ *vi* to be astonished; **E~** (**-s**) *nt* astonishment

erstaunlich *adj* astonishing

erst- [ˈeːrst] *zW*: **E~ausgabe** *f* first edition; **~beste(r, s)** *adj* first that comes along; **~e(r, s)** *adj* first

erstechen [ɛrˈʃtɛçən] (*unreg*) *vt* to stab (to death)

erstehen [ɛrˈʃteːən] (*unreg*) *vt* to buy ♦ *vi* to (a)rise

erstens [ˈeːrstəns] *adv* firstly, in the first place

ersticken [ɛrˈʃtɪkən] *vt* (*auch fig*) to stifle; (*Mensch*) to suffocate; (*Flammen*) to smother ♦ *vi* (*Mensch*) to suffocate; (*Feuer*) to be smothered; **in Arbeit ~** to be snowed under with work

erst- *zW*: **~klassig** *adj* first-class; **~malig** *adj* first; **~mals** *adv* for the first time

erstrebenswert [ɛrˈʃtreːbənsveːrt] *adj* desirable, worthwhile

erstrecken [ɛrˈʃtrɛkən] *vr* to extend, to stretch

ersuchen [ɛrˈzuːxən] *vt* to request

ertappen [ɛrˈtapən] *vt* to catch, to detect

erteilen [ɛrˈtaɪlən] *vt* to give

Ertrag [ɛrˈtraːk] (**-(e)s**, **ᵉe**) *m* yield; (*Gewinn*) proceeds *pl*

ertragen [ɛrˈtraːɡən] (*unreg*) *vt* to bear, to stand

erträglich [ɛrˈtrɛːklɪç] *adj* tolerable, bearable

ertrinken [ɛrˈtrɪŋkən] (*unreg*) *vi* to drown; **E~** (**-s**) *nt* drowning

erübrigen [ɛrˈyːbrɪɡən] *vt* to spare ♦ *vr* to be unnecessary

erwachen [ɛrˈvaxən] *vi* to awake

Rechtschreibreform: ▲ *neue Schreibung* △ *alte Schreibung (auslaufend)*

erwachsen [ɛr'vaksən] *adj* grown-up;
E~e(r) *f(m)* adult; E~enbildung *f* adult
education

erwägen [ɛr've:gən] *(unreg) vt* to consider;
Erwägung *f* ve:n] *zW:* ~en *vt* to mention;
consideration

erwähn- [ɛr've:n] *zW:* ~en *vt* to mention;
~enswert *adj* worth mentioning; E~ung *f*
mention

erwärmen [ɛr'vɛrmən] *vt* to warm, to heat
♦ *vr* to get warm, to warm up; **sich ~ für**
to warm to

Erwarten *nt:* **über meinen/unseren** *usw* ~
beyond my/our *etc* expectations; **wider** ~
contrary to expectations

erwarten [ɛr'vartən] *vt* to expect; *(warten
auf)* to wait for; **etw kaum ~ können** to be
hardly able to wait for sth

Erwartung *f* expectation

erwartungsgemäß *adv* as expected

erwartungsvoll *adj* expectant

erwecken [ɛr'vɛkən] *vt* to rouse, to awake;
den Anschein ~ to give the impression

Erweis [ɛr'vais] **(-es, -e)** *m* proof; e~en
(unreg) vt to prove ♦ *vr:* **sich e~en (als)** to
prove (to be); **jdm einen Gefallen/Dienst
e~en** to do sb a favour/service

Erwerb [ɛr'vɛrp] **(-(e)s, -e)** *m* acquisition;
(Beruf) trade; e~en [-bən] *(unreg) vt* to
acquire

erwerbs- *zW:* ~los *adj* unemployed;
E~quelle *f* source of income; ~tätig *adj*
(gainfully) employed

erwidern [ɛr'vi:dərn] *vt* to reply; *(vergelten)*
to return

erwischen [ɛr'vɪʃən] *(umg) vt* to catch, to
get

erwünscht [ɛr'vʏnʃt] *adj* desired

erwürgen [ɛr'vʏrgən] *vt* to strangle

Erz [e:rts] **(-es, -e)** *nt* ore

erzähl- [ɛr'tsɛ:l] *zW:* ~en *vt* to tell ♦ *vi:* **sie
kann gut ~en** she's a good story-teller;
E~er **(-s, -)** *m* narrator; E~ung *f* story, tale

Erzbischof *m* archbishop

erzeug- [ɛr'tsɔyg] *zW:* ~en *vt* to produce;
(Strom) to generate; E~nis **(-ses, -se)** *nt*
product, produce; E~ung *f* production;
generation

erziehen [ɛr'tsi:ən] *(unreg) vt* to bring up;
(bilden) to educate, to train; **Erzieher(in)**
(-s, -) *m(f) (Berufsbezeichnung)* teacher;
Erziehung *f* bringing up; *(Bildung)*
education; **Erziehungsbeihilfe** *f*
educational grant;
Erziehungsberechtigte(r) *f(m)* parent;
guardian

erzielen [ɛr'tsi:lən] *vt* to achieve, to obtain;
(Tor) to score

erzwingen [ɛr'tsvɪŋən] *(unreg) vt* to force, to
obtain by force

es [ɛs] *(nom, akk) pron* it

Esel ['e:zəl] **(-s, -)** *m* donkey, ass

Eskalation [ɛskalatsi'o:n] *f* escalation

ess- ▲ ['ɛs] *zW:* ~bar ['ɛsba:r] *adj* eatable,
edible; E~besteck *nt* knife, fork and
spoon; E~ecke *f* dining area

essen ['ɛsən] *(unreg) vt, vi* to eat; E~ **(-s, -)**
nt meal; food

Essig ['ɛsɪç] **(-s, -e)** *m* vinegar

Ess- ▲ *zW:* ~kastanie *f* sweet chestnut;
~löffel *m* tablespoon; ~tisch *m* dining
table; ~waren *pl* foodstuffs, provisions;
~zimmer *nt* dining room

etablieren [eta'bli:rən] *vr* to become
established; to set up in business

Etage [e'ta:ʒə] *f* floor, storey; ~nbetten *pl*
bunk beds; ~nwohnung *f* flat

Etappe [e'tapə] *f* stage

Etat [e'ta:] **(-s, -s)** *m* budget

etc *abk (= et cetera)* etc

Ethik ['e:tɪk] *f* ethics *sg;* **ethisch** *adj* ethical

Etikett [eti'kɛt] **(-(e)s, -e)** *nt* label; tag; ~e *f*
etiquette, manners *pl*

etliche ['ɛtlɪçə] *pron pl* some, quite a few; ~s
pron a thing or two

Etui [ɛt'vi:] **(-s, -s)** *nt* case

etwa ['ɛtva] *adv (ungefähr)* about; *(vielleicht)*
perhaps; *(beispielsweise)* for instance; **nicht**
~ by no means; ~ig ['ɛtvaɪç] *adj* possible

etwas *pron* something; anything; *(ein wenig)*
a little ♦ *adv* a little

euch [ɔyç] *pron (akk von ihr)* you; yourselves;
(dat von ihr) (to) you

euer ['ɔyər] *pron (gen von ihr)* of you ♦ *adj*
your

Spelling Reform: ▲ *new spelling* △ *old spelling (to be phased out)*

Eule ['ɔʏlə] f owl

eure ['ɔʏrə] adj f siehe **euer**

eure(r, s) ['ɔʏrə(r, s)] pron yours; **~rseits** adv on your part; **~s** adj nt siehe **euer**; **~sgleichen** pron people like you; **~twegen** adv (für euch) for your sakes; (wegen euch) on your account; **~twillen** adv: **um ~twillen** = **euretwegen**

eurige ['ɔʏrɪɡə] pron: **der/die/das ~** od E**~** yours

Euro ['ɔʏro] (-, -s) m (FIN) euro

Euro- zW: **~pa** [ɔʏ'ro:pa] nt Europe; **~päer(in)** [ɔʏro'pɛːər(ɪn)] m(f) European; **e~päisch** adj European; **~pameister** [ɔʏ'ro:pa-] m European champion; **~paparlament** nt European Parliament; **~scheck** m (FIN) eurocheque

Euter ['ɔʏtər] (-s, -) nt udder

ev. abk = **evangelisch**

evakuieren [evaku'iːrən] vt to evacuate

evangelisch [evaŋ'ɡeːlɪʃ] adj Protestant

Evangelium [evaŋ'ɡeːliʊm] nt gospel

eventuell [eventu'ɛl] adj possible ♦ adv possibly, perhaps

evtl. abk = **eventuell**

EWG [eːveː'ɡeː] (-) f abk (= Europäische Wirtschaftsgemeinschaft) EEC, Common Market

ewig ['eːvɪç] adj eternal; **E~keit** f eternity

EWU [eːveː'uː] f abk (= Europäische Währungsunion) EMU

exakt [ɛ'ksakt] adj exact

Examen [ɛ'ksaːmən] (-s, - od **Examina**) nt examination

Exemplar [ɛksɛm'plaːr] (-s, -e) nt specimen; (Buchexemplar) copy; **e~isch** adj exemplary

Exil [ɛ'ksiːl] (-s, -e) nt exile

Existenz [ɛksɪs'tɛnts] f existence; (Unterhalt) livelihood, living; (pej: Mensch) character; **~minimum** (-s) nt subsistence level

existieren [ɛksɪs'tiːrən] vi to exist

exklusiv [ɛksklu'ziːf] adj exclusive; **~e** adv exclusive of, not including ♦ präp +gen exclusive of, not including

exotisch [ɛ'ksoːtɪʃ] adj exotic

Expedition [ɛkspeditsi'oːn] f expedition

Experiment [ɛksperi'mɛnt] nt experiment;

e~ell [-'tɛl] adj experimental; **e~ieren** [-'tiːrən] vi to experiment

Experte [ɛks'pɛrtə] (-n, -n) m expert, specialist; **Expertin** f expert, specialist

explo- [ɛksplo] zW: **~dieren** [-'diːrən] vi to explode; **E~sion** [-zi'oːn] f explosion; **~siv** [-'ziːf] adj explosive

Export [ɛks'pɔrt] (-(e)s, -e) m export; **~eur** [-'tøːr] m exporter; **~handel** m export trade; **e~ieren** [-'tiːrən] vt to export; **~land** nt exporting country

Express- ▲ [ɛks'prɛs] zW: **~gut** nt express goods pl, express freight; **~zug** m express (train)

extra ['ɛkstra] adj inv (umg: gesondert) separate; (besondere) extra ♦ adv (gesondert) separately; (speziell) specially; (absichtlich) on purpose; (vor Adjektiven, zusätzlich) extra; **E~** (-s, -s) nt extra; **E~ausgabe** f special edition; **E~blatt** nt special edition

Extrakt [ɛks'trakt] (-(e)s, -e) m extract

extravagant [ɛkstrava'gant] adj extravagant

extrem [ɛks'treːm] adj extreme; **~istisch** [-'mɪstɪʃ] adj (POL) extremist; **E~itäten** [-mi'tɛːtən] pl extremities

exzentrisch [ɛks'tsɛntrɪʃ] adj eccentric

EZ nt abk = **Einzelzimmer**

EZB f abk (= Europäische Zentralbank) ECB

F, f

Fa. abk (= Firma) firm; (in Briefen) Messrs

Fabel ['faːbəl] (-, -n) f fable; **f~haft** adj fabulous, marvellous

Fabrik [fa'briːk] f factory; **~ant** [-'kant] m (Hersteller) manufacturer; (Besitzer) industrialist; **~arbeiter** m factory worker; **~at** [-'kaːt] (-(e)s, -e) nt manufacture, product; **~gelände** nt factory site

Fach [fax] (-(e)s, ⁻er) nt compartment; (Sachgebiet) subject; **ein Mann vom ~** an expert; **~arbeiter** m skilled worker; **~arzt** m (medical) specialist; **~ausdruck** m technical term

Fächer ['fɛçər] (-s, -) m fan

Fach- zW: **~geschäft** nt specialist shop;

~hochschule f technical college; **~kraft** f skilled worker, trained employee; **f~kundig** adj expert, specialist; **f~lich** adj professional; expert; **~mann** (pl **-leute**) m specialist; **f~männisch** adj professional; **~schule** f technical college; **f~simpeln** vi to talk shop; **~werk** nt timber frame

Fackel ['fakəl] (**-, -n**) f torch

fad(e) [fa:t, 'fa:də] adj insipid; (langweilig) dull

Faden ['fa:dən] (**-s, ¨**) m thread; **f~scheinig** adj (auch fig) threadbare

fähig ['fɛ:ɪç] adj: **~ (zu** od +gen) capable (of); able (to); **F~keit** f ability

fahnden ['fa:ndən] vi: **~ nach** to search for; **Fahndung** f search

Fahndungsliste f list of wanted criminals, wanted list

Fahne ['fa:nə] f flag, standard; **eine ~ haben** (umg) to smell of drink; **~nflucht** f desertion

Fahr- zW: **~ausweis** m ticket; **~bahn** f carriageway (BRIT), roadway

Fähre ['fɛ:rə] f ferry

fahren ['fa:rən] (unreg) vt to drive; (Rad) to ride; (befördern) to drive, to take; (Rennen) to drive in ♦ vi (sich bewegen) to go; (Schiff) to sail; (abfahren) to leave; **mit dem Auto/ Zug ~** to go od travel by car/train; **mit der Hand ~ über** +akk to pass one's hand over

Fahr- zW: **~er(in)** (**-s, -**) m(f) driver; **~erflucht** f hit-and-run; **~gast** m passenger; **~geld** nt fare; **~karte** f ticket; **~kartenausgabe** f ticket office; **~kartenautomat** m ticket machine; **~kartenschalter** m ticket office; **f~lässig** adj negligent; **f~lässige Tötung** manslaughter; **~lehrer** m driving instructor; **~plan** m timetable; **f~planmäßig** adj scheduled; **~preis** m fare; **~prüfung** f driving test; **~rad** nt bicycle; **~radweg** m cycle lane; **~schein** m ticket; **~scheinentwerter** m (automatic) ticket stamping machine

Fährschiff ['fɛ:rʃɪf] nt ferry(boat)

Fahr- zW: **~schule** f driving school; **~spur** f lane; **~stuhl** m lift (BRIT), elevator (US)

Fahrt [fa:rt] (**-, -en**) f journey; (kurz) trip;

(AUT) drive; (Geschwindigkeit) speed; **gute ~!** have a good journey

Fährte ['fɛ:rtə] f track, trail

Fahrt- zW: **~kosten** pl travelling expenses; **~richtung** f course, direction

Fahrzeit f time for the journey

Fahrzeug nt vehicle; **~brief** m log book; **~papiere** pl vehicle documents

fair [fɛ:r] adj fair

Fakt [fakt] (**-(e)s, -en**) m fact

Faktor ['faktɔr] m factor

Fakultät [fakʊl'tɛ:t] f faculty

Falke ['falkə] (**-n, -n**) m falcon

Fall [fal] (**-(e)s, ¨e**) m (Sturz) fall; (Sachverhalt, JUR, GRAM) case; **auf jeden ~, auf alle Fälle** in any case; (bestimmt) definitely; **auf keinen ~!** no way!

Falle f trap

fallen (unreg) vi to fall; **etw ~ lassen** to drop sth; (Bemerkung) to make sth; (Plan) to abandon sth, to drop sth

fällen ['fɛlən] vt (Baum) to fell; (Urteil) to pass

fällig ['fɛlɪç] adj due

falls [fals] adv in case, if

Fallschirm m parachute; **~springer** m parachutist

falsch [falʃ] adj false; (unrichtig) wrong

fälschen ['fɛlʃən] vt to forge

fälsch- zW: **~lich** adj false; **~licherweise** adv mistakenly; **F~ung** f forgery

Falte ['faltə] f (Knick) fold, crease; (Hautfalte) wrinkle; (Rockfalte) pleat; **f~n** vt to fold; (Stirn) to wrinkle

faltig ['faltɪç] adj (Hände, Haut) wrinkled; (zerknittert: Rock) creased

familiär [famili'ɛ:r] adj familiar

Familie [fa'mi:liə] f family

Familien- zW: **~betrieb** m family business; **~kreis** m family circle; **~mitglied** nt member of the family; **~name** m surname; **~stand** m marital status

Fanatiker [fa'na:tikər] (**-s, -**) m fanatic; **fanatisch** adj fanatical

fand etc [fant] vb siehe **finden**

Fang [faŋ] (**-(e)s, ¨e**) m catch; (Jagen) hunting; (Kralle) talon, claw; **f~en** (unreg) vt to catch ♦ vr to get caught; (Flugzeug) to level out; (*Mensch: nicht fallen*) to steady o.s.; (*fig*) to compose o.s.; (*in Leistung*) to get back on form

Fantasie ▲ [fanta'zi:] *f* imagination; **f~los** *adj* unimaginative; **f~ren** *vi* to fantasize; **f~voll** *adj* imaginative

fantastisch ▲ [fan'tastɪʃ] *adj* fantastic

Farb- [farb] *zW:* **~abzug** *m* colour print; **~aufnahme** *f* colour photograph; **~band** *m* typewriter ribbon; **~e** *f* colour; (*zum Malen etc*) paint; (*Stoffarbe*) dye; **f~echt** *adj* colourfast

färben ['fɛrbən] *vt* to colour; (*Stoff, Haar*) to dye

farben- ['farbən] *zW:* **~blind** *adj* colour-blind; **~freudig** *adj* colourful; **~froh** *adj* colourful, gay

Farb- *zW:* **~fernsehen** *nt* colour television; **~film** *m* colour film; **~foto** *nt* colour photograph; **f~ig** *adj* coloured; **~ige(r)** *f(m)* coloured (person); **~kasten** *m* paintbox; **f~lich** *adj* colour; **f~los** *adj* colourless; **~stift** *m* coloured pencil; **~stoff** *m* dye; **~ton** *m* hue, tone

Färbung ['fɛrbʊŋ] *f* colouring; (*Tendenz*) bias

Farn [farn] (**-(e)s, -e**) *m* fern; bracken

Fasan [fa'za:n] (**-(e)s, -e(n)**) *m* pheasant

Fasching ['faʃɪŋ] (**-s, -e** *od* **-s**) *m* carnival

Faschismus [fa'ʃɪsmʊs] *m* fascism

Faschist *m* fascist

Faser ['fa:zər] (**-, -n**) *f* fibre; **f~n** *vi* to fray

Fass ▲ [fas] (**-es, ⁻er**) *nt* vat, barrel; (*für Öl*) drum; **Bier vom ~** draught beer

Fassade [fa'sa:də] *f* façade

fassen ['fasən] *vt* (*ergreifen*) to grasp, to take; (*inhaltlich*) to hold; (*Entschluss etc*) to take; (*verstehen*) to understand; (*Ring etc*) to set; (*formulieren*) to formulate, to phrase ♦ *vr* to calm down; **nicht zu ~** unbelievable

Fassung ['fasʊŋ] *f* (*Umrahmung*) mounting; (*Lampenfassung*) socket; (*Wortlaut*) version; (*Beherrschung*) composure; **jdn aus der ~ bringen** to upset sb; **f~slos** *adj* speechless

fast [fast] *adv* almost, nearly

fasten ['fastən] *vi* to fast; **F~zeit** *f* Lent

Fastnacht *f* Shrove Tuesday; carnival

faszinieren [fastsi'ni:rən] *vt* to fascinate

fatal [fa'ta:l] *adj* fatal; (*peinlich*) embarrassing

faul [faʊl] *adj* rotten; (*Person*) lazy; (*Ausreden*) lame; **daran ist etwas ~** there's something fishy about it; **~en** *vi* to rot; **~enzen** *vi* to idle; **F~enzer** (**-s, -**) *m* idler, loafer; **F~heit** *f* laziness; **~ig** *adj* putrid

Faust ['faʊst] (**-, Fäuste**) *f* fist; **auf eigene ~** off one's own bat; **~handschuh** *m* mitten

Favorit [favo'ri:t] (**-en, -en**) *m* favourite

Fax [faks] (**-, -(e)**) *nt* fax

faxen ['faksən] *vt* to fax; **jdm etw ~** to fax sth to sb

FCKW *m abk* (= *Fluorchlorkohlenwasserstoff*) CFC

Februar ['fe:brua:r] (**-(s), -e**) *m* February

fechten ['fɛçtən] (*unreg*) *vi* to fence

Feder ['fe:dər] (**-, -n**) *f* feather; (*Schreibfeder*) pen nib; (*TECH*) spring; **~ball** *m* shuttlecock; **~bett** *nt* continental quilt; **~halter** *m* penholder, pen; **f~leicht** *adj* light as a feather; **f~n** *vi* (*nachgeben*) to be springy; (*sich bewegen*) to bounce ♦ *vt* to spring; **~ung** *f* (*AUT*) suspension

Fee [fe:] *f* fairy

fegen ['fe:gən] *vt* to sweep

fehl [fe:l] *adj:* **~ am Platz** *od* **Ort** out of place; **F~betrag** *m* deficit; **~en** *vi* to be wanting *od* missing; (*abwesend sein*) to be absent; **etw ~t jdm** sb lacks sth; **du ~st mir** I miss you; **was ~t ihm?** what's wrong with him?; **F~er** (**-s, -**) *m* mistake, error; (*Mangel, Schwäche*) fault; **~erfrei** *adj* faultless; without any mistakes; **~erhaft** *adj* incorrect; faulty; **~erlos** *adj* flawless, perfect; **F~geburt** *f* miscarriage; **~gehen** (*unreg*) *vi* to go astray; **F~griff** *m* blunder; **F~konstruktion** *f* badly designed thing; **~schlagen** (*unreg*) *vi* to fail; **F~start** *m* (*SPORT*) false start; **F~zündung** *f* (*AUT*) misfire, backfire

Feier ['faɪər] (**-, -n**) *f* celebration; **~abend** *m* time to stop work; **~abend machen** to stop, to knock off; **jetzt ist ~abend!** that's enough!; **f~lich** *adj* solemn; **~lichkeit** *f* solemnity; **~lichkeiten** *pl* (*Veranstaltungen*) festivities; **f~n** *vt, vi* to celebrate; **~tag** *m* holiday

feig(e) [faɪk, 'faɪgə] *adj* cowardly

Feige ['faɪgə] *f* fig

Feigheit *f* cowardice

Feigling *m* coward

Feile ['faɪlə] *f* file

feilschen ['faɪlʃən] *vi* to haggle

fein [faɪn] *adj* fine; (*vornehm*) refined; (*Gehör etc*) keen; **~!** great!

Feind [faɪnt] **(-(e)s, -e)** *m* enemy; **f~lich** *adj* hostile; **~schaft** *f* enmity; **f~selig** *adj* hostile

Fein- *zW*: **f~fühlig** *adj* sensitive; **~gefühl** *nt* delicacy, tact; **~heit** *f* fineness; refinement; keenness; **~kostgeschäft** *nt* delicatessen (shop); **~schmecker (-s, -)** *m* gourmet; **~wäsche** *f* delicate clothing (*when washing*); **~waschmittel** *nt* mild detergent

Feld [fɛlt] **(-(e)s, -er)** *nt* field; (*SCHACH*) square; (*SPORT*) pitch; **~herr** *m* commander; **~stecher (-s, -)** *m* binoculars *pl*; **~weg** *m* path; **~zug** *m* (*fig*) campaign

Felge ['fɛlgə] *f* (wheel) rim

Fell [fɛl] **(-(e)s, -e)** *nt* fur; coat; (*von Schaf*) fleece; (*von toten Tieren*) skin

Fels [fɛls] **(-en, -en)** *m* rock; (*Klippe*) cliff

Felsen ['fɛlzən] **(-s, -)** *m* = **Fels**; **f~fest** *adj* firm

feminin [femi'niːn] *adj* feminine

Fenster ['fɛnstər] **(-s, -)** *nt* window; **~bank** *f* windowsill; **~laden** *m* shutter; **~leder** *nt* chamois (leather); **~scheibe** *f* windowpane

Ferien ['feːriən] *pl* holidays, vacation *sg* (*US*); **~ haben** to be on holiday; **~bungalow** [-bʊŋgalo] **(-s, -s)** *m* holiday bungalow; **~haus** *nt* holiday home; **~kurs** *m* holiday course; **~lager** *nt* holiday camp; **~reise** *f* holiday; **~wohnung** *f* holiday apartment

Ferkel ['fɛrkəl] **(-s, -)** *nt* piglet

fern [fɛrn] *adj, adv* far-off, distant; **~ von hier** a long way (away) from here; **der F~e Osten** the Far East; **~ halten** to keep away; **F~bedienung** *f* remote control; **F~e** *f* distance; **~er** *adj* further ♦ *adv* further; (*weiterhin*) in future; **F~gespräch** *nt* trunk call; **F~glas** *nt* binoculars *pl*; **F~licht** *nt* (*AUT*) full beam; **F~rohr** *nt* telescope; **F~ruf** *m* (*förmlich*) telephone number; **F~schreiben** *nt* telex; **F~sehapparat** *m* television set; **F~sehen (-s)** *nt* television; **im F~sehen** on television; **~sehen** (*unreg*) *vi* to watch television; **F~seher** *m* television; **F~sehturm** *m* television tower; **F~sprecher** *m* telephone; **F~steuerung** *f* remote control; **F~straße** *f* ≈ 'A' road (*BRIT*), highway (*US*); **F~verkehr** *m* long-distance traffic

Ferse ['fɛrzə] *f* heel

fertig ['fɛrtɪç] *adj* (*bereit*) ready; (*beendet*) finished; (*gebrauchsfertig*) ready-made; **~ bringen** (*fähig sein*) to be capable of; **~ machen** (*beenden*) to finish; (*umg: Person*) to finish; (*: körperlich*) to exhaust; (*: moralisch*) to get down; **sich ~ machen** to get ready; **~ stellen** to complete; **F~gericht** *nt* precooked meal; **F~haus** *nt* kit house, prefab; **F~keit** *f* skill

Fessel ['fɛsəl] **(-, -n)** *f* fetter; **f~n** *vt* to bind; (*mit ~n*) to fetter; (*fig*) to spellbind; **f~nd** *adj* fascinating, captivating

Fest (-(e)s, -e) *nt* party; festival; **frohes ~!** Happy Christmas!

fest [fɛst] *adj* firm; (*Nahrung*) solid; (*Gehalt*) regular; **~e Kosten** fixed cost ♦ *adv* (*schlafen*) soundly; **~ angestellt** permanently employed; **~binden** (*unreg*) *vt* to tie, to fasten; **~bleiben** (*unreg*) *vi* to stand firm; **F~essen** *nt* banquet; **~halten** (*unreg*) *vt* to seize, to hold fast; (*Ereignis*) to record ♦ *vr*: **sich ~halten (an** +*dat*) to hold on (to); **~igen** *vt* to strengthen; **F~igkeit** *f* strength; **F~ival** ['fɛstival] **(-s, -s)** *nt* festival; **F~land** *nt* mainland; **~legen** *vt* to fix ♦ *vr* to commit o.s.; **~lich** *adj* festive; **~liegen** (*unreg*) *vi* (*~stehen: Termin*) to be confirmed, be fixed; **~machen** *vt* to fasten; (*Termin etc*) to fix; **F~nahme** *f* arrest; **~nehmen** (*unreg*) *vt* to arrest; **F~preis** *m* (*COMM*) fixed price; **F~rede** *f* address; **~setzen** *vt* to fix, to settle; **F~spiele** *pl* (*Veranstaltung*) festival *sg*; **~stehen** (*unreg*) *vi* to be certain; **~stellen** *vt* to establish; (*sagen*) to remark; **F~tag** *m*

feast day, holiday; **F~ung** *f* fortress;
F~wochen *pl* festival *sg*
Fett [fɛt] **(-(e)s, -e)** *nt* fat, grease
fett *adj* fat; (*Essen etc*) greasy; (*TYP*) bold;
~arm *adj* low fat; **~en** *vt* to grease;
F~fleck *m* grease stain; **~ig** *adj* greasy,
fatty
Fetzen ['fɛtsən] **(-s, -)** *m* scrap
feucht [fɔʏçt] *adj* damp; (*Luft*) humid;
F~igkeit *f* dampness; humidity;
F~igkeitscreme *f* moisturizing cream
Feuer ['fɔʏər] **(-s, -)** *nt* fire; (*zum Rauchen*) a
light; (*fig: Schwung*) spirit; **~alarm** *m* fire
alarm; **f~fest** *adj* fireproof; **~gefahr** *f*
danger of fire; **f~gefährlich** *adj*
inflammable; **~leiter** *f* fire escape ladder;
~löscher **(-s, -)** *m* fire extinguisher;
~melder **(-s, -)** *m* fire alarm; **f~n** *vt, vi*
(*auch fig*) to fire; **~stein** *m* flint; **~treppe** *f*
fire escape; **~wehr** **(-, -en)** *f* fire brigade;
~wehrauto *nt* fire engine; **~wehrfrau** *f*
firewoman; **~wehrmann** *m* fireman;
~werk *nt* fireworks *pl*; **~zeug** *nt*
(cigarette) lighter
Fichte ['fɪçtə] *f* spruce, pine
Fieber ['fiːbər] **(-s, -)** *nt* fever, temperature;
f~haft *adj* feverish; **~thermometer** *nt*
thermometer; **fiebrig** *adj* feverish
fiel *etc* [fiːl] *vb siehe* **fallen**
fies [fiːs] (*umg*) *adj* nasty
Figur [fi'guːr] **(-, -en)** *f* figure; (*Schachfigur*)
chessman, chess piece
Filet [fi'leː] **(-s, -s)** *nt* (*KOCH*) fillet
Filiale [fili'aːlə] *f* (*COMM*) branch
Film [fɪlm] **(-(e)s, -e)** *m* film; **~aufnahme** *f*
shooting; **f~en** *vt, vi* to film; **~kamera** *f*
cine camera
Filter ['fɪltər] **(-s, -)** *m* filter; **f~n** *vt* to filter;
~papier *nt* filter paper; **~zigarette** *f*
tipped cigarette
Filz [fɪlts] **(-es, -e)** *m* felt; **f~en** *vt* (*umg*) to
frisk ♦ *vi* (*Wolle*) to mat; **~stift** *m* felt-tip
pen
Finale [fi'naːlə] **(-s, -(s))** *nt* finale; (*SPORT*)
final(s)
Finanz [fi'nants] *f* finance; **~amt** *nt* Inland
Revenue office; **~beamte(r)** *m* revenue

officer, **f~iell** [-tsi'ɛl] *adj* financial; **f~ieren**
[-'tsiːrən] *vt* to finance; **f~kräftig** *adj*
financially strong; **~minister** *m* Chancellor
of the Exchequer (*BRIT*), Minister of Finance
Find- [fɪnd] *zW:* **f~en** (*unreg*) *vt* to find;
(*meinen*) to think ♦ *vr* to be (found); (*sich
fassen*) to compose o.s.; **ich f~e nichts
dabei, wenn ...** I don't see what's wrong if
...; **das wird sich f~en** things will work
out; **~er** **(-s, -)** *m* finder; **~erlohn** *m*
reward (*for sb who finds sth*); **f~ig** *adj*
resourceful
fing *etc* [fɪŋ] *vb siehe* **fangen**
Finger ['fɪŋər] **(-s, -)** *m* finger; **~abdruck** *m*
fingerprint; **~nagel** *m* fingernail; **~spitze** *f*
fingertip
fingiert *adj* made-up, fictitious
Fink ['fɪŋk] **(-en, -en)** *m* finch
Finn- [fɪn] *zW:* **~e** **(-n, -n)** *m* Finn; **~in** *f*
Finn; **f~isch** *adj* Finnish; **~land** *nt* Finland
finster ['fɪnstər] *adj* dark, gloomy;
(*verdächtig*) dubious; (*verdrossen*) grim;
(*Gedanke*) dark; **F~nis** **(-)** *f* darkness, gloom
Firma ['fɪrma] **(-, -men)** *f* firm
Firmen- ['fɪrmən] *zW:* **~inhaber** *m* owner
of firm; **~schild** *nt* (shop) sign; **~wagen**
m company car; **~zeichen** *nt* trademark
Fisch [fɪʃ] **(-(e)s, -e)** *m* fish; **~e** *pl* (*ASTROL*)
Pisces *sg*; **f~en** *vt, vi* to fish; **~er** **(-s, -)** *m*
fisherman; **~e'rei** *f* fishing, fishery; **~fang**
m fishing; **~geschäft** *nt* fishmonger's
(shop); **~gräte** *f* fishbone; **~stäbchen**
[-stɛːpçən] *nt* fish finger (*BRIT*), fish stick (*US*)
fit [fɪt] *adj* fit; **'F~ness** ▲ **(-, -)** *f* (physical)
fitness
fix [fɪks] *adj* fixed; (*Person*) alert, smart; **~ und
fertig** finished; (*erschöpft*) done in;
F~er(in) *m(f)* (*umg*) junkie; **F~erstube** *f*
(*umg*) junkies centre; **~ieren** [fɪ'ksiːrən] *vt*
to fix; (*anstarren*) to stare at
flach [flax] *adj* flat; (*Gefäß*) shallow
Fläche ['flɛçə] *f* area; (*Oberfläche*) surface
Flachland *nt* lowland
flackern ['flakərn] *vi* to flare, to flicker
Flagge ['flagə] *f* flag; **f~n** *vi* to fly a flag
flämisch ['flɛːmɪʃ] *adj* (*LING*) Flemish
Flamme ['flamə] *f* flame

Flandern ['flandərn] nt Flanders

Flanke ['flaŋkə] f flank; (SPORT: Seite) wing

Flasche ['flaʃə] f bottle; (umg: Versager) wash-out

Flaschen- zW: **~bier** nt bottled beer; **~öffner** m bottle opener; **~zug** m pulley

flatterhaft adj flighty, fickle

flattern ['flatərn] vi to flutter

flau [flau] adj weak, listless; (Nachfrage) slack; **jdm ist ~** sb feels queasy

Flaum [flaum] (-(e)s) m (Feder) down; (Haare) fluff

flauschig ['flauʃɪç] adj fluffy

Flaute ['flautə] f calm; (COMM) recession

Flechte ['flɛçtə] f plait; (MED) dry scab; (BOT) lichen; **f~n** (unreg) vt to plait; (Kranz) to twine

Fleck [flɛk] (-(e)s, -e) m spot; (Schmutzfleck) stain; (Stofffleck) patch; (Makel) blemish; **nicht vom ~ kommen** (auch fig) not to get any further; **vom ~ weg** straight away

Flecken (-s, -) m = **Fleck**; **f~los** adj spotless; **~mittel** nt stain remover; **~wasser** nt stain remover

fleckig adj spotted; stained

Fledermaus ['fle:dərmaus] f bat

Flegel ['fle:gəl] (-s, -) m (Mensch) lout; **f~haft** adj loutish, unmannerly; **~jahre** pl adolescence sg

flehen ['fle:ən] vi to implore; **~tlich** adj imploring

Fleisch [flaɪʃ] (-(e)s) nt flesh; (Essen) meat; **~brühe** f beef tea, meat stock; **~er** (-s, -) m butcher; **~e'rei** f butcher's (shop); **f~ig** adj fleshy; **f~los** adj meatless, vegetarian

Fleiß [flaɪs] (-es) m diligence, industry; **f~ig** adj diligent, industrious

fletschen ['flɛtʃən] vt (Zähne) to show

flexibel [flɛ'ksi:bəl] adj flexible

Flicken ['flɪkən] (-s, -) m patch; **f~** vt to mend

Flieder ['fli:dər] (-s, -) m lilac

Fliege ['fli:gə] f fly; (Kleidung) bow tie; **f~n** (unreg) vt, vi to fly; **auf jdn/etw f~n** (umg) to be mad about sb/sth; **~npilz** m toadstool; **~r** (-s, -) m flier, airman

fliehen ['fli:ən] (unreg) vi to flee

Fliese ['fli:zə] f tile

Fließ- ['fli:s] zW: **~band** nt production od assembly line; **f~en** (unreg) vi to flow; **f~end** adj flowing; (Rede, Deutsch) fluent; (Übergänge) smooth

flimmern ['flɪmərn] vi to glimmer

flink [flɪŋk] adj nimble, lively

Flinte ['flɪntə] f rifle; shotgun

Flitterwochen pl honeymoon sg

flitzen ['flɪtsən] vi to flit

Flocke ['flɔkə] f flake

flog etc [flo:k] vb siehe **fliegen**

Floh [flo:] (-(e)s, ⁓e) m flea; **~markt** m flea market

florieren [flo'ri:rən] vi to flourish

Floskel ['flɔskəl] (-, -n) f set phrase

Floß [flɔs] (-es, ⁓e) nt raft, float

floss ▲ etc vb siehe **fließen**

Flosse ['flɔsə] f fin

Flöte ['flø:tə] f flute; (Blockflöte) recorder

flott [flɔt] adj lively; (elegant) smart; (NAUT) afloat; **F~e** f fleet, navy

Fluch [flu:x] (-(e)s, ⁓e) m curse; **f~en** vi to curse, to swear

Flucht [flʊxt] (-, -en) f flight; (Fensterflucht) row; (Zimmerflucht) suite; **f~artig** adj hasty

flücht- ['flʏçt] zW: **~en** vi, vr to flee, to escape; (vergänglich) transitory; (oberflächlich) superficial; (eilig) fleeting; **F~igkeitsfehler** m careless slip; **F~ling** m fugitive, refugee

Flug [flu:k] (-(e)s, ⁓e) m flight; **~blatt** nt pamphlet

Flügel ['fly:gəl] (-s, -) m wing; (MUS) grand piano

Fluggast m airline passenger

Flug- zW: **~gesellschaft** f airline (company); **~hafen** m airport; **~lärm** m aircraft noise; **~linie** f airline; **~plan** m flight schedule; **~platz** m airport; (klein) airfield; **~reise** f flight; **~schein** m (Ticket) plane ticket; (Pilotenschein) pilot's licence; **~steig** [-staɪk] (-(e)s, -e) m gate; **~verbindung** f air connection; **~verkehr** m air traffic; **~zeug** nt (aero)plane, airplane (US); **~zeugentführung** f hijacking of a plane; **~zeughalle** f hangar; **~zeugträger**

m aircraft carrier

Flunder ['flʊndər] (-, -n) *f* flounder

flunkern ['flʊŋkərn] *vi* to fib, to tell stories

Fluor ['fluːɔr] (-s) *nt* fluorine

Flur [fluːr] (-(e)s, -e) *m* hall; (*Treppenflur*) staircase

Fluss ▲ [flʊs] (-es, ⁺e) *m* river; (*Fließen*) flow

flüssig ['flʏsɪç] *adj* liquid; ~ **machen** (*Geld*) to make available; **F~keit** *f* liquid; (*Zustand*) liquidity

flüstern ['flʏstərn] *vt, vi* to whisper

Flut [fluːt] (-, -en) *f* (*auch fig*) flood; (*Gezeiten*) high tide; **f~en** *vi* to flood; **~licht** *nt* floodlight

Fohlen ['foːlən] (-s, -) *nt* foal

Föhn¹ [føːn] (-(e)s, -e) *m* (*warmer Fallwind*) föhn

Föhn² (-(e)s, -e) ▲ (*Haartrockner*) hairdryer; **f~en** ▲ *vt* to (blow) dry; **~frisur** ▲ *f* blow-dry hairstyle

Folge ['fɔlɡə] *f* series, sequence; (*Fortsetzung*) instalment; (*Auswirkung*) result; **in rascher ~** in quick succession; **etw zur ~ haben** to result in sth; **~n haben** to have consequences; **einer Sache** *dat* **~ leisten** to comply with sth; **f~n** *vi* +*dat* to follow; (*gehorchen*) to obey; **jdm f~n können** (*fig*) to follow *od* understand sb; **f~nd** *adj* following; **f~ndermaßen** *adv* as follows, in the following way; **f~rn** *vt*: **f~rn (aus)** to conclude (from); **~rung** *f* conclusion

folglich ['fɔlklɪç] *adv* consequently

folgsam ['fɔlkzaːm] *adj* obedient

Folie ['foːliə] *f* foil

Folklore ['fɔlkloːər] *f* folklore

Folter ['fɔltər] (-, -n) *f* torture; (*Gerät*) rack; **f~n** *vt* to torture

Fön [føːn] (-(e)s, -e) ® *m* hair dryer

Fondue [fõdyː] (-s, -s *od* -, -s) *nt od f* (*KOCH*) fondue

fönen △ *vt siehe* **föhnen**

Fönfrisur △ *f siehe* **Föhnfrisur**

Fontäne [fɔnˈtɛːnə] *f* fountain

Förder- ['fœrdər] *zW:* **~band** *nt* conveyor belt; **~korb** *m* pit cage; **f~lich** *adj* beneficial

fordern ['fɔrdərn] *vt* to demand

fördern ['fœrdərn] *vt* to promote; (*unterstützen*) to help; (*Kohle*) to extract

Forderung ['fɔrdərʊŋ] *f* demand

Förderung ['fœrdərʊŋ] *f* promotion; help; extraction

Forelle [foˈrɛlə] *f* trout

Form [fɔrm] (-, -en) *f* shape; (*Gestaltung*) form; (*Gussform*) mould; (*Backform*) baking tin; **in ~ sein** to be in good form *od* shape; **in ~ von** in the shape of

Formali'tät *f* formality

Format [fɔrˈmaːt] (-(e)s, -e) *nt* format; (*fig*) distinction

formbar *adj* malleable

Formblatt *nt* form

Formel (-, -n) *f* formula

formell [fɔrˈmɛl] *adj* formal

formen *vt* to form, to shape

Formfehler *m* faux pas, gaffe; (*JUR*) irregularity

formieren [fɔrˈmiːrən] *vt* to form ♦ *vr* to form up

förmlich ['fœrmlɪç] *adj* formal; (*umg*) real; **F~keit** *f* formality

formlos *adj* shapeless; (*Benehmen etc*) informal

Formular [fɔrmuˈlaːr] (-s, -e) *nt* form

formulieren [fɔrmuˈliːrən] *vt* to formulate

forsch [fɔrʃ] *adj* energetic, vigorous

forsch- *zW:* **~en** *vi:* **~en (nach)** to search (for); (*wissenschaftlich*) to (do) research; **~end** *adj* searching; **F~er** (-s, -) *m* research scientist; (*Naturforscher*) explorer; **F~ung** *f* research

Forst [fɔrst] (-(e)s, -e) *m* forest

Förster ['fœrstər] (-s, -) *m* forester; (*für Wild*) gamekeeper

fort [fɔrt] *adv* away; (*verschwunden*) gone; (*vorwärts*) on; **und so ~** and so on; **in einem ~** on and on; **~bestehen** (*unreg*) *vi* to survive; **~bewegen** *vt, vr* to move away; **~bilden** *vr* to continue one's education; **~bleiben** (*unreg*) *vi* to stay away; **F~dauer** *f* continuance; **~fahren** (*unreg*) *vi* to depart; (*~setzen*) to go on, to continue; **~führen** *vt* to continue, to carry on; **~gehen** (*unreg*) *vi* to go away;

~**geschritten** adj advanced; ~**pflanzen** vr to reproduce; **F~pflanzung** f reproduction

fort- zW: ~**schaffen** vt to remove; ~**schreiten** (unreg) vi to advance

Fortschritt ['fɔrtʃrɪt] m advance; ~**e machen** to make progress; **f~lich** adj progressive

fort- zW: ~**setzen** vt to continue; **F~setzung** f continuation; (folgender Teil) instalment; **F~setzung folgt** to be continued; ~**während** adj incessant, continual

Foto ['fo:to] (-s, -s) nt photo(graph); ~**apparat** m camera; ~'**graf** m photographer; ~**gra'fie** f photography; (Bild) photograph; **f~gra'fieren** vt to photograph ♦ vi to take photographs; ~**kopie** f photocopy

Fr. abk (= Frau) Mrs, Ms

Fracht [fraxt] (-, -en) f freight; (NAUT) cargo; (Preis) carriage; ~ **zahlt Empfänger** (COMM) carriage forward; ~**er** (-s, -) m freighter, cargo boat; ~**gut** nt freight

Frack [frak] (-(e)s, ²e) m tails pl

Frage ['fra:gə] (-, -n) f question; **jdm eine ~ stellen** to ask sb a question, to put a question to sb; siehe **infrage**; ~**bogen** m questionnaire; **f~n** vt, vi to ask; ~**zeichen** nt question mark

fraglich adj questionable, doubtful

fraglos adv unquestionably

Fragment [fra'gmɛnt] nt fragment

fragwürdig ['fra:kvyrdɪç] adj questionable, dubious

Fraktion [fraktsi'o:n] f parliamentary party

frankieren [fraŋ'ki:rən] vt to stamp, to frank

franko ['fraŋko] adv post-paid; carriage paid

Frankreich ['fraŋkraɪç] (-s) nt France

Franzose [fran'tso:zə] m Frenchman; **Französin** [fran'tsø:zɪn] f Frenchwoman; **französisch** adj French

fraß etc [fra:s] vb siehe **fressen**

Fratze ['fratsə] f grimace

Frau [frau] (-, -en) f woman; (Ehefrau) wife; (Anrede) Mrs, Ms; ~ **Doktor** Doctor

Frauen- zW: ~**arzt** m gynaecologist; ~**bewegung** f feminist movement; ~**haus** nt women's refuge; ~**zimmer** nt female, broad (US)

Fräulein ['frɔylaɪn] nt young lady; (Anrede) Miss, Ms

fraulich ['fraulɪç] adj womanly

frech [frɛç] adj cheeky, impudent; **F~heit** f cheek, impudence

frei [fraɪ] adj free; (Stelle, Sitzplatz) free, vacant; (Mitarbeiter) freelance; (unbekleidet) bare; **von etw ~ sein** to be free of sth; **im F~en** in the open air; ~ **sprechen** to talk without notes; ~ **Haus** (COMM) carriage paid; ~**er Wettbewerb** (COMM) fair/open competition; **F~bad** nt open-air swimming pool; ~**bekommen** (unreg) vt: **einen Tag ~bekommen** to get a day off; ~**beruflich** adj self-employed; ~**gebig** adj generous; ~**halten** (unreg) vt to keep free; ~**händig** adv (fahren) with no hands; **F~heit** f freedom; ~**heitlich** adj liberal; **F~heitsstrafe** f prison sentence; **F~karte** f free ticket; ~**lassen** (unreg) vt to (set) free; ~**legen** vt to expose; ~**lich** adv certainly, admittedly; **ja ~lich** yes of course; **F~lichtbühne** f open-air theatre; **F~lichtmuseum** nt open-air museum; ~**machen** vt (Post) to frank ♦ vr to arrange to be free; (entkleiden) to undress; **Tage ~machen** to take days off; ~**nehmen** ▲ (unreg) vt: **sich** dat **einen Tag ~nehmen** to take a day off; ~**sprechen** (unreg) vt: ~**sprechen (von)** to acquit (of); **F~spruch** m acquittal; ~**stehen** (unreg) vi: **es steht dir ~, das zu tun** you're free to do that; (leer stehen: Wohnung, Haus) to lie/stand empty; ~**stellen** vt: **jdm etw ~stellen** to leave sth (up) to sb; **F~stoß** m free kick

Freitag m Friday; ~**s** adv on Fridays

frei- zW: ~**willig** adj voluntary; **F~zeit** f spare od free time; **F~zeitpark** m amusement park; **F~zeitzentrum** nt leisure centre; ~**zügig** adj liberal, broad-minded; (mit Geld) generous

fremd [frɛmt] adj (unvertraut) strange; (ausländisch) foreign; (nicht eigen) someone else's; **etw ist jdm ~** sth is foreign to sb; ~**artig** adj strange; **F~enführer** ['frɛmdən-]

m (tourist) guide; **F~enverkehr** *m* tourism; **F~enverkehrsamt** *nt* tourist board; **F~enzimmer** *nt* guest room; **F~körper** *m* foreign body; **~ländisch** *adj* foreign; **F~sprache** *f* foreign language; **F~wort** *nt* foreign word

Frequenz [fre'kvɛnts] *f* (*RADIO*) frequency

fressen ['frɛsən] (*unreg*) *vt, vi* to eat

Freude ['frɔydə] *f* joy, delight

freudig *adj* joyful, happy

freuen ['frɔyən] *vt unpers* to make happy *od* pleased ♦ *vr* to be glad *od* happy; **freut mich!** pleased to meet you; **sich auf etw** *akk* ~ to look forward to sth; **sich über etw** *akk* ~ to be pleased about sth

Freund ['frɔynt] (**-(e)s, -e**) *m* friend; boyfriend; **~in** [-dɪn] *f* friend; girlfriend; **f~lich** *adj* kind, friendly; **f~licherweise** *adv* kindly; **~lichkeit** *f* friendliness, kindness; **~schaft** *f* friendship; **f~schaftlich** *adj* friendly

Frieden ['friːdən] (**-s, -**) *m* peace; **im ~** in peacetime

Friedens- *zW*: **~schluss** ▲ *m* peace agreement; **~vertrag** *m* peace treaty; **~zeit** *f* peacetime

fried- ['friːt] *zW*: **~fertig** *adj* peaceable; **F~hof** *m* cemetery; **~lich** *adj* peaceful

frieren ['friːrən] (*unreg*) *vt, vi* to freeze; **ich friere, es friert mich** I'm freezing, I'm cold

Frikadelle [frika'dɛlə] *f* rissole

Frikassee [frika'seː] (**-s, -s**) *nt* (*KOCH*) fricassee

frisch [frɪʃ] *adj* fresh; (*lebhaft*) lively; **~ gestrichen!** wet paint!; **sich ~ machen** to freshen (o.s.) up; **F~e** *f* freshness, liveliness; **F~haltefolie** *f* cling film

Friseur [fri'zøːr] *m* hairdresser

Friseuse [fri'zøːzə] *f* hairdresser

frisieren [fri'ziːrən] *vt* to do (one's hair); (*fig: Abrechnung*) to fiddle, to doctor ♦ *vr* to do one's hair

Frisiersalon *m* hairdressing salon

frisst ▲ [frɪst] *vb siehe* **fressen**

Frist [frɪst] (**-, -en**) *f* period; (*Termin*) deadline; **f~gerecht** *adj* within the stipulated time *od* period; **f~los** *adj*

(*Entlassung*) instant

Frisur [fri'zuːr] *f* hairdo, hairstyle

frivol [fri'voːl] *adj* frivolous

froh [froː] *adj* happy, cheerful; **ich bin ~, dass ...** I'm glad that ...

fröhlich ['frøːlɪç] *adj* merry, happy; **F~keit** *f* merriness, gaiety

fromm [frɔm] *adj* pious, good; (*Wunsch*) idle; **Frömmigkeit** ['frœmɪçkaɪt] *f* piety

Fronleichnam [froːn'laɪçnaːm] (**-(e)s**) *m* Corpus Christi

Front [frɔnt] (**-, -en**) *f* front; **f~al** [frɔn'taːl] *adj* frontal

fror *etc* [froːr] *vb siehe* **frieren**

Frosch [frɔʃ] (**-(e)s, ⁻e**) *m* frog; (*Feuerwerk*) squib; **~mann** *m* frogman; **~schenkel** *m* frog's leg

Frost [frɔst] (**-(e)s, ⁻e**) *m* frost; **~beule** *f* chilblain

frösteln ['frœstəln] *vi* to shiver

frostig *adj* frosty

Frostschutzmittel *nt* antifreeze

Frottier(hand)tuch [frɔ'tiːr(hant)tuːx] *nt* towel

Frucht [frʊxt] (**-, ⁻e**) *f* (*auch fig*) fruit; (*Getreide*) corn; **f~bar** *adj* fruitful, fertile; **~barkeit** *f* fertility; **f~ig** *adj* (*Geschmack*) fruity; **f~los** *adj* fruitless; **~saft** *m* fruit juice

früh [fryː] *adj, adv* early; **heute ~** this morning; **F~aufsteher** (**-s, -**) *m* early riser; **F~e** *f* early morning; **~er** *adj* earlier; (*ehemalig*) former ♦ *adv* formerly; **~er war das anders** that used to be different; **~estens** *adv* at the earliest; **F~jahr** *nt*, **F~ling** *m* spring; **~reif** *adj* precocious; **F~stück** *nt* breakfast; **~stücken** *vi* to (have) breakfast; **F~stücksbüfett** *nt* breakfast buffet; **~zeitig** *adj* early; (*pej*) untimely

frustrieren [frʊs'triːrən] *vt* to frustrate

Fuchs [fʊks] (**-es, ⁻e**) *m* fox; **f~en** (*umg*) *vt* to rile, to annoy; **f~teufelswild** *adj* hopping mad

Fuge ['fuːgə] *f* joint; (*MUS*) fugue

fügen ['fyːgən] *vt* to place, to join ♦ *vr*: **sich ~ (in** +*dat*) to be obedient (to); (*anpassen*) to adapt oneself (to) ♦ *vr unpers* to happen

fühl- *zW*: **~bar** *adj* perceptible, noticeable; **~en** *vt, vi, vr* to feel; **F~er** (**-s, -**) *m* feeler

fuhr *etc* [fu:r] *vb siehe* **fahren**

führen ['fy:rən] *vt* to lead; (*Geschäft*) to run; (*Name*) to bear; (*Buch*) to keep ♦ *vi* to lead ♦ *vr* to behave

Führer ['fy:rər] (**-s, -**) *m* leader; (*Fremdenführer*) guide; **~schein** *m* driving licence

Führung ['fy:ruŋ] *f* leadership; (*eines Unternehmens*) management; (*MIL*) command; (*Benehmen*) conduct; (*Museumsführung*) conducted tour; **~szeugnis** *nt* certificate of good conduct

Fülle ['fylə] *f* wealth, abundance; **f~n** *vt* to fill; (*KOCH*) to stuff ♦ *vr* to fill (up)

Füll- *zW*: **~er** (**-s, -**) *m* fountain pen; **~federhalter** *m* fountain pen; **~ung** *f* filling; (*Holzfüllung*) panel

fummeln ['fuməln] (*umg*) *vi* to fumble

Fund [funt] (**-(e)s, -e**) *m* find

Fundament [fundaˈmɛnt] *nt* foundation; **fundamen'tal** *adj* fundamental

Fund- *zW*: **~büro** *nt* lost property office, lost and found (*US*); **~grube** *f* (*fig*) treasure trove

fundiert [funˈdiːrt] *adj* sound

fünf [fynf] *num* five; **~hundert** *num* five hundred; **~te(r, s)** *adj* fifth; **F~tel** (**-s, -**) *nt* fifth; **~zehn** *num* fifteen; **~zig** *num* fifty

Funk [fuŋk] (**-s**) *m* radio, wireless; **~e** (**-ns, -n**) *m* (*auch fig*) spark; **f~eln** *vi* to sparkle; **~en** (**-s, -**) *m* (*auch fig*) spark; **f~en** *vi* (*durch Funk*) to signal, to radio; (*umg: richtig funktionieren*) to work ♦ *vt* (*Funken sprühen*) to shower with sparks; **~er** (**-s, -**) *m* radio operator; **~gerät** *nt* radio set; **~rufempfänger** *m* pager, paging device; **~streife** *f* police radio patrol; **~telefon** *nt* cellphone

Funktion [fuŋktsiˈoːn] *f* function; **f~ieren** [-ˈniːrən] *vi* to work, to function

für [fyːr] *präp +akk* for; **was ~** what kind *od* sort of; **das F~ und Wider** the pros and cons *pl*; **Schritt ~ Schritt** step by step

Furche ['furçə] *f* furrow

Furcht [furçt] (**-**) *f* fear; **f~bar** *adj* terrible, frightful

fürchten ['fyrçtən] *vt* to be afraid of, to fear ♦ *vr*: **sich ~ (vor +dat)** to be afraid (of)

fürchterlich *adj* awful

furchtlos *adj* fearless

füreinander [fyːraɪˈnandər] *adv* for each other

Furnier [furˈniːr] (**-s, -e**) *nt* veneer

fürs [fyːrs] = **für das**

Fürsorge ['fyːrzɔrgə] *f* care; (*Sozialfürsorge*) welfare; **~r(in)** (**-s, -**) *m(f)* welfare worker; **~unterstützung** *f* social security, welfare benefit (*US*); **fürsorglich** *adj* attentive, caring

Fürsprache *f* recommendation; (*um Gnade*) intercession

Fürsprecher *m* advocate

Fürst [fyrst] (**-en, -en**) *m* prince; **~entum** *nt* principality; **~in** *f* princess; **f~lich** *adj* princely

Fuß [fuːs] (**-es, ²e**) *m* foot; (*von Glas, Säule etc*) base; (*von Möbel*) leg; **zu ~** on foot; **~ball** *m* football; **~ballplatz** *m* football pitch; **~ballspiel** *nt* football match; **~ballspieler** *m* footballer; **~boden** *m* floor; **~bremse** *f* (*AUT*) footbrake; **~ende** *nt* foot; **~gänger(in)** (**-s, -**) *m(f)* pedestrian; **~gängerzone** *f* pedestrian precinct; **~nagel** *m* toenail; **~note** *f* footnote; **~spur** *f* footprint; **~tritt** *m* kick; (*Spur*) footstep; **~weg** *m* footpath

Futter ['futər] (**-s, -**) *nt* fodder, feed; (*Stoff*) lining; **~al** [-ˈraːl] (**-s, -e**) *nt* case

füttern ['fytərn] *vt* to feed; (*Kleidung*) to line

Futur [fuˈtuːr] (**-s, -e**) *nt* future

G, g

g *abk* = **Gramm**

gab *etc* [gaːp] *vb siehe* **geben**

Gabe ['gaːbə] *f* gift

Gabel ['gaːbəl] (**-, -n**) *f* fork; **~ung** *f* fork

gackern ['gakərn] *vi* to cackle

gaffen ['gafən] *vi* to gape

Gage ['gaːʒə] *f* fee; salary

gähnen ['gɛːnən] *vi* to yawn

Galerie [galə'ri:] f gallery

Galgen ['galgən] **(-s, -)** m gallows sg; ~**frist** f respite; ~**humor** m macabre humour

Galle ['galə] f gall; (Organ) gall bladder; ~**nstein** m gallstone

gammeln ['gaməln] (umg) vi to bum around; **Gammler(in) (-s, -)** (pej) m(f) layabout, loafer (inf)

Gämse ▲ ['gɛmzə] f chamois

Gang [gaŋ] **(-(e)s, ‿e)** m walk; (Botengang) errand; (~art) gait; (Abschnitt eines Vorgangs) operation; (Essensgang, Ablauf) course; (Flur etc) corridor; (Durchgang) passage; (TECH) gear; **in ~ bringen** to start up; (fig) to get off the ground; **in ~ sein** to be in operation; (fig) to be under way

gang adj: ~ **und gäbe** usual, normal

gängig ['gɛŋɪç] adj common, current; (Ware) in demand, selling well

Gangschaltung f gears pl

Ganove [ga'no:və] **(-n, -n)** (umg) m crook

Gans [gans] **(-, ‿e)** f goose

Gänse- ['gɛnzə] zW: ~**blümchen** nt daisy; ~**füßchen** (umg) pl (Anführungszeichen) inverted commas; ~**haut** f goose pimples pl; ~**marsch** m: **im ~marsch** in single file; ~**rich (-s, -e)** m gander

ganz [gants] adj whole; (vollständig) complete ♦ adv quite; (völlig) completely; ~ **Europa** all Europe; **sein ~es Geld** all his money; ~ **und gar nicht** not at all; **es sieht ~ so aus** it really looks like it; **aufs G~e gehen** to go for the lot

gänzlich ['gɛntslɪç] adj complete, entire ♦ adv completely, entirely

Ganztagsschule f all-day school

gar [ga:r] adj cooked, done ♦ adv quite; ~ **nicht/nichts/keiner** not/nothing/nobody at all; ~ **nicht schlecht** not bad at all

Garage [ga'ra:ʒə] f garage

Garantie [garan'ti:] f guarantee; **g~ren** vt to guarantee; **er kommt g~rt** he's guaranteed to come

Garbe ['garbə] f sheaf

Garde ['gardə] f guard

Garderobe [gardə'ro:bə] f wardrobe; (Abgabe) cloakroom; ~**nfrau** f cloakroom attendant

Gardine [gar'di:nə] f curtain

garen ['ga:rən] vt, vi to cook

gären ['gɛ:rən] (unreg) vi to ferment

Garn [garn] **(-(e)s, -e)** nt thread; yarn (auch fig)

Garnele [gar'ne:lə] f shrimp, prawn

garnieren [gar'ni:rən] vt to decorate; (Speisen, fig) to garnish

Garnison [garni'zo:n] **(-, -en)** f garrison

Garnitur [garni'tu:r] f (Satz) set; (Unterwäsche) set of (matching) underwear; **erste ~** (fig) top rank; **zweite ~** (fig) second rate

garstig ['garstɪç] adj nasty, horrid

Garten ['gartən] **(-s, ‿)** m garden; ~**arbeit** f gardening; ~**gerät** nt gardening tool; ~**lokal** nt beer garden; ~**tür** f garden gate

Gärtner(in) ['gɛrtnər(m)] **(-s, -)** m(f) gardener; ~**ei** [-'rai] f nursery; (Gemüsegärtnerei) market garden (BRIT), truck farm (US)

Gärung ['gɛ:rʊŋ] f fermentation

Gas [ga:s] **(-es, -e)** nt gas; ~ **geben** (AUT) to accelerate, to step on the gas; ~**hahn** m gas tap; ~**herd** m gas cooker; ~**kocher** m gas cooker; ~**leitung** f gas pipe; ~**pedal** nt accelerator, gas pedal

Gasse ['gasə] f lane, alley

Gast [gast] **(-es, ‿e)** m guest; (in Lokal) patron; **bei jdm zu ~ sein** to be sb's guest; ~**arbeiter(in)** m(f) foreign worker

Gäste- ['gɛstə] zW: ~**buch** nt visitors' book, guest book; ~**zimmer** nt guest od spare room

Gast- zW: **g~freundlich** adj hospitable; ~**geber (-s, -)** m host; ~**geberin** f hostess; ~**haus** nt hotel, inn; ~**hof** m hotel, inn; **g~ieren** [-'ti:rən] vi (THEAT) to (appear as a) guest; **g~lich** adj hospitable; ~**rolle** f guest role; ~**spiel** nt (THEAT) guest performance; ~**stätte** f restaurant; pub; ~**wirt** m innkeeper; ~**wirtschaft** f hotel, inn

Gaswerk nt gasworks sg

Gaszähler m gas meter

Gatte ['gatə] **(-n, -n)** m husband, spouse

Gattin f wife, spouse

Rechtschreibreform: ▲ *neue Schreibung* △ *alte Schreibung (auslaufend)*

Gattung ['gatʊŋ] *f* genus; kind

Gaudi ['gaʊdi] (*umg: SÜDD, ÖSTERR*) *nt od f* fun

Gaul [gaʊl] (**-(e)s, Gäule**) *m* horse; nag

Gaumen ['gaʊmən] (**-s, -**) *m* palate

Gauner ['gaʊnər] (**-s, -**) *m* rogue;~**ei** [-'raɪ] *f* swindle

geb. *abk* = **geboren**

Gebäck [gə'bɛk] (**-(e)s, -e**) *nt* pastry

gebacken [gə'bakən] *adj* baked; (*gebraten*) fried

Gebälk [gə'bɛlk] (**-(e)s**) *nt* timberwork

Gebärde [gə'bɛːrdə] *f* gesture;~**n** *vr* to behave

gebären [gə'bɛːrən] (*unreg*) *vt* to give birth to, to bear

Gebärmutter *f* uterus, womb

Gebäude [gə'bɔydə] (**-s, -**) *nt* building; ~**komplex** *m* (building) complex

geben ['geːbən] (*unreg*) *vt, vi* to give; (*Karten*) to deal ♦ *vb unpers:* **es gibt** there is/are; there will be ♦ *vr* (*sich verhalten*) to behave, to act; (*aufhören*) to abate; **jdm etw** ~ to give sb sth *od* sth to sb; **was gibts?** what's up?; **was gibt es im Kino?** what's on at the cinema?; **sich geschlagen** ~ to admit defeat; **das wird sich schon** ~ that'll soon sort itself out

Gebet [gə'beːt] (**-(e)s, -e**) *nt* prayer

gebeten [gə'beːtən] *vb siehe* **bitten**

Gebiet [gə'biːt] (**-(e)s, -e**) *nt* area; (*Hoheitsgebiet*) territory; (*fig*) field;g~**en** (*unreg*) *vt* to command, to demand; g~**erisch** *adj* imperious

Gebilde [gə'bɪldə] (**-s, -**) *nt* object

gebildet *adj* cultured, educated

Gebirge [gə'bɪrgə] (**-s, -**) *nt* mountain chain

Gebiss [gə'bɪs] (**-es, -e**) *nt* teeth *pl*; (*künstlich*) dentures *pl*

gebissen *vb siehe* **beißen**

geblieben [gə'bliːbən] *vb siehe* **bleiben**

geblümt [gə'blyːmt] *adj* (*Kleid, Stoff, Tapete*) floral

geboren [gə'boːrən] *adj* born; (*Frau*) née

geborgen [gə'bɔrgən] *adj* secure, safe

Gebot [gə'boːt] (**-(e)s, -e**) *nt* command; (*REL*) commandment; (*bei Auktion*) bid

geboten [gə'boːtən] *vb siehe* **bieten**

Gebr. *abk* (= *Gebrüder*) Bros.

gebracht [gə'braxt] *vb siehe* **bringen**

gebraten [gə'braːtən] *adj* fried

Gebrauch [gə'braʊx] (**-(e)s, Gebräuche**) *m* use; (*Sitte*) custom;g~**en** *vt* to use

gebräuchlich [gə'brɔyçlɪç] *adj* usual, customary

Gebrauchs- *zW:*~**anweisung** *f* directions *pl* for use;g~**fertig** *adj* ready for use; ~**gegenstand** *m* commodity

gebraucht [gə'braʊxt] *adj* used;G~**wagen** *m* secondhand *od* used car

gebrechlich [gə'brɛçlɪç] *adj* frail

Gebrüder [gə'bryːdər] *pl* brothers

Gebrüll [gə'brʏl] (**-(e)s**) *nt* roaring

Gebühr [gə'byːr] (**-, -en**) *f* charge, fee; **nach** ~ fittingly; **über** ~ unduly;g~**en** *vi:* **jdm** **g~en** to be sb's due *od* due to sb ♦ *vr* to be fitting;g~**end** *adj* fitting, appropriate ♦ *adv* fittingly, appropriately

Gebühren- *zW:*~**einheit** *f* (*TEL*) unit; ~**erlass** ▲ *m* remission of fees; ~**ermäßigung** *f* reduction of fees;g~**frei** *adj* free of charge;~**ordnung** *f* scale of charges, tariff;g~**pflichtig** *adj* subject to a charge

gebunden [gə'bʊndən] *vb siehe* **binden**

Geburt [gə'buːrt] (**-, -en**) *f* birth

Geburtenkontrolle *f* birth control

Geburtenregelung *f* birth control

gebürtig [gə'bʏrtɪç] *adj* born in, native of; ~**e Schweizerin** native of Switzerland

Geburts- *zW:*~**anzeige** *f* birth notice; ~**datum** *nt* date of birth;~**jahr** *nt* year of birth;~**ort** *m* birthplace;~**tag** *m* birthday; ~**urkunde** *f* birth certificate

Gebüsch [gə'bʏʃ] (**-(e)s, -e**) *nt* bushes *pl*

gedacht [gə'daxt] *vb siehe* **denken**

Gedächtnis [gə'dɛçtnɪs] (**-ses, -se**) *nt* memory;~**feier** *f* commemoration

Gedanke [gə'daŋkə] (**-ns, -n**) *m* thought; **sich über etw** *akk* ~**n machen** to think about sth

Gedanken- *zW:*~**austausch** *m* exchange of ideas;g~**los** *adj* thoughtless;~**strich** *m* dash;~**übertragung** *f* thought transference, telepathy

Gedeck [gə'dɛk] **(-(e)s, -e)** *nt* cover(ing); (*Speisenfolge*) menu; **ein ~ auflegen** to lay a place

gedeihen [gə'daɪən] (*unreg*) *vi* to thrive, to prosper

Gedenken *nt*: **zum ~ an jdn** in memory of sb

gedenken [gə'dɛŋkən] (*unreg*) *vi* +*gen* (*beabsichtigen*) to intend; (*sich erinnern*) to remember

Gedenk- *zW*: **~feier** *f* commemoration; **~minute** *f* minute's silence; **~stätte** *f* memorial; **~tag** *m* remembrance day

Gedicht [gə'dɪçt] **(-(e)s, -e)** *nt* poem

gediegen [gə'diːgən] *adj* (good) quality; (*Mensch*) reliable, honest

Gedränge [gə'drɛŋə] **(-s)** *nt* crush, crowd

gedrängt *adj* compressed; **~ voll** packed

gedrückt [gə'drʏkt] *adj* (*deprimiert*) low, depressed

gedrungen [gə'drʊŋən] *adj* thickset, stocky

Geduld [gə'dʊlt] *f* patience; **g~en** [gə'dʊldən] *vr* to be patient; **g~ig** *adj* patient, forbearing; **~sprobe** *f* trial of (one's) patience

gedurft [gə'dʊrft] *vb siehe* **dürfen**

geehrt [gə'|eːrt] *adj*: **Sehr ~e Frau X!** Dear Mrs X

geeignet [gə'|aɪgnət] *adj* suitable

Gefahr [gə'faːr] **(-, -en)** *f* danger; **~ laufen, etw zu tun** to run the risk of doing sth; **auf eigene ~** at one's own risk

gefährden [gə'fɛːrdən] *vt* to endanger

Gefahren- *zW*: **~quelle** *f* source of danger; **~zulage** *f* danger money

gefährlich [gə'fɛːrlıç] *adj* dangerous

Gefährte [gə'fɛːrtə] **(-n, -n)** *m* companion; (*Lebenspartner*) partner

Gefährtin [gə'fɛːrtın] *f* (female) companion; (*Lebenspartner*) (female) partner

Gefälle [gə'fɛlə] **(-s, -)** *nt* gradient, incline

Gefallen¹ [gə'falən] **(-s, -)** *m* favour

Gefallen² [gə'falən] **(-s)** *nt* pleasure; **an etw** *dat* **~finden** to derive pleasure from sth

gefallen *pp von* **fallen** ♦ *vi*: **jdm ~** to please

sb; **er/es gefällt mir** I like him/it; **das gefällt mir an ihm** that's one thing I like about him; **sich** *dat* **etw ~ lassen** to put up with sth

gefällig [gə'fɛlıç] *adj* (*hilfsbereit*) obliging; (*erfreulich*) pleasant; **G~keit** *f* favour; helpfulness; **etw aus G~keit tun** to do sth out of the goodness of one's heart

gefangen [gə'faŋən] *adj* captured; (*fig*) captivated; **~ halten** to keep prisoner; **~ nehmen** to take prisoner; **G~e(r)** *f(m)* prisoner, captive; **G~nahme** *f* capture; **G~schaft** *f* captivity

Gefängnis [gə'fɛŋnıs] **(-ses, -se)** *nt* prison; **~strafe** *f* prison sentence; **~wärter** *m* prison warder; **~zelle** *f* prison cell

Gefäß [gə'fɛːs] **(-es, -e)** *nt* vessel; (*auch* ANAT) container

gefasst ▲ [gə'fast] *adj* composed, calm; **auf etw** *akk* **~ sein** to be prepared *od* ready for sth

Gefecht [gə'fɛçt] **(-(e)s, -e)** *nt* fight; (MIL) engagement

Gefieder [gə'fiːdər] **(-s, -)** *nt* plumage, feathers *pl*

gefleckt [gə'flɛkt] *adj* spotted, mottled

geflogen [gə'floːgən] *vb siehe* **fliegen**

geflossen [gə'flɔsən] *vb siehe* **fließen**

Geflügel [gə'flyːgəl] **(-s)** *nt* poultry

Gefolgschaft [gə'fɔlkʃaft] *f* following

gefragt [gə'fraːkt] *adj* in demand

gefräßig [gə'frɛːsıç] *adj* voracious

Gefreite(r) [gə'fraɪtə(r)] *m* lance corporal; (NAUT) able seaman; (AVIAT) aircraftman

Gefrierbeutel [gə'friːr-] *m* freezer bag

gefrieren [gə'friːrən] (*unreg*) *vi* to freeze

Gefrier- *zW*: **~fach** *nt* icebox; **~fleisch** *nt* frozen meat; **g~getrocknet** [-gətrɔknət] *adj* freeze-dried; **~punkt** *m* freezing point; **~schutzmittel** *nt* antifreeze; **~truhe** *f* deep-freeze

gefroren [gə'froːrən] *vb siehe* **frieren**

Gefühl [gə'fyːl] **(-(e)s, -e)** *nt* feeling; **etw im ~ haben** to have a feel for sth; **g~los** *adj* unfeeling

gefühls- *zW*: **~betont** *adj* emotional; **G~duselei** [-duːzə'laɪ] *f* over-sentimentality;

~mäßig adj instinctive

gefüllt [gə'fʏlt] adj (KOCH) stuffed

gefunden [gə'fʊndən] vb siehe **finden**

gegangen [gə'gaŋən] vb siehe **gehen**

gegeben [gə'ge:bən] vb siehe **geben ♦** adj given; **zu ~er Zeit** in good time

gegebenenfalls [gə'ge:bənənfals] adv if need be

SCHLÜSSELWORT

gegen ['ge:gən] präp +akk 1 against; **nichts gegen jdn haben** to have nothing against sb; **X gegen Y** (SPORT, JUR) X versus Y; **ein Mittel gegen Schnupfen** something for colds

2 (in Richtung auf) towards; **gegen Osten** to(wards) the east; **gegen Abend** towards evening; **gegen einen Baum fahren** to drive into a tree

3 (ungefähr) round about; **gegen 3 Uhr** around 3 o'clock

4 (gegenüber) towards; (ungefähr) around; **gerecht gegen alle** fair to all

5 (im Austausch für) for; **gegen bar** for cash; **gegen Quittung** against a receipt

6 (verglichen mit) compared with

Gegenangriff m counter-attack

Gegenbeweis m counter-evidence

Gegend ['ge:gənt] (-, -en) f area, district

Gegen- zW: **g~ei'nander** adv against one another; **~fahrbahn** f oncoming carriageway; **~frage** f counter-question; **~gewicht** nt counterbalance; **~gift** nt antidote; **~leistung** f service in return; **~maßnahme** f countermeasure; **~mittel** nt antidote, cure; **~satz** m contrast; **~sätze überbrücken** to overcome differences; **g~sätzlich** adj contrary, opposite; (widersprüchlich) contradictory; **g~seitig** adj mutual, reciprocal; **sich g~seitig helfen** to help each other; **~spieler** m opponent; **~sprechanlage** f (two-way) intercom; **~stand** m object; **~stimme** f vote against; **~stoß** m counterblow; **~stück** nt counterpart; **~teil** nt opposite; **im ~teil** on the contrary; **g~teilig** adj opposite, contrary

gegenüber [ge:gən'|y:bər] präp +dat opposite; (zu) to(wards); (angesichts) in the face of **♦** adv opposite; **G~ (-s, -)** nt person opposite; **~liegen** (unreg) vr to face each other; **~stehen** (unreg) vr to be opposed (to each other); **~stellen** vt to confront; (fig) to contrast; **G~stellung** f confrontation; (fig) contrast; **~treten** (unreg) vi +dat to face

Gegen- zW: **~verkehr** m oncoming traffic; **~vorschlag** m counterproposal; **~wart** f present; **g~wärtig** adj present **♦** adv at present; **das ist mir nicht mehr g~wärtig** that has slipped my mind; **~wert** m equivalent; **~wind** m headwind; **g~zeichnen** vt, vi to countersign

gegessen [gə'gesən] vb siehe **essen**

Gegner ['ge:gnər] (-s, -) m opponent; **g~isch** adj opposing

gegr. abk (= gegründet) est.

gegrillt [gə'grɪlt] adj grilled

Gehackte(s) [gə'haktə(s)] nt mince(d meat)

Gehalt¹ [gə'halt] (-(e)s, -e) m content

Gehalt² [gə'halt] (-(e)s, ⁺er) nt salary

Gehalts- zW: **~empfänger** m salary earner; **~erhöhung** f salary increase; **~zulage** f salary increment

gehaltvoll [gə'haltfɔl] adj (nahrhaft) nutritious

gehässig [gə'hɛsɪç] adj spiteful, nasty

Gehäuse [gə'hɔyzə] (-s, -) nt case; casing; (von Apfel etc) core

Gehege [gə'he:gə] (-s, -) nt reserve; (im Zoo) enclosure

geheim [gə'haɪm] adj secret; **~ halten** to keep secret; **G~dienst** m secret service, intelligence service; **G~nis** (-ses, -se) nt secret; mystery; **~nisvoll** adj mysterious; **G~polizei** f secret police

gehemmt [gə'hɛmt] adj inhibited, self-conscious

gehen ['ge:ən] (unreg) vt, vi to go; (zu Fuß ~) to walk **♦** vb unpers: **wie geht es (dir)?** how are you od things?; **~ nach** (Fenster) to face; **mir/ihm geht es gut** I'm/he's (doing) fine; **geht das?** is that possible?; **gehts**

noch? can you manage?; **es geht** not too bad, O.K.; **das geht nicht** that's not on; **es geht um etw** it has to do with sth, it's about sth; **sich ~ lassen** (*unbeherrscht sein*) to lose control (of o.s.); **jdn ~ lassen** to let/leave sb alone; **lass mich ~!** leave me alone!

geheuer [gəˈhɔyər] *adj:* **nicht ~** eerie; (*fragwürdig*) dubious

Gehilfe [gəˈhɪlfə] (**-n, -n**) *m* assistant; **Gehilfin** *f* assistant

Gehirn [gəˈhɪrn] (**-(e)s, -e**) *nt* brain; **~erschütterung** *f* concussion; **~hautentzündung** *f* meningitis

gehoben [gəˈhoːbən] *pp von* **heben** ♦ *adj* (*Position*) elevated; high

geholfen [gəˈhɔlfən] *vb siehe* **helfen**

Gehör [gəˈhøːr] (**-(e)s**) *nt* hearing; **musikalisches ~** ear; **~ finden** to gain a hearing; **jdm ~ schenken** to give sb a hearing

gehorchen [gəˈhɔrçən] *vi +dat* to obey

gehören [gəˈhøːrən] *vi* to belong ♦ *vr unpers* to be right *od* proper

gehörig *adj* proper; **~ zu** *od +dat* belonging to; part of

gehörlos *adj* deaf

gehorsam [gəˈhoːrzaːm] *adj* obedient; **G~** (**-s**) *m* obedience

Geh- [ˈgeː-] *zW:* **~steig** *m* pavement, sidewalk (*US*); **~weg** *m* pavement, sidewalk (*US*)

Geier [ˈgaɪər] (**-s, -**) *m* vulture

Geige [ˈgaɪgə] *f* violin; **~r** (**-s, -**) *m* violinist

geil [gaɪl] *adj* randy (*BRIT*), horny (*US*)

Geisel [ˈgaɪzəl] (**-, -n**) *f* hostage

Geist [gaɪst] (**-(e)s, -er**) *m* spirit; (*Gespenst*) ghost; (*Verstand*) mind

geisterhaft *adj* ghostly

Geistes- *zW:* **g~abwesend** *adj* absent-minded; **~blitz** *m* brainwave; **~gegenwart** *f* presence of mind; **g~krank** *adj* mentally ill; **~kranke(r)** *f(m)* mentally ill person; **~krankheit** *f* mental illness; **~wissenschaften** *pl* the arts; **~zustand** *m* state of mind

geist- *zW:* **~ig** *adj* intellectual; mental;

(*Getränke*) alcoholic; **~ig behindert** mentally handicapped; **~lich** *adj* spiritual, religious; clerical; **G~liche(r)** *m* clergyman; **G~lichkeit** *f* clergy; **~los** *adj* uninspired, dull; **~reich** *adj* clever; witty; **~voll** *adj* intellectual; (*weise*) wise

Geiz [gaɪts] (**-es**) *m* miserliness, meanness; **g~en** *vi* to be miserly; **~hals** *m* miser; **g~ig** *adj* miserly, mean; **~kragen** *m* miser

gekannt [gəˈkant] *vb siehe* **kennen**

gekonnt [gəˈkɔnt] *adj* skilful ♦ *vb siehe* **können**

gekünstelt [gəˈkʏnstəlt] *adj* artificial, affected

Gel [geːl] (**-s, -e**) *nt* gel

Gelächter [gəˈlɛçtər] (**-s, -**) *nt* laughter

geladen [gəˈlaːdən] *adj* loaded; (*ELEK*) live; (*fig*) furious

gelähmt [gəˈlɛːmt] *adj* paralysed

Gelände [gəˈlɛndə] (**-s, -**) *nt* land, terrain; (*von Fabrik, Sportgelände*) grounds *pl*; (*Bau~*) site; **~lauf** *m* cross-country race

Geländer [gəˈlɛndər] (**-s, -**) *nt* railing; (*Treppengeländer*) banister(s)

gelangen [gəˈlaŋən] *vi:* **~ (an** +*akk od* **zu)** to reach; (*erwerben*) to attain; **in jds Besitz** *akk* **~** to come into sb's possession

gelangweilt [gəˈlaŋvaɪlt] *adj* bored

gelassen [gəˈlasən] *adj* calm, composed; **G~heit** *f* calmness, composure

Gelatine [ʒelaˈtiːnə] *f* gelatine

geläufig [gəˈlɔʏfɪç] *adj* (*üblich*) common; **das ist mir nicht ~** I'm not familiar with that

gelaunt [gəˈlaʊnt] *adj:* **schlecht/gut ~** in a bad/good mood; **wie ist er ~?** what sort of mood is he in?

gelb [gɛlp] *adj* yellow; (*Ampellicht*) amber; **~lich** *adj* yellowish; **G~sucht** *f* jaundice

Geld [gɛlt] (**-(e)s, -er**) *nt* money; **etw zu ~ machen** to sell sth off; **~anlage** *f* investment; **~automat** *m* cash dispenser; **~beutel** *m* purse; **~börse** *f* purse; **~geber** (**-s, -**) *m* financial backer; **g~gierig** *adj* avaricious; **~schein** *m* banknote; **~schrank** *m* safe, strongbox; **~strafe** *f* fine; **~stück** *nt* coin; **~wechsel**

m exchange (of money)

Gelee [ʒeˈleː] (**-s, -s**) *nt od m* jelly

gelegen [gəˈleːgən] *adj* situated; (*passend*) convenient, opportune ♦ *vb siehe* **liegen**; **etw kommt jdm ~** sth is convenient for sb

Gelegenheit [gəˈleːgənhaɪt] *f* opportunity; (*Anlaß*) occasion; **bei jeder ~** at every opportunity; **~arbeit** *f* casual work; **~skauf** *m* bargain

gelegentlich [gəˈleːgəntlɪç] *adj* occasional ♦ *adv* occasionally; (*bei Gelegenheit*) some time (or other) ♦ *präp +gen* on the occasion of

gelehrt [gəˈleːrt] *adj* learned; **G~e(r)** *f(m)* scholar; **G~heit** *f* scholarliness

Geleise [gəˈlaɪzə] (**-s, -**) *nt* = **Gleis**

Geleit [gəˈlaɪt] (**-(e)s, -e**) *nt* escort; **g~en** *vt* to escort

Gelenk [gəˈlɛŋk] (**-(e)s, -e**) *nt* joint; **g~ig** *adj* supple

gelernt [gəˈlɛrnt] *adj* skilled

Geliebte(r) [gəˈliːptə(r)] *f(m)* sweetheart, beloved

geliehen [gəˈliːən] *vb siehe* **leihen**

gelind(e) [gəˈlɪnd(ə)] *adj* mild, light; (*fig: Wut*) fierce; **~ gesagt** to put it mildly

gelingen [gəˈlɪŋən] (*unreg*) *vi* to succeed; **es ist mir gelungen, etw zu tun** I succeeded in doing sth

geloben [gəˈloːbən] *vt, vi* to vow, to swear

gelten [ˈgɛltən] (*unreg*) *vt* (*wert sein*) to be worth (*gültig sein*) to be valid; (*erlaubt sein*) to be allowed ♦ *vb unpers:* **es gilt, etw zu tun** it is necessary to do sth; **jdm viel/ wenig ~** to mean a lot/not to mean much to sb; **was gilt die Wette?** what do you bet?; **etw ~ lassen** to accept sth; **als** *od* **für etw ~** to be considered to be sth; **jdm** *od* **für jdn ~** (*betreffen*) to apply to *od* for sb; **~d** *adj* prevailing; **etw ~d machen** to assert sth; **sich ~d machen** to make itself/ o.s. felt

Geltung [ˈgɛltʊŋ] *f:* **~ haben** to have validity; **sich/etw** *dat* **~ verschaffen** to establish one's position/the position of sth; **etw zur ~ bringen** to show sth to its best advantage; **zur ~ kommen** to be seen/

heard *etc* to its best advantage

Geltungsbedürfnis *nt* desire for admiration

Gelübde [gəˈlʏpdə] (**-s, -**) *nt* vow

gelungen [gəˈlʊŋən] *adj* successful

gemächlich [gəˈmɛːçlɪç] *adj* leisurely

Gemahl [gəˈmaːl] (**-(e)s, -e**) *m* husband; **~in** *f* wife

Gemälde [gəˈmɛːldə] (**-s, -**) *nt* picture, painting

gemäß [gəˈmɛːs] *präp +dat* in accordance with ♦ *adj (+dat)* appropriate (to)

gemäßigt *adj* moderate; (*Klima*) temperate

gemein [gəˈmaɪn] *adj* common; (*niederträchtig*) mean; **etw ~ haben (mit)** to have sth in common (with)

Gemeinde [gəˈmaɪndə] *f* district, community; (*Pfarrgemeinde*) parish; (*Kirchengemeinde*) congregation; **~steuer** *f* local rates *pl*; **~verwaltung** *f* local administration; **~wahl** *f* local election

Gemein- *zW:* **g~gefährlich** *adj* dangerous to the public; **~heit** *f* commonness; mean thing to do/to say; **g~nützig** *adj* charitable; **g~nütziger Verein** non-profit-making organization; **g~sam** *adj* joint, common (*AUCH MATH*) ♦ *adv* together, jointly; **g~same Sache mit jdm machen** to be in cahoots with sb; **etw g~sam haben** to have sth in common; **~samkeit** *f* community, having in common; **~schaft** *f* community; **in ~schaft mit** jointly *od* together with; **g~schaftlich** *adj* = **gemeinsam**; **~schaftsarbeit** *f* teamwork; team effort; **~sinn** *m* public spirit

Gemenge [gəˈmɛŋə] (**-s, -**) *nt* mixture; (*Handgemenge*) scuffle

gemessen [gəˈmɛsən] *adj* measured

Gemetzel [gəˈmɛtsəl] (**-s, -**) *nt* slaughter, carnage, butchery

Gemisch [gəˈmɪʃ] (**-es, -e**) *nt* mixture; **g~t** *adj* mixed

gemocht [gəˈmɔxt] *vb siehe* **mögen**

Gemse △ [ˈgɛmzə] *f siehe* **Gämse**

Gemurmel [gəˈmʊrməl] (**-s**) *nt* murmur(ing)

Gemüse [gəˈmyːzə] (**-s, -**) *nt* vegetables *pl*; **~garten** *m* vegetable garden; **~händler** *m* greengrocer

gemusst ▲ [gəˈmʊst] *vb siehe* **müssen**

gemustert [gəˈmʊstərt] *adj* patterned

Gemüt [gəˈmyːt] (**-(e)s, -er**) *nt* disposition, nature; person; **sich** *dat* **etw zu ~e führen** (*umg*) to indulge in sth; **die ~er erregen** to arouse strong feelings; **g~lich** *adj* comfortable, cosy; (*Person*) good-natured; **~lichkeit** *f* comfortableness, cosiness; amiability

Gemüts- *zW:* **~mensch** *m* sentimental person; **~ruhe** *f* composure; **~zustand** *m* state of mind

Gen [geːn] (**-s, -e**) *nt* gene

genannt [gəˈnant] *vb siehe* **nennen**

genau [gəˈnau] *adj* exact, precise ♦ *adv* exactly, precisely; **etw ~ nehmen** to take sth seriously; **~ genommen** strictly speaking; **G~igkeit** *f* exactness, accuracy; **~so** *adv* just the same; **~so gut** just as good

genehm [gəˈneːm] *adj* agreeable, acceptable; **~igen** *vt* to approve, to authorize; **sich** *dat* **etw ~igen** to indulge in sth; **G~igung** *f* approval, authorization; (*Schriftstück*) permit

General [geneˈraːl] (**-s, -e** *od* **⁺e**) *m* general; **~direktor** *m* director general; **~konsulat** *nt* consulate general; **~probe** *f* dress rehearsal; **~streik** *m* general strike; **g~überholen** *vt* to overhaul thoroughly; **~versammlung** *f* general meeting

Generation [generatsiˈoːn] *f* generation

Generator [geneˈraːtɔr] *m* generator, dynamo

generell [genəˈrɛl] *adj* general

genesen [geˈneːzən] (*unreg*) *vi* to convalesce, to recover; **Genesung** *f* recovery, convalescence

genetisch [geˈneːtɪʃ] *adj* genetic

Genf [ˈɡɛnf] *nt* Geneva; **der ~er See** Lake Geneva

genial [geniˈaːl] *adj* brilliant

Genick [gəˈnɪk] (**-(e)s, -e**) *nt* (back of the) neck

Genie [ʒeˈniː] (**-s, -s**) *nt* genius

genieren [ʒeˈniːrən] *vt* to bother ♦ *vr* to feel

awkward *od* self-conscious

genieß- *zW:* **~bar** *adj* edible; drinkable; **~en** [gəˈniːsən] (*unreg*) *vt* to enjoy; to eat; to drink; **G~er** (**-s, -**) *m* epicure; pleasure lover; **~erisch** *adj* appreciative ♦ *adv* with relish

genmanipuliert [ˈgɛnmanipuliːrt] *adj* genetically modified

genommen [gəˈnɔmən] *vb siehe* **nehmen**

Genosse [gəˈnɔsə] (**-n, -n**) *m* (*bes POL*) comrade, companion; **~nschaft** *f* cooperative (association)

Genossin *f* (*bes POL*) comrade, companion

Gentechnik [ˈgeːntɛçnɪk] *f* genetic engineering

genug [gəˈnuːk] *adv* enough

Genüge [gəˈnyːgə] *f:* **jdm/etw ~ tun** *od* **leisten** to satisfy sb/sth; **g~n** *vi* (*+dat*) to be enough (for); **g~nd** *adj* sufficient

genügsam [gəˈnyːkzaːm] *adj* modest, easily satisfied; **G~keit** *f* moderation

Genugtuung [gəˈnuːktuːʊŋ] *f* satisfaction

Genuss ▲ [gəˈnʊs] (**-es, ⁺e**) *m* pleasure; (*Zusichnehmen*) consumption; **in den ~ von etw kommen** to receive the benefit of sth

genüsslich ▲ [gəˈnʏslɪç] *adv* with relish

Genussmittel ▲ *pl* (semi-)luxury items

geöffnet [gəˈœfnət] *adj* open

Geograf ▲ [geoˈgraːf] (**-en, -en**) *m* geographer; **Geograˈfie** ▲ *f* geography; **g~isch** *adj* geographical

Geologe [geoˈloːgə] (**-n, -n**) *m* geologist; **Geoloˈgie** *f* geology

Geometrie [geomeˈtriː] *f* geometry

Gepäck [gəˈpɛk] (**-(e)s**) *nt* luggage, baggage; **~abfertigung** *f* luggage office; **~annahme** *f* luggage office; **~aufbewahrung** *f* left-luggage office (*BRIT*), baggage check (*US*); **~aufgabe** *f* luggage office; **~ausgabe** *f* luggage office; (*AVIAT*) luggage reclaim; **~netz** *nt* luggage rack; **~träger** *m* porter; (*Fahrrad*) carrier; **~versicherung** *f* luggage insurance; **~wagen** *m* luggage van (*BRIT*), baggage car (*US*)

gepflegt [gəˈpfleːkt] *adj* well-groomed; (*Park etc*) well looked after

---

Rechtschreibreform: ▲ *neue Schreibung* △ *alte Schreibung (auslaufend)*

Gerade [gə'ra:də] f straight line; **g~'aus** adv straight ahead; **g~he'raus** adv straight out, bluntly; **g~stehen** (unreg) vi: **für jdn/etw g~stehen** to be answerable for sb('s actions)/sth; **g~wegs** adv direct, straight; **g~zu** adv (beinahe) virtually, almost

SCHLÜSSELWORT

gerade [gə'ra:də] adj straight; (aufrecht) upright; **eine gerade Zahl** an even number
♦ adv 1 (genau) just, exactly; (speziell) especially; **gerade deshalb** that's just od exactly why; **das ist es ja gerade!** that's just it!; **gerade du** you especially; **warum gerade ich?** why me (of all people)?; **jetzt gerade nicht!** not now!; **gerade neben** right next to
2 (eben, soeben) just; **er wollte gerade aufstehen** he was just about to get up; **gerade erst** only just; **gerade noch** (only) just

gerannt [gə'rant] vb siehe **rennen**
Gerät [gə're:t] (-(e)s, -e) nt device; (Werkzeug) tool; (SPORT) apparatus; (Zubehör) equipment no pl
geraten [gə'ra:tən] (unreg) vi (gedeihen) to thrive; (gelingen): **(jdm) ~** to turn out well (for sb); **gut/schlecht ~** to turn out well/badly; **an jdn ~** to come across sb; **in etw akk ~** to get into sth; **nach jdm ~** to take after sb
Geratewohl [gəra:tə'vo:l] nt: **aufs ~** on the off chance; (bei Wahl) at random
geräuchert [gə'rɔʏçərt] adj smoked
geräumig [gə'rɔʏmɪç] adj roomy
Geräusch [gə'rɔʏʃ] (-(e)s, -e) nt sound, noise; **g~los** adj silent
gerben ['gɛrbən] vt to tan
gerecht [gə'rɛçt] adj just, fair; **jdm/etw ~ werden** to do justice to sb/sth; **G~igkeit** f justice, fairness
Gerede [gə're:də] (-s) nt talk, gossip
geregelt [gə're:gəlt] adj (Arbeit) steady, regular; (Mahlzeiten) regular, set

gereizt [gə'raɪtst] adj irritable; **G~heit** f irritation
Gericht [gə'rɪçt] (-(e)s, -e) nt court; (Essen) dish; **mit jdm ins ~ gehen** (fig) to judge sb harshly; **das Jüngste ~** the Last Judgement; **g~lich** adj judicial, legal ♦ adv judicially, legally
Gerichts- zW: **~barkeit** f jurisdiction; **~hof** m court (of law); **~kosten** pl (legal) costs; **~medizin** f forensic medicine; **~saal** m courtroom; **~verfahren** nt legal proceedings pl; **~verhandlung** f trial; **~vollzieher** m bailiff
gerieben [gə'ri:bən] adj grated; (umg: schlau) smart, wily ♦ vb siehe **reiben**
gering [gə'rɪŋ] adj slight, small; (niedrig) low; (Zeit) short; **~fügig** adj slight, trivial; **~schätzig** adj disparaging
geringste(r, s) adj slightest, least; **~nfalls** adv at the very least
gerinnen [gə'rɪnən] (unreg) vi to congeal; (Blut) to clot; (Milch) to curdle
Gerippe [gə'rɪpə] (-s, -) nt skeleton
gerissen [gə'rɪsən] adj wily, smart
geritten [gə'rɪtən] vb siehe **reiten**
gern(e) ['gɛrn(ə)] adv willingly, gladly; **~ haben, ~ mögen** to like; **etwas ~ tun** to like doing something; **ich möchte ~ ...** I'd like ...; **ja, ~** yes, please; yes, I'd like to; **~ geschehen** it's a pleasure
gerochen [gə'rɔxən] vb siehe **riechen**
Geröll [gə'rœl] (-(e)s, -e) nt scree
Gerste ['gɛrstə] f barley; **~nkorn** nt (im Auge) stye
Geruch [gə'rux] (-(e)s, ⁺e) m smell, odour; **g~los** adj odourless
Gerücht [gə'rʏçt] (-(e)s, -e) nt rumour
geruhsam [gə'ru:za:m] adj (Leben) peaceful; (Nacht, Zeit) peaceful, restful; (langsam: Arbeitsweise, Spaziergang) leisurely
Gerümpel [gə'rʏmpəl] (-s) nt junk
Gerüst [gə'rʏst] (-(e)s, -e) nt (Baugerüst) scaffold(ing); frame
gesalzen [gə'zaltsən] pp von **salzen** ♦ adj (umg: Preis, Rechnung) steep
gesamt [gə'zamt] adj whole, entire; (Kosten) total; (Werke) complete; **im G~en** all in all;

Spelling Reform: ▲ *new spelling* △ *old spelling (to be phased out)*

~deutsch *adj* all-German; **G~eindruck** *m* general impression; **G~heit** *f* totality, whole; **G~schule** *f* ≈ comprehensive school

---

Gesamtschule

i The **Gesamtschule** is a comprehensive school for pupils of different abilities. Traditionally pupils go to either a **Gymnasium**, **Realschule** or **Hauptschule**, depending on ability. The **Gesamtschule** seeks to avoid the elitism of many Gymnasien. However, these schools are still very controversial, with many parents still preferring the traditional education system.

---

gesandt [gə'zant] *vb siehe* **senden**
Gesandte(r) [gə'zantə(r)] *m* envoy
Gesandtschaft [gə'zantʃaft] *f* legation
Gesang [gə'zaŋ] **(-(e)s, ⁻e)** *m* song; (*Singen*) singing; **~buch** *nt* (*REL*) hymn book
Gesäß [gə'zɛːs] **(-es, -e)** *nt* seat, bottom
Geschäft [gə'ʃɛft] **(-(e)s, -e)** *nt* business; (*Laden*) shop; (*~sabschluß*) deal; **g~ig** *adj* active, busy; (*pej*) officious; **g~lich** *adj* commercial ♦ *adv* on business
Geschäfts- *zW:* **~bedingungen** *pl* terms *pl* of business; **~bericht** *m* financial report; **~frau** *f* businesswoman; **~führer** *m* manager; (*Klub*) secretary; **~geheimnis** *nt* trade secret; **~jahr** *nt* financial year; **~lage** *f* business conditions *pl*; **~mann** *m* businessman; **g~mäßig** *adj* businesslike; **~partner** *m* business partner; **~reise** *f* business trip; **~schluss** ▲ *m* closing time; **~stelle** *f* office, place of business; **g~tüchtig** *adj* business-minded; **~viertel** *nt* business quarter; shopping centre; **~wagen** *m* company car; **~zeit** *f* business hours *pl*
geschehen [gə'ʃeːən] (*unreg*) *vi* to happen; **es war um ihn ~** that was the end of him
gescheit [gə'ʃait] *adj* clever
Geschenk [gə'ʃɛŋk] **(-(e)s, -e)** *nt* present, gift
Geschichte [gə'ʃɪçtə] *f* story; (*Sache*) affair;

(*Historie*) history
geschichtlich *adj* historical
Geschick [gə'ʃɪk] **(-(e)s, -e)** *nt* aptitude; (*Schicksal*) fate; **~lichkeit** *f* skill, dexterity; **g~t** *adj* skilful
geschieden [gə'ʃiːdən] *adj* divorced
geschienen [gə'ʃiːnən] *vb siehe* **scheinen**
Geschirr [gə'ʃɪr] **(-(e)s, -e)** *nt* crockery; pots and pans *pl*; (*Pferdegeschirr*) harness; **~spülmaschine** *f* dishwasher; **~spülmittel** *nt* washing-up liquid; **~tuch** *nt* dish cloth
Geschlecht [gə'ʃlɛçt] **(-(e)s, -er)** *nt* sex; (*GRAM*) gender; (*Gattung*) race; family; **g~lich** *adj* sexual
Geschlechts- *zW:* **~krankheit** *f* venereal disease; **~teil** *nt* genitals *pl*; **~verkehr** *m* sexual intercourse
geschlossen [gə'ʃlɔsən] *adj* shut ♦ *vb siehe* **schließen**
Geschmack [gə'ʃmak] **(-(e)s, ⁻e)** *m* taste; **nach jds ~** to sb's taste; **~ finden an etw** *dat* to (come to) like sth; **g~los** *adj* tasteless; (*fig*) in bad taste; **~ssinn** *m* sense of taste; **g~voll** *adj* tasteful
geschmeidig [gə'ʃmaidɪç] *adj* supple; (*formbar*) malleable
Geschnetzelte(s) [gə'ʃnɛtsəltə(s)] *nt* (*KOCH*) strips of meat stewed to produce a thick sauce
geschnitten [gə'ʃnɪtən] *vb siehe* **schneiden**
Geschöpf [gə'ʃœpf] **(-(e)s, -e)** *nt* creature
Geschoss ▲ [gə'ʃɔs] **(-es, -e)** *nt* (*MIL*) projectile, missile; (*Stockwerk*) floor
geschossen [gə'ʃɔsən] *vb siehe* **schießen**
geschraubt [gə'ʃraupt] *adj* stilted, artificial
Geschrei [gə'ʃrai] **(-s)** *nt* cries *pl*, shouting; (*fig: Aufheben*) noise, fuss
geschrieben [gə'ʃriːbən] *vb siehe* **schreiben**
Geschütz [gə'ʃʏts] **(-es, -e)** *nt* gun, cannon; **ein schweres ~ auffahren** (*fig*) to bring out the big guns
geschützt *adj* protected
Geschw. *abk siehe* **Geschwister**
Geschwätz [gə'ʃvɛts] **(-es)** *nt* chatter, gossip; **g~ig** *adj* talkative
geschweige [gə'ʃvaigə] *adv*: **~ (denn)** let

---

alone, not to mention

geschwind [gə'ʃvɪnt] *adj* quick, swift;
G~igkeit [-dɪçkaɪt] *f* speed, velocity;
G~igkeitsbeschränkung *f* speed limit;
G~igkeitsüberschreitung *f* exceeding
the speed limit

Geschwister [gə'ʃvɪstər] *pl* brothers and
sisters

geschwommen [gə'ʃvɔmən] *vb siehe*
schwimmen

Geschworene(r) [gə'ʃvo:rənə(r)] *f(m)* juror;
~n *pl* jury

Geschwulst [gə'ʃvʊlst] (-, ¨e) *f* swelling,
growth, tumour

geschwungen [gə'ʃvʊŋən] *pp von*
schwingen ♦ *adj* curved, arched

Geschwür [gə'ʃvy:r] (-(e)s, -e) *nt* ulcer

Gesell- [gə'zɛl] *zW*: **~e** (-n, -n) *m* fellow;
(*Handwerksgeselle*) journeyman; **g~ig** *adj*
sociable; **~igkeit** *f* sociability; **~schaft** *f*
society; (*Begleitung, COMM*) company;
(*Abendgesellschaft etc*) party; **g~schaftlich**
adj social; **~schaftsordnung** *f* social
structure; **~schaftsschicht** *f* social
stratum

gesessen [gə'zɛsən] *vb siehe* **sitzen**

Gesetz [gə'zɛts] (-es, -e) *nt* law; **~buch** *nt*
statute book; **~entwurf** *m* (draft) bill;
~gebung *f* legislation; **g~lich** *adj* legal,
lawful; **g~licher Feiertag** statutory holiday;
g~los *adj* lawless; **g~mäßig** *adj* lawful;
g~t *adj* (*Mensch*) sedate; **g~widrig** *adj*
illegal, unlawful

Gesicht [gə'zɪçt] (-(e)s, -er) *nt* face; **das
zweite ~** second sight; **das ist mir nie zu
~ gekommen** I've never laid eyes on that

Gesichts- *zW*: **~ausdruck** *m* (facial)
expression; **~creme** *f* face cream; **~farbe**
f complexion; **~punkt** *m* point of view;
~wasser *nt* face lotion; **~züge** *pl* features

Gesindel [gə'zɪndəl] (-s) *nt* rabble

gesinnt [gə'zɪnt] *adj* disposed, minded

Gesinnung [gə'zɪnʊŋ] *f* disposition; (*Ansicht*)
views *pl*

gesittet [gə'zɪtət] *adj* well-mannered

Gespann [gə'ʃpan] (-(e)s, -e) *nt* team;
(*umg*) couple

gespannt *adj* tense, strained; (*begierig*)
eager; **ich bin ~, ob** I wonder if *od*
whether; **auf etw/jdn ~ sein** to look
forward to sth/meeting sb

Gespenst [gə'ʃpɛnst] (-(e)s, -er) *nt* ghost,
spectre

gesperrt [gə'ʃpɛrt] *adj* closed off

Gespött [gə'ʃpœt] (-(e)s) *nt* mockery; **zum ~
werden** to become a laughing stock

Gespräch [gə'ʃprɛ:ç] (-(e)s, -e) *nt*
conversation; discussion(s); (*Anruf*) call;
g~ig *adj* talkative

gesprochen [gə'ʃprɔxən] *vb siehe* **sprechen**

gesprungen [gə'ʃprʊŋən] *vb siehe* **springen**

Gespür [gə'ʃpy:r] (-s) *nt* feeling

Gestalt [gə'ʃtalt] (-, -en) *f* form, shape;
(*Person*) figure; **in ~ von** in the form of; **~
annehmen** to take shape; **g~en** *vt* (*formen*)
to shape, to form; (*organisieren*) to arrange,
to organize ♦ *vr*: **sich g~en (zu)** to turn out
(to be); **~ung** *f* formation; organization

gestanden [gəʃtandən] *vb siehe* **stehen**

Geständnis [gə'ʃtɛntnɪs] (-ses, -se) *nt*
confession

Gestank [gə'ʃtaŋk] (-(e)s) *m* stench

gestatten [gə'ʃtatən] *vt* to permit, to allow;
~ Sie? may I?; **sich** *dat* **~, etw zu tun** to
take the liberty of doing sth

Geste ['gɛstə] *f* gesture

gestehen [gə'ʃte:ən] (*unreg*) *vt* to confess

Gestein [gə'ʃtaɪn] (-(e)s, -e) *nt* rock

Gestell [gə'ʃtɛl] (-(e)s, -e) *nt* frame; (*Regal*)
rack, stand

gestern ['gɛstərn] *adv* yesterday; **~ Abend/
Morgen** yesterday evening/morning

Gestirn [gə'ʃtɪrn] (-(e)s, -e) *nt* star;
(*Sternbild*) constellation

gestohlen [gə'ʃto:lən] *vb siehe* **stehlen**

gestorben [gə'ʃtɔrbən] *vb siehe* **sterben**

gestört [gə'ʃtø:rt] *adj* disturbed

gestreift [gə'ʃtraɪft] *adj* striped

gestrichen [gə'ʃtrɪçən] *adj* cancelled

gestrig ['gɛstrɪç] *adj* yesterday's

Gestrüpp [gə'ʃtrʏp] (-(e)s, -e) *nt*
undergrowth

Gestüt [gə'ʃty:t] (-(e)s, -e) *nt* stud farm

Gesuch [gə'zu:x] (-(e)s, -e) *nt* petition;

Spelling Reform: ▲ *new spelling* △ *old spelling (to be phased out)*

(Antrag) application; **g~t** adj (COMM) in demand; wanted; (fig) contrived

gesund [gəˈzʊnt] adj healthy; **wieder ~ werden** to get better; **G~heit** f health(iness); **G~heit!** bless you!; **~heitlich** adj health attrib, physical ♦ adv: **wie geht es Ihnen ~heitlich?** how's your health?; **~heitsschädlich** adj unhealthy; **G~heitswesen** nt health service; **G~heitszustand** m state of health

gesungen [gəˈzʊŋən] vb siehe **singen**

getan [gəˈtaːn] vb siehe **tun**

Getöse [gəˈtøːzə] (-s) nt din, racket

Getränk [gəˈtrɛŋk] (-(e)s, -e) nt drink; **~ekarte** f wine list

getrauen [gəˈtraʊən] vr to dare, to venture

Getreide [gəˈtraɪdə] (-s, -) nt cereals pl, grain; **~speicher** m granary

getrennt [gəˈtrɛnt] adj separate

Getriebe [gəˈtriːbə] (-s, -) nt (Leute) bustle; (AUT) gearbox

getrieben vb siehe **treiben**

getroffen [gəˈtrɔfən] vb siehe **treffen**

getrost [gəˈtroːst] adv without any bother

getrunken [gəˈtrʊŋkən] vb siehe **trinken**

Getue [gəˈtuːə] (-s) nt fuss

geübt [gəˈyːpt] adj experienced

Gewächs [gəˈvɛks] (-es, -e) nt growth; (Pflanze) plant

gewachsen [gəˈvaksən] adj: **jdm/etw ~ sein** to be sb's equal/equal to sth

Gewächshaus nt greenhouse

gewagt [gəˈvaːkt] adj daring, risky

gewählt [gəˈvɛːlt] adj (Sprache) refined, elegant

Gewähr [gəˈvɛːr] (-) f guarantee; **keine ~ übernehmen für** to accept no responsibility for; **g~en** vt to grant; (geben) to provide; **g~leisten** vt to guarantee

Gewahrsam [gəˈvaːrzaːm] (-s, -e) m safekeeping; (Polizeigewahrsam) custody

Gewalt [gəˈvalt] (-, -en) f power; (große Kraft) force; (~taten) violence; **mit aller ~** with all one's might; **~anwendung** f use of force; **g~ig** adj tremendous; (Irrtum) huge; **~marsch** m forced march; **g~sam** adj forcible; **g~tätig** adj violent

Gewand [gəˈvant] (-(e)s, ⁻er) nt gown, robe

gewandt [gəˈvant] adj deft, skilful; (erfahren) experienced; **G~heit** f dexterity, skill

gewann etc [gəˈvan] vb siehe **gewinnen**

Gewässer [gəˈvɛsər] (-s, -) nt waters pl

Gewebe [gəˈveːbə] (-s, -) nt (Stoff) fabric; (BIOL) tissue

Gewehr [gəˈveːr] (-(e)s, -e) nt gun; rifle; **~lauf** m rifle barrel

Geweih [gəˈvaɪ] (-(e)s, -e) nt antlers pl

Gewerb- [gəˈvɛrb] zW: **~e** (-s, -) nt trade, occupation; **Handel und ~e** trade and industry; **~eschule** f technical school; **~ezweig** m line of trade

Gewerkschaft [gəˈvɛrkʃaft] f trade union; **~ler** (-s, -) m trade unionist; **~sbund** m trade unions federation

gewesen [gəˈveːzən] pp von **sein**

Gewicht [gəˈvɪçt] (-(e)s, -e) nt weight; (fig) importance

gewieft [gəˈviːft] adj shrewd, cunning

gewillt [gəˈvɪlt] adj willing, prepared

Gewimmel [gəˈvɪməl] (-s) nt swarm

Gewinde [gəˈvɪndə] (-s, -) nt (Kranz) wreath; (von Schraube) thread

Gewinn [gəˈvɪn] (-(e)s, -e) m profit; (bei Spiel) winnings pl; **~ bringend** profitable; **etw mit ~ verkaufen** to sell sth at a profit; **~- und Verlustrechnung** (COMM) profit and loss account; **~beteiligung** f profit-sharing; **g~en** (unreg) vt to win; (erwerben) to gain; (Kohle, Öl) to extract ♦ vi to win; (profitieren) to gain; **an etw** dat **g~en** to gain (in) sth; **g~end** adj (Lächeln, Aussehen) winning, charming; **~er(in)** (-s, -) m(f) winner; **~spanne** f profit margin; **~ung** f winning, gaining; (von Kohle etc) extraction

Gewirr [gəˈvɪr] (-(e)s, -e) nt tangle; (von Straßen) maze

gewiss ▲ [gəˈvɪs] adj certain ♦ adv certainly

Gewissen [gəˈvɪsən] (-s, -) nt conscience; **g~haft** adj conscientious; **g~los** adj unscrupulous

Gewissens- zW: **~bisse** pl pangs of conscience, qualms; **~frage** f matter of conscience; **~konflikt** m moral conflict

gewissermaßen [gəvɪsərˈmaːsən] adv more

or less, in a way

Gewissheit ▲ [gəˈvɪshaɪt] f certainty

Gewitter [gəˈvɪtər] **(-s, -)** nt thunderstorm; **g~n** vi unpers: **es g~t** there's a thunderstorm

gewitzt [gəˈvɪtst] adj shrewd, cunning

gewogen [gəˈvoːɡən] adj (+dat) well-disposed (towards)

gewöhnen [gəˈvøːnən] vt: **jdn an etw** akk ~ to accustom sb to sth; (erziehen zu) to teach sb sth ♦ vr: **sich an etw** akk ~ to get used od accustomed to sth

Gewohnheit [gəˈvoːnhaɪt] f habit; (Brauch) custom; **aus** ~ from habit; **zur** ~ **werden** to become a habit

Gewohnheits- zW: **~mensch** m creature of habit; **~recht** nt common law

gewöhnlich [gəˈvøːnlɪç] adj usual; ordinary; (pej) common; **wie** ~ as usual

gewohnt [gəˈvoːnt] adj usual; **etw** ~ **sein** to be used to sth

Gewöhnung f: ~ **(an** +akk) getting accustomed (to)

Gewölbe [gəˈvœlbə] **(-s, -)** nt vault

gewollt [gəˈvɔlt] adj affected, artificial

gewonnen [gəˈvɔnən] vb siehe **gewinnen**

geworden [gəˈvɔrdən] vb siehe **werden**

geworfen [gəˈvɔrfər] vb siehe **werfen**

Gewühl [gəˈvyːl] **(-(e)s)** nt throng

Gewürz [gəˈvʏrts] **(-es, -e)** nt spice, seasoning; **g~t** adj spiced

gewusst ▲ [gəˈvʊst] vb siehe **wissen**

Gezeiten [gəˈtsaɪtən] pl tides

gezielt [gəˈtsiːlt] adj with a particular aim in mind, purposeful; (Kritik) pointed

gezogen [gəˈtsoːɡən] vb siehe **ziehen**

Gezwitscher [gəˈtsvɪtʃər] **(-s)** nt twitter(ing), chirping

gezwungen [gəˈtsvʊŋən] adj forced; **~ermaßen** adv of necessity

ggf. abk von **gegebenenfalls**

gibst etc [giːpst] vb siehe **geben**

Gicht [gɪçt] **(-)** f gout

Giebel [ˈgiːbəl] **(-s, -)** m gable; **~dach** nt gable(d) roof; **~fenster** nt gable window

Gier [giːr] **(-)** f greed; **g~ig** adj greedy

gießen [ˈgiːsən] (unreg) vt to pour; (Blumen)

to water; (Metall) to cast; (Wachs) to mould

Gießkanne f watering can

Gift [gɪft] **(-(e)s, -e)** nt poison; **g~ig** adj poisonous; (fig: boshaft) venomous; **~müll** m toxic waste; **~stoff** m toxic substance; **~zahn** m fang

ging etc [gɪŋ] vb siehe **gehen**

Gipfel [ˈgɪpfəl] **(-s, -)** m summit, peak; (fig: Höhepunkt) height; **g~n** vi to culminate; **~treffen** nt summit (meeting)

Gips [gɪps] **(-es, -e)** m plaster; (MED) plaster (of Paris); **~abdruck** m plaster cast; **g~en** vt to plaster; **~verband** m plaster (cast)

Giraffe [giˈrafə] f giraffe

Girlande [gɪrˈlandə] f garland

Giro [ˈʒiːro] **(-s, -s)** nt giro; **~konto** nt current account

Gitarre [giˈtarə] f guitar

Gitter [ˈgɪtər] **(-s, -)** nt grating, bars pl; (für Pflanzen) trellis; (Zaun) railing(s); **~bett** nt cot; **~fenster** nt barred window; **~zaun** m railing(s)

Glanz [glants] **(-es)** m shine, lustre; (fig) splendour

glänzen [ˈglɛntsən] vi to shine (also fig), to gleam ♦ vt to polish; **~d** adj shining; (fig) brilliant

Glanz- zW: **~leistung** f brilliant achievement; **g~los** adj dull; **~zeit** f heyday

Glas [glaːs] **(-es, ⁱer)** nt glass; **~er (-s, -)** m glazier; **~faser** f fibreglass; **g~ieren** [glaˈziːrən] vt to glaze; **g~ig** adj glassy; **~scheibe** f pane; **~ur** [glaˈzuːr] f glaze; (KOCH) icing

glatt [glat] adj smooth; (rutschig) slippery; (Absage) flat; (Lüge) downright; **Glätte** f smoothness; slipperiness

Glatteis nt (black) ice; **jdn aufs** ~ **führen** (fig) to take sb for a ride

glätten vt to smooth out

Glatze [ˈglatsə] f bald head; **eine** ~ **bekommen** to go bald

Glaube [ˈglaʊbə] **(-ns, -n)** m: ~ **(an** +akk) faith (in); belief (in); **g~n** vt, vi to believe; to think; **jdm g~n** to believe sb; **an etw** akk **g~n** to believe in sth; **daran g~n müssen**

Spelling Reform: ▲ new spelling △ old spelling (to be phased out)

(umg) to be for it
glaubhaft ['glaʊbhaft] *adj* credible
gläubig ['glɔʏbɪç] *adj* (*REL*) devout;
(*vertrauensvoll*) trustful; **G~e(r)** *f(m)*
believer; **die G~en** the faithful; **G~er** (**-s, -**)
m creditor
glaubwürdig ['glaʊbvʏrdɪç] *adj* credible;
(*Mensch*) trustworthy; **G~keit** *f* credibility;
trustworthiness
gleich [glaɪç] *adj* equal; (*identisch*) (the)
same, identical ♦ *adv* equally; (*sofort*)
straight away; (*bald*) in a minute; **es ist
mir ~** it's all the same to me; **~ bleibend**
constant; **~ gesinnt** like-minded; **2 mal 2 =
4** 2 times 2 is *od* equals 4; **~ groß** the same
size; **~ nach/an** right after/at; **~altrig** *adj*
of the same age; **~artig** *adj* similar;
~bedeutend *adj* synonymous;
G~berechtigung *f* equal rights *pl*; **~en**
(*unreg*) *vi*: **jdm/etw ~en** to be like sb/sth
♦ *vr* to be alike; **~falls** *adv* likewise; **danke
~falls!** the same to you; **G~förmigkeit** *f*
uniformity; **G~gewicht** *nt* equilibrium,
balance; **~gültig** *adj* indifferent;
(*unbedeutend*) unimportant; **G~gültigkeit** *f*
indifference; **G~heit** *f* equality; **~kommen**
(*unreg*) *vi* +*dat* to be equal to; **~mäßig** *adj*
even, equal; **~sam** *adv* as it were;
G~schritt *m*: **im G~schritt gehen** to walk
in step; **~stellen** *vt* (*rechtlich etc*) to treat as
(an) equal; **G~strom** *m* (*ELEK*) direct
current; **~tun** (*unreg*) *vi*: **es jdm ~tun** to
match sb; **G~ung** *f* equation; **~viel** *adv* no
matter; **~wertig** *adj* (*Geld*) of the same
value; (*Gegner*) evenly matched; **~zeitig** *adj*
simultaneous
Gleis [glaɪs] (**-es, -e**) *nt* track, rails *pl*;
(*Bahnsteig*) platform
gleiten ['glaɪtən] (*unreg*) *vi* to glide;
(*rutschen*) to slide
Gleitzeit *f* flex(i)time
Gletscher ['glɛtʃər] (**-s, -**) *m* glacier;
~spalte *f* crevasse
Glied [gliːt] (**-(e)s, -er**) *nt* member; (*Arm,
Bein*) limb; (*von Kette*) link; (*MIL*) rank(s);
g~ern [-dərn] *vt* to organize, to structure;
~erung *f* structure, organization

glimmen ['glɪmən] (*unreg*) *vi* to glow, to
gleam
glimpflich ['glɪmpflɪç] *adj* mild, lenient; **~
davonkommen** to get off lightly
glitschig ['glɪtʃɪç] *adj* (*Fisch, Weg*) slippery
glitzern ['glɪtsərn] *vi* to glitter; to twinkle
global [glo'baːl] *adj* global
Globus ['gloːbʊs] (**- od -ses, Globen** *od* **-se**)
m globe
Glocke ['glɔkə] *f* bell; **etw an die große ~
hängen** (*fig*) to shout sth from the rooftops
Glocken- *zW*: **~blume** *f* bellflower;
~geläut *nt* peal of bells; **~spiel** *nt*
chime(s); (*MUS*) glockenspiel; **~turm** *m* bell
tower
Glosse ['glɔsə] *f* comment
glotzen ['glɔtsən] (*umg*) *vi* to stare
Glück [glʏk] (**-(e)s**) *nt* luck, fortune; (*Freude*)
happiness; **~ haben** to be lucky; **viel ~!**
good luck!; **zum ~** fortunately; **g~en** *vi* to
succeed; **es g~te ihm, es zu bekommen**
he succeeded in getting it
gluckern ['glʊkərn] *vi* to glug
glück- *zW*: **~lich** *adj* fortunate; (*froh*)
happy; **~licherweise** *adv* fortunately;
~'selig *adj* blissful
Glücks- *zW*: **~fall** *m* stroke of luck; **~kind**
nt lucky person; **~sache** *f* matter of luck;
~spiel *nt* game of chance
Glückwunsch *m* congratulations *pl*, best
wishes *pl*
Glüh- ['glyː] *zW*: **~birne** *f* light bulb; **g~en**
vi to glow; **~wein** *m* mulled wine;
~würmchen *nt* glow-worm
Glut [gluːt] (**-, -en**) *f* (*Röte*) glow; (*Feuersglut*)
fire; (*Hitze*) heat; (*fig*) ardour
GmbH [geːʔɛmbeːˈhaː] *f abk* (= *Gesellschaft mit
beschränkter Haftung*) limited company, Ltd
Gnade ['gnaːdə] *f* (*Gunst*) favour; (*Erbarmen*)
mercy; (*Milde*) clemency
Gnaden- *zW*: **~frist** *f* reprieve, respite;
g~los *adj* merciless; **~stoß** *m* coup de
grâce
gnädig ['gnɛːdɪç] *adj* gracious; (*voll Erbarmen*)
merciful
Gold [gɔlt] (**-(e)s**) *nt* gold; **g~en** *adj* golden;
~fisch *m* goldfish; **~grube** *f* goldmine;

g~ig ['gɔldɪç] (umg) adj (fig: allerliebst) sweet, adorable; ~**regen** m laburnum; ~**schmied** m goldsmith

Golf¹ [gɔlf] (-(e)s, -e) m gulf

Golf² [gɔlf] (-s) nt golf; ~**platz** m golf course; ~**schläger** m golf club

Golfstrom m Gulf Stream

Gondel ['gɔndəl] (-, -n) f gondola; (Seilbahn) cable car

gönnen ['gœnən] vt: **jdm etw** ~ not to begrudge sb sth; **sich** dat **etw** ~ to allow o.s. sth

Gönner (-s, -) m patron; **g~haft** adj patronizing

Gosse ['gɔsə] f gutter

Gott [gɔt] (-(e)s, -er) m god; **mein ~!** for heaven's sake!; **um ~es Willen!** for heaven's sake!; **grüß ~!** hello; ~ **sei Dank!** thank God!; ~**heit** f deity

Göttin ['gœtɪn] f goddess

göttlich adj divine

gottlos adj godless

Götze ['gœtsə] (-n, -n) m idol

Grab [graːp] (-(e)s, -er) m grave; **g~en** ['graːbən] (unreg) vt to dig; ~**en** (-s, -) m ditch; (MIL) trench; ~**stein** m gravestone

Grad [graːt] (-(e)s, -e) m degree

Graf [graːf] (-en, -en) m count, earl

Grafiker(in) ▲ ['graːfɪkər(ɪn)] (-s, -) m(f) graphic designer

grafisch ▲ ['graːfɪʃ] adj graphic

Gram [graːm] (-(e)s) m grief, sorrow

grämen ['grɛːmən] vr to grieve

Gramm [gram] (-s, -e) nt gram(me)

Grammatik [gra'matɪk] f grammar

Granat [gra'naːt] (-(e)s, -e) m (Stein) garnet

Granate f (MIL) shell; (Handgranate) grenade

Granit [gra'niːt] (-s, -e) m granite

Gras [graːs] (-es, -er) nt grass; **g~en** ['graːzən] vi to graze; ~**halm** m blade of grass

grassieren [gra'siːrən] vi to be rampant, to rage

grässlich ▲ ['grɛslɪç] adj horrible

Grat [graːt] (-(e)s, -e) m ridge

Gräte ['grɛːtə] f fishbone

gratis ['graːtɪs] adj, adv free (of charge);

G~probe f free sample

Gratulation [gratulatsi'oːn] f congratulation(s)

gratulieren [gratu'liːrən] vi: **jdm** ~ **(zu etw)** to congratulate sb (on sth); **(ich) gratuliere!** congratulations!

grau [graʊ] adj grey

Gräuel ▲ ['grɔʏəl] (-s, -) m horror, revulsion; **etw ist jdm ein** ~ sb loathes sth

Grauen (-s) nt horror; **g~** vi unpers: **es graut jdm vor etw** sb dreads sth, sb is afraid of sth ♦ vr: **sich vor** ~ to dread, to have a horror of; **g~haft** adj horrible

grauhaarig adj grey-haired

gräulich ▲ ['grɔʏlɪç] adj horrible

grausam ['graʊzaːm] adj cruel; **G~keit** f cruelty

Grausen ['graʊzən] (-s) nt horror; **g~** vb = **grauen**

gravieren [gra'viːrən] vt to engrave; ~**d** adj grave

graziös [gratsi'øːs] adj graceful

greifbar adj tangible, concrete; **in ~er Nähe** within reach

greifen ['graɪfən] (unreg) vt to seize; to grip; **nach etw** ~ to reach for sth; **um sich** ~ (fig) to spread; **zu etw** ~ (fig) to turn to sth

Greis [graɪs] (-es, -e) m old man; **g~enhaft** adj senile; ~**in** f old woman

grell [grɛl] adj harsh

Grenz- ['grɛnts] zW: ~**beamte(r)** m frontier official; ~**e** f boundary; (Staatsgrenze) frontier; (Schranke) limit; **g~en** vi: **g~en (an** +akk) to border (on); **g~enlos** adj boundless; ~**fall** m borderline case; ~**kontrolle** f border control; ~**übergang** m frontier crossing

Greuel △ ['grɔʏəl] (-s, -) m siehe **Gräuel**

greulich △ adj siehe **gräulich**

Griech- ['griːç] zW: ~**e** (-n, -n) m Greek; ~**enland** nt Greece; ~**in** f Greek; **g~isch** adj Greek

griesgrämig ['griːsgrɛːmɪç] adj grumpy

Grieß [griːs] (-es, -e) m (KOCH) semolina

Griff [grɪf] (-(e)s, -e) m grip; (Vorrichtung) handle; **g~bereit** adj handy

Grill [grɪl] m grill; ~**e** f cricket; **g~en** vt to

grill; **~fest** nt barbecue party

Grimasse [grɪˈmasə] f grimace

grimmig [ˈgrɪmɪç] adj furious; (*heftig*) fierce, severe

grinsen [ˈgrɪnzən] vi to grin

Grippe [ˈgrɪpə] f influenza, flu

grob [groːp] adj coarse, gross; (*Fehler, Verstoß*) gross; **G~heit** f coarseness; coarse expression

grölen [ˈgrøːlən] (*pej*) vt to bawl, to bellow

Groll [grɔl] **(-(e)s)** m resentment; **g~en** vi (*Donner*) to rumble; **g~en (mit** od **+dat)** to bear ill will (towards)

groß [groːs] adj big, large; (*hoch*) tall; (*fig*) great ♦ adv greatly; **im G~en und Ganzen** on the whole; **bei jdm ~ geschrieben werden** to be high on sb's list of priorities; **~artig** adj great, splendid; **G~aufnahme** f (*CINE*) close-up; **G~britannien** nt Great Britain

Größe [ˈgrøːsə] f size; (*Höhe*) height; (*fig*) greatness

Groß- zW: **~einkauf** m bulk purchase; **~eltern** pl grandparents; **g~enteils** adv mostly; **~format** nt large size; **~handel** m wholesale trade; **~händler** m wholesaler; **~macht** f great power; **~mutter** f grandmother; **~rechner** m mainframe (computer); **g~schreiben** (*unreg*) vt (*Wort*) to write in block capitals; *siehe* **groß**; **g~spurig** adj pompous; **~stadt** f city, large town

größte(r, s) [ˈgrøːstə(r, s)] adj superl von **groß**; **größtenteils** adv for the most part

Groß- zW: **g~tun** (*unreg*) vi to boast; **~vater** m grandfather; **g~ziehen** (*unreg*) vt to raise; **g~zügig** adj generous; (*Planung*) on a large scale

grotesk [groˈtɛsk] adj grotesque

Grotte [ˈgrɔtə] f grotto

Grübchen [ˈgryːpçən] nt dimple

Grube [ˈgruːbə] f pit; mine

grübeln [ˈgryːbəln] vi to brood

Gruft [gruft] **(-, ¨e)** f tomb, vault

grün [gryːn] adj green; **der ~e Punkt** green spot symbol on recyclable packaging

grüner Punkt

*The **grüner Punkt** is a green spot which appears on packaging that should be kept separate from normal household refuse to be recycled through the recycling company, **DSD** (Duales System Deutschland). The recycling is financed by licences bought by the packaging manufacturer from **DSD**. These costs are often passed on to the consumer.*

Grünanlage f park

Grund [grunt] **(-(e)s, ¨e)** m ground; (*von See, Gefäß*) bottom; (*fig*) reason; **im ~e genommen** basically; *siehe* **aufgrund**; **~ausbildung** f basic training; **~besitz** m land(ed property), real estate; **~buch** nt land register

gründen [ˈgrʏndən] vt to found ♦ vr: **sich ~ (auf +dat)** to be based (on); **~ auf +akk** to base on; **Gründer (-s, -)** m founder

Grund- zW: **~gebühr** f basic charge; **~gesetz** nt constitution; **~lage** f foundation; **g~legend** adj fundamental

gründlich adj thorough

Grund- zW: **g~los** adj groundless; **~regel** f basic rule; **~riss** ▲ m plan; (*fig*) outline; **~satz** m principle; **g~sätzlich** adj fundamental; (*Frage*) of principle ♦ adv fundamentally; (*prinzipiell*) on principle; **~schule** f elementary school; **~stein** m foundation stone; **~stück** nt estate; plot

Grundwasser nt ground water

Grundschule

*The **Grundschule** is a primary school which children attend for 4 years from the age of 6 to 10. There are no formal examinations in the **Grundschule** but parents receive a report on their child's progress twice a year. Many children attend a **Kindergarten** from 3-6 years before going to the **Grundschule**, though no formal instruction takes place in the **Kindergarten**.*

Grünstreifen m central reservation

grunzen ['grʊntsən] vi to grunt

Gruppe ['grʊpə] f group; **~nermäßigung** f group reduction; **g~nweise** adv in groups

gruppieren [grʊ'piːrən] vt, vr to group

gruselig adj creepy

gruseln ['gruːzəln] vi unpers: **es gruselt jdm vor etw** sth gives sb the creeps ♦ vr to have the creeps

Gruß [gruːs] (-es, ⁺e) m greeting; (MIL) salute; **viele Grüße** best wishes; **mit freundlichen Grüßen** yours sincerely; **Grüße an** +akk regards to

grüßen ['gryːsən] vt to greet; (MIL) to salute; **jdn von jdm ~** to give sb sb's regards; **jdn ~ lassen** to send sb one's regards

gucken ['gʊkən] vi to look

gültig ['gʏltɪç] adj valid; **G~keit** f validity

Gummi ['gʊmi] (-s, -s) nt od m rubber; (~harze) gum; **~band** nt rubber od elastic band; (Hosenband) elastic; **~bärchen** nt ≈ jelly baby (BRIT); **~baum** m rubber plant; **g~eren** [gʊ'miːrən] vt to gum; **~stiefel** m rubber boot

günstig ['gʏnstɪç] adj convenient; (Gelegenheit) favourable; **das habe ich ~ bekommen** it was a bargain

Gurgel ['gʊrgəl] (-, -n) f throat; **g~n** vi to gurgle; (im Mund) to gargle

Gurke ['gʊrkə] f cucumber; **saure ~** pickled cucumber, gherkin

Gurt [gʊrt] (-(e)s, -e) m belt

Gürtel ['gʏrtəl] (-s, -) m belt; (GEOG) zone; **~reifen** m radial tyre

GUS f abk (= Gemeinschaft unabhängiger Staaten) CIS

Guss ▲ [gʊs] (-es, ⁺e) m casting; (Regenguss) downpour; (KOCH) glazing; **~eisen** nt cast iron

SCHLÜSSELWORT

gut adj good; **alles Gute** all the best; **also gut** all right then

♦ adv well; **gut gehen** to work, to come off; **es geht jdm gut** sb's doing fine; **gut gemeint** well meant; **gut schmecken** to

taste good; **jdm gut tun** to do sb good; **gut, aber ...** OK, but ...; **(na) gut, ich komme** all right, I'll come; **gut drei Stunden** a good three hours; **das kann gut sein** that may well be; **lass es gut sein** that'll do

Gut [guːt] (-(e)s, ⁺er) nt (Besitz) possession; **Güter** pl (Waren) goods; **~achten** (-s, -) nt (expert) opinion; **~achter** (-s, -) m expert; **g~artig** adj good-natured; (MED) benign; **g~bürgerlich** adj (Küche) (good) plain; **~dünken** nt: **nach ~dünken** at one's discretion

Güte ['gyːtə] f goodness, kindness; (Qualität) quality

Güter- zW: **~abfertigung** f (EISENB) goods office; **~bahnhof** m goods station; **~wagen** m goods waggon (BRIT), freight car (US); **~zug** m goods train (BRIT), freight train (US)

Gütezeichen nt quality mark; ≈ kite mark

gut- zW: **~gehen** △ (unreg) vi unpers siehe **gut**; **~gemeint** △ adj siehe **gut**; **~gläubig** adj trusting; **G~haben** (-s) nt credit; **~heißen** (unreg) vt to approve (of)

gütig ['gyːtɪç] adj kind

Gut- zW: **g~mütig** adj good-natured; **~schein** m voucher; **g~schreiben** (unreg) vt to credit; **~schrift** f (Betrag) credit; **g~tun** △ (unreg) vi siehe **gut**; **g~willig** adj willing

Gymnasium [gʏm'naːziʊm] nt grammar school (BRIT), high school (US)

Gymnasium

ⓘ The **Gymnasium** is a selective secondary school. After nine years of study pupils sit the **Abitur** so they can go on to higher education. Pupils who successfully complete six years at a **Gymnasium** automatically gain the **mittlere Reife**.

Gymnastik [gʏm'nastɪk] f exercises pl, keep fit

H, h

Haag [ha:k] *m*: **Den ~** the Hague

Haar [ha:r] (-(e)s, -e) *nt* hair; **um ein ~** nearly; **an den ~en herbeigezogen** (*umg*: *Vergleich*) very far-fetched; **~bürste** *f* hairbrush; **h~en** *vi*, *vr* to lose hair; **~esbreite** *f*: **um ~esbreite** by a hair's-breadth; **~festiger** (-s, -) *m* (hair) setting lotion; **h~genau** *adv* precisely; **h~ig** *adj* hairy; (*fig*) nasty; **~klammer** *f* hairgrip; **~nadel** *f* hairpin; **h~scharf** *adv* (*beobachten*) very sharply; (*daneben*) by a hair's breadth; **~schnitt** *m* haircut; **~spange** *f* hair slide; **h~sträubend** *adj* hair-raising; **~teil** *nt* hairpiece; **~waschmittel** *nt* shampoo

Habe ['ha:bə] (-) *f* property

haben ['ha:bən] (*unreg*) *vt*, *vb aux* to have; **Hunger / Angst ~** to be hungry/afraid; **woher hast du das?** where did you get that from?; **was hast du denn?** what's the matter (with you)?; **du hast zu schweigen** you're to be quiet; **ich hätte gern** I would like; **H~** (-s, -) *nt* credit

Habgier *f* avarice; **h~ig** *adj* avaricious

Habicht ['ha:bıçt] (-s, -e) *m* hawk

Habseligkeiten ['ha:pze:lıçkaıtən] *pl* belongings

Hachse ['haksə] *f* (*KOCH*) knuckle

Hacke ['hakə] *f* hoe; (*Ferse*) heel; **h~n** *vt* to hack, to chop; (*Erde*) to hoe

Hackfleisch *nt* mince, minced meat

Hafen ['ha:fən] (-s, ⁺) *m* harbour, port; **~arbeiter** *m* docker; **~rundfahrt** *f* boat trip round the harbour; **~stadt** *f* port

Hafer ['ha:fər] (-s, -) *m* oats *pl*; **~flocken** *pl* rolled oats; **~schleim** *m* gruel

Haft [haft] (-) *f* custody; **h~bar** *adj* liable, responsible; **~befehl** *m* warrant (for arrest); **h~en** *vi* to stick, to cling; **h~en für** to be liable *od* responsible for; **h~en bleiben (an** +*dat*) to stick (to); **Häftling** *m* prisoner; **~pflicht** *f* liability; **~pflichtversicherung** *f* (*AUT*) third party

insurance; **~schalen** *pl* contact lenses; **~ung** *f* liability; **~ungsbeschränkung** *f* limitation of liability

Hagebutte ['ha:gəbutə] *f* rose hip

Hagel ['ha:gəl] (-s) *m* hail; **h~n** *vi unpers* to hail

hager ['ha:gər] *adj* gaunt

Hahn [ha:n] (-(e)s, ⁺e) *m* cock; (*Wasserhahn*) tap, faucet (*US*)

Hähnchen ['hɛːnçən] *nt* cockerel; (*KOCH*) chicken

Hai(fisch) ['haı(fıʃ)] (-(e)s, -e) *m* shark

häkeln ['hɛːkəln] *vt* to crochet

Haken ['ha:kən] (-s, -) *m* hook; (*fig*) catch; **~kreuz** *nt* swastika; **~nase** *f* hooked nose

halb [halp] *adj* half; **~ eins** half past twelve; **~ offen** half-open; **ein ~es Dutzend** half a dozen; **H~dunkel** *nt* semi-darkness

halber ['halbər] *präp* +*gen* (*wegen*) on account of; (*für*) for the sake of

Halb- *zW*: **~heit** *f* half-measure; **h~ieren** *vt* to halve; **~insel** *f* peninsula; **~jahr** *nt* six months; (*auch*: *COMM*) half-year; **h~jährlich** *adj* half-yearly; **~kreis** *m* semicircle; **~leiter** *m* semiconductor; **~mond** *m* half-moon; (*fig*) crescent; **~pension** *f* half-board; **~schuh** *m* shoe; **h~tags** *adv*: **h~tags arbeiten** to work part-time, to work mornings/afternoons; **h~wegs** *adv* halfway; **h~wegs besser** more or less better; **~zeit** *f* (*SPORT*) half; (*Pause*) half-time

Halde ['haldə] *f* (*Kohlen*) heap

half [half] *vb siehe* **helfen**

Hälfte ['hɛlftə] *f* half

Halfter ['halftər] (-s, -) *m od nt* (*für Tiere*) halter

Halle ['halə] *f* hall; (*AVIAT*) hangar; **h~n** *vi* to echo, to resound; **~nbad** *nt* indoor swimming pool

hallo [ha'lo:] *excl* hello

Halluzination [halutsinatsi'o:n] *f* hallucination

Halm ['halm] (-(e)s, -e) *m* blade; stalk

Halogenlampe [halo'ge:nlampə] *f* halogen lamp

Rechtschreibreform: ▲ *neue Schreibung* △ *alte Schreibung (auslaufend)*

Hals [hals] (**-es**, **ᵘe**) m neck; (*Kehle*) throat; ~ **über Kopf** in a rush; ~**band** nt (*von Hund*) collar; ~**kette** f necklace; ~~**Nasen-Ohren-Arzt** m ear, nose and throat specialist; ~**schmerzen** pl sore throat sg; ~**tuch** nt scarf

Halt [halt] (**-(e)s**, **-e**) m stop; (*fester* ~) hold; (*innerer* ~) stability; ~ **od h~!** stop!, halt!; ~ **machen** to stop; **h~bar** adj durable; (*Lebensmittel*) non-perishable; (*MIL, fig*) tenable; ~**barkeit** f durability; (non-)perishability

halten ['haltən] (*unreg*) vt to keep; (*festhalten*) to hold ♦ vi to hold; (*frisch bleiben*) to keep; (*stoppen*) to stop ♦ vr (*frisch bleiben*) to keep; (*sich behaupten*) to hold out; ~ **für** to regard as; ~ **von** to think of; **an sich** ~ to restrain o.s.; **sich rechts/links** ~ to keep to the right/left

Halte- zW: ~**stelle** f stop; ~**verbot** nt: **hier ist ~verbot** there's no waiting here

Halt- zW: **h~los** adj unstable; **h~machen** △ vi siehe **Halt**; ~**ung** f posture; (*fig*) attitude; (*Selbstbeherrschung*) composure

Halunke [ha'luŋkə] (**-n**, **-n**) m rascal

hämisch ['hɛːmɪʃ] adj malicious

Hammel ['haməl] (**-s**, **ᵘ od -**) m wether; ~**fleisch** nt mutton

Hammer ['hamər] (**-s**, **ᵘ**) m hammer

hämmern ['hɛmərn] vt, vi to hammer

Hämorr(ho)iden [hɛmɔro'iːdən, hɛmɔ'riːdn] pl haemorrhoids

Hamster ['hamstər] (**-s**, **-**) m hamster; ~**ei** [-'raɪ] f hoarding; **h~n** vi to hoard

Hand [hant] (**-**, **ᵘe**) f hand; ~**arbeit** f manual work; (*Nadelarbeit*) needlework; ~**ball** m (*SPORT*) handball; ~**bremse** f handbrake; ~**buch** nt handbook, manual

Händedruck ['hɛndədrʊk] m handshake

Handel ['handəl] (**-s**) m trade; (*Geschäft*) transaction

Handeln ['handəln] (**-s**) nt action

handeln vi to trade; (*agieren*) to act ♦ vr unpers: **sich** ~ **um** to be a question of, to be about; ~ **von** to be about

Handels- zW: ~**bilanz** f balance of trade;

~**kammer** f chamber of commerce; ~**reisende(r)** m commercial traveller; ~**schule** f business school; **h~üblich** adj customary; (*Preis*) going attrib; ~**vertreter** m sales representative

Hand- zW: ~**feger** (**-s**, **-**) m hand brush; **h~fest** adj hefty; **h~gearbeitet** adj handmade; ~**gelenk** nt wrist; ~**gemenge** nt scuffle; ~**gepäck** nt hand luggage; **h~geschrieben** adj handwritten; **h~greiflich** adj palpable; **h~greiflich werden** to become violent; ~**griff** m flick of the wrist; **h~haben** vt insep to handle

Händler ['hɛndlər] (**-s**, **-**) m trader, dealer

handlich ['hantlɪç] adj handy

Handlung ['handlʊŋ] f act(ion); (*in Buch*) plot; (*Geschäft*) shop

Hand- zW: ~**schelle** f handcuff; ~**schrift** f handwriting; (*Text*) manuscript; ~**schuh** m glove; ~**stand** m (*SPORT*) handstand; ~**tasche** f handbag; ~**tuch** nt towel; ~**umdrehen** nt: **im ~umdrehen** in the twinkling of an eye; ~**werk** nt trade, craft; ~**werker** (**-s**, **-**) m craftsman, artisan; ~**werkzeug** nt tools pl

Handy ['hændɪ] (**-s**, **-s**) nt mobile (telephone)

Hanf [hanf] (**-(e)s**) m hemp

Hang [haŋ] (**-(e)s**, **ᵘe**) m inclination; (*Abhang*) slope

Hänge- ['hɛŋə] in zW hanging; ~**brücke** f suspension bridge; ~**matte** f hammock

hängen ['hɛŋən] (*unreg*) vi to hang ♦ vt: **etw (an etw** akk) ~ to hang sth (on sth); ~ **an** +dat (*fig*) to be attached to; **sich** ~ **an** +akk to hang on to, to cling to; ~ **bleiben** to be caught; (*fig*) to remain, to stick; ~ **bleiben an** +dat to catch od get caught on; ~ **lassen** (*vergessen*) to leave; **den Kopf ~ lassen** to get downhearted

Hannover [ha'noːfər] (**-s**) nt Hanover

hänseln ['hɛnzəln] vt to tease

Hansestadt ['hanzəʃtat] f Hanse town

hantieren [han'tiːrən] vi to work, to be busy; **mit etw** ~ to handle sth

hapern ['haːpərn] vi unpers: **es hapert an etw** dat there is a lack of sth

Happen ['hapən] **(-s, -)** *m* mouthful

Harfe ['harfə] *f* harp

Harke ['harkə] *f* rake; **h~n** *vt, vi* to rake

harmlos ['harmlo:s] *adj* harmless; **H~igkeit** *f* harmlessness

Harmonie [harmo'ni:] *f* harmony; **h~ren** *vi* to harmonize

harmonisch [har'mo:nɪʃ] *adj* harmonious

Harn ['harn] **(-(e)s, -e)** *m* urine; **~blase** *f* bladder

Harpune [har'pu:nə] *f* harpoon

harren ['harən] *vi:* **~ (auf** +*akk*) to wait (for)

hart [hart] *adj* hard; (*fig*) harsh; **~ gekocht** hard-boiled

Härte ['hɛrtə] *f* hardness; (*fig*) harshness

hart- *zW:* **~herzig** *adj* hard-hearted; **~näckig** *adj* stubborn

Harz [ha:rts] **(-es, -e)** *nt* resin

Haschee [ha'ʃe:] **(-s, -s)** *nt* hash

Haschisch ['haʃɪʃ] **(-)** *nt* hashish

Hase ['ha:zə] **(-n, -n)** *m* hare

Haselnuss ▲ ['ha:zəlnʊs] *f* hazelnut

Hasenscharte *f* harelip

Hass [has] **(-es)** *m* hate, hatred

hassen ['hasən] *vt* to hate

hässlich ▲ ['hɛslɪç] *adj* ugly; (*gemein*) nasty; **H~keit** *f* ugliness; nastiness

Hast [hast] *f* haste

hast *vb siehe* **haben**

hasten *vi* to rush

hastig *adj* hasty

hat [hat] *vb siehe* **haben**

hatte *etc* ['hatə] *vb siehe* **haben**

Haube ['haubə] *f* hood; (*Mütze*) cap; (*AUT*) bonnet, hood (*US*)

Hauch [haux] **(-(e)s, -e)** *m* breath; (*Lufthauch*) breeze; (*fig*) trace; **h~dünn** *adj* extremely thin

Haue ['hauə] *f* hoe, pick; (*umg*) hiding; **h~n** (*unreg*) *vt* to hew, to cut; (*umg*) to thrash

Haufen ['haufən] **(-s, -)** *m* heap; (*Leute*) crowd; **ein ~ (x)** (*umg*) loads *od* a lot (of x); **auf einem ~** in one heap

häufen ['hɔyfən] *vt* to pile up ♦ *vr* to accumulate

haufenweise *adv* in heaps; in droves; **etw ~ haben** to have piles of sth

häufig ['hɔyfɪç] *adj* frequent ♦ *adv* frequently; **H~keit** *f* frequency

Haupt [haupt] **(-(e)s, Häupter)** *nt* head; (*Oberhaupt*) chief ♦ *in zW* main; **~bahnhof** *m* central station; **h~beruflich** *adv* as one's main occupation; **~darsteller(in)** *m(f)* leading actor (actress); **~fach** *nt* (*SCH, UNIV*) main subject, major (*US*); **~gericht** *nt* (*KOCH*) main course

Häuptling ['hɔyptlɪŋ] *m* chief(tain)

Haupt- *zW:* **~mann** (*pl* **-leute**) *m* (*MIL*) captain; **~person** *f* central figure; **~quartier** *nt* headquarters *pl*; **~rolle** *f* leading part; **~sache** *f* main thing; **h~sächlich** *adj* chief ♦ *adv* chiefly; **~saison** *f* high season, peak season; **~schule** *f* ≈ secondary school; **~stadt** *f* capital; **~straße** *f* main street; **~verkehrszeit** *f* rush-hour, peak traffic hours *pl*

Hauptschule

i The **Hauptschule** *is a non-selective school which pupils attend after the* **Grundschule**. *They complete five years of study and most go on to do some vocational training.*

Haus [haus] **(-es, Häuser)** *nt* house; **~ halten** (*sparen*) to economize; **nach ~e** home; **zu ~e** at home; **~apotheke** *f* medicine cabinet; **~arbeit** *f* housework; (*SCH*) homework; **~arzt** *m* family doctor; **~aufgabe** *f* (*SCH*) homework; **~besitzer(in)** *m(f)* house owner; **~besuch** *m* (*von Arzt*) house call; **~durchsuchung** *f* police raid; **h~eigen** *adj* belonging to a/the hotel/firm

Häuser- ['hɔyzər] *zW:* **~block** *m* block (of houses); **~makler** *m* estate agent (*BRIT*), real estate agent (*US*)

Haus- *zW:* **~flur** *m* hallway; **~frau** *f* housewife; **h~gemacht** *adj* home-made; **~halt** *m* household; (*POL*) budget; **h~halten** (*unreg*) *vi* △ *siehe* **Haus**; **~hälterin** *f* housekeeper; **~haltsgeld** *nt* housekeeping (money); **~haltsgerät** *nt*

domestic appliance; **~herr** m host; (*Vermieter*) landlord; **h~hoch** adv: **h~hoch verlieren** to lose by a mile

hausieren [hau'ziːrən] vi to peddle

Hausierer (-s, -) m pedlar (*BRIT*), peddler (*US*)

häuslich ['hɔyslɪç] adj domestic

Haus- zW: **~meister** m caretaker, janitor; **~nummer** f street number; **~ordnung** f house rules pl; **~putz** m house cleaning; **~schlüssel** m front door key; **~schuh** m slipper; **~tier** nt pet; **~tür** f front door; **~wirt** m landlord; **~wirtschaft** f domestic science; **~zelt** nt frame tent

Haut [haut] (-, Häute) f skin; (*Tierhaut*) hide; **~creme** f skin cream; **h~eng** adj skin-tight; **~farbe** f complexion; **~krebs** m skin cancer

Haxe ['haksə] f = **Hachse**

Hbf. abk = **Hauptbahnhof**

Hebamme ['heːplamə] f midwife

Hebel ['heːbəl] (-s, -) m lever

heben ['heːbən] (*unreg*) vt to raise, to lift

Hecht [hɛçt] (-(e)s, -e) m pike

Heck [hɛk] (-(e)s, -e) nt stern; (*von Auto*) rear

Hecke ['hɛkə] f hedge

Heckenschütze m sniper

Heckscheibe f rear window

Heer [heːr] (-(e)s, -e) nt army

Hefe ['heːfə] f yeast

Heft ['hɛft] (-(e)s, -e) nt exercise book; (*Zeitschrift*) number; (*von Messer*) haft; **h~en** vt: **h~en (an** +akk) to fasten (to); (*nähen*) to tack ((on) to); **etw an etw** akk **h~en** to fasten sth to sth; **~er** (-s, -) m folder

heftig adj fierce, violent; **H~keit** f fierceness, violence

Heft- zW: **~klammer** f paper clip; **~pflaster** nt sticking plaster; **~zwecke** f drawing pin

hegen ['heːgən] vt (*Wild, Bäume*) to care for, to tend; (*fig, geh: empfinden: Wunsch*) to cherish; (: *Misstrauen*) to feel

Hehl [heːl] m od nt: **kein(en) ~ aus etw machen** to make no secret of sth; **~er** (-s, -) m receiver (of stolen goods), fence

Heide[1] ['haɪdə] (-n, -n) m heathen, pagan

Heide[2] ['haɪdə] f heath, moor; **~kraut** nt heather

Heidelbeere f bilberry

Heidentum nt paganism

Heidin f heathen, pagan

heikel ['haɪkəl] adj awkward, thorny

Heil [haɪl] (-(e)s) nt well-being; (*Seelenheil*) salvation; **h~** adj in one piece, intact; **~and** (-(e)s, -e) m saviour; **h~bar** adj curable; **h~en** vt to cure ♦ vi to heal; **h~froh** adj very relieved

heilig ['haɪlɪç] adj holy; **~ sprechen** to canonize; **H~abend** m Christmas Eve; **H~e(r)** f(m) saint; **~en** vt to sanctify, to hallow; **H~enschein** m halo; **H~keit** f holiness; **H~tum** nt shrine; (*Gegenstand*) relic

Heil- zW: **h~los** adj unholy; (*fig*) hopeless; **~mittel** nt remedy; **~praktiker(in)** m(f) non-medical practitioner; **h~sam** adj (*fig*) salutary; **~sarmee** f Salvation Army; **~ung** f cure

Heim [haɪm] (-(e)s, -e) nt home; **h~** adv home

Heimat ['haɪmaːt] (-, -en) f home (town/country etc); **~land** nt homeland; **h~lich** adj native, home attrib; (*Gefühle*) nostalgic; **h~los** adj homeless; **~ort** m home town/area

Heim- zW: **~computer** m home computer; **h~fahren** (*unreg*) vi to drive home; **~fahrt** f journey home; **h~gehen** (*unreg*) vi to go home; (*sterben*) to pass away; **h~isch** adj (*gebürtig*) native; **sich ~isch fühlen** to feel at home; **~kehr** (-, -en) f homecoming; **h~kehren** vi to return home; **h~lich** adj secret; **~lichkeit** f secrecy; **~reise** f journey home; **~spiel** nt (*SPORT*) home game; **h~suchen** vt to afflict; (*Geist*) to haunt; **~trainer** m exercise bike; **h~tückisch** adj malicious; **~weg** m way home; **~weh** nt homesickness; **~werker** (-s, -) m handyman; **h~zahlen** vt: **jdm etw h~zahlen** to pay sb back for sth

Heirat ['haɪraːt] (-, -en) f marriage; **h~en** vt

to marry ♦ *vi* to marry, to get married ♦ *vr* to get married; **~santrag** *m* proposal

heiser ['haɪzər] *adj* hoarse; **H~keit** *f* hoarseness

heiß [haɪs] *adj* hot; **~e(s) Eisen** (*umg*) hot potato; **~blütig** *adj* hot-blooded

heißen ['haɪsən] (*unreg*) *vi* to be called; (*bedeuten*) to mean ♦ *vt* to command; (*nennen*) to name ♦ *vi unpers*: **es heißt** it says; it is said; **das heißt** that is (to say)

Heiß- *zW*: **~hunger** *m* ravenous hunger; **h~laufen** (*unreg*) *vi, vr* to overheat

heiter ['haɪtər] *adj* cheerful; (*Wetter*) bright; **H~keit** *f* cheerfulness; (*Belustigung*) amusement

Heiz- *zW*: **h~bar** *adj* heated; (*Raum*) with heating; **h~en** *vt* to heat; **~körper** *m* radiator; **~öl** *nt* fuel oil; **~sonne** *f* electric fire; **~ung** *f* heating

hektisch ['hɛktɪʃ] *adj* hectic

Held [hɛlt] **(-en, -en)** *m* hero; **h~enhaft** *adj* heroic; **~in** *f* heroine

helfen ['hɛlfən] (*unreg*) *vi* to help; (*nützen*) to be of use ♦ *vb unpers*: **es hilft nichts, du musst ...** it's no use, you'll have to ...; **jdm (bei etw) ~** to help sb (with sth); **sich** *dat* **zu ~ wissen** to be resourceful

Helfer (-s, -) *m* helper, assistant; **~shelfer** *m* accomplice

hell [hɛl] *adj* clear, bright; (*Farbe, Bier*) light; **~blau** *adj* light blue; **~blond** *adj* ash blond; **H~e (-)** *f* clearness, brightness; **~hörig** *adj* (*Wand*) paper-thin; **~hörig werden** (*fig*) to prick up one's ears; **H~seher** *m* clairvoyant; **~wach** *adj* wide-awake

Helm ['hɛlm] **(-(e)s, -e)** *m* (*auf Kopf*) helmet

Hemd [hɛmt] **(-(e)s, -en)** *nt* shirt; (*Unterhemd*) vest; **~bluse** *f* blouse

hemmen ['hɛmən] *vt* to check, to hold up; **gehemmt sein** to be inhibited; **Hemmung** *f* check; (*PSYCH*) inhibition; **hemmungslos** *adj* unrestrained, without restraint

Hengst [hɛŋst] **(-es, -e)** *m* stallion

Henkel ['hɛŋkəl] **(-s, -)** *m* handle

Henker (-s, -) *m* hangman

Henne ['hɛnə] *f* hen

SCHLÜSSELWORT

her [heːr] *adv* **1** (*Richtung*): **komm her zu mir** come here (to me); **von England her** from England; **von weit her** from a long way away; **her damit!** hand it over!; **wo hat er das her?** where did he get that from?

2 (*Blickpunkt*): **von der Form her** as far as the form is concerned

3 (*zeitlich*): **das ist 5 Jahre her** that was 5 years ago; **wo bist du her?** where do you come from?; **ich kenne ihn von früher her** I know him from before

herab [hɛˈrap] *adv* down(ward(s)); **~hängen** (*unreg*) *vi* to hang down; **~lassen** (*unreg*) *vt* to let down ♦ *vr* to condescend; **~lassend** *adj* condescending; **~setzen** *vt* to lower, to reduce; (*fig*) to belittle, to disparage

heran [hɛˈran] *adv*: **näher ~!** come up closer!; **~ zu mir!** come up to me!; **~bringen** (*unreg*) *vt*: **~bringen (an +***akk*) to bring up (to); **~fahren** (*unreg*) *vi*: **~fahren (an +***akk*) to drive up (to); **~kommen** (*unreg*) *vi*: **(an jdn/etw) ~kommen** to approach (sb/sth), to come near (to sb/ sth); **~machen** *vr*: **sich an jdn ~machen** to make up to sb; **~treten** (*unreg*) *vi*: **mit etw an jdn ~treten** to approach sb with sth; **~wachsen** (*unreg*) *vi* to grow up; **~ziehen** (*unreg*) *vt* to pull nearer; (*aufziehen*) to raise; (*ausbilden*) to train; **jdn zu etw ~ziehen** to call upon sb to help in sth

herauf [hɛˈrauf] *adv* up(ward(s)), up here; **~beschwören** (*unreg*) *vt* to conjure up, to evoke; **~bringen** (*unreg*) *vt* to bring up; **~setzen** *vt* (*Preise, Miete*) to raise, put up

heraus [hɛˈraus] *adv* out; **~bekommen** (*unreg*) *vt* to get out; (*fig*) to find *od* figure out; **~bringen** (*unreg*) *vt* to bring out; (*Geheimnis*) to elicit; **~finden** (*unreg*) *vt* to find out; **~fordern** *vt* to challenge; **H~forderung** *f* challenge; provocation; **~geben** (*unreg*) *vt* to hand over, to surrender; (*zurückgeben*) to give back; (*Buch*) to edit; (*veröffentlichen*) to publish; **H~geber** (**-s, -**) *m* editor; (*Verleger*) publisher; **~gehen** (*unreg*) *vi*: **aus sich ~gehen** to come out of one's shell; **~halten** (*unreg*) *vr*: **sich aus etw ~halten** to keep out of sth; **~hängen¹** *vt* to hang out; **~hängen²** (*unreg*) *vi* to hang up; **~holen** *vt*: **~holen (aus)** to get out (of); **~kommen** (*unreg*) *vi* to come out; **dabei kommt nichts ~** nothing will come of it; **~nehmen** (*unreg*) *vt* to remove (from), take out (of); **sich** *dat* **etw ~nehmen** to take liberties; **~reißen** (*unreg*) *vt* to tear out; to pull out; **~rücken** *vt* (*Geld*) to fork out, to hand over; **mit etw ~rücken** (*fig*) to come out with sth; **~stellen** *vr*: **sich ~stellen (als)** to turn out (to be); **~suchen** *vt*: **sich** *dat* **jdn/etw ~suchen** to pick sb/sth out; to extract

herb [hɛrp] *adj* (slightly) bitter, acid; (*Wein*) dry; (*fig*: *schmerzlich*) bitter

herbei [hɛrˈbaɪ] *adv* (over) here; **~führen** *vt* to bring about; **~schaffen** *vt* to procure

herbemühen [ˈheːrbəmyːən] *vr* to take the trouble to come

Herberge [ˈhɛrbɛrɡə] *f* shelter; hostel, inn

Herbergsmutter *f* warden

Herbergsvater *m* warden

herbitten (*unreg*) *vt* to ask to come (here)

Herbst [hɛrpst] (**-(e)s, -e**) *m* autumn, fall (*US*); **h~lich** *adj* autumnal

Herd [heːrt] (**-(e)s, -e**) *m* cooker; (*fig, MED*) focus, centre

Herde [ˈheːrdə] *f* herd; (*Schafherde*) flock

herein [hɛˈraɪn] *adv* in (here), here; **~!** come in!; **~bitten** (*unreg*) *vt* to ask sb in; **~brechen** (*unreg*) *vi* to set in; **~bringen** (*unreg*) *vt* to bring in; **~fallen** (*unreg*) *vi* to be caught, to be taken in; **~fallen auf** +*akk* to fall for; **~kommen** (*unreg*) *vi* to come in; **~lassen** (*unreg*) *vt* to admit; **~legen** *vt*: **jdn ~legen** to take sb in; **~platzen** (*umg*) *vi* to burst in

Her- *zW*: **~fahrt** *f* journey here; **h~fallen** (*unreg*) *vi*: **h~fallen über** +*akk* to fall upon; **~gang** *m* course of events; **h~geben**

(*unreg*) *vt* to give, to hand (over); **sich zu etw h~geben** to lend one's name to sth; **h~gehen** (*unreg*) *vi*: **hinter jdm h~gehen** to follow sb; **es geht hoch h~** there are a lot of goings-on; **h~halten** (*unreg*) *vt* to hold out; **h~halten müssen** (*umg*) to have to suffer; **h~hören** *vi* to listen

Hering [ˈheːrɪŋ] (**-s, -e**) *m* herring

her- [heːr] *zW*: **~kommen** (*unreg*) *vi* to come; **komm mal ~!** come here!; **~kömmlich** *adj* traditional; **H~kunft** (**-, -künfte**) *f* origin; **H~kunftsland** *nt* country of origin; **H~kunftsort** *m* place of origin; **~laufen** (*unreg*) *vi*: **~laufen hinter** +*dat* to run after

hermetisch [hɛrˈmeːtɪʃ] *adj* hermetic ♦ *adv* hermetically

her'nach *adv* afterwards

Heroin [heroˈiːn] (**-s**) *nt* heroin

Herr [hɛr] *zW*: **~(e)n, -en**) *m* master; (*Mann*) gentleman; (*REL*) Lord; (*vor Namen*) Mr.; **mein ~!** sir!; **meine ~en!** gentlemen!

Herren- *zW*: **~haus** *nt* mansion; **~konfektion** *f* menswear; **h~los** *adj* ownerless; **~toilette** *f* men's toilet *od* restroom (*US*)

herrichten [ˈheːrrɪçtən] *vt* to prepare

Herr- *zW*: **~in** *f* mistress; **h~isch** *adj* domineering; **h~lich** *adj* marvellous, splendid; **~lichkeit** *f* splendour, magnificence; **~schaft** *f* power, rule; (**~ und ~in**) master and mistress; **meine ~schaften!** ladies and gentlemen!

herrschen [ˈhɛrʃən] *vi* to rule; (*bestehen*) to prevail, to be

Herrscher(in) (**-s, -**) *m(f)* ruler

her- *zW*: **~rühren** *vi* to arise, to originate; **~sagen** *vt* to recite; **~stellen** *vt* to make, to manufacture; **H~steller** (**-s, -**) *m* manufacturer; **H~stellung** *f* manufacture

herüber [heˈryːbər] *adv* over (here), across

herum [heˈrʊm] *adv* about, (a)round; **um etw ~** around sth; **~führen** *vt* to show around; **~gehen** (*unreg*) *vi* to walk about; **um etw ~gehen** to walk *od* go round sth; **~kommen** (*unreg*) *vi* (*um Kurve etc*) to come round, to turn (round); **~kriegen**

(*umg*) *vt* to bring *od* talk around; **~lungern** (*umg*) *vt* to hang about *od* around; **~sprechen** (*unreg*) *vr* to get around, to be spread; **~treiben** *vi, vr* to drift about; **~ziehen** *vi, vr* to wander about

herunter [hɛˈrʊntər] *adv* downward(s), down (there); **~gekommen** *adj* run-down; **~kommen** (*unreg*) *vi* to come down; (*fig*) to come down in the world; **~laden** *unreg vt* (COMPUT) to download; **~machen** *vt* to take down; (*schimpfen*) to have a go at

hervor [hɛrˈfoːr] *adv* out, forth; **~bringen** (*unreg*) *vt* to produce; (*Wort*) to utter; **~gehen** (*unreg*) *vi* to emerge, to result; **~heben** (*unreg*) *vt* to stress; (*als Kontrast*) to set off; **~ragend** *adj* (*fig*) excellent; **~rufen** (*unreg*) *vt* to cause, to give rise to; **~treten** (*unreg*) *vi* to come out (from behind/ between/below); (*Adern*) to be prominent

Herz [hɛrts] (**-ens, -en**) *nt* heart; (KARTEN) hearts *pl*; **~anfall** *m* heart attack; **~fehler** *m* heart defect; **h~haft** *adj* hearty

herziehen [ˈheːrtsiːən] (*unreg*) *vi*: **über jdn/ etw ~** (*umg*) to pull sb/sth to pieces (*inf*)

Herz- *zW*: **~infarkt** *m* heart attack; **~klopfen** *nt* palpitation; **h~lich** *adj* cordial; **h~lichen Glückwunsch** congratulations *pl*; **h~liche Grüße** best wishes; **h~los** *adj* heartless

Herzog [ˈhɛrtsoːk] (**-(e)s, ⁺e**) *m* duke; **~tum** *nt* duchy

Herz- *zW*: **~schlag** *m* heartbeat; (MED) heart attack; **~stillstand** *m* cardiac arrest; **h~zerreißend** *adj* heartrending

Hessen [ˈhɛsən] (**-s**) *nt* Hesse

hessisch *adj* Hessian

Hetze [ˈhɛtsə] *f* (*Eile*) rush; **h~n** *vt* to hunt; (*verfolgen*) to chase ♦ *vi* (*eilen*) to rush; **jdn/etw auf jdn/etw h~n** to set sb/sth on sb/sth; **h~n gegen** to stir up feeling against; **h~n zu** to agitate for

Heu [hɔy] (**-(e)s**) *nt* hay; **Geld wie ~** stacks of money

Heuch- [ˈhɔyç] *zW*: **~elei** [-əˈlaɪ] *f* hypocrisy; **h~eln** *vt* to pretend, to feign ♦ *vi* to be hypocritical; **~ler(in)** (**-s, -**) *m(f)* hypocrite; **h~lerisch** *adj* hypocritical

heulen [ˈhɔylən] *vi* to howl; to cry

Heurige(r) [ˈhɔyrɪɡə(r)] *m* new wine

Heu- *zW*: **~schnupfen** *m* hay fever; '**~schrecke** *f* grasshopper; locust

heute [ˈhɔytə] *adv* today; **~ Abend/früh** this evening/morning

heutig [ˈhɔytɪç] *adj* today's

heutzutage [ˈhɔyttsutaːɡə] *adv* nowadays

Hexe [ˈhɛksə] *f* witch; **h~n** *vi* to practise witchcraft; **ich kann doch nicht h~n** I can't work miracles; **~nschuss** ▲ *m* lumbago; **~'rei** *f* witchcraft

Hieb [hiːp] (**-(e)s, -e**) *m* blow; (*Wunde*) cut, gash; (*Stichelei*) cutting remark; **~e bekommen** to get a thrashing

hielt *etc* [hiːlt] *vb siehe* **halten**

hier [hiːr] *adv* here; **~ behalten** to keep here; **~ bleiben** to stay here; **~ lassen** to leave here; **~auf** *adv* thereupon; (*danach*) after that; **~bei** *adv* herewith, enclosed; **~durch** *adv* by this means; (*örtlich*) through here; **~her** *adv* this way, here; **~hin** *adv* here; **~mit** *adv* hereby; **~nach** *adv* hereafter; **~von** *adv* about this, hereof; **~zulande, ~ zu Lande** *adv* in this country

hiesig [ˈhiːzɪç] *adj* of this place, local

hieß *etc* [hiːs] *vb siehe* **heißen**

Hilfe [ˈhɪlfə] *f* help; aid; **erste ~** first aid; **~!** help!

Hilf- *zW*: **h~los** *adj* helpless; **~losigkeit** *f* helplessness; **h~reich** *adj* helpful

Hilfs- *zW*: **~arbeiter** *m* labourer; **h~bedürftig** *adj* needy; **h~bereit** *adj* ready to help; **~kraft** *f* assistant, helper

hilfst [hɪlfst] *vb siehe* **helfen**

Himbeere [ˈhɪmbeːrə] *f* raspberry

Himmel [ˈhɪməl] (**-s, -**) *m* sky; (REL, *auch fig*) heaven; **~bett** *nt* four-poster bed; **h~blau** *adj* sky-blue; **~fahrt** *f* Ascension; **~srichtung** *f* direction

himmlisch [ˈhɪmlɪʃ] *adj* heavenly

SCHLÜSSELWORT

hin [hɪn] *adv* **1** (*Richtung*): **hin und zurück** there and back; **hin und her** to and fro; **bis zur Mauer hin** up to the wall; **wo ist**

er hin? where has he gone?; **Geld hin, Geld her** money or no money

2 (auf ... hin): **auf meine Bitte hin** at my request; **auf seinen Rat hin** on the basis of his advice

3 : **mein Glück ist hin** my happiness has gone

hinab [hɪˈnap] adv down; **~gehen** (unreg) vi to go down; **~sehen** (unreg) vi to look down

hinauf [hɪˈnauf] adv up; **~arbeiten** vr to work one's way up; **~steigen** (unreg) vi to climb

hinaus [hɪˈnaus] adv out; **~gehen** (unreg) vi to go out; **~gehen über** +akk to exceed; **~laufen** (unreg) vi to run out; **~laufen auf** +akk to come to, to amount to; **~schieben** (unreg) vt to put off, to postpone; **~werfen** (unreg) vt (Gegenstand, Person) to throw out; **~wollen** vi to want to go out; **~wollen auf** +akk to drive at, to get at

Hinblick [ˈhɪnblɪk] m: **in** od **im ~ auf** +akk in view of

hinder- [ˈhɪndər] zW: **~lich** adj: **~lich sein** to be a hindrance od nuisance; **~n** vt to hinder, to hamper; **jdn an etw** dat **~n** to prevent sb from doing sth; **H~nis** (-ses, -se) nt obstacle; **H~nisrennen** nt steeplechase

hindeuten [ˈhɪndɔytən] vi: **~ auf** +akk to point to

hindurch [hɪnˈdʊrç] adv through; across; (zeitlich) through(out)

hinein [hɪˈnaɪn] adv in; **~fallen** (unreg) vi to fall in; **~fallen in** +akk to fall into; **~gehen** (unreg) vi to go in; **~gehen in** +akk to go into, to enter; **~geraten** (unreg) vi: **~geraten in** +akk to get into; **~passen** vi to fit in; **~passen in** +akk to fit into; **~steigern** vr to get worked up; **~versetzen** vr: **sich ~versetzen in** +akk to put o.s. in the position of; **~ziehen** (unreg) vt to pull in ♦ vi to go in

hin- [ˈhɪn] zW: **~fahren** (unreg) vi to go; to drive ♦ vt to take; to drive; **H~fahrt** f

journey there; **~fallen** (unreg) vi to fall (down); **~fällig** adj frail; (fig: ungültig) invalid; **H~flug** m outward flight; **H~gabe** f devotion; **~geben** (unreg) vr +dat to give o.s. up to, to devote o.s. to; **~gehen** (unreg) vi to go; (Zeit) to pass; **~halten** (unreg) vt to hold out; (warten lassen) to put off, to stall

hinken [ˈhɪŋkən] vi to limp; (Vergleich) to be unconvincing

hinkommen (unreg) vi (an Ort) to arrive

hin- [ˈhɪn] zW: **~legen** vt to put down ♦ vr to lie down; **~nehmen** (unreg) vt (fig) to put up with, to take; **H~reise** f journey out; **~reißen** (unreg) vt to carry away, to enrapture; **sich ~reißen lassen, etw zu tun** to get carried away and do sth; **~richten** vt to execute; **H~richtung** f execution; **~setzen** vt to put down ♦ vr to sit down; **~sichtlich** präp +gen with regard to; **~stellen** vt to put (down) ♦ vr to place o.s.

hinten [ˈhɪntən] adv at the back; behind; **~herum** adv round the back; (fig) secretly

hinter [ˈhɪntər] präp (+dat od akk) behind; (: nach) after; **~ jdm her sein** to be after sb; **H~achse** f rear axle; **H~bliebene(r)** f(m) surviving relative; **~e(r, s)** adj rear, back; **~einander** adv one after the other; **H~gedanke** m ulterior motive; **~gehen** (unreg) vt to deceive; **H~grund** m background; **H~halt** m ambush; **~hältig** adj underhand, sneaky; **~her** adv afterwards, after; **H~hof** m backyard; **H~kopf** m back of one's head; **~lassen** (unreg) vt to leave; **~legen** vt to deposit; **H~list** f cunning, trickery; (Handlung) trick, dodge; **~listig** adj cunning, crafty; **H~mann** m person behind; **H~rad** nt back wheel; **H~radantrieb** m (AUT) rear wheel drive; **~rücks** adv from behind; **H~tür** f back door; (fig: Ausweg) loophole; **~ziehen** (unreg) vt (Steuern) to evade

hinüber [hɪˈnyːbər] adv across, over; **~gehen** (unreg) vi to go over od across

hinunter [hɪˈnʊntər] adv down; **~bringen** (unreg) vt to take down; **~schlucken** vt *(auch fig)* to swallow; **~steigen** *(unreg)* vi to descend

Hinweg ['hɪnveːk] *m* journey out

hinweghelfen [hɪn'vɛk-] *(unreg)* vi: **jdm über etw** akk **~** to help sb to get over sth

hinwegsetzen [hɪn'vɛk-] vr: **sich ~ über** +akk to disregard

hin- ['hɪn] zW: **H~weis** **(-es, -e)** *m (Andeutung)* hint; *(Anweisung)* instruction; *(Verweis)* reference; **~weisen** *(unreg)* vi: **~weisen auf** +akk *(anzeigen)* to point to; *(sagen)* to point out, to refer to; **~werfen** *(unreg)* vt to throw down; **~ziehen** *(unreg)* vr *(fig)* to drag on

hinzu [hɪn'tsuː] adv in addition; **~fügen** vt to add; **~kommen** *(unreg)* vi *(Mensch)* to arrive, to turn up; *(Umstand)* to ensue

Hirn [hɪrn] **(-(e)s, -e)** nt brain(s); **~gespinst** **(-(e)s, -e)** nt fantasy

Hirsch [hɪrʃ] **(-(e)s, -e)** *m* stag

Hirt ['hɪrt] **(-en, -en)** *m* herdsman; *(Schafhirt, fig)* shepherd

hissen ['hɪsən] vt to hoist

Historiker [hɪs'toːrikər] **(-s, -)** *m* historian

historisch [hɪs'toːrɪʃ] adj historical

Hitze ['hɪtsə] **(-)** f heat; **h~beständig** adj heat-resistant; **h~frei** adj: **h~frei haben** to have time off school because of excessively hot weather; **~welle** f heat wave

hitzig ['hɪtsɪç] adj hot-tempered; *(Debatte)* heated

Hitzkopf *m* hothead

Hitzschlag *m* heatstroke

hl. abk von **heilig**

H-Milch ['haːmɪlç] f long-life milk

Hobby ['hɔbi] **(-s, -s)** nt hobby

Hobel ['hoːbəl] **(-s, -)** *m* plane; **~bank** f carpenter's bench; **h~n** vt, vi to plane; **~späne** pl wood shavings

Hoch **(-s, -s)** nt *(Ruf)* cheer; *(MET)* anticyclone

hoch [hoːx] *(attrib* **hohe(r, s))** adj high; **♦** adv: **~ achten** to respect; **~ begabt** extremely gifted; **~ dotiert** highly paid; **H~achtung** f respect, esteem; **~achtungsvoll** adv yours faithfully; **H~amt** nt high mass; **~arbeiten** vr to

work one's way up; **H~betrieb** *m* intense activity; *(COMM)* peak time; **H~burg** f stronghold; **H~deutsch** nt High German; **H~druck** *m* high pressure; **H~ebene** f plateau; **H~form** f top form; **H~gebirge** nt high mountains pl; **H~glanz** *m (PHOT)* high gloss print; **etw auf H~glanz bringen** to make sth sparkle like new; **~halten** *(unreg)* vt to hold up; *(fig)* to cherish; **H~haus** nt multi-storey building; **~heben** *(unreg)* vt to lift (up); **H~konjunktur** f boom; **H~land** nt highlands pl; **~leben** vi: **jdn ~leben lassen** to give sb three cheers; **H~mut** *m* pride; **~mütig** adj proud, haughty; **~näsig** adj stuck-up, snooty; **H~ofen** *m* blast furnace; **~prozentig** adj *(Alkohol)* strong; **H~rechnung** f projection; **H~saison** f high season; **H~schule** f college; university; **H~sommer** *m* middle of summer; **H~spannung** f high tension; **H~sprung** *m* high jump

höchst [høːçst] adv highly, extremely

Hochstapler ['hoːxstaːplər] **(-s, -)** *m* swindler

höchste(r, s) adj highest; *(äußerste)* extreme

Höchst- zW: **h~ens** adv at the most; **~geschwindigkeit** f maximum speed; **h~persönlich** adv in person; **~preis** *m* maximum price; **h~wahrscheinlich** adv most probably

Hoch- zW: **~verrat** *m* high treason; **~wasser** nt high water; *(Überschwemmung)* floods pl

Hochzeit ['hɔxtsaɪt] **(-, -en)** f wedding; **~sreise** f honeymoon

hocken ['hɔkən] vi, vr to squat, to crouch

Hocker **(-s, -)** *m* stool

Höcker ['hœkər] **(-s, -)** *m* hump

Hoden ['hoːdən] **(-s, -)** *m* testicle

Hof [hoːf] **(-(e)s, ᵉe)** *m (Hinterhof)* yard; *(Bauernhof)* farm; *(Königshof)* court

hoff- ['hɔf] zW: **~en** vi: **~en (auf** +akk) to hope (for); **~entlich** adv I hope, hopefully; **H~nung** f hope

Hoffnungs- zW: **h~los** adj hopeless;

~losigkeit f hopelessness; **h~voll** adj hopeful

höflich ['hø:flɪç] adj polite, courteous; **H~keit** f courtesy, politeness

hohe(r, s) ['ho:ə(r, s)] adj attrib siehe **hoch**

Höhe ['hø:ə] f height; (Anhöhe) hill

Hoheit ['ho:haɪt] f (POL) sovereignty; (Titel) Highness

Hoheits- zW: **~gebiet** nt sovereign territory; **~gewässer** nt territorial waters pl

Höhen- ['hø:ən] zW: **~luft** f mountain air; **~messer** (-s, -) m altimeter; **~sonne** f sun lamp; **~unterschied** m difference in altitude

Höhepunkt m climax

höher adj, adv higher

hohl [ho:l] adj hollow

Höhle ['hø:lə] f cave, hole; (Mundhöhle) cavity; (fig, ZOOL) den

Hohlmaß nt measure of volume

Hohn [ho:n] (-(e)s) m scorn

höhnisch adj scornful, taunting

holen ['ho:lən] vt to get, to fetch; (Atem) to take; **jdn/etw ~ lassen** to send for sb/sth

Holland ['hɔlant] nt Holland; **Holländer** ['hɔlɛndər] m Dutchman; **holländisch** adj Dutch

Hölle ['hœlə] f hell

höllisch ['hœlɪʃ] adj hellish, infernal

holperig ['hɔlpərɪç] adj rough, bumpy

Holunder [ho'lundər] (-s, -) m elder

Holz [hɔlts] (-es, ⁻er) nt wood

hölzern ['hœltsərn] adj (auch fig) wooden

Holz- zW: **~fäller** (-s, -) m lumberjack, woodcutter; **h~ig** adj woody; **~kohle** f charcoal; **~schuh** m clog; **~weg** m (fig) wrong track; **~wolle** f fine wood shavings pl

Homöopathie [homøopa'ti:] f homeopathy

homosexuell [homozɛksu'ɛl] adj homosexual

Honig ['ho:nɪç] (-s, -e) m honey; **~melone** f (BOT, KOCH) honeydew melon; **~wabe** f honeycomb

Honorar [hono'ra:r] (-s, -e) nt fee

Hopfen ['hɔpfən] (-s, -) m hops pl

hopsen ['hɔpsən] vi to hop

Hörapparat m hearing aid

hörbar adj audible

horchen ['hɔrçən] vi to listen; (pej) to eavesdrop

Horde ['hɔrdə] f horde

hör- ['hø:r] zW: **~en** vt, vi to hear; **Musik/ Radio ~en** to listen to music/the radio; **H~er** (-s, -) m hearer; (RADIO) listener; (UNIV) student; (Telefonhörer) receiver; **H~funk** (-s) m radio; **~geschädigt** [-gəʃɛːdɪçt] adj hearing-impaired

Horizont [hori'tsɔnt] (-(e)s, -e) m horizon; **h~al** [-'ta:l] adj horizontal

Hormon [hɔr'mo:n] (-s, -e) nt hormone

Hörmuschel f (TEL) earpiece

Horn [hɔrn] (-(e)s, ⁻er) nt horn; **~haut** f horny skin

Hornisse [hɔr'nɪsə] f hornet

Horoskop [horo'sko:p] (-s, -e) nt horoscope

Hörspiel nt radio play

Hort [hɔrt] (-(e)s, -e) m (SCH) day centre for schoolchildren whose parents are at work

horten ['hɔrtən] vt to hoard

Hose ['ho:zə] f trousers pl, pants pl (US)

Hosen- zW: **~anzug** m trouser suit; **~rock** m culottes pl; **~tasche** f (trouser) pocket; **~träger** m braces pl (BRIT), suspenders pl (US)

Hostie ['hɔstiə] f (REL) host

Hotel [ho'tɛl] (-s, -s) nt hotel; **~ier** (-s, -s) [hoteli'e:] m hotelkeeper, hotelier; **~verzeichnis** nt hotel register

Hubraum ['hu:p-] m (AUT) cubic capacity

hübsch [hypʃ] adj pretty, nice

Hubschrauber ['hu:pʃraubər] (-s, -) m helicopter

Huf ['hu:f] (-(e)s, -e) m hoof; **~eisen** nt horseshoe

Hüft- ['hʏft] zW: **~e** f hip; **~gürtel** m girdle; **~halter** (-s, -) m girdle

Hügel ['hy:gəl] (-s, -) m hill; **h~ig** adj hilly

Huhn [hu:n] (-(e)s, ⁻er) nt hen; (KOCH) chicken

Hühner- ['hy:nər] zW: **~auge** nt corn; **~brühe** f chicken broth

Hülle ['hʏlə] f cover(ing); wrapping; **in ~**

und Fülle galore; **h~n** vt: **h~n (in** +akk**)** to cover (with); to wrap (in)

Hülse ['hʏlzə] f husk, shell; **~frucht** f pulse

human [hu'maːn] adj humane; **~i'tär** adj humanitarian; **H~i'tät** f humanity

Hummel ['hʊməl] (**-, -n**) f bumblebee

Hummer ['hʊmər] (**-s, -**) m lobster

Humor [hu'moːr] (**-s, -e**) m humour; **~ haben** to have a sense of humour; **~ist** [-'rɪst] m humorist; **h~voll** adj humorous

humpeln ['hʊmpəln] vi to hobble

Humpen ['hʊmpən] (**-s, -**) m tankard

Hund [hʊnt] (**-(e)s, -e**) m dog

Hunde- [hʊndə] zW: **~hütte** f (dog) kennel; **h~müde** (umg) adj dog-tired

hundert ['hʊndərt] num hundred; **H~'jahrfeier** f centenary; **~prozentig** adj, adv one hundred per cent

Hundesteuer f dog licence fee

Hündin ['hʏndɪn] f bitch

Hunger ['hʊŋər] (**-s**) m hunger; **~ haben** to be hungry; **h~n** vi to starve; **~snot** f famine

hungrig ['hʊŋrɪç] adj hungry

Hupe ['huːpə] f horn; **h~n** vi to hoot, to sound one's horn

hüpfen ['hʏpfən] vi to hop; to jump

Hürde ['hʏrdə] f hurdle; (für Schafe) pen; **~nlauf** m hurdling

Hure ['huːrə] f whore

hurtig ['hʊrtɪç] adj brisk, quick ♦ adv briskly, quickly

huschen ['hʊʃən] vi to flit; to scurry

Husten ['huːstən] (**-s**) m cough; **h~** vi to cough; **~anfall** m coughing fit; **~bonbon** m od nt cough drop; **~saft** m cough mixture

Hut¹ [huːt] (**-(e)s, ⁿe**) m hat

Hut² [huːt] (**-**) f care; **auf der ~ sein** to be on one's guard

hüten ['hyːtən] vt to guard ♦ vr to watch out; **sich ~, zu** to take care not to; **sich ~ (vor)** to beware (of); to be on one's guard (against)

Hütte ['hʏtə] f hut; cottage; (Eisen~) forge

Hütten- zW: **~käse** m (KOCH) cottage cheese; **~schuh** m slipper sock

Hydrant [hy'drant] m hydrant

hydraulisch [hy'draulɪʃ] adj hydraulic

Hygiene [hygi'eːnə] (**-**) f hygiene

hygienisch [hygi'eːnɪʃ] adj hygienic

Hymne ['hʏmnə] f hymn; anthem

Hypno- [hʏp'noː] zW: **~se** f hypnosis; **h~tisch** adj hypnotic; **~tiseur** [-ti'zøːr] m hypnotist; **h~ti'sieren** vt to hypnotize

Hypothek [hypo'teːk] (**-, -en**) f mortgage

Hypothese [hypo'teːzə] f hypothesis

Hysterie [hyste'riː] f hysteria

hysterisch [hʏs'teːrɪʃ] adj hysterical

I, i

ICE [iːtseː'leː] m abk = **Intercity-Expresszug**

Ich (**-(s), -(s)**) nt self; (PSYCH) ego

ich [ɪç] pron I; **~ bin's!** it's me!

Icon ['aɪkɔn] (**-s, -s**) nt (COMPUT) icon

Ideal [ide'aːl] (**-s, -e**) nt ideal; **ideal** adj ideal; **idealistisch** [-'lɪstɪʃ] adj idealistic

Idee [i'deː, pl i'deːən] f idea

identifizieren [identifi'tsiːrən] vt to identify

identisch [i'dentɪʃ] adj identical

Identität [identi'tɛːt] f identity

Ideo- [ideo] zW: **~loge** [-'loːgə] (**-n, -n**) m ideologist; **~logie** [-lo'giː] f ideology; **ideologisch** [-'loːgɪʃ] adj ideological

Idiot [idi'oːt] (**-en, -en**) m idiot; **idiotisch** adj idiotic

idyllisch [i'dʏlɪʃ] adj idyllic

Igel ['iːgəl] (**-s, -**) m hedgehog

ignorieren [ɪgno'riːrən] vt to ignore

ihm [iːm] (dat von er, es) pron (to) him; (to) it

ihn [iːn] (akk von er, es) pron him; it; **~en** (dat von sie pl) pron (to) them; **Ihnen** (dat von Sie pl) pron (to) you

SCHLÜSSELWORT

ihr [iːr] pron 1 (nom pl) you; **ihr seid es** it's you

2 (dat von sie) to her; **gib es ihr** give it to her; **er steht neben ihr** he is standing beside her

♦ possessiv pron 1 (sg) her; (: bei Tieren,

Dingen) its; **ihr Mann** her husband
2 (*pl*) their; **die Bäume und ihre Blätter**
the trees and their leaves

ihr(e) [iːr] *adj* (*sg*) her, its; (*pl*) their; **Ihr(e)**
adj your

ihre(r, s) *pron* (*sg*) hers, its; (*pl*) theirs;
Ihre(r, s) *pron* yours; **~r** (*gen von* **sie** *sg/pl*)
pron of her/them; **Ihrer** (*gen von* **Sie**)
pron of you; **~rseits** *adv* for her/their part;
~sgleichen *pron* people like her/them;
(*von Dingen*) others like it; **~twegen** *adv*
(*für sie*) for her/its/their sake; (*wegen ihr*) on
her/its/their account; **~twillen** *adv:* **um**
~twillen = ihretwegen

ihrige *pron:* **der/die/das ~** *od* **I~**
hers; its; theirs

illegal [ˈɪlegaːl] *adj* illegal
Illusion [ɪluziˈoːn] *f* illusion
illusorisch [ɪluˈzoːrɪʃ] *adj* illusory
illustrieren [ɪlʊsˈtriːrən] *vt* to illustrate
Illustrierte *f* magazine
im [ɪm] = **in dem**
Imbiss ▲ [ˈɪmbɪs] (**-es, -e**) *m* snack;
~stube *f* snack bar
imitieren [imiˈtiːrən] *vt* to imitate
Imker [ˈɪmkər] (**-s, -**) *m* beekeeper
immatrikulieren [ɪmatrikuˈliːrən] *vi, vr* to
register
immer [ˈɪmər] *adv* always; **~ wieder** again
and again; **~ noch** still; **~ noch nicht** still
not; **für ~** forever; **~ wenn ich ...** every
time I ...; **~ schöner/trauriger** more and
more beautiful/sadder and sadder; **was/**
wer (*auch*) **~** whatever/whoever; **~hin** *adv*
all the same; **~zu** *adv* all the time
Immobilien [ɪmoˈbiːliən] *pl* real estate *sg*;
~makler *m* estate agent (*BRIT*), realtor (*US*)
immun [ɪˈmuːn] *adj* immune; **Immunität**
[-iˈtɛːt] *f* immunity; **Immunsystem** *nt*
immune system
Imperfekt [ˈɪmpɛrfɛkt] (**-s, -e**) *nt* imperfect
(tense)
Impf- [ˈɪmpf] *zW:* **impfen** *vt* to vaccinate;
~stoff *m* vaccine, serum; **~ung** *f*
vaccination
imponieren [ɪmpoˈniːrən] *vi* +*dat* to impress

Import [ɪmˈpɔrt] (**-(e)s, -e**) *m* import; **~eur**
m importer; **importieren** *vt* to import
imposant [ɪmpoˈzant] *adj* imposing
impotent [ˈɪmpotɛnt] *adj* impotent
imprägnieren [ɪmprɛˈgniːrən] *vt* to
(water)proof
improvisieren [ɪmproviˈziːrən] *vt, vi* to
improvise
Impuls [ɪmˈpʊls] (**-es, -e**) *m* impulse;
impulsiv [-ˈziːf] *adj* impulsive
imstande, im Stande [ɪmˈʃtandə] *adj:* **~**
sein to be in a position; (*fähig*) to be able

SCHLÜSSELWORT

in [ɪn] *präp* +*akk* **1** (*räumlich: wohin?*) in, into;
in die Stadt into town; **in die Schule**
gehen to go to school
2 (*zeitlich*): **bis ins 20. Jahrhundert** into *od*
up to the 20th century
♦ *präp* +*dat* **1** (*räumlich: wo*) in; **in der Stadt**
in town; **in der Schule sein** to be at
school
2 (*zeitlich: wann*): **in diesem Jahr** this year;
(*in jenem Jahr*) in that year; **heute in zwei**
Wochen two weeks today

Inanspruchnahme [ɪnˈʔanʃpruxnaːmə] *f*
(+*gen*) demands *pl* (on)
Inbegriff [ˈɪnbəɡrɪf] *m* embodiment,
personification; **inbegriffen** *adv* included
indem [ɪnˈdeːm] *konj* while; **~ man etw**
macht (*dadurch*) by doing sth
Inder(in) [ˈɪndər(ɪn)] *m(f)* Indian
indes(sen) [ɪnˈdes(ən)] *adv* however;
(*inzwischen*) meanwhile ♦ *konj* while
Indianer(in) [ɪndiˈaːnər(ɪn)] (**-s, -**) *m(f)*
American Indian, native American;
indianisch *adj* Red Indian
Indien [ˈɪndiən] *nt* India
indirekt [ˈɪndirɛkt] *adj* indirect
indisch [ˈɪndɪʃ] *adj* Indian
indiskret [ˈɪndɪskreːt] *adj* indiscreet
indiskutabel [ˈɪndɪskutaːbəl] *adj* out of the
question
individuell [ɪndividuˈɛl] *adj* individual
Individuum [ɪndiˈviːduʊm] (**-s, -en**) *nt*
individual

Spelling Reform: ▲ *new spelling* △ *old spelling (to be phased out)*

Indiz [ɪn'diːts] (**-es, -ien**) *nt* (*JUR*) clue; ~ **(für)** sign (of)

industrialisieren [ɪndʊstriali'ziːrən] *vt* to industrialize

Industrie [ɪndʊs'triː] *f* industry ♦ *in zW* industrial; ~**gebiet** *nt* industrial area; ~**und Handelskammer** *f* chamber of commerce; ~**zweig** *m* branch of industry

ineinander [ɪn|aɪ'nandər] *adv* in(to) one another *od* each other

Infarkt [ɪn'farkt] (**-(e)s, -e**) *m* coronary (thrombosis)

Infektion [ɪnfɛktsi'oːn] *f* infection; ~**skrankheit** *f* infectious disease

Infinitiv ['ɪnfinitiːf] (**-s, -e**) *m* infinitive

infizieren [ɪnfi'tsiːrən] *vt* to infect ♦ *vr*: **sich (bei jdm)** ~ to be infected (by sb)

Inflation [ɪnflatsi'oːn] *f* inflation

inflationär [ɪnflatsio'nɛːr] *adj* inflationary

infolge [ɪn'fɔlgə] *präp +gen* as a result of, owing to; ~**dessen** [-'dɛsən] *adv* consequently

Informatik [ɪnfɔr'maːtɪk] *f* information studies *pl*

Information [ɪnfɔrmatsi'oːn] *f* information *no pl*

informieren [ɪnfɔr'miːrən] *vt* to inform ♦ *vr*: **sich ~ (über** +*akk*) to find out (about)

infrage, in Frage *adv*: ~ **stellen** to question sth; **nicht ~ kommen** to be out of the question

Ingenieur [ɪnʒeni'øːr] *m* engineer; ~**schule** *f* school of engineering

Ingwer ['ɪŋvər] (**-s**) *m* ginger

Inh. *abk* (= *Inhaber*) prop.; (= *Inhalt*) contents

Inhaber(in) ['ɪnhaːbər(ɪn)] (**-s, -**) *m(f)* owner; (*Hausinhaber*) occupier; (*Lizenzinhaber*) licensee, holder; (*FIN*) bearer

inhaftieren [ɪnhaf'tiːrən] *vt* to take into custody

inhalieren [ɪnha'liːrən] *vt, vi* to inhale

Inhalt ['ɪnhalt] (**-(e)s, -e**) *m* contents *pl*; (*eines Buchs etc*) content; (*MATH*) area; volume; **inhaltlich** *adj* as regards content

Inhalts- *zW*: ~**angabe** *f* summary; ~**verzeichnis** *nt* table of contents

inhuman ['ɪnhumaːn] *adj* inhuman

Initiative [initsia'tiːvə] *f* initiative

inklusive [ɪnklu'ziːvə] *präp +gen* inclusive of ♦ *adv* inclusive

In-Kraft-Treten [ɪn'krafttreːtən] (**-s**) *nt* coming into force

Inland ['ɪnlant] (**-(e)s**) *nt* (*GEOG*) inland; (*POL, COMM*) home (country); ~**flug** *m* domestic flight

inmitten [ɪn'mɪtən] *präp +gen* in the middle of; ~ **von** amongst

innehaben ['ɪnəhaːbən] (*unreg*) *vt* to hold

innen ['ɪnən] *adv* inside; **Innenarchitekt** *m* interior designer; **Inneneinrichtung** *f* (interior) furnishings *pl*; **Innenhof** *m* inner courtyard; **Innenminister** *m* minister of the interior, Home Secretary (*BRIT*); **Innenpolitik** *f* domestic policy; ~**politisch** *adj* (*Entwicklung, Lage*) internal, domestic; **Innenstadt** *f* town/city centre

inner- ['ɪnər] *zW*: ~**e(r, s)** *adj* inner; (*im Körper, inländisch*) internal; **Innere(s)** *nt* inside; (*Mitte*) centre; (*fig*) heart; **Innereien** [-'raɪən] *pl* innards; ~**halb** *adv* within; (*räumlich*) inside ♦ *präp +gen* within; inside; ~**lich** *adj* internal; (*geistig*) inward; ~**ste(r, s)** *adj* innermost; **Innerste(s)** *nt* heart

innig ['ɪnɪç] *adj* (*Freundschaft*) close

inoffiziell ['ɪnʔɔfitsiɛl] *adj* unofficial

ins [ɪns] = **in das**

Insasse ['ɪnzasə] (**-n, -n**) *m* (*Anstalt*) inmate; (*AUT*) passenger

Insassenversicherung *f* passenger insurance

insbesondere [ɪnsbə'zɔndərə] *adv* (e)specially

Inschrift ['ɪnʃrɪft] *f* inscription

Insekt [ɪn'zɛkt] (**-(e)s, -en**) *nt* insect

Insektenschutzmittel *nt* insect repellent

Insel ['ɪnzəl] (**-, -n**) *f* island

Inser- *zW*: ~**at** [ɪnze'raːt] (**-(e)s, -e**) *nt* advertisement; ~**ent** [ɪnze'rɛnt] *m* advertiser; **inserieren** [ɪnze'riːrən] *vt, vi* to advertise

insgeheim [ɪnsgə'haɪm] *adv* secretly

insgesamt [ɪnsgə'zamt] *adv* altogether, all in all

insofern [ɪnzo'fɛrn] *adv* in this respect ♦ *konj* if; (*deshalb*) (and) so; ~ **als** in so far as

insoweit [ɪnzo'vaɪt] = **insofern**

Installateur [ɪnstala'tøːr] *m* electrician; plumber

Instandhaltung [ɪn'ʃtanthaltʊŋ] *f* maintenance

inständig [ɪn'ʃtɛndɪç] *adj* urgent

Instandsetzung [ɪn'ʃtant-] *f* overhaul; (*eines Gebäudes*) restoration

Instanz [ɪn'stants] *f* authority; (*JUR*) court

Instinkt [ɪn'stɪŋkt] (**-(e)s, -e**) *m* instinct; **instinktiv** [-'tiːf] *adj* instinctive

Institut [ɪnsti'tuːt] (**-(e)s, -e**) *nt* institute

Instrument [ɪnstru'mɛnt] *nt* instrument

Intell- [ɪntɛl] *zW:* **intellektuell** [-ɛktu'ɛl] *adj* intellectual; **intelligent** [-i'gɛnt] *adj* intelligent; **~igenz** [-i'gɛnts] *f* intelligence; (*Leute*) intelligentsia *pl*

Intendant [ɪntɛn'dant] *m* director

intensiv [ɪntɛn'ziːf] *adj* intensive; **Intensivstation** *f* intensive care unit

Intercity- [ɪntɐ'sɪti] *zW:* **~-Expresszug** ▲ *m* high-speed train; **~-Zug** *m* intercity (train); **~-Zuschlag** *m* intercity supplement

Interess- *zW:* **i~ant** [ɪntere'sant] *adj* interesting; **i~anterweise** *adv* interestingly enough; **~e** [ɪnte'resə] (**-s, -n**) *nt* interest; **~e haben an** +*dat* to be interested in; **~ent** [ɪntere'sɛnt] *m* interested party; **i~ieren** [ɪntere'siːrən] *vt* to interest ♦ *vr:* **sich i~ieren für** to be interested in

intern [ɪn'tɛrn] *adj* (*Angelegenheiten, Regelung*) internal; (*Besprechung*) private

Internat [ɪntɐ'naːt] (**-(e)s, -e**) *nt* boarding school

inter- [ɪntɐ] *zW:* **~national** [-natsio'naːl] *adj* international; **I~net** ['ɪntɐnɛt] (**-s**) *nt:* **das I~net** the Internet; **I~net-Anbieter** *m* Internet Service Provider, ISP; **I~net-Café** *nt* Internet café; **~pretieren** [-pre'tiːrən] *vt* to interpret; **I~vall** [-'val] (**-s, -e**) *nt* interval; **I~view** [-'vjuː] (**-s, -s**) *nt* interview; **~viewen** [-'vjuːən] *vt* to interview

intim [ɪn'tiːm] *adj* intimate; **Intimität** *f* intimacy

intolerant ['ɪntolerant] *adj* intolerant

Intrige [ɪn'triːgə] *f* intrigue, plot

Invasion [ɪnvazi'oːn] *f* invasion

Inventar [ɪnvɛn'taːr] (**-s, -e**) *nt* inventory

Inventur [ɪnvɛn'tuːr] *f* stocktaking; **~ machen** to stocktake

investieren [ɪnvɛs'tiːrən] *vt* to invest

inwie- [ɪnvi'] *zW:* **~fern** *adv* how far, to what extent; **~weit** *adv* how far, to what extent

inzwischen [ɪn'tsvɪʃən] *adv* meanwhile

Irak [i'raːk] (**-s**) *m:* **der ~** Iraq; **irakisch** *adj* Iraqi

Iran [i'raːn] (**-s**) *m:* **der ~** Iran; **iranisch** *adj* Iranian

irdisch ['ɪrdɪʃ] *adj* earthly

Ire ['iːrə] (**-n, -n**) *m* Irishman

irgend ['ɪrgənt] *adv* at all; **wann/was/wer ~** whenever/whatever/whoever; **~etwas** *pron* something/anything; **~jemand** *pron* somebody/anybody; **~ein(e, s)** *adj* some, any; **~einmal** *adv* sometime or other; (*fragend*) ever; **~wann** *adv* sometime; **~wie** *adv* somehow; **~wo** *adv* somewhere; anywhere; **~wohin** *adv* somewhere; anywhere

Irin ['iːrɪn] *f* Irishwoman

Irland ['ɪrlant] (**-s**) *nt* Ireland

Ironie [iro'niː] *f* irony; **ironisch** [i'roːnɪʃ] *adj* ironic(al)

irre ['ɪrə] *adj* crazy, mad; **Irre(r)** *f(m)* lunatic; **~führen** *vt* to mislead; **~machen** *vt* to confuse; **~n** *vi* to be mistaken; (*umherirren*) to wander, to stray ♦ *vr* to be mistaken; **Irrenanstalt** *f* lunatic asylum

Irr- *zW:* **~garten** *m* maze; **i~ig** ['ɪrɪç] *adj* incorrect, wrong; **i~itieren** [ɪri'tiːrən] *vt* (*verwirren*) to confuse; (*ärgern*) to irritate; (*stören*) to annoy; **irrsinnig** *adj* mad, crazy; (*umg*) terrific; **~tum** (**-s, -tümer**) *m* mistake, error; **irrtümlich** *adj* mistaken

Island ['iːslant] (**-s**) *nt* Iceland

Isolation [izolatsi'oːn] *f* isolation; (*ELEK*) insulation

Isolier- [izo'liːr] *zW:* **~band** *nt* insulating tape; **isolieren** *vt* to isolate; (*ELEK*) to insulate; **~station** *f* (*MED*) isolation ward;

~ung f isolation; (ELEK) insulation
Israel ['ɪsraeːl] (-s) nt Israel; **~i** (-s, -s) [-'eːli] m Israeli; **israelisch** adj Israeli
isst ▲ [ɪst] vb siehe **essen**
ist [ɪst] vb siehe **sein**
Italien [i'taːliən] (-s) nt Italy; **~er(in)** (-s) m(f) Italian; **italienisch** adj Italian
i. V. abk = **in Vertretung**

J, j

SCHLÜSSELWORT

ja [jaː] adv 1 yes; **haben Sie das gesehen? - ja** did you see it? - yes(, I did); **ich glaube ja** (yes) I think so
2 (fragend) really?; **ich habe gekündigt - ja?** I've quit - have you?; **du kommst, ja?** you're coming, aren't you?
3: **sei ja vorsichtig** do be careful; **Sie wissen ja, dass ...** as you know, ...; **tu das ja nicht!** don't do that!; **ich habe es ja gewusst** I just knew it; **ja, also ...** well you see ...

Jacht [jaxt] (-, -en) f yacht
Jacke ['jakə] f jacket; (Wolljacke) cardigan
Jackett [ʒa'kɛt] (-s, -s od -e) nt jacket
Jagd [jaːkt] (-, -en) f hunt; (Jagen) hunting; **~beute** f kill; **~flugzeug** nt fighter; **~hund** m hunting dog
jagen ['jaːɡən] vi to hunt; (eilen) to race ♦ vt to hunt; (wegjagen) to drive (off); (verfolgen) to chase
Jäger ['jeːɡər] (-s, -) m hunter; **~schnitzel** nt (KOCH) pork in a spicy sauce with mushrooms
jäh [jeː] adj sudden, abrupt; (steil) steep, precipitous
Jahr [jaːr] (-(e)s, -e) nt year; **j~elang** adv for years
Jahres- zW: **~abonnement** nt annual subscription; **~abschluss** ▲ m end of the year; (COMM) annual statement of account; **~beitrag** m annual subscription; **~karte** f

yearly season ticket; **~tag** m anniversary; **~wechsel** m turn of the year; **~zahl** f date; year; **~zeit** f season
Jahr- zW: **~gang** m age group; (von Wein) vintage; **~'hundert** (-s, -e) nt century; **jährlich** ['jeːrlɪç] adj, adv yearly; **~markt** m fair; **~tausend** nt millennium; **~'zehnt** nt decade
Jähzorn ['jeːtsɔrn] m sudden anger; hot temper; **j~ig** adj hot-tempered
Jalousie [ʒaluˈziː] f venetian blind
Jammer ['jamər] (-s) m misery; **es ist ein ~, dass ...** it is a crying shame that ...
jämmerlich ['jɛmərlɪç] adj wretched, pathetic
jammern vi to wail ♦ vt unpers: **es jammert jdn** it makes sb feel sorry
Januar ['januaːr] (-(s), -e) m January
Japan ['jaːpan] (-s) nt Japan; **~er(in)** [-'paːnər(ɪn)] (-s) m(f) Japanese; **j~isch** adj Japanese
jäten ['jeːtən] vt: **Unkraut ~** to weed
jauchzen ['jaʊxtsən] vi to rejoice
jaulen ['jaʊlən] vi to howl
jawohl [ja'voːl] adv yes (of course)
Jawort ['jaːvɔrt] nt consent
Jazz [dʒæz] (-) m Jazz

SCHLÜSSELWORT

je [jeː] adv 1 (jemals) ever; **hast du so was je gesehen?** did you ever see anything like it?
2 (jeweils) every; each; **sie zahlten je 3 Mark** they paid 3 marks each
♦ konj 1: **je nach** depending on; **je nachdem** it depends; **je nachdem, ob ...** depending on whether ...
2: **je eher, desto** od **umso besser** the sooner the better

Jeans [dʒiːnz] pl jeans
jede(r, s) ['jeːdə(r, s)] adj every, each ♦ pron everybody; (~ Einzelne) each; **~s Mal** every time, each time; **ohne ~ x** without any x
jedenfalls adv in any case
jedermann pron everyone
jederzeit adv at any time

jedoch [je'dɔx] adv however

jeher ['je:he:r] adv: **von/seit ~** always

jemals ['je:ma:ls] adv ever

jemand ['je:mant] pron somebody; anybody

jene(r, s) ['je:nə(r, s)] adj that ♦ pron that one

jenseits ['je:nzaɪts] adv on the other side ♦ präp +gen on the other side of, beyond

Jenseits nt: **das ~** the hereafter, the beyond

jetzig ['jetsɪç] adj present

jetzt [jetst] adv now

jeweilig adj respective

jeweils adv: **~ zwei zusammen** two at a time; **zu ~ 5 Euros** at 5 euros each; **~ das Erste** the first each time

Jh. abk = **Jahrhundert**

Job [dʒɔp] (**-s, -s**) m (umg) job; j~ben ['dʒɔbən] vi (umg) to work

Jockei ['dʒɔke] (**-s, -s**) m jockey

Jod [jo:t] (**-(e)s**) nt iodine

jodeln ['jo:dəln] vi to yodel

joggen ['dʒɔgən] vi to jog

Jog(h)urt ['jo:gurt] (**-s, -s**) m od nt yogurt

Johannisbeere [jo'hanisbe:rə] f redcurrant; **schwarze ~** blackcurrant

johlen ['jo:lən] vi to yell

jonglieren [ʒõ'gli:rən] vi to juggle

Journal- [ʒurnal] zW: ~ismus [-'lɪsmʊs] m journalism; ~ist(in) [-'lɪst(ɪn)] m(f) journalist; journa'listisch adj journalistic

Jubel ['ju:bəl] (**-s**) m rejoicing; j~n vi to rejoice

Jubiläum [jubi'lɛ:ʊm] (**-s, Jubiläen**) nt anniversary; jubilee

jucken ['jʊkən] vi to itch ♦ vt: **es juckt mich am Arm** my arm is itching

Juckreiz ['jʊkraɪts] m itch

Jude ['ju:də] (**-n, -n**) m Jew

Juden- zW: ~tum (**-**) nt Judaism; Jewry; ~verfolgung f persecution of the Jews

Jüdin ['jy:dɪn] f Jewess

jüdisch ['jy:dɪʃ] adj Jewish

Jugend ['ju:gənt] (**-**) f youth; j~frei adj (CINE) U (BRIT), G (US), suitable for children; ~herberge f youth hostel; ~herbergsausweis m youth hostelling

card; j~lich adj youthful; ~liche(r) f(m) teenager, young person

Jugoslaw- [jugo'sla:v] zW: ~ien (**-s**) nt Yugoslavia; j~isch adj Yugoslavian

Juli ['ju:li] (**-(s), -s**) m July

jun. abk (= junior) jr.

jung [jʊŋ] adj young; J~e (**-n, -n**) m boy, lad ♦ nt young animal; J~en pl (von Tier) young pl

Jünger ['jʏŋər] (**-s, -**) m disciple

jünger adj younger

Jung- zW: ~frau f virgin; (ASTROL) Virgo; ~geselle m bachelor; ~gesellin f unmarried woman

jüngst [jʏŋst] adv lately, recently; ~e(r, s) adj youngest; (neuste) latest

Juni ['ju:ni] (**-(s), -s**) m June

Junior ['ju:niɔr] (**-s, -en**) m junior

Jurist [ju'rɪst] m jurist, lawyer; j~isch adj legal

Justiz [jʊs'ti:ts] (**-**) f justice; ~beamte(r) m judicial officer; ~irrtum m miscarriage of justice; ~minister m ≈ Lord (High) Chancellor (BRIT), ≈ Attorney General (US)

Juwel [ju've:l] (**-s, -en**) nt od m jewel

Juwelier [juve'li:r] (**-s, -e**) m jeweller; ~geschäft nt jeweller's (shop)

Jux [jʊks] (**-es, -e**) m joke, lark

K, k

Kabarett [kaba'rɛt] (**-s, -e** od **-s**) nt cabaret; ~ist [-'tɪst] m cabaret artiste

Kabel ['ka:bəl] (**-s, -**) nt (ELEK) wire; (stark) cable; ~fernsehen nt cable television

Kabeljau ['ka:bəljaʊ] (**-s, -e** od **-s**) m cod

Kabine [ka'bi:nə] f cabin; (Zelle) cubicle

Kabinenbahn f cable railway

Kabinett [kabi'nɛt] (**-s, -e**) nt (POL) cabinet

Kachel ['kaxəl] (**-, -n**) f tile; k~n vt to tile; ~ofen m tiled stove

Käfer ['kɛːfər] (**-s, -**) m beetle

Kaffee ['kafe] (**-s, -s**) m coffee; ~haus nt café; ~kanne f coffeepot; ~löffel m coffee spoon

Käfig ['kɛːfɪç] (**-s, -e**) m cage

kahl [kaːl] *adj* bald; **~ geschoren** shaven, shorn; **~köpfig** *adj* bald-headed

Kahn [kaːn] **(-(e)s, ᵘe)** *m* boat, barge

Kai [kaɪ] **(-s, -e od -s)** *m* quay

Kaiser ['kaɪzər] **(-s, -)** *m* emperor; **~in** *f* empress; **k~lich** *adj* imperial; **k~reich** *nt* empire; **~schnitt** *m* (*MED*) Caesarian (section)

Kakao [kaˈkaːo] **(-s, -s)** *m* cocoa

Kaktee [kakˈteː(ə)] **(-, -n)** *f* cactus

Kaktus ['kaktʊs] **(-, -teen)** *m* cactus

Kalb [kalp] **(-(e)s, ᵘer)** *nt* calf; **k~en** ['kalbən] *vi* to calve; **~fleisch** *nt* veal; **~sleder** *nt* calf(skin)

Kalender [kaˈlɛndər] **(-s, -)** *m* calendar; (*Taschenkalender*) diary

Kaliber [kaˈliːbər] **(-s, -)** *nt* (*auch fig*) calibre

Kalk [kalk] **(-(e)s, -e)** *m* lime; (*BIOL*) calcium; **~stein** *m* limestone

kalkulieren [kalkuˈliːrən] *vt* to calculate

Kalorie [kaloˈriː] *f* calorie

kalt [kalt] *adj* cold; **mir ist (es) ~** I am cold; **~ bleiben** (*fig*) to remain unmoved; **~ stellen** to chill; **~blütig** *adj* cold-blooded; (*ruhig*) cool

Kälte ['kɛltə] **(-)** *f* cold; coldness; **~grad** *m* degree of frost *od* below zero; **~welle** *f* cold spell

kalt- *zW*: **~herzig** *adj* cold-hearted; **~schnäuzig** *adj* cold, unfeeling; **~stellen** *vt* (*fig*) to leave out in the cold

kam *etc* [kaːm] *vb siehe* **kommen**

Kamel [kaˈmeːl] **(-(e)s, -e)** *nt* camel

Kamera ['kamera] **(-, -s)** *f* camera

Kamerad [kaməˈraːt] **(-en, -en)** *m* comrade, friend; **~schaft** *f* comradeship; **k~schaftlich** *adj* comradely

Kameramann **(-(e)s, -männer)** *m* cameraman

Kamille [kaˈmɪlə] *f* camomile; **~ntee** *m* camomile tea

Kamin [kaˈmiːn] **(-s, -e)** *m* (*außen*) chimney; (*innen*) fireside, fireplace; **~kehrer (-s, -)** *m* chimney sweep

Kamm [kam] **(-(e)s, ᵘe)** *m* comb; (*Bergkamm*) ridge; (*Hahnenkamm*) crest

kämmen ['kɛmən] *vt* to comb ♦ *vr* to comb one's hair

Kammer ['kamər] **(-, -n)** *f* chamber; small bedroom

Kammerdiener *m* valet

Kampagne [kamˈpanjə] *f* campaign

Kampf [kampf] **(-(e)s, ᵘe)** *m* fight, battle; (*Wettbewerb*) contest; (*fig: Anstrengung*) struggle; **k~bereit** *adj* ready for action

kämpfen ['kɛmpfən] *vi* to fight

Kämpfer (-s, -) *m* fighter, combatant

Kampf- *zW*: **~handlung** *f* action; **k~los** *adj* without a fight; **~richter** *m* (*SPORT*) referee; (*TENNIS*) umpire; **~stoff** *m*: **chemischer/biologischer ~stoff** chemical/biological weapon

Kanada ['kanada] **(-s)** *nt* Canada; **Kanadier(in) (-s, -)** [kəˈnaːdiər(ın)] *m(f)* Canadian; **kaˈnadisch** *adj* Canadian

Kanal [kaˈnaːl] **(-s, Kanäle)** *m* (*Fluss*) canal; (*Rinne, Ärmelkanal*) channel; (*für Abfluss*) drain; **~inseln** *pl* Channel Islands; **~isation** [-izatsiˈoːn] *f* sewage system; **~tunnel** *m*: **der ~tunnel** the Channel Tunnel

Kanarienvogel [kaˈnaːrienfoːgəl] *m* (*ZOOL*) canary

kanarisch [kaˈnaːrɪʃ] *adj*: **K~e Inseln** Canary Islands, Canaries

Kandi- [kandi] *zW*: **~dat** [-ˈdaːt] **(-en, -en)** *m* candidate; **~datur** [-daˈtuːr] *f* candidature, candidacy; **k~dieren** [-ˈdiːrən] *vi* to stand, to run

Kandis(zucker) ['kandɪs(tsʊkər)] **(-)** *m* candy

Känguru ▲ ['kɛnguru] **(-s, -s)** *nt* kangaroo

Kaninchen [kaˈniːnçən] *nt* rabbit

Kanister [kaˈnɪstər] **(-s, -)** *m* can, canister

Kännchen ['kɛnçən] *nt* pot

Kanne ['kanə] *f* (*Krug*) jug; (*Kaffeekanne*) pot; (*Milchkanne*) churn; (*Gießkanne*) can

kannst *etc* [kanst] *vb siehe* **können**

Kanone [kaˈnoːnə] *f* gun; (*HIST*) cannon; (*fig: Mensch*) ace

Kantate [kanˈtaːtə] *f* cantata

Kante ['kantə] *f* edge

Kantine [kanˈtiːnə] *f* canteen

Kanton [kanˈtoːn] **(-s, -e)** *m* canton

Kanton

ℹ️ **Kanton** is the term for a state or region of Switzerland. Under the Swiss constitution the **Kantone** enjoy considerable autonomy. The Swiss **Kantone** are Aargau, Appenzell, Basel, Bern, Fribourg, Geneva, Glarus, Graubünden, Luzern, Neuchâtel, St. Gallen, Schaffhausen, Schwyz, Solothurn, Ticino, Thurgau, Unterwalden, Uri, Valais, Vaud, Zug and Zürich.

Kanu ['ka:nu] (**-s, -s**) *nt* canoe
Kanzel ['kantsəl] (**-, -n**) *f* pulpit
Kanzler ['kantslər] (**-s, -**) *m* chancellor
Kap [kap] (**-s, -s**) *nt* cape (GEOG)
Kapazität [kapatsi'tɛːt] *f* capacity; (*Fachmann*) authority
Kapelle [ka'pɛlə] *f* (*Gebäude*) chapel; (MUS) band
kapieren [ka'piːrən] (*umg*) *vt, vi* to get, to understand
Kapital [kapi'taːl] (**-s, -e** *od* **-ien**) *nt* capital; ~**anlage** *f* investment; ~**ismus** [-'lɪsmʊs] *m* capitalism; ~**ist** [-'lɪst] *m* capitalist; **k~istisch** *adj* capitalist
Kapitän [kapi'tɛːn] (**-s, -e**) *m* captain
Kapitel [ka'pɪtəl] (**-s, -**) *nt* chapter
Kapitulation [kapitulatsi'oːn] *f* capitulation
kapitulieren [kapitu'liːrən] *vi* to capitulate
Kappe [ka'pə] *f* cap; (*Kapuze*) hood
kappen *vt* to cut
Kapsel ['kapsəl] (**-, -n**) *f* capsule
kaputt [ka'pʊt] (*umg*) *adj* kaput, broken; (*Person*) exhausted, finished; **am Auto ist etwas ~** there's something wrong with the car; ~**gehen** (*unreg*) *vi* to break; (*Schuhe*) to fall apart; (*Firma*) to go bust; (*Stoff*) to wear out; (*sterben*) to cop it (*umg*); ~**machen** *vt* to break; (*Mensch*) to exhaust, to wear out
Kapuze [ka'puːtsə] *f* hood
Karamell ▲ [kara'mɛl] (**-s**) *m* caramel; ~**bonbon** *m od nt* toffee
Karate [ka'raːtə] (**-s**) *nt* karate
Karawane [kara'vaːnə] *f* caravan

Kardinal [kardi'naːl] (**-s, Kardinäle**) *m* cardinal; ~**zahl** *f* cardinal number
Karfreitag [kar'fraitaːk] *m* Good Friday
karg [kark] *adj* (*Landschaft, Boden*) barren; (*Lohn*) meagre
kärglich ['kɛrklɪç] *adj* poor, scanty
Karibik [ka'riːbɪk] (**-**) *f*: **die ~** the Caribbean
karibisch [ka'riːbɪʃ] *adj*: **K~e Inseln** Caribbean Islands
kariert [ka'riːrt] *adj* (*Stoff*) checked; (*Papier*) squared
Karies ['kaːries] (**-**) *f* caries
Karikatur [karika'tuːr] *f* caricature; ~**ist** [-'rɪst] *m* cartoonist
Karneval ['karnəval] (**-s, -e** *od* **-s**) *m* carnival

Karneval

ℹ️ **Karneval** is the time immediately before Lent when people gather to eat, drink and generally have fun before the fasting begins. **Rosenmontag**, the day before Shrove Tuesday, is the most important day of **Karneval** on the Rhine. Most firms take a day's holiday on that day to enjoy the celebrations. In South Germany and Austria **Karneval** is called **Fasching**.

Karo ['kaːro] (**-s, -s**) *nt* square; (KARTEN) diamonds
Karosserie [karɔsə'riː] *f* (AUT) body(work)
Karotte [ka'rɔtə] *f* carrot
Karpfen ['karpfən] (**-s, -**) *m* carp
Karre ['karə] *f* cart, barrow
Karren (**-s, -**) *m* cart, barrow
Karriere [kari'ɛːrə] *f* career; **~ machen** to get on, to get to the top; ~**macher** (**-s, -**) *m* careerist
Karte ['kartə] *f* card; (*Landkarte*) map; (*Speisekarte*) menu; (*Eintrittskarte, Fahrkarte*) ticket; **alles auf eine ~ setzen** to put all one's eggs in one basket
Kartei [kar'tai] *f* card index; ~**karte** *f* index card
Kartell [kar'tɛl] (**-s, -e**) *nt* cartel
Karten- *zW*: ~**spiel** *nt* card game; pack of cards; ~**telefon** *nt* cardphone;

Spelling Reform: ▲ *new spelling* △ *old spelling (to be phased out)*

~vorverkauf *m* advance booking office

Kartoffel [kar'tɔfəl] (-, -n) *f* potato; **~brei** *m* mashed potatoes *pl*; **~mus** *nt* mashed potatoes *pl*; **~püree** *nt* mashed potatoes *pl*; **~salat** *m* potato salad

Karton [kar'tõ:] (-s, -s) *m* cardboard; (*Schachtel*) cardboard box; **k~iert** [karto'ni:rt] *adj* hardback

Karussell [karʊ'sɛl] (-s, -s) *nt* roundabout (*BRIT*), merry-go-round

Karwoche ['ka:rvɔxə] *f* Holy Week

Käse ['kɛ:zə] (-s, -) *m* cheese; **~glocke** *f* cheese (plate) cover; **~kuchen** *m* cheesecake

Kaserne [ka'zɛrnə] *f* barracks *pl*; **~nhof** *m* parade ground

Kasino [ka'zi:no] (-s, -s) *nt* club; (*MIL*) officers' mess; (*Spielkasino*) casino

Kaskoversicherung ['kasko-] *f* (*Teilkasko*) ≈ third party, fire and theft insurance; (*Vollkasko*) ≈ fully comprehensive insurance

Kasse ['kasə] *f* (*Geldkasten*) cashbox; (*in Geschäft*) till, cash register; cash desk, checkout; (*Kinokasse, Theaterkasse etc*) box office; ticket office; (*Krankenkasse*) health insurance; (*Sparkasse*) savings bank; **~machen** to count the money; **getrennte ~ führen** to pay separately; **an der ~** (*in Geschäft*) at the desk; **gut bei ~ sein** to be in the money

Kassen- *zW*: **~arzt** *m* panel doctor (*BRIT*); **~bestand** *m* cash balance; **~patient** *m* panel patient (*BRIT*); **~prüfung** *f* audit; **~sturz** *m*: **~sturz machen** to check one's money; **~zettel** *m* receipt

Kassette [ka'sɛtə] *f* small box; (*Tonband, PHOT*) cassette; (*Bücherkassette*) case

Kassettenrekorder (-s, -) *m* cassette recorder

kassieren [ka'si:rən] *vt* to take ♦ *vi*: **darf ich ~?** would you like to pay now?

Kassierer [ka'si:rər] (-s, -) *m* cashier; (*von Klub*) treasurer

Kastanie [kas'ta:niə] *f* chestnut; (*Baum*) chestnut tree

Kasten ['kastən] (-s, ⸚) *m* (*auch SPORT*) box; case; (*Truhe*) chest

kastrieren [kas'tri:rən] *vt* to castrate

Katalog [kata'lo:k] (-(e)s, -e) *m* catalogue

Katalysator [kataly'za:tɔr] *m* catalyst; (*AUT*) catalytic converter

katastrophal [katastro'fa:l] *adj* catastrophic

Katastrophe [kata'stro:fə] *f* catastrophe, disaster

Kat-Auto ['kat|auto] *nt* car fitted with a catalytic converter

Kategorie [katego'ri:] *f* category

kategorisch [kate'go:rɪʃ] *adj* categorical

Kater ['ka:tər] (-s, -) *m* tomcat; (*umg*) hangover

kath. *abk* (= *katholisch*) Cath.

Kathedrale [kate'dra:lə] *f* cathedral

Katholik [kato'li:k] (-en, -en) *m* Catholic

katholisch [ka'to:lɪʃ] *adj* Catholic

Kätzchen ['kɛtsçən] *nt* kitten

Katze ['katsə] *f* cat; **für die Katz** (*umg*) in vain, for nothing

Katzen- *zW*: **~auge** *nt* cat's eye; (*Fahrrad*) rear light; **~sprung** (*umg*) *m* stone's throw; short journey

Kauderwelsch ['kaudərvɛlʃ] (-(s)) *nt* jargon; (*umg*) double Dutch

kauen ['kauən] *vt, vi* to chew

kauern ['kauərn] *vi* to crouch down; (*furchtsam*) to cower

Kauf [kauf] (-(e)s, Käufe) *m* purchase, buy; (*~en*) buying; **ein guter ~** a bargain; **etw in ~ nehmen** to put up with sth; **k~en** *vt* to buy

Käufer(in) ['kɔyfər(in)] (-s, -) *m(f)* buyer

Kauf- *zW*: **~frau** *f* businesswoman; **~haus** *nt* department store; **~kraft** *f* purchasing power

käuflich ['kɔyflɪç] *adj* purchasable, for sale; (*pej*) venal ♦ *adv*: **~ erwerben** to purchase

Kauf- *zW*: **k~lustig** *adj* interested in buying; **~mann** (*pl* **-leute**) *m* businessman; shopkeeper; **k~männisch** *adj* commercial; **k~männischer Angestellter** office worker; **~preis** *m* purchase price; **~vertrag** *m* bill of sale

Kaugummi ['kaugumi] *m* chewing gum

Kaulquappe ['kaulkvapə] *f* tadpole

kaum [kaum] *adv* hardly, scarcely

Kaution [kaʊtsiˈoːn] f deposit; (JUR) bail

Kauz [kaʊts] (-es, Käuze) m owl; (fig) queer fellow

Kavalier [kavaˈliːr] (-s, -e) m gentleman, cavalier; **~sdelikt** nt peccadillo

Kaviar [ˈkaːviar] m caviar

keck [kɛk] adj daring, bold

Kegel [ˈkeːgəl] (-s, -) m skittle; (MATH) cone; **~bahn** f skittle alley; bowling alley; **k~n** vi to play skittles

Kehle [ˈkeːlə] f throat

Kehlkopf m larynx

Kehre [ˈkeːrə] f turn(ing), bend; **k~n** vt, vi (wenden) to turn; (mit Besen) to sweep; **sich an etw** dat **nicht k~n** not to heed sth

Kehricht [ˈkeːrɪçt] (-s) m sweepings pl

Kehrseite f reverse, other side; wrong side; bad side

kehrtmachen vi to turn about, to about-turn

keifen [ˈkaɪfən] vi to scold, to nag

Keil [kaɪl] (-(e)s, -e) m wedge; (MIL) arrowhead; **~riemen** m (AUT) fan belt

Keim [kaɪm] (-(e)s, -e) m bud; (MED, fig) germ; **k~en** vi to germinate; **k~frei** adj sterile; **~zelle** f (fig) nucleus

kein [kaɪn] adj no, not ... any; **~e(r, s)** pron no one, nobody; none; **~erlei** adj attrib no ... whatsoever

keinesfalls adv on no account

keineswegs adv by no means

keinmal adv not once

Keks [keːks] (-es, -e) m od nt biscuit

Kelch [kɛlç] (-(e)s, -e) m cup, goblet, chalice

Kelle [ˈkɛlə] f (Suppenkelle) ladle; (Maurerkelle) trowel

Keller [ˈkɛlər] (-s, -) m cellar

Kellner(in) [ˈkɛlnər(ɪn)] (-s, -) m(f) waiter (-tress)

keltern [ˈkɛltərn] vt to press

kennen [ˈkɛnən] (unreg) vt to know; **~ lernen** ▲ to get to know; **sich ~ lernen** to get to know each other; (zum ersten Mal) to meet

Kenner (-s, -) m connoisseur

kenntlich adj distinguishable, discernible;

etw ~ machen to mark sth

Kenntnis (-, -se) f knowledge no pl; **etw zur ~ nehmen** to note sth; **von etw ~ nehmen** to take notice of sth; **jdn in ~ setzen** to inform sb

Kenn- zW: **~zeichen** nt mark, characteristic; **k~zeichnen** vt insep to characterize; **~ziffer** f reference number

kentern [ˈkɛntərn] vi to capsize

Keramik [keˈraːmɪk] (-, -en) f ceramics pl, pottery

Kerbe [ˈkɛrbə] f notch, groove

Kerker [ˈkɛrkər] (-s, -) m prison

Kerl [kɛrl] (-s, -e) m chap, bloke (BRIT), guy

Kern [kɛrn] (-(e)s, -e) m (Obstkern) pip, stone; (Nusskern) kernel; (Atomkern) nucleus; (fig) heart, core; **~energie** f nuclear energy; **~forschung** f nuclear research; **~frage** f central issue; **k~gesund** adj thoroughly healthy, fit as a fiddle; **k~ig** adj (kraftvoll) robust; (Ausspruch) pithy; **~kraftwerk** nt nuclear power station; **k~los** adj seedless, without pips; **~physik** f nuclear physics sg; **~spaltung** f nuclear fission; **~waffen** pl nuclear weapons

Kerze [ˈkɛrtsə] f candle; (Zündkerze) plug; **k~ngerade** adj straight as a die; **~nständer** m candle holder

kess ▲ [kɛs] adj saucy

Kessel [ˈkɛsəl] (-s, -) m kettle; (von Lokomotive etc) boiler; (GEOG) depression; (MIL) encirclement

Kette [ˈkɛtə] f chain; **k~n** vt to chain; **~nrauchen** (-s) nt chain smoking; **~nreaktion** f chain reaction

Ketzer [ˈkɛtsər] (-s, -) m heretic

keuchen [ˈkɔʏçən] vi to pant, to gasp

Keuchhusten m whooping cough

Keule [ˈkɔʏlə] f club; (KOCH) leg

keusch [kɔʏʃ] adj chaste; **K~heit** f chastity

kfm. abk = kaufmännisch

Kfz [kaːʔɛfˈtseːt] nt abk = **Kraftfahrzeug**

KG [kaːˈgeː] (-, -s) f abk (= Kommanditgesellschaft) limited partnership

kg abk = **Kilogramm**

kichern [ˈkɪçərn] vi to giggle

kidnappen ['kɪtnɛpən] vt to kidnap

Kiefer¹ ['ki:fər] (-s, -) m jaw

Kiefer² ['ki:fər] (-, -n) f pine; **~nzapfen** m pine cone

Kiel [ki:l] (-(e)s, -e) m (Federkiel) quill; (NAUT) keel

Kieme ['ki:mə] f gill

Kies [ki:s] (-es, -e) m gravel

Kilo ['ki:lo] nt kilo; **~gramm** [kilo'gram] nt kilogram; **~meter** [kilo'me:tər] m kilometre; **~meterzähler** m milometer

Kind [kɪnt] (-(e)s, -er) nt child; **von ~ auf** from childhood

Kinder- ['kɪndər] zW: **~betreuung** f crèche; **~ei** [-'raɪ] f childishness; **~garten** m nursery school, playgroup; **~gärtnerin** f nursery school teacher; **~geld** nt child benefit (BRIT); **~heim** nt children's home; **~krippe** f crèche; **~lähmung** f poliomyelitis; **k~leicht** adj childishly easy; **k~los** adj childless; **~mädchen** nt nursemaid; **k~reich** adj with a lot of children; **~sendung** f (RADIO, TV) children's programme; **~sicherung** f (AUT) childproof safety catch; **~spiel** nt (fig) child's play; **~tagesstätte** f day nursery; **~wagen** m pram, baby carriage (US); **~zimmer** nt (für ~) children's room; (für Säugling) nursery

---

Kindergarten

ⓘ A **Kindergarten** is a nursery school for children aged between 3 and 6 years. The children sing and play but do not receive any formal instruction. Most Kindergärten are financed by the town or the church with parents paying a monthly contribution towards the cost.

Kind- zW: **~heit** f childhood; **k~isch** adj childish; **k~lich** adj childlike

Kinn [kɪn] (-(e)s, -e) nt chin; **~haken** m (BOXEN) uppercut

Kino ['ki:no] (-s, -s) nt cinema; **~besucher** m cinema-goer; **~programm** nt film programme

Kiosk [ki'ɔsk] (-(e)s, -e) m kiosk

Kippe ['kɪpə] f cigarette end; (umg) fag; **auf der ~ stehen** (fig) to be touch and go

kippen vi to topple over, to overturn ♦ vt to tilt

Kirch- ['kɪrç] zW: **~e** f church; **~enlied** nt hymn; **~ensteuer** f church tax; **~gänger** (-s, -) m churchgoer; **~hof** m churchyard; **k~lich** adj ecclesiastical

Kirmes ['kɪrməs] (-, -sen) f fair

Kirsche ['kɪrʃə] f cherry

Kissen ['kɪsən] (-s, -) nt cushion; (Kopfkissen) pillow; **~bezug** m pillowslip

Kiste ['kɪstə] f box; chest

Kitsch [kɪtʃ] (-(e)s) m kitsch; **k~ig** adj kitschy

Kitt [kɪt] (-(e)s, -e) m putty

Kittel (-s, -) m overall, smock

kitten vt to putty; (fig: Ehe etc) to cement

kitzelig ['kɪtsəlɪç] adj (auch fig) ticklish

kitzeln vi to tickle

Kiwi ['ki:vi] (-, -s) f (BOT, KOCH) kiwi fruit

KKW [ka:ka:'ve:] nt abk = **Kernkraftwerk**

Klage ['kla:gə] f complaint; (JUR) action; **k~n** vi (wehklagen) to lament, to wail; (sich beschweren) to complain; (JUR) to take legal action

Kläger(in) ['klɛ:gər(ɪn)] (-s, -) m(f) plaintiff

kläglich ['klɛ:klɪç] adj wretched

klamm [klam] adj (Finger) numb; (feucht) damp

Klammer ['klamər] (-, -n) f clamp; (in Text) bracket; (Büro~) clip; (Wäsche~) peg; (Zahn~) brace; **k~n** vr: **sich k~n an** +akk to cling to

Klang [klaŋ] (-(e)s, ⁻e) m sound; **k~voll** adj sonorous

Klappe ['klapə] f valve; (Ofen~) damper; (umg: Mund) trap; **k~n** vi (Geräusch) to click; (Sitz etc) to tip ♦ vt to tip ♦ vb unpers to work

Klapper ['klapər] (-, -n) f rattle; **k~ig** adj run-down, worn-out; **k~n** vi to clatter, to rattle; **~schlange** f rattlesnake; **~storch** m stork

Klapp- zW: **~messer** nt jackknife; **~rad** nt collapsible bicycle; **~stuhl** m folding chair; **~tisch** m folding table

Klaps [klaps] (-es, -e) m slap

---

klar [klaːr] *adj* clear; (*NAUT*) ready for sea; (*MIL*) ready for action; **sich** *dat* (**über etw** *akk*) ~ **werden** to get (sth) clear in one's mind; **sich** *dat* **im K~en sein über** +*akk* to be clear about; **ins K~e kommen** to get clear; (**na**) ~! of course!; ~ **sehen** to see clearly

Kläranlage *f* purification plant

klären ['klɛːrən] *vt* (*Flüssigkeit*) to purify; (*Probleme*) to clarify ♦ *vr* to clear (itself) up

Klarheit *f* clarity

Klarinette [klari'nɛtə] *f* clarinet

klar- *zW*: ~**legen** *vt* to clear up, to explain; ~**machen** *vt* (*Schiff*) to get ready for sea; **jdm etw ~machen** to make sth clear to sb; ~**sehen** △ (*unreg*) *vi siehe* **klar**; **K~sichtfolie** *f* transparent film; ~**stellen** *vt* to clarify

Klärung ['klɛːrʊŋ] *f* (*von Flüssigkeit*) purification; (*von Probleme*) clarification

klarwerden △ (*unreg*) *vi siehe* **klar**

Klasse ['klasə] *f* class; (*SCH*) class, form

klasse (*umg*) *adj* smashing

Klassen- *zW*: ~**arbeit** *f* test; ~**gesellschaft** *f* class society; ~**lehrer** *m* form master; **k~los** *adj* classless; ~**sprecher(in)** *m(f)* form prefect; ~**zimmer** *nt* classroom

klassifizieren [klasifi'tsiːrən] *vt* to classify

Klassik ['klasɪk] *f* (*Zeit*) classical period; (*Stil*) classicism; ~**er** (**-s, -**) *m* classic

klassisch *adj* (*auch fig*) classical

Klatsch [klatʃ] (**-(e)s, -e**) *m* smack, crack; (*Gerede*) gossip; ~**base** *f* gossip, scandalmonger; ~**e** (*umg*) *f* crib; **k~en** *vi* (*Geräusch*) to clash; (*reden*) to gossip; (*applaudieren*) to applaud, to clap ♦ *vt*: **jdm Beifall k~en** to applaud sb; ~**mohn** *m* (*corn*) poppy; **k~nass** ▲ *adj* soaking wet

Klaue ['klaʊə] *f* claw; (*umg*: *Schrift*) scrawl; **k~n** (*umg*) *vt* to pinch

Klausel ['klaʊzəl] (**-, -n**) *f* clause

Klausur [klaʊ'zuːr] *f* seclusion; ~**arbeit** *f* examination paper

Klavier [kla'viːr] (**-s, -e**) *nt* piano

Kleb- ['kleːb] *zW*: **k~en** ['kleːbən] *vt*, *vi*: **k~en (an** +*akk*) to stick (to); **k~rig** *adj*

sticky; ~**stoff** *m* glue; ~**streifen** *m* adhesive tape

kleckern ['klɛkərn] *vi* to make a mess ♦ *vt* to spill

Klecks [klɛks] (**-es, -e**) *m* blot, stain

Klee [kleː] (**-s**) *m* clover; ~**blatt** *nt* cloverleaf; (*fig*) trio

Kleid [klaɪt] (**-(e)s, -er**) *nt* garment; (*Frauenkleid*) dress; ~**er** *pl* (*~ung*) clothes; **k~en** ['klaɪdən] *vt* to clothe, to dress; to suit ♦ *vr* to dress

Kleider- ['klaɪdər] *zW*: ~**bügel** *m* coat hanger; ~**bürste** *f* clothes brush; ~**schrank** *m* wardrobe

Kleid- *zW*: **k~sam** *adj* flattering; ~**ung** *f* clothing; ~**ungsstück** *nt* garment

klein [klaɪn] *adj* little, small; ~ **hacken** to chop, to mince; ~ **schneiden** to chop up; **K~e(r, s)** *mf* little one; **K~format** *nt* small size; **im K~format** small-scale; **K~geld** *nt* small change; **K~igkeit** *f* trifle; **K~kind** *nt* infant; **K~kram** *m* details *pl*; ~**laut** *adj* dejected, quiet; ~**lich** *adj* petty, paltry; **K~od** ['klaɪnoːt] (**-s, -odien**) *nt* gem, jewel; treasure; **K~stadt** *f* small town; ~**städtisch** *adj* provincial; ~**stmöglich** *adj* smallest possible

Kleister ['klaɪstər] (**-s, -**) *m* paste

Klemme ['klɛmə] *f* clip; (*MED*) clamp; (*fig*) jam; **k~n** *vt* (*festhalten*) to jam; (*quetschen*) to pinch, to nip ♦ *vt* to catch o.s.; (*sich hineinzwängen*) to squeeze o.s. ♦ *vi* (*Tür*) to stick, to jam; **sich hinter jdn/etw k~n** to get on to sb/down to sth

Klempner ['klɛmpnər] (**-s, -**) *m* plumber

Klerus ['kleːrʊs] (**-**) *m* clergy

Klette ['klɛtə] *f* burr

Kletter- ['klɛtər] *zW*: ~**er** (**-s, -**) *m* climber; **k~n** *vi* to climb; ~**pflanze** *f* creeper

klicken ['klɪkən] *vi* (*COMPUT*) to click

Klient(in) [kli'ɛnt(ɪn)] *m(f)* client

Klima ['kliːma] (**-s, -s** *od* **-te**) *nt* climate; ~**anlage** *f* air conditioning; ~**wechsel** *m* change of air

klimpern ['klɪmpərn] (*umg*) *vi* (*mit Münzen, Schlüsseln*) to jingle; (*auf Klavier*) to plonk (away)

Klinge ['klɪŋə] f blade; sword

Klingel ['klɪŋəl] (-, -n) f bell; **~beutel** m collection bag; **k~n** vi to ring

klingen ['klɪŋən] (*unreg*) vi to sound; (*Gläser*) to clink

Klinik ['kliːnɪk] f hospital, clinic

Klinke ['klɪŋkə] f handle

Klippe ['klɪpə] f cliff; (*im Meer*) reef; (*fig*) hurdle

klipp und klar ['klɪp|ʊntklaːr] adj clear and concise

klirren ['klɪrən] vi to clank, to jangle; (*Gläser*) to clink; **~de Kälte** biting cold

Klischee [klɪ'ʃeː] (-s, -s) nt (*Druckplatte*) plate, block; (*fig*) cliché; **~vorstellung** f stereotyped idea

Klo [kloː] (-s, -s) (*umg*) nt loo (*BRIT*), john (*US*)

Kloake [klo'aːkə] f sewer

klobig ['kloːbɪç] adj clumsy

Klon [kloːn] (-s, -e) m clone

klonen ['kloːnən] vti to clone

Klopapier (*umg*) nt loo paper (*BRIT*)

klopfen ['klɔpfən] vi to knock; (*Herz*) to thump ♦ vt to beat; **es klopft** somebody's knocking; **jdm auf die Schulter ~** to tap sb on the shoulder

Klopfer (-s, -) m (*Teppichklopfer*) beater; (*Türklopfer*) knocker

Klops [klɔps] (-es, -e) m meatball

Klosett [klo'zɛt] (-s, -e *od* -s) nt lavatory, toilet; **~papier** nt toilet paper

Kloß [kloːs] (-es, ⁻e) m (*im Hals*) lump; (*KOCH*) dumpling

Kloster ['kloːstər] (-s, ⁻) nt (*Männerkloster*) monastery; (*Frauenkloster*) convent; **klösterlich** ['kløːstərlɪç] adj monastic; convent cpd

Klotz [klɔts] (-es, ⁻e) m log; (*Hackklotz*) block; **ein ~ am Bein** (*fig*) a drag, a millstone round (sb's) neck

Klub [klʊp] (-s, -s) m club; **~sessel** m easy chair

Kluft [klʊft] (-, ⁻e) f cleft, gap; (*GEOG*) gorge, chasm

klug [kluːk] adj clever, intelligent; **K~heit** f cleverness, intelligence

Klumpen ['klʊmpən] (-s, -) m (*Erd~*) clod;

(*Blut~*) clot; (*Gold~*) nugget; (*KOCH*) lump

km abk = **Kilometer**

knabbern ['knabərn] vt, vi to nibble

Knabe ['knaːbə] (-n, -n) m boy

Knäckebrot ['knɛkəbroːt] nt crispbread

knacken ['knakən] vt, vi (*auch fig*) to crack

Knacks [knaks] (-es, -e) m crack; (*fig*) defect

Knall [knal] (-(e)s, -e) m bang; (*Peitschenknall*) crack; **~ und Fall** (*umg*) unexpectedly; **~bonbon** nt cracker; **k~en** vi to bang; to crack; **k~rot** adj bright red

knapp [knap] adj tight; (*Geld*) scarce; (*Sprache*) concise; **eine ~e Stunde** just under an hour; **~ unter/neben** just under/by; **K~heit** f tightness; scarcity; conciseness

knarren ['knarən] vi to creak

Knast [knast] (-(e)s) (*umg*) m (*Haftstrafe*) porridge (*inf*), time (*inf*); (*Gefängnis*) slammer (*inf*), clink (*inf*)

knattern ['knatərn] vi to rattle; (*Maschinengewehr*) to chatter

Knäuel ['knɔʏəl] (-s, -) m od nt (*Wollknäuel*) ball; (*Menschenknäuel*) knot

Knauf [knauf] (-(e)s, Knäufe) m knob; (*Schwertknauf*) pommel

Knebel ['kneːbəl] (-s, -) m gag

kneifen ['knaɪfən] (*unreg*) vt to pinch ♦ vi to pinch; (*sich drücken*) to back out; **vor etw ~** to dodge sth

Kneipe ['knaɪpə] (*umg*) f pub

kneten ['kneːtən] vt to knead; (*Wachs*) to mould

Knick [knɪk] (-(e)s, -e) m (*Sprung*) crack; (*Kurve*) bend; (*Falte*) fold; **k~en** vt, vi (*springen*) to crack; (*brechen*) to break; (*Papier*) to fold; **geknickt sein** to be downcast

Knicks [knɪks] (-es, -e) m curtsey

Knie [kniː] (-s, -) nt knee; **~beuge** f knee bend; **~bundhose** m knee breeches; **~gelenk** nt knee joint; **~kehle** f back of the knee; **k~n** vi to kneel; **~scheibe** f kneecap; **~strumpf** m knee-length sock

Kniff [knɪf] (-(e)s, -e) m (*fig*) trick, knack; **k~elig** adj tricky

knipsen ['knɪpsən] *vt* (*Fahrkarte*) to punch; (*PHOT*) to take a snap of, to snap ♦ *vi* to take a snap *od* snaps

Knirps [knɪrps] (**-es, -e**) *m* little chap; (®: *Schirm*) telescopic umbrella

knirschen ['knɪrʃən] *vi* to crunch; **mit den Zähnen ~** to grind one's teeth

knistern ['knɪstərn] *vi* to crackle

Knitter- ['knɪtər] *zW:* **~falte** *f* crease; **k~frei** *adj* non-crease; **k~n** *vi* to crease

Knoblauch ['kno:plaʊx] (**-(e)s**) *m* garlic; **~zehe** *f* (*KOCH*) clove of garlic

Knöchel ['knœçəl] (**-s, -**) *m* knuckle; (*Fußknöchel*) ankle

Knochen ['knɔxən] (**-s, -**) *m* bone; **~bruch** *m* fracture; **~gerüst** *nt* skeleton; **~mark** *nt* bone marrow

knöchern ['knœçərn] *adj* bone

knochig ['knɔxɪç] *adj* bony

Knödel ['knø:dəl] (**-s, -**) *m* dumpling

Knolle ['knɔlə] *f* tuber

Knopf [knɔpf] (**-(e)s, ̈e**) *m* button; (*Kragenknopf*) stud

knöpfen ['knœpfən] *vt* to button

Knopfloch *nt* buttonhole

Knorpel ['knɔrpəl] (**-s, -**) *m* cartilage, gristle; **k~ig** *adj* gristly

Knospe ['knɔspə] *f* bud

Knoten ['kno:tən] (**-s, -**) *m* knot; (*BOT*) node; (*MED*) lump; **k~** *vt* to knot; **~punkt** *m* junction

Knüller ['knʏlər] (**-s, -**) (*umg*) *m* hit; (*Reportage*) scoop

knüpfen ['knʏpfən] *vt* to tie; (*Teppich*) to knot; (*Freundschaft*) to form

Knüppel ['knʏpəl] (**-s, -**) *m* cudgel; (*Polizeiknüppel*) baton, truncheon; (*AVIAT*) (joy)stick

knurren ['knʊrən] *vi* (*Hund*) to snarl, to growl; (*Magen*) to rumble; (*Mensch*) to mutter

knusperig ['knʊspərɪç] *adj* crisp; (*Keks*) crunchy

k. o. [ka:'o:] *adj* knocked out; (*fig*) done in

Koalition [koalitsi'o:n] *f* coalition

Kobold ['ko:bɔlt] (**-(e)s, -e**) *m* goblin, imp

Koch [kɔx] (**-(e)s, ̈e**) *m* cook; **~buch** *nt*

cook(ery) book; **k~en** *vt, vi* to cook; (*Wasser*) to boil; **~er** (**-s, -**) *m* stove, cooker; **~gelegenheit** *f* cooking facilities *pl*

Köchin ['kœçɪn] *f* cook

Koch- *zW:* **~löffel** *m* kitchen spoon; **~nische** *f* kitchenette; **~platte** *f* hotplate; **~salz** *nt* cooking salt; **~topf** *m* saucepan, pot

Köder ['kø:dər] (**-s, -**) *m* bait, lure

ködern *vt* (*Tier*) to trap with bait; (*Person*) to entice, to tempt

Koexistenz [koɛksɪs'tɛnts] *f* coexistence

Koffein [kɔfe'i:n] (**-s**) *nt* caffeine; **k~frei** *adj* decaffeinated

Koffer ['kɔfər] (**-s, -**) *m* suitcase; (*Schrankkoffer*) trunk; **~kuli** *m* (luggage) trolley; **~radio** *nt* portable radio; **~raum** *m* (*AUT*) boot (*BRIT*), trunk (*US*)

Kognak ['kɔnjak] (**-s, -s**) *m* brandy, cognac

Kohl [ko:l] (**-(e)s, -e**) *m* cabbage

Kohle ['ko:lə] *f* coal; (*Holzkohle*) charcoal; (*CHEM*) carbon; **~hydrat** (**-(e)s, -e**) *nt* carbohydrate

Kohlen- *zW:* **~dioxid** (**-(e)s, -e**) *nt* carbon dioxide; **~händler** *m* coal merchant, coalman; **~säure** *f* carbon dioxide; **~stoff** *m* carbon

Kohlepapier *nt* carbon paper

Koje ['ko:jə] *f* cabin; (*Bett*) bunk

Kokain [koka'i:n] (**-s**) *nt* cocaine

kokett [ko'kɛt] *adj* coquettish, flirtatious

Kokosnuss ▲ ['ko:kɔsnʊs] *f* coconut

Koks [ko:ks] (**-es, -e**) *m* coke

Kolben ['kɔlbən] (**-s, -**) *m* (*Gewehrkolben*) rifle butt; (*Keule*) club; (*CHEM*) flask; (*TECH*) piston; (*Maiskolben*) cob

Kolik ['ko:lɪk] *f* colic, the gripes *pl*

Kollaps [kɔ'laps] (**-es, -e**) *m* collapse

Kolleg [kɔl'e:k] (**-s, -s** *od* **-ien**) *nt* lecture course; **~e** [kɔ'le:gə] (**-n, -n**) *m* colleague; **~in** *f* colleague; **~ium** *nt* working party; (*SCH*) staff

Kollekte [kɔ'lɛktə] *f* (*REL*) collection

kollektiv [kɔlɛk'ti:f] *adj* collective

Köln [kœln] (**-s**) *nt* Cologne

Kolonie [kolo'ni:] *f* colony

kolonisieren [koloni'ʦiːrən] *vt* to colonize

Kolonne [ko'lɔnə] *f* column; (*von Fahrzeugen*) convoy

Koloss ▲ [ko'lɔs] (**-es, -e**) *m* colossus; **kolo'ssal** *adj* colossal

Kölsch [kœlʃ] (**-, -**) *nt* (*Bier*) ≈ (strong) lager

Kombi- [ˈkɔmbi] *zW:* **~nation** [-natsiˈoːn] *f* combination; (*Vermutung*) conjecture; (*Hemdhose*) combinations *pl*; **k~nieren** [-ˈniːrən] *vt* to combine ♦ *vi* to deduce, to work out; (*vermuten*) to guess; **~wagen** *m* station wagon; **~zange** *f* (pair of) pliers *pl*

Komet [koˈmeːt] (**-en, -en**) *m* comet

Komfort [kɔmˈfoːr] (**-s**) *m* luxury

Komik [ˈkoːmɪk] *f* humour, comedy; **~er** (**-s, -**) *m* comedian

komisch [ˈkoːmɪʃ] *adj* funny

Komitee [komiˈteː] (**-s, -s**) *nt* committee

Komma [ˈkɔma] (**-s, -s** *od* **-ta**) *nt* comma; **2 ~ 3** 2 point 3

Kommand- [kɔˈmand] *zW:* **~ant** [-ˈdant] *m* commander, commanding officer; **k~ieren** [-ˈdiːrən] *vt, vi* to command; **~o** (**-s, -s**) *nt* command, order; (*Truppe*) detachment, squad; **auf ~o** to order

kommen [ˈkɔmən] (*unreg*) *vi* to come; (*näher kommen*) to approach; (*passieren*) to happen; (*gelangen, geraten*) to get; (*Blumen, Zähne, Tränen etc*) to appear; (*in die Schule, das Zuchthaus etc*) to go; **~ lassen** to send for; **das kommt in den Schrank** that goes in the cupboard; **zu sich ~** to come round *od* to; **zu etw ~** to acquire sth; **um etw ~** to lose sth; **nichts auf jdn/etw ~ lassen** to have nothing said against sb/sth; **jdm frech ~** to get cheeky with sb; **auf jeden vierten kommt ein Platz** there's one place for every fourth person; **wer kommt zuerst?** who's first?; **unter ein Auto ~** to be run over by a car; **wie hoch kommt das?** what does that cost?; **komm gut nach Hause!** safe journey (home); **~den Sonntag** next Sunday; **K~** (**-s**) *nt* coming

Kommentar [kɔmɛnˈtaːr] *m* commentary; **kein ~** no comment; **k~los** *adj* without comment

Kommentator [kɔmɛnˈtaːtɔr] *m* (*TV*) commentator

kommentieren [kɔmɛnˈtiːrən] *vt* to comment on

kommerziell [kɔmɛrʦiˈɛl] *adj* commercial

Kommilitone [kɔmiliˈtoːnə] (**-n, -n**) *m* fellow student

Kommissar [kɔmɪˈsaːr] *m* police inspector

Kommission [kɔmɪsiˈoːn] *f* (*COMM*) commission; (*Ausschuss*) committee

Kommode [kɔˈmoːdə] *f* (chest of) drawers

kommunal [kɔmuˈnaːl] *adj* local; (*von Stadt auch*) municipal

Kommune [kɔˈmuːnə] *f* commune

Kommunikation [kɔmunikatsiˈoːn] *f* communication

Kommunion [kɔmuniˈoːn] *f* communion

Kommuniqué, Kommunikee ▲ [kɔmyniˈkeː] (**-s, -s**) *nt* communiqué

Kommunismus [kɔmuˈnɪsmʊs] *m* communism

Kommunist(in) [kɔmuˈnɪst(ɪn)] *m(f)* communist; **k~isch** *adj* communist

kommunizieren [kɔmuniˈʦiːrən] *vi* to communicate

Komödie [koˈmøːdiə] *f* comedy

Kompagnon [kɔmpanˈjõː] (**-s, -s**) *m* (*COMM*) partner

kompakt [kɔmˈpakt] *adj* compact

Kompanie [kɔmpaˈniː] *f* company

Kompass ▲ [ˈkɔmpas] (**-es, -e**) *m* compass

kompatibel [kɔmpaˈtiːbəl] *adj* compatible

kompetent [kɔmpeˈtɛnt] *adj* competent

Kompetenz *f* competence, authority

komplett [kɔmˈplɛt] *adj* complete

Komplex [kɔmˈpleks] (**-es, -e**) *m* (*Gebäudekomplex*) complex

Komplikation [kɔmplikatsiˈoːn] *f* complication

Kompliment [kɔmpliˈmɛnt] *nt* compliment

Komplize [kɔmˈpliːʦə] (**-n, -n**) *m* accomplice

kompliziert [kɔmpliˈʦiːrt] *adj* complicated

komponieren [kɔmpoˈniːrən] *vt* to compose

Komponist [kɔmpoˈnɪst(ɪn)] *m* composer

Komposition [kɔmpoʦitsiˈoːn] *f* composition

Kompost [kɔmˈpɔst] (**-(e)s, -e**) *m* compost

Kompott [kɔm'pɔt] **(-(e)s, -e)** nt stewed fruit

Kompromiss ▲ [kɔmpro'mɪs] **(-es, -e)** m compromise; **k~bereit** adj willing to compromise

Kondens- [kɔn'dɛns] zW: **~ation** [kɔndɛnzatsi'oːn] f condensation; **k~ieren** [kɔndɛn'ziːrən] vt to condense; **~milch** f condensed milk

Kondition [kɔnditsi'oːn] f (COMM, FIN) condition; (Durchhaltevermögen) stamina; (körperliche Verfassung) physical condition, state of health

Konditionstraining [kɔnditsi'oːnstreːnɪŋ] nt fitness training

Konditor [kɔn'diːtɔr] m pastry cook; **~ei** [-'raɪ] f café; cake shop

Kondom [kɔn'doːm] **(-s, -e)** nt condom

Konferenz [kɔnfe'rɛnts] f conference, meeting

Konfession [kɔnfesi'oːn] f (religious) denomination; **k~ell** [-'nɛl] adj denominational; **k~slos** adj non-denominational

Konfirmand [kɔnfɪr'mant] m candidate for confirmation

Konfirmation [kɔnfɪrmatsi'oːn] f (REL) confirmation

konfirmieren [kɔnfɪr'miːrən] vt to confirm

konfiszieren [kɔnfɪs'tsiːrən] vt to confiscate

Konfitüre [kɔnfi'tyːrə] f jam

Konflikt [kɔn'flɪkt] **(-(e)s, -e)** m conflict

konfrontieren [kɔnfrɔn'tiːrən] vt to confront

konfus [kɔn'fuːs] adj confused

Kongress ▲ [kɔn'grɛs] **(-es, -e)** m congress; **~zentrum** nt conference centre

Kongruenz [kɔngru'ɛnts] f agreement, congruence

König ['køːnɪç] **(-(e)s, -e)** m king; **~in** ['køːnɪgɪn] f queen; **k~lich** adj royal; **~reich** nt kingdom

Konjugation [kɔnjugatsi'oːn] f conjugation

konjugieren [kɔnju'giːrən] vt to conjugate

Konjunktion [kɔnjʊŋktsi'oːn] f conjunction

Konjunktiv ['kɔnjʊŋktiːf] **(-s, -e)** m subjunctive

Konjunktur [kɔnjʊŋk'tuːr] f economic

situation; (Hochkonjunktur) boom

konkret [kɔn'kreːt] adj concrete

Konkurrent(in) [kɔnku'rɛnt(ɪn)] m(f) competitor

Konkurrenz [kɔnku'rɛnts] f competition; **k~fähig** adj competitive; **~kampf** m competition; rivalry, competitive situation

konkurrieren [kɔnku'riːrən] vi to compete

Konkurs [kɔn'kʊrs] **(-es, -e)** m bankruptcy

Können (-s) nt ability

SCHLÜSSELWORT

können ['kœnən] (pt **konnte**, pp **gekonnt** od (als Hilfsverb) **können**) vt, vi 1 to be able to; **ich kann es machen** I can do it, I am able to do it; **ich kann es nicht machen** I can't do it, I'm not able to do it; **ich kann nicht ...** I can't ..., I cannot ...; **ich kann nicht mehr** I can't go on

2 (wissen, beherrschen) to know; **können Sie Deutsch?** can you speak German?; **er kann gut Englisch** he speaks English well; **sie kann keine Mathematik** she can't do mathematics

3 (dürfen) to be allowed to; **kann ich gehen?** can I go?; **könnte ich ...?** could I ...?; **kann ich mit?** (umg) can I come with you?

4 (möglich sein): **Sie könnten Recht haben** you may be right; **das kann sein** that's possible; **kann sein** maybe

---

Könner m expert

konnte etc ['kɔntə] vb siehe **können**

konsequent [kɔnze'kvɛnt] adj consistent

Konsequenz [kɔnze'kvɛnts] f consistency; (Folgerung) conclusion

Konserv- [kɔn'zɛrv] zW: **k~ativ** [-a'tiːf] adj conservative; **~ative(r)** [-a'tiːvə(r)] f(m) (POL) conservative; **~e** f tinned food; **~enbüchse** f tin, can; **k~ieren** [-'viːrən] vt to preserve; **~ierung** f preservation; **~ierungsstoff** m preservatives

Konsonant [kɔnzo'nant] m consonant

konstant [kɔn'stant] adj constant

konstru- zW: **~ieren** [kɔnstru'iːrən] vt to construct; **K~kteur** [kɔnstrʊk'tøːr] m

---

designer; **K~ktion** [kɔnstrʊktsi'oːn] *f*
construction; **~ktiv** [kɔnstrʊk'tiːf] *adj*
constructive

Konsul ['kɔnzʊl] (**-s, -n**) *m* consul; **~at** [-'laːt]
nt consulate

konsultieren [kɔnzʊl'tiːrən] *vt* to consult

Konsum [kɔn'zuːm] (**-s**) *m* consumption;
~artikel *m* consumer article; **~ent** [-'mɛnt]
m consumer; **k~ieren** [-'miːrən] *vt* to
consume

Kontakt [kɔn'takt] (**-(e)s, -e**) *m* contact;
k~arm *adj* unsociable; **k~freudig** *adj*
sociable; **~linsen** *pl* contact lenses

kontern ['kɔntərn] *vt, vi* to counter

Kontinent [kɔnti'nɛnt] *m* continent

Kontingent [kɔntɪŋ'gɛnt] (**-(e)s, -e**) *nt*
quota; (*Truppenkontingent*) contingent

kontinuierlich [kɔntinu'iːrlɪç] *adj*
continuous

Konto ['kɔnto] (**-s, Konten**) *nt* account;
~auszug *m* statement (of account);
~inhaber(in) *m(f)* account holder; **~stand**
m balance

Kontra ['kɔntra] (**-s, -s**) *nt* (*KARTEN*) double;
jdm ~ geben (*fig*) to contradict sb;
~bass ▲ *m* double bass; **~hent** *m* (*COMM*)
contracting party; **~punkt** *m* counterpoint

Kontrast [kɔn'trast] (**-(e)s, -e**) *m* contrast

Kontroll- [kɔn'trɔl] *zW:* **~e** *f* control,
supervision; (*Passkontrolle*) passport control;
~eur [-'løːr] *m* inspector; **k~ieren** [-'liːrən]
vt to control, to supervise; (*nachprüfen*) to
check

Konvention [kɔnvɛntsi'oːn] *f* convention;
k~ell [-'nɛl] *adj* conventional

Konversation [kɔnvɛrzatsi'oːn] *f*
conversation; **~slexikon** *nt*
encyclop(a)edia

Konvoi ['kɔnvɔy] (**-s, -s**) *m* convoy

Konzentration [kɔntsɛntratsi'oːn] *f*
concentration

Konzentrationslager *nt* concentration
camp

konzentrieren [kɔntsɛn'triːrən] *vt, vr* to
concentrate

konzentriert *adj* concentrated ♦ *adv*
(*zuhören, arbeiten*) intently

Konzern [kɔn'tsɛrn] (**-s, -e**) *m* combine

Konzert [kɔn'tsɛrt] (**-(e)s, -e**) *nt* concert;
(*Stück*) concerto; **~saal** *m* concert hall

Konzession [kɔntsesi'oːn] *f* licence;
(*Zugeständnis*) concession

Konzil [kɔn'tsiːl] (**-s, -e** *od* **-ien**) *nt* council

kooperativ [ko|opera'tiːf] *adj* cooperative

koordinieren [ko|ɔrdi'niːrən] *vt* to
coordinate

Kopf [kɔpf] (**-(e)s, ⁼e**) *m* head; **~haut** *f*
scalp; **~hörer** *m* headphones *pl*; **~kissen**
nt pillow; **k~los** *adj* panic-stricken;
k~rechnen *vt* to do mental arithmetic;
~salat *m* lettuce; **~schmerzen** *pl*
headache *sg*; **~sprung** *m* header, dive;
~stand *m* headstand; **~stütze** *f* (*im Auto
etc*) headrest, head restraint; **~tuch** *nt*
headscarf; **~weh** *nt* headache;
~zerbrechen *nt:* **jdm ~zerbrechen
machen** to be a headache for sb

Kopie [ko'piː] *f* copy; **k~ren** *vt* to copy

Kopiergerät *nt* photocopier

Koppel¹ ['kɔpəl] (**-, -n**) *f* (*Weide*) enclosure

Koppel² ['kɔpəl] (**-s, -**) *nt* (*Gürtel*) belt

koppeln *vt* to couple

Koppelung *f* coupling

Koralle [ko'ralə] *f* coral

Korb [kɔrp] (**-(e)s, ⁼e**) *m* basket; **jdm einen
~ geben** (*fig*) to turn sb down; **~ball** *m*
basketball; **~stuhl** *m* wicker chair

Kord [kɔrt] (**-(e)s, -e**) *m* cord, corduroy

Kordel ['kɔrdəl] (**-, -n**) *f* cord, string

Kork [kɔrk] (**-(e)s, -e**) *m* cork; **~en** (**-s, -**) *m*
stopper, cork; **~enzieher** (**-s, -**) *m*
corkscrew

Korn [kɔrn] (**-(e)s, ⁼er**) *nt* corn, grain;
(*Gewehr*) sight

Körper ['kœrper] (**-s, -**) *m* body; **~bau** *m*
build; **k~behindert** *adj* disabled; **~geruch**
m body odour; **~gewicht** *nt* weight;
~größe *f* height; **k~lich** *adj* physical;
~pflege *f* personal hygiene; **~schaft** *f*
corporation; **~schaftsteuer** *f* corporation
tax; **~teil** *m* part of the body;
~verletzung *f* bodily *od* physical injury

korpulent [kɔrpu'lɛnt] *adj* corpulent

korrekt [kɔ'rɛkt] *adj* correct; **K~ur** [-'tuːr] *f*

(*eines Textes*) proofreading; (*Text*) proof; (*SCH*) marking, correction

Korrespond- [kɔrɛspɔnd] *zW:* **~ent(in)** [-'dɛnt(ɪn)] *m(f)* correspondent; **~enz** [-'dɛnts] *f* correspondence; **k~ieren** [-'diːrən] *vi* to correspond

Korridor ['kɔridoːr] (**-s, -e**) *m* corridor

korrigieren [kɔri'giːrən] *vt* to correct

Korruption [kɔruptsi'oːn] *f* corruption

Kose- ['koːzə] *zW:* **~form** *f* pet form; **~name** *m* pet name; **~wort** *nt* term of endearment

Kosmetik [kɔs'meːtɪk] *f* cosmetics *pl*; **~erin** *f* beautician

kosmetisch *adj* cosmetic; (*Chirurgie*) plastic

kosmisch ['kɔsmɪʃ] *adj* cosmic

Kosmo- ['kɔsmo] *zW:* **~naut** [-'naut] (**-en, -en**) *m* cosmonaut; **k~politisch** *adj* cosmopolitan; **~s** (**-**) *m* cosmos

Kost [kɔst] (**-**) *f* (*Nahrung*) food; (*Verpflegung*) board; **k~bar** *adj* precious; (*teuer*) costly, expensive; **~barkeit** *f* preciousness; costliness, expensiveness; (*Wertstück*) valuable

Kosten *pl* cost(s); (*Ausgaben*) expenses; **auf ~ von** at the expense of; **k~** *vt* to cost; (*versuchen*) to taste; **was kostet ...?** what does ... cost?, how much is ...?; **~anschlag** *m* estimate; **k~los** *adj* free (of charge)

köstlich ['kœstlɪç] *adj* precious; (*Einfall*) delightful; (*Essen*) delicious; **sich ~ amüsieren** to have a marvellous time

Kostprobe *f* taste; (*fig*) sample

kostspielig *adj* expensive

Kostüm [kɔs'tyːm] (**-s, -e**) *nt* costume; (*Damenkostüm*) suit; **~fest** *nt* fancy-dress party; **k~ieren** [kɔsty'miːrən] *vt, vr* to dress up; **~verleih** *m* costume agency

Kot [koːt] (**-(e)s**) *m* excrement

Kotelett [kɔtə'lɛt] (**-(e)s, -e** *od* **-s**) *nt* cutlet, chop; **~en** *pl* (*Bart*) sideboards

Köter ['køːtər] (**-s, -**) *m* cur

Kotflügel *m* (*AUT*) wing

kotzen ['kɔtsən] (*umg!*) *vi* to puke (*umg*), to throw up (*umg*)

Krabbe ['krabə] *f* shrimp; **k~ln** *vi* to crawl

Krach [krax] (**-(e)s, -s** *od* **-e**) *m* crash; (*andauernd*) noise; (*umg: Streit*) quarrel, argument; **k~en** *vi* to crash; (*beim Brechen*) to crack ♦ *vr* (*umg*) to argue, to quarrel

krächzen ['krɛçtsən] *vi* to croak

Kraft [kraft] (**-, ⁻e**) *f* strength; power; force; (*Arbeitskraft*) worker; **in ~ treten** to come into force; **k~** *präp +gen* by virtue of; **~fahrer** *m* (motor) driver; **~fahrzeug** *nt* motor vehicle; **~fahrzeugbrief** *m* logbook; **~fahrzeugsteuer** *f* ≃ road tax; **~fahrzeugversicherung** *f* car insurance

kräftig ['krɛftɪç] *adj* strong; **~en** *vt* to strengthen

Kraft- *zW:* **k~los** *adj* weak; powerless; (*JUR*) invalid; **~probe** *f* trial of strength; **~stoff** *m* fuel; **k~voll** *adj* vigorous; **~werk** *nt* power station

Kragen ['kraːgən] (**-s, -**) *m* collar; **~weite** *f* collar size

Krähe ['krɛːə] *f* crow; **k~n** *vi* to crow

Kralle ['kralə] *f* claw; (*Vogelkralle*) talon; **k~n** *vt* to clutch; (*krampfhaft*) to claw

Kram [kraːm] (**-(e)s**) *m* stuff, rubbish; **k~en** *vi* to rummage; **~laden** (*pej*) *m* small shop

Krampf [krampf] (**-(e)s, ⁻e**) *m* cramp; (*zuckend*) spasm; **~ader** *f* varicose vein; **k~haft** *adj* convulsive; (*fig: Versuche*) desperate

Kran [kraːn] (**-(e)s, ⁻e**) *m* crane; (*Wasserkran*) tap, faucet (*US*)

krank [kraŋk] *adj* ill, sick; **K~e(r)** *f(m)* sick person, invalid; patient; **~en** *vi:* **an etw** *dat* **~en** (*fig*) to suffer from sth

kränken ['krɛŋkən] *vt* to hurt

Kranken- *zW:* **~geld** *nt* sick pay; **~gymnastik** *f* physiotherapy; **~haus** *nt* hospital; **~kasse** *f* health insurance; **~pfleger** *m* nursing orderly; **~schein** *m* health insurance card; **~schwester** *f* nurse; **~versicherung** *f* health insurance; **~wagen** *m* ambulance

Krank- *zW:* **k~haft** *adj* diseased; (*Angst etc*) morbid; **~heit** *f* illness; disease; **~heitserreger** *m* disease-causing agent

kränklich ['krɛŋklɪç] *adj* sickly

Kränkung *f* insult, offence

Spelling Reform: ▲ *new spelling* △ *old spelling (to be phased out)*

Kranz [krants] (-es, ⁼e) m wreath, garland

krass ▲ [kras] adj crass

Krater ['kra:tər] (-s, -) m crater

Kratz- ['krats] zW: **~bürste** f (fig) crosspatch; **k~en** vt, vi to scratch; **~er** (-s, -) m scratch; (Werkzeug) scraper

Kraul [kraʊl] (-s) nt crawl; **~ schwimmen** to do the crawl; **k~en** vi (schwimmen) to do the crawl ♦ vt (streicheln) to fondle

kraus [kraʊs] adj crinkly; (Haar) frizzy; (Stirn) wrinkled

Kraut [kraʊt] (-(e)s, Kräuter) nt plant; (Gewürz) herb; (Gemüse) cabbage

Krawall [kra'val] (-s, -e) m row, uproar

Krawatte [kra'vatə] f tie

kreativ [krea'ti:f] adj creative

Krebs [kre:ps] (-es, -e) m crab; (MED, ASTROL) cancer; **k~krank** adj suffering from cancer

Kredit [kre'di:t] (-(e)s, -e) m credit; **~institut** nt bank; **~karte** f credit card

Kreide ['kraɪdə] f chalk; **k~bleich** adj as white as a sheet

Kreis [kraɪs] (-es, -e) m circle; (Stadtkreis etc) district; **im ~ gehen** (auch fig) to go round in circles

kreischen ['kraɪʃən] vi to shriek, to screech

Kreis- zW: **~el** ['kraɪzəl] (-s, -) m top; (~verkehr) roundabout (BRIT), traffic circle (US); **k~en** ['kraɪzən] vi to spin; **~lauf** m (MED) circulation; (fig: der Natur etc) cycle; **~säge** f circular saw; **~stadt** f county town; **~verkehr** m roundabout traffic

Krematorium [krema'to:riʊm] nt crematorium

Kreml ['kre:ml] (-s) m Kremlin

krepieren [kre'pi:rən] (umg) vi (sterben) to die, to kick the bucket

Krepp [krɛp] (-s, -s od -e) m crepe; **~papier** ▲ nt crepe paper

Kresse ['krɛsə] f cress

Kreta ['kre:ta] (-s) nt Crete

Kreuz [krɔʏts] (-es, -e) nt cross; (ANAT) small of the back; (KARTEN) clubs; **k~en** vt, vr to cross ♦ vi (NAUT) to cruise; **~er** (-s, -) m (Schiff) cruiser; **~fahrt** f cruise; **~feuer** nt (fig): **ins ~feuer geraten** to be under fire from all sides; **~gang** m cloisters pl;

k~igen vt to crucify; **~igung** f crucifixion; **~ung** f (Verkehrskreuzung) crossing, junction; (Züchten) cross; **~verhör** nt cross-examination; **~weg** m crossroads; (REL) Way of the Cross; **~worträtsel** nt crossword puzzle; **~zug** m crusade

Kriech- ['kri:ç] zW: **k~en** (unreg) vi to crawl, to creep; (pej) to grovel, to crawl; **~er** (-s, -) m crawler; **~spur** f crawler lane; **~tier** nt reptile

Krieg [kri:k] (-(e)s, -e) m war

kriegen ['kri:gən] (umg) vt to get

Kriegs- zW: **~erklärung** f declaration of war; **~fuß** m: **mit jdm/etw auf ~fuß stehen** to be at loggerheads with sb/to have difficulties with sth; **~gefangene(r)** m prisoner of war; **~gefangenschaft** f captivity; **~gericht** nt court-martial; **~schiff** nt warship; **~verbrecher** m war criminal; **~versehrte(r)** m person disabled in the war; **~zustand** m state of war

Krim [krɪm] (-) f Crimea

Krimi ['kri:mi] (-s, -s) (umg) m thriller

Kriminal- [krimi'na:l] zW: **~beamte(r)** m detective; **~ität** f criminality; **~'polizei** f ≈ Criminal Investigation Department (BRIT), Federal Bureau of Investigation (US); **~roman** m detective story

kriminell [krimi'nɛl] adj criminal; **K~e(r)** m criminal

Krippe ['krɪpə] f crib; (Kinderkrippe) crèche

Krise ['kri:zə] f crisis; **k~ln** vi: **es k~lt** there's a crisis

Kristall [krɪs'tal] (-s, -e) m crystal ♦ nt (Glas) crystal

Kriterium [kri'te:riʊm] nt criterion

Kritik [kri'ti:k] f criticism; (Zeitungskritik) review, write-up; **~er** ['kri:tikər] (-s, -) m critic; **k~los** adj uncritical

kritisch ['kri:tɪʃ] adj critical

kritisieren [kriti'zi:rən] vt, vi to criticize

kritzeln ['krɪtsəln] vt, vi to scribble, to scrawl

Kroatien [kro'a:tsiən] nt Croatia

Krokodil [kroko'di:l] (-s, -e) nt crocodile

Krokus ['kro:kʊs] (-, - od -se) m crocus

Krone ['kro:nə] f crown; (Baumkrone) top

krönen ['krø:nən] vt to crown

Rechtschreibreform: ▲ neue Schreibung △ alte Schreibung (auslaufend)

Kron- *zW:* **~korken** *m* bottle top; **~leuchter** *m* chandelier; **~prinz** *m* crown prince

Krönung ['krøːnʊŋ] *f* coronation

Kropf [krɔpf] **(-(e)s, -̈e)** *m* (MED) goitre; (von Vogel) crop

Kröte ['krøːtə] *f* toad

Krücke ['krʏkə] *f* crutch

Krug [kruːk] **(-(e)s, -̈e)** *m* jug; (Bierkrug) mug

Krümel ['kryːməl] **(-s, -)** *m* crumb; **k~n** *vt, vi* to crumble

krumm [krʊm] *adj* (auch fig) crooked; (kurvig) curved; **jdm etw ~ nehmen** to take sth amiss; **~beinig** *adj* bandy-legged; **~lachen** (umg) *vr* to laugh o.s. silly

Krümmung ['krʏmʊŋ] *f* bend, curve

Krüppel ['krʏpəl] **(-s, -)** *m* cripple

Kruste ['krʊstə] *f* crust

Kruzifix [krutsiˈfɪks] **(-es, -e)** *nt* crucifix

Kübel ['kyːbəl] **(-s, -)** *m* tub; (Eimer) pail

Kubikmeter [kuˈbiːkmeːtər] *m* cubic metre

Küche ['kʏçə] *f* kitchen; (Kochen) cooking, cuisine

Kuchen ['kuːxən] **(-s, -)** *m* cake; **~form** *f* baking tin; **~gabel** *f* pastry fork

Küchen- *zW:* **~herd** *m* cooker, stove; **~schabe** *f* cockroach; **~schrank** *m* kitchen cabinet

Kuckuck ['kʊkʊk] **(-s, -e)** *m* cuckoo; **~suhr** *f* cuckoo clock

Kugel ['kuːgəl] **(-, -n)** *f* ball; (MATH) sphere; (MIL) bullet; (Erdkugel) globe; (SPORT) shot; **k~förmig** *adj* spherical; **~lager** *nt* ball bearing; **k~rund** *adj* (Gegenstand) round; (umg: Person) tubby; **~schreiber** *m* ballpoint (pen), Biro ®; **k~sicher** *adj* bulletproof; **~stoßen** **(-s)** *nt* shot put

Kuh [kuː] **(-, -̈e)** *f* cow

kühl [kyːl] *adj* (auch fig) cool; **K~anlage** *f* refrigeration plant; **K~e (-)** *f* coolness; **~en** *vt* to cool; **K~er (-s, -)** *m* (AUT) radiator; **K~erhaube** *f* (AUT) bonnet (BRIT), hood (US); **K~raum** *m* cold storage chamber; **K~schrank** *m* refrigerator; **K~truhe** *f* freezer; **K~ung** *f* cooling; **K~wasser** *nt* radiator water

kühn [kyːn] *adj* bold, daring; **K~heit** *f* boldness

Kuhstall *m* byre, cattle shed

Küken ['kyːkən] **(-s, -)** *nt* chicken

kulant [kuˈlant] *adj* obliging

Kuli ['kuːli] **(-s, -s)** *m* coolie; (umg: Kugelschreiber) Biro ®

Kulisse [kuˈlɪsə] *f* scenery

kullern ['kʊlərn] *vi* to roll

Kult [kʊlt] **(-(e)s, -e)** *m* worship, cult; **mit etw einen ~ treiben** to make a cult out of sth

kultivieren [kʊltiˈviːrən] *vt* to cultivate

kultiviert *adj* cultivated, refined

Kultur [kʊlˈtuːr] *f* culture; civilization; (des Bodens) cultivation; **~banause** (umg) *m* philistine, low-brow; **~beutel** *m* toilet bag; **k~ell** [-uˈrɛl] *adj* cultural; **~ministerium** *nt* ministry of education and the arts

Kümmel ['kʏməl] **(-s, -)** *m* caraway seed; (Branntwein) kümmel

Kummer ['kʊmər] **(-s)** *m* grief, sorrow

kümmerlich ['kʏmərlɪç] *adj* miserable, wretched

kümmern ['kʏmərn] *vt* to concern ♦ *vr:* **sich um jdn ~** to look after sb; **das kümmert mich nicht** that doesn't worry me; **sich um etw ~** to see to sth

Kumpel ['kʊmpəl] **(-s, -)** (umg) *m* mate

kündbar ['kʏntbaːr] *adj* redeemable, recallable; (Vertrag) terminable

Kunde¹ ['kʊndə] **(-n, -n)** *m* customer

Kunde² ['kʊndə] *f* (Botschaft) news

Kunden- *zW:* **~dienst** *m* after-sales service; **~konto** *nt* charge account; **~nummer** *f* customer number

Kund- *zW:* **k~geben** (unreg) *vt* to announce; **~gebung** *f* announcement; (Versammlung) rally

Künd- ['kʏnd] *zW:* **k~igen** *vi* to give in one's notice ♦ *vt* to cancel; **jdm k~igen** to give sb his notice; **die Stellung/Wohnung k~igen** to give notice that one is leaving one's job/house; **jdm die Stellung/Wohnung k~igen** to give sb notice to leave his/her job/house; **~igung** *f* notice; **~igungsfrist** *f* period of notice; **~igungsschutz** *m* protection against

wrongful dismissal
Kundin *f* customer
Kundschaft *f* customers *pl*, clientele
künftig ['kʏnftɪç] *adj* future ♦ *adv* in future
Kunst [kʊnst] (**-, ⸚e**) *f* art; (*Können*) skill; **das ist doch keine ~** it's easy; **~dünger** *m* artificial manure; **~faser** *f* synthetic fibre; **~fertigkeit** *f* skilfulness; **~gegenstand** *m* art object; **~gerecht** *adj* skilful; **~geschichte** *f* history of art; **~gewerbe** *nt* arts and crafts *pl*; **~griff** *m* trick, knack; **~händler** *m* art dealer
Künstler(in) ['kʏnstlər(ɪn)] (**-s, -**) *m(f)* artist; **k~isch** *adj* artistic; **~name** *m* pseudonym
künstlich ['kʏnstlɪç] *adj* artificial
Kunst- *zW*: **~sammler** (**-s, -**) *m* art collector; **~seide** *f* artificial silk; **~stoff** *m* synthetic material; **~stück** *nt* trick; **~turnen** *nt* gymnastics *sg*; **k~voll** *adj* artistic; **~werk** *nt* work of art
kunterbunt ['kʊntərbʊnt] *adj* higgledy-piggledy
Kupee ▲ [ku'pe:] (**-s, -s**) *nt* coupé
Kupfer ['kʊpfər] (**-s**) *nt* copper; **k~n** *adj* copper
Kupon [ku'põ:, ku'pɔŋ] (**-s, -s**) *m* coupon; (*Stoff~*) length of cloth
Kuppe ['kʊpə] *f* (*Bergkuppe*) top; (*Fingerkuppe*) tip
Kuppel (**-, -n**) *f* dome; **k~n** *vi* (*JUR*) to procure; (*AUT*) to declutch ♦ *vt* to join
Kupplung *f* coupling; (*AUT*) clutch
Kur [ku:r] (**-, -en**) *f* cure, treatment
Kür [ky:r] (**-, -en**) *f* (*SPORT*) free exercises *pl*
Kurbel ['kʊrbəl] (**-, -n**) *f* crank, winder; (*AUT*) starting handle; **~welle** *f* crankshaft
Kürbis ['kʏrbɪs] (**-ses, -se**) *m* pumpkin; (*exotisch*) gourd
Kurgast *m* visitor (to a health resort)
kurieren [ku'ri:rən] *vt* to cure
kurios [kuri'o:s] *adj* curious, odd; **K~i'tät** *f* curiosity
Kurort *m* health resort
Kurs [kʊrs] (**-es, -e**) *m* course; (*FIN*) rate; **~buch** *nt* timetable; **k~ieren** [kʊr'zi:rən] *vi* to circulate; **k~iv** [kʊr'zi:f] *adv* in italics; **~us** ['kʊrzʊs] (**-, Kurse**) *m* course; **~wagen** *m* (*EISENB*) through carriage
Kurtaxe [-taksə] (**-, -n**) *f* visitors' tax (at health resort or spa)
Kurve ['kʊrvə] *f* curve; (*Straßenkurve*) curve, bend; **kurvig** *adj* (*Straße*) bendy
kurz [kʊrts] *adj* short; **~ gesagt** in short; **~ halten** to keep short; **zu ~ kommen** to come off badly; **den Kürzeren ziehen** to get the worst of it; **K~arbeit** *f* short-time work; **~ärm(e)lig** *adj* short-sleeved
Kürze ['kʏrtsə] *f* shortness, brevity; **k~n** *vt* to cut short; (*in der Länge*) to shorten; (*Gehalt*) to reduce
kurz- *zW*: **~erhand** *adv* on the spot; **~fristig** *adj* short-term; **K~geschichte** *f* short story; **~halten** △ (*unreg*) *vt siehe* **kurz**; **~lebig** *adj* short-lived
kürzlich ['kʏrtslɪc] *adv* lately, recently
Kurz- *zW*: **~schluss** ▲ *m* (*ELEK*) short circuit; **k~sichtig** *adj* short-sighted
Kürzung *f* (*eines Textes*) abridgement; (*eines Theaterstück, des Gehalts*) cut
Kurzwelle *f* short wave
kuscheln ['kʊʃəln] *vr* to snuggle up
Kusine [ku'zi:nə] *f* cousin
Kuss ▲ [kʊs] (**-es, ⸚e**) *m* kiss
küssen ['kʏsən] *vt, vr* to kiss
Küste ['kʏstə] *f* coast, shore
Küstenwache *f* coastguard
Küster ['kʏstər] (**-s, -**) *m* sexton, verger
Kutsche ['kʊtʃə] *f* coach, carriage; **~r** (**-s, -**) *m* coachman
Kutte ['kʊtə] *f* habit
Kuvert [ku'vɛrt] (**-s, -e** *od* **-s**) *nt* envelope; cover
KZ *nt abk von* **Konzentrationslager**

L, l

l *abk* = **Liter**
labil [la'bi:l] *adj* (*MED*: *Konstitution*) delicate
Labor [la'bo:r] (**-s, -e** *od* **-s**) *nt* lab; **~ant(in)** *m(f)* lab(oratory) assistant
Labyrinth [laby'rɪnt] (**-s, -e**) *nt* labyrinth
Lache ['laxə] *f* (*Flüssigkeit*) puddle; (*von Blut, Benzin etc*) pool

lächeln ['lɛçəln] *vi* to smile; **L~** **(-s)** *nt* smile

lachen ['laxən] *vi* to laugh

lächerlich ['lɛçərlɪç] *adj* ridiculous

Lachgas *nt* laughing gas

lachhaft *adj* laughable

Lachs [laks] **(-es, -e)** *m* salmon

Lack [lak] **(-(e)s, -e)** *m* lacquer, varnish; (*von Auto*) paint; **l~ieren** [la'ki:rən] *vt* to varnish; (*Auto*) to spray; **~ierer** [la'ki:rər] **(-s, -)** *m* varnisher

Laden ['la:dən] **(-s, ⸚)** *m* shop; (*Fensterladen*) shutter

laden ['la:dən] (*unreg*) *vt* (*Lasten*) to load; (*JUR*) to summon; (*einladen*) to invite

Laden- *zW:* **~dieb** *m* shoplifter; **~diebstahl** *m* shoplifting; **~schluss** ▲ *m* closing time; **~tisch** *m* counter

Laderaum *m* freight space; (*AVIAT, NAUT*) hold

Ladung ['la:duŋ] *f* (*Last*) cargo, load; (*Beladen*) loading; (*JUR*) summons; (*Einladung*) invitation; (*Sprengladung*) charge

Lage ['la:gə] *f* position, situation; (*Schicht*) layer; **in der ~ sein** to be in a position

Lageplan *m* ground plan

Lager ['la:gər] **(-s, -)** *nt* camp; (*COMM*) warehouse; (*Schlaflager*) bed; (*von Tier*) lair; (*TECH*) bearing; **~bestand** *m* stocks *pl*; **~feuer** *nt* campfire; **~haus** *nt* warehouse, store

lagern ['la:gərn] *vi* (*Dinge*) to be stored; (*Menschen*) to camp ♦ *vt* to store; (*betten*) to lay down; (*Maschine*) to bed

Lagune [la'gu:nə] *f* lagoon

lahm [la:m] *adj* lame; **~ legen** to paralyse; **~en** *vi* to be lame

Lähmung *f* paralysis

Laib [laɪp] **(-s, -e)** *m* loaf

Laie ['laɪə] **(-n, -n)** *m* layman; **l~nhaft** *adj* amateurish

Laken ['la:kən] **(-s, -)** *nt* sheet

Lakritze [la'krɪtsə] *f* liquorice

lallen ['lalən] *vt, vi* to slur; (*Baby*) to babble

Lamelle [la'mɛlə] *f* lamella; (*ELEK*) lamina; (*TECH*) plate

Lametta [la'mɛta] **(-s)** *nt* tinsel

Lamm [lam] **(-(e)s, ⸚er)** *nt* lamb

Lampe ['lampə] *f* lamp

Lampen- *zW:* **~fieber** *nt* stage fright; **~schirm** *m* lampshade

Lampion [lampi'õ:] **(-s, -s)** *m* Chinese lantern

Land [lant] **(-(e)s, ⸚er)** *nt* land; (*Nation, nicht Stadt*) country; (*Bundesland*) state; **auf dem ~(e)** in the country; *siehe* **hierzulande**; **~besitz** *m* landed property; **~ebahn** *f* runway; **l~en** ['landən] *vt, vi* to land

---
Land

ⓘ A **Land** (*plural* **Länder**) is a member state of the **BRD** and of Austria. There are 16 **Länder** in Germany, namely Baden-Württemberg, Bayern, Berlin, Brandenburg, Bremen, Hamburg, Hessen, Mecklenburg-Vorpommern, Niedersachsen, Nordrhein-Westfalen, Rheinland-Pfalz, Saarland, Sachsen, Sachsen-Anhalt, Schleswig-Holstein and Thüringen. Each **Land** has its own parliament and constitution. The 9 **Länder** of Austria are Vorarlberg, Tirol, Salzburg, Oberösterreich, Niederösterreich, Kärnten, Steiermark, Burgenland and Wien.

Landes- ['landəs] *zW:* **~farben** *pl* national colours; **~innere(s)** *nt* inland region; **~sprache** *f* national language; **l~üblich** *adj* customary; **~verrat** *m* high treason; **~währung** *f* national currency; **l~weit** *adj* nationwide

Land- *zW:* **~haus** *nt* country house; **~karte** *f* map; **~kreis** *m* administrative region; **l~läufig** *adj* customary

ländlich ['lɛntlɪç] *adj* rural

Land- *zW:* **~schaft** *f* countryside; (*KUNST*) landscape; **~schaftsschutzgebiet** *nt* nature reserve; **~sitz** *m* country seat; **~straße** *f* country road; **~streicher** **(-s, -)** *m* tramp; **~strich** *m* region

Landung ['landuŋ] *f* landing; **~sbrücke** *f* jetty, pier

Land- *zW:* **~weg** *m:* **etw auf dem ~weg befördern** to transport sth by land; **~wirt**

m farmer; **~wirtschaft** *f* agriculture;
~zunge *f* spit

lang [laŋ] *adj* long; (*Mensch*) tall; **~atmig** *adj*
long-winded; **~e** *adv* for a long time;
(*dauern, brauchen*) a long time

Länge ['lɛŋə] *f* length; (*GEOG*) longitude

langen ['laŋən] *vi* (*ausreichen*) to do, to
suffice; (*fassen*): **~ (nach)** to reach (for)
♦ *vt*: **jdm etw ~** to hand *od* pass sb sth; **es
langt mir** I've had enough

Längengrad *m* longitude

Längenmaß *nt* linear measure

lang- *zW*: **L~eweile** *f* boredom; **~fristig**
adj long-term; **~jährig** *adj* (*Freundschaft,
Gewohnheit*) long-standing; **L~lauf** *m* (*SKI*)
cross-country skiing

länglich *adj* longish

längs [lɛŋs] *präp* (+*gen od dat*) along ♦ *adv*
lengthwise

lang- *zW*: **~sam** *adj* slow; **L~samkeit** *f*
slowness; **L~schläfer(in)** *m(f)* late riser

längst [lɛŋst] *adv*: **das ist ~ fertig** that was
finished a long time ago, that has been
finished for a long time; **~e(r, s)** *adj*
longest

lang- *zW*: **~weilen** *vt* to bore ♦ *vr* to be
bored; **~weilig** *adj* boring, tedious;
L~welle *f* long wave; **~wierig** *adj* lengthy,
long-drawn-out

Lanze ['lantsə] *f* lance

Lappalie [la'pa:liə] *f* trifle

Lappen ['lapən] (**-s, -**) *m* cloth, rag; (*ANAT*)
lobe

läppisch ['lɛpɪʃ] *adj* foolish

Lapsus ['lapsʊs] (**-, -**) *m* slip

Laptop ['lɛptɔp] (**-s, -s**) *m* laptop
(computer)

Lärche ['lɛrçə] *f* larch

Lärm [lɛrm] (**-(e)s**) *m* noise; **l~en** *vi* to be
noisy, to make a noise

Larve ['larfə] *f* (*BIOL*) larva

lasch [laʃ] *adj* slack

Laser ['le:zər] (**-s, -**) *m* laser

SCHLÜSSELWORT
---

lassen ['lasən] (*pt* **ließ**, *pp* **gelassen** *od* (*als
Hilfsverb*) **lassen**) *vt* **1** (*unterlassen*) to stop;

(*momentan*) to leave; **lass das (sein)!** don't
(do it)!; (*hör auf*) stop it!; **lass mich!** leave
me alone; **lassen wir das!** let's leave it; **er
kann das Trinken nicht lassen** he can't
stop drinking

2 (*zurücklassen*) to leave; **etw lassen, wie
es ist** to leave sth (just) as it is

3 (*überlassen*): **jdn ins Haus lassen** to let
sb into the house
♦ *vi*: **lass mal, ich mache das schon** leave
it, I'll do it

♦ *Hilfsverb* **1** (*veranlassen*): **etw machen
lassen** to have *od* get sth done; **sich** *dat*
etw schicken lassen to have sth sent (to
one)

2 (*zulassen*): **jdn etw wissen lassen** to let
sb know sth; **das Licht brennen lassen** to
leave the light on; **jdn warten lassen** to
keep sb waiting; **das lässt sich machen**
that can be done

3: **lass uns gehen** let's go

---

lässig ['lɛsɪç] *adj* casual; **L~keit** *f* casualness

Last [last] (**-, -en**) *f* load, burden; (*NAUT,
AVIAT*) cargo; (*meist pl*: *Gebühr*) charge; **jdm
zur ~ fallen** to be a burden to sb; **~auto**
nt lorry, truck; **l~en** *vi*: **l~en auf** +*dat* to
weigh on; **~enaufzug** *m* goods lift *od*
elevator (*US*)

Laster ['lastər] (**-s, -**) *nt* vice

lästern ['lɛstərn] *vt, vi* (*Gott*) to blaspheme;
(*schlecht sprechen*) to mock

Lästerung *f* jibe; (*Gotteslästerung*)
blasphemy

lästig ['lɛstɪç] *adj* troublesome, tiresome

Last- *zW*: **~kahn** *m* barge; **~kraftwagen**
m heavy goods vehicle; **~schrift** *f* debit;
~wagen *m* lorry, truck; **~zug** *m* articulated
lorry

Latein [la'taɪn] (**-s**) *nt* Latin; **~amerika** *nt*
Latin America

latent [la'tɛnt] *adj* latent

Laterne [la'tɛrnə] *f* lantern; (*Straßenlaterne*)
lamp, light; **~npfahl** *m* lamppost

latschen ['la:tʃən] (*umg*) *vi* (*gehen*) to
wander, to go; (*lässig*) to slouch

Latte ['latə] *f* lath; (*SPORT*) goalpost; (*quer*)

crossbar

Latzhose ['latsho:zə] f dungarees pl

lau [lao] adj (Nacht) balmy; (Wasser) lukewarm

Laub [laop] (-(e)s) nt foliage;~**baum** m deciduous tree;~**frosch** m tree frog; ~**säge** f fretsaw

Lauch [laox] (-(e)s, -e) m leek

Lauer ['laoər] f: **auf der ~ sein** od **liegen** to lie in wait;**l~n** vi to lie in wait; (Gefahr) to lurk

Lauf [laof] (-(e)s, Läufe) m run (Wettlauf) race; (Entwicklung, ASTRON) course; (Gewehrlauf) barrel; **einer Sache** dat **ihren ~ lassen** to let sth take its course;~**bahn** f career

laufen ['laofən] (unreg) vt, vi to run; (umg: gehen) to walk;~**d** adj running; (Monat, Ausgaben) current; **auf dem ~den sein/ halten** to be/keep up to date; **am ~den Band** (fig) continuously

Läufer ['lɔyfər] (-s, -) m (Teppich, SPORT) runner; (Fußball) half-back; (Schach) bishop

Lauf- zW:~**masche** f run, ladder (BRIT); ~**pass** ▲ m: **jdm den ~pass geben** (umg) to send sb packing (inf);~**stall** m playpen; ~**steg** m catwalk;~**werk** nt (COMPUT) disk drive

Lauge ['laogə] f soapy water; (CHEM) alkaline solution

Laune ['laonə] f mood, humour; (Einfall) caprice; (schlechte) temper;**l~nhaft** adj capricious, changeable

launisch adj moody; bad-tempered

Laus [laos] (-, Läuse) f louse

lauschen ['laoʃən] vi to eavesdrop, to listen in

lauschig ['laoʃɪç] adj snug

lausig ['laozɪç] (umg: pej) adj measly; (Kälte) perishing

laut [laot] adj loud ♦ adv loudly; (lesen) aloud ♦ präp (+gen od dat) according to;**L~** (-(e)s, -e) m sound

Laute ['laotə] f lute

lauten ['laotən] vi to say; (Urteil) to be

läuten ['lɔytən] vt, vi to ring, to sound

lauter ['laotər] adj (Wasser) clear, pure;

(Wahrheit, Charakter) honest ♦ adj inv (Freude, Dummheit etc) sheer ♦ adv nothing but, only

laut- zW:~**hals** adv at the top of one's voice;~**los** adj noiseless, silent;**L~schrift** f phonetics pl;**L~sprecher** m loudspeaker; ~**stark** adj vociferous;**L~stärke** f (RADIO) volume

lauwarm ['laovarm] adj (auch fig) lukewarm

Lavendel [la'vɛndəl] (-s, -) m lavender

Lawine [la'vi:nə] f avalanche;~**ngefahr** f danger of avalanches

lax [laks] adj lax

Lazarett [latsa'rɛt] (-(e)s, -e) nt (MIL) hospital, infirmary

leasen ['li:zən] vt to lease

Leben (-s, -) nt life

leben ['le:bən] vt, vi to live;~**d** adj living; ~**dig** [le'bɛndɪç] adj living, alive; (lebhaft) lively;**L~digkeit** f liveliness

Lebens- zW:~**art** f way of life; ~**erwartung** f life expectancy;**l~fähig** adj able to live;~**freude** f zest for life; ~**gefahr** f: ~**gefahr**! danger!; **in ~gefahr** dangerously ill;**l~gefährlich** adj dangerous; (Verletzung) critical; ~**haltungskosten** pl cost of living sg; ~**jahr** nt year of life;**l~länglich** adj (Strafe) for life;~**lauf** m curriculum vitae;~**mittel** pl food sg;~**mittelgeschäft** nt grocer's (shop);~**mittelvergiftung** f (MED) food poisoning;**l~müde** adj tired of life; ~**retter** m lifesaver;~**standard** m standard of living;~**unterhalt** m livelihood;~**versicherung** f life insurance; ~**wandel** m way of life;~**weise** f lifestyle, way of life;**l~wichtig** adj vital, essential; ~**zeichen** nt sign of life

Leber ['le:bər] (-, -n) f liver;~**fleck** m mole; ~**tran** m cod-liver oil;~**wurst** f liver sausage

Lebewesen nt creature

leb- ['le:p] zW:~**haft** adj lively, vivacious; **L~kuchen** m gingerbread;~**los** adj lifeless

Leck [lɛk] (-(e)s, -e) nt leak;**l~** adj leaky, leaking;**l~en** vi (Loch haben) to leak; (schlecken) to lick ♦ vt to lick

lecker ['lɛkər] *adj* delicious, tasty; **L~bissen** *m* dainty morsel

Leder ['le:dər] *(-s, -) nt* leather; **~hose** *f* lederhosen; **l~n** *adj* leather; **~waren** *pl* leather goods

ledig ['le:dɪç] *adj* single; **einer Sache** *gen* ~ **sein** to be free of sth; **~lich** *adv* merely, solely

leer [le:r] *adj* empty; vacant; **~ machen** to empty; **~ stehend** empty; **L~e (-)** *f* emptiness; **~en** *vt, vr* to empty; **L~gewicht** *nt* weight when empty; **L~gut** *nt* empties *pl*; **L~lauf** *m* neutral; **L~ung** *f* emptying; *(Post)* collection

legal [le'ga:l] *adj* legal, lawful; **~i'sieren** *vt* to legalize

legen ['le:gən] *vt* to lay, to put, to place; *(Ei)* to lay ♦ *vr* to lie down; *(fig)* to subside

Legende [le'gɛndə] *f* legend

leger [le'ʒe:r] *adj* casual

Legierung [le'gi:rʊŋ] *f* alloy

Legislative [legɪsla'ti:və] *f* legislature

legitim [legi'ti:m] *adj* legitimate

legitimieren [legiti'mi:rən] *vt* to legitimate ♦ *vr* to prove one's identity

Lehm [le:m] *(-(e)s, -e) m* loam; **l~ig** *adj* loamy

Lehne ['le:nə] *f* arm; back; **l~n** *vt, vr* to lean

Lehnstuhl *m* armchair

Lehr- *zW:* **~amt** *nt* teaching profession; **~buch** *nt* textbook

Lehre ['le:rə] *f* teaching, doctrine; *(beruflich)* apprenticeship; *(moralisch)* lesson; *(TECH)* gauge; **l~n** *vt* to teach

Lehrer(in) (-s, -) *m(f)* teacher; **~zimmer** *nt* staff room

Lehr- *zW:* **~gang** *m* course; **~jahre** *pl* apprenticeship *sg*; **~kraft** *f (förmlich)* teacher; **~ling** *m* apprentice; **~plan** *m* syllabus; **l~reich** *adj* instructive; **~stelle** *f* apprenticeship; **~zeit** *f* apprenticeship

Leib [laɪp] *(-(e)s, -er) m* body; **halt ihn mir vom ~!** keep him away from me!; **l~haftig** *adj* personified; *(Teufel)* incarnate; **l~lich** *adj* bodily; *(Vater etc)* own; **~schmerzen** *pl* stomach pains; **~wache** *f* bodyguard

Leiche ['laɪçə] *f* corpse; **~nhalle** *f* mortuary;

~nwagen *m* hearse

Leichnam ['laɪçna:m] *(-(e)s, -e) m* corpse

leicht [laɪçt] *adj* light; *(einfach)* easy; **jdm ~ fallen** to be easy for sb; **es sich** *dat* ~ **machen** to make things easy for o.s.; **L~athletik** *f* athletics *sg*; **~fertig** *adj* frivolous; **~gläubig** *adj* gullible, credulous; **~hin** *adv* lightly; **L~igkeit** *f* easiness; **mit L~igkeit** with ease; **L~sinn** *m* carelessness; **~sinnig** *adj* careless

Leid [laɪt] *(-(e)s) nt* grief, sorrow; **es tut mir/ihm ~** I am/he is sorry; **er/das tut mir ~** I am sorry for him/it; **l~ adj: etw l~ haben** *od* **sein** to be tired of sth; **l~en** *(unreg) vt* to suffer; *(erlauben)* to permit ♦ *vi* to suffer; **jdn/etw nicht l~en können** not to be able to stand sb/sth; **~en** ['laɪdən] *(-s, -) nt* suffering; *(Krankheit)* complaint; **~enschaft** *f* passion; **l~enschaftlich** *adj* passionate

leider ['laɪdər] *adv* unfortunately; **ja, ~** yes, I'm afraid so; **~ nicht** I'm afraid not

leidig ['laɪdɪç] *adj* worrying, troublesome

leidlich ['laɪtlɪç] *adj* tolerable ♦ *adv* tolerably

Leid- *zW:* **~tragende(r)** *f(m)* bereaved; *(Benachteiligter)* one who suffers; **~wesen** *nt:* **zu jds ~wesen** to sb's disappointment

Leier ['laɪər] *(-, -n) f* lyre; *(fig)* old story; **~kasten** *m* barrel organ

Leihbibliothek *f* lending library

Leihbücherei *f* lending library

leihen ['laɪən] *(unreg) vt* to lend; **sich** *dat* **etw ~** to borrow sth

Leih- *zW:* **~gebühr** *f* hire charge; **~haus** *nt* pawnshop; **~wagen** *m* hired car

Leim [laɪm] *(-(e)s, -e) m* glue; **l~en** *vt* to glue

Leine ['laɪnə] *f* line, cord; *(Hundeleine)* leash, lead

Leinen *nt* linen; **l~ adj** linen

Leinwand *f (KUNST)* canvas; *(CINE)* screen

leise ['laɪzə] *adj* quiet; *(sanft)* soft, gentle

Leiste ['laɪstə] *f* ledge; *(Zierleiste)* strip; *(ANAT)* groin

leisten ['laɪstən] *vt (Arbeit)* to do; *(Gesellschaft)* to keep; *(Ersatz)* to supply; *(vollbringen)* to achieve; **sich** *dat* **etw ~**

können to be able to afford sth
Leistung f performance; (gute) achievement; **~sdruck** m pressure; **l~sfähig** adj efficient
Leitartikel m leading article
Leitbild nt model
leiten ['laɪtən] vt to lead; (Firma) to manage; (in eine Richtung) to direct; (ELEK) to conduct
Leiter[1] ['laɪtər] (-s, -) m leader, head; (ELEK) conductor
Leiter[2] ['laɪtər] (-, -n) f ladder
Leitfaden m guide
Leitplanke f crash barrier
Leitung f (Führung) direction; (CINE, THEAT etc) production; (von Firma) management; directors pl; (Wasserleitung) pipe; (Kabel) cable; **eine lange ~ haben** to be slow on the uptake
Leitungs- zW: **~draht** m wire; **~rohr** nt pipe; **~wasser** nt tap water
Lektion [lɛktsi'oːn] f lesson
Lektüre [lɛk'tyːrə] f (Lesen) reading; (Lesestoff) reading matter
Lende ['lɛndə] f loin; **~nstück** nt fillet
lenk- ['lɛŋk] zW: **~bar** adj (Fahrzeug) steerable; (Kind) manageable; **~en** vt to steer; (Kind) to guide; (Blick, Aufmerksamkeit): **~en (auf** +akk) to direct (at); **L~rad** nt steering wheel; **L~radschloss** ▲ nt steering (wheel) lock; **L~stange** f handlebars pl; **L~ung** f steering
Lepra ['leːpra] (-) f leprosy
Lerche ['lɛrçə] f lark
lernbegierig adj eager to learn
lernen ['lɛrnən] vt to learn
lesbar ['leːsbaːr] adj legible
Lesbierin ['lɛsbiərɪn] f lesbian
lesbisch ['lɛsbɪʃ] adj lesbian
Lese ['leːzə] f (Wein) harvest
Lesebrille f reading glasses
Lesebuch nt reading book, reader
lesen (unreg) vt, vi to read; (ernten) to gather, to pick
Leser(in) ['leːzə] (-s, -) m(f) reader; **~brief** m reader's letter; **l~lich** adj legible
Lesezeichen nt bookmark

Lesung ['leːzʊŋ] f (PARL) reading
letzte(r, s) ['lɛtstə(r, s)] adj last; (neueste) latest; **zum ~n Mal** for the last time; **~ns** adv lately; **~re(r, s)** adj latter
Leuchte ['lɔʏçtə] f lamp, light; **l~n** vi to shine, to gleam; **~r (-s, -)** m candlestick
Leucht- zW: **~farbe** f fluorescent colour; **~rakete** f flare; **~reklame** f neon sign; **~röhre** f strip light; **~turm** m lighthouse
leugnen ['lɔʏɡnən] vt to deny
Leukämie [lɔʏkɛ'miː] f leukaemia
Leukoplast [lɔʏko'plast] (®; -(e)s, -e) nt Elastoplast ®
Leumund ['lɔʏmʊnt] (-(e)s, -e) m reputation
Leumundszeugnis nt character reference
Leute ['lɔʏtə] pl people pl
Leutnant ['lɔʏtnant] (-s, -s od -e) m lieutenant
leutselig ['lɔʏtseːlɪç] adj amiable
Lexikon ['lɛksikɔn] (-s, Lexiken od Lexika) nt encyclop(a)edia
Libelle [li'bɛlə] f dragonfly; (TECH) spirit level
liberal [libe'raːl] adj liberal; **L~e(r)** f(m) liberal
Licht [lɪçt] (-(e)s, -er) nt light; **~bild** nt photograph; (Dia) slide; **~blick** m cheering prospect; **l~empfindlich** adj sensitive to light; **l~en** vt to clear; (Anker) to weigh ♦ vr to clear up; (Haar) to thin; **l~erloh** adv: **l~erloh brennen** to be ablaze; **~hupe** f flashing of headlights; **~jahr** nt light year; **~maschine** f dynamo; **~schalter** m light switch; **~schutzfaktor** m protection factor
Lichtung f clearing, glade
Lid [liːt] (-(e)s, -er) nt eyelid; **~schatten** m eyeshadow
lieb [liːp] adj dear; **das ist ~ von dir** that's kind of you; **~ gewinnen** to get fond of; **~ haben** to be fond of; **~äugeln** ['liːbɔʏɡəln] vi insep: **mit etw ~äugeln** to have one's eye on sth; **mit dem Gedanken ~äugeln, etw zu tun** to toy with the idea of doing sth
Liebe ['liːbə] f love; **l~bedürftig** adj: **l~bedürftig sein** to need love; **l~n** vt to love; to like

Spelling Reform: ▲ *new spelling* △ *old spelling (to be phased out)*

liebens- *zW:* **~wert** *adj* loveable; **~würdig** *adj* kind; **~würdigerweise** *adv* kindly; **L~würdigkeit** *f* kindness

lieber ['liːbər] *adv* rather, preferably; **ich gehe ~ nicht** I'd rather not go; *siehe auch* **gern**; **lieb**

Liebes- *zW:* **~brief** *m* love letter; **~kummer** *m:* **~kummer haben** to be lovesick; **~paar** *nt* courting couple, lovers *pl*

liebevoll *adj* loving

lieb- [liːp] *zW:* **~gewinnen** △ *(unreg) vt siehe* **lieb**; **~haben** △ *(unreg) vt siehe* **lieb**; **L~haber (-s, -)** *m* lover; **L~habe'rei** *f* hobby; **~kosen** ['liːpkoːzən] *vt insep* to caress; **~lich** *adj* lovely, charming; **L~ling** *m* darling; **L~lings-** *in zW* favourite; **~los** *adj* unloving; **L~schaft** *f* love affair

Lied [liːt] **(-(e)s, -er)** *nt* song; *(REL)* hymn; **~erbuch** ['liːdər-] *nt* songbook; hymn book

liederlich ['liːdərlɪç] *adj* slovenly; *(Lebenswandel)* loose, immoral; **L~keit** *f* slovenliness; immorality

lief *etc* [liːf] *vb siehe* **laufen**

Lieferant [liːfə'rant] *m* supplier

Lieferbedingungen *pl* terms of delivery

liefern ['liːfərn] *vt* to deliver; *(versorgen mit)* to supply; *(Beweis)* to produce

Liefer- *zW:* **~schein** *m* delivery note; **~termin** *m* delivery date; **~ung** *f* delivery; supply; **~wagen** *m* van; **~zeit** *f* delivery period

Liege ['liːgə] *f* bed

liegen ['liːgən] *(unreg) vi* to lie; *(sich befinden)* to be; **mir liegt nichts/viel daran** it doesn't matter to me/it matters a lot to me; **es liegt bei Ihnen, ob ...** it's up to you whether ...; **Sprachen ~ mir nicht** languages are not my line; **woran liegt es?** what's the cause?; **~ bleiben** *(im Bett)* to stay in bed; *(nicht aufstehen)* to stay lying down; *(vergessen werden)* to be left (behind); **~ lassen** *(vergessen)* to leave behind

Liege- *zW:* **~sitz** *m (AUT)* reclining seat; **~stuhl** *m* deck chair; **~wagen** *m (EISENB)* couchette

Lift [lɪft] **(-(e)s, -e** *od* **-s)** *m* lift

Likör [li'køːr] **(-s, -e)** *m* liqueur

lila ['liːla] *adj inv* purple, lilac; **L~ (-s, -s)** *nt (Farbe)* purple, lilac

Lilie ['liːliə] *f* lily

Limonade [limo'naːdə] *f* lemonade

Limone [li'moːnə] *f* lime

Linde ['lɪndə] *f* lime tree, linden

lindern ['lɪndərn] *vt* to alleviate, to soothe; **Linderung** *f* alleviation

Lineal [line'aːl] **(-s, -e)** *nt* ruler

Linie ['liːniə] *f* line

Linien- *zW:* **~blatt** *nt* ruled sheet; **~flug** *m* scheduled flight; **~richter** *m* linesman

linieren [li'niːrən] *vt* to line

Linke ['lɪŋkə] *f* left side; left hand; *(POL)* left

linkisch *adj* awkward, gauche

links [lɪŋks] *adv* left; to *od* on the left; **~ von mir** on *od* to my left; **L~händer(in) (-s, -)** *m(f)* left-handed person; **L~kurve** *f* left-hand bend; **L~verkehr** *m* driving on the left

Linoleum [li'noːleʊm] **(-s)** *nt* lino(leum)

Linse ['lɪnzə] *f* lentil; *(optisch)* lens *sg*

Lippe ['lɪpə] *f* lip; **~nstift** *m* lipstick

lispeln ['lɪspəln] *vi* to lisp

Lissabon ['lɪsabɔn] **(-s)** *nt* Lisbon

List [lɪst] **(-, -en)** *f* cunning; trick, ruse

Liste ['lɪstə] *f* list

listig ['lɪstɪç] *adj* cunning, sly

Liter ['liːtər] **(-s, -)** *nt od m* litre

literarisch [lite'raːrɪʃ] *adj* literary

Literatur [lɪtera'tuːr] *f* literature

Litfaßsäule ['lɪtfaszɔylə] *f* advertising pillar

Liturgie [lɪtʊr'giː] *f* liturgy

liturgisch [li'tʊrgɪʃ] *adj* liturgical

Litze ['lɪtsə] *f* braid; *(ELEK)* flex

Lizenz [li'tsɛnts] *f* licence

Lkw [ɛlkaː'veː] **(-(s), -(s))** *m abk =* **Lastkraftwagen**

Lob [loːp] **(-(e)s)** *nt* praise

Lobby ['lɔbi] *f* lobby

loben ['loːbən] *vt* to praise; **~swert** *adj* praiseworthy

löblich ['løːplɪç] *adj* praiseworthy, laudable

Loch [lɔx] **(-(e)s, ̈er)** *nt* hole; **l~en** *vt* to punch holes in; **~er (-s, -)** *m* punch

---

Rechtschreibreform: ▲ *neue Schreibung* △ *alte Schreibung (auslaufend)*

löcherig ['lœçərɪç] *adj* full of holes
Lochkarte *f* punch card
Lochstreifen *m* punch tape
Locke ['lɔkə] *f* lock, curl; **l~n** *vt* to entice; (*Haare*) to curl; **~nwickler (-s, -)** *m* curler
locker ['lɔkər] *adj* loose; **~lassen** (*unreg*) *vi:* **nicht ~lassen** not to let up; **~n** *vt* to loosen
lockig ['lɔkɪç] *adj* curly
lodern ['lo:dərn] *vi* to blaze
Löffel ['lœfəl] **(-s, -)** *m* spoon
löffeln *vt* to spoon
Loge ['lo:ʒə] *f* (*THEAT*) box; (*Freimaurer*) (masonic) lodge; (*Pförtnerloge*) office
Logik ['lo:gɪk] *f* logic
logisch ['lo:gɪʃ] *adj* logical
Logopäde [logo'pɛ:də] **(-n, -n)** *m* speech therapist
Lohn [lo:n] **(-(e)s, ⁼e)** *m* reward; (*Arbeitslohn*) pay, wages *pl*; **~büro** *nt* wages office; **~empfänger** *m* wage earner
lohnen ['lo:nən] *vr unpers* to be worth it ♦ *vt:* (**jdm etw**) **~** to reward (sb for sth); **~d** *adj* worthwhile
Lohn- *zW:* **~erhöhung** *f* pay rise; **~steuer** *f* income tax; **~steuerkarte** *f* (income) tax card; **~streifen** *m* pay slip; **~tüte** *f* pay packet
Lokal [lo'ka:l] **(-(e)s, -e)** *nt* pub(lic house)
lokal *adj* local; **~isieren** *vt* to localize
Lokomotive [lokomo'ti:və] *f* locomotive
Lokomotivführer *m* engine driver
Lorbeer ['lɔrbe:r] **(-s, -en)** *m* (*auch fig*) laurel; **~blatt** *nt* (*KOCH*) bay leaf
Los [lo:s] **(-es, -e)** *nt* (*Schicksal*) lot, fate; (*Lotterielos*) lottery ticket
los [lo:s] *adj* (*locker*) loose; **~!** go on!; **etw ~ sein** to be rid of sth; **was ist ~?** what's the matter?; **dort ist nichts/viel ~** there's nothing/a lot going on there; **~binden** (*unreg*) *vt* to untie
Löschblatt ['lœʃblat] *nt* sheet of blotting paper
löschen ['lœʃən] *vt* (*Feuer, Licht*) to put out, to extinguish; (*Durst*) to quench; (*COMM*) to cancel; (*COMPUT*) to delete; (*Tonband*) to erase; (*Fracht*) to unload ♦ *vi* (*Feuerwehr*) to

put out a fire; (*Tinte*) to blot
Lösch- *zW:* **~fahrzeug** *nt* fire engine; fire boat; **~gerät** *nt* fire extinguisher; **~papier** *nt* blotting paper
lose ['lo:zə] *adj* loose
Lösegeld *nt* ransom
losen ['lo:zən] *vi* to draw lots
lösen ['lø:zən] *vt* to loosen; (*Rätsel etc*) to solve; (*Verlobung*) to call off; (*CHEM*) to dissolve; (*Partnerschaft*) to break up; (*Fahrkarte*) to buy ♦ *vr* (*aufgehen*) to come loose; (*Zucker etc*) to dissolve; (*Problem, Schwierigkeit*) to (re)solve itself
los- *zW:* **~fahren** (*unreg*) *vi* to leave; **~gehen** (*unreg*) *vi* to set out; (*anfangen*) to start; (*Bombe*) to go off; **auf jdn ~gehen** to go for sb; **~kaufen** *vt* (*Gefangene, Geißeln*) to pay ransom for; **~kommen** (*unreg*) *vi:* **von etw ~kommen** to get away from sth; **~lassen** (*unreg*) *vt* (*Seil*) to let go of; (*Schimpfe*) to let loose; **~laufen** (*unreg*) *vi* to run off
löslich ['lø:slɪç] *adj* soluble; **L~keit** *f* solubility
los- *zW:* **~lösen** *vt:* (**sich**) **~lösen** to free (o.s.); **~machen** to loosen; (*Boot*) to unmoor *vr* to get away; **~schrauben** *vt* to unscrew
Losung ['lo:zʊŋ] *f* watchword, slogan
Lösung ['lø:zʊŋ] *f* (*Lockermachen*) loosening; (*eines Rätsels, CHEM*) solution; **~smittel** *nt* solvent
los- *zW:* **~werden** (*unreg*) *vt* to get rid of; **~ziehen** (*unreg*) (*umg*) *vi* (*sich aufmachen*) to set off
Lot [lo:t] **(-(e)s, -e)** *nt* plumbline; **im ~** vertical; (*fig*) on an even keel
löten ['lø:tən] *vt* to solder
Lothringen ['lo:trɪŋən] **(-s)** *nt* Lorraine
Lotse ['lo:tsə] **(-n, -n)** *m* pilot; (*AVIAT*) air traffic controller; **l~n** *vt* to pilot; (*umg*) to lure
Lotterie [lɔtə'ri:] *f* lottery
Lotto ['lɔto] **(-s, -s)** *nt* national lottery; **~zahlen** *pl* winning lottery numbers
Löwe ['lø:və] **(-n, -n)** *m* lion; (*ASTROL*) Leo; **~nanteil** *m* lion's share; **~nzahn** *m*

dandelion

loyal [loa'jaːl] *adj* loyal; **L~ität** *f* loyalty

Luchs [lʊks] **(-es, -e)** *m* lynx

Lücke ['lʏkə] *f* gap

Lücken- *zW:* **~büßer (-s, -)** *m* stopgap; **l~haft** *adj* full of gaps; *(Versorgung, Vorräte etc)* inadequate; **l~los** *adj* complete

Luft [lʊft] **(-, ¨e)** *f* air; *(Atem)* breath; **in der ~ liegen** to be in the air; **jdn wie ~ behandeln** to ignore sb; **~angriff** *m* air raid; **~ballon** *m* balloon; **~blase** *f* air bubble; **l~dicht** *adj* airtight; **~druck** *m* atmospheric pressure

lüften ['lʏftən] *vt* to air; *(Hut)* to lift, to raise ♦ *vi* to let some air in

Luft- *zW:* **~fahrt** *f* aviation; **~fracht** *f* air freight; **l~gekühlt** *adj* air-cooled; **~gewehr** *nt* air rifle, airgun; **l~ig** *adj (Ort)* breezy; *(Raum)* airy; *(Kleider)* summery; **~kissenfahrzeug** *nt* hovercraft; **~kurort** *m* health resort; **l~leer** *adj:* **l~leerer Raum** vacuum; **~linie** *f:* **in der ~linie** as the crow flies; **~loch** *nt* air hole; *(AVIAT)* air pocket; **~matratze** *f* Lilo ® *(BRIT)*, air mattress; **~pirat** *m* hijacker; **~post** *f* airmail; **~pumpe** *f* air pump; **~röhre** *f (ANAT)* windpipe; **~schlange** *f* streamer; **~schutzkeller** *m* air-raid shelter; **~verkehr** *m* air traffic; **~verschmutzung** *f* air pollution; **~waffe** *f* air force; **~zug** *m* draught

Lüge ['lyːgə] *f* lie; **jdn/etw ~n strafen** to give the lie to sb/sth; **l~n** *(unreg)* *vi* to lie

Lügner(in) **(-s, -)** *m(f)* liar

Luke ['luːkə] *f* dormer window; hatch

Lump [lʊmp] **(-en, -en)** *m* scamp, rascal

Lumpen ['lʊmpən] **(-s, -)** *m* rag

lumpen ['lʊmpən] *vi:* **sich nicht ~ lassen** not to be mean

lumpig ['lʊmpɪç] *adj* shabby

Lupe ['luːpə] *f* magnifying glass; **unter die ~ nehmen** *(fig)* to scrutinize

Lust [lʊst] **(-, ¨e)** *f* joy, delight; *(Neigung)* desire; **~ haben zu** *od* **auf etw** *akk* **/etw zu tun** to feel like sth/doing sth

lüstern ['lʏstərn] *adj* lustful, lecherous

lustig ['lʊstɪç] *adj (komisch)* amusing, funny;

(fröhlich) cheerful

Lust- *zW:* **~los** *adj* unenthusiastic; **~mord** *m* sex(ual) murder; **~spiel** *nt* comedy

lutschen ['lʊtʃən] *vt, vi* to suck; **am Daumen ~** to suck one's thumb

Lutscher (-s, -) *m* lollipop

luxuriös [lʊksuri'øːs] *adj* luxurious

Luxus ['lʊksʊs] **(-)** *m* luxury; **~artikel** *pl* luxury goods; **~hotel** *nt* luxury hotel

Luzern [lu'tsɛrn] **(-s)** *nt* Lucerne

Lymphe ['lʏmfə] *f* lymph

lynchen ['lʏnçən] *vt* to lynch

Lyrik ['lyːrɪk] *f* lyric poetry; **~er (-s, -)** *m* lyric poet

lyrisch ['lyːrɪʃ] *adj* lyrical

M, m

m *abk* = **Meter**

Machart *f* make

machbar *adj* feasible

─────────────
SCHLÜSSELWORT
─────────────

machen ['maxən] *vt* **1** to do; *(herstellen, zubereiten)* to make; **was machst du da?** what are you doing (there)?; **das ist nicht zu machen** that can't be done; **das Radio leiser machen** to turn the radio down; **aus Holz gemacht** made of wood

2 *(verursachen, bewirken)* to make; **jdm Angst machen** to make sb afraid; **das macht die Kälte** it's the cold that does that

3 *(ausmachen)* to matter; **das macht nichts** that doesn't matter; **die Kälte macht mir nichts** I don't mind the cold

4 *(kosten, ergeben)* to be; **3 und 5 macht 8** 3 and 5 is *od* are 8; **was** *od* **wie viel macht das?** how much does that make?

5 was macht die Arbeit? how's the work going?; **was macht dein Bruder?** how is your brother doing?; **das Auto machen lassen** to have the car done; **machs gut!** take care!; *(viel Glück)* good luck!

♦ *vi:* **mach schnell!** hurry up!; **Schluss machen** to finish (off); **mach schon!** come

on!; **das macht müde** it makes you tired;
in etw *dat* **machen** to be *od* deal in sth
♦ *vr* to come along (nicely); **sich an etw**
akk **machen** to set about sth; **sich
verständlich machen** to make o.s.
understood; **sich** *dat* **viel aus jdm/etw
machen** to like sb/sth

Macht [maxt] (-, ̈e) *f* power; ~**haber** (-s, -)
m ruler
mächtig [ˈmɛçtɪç] *adj* powerful, mighty;
(*umg:* *ungeheuer*) enormous
Macht- *zW:* **m~los** *adj* powerless; ~**probe**
f trial of strength; ~**wort** *nt:* **ein ~wort
sprechen** to exercise one's authority
Mädchen [ˈmɛːtçən] *nt* girl; **m~haft** *adj*
girlish; ~**name** *m* maiden name
Made [ˈmaːdə] *f* maggot
madig [ˈmaːdɪç] *adj* maggoty; **jdm etw ~
machen** to spoil sth for sb
mag *etc* [maːk] *vb siehe* **mögen**
Magazin [magaˈtsiːn] (-s, -e) *nt* magazine
Magen [ˈmaːgən] (-s, -*od* ̈) *m* stomach;
~**geschwür** *nt* (MED) stomach ulcer;
~**schmerzen** *pl* stomachache *sg*
mager [ˈmaːgər] *adj* lean; (*dünn*) thin;
M~keit *f* leanness; thinness
Magie [maˈgiː] *f* magic
magisch [ˈmaːgɪʃ] *adj* magical
Magnet [maˈgneːt] (-s *od* -en, -en) *m*
magnet; **m~isch** *adj* magnetic; ~**nadel** *f*
magnetic needle
mähen [ˈmɛːən] *vt, vi* to mow
Mahl [maːl] (-(e)s, -e) *nt* meal; **m~en**
(*unreg*) *vt* to grind; ~**zeit** *f* meal ♦ *excl*
enjoy your meal
Mahnbrief *m* reminder
Mähne [ˈmɛːnə] *f* mane
mahn- [ˈmaːn] *zW:* ~**en** *vt* to remind;
(*warnend*) to warn; (*wegen Schuld*) to
demand payment from; **M~mal** *nt*
memorial; **M~ung** *f* reminder; admonition,
warning
Mai [mai] (-(e)s, -e) *m* May; ~**glöckchen** *nt*
lily of the valley
Mailand [ˈmailant] *nt* Milan
mailändisch *adj* Milanese

mailen [ˈmeːlən] *vti* to e-mail
Mais [mais] (-es, -e) *m* maize, corn (US);
~**kolben** *m* corncob; ~**mehl** *nt* (KOCH)
corn meal
Majestät [majɛsˈtɛːt] *f* majesty; **m~isch** *adj*
majestic
Majonäse ▲ [majoˈnɛːzə] *f* mayonnaise
Major [maˈjoːr] (-s, -e) *m* (MIL) major; (AVIAT)
squadron leader
Majoran [majoˈraːn] (-s, -e) *m* marjoram
makaber [maˈkaːbər] *adj* macabre
Makel [ˈmaːkəl] (-s, -) *m* blemish; (*moralisch*)
stain; **m~los** *adj* immaculate, spotless
mäkeln [ˈmɛːkəln] *vi* to find fault
Makler(in) [ˈmaːklər(ɪn)] (-s, -) *m(f)* broker
Makrele [maˈkreːlə] *f* mackerel
Mal [maːl] (-(e)s, -e) *nt* mark, sign;
(*Zeitpunkt*) time; **ein für alle ~** once and for
all; **m~** *adv* times; (*umg*) *siehe* **einmal**
♦ *suffix:* **-m~** -times
malen *vt, vi* to paint
Maler (-s, -) *m* painter; **Male~rei** *f*
painting; **m~isch** *adj* picturesque
Malkasten *m* paintbox
Mallorca [maˈjɔrka, maˈlɔrka] (-s) *nt* Majorca
malnehmen (*unreg*) *vt, vi* to multiply
Malz [malts] (-es) *nt* malt; ~**bier** *nt* (KOCH)
malt beer; ~**bonbon** *nt* cough drop;
~**kaffee** *m* malt coffee
Mama [ˈmamaː] (-, -s) (*umg*) *f* mum(my)
(BRIT), mom(my) (US)
Mami [ˈmami] (-, -s) = **Mama**
Mammut [ˈmamʊt] (-s, -e *od* -s) *nt*
mammoth
man [man] *pron* one, you; **~ sagt, ...** they *od*
people say ...; **wie schreibt ~ das?** how
do you write it?, how is it written?
Manager(in) [ˈmɛnɪdʒər(ɪn)] (-s, -) *m(f)*
manager
manch [manç] (*unver*) *pron* many a
manche(r, s) [ˈmançə(r, s)] *adj* many a; (*pl:*
einige) a number of ♦ *pron* some
mancherlei [mançərˈlai] *adj inv* various
♦ *pron inv* a variety of things
manchmal *adv* sometimes
Mandant(in) [manˈdant(ɪn)] *m(f)* (JUR) client
Mandarine [mandaˈriːnə] *f* mandarin,

tangerine

Mandat [man'da:t] **(-(e)s, -e)** *nt* mandate

Mandel ['mandəl] **(-, -n)** *f* almond; (*ANAT*) tonsil; **~entzündung** *f* (*MED*) tonsillitis

Manege [ma'ne:ʒə] *f* ring, arena

Mangel ['maŋəl] **(-s, ⸚)** *m* lack; (*Knappheit*) shortage; (*Fehler*) defect, fault; **~ an** +*dat* shortage of; **~erscheinung** *f* deficiency symptom; **m~haft** *adj* poor; (*fehlerhaft*) defective, faulty; **m~n** *vi unpers*: **es m~t jdm an etw** *dat* sb lacks sth ♦ *vt* (*Wäsche*) to mangle

mangels *präp* +*gen* for lack of

Manie [ma'ni:] *f* mania

Manier [ma'ni:r] **(-)** *f* manner; style; (*pej*) mannerism; **~en** *pl* (*Umgangsformen*) manners; **m~lich** *adj* well-mannered

Manifest [mani'fɛst] **(-es, -e)** *nt* manifesto

Maniküre [mani'ky:rə] *f* manicure

manipulieren [manipu'li:rən] *vt* to manipulate

Manko ['maŋko] **(-s, -s)** *nt* deficiency; (*COMM*) deficit

Mann [man] **(-(e)s, ⸚er)** *m* man; (*Ehemann*) husband; (*NAUT*) hand; **seinen ~ stehen** to hold one's own

Männchen ['mɛnçən] *nt* little man; (*Tier*) male

Mannequin [manə'kɛ̃:] **(-s, -s)** *nt* fashion model

männlich ['mɛnlıç] *adj* (*BIOL*) male; (*fig, GRAM*) masculine

Mannschaft *f* (*SPORT, fig*) team; (*AVIAT, NAUT*) crew; (*MIL*) other ranks *pl*

Manöver [ma'nø:vər] **(-s, -)** *nt* manoeuvre

manövrieren [manø'vri:rən] *vt, vi* to manoeuvre

Mansarde [man'zardə] *f* attic

Manschette [man'ʃɛtə] *f* cuff; (*TECH*) collar; sleeve; **~nknopf** *m* cufflink

Mantel ['mantəl] **(-s, ⸚)** *m* coat; (*TECH*) casing, jacket

Manuskript [manu'skrıpt] **(-(e)s, -e)** *nt* manuscript

Mappe ['mapə] *f* briefcase; (*Aktenmappe*) folder

Märchen ['mɛ:rçən] *nt* fairy tale; **m~haft** *adj* fabulous; **~prinz** *m* Prince Charming

Margarine [marga'ri:nə] *f* margarine

Margerite [marga'ri:tə] *f* (*BOT*) marguerite

Marienkäfer [ma'ri:ənkɛːfər] *m* ladybird

Marine [ma'ri:nə] *f* navy; **m~blau** *adj* navy blue

marinieren [mari'ni:rən] *vt* to marinate

Marionette [mario'nɛtə] *f* puppet

Mark¹ [mark] **(-, -)** *f* (*Münze*) mark

Mark² [mark] **(-(e)s)** *nt* (*Knochenmark*) marrow; **jdm durch ~ und Bein gehen** to go right through sb

markant [mar'kant] *adj* striking

Marke ['markə] *f* mark; (*Warensorte*) brand; (*Fabrikat*) make; (*Rabatt~, Brief~*) stamp; (*Essen~*) ticket; (*aus Metall etc*) token, disc

Markenartikel *m* proprietary article

markieren [mar'ki:rən] *vt* to mark; (*umg*) to act ♦ *vi* (*umg*) to act it

Markierung *f* marking

Markise [mar'ki:zə] *f* awning

Markstück *nt* one-mark piece

Markt [markt] **(-(e)s, ⸚e)** *m* market; **~forschung** *f* market research; **~lücke** *f* (*COMM*) opening, gap in the market; **~platz** *m* market place; **m~üblich** *adj* (*Preise, Mieten*) standard, usual; **~wert** *m* (*COMM*) market value; **~wirtschaft** *f* market economy

Marmelade [marmə'la:də] *f* jam

Marmor ['marmɔr] **(-s, -e)** *m* marble; **m~ieren** [-'ri:rən] *vt* to marble

Marokko [ma'rɔko] **(-s)** *nt* Morocco

Marone [ma'ro:nə] **(-, -n** *od* **Maroni)** *f* chestnut

Marotte [ma'rɔtə] *f* fad, quirk

Marsch¹ [marʃ] **(-, -en)** *f* marsh

Marsch² [marʃ] **(-(e)s, ⸚e)** *m* march ♦ *excl* march!; **~befehl** *m* marching orders *pl*; **m~bereit** *adj* ready to move; **m~ieren** [mar'ʃi:rən] *vi* to march

Märtyrer(in) ['mɛrtyrər(ın)] **(-s, -)** *m(f)* martyr

März [mɛrts] **(-(es), -e)** *m* March

Marzipan [martsi'pa:n] **(-s, -e)** *nt* marzipan

Masche ['maʃə] *f* mesh; (*Strickmasche*) stitch; **das ist die neueste ~** that's the

latest thing; **~ndraht** m wire mesh;
m~nfest adj run-resistant
Maschine [ma'ʃiːnə] f machine; (Motor)
engine; (Schreibmaschine) typewriter; **~
schreiben** to type; **m~ll** [maʃi'nɛl] adj
machine(-); mechanical
Maschinen- zW: **~bauer** m mechanical
engineer; **~gewehr** nt machine gun;
~pistole f submachine gun; **~schaden** m
mechanical fault; **~schlosser** m fitter;
~schrift f typescript
Maschinist [maʃi'nɪst] m engineer
Maser ['maːzər] (**-, -n**) f (von Holz) grain; **~n**
pl (MED) measles sg
Maske ['maskə] f mask; **~nball** m fancy-
dress ball
maskieren [mas'kiːrən] vt to mask;
(verkleiden) to dress up ♦ vr to disguise o.s.;
to dress up
Maskottchen [mas'kɔtçən] nt (lucky)
mascot
Maß¹ [maːs] (**-es, -e**) nt measure;
(Mäßigung) moderation; (Grad) degree,
extent; **~ halten** to exercise moderation
Maß² [maːs] (**-, -(e))** f litre of beer
Massage [ma'saːʒə] f massage
Maßanzug m made-to-measure suit
Maßarbeit f (fig) neat piece of work
Masse ['masə] f mass
Maßeinheit f unit of measurement
Massen- zW: **~artikel** m mass-produced
article; **~grab** nt mass grave; **m~haft** adj
loads of; **~medien** pl mass media pl;
~veranstaltung f mass meeting;
m~weise adv on a large scale
Masseur [ma'søːr] m masseur; **~in** f
masseuse
maßgebend adj authoritative
maßhalten △ (unreg) vi siehe **Maß¹**
massieren [ma'siːrən] vt to massage; (MIL)
to mass
massig ['masɪç] adj massive; (umg) massive
amount of
mäßig ['mɛːsɪç] adj moderate; **~en**
['mɛːsɪɡən] vt to restrain, to moderate;
M~keit f moderation
Massiv (**-s, -e**) nt massif

massiv [ma'siːf] adj solid; (fig) heavy, rough
Maß- zW: **~krug** m tankard; **m~los** adj
extreme; **~nahme** f measure, step; **~stab**
m rule, measure; (fig) standard; (GEOG)
scale; **m~voll** adj moderate
Mast [mast] (**-(e)s, -e(n))** m mast; (ELEK)
pylon
mästen ['mɛstən] vt to fatten
Material [materi'aːl] (**-s, -ien**) nt material(s);
~fehler m material defect; **~ismus** [-
'lɪsmʊs] m materialism; **m~istisch** [-'lɪstɪʃ]
adj materialistic
Materie [ma'teːriə] f matter, substance
materiell [materi'ɛl] adj material
Mathematik [matema'tiːk] f mathematics
sg; **~er(in)** [mate'maːtikər(ɪn)] (**-s, -**) m(f)
mathematician
mathematisch [mate'maːtɪʃ] adj
mathematical
Matjeshering ['matjəsheːrɪŋ] m (KOCH)
young herring
Matratze [ma'tratsə] f mattress
Matrixdrucker ['maːtrɪks-] m dot-matrix
printer
Matrose [ma'troːzə] (**-n, -n**) m sailor
Matsch [matʃ] (**-(e)s**) m mud;
(Schneematsch) slush; **m~ig** adj muddy;
slushy
matt [mat] adj weak; (glanzlos) dull; (PHOT)
matt; (SCHACH) mate
Matte ['matə] f mat
Mattscheibe f (TV) screen
Mauer ['mauər] (**-, -n**) f wall; **m~n** vi to
build; to lay bricks ♦ vt to build
Maul [maul] (**-(e)s, Mäuler**) nt mouth;
m~en (umg) vi to grumble; **~esel** m mule;
~korb m muzzle; **~sperre** f lockjaw;
~tasche f (KOCH) pasta envelopes stuffed
and used in soup; **~tier** nt mule; **~wurf** m
mole
Maurer ['maurər] (**-s, -**) m bricklayer
Maus [maus] (**-, Mäuse**) f (auch COMPUT)
mouse
Mause- ['mauzə] zW: **~falle** f mousetrap;
m~n vi to catch mice ♦ vt (umg) to pinch;
m~tot adj stone dead
Maut- ['maut] zW: **~gebühr** f toll (charge);

~**straße** f toll road
maximal [maksi'ma:l] adj maximum ♦ adv at most
Mayonnaise [majɔ'nɛ:zə] f mayonnaise
Mechan- [me'ça:n] zW: ~**ik** f mechanics sg; (Getriebe) mechanics pl; ~**iker** (-s, -) m mechanic, engineer; **m~isch** adj mechanical; ~**ismus** m mechanism
meckern ['mɛkərn] vi to bleat; (umg) to moan
Medaille [me'daljə] f medal
Medaillon [medal'jõ:] (-s, -s) nt (Schmuck) locket
Medikament [medika'mɛnt] nt medicine
Meditation [meditatsi'o:n] f meditation
meditieren [medi'ti:rən] vi to meditate
Medizin [medi'tsi:n] (-, -en) f medicine; **m~isch** adj medical
Meer [me:r] (-(e)s, -e) nt sea; ~**enge** f straits pl; ~**esfrüchte** pl seafood sg; ~**esspiegel** m sea level; ~**rettich** m horseradish; ~**schweinchen** nt guinea-pig
Mehl [me:l] (-(e)s, -e) nt flour; **m~ig** adj floury; ~**schwitze** f (KOCH) roux; ~**speise** f (KOCH) flummery
mehr [me:r] adj, adv more; ~**deutig** adj ambiguous; ~**ere** adj several; ~**eres** pron several things; ~**fach** adj multiple; (wiederholt) repeated; **M~fahrtenkarte** f multi-journey ticket; **M~heit** f majority; ~**malig** adj repeated; ~**mals** adv repeatedly; ~**stimmig** adj for several voices; ~**stimmig singen** to harmonize; **M~wertsteuer** f value added tax; **M~zahl** f majority; (GRAM) plural
Mehrzweck- in zW multipurpose
meiden ['maɪdən] (unreg) vt to avoid
Meile ['maɪlə] f mile; ~**nstein** m milestone; **m~nweit** adv for miles
mein(e) [maɪn] adj my; ~**e(r, s)** pron mine
Meineid ['maɪnʔaɪt] m perjury
meinen ['maɪnən] vi to think ♦ vt to think; (sagen) to say; (sagen wollen) to mean; **das will ich ~** I should think so
mein- zW: ~**erseits** adv for my part; ~**etwegen** adv (für mich) for my sake; (wegen mir) on my account; (von mir aus) as

far as I'm concerned; I don't care od mind; ~**etwillen** adv: **um ~etwillen** for my sake, on my account
Meinung ['maɪnʊŋ] f opinion; **ganz meine ~** I quite agree; **jdm die ~ sagen** to give sb a piece of one's mind
Meinungs- zW: ~**austausch** m exchange of views; ~**umfrage** f opinion poll; ~**verschiedenheit** f difference of opinion
Meise ['maɪzə] f tit(mouse)
Meißel ['maɪsəl] (-s, -) m chisel
meist [maɪst] adj most ♦ adv mostly; **am ~en** the most; ~**ens** adv generally, usually
Meister ['maɪstər] (-s, -) m master; (SPORT) champion; **m~haft** adj masterly; **m~n** vt (Schwierigkeiten etc) to overcome, conquer; ~**schaft** f mastery; (SPORT) championship; ~**stück** nt masterpiece; ~**werk** nt masterpiece
Melancholie [melaŋko'li:] f melancholy; **melancholisch** [melaŋ'ko:lɪʃ] adj melancholy
Melde- ['mɛldə] zW: ~**frist** f registration period; **m~n** vt to report ♦ vr to report; (SCH) to put one's hand up; (freiwillig) to volunteer; (auf etw, am Telefon) to answer; **sich m~n bei** to report to; to register with; **sich zu Wort m~n** to ask to speak; ~**pflicht** f obligation to register with the police; ~**schluss** ▲ m closing date; ~**stelle** f registration office
Meldung ['mɛldʊŋ] f announcement; (Bericht) report
meliert [me'li:rt] adj (Haar) greying; (Wolle) flecked
melken ['mɛlkən] (unreg) vt to milk
Melodie [melo'di:] f melody, tune
melodisch [me'lo:dɪʃ] adj melodious, tuneful
Melone [me'lo:nə] f melon; (Hut) bowler (hat)
Membran [mɛm'bra:n] (-, -en) f (TECH) diaphragm
Memoiren [memo'a:rən] pl memoirs
Menge ['mɛŋə] f quantity; (Menschenmenge) crowd; (große Anzahl) lot (of); **m~n** vt to mix ♦ vr: **sich m~n in** +akk to meddle

with; **~nlehre** f (*MATH*) set theory;
~nrabatt m bulk discount

Mensch [mɛnʃ] (**-en, -en**) m human being,
man; person ♦ excl heyl; **kein ~** nobody

Menschen- zW: **~affe** m (*ZOOL*) ape;
m~freundlich adj philanthropical;
~kenner m judge of human nature;
m~leer adj deserted; **m~möglich** adj
humanly possible; **~rechte** pl human
rights; **m~unwürdig** adj beneath human
dignity; **~verstand** m: **gesunder
~verstand** common sense

Mensch- zW: **~heit** f humanity, mankind;
m~lich adj human; (*human*) humane;
~lichkeit f humanity

Menstruation [mɛnstruatsi'oːn] f
menstruation

Mentalität [mɛntali'tɛːt] f mentality

Menü [me'nyː] (**-s, -s**) nt (*auch COMPUT*)
menu

Merk- ['mɛrk] zW: **~blatt** nt instruction
sheet od leaflet; **m~en** vt to notice; **sich**
dat **etw m~en** to remember sth; **m~lich**
adj noticeable; **~mal** nt sign, characteristic;
m~würdig adj odd

messbar ▲ ['mɛsbaːr] adj measurable

Messbecher ▲ m measuring jug

Messe ['mɛsə] f fair; (*ECCL*) mass; **~gelände**
nt exhibition centre; **~halle** f pavilion at a
fair

messen (*unreg*) vt to measure ♦ vr to
compete

Messer (**-s, -**) nt knife; **~spitze** f knife
point; (*in Rezept*) pinch

Messestand m stall at a fair

Messgerät ▲ nt measuring device, gauge

Messing ['mɛsɪŋ] (**-s**) nt brass

Metall [me'tal] (**-s, -e**) nt metal; **m~isch** adj
metallic

Meter ['meːtər] (**-s, -**) nt od m metre; **~maß**
nt tape measure

Methode [me'toːdə] f method;
methodisch adj methodical

Metropole [metro'poːlə] f metropolis

Metzger ['mɛtsgər] (**-s, -**) m butcher; **~ei**
[-'rai] f butcher's (shop)

Meute ['mɔytə] f pack; **~'rei** f mutiny;

m~rn vi to mutiny

miauen [mi'auən] vi to miaow

mich [mɪç] (*akk von* **ich**) pron me; myself

Miene ['miːnə] f look, expression

mies [miːs] (*umg*) adj lousy

Miet- ['miːt] zW: **~auto** nt hired car; **~e** f
rent; **zur ~e wohnen** to live in rented
accommodation; **m~en** vt to rent; (*Auto*)
to hire; **~er(in)** (**-s, -**) m(f) tenant; **~shaus**
nt tenement, block of (rented) flats;
~vertrag m lease

Migräne [mi'grɛːnə] f migraine

Mikro- ['mikro] zW: **~fon, ~phon**
[-'foːn] (**-s, -e**) nt microphone; **~skop**
[-'skoːp] (**-s, -e**) nt microscope;
m~skopisch adj microscopic;
~wellenherd m microwave (oven)

Milch [mɪlç] (**-**) f milk; **~glas** nt frosted
glass; **m~ig** adj milky; **~kaffee** m white
coffee; **~mann** (pl **-männer**) m milkman;
~mixgetränk nt (*KOCH*) milkshake;
~pulver nt powdered milk; **~straße** f
Milky Way; **~zahn** m milk tooth

mild [mɪlt] adj mild; (*Richter*) lenient;
(*freundlich*) kind, charitable; **M~e** f
mildness; leniency; **~ern** vt to mitigate, to
soften; (*Schmerz*) to alleviate; **~ernde
Umstände** extenuating circumstances

Milieu [mili'øː] (**-s, -s**) nt background,
environment; **m~geschädigt** adj
maladjusted

Mili- [mili] zW: **m~tant** [-'tant] adj militant;
~tär [-'tɛːr] (**-s**) nt military, army;
~'tärgericht nt military court; **m~'tärisch**
adj military

Milli- ['mili] zW: **~ardär** [-ar'dɛːr] m
multimillionaire; **~arde** [-'ardə] f milliard;
billion (*BES US*); **~meter** m millimetre;
~meterpapier nt graph paper

Million [mɪli'oːn] (**-, -en**) f million; **~är**
[-o'nɛːr] m millionaire

Milz [mɪlts] (**-, -en**) f spleen

Mimik ['miːmɪk] f mime

Mimose [mi'moːzə] f mimosa; (*fig*) sensitive
person

minder ['mɪndər] adj inferior ♦ adv less;
M~heit f minority; **~jährig** adj minor;

M~jährige(r) *f(m)* minor; **~n** *vt, vr* to decrease, to diminish; **M~ung** *f* decrease; **~wertig** *adj* inferior; **M~wertigkeitskomplex** *m* inferiority complex

Mindest- ['mɪndəst] *zW:* **~alter** *nt* minimum age; **~betrag** *m* minimum amount; **m~e(r, s)** *adj* least; **zum ~en** *od* **m~ens** *adv* at least; **m~ens** *adv* at least; **~haltbarkeitsdatum** *nt* best-before date; **~lohn** *m* minimum wage; **~maß** *nt* minimum

Mine ['miːnə] *f* mine; *(Bleistiftmine)* lead; *(Kugelschreibermine)* refill

Mineral [mine'raːl] **(-s, -e** *od* **-ien)** *nt* mineral; **m~isch** *adj* mineral; **~wasser** *nt* mineral water

Miniatur [minia'tuːr] *f* miniature

Mini- *zW:* **~golf** ['mɪnɪgɔlf] *nt* miniature golf, crazy golf; **m~mal** [mini'maːl] *adj* minimal; **m~mum** ['miːnimʊm] *nt* minimum; **~rock** *nt* miniskirt

Minister [mi'nɪstər] **(-s, -)** *m* minister; **m~iell** *adj* ministerial; **~ium** *nt* ministry; **~präsident** *m* prime minister

Minus ['miːnʊs] **(-, -)** *nt* deficit

minus *adv* minus; **M~zeichen** *nt* minus sign

Minute [mi'nuːtə] *f* minute

Minze ['mɪntsə] *f* mint

mir [miːr] *(dat von* **ich)** *pron* (to) me; **~ nichts, dir nichts** just like that

Misch- ['mɪʃ] *zW:* **~brot** *nt* bread made from more than one kind of flour; **~ehe** *f* mixed marriage; **m~en** *vt* to mix; **~ling** *m* half-caste; **~ung** *f* mixture

miserabel [mizə'raːbəl] *(umg) adj (Essen, Film)* dreadful

Miss- ▲ ['mɪs] *zW:* **~behagen** *nt* discomfort, uneasiness; **~bildung** *f* deformity; **m~billigen** *vt insep* to disapprove of; **~brauch** *m* abuse; *(falscher Gebrauch)* misuse; **m~'brauchen** *vt insep* to abuse; **jdn zu** *od* **für etw m~brauchen** to use sb for *od* to do sth; **~erfolg** *m* failure; **~fallen (-s)** *nt* displeasure; **m~'fallen** *(unreg) vi insep:* **jdm m~fallen**

to displease sb; **~geschick** *nt* misfortune; **m~glücken** [mɪs'ɡlʏkən] *vi insep* to fail; **jdm m~glückt etw** sb does not succeed with sth; **~griff** *m* mistake; **~gunst** *f* envy; **m~günstig** *adj* envious; **m~'handeln** *vt insep* to ill-treat; **~'handlung** *f* ill-treatment

Mission [mɪsi'oːn] *f* mission; **~ar(in)** *m(f)* missionary

Miss- ▲ *zW:* **~klang** *m* discord; **~kredit** *m* discredit; **m~lingen** [mɪs'lɪŋən] *(unreg) vi insep* to fail; **~mut** *m* sullenness; **m~mutig** *adj* sullen; **m~'raten** *(unreg) vi insep* to turn out badly ♦ *adj* ill-bred; **~stand** *m* bad state of affairs; abuse; **m~'trauen** *vi insep* to mistrust; **~trauen (-s)** *nt* distrust, suspicion; **~trauensantrag** *m (POL)* motion of no confidence; **m~trauisch** *adj* distrustful, suspicious; **~verhältnis** *nt* disproportion; **~verständnis** *nt* misunderstanding; **m~verstehen** *(unreg) vt insep* to misunderstand; **~wirtschaft** *f* mismanagement

Mist [mɪst] **(-(e)s)** *m* dung; dirt; *(umg)* rubbish

Mistel (-, -n) *f* mistletoe

Misthaufen *m* dungheap

mit [mɪt] *präp +dat* with; *(~tels)* by ♦ *adv* along, too; **~ der Bahn** by train; **~ 10 Jahren** at the age of 10; **wollen Sie ~?** do you want to come along?

Mitarbeit ['mɪtʔarbaɪt] *f* cooperation; **m~en** *vi* to cooperate, to collaborate; **~er(in)** *m(f)* collaborator; co-worker ♦ *pl (Personal)* staff

Mit- *zW:* **~bestimmung** *f* participation in decision-making; **m~bringen** *(unreg) vt* to bring along

miteinander [mɪtʔaɪ'nandər] *adv* together, with one another

miterleben *vt* to see, to witness

Mitesser ['mɪtʔɛsər] **(-s, -)** *m* blackhead

mitfahr- *zW:* **~en** *vi* to accompany; *(auf Reise auch)* to travel with; **M~gelegenheit** *f* lift; **M~zentrale** *f* agency for arranging lifts

mitfühlend *adj* sympathetic, compassionate

Mit- *zW*: **m~geben** (*unreg*) *vt* to give;
~gefühl *nt* sympathy; **m~gehen** (*unreg*) *vi*
to go/come along; **m~genommen** *adj*
done in, in a bad way; **~gift** *f* dowry

Mitglied ['mɪtɡliːt] *nt* member; **~sbeitrag**
m membership fee; **~schaft** *f* membership

Mit- *zW*: **m~halten** (*unreg*) *vi* to keep up;
m~helfen (*unreg*) *vi* to help; **~hilfe** *f* help,
assistance; **m~hören** *vt* to listen in to;
m~kommen (*unreg*) *vi* to come along;
(*verstehen*) to keep up, to follow; **~läufer**
m hanger-on; (*POL*) fellow traveller

Mitleid *nt* sympathy; (*Erbarmen*)
compassion; **m~ig** *adj* sympathetic;
m~slos *adj* pitiless, merciless

Mit- *zW*: **m~machen** *vt* to join in, to take
part in; **~mensch** *m* fellow man;
m~nehmen (*unreg*) *vt* to take along/away;
(*anstrengen*) to wear out, to exhaust; **zum**
~nehmen to take away; **m~reden** *vi*: **bei**
etw m~reden to have a say in sth;
m~reißen (*unreg*) *vt* to carry away/along;
(*fig*) to thrill, captivate

mitsamt [mɪt'zamt] *präp +dat* together with

Mitschuld *f* complicity; **m~ig** *adj*: **m~ig**
(**an** +*dat*) implicated (in); (*an Unfall*) partly
responsible (for)

Mit- *zW*: **~schüler(in)** *m(f)* schoolmate;
m~spielen *vi* to join in, to take part;
~spieler(in) *m(f)* partner

Mittag ['mɪtaːk] (**-(e)s, -e**) *m* midday,
lunchtime; (**zu**) **~ essen** to have lunch;
heute/morgen ~ today/tomorrow at
lunchtime *od* noon; **~essen** *nt* lunch,
dinner

mittags *adv* at lunchtime *od* noon;
M~pause *f* lunch break; **M~schlaf** *m*
early afternoon nap, siesta

Mittäter(in) ['mɪttɛːtər(ɪn)] *m(f)* accomplice

Mitte ['mɪtə] *f* middle; (*POL*) centre; **aus**
unserer ~ from our midst

mitteilen ['mɪttaɪlən] *vt*: **jdm etw ~** to
inform sb of sth, to communicate sth to sb

Mitteilung *f* communication

Mittel ['mɪtəl] (**-s -**) *nt* means; method;
(*MATH*) average; (*MED*) medicine; **ein ~ zum**
Zweck a means to an end; **~alter** *nt*

Middle Ages *pl*; **m~alterlich** *adj*
mediaeval; **~ding** *nt* cross; **~europa** *nt*
Central Europe; **~gebirge** *nt* low mountain
range; **m~mäßig** *adj* mediocre, middling;
~mäßigkeit *f* mediocrity; **~meer** *nt*
Mediterranean; **~ohrentzündung** *f*
inflammation of the middle ear; **~punkt** *m*
centre; **~stand** *m* middle class; **~streifen**
m central reservation; **~stürmer** *m* centre-
forward; **~weg** *m* middle course; **~welle** *f*
(*RADIO*) medium wave

mitten ['mɪtən] *adv* in the middle; **~ auf der**
Straße/in der Nacht in the middle of the
street/night

Mitternacht ['mɪtərnaxt] *f* midnight

mittlere(r, s) ['mɪtlərə(r, s)] *adj* middle;
(*durchschnittlich*) medium, average; **~ Reife**
≃ O-levels

---

mittlere Reife

ⓘ   The **mittlere Reife** *is the standard*
certificate gained at a **Realschule** *or*
Gymnasium *on successful completion of 6*
years' education there. If a pupil at a
Realschule *attains good results in several*
subjects he is allowed to enter the 11th
class of a **Gymnasium** *to study for the*
Abitur.

---

mittlerweile ['mɪtlər'vaɪlə] *adv* meanwhile

Mittwoch ['mɪtvɔx] (**-(e)s, -e**) *m*
Wednesday; **m~s** *adv* on Wednesdays

mitunter [mɪt'ʊntər] *adv* occasionally,
sometimes

Mit- *zW*: **m~verantwortlich** *adj* jointly
responsible; **m~wirken** *vi*: **m~wirken (bei)**
to contribute (to); (*THEAT*) to take part (in);
~wirkung *f* contribution; participation

Mobbing ['mɔbɪŋ] (**-s**) *nt* workplace
bullying

Möbel ['møːbəl] *pl* furniture *sg*; **~wagen** *m*
furniture *od* removal van

mobil [mo'biːl] *adj* mobile; (*MIL*) mobilized;
M~iar [mobili'aːr] (**-s, -e**) *nt* furnishings *pl*;
M~machung *f* mobilization; **M~telefon**
nt mobile phone

möblieren [mø'bliːrən] *vt* to furnish;

möbliert wohnen to live in furnished accommodation
möchte etc ['mœçtə] vb siehe **mögen**
Mode ['mo:də] f fashion
Modell [mo'dɛl] (-s, -e) nt model; **m~ieren** [-'li:rən] vt to model
Modenschau f fashion show
moderig ['mo:dərɪç] adj (Keller) musty; (Luft) stale
modern [mo'dɛrn] adj modern; (modisch) fashionable; **~i'sieren** vt to modernize
Mode- zW: **~schau** f fashion show; **~schmuck** m fashion jewellery; **~schöpfer(in)** m(f) fashion designer; **~wort** nt fashionable word, buzz word
modisch ['mo:dɪʃ] adj fashionable
Mofa ['mo:fa] (-s, -s) nt small moped
mogeln ['mo:gəln] (umg) vi to cheat

SCHLÜSSELWORT

---

mögen ['mø:gən] (pt mochte, pp gemocht od (als Hilfsverb) mögen) vt, vi to like; **magst du/mögen Sie ihn?** do you like him?; **ich möchte ...** I would like ..., I'd like ...; **er möchte in die Stadt** he'd like to go into town; **ich möchte nicht, dass du ...** I wouldn't like you to ...; **ich mag nicht mehr** I've had enough
♦ Hilfsverb to like to; (wollen) to want; **möchtest du etwas essen?** would you like something to eat?; **sie mag nicht bleiben** she doesn't want to stay; **das mag wohl sein** that may well be; **was mag das heißen?** what might that mean?; **Sie möchten zu Hause anrufen** could you please call home?

---

möglich ['mø:klɪç] adj possible; **~erweise** adv possibly; **M~keit** f possibility; **nach M~keit** if possible; **~st** adv as ... as possible
Mohn [mo:n] (-(e)s, -e) m (~blume) poppy; (~samen) poppy seed
Möhre ['mø:rə] f carrot
Mohrrübe ['mo:rry:bə] f carrot
mokieren [mo'ki:rən] vr: **sich ~ über** +akk to make fun of
Mole ['mo:lə] f (harbour) mole

Molekül [mole'ky:l] (-s, -e) nt molecule
Molkerei [mɔlkə'raɪ] f dairy
Moll [mɔl] (-, -) nt (MUS) minor (key)
mollig adj cosy; (dicklich) plump
Moment [mo'mɛnt] (-(e)s, -e) m moment
♦ nt factor; **im ~** at the moment; **~ (mal)!** just a moment; **m~an** [-'ta:n] adj momentary ♦ adv at the moment
Monarch [mo'narç] (-en, -en) m monarch; **~ie** [monar'çi:] f monarchy
Monat ['mo:nat] (-(e)s, -e) m month; **m~elang** adv for months; **m~lich** adj monthly
Monats- zW: **~gehalt** nt: **das dreizehnte ~gehalt** Christmas bonus (of one month's salary); **~karte** f monthly ticket
Mönch [mœnç] (-(e)s, -e) m monk
Mond [mo:nt] (-(e)s, -e) m moon; **~finsternis** f eclipse of the moon; **m~hell** adj moonlit; **~landung** f moon landing; **~schein** m moonlight
Mono- [mono] in zW mono; **~log** [-'lo:k] (-s, -e) m monologue; **~pol** [-'po:l] (-s, -e) nt monopoly; **m~polisieren** [-poli'zi:rən] vt to monopolize; **m~ton** [-'to:n] adj monotonous; **~tonie** [-to'ni:] f monotony
Montag ['mo:nta:k] (-(e)s, -e) m Monday
Montage [mɔn'ta:ʒə] f (PHOT etc) montage; (TECH) assembly; (Einbauen) fitting
Monteur [mɔn'tø:r] m fitter
montieren [mɔn'ti:rən] vt to assemble
Monument [monu'mɛnt] nt monument; **m~al** [-'ta:l] adj monumental
Moor [mo:r] (-(e)s, -e) nt moor
Moos [mo:s] (-es, -e) nt moss
Moped ['mo:pɛt] (-s, -s) nt moped
Moral [mo'ra:l] (-, -en) f morality; (einer Geschichte) moral; **m~isch** adj moral
Morast [mo'rast] (-(e)s, -e) m morass, mire; **m~ig** adj boggy
Mord [mɔrt] (-(e)s, -e) m murder; **~anschlag** m murder attempt
Mörder(in) ['mœrdər(ɪn)] (-s, -) m(f) murderer (murderess)
mörderisch adj (fig: schrecklich) terrible, dreadful ♦ adv (umg: entsetzlich) terribly, dreadfully

---

Mord- zW: **~kommission** f murder squad; **~sglück** (umg) nt amazing luck; **m~smäßig** (umg) adj terrific, enormous; **~verdacht** m suspicion of murder; **~waffe** f murder weapon

morgen ['mɔrgən] adv tomorrow; **~ früh** tomorrow morning; **M~ (-s, -)** m morning; **M~mantel** m dressing gown; **M~rock** m dressing gown; **M~röte** f dawn; **~s** adv in the morning

morgig ['mɔrgɪç] adj tomorrow's; **der ~e Tag** tomorrow

Morphium ['mɔrfiʊm] nt morphine

morsch [mɔrʃ] adj rotten

Morsealphabet ['mɔrzəlalfabeːt] nt Morse code

morsen vi to send a message by Morse code

Mörtel ['mœrtəl] **(-s, -)** m mortar

Mosaik [moza'iːk] **(-s, -en** od **-e)** nt mosaic

Moschee [mɔ'ʃeː] **(-, -n)** f mosque

Moskito [mɔs'kiːto] **(-s, -s)** m mosquito

Most [mɔst] **(-(e)s, -e)** m (unfermented) fruit juice; (Apfelwein) cider

Motel [mo'tel] **(-s, -s)** nt motel

Motiv [mo'tiːf] **(-s, -e)** nt motive; (MUS) theme; **~ation** [-vatsi'oːn] f motivation; **m~ieren** [moti'viːrən] vt to motivate

Motor ['moːtɔr, pl mo'toːrən] **(-s, -en)** m engine; (bes ELEK) motor; **~boot** nt motorboat; **~haube** f (von Auto) bonnet (BRIT), hood (US); **m~isieren** vt to motorize; **~öl** nt engine oil; **~rad** nt motorcycle; **~roller** m (motor) scooter; **~schaden** m engine trouble od failure

Motte ['mɔtə] f moth; **~nkugel** f mothball(s)

Motto ['mɔto] **(-s, -s)** nt motto

Möwe ['møːvə] f seagull

Mücke ['mʏkə] f midge, gnat; **~nstich** m midge od gnat bite

müde ['myːdə] adj tired

Müdigkeit ['myːdɪçkaɪt] f tiredness

Muffel (-s, -) (umg) m killjoy, sourpuss

muffig adj (Luft) musty

Mühe ['myːə] f trouble, pains pl; **mit Müh und Not** with great difficulty; **sich** dat **~**

geben to go to a lot of trouble; **m~los** adj without trouble, easy; **m~voll** adj laborious, arduous

Mühle ['myːlə] f mill; (Kaffeemühle) grinder

Müh- zW: **~sal (-, -e)** f tribulation; **m~sam** adj arduous, troublesome; **m~selig** adj arduous, laborious

Mulde ['mʊldə] f hollow, depression

Mull [mʊl] **(-(e)s, -e)** m thin muslin

Müll [mʏl] **(-(e)s, -e)** m refuse; **~abfuhr** f rubbish disposal; (Leute) dustmen pl; **~abladeplatz** m rubbish dump; **~binde** f gauze bandage; **~eimer** m dustbin, garbage can (US); **~haufen** m rubbish heap; **~schlucker (-s, -)** m garbage disposal unit; **~tonne** f dustbin; **~verbrennungsanlage** f incinerator

mulmig ['mʊlmɪç] adj rotten; (umg) dodgy; **jdm ist ~** sb feels funny

multiplizieren [mʊltipli'tsiːrən] vt to multiply

Mumie ['muːmiə] f mummy

Mumm [mʊm] **(-s)** (umg) m gumption, nerve

Mumps [mʊmps] **(-)** m od f (MED) mumps

München ['mʏnçən] **(-s)** nt Munich

Mund [mʊnt] **(-(e)s, ⸚er)** m mouth; **~art** f dialect

münden ['mʏndən] vi: **~ in** +akk to flow into

Mund- zW: **m~faul** adj taciturn; **~geruch** m bad breath; **~harmonika** f mouth organ

mündig ['mʏndɪç] adj of age; **M~keit** f majority

mündlich ['mʏntlɪç] adj oral

Mundstück nt mouthpiece; (Zigarettenmundstück) tip

Mündung ['mʏndʊŋ] f (von Fluss) mouth; (Gewehr) muzzle

Mund- zW: **~wasser** nt mouthwash; **~werk** nt: **ein großes ~werk haben** to have a big mouth; **~winkel** m corner of the mouth

Munition [munitsi'oːn] f ammunition; **~slager** nt ammunition dump

munkeln ['mʊŋkəln] vi to whisper, to

mutter

Münster ['mʏnstər] (**-s, -**) *nt* minster

munter ['mʊntər] *adj* lively

Münze ['mʏntsə] *f* coin; **m~n** *vt* to coin, to mint; **auf jdn gemünzt sein** to be aimed at sb

Münzfernsprecher ['mʏntsfɛrnʃprɛçər] *m* callbox (*BRIT*), pay phone

mürb(e) ['mʏrb(ə)] *adj* (*Gestein*) crumbly; (*Holz*) rotten; (*Gebäck*) crisp; **jdn ~ machen** to wear sb down; **M~eteig** ['mʏrbataɪç] *m* shortcrust pastry

murmeln ['mʊrməln] *vt, vi* to murmur, to mutter

murren ['mʊrən] *vi* to grumble, to grouse

mürrisch ['mʏrɪʃ] *adj* sullen

Mus [muːs] (**-es, -e**) *nt* purée

Muschel ['mʊʃəl] (**-, -n**) *f* mussel; (*~schale*) shell; (*Telefonmuschel*) receiver

Muse ['muːzə] *f* muse

Museum [mu'zeːʊm] (**-s, Museen**) *nt* museum

Musik [mu'ziːk] *f* music; (*Kapelle*) band; **m~alisch** [-ka:lɪʃ] *adj* musical; **~ant(in)** [-'kant(ɪn)] *m(f)* musician; **~box** *f* jukebox; **~er** (**-s, -**) *m* musician; **~hochschule** *f* college of music; **~instrument** *nt* musical instrument

musisch ['muːzɪʃ] *adj* (*Mensch*) artistic

musizieren [muzi'tsiːrən] *vi* to make music

Muskat [mʊs'kaːt] (**-(e)s, -e**) *m* nutmeg

Muskel ['mʊskəl] (**-s, -n**) *m* muscle; **~kater** *m*: **~kater haben** to be stiff

Muskulatur [mʊskula'tuːr] *f* muscular system

muskulös [mʊsku'løːs] *adj* muscular

Müsli ['myːsli] (**-s, -**) *nt* (*KOCH*) muesli

Muss ▲ [mʊs] (**-**) *nt* necessity, must

Muße ['muːsə] (**-**) *f* leisure

SCHLÜSSELWORT

müssen ['mʏsən] (*pt* **musste**, *pp* **gemusst** *od* (*als Hilfsverb*) **müssen**) *vi* **1** (*Zwang*) must (*nur im Präsens*), to have to; **ich muss es tun** I must do it, I have to do it; **ich musste es tun** I had to do it; **er muss es**

nicht tun he doesn't have to do it; **muss ich?** must I?, do I have to?; **wann müsst ihr zur Schule?** when do you have to go to school?; **er hat gehen müssen** he (has) had to go; **muss das sein?** is that really necessary?; **ich muss mal** (*umg*) I need the toilet

2 (*sollen*): **das musst du nicht tun!** you oughtn't to *od* shouldn't do that; **Sie hätten ihn fragen müssen** you should have asked him

3: **es muss geregnet haben** it must have rained; **es muss nicht wahr sein** it needn't be true

---

müßig ['myːsɪç] *adj* idle

Muster ['mʊstər] (**-s, -**) *nt* model; (*Dessin*) pattern; (*Probe*) sample; **m~gültig** *adj* exemplary; **m~n** *vt* (*Tapete*) to pattern; (*fig, MIL*) to examine; (*Truppen*) to inspect; **~ung** *f* (*von Stoff*) pattern; (*MIL*) inspection

Mut [muːt] *m* courage; **nur ~!** cheer up!; **jdm ~ machen** to encourage sb; **m~ig** *adj* courageous; **m~los** *adj* discouraged, despondent

mutmaßlich ['muːtmaːslɪç] *adj* presumed ♦ *adv* probably

Mutprobe *f* test *od* trial of courage

Mutter¹ ['mʊtər] (**-, ¨**) *f* mother

Mutter² ['mʊtər] (**-, -n**) *f* (*Schraubenmutter*) nut

mütterlich ['mʏtərlɪç] *adj* motherly; **~erseits** *adv* on the mother's side

Mutter- *zW*: **~liebe** *f* motherly love; **~mal** *nt* birthmark; **~milch** *f* mother's milk; **~schaft** *f* motherhood, maternity; **~schutz** *m* maternity regulations; **'~seelena|llein** *adj* all alone; **~sprache** *f* native language; **~tag** *m* Mother's Day

Mutti ['mʊti] (**-, -s**) *f* mum(my) (*BRIT*), mom(my) (*US*)

mutwillig ['muːtvɪlɪç] *adj* malicious, deliberate

Mütze ['mʏtsə] *f* cap

MwSt *abk* (= *Mehrwertsteuer*) VAT

mysteriös [mʏsteri'øːs] *adj* mysterious

Mythos ['myːtɔs] (**-, Mythen**) *m* myth

Rechtschreibreform: ▲ *neue Schreibung* △ *alte Schreibung (auslaufend)*

N, n

na [na] *excl* well; **~ gut** okay then
Nabel ['na:bəl] (**-s, -**) *m* navel; **~schnur** *f* umbilical cord

SCHLÜSSELWORT

nach [na:x] *präp +dat* **1** (*örtlich*) to; **nach Berlin** to Berlin; **nach links/rechts** (to the) left/right; **nach oben/hinten** up/back
2 (*zeitlich*) after; **einer nach dem anderen** one after the other; **nach Ihnen!** after you!; **zehn (Minuten) nach drei** ten (minutes) past three
3 (*gemäß*) according to; **nach dem Gesetz** according to the law; **dem Namen nach** judging by his/her name; **nach allem, was ich weiß** as far as I know
♦ *adv*: **ihm nach!** after him!; **nach und nach** gradually, little by little; **nach wie vor** still

nachahmen ['na:xʔa:mən] *vt* to imitate
Nachbar(in) ['naxbaːr(ɪn)] (**-s, -n**) *m(f)* neighbour; **~haus** *nt*: **im ~haus** next door; **n~lich** *adj* neighbourly; **~schaft** *f* neighbourhood; **~staat** *m* neighbouring state
nach- *zW*: **~bestellen** *vt*: **50 Stück ~bestellen** to order another 50; **N~bestellung** *f* (*COMM*) repeat order; **N~bildung** *f* imitation, copy; **~blicken** *vi* to gaze after; **~datieren** *vt* to postdate
nachdem [na:x'de:m] *konj* after; (*weil*) since; **je ~** it depends (whether)
nachdenken (*unreg*) *vi*: **~ über** *+akk* to think about; **N~** (**-s**) *nt* reflection, meditation
nachdenklich *adj* thoughtful, pensive
Nachdruck ['na:xdrʊk] *m* emphasis; (*TYP*) reprint, reproduction
nachdrücklich ['na:xdrʏklɪç] *adj* emphatic
nacheinander [na:xʔaɪ'nandər] *adv* one after the other
nachempfinden ['na:xʔɛmpfɪndən] (*unreg*)

vt: **jdm etw ~** to feel sth with sb
Nacherzählung ['na:xʔɛrtseːlʊŋ] *f* reproduction (of a story)
Nachfahr ['na:xfaːr] (**-s, -en**) *m* descendant
Nachfolge ['na:xfɔlgə] *f* succession; **n~n** *vi* +*dat* to follow; **~r(in)** (**-s, -**) *m(f)* successor
nachforschen *vt, vi* to investigate
Nachforschung *f* investigation
Nachfrage ['na:xfra:gə] *f* inquiry; (*COMM*) demand; **n~n** *vi* to inquire
nach- *zW*: **~füllen** *vt* to refill; **~geben** (*unreg*) *vi* to give way, to yield; **N~gebühr** *f* (*POST*) excess postage
nachgehen ['na:xgeːən] (*unreg*) *vi* (+*dat*) to follow; (*erforschen*) to inquire (into); (*Uhr*) to be slow
Nachgeschmack ['na:xgəʃmak] *m* aftertaste
nachgiebig ['na:xgiːbɪç] *adj* soft, accommodating; **N~keit** *f* softness
nachhaltig ['na:xhaltɪç] *adj* lasting; (*Widerstand*) persistent
nachhause *adv* (*österreichisch, schweizerisch*) home
nachhelfen ['na:xhɛlfən] (*unreg*) *vi* +*dat* to assist, to help
nachher [na:x'he:r] *adv* afterwards
Nachhilfeunterricht ['na:xhɪlfəʔʊntərrɪçt] *m* extra tuition
nachholen ['na:xhoːlən] *vt* to catch up with; (*Versäumtes*) to make up for
Nachkomme ['na:xkɔmə] (**-, -n**) *m* descendant
nachkommen (*unreg*) *vi* to follow; (*einer Verpflichtung*) to fulfil; **N~schaft** *f* descendants *pl*
Nachkriegszeit *f* postwar period
Nach- *zW*: **~lass** ▲ (**-es, -lässe**) *m* (*COMM*) discount, rebate; (*Erbe*) estate; **n~lassen** (*unreg*) *vt* (*Strafe*) to remit; (*Summe*) to take off; (*Schulden*) to cancel ♦ *vi* to decrease, to ease off; (*Sturm*) to die down, to ease off; (*schlechter werden*) to deteriorate; **er hat n~gelassen** he has got worse; **n~lässig** *adj* negligent, careless
nachlaufen ['na:xlaʊfən] (*unreg*) *vi* +*dat* to run after, to chase

Spelling Reform: ▲ *new spelling* △ *old spelling (to be phased out)*

nachlösen ['na:xløːzən] vi (*Zuschlag*) to pay on the train, pay at the other end; (*zur Weiterfahrt*) to pay the supplement

nachmachen ['na:xmaxən] vt to imitate, to copy; (*fälschen*) to counterfeit

Nachmittag ['na:xmɪta:k] m afternoon; **am ~** in the afternoon; **n~s** adv in the afternoon

Nach- zW: **~nahme** f cash on delivery; **per ~nahme** C.O.D.; **~name** m surname; **~porto** nt excess postage

nachprüfen ['na:xpryːfən] vt to check, to verify

nachrechnen ['na:xrɛçnən] vt to check

nachreichen ['na:xraɪçən] vt (*Unterlagen*) to hand in later

Nachricht ['na:xrɪçt] (-, -en) f (piece of) news; (*Mitteilung*) message; **~en** pl (*Neuigkeiten*) news

Nachrichten- zW: **~agentur** f news agency; **~dienst** m (MIL) intelligence service; **~sprecher(in)** m(f) newsreader; **~technik** f telecommunications sg

Nachruf ['na:xruːf] m obituary

nachsagen ['na:xza:gən] vt to repeat; **jdm etw ~** to say sth of sb

Nachsaison ['na:xzɛzɔ̃ː] f off-season

nachschicken ['na:xʃɪkən] vt to forward

nachschlagen ['na:xʃlaːgən] (*unreg*) vt to look up

Nachschlagewerk nt reference book

Nachschlüssel m duplicate key

Nachschub ['na:xʃuːp] m supplies pl; (*Truppen*) reinforcements pl

nachsehen ['na:xzeːən] (*unreg*) vt (*prüfen*) to check ♦ vi (*erforschen*) to look and see; **jdm etw ~** to forgive sb sth; **das N~ haben** to come off worst

Nachsendeantrag m application to have one's mail forwarded

nachsenden ['na:xzɛndən] (*unreg*) vt to send on, to forward

nachsichtig adj indulgent, lenient

nachsitzen ['na:xzɪtsən] (*unreg*) vi: **~ (müssen)** (SCH) to be kept in

Nachspeise ['na:xʃpaɪzə] f dessert, sweet, pudding

Nachspiel ['na:xʃpiːl] nt epilogue; (*fig*) sequel

nachsprechen ['na:xʃprɛçən] (*unreg*) vt: **(jdm) ~** to repeat (after sb)

nächst [nɛːçst] präp +dat (*räumlich*) next to; (*außer*) apart from; **~beste(r, s)** adj first that comes along; (*zweitbeste*) next best; **N~e(r)** f(m) neighbour; **~e(r, s)** adj next; (*~gelegen*) nearest

nachstellen ['na:xʃtɛlən] vt (TECH: *neu einstellen*) to adjust

nächst zW: **N~enliebe** f love for one's fellow men; **~ens** adv shortly, soon; **~liegend** adj nearest; (*fig*) obvious; **~möglich** adj next possible

Nacht [naxt] (-, ⁈e) f night; **~dienst** m night shift

Nachteil ['na:xtaɪl] m disadvantage; **n~ig** adj disadvantageous

Nachthemd nt (*Herrennachthemd*) nightshirt; (*Damennachthemd*) nightdress

Nachtigall ['naxtɪgal] (-, -en) f nightingale

Nachtisch ['na:xtɪʃ] m = **Nachspeise**

Nachtklub m night club

Nachtleben nt nightlife

nächtlich ['nɛçtlɪç] adj nightly

Nachtlokal nt night club

Nach- zW: **~trag** (-(e)s, -träge) m supplement; **n~tragen** (*unreg*) vt to carry; (*zufügen*) to add; **jdm etw n~tragen** to hold sth against sb; **n~träglich** adj later, subsequent; additional ♦ adv later, subsequently; additionally; **n~trauern** vi: **jdm/etw n~trauern** to mourn the loss of sb/sth

Nacht- zW: **n~s** adv at od by night; **~schicht** f nightshift; **~schwester** f night nurse; **~tarif** m off-peak tariff; **~tisch** m bedside table; **~wächter** m night watchman

Nach- zW: **~untersuchung** f checkup; **n~wachsen** (*unreg*) vi to grow again; **~wahl** f (POL) ≈ by-election

Nachweis ['na:xvaɪs] (-es, -e) m proof; **n~bar** adj provable, demonstrable; **n~en** (*unreg*) vt to prove; **jdm etw n~en** to point sth out to sb; **n~lich** adj evident, demonstrable

nach- *zW:* **~wirken** *vi* to have after-effects; **N~wirkung** *f* aftereffect; **N~wort** *nt* epilogue; (*beruflich etc*) new recruits *pl;* **~zahlen** *vt, vi* to pay extra; **N~zahlung** *f* additional payment; (*zurückdatiert*) back pay; **~ziehen** (*unreg*) *vt* (*hinter sich herziehen: Bein*) to drag; **N~zügler** (**-s, -**) *m* straggler

Nacken ['nakən] (**-s, -**) *m* nape of the neck

nackt [nakt] *adj* naked; (*Tatsachen*) plain, bare; **N~badestrand** *m* nudist beach; **N~heit** *f* nakedness

Nadel ['na:dəl] (**-, -n**) *f* needle; (*Stecknadel*) pin; **~öhr** *nt* eye of a needle; **~wald** *m* coniferous forest

Nagel ['na:gəl] (**-s, ¨**) *m* nail; **~bürste** *f* nailbrush; **~feile** *f* nailfile; **~lack** *m* nail varnish *od* polish (*BRIT*); **n~n** *vt, vi* to nail; **n~neu** *adj* brand-new; **~schere** *f* nail scissors *pl*

nagen ['na:gən] *vt, vi* to gnaw

Nagetier ['na:gəti:r] *nt* rodent

nah(e) ['na:(ə)] *adj* (*räumlich*) near(by); (*Verwandte*) near; (*Freunde*) close; (*zeitlich*) near, close ♦ *adv* near(by); near, close; (*verwandt*) closely ♦ *präp* (+*dat*) near (to), close to; **der Nahe Osten** the Near East; **~ gehen** (+*dat*) to grieve; **~ kommen** (+*dat*) to get close (to); **jdm etw ~ legen** to suggest sth to sb; **~ liegen** to be obvious; **~ liegend** obvious; **~ stehen** (+*dat*) to be close (to); **einer Sache ~ stehen** to sympathize with sth; **~ stehend** close; **jdm (zu) ~ treten** to offend sb

Nahaufnahme *f* close-up

Nähe ['nɛ:ə] (**-**) *f* nearness, proximity; (*Umgebung*) vicinity; **in der ~** close by; at hand; **aus der ~** from close to

nah(e)bei *adv* nearby

nahen *vi, vr* to approach, to draw near

nähen ['nɛ:ən] *vt, vi* to sew

näher *adj, adv* nearer; (*Erklärung, Erkundigung*) more detailed; **(sich) ~ kommen** to get closer; **N~e(s)** *nt* details *pl*, particulars *pl*

Naherholungsgebiet *nt* recreational area

(*close to a town*)

nähern *vr* to approach

nahezu *adv* nearly

Nähgarn *nt* thread

Nahkampf *m* hand-to-hand fighting

Nähkasten *m* sewing basket, workbox

nahm *etc* [na:m] *vb siehe* **nehmen**

Nähmaschine *f* sewing machine

Nähnadel *f* needle

nähren ['nɛ:rən] *vt* to feed ♦ *vr* (*Person*) to feed o.s.; (*Tier*) to feed

nahrhaft ['na:rhaft] *adj* nourishing, nutritious

Nahrung ['na:rʊŋ] *f* food; (*fig auch*) sustenance

Nahrungs- *zW:* **~mittel** *nt* foodstuffs *pl;* **~mittelindustrie** *f* food industry; **~suche** *f* search for food

Nährwert *m* nutritional value

Naht [na:t] (**-, ¨e**) *f* seam; (*MED*) suture; (*TECH*) join; **n~los** *adj* seamless; **n~los ineinander übergehen** to follow without a gap

Nah- *zW:* **~verkehr** *m* local traffic; **~verkehrszug** *m* local train; **~ziel** *nt* immediate objective

Name ['na:mə] (**-ns, -n**) *m* name; **im ~n** on behalf of; **n~ns** *adv* by the name of; **~nstag** *m* name day, saint's day; **n~ntlich** *adj* by name ♦ *adv* particularly, especially

Namenstag

i In Catholic areas of Germany the **Namenstag** is often a more important celebration than a birthday. This is the day dedicated to the saint after whom a person is called, and on that day the person receives presents and invites relatives and friends round to celebrate.

namhaft ['na:mhaft] *adj* (*berühmt*) famed, renowned; (*beträchtlich*) considerable; **~ machen** to name

nämlich ['nɛ:mlɪç] *adv* that is to say, namely; (*denn*) since

nannte *etc* ['nantə] *vb siehe* **nennen**

Napf [napf] (**-(e)s, ¨e**) *m* bowl, dish

Narbe ['narbə] f scar; **narbig** adj scarred
Narkose [nar'ko:zə] f anaesthetic
Narr [nar] (-en, -en) m fool; **n~en** vt to fool; **Närrin** ['nɛrɪn] f fool; **närrisch** adj foolish, crazy
Narzisse [nar'tsɪsə] f narcissus; daffodil
naschen ['naʃən] vt, vi to nibble; (*heimlich kosten*) to pinch a bit
naschhaft adj sweet-toothed
Nase ['na:zə] f nose
Nasen- zW: **~bluten** (-s) nt nosebleed; **~loch** nt nostril; **~tropfen** pl nose drops
naseweis adj pert, cheeky; (*neugierig*) nosey
Nashorn ['na:shɔrn] nt rhinoceros
nass [nas] adj wet
Nässe ['nɛsə] (-) f wetness; **n~n** vt to wet
nasskalt ▲ adj wet and cold
Nassrasur ▲ f wet shave
Nation [natsi'o:n] f nation
national [natsio'na:l] adj national; **N~feiertag** m national holiday; **N~hymne** f national anthem; **~isieren** [-i'zi:rən] vt to nationalize; **N~ismus** [-'lɪsmʊs] m nationalism; **~istisch** [-'lɪstɪʃ] adj nationalistic; **N~i'tät** f nationality; **N~mannschaft** f national team; **N~sozialismus** m national socialism
Natron ['na:trɔn] (-s) nt soda
Natter ['natər] (-, -n) f adder
Natur [na'tu:r] f nature; (*körperlich*) constitution; **~ell** (-es, -e) nt disposition; **~erscheinung** f natural phenomenon od event; **n~farben** adj natural coloured; **n~gemäß** adj natural; **~gesetz** nt law of nature; **n~getreu** adj true to life; **~katastrophe** f natural disaster
natürlich [na'ty:rlɪç] adj natural ♦ adv naturally; **ja, ~!** yes, of course; **N~keit** f naturalness
Natur- zW: **~park** m ≃ national park; **~produkt** nt natural product; **n~rein** adj natural, pure; **~schutz** m nature conservation; **unter ~schutz stehen** to be legally protected; **~schutzgebiet** nt nature reserve; **~wissenschaft** f natural science; **~wissenschaftler(in)** m(f)

scientist
nautisch ['nautɪʃ] adj nautical
Nazi ['na:tsi] (-s, -s) m Nazi
NB abk (= *nota bene*) nb
n. Chr. abk (= *nach Christus*) A.D.
Nebel ['ne:bəl] (-s, -) m fog, mist; **n~ig** adj foggy, misty; **~scheinwerfer** m fog lamp
neben ['ne:bən] präp (+akk od dat) next to; (+dat: *außer*) apart from, besides; **~an** [ne:bən'an] adv next door; **N~anschluss** ▲ m (*TEL*) extension; **N~ausgang** m side exit; **~bei** [ne:bən'bai] adv at the same time; (*außerdem*) additionally; (*beiläufig*) incidentally; **N~beruf** m second job; **N~beschäftigung** f second job; **N~buhler(in)** (-s, -) m(f) rival; **~einander** [ne:bən|ai'nandər] adv side by side; **~einander legen** to put next to each other; **N~eingang** m side entrance; **N~fach** nt subsidiary subject; **N~fluss** ▲ m tributary; **N~gebäude** nt annexe; **N~geräusch** nt (*RADIO*) atmospherics pl, interference; **~her** [ne:bən'he:r] adv (*zusätzlich*) besides; (*gleichzeitig*) at the same time; (*daneben*) alongside; **N~kosten** pl extra charges, extras; **N~produkt** nt by-product; **N~sache** f trifle, side issue; **~sächlich** adj minor, peripheral; **N~saison** f low season; **N~straße** f side street; **N~verdienst** m secondary income; **N~wirkung** f side effect; **N~zimmer** nt adjoining room
neblig ['ne:blɪç] adj foggy, misty
Necessaire [nesɛ'sɛ:r] (-s, -s) nt (*Nähnecessaire*) needlework box; (*Nagelnecessaire*) manicure case
necken ['nɛkən] vt to tease
Neckerei [nɛkə'rai] f teasing
Neffe ['nɛfə] (-n, -n) m nephew
negativ ['ne:gati:f] adj negative; **N~** (-s, -e) nt (*PHOT*) negative
Neger ['ne:gər] (-s, -) m negro; **~in** f negress
nehmen ['ne:mən] (*unreg*) vt to take; **jdn zu sich ~** to take sb in; **sich ernst ~** to take o.s. seriously; **nimm dir doch bitte** please help yourself

Neid [naɪt] *(-(e)s)* *m* envy; **~er** *(-s, -)* *m* envier; **n~isch** ['naɪdɪʃ] *adj* envious, jealous

neigen ['naɪgən] *vt* to incline, to lean; *(Kopf)* to bow ♦ *vi*: **zu etw ~** to tend to sth

Neigung *f (des Geländes)* slope; *(Tendenz)* tendency, inclination; *(Vorliebe)* liking; *(Zuneigung)* affection

nein [naɪn] *adv* no

Nektarine [nɛktaˈriːnə] *f (Frucht)* nectarine

Nelke ['nɛlkə] *f* carnation, pink; *(Gewürz)* clove

Nenn- ['nɛn] *zW*: **n~en** *(unreg)* *vt* to name; *(mit Namen)* to call; **wie n~t man ...?** what do you call ...?; **n~enswert** *adj* worth mentioning; **~er** *(-s, -)* *m* denominator; **~wert** *m* nominal value; *(COMM)* par

Neon ['neːɔn] *(-s)* *nt* neon; **~licht** *nt* neon light; **~röhre** *f* neon tube

Nerv [nɛrf] *(-s, -en)* *m* nerve; **jdm auf die ~en gehen** to get on sb's nerves; **n~enaufreibend** *adj* nerve-racking; **~enbündel** *nt* bundle of nerves; **~enheilanstalt** *f* mental home; **n~enkrank** *adj* mentally ill; **~ensäge** *(umg)* *f* pain (in the neck) *(umg)*; **~ensystem** *nt* nervous system; **~enzusammenbruch** *m* nervous breakdown; **n~lich** *adj (Belastung)* affecting the nerves; **n~ös** [nɛrˈvøːs] *adj* nervous; **~osi'tät** *f* nervousness; **n~tötend** *adj* nerve-racking; *(Arbeit)* soul-destroying

Nerz [nɛrts] *(-es, -e)* *m* mink

Nessel ['nɛsəl] *(-, -n)* *f* nettle

Nessessär ▲ [nesɛˈsɛːr] *(-s, -s)* *nt* = **Necessaire**

Nest [nɛst] *(-(e)s, -er)* *nt* nest; *(umg: Ort)* dump

nett [nɛt] *adj* nice; *(freundlich)* nice, kind; **~erweise** *adv* kindly

netto ['nɛtoː] *adv* net

Netz [nɛts] *(-es, -e)* *m* net; *(Gepäcknetz)* rack; *(Einkaufsnetz)* string bag; *(Spinnennetz)* web; *(System)* network; **jdm ins ~ gehen** *(fig)* to fall into sb's trap; **~anschluss** ▲ *m* mains connection

Netzhaut *f* retina

neu [nɔy] *adj* new; *(Sprache, Geschichte)* modern; **seit ~estem** (since) recently; **die ~esten Nachrichten** the latest news; **~ schreiben** to rewrite, to write again; **N~anschaffung** *f* new purchase *od* acquisition; **~artig** *adj* new kind of; **N~bau** *m* new building; **N~e(r)** *f(m)* the new man/woman; **~erdings** *adv (kürzlich)* (since) recently; *(von ~em)* again; **N~erscheinung** *f (Buch)* new publication; *(Schallplatte)* new release; **N~erung** *f* innovation, new departure; **N~gier** *f* curiosity; **~gierig** *adj* curious; **N~heit** *f* newness; novelty; **N~igkeit** *f* news *sg*; **N~jahr** *nt* New Year; **~lich** *adv* recently, the other day; **N~ling** *m* novice; **N~mond** *m* new moon

neun [nɔyn] *num* nine; **~zehn** *num* nineteen; **~zig** *num* ninety

neureich *adj* nouveau riche; **N~e(r)** *f(m)* nouveau riche

neurotisch *adj* neurotic

Neuseeland [nɔyˈzeːlant] *nt* New Zealand; **Neuseeländer(in)** [nɔyˈzeːlɛndər(ɪn)] *m(f)* New Zealander

neutral [nɔyˈtraːl] *adj* neutral; **~i'sieren** *vt* to neutralize

Neutrum ['nɔytrʊm] *(-s, -a od -en)* *nt* neuter

Neu- *zW*: **~wert** *m* purchase price; **n~wertig** *adj* (as) new, not used; **~zeit** *f* modern age; **n~zeitlich** *adj* modern, recent

SCHLÜSSELWORT

nicht [nɪçt] *adv* **1** *(Verneinung)* not; **er ist es nicht** it's not him, it isn't him; **er raucht nicht** *(gerade)* he isn't smoking; *(gewöhnlich)* he doesn't smoke; **ich kann das nicht - ich auch nicht** I can't do it - neither *od* nor can I; **es regnet nicht mehr** it's not raining any more; **nicht rostend** stainless

2 *(Bitte, Verbot)*: **nicht!** don't!, no!; **nicht berühren!** do not touch!; **nicht doch!** don't!

3 *(rhetorisch)*: **du bist müde, nicht (wahr)?** you're tired, aren't you?; **das ist schön,**

nicht (wahr)? it's nice, isn't it?
4: was du nicht sagst! the things you say!

Nichtangriffspakt [nɪçt'|angrɪfspakt] *m* non-aggression pact
Nichte ['nɪçtə] *f* niece
nichtig ['nɪçtɪç] *adj* (*ungültig*) null, void; (*wertlos*) futile
Nichtraucher(in) *m(f)* non-smoker
nichts [nɪçts] *pron* nothing; **für ~ und wieder ~** for nothing at all; **~ sagend** meaningless; **N~ (-)** *nt* nothingness; (*pej:* Person) nonentity
Nichtschwimmer *m* non-swimmer
nichts- *zW:* **~desto'weniger** *adv* nevertheless; **N~nutz (-es, -e)** *m* good-for-nothing; **~nutzig** *adj* worthless, useless; **N~tun (-s)** *nt* idleness
Nichtzutreffende(s) *nt:* **~s od nicht Zutreffendes (bitte) streichen!** (please) delete where appropriate
Nickel ['nɪkəl] (**-s**) *nt* nickel
nicken ['nɪkən] *vi* to nod
Nickerchen ['nɪkərçən] *nt* nap
nie [niː] *adv* never; **~ wieder** *od* **mehr** never again; **~ und nimmer** never ever
nieder ['niːdər] *adj* low; (*gering*) inferior ♦ *adv* down; **N~gang** *m* decline; **~gedrückt** *adj* (*deprimiert*) dejected, depressed; **~gehen** (*unreg*) *vi* to descend; (*AVIAT*) to come down; (*Regen*) to fall; (*Boxer*) to go down; **~geschlagen** *adj* depressed, dejected; **N~lage** *f* defeat; **N~lande** *pl* Netherlands; **N~länder(in)** *m(f)* Dutchman(-woman); **~ländisch** *adj* Dutch; **~lassen** (*unreg*) *vr* (*sich setzen*) to sit down; (*an Ort*) to settle (down); (*Arzt, Rechtsanwalt*) to set up a practice; **N~lassung** *f* settlement; (*COMM*) branch; **~legen** *vt* to lay down; (*Arbeit*) to stop; (*Amt*) to resign; **N~sachsen** *nt* Lower Saxony; **N~schlag** *m* (*MET*) precipitation; rainfall; **~schlagen** (*unreg*) *vt* (*Gegner*) to beat down; (*Gegenstand*) to knock down; (*Augen*) to lower; (*Aufstand*) to put down ♦ *vr* (*CHEM*) to precipitate; **~trächtig** *adj* base, mean; **N~trächtigkeit** *f* meanness,

baseness; outrage; **N~ung** *f* (*GEOG*) depression; (*Mündungsgebiet*) flats *pl*
niedlich ['niːtlɪç] *adj* sweet, cute
niedrig ['niːdrɪç] *adj* low; (*Stand*) lowly, humble; (*Gesinnung*) mean
niemals ['niːmaːls] *adv* never
niemand ['niːmant] *pron* nobody, no-one
Niemandsland ['niːmantslant] *nt* no-man's-land
Niere ['niːrə] *f* kidney
nieseln ['niːzəln] *vi* to drizzle
niesen ['niːzən] *vi* to sneeze
Niete ['niːtə] *f* (*TECH*) rivet; (*Los*) blank; (*Reinfall*) flop; (*Mensch*) failure; **n~n** *vt* to rivet

---
St. Nikolaus

ⓘ On December 6th, **St. Nikolaus** visits German children to reward those who have been good by filling shoes they have left out with sweets and small presents.

Nikotin [niko'tiːn] (**-s**) *nt* nicotine
Nilpferd [niːl-] *nt* hippopotamus
Nimmersatt ['nɪmərzat] (**-(e)s, -e**) *m* glutton
nimmst *etc* [nɪmst] *vb siehe* **nehmen**
nippen ['nɪpən] *vt, vi* to sip
nirgend- ['nɪrgənt] *zW:* **~s** *adv* nowhere; **~wo** *adv* nowhere; **~wohin** *adv* nowhere
Nische ['niːʃə] *f* niche
nisten ['nɪstən] *vi* to nest
Niveau [ni'voː] (**-s, -s**) *nt* level
Nixe ['nɪksə] *f* water nymph
nobel ['noːbəl] *adj* (*großzügig*) generous; (*elegant*) posh (*inf*)

SCHLÜSSELWORT
---

noch [nɔx] *adv* **1** (*weiterhin*) still; **noch nicht** not yet; **noch nie** never (yet); **noch immer** *od* **immer noch** still; **bleiben Sie doch noch** stay a bit longer
2 (*in Zukunft*) still, yet; **das kann noch passieren** that might still happen; **er wird noch kommen** he'll come (yet)
3 (*nicht später als*): **noch vor einer Woche** only a week ago; **noch am selben Tag** the

very same day; **noch im 19. Jahrhundert**
as late as the 19th century; **noch heute**
today

4 (*zusätzlich*): **wer war noch da?** who else
was there?; **noch einmal** once more,
again; **noch dreimal** three more times;
noch einer another one

5 (*bei Vergleichen*): **noch größer** even
bigger; **das ist noch besser** that's better
still; **und wenn es noch so schwer ist**
however hard it is

6: **Geld noch und noch** heaps (and heaps)
of money; **sie hat noch und noch
versucht, ...** she tried again and again
to ...

♦ *konj*: **weder A noch B** neither A nor B

noch- *zW*: **~mal** ['nɔxmaːl] *adv* again, once
more; **~malig** ['nɔxmaːlɪç] *adj* repeated;
~mals *adv* again, once more
Nominativ ['noːminatiːf] (**-s, -e**) *m*
nominative
nominell [nomi'nɛl] *adj* nominal
Nonne ['nɔnə] *f* nun
Nord(en) ['nɔrd(ən)] (**-s**) *m* north
Nordirland *nt* Northern Ireland
nordisch *adj* northern
nördlich ['nœrtlɪç] *adj* northerly, northern
♦ *präp* +*gen* (to the) north of; **~ von** (to
the) north of
Nord- *zW*: **~pol** *m* North Pole; **~rhein-
Westfalen** *nt* North Rhine-Westphalia;
~see *f* North Sea; **n~wärts** *adv*
northwards
nörgeln ['nœrgəln] *vi* to grumble; **Nörgler**
(**-s, -**) *m* grumbler
Norm [nɔrm] (**-, -en**) *f* norm;
(*Größenvorschrift*) standard; **n~al** [nɔr'maːl]
adj normal; **~al(benzin)** *nt* ≈ 2-star petrol
(*BRIT*), regular petrol (*US*); **n~alerweise**
adv normally; **n~alisieren** *vt* to normalize
♦ *vr* to return to normal
normen *vt* to standardize
Norwegen ['nɔrveːgən] *nt* Norway;
norwegisch *adj* Norwegian
Nostalgie [nɔstal'giː] *f* nostalgia
Not [noːt] (**-, ⁺e**) *f* need; (*Mangel*) want;

(*Mühe*) trouble; (*Zwang*) necessity; **~
leidend** needy; **zur ~** if necessary; (*gerade
noch*) just about
Notar [no'taːr] (**-s, -e**) *m* notary; **n~i'ell** *adj*
notarial
Not- *zW*: **~arzt** *m* emergency doctor;
~ausgang *m* emergency exit; **~behelf**
(**-s, -e**) *m* makeshift; **~bremse** *f* emergency brake; **~dienst** *m* (*Bereitschaftsdienst*)
emergency service; **n~dürftig** *adj* scanty;
(*behelfsmäßig*) makeshift
Note ['noːtə] *f* note; (*SCH*) mark (*BRIT*), grade
(*US*)
Noten- *zW*: **~blatt** *nt* sheet of music;
~schlüssel *m* clef; **~ständer** *m* music
stand
Not- *zW*: **~fall** *m* (case of) emergency;
n~falls *adv* if need be; **n~gedrungen** *adj*
necessary, unavoidable; **etw n~gedrungen
machen** to be forced to do sth
notieren [no'tiːrən] *vt* to note; (*COMM*) to
quote
Notierung *f* (*COMM*) quotation
nötig ['nøːtɪç] *adj* necessary; **etw ~ haben** to
need sth; **~en** [-gən] *vt* to compel, to force;
~enfalls *adv* if necessary
Notiz [no'tiːts] (**-, -en**) *f* note; (*Zeitungsnotiz*)
item; **~ nehmen** to take notice; **~block** *m*
notepad; **~buch** *nt* notebook
Not- *zW*: **~lage** *f* crisis, emergency;
n~landen *vi* to make a forced *od*
emergency landing; **n~leidend** △ *adj*
siehe **Not**; **~lösung** *f* temporary solution;
~lüge *f* white lie
notorisch [no'toːrɪʃ] *adj* notorious
Not- *zW*: **~ruf** *m* emergency call;
~rufsäule *f* emergency telephone;
~stand *m* state of emergency;
~unterkunft *f* emergency
accommodation; **~verband** *m* emergency
dressing; **~wehr** (**-**) *f* self-defence;
n~wendig *adj* necessary; **~wendigkeit** *f*
necessity
Novelle [no'vɛlə] *f* short novel; (*JUR*)
amendment
November [no'vɛmbər] (**-s, -**) *m* November
Nu [nuː] *m*: **im ~** in an instant

Nuance [ny'ã:sə] f nuance
nüchtern ['nʏçtərn] adj sober; (*Magen*) empty; (*Urteil*) prudent; **N~heit** f sobriety
Nudel ['nu:dəl] (-, -n) f noodle; **~n** pl (*Teigwaren*) pasta sg; (*in Suppe*) noodles
Null [nʊl] (-, -en) f nought, zero; (*pej: Mensch*) washout; **n~** num zero; (*Fehler*) no; **n~ Uhr** midnight; **n~ und nichtig** null and void; **~punkt** m zero; **auf dem ~punkt** at zero
numerisch [nu'me:rɪʃ] adj numerical
Nummer ['nʊmər] (-, -n) f number; (*Größe*) size; **n~ieren** ▲ vt to number; **~nschild** nt (*AUT*) number od license (*US*) plate
nun [nu:n] adv now ♦ excl well; **das ist ~ mal so** that's the way it is
nur [nu:r] adv just, only; **wo bleibt er ~?** (just) where is he?
Nürnberg ['nʏrnbɛrk] (-s) nt Nuremberg
Nuss ▲ [nʊs] (-, ⁻e) f nut; **~baum** m walnut tree; **~knacker** (-s, -) m nutcracker
nutz [nʊts] adj: **zu nichts ~ sein** to be no use for anything; **~bringend** adj (*Verwendung*) profitable
nütze ['nʏtsə] adj = **nutz**
Nutzen (-s) m usefulness; (*Gewinn*) profit; **von ~ useful; n~** vi to be of use ♦ vt: **etw zu etw n~** to use sth for sth; **was nutzt es?** what's the use?, what use is it?
nützen vi, vt = **nutzen**
nützlich ['nʏtslɪç] adj useful; **N~keit** f usefulness
Nutz- zW: **n~los** adj useless; **~losigkeit** f uselessness; **~nießer** (-s, -) m beneficiary
Nylon ['naɪlɔn] (-(s)) nt nylon

O, o

Oase [o'a:zə] f oasis
ob [ɔp] konj if, whether; **~ das wohl wahr ist?** can that be true?; **und ~!** you bet!
obdachlos adj homeless
Obdachlose(r) f(m) homeless person; **~nasyl** nt shelter for the homeless
Obduktion [ɔpdʊkts'oːn] f post-mortem
obduzieren [ɔpdu'tsiːrən] vt to do a post-

mortem on
O-Beine ['oːbaɪnə] pl bow od bandy legs
oben ['oːbən] adv above; (*in Haus*) upstairs; **~ erwähnt, ~ genannt** above-mentioned; **nach ~** up; **von ~** down; **~ ohne** topless; **jdn von ~ bis unten ansehen** to look sb up and down; **~an** adv at the top; **~auf** adv up above, on the top ♦ adj (*munter*) in form; **~drein** adv into the bargain
Ober ['oːbər] (-s, -) m waiter; **die ~en** pl (*umg*) the bosses; (*ECCL*) the superiors; **~arm** m upper arm; **~arzt** m senior physician; **~aufsicht** f supervision; **~bayern** nt Upper Bavaria; **~befehl** m supreme command; **~befehlshaber** m commander-in-chief; **~bekleidung** f outer clothing; **~'bürgermeister** m lord mayor; **~deck** nt od top deck; **o~e(r, s)** adj upper; **~fläche** f surface; **o~flächlich** adj superficial; **~geschoss** ▲ nt upper storey; **o~halb** adv above ♦ präp +gen above; **~haupt** nt head, chief; **~haus** nt (*POL*) upper house, House of Lords (*BRIT*); **~hemd** nt shirt; **~herrschaft** f supremacy, sovereignty; **~in** f matron; (*ECCL*) Mother Superior; **~kellner** m head waiter; **~kiefer** m upper jaw; **~körper** m upper part of body; **~leitung** f direction; (*ELEK*) overhead cable; **~licht** nt skylight; **~lippe** f upper lip; **~schenkel** m thigh; **~schicht** f upper classes pl; **~schule** f grammar school (*BRIT*), high school (*US*); **~schwester** f (*MED*) matron
Oberst ['oːbərst] (-en od -s, -en od -e) m colonel; **o~e(r, s)** adj very top, topmost
Ober- zW: **~stufe** f upper school; **~teil** nt upper part; **~weite** f bust/chest measurement
obgleich [ɔp'glaɪç] konj although
Obhut ['ɔphuːt] (-) f care, protection; **in jds ~ sein** to be in sb's care
obig ['oːbɪç] adj above
Objekt [ɔp'jɛkt] (-(e)s, -e) nt object; **~iv** [-'tiːf] (-s, -e) nt lens; **o~iv** adj objective; **~ivi'tät** f objectivity
Oblate [o'blaːtə] f (*Gebäck*) wafer; (*ECCL*) host

obligatorisch [obliga'to:rɪʃ] adj compulsory, obligatory

Obrigkeit ['o:brɪçkaɪt] f (Behörden) authorities pl, administration; (Regierung) government

obschon [ɔp'ʃo:n] konj although

Observatorium [ɔpzɛrva'to:riʊm] nt observatory

obskur [ɔps'ku:r] adj obscure; (verdächtig) dubious

Obst [o:pst] (-(e)s) nt fruit; ~baum m fruit tree; ~garten m orchard; ~händler m fruiterer, fruit merchant; ~kuchen m fruit tart

obszön [ɔps'tsø:n] adj obscene; O~ität f obscenity

obwohl [ɔp'vo:l] konj although

Ochse ['ɔksə] (-n, -n) m ox; o~n (umg) vt, vi to cram, to swot (BRIT)

Ochsenschwanzsuppe f oxtail soup

Ochsenzunge f oxtongue

öd(e) ['ø:d(ə)] adj (Land) waste, barren; (fig) dull; Ö~ f desert, waste(land); (fig) tedium

oder ['o:dər] konj or; das stimmt, ~? that's right, isn't it?

Ofen ['o:fən] (-s, ꙩ) m oven; (Heizofen) fire, heater; (Kohlenofen) stove; (Hochofen) furnace; (Herd) cooker, stove; ~rohr nt stovepipe

offen ['ɔfən] adj open; (aufrichtig) frank; (Stelle) vacant; ~ bleiben (Fenster) to stay open; (Frage, Entscheidung) to remain open; ~ halten to keep open; ~ lassen to leave open; ~ stehen to be open; (Rechnung) to be unpaid; es steht Ihnen ~, es zu tun you are at liberty to do it; ~ gesagt to be honest; ~bar adj obvious; ~baren [ɔfən'ba:rən] vt to reveal, to manifest; O~'barung f (REL) revelation; O~heit f candour, frankness; ~herzig adj candid, frank; (Kleid) revealing; ~kundig adj well-known; (klar) evident; ~sichtlich adj evident, obvious

offensiv [ɔfɛn'zi:f] adj offensive; O~e [-'zi:və] f offensive

öffentlich ['œfəntlɪç] adj public; Ö~keit f (Leute) public; (einer Versammlung etc) public nature; in aller Ö~keit in public; an die Ö~keit dringen to reach the public ear

offiziell [ɔfitsi'ɛl] adj official

Offizier [ɔfi'tsi:r] (-s, -e) m officer; ~skasino nt officers' mess

öffnen ['œfnən] vt, vr to open; jdm die Tür ~ to open the door for sb

Öffner ['œfnər] (-s, -) m opener

Öffnung ['œfnʊŋ] f opening; ~szeiten pl opening times

oft [ɔft] adv often

öfter ['œftər] adv more often od frequently; ~s adv often, frequently

oh [o:] excl oh; ~ je! oh dear

OHG abk (= Offene Handelsgesellschaft) general partnership

ohne ['o:nə] präp +akk without ♦ konj without; das ist nicht ~ (umg) it's not bad; ~ weiteres without a second thought; (sofort) immediately; ~ zu fragen without asking; ~ dass er es wusste without him knowing it; ~dies [o:nə'di:s] adv anyway; ~gleichen [o:nə'glaɪçən] adj unsurpassed, without equal; ~hin [o:nə'hɪn] adv anyway, in any case

Ohnmacht ['o:nmaxt] f faint; (fig) impotence; in ~ fallen to faint

ohnmächtig ['o:nmɛçtɪç] adj in a faint, unconscious; (fig) weak, impotent; sie ist ~ she has fainted

Ohr [o:r] (-(e)s, -en) nt ear

Öhr [ø:r] (-(e)s, -e) nt eye

Ohren- zW: ~arzt m ear specialist; o~betäubend adj deafening; ~schmalz nt earwax; ~schmerzen pl earache sg

Ohr- zW: ~feige f slap on the face; box on the ears; o~feigen vt: jdn o~feigen to slap sb's face; to box sb's ears; ~läppchen nt ear lobe; ~ring m earring; ~wurm m earwig; (MUS) catchy tune

Öko- [øko] zW: ~laden m wholefood shop; ö~logisch [-'lo:gɪʃ] adj ecological; ö~nomisch [-'no:mɪʃ] adj economical

Oktober [ɔk'to:bər] (-s, -) m October; ~fest nt Munich beer festival

---

Oktoberfest

The annual beer festival, the Oktoberfest, takes place in Munich at the end of September in a huge area where beer tents and various amusements are set up. People sit at long wooden tables, drink beer from enormous beer mugs, eat pretzels and listen to brass bands. It is a great attraction for tourists and locals alike.

ökumenisch [øku'meːnɪʃ] *adj* ecumenical
Öl [øːl] (-(e)s, -e) *nt* oil; **~baum** *m* olive tree; **ö~en** *vt* to oil; (*TECH*) to lubricate; **~farbe** *f* oil paint; **~feld** *nt* oilfield; **~film** *m* film of oil; **~heizung** *f* oil-fired central heating; **ö~ig** *adj* oily; **~industrie** *f* oil industry
oliv [o'liːf] *adj* olive-green; **O~e** *f* olive
Öl- *zW:* **~messstab** ▲ *m* dipstick; **~sardine** *f* sardine; **~stand** *m* oil level; **~standanzeiger** *m* (*AUT*) oil gauge; **~tanker** *m* oil tanker; **~ung** *f* lubrication; oiling; (*ECCL*) anointment; **die Letzte ~ung** Extreme Unction; **~wechsel** *m* oil change
Olymp- [o'lʏmp] *zW:* **~iade** [olʏmpi'aːdə] *f* Olympic Games *pl*; **~iasieger(in)** [-iaːziːgər(ɪn)] *m(f)* Olympic champion; **~iateilnehmer(in)** *m(f)* Olympic competitor; **o~isch** *adj* Olympic
Ölzeug *nt* oilskins *pl*
Oma ['oːma] (-, -s) (*umg*) *f* granny
Omelett [ɔm(ə)'let] (-(e)s, -s) *nt* omelet(te)
ominös [omi'nøːs] *adj* (*unheilvoll*) ominous
Onanie [ona'niː] *f* masturbation; **o~ren** *vi* to masturbate
Onkel ['ɔŋkəl] (-s, -) *m* uncle
Opa ['oːpa] (-s, -s) (*umg*) *m* grandpa
Oper ['oːpər] (-, -n) *f* opera; opera house
Operation [operatsi'oːn] *f* operation; **~ssaal** *m* operating theatre
Operette [ope'retə] *f* operetta
operieren [ope'riːrən] *vt* to operate on ♦ *vi* to operate
Opern- *zW:* **~glas** *nt* opera glasses *pl*; **~haus** *nt* opera house
Opfer ['ɔpfər] (-s, -) *nt* sacrifice; (*Mensch*)

victim; **o~n** *vt* to sacrifice; **~ung** *f* sacrifice
opponieren [ɔpo'niːrən] *vi:* **gegen jdn/etw ~** to oppose sb/sth
Opportunist [ɔpɔrtu'nɪst] *m* opportunist
Opposition [ɔpozitsi'oːn] *f* opposition; **o~ell** *adj* opposing
Optik ['ɔptɪk] *f* optics *sg;* **~er** (-s, -) *m* optician
optimal [ɔpti'maːl] *adj* optimal, optimum
Optimismus [ɔpti'mɪsmʊs] *m* optimism
Optimist [ɔpti'mɪst] *m* optimist; **o~isch** *adj* optimistic
optisch ['ɔptɪʃ] *adj* optical
Orakel [o'raːkəl] (-s, -) *nt* oracle
oral [o'raːl] *adj* (*MED*) oral
Orange [o'rãːʒə] *f* orange; **o~** *adj* orange; **~ade** [orã'ʒaːdə] *f* orangeade; **~at** [orã'ʒaːt] (-s, -e) *nt* candied peel
Orchester [ɔr'kɛstər] (-s, -) *nt* orchestra
Orchidee [ɔrçi'deːə] *f* orchid
Orden ['ɔrdən] (-s, -) *m* (*ECCL*) order; (*MIL*) decoration; **~sschwester** *f* nun
ordentlich ['ɔrdəntlɪç] *adj* (*anständig*) decent, respectable; (*geordnet*) tidy, neat; (*umg: annehmbar*) not bad; (: *tüchtig*) real, proper ♦ *adv* properly; **~er Professor** (full) professor; **O~keit** *f* respectability; tidiness, neatness
ordinär [ɔrdi'nɛːr] *adj* common, vulgar
ordnen ['ɔrdnən] *vt* to order, to put in order
Ordner (-s, -) *m* steward; (*COMM*) file
Ordnung *f* order; (*Ordnen*) ordering; (*Geordnetsein*) tidiness; **~ machen** to tidy up; **in ~!** okay!
Ordnungs- *zW:* **o~gemäß** *adj* proper, according to the rules; **o~liebend** *adj* orderly, methodical; **~strafe** *f* fine; **o~widrig** *adj* contrary to the rules, irregular; **~widrigkeit** [-vɪdrɪçkaɪt] *f* infringement (*of law or rule*); **~zahl** *f* ordinal number
Organ [ɔr'gaːn] (-s, -e) *nt* organ; (*Stimme*) voice; **~isation** [-izatsi'oːn] *f* organization; **~isator** [i'zaːtɔr] *m* organizer; **o~isch** *adj* organic; **o~isieren** [-i'ziːrən] *vt* to organize, to arrange; (*umg: beschaffen*) to acquire ♦ *vr* to organize; **~ismus** [-'nɪsmʊs] *m*

Rechtschreibreform: ▲ *neue Schreibung* △ *alte Schreibung (auslaufend)*

organism; ~**ist** [-'nɪst] *m* organist;
~**spende** *f* organ donation;
~**spenderausweis** *m* donor card
Orgasmus [ɔr'ɡasmʊs] *m* orgasm
Orgel ['ɔrɡəl] (-, -n) *f* organ
Orgie ['ɔrɡiə] *f* orgy
Orient ['oːriɛnt] (-s) *m* Orient, east;
o~alisch [-'taːlɪʃ] *adj* oriental
orientier- *zW:* ~**en** [-'tiːrən] *vt* (*örtlich*) to
locate; (*fig*) to inform ♦ *vr* to find one's way
od bearings; to inform o.s.; **O~ung** [-'tiːrʊŋ]
f orientation; (*fig*) information;
O~ungssinn *m* sense of direction;
O~ungsstufe *f* period during which pupils
are selected for different schools

Orientierungsstufe

ⓘ The **Orientierungsstufe** is the name
given to the first two years spent in a
Realschule or **Gymnasium**, during which
a child is assessed as to his or her
suitability for that type of school. At the
end of two years it may be decided to
transfer the child to a school more suited to
his or her ability.

---

original [oriɡi'naːl] *adj* original; **O~** (-s, -e)
nt original; **O~fassung** *f* original version;
O~i̍tät *f* originality
originell [oriɡi'nɛl] *adj* original
Orkan [ɔr'kaːn] (-(e)s, -e) *m* hurricane;
o~artig *adj* (*Wind*) gale-force; (*Beifall*)
thunderous
Ornament [ɔrna'mɛnt] *nt* decoration,
ornament; **o~al** [-'taːl] *adj* decorative,
ornamental
Ort [ɔrt] (-(e)s, -e *od* ʉe) *m* place; **an ~ und
Stelle** on the spot; **o~en** *vt* to locate
ortho- [ɔrto] *zW:* ~**dox** [-'dɔks] *adj* orthodox;
O~grafie ▲ [-ɡraː'fiː] *f* spelling,
orthography; ~'**grafisch** ▲ *adj*
orthographic; **O~päde** [-'pɛːdə] (-n, -n) *m*
orthopaedist; **O~pädie** [-pɛ'diː] *f*
orthopaedics *sg*; ~'**pädisch** *adj*
orthopaedic
örtlich ['œrtlɪç] *adj* local; **Ö~keit** *f* locality
ortsansässig *adj* local

Ortschaft *f* village, small town
Orts- *zW:* **o~fremd** *adj* non-local;
~**gespräch** *nt* local (phone)call; ~**name**
m place name; ~**netz** *nt* (*TEL*) local
telephone exchange area; ~**tarif** *m* (*TEL*)
tariff for local calls; ~**zeit** *f* local time
Ortung *f* locating
Öse ['øːzə] *f* loop, eye
Ostasien [ɔst'taːziən] *nt* Eastern Asia
Osten ['ɔstən] (-s) *m* east
Oster- ['oːstər] *zW:* ~**ei** *nt* Easter egg; ~**fest**
nt Easter; ~**glocke** *f* daffodil; ~**hase** *m*
Easter bunny; ~**montag** *m* Easter Monday;
~**n** (-s, -) *nt* Easter
Österreich ['øːstəraɪç] (-s) *nt* Austria;
~**er(in)** (-s, -) *m(f)* Austrian; **ö~isch** *adj*
Austrian
Ostküste *f* east coast
östlich ['œstlɪç] *adj* eastern, easterly
Ostsee *f:* **die ~** the Baltic (Sea)
Ouvertüre [uver'tyːrə] *f* overture
oval [o'vaːl] *adj* oval
Ovation [ovatsi'oːn] *f* ovation
Oxid, Oxyd [ɔ'ksyːt] (-(e)s, -e) *nt* oxide;
o~ieren *vt, vi* to oxidize; ~**ierung** *f*
oxidization
Ozean ['oːtseaːn] (-s, -e) *m* ocean;
~**dampfer** *m* (ocean-going) liner
Ozon [o'tsoːn] (-s) *nt* ozone; ~**loch** *nt* ozone
hole; ~**schicht** *f* ozone layer

P, p

Paar [paːr] (-(e)s, -e) *nt* pair; (*Ehepaar*)
couple; **ein p~** a few; **ein p~ Mal** a few
times; **p~en** *vt, vr* to couple; (*Tiere*) to
mate; ~**lauf** *m* pair skating; ~**ung** *f*
combination; mating; **p~weise** *adv* in
pairs; in couples
Pacht [paxt] (-, -en) *f* lease; **p~en** *vt* to
lease
Pächter ['pɛçtər] (-s, -) *m* leaseholder,
tenant
Pack¹ [pak] (-(e)s, -e *od* ʉe) *m* bundle,
pack
Pack² [pak] (-(e)s) *nt* (*pej*) mob, rabble

Spelling Reform: ▲ *new spelling* △ *old spelling (to be phased out)*

Päckchen ['pɛkçən] *nt* small package; (*Zigaretten*) packet; (*Postpäckchen*) small parcel

Pack- *zW:* **p~en** *vt* to pack; (*fassen*) to grasp, to seize; (*umg: schaffen*) to manage; (*fig: fesseln*) to grip; **~en** (**-s, -**) *m* bundle; (*fig: Menge*) heaps of; **~esel** *m* (*auch fig*) packhorse; **~papier** *nt* brown paper, wrapping paper; **~ung** *f* packet; (*Pralinenpackung*) box; (*MED*) compress; **~ungsbeilage** *f* enclosed instructions *pl* for use

Pädagog- [pɛda'goːg] *zW:* **~e** (**-n, -n**) *m* teacher; **~ik** *f* education; **p~isch** *adj* educational, pedagogical

Paddel ['padəl] (**-s, -**) *nt* paddle; **~boot** *nt* canoe; **p~n** *vi* to paddle

Page ['paːʒə] (**-n, -n**) *m* page

Paket [pa'keːt] (**-(e)s, -e**) *nt* packet; (*Postpaket*) parcel; **~karte** *f* dispatch note; **~post** *f* parcel post; **~schalter** *m* parcels counter

Pakt [pakt] (**-(e)s, -e**) *m* pact

Palast [pa'last] (**-es, Paläste**) *m* palace

Palästina [palɛ'stiːna] (**-s**) *nt* Palestine

Palme ['palmə] *f* palm (tree)

Pampelmuse ['pampəlmuːzə] *f* grapefruit

panieren [pa'niːrən] *vt* (*KOCH*) to bread

Paniermehl [pa'niːrmeːl] *nt* breadcrumbs *pl*

Panik ['paːnɪk] *f* panic

panisch ['paːnɪʃ] *adj* panic-stricken

Panne ['panə] *f* (*AUT etc*) breakdown; (*Missgeschick*) slip; **~nhilfe** *f* breakdown service

panschen ['panʃən] *vi* to splash about ♦ *vt* to water down

Pantoffel [pan'tɔfəl] (**-s, -n**) *m* slipper

Pantomime [panto'miːmə] *f* mime

Panzer ['pantsər] (**-s, -**) *m* armour; (*Platte*) armour plate; (*Fahrzeug*) tank; **~glas** *nt* bulletproof glass; **p~n** *vt* to armour ♦ *vr* (*fig*) to arm o.s.

Papa [pa'paː] (**-s, -s**) (*umg*) *m* dad, daddy

Papagei [papa'gaɪ] (**-s, -en**) *m* parrot

Papier [pa'piːr] (**-s, -e**) *nt* paper; (*Wertpapier*) security; **~fabrik** *f* paper mill; **~geld** *nt* paper money; **~korb** *m* wastepaper basket; **~taschentuch** *nt* tissue

Papp- ['pap] *zW:* **~deckel** *m* cardboard; **~e** *f* cardboard; **~el** (**-, -n**) *f* poplar; **p~en** (*umg*) *vt, vi* to stick; **p~ig** *adj* sticky

Paprika ['paprika] (**-s, -s**) *m* (*Gewürz*) paprika; (*~schote*) pepper

Papst [paːpst] (**-(e)s, -̈e**) *m* pope

päpstlich ['pɛːpstlɪç] *adj* papal

Parabel [pa'raːbəl] (**-, -n**) *f* parable; (*MATH*) parabola

Parabolantenne [parabo'lantenə] *f* satellite dish

Parade [pa'raːdə] *f* (*MIL*) parade, review; (*SPORT*) parry

Paradies [para'diːs] (**-es, -e**) *nt* paradise; **p~isch** *adj* heavenly

Paradox [para'dɔks] (**-es, -e**) *nt* paradox; **p~** *adj* paradoxical

Paragraf [para'graːf] (**-en, -en**) *m* paragraph; (*JUR*) section

parallel [para'leːl] *adj* parallel; **P~e** *f* parallel

Parasit [para'ziːt] (**-en, -en**) *m* (*auch fig*) parasite

parat [pa'raːt] *adj* ready

Pärchen ['pɛːrçən] *nt* couple

Parfüm [par'fyːm] (**-s, -s** *od* **-e**) *nt* perfume; **~erie** [-ə'riː] *f* perfumery; **p~frei** *adj* non-perfumed; **p~ieren** *vt* to scent, to perfume

parieren [pa'riːrən] *vt* to parry ♦ *vi* (*umg*) to obey

Paris [pa'riːs] (**-**) *nt* Paris; **~er** *adj* Parisian ♦ *m* Parisian; **~erin** *f* Parisian

Park [park] (**-s, -s**) *m* park; **~anlage** *f* park; (*um Gebäude*) grounds *pl*; **p~en** *vt, vi* to park; **~ett** (**-(e)s, -e**) *nt* parquet (floor); (*THEAT*) stalls *pl*; **~gebühr** *f* parking fee; **~haus** *nt* multi-storey car park; **~lücke** *f* parking space; **~platz** *m* parking place; car park, parking lot (*US*); **~scheibe** *f* parking disc; **~schein** *m* car park ticket; **~uhr** *f* parking meter; **~verbot** *nt* parking ban

Parlament [parla'mɛnt] *nt* parliament; **~arier** [-'taːriər] (**-s, -**) *m* parliamentarian; **p~arisch** [-'taːrɪʃ] *adj* parliamentary

Parlaments- *zW:* **~beschluss** ▲ *m* vote of parliament; **~mitglied** *nt* member of parliament; **~sitzung** *f* sitting (of parliament)

Parodie [paro'di:] f parody; **p~ren** vt to parody

Parole [pa'ro:lə] f password; (*Wahlspruch*) motto

Partei [par'tai] f party; **~ ergreifen für jdn** to take sb's side; **p~isch** adj partial, bias(s)ed; **p~los** adj neutral, impartial; **~mitglied** nt party member; **~programm** nt (party) manifesto; **~tag** m party conference

Parterre [par'tɛr] (**-s, -s**) nt ground floor; (*THEAT*) stalls pl

Partie [par'ti:] f part; (*Spiel*) game; (*Ausflug*) outing; (*Mann, Frau*) catch; (*COMM*) lot; **mit von der ~ sein** to join in

Partizip [parti'tsi:p] (**-s, -ien**) nt participle

Partner(in) ['partnər(ın)] (**-s, -**) m(f) partner; **~schaft** f partnership; (*von Städten*) twinning; **p~schaftlich** adj as partners; **~stadt** f twin town

Party ['pa:rti] (**-, -s**) f party

Pass ▲ [pas] (**-es, ⁼e**) m pass; (*Ausweis*) passport

passabel [pa'sa:bəl] adj passable, reasonable

Passage [pa'sa:ʒə] f passage

Passagier [pasa'ʒi:r] (**-s, -e**) m passenger; **~flugzeug** nt airliner

Passamt ▲ nt passport office

Passant [pa'sant] m passer-by

Passbild ▲ nt passport photograph

passen ['pasən] vi to fit; (*Farbe*) to go; (*auf Frage, KARTEN, SPORT*) to pass; **das passt mir nicht** that doesn't suit me; **~ zu** (*Farbe, Kleider*) to go with; **er passt nicht zu dir** he's not right for you; **~d** adj suitable; (*zusammenpassend*) matching; (*angebracht*) fitting; (*Zeit*) convenient

passier- [pa'si:r] zW: **~bar** adj passable; **~en** vt to pass; (*durch Sieb*) to strain ♦ vi to happen; **P~schein** m pass, permit

Passion [pasi'o:n] f passion; **p~iert** [-'ni:rt] adj enthusiastic, passionate; **~sspiel** nt Passion Play

passiv ['pasi:f] adj passive; **P~** (**-s, -e**) nt passive; **P~a** pl (*COMM*) liabilities; **P~i'tät** f

passiveness; **P~rauchen** nt passive smoking

Pass- ▲ zW: **~kontrolle** f passport control; **~stelle** f passport office; **~straße** f (mountain) pass

Paste ['pastə] f paste

Pastete [pas'te:tə] f pie

pasteurisieren [pastøri'zi:rən] vt to pasteurize

Pastor ['pastɔr] m vicar; pastor, minister

Pate ['pa:tə] (**-n, -n**) m godfather; **~nkind** nt godchild

Patent [pa'tɛnt] (**-(e)s, -e**) nt patent; (*MIL*) commission; **p~** adj clever; **~amt** nt patent office

Patentante f godmother

patentieren [paten'ti:rən] vt to patent

Patentinhaber m patentee

pathetisch [pa'te:tɪʃ] adj emotional; bombastic

Pathologe [pato'lo:gə] (**-n, -n**) m pathologist

pathologisch adj pathological

Pathos ['pa:tɔs] (**-**) nt emotiveness, emotionalism

Patient(in) [patsi'ɛnt(ın)] m(f) patient

Patin ['pa:tın] f godmother

Patriot [patri'o:t] (**-en, -en**) m patriot; **p~isch** adj patriotic; **~ismus** [-'tɪsmus] m patriotism

Patrone [pa'tro:nə] f cartridge

Patrouille [pa'truljə] f patrol

patrouillieren [patrul'ji:rən] vi to patrol

patsch [patʃ] excl splash; **P~e** (*umg*) f (*Bedrängnis*) mess, jam; **~en** vi to smack, to slap; (*im Wasser*) to splash; **~nass** ▲ adj soaking wet

patzig ['patsıç] (*umg*) adj cheeky, saucy

Pauke ['paukə] f kettledrum; **auf die ~ hauen** to live it up

pauken vt (*intensiv lernen*) to swot up (*inf*) ♦ vi to swot (*inf*), cram (*inf*)

pausbäckig ['pausbɛkıç] adj chubby-cheeked

pauschal [pau'ʃa:l] adj (*Kosten*) inclusive; (*Urteil*) sweeping; **P~e** f flat rate; **P~gebühr** f flat rate; **P~preis** m all-in

Spelling Reform: ▲ new spelling △ old spelling (to be phased out)

price; **P~reise** f package tour; **P~summe** f lump sum

Pause ['pauzə] f break; (*THEAT*) interval; (*Innehalten*) pause; (*Kopie*) tracing

pausen vt to trace; **~los** adj non-stop; **P~zeichen** nt call sign; (*MUS*) rest

Pauspapier ['pauspapiːr] nt tracing paper

Pavillon ['paviljõ] (**-s, -s**) m pavilion

Pazif- [pa'tsiːf] zW: **~ik** (**-s**) m Pacific; **p~istisch** adj pacifist

Pech [peç] (**-s, -e**) nt pitch; (*fig*) bad luck; **~ haben** to be unlucky; **p~schwarz** adj pitch-black; **~strähne** (*umg*) m unlucky patch; **~vogel** (*umg*) m unlucky person

Pedal [pe'daːl] (**-s, -e**) nt pedal

Pedant [pe'dant] m pedant; **~e'rie** f pedantry; **p~isch** adj pedantic

Pediküre [pedi'kyːrə] f (*Fußpflege*) pedicure

Pegel ['peːɡəl] (**-s, -**) m water gauge; **~stand** m water level

peilen ['pailən] vt to get a fix on

Pein [pain] (**-**) f agony, pain; **p~igen** vt to torture; (*plagen*) to torment; **p~lich** adj (*unangenehm*) embarrassing, awkward, painful; (*genau*) painstaking

Peitsche ['paitʃə] f whip; **p~n** vt to whip; (*Regen*) to lash

Pelle ['pɛlə] f skin; **p~n** vt to skin, to peel

Pellkartoffeln pl jacket potatoes

Pelz [pɛlts] (**-es, -e**) m fur

Pendel ['pɛndəl] (**-s, -**) nt pendulum; **p~n** vi (*Zug, Fähre etc*) to operate a shuttle service; (*Mensch*) to commute; **~verkehr** m shuttle traffic; (*für Pendler*) commuter traffic

Pendler ['pɛndlər] (**-s, -**) m commuter

penetrant [pene'trant] adj sharp; (*Person*) pushing

Penis ['peːnɪs] (**-, -se**) m penis

pennen ['pɛnən] (*umg*) vi to kip

Penner (*umg: pej*) m (*Landstreicher*) tramp

Pension [panzi'oːn] f (*Geld*) pension; (*Ruhestand*) retirement; (*für Gäste*) boarding od guesthouse; **~är(in)** [-'nɛːr(ɪn)] (**-s, -e**) m(f) pensioner; **p~ieren** vt to pension off; **p~iert** adj retired; **~ierung** f retirement; **~sgast** m boarder, paying guest

Pensum ['pɛnzʊm] (**-s, Pensen**) nt quota; (*SCH*) curriculum

per [pɛr] präp +akk by, per; (*pro*) per; (*bis*) by

Perfekt ['pɛrfɛkt] (**-(e)s, -e**) nt perfect; **p~** adj perfect

perforieren [pɛrfo'riːrən] vt to perforate

Pergament [pɛrɡa'mɛnt] nt parchment; **~papier** nt greaseproof paper

Periode [peri'oːdə] f period; **periodisch** adj periodic; (*dezimal*) recurring

Perle ['pɛrlə] f (*auch fig*) pearl; **p~n** vi to sparkle; (*Tropfen*) to trickle

Perl- ['pɛrl] zW: **~mutt** (**-s**) nt mother-of-pearl; **~wein** m sparkling wine

perplex [pɛr'plɛks] adj dumbfounded

Person [pɛr'zoːn] (**-, -en**) f person; **ich für meine ~ ...** personally I ...

Personal [pɛrzo'naːl] (**-s**) nt personnel; (*Bedienung*) servants pl; **~ausweis** m identity card; **~computer** m personal computer; **~ien** [-iən] pl particulars; **~mangel** m undermanning; **~pronomen** nt personal pronoun

personell [pɛrzo'nɛl] adj (*Veränderungen*) personnel

Personen- zW: **~aufzug** m lift, elevator (*US*); **~kraftwagen** m private motorcar; **~schaden** m injury to persons; **~zug** m stopping train; passenger train

personifizieren [pɛrzonifi'tsiːrən] vt to personify

persönlich [pɛr'zøːnlɪç] adj personal ♦ adv in person; personally; **P~keit** f personality

Perspektive [pɛrspɛk'tiːvə] f perspective

Perücke [pe'rʏkə] f wig

pervers [pɛr'vɛrs] adj perverse

Pessimismus [pɛsi'mɪsmʊs] m pessimism

Pessimist [pɛsi'mɪst] m pessimist; **p~isch** adj pessimistic

Pest [pɛst] (**-**) f plague

Petersilie [petər'ziːliə] f parsley

Petroleum [pe'troːleʊm] (**-s**) nt paraffin, kerosene (*US*)

Pfad [pfaːt] (**-(e)s, -e**) m path; **~finder** (**-s, -**) m boy scout; **~finderin** f girl guide

Pfahl [pfaːl] (**-(e)s, ⁿe**) m post, stake

Pfand [pfant] (**-(e)s, ⁿer**) nt pledge, security; (*Flaschenpfand*) deposit; (*im Spiel*) forfeit;

Rechtschreibreform: ▲ *neue Schreibung* △ *alte Schreibung (auslaufend)*

~brief m bond

pfänden ['pfɛndən] vt to seize, to distrain

Pfänderspiel nt game of forfeits

Pfandflasche f returnable bottle

Pfandschein m pawn ticket

Pfändung ['pfɛnduŋ] f seizure, distraint

Pfanne ['pfanə] f (frying) pan

Pfannkuchen m pancake; (Berliner) doughnut

Pfarr- ['pfar] zW: ~ei f parish; ~er (-s, -) m priest; (evangelisch) vicar; minister; ~haus nt vicarage; manse

Pfau [pfau] (-(e)s), -en m peacock; ~enauge nt peacock butterfly

Pfeffer ['pfɛfər] (-s, -) m pepper; ~kuchen m gingerbread; ~minz (-es, -e) nt peppermint; ~mühle f pepper mill; p~n vt to pepper; (umg: werfen) to fling; gepfefferte Preise/Witze steep prices/spicy jokes

Pfeife ['pfaifə] f whistle; (Tabakpfeife, Orgelpfeife) pipe; p~n (unreg) vt, vi to whistle; ~r (-s, -) m piper

Pfeil [pfail] (-(e)s, -e) m arrow

Pfeiler ['pfailər] (-s, -) m pillar, prop; (Brückenpfeiler) pier

Pfennig ['pfɛnɪç] (-(e)s, -e) m (HIST) pfennig (hundredth part of a mark)

Pferd [pfe:rt] (-(e)s, -e) nt horse

Pferde- ['pfe:rdə] zW: ~rennen nt horse race; horse racing; ~schwanz m (Frisur) ponytail; ~stall m stable

Pfiff [pfɪf] (-(e)s, -e) m whistle

Pfifferling ['pfɪfərlɪŋ] m yellow chanterelle (mushroom); keinen ~ wert not worth a thing

pfiffig adj sly, sharp

Pfingsten ['pfɪŋstən] (-, -) nt Whitsun (BRIT), Pentecost

Pfirsich ['pfɪrzɪç] (-s, -e) m peach

Pflanz- ['pflants] zW: ~e f plant; p~en vt to plant; ~enfett nt vegetable fat; p~lich adj vegetable; ~ung f plantation

Pflaster ['pflastər] (-s, -) nt plaster; (Straße) pavement; p~n vt to pave; ~stein m paving stone

Pflaume ['pflaumə] f plum

Pflege ['pfle:gə] f care; (von Idee) cultivation; (Krankenpflege) nursing; in ~ sein (Kind) to be fostered out; p~bedürftig adj needing care; ~eltern pl foster parents; ~heim nt nursing home; ~kind nt foster child; p~leicht adj easy-care; ~mutter f foster mother; p~n vt to look after; (Kranke) to nurse; (Beziehungen) to foster; p~r (-s, -) m orderly; male nurse; ~rin f nurse, attendant; ~vater m foster father

Pflicht [pflɪçt] (-, -en) f duty; (SPORT) compulsory section; p~bewusst ▲ adj conscientious; ~fach nt (SCH) compulsory subject; ~gefühl nt sense of duty; p~gemäß adj dutiful ♦ adv as in duty bound; ~versicherung f compulsory insurance

pflücken ['pflʏkən] vt to pick; (Blumen) to pick, to pluck

Pflug [pflu:k] (-(e)s, ⁼e) m plough

pflügen ['pfly:gən] vt to plough

Pforte ['pfɔrtə] f gate; door

Pförtner ['pfœrtnər] (-s, -) m porter, doorkeeper, doorman

Pfosten ['pfɔstən] (-s, -) m post

Pfote ['pfo:tə] f paw; (umg: Schrift) scrawl

Pfropfen (-s, -) m (Flaschenpfropfen) stopper; (Blutpfropfen) clot

pfui [pfui] excl ugh!

Pfund [pfunt] (-(e)s, -e) nt pound

pfuschen ['pfuʃən] (umg) vi to be sloppy; jdm ins Handwerk ~ to interfere in sb's business

Pfuscher ['pfuʃər] (-s, -) (umg) m sloppy worker; (Kurpfuscher) quack; ~ei (umg) f sloppy work; quackery

Pfütze ['pfʏtsə] f puddle

Phänomen [fɛno'me:n] (-s, -e) nt phenomenon

phänomenal [-'na:l] adj phenomenal

Phantasie etc [fanta'zi:] f = Fantasie etc

phantastisch [fan'tastɪʃ] adj = fantastisch

Phase ['fa:zə] f phase

Philologie [filolo'gi:] f philology

Philosoph [filo'zo:f] (-en, -en) m philosopher; ~ie [-'fi:] f philosophy; p~isch adj philosophical

phlegmatisch [flɛˈgmaːtɪʃ] adj lethargic

Phonetik [foˈneːtɪk] f phonetics sg

phonetisch adj phonetic

Phosphor [ˈfɔsfɔr] (-s) m phosphorus

Photo etc [ˈfoːto] (-s, -s) nt = **Foto** etc

Phrase [ˈfraːzə] f phrase; (pej) hollow phrase

pH-Wert [peːˈhaːveːrt] m pH-value

Physik [fyˈziːk] f physics sg; **p~alisch** [-ˈkaːlɪʃ] adj of physics; **~er(in)** [ˈfyːzɪkər(ɪn)] (-s, -) m(f) physicist

Physiologie [fyzioloˈgiː] f physiology

physisch [ˈfyːzɪʃ] adj physical

Pianist(in) [piaˈnɪst(ɪn)] m(f) pianist

Pickel [ˈpɪkəl] (-s, -) m pimple; (Werkzeug) pickaxe; (Bergpickel) ice axe; **p~ig** adj pimply, spotty

picken [ˈpɪkən] vi to pick, to peck

Picknick [ˈpɪknɪk] (-s, -e od -s) nt picnic; ~ **machen** to have a picnic

piepen [ˈpiːpən] vi to chirp

piepsen [ˈpiːpsən] vi to chirp

Piepser (umg) m pager, paging device

Pier [piːər] (-s, -s od -e) m od f pier

Pietät [pieˈtɛːt] f piety, reverence; **p~los** adj impious, irreverent

Pigment [pɪgˈmɛnt] nt pigment

Pik [piːk] (-s, -s) nt (KARTEN) spades

pikant [piˈkant] adj spicy, piquant; (anzüglich) suggestive

Pilger [ˈpɪlgər] (-s, -) m pilgrim; **~fahrt** f pilgrimage

Pille [ˈpɪlə] f pill

Pilot [piˈloːt] (-en, -en) m pilot

Pilz [pɪlts] (-es, -e) m fungus; (essbar) mushroom; (giftig) toadstool; **~krankheit** f fungal disease

Pinguin [ˈpɪŋguiːn] (-s, -e) m penguin

Pinie [ˈpiːniə] f pine

pinkeln [ˈpɪŋkəln] (umg) vi to pee

Pinnwand [ˈpɪnvant] f noticeboard

Pinsel [ˈpɪnzəl] (-s, -) m paintbrush

Pinzette [pɪnˈtsetə] f tweezers pl

Pionier [pioˈniːr] (-s, -e) m pioneer; (MIL) sapper, engineer

Pirat [piˈraːt] (-en, -en) m pirate

Piste [ˈpɪstə] f (SKI) run, piste; (AVIAT) runway

Pistole [pɪsˈtoːlə] f pistol

Pizza [ˈpɪtsa] (-, -s) f pizza

Pkw [peːkaːˈveː] (-(s), -(s)) m abk = **Personenkraftwagen**

plädieren [plɛˈdiːrən] vi to plead

Plädoyer [plɛdoaˈjeː] (-s, -s) nt speech for the defence; (fig) plea

Plage [ˈplaːgə] f plague; (Mühe) nuisance; **~geist** m pest, nuisance; **p~n** vt to torment ♦ vr to toil, to slave

Plakat [plaˈkaːt] (-(e)s, -e) nt placard; poster

Plan [plaːn] (-(e)s, ⁼e) m plan; (Karte) map

Plane f tarpaulin

planen vt to plan; (Mord etc) to plot

Planer (-s, -) m planner

Planet [plaˈneːt] (-en, -en) m planet

planieren [plaˈniːrən] vt to plane, to level

Planke [ˈplaŋkə] f plank

plan- [ˈplaːn] zW: **~los** adj (Vorgehen) unsystematic; (Umherlaufen) aimless; **~mäßig** adj according to plan; systematic; (EISENB) scheduled

Plansoll (-s) nt output target

Plantage [planˈtaːʒə] f plantation

Plan(t)schbecken [ˈplan(t)ʃbekən] nt paddling pool

plan(t)schen [ˈplan(t)ʃən] vi to splash

Planung f planning

Planwirtschaft f planned economy

plappern [ˈplapərn] vi to chatter

plärren [ˈplɛrən] vi (Mensch) to cry, to whine; (Radio) to blare

Plasma [ˈplasma] (-s, **Plasmen**) nt plasma

Plastik¹ [ˈplastɪk] f sculpture

Plastik² [ˈplastɪk] (-s) nt (Kunststoff) plastic; **~beutel** m plastic bag, carrier bag; **~folie** f plastic film

plastisch [ˈplastɪʃ] adj plastic; **stell dir das ~ vor!** just picture it!

Platane [plaˈtaːnə] f plane (tree)

Platin [ˈplaːtiːn] (-s) nt platinum

platonisch [plaˈtoːnɪʃ] adj platonic

platsch [platʃ] excl splash; **~en** vi to splash

plätschern [ˈplɛtʃərn] vi to babble

platschnass ▲ adj drenched

platt [plat] adj flat; (umg: überrascht) flabbergasted; (fig: geistlos) flat, boring; **~deutsch** adj low German; **P~e** f

(*Speisenplatte, PHOT, TECH*) plate; (*Steinplatte*) flag; (*Kachel*) tile; (*Schallplatte*) record; **P~enspieler** *m* record player; **P~enteller** *m* turntable

Platz [plats] **(-es, ˝e)** *m* place; (*Sitzplatz*) seat; (*Raum*) space, room; (*in Stadt*) square; (*Sportplatz*) playing field; **~ nehmen** to take a seat; **jdm ~ machen** to make room for sb; **~angst** *f* claustrophobia; **~anweiser(in)** **(-s, -)** *m(f)* usher(ette)

Plätzchen ['plɛtsçən] *nt* spot; (*Gebäck*) biscuit

platzen *vi* to burst; (*Bombe*) to explode; **vor Wut p~en** (*umg*) to be bursting with anger

platzieren ▲ [pla'tsiːrən] *vt* to place ♦ *vr* (*SPORT*) to be placed; (*TENNIS*) to be seeded

Platz- *zW:* **~karte** *f* seat reservation; **~mangel** *m* lack of space; **~patrone** *f* blank cartridge; **~regen** *m* downpour; **~reservierung** [-rezɛrviːrʊŋ] *f* seat reservation; **~wunde** *f* cut

Plauderei [plaʊdəˈraɪ] *f* chat, conversation; (*RADIO*) talk

plaudern ['plaʊdərn] *vi* to chat, to talk

plausibel [plaʊˈziːbəl] *adj* plausible

plazieren △ [plaˈtsiːrən] *vt, vr siehe* **platzieren**

Pleite ['plaɪtə] *f* bankruptcy; (*umg: Reinfall*) flop; **~ machen** to go bust; **p~** (*umg*) *adj* broke

Plenum ['pleːnʊm] **(-s)** *nt* plenum

Plombe ['plɔmbə] *f* lead seal; (*Zahnplombe*) filling

plombieren [plɔmˈbiːrən] *vt* to seal; (*Zahn*) to fill

plötzlich ['plœtslɪç] *adj* sudden ♦ *adv* suddenly

plump [plʊmp] *adj* clumsy; (*Hände*) coarse; (*Körper*) shapeless; **~sen** (*umg*) *vi* to plump down, to fall

Plunder ['plʊndər] **(-s)** *m* rubbish

plündern ['plʏndərn] *vt* to plunder; (*Stadt*) to sack ♦ *vi* to plunder; **Plünderung** *f* plundering, sack, pillage

Plural ['pluːraːl] **(-s, -e)** *m* plural; **p~istisch** *adj* pluralistic

Plus [plʊs] **(-, -)** *nt* plus; (*FIN*) profit; (*Vorteil*) advantage; **p~** *adv* plus

Plüsch [plyːʃ] **(-(e)s, -e)** *m* plush

Plus- [plʊs] *zW:* **~pol** *m* (*ELEK*) positive pole; **~punkt** *m* point; (*fig*) point in sb's favour

Plutonium [pluˈtoːniʊm] **(-s)** *nt* plutonium

PLZ *abk =* **Postleitzahl**

Po [poː] **(-s, -s)** (*umg*) *m* bottom, bum

Pöbel ['pøːbəl] **(-s)** *m* mob, rabble; **~ei** *f* vulgarity; **p~haft** *adj* low, vulgar

pochen ['pɔxən] *vi* to knock; (*Herz*) to pound; **auf etw** *akk* **~** (*fig*) to insist on sth

Pocken ['pɔkən] *pl* smallpox *sg*

Podium ['poːdiʊm] *nt* podium; **~sdiskussion** *f* panel discussion

Poesie [poeˈziː] *f* poetry

Poet [poˈeːt] **(-en, -en)** *m* poet; **p~isch** *adj* poetic

Pointe [poˈɛ̃ːtə] *f* point

Pokal [poˈkaːl] **(-s, -e)** *m* goblet; (*SPORT*) cup; **~spiel** *nt* cup tie

pökeln ['pøːkəln] *vt* to pickle, to salt

Poker ['poːkər] **(-s)** *nt od m* poker

Pol [poːl] **(-s, -e)** *m* pole; **p~ar** *adj* polar; **~arkreis** *m* Arctic circle

Pole ['poːlə] **(-n, -n)** *m* Pole

polemisch [poˈleːmɪʃ] *adj* polemical

Polen ['poːlən] **(-s)** *nt* Poland

Police [poˈliːs(ə)] *f* insurance policy

Polier [poˈliːr] **(-s, -e)** *m* foreman

polieren *vt* to polish

Poliklinik [poliˈkliːnɪk] *f* outpatients (department) *sg*

Polin *f* Pole

Politik [poliˈtiːk] *f* politics *sg*; (*eine bestimmte*) policy; **~er(in)** [poliˈtiːkər(ɪn)] **(-s, -)** *m(f)* politician

politisch [poˈliːtɪʃ] *adj* political

Politur [poliˈtuːr] *f* polish

Polizei [poliˈtsaɪ] *f* police; **~beamte(r)** *m* police officer; **p~lich** *adj* police; **sich p~lich melden** to register with the police; **~revier** *nt* police station; **~staat** *m* police state; **~streife** *f* police patrol; **~stunde** *f* closing time; **~wache** *f* police station

Polizist(in) [poliˈtsɪst(ɪn)] **(-en, -en)** *m(f)* policeman(-woman)

Pollen ['pɔlən] **(-s, -)** *m* pollen; ~flug *m* pollen count

polnisch ['pɔlnɪʃ] *adj* Polish

Polohemd ['po:lohɛmt] *nt* polo shirt

Polster ['pɔlstər] **(-s, -)** *nt* cushion; (~*ung*) upholstery; (*in Kleidung*) padding; (*fig: Geld*) reserves *pl*; ~er **(-s, -)** *m* upholsterer; ~möbel *pl* upholstered furniture *sg*; p~n *vt* to upholster; to pad

Polterabend ['pɔltəra:bənt] *m* party on eve of wedding

poltern *vi* (*Krach machen*) to crash; (*schimpfen*) to rant

Polyp [po'ly:p] **(-en, -en)** *m* polyp; (*umg*) cop; ~en *pl* (*MED*) adenoids

Pomade [po'ma:də] *f* pomade

Pommes frites [pɔm'frɪt] *pl* chips, French fried potatoes

Pomp [pɔmp] **(-(e)s)** *m* pomp; p~ös [pɔm'pø:s] *adj* (*Auftritt, Fest, Haus*) ostentatious, showy

Pony ['pɔni] **(-s, -s)** *nt* (*Pferd*) pony ♦ *m* (*Frisur*) fringe

Popmusik ['pɔpmuzi:k] *f* pop music

Popo [po'po:] **(-s, -s)** (*umg*) *m* bottom, bum

poppig ['pɔpɪç] *adj* (*Farbe etc*) gaudy

populär [popu'lɛ:r] *adj* popular

Popularität [populari'tɛ:t] *f* popularity

Pore ['po:rə] *f* pore

Pornografie ▲ [pɔrnogra'fi:] *f* pornography; **pornografisch** ▲ [pɔrno'gra:fɪʃ] *adj* pornographic

porös [po'rø:s] *adj* porous

Porree ['pɔre] **(-s, -s)** *m* leek

Portefeuille [pɔrt(ə)'fø:j] *nt* (*POL, FIN*) portfolio

Portemonnaie [pɔrtmɔ'ne:] **(-s, -s)** *nt* purse

Portier [pɔrti'e:] **(-s, -s)** *m* porter

Portion [pɔrtsi'o:n] *f* portion, helping; (*umg: Anteil*) amount

Portmonee ▲ [pɔrtmɔ'ne:] **(-s, -s)** *nt* = **Portemonnaie**

Porto ['pɔrto] **(-s, -s)** *nt* postage; p~frei *adj* post-free, (*postage*) prepaid

Portrait [pɔr'trɛ:] **(-s, -s)** *nt* = **Porträt**; p~ieren *vt* = **porträtieren**

Porträt [pɔr'trɛ:] **(-s, -s)** *nt* portrait; p~ieren *vt* to paint, to portray

Portugal ['pɔrtugal] **(-s)** *nt* Portugal; **Portugiese** [pɔrtu'gi:zə] **(-n, -n)** *m* Portuguese; **Portugiesin** *f* Portuguese; **portu'giesisch** *adj* Portuguese

Porzellan [pɔrtse'la:n] **(-s, -e)** *nt* china, porcelain; (*Geschirr*) china

Posaune [po'zaunə] *f* trombone

Pose ['po:zə] *f* pose

Position [pozitsi'o:n] *f* position

positiv ['po:ziti:f] *adj* positive; **P~ (-s, -e)** *nt* (*PHOT*) positive

possessiv ['pɔsesi:f] *adj* possessive; **P~pronomen (-s, -e)** *nt* possessive pronoun

possierlich [pɔ'si:rlɪç] *adj* funny

Post [pɔst] **(-, -en)** *f* post (*office*); (*Briefe*) mail; ~amt *nt* post office; ~anweisung *f* postal order, money order; ~bote *m* postman; ~en **(-s, -)** *m* post, position; (*COMM*) item; (*auf Liste*) entry; (*MIL*) sentry; (*Streikposten*) picket; ~er **(-s, -(s))** *nt* poster; ~fach *nt* post office box; ~karte *f* postcard; p~lagernd *adv* poste restante (*BRIT*), general delivery (*US*); ~leitzahl *f* postal code; ~scheckkonto *nt* postal giro account; ~sparbuch *nt* post office savings book; ~sparkasse *f* post office savings bank; ~stempel *m* postmark; p~wendend *adv* by return of post; ~wertzeichen *nt* postage stamp

potent [po'tɛnt] *adj* potent

Potential △ [potɛntsi'a:l] **(-s, -e)** *nt* siehe **Potenzial**

potentiell △ [potɛntsi'ɛl] *adj* siehe **potenziell**

Potenz [po'tɛnts] *f* power; (*eines Mannes*) potency

Potenzial ▲ [potɛn'tsia:l] **(-s, -e)** *nt* potential

potenziell ▲ [potɛn'tsiɛl] *adj* potential

Pracht [praxt] **(-)** *f* splendour, magnificence; **prächtig** ['prɛçtɪç] *adj* splendid

Prachtstück *nt* showpiece

prachtvoll *adj* splendid, magnificent

Prädikat [predi'ka:t] **(-(e)s, -e)** *nt* title;

(GRAM) predicate; (Zensur) distinction

prägen ['prɛ:gən] vt to stamp; (Münze) to mint; (Ausdruck) to coin; (Charakter) to form

prägnant [prɛ'gnant] adj precise, terse

Prägung ['prɛ:gʊŋ] f minting; forming; (Eigenart) character, stamp

prahlen ['pra:lən] vi to boast, to brag; **Prahle·rei** f boasting

Praktik ['praktɪk] f practice; **p~abel** [-'ka:bəl] adj practicable; **~ant(in)** [-'kant(ɪn)] m(f) trainee; **~um** (-s, **Praktika** od **Praktiken**) nt practical training

praktisch ['praktɪʃ] adj practical, handy; **~er Arzt** general practitioner

praktizieren [praktɪ'tsi:rən] vt, vi to practise

Praline [pra'li:nə] f chocolate

prall [pral] adj firmly rounded; (Segel) taut; (Arme) plump; (Sonne) blazing; **~en** vi to bounce, to rebound; (Sonne) to blaze

Prämie ['prɛ:miə] f premium; (Belohnung) award, prize; **p~ren** vt to give an award to

Präparat [prɛpa'ra:t] (-(e)s, -e) nt (BIOL) preparation; (MED) medicine

Präposition [prɛpozitsi'o:n] f preposition

Prärie [prɛ'ri:] f prairie

Präsens ['prɛ:zɛns] (-) nt present tense

präsentieren [prɛzɛn'ti:rən] vt to present

Präservativ [prɛzɛrva'ti:f] (-s, -e) nt contraceptive

Präsident(in) [prɛzi'dɛnt(ɪn)] m(f) president; **~schaft** f presidency

Präsidium [prɛ'zi:dium] nt presidency, chair(manship); (Polizeipräsidium) police headquarters pl

prasseln ['prasəln] vi (Feuer) to crackle; (Hagel) to drum; (Wörter) to rain down

Praxis ['praksɪs] (-, **Praxen**) f practice; (Behandlungsraum) surgery; (von Anwalt) office

Präzedenzfall [prɛtse'dɛnts-] m precedent

präzis [prɛ'tsi:s] adj precise; **P~ion** [prɛtsizi'o:n] f precision

predigen ['prɛ:dɪgən] vt, vi to preach; **Prediger** (-s, -) m preacher

Predigt ['prɛ:dɪçt] (-, -en) f sermon

Preis [praɪs] (-es, -e) m price; (Siegespreis) prize; **um keinen ~** not at any price;

p~bewusst ▲ adj price-conscious

Preiselbeere f cranberry

preis- [praɪs] zW: **~en** (unreg) vi to praise; **~geben** (unreg) vt to abandon; (opfern) to sacrifice; (zeigen) to expose; **~gekrönt** adj prizewinning; **P~gericht** nt jury; **~günstig** adj inexpensive; **P~lage** f price range; **~lich** adj (Lage, Unterschied) price, in price; **P~liste** f price list; **P~richter** m judge (in a competition); **P~schild** nt price tag; **P~träger(in)** m(f) prizewinner; **~wert** adj inexpensive

Prell- [prɛl] zW: **~bock** m buffers pl; **p~en** vt to bump; (fig) to cheat, to swindle; **~ung** f bruise

Premiere [prəmi'ɛ:rə] f premiere

Premierminister [prəmi'e:mɪnɪstər] m prime minister, premier

Presse ['prɛsə] f press; **~agentur** f press agency; **~freiheit** f freedom of the press; **p~n** vt to press

Pressluft ▲ ['prɛslʊft] f compressed air; **~bohrer** m pneumatic drill

Prestige [prɛs'ti:ʒə] (-s) nt prestige

prickeln ['prɪkəln] vt, vi to tingle; to tickle

Priester ['pri:stər] (-s, -) m priest

prima adj inv first-class, excellent

primär [pri'mɛ:r] adj primary

Primel ['pri:məl] (-, -n) f primrose

primitiv [primi'ti:f] adj primitive

Prinz [prɪnts] (-en, -en) m prince; **~essin** f princess

Prinzip [prɪn'tsi:p] (-s, -ien) nt principle; **p~iell** [-i'ɛl] adj, adv on principle; **p~ienlos** adj unprincipled

Priorität [priori'tɛ:t] f priority

Prise ['pri:zə] f pinch

Prisma ['prɪsma] (-s, **Prismen**) nt prism

privat [pri'va:t] adj private; **P~besitz** m private property; **P~fernsehen** nt commercial television; **P~patient(in)** m(f) private patient; **P~schule** f public school

Privileg [privi'le:k] (-(e)s, -ien) nt privilege

Pro [pro:] (-) nt pro

pro präp +akk per

Probe ['pro:bə] f test; (Teststück) sample; (THEAT) rehearsal; **jdn auf die ~ stellen** to

---

Spelling Reform: ▲ *new spelling* △ *old spelling (to be phased out)*

put sb to the test; **~exemplar** nt specimen copy; **~fahrt** f test drive; **p~n** vt to try; (THEAT) to rehearse; **p~weise** adv on approval; **~zeit** f probation period

probieren [pro'biːrən] vt to try; (Wein, Speise) to taste, to sample ♦ vi to try; to taste

Problem [pro'bleːm] (**-s, -e**) nt problem; **~atik** [-'maːtɪk] f problem; **p~atisch** [-'maːtɪʃ] adj problematic; **p~los** adj problem-free

Produkt [pro'dʊkt] (**-(e)s, -e**) nt product; (AGR) produce no pl; **~ion** [prodʊktsi'oːn] f production; output; **p~iv** [-'tiːf] adj productive; **~ivität** f productivity

Produzent [produ'tsɛnt] m manufacturer; (Film) producer

produzieren [produ'tsiːrən] vt to produce

Professor [pro'fɛsɔr] m professor

Profi ['proːfi] (**-s**) m (umg, SPORT) pro

Profil [pro'fiːl] (**-s, -e**) nt profile; (fig) image

Profit [pro'fiːt] (**-(e)s, -e**) m profit; **p~ieren** vi: **p~ieren (von)** to profit (from)

Prognose [pro'gnoːzə] f prediction, prognosis

Programm [pro'gram] (**-s, -e**) nt programme; (COMPUT) program; **p~ieren** [-'miːrən] vt to programme; (COMPUT) to program; **~ierer(in)** (**-s, -**) m(f) programmer

progressiv [progrɛ'siːf] adj progressive

Projekt [pro'jɛkt] (**-(e)s, -e**) nt project; **~or** [pro'jɛktɔr] m projector

proklamieren [prokla'miːrən] vt to proclaim

Prokurist(in) [proku'rɪst(ɪn)] m(f) ≈ company secretary

Prolet [pro'leːt] (**-en, -en**) m prole, pleb; **~arier** [-'taːriər] (**-s, -**) m proletarian

Prolog [pro'loːk] (**-(e)s, -e**) m prologue

Promenade [promə'naːdə] f promenade

Promille [pro'mɪlə] (**-(s), -**) nt alcohol level

prominent [promi'nɛnt] adj prominent

Prominenz [promi'nɛnts] f VIPs pl

Promotion [promotsi'oːn] f doctorate, Ph.D.

promovieren [promo'viːrən] vi to do a doctorate od Ph.D.

prompt [prɔmpt] adj prompt

Pronomen [pro'noːmɛn] (**-s, -**) nt pronoun

Propaganda [propa'ganda] (**-**) f propaganda

Propeller [pro'pɛlər] (**-s, -**) m propeller

Prophet [pro'feːt] (**-en, -en**) m prophet

prophezeien [profe'tsaɪən] vt to prophesy; **Prophezeiung** f prophecy

Proportion [propɔrtsi'oːn] f proportion; **p~al** [-'naːl] adj proportional

proportioniert [propɔrtsio'niːrt] adj: **gut/schlecht ~** well-/badly-proportioned

Prosa ['proːza] (**-**) f prose; **p~isch** [pro'zaːɪʃ] adj prosaic

prosit ['proːzɪt] excl cheers

Prospekt [pro'spɛkt] (**-(e)s, -e**) m leaflet, brochure

prost [proːst] excl cheers

Prostituierte [prostitu'iːrtə] f prostitute

Prostitution [prostitutsi'oːn] f prostitution

Protest [pro'tɛst] (**-(e)s, -e**) m protest; **~ant(in)** [protɛs'tant(ɪn)] m(f) Protestant; **p~antisch** [protɛs'tantɪʃ] adj Protestant; **p~ieren** [protɛs'tiːrən] vi to protest

Prothese [pro'teːzə] f artificial limb; (Zahnprothese) dentures pl

Protokoll [proto'kɔl] (**-s, -e**) nt register; (von Sitzung) minutes pl; (diplomatisch) protocol; (Polizeiprotokoll) statement; **p~ieren** [-'liːrən] vt to take down in the minutes

protzen ['prɔtsən] vi to show off

Proviant [provi'ant] (**-s, -e**) m provisions pl, supplies pl

Provinz [pro'vɪnts] (**-, -en**) f province; **p~iell** adj provincial

Provision [provizi'oːn] f (COMM) commission

provisorisch [provi'zoːrɪʃ] adj provisional

Provokation [provokatsi'oːn] f provocation

provozieren [provo'tsiːrən] vt to provoke

Prozedur [protse'duːr] f procedure; (pej) carry-on

Prozent [pro'tsɛnt] (**-(e)s, -e**) nt per cent, percentage; **~satz** m percentage; **p~ual** [-u'aːl] adj percentage cpd; as a percentage

Prozess ▲ [pro'tsɛs] (**-es, -e**) m trial, case

Prozession [protsɛsi'oːn] f procession

prüde ['pryːdə] adj prudish; **P~rie** [-'riː] f prudery

Prüf- ['pry:f] *zW:* **p~en** *vt* to examine, to test; (*nachprüfen*) to check; **~er** (**-s, -**) *m* examiner; **~ling** *m* examinee; **~ung** *f* examination; checking; **~ungsaus-schuss** ▲ *m* examining board

Prügel ['pry:gəl] (**-s, -**) *m* cudgel ♦ *pl* (*Schläge*) beating; **~ei** [-'laɪ] *f* fight; **p~n** *vt* to beat ♦ *vr* to fight; **~strafe** *f* corporal punishment

Prunk [prʊŋk] (**-(e)s**) *m* pomp, show; **p~voll** *adj* splendid, magnificent

PS [peː'ɛs] *abk* (= *Pferdestärke*) H.P.

Psych- ['psyç] *zW:* **~iater** [-iˈaːtər] (**-s, -**) *m* psychiatrist; **p~iatrisch** *adj* (*MED*) psychiatric; **p~isch** *adj* psychological; **~oanalyse** [-o|anaˈlyːze] *f* psychoanalysis; **~ologe** (**-n, -n**) *m* psychologist; **~ologie** *f* psychology; **p~ologisch** *adj* psychological; **~otherapeut(in)** (**-en, -en**) *m(f)* psychotherapist

Pubertät [pubɛrˈtɛːt] *f* puberty

Publikum ['puːblikʊm] (**-s**) *nt* audience; (*SPORT*) crowd

publizieren [publiˈtsiːrən] *vt* to publish, to publicize

Pudding ['pʊdɪŋ] (**-s, -e** *od* **-s**) *m* blancmange

Pudel ['puːdəl] (**-s**) *m* poodle

Puder ['puːdər] (**-s, -**) *m* powder; **~dose** *f* powder compact; **p~n** *vt* to powder; **~zucker** *m* icing sugar

Puff¹ [pʊf] (**-s, -e**) *m* (*Wäschepuff*) linen basket; (*Sitzpuff*) pouf

Puff² [pʊf] (**-s, ⁻e**) (*umg*) *m* (*Stoß*) push

Puff³ [pʊf] (**-s, -**) (*umg*) *m od nt* (*Bordell*) brothel

Puffer (**-s, -**) *m* buffer

Pullover [pʊˈloːvər] (**-s, -**) *m* pullover, jumper

Puls [pʊls] (**-es, -e**) *m* pulse; **~ader** *f* artery; **p~ieren** *vi* to throb, to pulsate

Pult [pʊlt] (**-(e)s, -e**) *nt* desk

Pulver ['pʊlfər] (**-s, -**) *nt* powder; **p~ig** *adj* powdery; **~schnee** *m* powdery snow

pummelig ['pʊmǝlɪç] *adj* chubby

Pumpe ['pʊmpǝ] *f* pump; **p~n** *vt* to pump; (*umg*) to lend; to borrow

Punkt [pʊŋkt] (**-(e)s, -e**) *m* point; (*bei Muster*) dot; (*Satzzeichen*) full stop; **p~ieren** [-'tiːrən] *vt* to dot; (*MED*) to aspirate

pünktlich ['pʏŋktlɪç] *adj* punctual; **P~keit** *f* punctuality

Punktsieg *m* victory on points

Punktzahl *f* score

Punsch [pʊnʃ] (**-(e)s, -e**) *m* punch

Pupille [puˈpɪlǝ] *f* pupil

Puppe ['pʊpǝ] *f* doll; (*Marionette*) puppet; (*Insektenpuppe*) pupa, chrysalis

Puppen- *zW:* **~spieler** *m* puppeteer; **~stube** *f* doll's house; **~theater** *nt* puppet theatre

pur [puːr] *adj* pure; (*völlig*) sheer; (*Whisky*) neat

Püree [pyˈreː] (**-s, -s**) *nt* mashed potatoes *pl*

Purzelbaum ['pʊrtsǝlbaum] *m* somersault

purzeln ['pʊrtsǝln] *vi* to tumble

Puste ['puːstǝ] (**-**) (*umg*) *f* puff; (*fig*) steam; **p~n** *vi* to puff, to blow

Pute ['puːtǝ] *f* turkey hen; **~r** (**-s, -**) *m* turkey cock

Putsch [pʊtʃ] (**-(e)s, -e**) *m* revolt, putsch

Putz [pʊts] (**-es**) *m* (*Mörtel*) plaster, roughcast

putzen *vt* to clean; (*Nase*) to wipe, to blow ♦ *vr* to clean o.s.; to dress o.s. up

Putz- *zW:* **~frau** *f* charwoman; **p~ig** *adj* quaint, funny; **~lappen** *m* cloth

Puzzle ['pasǝl] (**-s, -s**) *nt* jigsaw

PVC *nt abk* PVC

Pyjama [piˈdʒaːma] (**-s, -s**) *m* pyjamas *pl*

Pyramide [pyraˈmiːdǝ] *f* pyramid

Pyrenäen [pyreˈnɛːǝn] *pl* Pyrenees

Q, q

Quacksalber ['kvakzalbǝr] (**-s, -**) *m* quack (doctor)

Quader ['kvaːdǝr] (**-s, -**) *m* square stone; (*MATH*) cuboid

Quadrat [kvaˈdraːt] (**-(e)s, -e**) *nt* square; **q~isch** *adj* square; **~meter** *m* square metre

quaken ['kvaːkǝn] *vi* to croak; (*Ente*) to

quack

quäken ['kvɛːkən] vi to screech

Qual [kvaːl] (-, -en) f pain, agony; (seelisch) anguish; **q~en** vt to torment ♦ vr to struggle; (geistig) to torment o.s.; **~erei** f torture, torment

Qualifikation [kvalifikatsi'oːn] f qualification

qualifizieren [kvalifi'tsiːrən] vt to qualify; (einstufen) to label ♦ vr to qualify

Qualität [kvali'tɛːt] f quality; **~sware** f article of high quality

Qualle ['kvalə] f jellyfish

Qualm [kvalm] (-(e)s) m thick smoke; **q~en** vt, vi to smoke

qualvoll ['kvaːlfɔl] adj excruciating, painful, agonizing

Quant- [kvant] zW: **~ität** [-i'tɛːt] f quantity; **q~itativ** [-ita'tiːf] adj quantitative; **~um** (-s) nt quantity, amount

Quarantäne [karan'tɛːnə] f quarantine

Quark [kvark] (-s) m curd cheese

Quartal [kvar'taːl] (-s, -e) nt quarter (year)

Quartier [kvar'tiːr] (-s, -e) nt accommodation; (MIL) quarters pl; (Stadtquartier) district

Quarz [kvaːrts] (-es, -e) m quartz

quasseln ['kvasəln] (umg) vi to natter

Quatsch [kvatʃ] (-es) m rubbish; **q~en** vi to chat, to natter

Quecksilber ['kvɛkzɪlbər] nt mercury

Quelle ['kvɛlə] f spring; (eines Flusses) source; **q~n** (unreg) vi (hervorquellen) to pour od gush forth; (schwellen) to swell

quer [kveːr] adv crossways, diagonally; (rechtwinklig) at right angles; **~ auf dem Bett** across the bed; **Q~balken** m crossbeam; **Q~flöte** f flute; **Q~format** nt (PHOT) oblong format; **Q~schnitt** m cross-section; **~schnittsgelähmt** adj paralysed below the waist; **Q~straße** f intersecting road

quetschen ['kvɛtʃən] vt to squash, to crush; (MED) to bruise

Quetschung f bruise, contusion

quieken ['kviːkən] vi to squeak

quietschen ['kviːtʃən] vi to squeak

Quintessenz f ['kvɪntɛsɛnts] f quintessence

Quirl [kvɪrl] (-(e)s, -e) m whisk

quitt [kvɪt] adj quits, even

Quitte f quince

quittieren [kvɪ'tiːrən] vt to give a receipt for; (Dienst) to leave

Quittung f receipt

Quiz [kvɪs] (-, -) nt quiz

quoll etc [kvɔl] vb siehe **quellen**

Quote ['kvoːtə] f number, rate

R, r

Rabatt [ra'bat] (-(e)s, -e) m discount

Rabattmarke f trading stamp

Rabe ['raːbə] (-n, -n) m raven

rabiat [rabi'aːt] adj furious

Rache ['raxə] (-) f revenge, vengeance

Rachen (-s, -) m throat

rächen ['rɛçən] vt to avenge, to revenge ♦ vr to take (one's) revenge; **das wird sich ~** you'll pay for that

Rad [raːt] (-(e)s, ⁻er) nt wheel; (Fahrrad) bike; **~ fahren** to cycle

Radar ['raːdaːr] (-s) m od nt radar; **~falle** f speed trap; **~kontrolle** f radar-controlled speed trap

Radau [ra'dau] (-s) (umg) m row

radeln ['raːdəln] (umg) vi to cycle

Radfahr- zW: **r~en** △ (unreg) vi siehe **Rad**; **~er(in)** m(f) cyclist; **~weg** m cycle track od path

Radier- [ra'diːr] zW: **r~en** vt to rub out, to erase; (KUNST) to etch; **~gummi** m rubber, eraser; **~ung** f etching

Radieschen [ra'diːsçən] nt radish

radikal [radi'kaːl] adj radical

Radio ['raːdio] (-s, -s) nt radio, wireless; **r~ak'tiv** adj radioactive; **~aktivi'tät** f radioactivity; **~apparat** m radio, wireless set

Radius ['raːdius] (-, **Radien**) m radius

Rad- zW: **~kappe** f (AUT) hub cap; **~ler(in)** (umg) m(f) cyclist; **~rennen** nt cycle race; cycle racing; **~sport** m cycling; **~weg** m cycleway

raffen ['rafən] vt to snatch, to pick up; (Stoff)

to gather (up); (*Geld*) to pile up, to rake in

raffi'niert *adj* crafty, cunning

ragen ['ra:gən] *vi* to tower, to rise

Rahm [ra:m] **(-s)** *m* cream

Rahmen **(-s, -)** *m* frame(work); **im ~ des Möglichen** within the bounds of possibility; **r~** *vt* to frame

räkeln ['rɛːkln] *vr* = **rekeln**

Rakete [ra'ke:tə] *f* rocket; **~nstützpunkt** *m* missile base

rammen ['ramən] *vt* to ram

Rampe ['rampə] *f* ramp; **~nlicht** *nt* (*THEAT*) footlights *pl*

ramponieren [rampo'ni:rən] (*umg*) *vt* to damage

Ramsch [ramʃ] **(-(e)s, -e)** *m* junk

ran [ran] (*umg*) *adv* = **heran**

Rand [rant] **(-(e)s, ⁻er)** *m* edge; (*von Brille, Tasse etc*) rim; (*Hutrand*) brim; (*auf Papier*) margin; (*Schmutzrand, unter Augen*) ring; (*fig*) verge, brink; **außer ~ und Band** wild; **am ~e bemerkt** mentioned in passing

randalieren [randa'li:rən] *vi* to (go on the) rampage

Rang [raŋ] **(-(e)s, ⁻e)** *m* rank; (*Stand*) standing; (*Wert*) quality; (*THEAT*) circle

Rangier- [rãʒiːr] *zW:* **~bahnhof** *m* marshalling yard; **r~en** *vt* (*EISENB*) to shunt, to switch (*US*) ♦ *vi* to rank, to be classed; **~gleis** *nt* siding

Ranke ['raŋkə] *f* tendril, shoot

ranzig ['rantsɪç] *adj* rancid

Rappen ['rapən] *m* (*FIN*) rappen, centime

rar [ra:r] *adj* rare; **sich ~ machen** (*umg*) to keep o.s. to o.s.; **R~i'tät** *f* rarity; (*Sammelobjekt*) curio

rasant [ra'zant] *adj* quick, rapid

rasch [raʃ] *adj* quick

rascheln *vi* to rustle

Rasen ['ra:zən] **(-s, -)** *m* lawn; grass

rasen *vi* to rave; (*schnell*) to race; **~d** *adj* furious; **~de Kopfschmerzen** a splitting headache

Rasenmäher **(-s, -)** *m* lawnmower

Rasier- [ra'ziːr] *zW:* **~apparat** *m* shaver; **~creme** *f* shaving cream; **r~en** *vt, vr* to shave; **~klinge** *f* razor blade; **~messer** *nt*

razor; **~pinsel** *m* shaving brush; **~schaum** *m* shaving foam; **~seife** *f* shaving soap *od* stick; **~wasser** *nt* shaving lotion

Rasse ['rasə] *f* race; (*Tierrasse*) breed; **~hund** *m* thoroughbred dog

rasseln ['rasəln] *vi* to clatter

Rassen- *zW:* **~hass** ▲ *m* race *od* racial hatred; **~trennung** *f* racial segregation

Rassismus [ra'sɪsmʊs] *m* racism

Rast [rast] **(-, -en)** *f* rest; **r~en** *vi* to rest; **~hof** *m* (*AUT*) service station; **r~los** *adj* tireless; (*unruhig*) restless; **~platz** *m* (*AUT*) layby; **~stätte** *f* (*AUT*) service station

Rasur [ra'zu:r] *f* shaving

Rat [ra:t] **(-(e)s, -schläge)** *m* advice *no pl*; **ein ~** a piece of advice; **keinen ~ wissen** not to know what to do; *siehe* **zurate**

Rate *f* instalment

raten (*unreg*) *vt, vi* to guess; (*empfehlen*): **jdm ~** to advise sb

Ratenzahlung *f* hire purchase

Ratgeber **(-s, -)** *m* adviser

Rathaus *nt* town hall

ratifizieren [ratifi'tsi:rən] *vt* to ratify

Ration [ratsi'o:n] *f* ration; **r~al** [-'na:l] *adj* rational; **r~ali'sieren** *vt* to rationalize; **r~ell** [-'nɛl] *adj* efficient; **r~ieren** [-'ni:rən] *vt* to ration

Rat- *zW:* **r~los** *adj* at a loss, helpless; **r~sam** *adj* advisable; **~schlag** *m* (piece of) advice

Rätsel ['rɛːtsəl] **(-s, -)** *nt* puzzle; (*Worträtsel*) riddle; **r~haft** *adj* mysterious; **es ist mir r~haft** it's a mystery to me

Ratte ['ratə] *f* rat; **~nfänger** **(-s, -)** *m* ratcatcher

rattern ['ratərn] *vi* to rattle, to clatter

rau ▲ [rau] *adj* rough, coarse; (*Wetter*) harsh

Raub [raup] **(-(e)s)** *m* robbery; (*Beute*) loot, booty; **~bau** *m* ruthless exploitation; **r~en** ['raubən] *vt* to rob; (*Mensch*) to kidnap, to abduct

Räuber ['rɔybər] **(-s, -)** *m* robber

Raub- *zW:* **~mord** *m* robbery with murder; **~tier** *nt* predator; **~überfall** *m* robbery with violence; **~vogel** *m* bird of prey

Rauch [raux] **(-(e)s)** *m* smoke; **r~en** *vt, vi* to

smoke; **~er(in)** **(-s, -)** *m(f)* smoker;
~erabteil *nt* (*EISENB*) smoker; **räuchern** *vt*
to smoke, to cure; **~fleisch** *nt* smoked
meat; **r~ig** *adj* smoky

rauf [raʊf] (*umg*) *adv* = **herauf**; **hinauf**

raufen *vt* (*Haare*) to pull out ♦ *vi*, *vr* to fight;
Raufe'rei *f* brawl, fight

rauh △ *etc* [raʊ] *adj siehe* **rau** *etc*

Raum [raʊm] **(-(e)s, Räume)** *m* space;
(*Zimmer*, *Platz*) room; (*Gebiet*) area

räumen ['rɔʏmən] *vt* to clear; (*Wohnung*,
Platz) to vacate; (*wegbringen*) to shift, to
move; (*in Schrank etc*) to put away

Raum- *zW*: **~fähre** *f* space shuttle; **~fahrt** *f*
space travel; **~inhalt** *m* cubic capacity,
volume

räumlich ['rɔʏmlɪç] *adj* spatial; **R~keiten** *pl*
premises

Raum- *zW*: **~pflegerin** *f* cleaner; **~schiff**
nt spaceship; **~schifffahrt** ▲ *f* space
travel

Räumung ['rɔʏmʊŋ] *f* vacating, evacuation;
clearing (away)

Räumungs- *zW*: **~arbeiten** *pl* clearance
operations; **~verkauf** *m* clearance sale; (*bei
Geschäftsaufgabe*) closing down sale

raunen ['raʊnən] *vt*, *vi* to whisper

Raupe ['raʊpə] *f* caterpillar; (*~nkette*)
(caterpillar) track

Raureif ▲ ['raʊraɪf] *m* hoarfrost

raus [raʊs] (*umg*) *adv* = **heraus**; **hinaus**

Rausch [raʊʃ] **(-(e)s, Räusche)** *m*
intoxication

rauschen *vi* (*Wasser*) to rush; (*Baum*) to
rustle; (*Radio etc*) to hiss; (*Mensch*) to
sweep, to sail; **~d** *adj* (*Beifall*) thunderous;
(*Fest*) sumptuous

Rauschgift *nt* drug; **~süchtige(r)** *f(m)*
drug addict

räuspern ['rɔʏspərn] *vr* to clear one's throat

Razzia ['ratsia] **(-, Razzien)** *f* raid

Reagenzglas [rea'gɛntsglaːs] *nt* test tube

reagieren [rea'giːrən] *vi*: **~ (auf** +*akk*) to
react (to)

Reakt- *zW*: **~ion** [reaktsi'oːn] *f* reaction;
r~io'när *adj* reactionary; **~or** [re'aktɔr] *m*
reactor

real [re'aːl] *adj* real, material

reali'sieren *vt* (*verwirklichen: Pläne*) to carry
out

Realismus [rea'lɪsmʊs] *m* realism

rea'listisch *adj* realistic

Realschule *f* secondary school

Realschule

i The **Realschule** is one of the secondary
schools a German schoolchild may
attend after the **Grundschule**. On the
successful completion of six years of
schooling in the **Realschule** pupils gain the
mittlere Reife and usually go on to
vocational training or further education.

Rebe ['reːbə] *f* vine

rebellieren [rebɛ'liːrən] *vi* to rebel;
Rebelli'on *f* rebellion; **re'bellisch** *adj*
rebellious

Rebhuhn ['rɛphuːn] *nt* (*KOCH*, *ZOOL*)
partridge

Rechen ['rɛçən] **(-s, -)** *m* rake

Rechen- *zW*: **~fehler** *m* miscalculation;
~maschine *f* calculating machine;
~schaft *f* account; **für etw ~schaft
ablegen** to account for sth; **~schieber** *m*
slide rule

Rech- ['rɛç] *zW*: **r~nen** *vt*, *vi* to calculate;
jdn/etw r~nen zu to count sb/sth among;
r~nen mit to reckon with; **r~nen auf** +*akk*
to count on; **~nen** *nt* arithmetic; **~ner** **(-s,
-)** *m* calculator; (*COMPUT*) computer; **~nung**
f calculation(s); (*COMM*) bill, check (*US*);
jdm/etw ~nung tragen to take sb/sth into
account; **~nungsbetrag** *m* total amount
of a bill/invoice; **~nungsjahr** *nt* financial
year; **~nungsprüfer** *m* auditor

Recht [rɛçt] **(-(e)s, -e)** *nt* right; (*JUR*) law;
mit ~ rightly, justly; **R~ haben** to be right;
jdm R~ geben to agree with sb; **von ~s
wegen** by rights

recht *adj* right ♦ *adv* (*vor Adjektiv*) really,
quite; **das ist mir ~** that suits me; **jetzt
erst ~** now more than ever

Rechte *f* right (hand); (*POL*) Right; **r~(r, s)**
adj right; (*POL*) right-wing; **ein ~r** a right-

---

winger; ~(s) nt right thing; **etwas/nichts ~s** something/nothing proper

recht- zW: **~eckig** adj rectangular; **~fertigen** vt insep to justify ♦ vr insep to justify o.s.; **R~fertigung** f justification; **~haberisch** (pej) adj (Mensch) opinionated; **~lich** adj (gesetzlich: Gleichstellung, Anspruch) legal; **~los** adj with no rights; **~mäßig** adj legal, lawful

rechts [reçts] adv on/to the right; **R~anwalt** m lawyer, barrister; **R~anwältin** f lawyer, barrister

Rechtschreibung f spelling

Rechts- zW: **~fall** m (law) case; **~händer** (-s, -) m right-handed person; **r~kräftig** adj valid, legal; **~kurve** f right-hand bend; **r~verbindlich** adj legally binding; **~verkehr** m driving on the right; **r~widrig** adj illegal; **~wissenschaft** f jurisprudence

rechtwinklig adj right-angled

rechtzeitig adj timely ♦ adv in time

Reck [rɛk] (-(e)s, -e) nt horizontal bar; **r~en** vt, vr to stretch

recyceln [riː'saɪkəln] vt to recycle; **Recycling** [riː'saɪklɪŋ] (-s) nt recycling

Redakteur [redak'tøːr] m editor

Redaktion [redaktsi'oːn] f editing; (Leute) editorial staff; (Büro) editorial office(s)

Rede ['reːdə] f speech; (Gespräch) talk; **jdn zur ~ stellen** to take sb to task; **~freiheit** f freedom of speech; **r~gewandt** adj eloquent; **r~n** vi to talk, to speak ♦ vt to say; (Unsinn etc) to talk; **~nsart** f set phrase

redlich ['reːtlɪç] adj honest

Redner (-s, -) m speaker, orator

redselig ['reːtzeːlɪç] adj talkative, loquacious

reduzieren [redu'tsiːrən] vt to reduce

Reede ['reːdə] f protected anchorage; **~r** (-s, -) m shipowner; **~'rei** f shipping line od firm

reell [re'ɛl] adj fair, honest; (MATH) real

Refer- zW: **~at** [refe'raːt] (-(e)s, -e) nt report; (Vortrag) paper; (Gebiet) section; **~ent** [refe'rɛnt] m speaker; (Berichterstatter) reporter; (Sachbearbeiter) expert; **r~ieren** [refe'riːrən] vi: **r~ieren über** +akk to speak

od talk on

reflektieren [reflɛk'tiːrən] vt (Licht) to reflect

Reflex [re'flɛks] (-es, -e) m reflex; **r~iv** [-'ksiːf] adj (GRAM) reflexive

Reform [re'fɔrm] (-, -en) f reform; **~ati'on** f reformation; **~ationstag** m Reformation Day; **~haus** nt health food shop; **r~ieren** [-'miːrən] vt to reform

Regal [re'gaːl] (-s, -e) nt (book)shelves pl, bookcase; stand, rack

rege ['reːgə] adj (lebhaft: Treiben) lively; (wach, lebendig: Geist) keen

Regel ['reːgəl] (-, -n) f rule; (MED) period; **r~mäßig** adj regular; **~mäßigkeit** f regularity; **r~n** vt to regulate, to control; (Angelegenheit) to settle ♦ vr: **sich von selbst r~n** to take care of itself; **r~recht** adj regular, proper, thorough; **~ung** f regulation; settlement; **r~widrig** adj irregular, against the rules

Regen ['reːgən] (-s, -) m rain; **~bogen** m rainbow; **~bogenpresse** f tabloids pl

regenerierbar [regene'riːrbaːr] adj renewable

Regen- zW: **~mantel** m raincoat, mac(kintosh); **~schauer** m shower (of rain); **~schirm** m umbrella; **~wald** m (GEOG) rainforest; **~wurm** m earthworm; **~zeit** f rainy season

Regie [re'ʒiː] f (Film etc) direction; (THEAT) production

Regier- [re'giːr] zW: **r~en** vt, vi to govern, to rule; **~ung** f government; (Monarchie) reign; **~ungssitz** m seat of government; **~ungswechsel** m change of government; **~ungszeit** f period in government; (von König) reign

Regiment [regi'mɛnt] (-s, -er) nt regiment

Region [regi'oːn] f region

Regisseur [reʒɪ'søːr] m director; (THEAT) (stage) producer

Register [re'gɪstər] (-s, -) nt register; (in Buch) table of contents, index

registrieren [regɪs'triːrən] vt to register

Regler ['reːglər] (-s, -) m regulator, governor

reglos ['reːkloːs] adj motionless

regnen ['reːgnən] vi unpers to rain

regnerisch *adj* rainy

regulär [regu'lɛːr] *adj* regular

regulieren [regu'liːrən] *vt* to regulate; (*COMM*) to settle

Regung ['reːgʊŋ] *f* motion; (*Gefühl*) feeling, impulse; **r~slos** *adj* motionless

Reh [reː] **(-(e)s, -e)** *nt* deer, roe; **~bock** *m* roebuck; **~kitz** *nt* fawn

Reib- ['raɪb] *zW*: **~e** *f* grater; **~eisen** *nt* grater; **r~en** (*unreg*) *vt* to rub; (*KOCH*) to grate; **~fläche** *f* rough surface; **~ung** *f* friction; **r~ungslos** *adj* smooth

Reich **(-(e)s, -e)** *nt* empire, kingdom; (*fig*) realm; **das Dritte R~** the Third Reich

reich [raɪç] *adj* rich

reichen *vi* to reach; (*genügen*) to be enough *od* sufficient ♦ *vt* to hold out; (*geben*) to pass, to hand; (*anbieten*) to offer; **jdm ~** to be enough *od* sufficient for sb

reich- *zW*: **~haltig** *adj* ample, rich; **~lich** *adj* ample, plenty of; **R~tum (-s)** *m* wealth; **R~weite** *f* range

Reif **(-(e)s, -e)** *m* (*Ring*) ring, hoop

reif [raɪf] *adj* ripe; (*Mensch, Urteil*) mature

Reife (-) *f* ripeness; maturity; **r~n** *vi* to mature; to ripen

Reihe ['raɪə] *f* row; (*von Tagen etc, umg: Anzahl*) series *sg*; **der ~ nach** in turn; **er ist an der ~** it's his turn; **an die ~ kommen** to have one's turn

Reihen- *zW*: **~folge** *f* sequence; **alphabetische ~folge** alphabetical order; **~haus** *nt* terraced house

reihum [raɪ'ʊm] *adv*: **es geht/wir machen das ~** we take turns

Reim [raɪm] **(-(e)s, -e)** *m* rhyme; **r~en** *vt* to rhyme

rein¹ [raɪn] (*umg*) *adv* = **herein; hinein**

rein² [raɪn] *adj* pure; (*sauber*) clean ♦ *adv* purely; **etw ins R~e schreiben** to make a fair copy of sth; **etw ins R~e bringen** to clear up sth; **R~fall** (*umg*) *m* let-down; **R~gewinn** *m* net profit; **R~heit** *f* purity; cleanness; **r~igen** *vt* to clean; (*Wasser*) to

purify; **R~igung** *f* cleaning; purification; (*Geschäft*) cleaner's; **chemische R~igung** dry cleaning; dry cleaner's; **R~igungsmittel** *nt* cleansing agent; **~rassig** *adj* pedigree; **R~schrift** *f* fair copy

Reis [raɪs] **(-es, -e)** *m* rice

Reise ['raɪzə] *f* journey; (*Schiffsreise*) voyage; **~n** *pl* (*Herumreisen*) travels; **gute ~!** have a good journey; **~apotheke** *f* first-aid kit; **~büro** *nt* travel agency; **r~fertig** *adj* ready to start; **~führer** *m* guide(book); (*Mensch*) travel guide; **~gepäck** *nt* luggage; **~gesellschaft** *f* party of travellers; **~kosten** *pl* travelling expenses; **~leiter** *m* courier; **~lektüre** *f* reading matter for the journey; **r~n** *vi* to travel; **r~n nach** to go to; **~nde(r)** *f(m)* traveller; **~pass** ▲ *m* passport; **~proviant** *m* food and drink for the journey; **~route** *f* route, itinerary; **~ruf** *m* personal message; **~scheck** *m* traveller's cheque; **~veranstalter** *m* tour operator; **~versicherung** *f* travel insurance; **~ziel** *nt* destination

Reißbrett *nt* drawing board

reißen ['raɪsən] (*unreg*) *vt* to tear; (*ziehen*) to pull, to drag; (*Witz*) to crack ♦ *vi* to tear; to pull, to drag; **etw an sich ~** to snatch sth up; (*fig*) to take over sth; **sich um etw ~** to scramble for sth; **~d** *adj* (*Fluss*) raging; (*WIRTS: Verkauf*) rapid

Reiß- *zW*: **~verschluss** ▲ *m* zip(per), zip fastener; **~zwecke** *m* drawing pin (*BRIT*), thumbtack (*US*)

Reit- ['raɪt] *zW*: **r~en** (*unreg*) *vt, vi* to ride; **~er (-s, -)** *m* rider; (*MIL*) cavalryman, trooper; **~erin** *f* rider; **~hose** *f* riding breeches *pl*; **~pferd** *nt* saddle horse; **~stiefel** *m* riding boot; **~weg** *n* bridle path; **~zeug** *nt* riding outfit

Reiz [raɪts] **(-es, -e)** *m* stimulus; (*angenehm*) charm; (*Verlockung*) attraction; **r~bar** *adj* irritable; **~barkeit** *f* irritability; **r~en** *vt* to stimulate; (*unangenehm*) to irritate; (*verlocken*) to appeal to, to attract; **r~end** *adj* charming; **r~voll** *adj* attractive

rekeln ['reːkəln] *vr* to stretch out; (*lümmeln*)

to lounge *od* loll about

Reklamation [reklamatsiˈoːn] *f* complaint

Reklame [reˈklaːmə] *f* advertising; advertisement; ~ **machen für etw** to advertise sth

rekonstruieren [rekɔnstruˈiːrən] *vt* to reconstruct

Rekord [reˈkɔrt] (**-(e)s, -e**) *m* record; ~**leistung** *f* record performance

Rektor [ˈrektɔr] *m* (UNIV) rector, vice-chancellor; (SCH) headteacher (BRIT), principal (US); ~**at** [-ˈraːt] (**-(e)s, -e**) *nt* rectorate, vice-chancellorship; headship; (Zimmer) rector's *etc* office

Relais [rəˈleː] (**-, -**) *nt* relay

relativ [relaˈtiːf] *adj* relative; **R~ität** [relativiˈtɛːt] *f* relativity

relevant [releˈvant] *adj* relevant

Relief [reliˈɛf] (**-s, -s**) *nt* relief

Religion [religiˈoːn] *f* religion

religiös [religiˈøːs] *adj* religious

Reling [ˈreːlɪŋ] (**-, -s**) *f* (NAUT) rail

Remoulade [remuˈlaːdə] *f* remoulade

Rendezvous [rãdeˈvuː] (**-, -**) *nt* rendezvous

Renn- [ˈren] *zW:* ~**bahn** *f* racecourse; (AUT) circuit, race track; **r~en** (unreg) *vt, vi* to run, to race; ~**en** (**-s, -**) *nt* running; (Wettbewerb) race; ~**fahrer** *m* racing driver; ~**pferd** *nt* racehorse; ~**wagen** *m* racing car

renommiert [renɔˈmiːrt] *adj* renowned

renovieren [renoˈviːrən] *vt* to renovate; **Renovierung** *f* renovation

rentabel [renˈtaːbəl] *adj* profitable, lucrative

Rentabilität [rentabiliˈtɛːt] *f* profitability

Rente [ˈrentə] *f* pension

Rentenversicherung *f* pension scheme

rentieren [renˈtiːrən] *vr* to pay, to be profitable

Rentner(in) [ˈrentnər(ɪn)] (**-s, -**) *m(f)* pensioner

Reparatur [reparaˈtuːr] *f* repairing; repair; ~**werkstatt** *f* repair shop; (AUT) garage

reparieren [repaˈriːrən] *vt* to repair

Reportage [repɔrˈtaːʒə] *f* (on-the-spot) report; (TV, RADIO) live commentary *od* coverage

Reporter [reˈpɔrtər] (**-s, -**) *m* reporter, commentator

repräsentativ [reprezɛntaˈtiːf] *adj* (stellvertretend, typisch: Menge, Gruppe) representative; (beeindruckend: Haus, Auto etc) impressive

repräsentieren [reprezɛnˈtiːrən] *vt* (Staat, Firma) to represent; (darstellen: Wert) to constitute ♦ *vi* (gesellschaftlich) to perform official duties

Repressalie [represˈaːliə] *f* reprisal

Reprivatisierung [reprivatiˈziːrʊŋ] *f* denationalization

Reproduktion [reprodʊktsiˈoːn] *f* reproduction

reproduzieren [reprodʊˈtsiːrən] *vt* to reproduce

Reptil [repˈtiːl] (**-s, -ien**) *nt* reptile

Republik [repuˈbliːk] *f* republic; **r~anisch** *adj* republican

Reservat [rezɛrˈvaːt] (**-(e)s, -e**) *nt* reservation

Reserve [reˈzɛrvə] *f* reserve; ~**rad** *nt* (AUT) spare wheel; ~**spieler** *m* reserve; ~**tank** *m* reserve tank

reservieren [rezɛrˈviːrən] *vt* to reserve

Reservoir [rezɛrvoˈaːr] (**-s, -e**) *nt* reservoir

Residenz [reziˈdents] *f* residence, seat

resignieren [reziˈgniːrən] *vi* to resign

resolut [rezoˈluːt] *adj* resolute

Resonanz [rezoˈnants] *f* resonance; (fig) response

Resozialisierung [rezotsiali ziˈrʊŋ] *f* rehabilitation

Respekt [reˈspekt] (**-(e)s**) *m* respect; **r~ieren** [-ˈtiːrən] *vt* to respect; **r~los** *adj* disrespectful; **r~voll** *adj* respectful

Ressort [reˈsoːr] (**-s, -s**) *nt* department

Rest [rest] (**-(e)s, -e**) *m* remainder, rest; (Überrest) remains *pl*

Restaurant [restoˈrãː] (**-s, -s**) *nt* restaurant

restaurieren [restauˈriːrən] *vt* to restore

Rest- *zW:* ~**betrag** *m* remainder, outstanding sum; **r~lich** *adj* remaining; **r~los** *adj* complete

Resultat [rezʊlˈtaːt] (**-(e)s, -e**) *nt* result

Retorte [reˈtɔrtə] *f* retort

Spelling Reform: ▲ *new spelling* △ *old spelling (to be phased out)*

Retouren [re'tuːrən] *pl* (*COMM*) returns
retten ['rɛtən] *vt* to save, to rescue
Retter(in) *m(f)* rescuer
Rettich ['rɛtɪç] **(-s, -e)** *m* radish
Rettung *f* rescue; (*Hilfe*) help; **seine letzte ~** his last hope
Rettungs- *zW*: **~boot** *nt* lifeboat; **~dienst** *m* rescue service; **r~los** *adj* hopeless; **~ring** *m* lifebelt, life preserver (*US*); **~wagen** *m* ambulance
retuschieren [retu'ʃiːrən] *vt* (*PHOT*) to retouch
Reue ['rɔyə] **(-)** *f* remorse; (*Bedauern*) regret; **r~n** *vt*: **es reut ihn** he regrets (it) *od* is sorry (about it)
Revanche [re'vãːʃə] *f* revenge; (*SPORT*) return match
revanchieren [revã'ʃiːrən] *vr* (*sich rächen*) to get one's own back, to have one's revenge; (*erwidern*) to reciprocate, to return the compliment
Revier [re'viːr] **(-s, -e)** *nt* district; (*Jagdrevier*) preserve; (*Polizeirevier*) police station; beat
Revolte [re'vɔltə] *f* revolt
revol'tieren *vi* (*gegen jdn/etw*) to rebel
Revolution [revolutsi'oːn] *f* revolution; **~är** [-'nɛːr] **(-s, -e)** *m* revolutionary; **r~ieren** [-'niːrən] *vt* to revolutionize
Rezept [re'tsɛpt] **(-(e)s, -e)** *nt* recipe; (*MED*) prescription; **r~frei** *adj* available without prescription; **~ion** *f* reception; **r~pflichtig** *adj* available only on prescription
R-Gespräch ['ɛrgəʃprɛːç] *nt* reverse charge call (*BRIT*), collect call (*US*)
Rhabarber [ra'barbar] **(-s)** *m* rhubarb
Rhein [raɪn] **(-s)** *m* Rhine; **r~isch** *adj* Rhenish
Rheinland-Pfalz *nt* (*GEOG*) Rheinland-Pfalz, Rhineland-Palatinate
Rhesusfaktor ['reːzusfaktɔr] *m* rhesus factor
rhetorisch [re'toːrɪʃ] *adj* rhetorical
Rheuma ['rɔyma] **(-s)** *nt* rheumatism; **r~tisch** [-'maːtɪʃ] *adj* rheumatic
rhythmisch ['rʏtmɪʃ] *adj* rhythmical
Rhythmus ['rʏtmʊs] *m* rhythm
richt- ['rɪçt] *zW*: **~en** *vt* to direct; (*Waffe*) to aim; (*einstellen*) to adjust; (*instandsetzen*) to

repair; (*zurechtmachen*) to prepare; (*bestrafen*) to pass judgement on ♦ *vr*: **sich ~en nach** to go by; **~en an** +*akk* to direct at; (*fig*) to direct to; **~en auf** +*akk* to aim at; **R~er(in)** **(-s, -)** *m(f)* judge; **~erlich** *adj* judicial; **R~geschwindigkeit** *f* recommended speed
richtig *adj* right, correct; (*echt*) proper ♦ *adv* (*umg: sehr*) really; **bin ich hier ~?** am I in the right place?; **der/die R~e** the right one/person; **das R~e** the right thing; **etw ~ stellen** to correct sth; **R~keit** *f* correctness
Richt- *zW*: **~linie** *f* guideline; **~preis** *m* recommended price
Richtung *f* direction; tendency, orientation
rieb *etc* [riːp] *vb siehe* **reiben**
riechen ['riːçən] (*unreg*) *vt, vi* to smell; **an etw** *dat* **~** to smell sth; **nach etw ~** to smell of sth; **ich kann das/ihn nicht ~** (*umg*) I can't stand it/him
rief *etc* [riːf] *vb siehe* **rufen**
Riegel ['riːgəl] **(-s, -)** *m* bolt; (*Schokolade usw*) bar
Riemen ['riːmən] **(-s, -)** *m* strap; (*Gürtel, TECH*) belt; (*NAUT*) oar
Riese ['riːzə] **(-n, -n)** *m* giant
rieseln *vi* to trickle; (*Schnee*) to fall gently
Riesen- *zW*: **~erfolg** *m* enormous success; **r~groß** *adj* colossal, gigantic, huge; **~rad** *nt* big wheel
riesig ['riːzɪç] *adj* enormous, huge, vast
riet *etc* [riːt] *vb siehe* **raten**
Riff [rɪf] **(-(e)s, -e)** *nt* reef
Rille ['rɪlə] *f* groove
Rind [rɪnt] **(-(e)s, -er)** *nt* ox; cow; cattle *pl*; (*KOCH*) beef
Rinde ['rɪndə] *f* rind; (*Baumrinde*) bark; (*Brotrinde*) crust
Rind- *zW*: **~fleisch** *nt* beef; **~vieh** *nt* cattle *pl*; (*umg*) blockhead, stupid oaf
Ring [rɪŋ] **(-(e)s, -e)** *m* ring; **~buch** *nt* ring binder; **r~en** (*unreg*) *vi* to wrestle; **~en** **(-s)** *nt* wrestling; **~finger** *m* ring finger; **~kampf** *m* wrestling bout; **~richter** *m* referee; **r~s** *adv*: **r~s um** round; **r~sherum** *adv* round about; **~straße** *f*

ring road; **r~sum** *adv* (*rundherum*) round about; (*überall*) all round; **r~sumher =** **ringsum**

Rinn- ['rɪn] *zW:* **~e** *f* gutter, drain; **r~en** (*unreg*) *vi* to run, to trickle; **~stein** *m* gutter

Rippchen ['rɪpçən] *nt* small rib; cutlet

Rippe ['rɪpə] *f* rib

Risiko ['riːziko] (**-s, -s** *od* **Risiken**) *nt* risk

riskant [rɪs'kant] *adj* risky, hazardous

riskieren [rɪs'kiːrən] *vt* to risk

Riss ▲ [rɪs] (**-es, -e**) *m* tear; (*in Mauer, Tasse etc*) crack; (*in Haut*) scratch; (*TECH*) design

rissig ['rɪsɪç] *adj* torn; cracked; scratched

Ritt [rɪt] (**-(e)s, -e**) *m* ride

ritt *etc vb siehe* **reiten**

Ritter (**-s, -**) *m* knight; **r~lich** *adj* chivalrous

Ritze ['rɪtsə] *f* crack, chink

Rivale [ri'vaːlə] (**-n, -n**) *m* rival

Rivalität [rivali'tɛːt] *f* rivalry

Robbe ['rɔbə] *f* seal

Roboter ['rɔbɔtər] (**-s, -**) *m* robot

robust [ro'bʊst] *adj* (*kräftig: Mensch, Gesundheit*) robust

roch *etc vb siehe* **riechen**

Rock [rɔk] (**-(e)s, ⸚e**) *m* skirt; (*Jackett*) jacket; (*Uniformrock*) tunic

Rodel ['roːdəl] (**-s, -**) *m* toboggan; **~bahn** *f* toboggan run; **r~n** *vi* to toboggan

Rogen ['roːgən] (**-s, -**) *m* roe, spawn

Roggen ['rɔgən] (**-s, -**) *m* rye; **~brot** *nt* (*KOCH*) rye bread

roh [roː] *adj* raw; (*Mensch*) coarse, crude; **R~bau** *m* shell of a building; **R~material** *nt* raw material; **R~öl** *nt* crude oil

Rohr [roːr] (**-(e)s, -e**) *nt* pipe, tube; (*BOT*) cane; (*Schilf*) reed; (*Gewehrrohr*) barrel; **~bruch** *m* burst pipe

Röhre ['røːrə] *f* tube, pipe; (*RADIO etc*) valve; (*Backröhre*) oven

Rohr- *zW:* **~leitung** *f* pipeline; **~zucker** *m* cane sugar

Rohstoff *m* raw material

Rokoko ['rɔkoko] (**-s**) *nt* rococo

Rolladen △ *m siehe* **Rollladen**

Rollbahn ['rɔlbaːn] *f* (*AVIAT*) runway

Rolle ['rɔlə] *f* roll; (*THEAT, soziologisch*) role; (*Garnrolle etc*) reel, spool; (*Walze*) roller;

(*Wäscherolle*) mangle; **keine ~ spielen** not to matter; **eine (wichtige) ~ spielen bei** to play a (major) part *od* role in; **r~n** *vt, vi* to roll; (*AVIAT*) to taxi; **~r** (**-s, -**) *m* scooter; (*Welle*) roller

Roll- *zW:* **~kragen** *m* rollneck, polo neck; **~laden ▲** *m* shutter; **~mops** *m* pickled herring; **~schuh** *m* roller skate; **~stuhl** *m* wheelchair; **~stuhlfahrer(in)** *m(f)* wheelchair user; **~treppe** *f* escalator

Rom [roːm] (**-s**) *nt* Rome

Roman [ro'maːn] (**-s, -e**) *m* novel; **~tik** *f* romanticism; **~tiker** [ro'mantikər] (**-s, -**) *m* romanticist; **r~tisch** [ro'mantɪʃ] *adj* romantic; **~ze** [ro'mantsə] *f* romance

Römer ['røːmər] (**-s, -**) *m* wineglass; (*Mensch*) Roman

römisch ['røːmɪʃ] *adj* Roman; **~-katholisch** *adj* (*REL*) Roman Catholic

röntgen ['rœntgən] *vt* to X-ray; **R~bild** *nt* X-ray; **R~strahlen** *pl* X-rays

rosa ['roːza] *adj inv* pink, rose(-coloured)

Rose ['roːzə] *f* rose

Rosen- *zW:* **~kohl** *m* Brussels sprouts *pl*; **~kranz** *m* rosary; **~montag** *m* Monday before Ash Wednesday

rosig ['roːzɪç] *adj* rosy

Rosine [ro'ziːnə] *f* raisin, currant

Ross ▲ [rɔs] (**-es, -e**) *nt* horse, steed; **~kastanie** *f* horse chestnut

Rost [rɔst] (**-(e)s, -e**) *m* rust; (*Gitter*) grill, gridiron; (*Bettrost*) springs *pl*; **~braten** *m* roast(ed) meat, roast; **r~en** *vi* to rust

rösten ['røːstən] *vt* to roast; to toast; to grill

Rost- *zW:* **r~frei** *adj* rust-free; rustproof; stainless; **r~ig** *adj* rusty; **~schutz** *m* rust-proofing

rot [roːt] *adj* red; **in den ~en Zahlen** in the red

Röte ['røːtə] (**-**) *f* redness; **~ln** *pl* German measles *sg*; **r~n** *vt, vr* to redden

rothaarig *adj* red-haired

rotieren [ro'tiːrən] *vi* to rotate

Rot- *zW:* **~kehlchen** *nt* robin; **~stift** *m* red pencil; **~wein** *m* red wine

Rouge [ruːʒ] *nt* blusher

Roulade [ru'laːdə] *f* (*KOCH*) beef olive

Route ['ru:tə] f route

Routine [ru'ti:nə] f experience; routine

Rübe ['ry:bə] f turnip; **Gelbe ~** carrot; **Rote ~** beetroot (*BRIT*), beet (*US*)

rüber ['ry:bɐ] (*umg*) adv = **herüber; hinüber**

Rubrik [ru'bri:k] f heading; (*Spalte*) column

Ruck [rʊk] (**-(e)s, -e**) m jerk, jolt

Rück- ['rʏk] zW: **~antwort** f reply, answer; **r~bezüglich** adj reflexive

Rücken ['rʏkən] (**-s, -**) m back; (*Bergrücken*) ridge

rücken vt, vi to move

Rücken- zW: **~mark** nt spinal cord; **~schwimmen** nt backstroke

Rück- zW: **~erstattung** f return, restitution; **~fahrkarte** f return (ticket); **~fahrt** f return journey; **~fall** m relapse; **r~fällig** adj relapsing; **r~fällig werden** to relapse; **~flug** m return flight; **~frage** f question; **r~fragen** vi to check, to inquire (further); **~gabe** f return; **~gaberecht** nt right of return; **~gang** m decline, fall; **r~gängig** adj: **etw r~gängig machen** to cancel sth; **~grat** (**-(e)s, -e**) nt spine, backbone; **~halt** m (*Unterstützung*) backing, support; **~kehr** (**-, -en**) f return; **~licht** nt back light; **r~lings** adv from behind; backwards; **~nahme** f taking back; **~porto** nt return postage; **~reise** f return journey; (*NAUT*) home voyage; **~reiseverkehr** m homebound traffic; **~ruf** m recall

Rucksack ['rʊkzak] m rucksack; **~tourist(in)** m(f) backpacker

Rück- zW: **~schau** f reflection; **~schlag** m (*plötzliche Verschlechterung*) setback; **~schluss** ▲ m conclusion; **~schritt** m retrogression; **r~schrittlich** adj reactionary; retrograde; **~seite** f back; (*von Münze etc*) reverse; **~sicht** f consideration; **~sicht nehmen auf** +*akk* to show consideration for; **r~sichtslos** adj inconsiderate; (*Fahren*) reckless; (*unbarmherzig*) ruthless; **r~sichtsvoll** adj considerate; **~sitz** m back seat; **~spiegel** m (*AUT*) rear-view mirror; **~spiel** nt return match; **~sprache** f further discussion od talk; **~stand** m arrears pl; **r~ständig** adj

backward, out-of-date; (*Zahlungen*) in arrears; **~strahler**(**-s, -**) m rear reflector; **~tritt** m resignation; **~trittbremse** f pedal brake; **~vergütung** f repayment; (*COMM*) refund; **~versicherung** f reinsurance; **r~wärtig** adj rear; **r~wärts** adv backward(s), back; **~wärtsgang** m (*AUT*) reverse gear; **~weg** m return journey, way back; **r~wirkend** adj retroactive; **~wirkung** f reaction; retrospective effect; **~zahlung** f repayment; **~zug** m retreat

Rudel ['ru:dəl] (**-s, -**) nt pack; herd

Ruder ['ru:dɐ] (**-s, -**) nt oar; (*Steuer*) rudder; **~boot** nt rowing boat; **r~n** vt, vi to row

Ruf [ru:f] (**-(e)s, -e**) m call, cry; (*Ansehen*) reputation; **r~en** (*unreg*) vt, vi to call; to cry; **~name** m usual (first) name; **~nummer** f (tele)phone number; **~säule** f (*an Autobahn*) emergency telephone; **~zeichen** nt (*RADIO*) call sign; (*TEL*) ringing tone

rügen ['ry:gən] vt to rebuke

Ruhe ['ru:ə] (**-**) f rest; (*Ungestörtheit*) peace, quiet; (*Gelassenheit, Stille*) calm; (*Schweigen*) silence; **jdn in ~ lassen** to leave sb alone; **sich zur ~ setzen** to retire; **~! be quiet!**, silence!; **r~n** vi to rest; **~pause** f break; **~stand** m retirement; **~stätte** f: **letzte ~stätte** final resting place; **~störung** f breach of the peace; **~tag** m (*von Geschäft*) closing day

ruhig ['ru:ɪç] adj quiet; (*bewegungslos*) still; (*Hand*) steady; (*gelassen, friedlich*) calm; (*Gewissen*) clear; **kommen Sie ~ herein** just come on in; **tu das ~** feel free to do that

Ruhm [ru:m] (**-(e)s**) m fame, glory

rühmen ['ry:mən] vt to praise ♦ vr to boast

Rühr- [ry:r] zW: **~ei** nt scrambled egg; **r~en** vt, vr (*auch fig*) to move, to stir ♦ vi: **r~en von** to come od stem from; **r~en an** +*akk* to touch; (*fig*) to touch on; **r~end** adj touching, moving; **r~selig** adj sentimental, emotional; **~ung** f emotion

Ruin [ru'i:n] (**-s, -e**) m ruin; **~e** f ruin; **r~ieren** [-'ni:rən] vt to ruin

rülpsen ['rʏlpsən] vi to burp, to belch

Rum [rʊm] (**-s, -s**) m rum

Rumän- [ru'mɛːn] *zW:* **~ien (-s)** *nt* Ro(u)mania; **r~isch** *adj* Ro(u)manian

Rummel ['rʊməl] **(-s)** *(umg)* *m* hubbub; *(Jahrmarkt)* fair; **~platz** *m* fairground, fair

Rumpf [rʊmpf] **(-(e)s, ⁓e)** *m* trunk, torso; *(AVIAT)* fuselage; *(NAUT)* hull

rümpfen ['rʊmpfən] *vt (Nase)* to turn up

rund [rʊnt] *adj* round ♦ *adv (etwa)* around; **~ um etw** round sth; **R~brief** *m* circular; **R~e** ['rʊndə] *f* round; *(in Rennen)* lap; *(Gesellschaft)* circle; **R~fahrt** *f* (round) trip

Rundfunk ['rʊntfʊŋk] **(-(e)s)** *m* broadcasting; **im ~** on the radio; **~gerät** *nt* wireless set; **~sendung** *f* broadcast, radio programme

Rund- *zW:* **r~heraus** *adv* straight out, bluntly; **r~herum** *adv* round about; all round; **r~lich** *adj* plump, rounded; **~reise** *f* round trip; **~schreiben** *nt (COMM)* circular; **~(wander)weg** *m* circular path *od* route

runter ['rʊntər] *(umg)* *adv* = **herunter; hinunter**

Runzel ['rʊntsəl] **(-, -n)** *f* wrinkle; **r~ig** *adj* wrinkled; **r~n** *vt* to wrinkle; **die Stirn r~n** to frown

rupfen ['rʊpfən] *vt* to pluck

ruppig ['rʊpɪç] *adj* rough, gruff

Rüsche ['ryːʃə] *f* frill

Ruß [ruːs] **(-es)** *m* soot

Russe ['rʊsə] **(-n, -n)** *m* Russian

Rüssel ['rʊsəl] **(-s, -)** *m* snout; *(Elefantenrüssel)* trunk

rußig ['ruːsɪç] *adj* sooty

Russin ['rʊsɪn] *f* Russian

russisch *adj* Russian

Russland ▲ ['rʊslant] **(-s)** *nt* Russia

rüsten ['rʊstən] *vt* to prepare ♦ *vi* to prepare; *(MIL)* to arm ♦ *vr* to prepare (o.s.); to arm o.s.

rüstig ['rʊstɪç] *adj* sprightly, vigorous

Rüstung ['rʊstʊŋ] *f* preparation; arming; *(Ritterrüstung)* armour; *(Waffen etc)* armaments *pl*; **~skontrolle** *f* arms control

Rute ['ruːtə] *f* rod

Rutsch [rʊtʃ] **(-(e)s, -e)** *m* slide; *(Erdrutsch)* landslide; **~bahn** *f* slide; **r~en** *vi* to slide; .

(ausrutschen) to slip; **r~ig** *adj* slippery

rütteln ['rʊtəln] *vt, vi* to shake, to jolt

S, s

S. *abk (= Seite)* p.; = **Schilling**

s. *abk (= siehe)* see

Saal [zaːl] **(-(e)s, Säle)** *m* hall; room

Saarland ['zaːrlant] *nt:* **das ~** the Saar(land)

Saat [zaːt] **(-, -en)** *f* seed; *(Pflanzen)* crop; *(Säen)* sowing

Säbel ['zɛːbəl] **(-s, -)** *m* sabre, sword

Sabotage [zabo'taːʒə] *f* sabotage

Sach- ['zax] *zW:* **~bearbeiter** *m* specialist; **s~dienlich** *adj* relevant, helpful; **~e** *f* thing; *(Angelegenheit)* affair, business; *(Frage)* matter; *(Pflicht)* task; **zur ~e** to the point; **s~kundig** *adj* expert; **s~lich** *adj* matter-of-fact; objective; *(Irrtum, Angabe)* factual

sächlich ['zɛçlɪç] *adj* neuter

Sachschaden *m* material damage

Sachsen ['zaksən] **(-s)** *nt* Saxony

sächsisch ['zɛksɪʃ] *adj* Saxon

sacht(e) ['zaxt(ə)] *adv* softly, gently

Sachverständige(r) *f(m)* expert

Sack [zak] **(-(e)s, ⁓e)** *m* sack; **~gasse** *f* cul-de-sac, dead-end street *(US)*

Sadismus [za'dɪsmʊs] *m* sadism

Sadist [za'dɪst] *m* sadist

säen ['zɛːən] *vt, vi* to sow

Safersex ▲, **Safer Sex** *m* safe sex

Saft [zaft] **(-(e)s, ⁓e)** *m* juice; *(BOT)* sap; **s~ig** *adj* juicy; **s~los** *adj* dry

Sage ['zaːgə] *f* saga

Säge ['zɛːgə] *f* saw; **~mehl** *nt* sawdust

sagen ['zaːgən] *vt, vi* to say; *(mitteilen)*: **jdm ~** to tell sb; **~ Sie ihm, dass ...** tell him ...

sägen *vt, vi* to saw

sagenhaft *adj* legendary; *(umg)* great, smashing

sah *etc* [zaː] *vb siehe* **sehen**

Sahne ['zaːnə] **(-)** *f* cream

Saison [zɛ'zõː] **(-, -s)** *f* season

Saite ['zaɪtə] *f* string

Sakko ['zako] **(-s, -s)** *m od nt* jacket

Sakrament [zakra'mɛnt] *nt* sacrament

Sakristei [zakrıs'taı] *f* sacristy

Salat [za'la:t] **(-(e)s, -e)** *m* salad; *(Kopfsalat)* lettuce; **~soße** *f* salad dressing

Salbe ['zalbə] *f* ointment

Salbei ['zalbaı] **(-s** *od* **-)** *m od nt* sage

Saldo ['zaldo] **(-s, Salden)** *m* balance

Salmiak [zalmi'ak] **(-s)** *m* sal ammoniac; **~geist** *m* liquid ammonia

Salmonellenvergiftung [zalmo'nɛlən-] *f* salmonella (poisoning)

salopp [za'lɔp] *adj* casual

Salpeter [zal'pe:tər] **(-s)** *m* saltpetre; **~säure** *f* nitric acid

Salz [zalts] **(-es, -e)** *nt* salt; **s~en** *(unreg)* *vt* to salt; **s~ig** *adj* salty; **~kartoffeln** *pl* boiled potatoes; **~säure** *f* hydrochloric acid; **~streuer** *m* salt cellar; **~wasser** *nt* *(Meerwasser)* salt water

Samen ['za:mən] **(-s, -)** *m* seed; *(ANAT)* sperm

Sammel- ['zaml] *zW:* **~band** *m* anthology; **~fahrschein** *m* multi-journey ticket; *(für mehrere Personen)* group ticket

sammeln ['zamln] *vt* to collect ♦ *vr* to assemble, to gather; *(konzentrieren)* to concentrate

Sammlung ['zamluŋ] *f* collection; assembly, gathering; concentration

Samstag ['zamsta:k] *m* Saturday; **s~s** *adv* (on) Saturdays

Samt [zamt] **(-(e)s, -e)** *m* velvet; **s~** *präp* +*dat* (along) with, together with; **s~ und sonders** each and every one (of them)

sämtlich ['zɛmtlıç] *adj* all (the), entire

Sand [zant] **(-(e)s, -e)** *m* sand

Sandale [zan'da:lə] *f* sandal

Sand- *zW:* **~bank** *f* sandbank; **s~ig** ['zandıç] *adj* sandy; **~kasten** *m* sandpit; **~kuchen** *m* Madeira cake; **~papier** *nt* sandpaper; **~stein** *m* sandstone; **s~strahlen** *vt, vi insep* to sandblast; **~strand** *m* sandy beach

sandte *etc* ['zantə] *vb siehe* **senden**

sanft [zanft] *adj* soft, gentle; **~mütig** *adj* gentle, meek

sang *etc* [zaŋ] *vb siehe* **singen**

Sänger(in) ['zɛŋər(ın)] **(-s, -)** *m(f)* singer

Sani- *zW:* **s~eren** [za'ni:rən] *vt* to redevelop; *(Betrieb)* to make financially sound ♦ *vr* to line one's pockets; to become financially sound; **s~tär** [zani'te:r] *adj* sanitary; **s~täre Anlagen** sanitation *sg;* **~täter** [zani'te:tər] **(-s, -)** *m* first-aid attendant; *(MIL)* (medical) orderly

sanktionieren [zaŋktsio'ni:rən] *vt* to sanction

Sardelle [zar'dɛlə] *f* anchovy

Sardine [zar'di:nə] *f* sardine

Sarg [zark] **(-(e)s, ⸚e)** *m* coffin

Sarkasmus [zar'kasmʊs] *m* sarcasm

saß *etc* [za:s] *vb siehe* **sitzen**

Satan ['za:tan] **(-s, -e)** *m* Satan; devil

Satellit [zate'li:t] **(-en, -en)** *m* satellite; **~enfernsehen** *nt* satellite television

Satire [za'ti:rə] *f* satire; **satirisch** *adj* satirical

satt [zat] *adj* full; *(Farbe)* rich, deep; **jdn/etw ~ sein** *od* **haben** to be fed up with sb/sth; **sich ~ hören/sehen an** +*dat* to hear/see enough of; **sich ~ essen** to eat one's fill; **~ machen** to be filling

Sattel ['zatl] **(-s, ⸚)** *m* saddle; *(Berg)* ridge; **s~n** *vt* to saddle; **~schlepper** *m* articulated lorry

sättigen ['zɛtıgən] *vt* to satisfy; *(CHEM)* to saturate

Satz [zats] **(-es, ⸚e)** *m* *(GRAM)* sentence; *(Nebensatz, Adverbialsatz)* clause; *(Theorem)* theorem; *(MUS)* movement; *(TENNIS: Briefmarken etc)* set; *(Kaffee)* grounds *pl;* *(COMM)* rate; *(Sprung)* jump; **~teil** *m* part of a sentence; **~ung** *f* *(Statut)* statute, rule; **~zeichen** *nt* punctuation mark

Sau [zau] **(-, Säue)** *f* sow; *(umg)* dirty pig

sauber ['zaubər] *adj* clean; *(ironisch)* fine; **~ halten** to keep clean; **S~keit** *f* cleanness; *(einer Person)* cleanliness

säuberlich ['zɔybərlıç] *adv* neatly

säubern *vt* to clean; *(POL etc)* to purge; **Säuberung** *f* cleaning; purge

Sauce ['zo:sə] *f* sauce, gravy

sauer ['zauər] *adj* sour; *(CHEM)* acid; *(umg)*

cross; **saurer Regen** acid rain; **S~braten** m braised beef marinated in vinegar

Sauerei [zauə'raɪ] (umg) f rotten state of affairs, scandal; (Schmutz etc) mess; (Unanständigkeit) obscenity

Sauerkraut nt sauerkraut, pickled cabbage

säuerlich ['zɔyərlɪç] adj (Geschmack) sour; (missvergnügt: Gesicht) dour

Sauer- zW: **~milch** f sour milk; **~rahm** m (KOCH) sour cream; **~stoff** m oxygen; **~teig** m leaven

saufen ['zaufən] (unreg) (umg) vt, vi to drink, to booze; **Säufer** ['zɔyfər] (-s, -) (umg) m boozer

saugen ['zaugən] (unreg) vt, vi to suck

säugen ['zɔygən] vt to suckle

Sauger ['zaugər] (-s, -) m dummy, comforter (US); (auf Flasche) teat

Säugetier ['zɔygə-] nt mammal

Säugling m infant, baby

Säule ['zɔylə] f column, pillar

Saum [zaum] (-(e)s, **Säume**) m hem; (Naht) seam

säumen ['zɔymən] vt to hem; to seam ♦ vi to delay, to hesitate

Sauna ['zauna] (-, -s) f sauna

Säure ['zɔyrə] f acid

sausen ['zauzən] vi to blow; (umg: eilen) to rush; (Ohren) to buzz; **etw ~ lassen** (umg) not to bother with sth

Saxofon, Saxophon [zakso'foːn] (-s, -e) nt saxophone

SB abk = **Selbstbedienung**

S-Bahn f abk (= Schnellbahn) high speed railway; (= Stadtbahn) suburban railway

schaben ['ʃaːbən] vt to scrape

schäbig ['ʃɛːbɪç] adj shabby

Schablone [ʃa'bloːnə] f stencil; (Muster) pattern; (fig) convention

Schach [ʃax] (-s, -s) nt chess; (Stellung) check; **~brett** nt chessboard; **~figur** f chessman; **'~'matt** adj checkmate; **~spiel** nt game of chess

Schacht [ʃaxt] (-(e)s, ᵉe) m shaft

Schachtel (-, -n) f box

schade ['ʃaːdə] adj a pity od shame ♦ excl: **(wie) ~!** (what a) pity od shame; **sich** dat

zu ~ sein für etw to consider o.s. too good for sth

Schädel ['ʃɛːdəl] (-s, -) m skull; **~bruch** m fractured skull

Schaden ['ʃaːdən] (-s, ᵉ) m damage; (Verletzung) injury; (Nachteil) disadvantage; **s~** vi +dat to hurt; **einer Sache s~** to damage sth; **~ersatz** m compensation, damages pl; **~freude** f malicious glee; **s~froh** adj (Mensch, Lachen) gloating; **~sfall** m: **im ~sfall** in the event of a claim

schadhaft ['ʃaːthaft] adj faulty, damaged

schäd- ['ʃɛːt] zW: **~igen** ['ʃɛːdɪgən] vt to damage; (Person) to do harm to, to harm; **~lich** adj: **~lich (für)** harmful (to); **S~lichkeit** f harmfulness; **S~ling** m pest

Schadstoff ['ʃaːtʃtɔf] m harmful substance; **s~arm** adj: **s~arm sein** to contain a low level of harmful substances

Schaf [ʃaːf] (-(e)s, -e) nt sheep

Schäfer ['ʃɛːfər] (-s, -e) m shepherd; **~hund** m Alsatian (dog) (BRIT), German shepherd (dog) (US)

Schaffen ['ʃafən] (-s) nt (creative) activity

schaffen¹ ['ʃafən] (unreg) vt to create; (Platz) to make

schaffen² ['ʃafən] vt (erreichen) to manage, to do; (erledigen) to finish; (Prüfung) to pass; (transportieren) to take ♦ vi (umg: arbeiten) to work; **sich** dat **etw ~** to get o.s. sth; **sich an etw** dat **zu ~ machen** to busy o.s. with sth

Schaffner(in) ['ʃafnər(ɪn)] (-s, -) m(f) (Busschaffner) conductor(-tress); (EISENB) guard

Schaft [ʃaft] (-(e)s, ᵉe) m shaft; (von Gewehr) stock; (von Stiefel) leg; (BOT) stalk; tree trunk

Schal [ʃaːl] (-s, -e od -s) m scarf

schal adj flat; (fig) insipid

Schälchen ['ʃɛːlçən] nt cup, bowl

Schale ['ʃaːlə] f skin; (abgeschält) peel; (Nussschale, Muschelschale, Eischale) shell; (Geschirr) dish, bowl

schälen ['ʃɛːlən] vt to peel; to shell ♦ vr to peel

Schall [ʃal] (-(e)s, -e) m sound; **~dämpfer** (-s, -) m (AUT) silencer; **s~dicht** adj soundproof; **s~en** vi to (re)sound; **~end** adj resounding, loud; **~mauer** f sound barrier; **~platte** f (gramophone) record

Schalt- [ʃalt] zW: **~bild** nt circuit diagram; **~brett** nt switchboard; **s~en** vt to switch, to turn ♦ vi (AUT) to change (gear); (umg: begreifen) to catch on; **~er** (**-s, -**) m counter; (an Gerät) switch; **~erbeamte(r)** m counter clerk; **~erstunden** pl hours of business; **~hebel** m switch; (AUT) gear lever; **~jahr** nt leap year; **~ung** f switching; (ELEK) circuit; (AUT) gear change

Scham [ʃaːm] (**-**) f shame; (~gefühl) modesty; (Organe) private parts pl

schämen [ˈʃɛːmən] vr to be ashamed

schamlos adj shameless

Schande [ˈʃandə] (**-**) f disgrace

schändlich [ˈʃɛntlɪç] adj disgraceful, shameful

Schändung [ˈʃɛndʊŋ] f violation, defilement

Schanze [ˈʃantsə] f (Sprungschanze) ski jump

Schar [ʃaːr] (**-, -en**) f band, company; (Vögel) flock; (Menge) crowd; **in ~en** in droves; **s~en** vr to assemble, to rally

scharf [ʃarf] adj sharp; (Essen) hot, spicy; (Munition) live; **~ nachdenken** to think hard; **auf etw** akk **~ sein** (umg) to be keen on sth

Schärfe [ˈʃɛrfə] f sharpness; (Strenge) rigour; **s~n** vt to sharpen

Scharf- zW: **s~machen** (umg) vt to stir up; **~richter** m executioner; **~schütze** m marksman, sharpshooter; **s~sinnig** adj astute, shrewd

Scharlach [ˈʃarlax] (**-s, -e**) m (~fieber) scarlet fever

Scharnier [ʃarˈniːr] (**-s, -e**) nt hinge

scharren [ˈʃarən] vt, vi to scrape, to scratch

Schaschlik [ˈʃaʃlɪk] (**-s, -s**) m od nt (shish) kebab

Schatten [ˈʃatən] (**-s, -**) m shadow; **~riss** ▲ m silhouette; **~seite** f shady side, dark side

schattieren [ʃaˈtiːrən] vt, vi to shade

schattig [ˈʃatɪç] adj shady

Schatulle [ʃaˈtʊlə] f casket; (Geldschatulle) coffer

Schatz [ʃats] (**-es, ⁻e**) m treasure; (Person) darling

schätz- [ʃɛts] zW: **~bar** adj assessable; **S~chen** nt darling, love; **~en** vt (abschätzen) to estimate; (Gegenstand) to value; (würdigen) to value, to esteem; (vermuten) to reckon; **S~ung** f estimate; estimation; valuation; **nach meiner S~ung ...** I reckon that ...

Schau [ʃaʊ] (**-**) f show; (Ausstellung) display, exhibition; **etw zur ~ stellen** to make a show of sth, to show sth off; **~bild** nt diagram

Schauder [ˈʃaʊdər] (**-s, -s**) m shudder; (wegen Kälte) shiver; **s~haft** adj horrible; **s~n** vi to shudder; to shiver

schauen [ˈʃaʊən] vi to look

Schauer [ˈʃaʊər] (**-s, -**) m (Regenschauer) shower; (Schreck) shudder; **~geschichte** f horror story; **s~lich** adj horrific, spine-chilling

Schaufel [ˈʃaʊfəl] (**-, -n**) f shovel; (NAUT) paddle; (TECH) scoop; **s~n** vt to shovel, to scoop

Schau- zW: **~fenster** nt shop window; **~fensterbummel** m window shopping (expedition); **~kasten** m showcase

Schaukel [ˈʃaʊkəl] (**-, -n**) f swing; **s~n** vi to swing, to rock; **~pferd** nt rocking horse; **~stuhl** m rocking chair

Schaulustige(r) [ˈʃaʊlʊstɪɡə(r)] f(m) onlooker

Schaum [ʃaʊm] (**-(e)s, Schäume**) m foam; (Seifenschaum) lather; **~bad** nt bubble bath

schäumen [ˈʃɔymən] vi to foam

Schaum- zW: **~festiger** (**-s, -**) m mousse; **~gummi** m foam (rubber); **s~ig** adj frothy, foamy; **~stoff** m foam material; **~wein** m sparkling wine

Schauplatz m scene

schaurig [ˈʃaʊrɪç] adj horrific, dreadful

Schauspiel nt spectacle; (THEAT) play; **~er(in)** m(f) actor (actress); **s~ern** vi insep to act; **Schauspielhaus** nt theatre

Scheck [ʃɛk] (**-s, -s**) m cheque; **~gebühr** f encashment fee; **~heft** nt cheque book; **~karte** f cheque card

---

Rechtschreibreform: ▲ neue Schreibung △ alte Schreibung (auslaufend)

scheffeln ['ʃefəln] *vt* to amass

Scheibe ['ʃaɪbə] *f* disc; (*Brot etc*) slice; (*Glasscheibe*) pane; (*MIL*) target

Scheiben- *zW*: **~bremse** *f* (*AUT*) disc brake; **~wischer** *m* (*AUT*) windscreen wiper

Scheide ['ʃaɪdə] *f* sheath; (*Grenze*) boundary; (*ANAT*) vagina; **s~n** (*unreg*) *vt* to separate; (*Ehe*) to dissolve ♦ *vi* to depart; to part; **sich s~n lassen** to get a divorce

Scheidung *f* (*Ehescheidung*) divorce

Schein [ʃaɪn] (**-(e)s, -e**) *m* light; (*Anschein*) appearance; (*Geld*) (bank)note; (*Bescheinigung*) certificate; **zum ~** in pretence; **s~bar** *adj* apparent; **s~en** (*unreg*) *vi* to shine; (*Anschein haben*) to seem; **s~heilig** *adj* hypocritical; **~werfer** (**-s, -**) *m* floodlight; spotlight; (*Suchscheinwerfer*) searchlight; (*AUT*) headlamp

Scheiß ['ʃaɪs] (*umg*) *in zW* bloody

Scheiße ['ʃaɪsə] (**-**) (*umg*) *f* shit

Scheitel ['ʃaɪtəl] (**-s, -**) *m* top; (*Haarscheitel*) parting; **s~n** *vt* to part

scheitern ['ʃaɪtərn] *vi* to fail

Schelle ['ʃelə] *f* small bell; **s~n** *vi* to ring

Schellfisch ['ʃelfɪʃ] *m* haddock

Schelm [ʃelm] (**-(e)s, -e**) *m* rogue; **s~isch** *adj* mischievous, roguish

Schelte ['ʃeltə] *f* scolding; **s~n** (*unreg*) *vt* to scold

Schema ['ʃeːma] (**-s, -s** *od* **-ta**) *nt* scheme, plan; (*Darstellung*) schema; **nach ~** quite mechanically; **s~tisch** [ʃeˈmaːtɪʃ] *adj* schematic; (*pej*) mechanical

Schemel ['ʃeːməl] (**-s, -**) *m* (foot)stool

Schenkel ['ʃeŋkəl] (**-s, -**) *m* thigh

schenken ['ʃeŋkən] *vt* (*auch fig*) to give; (*Getränk*) to pour; **sich** *dat* **etw ~** (*umg*) to skip sth; **das ist geschenkt!** (*billig*) that's a giveaway!; (*nichts wert*) that's worthless!

Scherbe ['ʃerbə] *f* broken piece, fragment; (*archäologisch*) potsherd

Schere ['ʃeːrə] *f* scissors *pl*; (*groß*) shears *pl*; **s~n** (*unreg*) *vt* to cut; (*Schaf*) to shear; (*kümmern*) to bother ♦ *vr* to care; **scher dich zum Teufel!** get lost!; **~'rei** (*umg*) *f* bother, trouble

Scherz [ʃerts] (**-es, -e**) *m* joke; fun; **~frage** *f* conundrum; **s~haft** *adj* joking, jocular

Scheu [ʃɔy] (**-**) *f* shyness; (*Angst*) fear; (*Ehrfurcht*) awe; **s~** *adj* shy; **s~en** *vr*: **sich s~en vor** +*dat* to be afraid of, to shrink from ♦ *vt* to shun ♦ *vi* (*Pferd*) to shy

scheuern ['ʃɔyərn] *vt* to scour, to scrub

Scheune ['ʃɔynə] *f* barn

Scheusal ['ʃɔyzaːl] (**-s, -e**) *nt* monster

scheußlich ['ʃɔyslɪç] *adj* dreadful, frightful

Schi [ʃiː] *m* = **Ski**

Schicht [ʃɪçt] (**-, -en**) *f* layer; (*Klasse*) class, level; (*in Fabrik etc*) shift; **~arbeit** *f* shift work; **s~en** *vt* to layer, to stack

schick [ʃɪk] *adj* stylish, chic

schicken ['ʃɪkən] *vt* to send ♦ *vr*: **sich ~ (in** +*akk*) to resign o.s. (to) ♦ *vb unpers* (*anständig sein*) to be fitting

schicklich *adj* proper, fitting

Schicksal (**-s, -e**) *nt* fate; **~sschlag** *m* great misfortune, blow

Schieb- ['ʃiːb] *zW*: **~edach** *nt* (*AUT*) sun roof; **s~en** (*unreg*) *vt* (*auch Drogen*) to push; (*Schuld*) to put ♦ *vi* to push; **~etür** *f* sliding door; **~ung** *f* fiddle

Schieds- ['ʃiːts] *zW*: **~gericht** *nt* court of arbitration; **~richter** *m* referee; umpire; (*Schlichter*) arbitrator

schief [ʃiːf] *adj* crooked; (*Ebene*) sloping; (*Turm*) leaning; (*Winkel*) oblique; (*Blick*) funny; (*Vergleich*) distorted ♦ *adv* crooked(ly); (*ansehen*) askance; **etw ~ stellen** to slope sth; **~ gehen** (*umg*) to go wrong

Schiefer ['ʃiːfər] (**-s, -**) *m* slate

schielen ['ʃiːlən] *vi* to squint; **nach etw ~** (*fig*) to eye sth

schien *etc* [ʃiːn] *vb siehe* **scheinen**

Schienbein *nt* shinbone

Schiene ['ʃiːnə] *f* rail; (*MED*) splint; **s~n** *vt* to put in splints

schier [ʃiːr] *adj* (*fig*) sheer ♦ *adv* nearly, almost

Schieß- ['ʃiːs] *zW*: **~bude** *f* shooting gallery; **s~en** (*unreg*) *vt* to shoot; (*Ball*) to kick; (*Geschoss*) to fire ♦ *vi* to shoot; (*Salat etc*) to run to seed; **s~en auf** +*akk* to shoot

at; **~e'rei** f shooting incident, shoot-out;
~pulver nt gunpowder; **~scharte** f
embrasure

Schiff [ʃɪf] (-(e)s, -e) nt ship, vessel;
(Kirchenschiff) nave; **s~bar** adj (Fluss)
navigable; **~bruch** m shipwreck;
s~brüchig adj shipwrecked; **~chen** nt
small boat; (Weben) shuttle; (Mütze) forage
cap; **~er** (-s, -) m bargeman, boatman;
~fahrt ▲ f shipping; (Reise) voyage

Schikane [ʃiˈkaːnə] f harassment; dirty trick;
mit allen ~n with all the trimmings

schikanieren [ʃikaˈniːrən] vt to harass, to
torment

Schikoree ▲ [ˈʃikoreː] (-s) m od f =
Chicorée

Schild¹ [ʃɪlt] (-(e)s, -e) m shield; **etw im ~e
führen** to be up to sth

Schild² [ʃɪlt] (-(e)s, -er) nt sign; nameplate;
(Etikett) label

Schilddrüse f thyroid gland

schildern [ˈʃɪldərn] vt to depict, to portray

Schildkröte f tortoise; (Wasserschildkröte)
turtle

Schilf [ʃɪlf] (-(e)s, -e) nt (Pflanze) reed;
(Material) reeds pl, rushes pl; **~rohr** nt
(Pflanze) reed

schillern [ˈʃɪlərn] vi to shimmer; **~d** adj
iridescent

Schilling [ˈʃɪlɪŋ] m schilling

Schimmel [ˈʃɪməl] (-s, -) m mould; (Pferd)
white horse; **s~ig** adj mouldy; **s~n** vi to
get mouldy

Schimmer [ˈʃɪmər] (-s) m (Lichtsein)
glimmer; (Glanz) shimmer; **s~n** vi to
glimmer, to shimmer

Schimpanse [ʃɪmˈpanzə] (-n, -n) m
chimpanzee

schimpfen [ˈʃɪmpfən] vt to scold ♦ vi to
curse, to complain; to scold

Schimpfwort nt term of abuse

schinden [ˈʃɪndən] (unreg) vt to maltreat, to
drive too hard ♦ vr: **sich ~ (mit)** to sweat
and strain (at), to toil away (at); **Eindruck
~** (umg) to create an impression

Schinde'rei f grind, drudgery

Schinken [ˈʃɪŋkən] (-s, -) m ham

Schirm [ʃɪrm] (-(e)s, -e) m (Regenschirm)
umbrella; (Sonnenschirm) parasol, sunshade;
(Wandschirm, Bildschirm) screen;
(Lampenschirm) (lamp)shade; (Mützenschirm)
peak; (Pilzschirm) cap; **~mütze** f peaked
cap; **~ständer** m umbrella stand

schizophren [ʃitsoˈfreːn] adj schizophrenic

Schlacht [ʃlaxt] (-, -en) f battle; **s~en** vt to
slaughter, to kill; **~er** (-s, -) m butcher;
~feld nt battlefield; **~hof** m
slaughterhouse, abattoir; **~schiff** nt
battleship; **~vieh** nt animals kept for meat;
beef cattle

Schlaf [ʃlaːf] (-(e)s) m sleep; **~anzug** m
pyjamas pl

Schläfe f (ANAT) temple

schlafen [ˈʃlaːfən] (unreg) vi to sleep; **~
gehen** to go to bed; **S~szeit** f bedtime

schlaff [ʃlaf] adj slack; (energielos) limp;
(erschöpft) exhausted

Schlaf- zW: **~gelegenheit** f sleeping
accommodation; **~lied** nt lullaby; **s~los**
adj sleepless; **~losigkeit** f sleeplessness,
insomnia; **~mittel** nt sleeping pill

schläfrig [ˈʃleːfrɪç] adj sleepy

Schlaf- zW: **~saal** m dormitory; **~sack** m
sleeping bag; **~tablette** f sleeping pill;
~wagen m sleeping car, sleeper;
s~wandeln vi insep to sleepwalk;
~zimmer nt bedroom

Schlag [ʃlaːk] (-(e)s, ⁀e) m (auch fig) blow;
(auch MED) stroke; (Pulsschlag, Herzschlag)
beat; (ELEK) shock; (Blitzschlag) bolt, stroke;
(Autotür) car door; (umg: Portion) helping;
(Art) kind, type; **Schläge** pl (Tracht Prügel)
beating sg; **mit einem ~** all at once; **~ auf
~** in rapid succession; **~ader** f artery;
~anfall m stroke; **s~artig** adj sudden,
without warning; **~baum** m barrier

Schlägel [ˈʃleːgəl] (-s, -) m (drum)stick;
(Hammer) mallet, hammer

schlagen [ˈʃlaːgən] (unreg) vt, vi to strike, to
hit; (wiederholt ~, besiegen) to beat;
(Glocke) to ring; (Stunde) to strike; (Sahne)
to whip; (Schlacht) to fight ♦ vr to fight;
nach jdm ~ (fig) to take after sb; **sich gut
~** (fig) to do well; **Schlager** [ˈʃlaːgər] (-s, -)

m (auch fig) hit

Schläger ['ʃlɛːgər] *m* brawler; (*SPORT*) bat; (*TENNIS etc*) racket; (*GOLF*) club; hockey stick; (*Waffe*) rapier; **Schläge'rei** *f* fight, punch-up

Schlagersänger(in) *m(f)* pop singer

Schlag- *zW:* **s~fertig** *adj* quick-witted; **~fertigkeit** *f* ready wit, quickness of repartee; **~loch** *nt* pothole; **~obers** (*ÖSTERR*) *nt* = **Schlagsahne; ~sahne** *f* (whipped) cream; **~seite** *f* (*NAUT*) list; **~wort** *nt* slogan, catch phrase; **~zeile** *f* headline; **~zeug** *nt* percussion; drums *pl*; **~zeuger** (**-s, -**) *m* drummer

Schlamassel [ʃlaˈmasəl] (**-s, -**) (*umg*) *m* mess

Schlamm [ʃlam] (**-(e)s, -e**) *m* mud; **s~ig** *adj* muddy

Schlamp- ['ʃlamp] *zW:* **~e** (*umg*) *f* slut; **s~en** (*umg*) *vi* to be sloppy; **~e'rei** (*umg*) *f* disorder, untidiness; sloppy work; **s~ig** (*umg*) *adj* (*Mensch, Arbeit*) sloppy, messy

Schlange ['ʃlaŋə] *f* snake; (*Menschenschlange*) queue (*BRIT*), line-up (*US*); **~ stehen** to (form a) queue, to line up

schlängeln ['ʃlɛŋəln] *vr* (*Schlange*) to wind; (*Weg*) to wind, twist; (*Fluss*) to meander

Schlangen- *zW:* **~biss** ▲ *m* snake bite; **~gift** *nt* snake venom; **~linie** *f* wavy line

schlank [ʃlaŋk] *adj* slim, slender; **S~heit** *f* slimness, slenderness; **S~heitskur** *f* diet

schlapp [ʃlap] *adj* limp; (*locker*) slack; **S~e** (*umg*) *f* setback

Schlaraffenland [ʃlaˈrafənlant] *nt* land of milk and honey

schlau [ʃlau] *adj* crafty, cunning

Schlauch [ʃlaux] (**-(e)s, Schläuche**) *m* hose; (*in Reifen*) inner tube; (*umg: Anstrengung*) grind; **~boot** *nt* rubber dinghy; **s~en** (*umg*) *vt* to tell on, to exhaust

Schläue ['ʃlɔyə] (**-**) *f* cunning

Schlaufe ['ʃlaufə] *f* loop; (*Aufhänger*) hanger

Schlauheit *f* cunning

schlecht [ʃlɛçt] *adj* bad ♦ *adv* badly; **~ gelaunt** in a bad mood; **~ und recht** after

a fashion; **jdm ist ~** sb feels sick *od* bad; **jdm geht es ~** sb is in a bad way; **~ machen** to run down; **S~igkeit** *f* badness; bad deed

schlecken ['ʃlɛkən] *vt, vi* to lick

Schlegel ['ʃleːgəl] (**-s, -**) *m* (*KOCH*) leg; *siehe* **Schlägel**

schleichen ['ʃlaiçən] (*unreg*) *vi* to creep, to crawl; **~d** *adj* gradual; creeping

Schleichwerbung *f* (*COMM*) plug

Schleier ['ʃlaiər] (**-s, -**) *m* veil; **s~haft** (*umg*) *adj:* **jdm s~haft sein** to be a mystery to sb

Schleif- ['ʃlaif] *zW:* **~e** *f* loop; (*Band*) bow; **s~en¹** *vt, vi* to drag; **s~en²** (*unreg*) *vt* to grind; (*Edelstein*) to cut; **~stein** *m* grindstone

Schleim [ʃlaim] (**-(e)s, -e**) *m* slime; (*MED*) mucus; (*KOCH*) gruel; **~haut** *f* (*ANAT*) mucous membrane; **s~ig** *adj* slimy

Schlemm- ['ʃlɛm] *zW:* **s~en** *vi* to feast; **~er** (**-s, -**) *m* gourmet; **~e'rei** *f* gluttony, feasting

schlendern ['ʃlɛndərn] *vi* to stroll

schlenkern ['ʃlɛŋkərn] *vt, vi* to swing, to dangle

Schlepp- ['ʃlɛp] *zW:* **~e** *f* train; **s~en** *vt* to drag; (*Auto, Schiff*) to tow; (*tragen*) to lug; **s~end** *adj* dragging, slow; **~er** (**-s, -**) *m* tractor; (*Schiff*) tug

Schlesien ['ʃleːziən] (**-s**) *nt* Silesia

Schleuder ['ʃlɔydər] (**-, -n**) *f* catapult; (*Wäscheschleuder*) spin-drier; (*Butterschleuder etc*) centrifuge; **s~gefahr** *f* risk of skidding; „**Achtung ~gefahr**" "slippery road ahead"; **s~n** *vt* to hurl; (*Wäsche*) to spin-dry ♦ *vi* (*AUT*) to skid; **~preis** *m* give-away price; **~sitz** *m* (*AVIAT*) ejector seat; (*fig*) hot seat; **~ware** *f* cheap *od* cut-price goods *pl*

schleunigst ['ʃlɔynɪçst] *adv* straight away

Schleuse ['ʃlɔyzə] *f* lock; (*~ntor*) sluice

schlicht [ʃlɪçt] *adj* simple, plain; **~en** *vt* (*glätten*) to smooth, to dress; (*Streit*) to settle; **S~er** (**-s, -**) *m* mediator, arbitrator; **S~ung** *f* settlement; arbitration

Schlick [ʃlɪk] (**-(e)s, -e**) *m* mud; (*Ölschlick*) slick

schlief *etc* [ʃliːf] *vb siehe* **schlafen**

Schließ- ['ʃliːs] zW: **s~en** (unreg) vt to close, to shut; (beenden) to close; (Freundschaft, Bündnis, Ehe) to enter into; (folgern): **s~en (aus)** to infer (from) ♦ vi, vr to close, to shut; **etw in sich s~en** to include sth; **~fach** nt locker; **s~lich** adv finally; **s~lich doch** after all

Schliff [ʃlɪf] (-(e)s, -e) m cut(ting); (fig) polish

schlimm [ʃlɪm] adj bad; **~er** adj worse; **~ste(r, s)** adj worst; **~stenfalls** adv at (the) worst

Schlinge ['ʃlɪŋə] f loop; (bes Henkersschlinge) noose; (Falle) snare; (MED) sling; **s~n** (unreg) vt to wind; (essen) to bolt, to gobble ♦ vi (essen) to bolt one's food, to gobble

schlingern vi to roll

Schlips [ʃlɪps] (-es, -e) m tie

Schlitten ['ʃlɪtən] (-s, -) m sledge, sleigh; **~fahren** (-s) nt tobogganing

schlittern ['ʃlɪtərn] vi to slide

Schlittschuh ['ʃlɪtʃuː] m skate; **~ laufen** to skate; **~bahn** f skating rink; **~läufer(in)** m(f) skater

Schlitz [ʃlɪts] (-es, -e) m slit; (für Münze) slot; (Hosenschlitz) flies pl; **s~äugig** adj slant-eyed

Schloss ▲ [ʃlɔs] (-es, ̈er) nt lock; (an Schmuck etc) clasp; (Bau) castle; chateau

schloss ▲ etc vb siehe **schließen**

Schlosser ['ʃlɔsər] (-s, -) m (Autoschlosser) fitter; (für Schlüssel etc) locksmith

Schlosserei [-'raɪ] f metal (working) shop

Schlot [ʃloːt] (-(e)s, -e) m chimney; (NAUT) funnel

schlottern ['ʃlɔtərn] vi to shake, to tremble; (Kleidung) to be baggy

Schlucht [ʃlʊxt] (-, -en) f gorge, ravine

schluchzen ['ʃlʊxtsən] vi to sob

Schluck [ʃlʊk] (-(e)s, -e) m swallow; (Menge) drop; **~auf** (-s, -s) m hiccups pl; **s~en** vt, vi to swallow

schludern ['ʃluːdərn] vi to skimp, to do sloppy work

schlug etc [ʃluːk] vb siehe **schlagen**

Schlummer ['ʃlʊmər] (-s) m slumber; **s~n** vi to slumber

Schlund [ʃlʊnt] (-(e)s, ̈e) m gullet; (fig) jaw

schlüpfen ['ʃlʏpfən] vi to slip; (Vogel etc) to hatch (out)

Schlüpfer ['ʃlʏpfər] (-s, -) m panties pl, knickers pl

schlüpfrig ['ʃlʏpfrɪç] adj slippery; (fig) lewd; **S~keit** f slipperiness; (fig) lewdness

schlurfen ['ʃlʊrfən] vi to shuffle

schlürfen ['ʃlʏrfən] vt, vi to slurp

Schluss ▲ [ʃlʊs] (-es, ̈e) m end; (~folgerung) conclusion; **am ~** at the end; **~ machen mit** to finish with

Schlüssel ['ʃlʏsəl] (-s, -) m (auch fig) key; (Schraubenschlüssel) spanner, wrench; (MUS) clef; **~bein** nt collarbone; **~blume** f cowslip, primrose; **~bund** m bunch of keys; **~dienst** m key cutting service; **~loch** nt keyhole; **~position** f key position; **~wort** nt keyword

schlüssig ['ʃlʏsɪç] adj conclusive

Schluss- ▲ zW: **~licht** nt taillight; (fig) tailender; **~strich** m (fig) final stroke; **~verkauf** m clearance sale

schmächtig ['ʃmɛçtɪç] adj slight

schmackhaft ['ʃmakhaft] adj tasty

schmal [ʃmaːl] adj narrow; (Person, Buch etc) slender, slim; (karg) meagre

schmälern ['ʃmɛːlərn] vt to diminish; (fig) to belittle

Schmalfilm m cine film

Schmalz [ʃmalts] (-es, -e) nt dripping, lard; (fig) sentiment, schmaltz; **s~ig** adj (fig) schmaltzy

schmarotzen [ʃma'rɔtsən] vi to sponge; (BOT) to be parasitic; **Schmarotzer** (-s, -) m parasite; sponger

Schmarren ['ʃmarən] (-s, -) m (ÖSTERR) small piece of pancake; (fig) rubbish, tripe

schmatzen ['ʃmatsən] vi to smack one's lips; to eat noisily

schmecken ['ʃmɛkən] vt, vi to taste; **es schmeckt ihm** he likes it

Schmeichel- ['ʃmaɪçəl] zW: **~ei** [-'laɪ] f flattery; **s~haft** adj flattering; **s~n** vi to flatter

schmeißen ['ʃmaɪsən] (unreg) (umg) vt to

throw, to chuck

Schmelz [ʃmɛlts] **(-es, -e)** m enamel; (*Glasur*) glaze; (*von Stimme*) melodiousness; **s~en** (*unreg*) vt to melt; (*Erz*) to smelt ♦ vi to melt; **~punkt** m melting point; **~wasser** nt melted snow

Schmerz [ʃmɛrts] **(-es, -en)** m pain; (*Trauer*) grief; **s~empfindlich** adj sensitive to pain; **s~en** vt, vi to hurt; **~ensgeld** nt compensation; **s~haft** adj painful; **s~lich** adj painful; **s~los** adj painless; **~mittel** nt painkiller; **~tablette** f painkiller

Schmetterling [ˈʃmɛtərlɪŋ] m butterfly

schmettern [ˈʃmɛtərn] vt (*werfen*) to hurl; (*TENNIS: Ball*) to smash; (*singen*) to belt out (*inf*)

Schmied [ʃmiːt] **(-(e)s, -e)** m blacksmith; **~e** [ˈʃmiːdə] f smithy, forge; **~eeisen** nt wrought iron; **s~en** vt to forge; (*Pläne*) to devise, to concoct

schmiegen [ˈʃmiːɡən] vt to press, to nestle ♦ vr: **sich ~ (an** +akk) to cuddle up (to), to nestle (up to)

Schmier- [ˈʃmiːr] zW: **~e** f grease; (*THEAT*) greasepaint, make-up; **s~en** vt to smear; (*ölen*) to lubricate, to grease; (*bestechen*) to bribe; (*schreiben*) to scrawl ♦ vi (*schreiben*) to scrawl; **~fett** nt grease; **~geld** nt bribe; **s~ig** adj greasy; **~seife** f soft soap

Schminke [ˈʃmɪŋkə] f make-up; **s~n** vt, vr to make up

schmirgeln [ˈʃmɪrɡəln] vt to sand (down)

Schmirgelpapier nt emery paper

schmollen [ˈʃmɔlən] vi to sulk, to pout

Schmorbraten m stewed od braised meat

schmoren [ˈʃmoːrən] vt to stew, to braise

Schmuck [ʃmʊk] **(-(e)s, -e)** m jewellery; (*Verzierung*) decoration

schmücken [ˈʃmʏkən] vt to decorate

Schmuck- zW: **s~los** adj unadorned, plain; **~sachen** pl jewels, jewellery sg

Schmuggel [ˈʃmʊɡəl] **(-s)** m smuggling; **s~n** vt, vi to smuggle

Schmuggler (-s, -) m smuggler

schmunzeln [ˈʃmʊntsəln] vi to smile benignly

schmusen [ˈʃmuːzən] (*umg*) vi (*zärtlich sein*)

to cuddle, to canoodle (*inf*)

Schmutz [ʃmʊts] **(-es)** m dirt, filth; **~fink** m filthy creature; **~fleck** m stain; **s~ig** adj dirty

Schnabel [ˈʃnaːbəl] **(-s, ⁀)** m beak, bill; (*Ausguss*) spout

Schnalle [ˈʃnalə] f buckle, clasp; **s~n** vt to buckle

Schnapp- [ˈʃnap] zW: **s~en** vt to grab, to catch ♦ vi to snap; **~schloss** ▲ nt spring lock; **~schuss** ▲ m (*PHOT*) snapshot

Schnaps [ʃnaps] **(-es, ⁀e)** m spirits pl; schnapps

schnarchen [ˈʃnarçən] vi to snore

schnattern [ˈʃnatərn] vi (*Gänse*) to gabble; (*Ente*) to quack

schnauben [ˈʃnaʊbən] vi to snort ♦ vr to blow one's nose

schnaufen [ˈʃnaʊfən] vi to puff, to pant

Schnauze f snout, muzzle; (*Ausguss*) spout; (*umg*) gob

schnäuzen ▲ [ˈʃnɔʏtsən] vr to blow one's nose

Schnecke [ˈʃnɛkə] f snail; **~nhaus** nt snail's shell

Schnee [ʃneː] **(-s)** m snow; (*Eischnee*) beaten egg white; **~ball** m snowball; **~flocke** f snowflake; **s~frei** adj free of snow; **~gestöber** nt snowstorm; **~glöckchen** nt snowdrop; **~grenze** f snow line; **~kette** f (*AUT*) snow chain; **~mann** m snowman; **~pflug** m snowplough; **~regen** m sleet; **~schmelze** f thaw; **~wehe** f snowdrift

Schneide [ˈʃnaɪdə] f edge; (*Klinge*) blade; **s~n** (*unreg*) vt to cut; (*kreuzen*) to cross, to intersect with ♦ vr to cut o.s.; to cross, to intersect; **s~nd** adj cutting; **~r (-s, -)** m tailor; **~rei** f (*Geschäft*) tailor's; **~rin** f dressmaker; **s~rn** vt to make ♦ vi to be a tailor; **~zahn** m incisor

schneien [ˈʃnaɪən] vi unpers to snow

Schneise [ˈʃnaɪzə] f clearing

schnell [ʃnɛl] adj quick, fast ♦ adv quick, quickly, fast; **S~hefter (-s, -)** m loose-leaf binder; **S~igkeit** f speed; **S~imbiss** ▲ m (*Lokal*) snack bar; **S~kochtopf** m

(*Dampfkochtopf*) pressure cooker;
S~reinigung *f* dry cleaner's; **~stens** *adv*
as quickly as possible; **S~straße** *f*
expressway; **S~zug** *m* fast *od* express train
schneuzen △ ['ʃnɔʏtsən] *vr siehe*
schnäuzen
schnippeln ['ʃnɪpəln] (*umg*) *vt:* **~ (an** +*dat*)
to snip (at)
schnippisch ['ʃnɪpɪʃ] *adj* sharp-tongued
Schnitt (**-(e)s, -e**) *m* cut(ting); (*~punkt*)
intersection; (*Querschnitt*) (cross) section;
(*Durchschnitt*) average; (*~muster*) pattern;
(*an Buch*) edge; (*umg: Gewinn*) profit
schnitt *etc vb siehe* **schneiden**
Schnitt- *zW:* **~blumen** *pl* cut flowers; **~e** *f*
slice; (*belegt*) sandwich; **~fläche** *f* section;
~lauch *m* chive; **~punkt** *m* (point of)
intersection; **~stelle** *f* (*COMPUT*) interface;
~wunde *f* cut
Schnitz- ['ʃnɪts] *zW:* **~arbeit** *f* wood
carving; **~el** (**-s, -**) *nt* chip; (*KOCH*)
escalope; **s~en** *vt* to carve; **~er** (**-s, -**) *m*
carver; (*umg*) blunder; **~e'rei** *f* carving;
carved woodwork
schnodderig ['ʃnɔdərɪç] (*umg*) *adj* snotty
Schnorchel ['ʃnɔrçəl] (**-s, -**) *m* snorkel
Schnörkel ['ʃnœrkəl] (**-s, -**) *m* flourish;
(*ARCHIT*) scroll
schnorren ['ʃnɔrən] *vt, vi* to cadge
schnüffeln ['ʃnʏfəln] *vi* to sniff
Schnüffler (**-s, -**) *m* snooper
Schnuller ['ʃnʊlər] (**-s, -**) *m* dummy,
comforter (*US*)
Schnupfen ['ʃnʊpfən] (**-s, -**) *m* cold
schnuppern ['ʃnʊpərn] *vi* to sniff
Schnur [ʃnuːr] (**-, ⁻e**) *f* string, cord; (*ELEK*)
flex
schnüren ['ʃnyːrən] *vt* to tie
schnurgerade *adj* straight (as a die)
Schnurrbart ['ʃnʊrbaːrt] *m* moustache
schnurren ['ʃnʊrən] *vi* to purr; (*Kreisel*) to
hum
Schnürschuh *m* lace-up (shoe)
Schnürsenkel *m* shoelace
schnurstracks *adv* straight (away)
Schock [ʃɔk] (**-(e)s, -e**) *m* shock; **s~ieren**
[ʃɔ'kiːrən] *vt* to shock, to outrage

Schöffe ['ʃœfə] (**-n, -n**) *m* lay magistrate;
Schöffin *f* lay magistrate
Schokolade [ʃokoˈlaːdə] *f* chocolate
Scholle ['ʃɔlə] *f* clod; (*Eisscholle*) ice floe;
(*Fisch*) plaice

SCHLÜSSELWORT

---

schon [ʃoːn] *adv* **1** (*bereits*) already; **er ist
schon da** he's there already, he's already
there; **ist er schon da?** is he there yet?;
warst du schon einmal da? have you ever
been there?; **ich war schon einmal da** I've
been there before; **das war schon immer
so** that has always been the case; **schon
oft** often; **hast du schon gehört?** have
you heard?
2 (*bestimmt*) all right; **du wirst schon
sehen** you'll see (all right); **das wird
schon noch gut** that'll be OK
3 (*bloß*) just; **allein schon das Gefühl ...**
just the very feeling ...; **schon der
Gedanke** the very thought; **wenn ich das
schon höre** I only have to hear that
4 (*einschränkend*): **ja schon, aber ...** yes
(well), but ...
5: schon möglich possible; **schon gut!**
OK!; **du weißt schon** you know; **komm
schon!** come on!

---

schön [ʃøːn] *adj* beautiful; (*nett*) nice; **~e
Grüße** best wishes; **~e Ferien** have a nice
holiday; **~en Dank** (many) thanks; **sich ~
machen** to make o.s. look nice
schonen ['ʃoːnən] *vt* to look after ♦ *vr* to
take it easy; **~d** *adj* careful, gentle
Schön- *zW:* **~heit** *f* beauty; **~heitsfehler**
m blemish, flaw; **~heitsoperation** *f*
cosmetic surgery
Schonkost (**-**) *f* light diet; (*Spezialdiät*)
special diet
Schon- *zW:* **~ung** *f* good care; (*Nachsicht*)
consideration; (*Forst*) plantation of young
trees; **s~ungslos** *adj* unsparing, harsh;
~zeit *f* close season
Schöpf- ['ʃœpf] *zW:* **s~en** *vt* to scoop, to
ladle; (*Mut*) to summon up; (*Luft*) to
breathe in; **~er** (**-s, -**) *m* creator; **s~erisch**

Rechtschreibreform: ▲ *neue Schreibung* △ *alte Schreibung (auslaufend)*

adj creative; **~kelle** *f* ladle; **~ung** *f* creation

Schorf [ʃɔrf] **(-(e)s, -e)** *m* scab

Schornstein ['ʃɔrnʃtain] *m* chimney; (*NAUT*) funnel; **~feger (-s, -)** *m* chimney sweep

Schoß [ʃoːs] **(-es, ᵘe)** *m* lap

schoss ▲ *etc vb siehe* **schießen**

Schoßhund *m* pet dog, lapdog

Schote ['ʃoːtə] *f* pod

Schotte ['ʃɔtə] *m* Scot, Scotsman

Schotter ['ʃɔtər] **(-s)** *m* broken stone, road metal; (*EISENB*) ballast

Schott- [ʃɔt] *zW:* **~in** *f* Scot, Scotswoman; **s~isch** *adj* Scottish, Scots; **~land** *nt* Scotland

schraffieren [ʃra'fiːrən] *vt* to hatch

schräg [ʃrɛːk] *adj* slanting, not straight; **etw ~ stellen** to put sth at an angle; **~ gegenüber** diagonally opposite; **S~e** ['ʃrɛːgə] *f* slant; **S~strich** *m* oblique stroke

Schramme ['ʃramə] *f* scratch; **s~n** *vt* to scratch

Schrank [ʃraŋk] **(-(e)s, ᵘe)** *m* cupboard; (*Kleiderschrank*) wardrobe; **~e** *f* barrier; **~koffer** *m* trunk

Schraube ['ʃraubə] *f* screw; **s~n** *vt* to screw; **~nschlüssel** *m* spanner; **~nzieher (-s, -)** *m* screwdriver

Schraubstock ['ʃraupʃtɔk] *m* (*TECH*) vice

Schreck [ʃrɛk] **(-(e)s, -e)** *m* terror; fright; **~en (-s, -)** *m* terror; fright; **s~en** *vt* to frighten; to scare; **~gespenst** *nt* spectre, nightmare; **s~haft** *adj* jumpy, easily frightened; **s~lich** *adj* terrible, dreadful

Schrei [ʃrai] **(-(e)s, -e)** *m* scream; (*Ruf*) shout

Schreib- ['ʃraib] *zW:* **~block** *m* writing pad; **s~en** (*unreg*) *vt, vi* to write; (*buchstabieren*) to spell; **~en (-s, -)** *nt* letter, communication; **s~faul** *adj* bad about writing letters; **~kraft** *f* typist; **~maschine** *f* typewriter; **~papier** *nt* notepaper; **~tisch** *m* desk; **~ung** *f* spelling; **~waren** *pl* stationery *sg*; **~weise** *f* spelling; way of writing; **~zentrale** *f* typing pool; **~zeug** *nt* writing materials *pl*

schreien ['ʃraiən] (*unreg*) *vt, vi* to scream; (*rufen*) to shout; **~d** *adj* (*fig*) glaring; (*Farbe*)

loud

Schrein [ʃrain] **(-(e)s, -e)** *m* shrine

Schreiner ['ʃrainər] **(-s, -)** *m* joiner; (*Zimmermann*) carpenter; (*Möbelschreiner*) cabinetmaker; **~ei** [-'rai] *f* joiner's workshop

schreiten ['ʃraitən] (*unreg*) *vi* to stride

schrieb *etc* [ʃriːp] *vb siehe* **schreiben**

Schrift [ʃrift] **(-, -en)** *f* writing; handwriting; (*~art*) script; (*Gedrucktes*) pamphlet, work; **~deutsch** *nt* written German; **~führer** *m* secretary; **s~lich** *adj* written ♦ *adv* in writing; **~sprache** *f* written language; **~steller(in) (-s, -)** *m(f)* writer; **~stück** *nt* document; **~wechsel** *m* correspondence

schrill [ʃril] *adj* shrill

Schritt [ʃrit] **(-(e)s, -e)** *m* step; (*Gangart*) walk; (*Tempo*) pace; (*von Hose*) crutch; **~ fahren** to drive at walking pace; **~macher (-s, -)** *m* pacemaker; **~tempo ▲** *nt*: **im ~tempo** at a walking pace

schroff [ʃrɔf] *adj* steep; (*zackig*) jagged; (*fig*) brusque

schröpfen ['ʃrœpfən] *vt* (*fig*) to fleece

Schrot [ʃroːt] **(-(e)s, -e)** *m od nt* (*Blei*) (small) shot; (*Getreide*) coarsely ground grain, groats *pl*; **~flinte** *f* shotgun

Schrott [ʃrɔt] **(-(e)s, -e)** *m* scrap metal; **~haufen** *m* scrap heap; **s~reif** *adj* ready for the scrap heap

schrubben ['ʃrubən] *vt* to scrub

Schrubber (-s, -) *m* scrubbing brush

schrumpfen ['ʃrumpfən] *vi* to shrink; (*Apfel*) to shrivel

Schub- ['ʃuːb] *zW:* **~fach** *nt* drawer; **~karren** *m* wheelbarrow; **~lade** *f* drawer

Schubs [ʃups] **(-es, -e)** (*umg*) *m* shove (*inf*), push

schüchtern ['ʃʏçtərn] *adj* shy; **S~heit** *f* shyness

Schuft [ʃuft] **(-(e)s, -e)** *m* scoundrel

schuften (*umg*) *vi* to graft, to slave away

Schuh [ʃuː] **(-(e)s, -e)** *m* shoe; **~band** *nt* shoelace; **~creme** *f* shoe polish; **~größe** *f* shoe size; **~löffel** *m* shoehorn; **~macher (-s, -)** *m* shoemaker

Schul- *zW:* **~arbeit** *f* homework (*no pl*); **~aufgaben** *pl* homework *sg*; **~besuch** *m*

school attendance;**~buch** nt school book

Schuld [ʃʊlt] (-, -en) f guilt; (FIN) debt; (Verschulden) fault; **~ haben (an** +dat) to be to blame (for); **er hat ~** it's his fault; **jdm ~ geben** to blame sb; siehe **zuschulden;s~** adj: **s~ sein (an** +dat) to be to blame (for); **er ist s~** it's his fault;**s~en** ['ʃʊldən] vt to owe;**s~enfrei** adj free from debt; **~gefühl** nt feeling of guilt;**s~ig** adj guilty; (gebührend) due; **s~ig an etw** dat **sein** to be guilty of sth; **jdm etw s~ig sein** to owe sb sth; **jdm etw s~ig bleiben** not to provide sb with sth;**s~los** adj innocent, without guilt;**~ner** (-s, -) m debtor; **~schein** m promissory note, IOU

Schule ['ʃuːlə] f school;**s~n** vt to train, to school

Schüler(in) ['ʃyːlər(ɪn)] (-s, -) m(f) pupil; **~austausch** m school od student exchange;**~ausweis** m (school) student card

Schul- zW:**~ferien** pl school holidays; **s~frei** adj: **s~freier Tag** holiday; **s~frei sein** to be a holiday; **~hof** m playground; **~jahr** nt school year;**~kind** nt schoolchild; **s~pflichtig** adj of school age;**~schiff** nt (NAUT) training ship;**~stunde** f period, lesson;**~tasche** f school bag

Schulter ['ʃʊltər] (-, -n) f shoulder;**~blatt** nt shoulder blade;**s~n** vt to shoulder

Schulung f education, schooling

Schulzeugnis nt school report

Schund [ʃʊnt] (-(e)s) m trash, garbage

Schuppe ['ʃʊpə] f scale; **~n** pl (Haarschuppen) dandruff sg

Schuppen (-s, -) m shed

schuppig ['ʃʊpɪç] adj scaly

Schur [ʃuːr] (-, -en) f shearing

schüren ['ʃyːrən] vt to rake; (fig) to stir up

schürfen ['ʃʏrfən] vt, vi to scrape, to scratch; (MIN) to prospect

Schurke ['ʃʊrkə] (-n, -n) m rogue

Schurwolle f: **"reine ~"** "pure new wool"

Schürze ['ʃʏrtsə] f apron

Schuss ▲ [ʃʊs] (-es, ⁻e) m shot; (WEBEN) woof;**~bereich** m effective range

Schüssel ['ʃʏsəl] (-, -n) f bowl

Schuss- ▲ zW:**~linie** f line of fire; **~verletzung** f bullet wound;**~waffe** f firearm

Schuster ['ʃuːstər] (-s, -) m cobbler, shoemaker

Schutt [ʃʊt] (-(e)s) m rubbish; (Bauschutt) rubble

Schüttelfrost m shivering

schütteln ['ʃʏtəln] vt, vr to shake

schütten ['ʃʏtən] vt to pour; (Zucker, Kies etc) to tip; (verschütten) to spill ♦ vi unpers to pour (down)

Schutthalde f dump

Schutthaufen m heap of rubble

Schutz [ʃʊts] (-es) m protection; (Unterschlupf) shelter; **jdn in ~ nehmen** to stand up for sb;**~anzug** m overalls pl; **~blech** nt mudguard

Schütze ['ʃʏtsə] (-n, -n) m gunman; (Gewehrschütze) rifleman; (Scharfschütze, Sportschütze) marksman; (ASTROL) Sagittarius

schützen ['ʃʏtsən] vt to protect; **~ vor** +dat od **gegen** to protect from

Schützenfest nt fair featuring shooting matches

Schutz- zW:**~engel** m guardian angel; **~gebiet** nt protectorate; (Naturschutzgebiet) reserve;**~hütte** f shelter, refuge;**~impfung** f immunisation

Schützling ['ʃʏtslɪŋ] m protégé(e); (bes Kind) charge

Schutz- zW:**s~los** adj defenceless;**~mann** m policeman;**~patron** m patron saint

Schwaben ['ʃvaːbən] nt Swabia; **schwäbisch** adj Swabian

schwach [ʃvax] adj weak, feeble

Schwäche ['ʃvɛçə] f weakness;**s~n** vt to weaken

Schwachheit f weakness

schwächlich adj weakly, delicate

Schwächling m weakling

Schwach- zW:**~sinn** m imbecility; **s~sinnig** adj mentally deficient; (Idee) idiotic;**~strom** m weak current

Schwächung ['ʃvɛçʊŋ] f weakening

Schwager ['ʃvaːgər] (-s, ⁻) m brother-in-law;

Schwägerin ['ʃvɛːgərɪn] f sister-in-law

Rechtschreibreform: ▲ neue Schreibung △ alte Schreibung (auslaufend)

Schwalbe ['ʃvalbə] f swallow

Schwall [ʃval] (-(e)s, -e) m surge; (Worte) flood, torrent

Schwamm [ʃvam] (-(e)s, ⁺e) m sponge; (Pilz) fungus

schwamm etc vb siehe **schwimmen**

schwammig adj spongy; (Gesicht) puffy

Schwan [ʃvaːn] (-(e)s, ⁺e) m swan

schwanger ['ʃvaŋər] adj pregnant; **S~schaft** f pregnancy

schwanken vi to sway; (taumeln) to stagger, to reel; (Preise, Zahlen) to fluctuate; (zögern) to hesitate, to vacillate

Schwankung f fluctuation

Schwanz [ʃvants] (-es, ⁺e) m tail

schwänzen ['ʃvɛntsən] (umg) vt to skip, to cut ♦ vi to play truant

Schwarm [ʃvarm] (-(e)s, ⁺e) m swarm; (umg) heart-throb, idol

schwärm- ['ʃvɛrm] zW: **~en** vi to swarm; **~en für** to be mad od wild about; **S~erei** [-ə'raɪ] f enthusiasm; **~erisch** adj impassioned, effusive

Schwarte ['ʃvartə] f hard skin; (Speckschwarte) rind

schwarz [ʃvarts] adj black; **~es Brett** notice board; **ins S~e treffen** (auch fig) to hit the bull's eye; **in den ~en Zahlen** in the black; **~ sehen** (umg) to see the gloomy side of things; **S~arbeit** f illicit work, moonlighting; **S~brot** nt black bread; **S~e(r)** f(m) black (man/woman)

Schwärze ['ʃvɛrtsə] f blackness; (Farbe) blacking; (Druckerschwärze) printer's ink; **s~n** vt to blacken

Schwarz- zW: **s~fahren** (unreg) vi to travel without paying; to drive without a licence; **~handel** m black market (trade); **~markt** m black market; **~wald** m Black Forest; **s~weiß, s~-weiß** adj black and white

schwatzen ['ʃvatsən] vi to chatter

schwätzen ['ʃvɛtsən] vi to chatter

Schwätzer ['ʃvɛtsər] (-s, -) m gasbag

schwatzhaft adj talkative, gossipy

Schwebe ['ʃveːbə] f: **in der ~** (fig) in abeyance; **~bahn** f overhead railway; **s~n** vi to drift; to float; (hoch) to soar

Schwed- ['ʃveːd] zW: **~e** m Swede; **~en** nt Sweden; **~in** f Swede; **s~isch** adj Swedish

Schwefel ['ʃveːfəl] (-s) m sulphur; **s~ig** adj sulphurous; **~säure** f sulphuric acid

Schweig- ['ʃvaɪg] zW: **~egeld** nt hush money; **~en** (-s) nt silence; **s~en** (unreg) vi to be silent; to stop talking; **~epflicht** f pledge of secrecy; (von Anwalt) requirement of confidentiality; **s~sam** ['ʃvaɪkzaːm] adj silent, taciturn; **~samkeit** f taciturnity, quietness

Schwein [ʃvaɪn] (-(e)s, -e) nt pig; (umg) (good) luck

Schweine- zW: **~fleisch** nt pork; **~'rei** f mess; (Gemeinheit) dirty trick; **~stall** m pigsty

schweinisch adj filthy

Schweinsleder nt pigskin

Schweiß [ʃvaɪs] (-es) m sweat, perspiration; **s~en** vt, vi to weld; **~er** (-s, -) m welder; **~füße** pl sweaty feet; **~naht** f weld

Schweiz [ʃvaɪts] f Switzerland; **~er(in)** m(f) Swiss; **s~erisch** adj Swiss

schwelgen ['ʃvɛlgən] vi to indulge

Schwelle ['ʃvɛlə] f (auch fig) threshold; doorstep; (EISENB) sleeper (BRIT), tie (US)

schwellen (unreg) vi to swell

Schwellung f swelling

Schwemme ['ʃvɛmə] f (WIRTS: Überangebot) surplus

Schwenk- ['ʃvɛŋk] zW: **s~bar** adj swivel-mounted; **s~en** vt to swing; (Fahne) to wave; (abspülen) to rinse ♦ vi to turn, to swivel; (MIL) to wheel; **~ung** f turn; wheel

schwer [ʃveːr] adj heavy; (schwierig) difficult, hard; (schlimm) serious, bad ♦ adv (sehr) very (much); (verletzt etc) seriously, badly; **~ erziehbar** difficult (to bring up); **jdm ~ fallen** to be difficult for sb; **jdm/sich etw ~ machen** to make sth difficult for sb/o.s.; **~ nehmen** to take to heart; **sich dat od akk ~ tun** to have difficulties; **~ verdaulich** indigestible, heavy; **~ wiegend** weighty, important; **S~arbeiter** m manual worker, labourer; **S~behinderte(r)** f(m) seriously handicapped person; **S~e** *f* weight, heaviness; (*PHYS*) gravity; **~elos** *adj* weightless; (*Kammer*) zero-G; **~fällig** *adj* ponderous; **S~gewicht** *nt* heavyweight; (*fig*) emphasis; **~hörig** *adj* hard of hearing; **S~industrie** *f* heavy industry; **S~kraft** *f* gravity; **S~kranke(r)** *f(m)* person who is seriously ill; **~lich** *adv* hardly; **~mütig** *adj* melancholy; **S~punkt** *m* centre of gravity; (*fig*) emphasis, crucial point

Schwert [ʃveːrt] **(-(e)s, -er)** *nt* sword; **~lilie** *f* iris

schwer- *zW:* **S~verbrecher(in)** *m(f)* criminal, serious offender; **S~verletzte(r)** *f(m)* serious casualty; (*bei Unfall usw auch*) seriously injured person

Schwester [ʃvestər] **(-, -n)** *f* sister; (*MED*) nurse; **~lich** *adj* sisterly

Schwieger- [ʃviːgər] *zW:* **~eltern** *pl* parents-in-law; **~mutter** *f* mother-in-law; **~sohn** *m* son-in-law; **~tochter** *f* daughter-in-law; **~vater** *m* father-in-law

schwierig [ʃviːrɪç] *adj* difficult, hard; **S~keit** *f* difficulty

Schwimm- [ʃvɪm] *zW:* **~bad** *nt* swimming baths *pl;* **~becken** *nt* swimming pool; **s~en** (*unreg*) *vi* to swim; (*treiben, nicht sinken*) to float; (*fig: unsicher sein*) to be all at sea; **~er (-s, -)** *m* swimmer; (*Angeln*) float; **~erin** *f* (female) swimmer; **~lehrer** *m* swimming instructor; **~weste** *f* life jacket

Schwindel [ʃvɪndəl] **(-s)** *m* giddiness; dizzy spell; (*Betrug*) swindle, fraud; (*Zeug*) stuff; **s~frei** *adj:* **s~frei sein** to have a good head for heights; **s~n** (*umg*) *vi* (*lügen*) to fib; **jdm s~t es** sb feels dizzy

schwinden [ʃvɪndən] (*unreg*) *vi* to disappear; (*sich verringern*) to decrease; (*Kräfte*) to decline

Schwindler [ʃvɪndlər] *m* swindler; (*Lügner*) liar

schwindlig *adj* dizzy; **mir ist ~** I feel dizzy

Schwing- [ʃvɪŋ] *zW:* **s~en** (*unreg*) *vt* to swing; (*Waffe etc*) to brandish ♦ *vi* to swing; (*vibrieren*) to vibrate; (*klingen*) to sound; **~tür** *f* swing door(s); **~ung** *f* vibration;

(*PHYS*) oscillation

Schwips [ʃvɪps] **(-es, -e)** *m:* **einen ~ haben** to be tipsy

schwirren [ʃvɪrən] *vi* to buzz

schwitzen [ʃvɪtsən] *vi* to sweat, to perspire

schwören [ʃvøːrən] (*unreg*) *vt, vi* to swear

schwul [ʃvuːl] (*umg*) *adj* gay, queer

schwül [ʃvyːl] *adj* sultry, close; **S~e (-)** *f* sultriness

Schwule(r) (*umg*) *f(m)* gay (man/woman)

Schwung [ʃvʊŋ] **(-(e)s, ⁻e)** *m* swing; (*Triebkraft*) momentum; (*fig: Energie*) verve, energy; (*umg: Menge*) batch; **s~haft** *adj* brisk, lively; **s~voll** *adj* vigorous

Schwur [ʃvuːr] **(-(e)s, ⁻e)** *m* oath; **~gericht** *nt* court with a jury

sechs [zɛks] *num* six; **~hundert** *num* six hundred; **~te(r, s)** *adj* sixth; **S~tel (-s, -)** *nt* sixth

sechzehn [zɛçtseːn] *num* sixteen

sechzig [zɛçtsɪç] *num* sixty

See¹ [zeː] **(-, -n)** *f* sea

See² [zeː] **(-s, -n)** *m* lake

See- [zeː] *zW:* **~bad** *nt* seaside resort; **~hund** *m* seal; **~igel** [zeːliːgəl] *m* sea urchin; **s~krank** *adj* seasick; **~krankheit** *f* seasickness; **~lachs** *m* rock salmon

Seele [zeːlə] *f* soul; **s~nruhig** *adv* calmly

Seeleute [zeːlɔytə] *pl* seamen

Seel- *zW:* **s~isch** *adj* mental; **~sorge** *f* pastoral duties *pl;* **~sorger (-s, -)** *m* clergyman

See- *zW:* **~macht** *f* naval power; **~mann** (*pl* **-leute**) *m* seaman, sailor; **~meile** *f* nautical mile; **~möwe** *f* (*ZOOL*) seagull; **~not** *f* distress; **~räuber** *m* pirate; **~rose** *f* water lily; **~stern** *m* starfish; **s~tüchtig** *adj* seaworthy; **~weg** *m* sea route; **auf dem ~weg** by sea; **~zunge** *f* sole

Segel [zeːgəl] **(-s, -)** *nt* sail; **~boot** *nt* yacht; **~fliegen (-s)** *nt* gliding; **~flieger** *m* glider pilot; **~flugzeug** *nt* glider; **s~n** *vt, vi* to sail; **~schiff** *nt* sailing vessel; **~sport** *m* sailing; **~tuch** *nt* canvas

Segen [zeːgən] **(-s, -)** *m* blessing

Segler [zeːglər] **(-s, -)** *m* sailor, yachtsman

segnen [zeːgnən] *vt* to bless

Seh- ['ze:] zW: **s~behindert** adj partially sighted; **s~en** (unreg) vt, vi to see; (in bestimmte Richtung) to look; **mal s~en(, ob ...)** let's see (if ...); **siehe Seite 5** see page 5; **s~enswert** adj worth seeing; **~enswürdigkeiten** pl sights (of a town); **~fehler** m sight defect

Sehne ['ze:nə] f sinew; (an Bogen) string

sehnen vr: **sich ~ nach** to long od yearn for

sehnig adj sinewy

Sehn- zW: **s~lich** adj ardent; **~sucht** f longing; **s~süchtig** adj longing

sehr [ze:r] adv very; (mit Verben) a lot, (very) much; **zu ~** too much; **~ geehrte(r) ...** dear ...

seicht [zaɪçt] adj (auch fig) shallow

Seide ['zaɪdə] f silk; **s~n** adj silk; **~npapier** nt tissue paper

seidig ['zaɪdɪç] adj silky

Seife ['zaɪfə] f soap

Seifen- zW: **~lauge** f soapsuds pl; **~schale** f soap dish; **~schaum** m lather

seihen ['zaɪən] vt to strain, to filter

Seil [zaɪl] (**-(e)s, -e**) nt rope; cable; **~bahn** f cable railway; **~hüpfen** (**-s**) nt skipping; **~springen** (**-s**) nt skipping; **~tänzer(in)** m(f) tightrope walker

---

SCHLÜSSELWORT

sein [zaɪn] (pt **war**, pp **gewesen**) vi **1** to be; **ich bin** I am; **du bist** you are; **er/sie/es ist** he/she/it is; **wir sind/ihr seid/sie sind** we/you/they are; **wir waren** we were; **wir sind gewesen** we have been

2: seien Sie nicht böse don't be angry; **sei so gut und ...** be so kind as to ...; **das wäre gut** that would od that'd be a good thing; **wenn ich Sie wäre** if I were od was you; **das wärs** that's all, that's it; **morgen bin ich in Rom** tomorrow I'll od I will od I shall be in Rome; **waren Sie mal in Rom?** have you ever been to Rome?

3: wie ist das zu verstehen? how is that to be understood?; **er ist nicht zu ersetzen** he cannot be replaced; **mit ihr ist nicht zu reden** you can't talk to her

4: mir ist kalt I'm cold; **was ist?** what's the matter?, what is it?; **ist was?** is something the matter?; **es sei denn, dass ...** unless ...; **wie dem auch sei** be that as it may; **wie wäre es mit ...?** how od what about ...?; **lass das sein!** stop that!

---

sein(e) ['zaɪn(ə)] adj his; its; **~e(r, s)** pron his; its; **~er** (gen von **er**) pron of him; **~erseits** adv for his part; **~erzeit** adv in those days, formerly; **~esgleichen** pron people like him; **~etwegen** adv (für ihn) for his sake; (wegen ihm) on his account; (von ihm aus) as far as he is concerned; **~etwillen** adv: **um ~etwillen = seinetwegen**; **~ige** pron: **der/die/das ~ige** od **S~ige** his

seit [zaɪt] präp +dat since ♦ konj since; **er ist ~ einer Woche hier** he has been here for a week; **~ langem** for a long time; **~dem** [zaɪt'de:m] adv, konj since

Seite ['zaɪtə] f side; (Buch~) page; (MIL) flank

Seiten- zW: **~airbag** m side-impact airbag; **~ansicht** f side view; **~hieb** m (fig) passing shot, dig; **s~s** präp +gen on the part of; **~schiff** nt aisle; **~sprung** m extramarital escapade; **~stechen** nt (a) stitch; **~straße** f side road; **~streifen** m verge; (der Autobahn) hard shoulder

seither [zaɪt'he:r] adv, konj since (then)

seit- zW: **~lich** adj on one od the side; side cpd; **~wärts** adv sidewards

Sekretär [zekre'tɛ:r] m secretary; (Möbel) bureau

Sekretariat [zekretari'a:t] (**-(e)s, -e**) nt secretary's office, secretariat

Sekretärin f secretary

Sekt [zɛkt] (**-(e)s, -e**) m champagne

Sekte ['zɛktə] f sect

Sekunde [ze'kʊndə] f second

selber ['zɛlbər] = **selbst**

Selbst [zɛlpst] (**-**) nt self

SCHLÜSSELWORT

selbst [zɛlpst] pron **1**: **ich/er/wir selbst** I myself/he himself/we ourselves; **sie ist die Tugend selbst** she's virtue itself; **er braut**

Spelling Reform: ▲ new spelling △ old spelling (to be phased out)

sein Bier selbst he brews his own beer; **wie gehts? - gut, und selbst?** how are things? - fine, and yourself? **2** (*ohne Hilfe*) alone, on my/his/one's *etc* own; **von selbst** by itself; **er kam von selbst** he came of his own accord; **selbst gemacht** home-made
♦ *adv* even; **selbst wenn** even if; **selbst Gott** even God (himself)

selbständig *etc* ['zɛlpʃtɛndɪç] = **selbst- ständig** *etc*
Selbst- *zW:* **~auslöser** *m* (PHOT) delayed-action shutter release; **~bedienung** *f* self-service; **~befriedigung** *f* masturbation; **~beherrschung** *f* self-control; **~bestimmung** *f* (POL) self-determination; **~beteiligung** *f* (VERSICHERUNG: *bei Kosten*) (voluntary) excess; **s~bewusst** ▲ *adj* (self-)confident; **~bewusstsein** ▲ *nt* self-confidence; **~erhaltung** *f* self-preservation; **~erkenntnis** *f* self-knowledge; **s~gefällig** *adj* smug, self-satisfied; **~gespräch** *nt* conversation with o.s.; **~kostenpreis** *m* cost price; **s~los** *adj* unselfish, selfless; **~mord** *m* suicide; **~mörder(in)** *m(f)* suicide; **s~mörderisch** *adj* suicidal; **s~sicher** *adj* self-assured; **s~ständig** ▲ *adj* independent; **~ständigkeit** ▲ *f* independence; **s~süchtig** *adj* (*Mensch*) selfish; **~versorger** (**-s, -**) *m* (*im Urlaub etc*) self-caterer; **s~verständlich** ['zɛlpstfɛrʃtɛntlɪç] *adj* obvious ♦ *adv* naturally; **ich halte das für s~verständlich** I take that for granted; **~verteidigung** *f* self-defence; **~vertrauen** *nt* self-confidence; **~verwaltung** *f* autonomy, self-government

selig ['ze:lɪç] *adj* happy, blissful; (REL) blessed; (*tot*) late; **S~keit** *f* bliss
Sellerie ['zɛlari:] (**-s, -(s)** *od* **-, -**) *m od f* celery
selten ['zɛltən] *adj* rare ♦ *adv* seldom, rarely; **S~heit** *f* rarity
Selterswasser ['zɛltərsvasər] *nt* soda water
seltsam ['zɛltza:m] *adj* strange, curious; **S~keit** *f* strangeness

Semester [ze'mɛstər] (**-s, -**) *nt* semester; **~ferien** *pl* vacation *sg*
Semi- [zemi] *in zW* semi-; **~kolon** [-'ko:lɔn] (**-s, -s**) *nt* semicolon
Seminar [zemi'na:r] (**-s, -e**) *nt* seminary; (*Kurs*) seminar; (UNIV: *Ort*) department building
Semmel ['zɛməl] (**-, -n**) *f* roll
Senat [ze'na:t] (**-(e)s, -e**) *m* senate, council
Sende- ['zɛndə] *zW:* **~bereich** *m* transmission range; **~folge** *f* (*Serie*) series; **s~n** (*unreg*) *vt* to send; (RADIO, TV) to transmit, to broadcast ♦ *vi* to transmit, to broadcast; **~r** (**-s, -**) *m* station; (*Anlage*) transmitter; **~reihe** *f* series (of broadcasts)
Sendung ['zɛndʊŋ] *f* consignment; (*Aufgabe*) mission; (RADIO, TV) transmission; (*Programm*) programme
Senf [zɛnf] (**-(e)s, -e**) *m* mustard
senil [ze'ni:l] (*pej*) *adj* senile
Senior(in) ['ze:niɔr(ɪn)] (**-s, -en**) *m(f)* (*Mensch im Rentenalter*) (old age) pensioner
Seniorenheim [zeni'o:rənhaɪm] *nt* old people's home
Senk- ['zɛŋk] *zW:* **~blei** *nt* plumb; **~e** *f* depression; **s~en** *vt* to lower ♦ *vr* to sink, to drop gradually; **s~recht** *adj* vertical, perpendicular; **~rechte** *f* perpendicular; **~rechtstarter** *m* (AVIAT) vertical take-off plane; (*fig*) high-flyer
Sensation [zɛnzatsi'o:n] *f* sensation; **s~ell** [-'nɛl] *adj* sensational
sensibel [zɛn'zi:bəl] *adj* sensitive
sentimental [zɛntimɛn'ta:l] *adj* sentimental; **S~i'tät** *f* sentimentality
separat [zepa'ra:t] *adj* separate
September [zɛp'tɛmbər] (**-(s), -**) *m* September
Serie ['ze:riə] *f* series
serien- *zW:* **~mäßig** *adj* standard; **S~mörder(in)** *m(f)* serial killer; **~weise** *adv* in series
seriös [zeri'ø:s] *adj* serious, bona fide
Service¹ [zɛr'vi:s] (**-(s), -**) *nt* (*Geschirr*) set, service
Service² (**-, -s**) *m* service
servieren [zɛr'vi:rən] *vt, vi* to serve

Rechtschreibreform: ▲ *neue Schreibung* △ *alte Schreibung (auslaufend)*

Serviererin [zɛr'viːrərɪn] f waitress
Serviette [zɛrvi'ɛtə] f napkin, serviette
Servo- ['zɛrvo] zW: **~bremse** f (AUT) servo(-assisted) brake; **~lenkung** f (AUT) power steering
Sessel ['zɛsəl] (**-s, -**) m armchair; **~lift** m chairlift
sesshaft ▲ ['zɛshaft] adj settled; (ansässig) resident
setzen ['zɛtsən] vt to put, to set; (Baum etc) to plant; (Segel, TYP) to set ♦ vr to settle; (Person) to sit down ♦ vi (springen) to leap; (wetten) to bet
Setz- ['zɛts] zW: **~er** (**-s, -**) m (TYP) compositor; **~ling** m young plant
Seuche ['zɔʏçə] f epidemic; **~ngebiet** nt infected area
seufzen ['zɔʏftsən] vt, vi to sigh
Seufzer ['zɔʏftsər] (**-s, -**) m sigh
Sex [zɛks] (**-(es)**) m sex; **~ualität** [-uali'tɛt] f sex, sexuality; **~ualkunde** [zɛksu'aːl-] f (SCH) sex education; **s~uell** [-u'ɛl] adj sexual
Shampoo [ʃam'puː] (**-s, -s**) nt shampoo
Sibirien [zi'biːriən] nt Siberia

⎡ *SCHLÜSSELWORT* ⎤

sich [zɪç] pron 1 (akk): **er/sie/es ... sich** he/she/it ... himself/herself/itself; **sie** pl/ **man ... sich** they/one ... themselves/ oneself; **Sie ... sich** you ... yourself/ yourselves pl; **sich wiederholen** to repeat oneself/itself
2 (dat): **er/sie/es ... sich** he/she/it ... to himself/herself/itself; **sie** pl/**man ... sich** they/one ... to themselves/oneself; **Sie ... sich** you ... to yourself/yourselves pl; **sie hat sich einen Pullover gekauft** she bought herself a jumper; **sich die Haare waschen** to wash one's hair
3 (mit Präposition): **haben Sie Ihren Ausweis bei sich?** do you have your pass on you?; **er hat nichts bei sich** he's got nothing on him; **sie bleiben gern unter sich** they keep themselves to themselves
4 (einander) each other, one another; **sie bekämpfen sich** they fight each other od

one another
5: **dieses Auto fährt sich gut** this car drives well; **hier sitzt es sich gut** it's good to sit here

---

Sichel ['zɪçəl] (**-, -n**) f sickle; (Mondsichel) crescent
sicher ['zɪçər] adj safe; (gewiss) certain; (zuverlässig) secure, reliable; (selbstsicher) confident; **vor jdm/etw ~ sein** to be safe from sb/sth; **ich bin nicht ~** I'm not sure od certain; **~ nicht** surely not; **aber ~!** of course!; **~gehen** (unreg) vi to make sure
Sicherheit ['zɪçərhaɪt] f safety; (auch FIN) security; (Gewissheit) certainty; (Selbstsicherheit) confidence
Sicherheits- zW: **~abstand** m safe distance; **~glas** nt safety glass; **~gurt** m safety belt; **s~halber** adv for safety; to be on the safe side; **~nadel** f safety pin; **~schloss** ▲ nt safety lock; **~vorkehrung** f safety precaution
sicher- zW: **~lich** adv certainly, surely; **~n** vt to secure; (schützen) to protect; (Waffe) to put the safety catch on; **jdm etw ~n** to secure sth for sb; **sich dat etw ~n** to secure sth (for o.s.); **~stellen** vt to impound; (COMPUT) to save; **S~ung** f (S~n) securing; (Vorrichtung) safety device; (an Waffen) safety catch; (ELEK) fuse; **S~ungskopie** f back-up copy
Sicht [zɪçt] (**-**) f sight; (Aussicht) view; **auf** od **nach ~** (FIN) at sight; **auf lange ~** on a long-term basis; **s~bar** adj visible; **s~en** vt to sight; (auswählen) to sort out; **s~lich** adj evident, obvious; **~verhältnisse** pl visibility sg; **~vermerk** m visa; **~weite** f visibility
sickern ['zɪkərn] vi to trickle, to seep
Sie [ziː] (nom, akk) pron you
sie [ziː] pron (sg: nom) she, it; (: akk) her, it; (pl: nom) they; (: akk) them
Sieb [ziːp] (**-(e)s, -e**) nt sieve; (KOCH) strainer; **s~en¹** ['ziːbən] vt to sift; (Flüssigkeit) to strain
sieben² num seven; **~hundert** num seven hundred; **S~sachen** pl belongings

Spelling Reform: ▲ *new spelling* △ *old spelling (to be phased out)*

siebte(r, s) ['zi:ptə(r, s)] *adj* seventh; **S~l** (**-s, -**) *nt* seventh

siebzehn ['zi:ptse:n] *num* seventeen

siebzig ['zi:ptsıç] *num* seventy

siedeln ['zi:dəln] *vi* to settle

sieden ['zi:dən] *vt, vi* to boil, to simmer

Siedepunkt *m* boiling point

Siedler (**-s, -**) *m* settler

Siedlung *f* settlement; (*Häusersiedlung*) housing estate

Sieg [zi:k] (**-(e)s, -e**) *m* victory

Siegel ['zi:gəl] (**-s, -**) *nt* seal; **~ring** *m* signet ring

Sieg- *zW*: **s~en** *vi* to be victorious; (*SPORT*) to win; **~er** (**-s, -**) *m* victor; (*SPORT etc*) winner; **s~reich** *adj* victorious

siehe *etc* ['zi:ə] *vb siehe* **sehen**

siezen ['zi:tsən] *vt* to address as "Sie"

Signal [zɪ'gna:l] (**-s, -e**) *nt* signal

Silbe ['zɪlbə] *f* syllable

Silber ['zɪlbər] (**-s**) *nt* silver; **~hochzeit** *f* silver wedding (anniversary); **s~n** *adj* silver; **~papier** *nt* silver paper

Silvester [zɪl'vestər] (**-s, -**) *nt* New Year's Eve, Hogmanay (*SCOTTISH*); **~abend** *m* = **Silvester**

Silvester

i **Silvester** *is the German word for New Year's Eve. Although not an official holiday most businesses close early and shops shut at midday. Most Germans celebrate in the evening, and at midnight they let off fireworks and rockets; the revelry usually lasts until the early hours of the morning.*

---

simpel ['zɪmpəl] *adj* simple

Sims [zɪms] (**-es, -e**) *nt od m* (*Kaminsims*) mantelpiece; (*Fenstersims*) (window)sill

simsen ['zɪmzn] *vti* to text

simulieren [zimu'li:rən] *vt* to simulate; (*vortäuschen*) to feign ♦ *vi* to feign illness

simultan [zimʊl'ta:n] *adj* simultaneous

Sinfonie [zɪnfo'ni:] *f* symphony

singen ['zɪŋən] (*unreg*) *vt, vi* to sing

Singular ['zɪŋgula:r] *m* singular

Singvogel ['zɪŋfo:gəl] *m* songbird

sinken ['zɪŋkən] (*unreg*) *vi* to sink; (*Preise etc*) to fall, to go down

Sinn [zɪn] (**-(e)s, -e**) *m* mind; (*Wahrnehmungssinn*) sense; (*Bedeutung*) sense, meaning; **~ für etw** sense of sth; **von ~en sein** to be out of one's mind; **es hat keinen ~** there's no point; **~bild** *nt* symbol; **s~en** (*unreg*) *vi* to ponder; **auf etw** *akk* **s~en** to contemplate sth; **~estäuschung** *f* illusion; **s~gemäß** *adj* faithful; (*Wiedergabe*) in one's own words; **s~ig** *adj* clever; **s~lich** *adj* sensual, sensuous; (*Wahrnehmung*) sensory; **~lichkeit** *f* sensuality; **s~los** *adj* senseless, meaningless; **~losigkeit** *f* senselessness; meaninglessness; **s~voll** *adj* meaningful; (*vernünftig*) sensible

Sintflut ['zɪntflu:t] *f* Flood

Sippe ['zɪpə] *f* clan, kin

Sippschaft ['zɪpʃaft] (*pej*) *f* relations *pl*, tribe; (*Bande*) gang

Sirene [zi're:nə] *f* siren

Sirup ['zi:rʊp] (**-s, -e**) *m* syrup

Sitt- ['zɪt] *zW*: **~e** *f* custom; **~en** *pl* (*~lichkeit*) morals; **~enpolizei** *f* vice squad; **s~sam** *adj* modest, demure

Situation [zituatsi'o:n] *f* situation

Sitz [zɪts] (**-es, -e**) *m* seat; **der Anzug hat einen guten ~** the suit is a good fit; **s~en** (*unreg*) *vi* to sit; (*Bemerkung, Schlag*) to strike home, to tell; (*Gelerntes*) to have sunk in; **s~en bleiben** to remain seated; (*SCH*) to have to repeat a year; **auf etw** *dat* **s~en bleiben** to be lumbered with sth; **s~en lassen** (*SCH*) to make (sb) repeat a year; (*Mädchen*) to jilt; (*Wartenden*) to stand up; **etw auf sich** *dat* **s~en lassen** to take sth lying down; **s~end** *adj* (*Tätigkeit*) sedentary; **~gelegenheit** *f* place to sit down; **~platz** *m* seat; **~streik** *m* sit-down strike; **~ung** *f* meeting

Sizilien [zi'tsi:liən] *nt* Sicily

Skala ['ska:la] (**-, Skalen**) *f* scale

Skalpell [skal'pel] (**-s, -e**) *nt* scalpel

Skandal [skan'da:l] (**-s, -e**) *m* scandal; **s~ös** [-'lø:s] *adj* scandalous

Skandinav- [skandi'na:v] *zW:* **~ien** *nt* Scandinavia; **~ier(in)** *m(f)* Scandinavian; **s~isch** *adj* Scandinavian

Skelett [ske'lɛt] **(-(e)s, -e)** *nt* skeleton

Skepsis ['skɛpsɪs] **(-)** *f* scepticism

skeptisch ['skɛptɪʃ] *adj* sceptical

Ski [ʃiː] **(-s, -er)** *m* ski; **~ laufen** *od* **fahren** to ski; **~fahrer** *m* skier; **~gebiet** *nt* ski(ing) area; **~läufer** *m* skier; **~lehrer** *m* ski instructor; **~lift** *m* ski-lift; **~springen** *nt* ski-jumping; **~stock** *m* ski-pole

Skizze ['skɪtsə] *f* sketch

skizzieren [skɪ'tsiːrən] *vt, vi* to sketch

Sklave ['skla:və] **(-n, -n)** *m* slave; **~'rei** *f* slavery; **Sklavin** *f* slave

Skorpion [skɔrpi'oːn] **(-s, -e)** *m* scorpion; *(ASTROL)* Scorpio

Skrupel ['skruːpəl] **(-s, -)** *m* scruple; **s~los** *adj* unscrupulous

Skulptur [skʊlp'tuːr] *f (Gegenstand)* sculpture

Slip [slɪp] **(-s, -s)** *m* (under)pants; **~einlage** *f* panty liner

Slowakei [slova'kaɪ] *f:* **die ~** Slovakia

Slowenien [slo'veːniən] *nt* Slovenia

Smaragd [sma'rakt] **(-(e)s, -e)** *m* emerald

Smoking ['smoːkɪŋ] **(-s, -s)** *m* dinner jacket

SMS *abbr (= Short Message Service)* text message

Snowboarding ['snoːbɔːbdɪŋ] *nt* snowboarding

SCHLÜSSELWORT

so [zoː] *adv* **1** *(so sehr)* so; **so groß/schön** *etc* so big/nice *etc;* **so groß/schön wie ...** as big/nice as ...; **so viel (wie)** as much as; **rede nicht so viel** don't talk so much; **so weit sein** to be ready; **so weit wie** *od* **als möglich** as far as possible; **ich bin so weit zufrieden** by and large I'm quite satisfied; **so wenig (wie)** as little (as); **das hat ihn so geärgert, dass ...** that annoyed him so much that ...; **so einer wie ich** somebody like me; **na so was!** well, well!

2 *(auf diese Weise)* like this; **mach es nicht so** don't do it like that; **so oder so** one way or the other; **und so weiter** and so on; **... oder so was** ... or something like

that; **das ist gut so** that's fine; **so genannt** so-called

3 *(umg: umsonst)*: **ich habe es so bekommen** I got it for nothing

♦ *konj:* **so dass, sodass** so that; **so wie es jetzt ist** as things are at the moment

♦ *excl:* **so?** really?; **so, das wärs** so, that's it then

---

s. o. *abk* **= siehe oben**

Socke ['zɔkə] *f* sock

Sockel ['zɔkəl] **(-s, -)** *m* pedestal, base

sodass ▲ [zo'das] *konj* so that

Sodawasser ['zoːdavasɐ] *nt* soda water

Sodbrennen ['zoːtbrɛnən] **(-s, -)** *nt* heartburn

soeben [zo'leːbən] *adv* just (now)

Sofa ['zoːfa] **(-s, -s)** *nt* sofa

sofern [zo'fɛrn] *konj* if, provided (that)

sofort [zo'fɔrt] *adv* immediately, at once; **~ig** *adj* immediate

Sog [zoːk] **(-(e)s, -e)** *m (Strömung)* undertow

sogar [zo'ga:r] *adv* even

sogleich [zo'glaɪç] *adv* straight away, at once

Sohle ['zoːlə] *f* sole; *(Talsohle etc)* bottom; *(MIN)* level

Sohn [zoːn] **(-(e)s, ⁺e)** *m* son

Solar- [zo'laːr] *in zW* solar; **~zelle** *f* solar cell

solch [zɔlç] *pron* such; **ein ~e(r, s) ...** such a ...

Soldat [zɔl'daːt] **(-en, -en)** *m* soldier

Söldner ['zœldnɐ] **(-s, -)** *m* mercenary

solidarisch [zoli'da:rɪʃ] *adj* in *od* with solidarity; **sich ~ erklären** to declare one's solidarity

Solidari'tät *f* solidarity

solid(e) [zo'liːd(ə)] *adj* solid; *(Leben, Person)* respectable

Solist(in) [zo'lɪst(ɪn)] *m(f)* soloist

Soll [zɔl] **(-(s), -(s))** *nt (FIN)* debit (side); *(Arbeitsmenge)* quota, target

---

SCHLÜSSELWORT

sollen ['zɔlən] *(pt* **sollte**, *pp* **gesollt** *od (als Hilfsverb)* **sollen)** *Hilfsverb* **1** *(Pflicht, Befehl)* to be supposed to; **du hättest nicht gehen**

---

sollen you shouldn't have gone, you oughtn't to have gone; **soll ich?** shall I?; **soll ich dir helfen?** shall I help you?; **sag ihm, er soll warten** tell him he's to wait; **was soll ich machen?** what should I do? 2 (*Vermutung*): **sie soll verheiratet sein** she's said to be married; **was soll das heißen?** what's that supposed to mean?; **man sollte glauben, dass ...** you would think that ...; **sollte das passieren, ...** if that should happen ...

♦ *vt, vi:* **was soll das?** what's all this?; **das sollst du nicht** you shouldn't do that; **was solls?** what the hell!

Solo ['zo:lo] (**-s, -s** *od* **Soli**) *nt* solo

somit [zo'mɪt] *konj* and so, therefore

Sommer ['zɔmər] (**-s, -**) *m* summer; **s~lich** *adj* summery; summer; **~reifen** *m* normal tyre; **~schlussverkauf ▲** *m* summer sale; **~sprossen** *pl* freckles

Sonde ['zɔndə] *f* probe

Sonder- ['zɔndər] *in zW* special; **~angebot** *nt* special offer; **s~bar** *adj* strange, odd; **~fahrt** *f* special trip; **~fall** *m* special case; **s~lich** *adj* particular; (*außergewöhnlich*) remarkable; (*eigenartig*) peculiar; **~marke** *f* special issue stamp; **s~n** *konj* but ♦ *vt* to separate; **nicht nur ..., s~n auch** not only ..., but also; **~preis** *m* special reduced price; **~zug** *m* special train

Sonnabend ['zɔn|a:bənt] *m* Saturday

Sonne ['zɔnə] *f* sun; **s~n** *vr* to sun o.s.

Sonnen- *zW*: **~aufgang** *m* sunrise; **s~baden** *vi* to sunbathe; **~brand** *m* sunburn; **~brille** *f* sunglasses *pl*; **~creme** *f* suntan lotion; **~energie** *f* solar energy, solar power; **~finsternis** *f* solar eclipse; **~kollektor** *m* solar panel; **~schein** *m* sunshine; **~schirm** *m* parasol, sunshade; **~schutzfaktor** *m* protection factor; **~stich** *m* sunstroke; **~uhr** *f* sundial; **~untergang** *m* sunset; **~wende** *f* solstice

sonnig ['zɔnɪç] *adj* sunny

Sonntag ['zɔnta:k] *m* Sunday

sonst [zɔnst] *adv* otherwise; (*mit pron, in Fragen*) else; (*zu anderer Zeit*) at other times,

normally ♦ *konj* otherwise; **~ noch etwas?** anything else?; **~ nichts** nothing else; **~ jemand** anybody (at all); **~ wo** somewhere else; **~ woher** from somewhere else; **~ wohin** somewhere else; **~ig** *adj* other

sooft [zo'ɔft] *konj* whenever

Sopran [zo'pra:n] (**-s, -e**) *m* soprano

Sorge ['zɔrgə] *f* care, worry

sorgen *vi:* **für jdn ~** to look after sb ♦ *vr:* **sich ~ (um)** to worry (about); **für etw ~** to take care of *od* see to sth; **s~frei** *adj* carefree; **s~voll** *adj* troubled, worried

Sorg- [zɔrk] *zW*: **~falt** (-) *f* care(fulness); **s~fältig** *adj* careful; **s~los** *adj* careless; (*ohne ~en*) carefree; **s~sam** *adj* careful

Sorte ['zɔrtə] *f* sort; (*Warensorte*) brand; **~n** *pl* (FIN) foreign currency *sg*

sortieren [zɔr'ti:rən] *vt* to sort (out)

Sortiment [zɔrti'mɛnt] *nt* assortment

sosehr [zo'ze:r] *konj* as much as

Soße ['zo:sə] *f* sauce; (*Bratensoße*) gravy

soufflieren [zu'fli:rən] *vt, vi* to prompt

Souterrain [zute'rɛ̃:] (**-s, -s**) *nt* basement

souverän [zuvə'rɛ:n] *adj* sovereign; (*überlegen*) superior

so- *zW*: **~viel** [zo'fi:l] *konj:* **~viel ich weiß** as far as I know; *siehe* **so**; **~weit** [zo'vart] *konj* as far as; *siehe* **so**; **~wenig** [zo've:nɪç] *konj* little as; *siehe* **so**; **~wie** [zo'vi:] *konj* (*~bald*) as soon as; (*ebenso*) as well as; **~wieso** [zovi'zo:] *adv* anyway

sowjetisch [zɔ'vjɛtɪʃ] *adj* Soviet

Sowjetunion *f* Soviet Union

sowohl [zo'vo:l] *konj:* **~ ... als** *od* **wie auch** both ... and

sozial [zotsi'a:l] *adj* social; **S~abgaben** *pl* national insurance contributions; **S~arbeiter(in)** *m(f)* social worker; **S~demokrat** *m* social democrat; **~demokratisch** *adj* social democratic; **S~hilfe** *f* income support (BRIT), welfare (aid) (US); **~i'sieren** *vt* to socialize; **S~ismus** [-'lɪsmʊs] *m* socialism; **S~ist** [-'lɪst] *m* socialist; **~istisch** *adj* socialist; **S~politik** *f* social welfare policy; **S~produkt** *nt* (net) national product;

S~staat m welfare state;
S~versicherung f national insurance
(*BRIT*), social security (*US*); **S~wohnung** f
council flat

soziologisch [zotsio'lo:gɪʃ] *adj* sociological
sozusagen [zotsu'za:gən] *adv* so to speak
Spachtel ['ʃpaxtəl] (**-s, -**) m spatula
spähen ['ʃpɛːən] vi to peep, to peek
Spalier [ʃpa'liːr] (**-s, -e**) nt (*Gerüst*) trellis;
(*Leute*) guard of honour
Spalt [ʃpalt] (**-(e)s, -e**) m crack; (*Türspalt*)
chink; (*fig: Kluft*) split; **~e** f crack, fissure;
(*Gletscherspalte*) crevasse; (*in Text*) column;
s~en vt, vr (*auch fig*) to split; **~ung** f
splitting
Span [ʃpaːn] (**-(e)s, ⁻e**) m shaving
Spanferkel nt sucking pig
Spange ['ʃpaŋə] f clasp; (*Haarspange*) hair
slide; (*Schnalle*) buckle
Spanien ['ʃpaːniən] nt Spain; **Spanier(in)**
m(f) Spaniard; **spanisch** *adj* Spanish
Spann- ['ʃpan] zW: **~beton** m prestressed
concrete; **~betttuch** ▲ nt fitted sheet; **~e**
f (*Zeitspanne*) space; (*Differenz*) gap; **s~en**
vt (*straffen*) to tighten, to tauten;
(*befestigen*) to brace ♦ vi to be tight;
s~end *adj* exciting, gripping; **~ung** f
tension; (*ELEK*) voltage; (*fig*) suspense;
(*unangenehm*) tension
Spar- ['ʃpaːr] zW: **~buch** nt savings book;
~büchse f money box; **s~en** vt, vi to
save; **sich** *dat* **etw s~en** to save o.s. sth;
(*Bemerkung*) to keep sth to o.s.; **mit etw**
s~en to be sparing with sth; **an etw** *dat*
s~en to economize on sth; **~er** (**-s, -**) m
saver
Spargel ['ʃpargəl] (**-s, -**) m asparagus
Sparkasse f savings bank
Sparkonto nt savings account
spärlich ['ʃpɛːrlɪç] *adj* meagre; (*Bekleidung*)
scanty
Spar- zW: **~preis** m economy price;
s~sam *adj* economical, thrifty; **~samkeit**
f thrift, economizing; **~schwein** nt piggy
bank
Sparte ['ʃpartə] f field; line of business;
(*PRESSE*) column

Spaß [ʃpaːs] (**-es, ⁻e**) m joke; (*Freude*) fun;
jdm ~ machen to be fun (for sb); **viel ~!**
have fun!; **s~en** vi to joke; **mit ihm ist**
nicht zu s~en you can't take liberties with
him; **s~haft** *adj* funny, droll; **s~ig** *adj*
funny, droll
spät [ʃpɛːt] *adj, adv* late; **wie ~ ist es?**
what's the time?
Spaten ['ʃpaːtən] (**-s, -**) m spade
später *adj, adv* later
spätestens *adv* at the latest
Spätvorstellung f late show
Spatz [ʃpats] (**-en, -en**) m sparrow
spazier- [ʃpa'tsiːr] zW: **~en** vi to stroll, to
walk; **~en fahren** to go for a drive; **~en**
gehen to go for a walk; **S~gang** m walk;
S~stock m walking stick; **S~weg** m path,
walk
Specht [ʃpɛçt] (**-(e)s, -e**) m woodpecker
Speck [ʃpɛk] (**-(e)s, -e**) m bacon
Spediteur [ʃpedi'tøːr] m carrier;
(*Möbelspediteur*) furniture remover
Spedition [ʃpeditsi'oːn] f carriage; (*~sfirma*)
road haulage contractor; removal firm
Speer [ʃpeːr] (**-(e)s, -e**) m spear; (*SPORT*)
javelin
Speiche ['ʃpaɪçə] f spoke
Speichel ['ʃpaɪçəl] (**-s**) m saliva, spit(tle)
Speicher ['ʃpaɪçər] (**-s, -**) m storehouse;
(*Dachspeicher*) attic, loft; (*Kornspeicher*)
granary; (*Wasserspeicher*) tank; (*TECH*) store;
(*COMPUT*) memory; **s~n** vt to store;
(*COMPUT*) to save
speien ['ʃpaɪən] (*unreg*) vt, vi to spit;
(*erbrechen*) to vomit; (*Vulkan*) to spew
Speise ['ʃpaɪzə] f food; **~eis** [-ʔaɪs] nt ice-
cream; **~kammer** f larder, pantry; **~karte**
f menu; **s~n** vt to feed; to eat ♦ vi to dine;
~röhre f gullet, oesophagus; **~saal** m
dining room; **~wagen** m dining car
Speku- [ʃpeku] zW: **~lant** m speculator;
~lation [-latsi'oːn] f speculation; **s~lieren**
[-'liːrən] vi (*fig*) to speculate; **auf etw** *akk*
s~lieren to have hopes of sth
Spelunke [ʃpe'lʊŋkə] f dive
Spende ['ʃpɛndə] f donation; **s~n** vt to
donate, to give; **~r** (**-s, -**) m donor,

donator

spendieren [ʃpɛnˈdiːrən] vt to pay for, to buy; **jdm etw ~** to treat sb to sth, to stand sb sth

Sperling [ˈʃpɛrlɪŋ] m sparrow

Sperma [ˈʃpɛrma] (-s, **Spermen**) nt sperm

Sperr- [ˈʃpɛr] zW: **~e** f barrier; (Verbot) ban; **s~en** vt to block; (SPORT) to suspend, to bar; (vom Ball) to obstruct; (einschließen) to lock; (verbieten) to ban ♦ vr to baulk, to jib(e); **~gebiet** nt prohibited area; **~holz** nt plywood; **s~ig** adj bulky; **~müll** m bulky refuse; **~sitz** m (THEAT) stalls pl; **~stunde** f closing time

Spesen [ˈʃpeːzən] pl expenses

Spezial- [ʃpetsiˈaːl] in zW special; **~gebiet** nt specialist field; **s~i'sieren** vr to specialize; **~i'sierung** f specialization; **~ist** [-ˈlɪst] m specialist; **~i'tät** f speciality

speziell [ʃpetsiˈɛl] adj special

spezifisch [ʃpeˈtsiːfɪʃ] adj specific

Sphäre [ˈsfɛːrə] f sphere

Spiegel [ˈʃpiːgəl] (-s, -) m mirror; (Wasserspiegel) level; (MIL) tab; **~bild** nt reflection; **s~bildlich** adj reversed; **~ei** nt fried egg; **s~n** vt to mirror, to reflect ♦ vr to be reflected ♦ vi to gleam; (widerspiegeln) to be reflective; **~ung** f reflection

Spiel [ʃpiːl] (-(e)s, -e) nt game; (Schauspiel) play; (Tätigkeit) play(ing); (KARTEN) deck; (TECH) (free) play; **s~en** vt, vi to play; (um Geld) to gamble; (THEAT) to perform, to act; **s~end** adv easily; **~er** (-s, -) m player; (um Geld) gambler; **~erei** f trifling pastime; **~feld** nt pitch, field; **~film** m feature film; **~kasino** nt casino; **~plan** m (THEAT) programme; **~platz** m playground; **~raum** m room to manoeuvre, scope; **~regel** f rule; **~sachen** pl toys; **~uhr** f musical box; **~verderber** (-s, -) m spoilsport; **~waren** pl toys; **~zeug** nt toy(s)

Spieß [ʃpiːs] (-es, -e) m spear; (Bratspieß) spit; **~bürger** m bourgeois; **~er** (-s, -) (umg) m bourgeois; **s~ig** (pej) adj (petit) bourgeois

Spinat [ʃpiˈnaːt] (-(e)s, -e) m spinach

Spind [ʃpɪnt] (-(e)s, -e) m od nt locker

Spinn- [ˈʃpɪn] zW: **~e** f spider; **s~en** (unreg) vt, vi to spin; (umg) to talk rubbish; (verrückt sein) to be crazy od mad; **~e'rei** f spinning mill; **~rad** nt spinning wheel; **~webe** f cobweb

Spion [ʃpiˈoːn] (-s, -e) m spy; (in Tür) spyhole; **~age** [ʃpioˈnaːʒə] f espionage; **s~ieren** [ʃpioˈniːrən] vi to spy; **~in** f (female) spy

Spirale [ʃpiˈraːlə] f spiral

Spirituosen [ʃpirituˈoːzən] pl spirits

Spiritus [ˈʃpiːritus] (-, -se) m (methylated) spirit

Spital [ʃpiˈtaːl] (-s, ̈er) nt hospital

spitz [ʃpɪts] adj pointed; (Winkel) acute; (fig: Zunge) sharp; (: Bemerkung) caustic

Spitze f point, tip; (Bergspitze) peak; (Bemerkung) taunt, dig; (erster Platz) lead, top; (meist pl: Gewebe) lace

Spitzel (-s, -) m police informer

spitzen vt to sharpen

Spitzenmarke f brand leader

spitzfindig adj (over)subtle

Spitzname m nickname

Splitter [ˈʃplɪtar] (-s, -) m splinter

sponsern [ˈʃpɔnzarn] vt to sponsor

spontan [ʃpɔnˈtaːn] adj spontaneous

Sport [ʃpɔrt] (-(e)s, -e) m sport; (fig) hobby; **~lehrer(in)** m(f) games od P.E. teacher; **~ler(in)** (-s, -) m(f) sportsman(-woman); **s~lich** adj sporting; (Mensch) sporty; **~platz** m playing od sports field; **~schuh** m (Turnschuh) training shoe, trainer; **~stadion** nt sports stadium; **~verein** m sports club; **~wagen** m sports car

Spott [ʃpɔt] (-(e)s) m mockery, ridicule; **s~billig** adj dirt-cheap; **s~en** vi to mock; **s~en (über** +akk) to mock (at), to ridicule

spöttisch [ˈʃpœtɪʃ] adj mocking

sprach etc [ʃpraːx] vb siehe **sprechen**

Sprach- zW: **s~begabt** adj good at languages; **~e** f language; **~enschule** f language school; **~fehler** m speech defect; **~führer** m phrasebook; **~gefühl** nt feeling for language; **~kenntnisse** pl linguistic proficiency sg; **~kurs** m language course; **~labor** nt language laboratory; **s~lich** adj

---

Rechtschreibreform: ▲ *neue Schreibung* △ *alte Schreibung (auslaufend)*

linguistic; **s~los** adj speechless
sprang etc [ʃpraŋ] vb siehe **springen**
Spray [spreː] (-s, -s) m od nt spray
Sprech- [ʃpreç] zW: **~anlage** f intercom;
s~en (unreg) vi to speak, to talk ♦ vt to say;
(Sprache) to speak; (Person) to speak to; **mit
jdm s~en** to speak to sb; **das spricht für
ihn** that's a point in his favour; **~er(in)** (-s,
-) m(f) speaker; (für Gruppe) spokesman(-
woman); (RADIO, TV) announcer; **~stunde** f
consultation (hour); (doctor's) surgery;
~stundenhilfe f (doctor's) receptionist;
~zimmer nt consulting room, surgery,
office (US)
spreizen [ʃpraɪtsən] vt (Beine) to open, to
spread; (Finger, Flügel) to spread
Spreng- [ʃpreŋ] zW: **s~en** vt to sprinkle;
(mit ~stoff) to blow up; (Gestein) to blast;
(Versammlung) to break up; **~stoff** m
explosive(s)
sprichst etc [ʃpriçst] vb siehe **sprechen**
Sprichwort nt proverb; **sprichwörtlich**
adj proverbial
Spring- [ʃpriŋ] zW: **~brunnen** m fountain;
s~en (unreg) vi to jump; (Glas) to crack;
(mit Kopfsprung) to dive; **~er** (-s, -) m
jumper; (Schach) knight
Sprit [ʃprit] (-(e)s, -e) (umg) m juice, gas
Spritz- [ʃprits] zW: **~e** f syringe; injection;
(an Schlauch) nozzle; **s~en** vt to spray;
(MED) to inject ♦ vi to splash;
(herausspritzen) to spurt; (MED) to give
injections; **~pistole** f spray gun; **~tour** f
(umg) spin
spröde [ʃprøːdə] adj brittle; (Person)
reserved, coy
Sprosse [ʃprɔsə] f rung
Sprössling ▲ [ʃprœslɪŋ] (umg) m (Kind)
offspring (pl inv)
Spruch [ʃprux] (-(e)s, ⁻e) m saying, maxim;
(JUR) judgement
Sprudel [ʃpruːdəl] (-s, -) m mineral water;
lemonade; **s~n** vi to bubble; **~wasser** nt
(KOCH) sparkling od fizzy mineral water
Sprüh- [ʃpryː] zW: **~dose** f aerosol (can);
s~en vi to spray; (fig) to sparkle ♦ vt to
spray; **~regen** m drizzle

Sprung [ʃpruŋ] (-(e)s, ⁻e) m jump; (Riss)
crack; **~brett** nt springboard; **s~haft** adj
erratic; (Aufstieg) rapid; **~schanze** f ski
jump
Spucke [ʃpukə] (-) f spit; **s~n** vt, vi to spit
Spuk [ʃpuːk] (-(e)s, -e) m haunting; (fig)
nightmare; **s~en** vi (Geist) to walk; **hier
s~t es** this place is haunted
Spülbecken [ʃpyːlbɛkən] nt (in Küche) sink
Spule [ʃpuːlə] f spool; (ELEK) coil
Spül- [ʃpyːl] zW: **~e** f (kitchen) sink; **s~en**
vt, vi to rinse; (Geschirr) to wash up;
(Toilette) to flush; **~maschine** f
dishwasher; **~mittel** nt washing-up liquid;
~stein m sink; **~ung** f rinsing; flush; (MED)
irrigation
Spur [ʃpuːr] (-, -en) f trace; (Fußspur, Radspur,
Tonbandspur) track; (Fährte) trail; (Fahrspur)
lane
spürbar adj noticeable, perceptible
spüren [ʃpyːrən] vt to feel
spurlos adv without (a) trace
Spurt [ʃpurt] (-(e)s, -s od -e) m spurt; **s~en**
vi to spurt
sputen [ʃpuːtən] vr to make haste
St. abk = **Stück**; (= Sankt) St.
Staat [ʃtaːt] (-(e)s, -en) m state; (Prunk)
show; (Kleidung) finery; **s~enlos** adj
stateless; **s~lich** adj state(-); state-run
Staats- zW: **~angehörige(r)** f(m) national;
~angehörigkeit f nationality; **~anwalt** m
public prosecutor; **~bürger** m citizen;
~dienst m civil service; **~examen** nt
(UNIV) state exam(ination); **s~feindlich** adj
subversive; **~mann** (pl -männer) m
statesman; **~oberhaupt** nt head of state
Stab [ʃtaːp] (-(e)s, ⁻e) m rod; (Gitterstab) bar;
(Menschen) staff; **~hochsprung** m pole
vault
stabil [ʃtaˈbiːl] adj stable; (Möbel) sturdy;
~i'sieren vt to stabilize
Stachel [ʃtaxəl] (-s, -n) m spike; (von Tier)
spine; (von Insekten) sting; **~beere** f
gooseberry; **~draht** m barbed wire; **s~ig**
adj prickly; **~schwein** nt porcupine
Stadion [ʃtaːdiɔn] (-s, **Stadien**) nt stadium
Stadium [ʃtaːdiʊm] nt stage, phase

Spelling Reform: ▲ *new spelling* △ *old spelling (to be phased out)*

Stadt [ʃtat] (-, ⁓e) f town; ~autobahn f urban motorway; ~bahn f suburban railway; ~bücherei f municipal library

Städt- ['ʃtɛːt] zW: ~ebau m town planning; ~epartnerschaft f town twinning; ~er(in) (-s, -) m(f) town dweller; s~isch adj municipal; (nicht ländlich) urban

Stadt- zW: ~kern m town centre, city centre; ~mauer f city wall(s); ~mitte f town centre; ~plan m street map; ~rand m outskirts pl; ~rat m (Behörde) town council, city council; ~rundfahrt f tour of a/the city; ~teil m district, part of town; ~zentrum nt town centre

Staffel ['ʃtafəl] (-, -n) f rung; (SPORT) relay (team); (AVIAT) squadron; ~lauf m (SPORT) relay (race); s~n vt to graduate

Stahl [ʃtaːl] (-(e)s, ⁓e) m steel

stahl etc vb siehe **stehlen**

stak etc [ʃtaːk] vb siehe **stecken**

Stall [ʃtal] (-(e)s, ⁓e) m stable; (Kaninchenstall) hutch; (Schweinestall) sty; (Hühnerstall) henhouse

Stamm [ʃtam] (-(e)s, ⁓e) m (Baumstamm) trunk; (Menschenstamm) tribe; (GRAM) stem; ~baum m family tree; (von Tier) pedigree; s~eln vt, vi to stammer; s~en vi: s~en von od aus to come from; ~gast m regular (customer)

stämmig ['ʃtɛmɪç] adj sturdy; (Mensch) stocky

Stammtisch ['ʃtamtɪʃ] m table for the regulars

stampfen ['ʃtampfən] vt, vi to stamp; (stapfen) to tramp; (mit Werkzeug) to pound

Stand [ʃtant] (-(e)s, ⁓e) m position; (Wasserstand, Benzinstand etc) level; (Stehen) standing position; (Zustand) state; (Spielstand) score; (Messestand etc) stand; (Klasse) class; (Beruf) profession; siehe **imstande, zustande**

stand etc vb siehe **stehen**

Standard ['ʃtandart] (-s, -s) m standard

Ständer ['ʃtɛndər] (-s, -) m stand

Standes- ['ʃtandəs] zW: ~amt nt registry office; ~beamte(r) m registrar; s~gemäß adj, adv according to one's social position;

~unterschied m social difference

Stand- zW: s~haft adj steadfast; s~halten (unreg) vi: (jdm/etw) s~halten to stand firm (against sb/sth), to resist (sb/sth)

ständig ['ʃtɛndɪç] adj permanent; (ununterbrochen) constant, continual

Stand- zW: ~licht nt sidelights pl, parking lights pl (US); ~ort m location; (MIL) garrison; ~punkt m standpoint; ~spur f hard shoulder

Stange ['ʃtaŋə] f stick; (Stab) pole, bar; rod; (Zigaretten) carton; (COMM) off the peg; **eine ~ Geld** (umg) quite a packet

Stängel ▲ ['ʃtɛŋəl] (-s, -) m stalk

Stapel ['ʃtaːpəl] (-s, -) m pile; (NAUT) stocks pl; ~lauf m launch; s~n vt to pile (up)

Star¹ [ʃtaːr] (-(e)s, -e) m starling; (MED) cataract

Star² [staːr] (-s, -s) m (Filmstar etc) star

starb etc [ʃtarp] vb siehe **sterben**

stark [ʃtark] adj strong; (heftig, groß) heavy; (Maßangabe) thick

Stärke ['ʃtɛrkə] f strength; heaviness; thickness; (KOCH: Wäschestärke) starch; s~n vt to strengthen; (Wäsche) to starch

Starkstrom m heavy current

Stärkung ['ʃtɛrkʊŋ] f strengthening; (Essen) refreshment

starr [ʃtar] adj stiff; (unnachgiebig) rigid; (Blick) staring; ~en vi to stare; ~en vor od von to be covered in; (Waffen) to be bristling with; S~heit f rigidity; ~köpfig adj stubborn; S~sinn m obstinacy

Start [ʃtart] (-(e)s, -e) m start; (AVIAT) takeoff; ~automatik f (AUT) automatic choke; ~bahn f runway; s~en vt to start ♦ vi to start; to take off; ~er (-s, -) m starter; ~erlaubnis f takeoff clearance; ~hilfekabel nt jump leads pl

Station [ʃtatsi'oːn] f station; hospital ward; s~är [ʃtatsio'nɛːr] adj (MED) in-patient attr; s~ieren [-'niːrən] vt to station

Statist [ʃta'tɪst] m extra, supernumerary

Statistik f statistics sg; ~er (-s, -) m statistician

statistisch adj statistical

Stativ [ʃta'tiːf] (-s, -e) nt tripod

statt [ʃtat] *konj* instead of ♦ *präp* (+gen od dat) instead of

Stätte [ˈʃtɛtə] *f* place

statt- *zW*: **~finden** (*unreg*) *vi* to take place; **~haft** *adj* admissible; **~lich** *adj* imposing, handsome

Statue [ˈʃtaːtuə] *f* statue

Status [ˈʃtaːtʊs] (-, -) *m* status

Stau [ʃtaʊ] (-(e)s, -e) *m* blockage; (*Verkehrsstau*) (traffic) jam

Staub [ʃtaʊp] (-(e)s) *m* dust; ~ **saugen** to vacuum, to hoover®; **s~ig** *adj* dusty; **s~saugen** *vi* to vacuum, to hoover®; **~sauger** *m* vacuum cleaner; **~tuch** *nt* duster

Staudamm *m* dam

Staude [ˈʃtaʊdə] *f* shrub

stauen [ˈʃtaʊən] *vt* (*Wasser*) to dam up; (*Blut*) to stop the flow ♦ *vr* (*Wasser*) to become dammed up; (*MED*: *Verkehr*) to become congested; (*Menschen*) to collect; (*Gefühle*) to build up

staunen [ˈʃtaʊnən] *vi* to be astonished; **S~** (-s) *nt* amazement

Stausee [ˈʃtaʊzeː] (-s, -n) *m* reservoir, man-made lake

Stauung [ˈʃtaʊʊŋ] *f* (*von Wasser*) damming-up; (*von Blut, Verkehr*) congestion

Std. *abk* (= *Stunde*) hr.

Steak [ʃteːk] *nt* steak

Stech- [ˈʃtɛç] *zW*: **s~en** (*unreg*) *vt* (*mit Nadel etc*) to prick; (*mit Messer*) to stab; (*mit Finger*) to poke; (*Biene etc*) to sting; (*Mücke*) to bite; (*Sonne*) to burn; (*KARTEN*) to play; (*ART*) to engrave; (*Torf, Spargel*) to cut; **in See s~en** to put to sea; **~en** (-s, -) *nt* (*SPORT*) play-off; jump-off; **s~end** *adj* piercing, stabbing; (*Geruch*) pungent; **~palme** *f* holly; **~uhr** *f* time clock

Steck- [ˈʃtɛk] *zW*: **~brief** *m* "wanted" poster; **~dose** *f* (wall) socket; **s~en** *vt* to put, to insert; (*Nadel*) to stick; (*Pflanzen*) to plant; (*beim Nähen*) to pin ♦ *vi* (*auch unreg*) to be; (*festsitzen*) to be stuck; (*Nadeln*) to stick; **s~en bleiben** to get stuck; **s~en lassen** to leave in; **~enpferd** *nt* hobbyhorse; **~er** (-s, -) *m* plug; **~nadel** *f* pin

Steg [ʃteːk] (-(e)s, -e) *m* small bridge; (*Anlegesteg*) landing stage; **~reif** *m*: **aus dem ~reif** just like that

stehen [ˈʃteːən] (*unreg*) *vi* to stand; (*sich befinden*) to be; (*in Zeitung*) to say; (*stillstehen*) to have stopped ♦ *vi unpers*: **es steht schlecht um jdn/etw** things are bad for sb/sth; **zu jdm/etw** ~ to stand by sb/ sth; **jdm** ~ to suit sb; **wie stehts?** how are things?; (*SPORT*) what's the score?; ~ **bleiben** to remain standing; (*Uhr*) to stop; (*Fehler*) to stay as it is; ~ **lassen** to leave; (*Bart*) to grow

Stehlampe [ˈʃteːlampə] *f* standard lamp

stehlen [ˈʃteːlən] (*unreg*) *vt* to steal

Stehplatz [ˈʃteːplats] *m* standing place

steif [ʃtaɪf] *adj* stiff; **S~heit** *f* stiffness

Steig- [ʃtaɪk] *zW*: **~bügel** *m* stirrup; **s~en** [ˈʃtaɪgən] (*unreg*) *vi* to rise; (*klettern*) to climb; **s~en in** +*akk*/**auf** +*akk* to get in/on; **s~ern** *vt* to raise; (*GRAM*) to compare ♦ *vi* (*Auktion*) to bid ♦ *vr* to increase; **~erung** *f* raising; (*GRAM*) comparison; **~ung** *f* incline, gradient, rise

steil [ʃtaɪl] *adj* steep; **S~küste** *f* steep coast; (*Klippen*) cliffs *pl*

Stein [ʃtaɪn] (-(e)s, -e) *m* stone; (*in Uhr*) jewel; **~bock** *m* (*ASTROL*) Capricorn; **~bruch** *m* quarry; **s~ern** *adj* (made of) stone; (*fig*) stony; **~gut** *nt* stoneware; **s~ig** [ˈʃtaɪnɪç] *adj* stony; **s~igen** *vt* to stone; **~kohle** *f* mineral coal; **~zeit** *f* Stone Age

Stelle [ˈʃtɛlə] *f* place; (*Arbeit*) post, job; (*Amt*) office; **an Ihrer/meiner** ~ in your/my place; *siehe* **anstelle**

stellen *vt* to put; (*Uhr etc*) to set; (*zur Verfügung* ~) to supply; (*fassen*: *Dieb*) to apprehend ♦ *vr* (*sich aufstellen*) to stand; (*sich einfinden*) to present o.s.; (*bei Polizei*) to give o.s. up; (*vorgeben*) to pretend (to be); **sich zu etw** ~ to have an opinion of sth

Stellen- *zW*: **~angebot** *nt* offer of a post; (*in Zeitung*) "vacancies"; **~anzeige** *f* job advertisement; **~gesuch** *nt* application for a post; **~vermittlung** *f* employment agency

Stell- *zW:* **~ung** *f* position; (*MIL*) line; **~ung nehmen zu** to comment on; **~ungnahme** *f* comment; **s~vertretend** *adj* deputy, acting; **~vertreter** *m* deputy

Stelze ['ʃtɛltsə] *f* stilt

stemmen ['ʃtɛmən] *vt* to lift (up); (*drücken*) to press; **sich ~ gegen** (*fig*) to resist, to oppose

Stempel ['ʃtɛmpəl] (**-s, -**) *m* stamp; (*BOT*) pistil; **~kissen** *nt* ink pad; **s~n** *vt* to stamp; (*Briefmarke*) to cancel; **s~n gehen** (*umg*) to be od go on the dole

Stengel △ ['ʃtɛŋəl] (**-s, -**) *m* = **Stängel**

Steno- [ʃteno] *zW:* **~gramm** [-'gram] *nt* shorthand report; **~grafie** ▲ [-gra'fi:] *f* shorthand; **s~grafieren** ▲ [-gra'fi:rən] *vt, vi* to write (in) shorthand; **~typist(in)** [-ty'pɪst(ɪn)] *m(f)* shorthand typist

Stepp- ['ʃtɛp] *zW:* **~decke** *f* quilt; **~e** *f* prairie; steppe; **s~en** *vt* to stitch ♦ *vi* to tap-dance

Sterb- ['ʃtɛrb] *zW:* **~efall** *m* death; **~ehilfe** *f* euthanasia; **s~en** (*unreg*) *vi* to die; **s~lich** ['ʃtɛrplɪç] *adj* mortal; **~lichkeit** *f* mortality; **~lichkeitsziffer** *f* death rate

stereo- ['ʃte:reo] *in zW* stereo(-); **S~anlage** *f* stereo (system); **~typ** [ʃtereo'ty:p] *adj* stereotype

steril [ʃte'ri:l] *adj* sterile; **~isieren** *vt* to sterilize; **S~i'sierung** *f* sterilization

Stern [ʃtɛrn] (**-(e)s, -e**) *m* star; **~bild** *nt* constellation; **~schnuppe** *f* meteor, falling star; **~stunde** *f* historic moment; **~zeichen** *nt* sign of the zodiac

stet [ʃte:t] *adj* steady; **~ig** *adj* constant, continual; **~s** *adv* continually, always

Steuer¹ ['ʃtɔyər] (**-s, -**) *nt* (*NAUT*) helm; (*~ruder*) rudder; (*AUT*) steering wheel

Steuer² ['ʃtɔyər] (**-, -n**) *f* tax; **~berater(in)** *m(f)* tax consultant

Steuerbord *nt* (*NAUT, AVIAT*) starboard

Steuer- ['ʃtɔyər] *zW:* **~erklärung** *f* tax return; **s~frei** *adj* tax-free; **~freibetrag** *m* tax allowance; **~klasse** *f* tax group; **~knüppel** *m* control column; (*AVIAT, COMPUT*) joystick; **~mann** (*pl* **-männer** *od* **-leute**) *m* helmsman; **s~n** *vt, vi* to steer;

(*Flugzeug*) to pilot; (*Entwicklung, Tonstärke*) to control; **s~pflichtig** [-pflɪçtɪç] *adj* taxable; **~rad** *nt* steering wheel; **~ung** *f* (*auch AUT*) steering; piloting; control; (*Vorrichtung*) controls *pl*; **~zahler** (**-s, -**) *m* taxpayer

Steward ['stju:ərt] (**-s, -s**) *m* steward; **~ess** ▲ ['stju:ərdɛs] (**-, -en**) *f* stewardess; air hostess

Stich [ʃtɪç] (**-(e)s, -e**) *m* (*Insektenstich*) sting; (*Messerstich*) stab; (*beim Nähen*) stitch; (*Färbung*) tinge; (*KARTEN*) trick; (*ART*) engraving; **jdn im ~ lassen** to leave sb in the lurch; **s~eln** *vi* (*fig*) to jibe; **s~haltig** *adj* sound, tenable; **~probe** *f* spot check; **~straße** *f* cul-de-sac; **~wahl** *f* final ballot; **~wort** *nt* cue; (*in Wörterbuch*) headword; (*für Vortrag*) note

sticken ['ʃtɪkən] *vt, vi* to embroider

Sticke'rei *f* embroidery

stickig *adj* stuffy, close

Stickstoff *m* nitrogen

Stief- ['ʃti:f] *in zW* step

Stiefel ['ʃti:fəl] (**-s, -**) *m* boot

Stief- *zW:* **~kind** *nt* stepchild; (*fig*) Cinderella; **~mutter** *f* stepmother; **~mütterchen** *nt* pansy; **s~mütterlich** *adj* (*fig*) **jdn/etw s~mütterlich behandeln** to pay little attention to sb/sth; **~vater** *m* stepfather

stiehlst *etc* [ʃti:lst] *vb siehe* **stehlen**

Stiel [ʃti:l] (**-(e)s, -e**) *m* handle; (*BOT*) stalk

Stier (**-(e)s, -e**) *m* bull; (*ASTROL*) Taurus

stieren *vi* to stare

Stierkampf *m* bullfight

Stierkämpfer *m* bullfighter

Stift [ʃtɪft] (**-(e)s, -e**) *m* peg; (*Nagel*) tack; (*Farbstift*) crayon; (*Bleistift*) pencil ♦ *nt* (*charitable*) foundation; (*ECCL*) religious institution; **s~en** *vt* to found; (*Unruhe*) to cause; (*spenden*) to contribute; **~er(in)** (**-s, -**) *m(f)* founder; **~ung** *f* donation; (*Organisation*) foundation; **~zahn** *m* post crown

Stil [ʃti:l] (**-(e)s, -e**) *m* style

still [ʃtɪl] *adj* quiet; (*unbewegt*) still; (*heimlich*) secret; **S~er Ozean** Pacific; **~ halten** to keep still; **~ stehen** to stand still; **S~e** *f*

stillness, quietness; **in aller S~e** quietly;
~en vt to stop; (*befriedigen*) to satisfy;
(*Säugling*) to breast-feed; **~legen** ▲ vt to
close down; **~schweigen** (*unreg*) vi to be
silent; **S~schweigen** nt silence;
~schweigend adj silent; (*Einverständnis*)
tacit ♦ adv silently; tacitly; **S~stand** m
standstill

Stimm- ['ʃtɪm] zW: **~bänder** pl vocal cords;
s~berechtigt adj entitled to vote; **~e** f
voice; (*Wahlstimme*) vote; **s~en** vt (*MUS*) to
tune ♦ vi to be right; **das s~te ihn traurig**
that made him feel sad; **s~en für/gegen**
to vote for/against; **s~t so!** that's right;
~enmehrheit f majority (of votes);
~enthaltung f abstention; **~gabel** f
tuning fork; **~recht** nt right to vote; **~ung**
f mood; atmosphere; **s~ungsvoll** adj
enjoyable; full of atmosphere; **~zettel** m
ballot paper

stinken ['ʃtɪŋkən] (*unreg*) vi to stink
Stipendium [ʃti'pɛndiʊm] nt grant
stirbst etc [ʃtɪrpst] vb siehe **sterben**
Stirn [ʃtɪrn] (-, -en) f forehead, brow;
(*Frechheit*) impudence; **~band** nt
headband; **~höhle** f sinus
stöbern ['ʃtøːbərn] vi to rummage
stochern ['ʃtɔxərn] vi to poke (about)
Stock¹ [ʃtɔk] (-(e)s, **¨e**) m stick; (*BOT*) stock
Stock² [ʃtɔk] (-(e)s, - od **Stockwerke**) m
storey
stocken vi to stop, to pause; **~d** adj halting
Stockung f stoppage
Stockwerk nt storey, floor
Stoff [ʃtɔf] (-(e)s, -e) m (*Gewebe*) material,
cloth; (*Materie*) matter; (*von Buch etc*)
subject (matter); **s~lich** adj material; **~tier**
nt soft toy; **~wechsel** m metabolism
stöhnen ['ʃtøːnən] vi to groan
Stollen ['ʃtɔlən] (-s, -) m (*MIN*) gallery;
(*KOCH*) cake eaten at Christmas; (*von
Schuhen*) stud
stolpern ['ʃtɔlpərn] vi to stumble, to trip
Stolz [ʃtɔlts] (-es) m pride; **s~** adj proud;
s~ieren [ʃtɔl'tsiːrən] vi to strut
stopfen ['ʃtɔpfən] vt (*hineinstopfen*) to stuff;
(*voll stopfen*) to fill (up); (*nähen*) to darn ♦ vi

(*MED*) to cause constipation
Stopfgarn nt darning thread
Stoppel ['ʃtɔpəl] (-, -n) f stubble
Stopp- ['ʃtɔp] zW: **s~en** vt to stop; (*mit Uhr*)
to time ♦ vi to stop; **~schild** nt stop sign;
~uhr f stopwatch
Stöpsel ['ʃtœpsəl] (-s, -) m plug; (*für
Flaschen*) stopper
Storch [ʃtɔrç] (-(e)s, **¨e**) m stork
Stör- ['ʃtøːr] zW: **s~en** vt to disturb;
(*behindern*, *RADIO*) to interfere with ♦ vr:
sich an etw dat **s~en** to let sth bother
one; **s~end** adj disturbing, annoying;
~enfried (-(e)s, -e) m troublemaker
stornieren [ʃtɔr'niːrən] vt (*Auftrag*) to
cancel; (*Buchung*) to reverse
Stornogebühr ['ʃtɔrno-] f cancellation fee
störrisch ['ʃtœrɪʃ] adj stubborn, perverse
Störung f disturbance; interference
Stoß [ʃtoːs] (-es, **¨e**) m (*Schub*) push; (*Schlag*)
blow; knock; (*mit Schwert*) thrust; (*mit Fuß*)
kick; (*Erdstoß*) shock; (*Haufen*) pile;
~dämpfer (-s, -) m shock absorber; **s~en**
(*unreg*) vt (*mit Druck*) to shove, to push; (*mit
Schlag*) to knock, to bump; (*mit Fuß*) to
kick; (*Schwert etc*) to thrust; (*anstoßen: Kopf
etc*) to bump ♦ vr to get a knock ♦ vi: **s~en
an** od **auf** +akk to bump into; (*finden*) to
come across; (*angrenzen*) to be next to;
sich s~en an +dat (*fig*) to take exception
to; **~stange** f (*AUT*) bumper
stottern ['ʃtɔtərn] vt, vi to stutter
Str. abk (= *Straße*) St.
Straf- ['ʃtraːf] zW: **~anstalt** f penal
institution; **~arbeit** f (*SCH*) punishment;
lines pl; **s~bar** adj punishable; **~e** f
punishment; (*JUR*) penalty; (*Gefängnisstrafe*)
sentence; (*Geldstrafe*) fine; **s~en** vt to
punish
straff [ʃtraf] adj tight; (*streng*) strict; (*Stil etc*)
concise; (*Haltung*) erect; **~en** vt to tighten,
to tauten
Strafgefangene(r) f(m) prisoner, convict
Strafgesetzbuch nt penal code
sträflich ['ʃtrɛːflɪç] adj criminal
Sträfling m convict
Straf- zW: **~porto** nt excess postage

Spelling Reform: ▲ *new spelling* △ *old spelling (to be phased out)*

(charge); **~predigt** f telling-off; **~raum** m
(*SPORT*) penalty area; **~recht** nt criminal
law; **~stoß** m (*SPORT*) penalty (kick); **~tat** f
punishable act; **~zettel** m ticket

Strahl [ʃtraːl] (**-s, -en**) m ray, beam;
(*Wasserstrahl*) jet; **s~en** vi to radiate; (*fig*)
to beam; **~ung** f radiation

Strähne [ˈʃtrɛːnə] f strand

stramm [ʃtram] adj tight; (*Haltung*) erect;
(*Mensch*) robust

strampeln [ˈʃtrampəln] vi to kick (about), to
fidget

Strand [ʃtrant] (**-(e)s, ˮe**) m shore; (*mit
Sand*) beach; **~bad** nt open-air swimming
pool, lido; **s~en** [ˈʃtrandən] vi to run
aground; (*fig: Mensch*) to fail; **~gut** nt
flotsam; **~korb** m beach chair

Strang [ʃtraŋ] (**-(e)s, ˮe**) m cord, rope;
(*Bündel*) skein

Strapaz- zW: **~e** [ʃtraˈpaːtsə] f strain,
exertion; **s~ieren** [ʃtrapaˈtsiːrən] vt
(*Material*) to treat roughly, to punish;
(*Mensch, Kräfte*) to wear out, to exhaust;
s~ierfähig adj hard-wearing; **s~iös**
[ʃtrapatsiˈøːs] adj exhausting, tough

Straße [ˈʃtraːsə] f street, road

Straßen- zW: **~bahn** f tram, streetcar (*US*);
~glätte f slippery road surface; **~karte** f
road map; **~kehrer (-s, -)** m roadsweeper;
~sperre f roadblock; **~verkehr** m (road)
traffic; **~verkehrsordnung** f highway
code

Strateg- [ʃtraˈteːg] zW: **~e (-n, -n)** m
strategist; **~ie** [ʃtrateˈgiː] f strategy; **s~isch**
adj strategic

sträuben [ˈʃtrɔʏbən] vt to ruffle ♦ vr to
bristle; (*Mensch*): **sich (gegen etw) ~** to
resist (sth)

Strauch [ʃtraʊx] (**-(e)s, Sträucher**) m bush,
shrub

Strauß¹ [ʃtraʊs] (**-es, Sträuße**) m bunch;
bouquet

Strauß² [ʃtraʊs] (**-es, -e**) m ostrich

Streb- [ˈʃtreːb] zW: **s~en** vi to strive, to
endeavour; **s~en nach** to strive for; **~er
(-s, -)** (*pej*) m pusher, climber; (*SCH*) swot
(*BRIT*)

Strecke [ˈʃtrɛkə] f stretch; (*Entfernung*)
distance; (*EISENB, MATH*) line; **s~n** vt to
stretch; (*Waffen*) to lay down; (*KOCH*) to eke
out ♦ vr to stretch (o.s.)

Streich [ʃtraɪç] (**-(e)s, -e**) m trick, prank;
(*Hieb*) blow; **s~eln** vt to stroke; **s~en**
(*unreg*) vt (*berühren*) to stroke; (*auftragen*) to
spread; (*anmalen*) to paint; (*durchstreichen*)
to delete; (*nicht genehmigen*) to cancel ♦ vi
(*berühren*) to brush; (*schleichen*) to prowl;
~holz nt match; **~instrument** nt string
instrument

Streif- [ʃtraɪf] zW: **~e** f patrol; **s~en** vt
(*leicht berühren*) to brush against, to graze;
(*Blick*) to skim over; (*Thema, Problem*) to
touch on; (*abstreifen*) to take off ♦ vi
(*gehen*) to roam; **~en (-s, -)** m (*Linie*) stripe;
(*Stück*) strip; (*Film*) film; **~enwagen** m
patrol car; **~schuss** ▲ m graze, grazing
shot; **~zug** m scouting trip

Streik [ʃtraɪk] (**-(e)s, -s**) m strike; **~brecher
(-s, -)** m blackleg, strikebreaker; **s~en** vi to
strike; **~posten** m (strike) picket

Streit [ʃtraɪt] (**-(e)s, -e**) m argument;
dispute; **s~en** (*unreg*) vi, vr to argue; to
dispute; **~frage** f point at issue; **s~ig** adj:
jdm etw s~ig machen to dispute sb's right
to sth; **~igkeiten** pl quarrel sg, dispute sg;
~kräfte pl (*MIL*) armed forces

streng [ʃtrɛŋ] adj severe; (*Lehrer, Maßnahme*)
strict; (*Geruch etc*) sharp; **~ genommen**
strictly speaking; **S~e (-)** f severity,
strictness, sharpness; **~gläubig** adj
orthodox, strict; **~stens** adv strictly

Stress ▲ [ʃtrɛs] (**-es, -e**) m stress

stressen vt to put under stress

streuen [ˈʃtrɔʏən] vt to strew, to scatter, to
spread

Strich [ʃtrɪç] (**-(e)s, -e**) m (*Linie*) line;
(*Federstrich, Pinselstrich*) stroke; (*von
Geweben*) nap; (*von Fell*) pile; **auf den ~
gehen** (*umg*) to walk the streets; **jdm
gegen den ~ gehen** to rub sb up the
wrong way; **einen ~ machen durch** to
cross out; (*fig*) to foil; **~kode** m (*auf Waren*)
bar code; **~mädchen** nt streetwalker;
s~weise adv here and there

Strick [ʃtrɪk] **(-(e)s, -e)** *m* rope; **s~en** *vt, vi* to knit; **~jacke** *f* cardigan; **~leiter** *f* rope ladder; **~nadel** *f* knitting needle; **~waren** *pl* knitwear *sg*

strikt [strɪkt] *adj* strict

strittig [ˈʃtrɪtɪç] *adj* disputed, in dispute

Stroh [ʃtroː] **(-(e)s)** *nt* straw; **~blume** *f* everlasting flower; **~dach** *nt* thatched roof; **~halm** *m* (drinking) straw

Strom [ʃtroːm] **(-(e)s, ⁓e)** *m* river; (*fig*) stream; (*ELEK*) current; **s~abwärts** *adv* downstream; **s~aufwärts** *adv* upstream; **~ausfall** *m* power failure

strömen [ˈʃtrøːmən] *vi* to stream, to pour

Strom- *zW:* **~kreis** *m* circuit; **s~linienförmig** *adj* streamlined; **~sperre** *f* power cut

Strömung [ˈʃtrøːmʊŋ] *f* current

Strophe [ˈʃtroːfə] *f* verse

strotzen [ˈʃtrɔtsən] *vi:* **~ vor** *od* **von** to abound in, to be full of

Strudel [ˈʃtruːdəl] **(-s, -)** *m* whirlpool, vortex; (*KOCH*) strudel

Struktur [ʃtrʊkˈtuːr] *f* structure

Strumpf [ʃtrʊmpf] **(-(e)s, ⁓e)** *m* stocking; **~band** *nt* garter; **~hose** *f* (pair of) tights

Stube [ˈʃtuːbə] *f* room

Stuben- *zW:* **~arrest** *m* confinement to one's room; (*MIL*) confinement to quarters; **~hocker** (*umg*) *m* stay-at-home; **s~rein** *adj* house-trained

Stuck [ʃtʊk] **(-(e)s)** *m* stucco

Stück [ʃtʏk] **(-(e)s, -e)** *nt* piece; (*etwas*) bit; (*THEAT*) play; **~chen** *nt* little piece; **~lohn** *m* piecework wages *pl*; **s~weise** *adv* bit by bit, piecemeal; (*COMM*) individually

Student(in) [ʃtuˈdɛnt(ɪn)] *m(f)* student; **s~isch** *adj* student, academic

Studie [ˈʃtuːdiə] *f* study

Studienfahrt *f* study trip

studieren [ʃtuˈdiːrən] *vt, vi* to study

Studio [ˈʃtuːdio] **(-s, -s)** *nt* studio

Studium [ˈʃtuːdiʊm] *nt* studies *pl*

Stufe [ˈʃtuːfə] *f* step; (*Entwicklungsstufe*) stage; **s~nweise** *adv* gradually

Stuhl [ʃtuːl] **(-(e)s, ⁓e)** *m* chair; **~gang** *m* bowel movement

stülpen [ˈʃtʏlpən] *vt* (*umdrehen*) to turn upside down; (*bedecken*) to put

stumm [ʃtʊm] *adj* silent; (*MED*) dumb

Stummel [ˈʃtʊməl] **(-s, -)** *m* stump; (*Zigarettenstummel*) stub

Stummfilm *m* silent film

Stümper [ˈʃtʏmpər] **(-s, -)** *m* incompetent, duffer; **s~haft** *adj* bungling, incompetent; **s~n** *vi* to bungle

Stumpf [ʃtʊmpf] **(-(e)s, ⁓e)** *m* stump; **s~** *adj* blunt; (*teilnahmslos, glanzlos*) dull; (*Winkel*) obtuse; **~sinn** *m* tediousness; **s~sinnig** *adj* dull

Stunde [ˈʃtʊndə] *f* hour; (*SCH*) lesson

stunden *vt:* **jdm etw ~** to give sb time to pay sth; **S~geschwindigkeit** *f* average speed per hour; **S~kilometer** *pl* kilometres per hour; **~lang** *adj* for hours; **S~lohn** *m* hourly wage; **~plan** *m* timetable; **~weise** *adj* by the hour; every hour

stündlich [ˈʃtʏntlɪç] *adj* hourly

Stups [ʃtʊps] **(-es, -e)** (*umg*) *m* push; **~nase** *f* snub nose

stur [ʃtuːr] *adj* obstinate, pigheaded

Sturm [ʃtʊrm] **(-(e)s, ⁓e)** *m* storm, gale; (*MIL etc*) attack, assault

stürm- [ˈʃtʏrm] *zW:* **~en** *vi* (*Wind*) to blow hard, to rage; (*rennen*) to storm ♦ *vt* (*MIL, fig*) to storm ♦ *vb unpers:* **es ~t** there's a gale blowing; **S~er (-s, -)** *m* (*SPORT*) forward, striker; **~isch** *adj* stormy

Sturmwarnung *f* gale warning

Sturz [ʃtʊrts] **(-es, ⁓e)** *m* fall; (*POL*) overthrow

stürzen [ˈʃtʏrtsən] *vt* (*werfen*) to hurl; (*POL*) to overthrow; (*umkehren*) to overturn ♦ *vr* to rush; (*hineinstürzen*) to plunge ♦ *vi* to fall; (*AVIAT*) to dive; (*rennen*) to dash

Sturzflug *m* nose dive

Sturzhelm *m* crash helmet

Stute [ˈʃtuːtə] *f* mare

Stützbalken *m* brace, joist

Stütze [ˈʃtʏtsə] *f* support; help

stutzen [ˈʃtʊtsən] *vt* to trim; (*Ohr, Schwanz*) to dock; (*Flügel*) to clip ♦ *vi* to hesitate; to become suspicious

stützen *vt* (*auch fig*) to support; (*Ellbogen*

etc) to prop up

stutzig *adj* perplexed, puzzled; (*misstrauisch*) suspicious

Stützpunkt *m* point of support; (*von Hebel*) fulcrum; (*MIL, fig*) base

Styropor [ʃtyroˈpoːr] (®; **-s**) *nt* polystyrene

s. u. *abk* = **siehe unten**

Subjekt [zʊpˈjɛkt] (**-(e)s, -e**) *nt* subject; **s~iv** [-ˈtiːf] *adj* subjective; **~ivität** *f* subjectivity

Subsidiarität *f* subsidiarity

Substantiv [zʊpstanˈtiːf] (**-s, -e**) *nt* noun

Substanz [zʊpˈstants] *f* substance

subtil [zʊpˈtiːl] *adj* subtle

subtrahieren [zʊptraˈhiːrən] *vt* to subtract

subtropisch [ˈzʊptroːpɪʃ] *adj* subtropical

Subvention [zʊpvɛntsiˈoːn] *f* subsidy; **s~ieren** *vt* to subsidize

Such- [ˈzuːx] *zW:* **~aktion** *f* search; **~e** *f* search; **s~en** *vt* to look (for), to seek; (*versuchen*) to try ♦ *vi* to seek, to search; **~er** (**-s, -**) *m* seeker, searcher; (*PHOT*) viewfinder; **~maschine** *f* (*COMPUT*) search engine

Sucht [zʊxt] (**-, ⁻e**) *f* mania; (*MED*) addiction, craving

süchtig [ˈzʏçtɪç] *adj* addicted; **S~e(r)** *f(m)* addict

Süd- [ˈzyːt] *zW:* **~en** [ˈzyːdən] (**-s**) *m* south; **~früchte** *pl* Mediterranean fruit *sg*; **s~lich** *adj* southern; **s~lich von** (to the) south of; **~pol** *m* South Pole; **s~wärts** *adv* southwards

süffig [ˈzʏfɪç] *adj* (*Wein*) pleasant to the taste

süffisant [zʏfiˈzant] *adj* smug

suggerieren [zʊɡeˈriːrən] *vt* to suggest

Sühne [ˈzyːnə] *f* atonement, expiation; **s~n** *vt* to atone for, to expiate

Sultan [ˈzʊltan] (**-s, -e**) *m* sultan; **~ine** [zʊltaˈniːnə] *f* sultana

Sülze [ˈzʏltsə] *f* brawn

Summe [ˈzʊmə] *f* sum, total

summen *vt, vi* to buzz; (*Lied*) to hum

Sumpf [zʊmpf] (**-(e)s, ⁻e**) *m* swamp, marsh; **s~ig** *adj* marshy

Sünde [ˈzʏndə] *f* sin; **~nbock** (*umg*) *m* scapegoat; **~r(in)** (**-s, -**) *m(f)* sinner; **sündigen** *vi* to sin

Super [ˈzuːpɐr] (**-s**) *nt* (*Benzin*) four star (petrol) (*BRIT*), premium (*US*); **~lativ** [-latiːf] (**-s, -e**) *m* superlative; **~macht** *f* superpower; **~markt** *m* supermarket

Suppe [ˈzʊpə] *f* soup; **~nteller** *m* soup plate

süß [zyːs] *adj* sweet; **S~e** (**-**) *f* sweetness; **~en** *vt* to sweeten; **S~igkeit** *f* sweetness; (*Bonbon etc*) sweet (*BRIT*), candy (*US*); **~lich** *adj* sweetish; (*fig*) sugary; **~sauer** *adj* (*Gurke*) pickled; (*Sauce etc*) sweet-and-sour; **S~speise** *f* pudding, sweet; **S~stoff** *m* sweetener; **S~waren** *pl* confectionery (*sing*); **S~wasser** *nt* fresh water

Symbol [zymˈboːl] (**-s, -e**) *nt* symbol; **s~isch** *adj* symbolic(al)

Symmetrie [zymeˈtriː] *f* symmetry

symmetrisch [zʏˈmeːtrɪʃ] *adj* symmetrical

Sympathie [zympaˈtiː] *f* liking, sympathy; **sympathisch** [zymˈpaːtɪʃ] *adj* likeable; **er ist mir sympathisch** I like him; **sympathisieren** *vi* to sympathize

Symphonie [zymfoˈniː] *f* (*MUS*) symphony

Symptom [zympˈtoːm] (**-s, -e**) *nt* symptom; **s~atisch** [zymptoˈmaːtɪʃ] *adj* symptomatic

Synagoge [zynaˈɡoːɡə] *f* synagogue

synchron [zynˈkroːn] *adj* synchronous; **~isieren** *vt* to synchronize; (*Film*) to dub

Synonym [zynoˈnyːm] (**-s, -e**) *nt* synonym; **s~** *adj* synonymous

Synthese [zynˈteːzə] *f* synthesis

synthetisch *adj* synthetic

System [zʏsˈteːm] (**-s, -e**) *nt* system; **s~atisch** *adj* systematic; **s~atisieren** *vt* to systematize

Szene [ˈstseːnə] *f* scene; **~rie** [stsenaˈriː] *f* scenery

T, t

t abk (= *Tonne*) t

Tabak [ˈtaːbak] (**-s, -e**) *m* tobacco

Tabell- [taˈbel] *zW:* **t~arisch** [tabeˈlaːrɪʃ] *adj* tabular; **~e** *f* table

Tablett [taˈblɛt] *nt* tray; **~e** *f* tablet, pill

Tabu [taˈbuː] *nt* taboo; **t~** *adj* taboo

Tachometer [taxoˈmeːtɐr] (**-s, -**) *m* (*AUT*)

speedometer

Tadel ['taːdəl] (-s, -) m censure; scolding; (Fehler) fault, blemish; t~los adj faultless, irreproachable; t~n vt to scold

Tafel ['taːfəl] (-, -n) f (auch MATH) table; (Anschlag~) board; (Wand~) blackboard; (Schiefer~) slate; (Gedenk~) plaque; (Illustration) plate; (Schalt~) panel; (Schokolade etc) bar

Tag [taːk] (-(e)s, -e) m day; daylight; unter/über ~e (MIN) underground/on the surface; an den ~ kommen to come to light; guten ~! good morning/afternoon!; siehe zutage; t~aus adv: t~aus, ~ein day in, day out; ~dienst m day duty

Tage- ['taːgə] zW: ~buch ['taːgəbuːx] nt diary, journal; ~geld nt daily allowance; t~lang adv for days; t~n vi to sit, to meet ♦ vb unpers: es tagt dawn is breaking

Tages- zW: ~ablauf m course of the day; ~anbruch m dawn; ~fahrt f day trip; ~karte f menu of the day; (Fahrkarte) day ticket; ~licht nt daylight; ~ordnung f agenda; ~zeit f time of day; ~zeitung f daily (paper)

täglich ['tɛːklɪç] adj, adv daily

tagsüber ['taːksˈyːbar] adv during the day

Tagung f conference

Taille ['taljə] f waist

Takt [takt] (-(e)s, -e) m tact; (MUS) time; ~gefühl nt tact

Taktik f tactics pl; taktisch adj tactical

Takt- zW: t~los adj tactless; ~losigkeit f tactlessness; ~stock m (conductor's) baton; t~voll adj tactful

Tal [taːl] (-(e)s, -er) nt valley

Talent [ta'lɛnt] (-(e)s, -e) nt talent; t~iert [talɛn'tiːrt] adj talented, gifted

Talisman ['taːlɪsman] (-s, -e) m talisman

Talkshow ['tɔːkʃoː] f chat show

Talsohle f bottom of a valley

Talsperre f dam

Tampon ['tampɔn] (-s, -s) m tampon

Tang [taŋ] (-(e)s, -e) m seaweed

Tank [taŋk] (-s, -s) m tank; ~anzeige f fuel gauge; t~en vi to fill up with petrol (BRIT) od gas (US); (AVIAT) to (re)fuel; ~er (-s, -) m tanker; ~schiff nt tanker; ~stelle f petrol

(BRIT) od gas (US) station; ~wart m petrol pump (BRIT) od gas station (US) attendant

Tanne ['tanə] f fir

Tannen- zW: ~baum m fir tree; ~zapfen m fir cone

Tante ['tantə] f aunt

Tanz [tants] (-es, -e) m dance; t~en vt, vi to dance

Tänzer(in) ['tɛntsər(ɪn)] (-s, -) m(f) dancer

Tanzfläche f (dance) floor

Tanzschule f dancing school

Tapete [ta'peːtə] f wallpaper; ~nwechsel m (fig) change of scenery

tapezieren [tape'tsiːrən] vt to (wall)paper; **Tapezierer** [tape'tsiːrər] (-s, -) m (interior) decorator

tapfer ['tapfər] adj brave; T~keit f courage, bravery

Tarif [ta'riːf] (-s, -e) m tariff, (scale of) fares od charges; ~lohn m standard wage rate; ~verhandlungen pl wage negotiations; ~zone f fare zone

Tarn- ['tarn] zW: t~en vt to camouflage; (Person, Absicht) to disguise; ~ung f camouflaging; disguising

Tasche ['taʃə] f pocket; handbag

Taschen- in zW pocket; ~buch nt paperback; ~dieb m pickpocket; ~geld nt pocket money; ~lampe f (electric) torch, flashlight (US); ~messer nt penknife; ~tuch nt handkerchief

Tasse ['tasə] f cup

Tastatur [tasta'tuːr] f keyboard

Taste ['tastə] f push-button control; (an Schreibmaschine) key; t~n vt to feel, to touch ♦ vi to feel, to grope ♦ vr to feel one's way

Tat [taːt] (-, -en) f act, deed, action; in der ~ indeed, as a matter of fact; t~ etc vb siehe tun; ~bestand m facts pl of the case; t~enlos adj inactive

Tät- ['tɛːt] zW: ~er(in) (-s, -) m(f) perpetrator, culprit; t~ig adj active; in einer Firma t~ig sein to work for a firm; ~igkeit f activity; (Beruf) occupation; t~lich adj violent; ~lichkeit f violence; ~lichkeiten pl (Schläge) blows

tätowieren [tɛto'viːrən] *vt* to tattoo

Tatsache *f* fact

tatsächlich *adj* actual ♦ *adv* really

Tau¹ [tau] (-(e)s, -e) *nt* rope

Tau² [tau] (-(e)s, -) *m* dew

taub [taup] *adj* deaf; (*Nuss*) hollow

Taube ['taubə] *f* dove; pigeon; **~nschlag** *m* dovecote; **hier geht es zu wie in einem ~nschlag** it's a hive of activity here

taub- *zW*: **T~heit** *f* deafness; **~stumm** *adj* deaf-and-dumb

Tauch- [taux] *zW*: **t~en** *vt* to dip ♦ *vi* to dive; (*NAUT*) to submerge; **~er** (-s, -) *m* diver; **~eranzug** *m* diving suit; **~erbrille** *f* diving goggles *pl*; **~sieder** (-s, -) *m* immersion coil (*for boiling water*)

tauen ['tauən] *vt*, *vi* to thaw ♦ *vb unpers*: **es taut** it's thawing

Tauf- ['tauf] *zW*: **~becken** *nt* font; **~e** *f* baptism; **t~en** *vt* to christen, to baptize; **~pate** *m* godfather; **~patin** *f* godmother; **~schein** *m* certificate of baptism

taug- ['taug] *zW*: **~en** *vi* to be of use; **~en für** to do for, to be good for; **nicht ~en** to be no good *od* useless; **T~enichts** (-es, -e) *m* good-for-nothing; **~lich** ['tauklɪç] *adj* suitable; (*MIL*) fit (for service)

Taumel ['tauməl] (-s) *m* dizziness; (*fig*) frenzy; **t~n** *vi* to reel, to stagger

Tausch [tauʃ] (-(e)s, -e) *m* exchange; **t~en** *vt* to exchange, to swap

täuschen ['tɔyʃən] *vt* to deceive ♦ *vi* to be deceptive ♦ *vr* to be wrong; **~d** *adj* deceptive

Tauschhandel *m* barter

Täuschung *f* deception; (*optisch*) illusion

tausend ['tauzənt] *num* (a) thousand

Tauwetter *nt* thaw

Taxi ['taksi] (-(s), -(s)) *nt* taxi; **~fahrer** *m* taxi driver; **~stand** *m* taxi rank

Tech- [tɛç] *zW*: **~nik** *f* technology; (*Methode, Kunstfertigkeit*) technique; **~niker** (-s, -) *m* technician; **t~nisch** *adj* technical; **~nolo'gie** *f* technology; **t~no'logisch** *adj* technological

Tee [teː] (-s, -s) *m* tea; **~beutel** *m* tea bag; **~kanne** *f* teapot; **~löffel** *m* teaspoon

Teer [teːr] (-(e)s, -e) *m* tar; **t~en** *vt* to tar

Teesieb *nt* tea strainer

Teich [taiç] (-(e)s, -e) *m* pond

Teig [taik] (-(e)s, -e) *m* dough; **t~ig** ['taigɪç] *adj* doughy; **~waren** *pl* pasta *sg*

Teil [tail] (-(e)s, -e) *m od nt* part; (*Anteil*) share; (*Bestandteil*) component; **zum ~** partly; **t~bar** *adj* divisible; **~betrag** *m* instalment; **~chen** *nt* (atomic) particle; **t~en** *vt*, *vr* to divide; (*mit jdm*) to share; **t~haben** (*unreg*) *vi*: **t~haben an** +*dat* to share in; **~haber** (-s, -) *m* partner; **~kaskoversicherung** *f* third party, fire and theft insurance; **t~möbliert** *adj* partially furnished; **~nahme** *f* participation; (*Mitleid*) sympathy; **t~nahmslos** *adj* disinterested, apathetic; **t~nehmen** (*unreg*) *vi*: **t~nehmen an** +*dat* to take part in; **~nehmer** (-s, -) *m* participant; **t~s** *adv* partly; **~ung** *f* division; **t~weise** *adv* partially, in part; **~zahlung** *f* payment by instalments; **~zeitarbeit** *f* part-time work

Teint [tɛ̃ː] (-s, -s) *m* complexion

Telearbeit ['teːleˌarbait] *f* teleworking

Telefax ['teːlefaks] *nt* fax

Telefon [tele'foːn] (-s, -e) *nt* telephone; **~anruf** *m* (tele)phone call; **~at** [telefo'naːt] (-(e)s, -e) *nt* (tele)phone call; **~buch** *nt* telephone directory; **~hörer** *m* (telephone) receiver; **t~ieren** *vi* to telephone; **t~isch** [-ɪʃ] *adj* telephone; (*Benachrichtigung*) by telephone; **~ist(in)** [telefo'nɪst(ɪn)] *m(f)* telephonist; **~karte** *f* phonecard; **~nummer** *f* (tele)phone number; **~zelle** *f* telephone kiosk, callbox; **~zentrale** *f* telephone exchange

Telegraf [tele'graːf] (-en, -en) *m* telegraph; **~enmast** *m* telegraph pole; **~ie** [-'fiː] *f* telegraphy; **t~ieren** [-'fiːrən] *vt*, *vi* to telegraph, to wire

Telegramm [tele'gram] (-s, -e) *nt* telegram, cable; **~adresse** *f* telegraphic address

Tele- *zW*: **~objektiv** ['teːleˌɔpjɛktiːf] *nt* telephoto lens; **t~pathisch** [tele'paːtɪʃ] *adj* telepathic; **~skop** [tele'skoːp] (-s, -e) *nt* telescope

Teller ['tɛlər] (**-s, -**) *m* plate; **~gericht** *nt* (*KOCH*) one-course meal

Tempel ['tɛmpəl] (**-s, -**) *m* temple

Temperament [tɛmpəra'mɛnt] *nt* temperament; (*Schwung*) vivacity, liveliness; **t~voll** *adj* high-spirited, lively

Temperatur [tɛmpəra'tuːr] *f* temperature

Tempo¹ ['tɛmpo] (**-s, Tempi**) *nt* (*MUS*) tempo

Tempo² ['tɛmpo] (**-s, -s**) *nt* speed, pace; **~!** get a move on!; **~limit** [-lɪmɪt] (**-s, -s**) *nt* speed limit; **~taschentuch** ® *nt* tissue

Tendenz [tɛn'dɛnts] *f* tendency; (*Absicht*) intention; **t~iös** [-i'øːs] *adj* biased, tendentious

tendieren [tɛn'diːrən] *vi*: **~ zu** to show a tendency to, to incline towards

Tennis ['tɛnɪs] (**-**) *nt* tennis; **~ball** *m* tennis ball; **~platz** *m* tennis court; **~schläger** *m* tennis racket; **~schuh** *m* tennis shoe; **~spieler(in)** *m(f)* tennis player

Tenor [te'noːr] (**-s, ⁺e**) *m* tenor

Teppich ['tɛpɪç] (**-s, -e**) *m* carpet; **~boden** *m* wall-to-wall carpeting

Termin [tɛr'miːn] (**-s, -e**) *m* (*Zeitpunkt*) date; (*Frist*) time limit, deadline; (*Arzttermin etc*) appointment; **~kalender** *m* diary, appointments book; **~planer** *m* personal organizer

Terrasse [tɛ'rasə] *f* terrace

Terrine [tɛ'riːnə] *f* tureen

territorial [tɛritori'aːl] *adj* territorial

Territorium [tɛri'toːriʊm] *nt* territory

Terror ['tɛrɔr] (**-s**) *m* terror; reign of terror; **t~isieren** [tɛrori'ziːrən] *vt* to terrorize; **~ismus** [-'rɪsmʊs] *m* terrorism; **~ist** [-'rɪst] *m* terrorist

Tesafilm ['teːzafɪlm] ® *m* Sellotape ® (*BRIT*), Scotch tape ® (*US*)

Tessin [tɛ'siːn] (**-s**) *nt*: **das ~** Ticino

Test [tɛst] (**-s, -s**) *m* test

Testament [tɛsta'mɛnt] *nt* will, testament; (*REL*) Testament; **t~arisch** [-'taːrɪʃ] *adj* testamentary

Testamentsvollstrecker *m* executor (of a will)

testen *vt* to test

Tetanus ['teːtanʊs] (**-**) *m* tetanus; **~impfung** *f* (anti-)tetanus injection

teuer ['tɔyər] *adj* dear, expensive; **T~ung** *f* increase in prices; **T~ungszulage** *f* cost of living bonus

Teufel ['tɔyfəl] (**-s, -**) *m* devil; **teuflisch** ['tɔyflɪʃ] *adj* fiendish, diabolical

Text [tɛkst] (**-(e)s, -e**) *m* text; (*Liedertext*) words *pl*; **t~en** *vi* to write the words

textil [tɛks'tiːl] *adj* textile; **T~ien** *pl* textiles; **T~industrie** *f* textile industry; **T~waren** *pl* textiles

Textverarbeitung *f* word processing

Theater [te'aːtər] (**-s, -**) *nt* theatre; (*umg*) fuss; **~ spielen** (*auch fig*) to playact; **~besucher** *m* playgoer; **~kasse** *f* box office; **~stück** *nt* (stage) play

Theke ['teːkə] *f* (*Schanktisch*) bar; (*Ladentisch*) counter

Thema ['teːma] (**-s, Themen** *od* **-ta**) *nt* theme, topic, subject

Themse ['tɛmzə] *f* Thames

Theo- [teo] *zW*: **~loge** [-'loːgə] (**-n, -n**) *m* theologian; **~logie** [-lo'giː] *f* theology; **t~logisch** [-'loːgɪʃ] *adj* theological; **~retiker** [-'reːtikar] (**-s, -**) *m* theorist; **t~retisch** [-'reːtɪʃ] *adj* theoretical; **~rie** [-'riː] *f* theory

Thera- [tera] *zW*: **~peut** [-'pɔyt] (**-en, -en**) *m* therapist; **t~peutisch** [-'pɔytɪʃ] *adj* therapeutic; **~pie** [-'piː] *f* therapy

Therm- *zW*: **~albad** [tɛr'maːlbaːt] *nt* thermal bath; thermal spa; **~odrucker** [tɛrmo-] *m* thermal printer; **~ometer** [tɛrmo'meːtər] (**-s, -**) *nt* thermometer; **~osflasche** ['tɛrmɔsflaʃə] ® *f* Thermos ® flask

These ['teːzə] *f* thesis

Thrombose [trɔm'boːzə] *f* thrombosis

Thron [troːn] (**-(e)s, -e**) *m* throne; **t~en** *vi* to sit enthroned; (*fig*) to sit in state; **~folge** *f* succession (to the throne); **~folger(in)** (**-s, -**) *m(f)* heir to the throne

Thunfisch ['tuːnfɪʃ] *m* tuna

Thüringen ['tyːrɪŋən] (**-s**) *nt* Thuringia

Thymian ['tyːmiaːn] (**-s, -e**) *m* thyme

Tick [tɪk] (**-(e)s, -s**) *m* tic; (*Eigenart*) quirk;

Spelling Reform: ▲ *new spelling* △ *old spelling (to be phased out)*

(Fimmel) craze

ticken *vi* to tick

tief [tiːf] *adj* deep; *(~sinnig)* profound; *(Ausschnitt, Preis, Ton)* low; **~ greifend** far-reaching; **~ schürfend** profound; **T~ (-s, -s)** *nt (MET)* depression; **T~druck** *m* low pressure; **T~e** *f* depth; **T~ebene** *f* plain; **T~enschärfe** *f (PHOT)* depth of focus; **T~garage** *f* underground garage; **~gekühlt** *adj* frozen; **T~kühlfach** *nt* deepfreeze compartment; **T~kühlkost** *f* (deep) frozen food; **T~kühltruhe** *f* deepfreeze, freezer; **T~punkt** *m* low point; *(fig)* low ebb; **T~schlag** *m (BOXEN, fig)* blow below the belt; **T~see** *f* deep sea; **~sinnig** *adj* profound; melancholy; **T~stand** *m* low level; **T~stwert** *m* minimum *od* lowest value

Tier [tiːr] **(-(e)s, -e)** *nt* animal; **~arzt** *m* vet(erinary surgeon); **~garten** *m* zoo(logical gardens *pl)*; **~heim** *nt* cat/dog home; **t~isch** *adj* animal; *(auch fig)* brutish; *(fig: Ernst etc)* deadly; **~kreis** *m* zodiac; **~kunde** *f* zoology; **t~liebend** *adj* fond of animals; **~park** *m* zoo; **~quälerei** [-kvɛːləˈraɪ] *f* cruelty to animals; **~schutzverein** *m* society for the prevention of cruelty to animals

Tiger(in) [ˈtiːɡər(ɪn)] **(-s, -)** *m(f)* tiger(-gress)

tilgen [ˈtɪlɡən] *vt* to erase; *(Sünden)* to expiate; *(Schulden)* to pay off

Tinte [ˈtɪntə] *f* ink

Tintenfisch *m* cuttlefish

Tipp ▲ [tɪp] *m* tip; **t~en** *vt, vi* to tap, to touch; *(umg: schreiben)* to type; *(im Lotto etc)* to bet (on); **auf jdn t~en** *(umg: raten)* to tip sb, to put one's money on sb *(fig)*

Tipp- [ˈtɪp] *zW:* **~fehler** *(umg) m* typing error; **t~topp** *(umg) adj* tip-top; **~zettel** *m* (pools) coupon

Tirol [tiˈroːl] *nt* the Tyrol; **~er(in)** *m(f)* Tyrolean; **t~isch** *adj* Tyrolean

Tisch [tɪʃ] **(-(e)s, -e)** *m* table; **bei ~** at table; **vor/nach ~** before/after eating; **unter den ~ fallen** *(fig)* to be dropped; **~decke** *f* tablecloth; **~ler (-s, -)** *m* carpenter, joiner; **~lerei** *f* joiner's workshop; *(Arbeit)*

carpentry, joinery; **t~lern** *vi* to do carpentry *etc*; **~rede** *f* after-dinner speech; **~tennis** *nt* table tennis; **~tuch** *nt* tablecloth

Titel [ˈtiːtəl] **(-s, -)** *m* title; **~bild** *nt* cover (picture); *(von Buch)* frontispiece; **~rolle** *f* title role; **~seite** *f* cover; *(Buchtitelseite)* title page; **~verteidiger** *m* defending champion, title holder

Toast [toːst] **(-(e)s, -s** *od* **-e)** *m* toast; **~brot** *nt* bread for toasting; **~er (-s, -)** *m* toaster

tob- [ˈtoːb] *zW:* **~en** *vi* to rage; *(Kinder)* to romp about; **~süchtig** *adj* maniacal

Tochter [ˈtɔxtər] **(-, ¨)** *f* daughter; **~gesellschaft** *f* subsidiary (company)

Tod [toːt] **(-(e)s, -e)** *m* death; **t~ernst** *adj* deadly serious ♦ *adv* in dead earnest

Todes- [ˈtoːdəs] *zW:* **~angst** [-aŋst] *f* mortal fear; **~anzeige** *f* obituary (notice); **~fall** *m* death; **~strafe** *f* death penalty; **~ursache** *f* cause of death; **~urteil** *nt* death sentence; **~verachtung** *f* utter disgust

todkrank *adj* dangerously ill

tödlich [ˈtøːtlɪç] *adj* deadly, fatal

tod- *zW:* **~müde** *adj* dead tired; **~schick** *(umg) adj* smart, classy; **~sicher** *(umg) adj* absolutely *od* dead certain; **T~sünde** *f* deadly sin

Toilette [toaˈlɛtə] *f* toilet, lavatory; *(Frisiertisch)* dressing table

Toiletten- *zW:* **~artikel** *pl* toiletries, toilet articles; **~papier** *nt* toilet paper; **~tisch** *m* dressing table

toi, toi, toi [ˈtɔʏˈtɔʏˈtɔʏ] *excl* touch wood

tolerant [toleˈrant] *adj* tolerant

Toleranz [toleˈrants] *f* tolerance

tolerieren [toleˈriːrən] *vt* to tolerate

toll [tɔl] *adj* mad; *(Treiben)* wild; *(umg)* terrific; **~en** *vi* to romp; **T~kirsche** *f* deadly nightshade; **~kühn** *adj* daring; **T~wut** *f* rabies

Tomate [toˈmaːtə] *f* tomato; **~nmark** *nt* tomato purée

Ton¹ [toːn] **(-(e)s, -e)** *m (Erde)* clay

Ton² [toːn] **(-(e)s, ¨e)** *m (Laut)* sound; *(MUS)* note; *(Redeweise)* tone; *(Farbton, Nuance)* shade; *(Betonung)* stress;

t~angebend *adj* leading; ~art *f* (musical) key; ~band *nt* tape; ~bandgerät *nt* tape recorder

tönen ['tø:nən] *vi* to sound ♦ *vt* to shade; (*Haare*) to tint

tönern ['tø:nərn] *adj* clay

Ton- *zW:* ~fall *m* intonation; ~film *m* sound film; ~leiter *f* (*MUS*) scale; t~los *adj* soundless

Tonne ['tɔnə] *f* barrel; (*Maß*) ton

Ton- *zW:* ~taube *f* clay pigeon; ~waren *pl* pottery *sg*, earthenware *sg*

Topf [tɔpf] (-(e)s, ⁺e) *m* pot; ~blume *f* pot plant

Töpfer ['tœpfər] (-s, -) *m* potter; ~ei [-'rai] *f* piece of pottery; potter's workshop; ~scheibe *f* potter's wheel

topografisch ▲ [topo'gra:fɪʃ] *adj* topographic

Tor¹ [to:r] (-en, -en) *m* fool

Tor² [to:r] (-(e)s, -e) *nt* gate; (*SPORT*) goal; ~bogen *m* archway

Torf [tɔrf] (-(e)s) *m* peat

Torheit *f* foolishness; foolish deed

töricht ['tø:rɪçt] *adj* foolish

torkeln ['tɔrkəln] *vi* to stagger, to reel

Torte ['tɔrtə] *f* cake; (*Obsttorte*) flan, tart

Tortur [tɔr'tu:r] *f* ordeal

Torwart (-(e)s, -e) *m* goalkeeper

tosen ['to:zən] *vi* to roar

tot [to:t] *adj* dead; ~ geboren stillborn; sich ~ stellen to pretend to be dead

total [to'ta:l] *adj* total; ~itär [totali'tɛ:r] *adj* totalitarian; T~schaden *m* (*AUT*) complete write-off

Tote(r) *f(m)* dead person

töten ['tø:tən] *vt, vi* to kill

Toten- *zW:* ~bett *nt* death bed; t~-blass ▲ *adj* deathly pale, white as a sheet; ~kopf *m* skull; ~schein *m* death certificate; ~stille *f* deathly silence

tot- *zW:* ~fahren (*unreg*) *vt* to run over; ~geboren △ *adj siehe* tot; ~lachen (*umg*) *vr* to laugh one's head off

Toto ['to:to] (-s, -s) *m od nt* pools *pl*; ~schein *m* pools coupon

tot- *zW:* T~schlag *m* manslaughter;

~schlagen (*unreg*) *vt* (*auch fig*) to kill; ~schweigen (*unreg*) *vt* to hush up; ~stellen △ *vr siehe* tot

Tötung ['tø:tʊŋ] *f* killing

Toupet [tu'pe:] (-s, -s) *nt* toupee

toupieren [tu'pi:rən] *vt* to backcomb

Tour [tu:r] (-, -en) *f* tour, trip; (*Umdrehung*) revolution; (*Verhaltensart*) way; in einer ~ incessantly; ~enzähler *m* rev counter; ~ismus [tu'rɪsmʊs] *m* tourism; ~ist [tu'rɪst] *m* tourist; ~istenklasse *f* tourist class; ~nee [tʊr'ne:] (-, -n) *f* (*THEAT etc*) tour; auf ~nee gehen to go on tour

Trab [tra:p] (-(e)s) *m* trot

Trabantenstadt *f* satellite town

traben ['tra:bən] *vi* to trot

Tracht [traxt] (-, -en) *f* (*Kleidung*) costume, dress; eine ~ Prügel a sound thrashing; t~en *vi*: t~en (nach) to strive (for); jdm nach dem Leben t~en to seek to kill sb; danach t~en, etw zu tun to strive *od* endeavour to do sth

trächtig ['trɛçtɪç] *adj* (*Tier*) pregnant

Tradition [traditsi'o:n] *f* tradition; t~ell [-'nɛl] *adj* traditional

traf *etc* [tra:f] *vb siehe* treffen

Tragbahre *f* stretcher

tragbar *adj* (*Gerät*) portable; (*Kleidung*) wearable; (*erträglich*) bearable

träge ['trɛ:gə] *adj* sluggish, slow; (*PHYS*) inert

tragen ['tra:gən] (*unreg*) *vt* to carry; (*Kleidung, Brille*) to wear; (*Namen, Früchte*) to bear; (*erdulden*) to endure ♦ *vi* (*schwanger sein*) to be pregnant; (*Eis*) to hold; sich mit einem Gedanken ~ to have an idea in mind; zum T~ kommen to have an effect

Träger ['trɛ:gər] (-s, -) *m* carrier; wearer; bearer; (*Ordensträger*) holder; (*an Kleidung*) (shoulder) strap; (*Körperschaft etc*) sponsor

Tragetasche *f* carrier bag

Tragfläche *f* (*AVIAT*) wing

Tragflügelboot *nt* hydrofoil

Trägheit ['trɛ:khait] *f* laziness; (*PHYS*) inertia

Tragik ['tra:gɪk] *f* tragedy; tragisch *adj* tragic

Tragödie [tra'gø:diə] *f* tragedy

Tragweite *f* range; (*fig*) scope

Train- ['tre:n] *zW:* **~er (-s, -)** *m* (*SPORT*) trainer, coach; (*Fußball*) manager; **t~ieren** [tre'ni:rən] *vt, vi* to train; (*Mensch*) to train, to coach; (*Übung*) to practise; **~ing (-s, -s)** *nt* training; **~ingsanzug** *m* track suit

Traktor ['traktɔr] *m* tractor; (*von Drucker*) tractor feed

trällern ['trɛlərn] *vt, vi* to trill, to sing

Tram [tram] **(-, -s)** *f* tram

trampeln ['trampəln] *vt, vi* to trample, to stamp

trampen ['trɛmpən] *vi* to hitch-hike

Tramper(in) [trɛmpər(ɪn)] **(-s, -)** *m(f)* hitch-hiker

Tran [tra:n] **(-(e)s, -e)** *m* train oil, blubber

tranchieren [trɑ̃'ʃi:rən] *vt* to carve

Träne ['trɛ:nə] *f* tear; **t~n** *vi* to water; **~ngas** *nt* teargas

trank *etc* [traŋk] *vb siehe* **trinken**

tränken ['trɛŋkən] *vt* (*Tiere*) to water

transchieren ▲ [tran'ʃi:rən] *vt* to carve

Trans- *zW:* **~formator** [transfɔr'ma:tɔr] *m* transformer; **~istor** [tran'zɪstɔr] *m* transistor; **~itverkehr** [tran'zɪt:ferke:r] *m* transit traffic; **~itvisum** *nt* transit visa; **t~parent** *adj* transparent; **~parent (-(e)s, -e)** *nt* (*Bild*) transparency; (*Spruchband*) banner; **~plantation** [transplantatsi'o:n] *f* transplantation; (*Hauttransplantation*) graft(ing)

Transport [trans'pɔrt] **(-(e)s, -e)** *m* transport; **t~ieren** [transpɔr'ti:rən] *vt* to transport; **~kosten** *pl* transport charges, carriage *sg*; **~mittel** *nt* means *sg* of transportation; **~unternehmen** *nt* carrier

Traube ['traubə] *f* grape; bunch (of grapes); **~nzucker** *m* glucose

trauen ['trauən] *vi:* **jdm/etw ~** to trust sb/ sth ♦ *vr* to dare ♦ *vt* to marry

Trauer ['trauər] **(-)** *f* sorrow; (*für Verstorbenen*) mourning; **~fall** *m* death, bereavement; **~feier** *f* funeral service; **~kleidung** *f* mourning; **t~n** *vi* to mourn; **um jdn t~n** to mourn (for) sb; **~rand** *m* black border; **~spiel** *nt* tragedy

traulich ['traulɪç] *adj* cosy, intimate

Traum [traum] **(-(e)s, Träume)** *m* dream

Trauma (-s, -men) *nt* trauma

träum- ['trɔym] *zW:* **~en** *vt, vi* to dream; **T~er (-s, -)** *m* dreamer; **T~e'rei** *f* dreaming; **~erisch** *adj* dreamy

traumhaft *adj* dreamlike; (*fig*) wonderful

traurig ['traurɪç] *adj* sad; **T~keit** *f* sadness

Trau- ['trau] *zW:* **~ring** *m* wedding ring; **~schein** *m* marriage certificate; **~ung** *f* wedding ceremony; **~zeuge** *m* witness (to a marriage); **~zeugin** *f* witness (to a marriage)

treffen ['trɛfən] (*unreg*) *vt* to strike, to hit; (*Bemerkung*) to hurt; (*begegnen*) to meet; (*Entscheidung etc*) to make; (*Maßnahmen*) to take ♦ *vi* to hit ♦ *vr* to meet; **er hat es gut getroffen** he did well; **~ auf** +*akk* to come across, to meet with; **es traf sich, dass ...** it so happened that ...; **es trifft sich gut** it's convenient; **wie es so trifft** as these things happen; **T~ (-s, -)** *nt* meeting; **~d** *adj* pertinent, apposite

Treffer (-s, -) *m* hit; (*Tor*) goal; (*Los*) winner

Treffpunkt *m* meeting place

Treib- ['traib] *zW:* **~eis** *nt* drift ice; **t~en** (*unreg*) *vt* to drive; (*Studien etc*) to pursue; (*Sport*) to do, to go in for ♦ *vi* (*Schiff etc*) to drift; (*Pflanzen*) to sprout; (*KOCH: aufgehen*) to rise; (*Tee, Kaffee*) to be diuretic; **~haus** *nt* greenhouse; **~hauseffekt** *m* greenhouse effect; **~hausgas** *nt* greenhouse gas; **~stoff** *m* fuel

trenn- ['trɛn] *zW:* **~bar** *adj* separable; **~en** *vt* to separate; (*teilen*) to divide ♦ *vr* to separate; **sich ~en von** to part with; **T~ung** *f* separation; **T~wand** *f* partition (wall)

Trepp- ['trɛp] *zW:* **t~ab** *adv* downstairs; **t~auf** *adv* upstairs; **~e** *f* stair(case); **~engeländer** *nt* banister; **~enhaus** *nt* staircase

Tresor [tre'zo:r] **(-s, -e)** *m* safe

Tretboot *nt* pedalo, pedal boat

treten ['tre:tən] (*unreg*) *vi* to step; (*Tränen, Schweiß*) to appear ♦ *vt* (*mit Fußtritt*) to kick; (*niedertreten*) to tread, to trample; **~ nach** to kick at; **~ in** +*akk* to step in(to); **in Verbindung ~** to get in contact; **in**

Erscheinung ~ to appear

treu [trɔʏ] *adj* faithful, true; **T~e** (-) *f* loyalty, faithfulness; **T~händer** (-s, -) *m* trustee; **T~handanstalt** *f* trustee organization; **T~handgesellschaft** *f* trust company; **~herzig** *adj* innocent; **~los** *adj* faithless

Treuhandanstalt

i The **Treuhandanstalt** was the organization set up in 1990 to take over the nationally-owned companies of the former **DDR**, break them down into smaller units and privatize them. It was based in Berlin and had nine branches. Many companies were closed down by the **Treuhandanstalt** because of their outdated equipment and inability to compete with Western firms which resulted in rising unemployment. Having completed its initial task, the **Treuhandanstalt** was closed down in 1995.

Tribüne [tri'byːnə] *f* grandstand; (*Rednertribüne*) platform
Trichter ['trɪçtər] (-s, -) *m* funnel; (*in Boden*) crater
Trick [trɪk] (-s, -e *od* -s) *m* trick; **~film** *m* cartoon
Trieb [triːp] (-(e)s, -e) *m* urge, drive; (*Neigung*) inclination; (*an Baum etc*) shoot; **t~** *etc vb siehe* **treiben**; **~kraft** *f* (*fig*) drive; **~täter** *m* sex offender; **~werk** *nt* engine
triefen ['triːfən] *vi* to drip
triffst *etc* [trɪfst] *vb siehe* **treffen**
triftig ['trɪftɪç] *adj* good, convincing
Trikot [tri'koː] (-s, -s) *nt* vest; (*SPORT*) shirt
Trimester [tri'mɛstər] (-s, -) *nt* term
trimmen ['trɪmən] *vt* to do keep fit exercises
trink- ['trɪŋk] *zW:* **~bar** *adj* drinkable; **~en** (*unreg*) *vt, vi* to drink; **T~er** (-s, -) *m* drinker; **T~geld** *nt* tip; **T~halle** *f* refreshment kiosk; **T~wasser** *nt* drinking water
Tripper ['trɪpər] (-s, -) *m* gonorrhoea
Tritt [trɪt] (-(e)s, -e) *m* step; (*Fußtritt*) kick; **~brett** *nt* (*EISENB*) step; (*AUT*) running board

Triumph [tri'ʊmf] (-(e)s, -e) *m* triumph; **~bogen** *m* triumphal arch; **t~ieren** [triʊm'fiːrən] *vi* to triumph; (*jubeln*) to exult
trocken ['trɔkən] *adj* dry; **T~element** *nt* dry cell; **T~haube** *f* hair dryer; **T~heit** *f* dryness; **t~legen** *vt* (*Sumpf*) to drain; (*Kind*) to put a clean nappy on; **T~milch** *f* dried milk; **T~rasur** *f* dry shave, electric shave
trocknen ['trɔknən] *vt, vi* to dry
Trödel ['trøːdəl] (-s) (*umg*) *m* junk; **~markt** *m* flea market; **t~n** (*umg*) *vi* to dawdle
Trommel ['trɔməl] (-, -n) *f* drum; **~fell** *nt* eardrum; **t~n** *vt, vi* to drum
Trompete [trɔm'peːtə] *f* trumpet; **~r** (-s, -) *m* trumpeter
Tropen ['troːpən] *pl* tropics; **~helm** *m* sun helmet
tröpfeln ['trœpfəln] *vi* to drop, to trickle
Tropfen ['trɔpfən] (-s, -) *m* drop; **t~** *vt, vi* to drip ♦ *vb unpers:* **es tropft** a few raindrops are falling; **t~weise** *adv* in drops
Tropfsteinhöhle *f* stalactite cave
tropisch ['troːpɪʃ] *adj* tropical
Trost [troːst] (-es) *m* consolation, comfort
trösten ['trøːstən] *vt* to console, to comfort
trost- *zW:* **~los** *adj* bleak; (*Verhältnisse*) wretched; **T~preis** *m* consolation prize; **~reich** *adj* comforting
Trott [trɔt] (-(e)s, -e) *m* trot; (*Routine*) routine; **~el** (-s, -) (*umg*) *m* fool, dope; **t~en** *vi* to trot
Trotz [trɔts] (-es) *m* pigheadedness; **etw aus ~ tun** to do sth just to show them; **jdm zum ~** in defiance of sb; **t~** *präp* (+gen *od* dat) in spite of; **t~dem** *adv* nevertheless, all the same ♦ *konj* although; **t~en** *vi* (+dat) to defy; (*der Kälte, Klima etc*) to withstand; (*der Gefahr*) to brave; (*t~ig sein*) to be awkward; **t~ig** *adj* defiant, pig-headed; **~kopf** *m* obstinate child
trüb [tryːp] *adj* dull; (*Flüssigkeit, Glas*) cloudy; (*fig*) gloomy
Trubel ['truːbəl] (-s) *m* hurly-burly
trüb- *zW:* **~en** ['tryːbən] *vt* to cloud ♦ *vr* to become clouded; **T~heit** *f* dullness; cloudiness; gloom; **T~sal** (-, -e) *f* distress; **~selig** *adj* sad, melancholy; **T~sinn** *m*

depression; **~sinnig** *adj* depressed, gloomy

Trüffel ['tryfəl] (**-, -n**) *f* truffle

trug *etc* [truːk] *vb siehe* **tragen**

trügen ['tryːgən] (*unreg*) *vt* to deceive ♦ *vi* to be deceptive

trügerisch *adj* deceptive

Trugschluss ▲ ['truːgʃlʊs] *m* false conclusion

Truhe ['truːə] *f* chest

Trümmer ['trʏmər] *pl* wreckage *sg*; (*Bautrümmer*) ruins; **~haufen** *m* heap of rubble

Trumpf [trʊmpf] (**-(e)s, ⁼e**) *m* (*auch fig*) trump; **t~en** *vt, vi* to trump

Trunk [trʊŋk] (**-(e)s, ⁼e**) *m* drink; **t~en** *adj* intoxicated; **~enheit** *f* intoxication; **~enheit am Steuer** drunken driving; **~sucht** *f* alcoholism

Trupp [trʊp] (**-s, -s**) *m* troop; **~e** *f* troop; (*Waffengattung*) force; (*Schauspieltruppe*) troupe; **~en** *pl* (*MIL*) troops; **~enübungsplatz** *m* training area

Truthahn ['truːthaːn] *m* turkey

Tschech- ['tʃɛç] *zW:* **~e** *m* Czech; **~ien** (**-s**) *nt* the Czech Republic; **~in** *f* Czech; **t~isch** *adj* Czech; **~oslowakei** [-oslova'kaɪ] *f:* **die ~oslowakei** Czechoslovakia; **t~oslowakisch** [-oslo'vaːkɪʃ] *adj* Czechoslovak(ian)

tschüs(s) [tʃʏs] *excl* cheerio

T-Shirt ['tiːʃəːt] *nt* T-shirt

Tube ['tuːbə] *f* tube

Tuberkulose [tubɛrku'loːzə] *f* tuberculosis

Tuch [tuːx] (**-(e)s, ⁼er**) *nt* cloth; (*Halstuch*) scarf; (*Kopftuch*) headscarf; (*Handtuch*) towel

tüchtig ['tʏçtɪç] *adj* efficient, (cap)able; (*umg: kräftig*) good, sound; **T~keit** *f* efficiency, ability

Tücke ['tʏkə] *f* (*Arglist*) malice; (*Trick*) trick; (*Schwierigkeit*) difficulty, problem

tückisch ['tʏkɪʃ] *adj* treacherous; (*böswillig*) malicious

Tugend ['tuːgənt] (**-, -en**) *f* virtue; **t~haft** *adj* virtuous

Tülle *f* spout

Tulpe ['tʊlpə] *f* tulip

Tumor ['tuːmɔr] (**-s, -e**) *m* tumour

Tümpel ['tʏmpəl] (**-s, -**) *m* pool, pond

Tumult [tu'mʊlt] (**-(e)s, -e**) *m* tumult

tun [tuːn] (*unreg*) *vt* (*machen*) to do; (*legen*) to put ♦ *vi* to act ♦ *vr:* **es tut sich etwas/ viel** something/a lot is happening; **jdm etw ~** (*antun*) to do sth to sb; **etw tut es auch** sth will do; **das tut nichts** that doesn't matter; **das tut nichts zur Sache** that's neither here nor there; **so ~ als ob** to act as if

tünchen ['tʏnçən] *vt* to whitewash

Tunfisch ▲ ['tuːnfɪʃ] *m* = **Thunfisch**

Tunke ['tʊŋkə] *f* sauce; **t~n** *vt* to dip, to dunk

tunlichst ['tuːnlɪçst] *adv* if at all possible; **~ bald** as soon as possible

Tunnel ['tʊnəl] (**-s, -s** *od* **-**) *m* tunnel

Tupfen ['tʊpfən] (**-s, -**) *m* dot, spot; **t~** *vt, vi* to dab; (*mit Farbe*) to dot

Tür [tyːr] (**-, -en**) *f* door

Turbine [tʊr'biːnə] *f* turbine

Türk- [tʏrk] *zW:* **~e** *m* Turk; **~ei** [tʏr'kaɪ] *f:* **die ~ei** Turkey; **~in** *f* Turk

Türkis [tʏr'kiːs] (**-es, -e**) *m* turquoise; **t~** *adj* turquoise

türkisch ['tʏrkɪʃ] *adj* Turkish

Türklinke *f* doorknob, door handle

Turm [tʊrm] (**-(e)s, ⁼e**) *m* tower; (*Kirchturm*) steeple; (*Sprungturm*) diving platform; (*SCHACH*) castle, rook

türmen ['tʏrmən] *vr* to tower up ♦ *vt* to heap up ♦ *vi* (*umg*) to scarper, to bolt

Turn- ['tʊrn] *zW:* **t~en** *vi* to do gymnastic exercises ♦ *vt* to perform; **~en** (**-s**) *nt* gymnastics; (*SCH*) physical education, P.E.; **~er(in)** (**-s, -**) *m(f)* gymnast; **~halle** *f* gym(nasium); **~hose** *f* gym shorts *pl*

Turnier [tʊr'niːr] (**-s, -e**) *nt* tournament

Turn- *zW:* **~schuh** *m* gym shoe; **~verein** *m* gymnastics club; **~zeug** *nt* gym things *pl*

Tusche ['tʊʃə] *f* Indian ink

tuscheln ['tʊʃəln] *vt, vi* to whisper

Tuschkasten *m* paintbox

Tüte ['tyːtə] *f* bag

tuten ['tuːtən] *vi* (*AUT*) to hoot (*BRIT*), to honk (*US*)

Rechtschreibreform: ▲ *neue Schreibung* △ *alte Schreibung (auslaufend)*

TÜV [tyf] **(-s, -s)** m abk (= Technischer Überwachungs-Verein) ≈ MOT

Typ [ty:p] **(-s, -en)** m type; **~e** f (TYP) type

Typhus ['ty:fʊs] **(-)** m typhoid (fever)

typisch ['ty:pɪʃ] adj: **~** typical (of)

Tyrann [ty'ran] **(-en, -en)** m tyrant; **~ei** [-'naɪ] f tyranny; **t~isch** adj tyrannical; **t~i'sieren** vt to tyrannize

U, u

u. a. abk = unter anderem

U-Bahn ['u:ba:n] f underground, tube

übel ['y:bəl] adj bad; (moralisch) bad, wicked; **jdm ist ~** sb feels sick; **~ gelaunt** bad-tempered; **jdm eine Bemerkung** etc **~ nehmen** to be offended at sb's remark etc; **Ü~ (-s, -)** nt evil; (Krankheit) disease; **Ü~keit** f nausea

üben ['y:bən] vt, vi to exercise, to practise

SCHLÜSSELWORT

über ['y:bər] präp +dat 1 (räumlich) over, above; **zwei Grad über null** two degrees above zero

2 (zeitlich) over; **über der Arbeit einschlafen** to fall asleep over one's work
♦ präp +akk 1 (räumlich) over; (hoch über auch) above; (quer über auch) across

2 (zeitlich) over; **über Weihnachten** over Christmas; **über kurz oder lang** sooner or later

3 (mit Zahlen): **Kinder über 12 Jahren** children over od above 12 years of age; **ein Scheck über 200 Mark** a cheque for 200 marks

4 (auf dem Wege) via; **nach Köln über Aachen** to Cologne via Aachen; **ich habe es über die Auskunft erfahren** I found out from information

5 (betreffend) about; **ein Buch über ...** a book about od on ...; **über jdn/etw lachen** to laugh about od at sb/sth

6: **Macht über jdn haben** to have power over sb; **sie liebt ihn über alles** she loves him more than everything

♦ adv over; **über und über** over and over; **den ganzen Tag über** all day long; **jdm in etw** dat **über sein** to be superior to sb in sth

---

überall [y:bər'|al] adv everywhere; **~'hin** adv everywhere

überanstrengen [y:bər'|anʃtrɛŋən] vt insep to overexert ♦ vr insep to overexert o.s.

überarbeiten [y:bər'|arbaɪtən] vt insep to revise, to rework ♦ vr insep to overwork (o.s.)

überaus ['y:bər|aʊs] adv exceedingly

überbelichten ['y:bərbəlɪçtən] vt (PHOT) to overexpose

über'bieten (unreg) vt insep to outbid; (übertreffen) to surpass; (Rekord) to break

Überbleibsel ['y:bərblaɪpsəl] **(-s, -)** nt residue, remainder

Überblick ['y:bərblɪk] m view; (fig: Darstellung) survey, overview; (Fähigkeit): **~ (über** +akk) grasp (of), overall view (of); **ü~en** [-'blɪkən] vt insep to survey

überbring- [y:bər'brɪŋ] zW: **~en** (unreg) vt insep to deliver, to hand over; **Ü~er (-s, -)** m bearer

überbrücken [y:bər'brʏkən] vt insep to bridge (over)

überbuchen ['y:bərbu:xən] vt insep to overbook

über'dauern vt insep to outlast

über'denken (unreg) vt insep to think over

überdies [y:bər'di:s] adv besides

überdimensional ['y:bərdimɛnziona:l] adj oversize

Überdruss ▲ ['y:bərdrʊs] **(-es)** m weariness; **bis zum ~** ad nauseam

überdurchschnittlich ['y:bərdʊrçʃnɪtlɪç] adj above-average ♦ adv exceptionally

übereifrig ['y:bər|aɪfrɪç] adj over-keen

übereilt [y:bər'|aɪlt] adj (over)hasty, premature

überein- [y:bər'|aɪn] zW: **~ander** [y:bər|aɪ'nandər] adv one upon the other; (sprechen) about each other; **~kommen** (unreg) vi to agree; **Ü~kunft (-, -künfte)** f agreement; **~stimmen** vi to agree;

Ü~stimmung *f* agreement

überempfindlich ['y:bər|ɛmpfɪntlɪç] *adj*
hypersensitive

überfahren [y:bər'fa:rən] (*unreg*) *vt insep*
(*AUT*) to run over; (*fig*) to walk all over

Überfahrt ['y:bərfa:rt] *f* crossing

Überfall ['y:bərfal] *m* (*Banküberfall, MIL*) raid;
(*auf jdn*) assault; **ü~en** [-'falən] (*unreg*) *vt
insep* to attack; (*Bank*) to raid; (*besuchen*) to
drop in on, to descend on

überfällig ['y:bərfɛlɪç] *adj* overdue

über'fliegen (*unreg*) *vt insep* to fly over, to
overfly; (*Buch*) to skim through

Überfluss ▲ ['y:bərflʊs] *m*: ~ **(an** +*dat*)
(super)abundance (of), excess (of)

überflüssig ['y:bərflʏsɪç] *adj* superfluous

über'fordern *vt insep* to demand too
much of; (*Kräfte etc*) to overtax

über'führen *vt insep* (*Leiche etc*) to
transport; (*Täter*) to have convicted

Über'führung *f* transport; conviction;
(*Brücke*) bridge, overpass

über'füllt *adj* (*Schulen, Straßen*)
overcrowded; (*Kurs*) oversubscribed

Übergabe ['y:bərga:bə] *f* handing over; (*MIL*)
surrender

Übergang ['y:bərgaŋ] *m* crossing; (*Wandel,
Überleitung*) transition

Übergangs- *zW*: **~lösung** *f* provisional
solution, stopgap; **~zeit** *f* transitional
period

über'geben (*unreg*) *vt insep* to hand over;
(*MIL*) to surrender ♦ *vr insep* to be sick

übergehen ['y:bərge:ən] (*unreg*) *vi* (*Besitz*) to
pass; (*zum Feind etc*) to go over, to defect;
~ **in** +*akk* to turn into; **über'gehen** (*unreg*)
vt insep to pass over, to omit

Übergewicht ['y:bərgəvɪçt] *nt* excess
weight; (*fig*) preponderance

überglücklich ['y:bərglʏklɪç] *adj* overjoyed

Übergröße ['y:bərgrø:sə] *f* oversize

überhaupt [y:bər'haupt] *adv* at all; (*im
Allgemeinen*) in general; (*besonders*)
especially; ~ **nicht/keine** not/none at all

überheblich [y:bər'he:plɪç] *adj* arrogant;
Ü~keit *f* arrogance

über'holen *vt insep* to overtake; (*TECH*) to

overhaul

über'holt *adj* out-of-date, obsolete

Überholverbot [y:bər'ho:lfɛrbo:t] *nt*
restriction on overtaking

über'hören *vt insep* not to hear;
(*absichtlich*) to ignore

überirdisch ['y:bər|ɪrdɪʃ] *adj* supernatural,
unearthly

über'laden (*unreg*) *vt insep* to overload
♦ *adj* (*fig*) cluttered

über'lassen (*unreg*) *vt insep*: **jdm etw ~** to
leave sth to sb ♦ *vr insep*: **sich einer Sache**
dat ~ to give o.s. over to sth

über'lasten *vt insep* to overload; (*Mensch*)
to overtax

überlaufen ['y:bərlaufən] (*unreg*) *vi*
(*Flüssigkeit*) to flow over; (*zum Feind etc*) to
go over, to defect; ~ **sein** to be inundated
od besieged; **über'laufen** (*unreg*) *vt insep*
(*Schauer etc*) to come over

über'leben *vt insep* to survive;
Über'lebende(r) *f(m)* survivor

über'legen *vt insep* to consider ♦ *adj*
superior; **ich muss es mir ~** I'll have to
think about it; **Über'legenheit** *f*
superiority

Über'legung *f* consideration, deliberation

über'liefern *vt insep* to hand down, to
transmit

Überlieferung *f* tradition

überlisten [y:bər'lɪstən] *vt insep* to outwit

überm ['y:bərm] = **über dem**

Übermacht ['y:bərmaxt] *f* superior force,
superiority; **übermächtig** ['y:bərmɛçtɪç] *adj*
superior (in strength); (*Gefühl etc*)
overwhelming

übermäßig ['y:bərmɛ:sɪç] *adj* excessive

Übermensch ['y:bərmɛnʃ] *m* superman;
ü~lich *adj* superhuman

übermitteln [y:bər'mɪtəln] *vt insep* to
convey

übermorgen [y:bər'mɔrgən] *adv* the day
after tomorrow

Übermüdung [y:bər'my:dʊŋ] *f* fatigue,
overtiredness

Übermut ['y:bərmu:t] *m* exuberance

übermütig ['y:bərmy:tɪç] *adj* exuberant,

high-spirited; **~ werden** to get overconfident

übernächste(r, s) [ˈyːbɐnɛːçstə(r, s)] *adj* (*Jahr*) next but one

übernacht- [yːbɐˈnaxt] *zW:* **~en** *vi insep:* (**bei jdm**) **~en** to spend the night (at sb's place); **Ü~ung** *f* overnight stay; **Ü~ung mit Frühstück** bed and breakfast; **Ü~ungsmöglichkeit** *f* overnight accommodation *no pl*

Übernahme [ˈyːbɐnaːmə] *f* taking over *od* on, acceptance

über'nehmen (*unreg*) *vt insep* to take on, to accept; (*Amt, Geschäft*) to take over ♦ *vr insep* to take on too much

über'prüfen *vt insep* to examine, to check

überqueren [yːbɐˈkveːrən] *vt insep* to cross

überragen [yːbɐˈraːgən] *vt insep* to tower above; (*fig*) to surpass

überraschen [yːbɐˈraʃən] *vt insep* to surprise

Überraschung *f* surprise

überreden [yːbɐˈreːdən] *vt insep* to persuade

überreichen [yːbɐˈraɪçən] *vt insep* to present, to hand over

'Überrest *m* remains, remnants

überrumpeln [yːbɐˈrʊmpəln] *vt insep* to take by surprise

überrunden [yːbɐˈrʊndən] *vt insep* to lap

übers [ˈyːbɐs] = **über das**

Überschall- [ˈyːbɐʃal] *zW:* **~flugzeug** *nt* supersonic jet; **~geschwindigkeit** *f* supersonic speed

über'schätzen *vt insep* to overestimate

'überschäumen *vi* (*Bier*) to foam over, bubble over; (*Temperament*) to boil over

Überschlag [ˈyːbɐʃlaːk] *m* (*FIN*) estimate; (*SPORT*) somersault; **ü~en** [-ˈʃlaːgən] (*unreg*) *vt insep* (*berechnen*) to estimate; (*auslassen: Seite*) to omit ♦ *vr insep* to somersault; (*Stimme*) to crack; (*AVIAT*) to loop the loop; **'überschlagen** (*unreg*) *vt* (*Beine*) to cross ♦ *vi* (*Wellen*) to break; (*Funken*) to flash

überschnappen [ˈyːbɐʃnapən] *vi* (*Stimme*) to crack; (*umg: Mensch*) to flip one's lid

über'schneiden (*unreg*) *vr insep* (*auch fig*) to overlap; (*Linien*) to intersect

über'schreiben (*unreg*) *vt insep* to provide with a heading; **jdm etw ~** to transfer *od* make over sth to sb

über'schreiten (*unreg*) *vt insep* to cross over; (*fig*) to exceed; (*verletzen*) to transgress

Überschrift [ˈyːbɐʃrɪft] *f* heading, title

Überschuss ▲ [ˈyːbɐʃʊs] *m:* **~ (an** +*dat*) surplus (of); **überschüssig** [ˈyːbɐʃʏsɪç] *adj* surplus, excess

über'schütten *vt insep:* **jdn/etw mit etw ~** to pour over sb/sth; **jdn mit etw ~** (*fig*) to shower sb with sth

überschwänglich ▲ [ˈyːbɐʃvɛŋlɪç] *adj* effusive

überschwemmen [yːbɐˈʃvɛmən] *vt insep* to flood

Überschwemmung *f* flood

Übersee [ˈyːbɐzeː] *f:* **nach/in ~** overseas; **ü~isch** *adj* overseas

über'sehen (*unreg*) *vt insep* to look (out) over; (*fig: Folgen*) to see, to get an overall view of; (: *nicht beachten*) to overlook

über'senden *vt insep* to send, to forward

übersetz- *zW:* **~en** [yːbɐˈzɛtsən] *vt insep* to translate; **'übersetzen** *vi* to cross; **Ü~er(in)** [-ˈzɛtsər(ɪn)] (**-s, -**) *m(f)* translator; **Ü~ung** [-ˈzɛtsʊŋ] *f* translation; (*TECH*) gear ratio

Übersicht [ˈyːbɐzɪçt] *f* overall view; (*Darstellung*) survey; **ü~lich** *adj* clear; (*Gelände*) open; **~lichkeit** *f* clarity, lucidity

übersiedeln [ˈyːbɐziːdəln] *vi sep* to move; **über'siedeln** *vt* to move

über'spannt *adj* eccentric; (*Idee*) wild, crazy

überspitzt [yːbɐˈʃpɪtst] *adj* exaggerated

über'springen (*unreg*) *vt insep* to jump over; (*fig*) to skip

überstehen (*unreg*) *vt insep* to overcome, to get over; (*Winter etc*) to survive, to get through; **'überstehen** (*unreg*) *vi* to project

über'steigen (*unreg*) *vt insep* to climb over; (*fig*) to exceed

---

Spelling Reform: ▲ *new spelling* △ *old spelling (to be phased out)*

über'stimmen vt insep to outvote
Überstunden ['y:bərʃtʊndən] pl overtime sg
über'stürzen vt insep to rush ♦ vr insep to follow (one another) in rapid succession
überstürzt adj (over)hasty
Übertrag ['y:bərtra:k] (-(e)s, -träge) m (COMM) amount brought forward; **ü~bar** [-'tra:kba:r] adj transferable; (MED) infectious; **ü~en** [-'tra:gən] (unreg) vt insep to transfer; (RADIO) to broadcast; (übersetzen) to render; (Krankheit) to transmit ♦ vr insep to spread ♦ adj figurative; **ü~en auf** +akk to transfer to; **jdm etw ü~en** to assign sth to sb; **sich ü~en auf** +akk to spread to; **~ung** [-'tra:gʊŋ] f transfer(ence); (RADIO) broadcast; rendering; transmission
über'treffen (unreg) vt insep to surpass
über'treiben (unreg) vt insep to exaggerate; **Übertreibung** f exaggeration
übertreten [y:bər'tre:tən] (unreg) vt insep to cross; (Gebot etc) to break; **'übertreten** (unreg) vi (über Linie, Gebiet) to step (over); (SPORT) to overstep; (zu anderem Glauben) to be converted; **übertreten (in** +akk) (POL) to go over (to)
Über'tretung f violation, transgression
übertrieben [y:bər'tri:bən] adj exaggerated, excessive
übervölkert [y:bər'fœlkərt] adj overpopulated
übervoll ['y:bərfɔl] adj overfull
übervorteilen [y:bər'fɔrtailən] vt insep to dupe, to cheat
über'wachen vt insep to supervise; (Verdächtigen) to keep under surveillance; **Überwachung** f supervision; surveillance
überwältigen [y:bər'vɛltigən] vt insep to overpower; **~d** adj overwhelming
überweisen [y:bər'vaizən] (unreg) vt insep to transfer
Überweisung f transfer; **~sauftrag** m (credit) transfer order
über'wiegen (unreg) vi insep to predominate; **~d** adj predominant
über'winden (unreg) vt insep to overcome ♦ vr insep to make an effort, to bring o.s. (to do sth)

Überwindung f effort, strength of mind
Überzahl ['y:bərtsa:l] f superiority, superior numbers pl; **in der ~ sein** to be numerically superior
überzählig ['y:bərtsɛ:lɪç] adj surplus
über'zeugen vt insep to convince; **~d** adj convincing
Überzeugung f conviction
überziehen ['y:bərtsi:ən] (unreg) vt to put on; **über'ziehen** (unreg) vt insep to cover; (Konto) to overdraw
Überziehungskredit m overdraft provision
Überzug ['y:bərtsu:k] m cover; (Belag) coating
üblich ['y:plɪç] adj usual
U-Boot ['u:bo:t] nt submarine
übrig ['y:brɪç] adj remaining; **für jdn etwas ~ haben** (umg) to be fond of sb; **die Ü~en** the others; **das Ü~e** the rest; **im Ü~en** besides; **~ bleiben** to remain, to be left (over); **~ lassen** to leave (over); **~ens** ['y:brigəns] adv besides; (nebenbei bemerkt) by the way
Übung ['y:bʊŋ] f practice; (Turnübung, Aufgabe etc) exercise; **~ macht den Meister** practice makes perfect
Ufer ['u:fər] (-s, -) nt bank; (Meeresufer) shore
Uhr [u:r] (-, -en) f clock; (Armbanduhr) watch; **wie viel ~ ist es?** what time is it?; **1 ~** 1 o'clock; **20 ~** 8 o'clock, 20.00 (twenty hundred) hours; **~(arm)band** nt watch strap; **~band** nt watch strap; **~macher** (-s, -) m watchmaker; **~werk** nt clockwork; works of a watch; **~zeiger** m hand; **~zeigersinn** m: **im ~zeigersinn** clockwise; **entgegen dem ~zeigersinn** anticlockwise; **~zeit** f time (of day)
Uhu ['u:hu] (-s, -s) m eagle owl
UKW [u:ka:'ve:] abk (= Ultrakurzwelle) VHF
ulkig ['ʊlkɪç] adj funny
Ulme ['ʊlmə] f elm
Ultimatum [ʊlti'ma:tʊm] (-s, **Ultimaten**) nt ultimatum
Ultra- ['ʊltra] zW: **~schall** m (PHYS) ultrasound; **u~violett** adj ultraviolet

SCHLÜSSELWORT

um [ʊm] *präp +akk* **1** (*um herum*) (a)round;
um Weihnachten around Christmas; **er
schlug um sich** he hit about him
2 (*mit Zeitangabe*) at; **um acht (Uhr)** at
eight (o'clock)
3 (*mit Größenangabe*) by; **etw um 4 cm
kürzen** to shorten sth by 4 cm; **um 10%
teurer** 10% more expensive; **um vieles
besser** better by far; **um nichts besser**
not in the least bit better
4: **der Kampf um den Titel** the battle for
the title; **um Geld spielen** to play for
money; **Stunde um Stunde** hour after
hour; **Auge um Auge** an eye for an eye
♦ *präp +gen*: **um ... willen** for the sake of
...; **um Gottes willen** for goodness' *od*
(*stärker*) God's sake
♦ *konj*: **um ... zu** (in order) to ...; **zu klug,
um zu ...** too clever to ...; *siehe* **umso**
♦ *adv* **1** (*ungefähr*) about; **um (die) 30
Leute** about *od* around 30 people
2 (*vorbei*): **die 2 Stunden sind um** the two
hours are up

umändern [ˈʊm|ɛndərn] *vt* to alter
Umänderung *f* alteration
umarbeiten [ˈʊm|arbaɪtən] *vt* to remodel;
(*Buch etc*) to revise, to rework
umarmen [ʊmˈarmən] *vt insep* to embrace
Umbau [ˈʊmbaʊ] **(-(e)s, -e** *od* **-ten)** *m*
reconstruction, alteration(s); **u~en** *vt* to
rebuild, to reconstruct
umbilden [ˈʊmbɪldən] *vt* to reorganize; (*POL:
Kabinett*) to reshuffle
umbinden [ˈʊmbɪndən] (*unreg*) *vt* (*Krawatte
etc*) to put on
umblättern [ˈʊmblɛtərn] *vt* to turn over
umblicken [ˈʊmblɪkən] *vr* to look around
umbringen [ˈʊmbrɪŋən] (*unreg*) *vt* to kill
umbuchen [ˈʊmbuːxən] *vi* to change one's
reservation/flight *etc* ♦ *vt* to change
umdenken [ˈʊmdɛŋkən] (*unreg*) *vi* to adjust
one's views
umdrehen [ˈʊmdreːən] *vt* to turn (round);
(*Hals*) to wring ♦ *vr* to turn (round)

Um'drehung *f* revolution; rotation
umeinander [ʊmaɪˈnandər] *adv* round one
another; (*füreinander*) for one another
umfahren [ˈʊmfaːrən] (*unreg*) *vt* to run over;
um'fahren (*unreg*) *vt insep* to drive round;
to sail round
umfallen [ˈʊmfalən] (*unreg*) *vi* to fall down
od over
Umfang [ˈʊmfaŋ] *m* extent; (*von Buch*) size;
(*Reichweite*) range; (*Fläche*) area; (*MATH*)
circumference; **u~reich** *adj* extensive;
(*Buch etc*) voluminous
um'fassen *vt insep* to embrace; (*umgeben*)
to surround; (*enthalten*) to include;
um'fassend *adj* comprehensive, extensive
umformen [ˈʊmfɔrmən] *vi* to transform
Umfrage [ˈʊmfraːgə] *f* poll
umfüllen [ˈʊmfʏlən] *vt* to transfer; (*Wein*) to
decant
umfunktionieren [ˈʊmfʊŋktsioniːrən] *vt* to
convert, to transform
Umgang [ˈʊmgaŋ] *m* company; (*mit jdm*)
dealings *pl*; (*Behandlung*) way of behaving
umgänglich [ˈʊmgɛŋlɪç] *adj* sociable
Umgangs- *zW*: **~formen** *pl* manners;
~sprache *f* colloquial language
umgeben [ʊmˈgeːbən] (*unreg*) *vt insep* to
surround
Umgebung *f* surroundings *pl*; (*Milieu*)
environment; (*Personen*) people in one's
circle
umgehen [ˈʊmgeːən] (*unreg*) *vi* to go
(a)round; **im Schlosse ~** to haunt the
castle; **mit jdm grob** *etc* **~** to treat sb
roughly *etc*; **mit Geld sparsam ~** to be
careful with one's money; **um'gehen** *vt
insep* to bypass; (*MIL*) to outflank; (*Gesetz
etc*) to circumvent; (*vermeiden*) to avoid;
'umgehend *adj* immediate
Um'gehung *f* bypassing; outflanking;
circumvention; avoidance; **~sstraße** *f*
bypass
umgekehrt [ˈʊmgəkeːrt] *adj* reverse(d);
(*gegenteilig*) opposite ♦ *adv* the other way
around; **und ~** and vice versa
umgraben [ˈʊmgraːbən] (*unreg*) *vt* to dig up
Umhang [ˈʊmhaŋ] *m* wrap, cape

Spelling Reform: ▲ *new spelling* △ *old spelling (to be phased out)*

umhauen ['ʊmhaʊən] *vt* to fell; (*fig*) to bowl over

umher [ʊm'heːr] *adv* about, around; **~gehen** (*unreg*) *vi* to walk about; **~ziehen** (*unreg*) *vi* to wander from place to place

umhinkönnen [ʊm'hɪnkœnən] (*unreg*) *vi*: **ich kann nicht umhin, das zu tun** I can't help doing it

umhören ['ʊmhøːrən] *vr* to ask around

Umkehr ['ʊmkeːr] (-) *f* turning back; (*Änderung*) change; **u~en** *vi* to turn back ♦ *vt* to turn round, to reverse; (*Tasche etc*) to turn inside out; (*Gefäß etc*) to turn upside down

umkippen ['ʊmkɪpən] *vt* to tip over ♦ *vi* to overturn; (*umg: Mensch*) to keel over; (*fig: Meinung ändern*) to change one's mind

Umkleide- ['ʊmklaɪdə] *zW*: **~kabine** *f* (*im Schwimmbad*) (changing) cubicle; **~raum** *m* changing *od* dressing room

umkommen ['ʊmkɔmən] (*unreg*) *vi* to die, to perish; (*Lebensmittel*) to go bad

Umkreis ['ʊmkraɪs] *m* neighbourhood; **im ~ von** within a radius of

Umlage ['ʊmlaːɡə] *f* share of the costs

Umlauf ['ʊmlaʊf] *m* (*Geldumlauf*) circulation; (*von Gestirn*) revolution; **~bahn** *f* orbit

Umlaut ['ʊmlaʊt] *m* umlaut

umlegen ['ʊmleːɡən] *vt* to put on; (*verlegen*) to move, to shift; (*Kosten*) to share out; (*umkippen*) to tip over; (*umg: töten*) to bump off

umleiten ['ʊmlaɪtən] *vt* to divert

Umleitung *f* diversion

umliegend ['ʊmliːɡənt] *adj* surrounding

um'randen *vt insep* to border, to edge

umrechnen ['ʊmrɛçnən] *vt* to convert

Umrechnung *f* conversion; **~skurs** *m* rate of exchange

um'reißen (*unreg*) *vt insep* to outline, to sketch

Umriss ▲ ['ʊmrɪs] *m* outline

umrühren ['ʊmryːrən] *vt, vi* to stir

ums [ʊms] = **um das**

Umsatz ['ʊmzats] *m* turnover; **~steuer** *f* sales tax

umschalten ['ʊmʃaltən] *vt* to switch

umschauen *vr* to look round

Umschlag ['ʊmʃlaːk] *m* cover; (*Buchumschlag auch*) jacket; (*MED*) compress; (*Briefumschlag*) envelope; (*Wechsel*) change; (*von Hose*) turn-up; **u~en** [-ɡən] (*unreg*) *vi* to change; (*NAUT*) to capsize ♦ *vt* to knock over; (*Ärmel*) to turn up; (*Seite*) to turn over; (*Waren*) to transfer; **~platz** *m* (*COMM*) distribution centre

umschreiben ['ʊmʃraɪbən] (*unreg*) *vt* (*neu schreiben*) to rewrite; (*übertragen*) to transfer; **~ auf** +*akk* to transfer to; **um'schreiben** (*unreg*) *vt insep* to paraphrase; (*abgrenzen*) to define

Umschweife ['ʊmʃvaɪfə] *pl*: **ohne ~** without beating about the bush, straight out

Umschwung ['ʊmʃvʊŋ] *m* change (around), revolution

umsehen ['ʊmzeːən] (*unreg*) *vr* to look around *od* about; (*suchen*): **sich ~ (nach)** to look out (for)

umseitig ['ʊmzaɪtɪç] *adv* overleaf

umsichtig ['ʊmzɪçtɪç] *adj* cautious, prudent

umso ▲ ['ʊmzoː] *konj*: **~ besser/schlimmer** so much the better/worse

umsonst [ʊm'zɔnst] *adv* in vain; (*gratis*) for nothing

umspringen ['ʊmʃprɪŋən] (*unreg*) *vi* to change; (*Wind auch*) to veer; **mit jdm ~** to treat sb badly

Umstand ['ʊmʃtant] *m* circumstance; **Umstände** *pl* (*fig: Schwierigkeiten*) fuss; **in anderen Umständen sein** to be pregnant; **Umstände machen** to go to a lot of trouble; **unter Umständen** possibly

umständlich ['ʊmʃtɛntlɪç] *adj* (*Methode*) cumbersome, complicated; (*Ausdrucksweise, Erklärung*) long-winded; (*Mensch*) ponderous

Umstandskleid *nt* maternity dress

Umstehende(n) ['ʊmʃteːəndə(n)] *pl* bystanders

umsteigen ['ʊmʃtaɪɡən] (*unreg*) *vi* (*EISENB*) to change

umstellen ['ʊmʃtɛlən] *vt* (*an anderen Ort*) to

change round, to rearrange; (*TECH*) to convert ♦ *vr* to adapt (o.s.); **sich auf etw** *akk* ~ to adapt to sth; **um'stellen** *vt insep* to surround

Umstellung ['ʊmʃtɛlʊŋ] *f* change; (*Umgewöhnung*) adjustment; (*TECH*) conversion

umstimmen ['ʊmʃtɪmən] *vt* (*MUS*) to retune; **jdn ~** to make sb change his mind

umstoßen ['ʊmʃtoːsən] (*unreg*) *vt* to overturn; (*Plan etc*) to change, to upset

umstritten [ʊm'ʃtrɪtən] *adj* disputed

Umsturz ['ʊmʃtʊrts] *m* overthrow

umstürzen ['ʊmʃtʏrtsən] *vt* (*umwerfen*) to overturn ♦ *vi* to collapse, to fall down; (*Wagen*) to overturn

Umtausch ['ʊmtaʊʃ] *m* exchange; **u~en** *vt* to exchange

Umverpackung ['ʊmfɛrpakʊŋ] *f* packaging

umwandeln ['ʊmvandəln] *vt* to change, to convert; (*ELEK*) to transform

umwechseln ['ʊmvɛksəln] *vt* to change

Umweg ['ʊmveːk] *m* detour, roundabout way

Umwelt ['ʊmvɛlt] *f* environment; **u~freundlich** *adj* not harmful to the environment, environment-friendly; **u~schädlich** *adj* ecologically harmful; **~schutz** *m* environmental protection; **~schützer** *m* environmentalist; **~verschmutzung** *f* environmental pollution

umwenden ['ʊmvɛndən] (*unreg*) *vt, vr* to turn (round)

umwerfen ['ʊmvɛrfən] (*unreg*) *vt* to upset, to overturn; (*fig: erschüttern*) to upset, to throw; **~d** (*umg*) *adj* fantastic

umziehen ['ʊmtsiːən] (*unreg*) *vt, vr* to change ♦ *vi* to move

Umzug ['ʊmtsuːk] *m* procession; (*Wohnungsumzug*) move, removal

unab- ['ʊnʔap] *zW:* **~änderlich** *adj* irreversible, unalterable; **~hängig** *adj* independent; **U~hängigkeit** *f* independence; **~kömmlich** *adj* indispensable; **zur Zeit ~kömmlich** not free at the moment; **~lässig** *adj* incessant,

constant; **~sehbar** *adj* immeasurable; (*Folgen*) unforeseeable; (*Kosten*) incalculable; **~sichtlich** *adj* unintentional; **~'wendbar** *adj* inevitable

unachtsam ['ʊnʔaxtzaːm] *adj* careless; **U~keit** *f* carelessness

unan- ['ʊnʔan] *zW:* **~'fechtbar** *adj* indisputable; **~gebracht** *adj* uncalled-for; **~gemessen** *adj* inadequate; **~genehm** *adj* unpleasant; **U~nehmlichkeit** *f* inconvenience; **U~nehmlichkeiten** *pl* (*Ärger*) trouble *sg*; **~sehnlich** *adj* unsightly; **~ständig** *adj* indecent, improper

unappetitlich ['ʊnʔapetiːtlɪç] *adj* unsavoury

Unart ['ʊnʔaːrt] *f* bad manners *pl*; (*Angewohnheit*) bad habit; **u~ig** *adj* naughty, badly behaved

unauf- ['ʊnʔaʊf] *zW:* **~fällig** *adj* unobtrusive; (*Kleidung*) inconspicuous; **~'findbar** *adj* not to be found; **~gefordert** *adj* unasked ♦ *adv* spontaneously; **~haltsam** *adj* irresistible; **~'hörlich** *adj* incessant, continuous; **~merksam** *adj* inattentive; **~richtig** *adj* insincere

unaus- ['ʊnʔaʊs] *zW:* **~geglichen** *adj* unbalanced; **~'sprechlich** *adj* inexpressible; **~'stehlich** *adj* intolerable

unbarmherzig ['ʊnbarmhɛrtsɪç] *adj* pitiless, merciless

unbeabsichtigt ['ʊnbəʔapzɪçtɪçt] *adj* unintentional

unbeachtet ['ʊnbəʔaxtət] *adj* unnoticed, ignored

unbedenklich ['ʊnbədɛŋklɪç] *adj* (*Plan*) unobjectionable

unbedeutend ['ʊnbədɔʏtənt] *adj* insignificant, unimportant; (*Fehler*) slight

unbedingt ['ʊnbədɪŋt] *adj* unconditional ♦ *adv* absolutely; **musst du ~ gehen?** do you really have to go?

unbefangen ['ʊnbəfaŋən] *adj* impartial, unprejudiced; (*ohne Hemmungen*) uninhibited; **U~heit** *f* impartiality; uninhibitedness

unbefriedigend ['ʊnbəfriːdɪgənt] *adj* unsatisfactory

unbefriedigt ['ʊnbəfriːdɪçt] *adj* unsatisfied,

Spelling Reform: ▲ *new spelling* △ *old spelling (to be phased out)*

dissatisfied

unbefugt ['ʊnbəfuːkt] *adj* unauthorized

unbegreiflich [ʊnbə'ɡraɪflɪç] *adj* inconceivable

unbegrenzt ['ʊnbəɡrɛntst] *adj* unlimited

unbegründet ['ʊnbəɡrʏndət] *adj* unfounded

Unbehagen ['ʊnbəhaːɡən] *nt* discomfort; **unbehaglich** ['ʊnbəhaːklɪç] *adj* uncomfortable; (*Gefühl*) uneasy

unbeholfen ['ʊnbəhɔlfən] *adj* awkward, clumsy

unbekannt ['ʊnbəkant] *adj* unknown

unbekümmert ['ʊnbəkʏmərt] *adj* unconcerned

unbeliebt ['ʊnbəliːpt] *adj* unpopular

unbequem ['ʊnbəkveːm] *adj* (*Stuhl*) uncomfortable; (*Mensch*) bothersome; (*Regelung*) inconvenient

unberechenbar [ʊnbə'rɛçənbaːr] *adj* incalculable; (*Mensch, Verhalten*) unpredictable

unberechtigt ['ʊnbərɛçtɪçt] *adj* unjustified; (*nicht erlaubt*) unauthorized

unberührt ['ʊnbəryːrt] *adj* untouched, intact; **sie ist noch ~** she is still a virgin

unbescheiden ['ʊnbəʃaɪdən] *adj* presumptuous

unbeschreiblich [ʊnbə'ʃraɪplɪç] *adj* indescribable

unbeständig ['ʊnbəʃtɛndɪç] *adj* (*Mensch*) inconstant; (*Wetter*) unsettled; (*Lage*) unstable

unbestechlich [ʊnbə'ʃtɛçlɪç] *adj* incorruptible

unbestimmt ['ʊnbəʃtɪmt] *adj* indefinite; (*Zukunft auch*) uncertain

unbeteiligt [ʊnbə'taɪlɪçt] *adj* unconcerned, indifferent

unbeweglich ['ʊnbəveːklɪç] *adj* immovable

unbewohnt ['ʊnbəvoːnt] *adj* uninhabited; (*Wohnung*) unoccupied

unbewusst ▲ ['ʊnbəvʊst] *adj* unconscious

unbezahlt ['ʊnbətsaːlt] *adj* (*Rechnung*) outstanding, unsettled; (*Urlaub*) unpaid

unbrauchbar ['ʊnbraʊxbaːr] *adj* (*Arbeit*) useless; (*Gerät auch*) unusable

und [ʊnt] *konj* and; **~ so weiter** and so on

Undank ['ʊndaŋk] *m* ingratitude; **u~bar** ungrateful

undefinierbar [ʊndefi'niːrbaːr] *adj* indefinable

undenkbar [ʊn'dɛŋkbaːr] *adj* inconceivable

undeutlich ['ʊndɔʏtlɪç] *adj* indistinct

undicht ['ʊndɪçt] *adj* leaky

Unding ['ʊndɪŋ] *nt* absurdity

undurch- ['ʊndʊrç] *zW*: **~führbar** [-'fyːrbaːr] *adj* impracticable; **~lässig** [-'lɛsɪç] *adj* waterproof, impermeable; **~sichtig** [-'zɪçtɪç] *adj* opaque; (*fig*) obscure

uneben ['ʊnʔeːbən] *adj* uneven

unecht ['ʊnʔɛçt] *adj* (*Schmuck*) fake; (*vorgetäuscht: Freundlichkeit*) false

unehelich ['ʊnʔeːəlɪç] *adj* illegitimate

uneinig ['ʊnʔaɪnɪç] *adj* divided; **~ sein** to disagree; **U~keit** *f* discord, dissension

uneins ['ʊnʔaɪns] *adj* at variance, at odds

unempfindlich ['ʊnʔɛmpfɪntlɪç] *adj* insensitive; (*Stoff*) practical

unendlich [ʊn'ʔɛntlɪç] *adj* infinite

unent- ['ʊnʔɛnt] *zW*: **~behrlich** [-'beːrlɪç] *adj* indispensable; **~geltlich** [-ɡɛltlɪç] *adj* free (of charge); **~schieden** [-'ʃiːdən] *adj* undecided; **~schieden enden** (*SPORT*) to end in a draw; **~schlossen** [-ʃlɔsən] *adj* undecided; irresolute; **~wegt** [-'veːkt] *adj* unswerving; (*unaufhörlich*) incessant

uner- ['ʊnʔer] *zW*: **~bittlich** [-'bɪtlɪç] *adj* unyielding, inexorable; **~fahren** [-faːrən] *adj* inexperienced; **~freulich** [-frɔʏlɪç] *adj* unpleasant; **~gründlich** *adj* unfathomable; **~hört** [-høːrt] *adj* unheard-of; (*Bitte*) outrageous; **~lässlich** ▲ [-'lɛslɪç] *adj* indispensable; **~laubt** *adj* unauthorized; **~messlich** ▲ *adj* immeasurable, immense; **~reichbar** *adj* (*Ziel*) unattainable; (*Ort*) inaccessible; (*telefonisch*) unobtainable; **~schöpflich** [-'ʃœpflɪç] *adj* inexhaustible; **~schwinglich** [-'ʃvɪŋlɪç] *adj* (*Preis*) exorbitant; too expensive; **~träglich** [-'trɛːklɪç] *adj* unbearable; (*Frechheit*) insufferable; **~wartet** *adj* unexpected; **~wünscht** *adj* undesirable, unwelcome

unfähig ['ʊnfɛːɪç] *adj* incapable, incompetent; **zu etw ~ sein** to be incapable of sth; **U~keit** f incapacity; incompetence

unfair ['ʊnfɛːr] adj unfair

Unfall ['ʊnfal] m accident; **~flucht** f hit-and-run (driving); **~schaden** m damages pl; **~station** f emergency ward; **~stelle** f scene of the accident; **~versicherung** f accident insurance

unfassbar ▲ [ʊn'fasbaːr] adj inconceivable

unfehlbar [ʊn'feːlbaːr] adj infallible ♦ adv inevitably; **U~keit** f infallibility

unförmig ['ʊnfœrmɪç] adj (formlos) shapeless

unfrei ['ʊnfraɪ] adj not free, unfree; (Paket) unfranked; **~willig** adj involuntary, against one's will

unfreundlich ['ʊnfrɔʏntlɪç] adj unfriendly; **U~keit** f unfriendliness

Unfriede(n) ['ʊnfriːdə(n)] m dissension, strife

unfruchtbar ['ʊnfrʊxtbaːr] adj infertile; (Gespräche) unfruitful; **U~keit** f infertility; unfruitfulness

Unfug ['ʊnfuːk] (-s) m (Benehmen) mischief; (Unsinn) nonsense; **grober ~** (JUR) gross misconduct; malicious damage

Ungar(in) ['ʊngar(ɪn)] m(f) Hungarian; **u~isch** adj Hungarian; **~n** nt Hungary

ungeachtet ['ʊngəʔaxtət] präp +gen notwithstanding

ungeahnt ['ʊngəʔaːnt] adj unsuspected, undreamt-of

ungebeten ['ʊngəbeːtən] adj uninvited

ungebildet ['ʊngəbɪldət] adj uneducated; uncultured

ungedeckt ['ʊngədɛkt] adj (Scheck) uncovered

Ungeduld ['ʊngədʊlt] f impatience; **u~ig** [-dɪç] adj impatient

ungeeignet ['ʊngəʔaɪgnət] adj unsuitable

ungefähr ['ʊngəfɛːr] adj rough, approximate; **das kommt nicht von ~** that's hardly surprising

ungefährlich ['ʊngəfɛːrlɪç] adj not dangerous, harmless

ungehalten ['ʊngəhaltən] adj indignant

ungeheuer ['ʊngəhɔʏər] adj huge ♦ adv (umg) enormously; **U~ (-s, -)** nt monster;

~lich [-'hɔʏərlɪç] adj monstrous

ungehörig ['ʊngəhøːrɪç] adj impertinent, improper

ungehorsam ['ʊngəhoːrzaːm] adj disobedient; **U~** m disobedience

ungeklärt ['ʊngəklɛːrt] adj not cleared up; (Rätsel) unsolved

ungeladen ['ʊngəlaːdən] adj not loaded; (Gast) uninvited

ungelegen ['ʊngəleːgən] adj inconvenient

ungelernt ['ʊngəlɛrnt] adj unskilled

ungelogen ['ʊngəloːgən] adv really, honestly

ungemein ['ʊngəmaɪn] adj uncommon

ungemütlich ['ʊngəmyːtlɪç] adj uncomfortable; (Person) disagreeable

ungenau ['ʊngənaʊ] adj inaccurate; **U~igkeit** f inaccuracy

ungenießbar ['ʊngəniːsbaːr] adj inedible; undrinkable; (umg) unbearable

ungenügend ['ʊngənyːgənt] adj insufficient, inadequate

ungepflegt ['ʊngəpfleːkt] adj (Garten etc) untended; (Person) unkempt; (Hände) neglected

ungerade ['ʊngəraːdə] adj uneven, odd

ungerecht ['ʊngərɛçt] adj unjust; **~fertigt** adj unjustified; **U~igkeit** f injustice, unfairness

ungern ['ʊngɛrn] adv unwillingly, reluctantly

ungeschehen ['ʊngəʃeːən] adj: **~ machen** to undo

Ungeschicklichkeit ['ʊngəʃɪklɪçkaɪt] f clumsiness

ungeschickt adj awkward, clumsy

ungeschminkt ['ʊngəʃmɪŋkt] adj without make-up; (fig) unvarnished

ungesetzlich ['ʊngəzɛtslɪç] adj illegal

ungestört ['ʊngəʃtøːrt] adj undisturbed

ungestraft ['ʊngəʃtraːft] adv with impunity

ungestüm ['ʊngəʃtyːm] adj impetuous; tempestuous

ungesund ['ʊngəzʊnt] adj unhealthy

ungetrübt ['ʊngətryːpt] adj clear; (fig) untroubled; (Freude) unalloyed

Ungetüm ['ʊngətyːm] (-(e)s, -e) nt monster

ungewiss ▲ ['ʊngəvɪs] adj uncertain;

U~heit *f* uncertainty

ungewöhnlich ['ʊngəvøːnlıç] *adj* unusual

ungewohnt ['ʊngəvoːnt] *adj* unaccustomed

Ungeziefer ['ʊngətsiːfər] **(-s)** *nt* vermin

ungezogen ['ʊngətsoːgən] *adj* rude, impertinent; U~heit *f* rudeness, impertinence

ungezwungen ['ʊngətsvʊŋən] *adj* natural, unconstrained

unglaublich [ʊnˈglaʊplıç] *adj* incredible

ungleich ['ʊnglaıç] *adj* dissimilar; unequal ♦ *adv* incomparably; ~artig *adj* different; U~heit *f* dissimilarity; inequality; ~mäßig *adj* irregular, uneven

Unglück ['ʊnglʏk] **(-(e)s, -e)** *nt* misfortune; (*Pech*) bad luck; (~*sfall*) calamity, disaster; (*Verkehrsunglück*) accident; u~lich *adj* unhappy; (*erfolglos*) unlucky; (*unerfreulich*) unfortunate; u~licherweise [-ˈvaɪzə] *adv* unfortunately; ~sfall *m* accident, calamity

ungültig ['ʊngʏltıç] *adj* invalid; U~keit *f* invalidity

ungünstig ['ʊngʏnstıç] *adj* unfavourable

ungut ['ʊnguːt] *adj* (*Gefühl*) uneasy; **nichts für** ~ no offence

unhaltbar ['ʊnhaltbaːr] *adj* untenable

Unheil ['ʊnhaıl] *nt* evil; (*Unglück*) misfortune; ~ **anrichten** to cause mischief; u~bar *adj* incurable

unheimlich ['ʊnhaımlıç] *adj* weird, uncanny ♦ *adv* (*umg*) tremendously

unhöflich ['ʊnhøːflıç] *adj* impolite; U~keit *f* impoliteness

unhygienisch ['ʊnhygieːnıʃ] *adj* unhygienic

Uni ['ʊni] **(-, -s)** (*umg*) *f* university

Uniform [uniˈfɔrm] *f* uniform; u~iert [-ˈmiːrt] *adj* uniformed

uninteressant ['ʊnɪnterɛsant] *adj* uninteresting

Uni- *zW:* ~**versität** [univɛrziˈtɛːt] *f* university; ~**versum** [uniˈvɛrzʊm] **(-s)** *nt* universe

unkenntlich ['ʊnkɛntlıç] *adj* unrecognizable

Unkenntnis ['ʊnkɛntnıs] *f* ignorance

unklar ['ʊnklaːr] *adj* unclear; **im U~en sein über** +*akk* to be in the dark about; U~heit *f* unclarity; (*Unentschiedenheit*) uncertainty

unklug ['ʊnkluːk] *adj* unwise

Unkosten ['ʊnkɔstən] *pl* expense(s); ~**beitrag** *m* contribution to costs *od* expenses

Unkraut ['ʊnkraʊt] *nt* weed; weeds *pl*

unkündbar ['ʊnkʏntbaːr] *adj* (*Stelle*) permanent; (*Vertrag*) binding

unlauter ['ʊnlaʊtər] *adj* unfair

unleserlich ['ʊnleːzərlıç] *adj* illegible

unlogisch ['ʊnloːgıʃ] *adj* illogical

unlösbar ['ʊnløːsbaːr] *adj* insoluble

Unlust ['ʊnlʊst] *f* lack of enthusiasm

Unmenge ['ʊnmɛŋə] *f* tremendous number, hundreds *pl*

Unmensch ['ʊnmɛnʃ] *m* ogre, brute; u~lich *adj* inhuman, brutal; (*ungeheuer*) awful

unmerklich [ʊnˈmɛrklıç] *adj* imperceptible

unmissverständlich ▲ ['ʊnmısfɛrʃtɛntlıç] *adj* unmistakable

unmittelbar ['ʊnmıtəlbaːr] *adj* immediate

unmodern ['ʊnmoːdɛrn] *adj* old-fashioned

unmöglich ['ʊnmøːklıç] *adj* impossible; U~keit *f* impossibility

unmoralisch ['ʊnmoraːlıʃ] *adj* immoral

Unmut ['ʊnmuːt] *m* ill humour

unnachgiebig ['ʊnnaːxgiːbıç] *adj* unyielding

unnahbar [ʊnˈnaːbaːr] *adj* unapproachable

unnötig ['ʊnnøːtıç] *adj* unnecessary

unnütz ['ʊnnʏts] *adj* useless

unordentlich ['ʊnɔrdəntlıç] *adj* untidy

Unordnung ['ʊnɔrdnʊŋ] *f* disorder

unparteiisch ['ʊnpartaıʃ] *adj* impartial; U~e(r) *f(m)* umpire; (*FUSSBALL*) referee

unpassend ['ʊnpasənt] *adj* inappropriate; (*Zeit*) inopportune

unpässlich ▲ ['ʊnpɛslıç] *adj* unwell

unpersönlich ['ʊnpɛrzøːnlıç] *adj* impersonal

unpolitisch ['ʊnpoliːtıʃ] *adj* apolitical

unpraktisch ['ʊnpraktıʃ] *adj* unpractical

unpünktlich ['ʊnpʏŋktlıç] *adj* unpunctual

unrationell ['ʊnratsionɛl] *adj* inefficient

unrealistisch ['ʊnrealıstıʃ] *adj* unrealistic

unrecht ['ʊnrɛçt] *adj* wrong; U~ *nt* wrong; **zu U~** wrongly; U~ **haben** to be wrong; ~**mäßig** *adj* unlawful, illegal

unregelmäßig ['ʊnreːgəlmɛːsıç] *adj* irregular; U~keit *f* irregularity

unreif ['ʊnraɪf] *adj* (*Obst*) unripe; (*fig*) immature

unrentabel ['ʊnrɛntaːbəl] *adj* unprofitable

unrichtig ['ʊnrɪçtɪç] *adj* incorrect, wrong

Unruhe ['ʊnruːə] *f* unrest; **~stifter** *m* troublemaker

unruhig ['ʊnruːɪç] *adj* restless

uns [ʊns] (*akk, dat von* **wir**) *pron* us; ourselves

unsachlich ['ʊnzaxlɪç] *adj* not to the point, irrelevant

unsagbar [ʊn'zaːkbaːr] *adj* indescribable

unsanft ['ʊnzanft] *adj* rough

unsauber ['ʊnzaʊbər] *adj* unclean, dirty; (*fig*) crooked; (*MUS*) fuzzy

unschädlich ['ʊnʃɛːtlɪç] *adj* harmless; **jdn/etw ~ machen** to render sb/sth harmless

unscharf ['ʊnʃarf] *adj* indistinct; (*Bild etc*) out of focus, blurred

unscheinbar ['ʊnʃaɪnbaːr] *adj* insignificant; (*Aussehen, Haus etc*) unprepossessing

unschlagbar [ʊn'ʃlaːkbaːr] *adj* invincible

unschön ['ʊnʃøːn] *adj* (*hässlich: Anblick*) ugly, unattractive; (*unfreundlich: Benehmen*) unpleasant, ugly

Unschuld ['ʊnʃʊlt] *f* innocence; **u~ig** [-dɪç] *adj* innocent

unselbst(st)ändig ['ʊnzɛlpʃtɛndɪç] *adj* dependent, over-reliant on others

unser(e) ['ʊnzər(ə)] *adj* our; **~e(r, s)** *pron* ours; **~einer** *pron* people like us; **~eins** *pron* = **unsereiner**; **~erseits** *adv* on our part; **~tegen** *adv* (*für uns*) for our sake; (*wegen uns*) on our account; **~twillen** *adv*: **um ~twillen** = **unsertwegen**

unsicher ['ʊnzɪçər] *adj* uncertain; (*Mensch*) insecure; **U~heit** *f* uncertainty; insecurity

unsichtbar ['ʊnzɪçtbaːr] *adj* invisible

Unsinn ['ʊnzɪn] *m* nonsense; **u~ig** *adj* nonsensical

Unsitte ['ʊnzɪtə] *f* deplorable habit

unsozial ['ʊnzotsiaːl] *adj* (*Verhalten*) antisocial

unsportlich ['ʊnʃpɔrtlɪç] *adj* not sporty; unfit; (*Verhalten*) unsporting

unsre ['ʊnzrə] = **unsere**

unsterblich ['ʊnʃtɛrplɪç] *adj* immortal

Unstimmigkeit ['ʊnʃtɪmɪçkaɪt] *f* inconsistency; (*Streit*) disagreement

unsympathisch ['ʊnzʏmpaːtɪʃ] *adj* unpleasant; **er ist mir ~** I don't like him

untätig ['ʊntɛːtɪç] *adj* idle

untauglich ['ʊntaʊklɪç] *adj* unsuitable; (*MIL*) unfit

unteilbar [ʊn'taɪlbaːr] *adj* indivisible

unten ['ʊntən] *adv* below; (*im Haus*) downstairs; (*an der Treppe etc*) at the bottom; **nach ~** down; **~ am Berg** *etc* at the bottom of the mountain *etc*; **ich bin bei ihm ~ durch** (*umg*) he's through with me

---

SCHLÜSSELWORT

unter ['ʊntər] *präp +dat* **1** (*räumlich, mit Zahlen*) under; (*drunter*) underneath, below; **unter 18 Jahren** under 18 years
2 (*zwischen*) among(st); **sie waren unter sich** they were by themselves; **einer unter ihnen** one of them; **unter anderem** among other things
♦ *präp +akk* under, below

Unterarm ['ʊntərarm] *m* forearm

unter- *zW:* **~belichten** *vt* (*PHOT*) to underexpose; **U~bewusstsein ▲** *nt* subconscious; **~bezahlt** *adj* underpaid

unterbieten [ʊntər'biːtən] (*unreg*) *vt insep* (*COMM*) to undercut; (*Rekord*) to lower

unterbrechen [ʊntər'brɛçən] (*unreg*) *vt insep* to interrupt

Unterbrechung *f* interruption

unterbringen ['ʊntərbrɪŋən] (*unreg*) *vt* (*in Koffer*) to stow; (*in Zeitung*) to place; (*Person: in Hotel etc*) to accommodate, to put up

unterdessen [ʊntər'dɛsən] *adv* meanwhile

Unterdruck ['ʊntərdrʊk] *m* low pressure

unterdrücken [ʊntər'drʏkən] *vt insep* to suppress; (*Leute*) to oppress

untere(r, s) ['ʊntərə(r, s)] *adj* lower

untereinander [ʊntər|aɪ'nandər] *adv* with each other; among themselves *etc*

unterentwickelt ['ʊntər|ɛntvɪkəlt] *adj* underdeveloped

Spelling Reform: ▲ *new spelling* △ *old spelling (to be phased out)*

unterernährt ['ʊntərʔɛrnɛːrt] *adj*
undernourished, underfed

Unterernährung *f* malnutrition

Unter'führung *f* subway, underpass

Untergang ['ʊntərɡaŋ] *m* (down)fall,
decline; (*NAUT*) sinking; (*von Gestirn*) setting

unter'geben *adj* subordinate

untergehen ['ʊntərɡeːən] (*unreg*) *vi* to go
down; (*Sonne auch*) to set; (*Staat*) to fall;
(*Volk*) to perish; (*Welt*) to come to an end;
(*im Lärm*) to be drowned

Untergeschoss ▲ ['ʊntərɡəʃɔs] *nt*
basement

'Untergewicht *nt* underweight

unter'gliedern *vt insep* to subdivide

Untergrund ['ʊntərɡrʊnt] *m* foundation;
(*POL*) underground; **~bahn** *f* underground,
tube, subway (*US*)

unterhalb ['ʊntərhalp] *präp +gen* below
♦ *adv* below; **~ von** below

Unterhalt ['ʊntərhalt] *m* maintenance;
u~en (*unreg*) *vt insep* to maintain;
(*belustigen*) to entertain ♦ *vr insep* to talk;
(*sich belustigen*) to enjoy o.s.; **u~sam** *adj*
(*Abend, Person*) entertaining, amusing;
~ung *f* maintenance; (*Belustigung*)
entertainment, amusement; (*Gespräch*) talk

Unterhändler ['ʊntərhɛntlər] *m* negotiator

Unter- *zW:* **~hemd** *nt* vest, undershirt (*US*);
~hose *f* underpants *pl;* **~kiefer** *m* lower
jaw

unterkommen ['ʊntərkɔmən] (*unreg*) *vi* to
find shelter; to find work; **das ist mir noch
nie untergekommen** I've never met with
that

unterkühlt [ʊntər'kyːlt] *adj* (*Körper*) affected
by hypothermia

Unterkunft ['ʊntərkʊnft] (**-, -künfte**) *f*
accommodation

Unterlage ['ʊntərlaːɡə] *f* foundation; (*Beleg*)
document; (*Schreibunterlage etc*) pad

unter'lassen (*unreg*) *vt insep* (*versäumen*) to
fail to do; (*sich enthalten*) to refrain from

unterlaufen [ʊntər'laʊfən] (*unreg*) *vi insep* to
happen ♦ *adj:* **mit Blut ~** suffused with
blood; (*Augen*) bloodshot

unterlegen ['ʊntərleːɡən] *vt* to lay *od* put

under; **unter'legen** *adj* inferior; (*besiegt*)
defeated

Unterleib ['ʊntərlaɪp] *m* abdomen

unter'liegen (*unreg*) *vi insep* (+*dat*) to be
defeated *od* overcome (by); (*unterworfen
sein*) to be subject (to)

Untermiete ['ʊntərmiːtə] *f:* **zur ~ wohnen**
to be a subtenant *od* lodger; **~r(in)** *m(f)*
subtenant, lodger

unter'nehmen (*unreg*) *vt insep* to
undertake; **Unter'nehmen** (**-s, -**) *nt*
undertaking, enterprise (*auch COMM*)

Unternehmer [ʊntər'neːmər] (**-s, -**) *m*
entrepreneur, businessman

'unterordnen ['ʊntərʔɔrdnən] *vr* +*dat* to
submit o.s. (to), to give o.s. second place
to

Unterredung [ʊntər'reːdʊŋ] *f* discussion,
talk

Unterricht ['ʊntərrɪçt] (**-(e)s, -e**) *m*
instruction, lessons *pl;* **u~en** [ʊntər'rɪçtən] *vt*
insep to instruct; (*SCH*) to teach ♦ *vr insep:*
sich u~en (über +*akk*) to inform o.s.
(about), to obtain information (about);
~sfach *nt* subject (on school *etc*
curriculum)

Unterrock ['ʊntərrɔk] *m* petticoat, slip

unter'sagen *vt insep* to forbid; **jdm etw ~**
to forbid sb to do sth

Untersatz ['ʊntərzats] *m* coaster, saucer

unter'schätzen *vt insep* to underestimate

unter'scheiden (*unreg*) *vt insep* to
distinguish ♦ *vr insep* to differ

Unter'scheidung *f* (*Unterschied*)
distinction; (*Unterscheiden*) differentiation

Unterschied ['ʊntərʃiːt] (**-(e)s, -e**) *m*
difference, distinction; **im ~ zu** as distinct
from; **u~lich** *adj* varying, differing;
(*diskriminierend*) discriminatory

unterschiedslos *adv* indiscriminately

unter'schlagen (*unreg*) *vt insep* to
embezzle; (*verheimlichen*) to suppress

Unter'schlagung *f* embezzlement

Unterschlupf ['ʊntərʃlʊpf] (**-(e)s,
-schlüpfe**) *m* refuge

unter'schreiben (*unreg*) *vt insep* to sign

Unterschrift ['ʊntərʃrɪft] *f* signature

Unterseeboot ['ʊntərzeːboːt] *nt* submarine

Untersetzer ['ʊntərzɛtsər] *m* tablemat; *(für Gläser)* coaster

untersetzt [ʊntər'zɛtst] *adj* stocky

unterste(r, s) ['ʊntərstə(r, s)] *adj* lowest, bottom

unterstehen [ʊntər'ʃteːən] *(unreg) vi insep (+dat)* to be under ♦ *vr insep* to dare; **'unterstehen** *(unreg) vi* to shelter

unterstellen [ʊntər'ʃtɛlən] *vt insep* to subordinate; *(fig)* to impute ♦ *vt (Auto)* to garage, to park ♦ *vr* to take shelter

unter'streichen *(unreg) vt insep (auch fig)* to underline

Unterstufe ['ʊntərʃtuːfə] *f* lower grade

unter'stützen *vt insep* to support

Unter'stützung *f* support, assistance

unter'suchen *vt insep (MED)* to examine; *(Polizei)* to investigate

Unter'suchung *f* examination; investigation, inquiry; **~sausschuss** ▲ *m* committee of inquiry; **~shaft** *f* imprisonment on remand

Untertasse ['ʊntərtasə] *f* saucer

untertauchen ['ʊntərtaʊxən] *vi* to dive; *(fig)* to disappear, to go underground

Unterteil ['ʊntərtaɪl] *nt od m* lower part, bottom; **u~en** [ʊntər'taɪlən] *vt insep* to divide up

Untertitel ['ʊntərtiːtəl] *m* subtitle

Unterwäsche ['ʊntərvɛʃə] *f* underwear

unterwegs [ʊntər'veːks] *adv* on the way

unter'werfen *(unreg) vt insep* to subject; *(Volk)* to subjugate ♦ *vr insep (+dat)* to submit (to)

unter'zeichnen *vt insep* to sign

unter'ziehen *(unreg) vt insep* to subject ♦ *vr insep (+dat)* to undergo; *(einer Prüfung)* to take

untragbar [ʊn'traːkbaːr] *adj* unbearable, intolerable

untreu ['ʊntrɔy] *adj* unfaithful; **U~e** *f* unfaithfulness

untröstlich [ʊn'trøːstlɪç] *adj* inconsolable

unüberlegt ['ʊnlyːbərleːkt] *adj* ill-considered ♦ *adv* without thinking

unübersichtlich *adj (Gelände)* broken;

(Kurve) blind

unumgänglich [ʊn|ʊm'gɛŋlɪç] *adj* indispensable, vital; absolutely necessary

ununterbrochen ['ʊn|ʊntərbrɔxən] *adj* uninterrupted

unver- ['ʊnfer] *zW:* **~änderlich** [-'ɛndərlɪç] *adj* unchangeable; **~antwortlich** [-'antvɔrtlɪç] *adj* irresponsible; *(unentschuldbar)* inexcusable; **~besserlich** *adj* incorrigible; **~bindlich** *adj* not binding; *(Antwort)* curt ♦ *adv (COMM)* without obligation; **~bleit** *adj (Benzin usw)* unleaded; **ich fahre ~bleit** I use unleaded; **~blümt** [-'blyːmt] *adj* plain, blunt ♦ *adv* plainly, bluntly; **~daulich** *adj* indigestible; **~einbar** *adj* incompatible; **~fänglich** [-'fɛŋlɪç] *adj* harmless; **~froren** *adj* impudent; **~gesslich** ▲ *adj (Tag, Erlebnis)* unforgettable; **~hofft** [-'hɔft] *adj* unexpected; **~meidlich** [-'maɪtlɪç] *adj* unavoidable; **~mutet** *adj* unexpected; **~nünftig** [-'nynftɪç] *adj* foolish; **~schämt** *adj* impudent; **U~schämtheit** *f* impudence, insolence; **~sehrt** *adj* uninjured; **~söhnlich** [-'zøːnlɪç] *adj* irreconcilable; **~ständlich** [-'ʃtɛntlɪç] *adj* unintelligible; **~träglich** *adj* quarrelsome; *(Meinungen, MED)* incompatible; **~zeihlich** *adj* unpardonable; **~züglich** [-'tsyːklɪç] *adj* immediate

unvollkommen ['ʊnfɔlkɔmən] *adj* imperfect

unvollständig *adj* incomplete

unvor- ['ʊnfoːr] *zW:* **~bereitet** *adj* unprepared; **~eingenommen** *adj* unbiased; **~hergesehen** [-'heːrgezeːən] *adj* unforeseen; **~sichtig** [-zɪçtɪç] *adj* careless, imprudent; **~stellbar** [-'ʃtɛlbaːr] *adj* inconceivable; **~teilhaft** *adj* disadvantageous

unwahr ['ʊnvaːr] *adj* untrue; **~scheinlich** *adj* improbable, unlikely ♦ *adv (umg)* incredibly

unweigerlich [ʊn'vaɪgərlɪç] *adj* unquestioning ♦ *adv* without fail

Unwesen ['ʊnveːzən] *nt* nuisance; *(Unfug)* mischief; **sein ~ treiben** to wreak havoc

unwesentlich *adj* inessential, unimportant; **~ besser** marginally better

Spelling Reform: ▲ *new spelling* △ *old spelling (to be phased out)*

Unwetter ['ʊnvɛtər] *nt* thunderstorm
unwichtig ['ʊnvɪçtɪç] *adj* unimportant
unwider- ['ʊnviːdər] *zW*: **~legbar** *adj* irrefutable; **~ruflich** *adj* irrevocable; **~stehlich** *adj* irresistible
unwill- ['ʊnvɪl] *zW*: **U~e(n)** *m* indignation; **~ig** *adj* indignant; (*widerwillig*) reluctant; **~kürlich** [-kyːrlɪç] *adj* involuntary ♦ *adv* instinctively; (*lachen*) involuntarily
unwirklich ['ʊnvɪrklɪç] *adj* unreal
unwirksam ['ʊnvɪrkzaːm] *adj* (*Mittel, Methode*) ineffective
unwirtschaftlich ['ʊnvɪrtʃaftlɪç] *adj* uneconomical
unwissen- ['ʊnvɪsən] *zW*: **~d** *adj* ignorant; **U~heit** *f* ignorance; **~tlich** *adv* unknowingly, unwittingly
unwohl ['ʊnvoːl] *adj* unwell, ill; **U~sein (-s)** *nt* indisposition
unwürdig ['ʊnvYrdɪç] *adj* unworthy
unzählig [ʊn'tseːlɪç] *adj* innumerable, countless
unzer- [ʊntsɛr] *zW*: **~brechlich** *adj* unbreakable; **~störbar** *adj* indestructible; **~trennlich** *adj* inseparable
Unzucht ['ʊntsʊxt] *f* sexual offence
unzüchtig ['ʊntsYçtɪç] *adj* immoral; lewd
unzu- ['ʊntsu] *zW*: **~frieden** *adj* dissatisfied; **U~friedenheit** *f* discontent; **~länglich** *adj* inadequate; **~lässig** *adj* inadmissible; **~rechnungsfähig** *adj* irresponsible; **~treffend** *adj* incorrect; **~verlässig** *adj* unreliable
unzweideutig ['ʊntsvaɪdɔytɪç] *adj* unambiguous
üppig ['Ypɪç] *adj* (*Frau*) curvaceous; (*Busen*) full, ample; (*Essen*) sumptuous; (*Vegetation*) luxuriant, lush
Ur- ['uːr] *in zW* original
uralt ['uːralt] *adj* ancient, very old
Uran [u'raːn] (**-s**) *nt* uranium
Ur- *zW*: **~aufführung** *f* first performance; **~einwohner** *m* original inhabitant; **~eltern** *pl* ancestors; **~enkel(in)** *m(f)* great-grandchild, great-grandson (-daughter); **~großeltern** *pl* great-grandparents; **~heber (-s, -)** *m* originator;

(*Autor*) author; **~heberrecht** *nt* copyright
Urin [u'riːn] (**-s, -e**) *m* urine
Urkunde ['uːrkʊndə] *f* document, deed
Urlaub ['uːrlaʊp] (**-(e)s, -e**) *m* holiday(s *pl*) (*BRIT*), vacation (*US*); (*MIL etc*) leave; **~er** [-'laʊbər] (**-s, -**) *m* holiday-maker (*BRIT*), vacationer (*US*); **~sort** *m* holiday resort; **~szeit** *f* holiday season
Urne ['ʊrnə] *f* urn
Ursache ['uːrzaxə] *f* cause; **keine ~** that's all right
Ursprung ['uːrʃprʊŋ] *m* origin, source; (*von Fluss*) source
ursprünglich ['uːrʃprʏŋlɪç] *adj* original ♦ *adv* originally
Ursprungsland *nt* country of origin
Urteil ['ʊrtaɪl] (**-s, -e**) *nt* opinion; (*JUR*) sentence, judgement; **u~en** *vi* to judge; **~sspruch** *m* sentence, verdict
Urwald *m* jungle
Urzeit *f* prehistoric times *pl*
USA [uː'ɛs|aː] *pl abk* (= *Vereinigte Staaten von Amerika*) USA
usw. *abk* (= *und so weiter*) etc
Utensilien [utɛn'ziːliən] *pl* utensils
Utopie [uto'piː] *f* pipe dream
utopisch [u'toːpɪʃ] *adj* utopian

V, v

vag(e) [vaːk, 'vaːgə] *adj* vague
Vagina [va'giːna] (**-, Vaginen**) *f* vagina
Vakuum ['vaːkuʊm] (**-s, Vakua** *od* **Vakuen**) *nt* vacuum
Vampir [vam'piːr] (**-s, -e**) *m* vampire
Vanille [va'nɪljə] (**-**) *f* vanilla
Variation [variatsi'oːn] *f* variation
variieren [vari'iːrən] *vt, vi* to vary
Vase ['vaːzə] *f* vase
Vater ['faːtər] (**-s, ̈**) *m* father; **~land** *nt* native country; Fatherland
väterlich ['fɛːtərlɪç] *adj* fatherly
Vaterschaft *f* paternity
Vaterunser (**-s, -**) *nt* Lord's prayer
Vati ['faːti] *m* daddy
v. Chr. *abk* (= *vor Christus*) B.C.

Vegetarier(in) [vege'ta:riər(ɪn)] **(-s, -)** m(f) vegetarian

vegetarisch [vege'ta:rɪʃ] adj vegetarian

Veilchen ['faɪlçən] nt violet

Vene ['ve:nə] f vein

Ventil [vɛn'ti:l] **(-s, -e)** nt valve

Ventilator [vɛntila'to:r] m ventilator

verab- [fɛr|ap] zW: **~reden** vt to agree, to arrange ♦ vr: **~reden sich mit jdm** to arrange to meet sb; **mit jdm ~redet sein** to have arranged to meet sb; **V~redung** f arrangement; (*Treffen*) appointment; **~scheuen** vt to detest, to abhor; **~schieden** vt (*Gäste*) to say goodbye to; (*entlassen*) to discharge; (*Gesetz*) to pass ♦ vr to take one's leave; **V~schiedung** f leave-taking; discharge; passing

ver- [fɛr] zW: **~achten** vt to despise; **~ächtlich** [-'lɛçtlɪç] adj contemptuous; (*~achtenswert*) contemptible; **jdn ~ächtlich machen** to run sb down; **V~achtung** f contempt

verallgemeinern [fɛr|algə'maɪnərn] vt to generalize; **Verallgemeinerung** f generalization

veralten [fɛr|altən] vi to become obsolete od out-of-date

Veranda [ve'randa] **(-, Veranden)** f veranda

veränder- [fɛr|ɛndər] zW: **~lich** adj changeable; **~n** vt, vr to change, to alter; **V~ung** f change, alteration

veran- [fɛr|an] zW: **~lagt** adj with a ... nature; **V~lagung** f disposition; **~lassen** vt to cause; **Maßnahmen ~lassen** to take measures; **sich ~lasst sehen** to feel prompted; **~schaulichen** vt to illustrate; **~schlagen** vt to estimate; **~stalten** vt to organize, to arrange; **V~stalter (-s, -)** m organizer; **V~staltung** f (*V~stalten*) organizing; (*Konzert etc*) event, function

verantwort- [fɛr|antvɔrt] zW: **~en** vt to answer for ♦ vr to justify o.s.; **~lich** adj responsible; **V~ung** f responsibility; **~ungsbewusst** ▲ adj responsible; **~ungslos** adj irresponsible

verarbeiten [fɛr|arbaɪtən] vt to process; (*geistig*) to assimilate; **etw zu etw ~** to

make sth into sth; **Verarbeitung** f processing; assimilation

verärgern [fɛr|ɛrgərn] vt to annoy

verausgaben [fɛr|ausga:bən] vr to run out of money; (*fig*) to exhaust o.s.

Verb [vɛrp] **(-s, -en)** nt verb

Verband [fɛr'bant] **(-(e)s, ¨e)** m (*MED*) bandage, dressing; (*Bund*) association, society; (*MIL*) unit; **~kasten** m medicine chest, first-aid box; **~zeug** nt bandage

verbannen [fɛr'banən] vt to banish

verbergen [fɛr'bɛrgən] (*unreg*) vt, vr: **(sich) ~ (vor +dat)** to hide (from)

verbessern [fɛr'bɛsərn] vt, vr to improve; (*berichtigen*) to correct (o.s.)

Verbesserung f improvement; correction

verbeugen [fɛr'bɔygən] vr to bow

Verbeugung f bow

ver'biegen (*unreg*) vi to bend

ver'bieten (*unreg*) vt to forbid; **jdm etw ~** to forbid sb to do sth

verbilligen [fɛr'bɪlɪgən] vt to reduce the cost of; (*Preis*) to reduce

ver'binden (*unreg*) vt to connect; (*kombinieren*) to combine; (*MED*) to bandage ♦ vr (*auch CHEM*) to combine, to join; **jdm die Augen ~** to blindfold sb

verbindlich [fɛr'bɪntlɪç] adj binding; (*freundlich*) friendly

Ver'bindung f connection; (*Zusammensetzung*) combination; (*CHEM*) compound; (*UNIV*) club

verbissen [fɛr'bɪsən] adj (*Kampf*) bitter; (*Gesichtsausdruck*) grim

ver'bitten (*unreg*) vt: **sich** dat **etw ~** not to tolerate sth, not to stand for sth

Verbleib [fɛr'blaɪp] **(-(e)s)** m whereabouts; **v~en** (*unreg*) vi to remain

verbleit [fɛr'blaɪt] adj (*Benzin*) leaded

verblüffen [fɛr'blʏfən] vt to stagger, to amaze; **Verblüffung** f stupefaction

ver'blühen vi to wither, to fade

ver'bluten vi to bleed to death

verborgen [fɛr'bɔrgən] adj hidden

Verbot [fɛr'bo:t] **(-(e)s, -e)** nt prohibition, ban; **v~en** adj forbidden; **Rauchen v~en!** no smoking; **~sschild** nt prohibitory sign

---

Spelling Reform: ▲ *new spelling* △ *old spelling (to be phased out)*

Verbrauch [fɛr'braux] **(-(e)s)** *m*
consumption; **v~en** *vt* to use up; **~er (-s, -)** *m* consumer; **v~t** *adj* used up, finished; (*Luft*) stale; (*Mensch*) worn-out

Verbrechen [fɛr'brɛçən] **(-s, -)** *nt* crime

Verbrecher [fɛr'brɛçər] **(-s, -)** *m* criminal; **v~isch** *adj* criminal

ver'breiten *vt, vr* to spread; **sich über etw** *akk* **~** to expound on sth

verbreitern [fɛr'braɪtərn] *vt* to broaden

Verbreitung *f* spread(ing), propagation

verbrenn- [fɛr'brɛn] *zW:* **~bar** *adj* combustible; **~en** (*unreg*) *vt* to burn; (*Leiche*) to cremate; **V~ung** *f* burning; (*in Motor*) combustion; (*von Leiche*) cremation; **V~ungsmotor** *m* internal combustion engine

verbringen [fɛr'brɪŋən] (*unreg*) *vt* to spend

verbrühen [fɛr'bryːən] *vt* to scald

verbuchen [fɛr'buːxən] *vt* (*FIN*) to register; (*Erfolg*) to enjoy; (*Misserfolg*) to suffer

verbunden [fɛr'bʊndən] *adj* connected; **jdm ~ sein** to be obliged or indebted to sb; **„falsch ~"** (*TEL*) "wrong number"

ver'bünden [fɛr'bʏndən] *vr* to ally o.s.; **Verbündete(r)** *f(m)* ally

ver'bürgen *vr:* **sich ~ für** to vouch for

ver'büßen *vt:* **eine Strafe ~** to serve a sentence

Verdacht [fɛr'daxt] **(-(e)s)** *m* suspicion

verdächtig [fɛr'dɛçtɪç] *adj* suspicious, suspect; **~en** [fɛr'dɛçtɪgən] *vt* to suspect

verdammen [fɛr'damən] *vt* to damn, to condemn; **verdammt!** damn!

verdammt (*umg*) *adj, adv* damned; **~ noch mal!** damn!, dammit!

ver'dampfen *vi* to vaporize, to evaporate

ver'danken *vt:* **jdm etw ~** to owe sb sth

verdau- [fɛr'dau] *zW:* **~en** *vt* (*auch fig*) to digest; **~lich** *adj* digestible; **das ist schwer ~lich** that is hard to digest; **V~ung** *f* digestion

Verdeck [fɛr'dɛk] **(-(e)s, -e)** *nt* (*AUT*) hood; (*NAUT*) deck; **v~en** *vt* to cover (up); (*verbergen*) to hide

Verderb- [fɛr'dɛrp] *zW:* **~en** [-'dɛrbən] **(-s)** *nt* ruin; **v~en** (*unreg*) *vt* to spoil; (*schädigen*)

to ruin; (*moralisch*) to corrupt ♦ *vi* (*Essen*) to spoil, to rot; (*Mensch*) to go to the bad; **es mit jdm v~en** to get into sb's bad books; **v~lich** *adj* (*Einfluss*) pernicious; (*Lebensmittel*) perishable

verdeutlichen [fɛr'dɔʏtlɪçən] *vt* to make clear

ver'dichten *vt, vr* to condense

ver'dienen *vt* to earn; (*moralisch*) to deserve

Ver'dienst (-(e)s, -e) *m* earnings *pl* ♦ *nt* merit; (*Leistung*): **~ (um)** service (to)

verdient [fɛr'diːnt] *adj* well-earned; (*Person*) deserving of esteem; **sich um etw ~ machen** to do a lot for sth

verdoppeln [fɛr'dɔpəln] *vt* to double

verdorben [fɛr'dɔrbən] *adj* spoilt; (*geschädigt*) ruined; (*moralisch*) corrupt

verdrängen [fɛr'drɛŋən] *vt* to oust, to displace (*auch PHYS*); (*PSYCH*) to repress

ver'drehen *vt* (*auch fig*) to twist; (*Augen*) to roll; **jdm den Kopf ~** (*fig*) to turn sb's head

verdrießlich [fɛr'driːslɪç] *adj* peevish, annoyed

Verdruss ▲ [fɛr'drʊs] **(-es, -e)** *m* annoyance, worry

verdummen [fɛr'dʊmən] *vt* to make stupid ♦ *vi* to grow stupid

verdunkeln [fɛr'dʊŋkəln] *vt* to darken; (*fig*) to obscure ♦ *vr* to darken

Verdunk(e)lung *f* blackout; (*fig*) obscuring

verdünnen [fɛr'dʏnən] *vt* to dilute

verdunsten [fɛr'dʊnstən] *vi* to evaporate

verdursten [fɛr'dʊrstən] *vi* to die of thirst

verdutzt [fɛr'dʊtst] *adj* nonplussed, taken aback

verehr- [fɛr'eːr] *zW:* **~en** *vt* to venerate, to worship (*auch REL*); **jdm etw ~en** to present sb with sth; **V~er(in) (-s, -)** *m(f)* admirer, worshipper (*auch REL*); **~t** *adj* esteemed; **V~ung** *f* respect; (*REL*) worship

Verein [fɛr'aɪn] **(-(e)s, -e)** *m* club, association; **v~bar** *adj* compatible; **v~baren** *vt* to agree upon; **~barung** *f* agreement; **v~en** *vt* (*Menschen, Länder*) to unite; (*Prinzipien*) to reconcile; **mit v~ten**

Kräften having pooled resources, having joined forces; **~te Nationen** United Nations; v~**fachen** vt to simplify; v~**heitlichen** [-haɪtlɪçən] vt to standardize; v~**igen** vt, vr to unite; ~**igung** f union; (*Verein*) association; v~**t** adj united; v~**zelt** adj isolated

ver'eitern vi to suppurate, to fester

verengen [fɛr|'ɛŋən] vr to narrow

vererb- [fɛr|'ɛrb] zW: ~**en** vt to bequeath; (*BIOL*) to transmit ♦ vr to be hereditary; **V~ung** f bequeathing; (*BIOL*) transmission; (*Lehre*) heredity

verewigen [fɛr|'e:vɪgən] vt to immortalize ♦ vr (*umg*) to immortalize o.s.

ver'fahren (*unreg*) vi to act ♦ vr to get lost ♦ adj tangled; ~ **mit** to deal with; **Ver'fahren (-s, -)** nt procedure; (*TECH*) process; (*JUR*) proceedings pl

Verfall [fɛr'fal] (-(e)s) m decline; (*von Haus*) dilapidation; (*FIN*) expiry; v~**en** (*unreg*) vi to decline; (*Haus*) to be falling down; (*FIN*) to lapse; **v~en in** +akk to lapse into; **v~en auf** +akk to hit upon; **einem Laster v~en sein** to be addicted to a vice; ~**sdatum** nt expiry date; (*der Haltbarkeit*) sell-by date

ver'färben vr to change colour

verfassen [fɛr'fasən] vt (*Rede*) to prepare, work out

Verfasser(in) [fɛr'fasər(ɪn)] (-s, -) m(f) author, writer

Verfassung f (*auch POL*) constitution

Verfassungs- zW: ~**gericht** nt constitutional court; v~**widrig** adj unconstitutional

ver'faulen vi to rot

ver'fehlen vt to miss; **etw für verfehlt halten** to regard sth as mistaken

verfeinern [fɛr'faɪnərn] vt to refine

ver'filmen vt to film

verflixt [fɛr'flɪkst] (*umg*) adj damned, damn

ver'fluchen vt to curse

verfolg- [fɛr'fɔlg] zW: ~**en** vt to pursue; (*gerichtlich*) to prosecute; (*grausam, bes POL*) to persecute; **V~er (-s, -)** m pursuer; **V~ung** f pursuit; prosecution; persecution

verfrüht [fɛr'fry:t] adj premature

verfüg- [fɛr'fy:g] zW: ~**bar** adj available; ~**en** vt to direct, to order ♦ vr to proceed ♦ vi: ~**en über** +akk to have at one's disposal; **V~ung** f direction, order; **zur V~ung** at one's disposal; **jdm zur V~ung stehen** to be available to sb

verführ- [fɛr'fy:r] zW: ~**en** vt to tempt; (*sexuell*) to seduce; **V~er** m tempter; seducer; ~**erisch** adj seductive; **V~ung** f seduction; (*Versuchung*) temptation

ver'gammeln (*umg*) vi to go to seed; (*Nahrung*) to go off

vergangen [fɛr'gaŋən] adj past; **V~heit** f past

vergänglich [fɛr'gɛŋlɪç] adj transitory

vergasen [fɛr'ga:zən] vt (*töten*) to gas

Vergaser (-s, -) m (*AUT*) carburettor

vergaß etc [fɛr'ga:s] vb siehe **vergessen**

vergeb- [fɛr'ge:b] zW: ~**en** (*unreg*) vt (*verzeihen*) to forgive; (*weggeben*) to give away; **jdm etw ~en** to forgive sb (for) sth; ~**ens** adv in vain; ~**lich** [fɛr'ge:plɪç] adv in vain ♦ adj vain, futile; **V~ung** f forgiveness

ver'gehen (*unreg*) vi to pass by od away ♦ vr to commit an offence; **jdm vergeht etw** sb loses sth; **sich an jdm ~** to (sexually) assault sb; **Ver'gehen (-s, -)** nt offence

ver'gelten (*unreg*) vt: **jdm etw ~** to pay sb back for sth, to repay sb for sth

Ver'geltung f retaliation, reprisal

vergessen [fɛr'gɛsən] (*unreg*) vt to forget; **V~heit** f oblivion

vergesslich ▲ [fɛr'gɛslɪç] adj forgetful; **V~keit** f forgetfulness

vergeuden [fɛr'gɔʏdən] vt to squander, to waste

vergewaltigen [fɛrgə'valtɪgən] vt to rape; (*fig*) to violate

Vergewaltigung f rape

vergewissern [fɛrgə'vɪsərn] vr to make sure

ver'gießen (*unreg*) vt to shed

vergiften [fɛr'gɪftən] vt to poison

Vergiftung f poisoning

Vergissmeinnicht ▲ [fɛr'gɪsmaɪnnɪçt] (-(e)s, -e) nt forget-me-not

vergisst ▲ etc [fɛr'gɪst] vb siehe **vergessen**

Spelling Reform: ▲ *new spelling* △ *old spelling (to be phased out)*

Vergleich [fɛr'glaɪç] (**-(e)s, -e**) *m*
comparison; (*JUR*) settlement; **im ~ mit** *od*
zu compared with *od* to; **v~bar** *adj*
comparable; **v~en** (*unreg*) *vt* to compare
♦ *vr* to reach a settlement

vergnügen [fɛr'gny:gən] *vr* to enjoy *od*
amuse o.s.; **V~** (**-s, -**) *nt* pleasure; **viel V~!**
enjoy yourself!

vergnügt [fɛr'gny:kt] *adj* cheerful

Vergnügung *f* pleasure, amusement;
~spark *m* amusement park

vergolden [fɛr'gɔldən] *vt* to gild

ver'graben *vt* to bury

ver'greifen (*unreg*) *vr*: **sich an jdm ~** to lay
hands on sb; **sich an etw ~** to
misappropriate sth; **sich im Ton ~** to say
the wrong thing

vergriffen [fɛr'grɪfən] *adj* (*Buch*) out of print;
(*Ware*) out of stock

vergrößern [fɛr'grø:sərn] *vt* to enlarge;
(*mengenmäßig*) to increase; (*Lupe*) to
magnify

Vergrößerung *f* enlargement; increase;
magnification; **~sglas** *nt* magnifying glass

Vergünstigung [fɛr'gʏnstɪgʊŋ] *f*
concession, privilege

Vergütung *f* compensation

verhaften [fɛr'haftən] *vt* to arrest

Verhaftung *f* arrest

ver'halten (*unreg*) *vr* to be, to stand; (*sich
benehmen*) to behave ♦ *vt* to hold *od* keep
back; (*Schritt*) to check; **sich ~ (zu)** (*MATH*)
to be in proportion (to); **Ver'halten** (**-s**) *nt*
behaviour

Verhältnis [fɛr'hɛltnɪs] (**-ses, -se**) *nt*
relationship; (*MATH*) proportion, ratio; **~se**
pl (*Umstände*) conditions; **über seine ~se
leben** to live beyond one's means;
v~mäßig *adj* relative, comparative ♦ *adv*
relatively, comparatively

verhandeln [fɛr'handəln] *vi* to negotiate;
(*JUR*) to hold proceedings ♦ *vt* to discuss;
(*JUR*) to hear; **über etw** *akk* **~** to negotiate
sth *od* about sth

Verhandlung *f* negotiation; (*JUR*)
proceedings *pl*; **~sbasis** *f* (*FIN*) basis for
negotiations

ver'hängen *vt* (*fig*) to impose, to inflict

Verhängnis [fɛr'hɛŋnɪs] (**-ses, -se**) *nt* fate,
doom; **jdm zum ~ werden** to be sb's
undoing; **v~voll** *adj* fatal, disastrous

verharmlosen [fɛr'harmlo:zən] *vt* to make
light of, to play down

verhärten [fɛr'hɛrtən] *vr* to harden

verhasst ▲ [fɛr'hast] *adj* odious, hateful

verhauen [fɛr'hauən] (*unreg; umg*) *vt*
(*verprügeln*) to beat up

verheerend [fɛr'he:rənt] *adj* disastrous,
devastating

verheimlichen [fɛr'haɪmlɪçən] *vt*: **jdm etw
~** to keep sth secret from sb

verheiratet [fɛr'haira:tət] *adj* married

ver'helfen (*unreg*) *vi*: **jdm ~ zu** to help sb
to get

ver'hindern *vt* to prevent; **verhindert sein**
to be unable to make it

verhöhnen [fɛr'hø:nən] *vt* to mock, to
sneer at

Verhör [fɛr'hø:r] (**-(e)s, -e**) *nt* interrogation;
(*gerichtlich*) (cross-)examination; **v~en** *vt* to
interrogate; to (cross-)examine ♦ *vr* to
misunderstand, to mishear

ver'hungern *vi* to starve, to die of hunger

ver'hüten *vt* to prevent, to avert

Ver'hütung *f* prevention; **~smittel** *nt*
contraceptive

verirren [fɛr'|ɪrən] *vr* to go astray

ver'jagen *vt* to drive away *od* out

verkalken [fɛr'kalkən] *vi* to calcify; (*umg*) to
become senile

Verkauf [fɛr'kauf] *m* sale; **v~en** *vt* to sell

Verkäufer(in) [fɛr'kɔyfər(ɪn)] (**-s, -**) *m(f)*
seller; salesman(-woman); (*in Laden*) shop
assistant

verkaufsoffen *adj*: **~er Samstag** *Saturday
when the shops stay open all day*

Verkehr [fɛr'ke:r] (**-s, -e**) *m* traffic; (*Umgang,
bes sexuell*) intercourse; (*Umlauf*) circulation;
v~en *vi* (*Fahrzeug*) to ply, to run ♦ *vt*, *vr* to
turn, to transform; **v~en mit** to associate
with; **bei jdm v~en** (*besuchen*) to visit sb
regularly

Verkehrs- *zW*: **~ampel** *f* traffic lights *pl*;
~aufkommen *nt* volume of traffic;

~**beruhigung** f traffic calming; ~**delikt** nt traffic offence; ~**funk** m radio traffic service; v~**günstig** adj convenient; ~**mittel** nt means of transport; ~**schild** nt road sign; ~**stau** m traffic jam, stoppage; ~**unfall** m traffic accident; ~**verein** m tourist information office; ~**zeichen** nt traffic sign

verkehrt adj wrong; (umgekehrt) the wrong way round

ver**'kennen** (unreg) vt to misjudge, not to appreciate

ver**'klagen** vt to take to court

ver**kleiden** [fɛr'klaɪdən] vr to disguise (o.s.); (sich kostümieren) to get dressed up ♦ vt (Wand) to cover

Verkleidung f disguise; (ARCHIT) wainscoting

ver**kleinern** [fɛr'klaɪnərn] vt to make smaller, to reduce in size

ver**'kneifen** (umg) vt: **sich** dat **etw** ~ (Lachen) to stifle sth; (Schmerz) to hide sth; (sich versagen) to do without sth

ver**knüpfen** [fɛr'knʏpfən] vt to tie (up), to knot; (fig) to connect

ver**'kommen** (unreg) vi to deteriorate, to decay; (Mensch) to go downhill, to come down in the world ♦ adj (moralisch) dissolute, depraved

ver**körpern** [fɛr'kœrpərn] vt to embody, to personify

ver**kraften** [fɛr'kraftən] vt to cope with

ver**'kriechen** (unreg) vr to creep away, to creep into a corner

ver**krüppelt** [fɛr'krʏpəlt] adj crippled

ver**'kühlen** vr to get a chill

ver**'kümmern** vi to waste away

ver**künden** [fɛr'kʏndən] vt to proclaim; (Urteil) to pronounce

ver**kürzen** [fɛr'kʏrtsən] vt to shorten; (Wort) to abbreviate; **sich** dat **die Zeit** ~ to while away the time

Verkürzung f shortening; abbreviation

ver**laden** [fɛr'laːdən] (unreg) vt (Waren, Vieh) to load; (Truppen: auf Schiff) to embark, (auf Zug) to entrain, (auf Flugzeug) to enplane

Verlag [fɛr'laːk] (-(e)s, -e) m publishing firm

ver**langen** [fɛr'laŋən] vt to demand; to desire ♦ vi: ~ **nach** to ask for, to desire; ~ **Sie Herrn X** ask for Mr X; V~ (-s, -) nt: V~ **(nach)** desire (for); **auf** jds **V~ (hin)** at sb's request

ver**längern** [fɛr'lɛŋərn] vt to extend; (länger machen) to lengthen

Verlängerung f extension; (SPORT) extra time; ~**sschnur** f extension cable

ver**langsamen** [fɛr'laŋzaːmən] vt, vr to decelerate, to slow down

Verlass ▲ [fɛr'las] m: **auf ihn/das ist kein** ~ he/it cannot be relied upon

ver**'lassen** (unreg) vt to leave ♦ vr: **sich** ~ **auf** +akk to depend on ♦ adj desolate; (Mensch) abandoned

ver**lässlich** ▲ [fɛr'lɛslɪç] adj reliable

Verlauf [fɛr'lauf] m course; v~**en** (unreg) vi (zeitlich) to pass; (Farben) to run ♦ vr to get lost; (Menschenmenge) to disperse

ver**'lauten** vi: **etw** ~ **lassen** to disclose sth; **wie verlautet** as reported

ver**'legen** vt to move; (verlieren) to mislay; (Buch) to publish ♦ vr: **sich auf etw** akk ~ to take up od to sth ♦ adj embarrassed; **nicht** ~ **um** never at a loss for;

Ver'legenheit f embarrassment; (Situation) difficulty, scrape

Verleger [fɛr'leːɡər] (-s, -) m publisher

Verleih [fɛr'laɪ] (-(e)s, -e) m hire service; v~**en** (unreg) vt to lend; (Kraft, Anschein) to confer, to bestow; (Preis, Medaille) to award; ~**ung** f lending; bestowal; award

ver**'leiten** vt to lead astray; ~ **zu** to talk into, to tempt into

ver**'lernen** vt to forget, to unlearn

ver**'lesen** (unreg) vt to read out; (aussondern) to sort out ♦ vr to make a mistake in reading

verletz- [fɛr'lɛts] zW: ~**en** vt (auch fig) to injure, to hurt; (Gesetz etc) to violate; ~**end** adj (fig: Worte) hurtful; ~**lich** adj vulnerable, sensitive; ~**te(r)** f(m) injured person; **V~ung** f injury; (Verstoß) violation, infringement

ver**leugnen** [fɛr'lɔɣnən] vt (Herkunft, Glauben) to belie; (Menschen) to disown

Spelling Reform: ▲ *new spelling* △ *old spelling (to be phased out)*

verleumden [fɛrˈlɔymdən] *vt* to slander;
  Verleumdung *f* slander, libel
ver'lieben *vr*: **sich ~ (in** +*akk*) to fall in love
  (with)
verliebt [fɛrˈliːpt] *adj* in love
verlieren [fɛrˈliːrən] (*unreg*) *vt, vi* to lose ♦ *vr*
  to get lost
Verlierer *m* loser
verlob- [fɛrˈloːb] *zW*: **~en** *vr*: **sich ~en (mit)**
  to get engaged (to); **V~te(r)** [fɛrˈloːptə(r)]
  f(m) fiancé *m*, fiancée *f*; **V~ung** *f*
  engagement
ver'locken *vt* to entice, to lure
Ver'lockung *f* temptation, attraction
verlogen [fɛrˈloːgən] *adj* untruthful
verlor *etc vb siehe* **verlieren**
verloren [fɛrˈloːrən] *adj* lost; (*Eier*) poached
  ♦ *vb siehe* **verlieren**; **etw ~ geben** to give
  sth up for lost; **~ gehen** to get lost
verlosen [fɛrˈloːzən] *vt* to raffle, to draw lots
  for; **Verlosung** *f* raffle, lottery
Verlust [fɛrˈlʊst] (**-(e)s, -e**) *m* loss; (*MIL*)
  casualty
ver'machen *vt* to bequeath, to leave
Vermächtnis [fɛrˈmɛçtnɪs] (**-ses, -se**) *nt*
  legacy
Vermählung [fɛrˈmɛːlʊŋ] *f* wedding,
  marriage
vermarkten [fɛrˈmarktən] *vt* (*COMM: Artikel*)
  to market
vermehren [fɛrˈmeːrən] *vt, vr* to multiply;
  (*Menge*) to increase
Vermehrung *f* multiplying; increase
ver'meiden (*unreg*) *vt* to avoid
vermeintlich [fɛrˈmaɪntlɪç] *adj* supposed
Vermerk [fɛrˈmɛrk] (**-(e)s, -e**) *m* note; (*in
  Ausweis*) endorsement; **v~en** *vt* to note
ver'messen (*unreg*) *vt* to survey ♦ *adj*
  presumptuous, bold; **Ver'messenheit** *f*
  presumptuousness; recklessness
Ver'messung *f* survey(ing)
vermiet- [fɛrˈmiːt] *zW*: **ver'mieten** *vt* to
  let, to rent (out); (*Auto*) to hire out, to rent;
  Ver'mieter(in) (**-s, -**) *m(f)* landlord(-lady);
  Ver'mietung *f* letting, renting (out); (*von
  Autos*) hiring (out)
vermindern [fɛrˈmɪndərn] *vt, vr* to lessen, to

decrease; (*Preise*) to reduce
Verminderung *f* reduction
ver'mischen *vt, vr* to mix, to blend
vermissen [fɛrˈmɪsən] *vt* to miss
vermitt- [fɛrˈmɪt] *zW*: **~eln** *vi* to mediate
  ♦ *vt* (*Gespräch*) to connect; **jdm etw ~eln** to
  help sb to obtain sth; **V~ler (-s, -)** *m*
  (*Schlichter*) agent, mediator; **V~lung** *f*
  procurement; (*Stellenvermittlung*) agency;
  (*TEL*) exchange; (*Schlichtung*) mediation;
  V~lungsgebühr *f* commission
ver'mögen (*unreg*) *vt* to be capable of; **~
  zu** to be able to; **Ver'mögen (-s, -)** *nt*
  wealth; (*Fähigkeit*) ability; **ein V~ kosten** to
  cost a fortune; **ver'mögend** *adj* wealthy
vermuten [fɛrˈmuːtən] *vt* to suppose, to
  guess; (*argwöhnen*) to suspect
vermutlich *adj* supposed, presumed ♦ *adv*
  probably
Vermutung *f* supposition; suspicion
vernachlässigen [fɛrˈnaːxlɛsɪgən] *vt* to
  neglect
ver'nehmen (*unreg*) *vt* to perceive, to hear;
  (*erfahren*) to learn; (*JUR*) to (cross-)examine;
  dem V~ nach from what I/we *etc* hear
Vernehmung *f* (cross-)examination
verneigen [fɛrˈnaɪgən] *vr* to bow
verneinen [fɛrˈnaɪnən] *vt* (*Frage*) to answer
  in the negative; (*ablehnen*) to deny; (*GRAM*)
  to negate; **~d** *adj* negative
Verneinung *f* negation
vernichten [fɛrˈnɪçtən] *vt* to annihilate, to
  destroy; **~d** *adj* (*fig*) crushing; (*Blick*)
  withering; (*Kritik*) scathing
Vernunft [fɛrˈnʊnft] (**-**) *f* reason,
  understanding
vernünftig [fɛrˈnʏnftɪç] *adj* sensible,
  reasonable
veröffentlichen [fɛrˈʔœfəntlɪçən] *vt* to
  publish; **Veröffentlichung** *f* publication
verordnen [fɛrˈʔɔrdnən] *vt* (*MED*) to
  prescribe
Verordnung *f* order, decree; (*MED*)
  prescription
ver'pachten *vt* to lease (out)
ver'packen *vt* to pack
Ver'packung *f* packing, wrapping;

~smaterial nt packing, wrapping

ver'passen vt to miss; **jdm eine Ohrfeige ~** (umg) to give sb a clip round the ear

verpfänden [fɛr'pfɛndən] vt (Besitz) to mortgage

ver'pflanzen vt to transplant

ver'pflegen vt to feed, to cater for

Ver'pflegung f feeding, catering; (Kost) food; (in Hotel) board

verpflichten [fɛr'pflɪçtən] vt to oblige, to bind; (anstellen) to engage ♦ vr to undertake; (MIL) to sign on ♦ vi to carry obligations; **jdm zu Dank verpflichtet sein** to be obliged to sb

Verpflichtung f obligation, duty

verpönt [fɛr'pøːnt] adj disapproved (of), taboo

ver'prügeln (umg) vt to beat up, to do over

Verputz [fɛr'pʊts] m plaster, roughcast; **v~en** vt to plaster; (umg: Essen) to put away

Verrat [fɛr'raːt] (-(e)s) m treachery; (POL) treason; **v~en** (unreg) vt to betray; (Geheimnis) to divulge ♦ vr to give o.s. away

Verräter [fɛr'rɛːtər] (-s, -) m traitor(-tress); **v~isch** adj treacherous

ver'rechnen vt: **~ mit** to set off against ♦ vr to miscalculate

Verrechnungsscheck [fɛr'rɛçnʊŋsʃɛk] m crossed cheque

verregnet [fɛr'reːgnət] adj spoilt by rain, rainy

ver'reisen vi to go away (on a journey)

verrenken [fɛr'rɛŋkən] vt to contort; (MED) to dislocate; **sich** dat **den Knöchel ~** to sprain one's ankle

ver'richten vt to do, to perform

verriegeln [fɛr'riːgəln] vt to bolt up, to lock

verringern [fɛr'rɪŋərn] vt to reduce ♦ vr to diminish

Verringerung f reduction; lessening

ver'rinnen (unreg) vi to run out od away; (Zeit) to elapse

ver'rosten vi to rust

verrotten [fɛr'rɔtən] vi to rot

ver'rücken vt to move, to shift

verrückt [fɛr'rʏkt] adj crazy, mad; **V~e(r)** f(m) lunatic; **V~heit** f madness, lunacy

Verruf [fɛr'ruːf] m: **in ~ geraten/bringen** to fall/bring into disrepute; **v~en** adj notorious, disreputable

Vers [fɛrs] (-es, -e) m verse

ver'sagen vt: **jdm/sich etw ~** to deny sb/ o.s. sth ♦ vi to fail; **Ver'sagen** (-s) nt failure

ver'salzen (unreg) vt to put too much salt in; (fig) to spoil

ver'sammeln vt, vr to assemble, to gather

Ver'sammlung f meeting, gathering

Versand [fɛr'zant] (-(e)s) m forwarding; dispatch; (~abteilung) dispatch department; **~haus** nt mail-order firm

versäumen [fɛr'zɔʏmən] vt to miss; (unterlassen) to neglect, to fail

ver'schaffen vt: **jdm/sich etw ~** to get od procure sth for sb/o.s.

verschämt [fɛr'ʃɛːmt] adj bashful

verschandeln [fɛr'ʃandəln] (umg) vt to spoil

verschärfen [fɛr'ʃɛrfən] vt to intensify; (Lage) to aggravate ♦ vr to intensify; to become aggravated

ver'schätzen vr to be out in one's reckoning

ver'schenken vt to give away

verscheuchen [fɛr'ʃɔʏçən] vt (Tiere) to chase off od away

ver'schicken vt to send off

ver'schieben (unreg) vt to shift; (EISENB) to shunt; (Termin) to postpone

verschieden [fɛr'ʃiːdən] adj different; (pl: mehrere) various; **sie sind ~ groß** they are of different sizes; **~tlich** adv several times

verschimmeln [fɛr'ʃɪməln] vi (Nahrungsmittel) to go mouldy

verschlafen [fɛr'ʃlaːfən] (unreg) vt to sleep through; (fig: versäumen) to miss ♦ vi, vr to oversleep ♦ adj sleepy

Verschlag [fɛr'ʃlaːk] m shed; **v~en** [-gən] (unreg) vt to board up ♦ adj cunning; **jdm den Atem v~en** to take sb's breath away; **an einen Ort v~en werden** to wind up in a place

verschlechtern [fɛrˈʃlɛçtərn] *vt* to make worse ♦ *vr* to deteriorate, to get worse; **Verschlechterung** *f* deterioration

Verschleiß [fɛrˈʃlaɪs] **(-es, -e)** *m* wear and tear; **v~en** *(unreg) vt* to wear out

ver'schleppen *vt* to carry off, to abduct; *(Krankheit)* to protract; *(zeitlich)* to drag out

ver'schleudern *vt* to squander; *(COMM)* to sell dirt-cheap

verschließbar *adj* lockable

verschließen [fɛrˈʃliːsən] *(unreg) vt* to close; to lock ♦ *vr:* **sich einer Sache** *dat* **~** to close one's mind to sth

verschlimmern [fɛrˈʃlɪmərn] *vt* to make worse, to aggravate ♦ *vr* to get worse, to deteriorate

verschlingen [fɛrˈʃlɪŋən] *(unreg) vt* to devour, to swallow up; *(Fäden)* to twist

verschlossen [fɛrˈʃlɔsən] *adj* locked; *(fig)* reserved; **V~heit** *f* reserve

ver'schlucken *vt* to swallow ♦ *vr* to choke

Verschluss ▲ [fɛrˈʃlʊs] *m* lock; *(von Kleid etc)* fastener; *(PHOT)* shutter; *(Stöpsel)* plug

verschlüsseln [fɛrˈʃlʏsəln] *vt* to encode

verschmieren [fɛrˈʃmiːrən] *vt* *(verstreichen: Gips, Mörtel)* to apply, spread on; *(schmutzig machen: Wand etc)* to smear

ver'schmutzen *vt* to soil; *(Umwelt)* to pollute

verschneit [fɛrˈʃnaɪt] *adj* snowed up, covered in snow

verschollen [fɛrˈʃɔlən] *adj* lost, missing

ver'schonen *vt:* **jdn mit etw ~** to spare sb sth

verschönern [fɛrˈʃøːnərn] *vt* to decorate; *(verbessern)* to improve

ver'schreiben *(unreg) vt* *(MED)* to prescribe ♦ *vr* to make a mistake (in writing); **sich einer Sache** *dat* **~** to devote o.s. to sth

verschreibungspflichtig *adj* *(Medikament)* available on prescription only

verschrotten [fɛrˈʃrɔtən] *vt* to scrap

verschuld- [fɛrˈʃʊld] *zW:* **~en** *vt* to be guilty of; **V~en (-s)** *nt* fault, guilt; **~et** *adj* in debt; **V~ung** *f* fault; *(Geld)* debts *pl*

ver'schütten *vt* to spill; *(zuschütten)* to fill; *(unter Trümmer)* to bury

ver'schweigen *(unreg) vt* to keep secret; **jdm etw ~** to keep sth from sb

verschwend- [fɛrˈʃvɛnd] *zW:* **~en** *vt* to squander; **V~er(-s, -)** *m* spendthrift; **~erisch** *adj* wasteful, extravagant; **V~ung** *f* waste; extravagance

verschwiegen [fɛrˈʃviːɡən] *adj* discreet; *(Ort)* secluded; **V~heit** *f* discretion; seclusion

ver'schwimmen *(unreg) vi* to grow hazy, to become blurred

ver'schwinden *(unreg) vi* to disappear, to vanish; **Ver'schwinden (-s)** *nt* disappearance

verschwitzt [fɛrˈʃvɪtst] *adj* *(Mensch)* sweaty

verschwommen [fɛrˈʃvɔmən] *adj* hazy, vague

verschwör- [fɛrˈʃvøːr] *zW:* **~en** *(unreg) vr* to plot, to conspire; **V~ung** *f* conspiracy, plot

ver'sehen *(unreg) vt* to supply, to provide; *(Pflicht)* to carry out; *(Amt)* to fill; *(Haushalt)* to keep ♦ *vr (fig)* to make a mistake; **ehe er (es) sich ~ hatte ...** before he knew it ...; **Ver'sehen (-s, -)** *nt* oversight; **aus V~** by mistake; **~tlich** *adv* by mistake

Versehrte(r) [fɛrˈzeːrtə(r)] *f(m)* disabled person

ver'senden *(unreg) vt* to forward, to dispatch

ver'senken *vt* to sink ♦ *vr:* **sich ~ in** *+akk* to become engrossed in

versessen [fɛrˈzɛsən] *adj:* **~ auf** *+akk* mad about

ver'setzen *vt* to transfer; *(verpfänden)* to pawn; *(umg)* to stand up ♦ *vr:* **sich in jdn** *od* **in jds Lage ~** to put o.s. in sb's place; **jdm einen Tritt/Schlag ~** to kick/hit sb; **etw mit etw ~** to mix sth with sth; **jdn in gute Laune ~** to put sb in a good mood

Ver'setzung *f* transfer

verseuchen [fɛrˈzɔʏçən] *vt* to contaminate

versichern [fɛrˈzɪçərn] *vt* to assure; *(mit Geld)* to insure

Versicherung *f* assurance; insurance

Versicherungs- *zW:* **~gesellschaft** *f* insurance company; **~karte** *f* insurance card; **die grüne ~karte** the green card;

~police f insurance policy

ver'sinken (unreg) vi to sink

versöhnen [fɛr'zøːnən] vt to reconcile ♦ vr to become reconciled

Versöhnung f reconciliation

ver'sorgen vt to provide, to supply; (Familie etc) to look after

Ver'sorgung f provision; (Unterhalt) maintenance; (Altersversorgung etc) benefit, assistance

verspäten [fɛr'ʃpɛːtən] vr to be late

verspätet adj (Zug, Abflug, Ankunft) late; (Glückwünsche) belated

Verspätung f delay; ~ haben to be late

ver'sperren vt to bar, to obstruct

verspielt [fɛr'ʃpiːlt] adj (Kind, Tier) playful

ver'spotten vt to ridicule, to scoff at

ver'sprechen (unreg) vt to promise; sich dat etw von etw ~ to expect sth from sth; Ver'sprechen (-s, -) nt promise

verstaatlichen [fɛr'ʃtaːtlɪçən] vt to nationalize

Verstand [fɛr'ʃtant] m intelligence; mind; den ~ verlieren to go out of one's mind; über jds ~ gehen to go beyond sb

verständig [fɛr'ʃtɛndɪç] adj sensible; ~en [fɛr'ʃtɛndɪgən] vt to inform ♦ vr to communicate; (sich einigen) to come to an understanding; V~ung f communication; (Benachrichtigung) informing; (Einigung) agreement

verständ- [fɛr'ʃtɛnt] zW: ~lich adj understandable, comprehensible; V~lichkeit f clarity, intelligibility; V~nis (-ses, -se) nt understanding; ~nislos adj uncomprehending; ~nisvoll adj understanding, sympathetic

verstärk- [fɛr'ʃtɛrk] zW: ~en vt to strengthen; (Ton) to amplify; (erhöhen) to intensify ♦ vr to intensify; V~er (-s, -) m amplifier; V~ung f strengthening; (Hilfe) reinforcements pl; (von Ton) amplification

verstauchen [fɛr'ʃtauxən] vt to sprain

verstauen [fɛr'ʃtauən] vt to stow away

Versteck [fɛr'ʃtɛk] (-(e)s, -e) nt hiding (place); v~en vt, vr to hide; v~t adj hidden

ver'stehen (unreg) vt to understand ♦ vr to get on; das versteht sich (von selbst) that goes without saying

versteigern [fɛr'ʃtaɪgərn] vt to auction; Versteigerung f auction

verstell- [fɛr'ʃtɛl] zW: ~bar adj adjustable, variable; ~en vt to move, to shift; (Uhr) to adjust; (versperren) to block; (fig) to disguise ♦ vr to pretend, to put on an act; V~ung f pretence

versteuern [fɛr'ʃtɔyərn] vt to pay tax on

verstimmt [fɛr'ʃtɪmt] adj out of tune; (fig) cross, put out; (Magen) upset

ver'stopfen vt to block, to stop up; (MED) to constipate

Ver'stopfung f obstruction; (MED) constipation

verstorben [fɛr'ʃtɔrbən] adj deceased, late

verstört [fɛr'ʃtøːrt] adj (Mensch) distraught

Verstoß [fɛr'ʃtoːs] m: ~ (gegen) infringement (of), violation (of); v~en (unreg) vt to disown, to reject ♦ vi: v~en gegen to offend against

ver'streichen (unreg) vt to spread ♦ vi to elapse

ver'streuen vt to scatter (about)

verstümmeln [fɛr'ʃtʏməln] vt to maim, to mutilate (auch fig)

verstummen [fɛr'ʃtʊmən] vi to go silent; (Lärm) to die away

Versuch [fɛr'zuːx] (-(e)s, -e) m attempt; (SCI) experiment; v~en vt to try; (verlocken) to tempt ♦ vr: sich an etw dat v~en to try one's hand at sth; ~skaninchen nt (fig) guinea-pig; ~ung f temptation

vertagen [fɛr'taːgən] vt, vi to adjourn

ver'tauschen vt to exchange; (versehentlich) to mix up

verteidig- [fɛr'taɪdɪg] zW: ~en vt to defend; V~er (-s, -) m defender; (JUR) defence counsel; V~ung f defence

ver'teilen vt to distribute; (Rollen) to assign; (Salbe) to spread

Verteilung f distribution, allotment

vertiefen [fɛr'tiːfən] vt to deepen ♦ vr: sich in etw akk ~ to become engrossed od absorbed in sth

Vertiefung f depression

vertikal [vɛrti'kaːl] *adj* vertical

vertilgen [fɛr'tɪlgən] *vt* to exterminate; (*umg*) to eat up, to consume

vertonen [fɛr'toːnən] *vt* to set to music

Vertrag [fɛr'traːk] (-(e)s, ⁻e) *m* contract, agreement; (*POL*) treaty; **v~en** [-gən] (*unreg*) *vt* to tolerate, to stand ♦ *vr* to get along; (*sich aussöhnen*) to become reconciled; **v~lich** *adj* contractual

verträglich [fɛr'trɛːklɪç] *adj* good-natured, sociable; (*Speisen*) easily digested; (*MED*) easily tolerated; **V~keit** *f* sociability; good nature; digestibility

Vertrags- *zW:* **~bruch** *m* breach of contract; **~händler** *m* appointed retailer; **~partner** *m* party to a contract; **~werkstatt** *f* appointed repair shop; **v~widrig** *adj* contrary to contract

vertrauen [fɛr'trauən] *vi:* **jdm ~** to trust sb; **~ auf** +*akk* to rely on; **V~ (-s)** *nt* confidence; **V~ erweckend** inspiring trust; **~svoll** *adj* trustful; **~swürdig** *adj* trustworthy

vertraulich [fɛr'traulɪç] *adj* familiar; (*geheim*) confidential

vertraut [fɛr'traut] *adj* familiar; **V~heit** *f* familiarity

ver'treiben (*unreg*) *vt* to drive away; (*aus Land*) to expel; (*COMM*) to sell; (*Zeit*) to pass

vertret- [fɛr'treːt] *zW:* **~en** (*unreg*) *vt* to represent; (*Ansicht*) to hold, to advocate; **sich** *dat* **die Beine ~en** to stretch one's legs; **V~er (-s, -)** *m* representative; (*Verfechter*) advocate; **V~ung** *f* representation; advocacy

Vertrieb [fɛr'triːp] (-(e)s, -e) *m* marketing (department)

ver'trocknen *vi* to dry up

ver'trösten *vt* to put off

vertun [fɛr'tuːn] (*unreg*) *vt* to waste ♦ *vr* (*umg*) to make a mistake

vertuschen [fɛr'tuʃən] *vt* to hush *od* cover up

verübeln [fɛr'|yːbəln] *vt:* **jdm etw ~** to be cross *od* offended with sb on account of sth

verüben [fɛr'|yːbən] *vt* to commit

verun- [fɛr'|ʊn] *zW:* **~glimpfen** *vt* to disparage; **~glücken** *vi* to have an accident; **tödlich ~glücken** to be killed in an accident; **~reinigen** *vt* to soil; (*Umwelt*) to pollute; **~sichern** *vt* to rattle; **~treuen** [-trɔyən] *vt* to embezzle

verur- [fɛr'|uːr] *zW:* **~sachen** *vt* to cause; **~teilen** [-tailən] *vt* to condemn; **V~teilung** *f* condemnation; (*JUR*) sentence

verviel- [fɛr'fiːl] *zW:* **~fachen** *vt* to multiply; **~fältigen** [-fɛltɪgən] *vt* to duplicate, to copy; **V~fältigung** *f* duplication, copying

vervollkommnen [fɛr'fɔlkɔmnən] *vt* to perfect

vervollständigen [fɛr'fɔlʃtɛndɪgən] *vt* to complete

ver'wackeln *vt* (*Foto*) to blur

ver'wählen *vr* (*TEL*) to dial the wrong number

verwahren [fɛr'vaːrən] *vt* to keep, to lock away ♦ *vr* to protest

verwalt- [fɛr'valt] *zW:* **~en** *vt* to manage; to administer; **V~er (-s, -)** *m* manager; (*Vermögensverwalter*) trustee; **V~ung** *f* administration; management

ver'wandeln *vt* to change, to transform ♦ *vr* to change; to be transformed; **Ver'wandlung** *f* change, transformation

verwandt [fɛr'vant] *adj:* **~ (mit)** related (to); **V~e(r)** *f(m)* relative, relation; **V~schaft** *f* relationship; (*Menschen*) relations *pl*

ver'warnen *vt* to caution

Ver'warnung *f* caution

ver'wechseln *vt:* **~ mit** to confuse with; to mistake for; **zum V~ ähnlich** as like as two peas

Ver'wechslung *f* confusion, mixing up

Verwehung [fɛr'veːʊŋ] *f* snowdrift; sand drift

verweichlicht [fɛr'vaiçlɪçt] *adj* effeminate, soft

ver'weigern *vt:* **jdm etw ~** to refuse sb sth; **den Gehorsam/die Aussage ~** to refuse to obey/testify

Ver'weigerung *f* refusal

Verweis [fɛr'vais] (-es, -e) *m* reprimand,

rebuke; *(Hinweis)* reference; **v~en** *(unreg) vt* to refer; **jdn von der Schule v~en** to expel sb (from school); **jdn des Landes v~en** to deport *od* expel sb

ver'welken *vi* to fade

verwend- [fɛr'vɛnd] *zW:* **~bar** [-'vɛntbaːr] *adj* usable; **ver'wenden** *(unreg) vt* to use; *(Mühe, Zeit, Arbeit)* to spend ♦ *vr* to intercede; **Ver'wendung** *f* use

ver'werfen *(unreg) vt* to reject

verwerflich [fɛr'vɛrflɪç] *adj* reprehensible

ver'werten *vt* to utilize

Ver'wertung *f* utilization

verwesen [fɛr'veːzən] *vi* to decay

ver'wickeln *vt* to tangle (up); *(fig)* to involve ♦ *vt* to get tangled (up); **jdn in etw** *akk* **~** to involve sb in sth; **sich in etw** *akk* **~** to get involved in sth

verwickelt [fɛr'vɪkəlt] *adj (Situation, Fall)* difficult, complicated

verwildern [fɛr'vɪldərn] *vi* to run wild

verwirklichen [fɛr'vɪrklɪçən] *vt* to realize, to put into effect

Verwirklichung *f* realization

verwirren [fɛr'vɪrən] *vt* to tangle (up); *(fig)* to confuse

Verwirrung *f* confusion

verwittern [fɛr'vɪtərn] *vi* to weather

verwitwet [fɛr'vɪtvət] *adj* widowed

verwöhnen [fɛr'vøːnən] *vt* to spoil

verworren [fɛr'vɔrən] *adj* confused

verwundbar [fɛr'vʊntbaːr] *adj* vulnerable

verwunden [fɛr'vʊndən] *vt* to wound

verwunder- [fɛr'vʊndər] *zW:* **~lich** *adj* surprising; **V~ung** *f* astonishment

Verwundete(r) *f(m)* injured person

Verwundung *f* wound, injury

ver'wünschen *vt* to curse

verwüsten [fɛr'vyːstən] *vt* to devastate

verzagen [fɛr'tsaːgən] *vi* to despair

ver'zählen *vr* to miscount

verzehren [fɛr'tseːrən] *vt* to consume

ver'zeichnen *vt* to list; *(Niederlage, Verlust)* to register

Verzeichnis [fɛr'tsaɪçnɪs] **(-ses, -se)** *nt* list, catalogue; *(in Buch)* index

verzeih- [fɛr'tsaɪ] *zW:* **~en** *(unreg) vt, vi* to

forgive; **jdm etw ~en** to forgive sb for sth; **~lich** *adj* pardonable; **V~ung** *f* forgiveness, pardon; **V~ung!** sorry!, excuse me!

verzichten [fɛr'tsɪçtən] *vi:* **~ auf** *+akk* to forgo, to give up

ver'ziehen *(unreg) vi* to move ♦ *vt* to put out of shape; *(Kind)* to spoil; *(Pflanzen)* to thin out ♦ *vr* to go out of shape; *(Gesicht)* to contort; *(verschwinden)* to disappear; **das Gesicht ~** to pull a face

verzieren [fɛr'tsiːrən] *vt* to decorate, to ornament

Verzierung *f* decoration

verzinsen [fɛr'tsɪnzən] *vt* to pay interest on

ver'zögern *vt* to delay

Ver'zögerung *f* delay, time lag; **~staktik** *f* delaying tactics *pl*

verzollen [fɛr'tsɔlən] *vt* to pay duty on

Verzug [fɛr'tsuːk] *m* delay

verzweif- [fɛr'tsvaɪf] *zW:* **~eln** *vi* to despair; **~elt** *adj* desperate; **V~lung** *f* despair

Veto ['veːto] **(-s, -s)** *nt* veto

Vetter ['fɛtər] **(-s, -n)** *m* cousin

vgl. *abk (= vergleiche)* cf.

v. H. *abk (= vom Hundert)* p.c.

vibrieren [vi'briːrən] *vi* to vibrate

Video ['viːdeo] *nt* video; **~gerät** *nt* video recorder; **~rekorder** *m* video recorder

Vieh [fiː] **(-(e)s)** *nt* cattle *pl*; **v~isch** *adj* bestial

viel [fiːl] *adj* a lot of, much ♦ *adv* a lot, much; **~ sagend** significant; **~ versprechend** promising; **~e** *pron pl* a lot of, many; **~ zu wenig** much too little; **~erlei** *adj* a great variety of; **~es** *pron* a lot; **~fach** *adj, adv* many times; **auf ~fachen Wunsch** at the request of many people; **V~falt (-)** *f* variety; **~fältig** *adj* varied, many-sided

vielleicht [fi'laɪçt] *adv* perhaps

viel- *zW:* **~mal(s)** *adv* many times; **danke ~mals** many thanks; **~mehr** *adv* rather, on the contrary; **~seitig** *adj* many-sided

vier [fiːr] *num* four; **V~eck (-(e)s, -e)** *nt* four-sided figure; *(gleichseitig)* square; **~eckig** *adj* four-sided; square; **V~takt-motor** *m* four-stroke engine; **~te(r, s)**

Spelling Reform: ▲ *new spelling* △ *old spelling (to be phased out)*

['fiːrtə(r, s)] *adj* fourth; **V~tel** ['fɪrtəl] (**-s, -**) *nt* quarter; **V~teljahr** *nt* quarter; **~teljährlich** *adj* quarterly; **~teln** *vt* to divide into four; (*Kuchen usw*) to divide into quarters; **V~telstunde** *f* quarter of an hour; **~zehn** ['fɪrtseːn] *num* fourteen; **in ~zehn Tagen** in a fortnight; **~zehntägig** *adj* fortnightly; **~zig** ['fɪrtsɪç] *num* forty

Villa ['vɪla] (**-, Villen**) *f* villa

violett [vio'lɛt] *adj* violet

Violin- [vio'liːn] *zW:* **~e** *f* violin; **~schlüssel** *m* treble clef

virtuell [vɪrtu'ɛl] *adj* (COMPUT) virtual; **~e Realität** virtual reality

Virus ['viːrʊs] (**-, Viren**) *m od nt* (*auch* COMPUT) virus

Visa ['viːza] *pl von* **Visum**

vis-a-vis ▲, **vis-à-vis** [viza'viː] *adv* opposite

Visen ['viːzən] *pl von* **Visum**

Visier [vi'ziːr] (**-s, -e**) *nt* gunsight; (*am Helm*) visor

Visite [vi'ziːtə] *f* (MED) visit; **~nkarte** *f* visiting card

Visum ['viːzʊm] (**-s, Visa od Visen**) *nt* visa

vital [vi'taːl] *adj* lively, full of life, vital

Vitamin [vita'miːn] (**-s, -e**) *nt* vitamin

Vogel ['foːɡəl] (**-s, ¨**) *m* bird; **einen ~ haben** (*umg*) to have bats in the belfry; **jdm den ~ zeigen** (*umg*) to tap one's forehead (*meaning that one thinks sb stupid*); **~bauer** *nt* birdcage; **~perspektive** *f* bird's-eye view; **~scheuche** *f* scarecrow

Vokabel [vo'kaːbəl] (**-, -n**) *f* word

Vokabular [vokabu'laːr] (**-s, -e**) *nt* vocabulary

Vokal [vo'kaːl] (**-s, -e**) *nt* vowel

Volk [fɔlk] (**-(e)s, ¨er**) *nt* people; nation

Völker- ['fœlkər] *zW:* **~recht** *nt* international law; **v~rechtlich** *adj* according to international law; **~verständigung** *f* international understanding

Volkshochschule

ⓘ The **Volkshochschule** (*VHS*) is an institution which offers Adult Education classes. No set qualifications are necessary

to attend. For a small fee adults can attend both vocational and non-vocational classes in the day-time or evening.

Volks- *zW:* **~entscheid** *m* referendum; **~fest** *nt* fair; **~hochschule** *f* adult education classes *pl*; **~lied** *nt* folksong; **~republik** *f* people's republic; **~schule** *f* elementary school; **~tanz** *m* folk dance; **~vertreter(in)** *m(f)* people's representative; **~wirtschaft** *f* economics *sg*

voll [fɔl] *adj* full; **etw ~ machen** to fill sth up; **~ tanken** to fill up; **~ und ganz** completely; **jdn für ~ nehmen** (*umg*) to take sb seriously; **~auf** *adv* amply; **V~bart** *m* full beard; **V~beschäftigung** *f* full employment; **~'bringen** (*unreg*) *vt insep* to accomplish; **~'enden** *vt insep* to finish, to complete; **~endet** *adj* (*~kommen*) completed; **~ends** ['fɔlɛnts] *adv* completely; **V~'endung** *f* completion

Volleyball ['vɔlibal] *m* volleyball

Vollgas *nt*: **mit ~** at full throttle; **~ geben** to step on it

völlig ['fœlɪç] *adj* complete ♦ *adv* completely

voll- *zW:* **~jährig** *adj* of age; **V~kaskoversicherung** ['fɔlkaskofɛrzɪçərʊŋ] *f* fully comprehensive insurance; **~'kommen** *adj* perfect, full; **V~'kommenheit** *f* perfection; **V~kornbrot** *nt* wholemeal bread; **V~macht** (**-, -en**) *f* authority, full powers *pl*; **V~milch** *f* (KOCH) full-cream milk; **V~mond** *m* full moon; **V~pension** *f* full board; **~'ständig** ['fɔlʃtɛndɪç] *adj* complete; **~'strecken** *vt insep* to execute; **~tanken** △ *vt, vi siehe* **voll**; **V~waschmittel** *nt* detergent; **V~wertkost** *f* wholefood; **~'zählig** ['fɔlsɛːlɪç] *adj* complete; in full number; **~'ziehen** (*unreg*) *vt insep* to carry out ♦ *vr insep* to happen; **V~'zug** *m* execution

Volumen [vo'luːmən] (**-s, - od Volumina**) *nt* volume

vom [fɔm] = **von dem**

SCHLÜSSELWORT

von [fɔn] *präp +dat* **1** (*Ausgangspunkt*) from;

von from ... to; **von morgens bis abends** from morning till night; **von ... nach ... from ... to ...;** **von ... an** from ...; **von ... aus** from ...; **von dort aus** from there; **etw von sich aus tun** to do sth of one's own accord; **von mir aus** (*umg*) if you like, I don't mind; **von wo/wann ...?** where/when ... from?

2 (*Ursache, im Passiv*) by; **ein Gedicht von Schiller** a poem by Schiller; **von etw müde** tired from sth

3 (*als Genitiv*) of; **ein Freund von mir** a friend of mine; **nett von dir** nice of you; **jeweils zwei von zehn** two out of every ten

4 (*über*) about; **er erzählte vom Urlaub** he talked about his holiday

5: **von wegen!** (*umg*) no way!

voneinander *adv* from each other

SCHLÜSSELWORT

vor [foːr] *präp +dat* 1 (*räumlich*) in front of; **vor der Kirche links abbiegen** turn left before the church

2 (*zeitlich*) before; **ich war vor ihm da** I was there before him; **vor 2 Tagen** 2 days ago; **5 (Minuten) vor 4** 5 (minutes) to 4; **vor kurzem** a little while ago

3 (*Ursache*) with; **vor Wut/Liebe** with rage/love; **vor Hunger sterben** to die of hunger; **vor lauter Arbeit** because of work

4: **vor allem, vor allen Dingen** most of all

♦ *präp +akk* (*räumlich*) in front of

♦ *adv*: **vor und zurück** backwards and forwards

Vorabend ['foːrʔaːbənt] *m* evening before, eve

voran [foˈran] *adv* before, ahead; **mach ~!** get on with it!; **~gehen** (*unreg*) *vi* to go ahead; **einer Sache** *dat* **~gehen** to precede sth; **~kommen** (*unreg*) *vi* to come along, to make progress

Voranschlag ['foːrʔanʃlaːk] *m* estimate

Vorarbeiter ['foːrʔarbaitər] *m* foreman

voraus [foˈraus] *adv* ahead; (*zeitlich*) in advance; **jdm ~ sein** to be ahead of sb; **im V~** in advance; **~gehen** (*unreg*) *vi* to go (on) ahead; (*fig*) to precede; **~haben** (*unreg*) *vt*: **jdm etw ~haben** to have the edge on sb in sth; **V~sage** *f* prediction; **~sagen** *vt* to predict; **~sehen** (*unreg*) *vt* to foresee; **~setzen** *vt* to assume; **~gesetzt, dass ...** provided that ...; **V~setzung** *f* requirement, prerequisite; **V~sicht** *f* foresight; **aller V~sicht nach** in all probability; **~sichtlich** *adv* probably

Vorbehalt ['foːrbəhalt] (*-(e)s, -e*) *m* reservation, proviso; **v~en** (*unreg*) *vt*: **sich/jdm etw v~en** to reserve sth (for o.s.)/for sb; **v~los** *adj* unconditional ♦ *adv* unconditionally

vorbei [fɔrˈbai] *adv* by, past; **das ist ~** that's over; **~gehen** (*unreg*) *vi* to pass by, to go past; **~kommen** (*unreg*) *vi*: **bei jdm ~kommen** to drop in *od* call in on sb

vor- *zW*: **~belastet** ['foːrbəlastət] *adj* (*fig*) handicapped; **~bereiten** *vt* to prepare; **V~bereitung** *f* preparation; **V~bestellung** *f* advance order; (*von Platz, Tisch etc*) advance booking; **~bestraft** ['foːrbəʃtraːft] *adj* previously convicted, with a record

vorbeugen ['foːrbɔygən] *vt, vr* to lean forward ♦ *vi +dat* to prevent; **~d** *adj* preventive

Vorbeugung *f* prevention; **zur ~ gegen** for the prevention of

Vorbild ['foːrbɪlt] *nt* model; **sich** *dat* **jdn zum ~ nehmen** to model o.s. on sb; **v~lich** *adj* model, ideal

vorbringen ['foːrbrɪŋən] (*unreg*) *vt* to advance, to state

Vorder- ['fɔrdər] *zW*: **~achse** *f* front axle; **v~e(r, s)** *adj* front; **~grund** *m* foreground; **~mann** (*pl* **-männer**) *m* man in front; **jdn auf ~mann bringen** (*umg*) to get sb to shape up; **~seite** *f* front (side); **v~ste(r, s)** *adj* front

vordrängen ['foːrdrɛŋən] *vr* to push to the front

voreilig ['foːrʔailɪç] *adj* hasty, rash

voreinander [foːrʔaiˈnandər] *adv* (*räumlich*)

Spelling Reform: ▲ *new spelling* △ *old spelling (to be phased out)*

in front of each other

voreingenommen ['fo:r|aingənɔmən] *adj* biased; **V~heit** *f* bias

vorenthalten ['fo:r|enthaltən] (*unreg*) *vt*: **jdm etw ~** to withhold sth from sb

vorerst ['fo:r|e:rst] *adv* for the moment *od* present

Vorfahr ['fo:rfa:r] (**-en, -en**) *m* ancestor

vorfahren (*unreg*) *vi* to drive (on) ahead; (*vors Haus etc*) to drive up

Vorfahrt *f* (*AUT*) right of way; **~ achten!** give way!

Vorfahrts- *zW*: **~regel** *f* right of way; **~schild** *nt* give way sign; **~straße** *f* major road

Vorfall ['fo:rfal] *m* incident; **v~en** (*unreg*) *vi* to occur

vorfinden ['fo:rfɪndən] (*unreg*) *vt* to find

Vorfreude ['fo:rfrɔydə] *f* (joyful) anticipation

vorführen ['fo:rfy:rən] *vt* to show, to display; **dem Gericht ~** to bring before the court

Vorgabe ['fo:rga:bə] *f* (*SPORT*) start, handicap ♦ *in zW* (*COMPUT*) default

Vorgang ['fo:rgaŋ] *m* course of events; (*bes SCI*) process

Vorgänger(in) ['fo:rgeŋər(ɪn)] (**-s, -**) *m(f)* predecessor

vorgeben ['fo:rge:bən] (*unreg*) *vt* to pretend, to use as a pretext; (*SPORT*) to give an advantage *od* a start of

vorgefertigt ['fo:rgəfertɪçt] *adj* prefabricated

vorgehen ['fo:rge:ən] (*unreg*) *vi* (*voraus*) to go (on) ahead; (*nach vorn*) to go up front; (*handeln*) to act, to proceed; (*Uhr*) to be fast; (*Vorrang haben*) to take precedence; (*passieren*) to go on

Vorgehen (-s) *nt* action

Vorgeschichte ['fo:rgəʃɪçtə] *f* past history

Vorgeschmack ['fo:rgəʃmak] *m* foretaste

Vorgesetzte(r) ['fo:rgəzetstə(r)] *f(m)* superior

vorgestern ['fo:rgestərn] *adv* the day before yesterday

vorhaben ['fo:rha:bən] (*unreg*) *vt* to intend; **hast du schon was vor?** have you got anything on?; **V~ (-s, -)** *nt* intention

vorhalten ['fo:rhaltən] (*unreg*) *vt* to hold *od* put up ♦ *vi* to last; **jdm etw ~** (*fig*) to reproach sb for sth

vorhanden [fo:r'handən] *adj* existing; (*erhältlich*) available

Vorhang ['fo:rhaŋ] *m* curtain

Vorhängeschloss ▲ ['fo:rheŋəʃlɔs] *nt* padlock

vorher [fo:r'he:r] *adv* before(hand); **~bestimmen** *vt* (*Schicksal*) to preordain; **~gehen** (*unreg*) *vi* to precede; **~ig** *adj* previous

Vorherrschaft ['fo:rherʃaft] *f* predominance, supremacy

vorherrschen ['fo:rherʃən] *vi* to predominate

vorher- [fo:r'he:r] *zW*: **V~sage** *f* forecast; **~sagen** *vt* to forecast, to predict; **~sehbar** *adj* predictable; **~sehen** (*unreg*) *vt* to foresee

vorhin [fo:r'hɪn] *adv* not long ago, just now; **V~ein** ▲ *adv*: **im V~ein** beforehand

vorig ['fo:rɪç] *adj* previous, last

Vorkämpfer(in) ['fo:rkempfər(ɪn)] *m(f)* pioneer

Vorkaufsrecht ['fo:rkaufsreçt] *nt* option to buy

Vorkehrung ['fo:rke:ruŋ] *f* precaution

vorkommen ['fo:rkɔmən] (*unreg*) *vi* to come forward; (*geschehen, sich finden*) to occur; (*scheinen*) to seem (to be); **sich** *dat* **dumm** *etc* **~** to feel stupid *etc*; **V~ (-s, -)** *nt* occurrence

Vorkriegs- ['fo:rkri:ks] *in zW* prewar

Vorladung ['fo:rla:duŋ] *f* summons *sg*

Vorlage ['fo:rla:gə] *f* model, pattern; (*Gesetzesvorlage*) bill; (*SPORT*) pass

vorlassen ['fo:rlasən] (*unreg*) *vt* to admit; (*vorgehen lassen*) to allow to go in front

vorläufig ['fo:rlɔyfɪç] *adj* temporary, provisional

vorlaut ['fo:rlaut] *adj* impertinent, cheeky

vorlesen ['fo:rle:zən] (*unreg*) *vt* to read (out)

Vorlesung *f* (*UNIV*) lecture

vorletzte(r, s) ['fo:rletstə(r, s)] *adj* last but one

vorlieb [fo:r'li:p] *adv*: **~ nehmen mit** to

make do with

Vorliebe ['foːrliːbə] f preference, partiality

vorliegen ['foːrliːgən] (unreg) vi to be (here); **etw liegt jdm vor** sb has sth; **~d** adj present, at issue

vormachen ['foːrmaxən] vt: **jdm etw ~** to show sb how to do sth; (fig) to fool sb; to have sb on

Vormachtstellung ['foːrmaxtʃtɛluŋ] f supremacy, hegemony

Vormarsch ['foːrmarʃ] m advance

vormerken ['foːrmɛrkən] vt to book

Vormittag ['foːrmɪtaːk] m morning; **v~s** adv in the morning, before noon

vorn [fɔrn] adv in front; **von ~ anfangen** to start at the beginning; **nach ~** to the front

Vorname ['foːrnaːmə] m first name, Christian name

vorne ['fɔrnə] adv = **vorn**

vornehm ['foːrneːm] adj distinguished; refined; elegant

vornehmen (unreg) vt (fig) to carry out; **sich** dat **etw ~** to start on sth; (beschließen) to decide to do sth; **sich** dat **jdn ~** to tell sb off

vornherein ['fɔrnhɛraɪn] adv: **von ~** from the start

Vorort ['foːrʔɔrt] m suburb

Vorrang ['foːrraŋ] m precedence, priority; **v~ig** adj of prime importance, primary

Vorrat ['foːrraːt] m stock, supply

vorrätig ['foːrrɛːtɪç] adj in stock

Vorratskammer f pantry

Vorrecht ['foːrrɛçt] nt privilege

Vorrichtung ['foːrrɪçtuŋ] f device, contrivance

vorrücken ['foːrrʏkən] vi to advance ♦ vt to move forward

Vorsaison ['foːrzɛzõː] f early season

Vorsatz ['foːrzats] m intention; (JUR) intent; **einen ~ fassen** to make a resolution

vorsätzlich ['foːrzɛtslɪç] adj intentional; (JUR) premeditated ♦ adv intentionally

Vorschau ['foːrʃau] f (RADIO, TV) (programme) preview; (Film) trailer

Vorschlag ['foːrʃlaːk] m suggestion, proposal; **v~en** (unreg) vt to suggest, to

propose

vorschreiben ['foːrʃraibən] (unreg) vt to prescribe, to specify

Vorschrift ['foːrʃrɪft] f regulation(s); rule(s); (Anweisungen) instruction(s); **Dienst nach ~** work-to-rule; **v~smäßig** adj as per regulations/instructions

Vorschuss ▲ ['foːrʃus] m advance

vorsehen ['foːrzeːən] (unreg) vt to provide for, to plan ♦ vr to take care, to be careful ♦ vi to be visible

Vorsehung f providence

Vorsicht ['foːrzɪçt] f caution, care; **~!** look out!, take care!; (auf Schildern) caution!, danger!; **~, Stufe!** mind the step!; **v~ig** adj cautious, careful; **v~shalber** adv just in case

Vorsilbe ['foːrzɪlbə] f prefix

vorsingen ['foːrzɪŋən] vt (vor Zuhörern) to sing (to); (in Prüfung, für Theater etc) to audition (for) ♦ vi to sing

Vorsitz ['foːrzɪts] m chair(manship); **~ende(r)** f(m) chairman(-woman)

Vorsorge ['foːrzɔrgə] f precaution(s), provision(s); **v~n** vi: **v~n für** to make provision(s) for; **~untersuchung** f check-up

vorsorglich ['foːrzɔrklɪç] adv as a precaution

Vorspeise ['foːrʃpaizə] f hors d'oeuvre, appetizer

Vorspiel ['foːrʃpiːl] nt prelude

vorspielen vt: **jdm etw ~** (MUS) to play sth for od to sb ♦ vi (zur Prüfung etc) to play for od to sb

vorsprechen ['foːrʃprɛçən] (unreg) vt to say out loud, to recite ♦ vi: **bei jdm ~** to call on sb

Vorsprung ['foːrʃpruŋ] m projection, ledge; (fig) advantage, start

Vorstadt ['foːrʃtat] f suburbs pl

Vorstand ['foːrʃtant] m executive committee; (COMM) board (of directors); (Person) director, head

vorstehen ['foːrʃteːən] (unreg) vi to project; **einer Sache** dat **~** (fig) to be the head of sth

vorstell- ['foːrʃtɛl] zW: **~bar** adj

conceivable; **~en** vt to put forward; (*bekannt machen*) to introduce; (*darstellen*) to represent; **~en vor** +akk to put in front of; **sich** dat **etw ~en** to imagine sth; **V~ung** f (*Bekanntmachung*) introduction; (*THEAT etc*) performance; (*Gedanke*) idea, thought

vorstoßen ['foːɐ̯ʃtoːsən] (*unreg*) vi (*ins Unbekannte*) to venture (forth)

Vorstrafe ['foːɐ̯ʃtraːfə] f previous conviction

Vortag ['foːɐ̯taːk] m: **am ~ einer Sache** gen on the day before sth

vortäuschen ['foːɐ̯tɔʏʃən] vt to feign, to pretend

Vorteil ['foːɐ̯taɪl] (**-s, -e**) m: **~ (gegenüber)** advantage (over); **im ~ sein** to have the advantage; **v~haft** adj advantageous

Vortrag ['foːɐ̯traːk] (**-(e)s, Vorträge**) m talk, lecture; **v~en** [-gən] (*unreg*) vt to carry forward; (*fig*) to recite; (*Rede*) to deliver; (*Lied*) to perform; (*Meinung etc*) to express

vortreten ['foːɐ̯treːtən] (*unreg*) vi to step forward; (*Augen etc*) to protrude

vorüber [fo'ryːbər] adv past, over; **~gehen** (*unreg*) vi to pass (by); **~gehen an** +dat (*fig*) to pass over; **~gehend** adj temporary, passing

Vorurteil ['foːɐ̯ʊrtaɪl] nt prejudice

Vorverkauf ['foːɐ̯fɛrkauf] m advance booking

Vorwahl ['foːɐ̯vaːl] f preliminary election; (*TEL*) dialling code

Vorwand ['foːɐ̯vant] (**-(e)s, Vorwände**) m pretext

vorwärts ['foːɐ̯vɛrts] adv forward; **~ gehen** to progress; **V~gang** m (*AUT etc*) forward gear; **~ kommen** to get on, to make progress

Vorwäsche f prewash

vorweg [foːɐ̯'vɛk] adv in advance; **~nehmen** (*unreg*) vt to anticipate

vorweisen ['foːɐ̯vaɪzən] (*unreg*) vt to show, to produce

vorwerfen ['foːɐ̯vɛrfən] (*unreg*) vt: **jdm etw ~** to reproach sb for sth, to accuse sb of sth; **sich** dat **nichts vorzuwerfen haben** to have nothing to reproach o.s. with

vorwiegend ['foːɐ̯viːgənt] adj predominant
♦ adv predominantly

vorwitzig ['foːɐ̯vɪtsɪç] adj (*Mensch, Bemerkung*) cheeky

Vorwort ['foːɐ̯vɔrt] (**-(e)s, -e**) nt preface

Vorwurf ['foːɐ̯vʊrf] m reproach; **jdm/sich Vorwürfe machen** to reproach sb/o.s.; **v~svoll** adj reproachful

vorzeigen ['foːɐ̯tsaɪgən] vt to show, to produce

vorzeitig ['foːɐ̯tsaɪtɪç] adj premature

vorziehen ['foːɐ̯tsiːən] (*unreg*) vt to pull forward; (*Gardinen*) to draw; (*lieber haben*) to prefer

Vorzimmer ['foːɐ̯tsɪmər] nt (*Büro*) outer office

Vorzug ['foːɐ̯tsuːk] m preference; (*gute Eigenschaft*) merit, good quality; (*Vorteil*) advantage

vorzüglich [foːɐ̯'tsyːklɪç] adj excellent

Vorzugspreis m special discount price

vulgär [vʊl'gɛːr] adj vulgar

Vulkan [vʊl'kaːn] (**-s, -e**) m volcano

W, w

Waage ['vaːgə] f scales pl; (*ASTROL*) Libra; **w~recht** adj horizontal

Wabe ['vaːbə] f honeycomb

wach [vax] adj awake; (*fig*) alert; **W~e** f guard, watch; **W~e halten** to keep watch; **W~e stehen** to stand guard; **~en** vi to be awake; (*Wache halten*) to guard

Wachs [vaks] (**-es, -e**) nt wax

wachsam ['vaxzaːm] adj watchful, vigilant, alert

wachsen (*unreg*) vi to grow

Wachstuch ['vakstuːx] nt oilcloth

Wachstum ['vakstuːm] (**-s**) nt growth

Wächter ['vɛçtər] (**-s, -**) m guard, warden, keeper; (*Parkplatzwächter*) attendant

wackel- ['vakəl] zW: **~ig** adj shaky, wobbly; **W~kontakt** m loose connection; **~n** vi to shake; (*fig: Position*) to be shaky

wacker ['vakər] adj valiant, stout ♦ adv well, bravely

Wade ['va:də] f (ANAT) calf

Waffe ['vafə] f weapon

Waffel ['vafəl] (-, -n) f waffle; wafer

Waffen- zW: **~schein** m gun licence; **~stillstand** m armistice, truce

Wagemut ['va:gəmu:t] m daring

wagen ['va:gən] vt to venture, to dare

Wagen ['va:gən] (-s, -) m vehicle; (Auto) car; (EISENB) carriage; (Pferdewagen) cart; **~heber** (-s, -) m jack

Waggon [va'gõ] (-s, -s) m carriage; (Güterwaggon) goods van, freight truck (US)

Wagnis ['va:knɪs] (-ses, -se) nt risk

Wagon ▲ ['va:gõ, va'go:n] (-s, -s) m = Waggon

Wahl [va:l] (-, -en) f choice; (POL) election; **zweite ~** (COMM) seconds pl

wähl- ['vɛ:l] zW: **~bar** adj eligible; **~en** vt, vi to choose; (POL) to elect, to vote (for); (TEL) to dial; **~er(in)** (-s, -) m(f) voter; **~erisch** adj fastidious, particular

Wahl- zW: **~fach** nt optional subject; **~gang** m ballot; **~kabine** f polling booth; **~kampf** m election campaign; **~kreis** m constituency; **~lokal** nt polling station; **w~los** adv at random; **~recht** nt franchise; **~spruch** m motto; **~urne** f ballot box

Wahn [va:n] (-(e)s) m delusion; folly; **~sinn** m madness; **w~sinnig** adj insane, mad ♦ adv (umg) incredibly

wahr [va:r] adj true

wahren vt to maintain, to keep

während ['vɛ:rənt] präp +gen during ♦ konj while; **~dessen** adv meanwhile

wahr- zW: **~haben** (unreg) vt: **etw nicht ~haben wollen** to refuse to admit sth; **~haft** adv (tatsächlich) truly; **~haftig** [va:r'haftɪç] adj true, real ♦ adv really; **W~heit** f truth; **~nehmen** (unreg) vt to perceive, to observe; **W~nehmung** f perception; **~sagen** vi to prophesy, to tell fortunes; **W~sager(in)** (-s, -) m(f) fortune teller; **~scheinlich** [va:r'ʃaɪnlɪç] adj probable ♦ adv probably; **W~'scheinlichkeit** f probability; **aller W~scheinlichkeit nach** in all probability

Währung ['vɛ:rʊŋ] f currency

Wahrzeichen nt symbol

Waise ['vaɪzə] f orphan; **~nhaus** nt orphanage

Wald [valt] (-(e)s, ¨er) m wood(s); (groß) forest; **~brand** m forest fire; **~sterben** nt trees dying due to pollution

Wales [weɪlz] (-) nt Wales

Wal(fisch) ['va:l(fɪʃ)] (-(e)s, -e) m whale

Waliser [va'li:zər] (-s, -) m Welshman; **Waliserin** [va'li:zərɪn] f Welshwoman; **walisisch** [va'li:zɪʃ] adj Welsh

Walkman ['wɔ:kman] (®; -s, Walkmen) m Walkman ®, personal stereo

Wall [val] (-(e)s, ¨e) m embankment; (Bollwerk) rampart

Wallfahr- zW: **~er(in)** m(f) pilgrim; **~t** f pilgrimage

Walnuss ▲ ['valnʊs] f walnut

Walross ▲ ['valrɔs] nt walrus

Walze ['valtsə] f (Gerät) cylinder; (Fahrzeug) roller; **w~n** vt to roll (out)

wälzen ['vɛltsən] vt to roll (over); (Bücher) to hunt through; (Probleme) to deliberate on ♦ vr to wallow; (vor Schmerzen) to roll about; (im Bett) to toss and turn

Walzer ['valtsər] (-s, -) m waltz

Wand [vant] (-, ¨e) f wall; (Trennwand) partition; (Bergwand) precipice

Wandel ['vandəl] (-s) m change; **w~bar** adj changeable, variable; **w~n** vt, vr to change ♦ vi (gehen) to walk

Wander- ['vandər] zW: **~er** (-s, -) m hiker, rambler; **~karte** f map of country walks; **w~n** vi to hike; (Blick) to wander; (Gedanken) to stray; **~schaft** f travelling; **~ung** f walk, hike; **~weg** m trail, walk

Wandlung f change, transformation

Wange ['vaŋə] f cheek

wanken ['vaŋkən] vi to stagger; (fig) to waver

wann [van] adv when

Wanne ['vanə] f tub

Wanze ['vantsə] f bug

Wappen ['vapən] (-s, -) nt coat of arms, crest; **~kunde** f heraldry

war etc [va:r] vb siehe **sein**

Ware ['va:rə] f ware

Waren- *zW:* **~haus** *nt* department store; **~lager** *nt* stock, store; **~muster** *nt* trade sample; **~probe** *f* sample; **~sendung** *f* trade sample (*sent by post*); **~zeichen** *nt*: **(eingetragenes) ~zeichen** (registered) trademark

warf *etc* [varf] *vb siehe* **werfen**

warm [varm] *adj* warm; (*Essen*) hot

Wärm- ['verm] *zW:* **~e** *f* warmth; **w~en** *vt, vr* to warm (up), to heat (up); **~flasche** *f* hot-water bottle

Warn- ['varn] *zW:* **~blinkanlage** *f* (*AUT*) hazard warning lights *pl;* **~dreieck** *nt* warning triangle; **w~en** *vt* to warn; **~ung** *f* warning

warten ['vartən] *vi:* **~ (auf** +*akk*) to wait (for); **auf sich ~ lassen** to take a long time

Wärter(in) ['vertər(ın)] **(-s, -)** *m(f)* attendant

Warte- ['vartə] *zW:* **~saal** *m* (*EISENB*) waiting room; **~zimmer** *nt* waiting room

Wartung *f* servicing; service; **~ und Instandhaltung** maintenance

warum [va'rʊm] *adv* why

Warze ['vartsə] *f* wart

was [vas] *pron* what; (*umg: etwas*) something; **~ für (ein) ...** what sort of ...

waschbar *adj* washable

Waschbecken *nt* washbasin

Wäsche ['vɛʃə] *f* wash(ing); (*Bettwäsche*) linen; (*Unterwäsche*) underclothing

waschecht *adj* colourfast; (*fig*) genuine

Wäsche- *zW:* **~klammer** *f* clothes peg (*BRIT*), clothespin (*US*); **~leine** *f* washing line (*BRIT*)

waschen ['vaʃən] (*unreg*) *vt, vi* to wash ♦ *vr* to (have a) wash; **sich** *dat* **die Hände ~** to wash one's hands

Wäscherei ['vɛʃərai] *f* laundry

Wasch- *zW:* **~gelegenheit** *f* washing facilities; **~küche** *f* laundry room; **~lappen** *m* face flannel, washcloth (*US*); (*umg*) sissy; **~maschine** *f* washing machine; **~mittel** *nt* detergent, washing powder; **~pulver** *nt* detergent, washing powder; **~raum** *m* washroom; **~salon** *m* Launderette ®

Wasser ['vasər] **(-s, -)** *nt* water; **~ball** *m* water polo; **w~dicht** *adj* waterproof; **~fall** *m* waterfall; **w~farbe** *f* watercolour; **~hahn** *m* tap, faucet (*US*); **~kraftwerk** *nt* hydroelectric power station; **~leitung** *f* water pipe; **~mann** *n* (*ASTROL*) Aquarius

wässern ['vesərn] *vt, vi* to water

Wasser- *zW:* **w~scheu** *adj* afraid of (the) water; **~ski** ['vasərʃiː] *nt* water-skiing; **~stoff** *m* hydrogen; **w~waage** *f* spirit level; **~zeichen** *nt* watermark

wässrig ▲ ['vesrıç] *adj* watery

Watt [vat] **(-(e)s, -en)** *nt* mud flats *pl*

Watte *f* cotton wool, absorbent cotton (*US*)

WC ['veːˈtseː] **(-s, -s)** *nt abk* W.C.

Web [vɛb] **(-s)** *nt* (*COMPUT*) **das ~** the Web

Web- ['veːb] *zW:* **w~en** (*unreg*) *vt* to weave; **~er** **(-s, -)** *m* weaver; **~e'rei** *f* (*Betrieb*) weaving mill

Website ['vɛbsaɪt] *f* (*COMPUT*) website

Webstuhl ['veːpʃtuːl] *m* loom

Wechsel ['vɛksəl] **(-s, -)** *m* change; (*COMM*) bill of exchange; **~geld** *nt* change; **w~haft** *adj* (*Wetter*) variable; **~jahre** *pl* change of life *sg;* **~kurs** *m* rate of exchange; **w~n** *vt* to change; (*Blicke*) to exchange ♦ *vi* to change; to vary; (*Geldwechseln*) to have change; **~strom** *m* alternating current; **~stube** *f* bureau de change; **~wirkung** *f* interaction

Weck- ['vɛk] *zW:* **~dienst** *m* alarm call service; **w~en** *vt* to wake (up); to call; **~er** **(-s, -)** *m* alarm clock

wedeln ['veːdəln] *vi* (*mit Schwanz*) to wag; (*mit Fächer etc*) to wave

weder ['veːdər] *konj* neither; **~ ... noch ...** neither ... nor ...

Weg [veːk] **(-(e)s, -e)** *m* way; (*Pfad*) path; (*Route*) route; **sich auf den ~ machen** to be on one's way; **jdm aus dem ~ gehen** to keep out of sb's way; *siehe* **zuwege**

weg [vɛk] *adv* away, off; **über etw** *akk* **~ sein** to be over sth; **er war schon ~** he had already left; **Finger ~!** hands off!

wegbleiben (*unreg*) *vi* to stay away

wegen ['veːgən] *präp* +*gen* (*umg:* +*dat*) because of

weg- ['vɛk] *zW:* **~fallen** (*unreg*) *vi* to be left

Rechtschreibreform: ▲ *neue Schreibung* △ *alte Schreibung (auslaufend)*

out; (*Ferien, Bezahlung*) to be cancelled; (*aufhören*) to cease; ~**gehen** (*unreg*) *vi* to go away; to leave; ~**lassen** (*unreg*) *vt* to leave out; ~**laufen** (*unreg*) *vi* to run away *od* off; ~**legen** *vt* to put aside; ~**machen** (*umg*) *vt* to get rid of; ~**müssen** (*unreg*; *umg*) *vi* to have to go; ~**nehmen** (*unreg*) *vt* to take away; ~**tun** (*unreg*) *vt* to put away; **W~weiser** (**-s, -**) *m* road sign, signpost; ~**werfen** (*unreg*) *vt* to throw away

weh [ve:] *adj* sore; ~(**e**) *excl*: ~(**e**), **wenn du ...** woe betide you if ...; **o ~!** oh dear!; ~**e!** just you dare!

wehen *vt, vi* to blow; (*Fahnen*) to flutter

weh- *zW*: ~**leidig** *adj* whiny, whining; ~**mütig** *adj* melancholy

Wehr [ve:r] (**-, -en**) *f*: **sich zur ~ setzen** to defend o.s.; ~**dienst** *m* military service; ~**dienstverweigerer** *m* ≈ conscientious objector; **w~en** *vr* to defend o.s.; **w~los** *adj* defenceless; ~**pflicht** *f* compulsory military service; **w~pflichtig** *adj* liable for military service

---

Wehrdienst

ⓘ **Wehrdienst** is military service which is still compulsory in Germany. All young men receive their call-up papers at 18 and all those pronounced physically fit are required to spend 10 months in the **Bundeswehr**. Conscientious objectors are allowed to do **Zivildienst** as an alternative, after presenting their case.

---

wehtun ▲ ['ve:tu:n] (*unreg*) *vt* to hurt, to be sore; **jdm/sich ~** to hurt sb/o.s.

Weib [vaip] (**-(e)s, -er**) *nt* woman, female; wife; ~**chen** *nt* female; **w~lich** *adj* feminine

weich [vaiç] *adj* soft; **W~e** *f* points *pl*; ~**en** (*unreg*) *vi* to yield, to give way; **W~heit** *f* softness; ~**lich** *adj* soft, namby-pamby

Weide ['vaidə] *f* (*Baum*) willow; (*Gras*) pasture; **w~n** *vi* to graze ♦ *vr*: **sich an etw** *dat* **w~n** to delight in sth

weigern ['vaigərn] *vr* to refuse

Weigerung ['vaigərʊŋ] *f* refusal

Weihe ['vaiə] *f* consecration; (*Priesterweihe*) ordination; **w~n** *vt* to consecrate; to ordain

Weihnacht- *zW*: ~**en** (**-**) *nt* Christmas; **w~lich** *adj* Christmas *cpd*

Weihnachts- *zW*: ~**abend** *m* Christmas Eve; ~**lied** *nt* Christmas carol; ~**mann** *m* Father Christmas, Santa Claus; ~**markt** *m* Christmas fair; ~**tag** *m* Christmas Day; **zweiter ~tag** Boxing Day

---

Weihnachtsmarkt

ⓘ The **Weihnachtsmarkt** is a market held in most large towns in Germany in the weeks prior to Christmas. People visit it to buy presents, toys and Christmas decorations, and to enjoy the festive atmosphere. Traditional Christmas food and drink can also be consumed there, for example, **Lebkuchen** and **Glühwein**.

Weihwasser *nt* holy water

weil [vail] *konj* because

Weile ['vailə] (**-**) *f* while, short time

Wein [vain] (**-(e)s, -e**) *m* wine; (*Pflanze*) vine; ~**bau** *m* cultivation of vines; ~**berg** *m* vineyard; ~**bergschnecke** *f* snail; ~**brand** *m* brandy

weinen *vt, vi* to cry; **das ist zum W~** it's enough to make you cry *od* weep

Wein- *zW*: ~**glas** *nt* wine glass; ~**karte** *f* wine list; ~**lese** *f* vintage; ~**probe** *f* winetasting; ~**rebe** *f* vine; **w~rot** *adj* burgundy, claret, wine-red; ~**stock** *m* vine; ~**stube** *f* wine bar; ~**traube** *f* grape

weise ['vaizə] *adj* wise

Weise *f* manner, way; (*Lied*) tune; **auf diese ~** in this way

weisen (*unreg*) *vt* to show

Weisheit ['vaishait] *f* wisdom; ~**szahn** *m* wisdom tooth

weiß [vais] *adj* white ♦ *vb siehe* **wissen**; **W~bier** *nt* weissbier (*light, fizzy beer made using top-fermentation yeast*); **W~brot** *nt* white bread; ~**en** *vt* to whitewash; **W~glut** *f* (*TECH*) incandescence; **jdn bis zur W~glut bringen** (*fig*) to make sb see red; **W~kohl**

---

m (white) cabbage; **W~wein** *m* white wine; **W~wurst** *f* veal sausage

weit [vaɪt] *adj* wide; *(Begriff)* broad; *(Reise, Wurf)* long ♦ *adv* far; **wie ~ ist es ...?** how far is it ...?; **in ~er Ferne** in the far distance; **~ blickend** far-seeing; **~ reichend** long-range; *(fig)* far-reaching; **~ verbreitet** widespread; **das geht zu ~** that's going too far; **~aus** *adv* by far; **~blickend** *adj* far-seeing; **W~e** *f* width; *(Raum)* space; *(von Entfernung)* distance; **~en** *vt, vr* to widen

weiter ['vaɪtər] *adj* wider; broader; farther (away); *(zusätzlich)* further ♦ *adv* further; **ohne ~es** without further ado; just like that; **~ nichts/niemand** nothing/nobody else; **~arbeiten** *vi* to go on working; **~bilden** *vr* to continue one's education; **~empfehlen** *(unreg) vt* to recommend (to others); **W~fahrt** *f* continuation of the journey; **~führen** *vi (Straße)* to lead on (to) ♦ *vt (fortsetzen)* to continue, carry on; **~gehen** *(unreg) vi* to go on; **~hin** *adv*: **etw ~hin tun** to go on doing sth; **~kommen** *(unreg) vi (fig: mit Arbeit)* to make progress; **~leiten** *vt* to pass on; **~machen** *vt, vi* to continue

weit- *zW*: **~gehend** *adj* considerable ♦ *adv* largely; **~läufig** *adj (Gebäude)* spacious; *(Erklärung)* lengthy; *(Verwandter)* distant; **~reichend** *adj* long-range; *(fig)* far-reaching; **~schweifig** *adj* long-winded; **~sichtig** *adj (MED)* long-sighted; *(fig)* far-sighted; **W~sprung** *m* long jump; **~verbreitet** *adj* widespread

Weizen ['vaɪtsən] *(-s, -) m* wheat

SCHLÜSSELWORT

welche(r, s) *interrogativ pron* which; **welcher von beiden?** which (one) of the two?; **welchen hast du genommen?** which (one) did you take?; **welche eine ...!** what a ...!; **welche Freude!** what joy!
♦ *indef pron* some; *(in Fragen)* any; **ich habe welche** I have some; **haben Sie welche?** do you have any?
♦ *relativ pron (bei Menschen)* who; *(bei Sachen)* which, that; **welche(r, s) auch immer** whoever/whichever/whatever

welk [vɛlk] *adj* withered; **~en** *vi* to wither

Welle ['vɛlə] *f* wave; *(TECH)* shaft

Wellen- *zW*: **~bereich** *m* waveband; **~länge** *f (auch fig)* wavelength; **~linie** *f* wavy line; **~sittich** *m* budgerigar

Welt [vɛlt] *(-, -en) f* world; **~all** *nt* universe; **~anschauung** *f* philosophy of life; **w~berühmt** *adj* world-famous; **~krieg** *m* world war; **w~lich** *adj* worldly; *(nicht kirchlich)* secular; **~macht** *f* world power; **~meister** *m* world champion; **~raum** *m* space; **~reise** *f* trip round the world; **~stadt** *f* metropolis; **w~weit** *adj* world-wide

wem [veːm] *(dat von wer) pron* to whom

wen [veːn] *(akk von wer) pron* whom

Wende ['vɛndə] *f* turn; *(Veränderung)* change; **~kreis** *m (GEOG)* tropic; *(AUT)* turning circle; **~ltreppe** *f* spiral staircase; **w~n** *(unreg) vt, vi, vr* to turn; **sich an jdn w~n** to go/come to sb

wendig ['vɛndɪç] *adj (Auto etc)* manœuvrable; *(fig)* agile

Wendung *f* turn; *(Redewendung)* idiom

wenig ['veːnɪç] *adj, adv* little; **~er** *adj* less; *(mit pl)* fewer ♦ *adv* less; **~ste(r, s)** *adj* least; **am ~sten** least; **~stens** *adv* at least

SCHLÜSSELWORT

wenn [vɛn] *konj* 1 *(falls, bei Wünschen)* if; **wenn auch ..., selbst wenn ...** even if ...; **wenn ich doch ...** if only I ...
2 *(zeitlich)* when; **immer wenn** whenever

wennschon ['vɛnʃoːn] *adv*: **na ~** so what?; **~, dennschon!** in for a penny, in for a pound

wer [veːr] *pron* who

Werbe- ['vɛrbə] *zW*: **~fernsehen** *nt* commercial television; **~geschenk** *nt* gift *(from company)*; *(zu Gekauftem)* free gift; **w~n** *(unreg) vt* to win; *(Mitglied)* to recruit ♦ *vi* to advertise; **um jdn/etw w~n** to try to win sb/sth; **für jdn/etw w~n** to promote sb/sth

Werbung f advertising; (von Mitgliedern) recruitment; **~ um jdn/etw** promotion of sb/sth

Werdegang ['veːɐdəgaŋ] m (Laufbahn) development; (beruflich) career

SCHLÜSSELWORT

werden ['veːɐdən] (pt **wurde**, pp **geworden** od (bei Passiv) **worden**) vi to become; **was ist aus ihm/aus der Sache geworden?** what became of him/it?; **es ist nichts/gut geworden** it came to nothing/turned out well; **es wird Nacht/Tag** it's getting dark/light; **mir wird kalt** I'm getting cold; **mir wird schlecht** I feel ill; **Erster werden** to come od be first; **das muss anders werden** that'll have to change; **rot/zu Eis werden** to turn red/to ice; **was willst du (mal) werden?** what do you want to be?; **die Fotos sind gut geworden** the photos have come out nicely

♦ als Hilfsverb **1** (bei Futur): **er wird es tun** he will od he'll do it; **er wird das nicht tun** he will not od he won't do it; **es wird gleich regnen** it's going to rain

2 (bei Konjunktiv): **ich würde ...** I would ...; **er würde gern ...** he would od he'd like to ...; **ich würde lieber ...** I would od I'd rather ...

3 (bei Vermutung): **sie wird in der Küche sein** she will be in the kitchen

4 (bei Passiv): **gebraucht werden** to be used; **er ist erschossen worden** he has od he's been shot; **mir wurde gesagt, dass ...** I was told that ...

werfen ['vɛrfən] (unreg) vt to throw

Werft [vɛrft] (-, -en) f shipyard, dockyard

Werk [vɛrk] (-(e)s, -e) nt work; (Tätigkeit) job; (Fabrik, Mechanismus) works pl; **ans ~ gehen** to set to work; **~statt** (-, **-stätten**) f workshop; (AUT) garage; **~tag** m working day; **w~tags** adv on working days; **w~tätig** adj working; **~zeug** nt tool

Wermut ['veːɐmuːt] (-(e)s) m wormwood;

(Wein) vermouth

Wert [veːɐt] (-(e)s, -e) m worth; (FIN) value; **~ legen auf** +akk to attach importance to; **es hat doch keinen ~** it's useless; **w~** adj worth; (geschätzt) dear; worthy; **das ist nichts/viel w~** it's not worth anything/it's worth a lot; **das ist es/er mir ~** it's/he's worth that to me; **~angabe** f declaration of value; **~brief** m registered letter (containing sth of value); **~en** vt to rate; **~gegenstände** mpl valuables; **w~los** adj worthless; **~papier** nt security; **w~voll** adj valuable

Wesen ['veːzən] (-s, -) nt (Geschöpf) being; (Natur, Charakter) nature; **w~tlich** adj significant; (beträchtlich) considerable

weshalb [vɛsˈhalp] adv why

Wespe ['vɛspə] f wasp

wessen ['vɛsən] (gen von **wer**) pron whose

Weste ['vɛstə] f waistcoat, vest (US); (Wollweste) cardigan

West- zW: **~en** (-s) m west; **~europa** nt Western Europe; **w~lich** adj western ♦ adv to the west

weswegen [vɛsˈveːgən] adv why

wett [vɛt] adj even; **W~bewerb** m competition; **W~e** f bet, wager; **~en** vt, vi to bet

Wetter ['vɛtɐ] (-s, -) nt weather; **~bericht** m weather report; **~dienst** m meteorological service; **~lage** f (weather) situation; **~vorhersage** f weather forecast; **~warte** f weather station

Wett- zW: **~kampf** m contest; **~lauf** m race; **w~machen** vt to make good

wichtig ['vɪçtɪç] adj important; **W~keit** f importance

wickeln ['vɪkəln] vt to wind; (Haare) to set; (Kind) to change; **jdn/etw in etw** akk **~** to wrap sb/sth in sth

Wickelraum m mothers' (and babies') room

Widder ['vɪdɐ] (-s, -) m ram; (ASTROL) Aries

wider ['viːdɐ] präp +akk against; **~'fahren** (unreg) vi to happen; **~legen** vt to refute

widerlich ['viːdɐlɪç] adj disgusting, repulsive

Spelling Reform: ▲ new spelling △ old spelling (to be phased out)

wider- ['viːdər] *zW:* **~rechtlich** *adj*
unlawful; **W~rede** *f* contradiction; **~'rufen**
(*unreg*) *vt insep* to retract; (*Anordnung*) to
revoke; (*Befehl*) to countermand; **~'setzen**
vr insep: **sich jdm/etw ~setzen** to oppose
sb/sth

widerspenstig ['viːdərʃpɛnstɪç] *adj* wilful

wider- ['viːdər] *zW:* **~spiegeln** *vt*
(*Entwicklung, Erscheinung*) to mirror, reflect
♦ *vr* to be reflected; **~'sprechen** (*unreg*) *vi*
insep: **jdm ~sprechen** to contradict sb

Widerspruch ['viːdərʃprʊx] *m*
contradiction; **w~slos** *adv* without arguing

Widerstand ['viːdərʃtant] *m* resistance

Widerstands- *zW:* **~bewegung** *f*
resistance (movement); **w~fähig** *adj*
resistant, tough; **w~los** *adj* unresisting

wider'stehen (*unreg*) *vi insep:* **jdm/etw ~**
to withstand sb/sth

wider- ['viːdər] *zW:* **~wärtig** *adj* nasty,
horrid; **W~wille** *m:* **W~wille (gegen)**
aversion (to); **~willig** *adj* unwilling,
reluctant

widmen ['vɪtmən] *vt* to dedicate; to devote
♦ *vr* to devote o.s.

widrig ['viːdrɪç] *adj* (*Umstände*) adverse

SCHLÜSSELWORT

wie [viː] *adv* how; **wie groß/schnell?** how
big/fast?; **wie wärs?** how about it?; **wie ist
er?** what's he like?; **wie gut du das
kannst!** you're very good at it; **wie bitte?**
pardon?; (*entrüstet*) I beg your pardon!;
und wie! and how!; **wie viel** how much;
wie viel Menschen how many people;
wie weit to what extent

♦ *konj* **1** (*bei Vergleichen*): **so schön wie ...**
as beautiful as ...; **wie ich schon sagte** as I
said; **wie du** like you; **singen wie ein ...** to
sing like a ...; **wie (zum Beispiel)** such as
(for example)

2 (*zeitlich*): **wie er das hörte, ging er**
when he heard that he left; **er hörte, wie
der Regen fiel** he heard the rain falling

---

wieder ['viːdər] *adv* again; **~ da sein** to be
back (again); **~ aufbereiten** to recycle; **~**
aufnehmen to resume; **~ erkennen** to
recognize; **~ gutmachen** to make up for;
(*Fehler*) to put right; **~ herstellen** (*Ruhe,
Frieden etc*) to restore; **~ vereinigen** to
reunite; (*POL*) to reunify; **~ verwerten** to
recycle; **gehst du schon ~?** are you off
again?; **~ ein(e) ...** another ...; **W~aufbau**
m rebuilding; **~bekommen** (*unreg*) *vt* to
get back; **W~gabe** *f* reproduction;
~geben (*unreg*) *vt* (*zurückgeben*) to return;
(*Erzählung etc*) to repeat; (*Gefühle etc*) to
convey; **W~'gutmachung** *f* reparation;
~'herstellen *vt* (*Gesundheit, Gebäude*) to
restore; **~'holen** *vt insep* to repeat;
W~'holung *f* repetition; **W~hören** *nt:* **auf
W~hören** (*TEL*) goodbye; **W~kehr** (*-*) *f*
return; (*von Vorfall*) repetition, recurrence;
~sehen (*unreg*) *vt* to see again; **auf
W~sehen** goodbye; **~um** *adv* again;
(*andererseits*) on the other hand;
W~vereinigung *f* (*POL*) reunification;
W~wahl *f* re-election

Wiege ['viːgə] *f* cradle; **w~n¹** *vt* (*schaukeln*)
to rock

wiegen² (*unreg*) *vt, vi* (*Gewicht*) to weigh

Wien [viːn] *nt* Vienna

Wiese ['viːzə] *f* meadow

Wiesel ['viːzəl] (*-s, -*) *nt* weasel

wieso [viːˈzoː] *adv* why

wieviel △ [viːˈfiːl] *adj siehe* **wie**

wievielmal [viːˈfiːlmaːl] *adv* how often

wievielte(r, s) *adj:* **zum ~n Mal?** how
many times?; **den W~n haben wir?** what's
the date?; **an ~r Stelle?** in what place?;
der ~ Besucher war er? how many
visitors were there before him?

wild [vɪlt] *adj* wild; **W~ (-(e)s)** *nt* game;
W~e(r) ['vɪldə(r)] *f(m)* savage; **~ern** *vi* to
poach; **~'fremd** (*umg*) *adj* quite strange *od*
unknown; **W~heit** *f* wildness; **W~leder** *nt*
suede; **W~nis** (*-, -se*) *f* wilderness;
W~schwein *nt* (wild) boar

will *etc* [vɪl] *vb siehe* **wollen**

Wille ['vɪlə] (*-ns, -n*) *m* will; **w~n** *präp +gen:*
um ... w~n for the sake of ...; **w~nsstark**
adj strong-willed

will- *zW:* **~ig** *adj* willing; **W~kommen**

[vɪl'kɔmən] **(-s, -)** *nt* welcome; **~kommen** *adj* welcome; **jdn ~kommen heißen** to welcome sb; **~kürlich** *adj* arbitrary; *(Bewegung)* voluntary

wimmeln ['vɪməln] *vi:* **~ (von)** to swarm (with)

wimmern ['vɪmərn] *vi* to whimper

Wimper ['vɪmpər] **(-, -n)** *f* eyelash

Wimperntusche *f* mascara

Wind [vɪnt] **(-(e)s, -e)** *m* wind; **~beutel** *m* cream puff; *(fig)* rake; **~e** *f (TECH)* winch, windlass; *(BOT)* bindweed; **~el** ['vɪndəl] **(-, -n)** *f* nappy, diaper *(US)*; **w~en** *vi unpers* to be windy ♦ *vt (unreg)* to wind; *(Kranz)* to weave; *(entwinden)* to twist ♦ *vr (unreg)* to wind; *(Person)* to writhe; **~energie** *f* wind energy; **w~ig** ['vɪndɪç] *adj* windy; *(fig)* dubious; **~jacke** *f* windcheater; **~mühle** *f* windmill; **~pocken** *pl* chickenpox *sg*; **~schutzscheibe** *f (AUT)* windscreen *(BRIT)*, windshield *(US)*; **~stärke** *f* wind force; **w~still** *adj (Tag)* still, windless; *(Platz)* sheltered; **~stille** *f* calm; **~stoß** *m* gust of wind

Wink [vɪŋk] **(-(e)s, -e)** *m (mit Hand)* wave; *(mit Kopf)* nod; *(Hinweis)* hint

Winkel ['vɪŋkəl] **(-s, -)** *m (MATH)* angle; *(Gerät)* set square; *(in Raum)* corner

winken ['vɪŋkən] *vt, vi* to wave

winseln ['vɪnzəln] *vi* to whine

Winter ['vɪntər] **(-s, -)** *m* winter; **w~fest** *adj (Pflanze)* hardy; **~garten** *m* conservatory; **w~lich** *adj* wintry; **~reifen** *m* winter tyre; **~sport** *m* winter sports *pl*

Winzer ['vɪntsər] **(-s, -)** *m* vine grower

winzig ['vɪntsɪç] *adj* tiny

Wipfel ['vɪpfəl] **(-s, -)** *m* treetop

wir [viːr] *pron* we; **~ alle** all of us, we all

Wirbel ['vɪrbəl] **(-s, -)** *m* whirl, swirl; *(Trubel)* hurly-burly; *(Aufsehen)* fuss; *(ANAT)* vertebra; **w~n** *vi* to whirl, to swirl; **~säule** *f* spine

wird [vɪrt] *vb siehe* **werden**

wirfst *etc* [vɪrfst] *vb siehe* **werfen**

wirken ['vɪrkən] *vi* to have an effect; *(erfolgreich sein)* to work; *(scheinen)* to seem ♦ *vt (Wunder)* to work

wirklich ['vɪrklɪç] *adj* real ♦ *adv* really;

W~keit *f* reality

wirksam ['vɪrkzaːm] *adj* effective

Wirkstoff *m (biologisch, chemisch, pflanzlich)* active substance

Wirkung ['vɪrkʊŋ] *f* effect; **w~slos** *adj* ineffective; **w~slos bleiben** to have no effect; **w~svoll** *adj* effective

wirr [vɪr] *adj* confused, wild; **W~warr (-s)** *m* disorder, chaos

wirst [vɪrst] *vb siehe* **werden**

Wirt(in) [vɪrt(ɪn)] **(-(e)s, -e)** *m(f)* landlord(lady); **~schaft** *f (Gaststätte)* pub; *(Haushalt)* housekeeping; *(eines Landes)* economy; *(umg: Durcheinander)* mess; **w~schaftlich** *adj* economical; *(POL)* economic

Wirtschafts- *zW:* **~krise** *f* economic crisis; **~politik** *f* economic policy; **~prüfer** *m* chartered accountant; **~wunder** *nt* economic miracle

Wirtshaus *nt* inn

wischen ['vɪʃən] *vt* to wipe

Wischer (-s, -) *m (AUT)* wiper

Wissbegier(de) ▲ ['vɪsbəgiːr(də)] *f* thirst for knowledge; **wissbegierig** ▲ *adj* inquisitive, eager for knowledge

wissen ['vɪsən] *(unreg) vt* to know; **was weiß ich!** I don't know!; **W~ (-s)** *nt* knowledge; **W~schaft** *f* science; **W~schaftler(in) (-s, -)** *m(f)* scientist; **~schaftlich** *adj* scientific; **~swert** *adj* worth knowing

wittern ['vɪtərn] *vt* to scent; *(fig)* to suspect

Witterung *f* weather; *(Geruch)* scent

Witwe ['vɪtvə] *f* widow; **~r (-s, -)** *m* widower

Witz [vɪts] **(-(e)s, -e)** *m* joke; **~bold (-(e)s, -e)** *m* joker, wit; **w~ig** *adj* funny

wo [voː] *adv* where; *(umg: irgendwo)* somewhere; **im Augenblick, ~ ...** the moment (that) ...; **die Zeit, ~ ...** the time when ...; **~anders** [voːˈandərs] *adv* elsewhere; **~bei** [-ˈbaɪ] *adv (relativ)* by/with which; *(interrogativ)* what ... in/by/with

Woche ['vɔxə] *f* week

Wochen- *zW:* **~ende** *nt* weekend; **w~lang** *adj, adv* for weeks; **~markt** *m* weekly market; **~schau** *f* newsreel

Spelling Reform: ▲ *new spelling* △ *old spelling (to be phased out)*

wöchentlich ['vϾçəntlɪç] adj, adv weekly

wodurch [vo'dʊrç] adv (relativ) through which; (interrogativ) what ... through

wofür [vo'fyːr] adv (relativ) for which; (interrogativ) what ... for

wog etc [voːk] vb siehe **wiegen**

wo- [voː] zW: **~'gegen** adv (relativ) against which; (interrogativ) what ... against; **~her** [-'heːr] adv where ... from; **~hin** [-'hɪn] adv where ... to

---
SCHLÜSSELWORT
---

wohl [voːl] adv 1: **sich wohl fühlen** (zufrieden) to feel happy; (gesundheitlich) to feel well; **jdm wohl tun** to do sb good; **wohl oder übel** whether one likes it or not 2 (wahrscheinlich) probably; (gewiss) certainly; (vielleicht) perhaps; **sie ist wohl zu Hause** she's probably at home; **das ist doch wohl nicht dein Ernst!** surely you're not serious!; **das mag wohl sein** that may well be; **ob das wohl stimmt?** I wonder if that's true; **er weiß das sehr wohl** he knows that perfectly well

Wohl [voːl] (-(e)s) nt welfare; **zum ~!** cheers!; **w~auf** adv well; **~behagen** nt comfort; **~fahrt** f welfare; **~fahrtsstaat** m welfare state; **w~habend** adj wealthy; **w~ig** adj contented, comfortable; **w~schmeckend** adj delicious; **~stand** m prosperity; **~standsgesellschaft** f affluent society; **~tat** f relief; act of charity; **~täter(in)** m(f) benefactor; **w~tätig** adj charitable; **~tätigkeits-** zW charity, charitable; **w~tun** (unreg) vi △ siehe **wohl**; **w~verdient** adj well-earned, well-deserved; **w~weislich** adv prudently; **~wollen** (-s) nt good will; **w~wollend** adj benevolent

wohn- ['voːn] zW: **~en** vi to live; **W~gemeinschaft** f (Menschen) people sharing a flat; **~haft** adj resident; **W~heim** nt (für Studenten) hall of residence; (für Senioren) home; (bes für Arbeiter) hostel; **~lich** adj comfortable; **W~mobil** (-s, -e) nt camper; **W~ort** m domicile; **W~sitz** m

place of residence; **W~ung** f house; (Etagenwohnung) flat, apartment (US); **W~wagen** m caravan; **W~zimmer** nt living room

wölben ['vœlbən] vt, vr to curve

Wolf [vɔlf] (-(e)s, ᵘe) m wolf

Wolke ['vɔlkə] f cloud; **~nkratzer** m skyscraper; **wolkig** ['vɔlkɪç] adj cloudy

Wolle ['vɔlə] f wool; **w~n¹** adj woollen

SCHLÜSSELWORT
---

wollen² ['vɔlən] (pt **wollte**, pp **gewollt** od (als Hilfsverb) **wollen**) vt, vi to want; **ich will nach Hause** I want to go home; **er will nicht** he doesn't want to; **er wollte das nicht** he didn't want it; **wenn du willst** if you like; **ich will, dass du mir zuhörst** I want you to listen to me ♦ Hilfsverb: **er will ein Haus kaufen** he wants to buy a house; **ich wollte, ich wäre ...** I wish I were ...; **etw gerade tun wollen** to be going to do sth

wollüstig ['vɔlʏstɪç] adj lusty, sensual

wo- zW: **~mit** adv (relativ) with which; (interrogativ) what ... with; **~möglich** adv probably, I suppose; **~nach** adv (relativ) after/for which; (interrogativ) what ... for/after; **~ran** adv (relativ) on/at which; (interrogativ) what ... on/at; **~rauf** adv (relativ) on which; (interrogativ) what ... on; **~raus** adv (relativ) from/out of which; (interrogativ) what ... from/out of; **~rin** adv (relativ) in which; (interrogativ) what ... in

Wort [vɔrt] (-(e)s, ᵘer od -e) nt word; **jdn beim ~ nehmen** to take sb at his word; **mit anderen ~en** in other words; **w~brüchig** adj not true to one's word

Wörterbuch ['vœrtərbuːx] nt dictionary

Wort- zW: **~führer** m spokesman; **w~karg** adj taciturn; **~laut** m wording

wörtlich ['vœrtlɪç] adj literal

Wort- zW: **w~los** adj mute; **w~reich** adj wordy, verbose; **~schatz** m vocabulary; **~spiel** nt play on words, pun

wo- zW: **~rüber** adv (relativ) over/about which; (interrogativ) what ... over/about;

~rum *adv* (*relativ*) about/round which; (*interrogativ*) what ... about/round; **~runter** *adv* (*relativ*) under which; (*interrogativ*) what ... under; **~von** *adv* (*relativ*) from which; (*interrogativ*) what ... from; **~vor** *adv* (*relativ*) in front of/before which; (*interrogativ*) in front of/before what; of what; **~zu** *adv* (*relativ*) to/for which; (*interrogativ*) what ... for/to; (*warum*) why

Wrack [vrak] (-(e)s, -s) *nt* wreck

Wucher ['vuːxər] (-s) *m* profiteering; **~er** (-s, -) *m* profiteer; **w~isch** *adj* profiteering; **w~n** *vi* (*Pflanzen*) to grow wild; **~ung** *f* (*MED*) growth, tumour

Wuchs [vuːks] (-es) *m* (*Wachstum*) growth; (*Statur*) build

Wucht [voxt] (-) *f* force

wühlen ['vyːlən] *vi* to scrabble; (*Tier*) to root; (*Maulwurf*) to burrow; (*umg: arbeiten*) to slave away ♦ *vt* to dig

Wulst [volst] (-es, ᵉe) *m* bulge; (*an Wunde*) swelling

wund [vont] *adj* sore, raw; **W~e** *f* wound

Wunder ['vondər] (-s, -) *nt* miracle; **es ist kein ~** it's no wonder; **w~bar** *adj* wonderful, marvellous; **~kerze** *f* sparkler; **~kind** *nt* infant prodigy; **w~lich** *adj* odd, peculiar; **w~n** *vr* to be surprised ♦ *vt* to surprise; **sich w~n über** +*akk* to be surprised at; **w~schön** *adj* beautiful; **w~voll** *adj* wonderful

Wundstarrkrampf ['vontʃtarkrampf] *m* tetanus, lockjaw

Wunsch [vonʃ] (-(e)s, ᵉe) *m* wish

wünschen ['vynʃən] *vt* to wish; **sich** *dat* **etw ~** to want sth, to wish for sth; **~swert** *adj* desirable

wurde *etc* ['vordə] *vb siehe* **werden**

Würde ['vyrdə] *f* dignity; (*Stellung*) honour; **w~voll** *adj* dignified

würdig ['vyrdıç] *adj* worthy; (*würdevoll*) dignified; **~en** *vt* to appreciate

Wurf [vorf] (-s, ᵉe) *m* throw; (*Junge*) litter

Würfel ['vyrfəl] (-s, -) *m* dice; (*MATH*) cube; **~becher** *m* (dice) cup; **w~n** *vi* to play dice ♦ *vt* to dice; **~zucker** *m* lump sugar

würgen ['vyrgən] *vt*, *vi* to choke

Wurm [vorm] (-(e)s, ᵉer) *m* worm; **w~stichig** *adj* worm-ridden

Wurst [vorst] (-, ᵉe) *f* sausage; **das ist mir ~** (*umg*) I don't care, I don't give a damn

Würstchen ['vyrstçən] *nt* sausage

Würze ['vyrtsə] *f* seasoning, spice

Wurzel ['vortsəl] (-, -n) *f* root

würzen ['vyrtsən] *vt* to season, to spice

würzig *adj* spicy

wusch *etc* [voʃ] *vb siehe* **waschen**

wusste ▲ *etc* ['vostə] *vb siehe* **wissen**

wüst [vyːst] *adj* untidy, messy; (*ausschweifend*) wild; (*öde*) waste; (*umg: heftig*) terrible; **W~e** *f* desert

Wut [vuːt] (-) *f* rage, fury; **~anfall** *m* fit of rage

wüten ['vyːtən] *vi* to rage; **~d** *adj* furious, mad

X, x

X-Beine ['ıksbaınə] *pl* knock-knees

x-beliebig [ıksbə'liːbıç] *adj* any (whatever)

xerokopieren [kseroko'piːrən] *vt* to xerox, to photocopy

x-mal ['ıksmaːl] *adv* any number of times, n times

Xylofon ▲, **Xylophon** [ksylo'foːn] (-s, -e) *nt* xylophone

Y, y

Yacht (-, -en) *f siehe* **Jacht**

Ypsilon ['ypsilɔn] (-(s), -s) *nt* the letter Y

Z, z

Zacke ['tsakə] *f* point; (*Bergzacke*) jagged peak; (*Gabelzacke*) prong; (*Kammzacke*) tooth

zackig ['tsakıç] *adj* jagged; (*umg*) smart; (*Tempo*) brisk

zaghaft ['tsaːkhaft] *adj* timid

zäh [tsɛː] *adj* tough; (*Mensch*) tenacious;

Spelling Reform: ▲ *new spelling* △ *old spelling (to be phased out)*

(*Flüssigkeit*) thick; (*schleppend*) sluggish;
Z~igkeit f toughness; tenacity
Zahl [tsaːl] (-, **-en**) f number; **z~bar** adj
payable; **z~en** vt, vi to pay; **z~en bitte!** the
bill please!
zählen ['tsɛːlən] vt, vi to count; **~ auf** +*akk*
to count on; **~ zu** to be numbered among
Zahlenschloss ▲ nt combination lock
Zähler ['tsɛːlər] (-s, -) m (*TECH*) meter;
(*MATH*) numerator
Zahl- zW: **z~los** adj countless; **z~reich** adj
numerous; **~tag** m payday; **~ung** f
payment; **~ungsanweisung** f giro
transfer order; **z~ungsfähig** adj solvent;
~wort nt numeral
zahm [tsaːm] adj tame
zähmen ['tsɛːmən] vt to tame; (*fig*) to curb
Zahn [tsaːn] (-(e)s, ⸚e) m tooth; **~arzt** m
dentist; **~ärztin** f (female) dentist;
~bürste f toothbrush; **~fleisch** nt gums
pl; **~pasta** f toothpaste; **~rad** nt
cog(wheel); **~schmerzen** pl toothache sg;
~stein m tartar; **~stocher** (-s, -) m
toothpick
Zange ['tsaŋə] f pliers pl; (*Zuckerzange etc*)
tongs pl; (*Beißzange, ZOOL*) pincers pl; (*MED*)
forceps pl
zanken ['tsaŋkən] vi, vr to quarrel
zänkisch ['tsɛŋkɪʃ] adj quarrelsome
Zäpfchen ['tsɛpfçən] nt (*ANAT*) uvula; (*MED*)
suppository
Zapfen ['tsapfən] (-s, -) m plug; (*BOT*) cone;
(*Eiszapfen*) icicle
zappeln ['tsapəln] vi to wriggle; to fidget
zart [tsart] adj (*weich, leise*) soft; (*Fleisch*)
tender; (*fein, schwächlich*) delicate; **Z~heit** f
softness; tenderness; delicacy
zärtlich ['tsɛːrtlɪç] adj tender, affectionate
Zauber ['tsaubər] (-s, -) m magic; (*~bann*)
spell; **~ei** [-'raɪ] f magic; **~er** (-s, -) m
magician; conjuror; **z~haft** adj magical,
enchanting; **~künstler** m conjuror;
~kunststück nt conjuring trick; **z~n** vi to
conjure, to practise magic
zaudern ['tsaudərn] vi to hesitate
Zaum [tsaum] (-(e)s, **Zäume**) m bridle; **etw
im ~ halten** to keep sth in check

Zaun [tsaun] (-(e)s, **Zäune**) m fence
z. B. abk (= *zum Beispiel*) e.g.
Zebra ['tseːbra] nt zebra; **~streifen** m zebra
crossing
Zeche ['tsɛçə] f (*Rechnung*) bill; (*Bergbau*)
mine
Zeh [tseː] (-s, **-en**) m toe
Zehe ['tseːə] f toe; (*Knoblauchzehe*) clove
zehn [tseːn] num ten; **~te(r, s)** adj tenth;
Z~tel (-s, -) nt tenth (part)
Zeich- ['tsaɪç] zW: **~en** (-s, -) nt sign;
z~nen vt to draw; (*kennzeichnen*) to mark;
(*unterzeichnen*) to sign ♦ vi to draw; to sign;
~ner (-s, -) m artist; **technischer ~ner**
draughtsman; **~nung** f drawing;
(*Markierung*) markings pl
Zeige- ['tsaɪgə] zW: **~finger** m index finger;
z~n vt to show ♦ vi to point ♦ vr to show
o.s.; **z~n auf** +*akk* to point to; to point at;
es wird sich z~n time will tell; **es zeigte
sich, dass ...** it turned out that ...; **~r** (-s,
-) m pointer; (*Uhrzeiger*) hand
Zeile ['tsaɪlə] f line; (*Häuserzeile*) row
Zeit [tsaɪt] (-, **-en**) f time; (*GRAM*) tense; **sich
dat ~ lassen** to take one's time; **von ~ zu ~**
from time to time; **siehe zurzeit**; **~alter** nt
age; **~ansage** f (*TEL*) speaking clock;
~arbeit f (*COMM*) temporary job;
z~gemäß adj in keeping with the times;
~genosse m contemporary; **z~ig** adj
early; **z~lich** adj temporal; **~lupe** f slow
motion; **z~raubend** adj time-consuming;
~raum m period; **~rechnung** f time, era;
nach/vor unserer ~rechnung A.D./B.C.;
~schrift f periodical; **~ung** f newspaper;
~vertreib m pastime, diversion; **z~weilig**
adj temporary; **z~weise** adv for a time;
~wort nt verb
Zelle ['tsɛlə] f cell; (*Telefonzelle*) callbox
Zellstoff m cellulose
Zelt [tsɛlt] (-(e)s, -e) nt tent; **z~en** vi to
camp; **~platz** m camp site
Zement [tse'mɛnt] (-(e)s, -e) m cement;
z~ieren vt to cement
zensieren [tsɛn'ziːrən] vt to censor; (*SCH*) to
mark
Zensur [tsɛn'zuːr] f censorship; (*SCH*) mark

Zentimeter [tsɛntiˈmeːtər] *m od nt* centimetre

Zentner [ˈtsɛntnər] (**-s, -**) *m* hundredweight

zentral [tsɛnˈtraːl] *adj* central; **Z~e** *f* central office; (*TEL*) exchange; **Z~heizung** *f* central heating

Zentrum [ˈtsɛntrʊm] (**-s, Zentren**) *nt* centre

zerbrechen [tsɛrˈbrɛçən] (*unreg*) *vt, vi* to break

zerbrechlich *adj* fragile

zer'drücken *vt* to squash, to crush; (*Kartoffeln*) to mash

Zeremonie [tseremoˈniː] *f* ceremony

Zerfall [tsɛrˈfal] *m* decay; **z~en** (*unreg*) *vi* to disintegrate, to decay; (*sich gliedern*): **z~en (in** +*akk*) to fall (into)

zer'gehen (*unreg*) *vi* to melt, to dissolve

zerkleinern [tsɛrˈklaɪnərn] *vt* to reduce to small pieces

zerlegbar [tsɛrˈleːkbaːr] *adj* able to be dismantled

zerlegen [tsɛrˈleːgən] *vt* to take to pieces; (*Fleisch*) to carve; (*Satz*) to analyse

zermürben [tsɛrˈmʏrbən] *vt* to wear down

zerquetschen [tsɛrˈkvɛtʃən] *vt* to squash

zer'reißen (*unreg*) *vt* to tear to pieces ♦ *vi* to tear, to rip

zerren [ˈtsɛrən] *vt* to drag ♦ *vi*: **~ (an** +*dat*) to tug (at)

zer'rinnen (*unreg*) *vi* to melt away

zerrissen [tsɛrˈrɪsən] *adj* torn, tattered; **Z~heit** *f* tattered state; (*POL*) disunion, discord; (*innere Z~heit*) disintegration

Zerrung *f* (*MED*): **eine ~** pulled muscle

zerrütten [tsɛrˈrʏtən] *vt* to wreck, to destroy

zer'schlagen (*unreg*) *vt* to shatter, to smash ♦ *vr* to fall through

zer'schneiden (*unreg*) *vt* to cut up

zer'setzen *vt, vr* to decompose, to dissolve

zer'springen (*unreg*) *vi* to shatter, to burst

Zerstäuber [tsɛrˈʃtɔybər] (**-s, -**) *m* atomizer

zerstören [tsɛrˈʃtøːrən] *vt* to destroy

Zerstörung *f* destruction

zerstreu- [tsɛrˈʃtrɔy] *zW*: **~en** *vt* to disperse, to scatter; (*unterhalten*) to divert; (*Zweifel etc*) to dispel ♦ *vr* to disperse, to scatter; to be dispelled; **~t** *adj* scattered; (*Mensch*)

absent-minded; **Z~theit** *f* absent-mindedness; **Z~ung** *f* dispersion; (*Ablenkung*) diversion

zerstückeln [tsɛrˈʃtʏkəln] *vt* to cut into pieces

zer'teilen *vt* to divide into parts

Zertifikat [tsɛrtifiˈkaːt] (**-(e)s, -e**) *nt* certificate

zer'treten (*unreg*) *vt* to crush underfoot

zertrümmern [tsɛrˈtrʏmərn] *vt* to shatter; (*Gebäude etc*) to demolish

Zettel [ˈtsɛtəl] (**-s, -**) *m* piece of paper, slip; (*Notizzettel*) note; (*Formular*) form

Zeug [tsɔyk] (**-(e)s, -e**) (*umg*) *nt* stuff; (*Ausrüstung*) gear; **dummes ~** (stupid) nonsense; **das ~ haben zu** to have the makings of; **sich ins ~ legen** to put one's shoulder to the wheel

Zeuge [ˈtsɔygə] (**-n, -n**) *m* witness; **z~n** *vi* to bear witness, to testify ♦ *vt* (*Kind*) to father; **es zeugt von ...** it testifies to ...; **~naussage** *f* evidence; **Zeugin** [ˈtsɔygɪn] *f* witness

Zeugnis [ˈtsɔygnɪs] (**-ses, -se**) *nt* certificate; (*SCH*) report; (*Referenz*) reference; (*Aussage*) evidence, testimony; **~ geben von** to be evidence of, to testify to

z. H(d). *abk* (= *zu Händen*) attn.

Zickzack [ˈtsɪktsak] (**-(e)s, -e**) *m* zigzag

Ziege [ˈtsiːgə] *f* goat

Ziegel [ˈtsiːgəl] (**-s, -**) *m* brick; (*Dachziegel*) tile

ziehen [ˈtsiːən] (*unreg*) *vt* to draw; (*zerren*) to pull; (*SCHACH etc*) to move; (*züchten*) to rear ♦ *vi* to draw; (*umziehen, wandern*) to move; (*Rauch, Wolke etc*) to drift; (*reißen*) to pull ♦ *vb unpers*: **es zieht** there is a draught, it's draughty ♦ *vr* (*Gummi*) to stretch; (*Grenze etc*) to run; (*Gespräche*) to be drawn out; **etw nach sich ~** to lead to sth, to entail sth

Ziehung [ˈtsiːʊŋ] *f* (*Losziehung*) drawing

Ziel [tsiːl] (**-(e)s, -e**) *nt* (*einer Reise*) destination; (*SPORT*) finish; (*MIL*) target; (*Absicht*) goal; **z~bewusst** ▲ *adj* decisive; **z~en** *vi*: **z~en (auf** +*akk*) to aim (at); **z~los** *adj* aimless; **~scheibe** *f* target; **z~strebig**

adj purposeful

ziemlich ['tsi:mlɪç] *adj* quite a; fair ♦ *adv* rather; quite a bit

zieren ['tsi:rən] *vr* to act coy

zierlich ['tsi:rlɪç] *adj* dainty

Ziffer ['tsɪfər] (-, -n) *f* figure, digit; ~**blatt** *nt* dial, clock-face

zig [tsɪk] (*umg*) *adj* umpteen

Zigarette [tsɪga'retə] *f* cigarette

Zigaretten- *zW*: ~**automat** *m* cigarette machine; ~**schachtel** *f* cigarette packet; ~**spitze** *f* cigarette holder

Zigarre [tsɪ'garə] *f* cigar

Zigeuner(in) [tsɪ'gɔynər(ɪn)] (-s, -) *m(f)* gipsy

Zimmer ['tsɪmər] (-s, -) *nt* room; ~**lautstärke** *f* reasonable volume; ~**mädchen** *nt* chambermaid; ~**mann** *m* carpenter; **z~n** *vt* to make (from wood); ~**nachweis** *m* accommodation office; ~**pflanze** *f* indoor plant; ~**service** *m* room service

zimperlich ['tsɪmpərlɪç] *adj* squeamish; (*pingelig*) fussy, finicky

Zimt [tsɪmt] (-(e)s, -e) *m* cinnamon

Zink [tsɪŋk] (-(e)s) *nt* zinc

Zinn [tsɪn] (-(e)s) *nt* (*Element*) tin; (*in ~waren*) pewter; ~**soldat** *m* tin soldier

Zins [tsɪns] (-es, -en) *m* interest; ~**eszins** *m* compound interest; ~**fuß** *m* rate of interest; **z~los** *adj* interest-free; ~**satz** *m* rate of interest

Zipfel ['tsɪpfəl] (-s, -) *m* corner; (*spitz*) tip; (*Hemdzipfel*) tail; (*Wurstzipfel*) end

zirka ['tsɪrka] *adv* (round) about

Zirkel ['tsɪrkəl] *m* circle; (*MATH*) pair of compasses

Zirkus ['tsɪrkʊs] (-, -se) *m* circus

zischen ['tsɪʃən] *vi* to hiss

Zitat [tsi'ta:t] (-(e)s, -e) *nt* quotation, quote

zitieren [tsi'ti:rən] *vt* to quote

Zitrone [tsi'tro:nə] *f* lemon; ~**nlimonade** *f* lemonade; ~**nsaft** *m* lemon juice

zittern ['tsɪtərn] *vi* to tremble

zivil [tsi'vi:l] *adj* civil; (*Preis*) moderate; **Z~** (-s) *nt* plain clothes *pl*; (*MIL*) civilian clothing; **Z~courage** *f* courage of one's convictions;

Z~dienst *m* community service; **Z~isation** [tsivilizatsi'o:n] *f* civilization; **Z~isationskrankheit** *f* disease peculiar to civilization; ~**i'sieren** *vt* to civilize

---

Zivildienst

i A young German has to complete his 13 months' **Zivildienst** or service to the community if he has opted out of military service as a conscientious objector. This is usually done in a hospital or old people's home. About 18% of young Germans choose to do this as an alternative to the **Wehrdienst**.

Zivilist [tsivi'lɪst] *m* civilian

zögern ['tsø:gərn] *vi* to hesitate

Zoll [tsɔl] (-(e)s, ⁻e) *m* customs *pl*; (*Abgabe*) duty; ~**abfertigung** *f* customs clearance; ~**amt** *nt* customs office; ~**beamte(r)** *m* customs official; ~**erklärung** *f* customs declaration; **z~frei** *adj* duty-free; ~**kontrolle** *f* customs check; **z~pflichtig** *adj* liable to duty, dutiable

Zone ['tso:nə] *f* zone

Zoo [tso:] (-s, -s) *m* zoo; ~**loge** [tsoo'lo:gə] (-n, -n) *m* zoologist; ~**lo'gie** *f* zoology; **z~logisch** *adj* zoological

Zopf [tsɔpf] (-(e)s, ⁻e) *m* plait; pigtail; **alter ~** antiquated custom

Zorn [tsɔrn] (-(e)s) *m* anger; **z~ig** *adj* angry

zottig ['tsɔtɪç] *adj* shaggy

z. T. *abk* = **zum Teil**

SCHLÜSSELWORT

zu [tsu:] *präp +dat* **1** (*örtlich*) to; **zum Bahnhof/Arzt gehen** to go to the station/ doctor; **zur Schule/Kirche gehen** to go to school/church; **sollen wir zu euch gehen?** shall we go to your place?; **sie sah zu ihm hin** she looked towards him; **zum Fenster herein** through the window; **zu meiner Linken** to *od* on my left

2 (*zeitlich*) at; **zu Ostern** at Easter; **bis zum 1. Mai** until May 1st; (*nicht später als*) by May 1st; **zu meiner Zeit** in my time

3 (*Zusatz*) with; **Wein zum Essen trinken**

---

to drink wine with one's meal; **sich zu jdm setzen** to sit down beside sb; **setz dich doch zu uns** (come and) sit with us; **Anmerkungen zu etw** notes on sth 4 (*Zweck*) for; **Wasser zum Waschen** water for washing; **Papier zum Schreiben** paper to write on; **etw zum Geburtstag bekommen** to get sth for one's birthday 5 (*Veränderung*) into; **zu etw werden** to turn into sth; **jdn zu etw machen** to make sb (into) sth; **zu Asche verbrennen** to burn to ashes 6 (*mit Zahlen*): **3 zu 2** (*SPORT*) 3-2; **das Stück zu 2 Mark** at 2 marks each; **zum ersten Mal** for the first time 7: **zu meiner Freude** *etc* to my joy *etc*; **zum Glück** luckily; **zu Fuß** on foot; **es ist zum Weinen** it's enough to make you cry ♦ *konj* to; **etw zu essen** sth to eat; **um besser sehen zu können** in order to see better; **ohne es zu wissen** without knowing it; **noch zu bezahlende Rechnungen** bills that are still to be paid ♦ *adv* 1 (*allzu*) too; **zu sehr** too much; **zu viel** too much; **zu wenig** too little 2 (*örtlich*) toward(s); **er kam auf mich zu** he came up to me 3 (*geschlossen*) shut, closed; **die Geschäfte haben zu** the shops are closed; „**auf/zu**" (*Wasserhahn etc*) "on/off" 4 (*umg: los*): **nur zu!** just keep on!; **mach zu!** hurry up!

zualler- [tsuʔalər] *zW*: **~erst** [-ʔeːrst] *adv* first of all; **~letzt** [-ʔletst] *adv* last of all
Zubehör ['tsuːbəhøːr] (**-(e)s, -e**) *nt* accessories *pl*
zubereiten ['tsuːbəraitən] *vt* to prepare
zubilligen ['tsuːbiligən] *vt* to grant
zubinden ['tsuːbindən] (*unreg*) *vt* to tie up
zubringen ['tsuːbriŋən] (*unreg*) *vt* (*Zeit*) to spend
Zubringer (**-s, -**) *m* (*Straße*) approach *od* slip road
Zucchini [tsuˈkiːniː] *pl* (*BOT, KOCH*) courgette (*BRIT*), zucchini (*US*)
Zucht [tsuxt] (**-, -en**) *f* (*von Tieren*) breeding;

(*von Pflanzen*) cultivation; (*Rasse*) breed; (*Erziehung*) raising; (*Disziplin*) discipline
züchten ['tsʏçtən] *vt* (*Tiere*) to breed; (*Pflanzen*) to cultivate, to grow; **Züchter** (**-s, -**) *m* breeder; grower
Zuchthaus *nt* prison, penitentiary (*US*)
züchtigen ['tsʏçtigən] *vt* to chastise
Züchtung *f* (*Zuchtart, Sorte: von Tier*) breed; (*: von Pflanze*) variety
zucken ['tsukən] *vi* to jerk, to twitch; (*Strahl etc*) to flicker ♦ *vt* (*Schultern*) to shrug
Zucker ['tsukər] (**-s, -**) *m* sugar; (*MED*) diabetes; **~guss** ▲ *m* icing; **z~krank** *adj* diabetic; **~krankheit** *f* (*MED*) diabetes; **z~n** *vt* to sugar; **~rohr** *nt* sugar cane; **~rübe** *f* sugar beet
Zuckung ['tsukuŋ] *f* convulsion, spasm; (*leicht*) twitch
zudecken ['tsuːdɛkən] *vt* to cover (up)
zudem [tsuˈdeːm] *adv* in addition (to this)
zudringlich ['tsuːdriŋliç] *adj* forward, pushing, obtrusive
zudrücken ['tsuːdrʏkən] *vt* to close; **ein Auge ~** to turn a blind eye
zueinander [tsuʔaiˈnandər] *adv* to one other; (*in Veranbindung*) together
zuerkennen ['tsuːʔɛrkɛnən] (*unreg*) *vt* to award; **jdm etw ~** to award sth to sb, to award sb sth
zuerst [tsuˈʔeːrst] *adv* first; (*zu Anfang*) at first; **~ einmal** first of all
Zufahrt ['tsuːfaːrt] *f* approach; **~sstraße** *f* approach road; (*von Autobahn etc*) slip road
Zufall ['tsuːfal] *m* chance; (*Ereignis*) coincidence; **durch ~** by accident; **so ein ~** what a coincidence; **z~en** (*unreg*) *vi* to close, to shut; (*Anteil, Aufgabe*) to fall
zufällig ['tsuːfɛliç] *adj* chance ♦ *adv* by chance; (*in Frage*) by any chance
Zuflucht ['tsuːfluxt] *f* recourse; (*Ort*) refuge
zufolge [tsuˈfɔlgə] *präp* (*+dat od gen*) judging by; (*laut*) according to
zufrieden [tsuˈfriːdən] *adj* content(ed), satisfied; **~ geben** to be content *od* satisfied (with); **~ stellen** to satisfy
zufrieren ['tsuːfriːrən] (*unreg*) *vi* to freeze up *od* over

Spelling Reform: ▲ *new spelling* △ *old spelling (to be phased out)*

zufügen ['tsuːfyːɡən] vt to add; (Leid etc): (jdm) etw ~ to cause (sb) sth

Zufuhr ['tsuːfuːr] (-, -en) f (Herbeibringen) supplying; (MET) influx

Zug [tsuːk] (-(e)s, ⸚e) m (EISENB) train; (Luftzug) draught; (Ziehen) pull(ing); (Gesichtszug) feature; (SCHACH etc) move; (Schriftzug) stroke; (Atemzug) breath; (Charakterzug) trait; (an Zigarette) puff, pull, drag; (Schluck) gulp; (Menschengruppe) procession; (von Vögeln) flight; (MIL) platoon; **etw in vollen Zügen genießen** to enjoy sth to the full

Zu- ['tsuː] zW: ~**gabe** f extra; (in Konzert etc) encore; ~**gang** m access, approach; **z~gänglich** adj accessible; (Mensch) approachable

zugeben ['tsuːɡeːbən] (unreg) vt (beifügen) to add, to throw in; (zugestehen) to admit; (erlauben) to permit

zugehen ['tsuːɡeːən] (unreg) vi (schließen) to shut; **es geht dort seltsam zu** there are strange goings-on there; **auf jdn/etw ~** to walk towards sb/sth; **dem Ende ~** to be finishing

Zugehörigkeit ['tsuːɡəhøːrɪçkaɪt] f: ~ **(zu)** membership (of), belonging (to)

Zügel ['tsyːɡəl] (-s, -) m rein(s); (fig) curb; **z~n** vt to curb; (Pferd) to rein in

zuge- ['tsuːɡə] zW: **Z~ständnis** (-ses, -se) nt concession; ~**stehen** (unreg) vt to admit; (Rechte) to concede

Zugführer m (EISENB) guard

zugig ['tsuːɡɪç] adj draughty

zügig ['tsyːɡɪç] adj speedy, swift

zugreifen ['tsuːɡraɪfən] (unreg) vi to seize or grab at; (helfen) to help; (beim Essen) to help o.s.

Zugrestaurant nt dining car

zugrunde, zu Grunde [tsuːˈɡrʊndə] adv: ~ **gehen** to collapse; (Mensch) to perish; **einer Sache** dat etw ~ **legen** to base sth on sth; **einer Sache** dat ~ **liegen** to be based on sth; ~ **richten** to ruin, to destroy

zugunsten, zu Gunsten [tsuːˈɡʊnstən] präp (+gen od dat) in favour of

zugute [tsuːˈɡuːtə] adv: **jdm etw ~ halten** to concede sth to sb; **jdm ~ kommen** to be of assistance to sb

Zugvogel m migratory bird

zuhalten ['tsuːhaltən] (unreg) vt to keep closed ♦ vi: **auf jdn/etw ~** to make a beeline for sb/sth

Zuhälter ['tsuːhɛltər] (-s, -) m pimp

Zuhause ['tsuːhauzə] (-) nt home

zuhause [tsuːˈhauzə] adv (österreichisch, schweizerisch) at home

zuhören ['tsuːhøːrən] vi to listen

Zuhörer (-s, -) m listener

zukleben ['tsuːkleːbən] vt to paste up

zukommen ['tsuːkɔmən] (unreg) vi to come up; **auf jdn ~** to come up to sb; **jdm etw ~ lassen** to give sb sth; **etw auf sich ~ lassen** to wait and see; **jdm ~** (sich gehören) to be fitting for sb

Zukunft ['tsuːkʊnft] (-, Zukünfte) f future; **zukünftig** ['tsuːkʏnftɪç] adj future ♦ adv in future; **mein zukünftiger Mann** my husband to be

Zulage ['tsuːlaːɡə] f bonus

zulassen ['tsuːlasən] (unreg) vt (hereinlassen) to admit; (erlauben) to permit; (Auto) to license; (umg: nicht öffnen) to (keep) shut

zulässig ['tsuːlɛsɪç] adj permissible, permitted

Zulassung f (amtlich) authorization; (von Kfz) licensing

zulaufen ['tsuːlaufən] (unreg) vi (subj: Mensch): ~ **auf jdn/etw** to run up to sb/sth; (: Straße): ~ **auf** to lead towards

zuleide, zu Leide [tsuːˈlaɪdə] adv: **jdm etw ~ tun** to hurt od harm sb

zuletzt [tsuːˈlɛtst] adv finally, at last

zuliebe [tsuːˈliːbə] adv: **jdm ~** to please sb

zum [tsʊm] = **zu dem**; ~ **dritten Mal** for the third time; ~ **Scherz** as a joke; ~ **Trinken** for drinking

zumachen ['tsuːmaxən] vt to shut; (Kleidung) to do up, to fasten ♦ vi to shut; (umg) to hurry up

zu- zW: ~**mal** [tsuːˈmaːl] konj especially (as); ~**meist** [tsuːˈmaɪst] adv mostly; ~**mindest** [tsuːˈmɪndəst] adv at least

---

Rechtschreibreform: ▲ *neue Schreibung* △ *alte Schreibung (auslaufend)*

zumutbar ['tsuːmuːtbaːr] *adj* reasonable

zumute, zu Mute [tsuˈmuːtə] *adv*: **wie ist ihm ~?** how does he feel?

zumuten ['tsuːmuːtən] *vt*: **(jdm) etw ~** to expect *od* ask sth (of sb)

Zumutung ['tsuːmuːtʊŋ] *f* unreasonable expectation *od* demand, impertinence

zunächst [tsuˈnɛːçst] *adv* first of all; **~ einmal** to start with

Zunahme ['tsuːnaːmə] *f* increase

Zuname ['tsuːnaːmə] *m* surname

Zünd- [tsʏnd] *zW*: **z~en** *vi* (*Feuer*) to light, to ignite; (*Motor*) to fire; (*begeistern*): **bei jdm z~en** to fire sb (with enthusiasm); **z~end** *adj* fiery; **~er** (**-s,** -) *m* fuse; (*MIL*) detonator; **~holz** *nt* match; **~kerze** *f* (*AUT*) spark(ing) plug; **~schloss** ▲ *nt* ignition lock; **~schlüssel** *m* ignition key; **~schnur** *f* fuse wire; **~stoff** *m* (*fig*) inflammatory stuff; **~ung** *f* ignition

zunehmen ['tsuːneːmən] (*unreg*) *vi* to increase, to grow; (*Mensch*) to put on weight

Zuneigung ['tsuːnaɪɡʊŋ] *f* affection

Zunft [tsʊnft] (**-,** ⁺e) *f* guild

zünftig ['tsʏnftɪç] *adj* proper, real; (*Handwerk*) decent

Zunge ['tsʊŋə] *f* tongue

zunichte [tsuˈnɪçtə] *adv*: **~ machen** to ruin, to destroy; **~ werden** to come to nothing

zunutze, zu Nutze [tsuˈnʊtsə] *adv*: **sich** *dat* **etw ~ machen** to make use of sth

zuoberst [tsuˈʔoːbərst] *adv* at the top

zupfen ['tsʊpfən] *vt* to pull, to pick, to pluck; (*Gitarre*) to pluck

zur [tsuːr] = **zu der**

zurate, zu Rate [tsuˈraːtə] *adv*: **jdn ~ ziehen** to consult sb

zurechnungsfähig ['tsuːrɛçnʊŋsfɛːɪç] *adj* responsible, accountable

zurecht- [tsuˈrɛçt] *zW*: **~finden** (*unreg*) *vr* to find one's way (about); **~kommen** (*unreg*) *vi* to (be able to) cope, to manage; **~legen** *vt* to get ready; (*Ausrede etc*) to have ready; **~machen** *vt* to prepare ♦ *vr* to get ready; **~weisen** (*unreg*) *vt* to reprimand

zureden ['tsuːreːdən] *vi*: **jdm ~** to persuade *od* urge sb

zurück [tsuˈrʏk] *adv* back; **~behalten** (*unreg*) *vt* to keep back; **~bekommen** (*unreg*) *vt* to get back; **~bleiben** (*unreg*) *vi* (*Mensch*) to remain behind; (*nicht nachkommen*) to fall behind, to lag; (*Schaden*) to remain; **~bringen** (*unreg*) *vt* to bring back; **~fahren** (*unreg*) *vi* to travel back; (*vor Schreck*) to recoil, to start ♦ *vt* to drive back; **~finden** (*unreg*) *vi* to find one's way back; **~fordern** *vt* to demand back; **~führen** *vt* to lead back; **etw auf etw** *akk* **~führen** to trace sth back to sth; **~geben** (*unreg*) *vt* to give back; (*antworten*) to retort with; **~geblieben** *adj* retarded; **~gehen** (*unreg*) *vi* to go back; (*fallen*) to go down, to fall; (*zeitlich*): **~gehen (auf** +*akk*) to date back (to); **~gezogen** *adj* retired, withdrawn; **~halten** (*unreg*) *vt* to hold back; (*Mensch*) to restrain; (*hindern*) to prevent ♦ *vr* (*reserviert sein*) to be reserved; (*im Essen*) to hold back; **~haltend** *adj* reserved; **Z~haltung** *f* reserve; **~kehren** *vi* to return; **~kommen** (*unreg*) *vi* to come back; **auf etw** *akk* **~kommen** to return to sth; **~lassen** (*unreg*) *vt* to leave behind; **~legen** *vt* to put back; (*Geld*) to put by; (*reservieren*) to keep back; (*Strecke*) to cover; **~nehmen** (*unreg*) *vt* to take back; **~stellen** *vt* to put back, to replace; (*aufschieben*) to put off, to postpone; (*Interessen*) to defer; (*Ware*) to keep; **~treten** (*unreg*) *vi* to step back; (*vom Amt*) to retire; **gegenüber etw** *od* **hinter etw** *dat* **~treten** to diminish in importance in view of sth; **~weisen** (*unreg*) *vt* to turn down; (*Mensch*) to reject; **~zahlen** *vt* to repay, to pay back; **~ziehen** (*unreg*) *vt* to pull back; (*Angebot*) to withdraw ♦ *vr* to retire

Zuruf ['tsuːruːf] *m* shout, cry

zurzeit [tsʊrˈtsaɪt] *adv* at the moment

Zusage ['tsuːzaːɡə] *f* promise; (*Annahme*) consent; **z~n** *vt* to promise ♦ *vi* to accept; **jdm z~n** (*gefallen*) to agree with *od* please sb

zusammen [tsuˈzamən] *adv* together;

Z~arbeit f cooperation; ~arbeiten vi to cooperate; ~beißen (unreg) vt (Zähne) to clench; ~brechen (unreg) vi to collapse; (Mensch auch) to break down; ~bringen (unreg) vt to bring od get together; (Geld) to get; (Sätze) to put together; Z~bruch m collapse; ~fassen vt to summarize; (vereinigen) to unite; Z~fassung f summary, résumé; ~fügen vt to join (together), to unite; ~halten (unreg) vi to stick together; Z~hang m connection; im/aus dem Z~hang in/out of context; ~hängen (unreg) vi to be connected od linked; ~kommen (unreg) vi to meet, to assemble; (sich ereignen) to occur at once od together; ~legen vt to put together; (stapeln) to pile up; (falten) to fold; (verbinden) to combine, to unite; (Termine, Fest) to amalgamate; (Geld) to collect; ~nehmen (unreg) vt to summon up ♦ vr to pull o.s. together; alles ~genommen all in all; ~passen vi to go well together, to match; ~schließen (unreg) vt, vr to join (together); Z~schluss ▲ m amalgamation; ~schreiben (unreg) vt to write as one word; (Bericht) to put together; Z~sein (-s) nt get-together; ~setzen vt to put together ♦ vr (Stoff) to be composed of; (Menschen) to get together; Z~setzung f composition; ~stellen vt to put together, to compile; Z~stoß m collision; ~stoßen (unreg) vi to collide; ~treffen (unreg) vi to coincide; (Menschen) to meet; Z~treffen nt coincidence; meeting; ~zählen vt to add up; ~ziehen (unreg) vt (verengern) to draw together; (vereinigen) to bring together; (addieren) to add up ♦ vr to shrink; (sich bilden) to form, to develop

zusätzlich ['tsu:zɛtslɪç] adj additional ♦ adv in addition

zuschauen ['tsu:ʃauən] vi to watch, to look on; **Zuschauer(in)** (-s, -) m(f) spectator ♦ pl (THEAT) audience sg

zuschicken ['tsu:ʃɪkən] vt: (jdm etw) ~ to send od to forward (sth to sb)

Zuschlag ['tsu:ʃla:k] m extra charge, surcharge; **z~en** (unreg) vt (Tür) to slam; (Ball) to hit; (bei Auktion) to knock down; (Steine etc) to knock into shape ♦ vi (Fenster, Tür) to shut; (Mensch) to hit, to punch; ~karte f (EISENB) surcharge ticket; **z~pflichtig** adj subject to surcharge

zuschneiden ['tsu:ʃnaidən] (unreg) vt to cut out; to cut to size

zuschrauben ['tsu:ʃraubən] vt to screw down od up

zuschreiben ['tsu:ʃraibən] (unreg) vt (fig) to ascribe, to attribute; (COMM) to credit

Zuschrift ['tsu:ʃrɪft] f letter, reply

zuschulden, zu Schulden [tsu'ʃuldən] adv: sich dat etw ~ kommen lassen to make o.s. guilty of sth

Zuschuss ▲ ['tsu:ʃus] m subsidy, allowance

zusehen ['tsu:ze:ən] (unreg) vi to watch; (dafür sorgen) to take care; jdm/etw ~ to watch sb/sth; ~ds adv visibly

zusenden ['tsu:zɛndən] (unreg) vt to forward, to send on

zusichern ['tsu:zɪçərn] vt: jdm etw ~ to assure sb of sth

zuspielen ['tsu:ʃpi:lən] vt, vi to pass

zuspitzen ['tsu:ʃpɪtsən] vt to sharpen ♦ vr (Lage) to become critical

zusprechen ['tsu:ʃprɛçən] (unreg) vt (zuerkennen) to award ♦ vi to speak; jdm etw ~ to award sb sth od sth to sb; jdm Trost ~ to comfort sb; dem Essen/ Alkohol ~ to eat/drink a lot

Zustand ['tsu:ʃtant] m state, condition

zustande, zu Stande [tsu'ʃtandə] adv: ~ bringen to bring about; ~ kommen to come about

zuständig ['tsu:ʃtɛndɪç] adj responsible; Z~keit f competence, responsibility

zustehen ['tsu:ʃte:ən] (unreg) vi: jdm ~ to be sb's right

zustellen ['tsu:ʃtɛlən] vt (verstellen) to block; (Post etc) to send

Zustellung f delivery

zustimmen ['tsu:ʃtɪmən] vi to agree

Zustimmung f agreement, consent

zustoßen ['tsu:ʃto:sən] (unreg) vi (fig) to happen

Rechtschreibreform: ▲ *neue Schreibung* △ *alte Schreibung (auslaufend)*

zutage, zu Tage [tsu'ta:gə] *adv*: **~ bringen** to bring to light; **~ treten** to come to light

Zutaten ['tsu:ta:tən] *pl* ingredients

zuteilen ['tsu:taɪlən] *vt* (*Arbeit, Rolle*) to designate, assign; (*Aktien, Wohnung*) to allocate

zutiefst [tsu'ti:fst] *adv* deeply

zutragen ['tsu:tra:gən] (*unreg*) *vt* to bring; (*Klatsch*) to tell ♦ *vr* to happen

zutrau- ['tsu:trau] *zW*: **Z~en (-s)** *nt*: **Z~en (zu)** trust (in); **~en** *vt*: **jdm etw ~en** to credit sb with sth; **~lich** *adj* trusting, friendly

zutreffen ['tsu:trɛfən] (*unreg*) *vi* to be correct; to apply; **~d** *adj* (*richtig*) accurate; **Z~des bitte unterstreichen** please underline where applicable

Zutritt ['tsu:trɪt] *m* access, admittance

Zutun ['tsu:tu:n] (-s) *nt* assistance

zuverlässig ['tsu:fɛrlɛsɪç] *adj* reliable; **Z~keit** *f* reliability

zuversichtlich ['tsu:fɛrzɪçtlɪç] *adj* confident

zuvor [tsu'fo:r] *adv* before, previously; **~kommen** (*unreg*) *vi* +*dat* to anticipate; **jdm ~kommen** to beat sb to it; **~kommend** *adj* obliging, courteous

Zuwachs ['tsu:vaks] (-es) *m* increase, growth; (*umg*) **~en** (*unreg*) *vi* to become overgrown; (*Wunde*) to heal (up)

zuwege, zu Wege [tsu've:gə] *adv*: **etw ~ bringen** to accomplish sth

zuweilen [tsu'vaɪlən] *adv* at times, now and then

zuweisen ['tsu:vaɪzən] (*unreg*) *vt* to assign, to allocate

zuwenden ['tsu:vɛndən] (*unreg*) *vt* (+*dat*) to turn (towards) ♦ *vr*: **sich jdm/etw ~** to devote o.s. to sb/sth; to turn to sb/sth

zuwider [tsu'vi:dər] *adv*: **etw ist jdm ~** sb loathes sth, sb finds sth repugnant; **~handeln** *vi*: **einer Sache** *dat* **~handeln** to act contrary to sth; **einem Gesetz ~handeln** to contravene a law

zuziehen ['tsu:tsi:ən] (*unreg*) *vt* (*schließen*: *Vorhang*) to draw, to close; (*herbeirufen*: *Experten*) to call in ♦ *vi* to move in, to

come; **sich** *dat* **etw ~** (*Krankheit*) to catch sth; (*Zorn*) to incur sth

zuzüglich ['tsu:tsy:klɪç] *präp* +*gen* plus, with the addition of

Zwang [tsvaŋ] **(-(e)s, ⁻e)** *m* compulsion, coercion

zwängen ['tsvɛŋən] *vt, vr* to squeeze

zwanglos *adj* informal

Zwangs- *zW*: **z~arbeit** *f* forced labour; (*Strafe*) hard labour; **~lage** *f* predicament, tight corner; **z~läufig** *adj* necessary, inevitable

zwanzig ['tsvantsɪç] *num* twenty

zwar [tsva:r] *adv* to be sure, indeed; **das ist ~ ..., aber ...** that may be ... but ...; **und ~ am Sonntag** on Sunday to be precise; **und ~ so schnell, dass ...** in fact so quickly that ...

Zweck [tsvɛk] **(-(e)s, -e)** *m* purpose, aim; **es hat keinen ~** there's no point; **z~dienlich** *adj* practical; expedient

Zwecke *f* hobnail; (*Heftzwecke*) drawing pin, thumbtack (*US*)

Zweck- *zW*: **z~los** *adj* pointless; **z~mäßig** *adj* suitable, appropriate; **z~s** *präp* +*gen* for the purpose of

zwei [tsvaɪ] *num* two; **Z~bettzimmer** *nt* twin room; **~deutig** *adj* ambiguous; (*unanständig*) suggestive; **~erlei** *adj*: **~erlei Stoff** two different kinds of material; **~erlei Meinung** of differing opinions; **~fach** *adj* double

Zweifel ['tsvaɪfəl] **(-s, -)** *m* doubt; **z~haft** *adj* doubtful, dubious; **z~los** *adj* doubtless; **z~n** *vi*: **(an etw** *dat*) **z~n** to doubt (sth)

Zweig [tsvaɪk] **(-(e)s, -e)** *m* branch; **~stelle** *f* branch (office)

zwei- *zW*: **~hundert** *num* two hundred; **~mal** *adv* twice; **~sprachig** *adj* bilingual; **~spurig** *adj* (*AUT*) two-lane; **~stimmig** *adj* for two voices

zweit [tsvaɪt] *adv*: **zu ~** together; (*bei mehreren Paaren*) in twos

zweitbeste(r, s) *adj* second best

zweite(r, s) *adj* second

zweiteilig ['tsvaɪtaɪlɪç] *adj* (*Gruppe*) two-piece; (*Fernsehfilm*) two-part; (*Kleidung*)

Spelling Reform: ▲ *new spelling* △ *old spelling (to be phased out)*

two-piece

zweit- *zW:* ~**ens** *adv* secondly; ~**größte(r, s)** *adj* second largest; ~**klassig** *adj* second-class; ~**letzte(r, s)** *adj* last but one, penultimate; ~**rangig** *adj* second-rate

Zwerchfell ['tsvɛrçfɛl] *nt* diaphragm

Zwerg [tsvɛrk] (-(e)s, -e) *m* dwarf

Zwetsch(g)e ['tsvɛtʃ(g)ə] *f* plum

Zwieback ['tsviːbak] (-(e)s, -e) *m* rusk

Zwiebel ['tsviːbəl] (-, -n) *f* onion; (*Blumenzwiebel*) bulb

Zwie- ['tsviː] *zW:* z~**lichtig** *adj* shady, dubious; z~**spältig** *adj* (*Gefühle*) conflicting; (*Charakter*) contradictory; ~**tracht** *f* discord, dissension

Zwilling ['tsvɪlɪŋ] (-s, -e) *m* twin; ~**e** *pl* (*ASTROL*) Gemini

zwingen ['tsvɪŋən] (*unreg*) *vt* to force; ~**d** *adj* (*Grund etc*) compelling

zwinkern ['tsvɪŋkərn] *vi* to blink; (*absichtlich*) to wink

Zwirn [tsvɪrn] (-(e)s, -e) *m* thread

zwischen ['tsvɪʃən] *präp* (+akk od dat)

between; Z~**bemerkung** *f* (incidental) remark; Z~**ding** *nt* cross; ~**durch** *adv* in between; (*räumlich*) here and there; Z~**ergebnis** *nt* intermediate result; Z~**fall** *m* incident; Z~**frage** *f* question; Z~**handel** *m* middlemen *pl*; middleman's trade; Z~**landung** *f* (*AVIAT*) stopover; ~**menschlich** *adj* interpersonal; Z~**raum** *m* space; Z~**ruf** *m* interjection; Z~**stecker** *m* adaptor (plug); Z~**zeit** *f* interval; **in der Z~zeit** in the interim, meanwhile

zwitschern ['tsvɪtʃərn] *vt, vi* to twitter, to chirp

zwo [tsvoː] *num* two

zwölf [tsvœlf] *num* twelve

Zyklus ['tsyːklʊs] (-, Zyklen) *m* cycle

Zylinder [tsiˈlɪndər] (-s, -) *m* cylinder; (*Hut*) top hat

Zyniker ['tsyːnikər] (-s, -) *m* cynic

zynisch ['tsyːnɪʃ] *adj* cynical

Zypern ['tsyːpərn] *nt* Cyprus

Zyste ['tsʏstə] *f* cyst

zz., zzt. *abk* = **zurzeit**

VERB TABLES

Introduction

The **Verb Tables** in the following section contain 52 tables of German verbs in alphabetical order. Each table shows you the following forms: **Present, Perfect, Future, Subjunctive, Imperfect, Conditional, Imperative** and the **Present** and **Past Participles**.

In order to help you use the verbs shown in the Verb Tables correctly, there are also a number of example phrases at the bottom of each page to show the verb as it is used in context.

In German there are **regular** verbs or **weak** verbs (their forms follow the normal rules) and **irregular** or **strong** verbs (their forms do not follow the normal rules) and **mixed** verbs (their forms have features of both **weak** and **strong** verbs).

The **Verb Tables** given show one **weak** verb – machen, Verb Table 27 and three **mixed** verbs – bringen, Verb Table 6; denken, Verb Table 7 and kennen Verb Table 20. The rest of the verbs shown are **strong** verbs.

For a further list of German **irregular** verb forms see pages 609–613.

▶ bieten (to offer)

PRESENT

ich	biete
du	bietest
er	bietet
wir	bieten
ihr	bietet
sie	bieten

PRESENT SUBJUNCTIVE

ich	biete
du	bietest
er	biete
wir	bieten
ihr	bietet
sie	bieten

PERFECT

ich	habe geboten
du	hast geboten
er	hat geboten
wir	haben geboten
ihr	habt geboten
sie	haben geboten

IMPERFECT

ich	bot
du	bot(e)st
er	bot
wir	boten
ihr	botet
sie	boten

FUTURE

ich	werde bieten
du	wirst bieten
er	wird bieten
wir	werden bieten
ihr	werdet bieten
sie	werden bieten

CONDITIONAL

ich	würde bieten
du	würdest bieten
er	würde bieten
wir	würden bieten
ihr	würdet bieten
sie	würden bieten

IMPERATIVE

biet(e)!/bieten wir!/bietet!
bieten Sie!

PAST PARTICIPLE

geboten

PRESENT PARTICIPLE

bietend

EXAMPLE PHRASES

*Er **bot** ihm die Hand.* He held out his hand to him.
*Für das Bild wurden 2000 Euro **geboten**.* There was a bid of 2000 euros for the painting.
*Diese Stadt hat nichts zu **bieten**.* This town has nothing to offer.

---

ich = I **du** = you **er** = he **wir** = we/one **ihr** = you **sie** = they

▶ **bitten** (to request)

PRESENT

ich	bitte
du	bittest
er	bittet
wir	bitten
ihr	bittet
sie	bitten

PRESENT SUBJUNCTIVE

ich	bitte
du	bittest
er	bitte
wir	bitten
ihr	bittet
sie	bitten

PERFECT

ich	habe gebeten
du	hast gebeten
er	hat gebeten
wir	haben gebeten
ihr	habt gebeten
sie	haben gebeten

IMPERFECT

ich	bat
du	bat(e)st
er	bat
wir	baten
ihr	batet
sie	baten

FUTURE

ich	werde bitten
du	wirst bitten
er	wird bitten
wir	werden bitten
ihr	werdet bitten
sie	werden bitten

CONDITIONAL

ich	würde bitten
du	würdest bitten
er	würde bitten
wir	würden bitten
ihr	würdet bitten
sie	würden bitten

IMPERATIVE

bitt(e)!/bitten wir!/bittet!
bitten Sie!

PAST PARTICIPLE

gebeten

PRESENT PARTICIPLE

bittend

EXAMPLE PHRASES

*Sie **bat** ihn um Hilfe.* She asked him for help
*Herr Müller lässt **bitten**.* Mr Müller will see you now.
*Man **hat** die Bevölkerung um Mithilfe **geboten**.* The public was asked for assistance.

ich = I **du** = you **er** = he **wir** = we/one **ihr** = you **sie** = they

▶ bleiben (to remain)

PRESENT

ich	bleibe
du	bleibst
er	bleibt
wir	bleiben
ihr	bleibt
sie	bleiben

PRESENT SUBJUNCTIVE

ich	bleibe
du	bleibest
er	bleibe
wir	bleiben
ihr	bleibet
sie	bleiben

PERFECT

ich	bin geblieben
du	bist geblieben
er	ist geblieben
wir	sind geblieben
ihr	seid geblieben
sie	sind geblieben

IMPERFECT

ich	blieb
du	bliebst
er	blieb
wir	blieben
ihr	bliebt
sie	blieben

FUTURE

ich	werde bleiben
du	wirst bleiben
er	wird bleiben
wir	werden bleiben
ihr	werdet bleiben
sie	werden bleiben

CONDITIONAL

ich	würde bleiben
du	würdest bleiben
er	würde bleiben
wir	würden bleiben
ihr	würdet bleiben
sie	würden bleiben

IMPERATIVE

bleib(e)!/bleiben wir!/bleibt!
bleiben Sie!

PAST PARTICIPLE

geblieben

PRESENT PARTICIPLE

bleibend

EXAMPLE PHRASES

*Hoffentlich **bleibt** das Wetter schön.* I hope the weather will stay fine.
*Vom Kuchen **ist** nur noch ein Stück **geblieben**.* There's only one piece of cake left.
*Dieses Erlebnis **blieb** in meiner Erinnerung.* This experience stayed with me.

ich = I **du** = you **er** = he **wir** = we/one **ihr** = you **sie** = they

▶ brechen (to break)

PRESENT

ich	breche
du	brichst
er	bricht
wir	brechen
ihr	brecht
sie	brechen

PRESENT SUBJUNCTIVE

ich	breche
du	brechest
er	breche
wir	brechen
ihr	brechet
sie	brechen

PERFECT

ich	habe gebrochen*
du	hast gebrochen
er	hat gebrochen
wir	haben gebrochen
ihr	habt gebrochen
sie	haben gebrochen

IMPERFECT

ich	brach
du	brachst
er	brach
wir	brachen
ihr	bracht
sie	brachen

FUTURE

ich	werde brechen
du	wirst brechen
er	wird brechen
wir	werden brechen
ihr	werdet brechen
sie	werden brechen

CONDITIONAL

ich	würde brechen
du	würdest brechen
er	würde brechen
wir	würden brechen
ihr	würdet brechen
sie	würden brechen

IMPERATIVE

brich!/brechen wir!/brecht!
brechen Sie!
OR: ich bin/wäre gebrochen
etc (when intransitive).

PAST PARTICIPLE

gebrochen

PRESENT PARTICIPLE

brechend

EXAMPLE PHRASES

*Mir **bricht** das Herz.* It breaks my heart.
*Der Sturz **brach** ihm fast den Arm.* The fall almost broke his arm.
*Sie **hat** ihr Versprechen **gebrochen**.* She broke her promise.

ich = I **du** = you **er** = he **wir** = we/one **ihr** = you **sie** = they

▶ bringen (to bring)

PRESENT

ich	bringe
du	bringst
er	bringt
wir	bringen
ihr	bringt
sie	bringen

PRESENT SUBJUNCTIVE

ich	bringe
du	bringest
er	bringe
wir	bringen
ihr	bringet
sie	bringen

PERFECT

ich	habe gebracht
du	hast gebracht
er	hat gebracht
wir	haben gebracht
ihr	habt gebracht
sie	haben gebracht

IMPERFECT

ich	brachte
du	brachtest
er	brachte
wir	brachten
ihr	brachtet
sie	brachten

FUTURE

ich	werde bringen
du	wirst bringen
er	wird bringen
wir	werden bringen
ihr	werdet bringen
sie	werden bringen

CONDITIONAL

ich	würde bringen
du	würdest bringen
er	würde bringen
wir	würden bringen
ihr	würdet bringen
sie	würden bringen

IMPERATIVE

bring(e)!/bringen wir!/bringt!
bringen Sie!

PAST PARTICIPLE

gebracht

PRESENT PARTICIPLE

bringend

EXAMPLE PHRASES

*Kannst du mich zum Flughafen **bringen**?* Can you take me to the airport?
*Max **hat** mir Blumen **gebracht**.* Max brought me flowers.
*Das **brachte** mich auf eine Idee.* It gave me an idea.

---

ich = I **du** = you **er** = he **wir** = we/one **ihr** = you **sie** = they

▶ denken (to think)

PRESENT

ich	denke
du	denkst
er	denkt
wir	denken
ihr	denkt
sie	denken

PRESENT SUBJUNCTIVE

ich	denke
du	denkest
er	denke
wir	denken
ihr	denket
sie	denken

PERFECT

ich	habe gedacht
du	hast gedacht
er	hat gedacht
wir	haben gedacht
ihr	habt gedacht
sie	haben gedacht

IMPERFECT

ich	dachte
du	dachtest
er	dachte
wir	dachten
ihr	dachtet
sie	dachten

FUTURE

ich	werde denken
du	wirst denken
er	wird denken
wir	werden denken
ihr	werdet denken
sie	werden denken

CONDITIONAL

ich	würde denken
du	würdest denken
er	würde denken
wir	würden denken
ihr	würdet denken
sie	würden denken

IMPERATIVE

denk(e)!/denken wir!/denkt!
denken Sie!

PAST PARTICIPLE

gedacht

PRESENT PARTICIPLE

denkend

EXAMPLE PHRASES

*Wie **denken** Sie darüber?* What do you think about it?
*Das war für ihn **gedacht**.* It was meant for him.
*Es war das Erste, woran ich **dachte**.* It was the first thing I thought of.

ich = I **du** = you **er** = he **wir** = we/one **ihr** = you **sie** = they

▶ dürfen (to be allowed to)

PRESENT

ich	darf
du	darfst
er	darf
wir	dürfen
ihr	dürft
sie	dürfen

PRESENT SUBJUNCTIVE

ich	dürfe
du	dürfest
er	dürfe
wir	dürfen
ihr	dürfet
sie	dürfen

PERFECT

ich	habe gedurft/dürfen
du	hast gedurft/dürfen
er	hat gedurft/dürfen
wir	haben gedurft/dürfen
ihr	habt gedurft/dürfen
sie	haben gedurft/dürfen

IMPERFECT

ich	durfte
du	durftest
er	durfte
wir	durften
ihr	durftet
sie	durften

FUTURE

ich	werde dürfen
du	wirst dürfen
er	wird dürfen
wir	werden dürfen
ihr	werdet dürfen
sie	werden dürfen

CONDITIONAL

ich	würde dürfen
du	würdest dürfen
er	würde dürfen
wir	würden dürfen
ihr	würdet dürfen
sie	würden dürfen

IMPERATIVE

PAST PARTICIPLE

gedurft/dürfen*

PRESENT PARTICIPLE

dürfend

*The second form is used when combined with an infinitive construction.

EXAMPLE PHRASES

Darf ich ins Kino? Can I go to the cinema?
Das **würde** *ich zu Hause nicht dürfen.* I wouldn't be allowed to do that at home.
Das **dürfen** *Sie mir glauben.* You can take my word for it.

---

ich = I **du** = you **er** = he **wir** = we/one **ihr** = you **sie** = they

▶ empfehlen (to recommend)

PRESENT

ich	empfehle
du	empfiehlst
er	empfiehlt
wir	empfehlen
ihr	empfehlt
sie	empfehlen

PRESENT SUBJUNCTIVE

ich	empfehle
du	empfehlest
er	empfehle
wir	empfehlen
ihr	empfehlet
sie	empfehlen

PERFECT

ich	habe empfohlen
du	hast empfohlen
er	hat empfohlen
wir	haben empfohlen
ihr	habt empfohlen
sie	haben empfohlen

IMPERFECT

ich	empfahl
du	empfahlst
er	empfahl
wir	empfahlen
ihr	empfahlt
sie	empfahlen

FUTURE

ich	werde empfehlen
du	wirst empfehlen
er	wird empfehlen
wir	werden empfehlen
ihr	werdet empfehlen
sie	werden empfehlen

CONDITIONAL

ich	würde empfehlen
du	würdest empfehlen
er	würde empfehlen
wir	würden empfehlen
ihr	würdet empfehlen
sie	würden empfehlen

IMPERATIVE

empfiehl!/empfehlen wir!
empfehlt!/empfehlen Sie!

PAST PARTICIPLE

empfohlen

PRESENT PARTICIPLE

empfehlend

EXAMPLE PHRASES

Ich würde Ihnen empfehlen, zu gehen. I would advise you to go.
Was empfiehlst du mir zu tun? What would you recommend I do?
Dieses Restaurant wurde uns empfohlen. This restaurant has been recommended to us.

ich = I **du** = you **er** = he **wir** = we/one **ihr** = you **sie** = they

▶ essen (to eat)

PRESENT		PRESENT SUBJUNCTIVE	
ich	esse	ich	esse
du	isst	du	essest
er	isst	er	esse
wir	essen	wir	essen
ihr	esst	ihr	esset
sie	essen	sie	essen

PERFECT		IMPERFECT	
ich	habe gegessen	ich	aß
du	hast gegessen	du	aßest
er	hat gegessen	er	aß
wir	haben gegessen	wir	aßen
ihr	habt gegessen	ihr	aßt
sie	haben gegessen	sie	aßen

FUTURE		CONDITIONAL	
ich	werde essen	ich	würde essen
du	wirst essen	du	würdest essen
er	wird essen	er	würde essen
wir	werden essen	wir	würden essen
ihr	werdet essen	ihr	würdet essen
sie	werden essen	sie	würden essen

IMPERATIVE

iss!/essen wir!/esst!/essen Sie!

PAST PARTICIPLE

gegessen

PRESENT PARTICIPLE

essend

EXAMPLE PHRASES

Ich esse kein Fleisch. I don't eat meat.
*Wir **haben** nichts **gegessen**.* We haven't had anything to eat.
Ich möchte was essen. I'd like something to eat.

---

ich = I   **du** = you   **er** = he   **wir** = we/one   **ihr** = you   **sie** = they

▶ **fahren** (to drive/to go)

PRESENT

ich	fahre
du	fährst
er	fährt
wir	fahren
ihr	fahrt
sie	fahren

PRESENT SUBJUNCTIVE

ich	fahre
du	fahrest
er	fahre
wir	fahren
ihr	fahret
sie	fahren

PERFECT

ich	bin gefahren*
du	bist gefahren
er	ist gefahren
wir	sind gefahren
ihr	seid gefahren
sie	sind gefahren

IMPERFECT

ich	fuhr
du	fuhrst
er	fuhr
wir	fuhren
ihr	fuhrt
sie	fuhren

FUTURE

ich	werde fahren
du	wirst fahren
er	wird fahren
wir	werden fahren
ihr	werdet fahren
sie	werden fahren

CONDITIONAL

ich	würde fahren
du	würdest fahren
er	würde fahren
wir	würden fahren
ihr	würdet fahren
sie	würden fahren

IIMPERATIVE

fahr(e)!/fahren wir!/fahrt!
fahren Sie!
OR: ich habe/hätte gefahren
etc (*when transitive*).

PAST PARTICIPLE

gefahren

PRESENT PARTICIPLE

fahrend

EXAMPLE PHRASES

Sie fahren mit dem Bus in die Schule. They go to school by bus.
Rechts fahren! Drive on the right!
Ich bin mit der Familie nach Spanien gefahren. I went to Spain with my family.

ich = I **du** = you **er** = he **wir** = we/one **ihr** = you **sie** = they

▶ **fallen** (to fall)

PRESENT

ich	falle
du	fällst
er	fällt
wir	fallen
ihr	fallt
sie	fallen

PRESENT SUBJUNCTIVE

ich	falle
du	fallest
er	falle
wir	fallen
ihr	fallet
sie	fallen

PERFECT

ich	bin gefallen
du	bist gefallen
er	ist gefallen
wir	sind gefallen
ihr	seid gefallen
sie	sind gefallen

IMPERFECT

ich	fiel
du	fielst
er	fiel
wir	fielen
ihr	fielt
sie	fielen

FUTURE

ich	werde fallen
du	wirst fallen
er	wird fallen
wir	werden fallen
ihr	werdet fallen
sie	werden fallen

CONDITIONAL

ich	würde fallen
du	würdest fallen
er	würde fallen
wir	würden fallen
ihr	würdet fallen
sie	würden fallen

IMPERATIVE

fall(e)!/fallen wir!/fallt!
fallen Sie!

PAST PARTICIPLE

gefallen

PRESENT PARTICIPLE

fallend

EXAMPLE PHRASES

*Er **fiel** vom Fahrrad.* He fell off his bike.
*Ich **bin** durch die Prüfung **gefallen**.* I failed my exam.
*Die Aktien **fielen** im Kurs.* Share prices went down.

ich = I **du** = you **er** = he **wir** = we/one **ihr** = you **sie** = they

▶ finden (to find)

PRESENT

ich	finde
du	findest
er	findet
wir	finden
ihr	findet
sie	finden

PRESENT SUBJUNCTIVE

ich	finde
du	findest
er	finde
wir	finden
ihr	findet
sie	finden

PERFECT

ich	habe gefunden
du	hast gefunden
er	hat gefunden
wir	haben gefunden
ihr	habt gefunden
sie	haben gefunden

IMPERFECT

ich	fand
du	fand(e)st
er	fand
wir	fanden
ihr	fandet
sie	fanden

FUTURE

ich	werde finden
du	wirst finden
er	wird finden
wir	werden finden
ihr	werdet finden
sie	werden finden

CONDITIONAL

ich	würde finden
du	würdest finden
er	würde finden
wir	würden finden
ihr	würdet finden
sie	würden finden

IMPERATIVE

find(e)!/finden wir!/findet!
finden Sie!

PAST PARTICIPLE

gefunden

PRESENT PARTICIPLE

findend

EXAMPLE PHRASES

***Hast** du deine Brieftasche **gefunden**?* Have you found your wallet?
*Er **fand** den Mut, sie zu fragen.* He found the courage to ask her.
*Ich **finde**, sie ist eine gute Lehrerin.* I think she's a good teacher.

ich = I **du** = you **er** = he **wir** = we/one **ihr** = you **sie** = they

▶ **fliegen** (to fly)

PRESENT

ich	fliege
du	fliegst
er	fliegt
wir	fliegen
ihr	fliegt
sie	fliegen

PRESENT SUBJUNCTIVE

ich	fliege
du	fliegest
er	fliege
wir	fliegen
ihr	flieget
sie	fliegen

PERFECT

ich	habe geflogen*
du	hast geflogen
er	hat geflogen
wir	haben geflogen
ihr	habt geflogen
sie	haben geflogen

IMPERFECT

ich	flog
du	flogst
er	flog
wir	flogen
ihr	flogt
sie	flogen

FUTURE

ich	werde fliegen
du	wirst fliegen
er	wird fliegen
wir	werden fliegen
ihr	werdet fliegen
sie	werden fliegen

CONDITIONAL

ich	würde fliegen
du	würdest fliegen
er	würde fliegen
wir	würden fliegen
ihr	würdet fliegen
sie	würden fliegen

IMPERATIVE

flieg(e)!/fliegen wir!/fliegt!
fliegen Sie!
OR: ich bin/wäre geflogen
etc (*when intransitive*).

PAST PARTICIPLE

geflogen

PRESENT PARTICIPLE

fliegend

EXAMPLE PHRASES

*Wir **flogen** zusammen nach Spanien.* We flew together to Spain.
*Die Zeit **fliegt**.* Time flies.
*Er **ist** von der Schule **geflogen**.* He was chucked out of school.

---

ich = I   **du** = you   **er** = he   **wir** = we/one   **ihr** = you   **sie** = they

▶ geben (to give)

PRESENT

ich	gebe
du	gibst
er	gibt
wir	geben
ihr	gebt
sie	geben

PRESENT SUBJUNCTIVE

ich	gebe
du	gebest
er	gebe
wir	geben
ihr	gebet
sie	geben

PERFECT

ich	habe gegeben
du	hast gegeben
er	hat gegeben
wir	haben gegeben
ihr	habt gegeben
sie	haben gegeben

IMPERFECT

ich	gab
du	gabst
er	gab
wir	gaben
ihr	gabt
sie	gaben

FUTURE

ich	werde geben
du	wirst geben
er	wird geben
wir	werden geben
ihr	werdet geben
sie	werden geben

CONDITIONAL

ich	würde geben
du	würdest geben
er	würde geben
wir	würden geben
ihr	würdet geben
sie	würden geben

IMPERATIVE

gib!/geben wir!/gebt!
geben Sie!

PAST PARTICIPLE

gegeben

PRESENT PARTICIPLE

gebend

EXAMPLE PHRASES

*Er **gab** mir das Geld für die Bücher.* He gave me the money for the books.
*Was **gibt** es im Kino?* What's on at the cinema?
*Wir **würden** alles darum **geben**, ins Finale zu kommen.* We would give anything
to reach the finals.

---

ich = I **du** = you **er** = he **wir** = we/one **ihr** = you **sie** = they

▶ gehen (to go)

PRESENT

ich	gehe
du	gehst
er	geht
wir	gehen
ihr	geht
sie	gehen

PRESENT SUBJUNCTIVE

ich	gehe
du	gehest
er	gehe
wir	gehen
ihr	gehet
sie	gehen

PERFECT

ich	bin gegangen
du	bist gegangen
er	ist gegangen
wir	sind gegangen
ihr	seid gegangen
sie	sind gegangen

IMPERFECT

ich	ging
du	gingst
er	ging
wir	gingen
ihr	gingt
sie	gingen

FUTURE

ich	werde gehen
du	wirst gehen
er	wird gehen
wir	werden gehen
ihr	werdet gehen
sie	werden gehen

CONDITIONAL

ich	würde gehen
du	würdest gehen
er	würde gehen
wir	würden gehen
ihr	würdet gehen
sie	würden gehen

IMPERATIVE

geh(e)!/gehen wir!/geht!
gehen Sie!

PAST PARTICIPLE

gegangen

PRESENT PARTICIPLE

gehend

EXAMPLE PHRASES

*Die Kinder **gingen** ins Haus.* The children went into the house.
*Wie **geht** es dir?* How are you?
*Wir **sind** gestern schwimmen **gegangen**.* We went swimming yesterday.

ich = I **du** = you **er** = he **wir** = we/one **ihr** = you **sie** = they

▶ **haben** (to have)

PRESENT

ich	habe
du	hast
er	hat
wir	haben
ihr	habt
sie	haben

PRESENT SUBJUNCTIVE

ich	habe
du	habest
er	habe
wir	haben
ihr	habet
sie	haben

PERFECT

ich	habe gehabt
du	hast gehabt
er	hat gehabt
wir	haben gehabt
ihr	habt gehabt
sie	haben gehabt

IMPERFECT

ich	hatte
du	hattest
er	hatte
wir	hatten
ihr	hattet
sie	hatten

FUTURE

ich	werde haben
du	wirst haben
er	wird haben
wir	werden haben
ihr	werdet haben
sie	werden haben

CONDITIONAL

ich	würde haben
du	würdest haben
er	würde haben
wir	würden haben
ihr	würdet haben
sie	würden haben

IMPERATIVE

hab(e)!/haben wir!/habt!
haben Sie!

PAST PARTICIPLE

gehabt

PRESENT PARTICIPLE

habend

EXAMPLE PHRASES

Hast du eine Schwester? Have you got a sister?
Er hatte Hunger. He was hungry.
Ich hätte gern ein Eis. I'd like an ice cream.
Sie hat heute Geburtstag. It's her birthday today.

ich = I **du** = you **er** = he **wir** = we/one **ihr** = you **sie** = they

▶ halten (to hold)

PRESENT

ich	halte
du	hältst
er	hält
wir	halten
ihr	haltet
sie	halten

PRESENT SUBJUNCTIVE

ich	halte
du	haltest
er	halte
wir	halten
ihr	haltet
sie	halten

PERFECT

ich	habe gehalten
du	hast gehalten
er	hat gehalten
wir	haben gehalten
ihr	habt gehalten
sie	haben gehalten

IMPERFECT

ich	hielt
du	hielt(e)st
er	hielt
wir	hielten
ihr	hieltet
sie	hielten

FUTURE

ich	werde halten
du	wirst halten
er	wird halten
wir	werden halten
ihr	werdet halten
sie	werden halten

CONDITIONAL

ich	würde halten
du	würdest halten
er	würde halten
wir	würden halten
ihr	würdet halten
sie	würden halten

IMPERATIVE

halt(e)!/halten wir!/haltet!
halten Sie!

PAST PARTICIPLE

gehalten

PRESENT PARTICIPLE

haltend

EXAMPLE PHRASES

*Kannst du das mal **halten**?* Can you hold that for a moment?
*Der Bus **hielt** vor dem Rathaus.* The bus stopped in front of the town hall.
*Ich **habe** sie für deine Mutter **gehalten**.* I took her for your mother.

---

ich = I **du** = you **er** = he **wir** = we/one **ihr** = you **sie** = they

▶ helfen (to help)

PRESENT

ich	helfe
du	hilfst
er	hilft
wir	helfen
ihr	helft
sie	helfen

PRESENT SUBJUNCTIVE

ich	helfe
du	helfest
er	helfe
wir	helfen
ihr	helfet
sie	helfen

PERFECT

ich	habe geholfen
du	hast geholfen
er	hat geholfen
wir	haben geholfen
ihr	habt geholfen
sie	haben geholfen

IMPERFECT

ich	half
du	halfst
er	half
wir	halfen
ihr	halft
sie	halfen

FUTURE

ich	werde helfen
du	wirst helfen
er	wird helfen
wir	werden helfen
ihr	werdet helfen
sie	werden helfen

CONDITIONAL

ich	würde helfen
du	würdest helfen
er	würde helfen
wir	würden helfen
ihr	würdet helfen
sie	würden helfen

IMPERATIVE

hilf!/helfen wir!/helft!
helfen Sie!

PAST PARTICIPLE

geholfen

PRESENT PARTICIPLE

helfend

EXAMPLE PHRASES

*Er **hat** mir dabei **geholfen**.* He helped me with it.
*Diese Arznei **hilft** gegen Kopfschmerzen.* This medicine is good for headaches.
*Sein Vorschlag **half** mir wenig.* His suggestion was not much help to me.

ich = I **du** = you **er** = he **wir** = we/one **ihr** = you **sie** = they

▶ **kennen** (to know) *(be acquainted with)*

PRESENT

ich	kenne
du	kennst
er	kennt
wir	kennen
ihr	kennt
sie	kennen

PRESENT SUBJUNCTIVE

ich	kenne
du	kennest
er	kenne
wir	kennen
ihr	kennet
sie	kennen

PERFECT

ich	habe gekannt
du	hast gekannt
er	hat gekannt
wir	haben gekannt
ihr	habt gekannt
sie	haben gekannt

IMPERFECT

ich	kannte
du	kanntest
er	kannte
wir	kannten
ihr	kanntet
sie	kannten

FUTURE

ich	werde kennen
du	wirst kennen
er	wird kennen
wir	werden kennen
ihr	werdet kennen
sie	werden kennen

CONDITIONAL

ich	würde kennen
du	würdest kennen
er	würde kennen
wir	würden kennen
ihr	würdet kennen
sie	würden kennen

IMPERATIVE

kenn(e)!/kennen wir!/kennt!
kennen Sie!

PAST PARTICIPLE

gekannt

PRESENT PARTICIPLE

kennend

EXAMPLE PHRASES

*Ich **kenne** ihn nicht.* I don't know him.
*Er **kannte** kein Erbarmen.* He knew no mercy.
***Kennst** du mich noch?* Do you remember me?

ich = I **du** = you **er** = he **wir** = we/one **ihr** = you **sie** = they

▶ **kommen** (to come)

PRESENT

ich	komme
du	kommst
er	kommt
wir	kommen
ihr	kommt
sie	kommen

PRESENT SUBJUNCTIVE

ich	komme
du	kommest
er	komme
wir	kommen
ihr	kommet
sie	kommen

PERFECT

ich	bin gekommen
du	bist gekommen
er	ist gekommen
wir	sind gekommen
ihr	seid gekommen
sie	sind gekommen

IMPERFECT

ich	kam
du	kamst
er	kam
wir	kamen
ihr	kamt
sie	kamen

FUTURE

ich	werde kommen
du	wirst kommen
er	wird kommen
wir	werden kommen
ihr	werdet kommen
sie	werden kommen

CONDITIONAL

ich	würde kommen
du	würdest kommen
er	würde kommen
wir	würden kommen
ihr	würdet kommen
sie	würden kommen

IMPERATIVE

komm(e)!/kommen wir!
kommt!/kommen Sie!

PAST PARTICIPLE

gekommen

PRESENT PARTICIPLE

kommend

EXAMPLE PHRASES

*Er **kam** die Straße entlang.* He was coming along the street.
*Ich **komme** zu deiner Party.* I'm coming to your party.
*Woher **kommst** du?* Where do you come from?

ich = I **du** = you **er** = he **wir** = we/one **ihr** = you **sie** = they

▶ **können** (to be able to)

PRESENT

ich	kann
du	kannst
er	kann
wir	können
ihr	könnt
sie	können

PRESENT SUBJUNCTIVE

ich	könne
du	könnest
er	könne
wir	können
ihr	könnet
sie	können

PERFECT

ich	habe gekonnt/können
du	hast gekonnt/können
er	hat gekonnt/können
wir	haben gekonnt/können
ihr	habt gekonnt/können
sie	haben gekonnt/können

IMPERFECT

ich	konnte
du	konntest
er	konnte
wir	konnten
ihr	konntet
sie	konnten

FUTURE

ich	werde können
du	wirst können
er	wird können
wir	werden können
ihr	werdet können
sie	werden können

CONDITIONAL

ich	würde können
du	würdest können
er	würde können
wir	würden können
ihr	würdet können
sie	würden können

IMPERATIVE

PAST PARTICIPLE

gekonnt/können*

PRESENT PARTICIPLE

könnend

The second form is used when combined with an infinitive construction.

EXAMPLE PHRASES

*Er **kann** gut schwimmen.* He can swim well.
*Sie **konnte** kein Wort Deutsch.* She couldn't speak a word of German.
***Kann** ich gehen?* Can I go?

---

ich = I **du** = you **er** = he **wir** = we/one **ihr** = you **sie** = they

▶ lassen (to leave; to allow)

PRESENT

ich	lasse
du	lässt
er	lässt
wir	lassen
ihr	lasst
sie	lassen

PRESENT SUBJUNCTIVE

ich	lasse
du	lassest
er	lasse
wir	lassen
ihr	lasset
sie	lassen

PERFECT

ich	habe gelassen
du	hast gelassen
er	hat gelassen
wir	haben gelassen
ihr	habt gelassen
sie	haben gelassen

IMPERFECT

ich	ließ
du	ließest
er	ließ
wir	ließen
ihr	ließt
sie	ließen

FUTURE

ich	werde lassen
du	wirst lassen
er	wird lassen
wir	werden lassen
ihr	werdet lassen
sie	werden lassen

CONDITIONAL

ich	würde lassen
du	würdest lassen
er	würde lassen
wir	würden lassen
ihr	würdet lassen
sie	würden lassen

IMPERATIVE

lass!/lassen wir!/lasst!
lassen Sie!

PAST PARTICIPLE

gelassen/lassen*

PRESENT PARTICIPLE

lassend

The second form is used when combined with an infinitive construction.

EXAMPLE PHRASES

*Sie **ließ** uns warten.* She kept us waiting.
*Ich **lasse** den Hund nicht auf das Sofa.* I won't let the dog get up on the sofa.
*Sie **haben** ihn allein im Auto **gelassen**.* They left him alone in the car.

ich = I **du** = you **er** = he **wir** = we/one **ihr** = you **sie** = they

▶ laufen (to run)

PRESENT		PRESENT SUBJUNCTIVE	
ich	laufe	ich	laufe
du	läufst	du	laufest
er	läuft	er	laufe
wir	laufen	wir	laufen
ihr	lauft	ihr	laufet
sie	laufen	sie	laufen

PERFECT		IMPERFECT	
ich	bin gelaufen	ich	lief
du	bist gelaufen	du	liefst
er	ist gelaufen	er	lief
wir	sind gelaufen	wir	liefen
ihr	seid gelaufen	ihr	lieft
sie	sind gelaufen	sie	liefen

FUTURE		CONDITIONAL	
ich	werde laufen	ich	würde laufen
du	wirst laufen	du	würdest laufen
er	wird laufen	er	würde laufen
wir	werden laufen	wir	würden laufen
ihr	werdet laufen	ihr	würdet laufen
sie	werden laufen	sie	würden laufen

IIMPERATIVE

lauf(e)!/laufen wir!/lauft!
laufen Sie!

PAST PARTICIPLE

gelaufen

PRESENT PARTICIPLE

laufend

EXAMPLE PHRASES

*Er **lief** so schnell er konnte.* He ran as fast as he could.
*Sie **läuft** ständig zur Polizei.* She's always going to the police.
*Das Schiff **ist** auf Grund **gelaufen**.* The ship ran aground.

ich = I **du** = you **er** = he **wir** = we/one **ihr** = you **sie** = they

▶ lesen (to read)

PRESENT

ich	lese
du	liest
er	liest
wir	lesen
ihr	lest
sie	lesen

PRESENT SUBJUNCTIVE

ich	lese
du	lesest
er	lese
wir	lesen
ihr	leset
sie	lesen

PERFECT

ich	habe gelesen
du	hast gelesen
er	hat gelesen
wir	haben gelesen
ihr	habt gelesen
sie	haben gelesen

IMPERFECT

ich	las
du	lasest
er	las
wir	lasen
ihr	last
sie	lasen

FUTURE

ich	werde lesen
du	wirst lesen
er	wird lesen
wir	werden lesen
ihr	werdet lesen
sie	werden lesen

CONDITIONAL

ich	würde lesen
du	würdest lesen
er	würde lesen
wir	würden lesen
ihr	würdet lesen
sie	würden lesen

IMPERATIVE

lies!/lesen wir!/lest!/lesen Sie!

PAST PARTICIPLE

gelesen

PRESENT PARTICIPLE

lesend

EXAMPLE PHRASES

Das habe ich in der Zeitung gelesen. I read it in the newspaper.
Es war in ihrem Gesicht zu lesen. It was written all over her face.
Dieses Buch liest sich gut. This book is a good read.

ich = I **du** = you **er** = he **wir** = we/one **ihr** = you **sie** = they

▶ liegen (to lie)

PRESENT

ich	liege
du	liegst
er	liegt
wir	liegen
ihr	liegt
sie	liegen

PRESENT SUBJUNCTIVE

ich	liege
du	liegest
er	liege
wir	liegen
ihr	lieget
sie	liegen

PERFECT

ich	habe gelegen
du	hast gelegen
er	hat gelegen
wir	haben gelegen
ihr	habt gelegen
sie	haben gelegen

IMPERFECT

ich	lag
du	lagst
er	lag
wir	lagen
ihr	lagt
sie	lagen

FUTURE

ich	werde liegen
du	wirst liegen
er	wird liegen
wir	werden liegen
ihr	werdet liegen
sie	werden liegen

CONDITIONAL

ich	würde liegen
du	würdest liegen
er	würde liegen
wir	würden liegen
ihr	würdet liegen
sie	würden liegen

IMPERATIVE

lieg(e)!/liegen wir!/liegt!
liegen Sie!

PAST PARTICIPLE

gelegen

PRESENT PARTICIPLE

liegend

EXAMPLE PHRASES

*Wir **lagen** den ganzen Tag am Strand.* We lay on the beach all day.
*Köln **liegt** am Rhein.* Cologne is on the Rhine.
*Es **hat** daran **gelegen**, dass ich krank war.* It was because I was ill.

ich = I **du** = you **er** = he **wir** = we/one **ihr** = you **sie** = they

▶ **machen** (to do *or* to make)

PRESENT

ich	mache
du	machst
er	macht
wir	machen
ihr	macht
sie	machen

PRESENT SUBJUNCTIVE

ich	mache
du	machest
er	mache
wir	machen
ihr	machet
sie	machen

PERFECT

ich	habe gemacht
du	hast gemacht
er	hat gemacht
wir	haben gemacht
ihr	habt gemacht
sie	haben gemacht

IMPERFECT

ich	machte
du	machtest
er	machte
wir	machten
ihr	machtet
sie	machten

FUTURE

ich	werde machen
du	wirst machen
er	wird machen
wir	werden machen
ihr	werdet machen
sie	werden machen

CONDITIONAL

ich	würde machen
du	würdest machen
er	würde machen
wir	würden machen
ihr	würdet machen
sie	würden machen

IMPERATIVE

mach!/macht!/machen Sie!

PAST PARTICIPLE

gemacht

PRESENT PARTICIPLE

machend

EXAMPLE PHRASES

*Was **machst** du?* What are you doing?
*Ich **habe** die Betten **gemacht**.* I made the beds.
*Ich **werde** es morgen **machen**.* I'll do it tomorrow.

ich = I **du** = you **er** = he **wir** = we/one **ihr** = you **sie** = they

▶ mögen (to like)

PRESENT

ich	mag
du	magst
er	mag
wir	mögen
ihr	mögt
sie	mögen

PRESENT SUBJUNCTIVE

ich	möge
du	mögest
er	möge
wir	mögen
ihr	möget
sie	mögen

PERFECT

ich	habe gemocht/mögen
du	hast gemocht/mögen
er	hat gemocht/mögen
wir	haben gemocht/mögen
ihr	habt gemocht/mögen
sie	haben gemocht/mögen

IMPERFECT

ich	mochte
du	mochtest
er	mochte
wir	mochten
ihr	mochtet
sie	mochten

FUTURE

ich	werde mögen
du	wirst mögen
er	wird mögen
wir	werden mögen
ihr	werdet mögen
sie	werden mögen

CONDITIONAL

ich	würde mögen
du	würdest mögen
er	würde mögen
wir	würden mögen
ihr	würdet mögen
sie	würden mögen

IMPERATIVE

PAST PARTICIPLE

gemocht/mögen

PRESENT PARTICIPLE

mögend

The second form is used when combined with an infinitive construction.

EXAMPLE PHRASES

*Ich **mag** gern Vanilleeis.* I like vanilla ice cream.
*Er **mochte** sie nicht danach fragen.* He didn't want to ask her about it.
*Ich **habe** ihn noch nie **gemocht**.* I never liked him.

ich = I **du** = you **er** = he **wir** = we/one **ihr** = you **sie** = they

▶ müssen (to have to)

PRESENT

ich	muss
du	musst
er	muss
wir	müssen
ihr	müsst
sie	müssen

PRESENT SUBJUNCTIVE

ich	müsse
du	müssest
er	müsse
wir	müssen
ihr	müsset
sie	müssen

PERFECT

ich	habe gemusst/müssen
du	hast gemusst/müssen
er	hat gemusst/müssen
wir	haben gemusst/müssen
ihr	habt gemusst/müssen
sie	haben gemusst/müssen

IMPERFECT

ich	musste
du	musstest
er	musste
wir	mussten
ihr	musstet
sie	mussten

FUTURE

ich	werde müssen
du	wirst müssen
er	wird müssen
wir	werden müssen
ihr	werdet müssen
sie	werden müssen

CONDITIONAL

ich	würde müssen
du	würdest müssen
er	würde müssen
wir	würden müssen
ihr	würdet müssen
sie	würden müssen

IMPERATIVE

PAST PARTICIPLE

gemusst/müssen*

PRESENT PARTICIPLE

müssend

*The second form is used when combined with an infinitive construction.

EXAMPLE PHRASES

*Ich **muss** aufs Klo.* I must go to the loo.
*Wir **müssen** jeden Abend unsere Hausaufgaben machen.* We have to do our homework every night.
*Sie **hat** abwaschen **müssen**.* She had to wash up.

ich = I **du** = you **er** = he **wir** = we/one **ihr** = you **sie** = they

▶ **nehmen** (to take)

PRESENT

ich	nehme
du	nimmst
er	nimmt
wir	nehmen
ihr	nehmt
sie	nehmen

PRESENT SUBJUNCTIVE

ich	nehme
du	nehmest
er	nehme
wir	nehmen
ihr	nehmet
sie	nehmen

PERFECT

ich	habe genommen
du	hast genommen
er	hat genommen
wir	haben genommen
ihr	habt genommen
sie	haben genommen

IMPERFECT

ich	nahm
du	nahmst
er	nahm
wir	nahmen
ihr	nahmt
sie	nahmen

FUTURE

ich	werde nehmen
du	wirst nehmen
er	wird nehmen
wir	werden nehmen
ihr	werdet nehmen
sie	werden nehmen

CONDITIONAL

ich	würde nehmen
du	würdest nehmen
er	würde nehmen
wir	würden nehmen
ihr	würdet nehmen
sie	würden nehmen

IMPERATIVE

nimm!/nehmen wir!/nehmt!
nehmen Sie!

PAST PARTICIPLE

genommen

PRESENT PARTICIPLE

nehmend

EXAMPLE PHRASES

Hast du den Bus in die Stadt genommen? Did you take the bus into town?
Wie viel nimmst du dafür? How much will you take for it?
Er nahm sich vom Brot. He helped himself to bread.

---

ich = I   **du** = you   **er** = he   **wir** = we/one   **ihr** = you   **sie** = they

▶ schlafen (to sleep)

PRESENT

ich	schlafe
du	schläfst
er	schläft
wir	schlafen
ihr	schlaft
sie	schlafen

PRESENT SUBJUNCTIVE

ich	schlafe
du	schlafest
er	schlafe
wir	schlafen
ihr	schlafet
sie	schlafen

PERFECT

ich	habe geschlafen
du	hast geschlafen
er	hat geschlafen
wir	haben geschlafen
ihr	habt geschlafen
sie	haben geschlafen

IMPERFECT

ich	schlief
du	schliefst
er	schlief
wir	schliefen
ihr	schlieft
sie	schliefen

FUTURE

ich	werde schlafen
du	wirst schlafen
er	wird schlafen
wir	werden schlafen
ihr	werdet schlafen
sie	werden schlafen

CONDITIONAL

ich	würde schlafen
du	würdest schlafen
er	würde schlafen
wir	würden schlafen
ihr	würdet schlafen
sie	würden schlafen

IMPERATIVE

schlaf(e)!/schlafen wir!/schlaft!
schlafen Sie!

PAST PARTICIPLE

geschlafen

PRESENT PARTICIPLE

schlafend

EXAMPLE PHRASES

*Sie **schläft** immer noch.* She's still asleep.
*Heute Nacht **wirst** du bestimmt gut **schlafen**.* I'm sure you'll sleep well tonight.
*Er **schlief** während des Unterrichts.* He slept during lessons.

ich = I **du** = you **er** = he **wir** = we/one **ihr** = you **sie** = they

▶ schneiden (to cut)

PRESENT

ich	schneide
du	schneidest
er	schneidet
wir	schneiden
ihr	schneidet
sie	schneiden

PRESENT SUBJUNCTIVE

ich	schneide
du	schneidest
er	schneide
wir	schneiden
ihr	schneidet
sie	schneiden

PERFECT

ich	habe geschnitten
du	hast geschnitten
er	hat geschnitten
wir	haben geschnitten
ihr	habt geschnitten
sie	haben geschnitten

IMPERFECT

ich	schnitt
du	schnittst
er	schnitt
wir	schnitten
ihr	schnittet
sie	schnitten

FUTURE

ich	werde schneiden
du	wirst schneiden
er	wird schneiden
wir	werden schneiden
ihr	werdet schneiden
sie	werden schneiden

CONDITIONAL

ich	würde schneiden
du	würdest schneiden
er	würde schneiden
wir	würden schneiden
ihr	würdet schneiden
sie	würden schneiden

IMPERATIVE

schneid(e)!/schneiden wir!
schneidet!/schneiden Sie!

PAST PARTICIPLE

geschnitten

PRESENT PARTICIPLE

schneidend

EXAMPLE PHRASES

*Sie **schneidet** ihm die Haare.* She cuts his hair.
*Ich **habe** mir in den Finger **geschnitten**.* I've cut my finger.
*Sie **schnitt** die Tomaten in Scheiben.* She sliced the tomatoes.

ich = I **du** = you **er** = he **wir** = we/one **ihr** = you **sie** = they

▶ schreiben (to write)

PRESENT

ich	schreibe
du	schreibst
er	schreibt
wir	schreiben
ihr	schreibt
sie	schreiben

PRESENT SUBJUNCTIVE

ich	schreibe
du	schreibest
er	schreibe
wir	schreiben
ihr	schreibet
sie	schreiben

PERFECT

ich	habe geschrieben
du	hast geschrieben
er	hat geschrieben
wir	haben geschrieben
ihr	habt geschrieben
sie	haben geschrieben

IMPERFECT

ich	schrieb
du	schriebst
er	schrieb
wir	schrieben
ihr	schriebt
sie	schrieben

FUTURE

ich	werde schreiben
du	wirst schreiben
er	wird schreiben
wir	werden schreiben
ihr	werdet schreiben
sie	werden schreiben

CONDITIONAL

ich	würde schreiben
du	würdest schreiben
er	würde schreiben
wir	würden schreiben
ihr	würdet schreiben
sie	würden schreiben

IMPERATIVE

schreib(e)!/schreiben wir!
schreibt!/schreiben Sie!

PAST PARTICIPLE

geschrieben

PRESENT PARTICIPLE

schreibend

EXAMPLE PHRASES

*Er **schrieb** das Wort an die Tafel.* He wrote the word on the blackboard.
*Wie **schreibst** du deinen Namen?* How do you spell your name?
*Sie **hat** mir einen Brief **geschrieben**.* She wrote me a letter.

ich = I **du** = you **er** = he **wir** = we/one **ihr** = you **sie** = they

▶ sehen (to see)

PRESENT

ich	sehe
du	siehst
er	sieht
wir	sehen
ihr	seht
sie	sehen

PRESENT SUBJUNCTIVE

ich	sehe
du	sehest
er	sehe
wir	sehen
ihr	sehet
sie	sehen

PERFECT

ich	habe gesehen
du	hast gesehen
er	hat gesehen
wir	haben gesehen
ihr	habt gesehen
sie	haben gesehen

IMPERFECT

ich	sah
du	sahst
er	sah
wir	sahen
ihr	saht
sie	sahen

FUTURE

ich	werde sehen
du	wirst sehen
er	wird sehen
wir	werden sehen
ihr	werdet sehen
sie	werden sehen

CONDITIONAL

ich	würde sehen
du	würdest sehen
er	würde sehen
wir	würden sehen
ihr	würdet sehen
sie	würden sehen

IMPERATIVE

sieh(e)!/sehen wir!/seht!
sehen Sie!

PAST PARTICIPLE

gesehen

PRESENT PARTICIPLE

sehend

EXAMPLE PHRASES

*Mein Vater **sieht** schlecht.* My father has bad eyesight.
*Ich **habe** diesen Film noch nicht **gesehen**.* I haven't seen this film yet.
*Er **sah** auf die Uhr.* He looked at his watch.

ich = I **du** = you **er** = he **wir** = we/one **ihr** = you **sie** = they

▶ sein (to be)

PRESENT

ich	bin
du	bist
er	ist
wir	sind
ihr	seid
sie	sind

PRESENT SUBJUNCTIVE

ich	sei
du	sei(e)st
er	sei
wir	seien
ihr	seiet
sie	seien

PERFECT

ich	bin gewesen
du	bist gewesen
er	ist gewesen
wir	sind gewesen
ihr	seid gewesen
sie	sind gewesen

IMPERFECT

ich	war
du	warst
er	war
wir	waren
ihr	wart
sie	waren

FUTURE

ich	werde sein
du	wirst sein
er	wird sein
wir	werden sein
ihr	werdet sein
sie	werden sein

CONDITIONAL

ich	würde sein
du	würdest sein
er	würde sein
wir	würden sein
ihr	würdet sein
sie	würden sein

IMPERATIVE

sei!/seien wir!/seid!/seien Sie!

PAST PARTICIPLE

gewesen

PRESENT PARTICIPLE

seiend

EXAMPLE PHRASES

*Er **ist** zehn Jahre alt.* He is ten years old.
*Mir **ist** kalt.* I'm cold.
*Wir **waren** gestern im Theater.* We were at the theatre yesterday.
***Seid** ruhig!* Be quiet!

ich = I **du** = you **er** = he **wir** = we/one **ihr** = you **sie** = they

▶ singen (to sing)

PRESENT

ich	singe
du	singst
er	singt
wir	singen
ihr	singt
sie	singen

PRESENT SUBJUNCTIVE

ich	singe
du	singest
er	singe
wir	singen
ihr	singet
sie	singen

PERFECT

ich	habe gesungen
du	hast gesungen
er	hat gesungen
wir	haben gesungen
ihr	habt gesungen
sie	haben gesungen

IMPERFECT

ich	sang
du	sangst
er	sang
wir	sangen
ihr	sangt
sie	sangen

FUTURE

ich	werde singen
du	wirst singen
er	wird singen
wir	werden singen
ihr	werdet singen
sie	werden singen

CONDITIONAL

ich	würde singen
du	würdest singen
er	würde singen
wir	würden singen
ihr	würdet singen
sie	würden singen

IMPERATIVE

sing(e)!/singen wir!/singt!
singen Sie!

PAST PARTICIPLE

gesungen

PRESENT PARTICIPLE

singend

EXAMPLE PHRASES

Sie sang das Kind in den Schlaf. She sang the child to sleep.
Er singt nicht gut. He's a bad singer.
Ich habe dieses Lied früher oft gesungen. I used to sing this song a lot.

ich = I **du** = you **er** = he **wir** = we/one **ihr** = you **sie** = they

▶ sitzen (to sit)

PRESENT

ich	sitze
du	sitzt
er	sitzt
wir	sitzen
ihr	sitzt
sie	sitzen

PRESENT SUBJUNCTIVE

ich	sitze
du	sitzest
er	sitze
wir	sitzen
ihr	sitzet
sie	sitzen

PERFECT

ich	habe gesessen
du	hast gesessen
er	hat gesessen
wir	haben gesessen
ihr	habt gesessen
sie	haben gesessen

IMPERFECT

ich	saß
du	saßest
er	saß
wir	saßen
ihr	saßt
sie	saßen

FUTURE

ich	werde sitzen
du	wirst sitzen
er	wird sitzen
wir	werden sitzen
ihr	werdet sitzen
sie	werden sitzen

CONDITIONAL

ich	würde sitzen
du	würdest sitzen
er	würde sitzen
wir	würden sitzen
ihr	würdet sitzen
sie	würden sitzen

IMPERATIVE

sitz(e)!/sitzen wir!/sitzt!
sitzen Sie!

PAST PARTICIPLE

gesessen

PRESENT PARTICIPLE

sitzend

EXAMPLE PHRASES

Er saß auf meinem Stuhl. He was sitting on my chair.
Deine Krawatte sitzt nicht richtig. Your tie isn't straight.
Ich habe zwei Jahre über dieser Arbeit gesessen. I've spent two years on this piece of work.

---

ich = I **du** = you **er** = he **wir** = we/one **ihr** = you **sie** = they

▶ sprechen (to speak)

PRESENT

ich	spreche
du	sprichst
er	spricht
wir	sprechen
ihr	sprecht
sie	sprechen

PRESENT SUBJUNCTIVE

ich	spreche
du	sprechest
er	spreche
wir	sprechen
ihr	sprechet
sie	sprechen

PERFECT

ich	habe gesprochen
du	hast gesprochen
er	hat gesprochen
wir	haben gesprochen
ihr	habt gesprochen
sie	haben gesprochen

IMPERFECT

ich	sprach
du	sprachst
er	sprach
wir	sprachen
ihr	spracht
sie	sprachen

FUTURE

ich	werde sprechen
du	wirst sprechen
er	wird sprechen
wir	werden sprechen
ihr	werdet sprechen
sie	werden sprechen

CONDITIONAL

ich	würde sprechen
du	würdest sprechen
er	würde sprechen
wir	würden sprechen
ihr	würdet sprechen
sie	würden sprechen

IMPERATIVE

sprich!/sprechen wir!/sprecht!
sprechen Sie!

PAST PARTICIPLE

gesprochen

PRESENT PARTICIPLE

sprechend

EXAMPLE PHRASES

*Er **spricht** kein Italienisch.* He doesn't speak Italian.
*Ich **würde** dich gern privat **sprechen.*** I would like to speak to you privately.
Hast** du mit ihr **gesprochen? Have you spoken to her?

---

ich = I **du** = you **er** = he **wir** = we/one **ihr** = you **sie** = they

▶ stehen (to stand)

PRESENT		PRESENT SUBJUNCTIVE	
ich	stehe	ich	stehe
du	stehst	du	stehest
er	steht	er	stehe
wir	stehen	wir	stehen
ihr	steht	ihr	stehet
sie	stehen	sie	stehen

PERFECT		IMPERFECT	
ich	habe gestanden	ich	stand
du	hast gestanden	du	stand(e)st
er	hat gestanden	er	stand
wir	haben gestanden	wir	standen
ihr	habt gestanden	ihr	standet
sie	haben gestanden	sie	standen

FUTURE		CONDITIONAL	
ich	werde stehen	ich	würde stehen
du	wirst stehen	du	würdest stehen
er	wird stehen	er	würde stehen
wir	werden stehen	wir	würden stehen
ihr	werdet stehen	ihr	würdet stehen
sie	werden stehen	sie	würden stehen

IMPERATIVE

steh(e)!/stehen wir!/steht!
stehen Sie!

PAST PARTICIPLE

gestanden

PRESENT PARTICIPLE

stehend

EXAMPLE PHRASES

*Wir **standen** an der Bushaltestelle.* We stood at the bus stop.
*Es **hat** in der Zeitung **gestanden**.* It was in the newspaper.
*Dieses Kleid **würde** dir gut **stehen**.* This dress would suit you.

ich = I **du** = you **er** = he **wir** = we/one **ihr** = you **sie** = they

▶ sterben (to die)

PRESENT

ich	sterbe
du	stirbst
er	stirbt
wir	sterben
ihr	sterbt
sie	sterben

PRESENT SUBJUNCTIVE

ich	sterbe
du	sterbest
er	sterbe
wir	sterben
ihr	sterbet
sie	sterben

PERFECT

ich	bin gestorben
du	bist gestorben
er	ist gestorben
wir	sind gestorben
ihr	seid gestorben
sie	sind gestorben

IMPERFECT

ich	starb
du	starbst
er	starb
wir	starben
ihr	starbt
sie	starben

FUTURE

ich	werde sterben
du	wirst sterben
er	wird sterben
wir	werden sterben
ihr	werdet sterben
sie	werden sterben

CONDITIONAL

ich	würde sterben
du	würdest sterben
er	würde sterben
wir	würden sterben
ihr	würdet sterben
sie	würden sterben

IMPERATIVE

stirb!/sterben wir!/sterbt!
sterben Sie!

PAST PARTICIPLE

gestorben

PRESENT PARTICIPLE

sterbend

EXAMPLE PHRASES

*Er **starb** eines natürlichen Todes.* He died a natural death.
*Shakespeare **ist** 1616 **gestorben**.* Shakespeare died in 1616.
*Daran **wirst** du nicht **sterben**!* It won't kill you!

---

ich = I **du** = you **er** = he **wir** = we/one **ihr** = you **sie** = they

▶ **tragen** (to wear, to carry)

PRESENT

ich	trage
du	trägst
er	trägt
wir	tragen
ihr	tragt
sie	tragen

PRESENT SUBJUNCTIVE

ich	trage
du	tragest
er	trage
wir	tragen
ihr	traget
sie	tragen

PERFECT

ich	habe getragen
du	hast getragen
er	hat getragen
wir	haben getragen
ihr	habt getragen
sie	haben getragen

IMPERFECT

ich	trug
du	trugst
er	trug
wir	trugen
ihr	trugt
sie	trugen

FUTURE

ich	werde tragen
du	wirst tragen
er	wird tragen
wir	werden tragen
ihr	werdet tragen
sie	werden tragen

CONDITIONAL

ich	würde tragen
du	würdest tragen
er	würde tragen
wir	würden tragen
ihr	würdet tragen
sie	würden tragen

IMPERATIVE

trag(e)!/tragen wir!/tragt!
tragen Sie!

PAST PARTICIPLE

getragen

PRESENT PARTICIPLE

tragend

EXAMPLE PHRASES

*Ich **trug** ihren Koffer zum Bahnhof.* I carried her case to the station.
*Du **trägst** die ganze Verantwortung dafür.* You bear the full responsibility for it.
*Ich **würde** meine Haare gern länger **tragen**.* I'd like to wear my hair longer.

ich = I **du** = you **er** = he **wir** = we/one **ihr** = you **sie** = they

▶ treffen (to meet)

PRESENT		PRESENT SUBJUNCTIVE	
ich	treffe	ich	treffe
du	triffst	du	treffest
er	trifft	er	treffe
wir	treffen	wir	treffen
ihr	trefft	ihr	treffet
sie	treffen	sie	treffen

PERFECT		IMPERFECT	
ich	habe getroffen	ich	traf
du	hast getroffen	du	trafst
er	hat getroffen	er	traf
wir	haben getroffen	wir	trafen
ihr	habt getroffen	ihr	traft
sie	haben getroffen	sie	trafen

FUTURE		CONDITIONAL	
ich	werde treffen	ich	würde treffen
du	wirst treffen	du	würdest treffen
er	wird treffen	er	würde treffen
wir	werden treffen	wir	würden treffen
ihr	werdet treffen	ihr	würdet treffen
sie	werden treffen	sie	würden treffen

IMPERATIVE

triff!/treffen wir!/trefft!
treffen Sie!

PAST PARTICIPLE

getroffen

PRESENT PARTICIPLE

treffend

EXAMPLE PHRASES

*Sie **trifft** sich zweimal pro Woche mit ihm.* She meets with him twice a week.
*Der Schuss **traf** ihn am Kopf.* The shot hit him in the head.
*Du **hast** das Ziel gut **getroffen**.* You hit the target well.

---

ich = I **du** = you **er** = he **wir** = we/one **ihr** = you **sie** = they

▶ **trinken** (to drink)

PRESENT

ich	trinke
du	trinkst
er	trinkt
wir	trinken
ihr	trinkt
sie	trinken

PRESENT SUBJUNCTIVE

ich	trinke
du	trinkest
er	trinke
wir	trinken
ihr	trinket
sie	trinken

PERFECT

ich	habe getrunken
du	hast getrunken
er	hat getrunken
wir	haben getrunken
ihr	habt getrunken
sie	haben getrunken

IMPERFECT

ich	trank
du	trankst
er	trank
wir	tranken
ihr	trankt
sie	tranken

FUTURE

ich	werde trinken
du	wirst trinken
er	wird trinken
wir	werden trinken
ihr	werdet trinken
sie	werden trinken

CONDITIONAL

ich	würde trinken
du	würdest trinken
er	würde trinken
wir	würden trinken
ihr	würdet trinken
sie	würden trinken

IMPERATIVE

trink(e)!/trinken wir!/trinkt!
trinken Sie!

PAST PARTICIPLE

getrunken

PRESENT PARTICIPLE

trinkend

EXAMPLE PHRASES

*Er **trank** die ganze Flasche leer.* He drank the whole bottle.
*Ich **habe** zu viel **getrunken**.* I've had too much to drink.
*Wollen wir etwas **trinken** gehen?* Shall we go for a drink?

---

ich = I **du** = you **er** = he **wir** = we/one **ihr** = you **sie** = they

▶ tun (to do)

PRESENT

ich	tue
du	tust
er	tut
wir	tun
ihr	tut
sie	tun

PRESENT SUBJUNCTIVE

ich	tue
du	tuest
er	tue
wir	tuen
ihr	tuet
sie	tuen

PERFECT

ich	habe getan
du	hast getan
er	hat getan
wir	haben getan
ihr	habt getan
sie	haben getan

IMPERFECT

ich	tat
du	tat(e)st
er	tat
wir	taten
ihr	tatet
sie	taten

FUTURE

ich	werde tun
du	wirst tun
er	wird tun
wir	werden tun
ihr	werdet tun
sie	werden tun

CONDITIONAL

ich	würde tun
du	würdest tun
er	würde tun
wir	würden tun
ihr	würdet tun
sie	würden tun

IMPERATIVE

tu(e)!/tun wir!/tut!/tun Sie!

PAST PARTICIPLE

getan

PRESENT PARTICIPLE

tuend

EXAMPLE PHRASES

*Ich **werde** das auf keinen Fall **tun**.* There is no way I'll do that.
*So etwas **tut** man nicht!* That is just not done!
*Sie **tat**, als ob sie schliefe.* She pretended to be sleeping.

---

ich = I **du** = you **er** = he **wir** = we/one **ihr** = you **sie** = they

▶ vergessen (to forget)

PRESENT

ich	vergesse
du	vergisst
er	vergisst
wir	vergessen
ihr	vergesst
sie	vergessen

PRESENT SUBJUNCTIVE

ich	vergesse
du	vergessest
er	vergesse
wir	vergessen
ihr	vergesset
sie	vergessen

PERFECT

ich	habe vergessen
du	hast vergessen
er	hat vergessen
wir	haben vergessen
ihr	habt vergessen
sie	haben vergessen

IMPERFECT

ich	vergaß
du	vergaßest
er	vergaß
wir	vergaßen
ihr	vergaßt
sie	vergaßen

FUTURE

ich	werde vergessen
du	wirst vergessen
er	wird vergessen
wir	werden vergessen
ihr	werdet vergessen
sie	werden vergessen

CONDITIONAL

ich	würde vergessen
du	würdest vergessen
er	würde vergessen
wir	würden vergessen
ihr	würdet vergessen
sie	würden vergessen

IMPERATIVE

vergiss!/vergessen wir!
vergesst!/vergessen Sie!

PAST PARTICIPLE

vergessen

PRESENT PARTICIPLE

vergessend

EXAMPLE PHRASES

*Ich **habe** seinen Namen **vergessen**.* I've forgotten his name.
*Sie **vergaß**, die Blumen zu gießen.* She forgot to water the flowers.
*Sie **vergisst** ständig ihre Bücher.* She always forgets to bring her books.

ich = I **du** = you **er** = he **wir** = we/one **ihr** = you **sie** = they

▶ **verlieren** (to lose)

PRESENT

ich	verliere
du	verlierst
er	verliert
wir	verlieren
ihr	verliert
sie	verlieren

PRESENT SUBJUNCTIVE

ich	verliere
du	verlierest
er	verliere
wir	verlieren
ihr	verlieret
sie	verlieren

PERFECT

ich	habe verloren
du	hast verloren
er	hat verloren
wir	haben verloren
ihr	habt verloren
sie	haben verloren

IMPERFECT

ich	verlor
du	verlorst
er	verlor
wir	verloren
ihr	verlort
sie	verloren

FUTURE

ich	werde verlieren
du	wirst verlieren
er	wird verlieren
wir	werden verlieren
ihr	werdet verlieren
sie	werden verlieren

CONDITIONAL

ich	würde verlieren
du	würdest verlieren
er	würde verlieren
wir	würden verlieren
ihr	würdet verlieren
sie	würden verlieren

IMPERATIVE

verlier(e)!/verlieren wir!
verliert!/verlieren Sie!

PAST PARTICIPLE

verloren

PRESENT PARTICIPLE

verlierend

EXAMPLE PHRASES

*Wenn du **verlierst**, musst du 10 Euro Strafe zahlen.* If you lose, you'll have to pay a 10 euro penalty.
*Wir **haben** drei Spiele hintereinander **verloren**.* We lost three matches in a row.
*Er **verlor** kein Wort darüber.* He didn't say a word about it.

---

ich = I **du** = you **er** = he **wir** = we/one **ihr** = you **sie** = they

▶ wachsen* (to grow)

PRESENT

ich	wachse
du	wächst
er	wächst
wir	wachsen
ihr	wachst
sie	wachsen

PRESENT SUBJUNCTIVE

ich	wachse
du	wachsest
er	wachse
wir	wachsen
ihr	wachset
sie	wachsen

PERFECT

ich	bin gewachsen
du	bist gewachsen
er	ist gewachsen
wir	sind gewachsen
ihr	seid gewachsen
sie	sind gewachsen

IMPERFECT

ich	wuchs
du	wuchsest
er	wuchs
wir	wuchsen
ihr	wuchst
sie	wuchsen

FUTURE

ich	werde wachsen
du	wirst wachsen
er	wird wachsen
wir	werden wachsen
ihr	werdet wachsen
sie	werden wachsen

CONDITIONAL

ich	würde wachsen
du	würdest wachsen
er	würde wachsen
wir	würden wachsen
ihr	würdet wachsen
sie	würden wachsen

IMPERATIVE

wachs(e)!/wachsen wir!
wachst!/wachsen Sie!
**Conjugated as a weak verb when
the meaning is "to wax".*

PAST PARTICIPLE

gewachsen

PRESENT PARTICIPLE

wachsend

EXAMPLE PHRASES

*Der Baum **wächst** nicht mehr.* The tree has stopped growing.
*Er ließ sich einen Bart **wachsen**.* He grew a beard.
*Sie **ist** gut **gewachsen**.* She has a good figure.

ich = I **du** = you **er** = he **wir** = we/one **ihr** = you **sie** = they

▶ waschen (to wash)

PRESENT

ich	wasche
du	wäschst
er	wäscht
wir	waschen
ihr	wascht
sie	waschen

PRESENT SUBJUNCTIVE

ich	wasche
du	waschest
er	wasche
wir	waschen
ihr	waschet
sie	waschen

PERFECT

ich	habe gewaschen
du	hast gewaschen
er	hat gewaschen
wir	haben gewaschen
ihr	habt gewaschen
sie	haben gewaschen

IMPERFECT

ich	wusch
du	wuschest
er	wusch
wir	wuschen
ihr	wuscht
sie	wuschen

FUTURE

ich	werde waschen
du	wirst waschen
er	wird waschen
wir	werden waschen
ihr	werdet waschen
sie	werden waschen

CONDITIONAL

ich	würde waschen
du	würdest waschen
er	würde waschen
wir	würden waschen
ihr	würdet waschen
sie	würden waschen

IMPERATIVE

wasch(e)!/waschen wir!
wascht!/waschen Sie!

PAST PARTICIPLE

gewaschen

PRESENT PARTICIPLE

waschend

EXAMPLE PHRASES

*Ich **habe** mir die Hände **gewaschen**.* I washed my hands.
*Er **wäscht** sich jeden Tag.* He washes every day.
*Die Katze **wusch** sich in der Sonne.* The cat was washing itself in the sunshine.

ich = I **du** = you **er** = he **wir** = we/one **ihr** = you **sie** = they

▶ **werden** (to become)

PRESENT

ich	werde
du	wirst
er	wird
wir	werden
ihr	werdet
sie	werden

PRESENT SUBJUNCTIVE

ich	werde
du	werdest
er	werde
wir	werden
ihr	werdet
sie	werden

PERFECT

ich	bin geworden/worden
du	bist geworden/worden
er	ist geworden/worden
wir	sind geworden/worden
ihr	seid geworden/worden
sie	sind geworden/worden

IMPERFECT

ich	wurde
du	wurdest
er	wurde
wir	wurden
ihr	wurdet
sie	wurden

FUTURE

ich	werde werden
du	wirst werden
er	wird werden
wir	werden werden
ihr	werdet werden
sie	werden werden

CONDITIONAL

ich	würde werden
du	würdest werden
er	würde werden
wir	würden werden
ihr	würdet werden
sie	würden werden

IMPERATIVE

werde!/werden wir!/werdet!
werden Sie!

PAST PARTICIPLE

geworden/worden*

PRESENT PARTICIPLE

werdend

The second form is used when combined with an infinitive construction.

EXAMPLE PHRASES

*Mir **wird** schlecht.* I feel ill.
*Ich will Lehrerin **werden**.* I want to be a teacher.
*Der Kuchen **ist** gut **geworden**.* The cake turned out well.

ich = I **du** = you **er** = he **wir** = we/one **ihr** = you **sie** = they

▶ **wissen** (to know)

PRESENT

ich	weiß
du	weißt
er	weiß
wir	wissen
ihr	wisst
sie	wissen

PRESENT SUBJUNCTIVE

ich	wisse
du	wissest
er	wisse
wir	wissen
ihr	wisset
sie	wissen

PERFECT

ich	habe gewusst
du	hast gewusst
er	hat gewusst
wir	haben gewusst
ihr	habt gewusst
sie	haben gewusst

IMPERFECT

ich	wusste
du	wusstest
er	wusste
wir	wussten
ihr	wusstet
sie	wussten

FUTURE

ich	werde wissen
du	wirst wissen
er	wird wissen
wir	werden wissen
ihr	werdet wissen
sie	werden wissen

CONDITIONAL

ich	würde wissen
du	würdest wissen
er	würde wissen
wir	würden wissen
ihr	würdet wissen
sie	würden wissen

IMPERATIVE

wisse!/wissen wir!/wisset!
wissen Sie!

PAST PARTICIPLE

gewusst

PRESENT PARTICIPLE

wissend

EXAMPLE PHRASES

*Ich **weiß** nicht.* I don't know.
*Er **hat** nichts davon **gewusst**.* He didn't know anything about it.
*Sie **wussten**, wo das Kino war.* They knew where the cinema was.

---

ich = I **du** = you **er** = he **wir** = we/one **ihr** = you **sie** = they

▶ wollen (to want)

PRESENT

ich	will
du	willst
er	will
wir	wollen
ihr	wollt
sie	wollen

PRESENT SUBJUNCTIVE

ich	wolle
du	wollest
er	wolle
wir	wollen
ihr	wollet
sie	wollen

PERFECT

ich	habe gewollt/wollen
du	hast gewollt/wollen
er	hat gewollt/wollen
wir	haben gewollt/wollen
ihr	habt gewollt/wollen
sie	haben gewollt/wollen

IMPERFECT

ich	wollte
du	wolltest
er	wollte
wir	wollten
ihr	wolltet
sie	wollten

FUTURE

ich	werde wollen
du	wirst wollen
er	wird wollen
wir	werden wollen
ihr	werdet wollen
sie	werden wollen

CONDITIONAL

ich	würde wollen
du	würdest wollen
er	würde wollen
wir	würden wollen
ihr	würdet wollen
sie	würden wollen

IMPERATIVE

wolle!/wollen wir!/wollt!
wollen Sie!

PAST PARTICIPLE

gewollt/wollen*

PRESENT PARTICIPLE

wollend

*The second form is used when combined with an infinitive construction.

EXAMPLE PHRASES

*Er **will** nach London gehen.* He wants to go to London.
*Das **habe** ich nicht **gewollt**.* I didn't want this to happen.
*Sie **wollten** nur mehr Geld.* All they wanted was more money.

ich = I **du** = you **er** = he **wir** = we/one **ihr** = you **sie** = they

▶ ziehen (to go/to pull)

PRESENT		PRESENT SUBJUNCTIVE	
ich	ziehe	ich	ziehe
du	ziehst	du	ziehest
er	zieht	er	ziehe
wir	ziehen	wir	ziehen
ihr	zieht	ihr	ziehet
sie	ziehen	sie	ziehen

PERFECT		IMPERFECT	
ich	bin/habe gezogen	ich	zog
du	bist/hast gezogen	du	zogst
er	ist/hat gezogen	er	zog
wir	sind/haben gezogen	wir	zogen
ihr	seid/habt gezogen	ihr	zogt
sie	sind/haben gezogen	sie	zogen

FUTURE		CONDITIONAL	
ich	werde ziehen	ich	würde ziehen
du	wirst ziehen	du	würdest ziehen
er	wird ziehen	er	würde ziehen
wir	werden ziehen	wir	würden ziehen
ihr	werdet ziehen	ihr	würdet ziehen
sie	werden ziehen	sie	würden ziehen

IMPERATIVE

zieh(e)!/ziehen wir!/zieht!
ziehen Sie!

PAST PARTICIPLE

gezogen

PRESENT PARTICIPLE

ziehend

EXAMPLE PHRASES

Sie **zog** *mich am Ärmel.* She pulled at my sleeve.
Seine Familie **ist** *nach München* **gezogen.** His family has moved to Munich.
In diesem Zimmer **zieht** *es.* There's a draught in this room.

ich = I **du** = you **er** = he **wir** = we/one **ihr** = you **sie** = they

ENGLISH – GERMAN
ENGLISCH – DEUTSCH

A, a

A [eɪ] n (MUS) A nt; **~ road**
Hauptverkehrsstraße f

KEYWORD

a [eɪ, ə] (before vowel or silent h: an) indef art 1
ein; eine; **a woman** eine Frau; **a book** ein
Buch; **an eagle** ein Adler; **she's a doctor**
sie ist Ärztin
2 (instead of the number "one") ein, eine; **a
year ago** vor einem Jahr; **a hundred /
thousand** etc **pounds** (ein) hundert/(ein)
tausend etc Pfund
3 (in expressing ratios, prices etc) pro; **3 a
day / week** 3 pro Tag/Woche, 3 am Tag/in
der Woche; **10 km an hour** 10 km pro
Stunde/in der Stunde

A.A. n abbr = **Alcoholics Anonymous**;
(BRIT) = **Automobile Association**

A.A.A. (US) n abbr = **American Automobile
Association**

aback [ə'bæk] adv: **to be taken ~** verblüfft
sein

abandon [ə'bændən] vt (give up) aufgeben;
(desert) verlassen ♦ n Hingabe f

abate [ə'beɪt] vi nachlassen, sich legen

abattoir ['æbətwɑːr] (BRIT) n Schlachthaus nt

abbey ['æbɪ] n Abtei f

abbot ['æbət] n Abt m

abbreviate [ə'briːvɪeɪt] vt abkürzen;
abbreviation [əbriːvɪ'eɪʃən] n Abkürzung f

abdicate ['æbdɪkeɪt] vt aufgeben ♦ vi
abdanken

abdomen ['æbdəmən] n Unterleib m

abduct [æb'dʌkt] vt entführen

aberration [æbə'reɪʃən] n (geistige)
Verwirrung f

abet [ə'bet] vt see **aid**

abeyance [ə'beɪəns] n: **in ~** in der Schwebe;
(disuse) außer Kraft

abide [ə'baɪd] vt vertragen; leiden; **~ by** vt
sich halten an +acc

ability [ə'bɪlɪtɪ] n (power) Fähigkeit f; (skill)
Geschicklichkeit f

abject ['æbdʒekt] adj (liar) übel; (poverty)
größte(r, s); (apology) zerknirscht

ablaze [ə'bleɪz] adj in Flammen

able ['eɪbl] adj geschickt, fähig; **to be ~ to
do sth** etw tun können; **~-bodied**
['eɪbl'bɔdɪd] adj kräftig; (seaman) Voll-; **ably**
['eɪblɪ] adv geschickt

abnormal [æb'nɔːməl] adj regelwidrig,
abnorm

aboard [ə'bɔːd] adv, prep an Bord +gen

abode [ə'bəud] n: **of no fixed ~** ohne festen
Wohnsitz

abolish [ə'bɔlɪʃ] vt abschaffen; **abolition**
[æbə'lɪʃən] n Abschaffung f

abominable [ə'bɔmɪnəbl] adj scheußlich

aborigine [æbə'rɪdʒɪnɪ] n Ureinwohner m

abort [ə'bɔːt] vt abtreiben; fehlgebären; **~ion**
[ə'bɔːʃən] n Abtreibung f; (miscarriage)
Fehlgeburt f; **~ive** adj misslungen

abound [ə'baund] vi im Überfluss vorhanden
sein; **to ~ in** Überfluss haben an +dat

KEYWORD

about [ə'baut] adv 1 (approximately) etwa,
ungefähr; **about a hundred / thousand** etc
etwa hundert/tausend etc; **at about 2
o'clock** etwa um 2 Uhr; **I've just about
finished** ich bin gerade fertig
2 (referring to place) herum, umher; **to
leave things lying about** Sachen
herumliegen lassen; **to run / walk** etc **about**
herumrennen/gehen etc
3: to be about to do sth im Begriff sein,
etw zu tun; **he was about to go to bed** er
wollte gerade ins Bett gehen
♦ prep 1 (relating to) über +acc; **a book**

about London ein Buch über London; **what is it about?** worum geht es?; (*book etc*) wovon handelt es?; **we talked about it** wir haben darüber geredet; **what** or **how about doing this?** wollen wir das machen? 2 (*referring to place*) um (... herum); **to walk about the town** in der Stadt herumgehen; **her clothes were scattered about the room** ihre Kleider waren über das ganze Zimmer verstreut

about-turn [ə'baut'tɜːn] n Kehrtwendung f
above [ə'bʌv] adv oben ♦ prep über; ~ **all** vor allem; ~ **board** adj offen, ehrlich
abrasive [ə'breɪzɪv] adj Abschleif-; (*personality*) zermürbend, aufreibend
abreast [ə'brest] adv nebeneinander; **to keep ~ of** Schritt halten mit
abroad [ə'brɔːd] adv (*be*) im Ausland; (*go*) ins Ausland
abrupt [ə'brʌpt] adj (*sudden*) abrupt, jäh; (*curt*) schroff; **~ly** adv abrupt
abscess ['æbsɪs] n Geschwür nt
abscond [əb'skɒnd] vi flüchten, sich davonmachen
abseil ['æbseɪl] vi (*also*: ~ **down**) sich abseilen
absence ['æbsəns] n Abwesenheit f
absent ['æbsənt] adj abwesend, nicht da; (*lost in thought*) geistesabwesend; **~-minded** adj zerstreut
absolute ['æbsəluːt] adj absolut; (*power*) unumschränkt; (*rubbish*) vollkommen, rein; **~ly** [æbsə'luːtlɪ] adv absolut, vollkommen; **~ly!** ganz bestimmt!
absolve [əb'zɒlv] vt entbinden; freisprechen
absorb [əb'zɔːb] vt aufsaugen, absorbieren; (*fig*) ganz in Anspruch nehmen, fesseln; **to be ~ed in a book** in ein Buch vertieft sein; **~ent cotton** (*US*) n Verbandwatte f; **~ing** adj aufsaugend; (*fig*) packend; **absorption** [əb'sɔːpʃən] n Aufsaugung f, Absorption f; (*fig*) Versunkenheit f
abstain [əb'steɪn] vi (*in vote*) sich enthalten; **to ~ from** (*keep from*) sich enthalten +gen
abstemious [əb'stiːmɪəs] adj enthaltsam
abstinence ['æbstɪnəns] n Enthaltsamkeit f

abstract ['æbstrækt] adj abstrakt
absurd [əb'sɜːd] adj absurd
abundance [ə'bʌndəns] n: ~ **(of)** Überfluss m (an +dat); **abundant** [ə'bʌndənt] adj reichlich
abuse [n ə'bjuːs, vb ə'bjuːz] n (*rude language*) Beschimpfung f; (*ill usage*) Missbrauch m; (*bad practice*) (Amts)missbrauch m ♦ vt (*misuse*) missbrauchen; **abusive** [ə'bjuːsɪv] adj beleidigend, Schimpf-
abysmal [ə'bɪzməl] adj scheußlich; (*ignorance*) bodenlos
abyss [ə'bɪs] n Abgrund m
AC abbr (= *alternating current*) Wechselstron, m
academic [ækə'demɪk] adj akademisch; (*theoretical*) theoretisch ♦ n Akademiker(in) m(f)
academy [ə'kædəmɪ] n (*school*) Hochschule f; (*society*) Akademie f
accelerate [æk'seləreɪt] vi schneller werden; (*AUT*) Gas geben ♦ vt beschleunigen; **acceleration** [ækselə'reɪʃən] n Beschleunigung f; **accelerator** [æk'seləreɪtə'] n Gas(pedal) nt
accent ['æksənt] n Akzent m, Tonfall m; (*mark*) Akzent m; (*stress*) Betonung f
accept [ək'sept] vt (*take*) annehmen; (*agree to*) akzeptieren; **~able** adj annehmbar; **~ance** n Annahme f
access ['ækses] n Zugang m; **~ible** [æk'sesəbl] adj (*easy to approach*) zugänglich; (*within reach*) (leicht) erreichbar
accessory [æk'sesərɪ] n Zubehörteil nt; **toilet accessories** Toilettenartikel pl
accident ['æksɪdənt] n Unfall m; (*coincidence*) Zufall m; **by ~** zufällig; **~al** [æksɪ'dentl] adj unbeabsichtigt; **~ally** [æksɪ'dentəlɪ] adv zufällig; ~ **insurance** n Unfallversicherung f; **~-prone** adj: **to be ~-prone** zu Unfällen neigen
acclaim [ə'kleɪm] vt zujubeln +dat ♦ n Beifall m
acclimatize [ə'klaɪmətaɪz] vt: **to become ~d (to)** sich gewöhnen (an +acc), sich akklimatisieren (in +dat)
accommodate [ə'kɒmədeɪt] vt

unterbringen; (*hold*) Platz haben für; (*oblige*) (aus)helfen +*dat*

accommodating [əˈkɔmədeɪtɪŋ] *adj* entgegenkommend

accommodation [əkɔməˈdeɪʃən] (*US* **accommodations**) *n* Unterkunft *f*

accompany [əˈkʌmpənɪ] *vt* begleiten

accomplice [əˈkʌmplɪs] *n* Helfershelfer *m*, Komplize *m*

accomplish [əˈkʌmplɪʃ] *vt* (*fulfil*) durchführen; (*finish*) vollenden; (*aim*) erreichen; **~ed** *adj* vollendet, ausgezeichnet; **~ment** *n* (*skill*) Fähigkeit *f*; (*completion*) Vollendung *f*; (*feat*) Leistung *f*

accord [əˈkɔːd] *n* Übereinstimmung *f* ♦ *vt* gewähren; **of one's own ~** freiwillig; **~ing to** nach, laut +*gen*; **~ance** *n*: **in ~ance with** in Übereinstimmung mit; **~ingly** *adv* danach, dementsprechend

accordion [əˈkɔːdɪən] *n* Akkordeon *nt*

accost [əˈkɔst] *vt* ansprechen

account [əˈkaʊnt] *n* (*bill*) Rechnung *f*; (*narrative*) Bericht *m*; (*report*) Rechenschaftsbericht *m*; (*in bank*) Konto *nt*; (*importance*) Geltung *f*; **~s** *npl* (FIN) Bücher *pl*; **on ~** auf Rechnung; **of no ~** ohne Bedeutung; **on no ~** keinesfalls; **on ~ of** wegen; **to take into ~** berücksichtigen; **~ for** *vt fus* (*expenditure*) Rechenschaft ablegen für; **how do you ~ for that?** wie erklären Sie (sich) das?; **~able** *adj* verantwortlich; **~ancy** [əˈkaʊntənsɪ] *n* Buchhaltung *f*; **~ant** [əˈkaʊntənt] *n* Wirtschaftsprüfer(in) *m(f)*; **~ number** *n* Kontonummer *f*

accumulate [əˈkjuːmjʊleɪt] *vt* ansammeln ♦ *vi* sich ansammeln

accuracy [ˈækjʊrəsɪ] *n* Genauigkeit *f*

accurate [ˈækjʊrɪt] *adj* genau; **~ly** *adv* genau, richtig

accusation [ækjuˈzeɪʃən] *n* Anklage *f*, Beschuldigung *f*

accuse [əˈkjuːz] *vt* anklagen, beschuldigen; **~d** *n* Angeklagte(r) *f(m)*

accustom [əˈkʌstəm] *vt*: **to ~ sb (to sth)** jdn (an etw *acc*) gewöhnen; **~ed** *adj* gewohnt

ace [eɪs] *n* Ass *nt*, (*inf*) Ass *nt*, Kanone *f*

ache [eɪk] *n* Schmerz *m* ♦ *vi* (*be sore*) schmerzen, wehtun

achieve [əˈtʃiːv] *vt* zustande *or* zu Stande bringen; (*aim*) erreichen; **~ment** *n* Leistung *f*; (*act*) Erreichen *nt*

acid [ˈæsɪd] *n* Säure *f* ♦ *adj* sauer, scharf; **~ rain** *n* saure(r) Regen *m*

acknowledge [əkˈnɔlɪdʒ] *vt* (*receipt*) bestätigen; (*admit*) zugeben; **~ment** *n* Anerkennung *f*; (*letter*) Empfangsbestätigung *f*

acne [ˈæknɪ] *n* Akne *f*

acorn [ˈeɪkɔːn] *n* Eichel *f*

acoustic [əˈkuːstɪk] *adj* akustisch; **~s** *npl* Akustik *f*

acquaint [əˈkweɪnt] *vt* vertraut machen; **to be ~ed with sb** mit jdm bekannt sein; **~ance** *n* (*person*) Bekannte(r) *f(m)*; (*knowledge*) Kenntnis *f*

acquire [əˈkwaɪəʳ] *vt* erwerben; **acquisition** [ækwɪˈzɪʃən] *n* Errungenschaft *f*; (*act*) Erwerb *m*

acquit [əˈkwɪt] *vt* (*free*) freisprechen; **to ~ o.s. well** sich bewähren; **~tal** *n* Freispruch *m*

acre [ˈeɪkəʳ] *n* Morgen *m*

acrid [ˈækrɪd] *adj* (*smell, taste*) bitter; (*smoke*) beißend

acrobat [ˈækrəbæt] *n* Akrobat *m*

across [əˈkrɔs] *prep* über +*acc* ♦ *adv* hinüber, herüber; **he lives ~ the river** er wohnt auf der anderen Seite des Flusses; **ten metres ~** zehn Meter breit; **he lives ~ from us** er wohnt uns gegenüber; **to run/swim ~** hinüberlaufen/schwimmen

acrylic [əˈkrɪlɪk] *adj* Acryl-

act [ækt] *n* (*deed*) Tat *f*; (JUR) Gesetz *nt*; (THEAT) Akt *m*; (: *turn*) Nummer *f* ♦ *vi* (*take ~ion*) handeln; (*behave*) sich verhalten; (*pretend*) vorgeben; (THEAT) spielen ♦ *vt* (*in play*) spielen; **to ~ as** fungieren als; **~ing** *adj* stellvertretend ♦ *n* Schauspielkunst *f*; (*performance*) Aufführung *f*

action [ˈækʃən] *n* (*deed*) Tat *f*; Handlung *f*; (*motion*) Bewegung *f*; (*way of working*) Funktionieren *nt*; (*battle*) Einsatz *m*, Gefecht *nt*; (*lawsuit*) Klage *f*, Prozess *m*; **out of ~**

(person) nicht einsatzfähig; *(thing)* außer Betrieb; **to take ~** etwas unternehmen; **~ replay** n *(TV)* Wiederholung f

activate ['æktɪveɪt] vt *(mechanism)* betätigen; *(CHEM, PHYS)* aktivieren

active ['æktɪv] adj *(brisk)* rege, tatkräftig; *(working)* aktiv; *(GRAM)* aktiv, Tätigkeits-; **~ly** adv aktiv; *(dislike)* offen

activity [æk'tɪvɪtɪ] n Aktivität f; *(doings)* Unternehmungen pl; *(occupation)* Tätigkeit f; **~ holiday** n Aktivurlaub m

actor ['æktər] n Schauspieler m

actress ['æktrɪs] n Schauspielerin f

actual ['æktjʊəl] adj wirklich; **~ly** adv tatsächlich; **~ly no** eigentlich nicht

acumen ['ækjʊmən] n Scharfsinn m

acute [ə'kjuːt] adj *(severe)* heftig, akut; *(keen)* scharfsinnig

ad [æd] n abbr = **advertisement**

A.D. adv abbr (= Anno Domini) n. Chr.

adamant ['ædəmənt] adj eisern; hartnäckig

adapt [ə'dæpt] vt anpassen ♦ vi: **to ~ (to)** sich anpassen (an +acc); **~able** adj anpassungsfähig; **~ation** [ædæp'teɪʃən] n *(THEAT etc)* Bearbeitung f; *(adjustment)* Anpassung f; **~er, ~or** n *(ELEC)* Zwischenstecker m

add [æd] vt *(join)* hinzufügen; *(numbers: also:* **~ up)** addieren; **~ up** vi *(make sense)* stimmen; **~ up to** vt fus ausmachen

adder ['ædər] n Kreuzotter f, Natter f

addict ['ædɪkt] n Süchtige(r) f(m); **~ed** [ə'dɪktɪd] adj: **~ed to** -süchtig; **~ion** [ə'dɪkʃən] n Sucht f; **~ive** [ə'dɪktɪv] adj: **to be ~ive** süchtig machen

addition [ə'dɪʃən] n Anhang m, Addition f; *(MATH)* Addition f, Zusammenzählen nt; **in ~** zusätzlich, außerdem; **~al** adj zusätzlich, weiter

additive ['ædɪtɪv] n Zusatz m

address [ə'drɛs] n Adresse f; *(speech)* Ansprache f ♦ vt *(letter)* adressieren; *(speak to)* ansprechen; *(make speech to)* eine Ansprache halten an +acc

adept ['ædɛpt] adj geschickt; **to be ~ at** gut sein in +dat

adequate ['ædɪkwɪt] adj angemessen

adhere [əd'hɪər] vi: **to ~ to** haften an +dat; *(fig)* festhalten an +dat

adhesive [əd'hiːzɪv] adj klebend; Kleb(e)- ♦ n Klebstoff m; **~ tape** n *(BRIT)* Klebestreifen m; *(US)* Heftpflaster nt

ad hoc [æd'hɔk] adj *(decision, committee)* Ad-hoc- ♦ adv ad hoc

adjacent [ə'dʒeɪsənt] adj benachbart; **~ to** angrenzend an +acc

adjective ['ædʒɛktɪv] n Adjektiv nt, Eigenschaftswort nt

adjoining [ə'dʒɔɪnɪŋ] adj benachbart, Neben-

adjourn [ə'dʒɜːn] vt vertagen ♦ vi abbrechen

adjudicate [ə'dʒuːdɪkeɪt] vi entscheiden, ein Urteil fällen

adjust [ə'dʒʌst] vt *(alter)* anpassen; *(put right)* regulieren, richtig stellen ♦ vi sich anpassen; **~able** adj verstellbar

ad-lib [æd'lɪb] vt, vi improvisieren ♦ adv: **ad lib** aus dem Stegreif

administer [əd'mɪnɪstər] vt *(manage)* verwalten; *(dispense)* ausüben; *(justice)* sprechen; *(medicine)* geben; **administration** [ədmɪnɪs'treɪʃən] n Verwaltung f; *(POL)* Regierung f; **administrative** [əd'mɪnɪstrətɪv] adj Verwaltungs-; **administrator** [əd'mɪnɪstreɪtər] n Verwaltungsbeamte(r) f(m)

Admiralty ['ædmərəltɪ] *(BRIT)* n Admiralität f

admiration [ædmə'reɪʃən] n Bewunderung f

admire [əd'maɪər] vt *(respect)* bewundern; *(love)* verehren; **~r** n Bewunderer m

admission [əd'mɪʃən] n *(entrance)* Einlass m; *(fee)* Eintritt(spreis m) m; *(confession)* Geständnis nt; **~ charge** n Eintritt(spreis) m

admit [əd'mɪt] vt *(let in)* einlassen; *(confess)* gestehen; *(accept)* anerkennen; **~tance** n Zulassung f; **~tedly** adv zugegebenermaßen

admonish [əd'mɔnɪʃ] vt ermahnen

ad nauseam [æd'nɔːsɪæm] adv *(repeat, talk)* endlos

ado [ə'duː] n: **without more ~** ohne weitere Umstände

adolescence [ædəu'lesns] *n* Jugendalter *nt*;
adolescent [ædəu'lesnt] *adj* jugendlich ♦ *n*
Jugendliche(r) *f(m)*

adopt [ə'dɒpt] *vt (child)* adoptieren; *(idea)*
übernehmen; **~ion** [ə'dɒpʃən] *n* Adoption *f*;
Übernahme *f*

adore [ə'dɔ:ʳ] *vt* anbeten; verehren

adorn [ə'dɔ:n] *vt* schmücken

Adriatic [eɪdrɪ'ætɪk] *n*: **the ~ (Sea)** die Adria

adrift [ə'drɪft] *adv* Wind und Wellen
preisgegeben

adult [ə'dʌlt] *n* Erwachsene(r) *f(m)*

adultery [ə'dʌltərɪ] *n* Ehebruch *m*

advance [əd'vɑ:ns] *n (progress)* Vorrücken
nt; *(money)* Vorschuss *m* ♦ *vt (move forward)*
vorrücken; *(money)* vorschießen; *(argument)*
vorbringen ♦ *vi* vorwärts gehen; **in ~** im
Voraus; **~ booking** *n* Vorverkauf *m*; **~d** *adj
(ahead)* vorgerückt; *(modern)*
fortgeschritten; *(study)* für Fortgeschrittene

advantage [əd'vɑ:ntɪdʒ] *n* Vorteil *m*; **to
have an ~ over sb** jdm gegenüber im
Vorteil sein; **to take ~ of** *(misuse)*
ausnutzen; *(profit from)* Nutzen ziehen aus;
~ous [ædvən'teɪdʒəs] *adj* vorteilhaft

advent [ædvənt] *n* Ankunft *f*; **A~** Advent *m*

adventure [əd'ventʃəʳ] *n* Abenteuer *nt*;
adventurous *adj* abenteuerlich, waghalsig

adverb [ædvɜ:b] *n* Adverb *nt*,
Umstandswort *nt*

adversary [ædvəsərɪ] *n* Gegner *m*

adverse [ædvɜ:s] *adj* widrig; **adversity**
[əd'vɜ:sɪtɪ] *n* Widrigkeit *f*, Missgeschick *nt*

advert [ædvɜ:t] *n* Anzeige *f*; **~ise** [ædvətaɪz]
vt werben für ♦ *vi* annoncieren; **to ~ise for
sth** etw (per Anzeige) suchen; **~isement**
[əd'vɜ:tɪsmənt] *n* Anzeige *f*, Inserat *nt*; **~iser**
n (in newspaper etc) Inserent *m*; **~ising** *n*
Werbung *f*

advice [əd'vaɪs] *n* Rat(schlag) *m*

advisable [əd'vaɪzəbl] *adj* ratsam

advise [əd'vaɪz] *vt*: **to ~ (sb)** (jdm) raten;
~dly [əd'vaɪzɪdlɪ] *adv (deliberately)* bewusst;
~r *n* Berater *m*; **advisory** [əd'vaɪzərɪ] *adj*
beratend, Beratungs-

advocate [*vb* ædvəkeɪt, *n* ædvəkət] *vt*
vertreten ♦ *n* Befürworter(in) *m(f)*

Aegean [i:'dʒi:ən] *n*: **the ~ (Sea)** die Ägäis

aerial ['ɛərɪəl] *n* Antenne *f* ♦ *adj* Luft-

aerobics [ɛə'rəubɪks] *n* Aerobic *nt*

aerodynamic ['ɛərəudaɪ'næmɪk] *adj*
aerodynamisch

aeroplane ['ɛərəpleɪn] *n* Flugzeug *nt*

aerosol ['ɛərəsɒl] *n* Aerosol *nt*; Sprühdose *f*

aesthetic [i:s'θetɪk] *adj* ästhetisch

afar [ə'fɑ:ʳ] *adv*: **from ~** aus der Ferne

affable ['æfəbl] *adj* umgänglich

affair [ə'fɛəʳ] *n (concern)* Angelegenheit *f*;
(event) Ereignis *nt*; *(love ~)* Verhältnis *nt*; **~s**
npl (business) Geschäfte *pl*

affect [ə'fekt] *vt (influence)* (ein)wirken auf
+*acc*; *(move deeply)* bewegen; **this change
doesn't ~ us** diese Änderung betrifft uns
nicht; **~ed** *adj* affektiert, gekünstelt

affection [ə'fekʃən] *n* Zuneigung *f*; **~ate** *adj*
liebevoll

affiliated [ə'fɪlɪeɪtɪd] *adj* angeschlossen

affinity [ə'fɪnɪtɪ] *n (attraction)* gegenseitige
Anziehung *f*; *(relationship)* Verwandtschaft *f*

affirmative [ə'fɜ:mətɪv] *adj* bestätigend

afflict [ə'flɪkt] *vt* quälen, heimsuchen

affluence ['æfluəns] *n (wealth)* Wohlstand
m; **affluent** *adj* wohlhabend, Wohlstands-

afford [ə'fɔ:d] *vt* sich *dat* leisten; *(yield)*
bieten, einbringen

afield [ə'fi:ld] *adv*: **far ~** weit fort

afloat [ə'fləut] *adj*: **to be ~** schwimmen

afoot [ə'fut] *adv* im Gang

afraid [ə'freɪd] *adj* ängstlich; **to be ~ of**
Angst haben vor +*dat*; **to be ~ to do sth**
sich scheuen, etw zu tun; **I am ~ I have ...**
ich habe leider ...; **I'm ~ so/not** leider
leider nicht; **I am ~ that ...** ich fürchte(,
dass) ...

afresh [ə'freʃ] *adv* von neuem

Africa ['æfrɪkə] *n* Afrika *nt*; **~n** *adj* afrikanisch
♦ *n* Afrikaner(in) *m(f)*

after ['ɑ:ftəʳ] *prep* nach; *(following, seeking)*
hinter ... *dat* ... her; *(in imitation)* nach, im
Stil von ♦ *adv*: **soon ~** bald danach ♦ *conj*
nachdem; **what are you ~?** was wollen
Sie?; **~ he left** nachdem er gegangen war;
~ you! nach Ihnen!; **~ all** letzten Endes; **~
having shaved** als er sich rasiert hatte;

~effects npl Nachwirkungen pl; ~math n Auswirkungen pl; ~noon n Nachmittag m; ~s (inf) n (dessert) Nachtisch m; ~sales service (BRIT) n Kundendienst m; ~shave (lotion) n Rasierwasser nt; ~sun n Aftersunlotion f; ~thought n nachträgliche(r) Einfall m; ~wards adv danach, nachher

again [ə'gɛn] adv wieder, noch einmal; (besides) außerdem, ferner; ~ **and** ~ immer wieder

against [ə'gɛnst] prep gegen

age [eɪdʒ] n (of person) Alter nt; (in history) Zeitalter nt ♦ vi altern, alt werden ♦ vt älter machen; **to come of** ~ mündig werden; **20 years of** ~ 20 Jahre alt; **it's been** ~s **since** ... es ist ewig her, seit ...

aged¹ [eɪdʒd] adj ... Jahre alt, -jährig

aged² [eɪdʒɪd] adj (elderly) betagt ♦ npl: **the** ~ **die Alten** pl

age group n Altersgruppe f

age limit n Altersgrenze f

agency [eɪdʒənsɪ] n Agentur f; Vermittlung f; (CHEM) Wirkung f; **through** or **by the** ~ **of** ... mithilfe or mit Hilfe von ...

agenda [ə'dʒɛndə] n Tagesordnung f

agent [eɪdʒənt] n (COMM) Vertreter m; (spy) Agent m

aggravate [ægrəveɪt] vt (make worse) verschlimmern; (irritate) reizen

aggregate [ægrɪgɪt] n Summe f

aggression [ə'grɛʃən] n Aggression f; **aggressive** [ə'grɛsɪv] adj aggressiv

aghast [ə'gɑːst] adj entsetzt

agile [ædʒaɪl] adj flink, agil; (mind) rege

agitate [ædʒɪteɪt] vt rütteln; **to** ~ **for** sich stark machen für

AGM n abbr (= annual general meeting) JHV f

ago [ə'gəʊ] adv: **two days** ~ vor zwei Tagen; **not long** ~ vor kurzem; **it's so long** ~ es ist schon so lange her

agog [ə'gɒg] adj gespannt

agonizing [ægənaɪzɪŋ] adj quälend

agony [ægənɪ] n Qual f; **to be in** ~ Qualen leiden

agree [ə'griː] vt (date) vereinbaren ♦ vi (have same opinion, correspond) übereinstimmen; (consent) zustimmen; (be in harmony) sich vertragen; **to** ~ **to sth** einer Sache dat zustimmen; **to** ~ **that** ... (admit) zugeben, dass ...; **to** ~ **to do sth** sich bereit erklären, etw zu tun; **garlic doesn't** ~ **with me** Knoblauch vertrage ich nicht; **I** ~ einverstanden, ich stimme zu; **to** ~ **on sth** sich auf etw acc einigen; ~**able** adj (pleasing) liebenswürdig; (willing to consent) einverstanden; ~**d** adj vereinbart; ~**ment** n (~ing) Übereinstimmung f; (contract) Vereinbarung f, Vertrag m; **to be in** ~**ment** übereinstimmen

agricultural [ægrɪ'kʌltʃərəl] adj landwirtschaftlich, Landwirtschafts-

agriculture [ægrɪkʌltʃəʳ] n Landwirtschaft f

aground [ə'graʊnd] adv: **to run** ~ auf Grund laufen

ahead [ə'hɛd] adv vorwärts; **to be** ~ voraus sein; ~ **of time** der Zeit voraus; **go right** or **straight** ~ gehen Sie geradeaus; fahren Sie geradeaus

aid [eɪd] n (assistance) Hilfe f, Unterstützung f; (person) Hilfe f; (thing) Hilfsmittel nt ♦ vt unterstützen, helfen +dat; **in** ~ **of** zugunsten or zu Gunsten +gen; **to** ~ **and abet sb** jdm Beihilfe leisten

aide [eɪd] n (person) Gehilfe m, (MIL) Adjutant m

AIDS [eɪdz] n abbr (= acquired immune deficiency syndrome) Aids nt; **AIDS-related** aidsbedingt

ailing [eɪlɪŋ] adj kränkelnd

ailment [eɪlmənt] n Leiden nt

aim [eɪm] vt (gun, camera) richten ♦ vi (with gun: also: **take** ~) zielen; (intend) beabsichtigen ♦ n (intention) Absicht f, Ziel nt; (pointing) Zielen nt, Richten nt; **to** ~ **at sth** auf etw dat richten; (fig) etw anstreben; **to** ~ **to do sth** vorhaben, etw zu tun; ~**less** adj ziellos; ~**lessly** adv ziellos

ain't [eɪnt] (inf) = **am not**; **are not**; **is not**; **has not**; **have not**

air [ɛəʳ] n Luft f; (manner) Miene f, Anschein m; (MUS) Melodie f ♦ vt lüften; (fig) an die Öffentlichkeit bringen ♦ cpd Luft-; **by** ~ (travel) auf dem Luftweg; **to be on the** ~

(RADIO, TV: programme) gesendet werden;
~bed (BRIT) n Luftmatratze f; **~-conditioned** adj mit Klimaanlage; **~-conditioning** n Klimaanlage f; **~craft** n Flugzeug nt, Maschine f; **~craft carrier** n Flugzeugträger m; **~field** n Flugplatz m; **~force** n Luftwaffe f; **~freshener** n Raumspray nt; **~gun** n Luftgewehr nt; **~hostess** (BRIT) n Stewardess f; **~ letter** (BRIT) n Luftpostbrief m; **~lift** n Luftbrücke f; **~line** n Luftverkehrsgesellschaft f; **~liner** n Verkehrsflugzeug nt; **~lock** n Luftblase f; **~mail** n: **by ~mail** mit Luftpost; **~ miles** npl ≈ Flugkilometer m; **~plane** (US) n Flugzeug nt; **~port** n Flughafen m, Flugplatz m; **~ raid** n Luftangriff m; **~sick** adj luftkrank; **~space** n Luftraum m; **~strip** n Landestreifen m; **~ terminal** n Terminal m; **~tight** adj luftdicht; **~ traffic controller** n Fluglotse m; **~y** adj luftig; (manner) leichtfertig

aisle [aɪl] n Gang m; **~ seat** n Sitz m am Gang

ajar [ə'dʒɑːʳ] adv angelehnt; einen Spalt offen

alarm [ə'lɑːm] n (warning) Alarm m; (bell etc) Alarmanlage f; (anxiety) Sorge f ♦ vt erschrecken; **~ call** n (in hotel etc) Weckruf m; **~ clock** n Wecker m

Albania [æl'beɪnɪə] n Albanien nt

albeit [ɔːl'biːɪt] conj obgleich

album [ˈælbəm] n Album nt

alcohol [ˈælkəhɒl] n Alkohol m; **~-free** adj alkoholfrei; **~ic** [ælkə'hɒlɪk] adj (drink) alkoholisch ♦ n Alkoholiker(in) m(f); **~ism** n Alkoholismus m

alert [ə'lɜːt] adj wachsam ♦ n Alarm m ♦ vt alarmieren; **to be on the ~** wachsam sein

Algeria [æl'dʒɪərɪə] n Algerien nt

alias [ˈeɪlɪəs] adv alias ♦ n Deckname m

alibi [ˈælɪbaɪ] n Alibi nt

alien [ˈeɪlɪən] n Ausländer m ♦ adj (foreign) ausländisch; (strange) fremd; **~ to** fremd +dat; **~ate** vt entfremden

alight [ə'laɪt] adj brennend; (of building) in Flammen ♦ vi (descend) aussteigen; (bird) sich setzen

align [ə'laɪn] vt ausrichten

alike [ə'laɪk] adj gleich, ähnlich ♦ adv gleich, ebenso; **to look ~** sich dat ähnlich sehen

alimony [ˈælɪmənɪ] n Unterhalt m, Alimente pl

alive [ə'laɪv] adj (living) lebend; (lively) lebendig, aufgeweckt; **~ (with)** (full of) voll (von), wimmelnd (von)

KEYWORD
---

all [ɔːl] adj alle(r, s); **all day/night** den ganzen Tag/die ganze Nacht; **all men are equal** alle Menschen sind gleich; **all five came** alle fünf kamen; **all the books/food** die ganzen Bücher/das ganze Essen; **all the time** die ganze Zeit (über); **all his life** sein ganzes Leben (lang)
♦ pron 1 alles; **I ate it all, I ate all of it** ich habe alles gegessen; **all of us/the boys went** wir gingen alle/alle Jungen gingen; **we all sat down** wir setzten uns alle
2 (in phrases): **above all** vor allem; **after all** schließlich; **at all: not at all** (in answer to question) überhaupt nicht; (in answer to thanks) gern geschehen; **I'm not at all tired** ich bin überhaupt nicht müde; **anything at all will do** es ist egal, welche(r, s); **all in all** alles in allem
♦ adv ganz; **all alone** ganz allein; **it's not as hard as all that** so schwer ist es nun auch wieder nicht; **all the more/the better** umso mehr/besser; **all but** fast; **the score is 2 all** es steht 2 zu 2

---

allay [ə'leɪ] vt (fears) beschwichtigen

all clear n Entwarnung f

allegation [ælɪ'geɪʃən] n Behauptung f

allege [ə'ledʒ] vt (declare) behaupten; (falsely) vorgeben; **~dly** adv angeblich

allegiance [ə'liːdʒəns] n Treue f

allergic [ə'lɜːdʒɪk] adj: **~ (to)** allergisch (gegen)

allergy [ˈælədʒɪ] n Allergie f

alleviate [ə'liːvɪeɪt] vt lindern

alley [ˈælɪ] n Gasse f, Durchgang m

alliance [ə'laɪəns] n Bund m, Allianz f

allied [ˈælaɪd] adj vereinigt; (powers) alliiert; **~ (to)** verwandt (mit)

all: ~~-in** (BRIT) *adj, adv* (*charge*) alles inbegriffen, Gesamt-; ~~-in wrestling** *n* Freistilringen *nt*; ~~-night** *adj* (*café, cinema*) die ganze Nacht geöffnet, Nacht-

allocate ['ælǝkeɪt] *vt* zuteilen

allot [ǝ'lɒt] *vt* zuteilen; ~**ment** *n* (*share*) Anteil *m*; (*plot*) Schrebergarten *m*

all-out ['ɔːlaut] *adj* total; **all out** *adv* mit voller Kraft

allow [ǝ'lau] *vt* (*permit*) erlauben, gestatten; (*grant*) bewilligen; (*deduct*) abziehen; (*concede*): **to** ~ **that ...** annehmen, dass ...; **to** ~ **sb sth** jdm etw erlauben, jdm etw gestatten; **to** ~ **sb to do sth** jdm erlauben *or* gestatten, etw zu tun; ~ **for** *vt fus* berücksichtigen, einplanen; ~**ance** *n* Beihilfe *f*; **to make** ~**ances for** berücksichtigen

alloy ['ælɔɪ] *n* Metalllegierung *f*

all: ~ **right** *adv* (*well*) gut; (*correct*) richtig; (*as answer*) okay; ~~-round** *adj* (*sportsman*) allseitig, Allround-; (*view*) Rundum-; ~~-time** *adj* (*record, high*) ... aller Zeiten, Höchst-

allude [ǝ'luːd] *vi:* **to** ~ **to** hinweisen auf +*acc*, anspielen auf +*acc*

alluring [ǝ'ljuǝrɪŋ] *adj* verlockend

ally [*n* 'ælaɪ, *vb* ǝ'laɪ] *n* Verbündete(r) *f(m)*; (*POL*) Alliierte(r) *f(m)* ♦ *vr:* **to** ~ **o.s. with** sich verbünden mit

almighty [ɔːl'maɪtɪ] *adj* allmächtig

almond ['ɑːmǝnd] *n* Mandel *f*

almost ['ɔːlmǝust] *adv* fast, beinahe

alms [ɑːmz] *npl* Almosen *nt*

alone [ǝ'lǝun] *adj, adv* allein; **to leave sth** ~ etw sein lassen; **let** ~ **...** geschweige denn ...

along [ǝ'lɒŋ] *prep* entlang, längs ♦ *adv* (*onward*) vorwärts, weiter; ~ **with** zusammen mit; **he was limping** ~ er humpelte einher; **all** ~ (*all the time*) die ganze Zeit; ~**side** *adv* (*walk*) nebenher; (*come*) nebendran; (*be*) daneben ♦ *prep* (*walk, compared with*) neben +*dat*; (*come*) neben +*acc*; (*be*) entlang, neben +*dat*; (*of ship*) längsseits +*gen*

aloof [ǝ'luːf] *adj* zurückhaltend ♦ *adv* fern; **to stand** ~ abseits stehen

aloud [ǝ'laud] *adv* laut

alphabet ['ælfǝbet] *n* Alphabet *nt*; ~**ical** [ælfǝ'betɪkl] *adj* alphabetisch

alpine ['ælpaɪn] *adj* alpin, Alpen-

Alps [ælps] *npl:* **the** ~ die Alpen *pl*

already [ɔːl'redɪ] *adv* schon, bereits

alright ['ɔːl'raɪt] (BRIT) *adv* = **all right**

Alsatian [æl'seɪʃǝn] *n* (*dog*) Schäferhund *m*

also ['ɔːlsǝu] *adv* auch, außerdem

altar ['ɔːltǝ] *n* Altar *m*

alter ['ɔːltǝ] *vt* ändern; (*dress*) umändern; ~**ation** [ɔːltǝ'reɪʃǝn] *n* Änderung *f*; Umänderung *f*; (*to building*) Umbau *m*

alternate [*adj* ɔl'tɜːnɪt, *vb* 'ɔltǝneɪt] *adj* abwechselnd ♦ *vi* abwechseln; **on** ~ **days** jeden zweiten Tag

alternating ['ɔltǝneɪtɪŋ] *adj:* ~ **current** Wechselstrom *m*; **alternative** [ɔl'tɜːnǝtɪv] *adj* andere(r, s) ♦ *n* Alternative *f*; **alternative medicine** Alternativmedizin *f*; **alternatively** *adv* im anderen Falle; **alternatively one could ...** oder man könnte ...; **alternator** ['ɔltǝneɪtǝ] *n* (AUT) Lichtmaschine *f*

although [ɔːl'ðǝu] *conj* obwohl

altitude ['æltɪtjuːd] *n* Höhe *f*

alto ['æltǝu] *n* Alt *m*

altogether [ɔːltǝ'geðǝ] *adv* (*on the whole*) im Ganzen genommen; (*entirely*) ganz und gar

aluminium [ælju'mɪnɪǝm] (BRIT) *n* Aluminium *nt*

aluminum [ǝ'luːmɪnǝm] (US) *n* Aluminium *nt*

always ['ɔːlweɪz] *adv* immer

Alzheimer's (disease) ['æltshaɪmǝz-] *n* (MED) Alzheimerkrankheit *f*

AM *n abbr* (= *Assembly Member*) Mitglied *nt* der walisischen Versammlung

am [æm] *see* **be**

a.m. *adv abbr* (= *ante meridiem*) vormittags

amalgamate [ǝ'mælgǝmeɪt] *vi* (*combine*) sich vereinigen ♦ *vt* (*mix*) amalgamieren

amass [ǝ'mæs] *vt* anhäufen

amateur ['æmǝtǝ] *n* Amateur *m*; (*pej*) Amateur *m*, Stümper *m*; ~**ish** (*pej*) *adj* dilettantisch, stümperhaft

amaze [ǝ'meɪz] *vt* erstaunen; **to be** ~**d (at)** erstaunt sein (über); ~**ment** *n* höchste(s)

Erstaunen nt; **amazing** adj höchst erstaunlich

Amazon ['æməzən] n (GEOG) Amazonas m

ambassador [æm'bæsədəʳ] n Botschafter m

amber ['æmbəʳ] n Bernstein m; **at ~** (BRIT: AUT) auf Gelb, gelb

ambiguous [æm'bɪgjuəs] adj zweideutig; (not clear) unklar

ambition [æm'bɪʃən] n Ehrgeiz m; **ambitious** adj ehrgeizig

amble ['æmbl] vi (usu: ~ along) schlendern

ambulance ['æmbjuləns] n Krankenwagen m; **~ man** (irreg) n Sanitäter m

ambush ['æmbuʃ] n Hinterhalt m ♦ vt (aus dem Hinterhalt) überfallen

amenable [ə'mi:nəbl] adj gefügig; **~ (to)** (reason) zugänglich (+dat); (flattery) empfänglich (für)

amend [ə'mɛnd] vt (law etc) abändern, ergänzen; **to make ~s** etw wieder gutmachen; **~ment** n Abänderung f

amenities [ə'mi:nɪtɪz] npl Einrichtungen pl

America [ə'mɛrɪkə] n Amerika nt; **~n** adj amerikanisch ♦ n Amerikaner(in) m(f)

amiable ['eɪmɪəbl] adj liebenswürdig

amicable ['æmɪkəbl] adj freundschaftlich; (settlement) gütlich

amid(st) [ə'mɪd(st)] prep mitten in or unter +dat

amiss [ə'mɪs] adv: **to take sth ~** etw übel nehmen; **there's something ~** da stimmt irgendetwas nicht

ammonia [ə'məunɪə] n Ammoniak nt

ammunition [æmju'nɪʃən] n Munition f

amnesia [æm'ni:zɪə] n Gedächtnisverlust m

amnesty ['æmnɪstɪ] n Amnestie f

amok [ə'mɔk] adv: **to run ~** Amok laufen

among(st) [ə'mʌŋ(st)] prep unter

amoral [æ'mɔrəl] adj unmoralisch

amorous ['æmərəs] adj verliebt

amount [ə'maunt] n (of money) Betrag m; (of water, sand) Menge f ♦ vi: **to ~ to** (total) sich belaufen auf +acc; **a great ~ of time / energy** ein großer Aufwand an Zeit/ Energie (dat); **this ~s to treachery** das kommt Verrat gleich; **he won't ~ to much** aus ihm wird nie was

amp(ere) [æmp(ɛəʳ)] n Ampere nt

amphibian [æm'fɪbɪən] n Amphibie f

ample ['æmpl] adj (portion) reichlich; (dress) weit, groß; **~ time** genügend Zeit

amplifier ['æmplɪfaɪəʳ] n Verstärker m

amuse [ə'mju:z] vt (entertain) unterhalten; (make smile) belustigen; **~ment** n (feeling) Unterhaltung f; (recreation) Zeitvertreib m; **~ment arcade** n Spielhalle f; **~ment park** n Vergnügungspark m

an [æn, ən] see **a**

anaemia [ə'ni:mɪə] n Anämie f; **anaemic** adj blutarm

anaesthetic [ænɪs'θɛtɪk] n Betäubungsmittel nt; **under ~** unter Narkose; **anaesthetist** [æ'ni:sθɪtɪst] n Anästhesist(in) m(f)

analgesic [ænæl'dʒi:sɪk] n schmerzlindernde(s) Mittel nt

analog(ue) ['ænəlɔg] adj Analog-

analogy [ə'nælədʒɪ] n Analogie f

analyse ['ænəlaɪz] (BRIT) vt analysieren

analyses [ə'næləsi:z] (BRIT) npl of **analysis**

analysis [ə'næləsɪs] (pl **analyses**) n Analyse f

analyst ['ænəlɪst] n Analytiker(in) m(f)

analytic(al) [ænə'lɪtɪk(l)] adj analytisch

analyze ['ænəlaɪz] (US) vt = **analyse**

anarchy ['ænəkɪ] n Anarchie f

anatomy [ə'nætəmɪ] n (structure) anatomische(r) Aufbau m; (study) Anatomie f

ancestor ['ænsɪstəʳ] n Vorfahr m

anchor ['æŋkəʳ] n Anker m ♦ vi (also: **to drop ~**) ankern, vor Anker gehen ♦ vt verankern; **to weigh ~** den Anker lichten

anchovy ['æntʃəvɪ] n Sardelle f

ancient ['eɪnʃənt] adj alt; (car etc) uralt

ancillary [æn'sɪlərɪ] adj Hilfs-

and [ænd] conj und; **~ so on** und so weiter; **try ~ come** versuche zu kommen; **better ~ better** immer besser

Andes ['ændi:z] npl: **the ~** die Anden pl

anemia etc [ə'ni:mɪə] (US) n = **anaemia** etc

anesthetic etc [ænɪs'θɛtɪk] (US) n = **anaesthetic** etc

anew [ə'nju:] adv von neuem

angel ['eɪndʒəl] n Engel m

anger ['æŋgəʳ] n Zorn m ♦ vt ärgern

angina [æn'dʒaɪnə] n Angina f

angle ['æŋgl] n Winkel m; (point of view) Standpunkt m

angler ['æŋglər] n Angler m

Anglican ['æŋglɪkən] adj anglikanisch ♦ n Anglikaner(in) m(f)

angling ['æŋglɪŋ] n Angeln nt

angrily ['æŋgrɪlɪ] adv ärgerlich, böse

angry ['æŋgrɪ] adj ärgerlich, ungehalten, böse; (wound) entzündet; **to be ~ with sb** auf jdn böse sein; **to be ~ at sth** über etw acc verärgert sein

anguish ['æŋgwɪʃ] n Qual f

angular ['æŋgjulər] adj eckig, winkelförmig; (face) kantig

animal ['ænɪməl] n Tier nt; (living creature) Lebewesen nt ♦ adj tierisch

animate [vb 'ænɪmeɪt, adj 'ænɪmɪt] vt beleben ♦ adj lebhaft; **~d** adj lebendig; (film) Zeichentrick-

animosity [ænɪ'mɔsɪtɪ] n Feindseligkeit f, Abneigung f

aniseed ['ænɪsiːd] n Anis m

ankle ['æŋkl] n (Fuß)knöchel m; **~ sock** n Söckchen nt

annex [n 'æneks, vb ə'neks] n (BRIT: also: ~e) Anbau m ♦ vt anfügen; (POL) annektieren, angliedern

annihilate [ə'naɪəleɪt] vt vernichten

anniversary [ænɪ'vɜːsərɪ] n Jahrestag m

announce [ə'nauns] vt ankündigen, anzeigen; **~ment** n Ankündigung f; (official) Bekanntmachung f; **~r** n Ansager(in) m(f)

annoy [ə'nɔɪ] vt ärgern; **don't get ~ed!** reg dich nicht auf!; **~ance** n Ärgernis nt, Störung f; **~ing** adj ärgerlich; (person) lästig

annual ['ænjuəl] adj jährlich; (salary) Jahres- ♦ n (plant) einjährige Pflanze f; (book) Jahrbuch nt; **~ly** adv jährlich

annul [ə'nʌl] vt aufheben, annullieren

annum ['ænəm] n see **per**

anonymous [ə'nɔnɪməs] adj anonym

anorak ['ænəræk] n Anorak m, Windjacke f

anorexia [ænə'reksɪə] n (MED) Magersucht f

another [ə'nʌðər] adj, pron (different) ein(e) andere(r, s); (additional) noch eine(r, s); see

also **one**

answer ['ɑːnsər] n Antwort f ♦ vi antworten; (on phone) sich melden ♦ vt (person) antworten +dat; (letter, question) beantworten; (telephone) gehen an +acc, abnehmen; (door) öffnen; **in ~ to your letter** in Beantwortung Ihres Schreibens; **to ~ the phone** ans Telefon gehen; **to ~ the bell** or **the door** aufmachen; **~ back** vi frech sein; **~ for** vt fus: **to ~ for sth** für etw verantwortlich sein; **~able** adj: **to be ~able to sb for sth** jdm gegenüber für etw verantwortlich sein; **~ing machine** n Anrufbeantworter m

ant [ænt] n Ameise f

antagonism [æn'tægənɪzəm] n Antagonismus m

antagonize [æn'tægənaɪz] vt reizen

Antarctic [ænt'ɑːktɪk] adj antarktisch ♦ n: **the ~** die Antarktis

antelope ['æntɪləup] n Antilope f

antenatal ['æntɪ'neɪtl] adj vor der Geburt; **~ clinic** n Sprechstunde f für werdende Mütter

antenna [æn'tenə] n (BIOL) Fühler m; (RAD) Antenne f

antennae [æn'teniː] npl of **antenna**

anthem ['ænθəm] n Hymne f; **national ~** Nationalhymne f

anthology [æn'θɔlədʒɪ] n Gedichtsammlung f, Anthologie f

anti- ['æntɪ] prefix Gegen-, Anti-

anti-aircraft ['æntɪ'eəkrɑːft] adj Flugabwehr-

antibiotic ['æntɪbaɪ'ɔtɪk] n Antibiotikum nt

antibody ['æntɪbɔdɪ] n Antikörper m

anticipate [æn'tɪsɪpeɪt] vt (expect: trouble, question) erwarten, rechnen mit; (look forward to) sich freuen auf +acc; (do first) vorwegnehmen, (foresee) ahnen, vorhersehen; **anticipation** [æntɪsɪ'peɪʃən] n Erwartung f; (foreshadowing) Vorwegnahme f

anticlimax ['æntɪ'klaɪmæks] n Ernüchterung f

anticlockwise ['æntɪ'klɔkwaɪz] adv entgegen dem Uhrzeigersinn

antics ['æntɪks] npl Possen pl

anti: ~**cyclone** n Hoch nt, Hochdruckgebiet nt; ~**depressant** n Antidepressivum nt; ~**dote** n Gegenmittel nt; ~**freeze** n Frostschutzmittel nt; ~**histamine** n Antihistamin nt

antiquated ['æntɪkweɪtɪd] adj antiquiert

antique [æn'tiːk] n Antiquität f ♦ adj antik; (old-fashioned) altmodisch; ~ **shop** n Antiquitätenladen m; **antiquity** [æn'tɪkwɪtɪ] n Altertum nt

antiseptic [æntɪ'septɪk] n Antiseptikum nt ♦ adj antiseptisch

antisocial ['æntɪ'səʊʃəl] adj (person) ungesellig; (law) unsozial

antlers ['æntləz] npl Geweih nt

anus ['eɪnəs] n After m

anvil ['ænvɪl] n Amboss m

anxiety [æŋ'zaɪətɪ] n Angst f; (worry) Sorge f; **anxious** ['æŋkʃəs] adj ängstlich; (worried) besorgt; **to be anxious to do sth** etw unbedingt tun wollen

---
KEYWORD
---

any ['enɪ] adj 1 (in questions etc): **have you any butter?** haben Sie (etwas) Butter?; **have you any children?** haben Sie Kinder?; **if there are any tickets left** falls noch Karten da sind

2 (with negative): **I haven't any money/ books** ich habe kein Geld/keine Bücher

3 (no matter which) jede(r, s) (beliebige); **any colour (at all)** jede beliebige Farbe; **choose any book you like** nehmen Sie ein beliebiges Buch

4 (in phrases): **in any case** in jedem Fall; **any day now** jeden Tag; **at any moment** jeden Moment; **at any rate** auf jeden Fall

♦ pron 1 (in questions etc): **have you got any?** haben Sie welche?; **can any of you sing?** kann (irgend)einer von euch singen?

2 (with negative): **I haven't any (of them)** ich habe keinen/keines (davon)

3 (no matter which one(s)): **take any of those books (you like)** nehmen Sie irgendeines dieser Bücher

♦ adv 1 (in questions etc): **do you want any more soup/sandwiches?** möchten Sie

noch Suppe/Brote?; **are you feeling any better?** fühlen Sie sich etwas besser?

2 (with negative): **I can't hear him any more** ich kann ihn nicht mehr hören

---

anybody ['enɪbɔdɪ] pron (no matter who) jede(r); (in questions etc) (irgend)jemand, (irgend)eine(r); (with negative): **I can't see** ~ ich kann niemanden sehen

anyhow ['enɪhaʊ] adv (at any rate): **I shall go** ~ ich gehe sowieso; (haphazardly): **do it** ~ machen Sie es, wie Sie wollen

anyone ['enɪwʌn] pron = **anybody**

KEYWORD
---

anything ['enɪθɪŋ] pron 1 (in questions etc) (irgend)etwas; **can you see anything?** können Sie etwas sehen?

2 (with negative): **I can't see anything** ich kann nichts sehen

3 (no matter what): **you can say anything you like** Sie können sagen, was Sie wollen; **anything will do** irgendetwas (wird genügen), irgendeine(r, s) (wird genügen); **he'll eat anything** er isst alles

---

anyway ['enɪweɪ] adv (at any rate) auf jeden Fall; (besides): ~, **I couldn't come even if I wanted to** jedenfalls könnte ich nicht kommen, selbst wenn ich wollte; **why are you phoning,** ~? warum rufst du überhaupt an?

anywhere ['enɪweəʳ] adv (in questions etc) irgendwo; (: with direction) irgendwohin; (no matter where) überall; (: with direction) überallhin; (with negative): **I can't see him** ~ ich kann ihn nirgendwo or nirgends sehen; **can you see him** ~? siehst du ihn irgendwo?; **put the books down** ~ leg die Bücher irgendwohin

apart [ə'pɑːt] adv (parted) auseinander; (away) beiseite, abseits; **10 miles** ~ 10 Meilen auseinander; **to take** ~ auseinander nehmen; ~ **from** prep außer

apartheid [ə'pɑːteɪt] n Apartheid f

apartment [ə'pɑːtmənt] (US) n Wohnung f; ~ **building** (US) n Wohnhaus nt

apathy ['æpəθɪ] n Teilnahmslosigkeit f,

Apathie f

ape [eɪp] n (Menschen)affe m ♦ vt nachahmen

aperitif [ə'perɪti:f] n Aperitif m

aperture ['æpətʃjuər] n Öffnung f; (PHOT) Blende f

APEX ['eɪpeks] n abbr (AVIAT: = advance purchase excursion) APEX (im Voraus reservierte(r) Fahrkarte/Flugschein zu reduzierten Preisen)

apex ['eɪpeks] n Spitze f

apiece [ə'pi:s] adv pro Stück; (per person) pro Kopf

apologetic [əpɒlə'dʒetɪk] adj entschuldigend; **to be ~** sich sehr entschuldigen

apologize [ə'pɒlədʒaɪz] vi: **to ~ (for sth to sb)** sich (für etw bei jdm) entschuldigen; **apology** n Entschuldigung f

apostle [ə'pɒsl] n Apostel m

apostrophe [ə'pɒstrəfɪ] n Apostroph m

appal [ə'pɔ:l] vt erschrecken; **~ling** adj schrecklich

apparatus [æpə'reɪtəs] n Gerät nt

apparel [ə'pærəl] (US) n Kleidung f

apparent [ə'pærənt] adj offenbar; **~ly** adv anscheinend

apparition [æpə'rɪʃən] n (ghost) Erscheinung f, Geist m

appeal [ə'pi:l] vi dringend ersuchen; (JUR) Berufung einlegen ♦ n Aufruf m; (JUR) Berufung f; **to ~ for** dringend bitten um; **to ~ to** sich wenden an +acc; (to public) appellieren an +acc; **it doesn't ~ to me** es gefällt mir nicht; **~ing** adj ansprechend

appear [ə'pɪər] vi (come into sight) erscheinen; (be seen) auftauchen; (seem) scheinen; **it would ~ that ...** anscheinend ...; **~ance** n (coming into sight) Erscheinen nt; (outward show) Äußere(s) nt

appease [ə'pi:z] vt beschwichtigen

appendices [ə'pendɪsi:z] npl of **appendix**

appendicitis [əpendɪ'saɪtɪs] n Blinddarmentzündung f

appendix [ə'pendɪks] (pl **appendices**) n (in book) Anhang m; (MED) Blinddarm m

appetite ['æpɪtaɪt] n Appetit m; (fig) Lust f

appetizer ['æpɪtaɪzər] n Appetitanreger m;

appetizing ['æpɪtaɪzɪŋ] adj appetitanregend

applaud [ə'plɔ:d] vi Beifall klatschen, applaudieren ♦ vt Beifall klatschen +dat;

applause [ə'plɔ:z] n Beifall m, Applaus m

apple ['æpl] n Apfel m; **~ tree** n Apfelbaum m

appliance [ə'plaɪəns] n Gerät nt

applicable [ə'plɪkəbl] adj anwendbar; (in forms) zutreffend

applicant ['æplɪkənt] n Bewerber(in) m(f)

application [æplɪ'keɪʃən] n (request) Antrag m; (for job) Bewerbung f; (putting into practice) Anwendung f; (hard work) Fleiß m; **~ form** n Bewerbungsformular nt

applied [ə'plaɪd] adj angewandt

apply [ə'plaɪ] vi (be suitable) zutreffen; (ask): **to ~ (to)** sich wenden (an +acc); (request): **to ~ for** sich melden für +acc ♦ vt (place on) auflegen; (cream) auftragen; (put into practice) anwenden; **to ~ for sth** sich um etw bewerben; **to ~ o.s. to sth** sich bei etw anstrengen

appoint [ə'pɔɪnt] vt (to office) ernennen, berufen; (settle) festsetzen; **~ment** n (meeting) Verabredung f; (at hairdresser etc) Bestellung f; (in business) Termin m; (choice for a position) Ernennung f; (UNIV) Berufung f

appraisal [ə'preɪzl] n Beurteilung f

appreciable [ə'pri:ʃəbl] adj (perceptible) merklich; (able to be estimated) abschätzbar

appreciate [ə'pri:ʃɪeɪt] vt (value) zu schätzen wissen; (understand) einsehen ♦ vi (increase in value) im Wert steigen; **appreciation** [əpri:ʃɪ'eɪʃən] n Wertschätzung f; (COMM) Wertzuwachs m; **appreciative** [ə'pri:ʃɪətɪv] adj (showing thanks) dankbar; (showing liking) anerkennend

apprehend [æprɪ'hend] vt (arrest) festnehmen; (understand) erfassen

apprehension [æprɪ'henʃən] n Angst f

apprehensive [æprɪ'hensɪv] adj furchtsam

apprentice [ə'prentɪs] n Lehrling m; **~ship** n Lehrzeit f

approach [ə'prəutʃ] vi sich nähern ♦ vt herantreten an +acc; (problem) herangehen

an +acc ♦ n Annäherung f; (to problem)
Ansatz m; (path) Zugang m, Zufahrt f;
~able adj zugänglich
appropriate [adj ə'prəuprɪɪt, vb ə'prəuprɪeɪt]
adj angemessen; (remark) angebracht ♦ vt
(take for o.s.) sich aneignen; (set apart)
bereitstellen
approval [ə'pru:vəl] n (show of satisfaction)
Beifall m; (permission) Billigung f; on ~
(COMM) bei Gefallen
approve [ə'pru:v] vt, vi billigen; I don't ~ of
it/him ich halte nichts davon/von ihm; ~d
school (BRIT) n Erziehungsheim nt
approximate [adj ə'prɔksɪmɪt, vb
ə'prɔksɪmeɪt] adj annähernd, ungefähr ♦ vt
nahe kommen +dat; ~ly adv rund,
ungefähr
apricot ['eɪprɪkɔt] n Aprikose f
April ['eɪprəl] n April m; ~ Fools' Day n der
erste April
apron ['eɪprən] n Schürze f
apt [æpt] adj (suitable) passend; (able)
begabt; (likely): to be ~ to do sth dazu
neigen, etw zu tun
aptitude ['æptɪtju:d] n Begabung f
aqualung ['ækwəlʌŋ] n
Unterwasseratmungsgerät nt
aquarium [ə'kweərɪəm] n Aquarium nt
Aquarius [ə'kweərɪəs] n Wassermann m
aquatic [ə'kwætɪk] adj Wasser-
Arab ['ærəb] n Araber(in) m(f)
Arabia [ə'reɪbɪə] n Arabien nt; ~n adj
arabisch
Arabic ['ærəbɪk] adj arabisch ♦ n Arabisch nt
arable ['ærəbl] adj bebaubar, Kultur-
arbitrary ['ɑːbɪtrərɪ] adj willkürlich
arbitration [ɑːbɪ'treɪʃən] n Schlichtung f
arc [ɑːk] n Bogen m
arcade [ɑː'keɪd] n Säulengang m; (with video
games) Spielhalle f
arch [ɑːtʃ] n Bogen m ♦ vt überwölben;
(back) krumm machen
archaeologist [ɑːkɪ'ɔlədʒɪst] n Archäologe
m
archaeology [ɑːkɪ'ɔlədʒɪ] n Archäologie f
archaic [ɑː'keɪɪk] adj altertümlich
archbishop [ɑːtʃ'bɪʃəp] n Erzbischof m

archenemy ['ɑːtʃ'enəmɪ] n Erzfeind m
archeology [ɑːkɪ'ɔlədʒɪ] (US) =
archaeology etc
archery ['ɑːtʃərɪ] n Bogenschießen nt
architect ['ɑːkɪtekt] n Architekt(in) m(f);
~ural [ɑːkɪ'tektʃərəl] adj architektonisch;
~ure n Architektur f
archives ['ɑːkaɪvz] npl Archiv nt
archway ['ɑːtʃweɪ] n Bogen m
Arctic ['ɑːktɪk] adj arktisch ♦ n: the ~ die
Arktis
ardent ['ɑːdənt] adj glühend
arduous ['ɑːdjuəs] adj mühsam
are [ɑːr] see be
area ['eərɪə] n Fläche f; (of land) Gebiet nt;
(part of sth) Teil m, Abschnitt m
arena [ə'riːnə] n Arena f
aren't [ɑːnt] = are not
Argentina [ɑːdʒən'tiːnə] n Argentinien nt;
Argentinian [ɑːdʒən'tɪnɪən] adj
argentinisch ♦ n Argentinier(in) m(f)
arguably ['ɑːgjuəblɪ] adv wohl
argue ['ɑːgjuː] vi diskutieren; (angrily)
streiten; argument n (theory) Argument nt;
(reasoning) Argumentation f; (row)
Auseinandersetzung f, Streit m; to have an
argument sich streiten; argumentative
[ɑːgju'mentətɪv] adj streitlustig
aria ['ɑːrɪə] n Arie f
Aries ['eərɪz] n Widder m
arise [ə'raɪz] (pt arose, pp arisen) vi
aufsteigen; (get up) aufstehen; (difficulties
etc) entstehen; (case) vorkommen; to ~
from sth herrühren von etw; ~n [ə'rɪzn] pp
of arise
aristocracy [ærɪs'tɔkrəsɪ] n Adel m,
Aristokratie f; aristocrat ['ærɪstəkræt] n
Adlige(r) f(m), Aristokrat(in) m(f)
arithmetic [ə'rɪθmətɪk] n Rechnen nt,
Arithmetik f
arm [ɑːm] n Arm m; (branch of military service)
Zweig m ♦ vt bewaffnen; ~s npl (weapons)
Waffen pl
armaments ['ɑːməmənts] npl Ausrüstung f
armchair ['ɑːmtʃeər] n Lehnstuhl m
armed [ɑːmd] adj (forces) Streit-, bewaffnet;
~ robbery n bewaffnete(r) Raubüberfall m

armistice ['ɑːmɪstɪs] *n* Waffenstillstand *m*

armour ['ɑːmər] *n* (*US* **armor**) *n* (*knight's*) Rüstung *f*; (*MIL*) Panzerplatte *f*; **~ed car** *n* Panzerwagen *m*

armpit ['ɑːmpɪt] *n* Achselhöhle *f*

armrest ['ɑːmrest] *n* Armlehne *f*

army ['ɑːmɪ] *n* Armee *f*, Heer *nt*; (*host*) Heer *nt*

aroma [ə'rəumə] *n* Duft *m*, Aroma *nt*; **~therapy** [ərəumə'θerəpɪ] *n* Aromatherapie *f*; **~tic** [ærə'mætɪk] *adj* aromatisch, würzig

arose [ə'rəuz] *pt of* **arise**

around [ə'raund] *adv* ringsherum; (*almost*) ungefähr ♦ *prep* um ... herum; **is he ~?** ist er hier?

arrange [ə'reɪndʒ] *vt* (*time, meeting*) festsetzen; (*holidays*) festlegen; (*flowers, hair, objects*) anordnen; **I ~d to meet him** ich habe mit ihm ausgemacht, ihn zu treffen; **it's all ~d** es ist alles arrangiert; **~ment** *n* (*order*) Reihenfolge *f*; (*agreement*) Vereinbarung *f*; **~ments** *npl* (*plans*) Pläne *pl*

array [ə'reɪ] *n* (*collection*) Ansammlung *f*

arrears [ə'rɪəz] *npl* (*of debts*) Rückstand *m*; (*of work*) Unerledigte(s) *nt*; **in ~** im Rückstand

arrest [ə'rest] *vt* (*person*) verhaften; (*stop*) aufhalten ♦ *n* Verhaftung *f*; **under ~** in Haft

arrival [ə'raɪvl] *n* Ankunft *f*

arrive [ə'raɪv] *vi* ankommen; **to ~ at** ankommen in +*dat*, ankommen bei

arrogance ['ærəgəns] *n* Überheblichkeit *f*, Arroganz *f*; **arrogant** ['ærəgənt] *adj* überheblich, arrogant

arrow ['ærəu] *n* Pfeil *m*

arse [ɑːs] (*inf!*) *n* Arsch *m* (*!*)

arsenal ['ɑːsɪnl] *n* Waffenlager *nt*, Zeughaus *nt*

arsenic ['ɑːsnɪk] *n* Arsen *nt*

arson ['ɑːsn] *n* Brandstiftung *f*

art [ɑːt] *n* Kunst *f*; **A~s** *npl* (*UNIV*) Geisteswissenschaften *pl*

artery ['ɑːtərɪ] *n* Schlagader *f*, Arterie *f*

art gallery *n* Kunstgalerie *f*

arthritis [ɑː'θraɪtɪs] *n* Arthritis *f*

artichoke ['ɑːtɪtʃəuk] *n* Artischocke *f*;

Jerusalem ~ Erdartischocke *f*

article ['ɑːtɪkl] *n* (*PRESS, GRAM*) Artikel *m*; (*thing*) Gegenstand *m*, Artikel *m*; (*clause*) Abschnitt *m*, Paragraf *m*; **~ of clothing** Kleidungsstück *nt*

articulate [*adj* ɑː'tɪkjulɪt, *vb* ɑː'tɪkjuleɪt] *adj* (*able to express o.s.*) redegewandt; (*speaking clearly*) deutlich, verständlich ♦ *vt* (*connect*) zusammenfügen, gliedern; **to be ~** sich gut ausdrücken können; **~d vehicle** *n* Sattelschlepper *m*

artificial [ɑːtɪ'fɪʃl] *adj* künstlich, Kunst-; **~ respiration** *n* künstliche Atmung *f*

artisan ['ɑːtɪzæn] *n* gelernte(r) Handwerker *m*

artist ['ɑːtɪst] *n* Künstler(in) *m(f)*; **~ic** [ɑː'tɪstɪk] *adj* künstlerisch; **~ry** *n* künstlerische(s) Können *nt*

art school *n* Kunsthochschule *f*

KEYWORD

---

as [æz] *conj* **1** (*referring to time*) als; **as the years went by** mit den Jahren; **he came in as I was leaving** als er hereinkam, ging ich gerade; **as from tomorrow** ab morgen

2 (*in comparisons*): **as big as** so groß wie; **twice as big as** zweimal so groß wie; **as much/many as** so viel/so viele wie; **as soon as** sobald

3 (*since, because*) da; **he left early as he had to be home by 10** er ging früher, da er um 10 zu Hause sein musste

4 (*referring to manner, way*) wie; **do as you wish** mach was du willst; **as she said** wie sie sagte

5 (*concerning*): **as for** *or* **to that** was das betrifft *or* angeht

6: as if *or* **though** als ob

♦ *prep* als; *see also* **long**; **he works as a driver** er arbeitet als Fahrer; *see also* **such**; **he gave it to me as a present** er hat es mir als Geschenk gegeben; *see also* **well**

---

a.s.a.p. *abbr =* **as soon as possible**

asbestos [æz'bestəs] *n* Asbest *m*

ascend [ə'send] *vi* aufsteigen ♦ *vt* besteigen; **ascent** *n* Aufstieg *m*; Besteigung *f* ascertain [æsə'teɪn] vt feststellen

ascribe [ə'skraɪb] vt: **to ~ sth to sth /sth to sb** etw einer Sache/jdm etw zuschreiben

ash [æʃ] n Asche f; (tree) Esche f

ashamed [ə'ʃeɪmd] adj beschämt; **to be ~ of sth** sich für etw schämen

ashen ['æʃən] adj (pale) aschfahl

ashore [ə'ʃɔːr] adv an Land

ashtray ['æʃtreɪ] n Aschenbecher m

Ash Wednesday n Aschermittwoch m

Asia ['eɪʃə] n Asien nt; **~n** adj asiatisch ♦ n Asiat(in) m(f)

aside [ə'saɪd] adv beiseite

ask [ɑːsk] vt fragen; (permission) bitten um; **~ him his name** frage ihn nach seinem Namen; **he ~ed to see you** er wollte dich sehen; **to ~ sb to do sth** jdn bitten, etw zu tun; **to ~ sb about sth** jdn nach etw fragen; **to ~ (sb) a question** (jdn) etwas fragen; **to ~ sb out to dinner** jdn zum Essen einladen; **~ after** vt fus fragen nach; **~ for** vt fus bitten um

askance [ə'skɑːns] adv: **to look ~ at sb** jdn schief ansehen

asking price ['ɑːskɪŋ-] n Verkaufspreis m

asleep [ə'sliːp] adj: **to be ~** schlafen; **to fall ~** einschlafen

asparagus [əs'pærəgəs] n Spargel m

aspect ['æspekt] n Aspekt m

aspersions [əs'pɜːʃənz] npl: **to cast ~ on sb/sth** sich abfällig über jdn/etw äußern

asphyxiation [æsfɪksɪ'eɪʃən] n Erstickung f

aspirations [æspə'reɪʃənz] npl: **to have ~ towards sth** etw anstreben

aspire [əs'paɪər] vi: **to ~ to** streben nach

aspirin ['æsprɪn] n Aspirin nt

ass [æs] n (also fig) Esel m; (US: inf!) Arsch m (!)

assailant [ə'seɪlənt] n Angreifer m

assassin [ə'sæsɪn] n Attentäter(in) m(f); **~ate** vt ermorden; **~ation** [əsæsɪ'neɪʃən] n (geglückte(s)) Attentat nt

assault [ə'sɔːlt] n Angriff m ♦ vt überfallen; (woman) herfallen über +acc

assemble [ə'sembl] vt versammeln; (parts) zusammensetzen ♦ vi sich versammeln; assembly n (meeting) Versammlung f; (construction) Zusammensetzung f, Montage f; **assembly line** n Fließband nt

assent [ə'sent] n Zustimmung f

assert [ə'sɜːt] vt erklären; **~ion** n Behauptung f

assess [ə'ses] vt schätzen; **~ment** n Bewertung f, Einschätzung f; **~or** n Steuerberater m

asset ['æset] n Vorteil m, Wert m; **~s** npl (FIN) Vermögen nt; (estate) Nachlass m

assign [ə'saɪn] vt zuweisen; **~ment** n Aufgabe f, Auftrag m

assimilate [ə'sɪmɪleɪt] vt sich aneignen, aufnehmen

assist [ə'sɪst] vt beistehen +dat; **~ance** n Unterstützung f, Hilfe f; **~ant** n Assistent(in) m(f), Mitarbeiter(in) m(f); (BRIT: also: **shop ~ant**) Verkäufer(in) m(f)

associate [n ə'səʊʃɪt, vb ə'səʊʃɪeɪt] n (partner) Kollege m, Teilhaber m; (member) außerordentliche(s) Mitglied nt ♦ vt verbinden ♦ vi (keep company) verkehren; **association** [əsəʊsɪ'eɪʃən] n Verband m, Verein m; (PSYCH) Assoziation f; (link) Verbindung f

assorted [ə'sɔːtɪd] adj gemischt

assortment [ə'sɔːtmənt] n Sammlung f; (COMM) **~ (of)** Sortiment nt (von), Auswahl f (an +dat)

assume [ə'sjuːm] vt (take for granted) annehmen; (put on) annehmen, sich geben; **~d name** n Deckname m

assumption [ə'sʌmpʃən] n Annahme f

assurance [ə'ʃʊərəns] n (firm statement) Versicherung f; (confidence) Selbstsicherheit f; (insurance) (Lebens)versicherung f

assure [ə'ʃʊər] vt (make sure) sicherstellen; (convince) versichern +dat; (life) versichern

asterisk ['æstərɪsk] n Sternchen nt

asthma ['æsmə] n Asthma nt

astonish [ə'stɒnɪʃ] vt erstaunen; **~ment** n Erstaunen nt

astound [ə'staʊnd] vt verblüffen

astray [ə'streɪ] adv in die Irre; auf Abwege; **to go ~** (go wrong) sich vertun; **to lead ~** irreführen

astride [ə'straɪd] adv rittlings ♦ prep rittlings

auf

astrologer [əˈstrɒlədʒəʳ] n Astrologe m, Astrologin f; **astrology** n Astrologie f

astronaut [ˈæstrənɔːt] n Astronaut(in) m(f)

astronomer [əsˈtrɒnəməʳ] n Astronom m

astronomical [æstrəˈnɒmɪkl] adj astronomisch; (success) riesig

astronomy [əsˈtrɒnəmɪ] n Astronomie f

astute [əsˈtjuːt] adj scharfsinnig; schlau, gerissen

asylum [əˈsaɪləm] n (home) Heim nt; (refuge) Asyl nt

KEYWORD

at [æt] prep **1** (referring to position, direction) an +dat, bei +dat; (with place) in +dat; **at the top** an der Spitze; **at home/school** zu Hause/in der Schule; **at the baker's** beim Bäcker; **to look at sth** auf etw acc blicken; **to throw sth at sb** etw nach jdm werfen
2 (referring to time): **at 4 o'clock** um 4 Uhr; **at night** bei Nacht; **at Christmas** zu Weihnachten; **at times** manchmal
3 (referring to rates, speed etc): **at £1 a kilo** zu £1 pro Kilo; **two at a time** zwei auf einmal; **at 50 km/h** mit 50 km/h
4 (referring to manner): **at a stroke** mit einem Schlag; **at peace** in Frieden
5 (referring to activity): **to be at work** bei der Arbeit sein; **to play at cowboys** Cowboy spielen; **to be good at sth** gut in etw dat sein
6 (referring to cause): **shocked/surprised/annoyed at sth** schockiert/überrascht/verärgert über etw acc; **I went at his suggestion** ich ging auf seinen Vorschlag hin

---

ate [eɪt] pt of **eat**

atheist [ˈeɪθɪɪst] n Atheist(in) m(f)

Athens [ˈæθɪnz] n Athen nt

athlete [ˈæθliːt] n Athlet m, Sportler m

athletic [æθˈletɪk] adj sportlich, athletisch; **~s** n Leichtathletik f

Atlantic [ətˈlæntɪk] adj atlantisch ♦ n: **the ~ (Ocean)** der Atlantik

atlas [ˈætləs] n Atlas m

ATM abbr (= automated teller machine) Geldautomat m

atmosphere [ˈætməsfɪəʳ] n Atmosphäre f

atom [ˈætəm] n Atom nt; (fig) bisschen nt; **~ic** [əˈtɒmɪk] adj atomar, Atom-; **~(ic) bomb** n Atombombe f

atomizer [ˈætəmaɪzəʳ] n Zerstäuber m

atone [əˈtəun] vi sühnen; **to ~ for sth** etw sühnen

atrocious [əˈtrəuʃəs] adj grässlich

atrocity [əˈtrɒsɪtɪ] n Scheußlichkeit f; (deed) Gräueltat f

attach [əˈtætʃ] vt (fasten) befestigen; **to be ~ed to sb/sth** an jdm/etw hängen; **to ~ importance** etc **to sth** Wichtigkeit etc auf etw acc legen, einer Sache dat Wichtigkeit etc beimessen

attaché case [əˈtæʃeɪ] n Aktenkoffer m

attachment [əˈtætʃmənt] n (tool) Zubehörteil nt; (love): **~ (to sb)** Zuneigung f (zu jdm)

attack [əˈtæk] vt angreifen ♦ n Angriff m; (MED) Anfall m; **~er** n Angreifer(in) m(f)

attain [əˈteɪn] vt erreichen; **~ments** npl Kenntnisse pl

attempt [əˈtempt] n Versuch m ♦ vt versuchen; **~ed murder** Mordversuch m

attend [əˈtend] vt (go to) teilnehmen an +dat); (lectures) besuchen; **to ~ to** (needs) nachkommen +dat; (person) sich kümmern um; **~ance** n (presence) Anwesenheit f; (people present) Besucherzahl f; **good ~ance** gute Teilnahme; **~ant** n (companion) Begleiter(in) m(f); Gesellschafter(in) m(f); (in car park etc) Wächter(in) m(f); (servant) Bedienstete(r) mf ♦ adj begleitend; (fig) damit verbunden

attention [əˈtenʃən] n Aufmerksamkeit f; (care) Fürsorge f; (for machine etc) Pflege f ♦ excl (MIL) Achtung!; **for the ~ of ...** zu Händen (von) ...

attentive [əˈtentɪv] adj aufmerksam

attic [ˈætɪk] n Dachstube f, Mansarde f

attitude [ˈætɪtjuːd] n (mental) Einstellung f

attorney [əˈtəːnɪ] n (solicitor) Rechtsanwalt m; **A~ General** n Justizminister m

attract [əˈtrækt] vt anziehen; (attention)

erregen; ~ion n Anziehungskraft f; (thing) Attraktion f; ~ive adj attraktiv

attribute [n ˈætrɪbjuːt, vb əˈtrɪbjuːt] n Eigenschaft f, Attribut nt ♦ vt zuschreiben

attrition [əˈtrɪʃən] n: **war of ~** Zermürbungskrieg m

aubergine [ˈəʊbəʒiːn] n Aubergine f

auburn [ˈɔːbən] adj kastanienbraun

auction [ˈɔːkʃən] n (also: **sale by ~**) Versteigerung f, Auktion f ♦ vt versteigern; ~eer [ɔːkʃəˈnɪə] n Versteigerer m

audacity [ɔːˈdæsɪtɪ] n (boldness) Wagemut m; (impudence) Unverfrorenheit f

audible [ˈɔːdɪbl] adj hörbar

audience [ˈɔːdɪəns] n Zuhörer pl, Zuschauer pl; (with queen) Audienz f

audiotypist [ˈɔːdɪəʊtaɪpɪst] n Phonotypistin f, Fonotypistin f

audiovisual [ɔːdɪəʊˈvɪzjuəl] adj audiovisuell

audit [ˈɔːdɪt] vt prüfen

audition [ɔːˈdɪʃən] n Probe f

auditor [ˈɔːdɪtə] n (accountant) Rechnungsprüfer(in) m(f), Buchprüfer m

auditorium [ɔːdɪˈtɔːrɪəm] n Zuschauerraum m

augment [ɔːgˈmɛnt] vt vermehren

augur [ˈɔːgə] vi bedeuten, voraussagen; **this ~s well** das ist ein gutes Omen

August [ˈɔːgəst] n August m

aunt [ɑːnt] n Tante f; ~ie n Tantchen nt; ~y n = **auntie**

au pair [ˈəʊˈpɛə] n (also: ~ **girl**) Aupairmädchen nt, Au-pair-Mädchen nt

aura [ˈɔːrə] n Nimbus m

auspicious [ɔːsˈpɪʃəs] adj günstig; verheißungsvoll

austere [ɔsˈtɪə] adj streng; (room) nüchtern; **austerity** [ɔsˈtɛrɪtɪ] n Strenge f; (POL) wirtschaftliche Einschränkung f

Australia [ɔsˈtreɪlɪə] n Australien nt; ~n adj australisch ♦ n Australier(in) m(f)

Austria [ˈɔstrɪə] n Österreich nt; ~n adj österreichisch ♦ n Österreicher(in) m(f)

authentic [ɔːˈθɛntɪk] adj echt, authentisch

author [ˈɔːθə] n Autor m, Schriftsteller m; (beginner) Urheber m, Schöpfer m

authoritarian [ɔːθɔrɪˈtɛərɪən] adj autoritär

authoritative [ɔːˈθɔrɪtətɪv] adj (account) maßgeblich; (manner) herrisch

authority [ɔːˈθɔrɪtɪ] n (power) Autorität f; (expert) Autorität f, Fachmann m; **the authorities** npl (ruling body) die Behörden pl

authorize [ˈɔːθəraɪz] vt bevollmächtigen; (permit) genehmigen

auto [ˈɔːtəʊ] (US) n Auto nt, Wagen m

autobiography [ɔːtəbaɪˈɔgrəfɪ] n Autobiografie f

autograph [ˈɔːtəgrɑːf] n (of celebrity) Autogramm nt ♦ vt mit Autogramm versehen

automatic [ɔːtəˈmætɪk] adj automatisch ♦ n (gun) Selbstladepistole f; (car) Automatik m; ~ally adv automatisch

automation [ɔːtəˈmeɪʃən] n Automatisierung f

automobile [ˈɔːtəməbiːl] (US) n Auto(mobil) nt

autonomous [ɔːˈtɔnəməs] adj autonom; **autonomy** n Autonomie f

autumn [ˈɔːtəm] n Herbst m

auxiliary [ɔːgˈzɪlɪərɪ] adj Hilfs-

Av. abbr = **avenue**

avail [əˈveɪl] vt: **to ~ o.s. of sth** sich einer Sache gen bedienen ♦ n: **to no ~** nutzlos

availability [əveɪləˈbɪlɪtɪ] n Erhältlichkeit f, Vorhandensein nt

available [əˈveɪləbl] adj erhältlich; zur Verfügung stehend; (person) erreichbar, abkömmlich

avalanche [ˈævəlɑːnʃ] n Lawine f

Ave. abbr = **avenue**

avenge [əˈvɛndʒ] vt rächen, sühnen

avenue [ˈævənjuː] n Allee f

average [ˈævərɪdʒ] n Durchschnitt m ♦ adj durchschnittlich, Durchschnitts- ♦ vt (figures) den Durchschnitt nehmen von; (perform) durchschnittlich leisten; (in car etc) im Schnitt fahren; **on ~** durchschnittlich, im Durchschnitt; ~ **out** vi: **to ~ out at** im Durchschnitt betragen

averse [əˈvəːs] adj: **to be ~ to doing sth** eine Abneigung dagegen haben, etw zu tun

avert [əˈvɜːt] vt (turn away) abkehren; (prevent) abwehren

aviary [ˈeɪvɪərɪ] n Vogelhaus nt

aviation [eɪvɪˈeɪʃən] n Luftfahrt f, Flugwesen nt

avid [ˈævɪd] adj: **~ (for)** gierig (auf +acc)

avocado [ævəˈkɑːdəu] n (BRIT: also: **~ pear**) Avocado(birne) f

avoid [əˈvɔɪd] vt vermeiden

await [əˈweɪt] vt erwarten, entgegensehen +dat

awake [əˈweɪk] (pt **awoke**, pp **awoken** or **awaked**) adj wach ♦ vt (auf)wecken ♦ vi aufwachen; **to be ~** wach sein; **~ning** n Erwachen nt

award [əˈwɔːd] n (prize) Preis m ♦ vt: **to ~ (sb sth)** (jdm etw) zuerkennen

aware [əˈwɛər] adj bewusst; **to be ~** sich bewusst sein; **~ness** n Bewusstsein nt

awash [əˈwɒʃ] adj überflutet

away [əˈweɪ] adv weg, fort; **two hours ~ by car** zwei Autostunden entfernt; **the holiday was two weeks ~** es war noch zwei Wochen bis zum Urlaub; **two kilometres ~** zwei Kilometer entfernt; **~ match** n (SPORT) Auswärtsspiel nt

awe [ɔː] n Ehrfurcht f; **~-inspiring** adj Ehrfurcht gebietend; **~some** adj Ehrfurcht gebietend

awful [ˈɔːfəl] adj (very bad) furchtbar; **~ly** adv furchtbar, sehr

awhile [əˈwaɪl] adv eine Weile

awkward [ˈɔːkwəd] adj (clumsy) ungeschickt, linkisch; (embarrassing) peinlich

awning [ˈɔːnɪŋ] n Markise f

awoke [əˈwəuk] pt of **awake**; **~n** pp of **awake**

awry [əˈraɪ] adv schief; (plans) schief gehen

axe [æks] (US **ax**) n Axt f, Beil nt ♦ vt (end suddenly) streichen

axes[1] [ˈæksɪz] npl of **axe**

axes[2] [ˈæksiːz] npl of **axis**

axis [ˈæksɪs] (pl **axes**) n Achse f

axle [ˈæksl] n Achse f

ay(e) [aɪ] excl (yes) ja

azalea [əˈzeɪlɪə] n Azalee f

B, b

B [biː] n (MUS) H nt; **~ road** (BRIT) Landstraße f

B.A. n abbr = **Bachelor of Arts**

babble [ˈbæbl] vi schwätzen

baby [ˈbeɪbɪ] n Baby nt; **~ carriage** (US) n Kinderwagen m; **~ food** n Babynahrung f; **~-sit** vi Kinder hüten, babysitten; **~-sitter** n Babysitter m; **~-sitting** n Babysitten nt, Babysitting nt; **~ wipe** n Ölpflegetuch nt

bachelor [ˈbætʃələr] n Junggeselle m; **B~ of Arts** Bakkalaureus m der philosophischen Fakultät; **B~ of Science** Bakkalaureus m der Naturwissenschaften

back [bæk] n (of person, horse) Rücken m; (of house) Rückseite f; (of train) Ende nt; (FOOTBALL) Verteidiger m ♦ vt (support) unterstützen; (wager) wetten auf +acc; (car) rückwärts fahren ♦ vi (go ~wards) rückwärts gehen or fahren ♦ adj hintere(r, s) ♦ adv zurück; (to the rear) nach hinten; **~ down** vi zurückstecken; **~ out** vi sich zurückziehen; (inf) kneifen; **~ up** vt (support) unterstützen; (car) zurücksetzen; (COMPUT) eine Sicherungskopie machen von; **~ache** n Rückenschmerzen pl; **~bencher** (BRIT) n Parlamentarier(in) m(f); **~bone** n Rückgrat nt; (support) Rückhalt m; **~cloth** n Hintergrund m; **~date** vt rückdatieren; **~drop** n (THEAT) = **backcloth**; (~ground) Hintergrund m; **~fire** vi (plan) fehlschlagen; (TECH) fehlzünden; **~ground** n Hintergrund m; (person's education) Vorbildung f; **family ~ground** Familienverhältnisse pl; **~hand** n (TENNIS: also: **~hand stroke**) Rückhand f; **~hander** (BRIT) n (bribe) Schmiergeld nt; **~ing** n (support) Unterstützung f; **~lash** n (fig) Gegenschlag m; **~log** n (of work) Rückstand m; **~ number** n (PRESS) alte Nummer f; **~pack** n Rucksack m; **~packer** n Rucksacktourist(in) m(f); **~ pain** n Rückenschmerzen pl; **~ pay** n (Gehalts- or Lohn)nachzahlung f; **~ payments** npl

Zahlungsrückstände pl; ~ seat n (AUT) Rücksitz m; ~side (inf) n Hintern m; ~stage adv hinter den Kulissen; ~stroke n Rückenschwimmen nt; ~up adj (COMPUT) Sicherungs- ♦ n (COMPUT) Sicherungskopie f; ~ward adj (less developed) zurückgeblieben; (primitive) rückständig; ~wards adv rückwärts; ~water n (fig) Kaff nt; ~yard n Hinterhof m

bacon ['beɪkən] n Schinkenspeck m

bacteria [bæk'tɪərɪə] npl Bakterien pl

bad [bæd] adj schlecht, schlimm; **to go ~** schlecht werden

bade [bæd] pt of **bid**

badge [bædʒ] n Abzeichen nt

badger ['bædʒə'] n Dachs m

badly ['bædlɪ] adv schlecht, schlimm; ~ **wounded** schwer verwundet; **he needs it ~** er braucht es dringend; **to be ~ off (for money)** dringend Geld nötig haben

badminton ['bædmɪntən] n Federball m, Badminton nt

bad-tempered ['bæd'tempəd] adj schlecht gelaunt

baffle ['bæfl] vt (puzzle) verblüffen

bag [bæg] n (sack) Beutel m; (paper) Tüte f; (handbag) Tasche f; (suitcase) Koffer m; (inf: old woman) alte Schachtel f ♦ vt (put in sack) in einen Sack stecken; (hunting) erlegen; ~s of (inf: lots of) eine Menge +acc; ~gage ['bægɪdʒ] n Gepäck nt; ~ allowance n Freigepäck nt; ~ reclaim n Gepäckausgabe f; ~gy ['bægɪ] adj bauschig, sackartig

bagpipes ['bægpaɪps] npl Dudelsack m

bail [beɪl] n (money) Kaution f ♦ vt (prisoner: usu: grant ~ to) gegen Kaution freilassen; (boat: also: ~ out) ausschöpfen; **on ~** (prisoner) gegen Kaution freigelassen; **to ~ sb out** die Kaution für jdn stellen; see also **bale**

bailiff ['beɪlɪf] n Gerichtsvollzieher(in) m(f)

bait [beɪt] n Köder m ♦ vt mit einem Köder versehen; (fig) ködern

bake [beɪk] vt, vi backen; **~d beans** gebackene Bohnen pl; **~d potatoes** npl in der Schale gebackene Kartoffeln pl; **~r** n

Bäcker m; **~ry** Bäckerei f; **baking** n Backen nt; **baking powder** n Backpulver nt

balance ['bæləns] n (scales) Waage f; (equilibrium) Gleichgewicht nt; (FIN: state of account) Saldo m; (difference) Bilanz f; (amount remaining) Restbetrag m ♦ vt (weigh) wägen; (make equal) ausgleichen; ~ **of trade/payments** Handels-/ Zahlungsbilanz f; **~d** adj ausgeglichen; ~ **sheet** n Bilanz f, Rechnungsabschluss m

balcony ['bælkənɪ] n Balkon m

bald [bɔːld] adj kahl; (statement) knapp

bale [beɪl] n Ballen m; **bale out** vi (from a plane) abspringen

ball [bɔːl] n Ball m; ~ **bearing** n Kugellager nt

ballet ['bæleɪ] n Ballett nt; ~ **dancer** n Balletttänzer(in) m(f); ~ **shoe** n Ballettschuh m

balloon [bə'luːn] n (Luft)ballon m

ballot ['bælət] n (geheime) Abstimmung f

ballpoint (pen) ['bɔːlpɔɪnt-] n Kugelschreiber m

ballroom ['bɔːlrum] n Tanzsaal m

Baltic ['bɔːltɪk] n: **the ~ (Sea)** die Ostsee

bamboo [bæm'buː] n Bambus m

ban [bæn] n Verbot nt ♦ vt verbieten

banana [bə'nɑːnə] n Banane f

band [bænd] n Band nt; (group) Gruppe f; (of criminals) Bande f; (MUS) Kapelle f, Band f; ~ **together** vi sich zusammentun

bandage ['bændɪdʒ] n Verband m; (elastic) Bandage f ♦ vt (cut) verbinden; (broken limb) bandagieren

Bandaid ['bændeɪd] (® US) n Heftpflaster nt

bandit ['bændɪt] n Bandit m, Räuber m

bandwagon ['bændwægən] n: **to jump on the ~** (fig) auf den fahrenden Zug aufspringen

bandy ['bændɪ] vt wechseln; **~-legged** adj o-beinig, O-beinig

bang [bæŋ] n (explosion) Knall m; (blow) Hieb m ♦ vt, vi knallen

Bangladesh [bæŋglə'deʃ] n Bangladesch nt

bangle ['bæŋgl] n Armspange f

bangs [bæŋz] (US) npl (fringe) Pony m

banish ['bænɪʃ] vt verbannen
banister(s) ['bænɪstə(z)] n(pl)
(Treppen)geländer nt
bank [bæŋk] n (raised ground) Erdwall m; (of
lake etc) Ufer nt; (FIN) Bank f ♦ vt (tilt: AVIAT)
in die Kurve bringen; (money) einzahlen; ~
on vt fus: **to ~ on sth** mit etw rechnen; ~
account n Bankkonto nt; ~ **card** n
Scheckkarte f; ~**er** n Bankier m; ~**er's**
card (BRIT) n = **bank card**; **B~ holiday**
(BRIT) n gesetzliche(r) Feiertag m; ~**ing** n
Bankwesen nt; ~**note** n Banknote f; ~ **rate**
n Banksatz m

---
bank holiday

ⓘ Als **bank holiday** wird in
Großbritannien ein gesetzlicher Feiertag
bezeichnet, an dem die Banken geschlossen
sind. Die meisten dieser Feiertage,
abgesehen von Weihnachten und Ostern,
fallen auf Montage im Mai und August. An
diesen langen Wochenenden (bank holiday
weekends) fahren viele Briten in Urlaub, so
dass dann auf den Straßen, Flughäfen und
bei der Bahn sehr viel Betrieb ist.

---

bankrupt ['bæŋkrʌpt] adj: **to be ~** bankrott
sein; **to go ~** Bankrott machen; ~**cy** n
Bankrott m
bank statement n Kontoauszug m
banned [bænd] adj: **he was ~ from driving**
(BRIT) ihm wurde Fahrverbot erteilt
banner ['bænə'] n Banner nt
banns [bænz] npl Aufgebot nt
baptism ['bæptɪzəm] n Taufe f
baptize [bæp'taɪz] vt taufen
bar [bɑ:'] n (rod) Stange f; (obstacle)
Hindernis nt; (of chocolate) Tafel f; (of soap)
Stück nt; (for food, drink) Buffet nt, Bar f;
(pub) Wirtschaft f; (MUS) Takt(strich) m ♦ vt
(fasten) verriegeln; (hinder) versperren;
(exclude) ausschließen; **behind ~s** hinter
Gittern; **the B~: to be called to the B~** als
Anwalt zugelassen werden; **~ none** ohne
Ausnahme
barbaric [bɑ:'bærɪk] adj primitiv, unkultiviert
barbecue ['bɑ:bɪkju:] n Barbecue nt

barbed wire ['bɑ:bd-] n Stacheldraht m
barber ['bɑ:bə'] n Herrenfriseur m
bar code n (COMM) Registrierkode f
bare [beə'] adj nackt; (trees, country) kahl;
(mere) bloß ♦ vt entblößen; ~**back** adv
ungesattelt; ~**faced** adj unverfroren; ~**foot**
adj, adv barfuß; ~**ly** adv kaum, knapp
bargain ['bɑ:gɪn] n (sth cheap) günstiger
Kauf; (agreement: written) Kaufvertrag m;
(: oral) Geschäft nt; **into the ~** obendrein;
~ **for** vt: **he got more than he ~ed for** er
erlebte sein blaues Wunder
barge [bɑ:dʒ] n Lastkahn m; ~ **in** vi
hereinplatzen; ~ **into** vt rennen gegen
bark [bɑ:k] n (of tree) Rinde f; (of dog) Bellen
nt ♦ vi (dog) bellen
barley ['bɑ:lɪ] n Gerste f; ~ **sugar** n
Malzbonbon nt
bar: ~**maid** n Bardame f; ~**man** (irreg) n
Barkellner m; ~ **meal** n einfaches Essen in
einem Pub
barn [bɑ:n] n Scheune f
barometer [bə'rɔmɪtə'] n Barometer nt
baron ['bærən] n Baron m; ~**ess** n Baronin f
barracks ['bærəks] npl Kaserne f
barrage ['bærɑ:ʒ] n (gunfire) Sperrfeuer nt;
(dam) Staudamm m; Talsperre f
barrel ['bærəl] n Fass nt; (of gun) Lauf m
barren ['bærən] adj unfruchtbar
barricade [bærɪ'keɪd] n Barrikade f ♦ vt
verbarrikadieren
barrier ['bærɪə'] n (obstruction) Hindernis nt;
(fence) Schranke f
barring ['bɑ:rɪŋ] prep außer im Falle +gen
barrister ['bærɪstə'] (BRIT) n Rechtsanwalt m
barrow ['bærəu] n (cart) Schubkarren m
bartender ['bɑ:tendə'] (US) n Barmann or -
kellner m
barter ['bɑ:tə'] vt handeln
base [beɪs] n (bottom) Boden m, Basis f; (MIL)
Stützpunkt m ♦ vt gründen; (opinion,
theory): **to be ~d on** basieren auf +dat ♦ adj
(low) gemein; **I'm ~d in London** ich wohne
in London; ~**ball** ['beɪsbɔ:l] n Baseball m;
~**ment** ['beɪsmənt] n Kellergeschoss nt
bases[1] ['beɪsɪz] npl of **base**
bases[2] ['beɪsi:z] npl of **basis**

bash [bæʃ] (*inf*) *vt* (heftig) schlagen

bashful ['bæʃful] *adj* schüchtern

basic ['beɪsɪk] *adj* grundlegend; **~s** *npl*: **the ~s** das Wesentliche *sg*; **~ally** *adv* im Grunde

basil ['bæzl] *n* Basilikum *nt*

basin ['beɪsn] *n* (*dish*) Schüssel *f*; (*for washing, also valley*) Becken *nt*; (*dock*) (Trocken)becken *nt*

basis ['beɪsɪs] (*pl* **bases**) *n* Basis *f*, Grundlage *f*

bask [bɑːsk] *vi*: **to ~ in the sun** sich sonnen

basket ['bɑːskɪt] *n* Korb *m*; **~ball** *n* Basketball *m*

bass [beɪs] *n* (*MUS, also instrument*) Bass *m*; (*voice*) Bassstimme *f*; **~ drum** *n* große Trommel

bassoon [bə'suːn] *n* Fagott *nt*

bastard ['bɑːstəd] *n* Bastard *m*; (*inf!*) Arschloch *nt* (!)

bat [bæt] *n* (*SPORT*) Schlagholz *nt*; Schläger *m*; (*ZOOL*) Fledermaus *f* ♦ *vt*: **he didn't ~ an eyelid** er hat nicht mit der Wimper gezuckt

batch [bætʃ] *n* (*of letters*) Stoß *m*; (*of samples*) Satz *m*

bated ['beɪtɪd] *adj*: **with ~ breath** mit angehaltenem Atem

bath [bɑːθ] *n* Bad *nt*; (*~ tub*) Badewanne *f* ♦ *vt* baden; **to have a ~** baden; *see also* **baths**

bathe [beɪð] *vt, vi* baden; **~r** *n* Badende(r) *f(m)*

bathing ['beɪðɪŋ] *n* Baden *nt*; **~ cap** *n* Badekappe *f*; **~ costume** *n* Badeanzug *m*; **~ suit** (*US*) *n* Badeanzug *m*; **~ trunks** (*BRIT*) *npl* Badehose *f*

bath: ~robe *n* Bademantel *m*; **~room** *n* Bad(ezimmer *nt*) *nt*; **~s** *npl* (Schwimm)bad *nt*; **~ towel** *n* Badetuch *nt*

baton ['bætən] *n* (*of police*) Gummiknüppel *m*; (*MUS*) Taktstock *m*

batter ['bætə'] *vt* verprügeln ♦ *n* Schlagteig *m*; (*for cake*) Biskuitteig *m*; **~ed** *adj* (*hat, pan*) verbeult

battery ['bætərɪ] *n* (*ELEC*) Batterie *f*; (*MIL*) Geschützbatterie *f*

battery farming *n* (Hühner- *etc*) batterien *pl*

battle ['bætl] *n* Schlacht *f*; (*small*) Gefecht *nt* ♦ *vi* kämpfen; **~field** *n* Schlachtfeld *nt*; **~ship** *n* Schlachtschiff *nt*

Bavaria [bə'veərɪə] *n* Bayern *nt*; **~n** *adj* bay(e)risch ♦ *n* (*person*) Bayer(in) *m(f)*

bawdy ['bɔːdɪ] *adj* unflätig

bawl [bɔːl] *vi* brüllen

bay [beɪ] *n* (*of sea*) Bucht *f* ♦ *vi* bellen; **to keep at ~** unter Kontrolle halten; **~ window** *n* Erkerfenster *nt*

bazaar [bə'zɑː'] *n* Basar *m*

B. & B. *abbr* = **bed and breakfast**

BBC *n abbr* (= *British Broadcasting Corporation*) BBC *f or m*

B.C. *adv abbr* (= *before Christ*) v. Chr.

KEYWORD

---

be [biː] (*pt* **was, were**, *pp* **been**) *aux vb*
1 (*with present participle: forming continuous tenses*): **what are you doing?** was machst du (gerade)?; **it is raining** es regnet; **I've been waiting for you for hours** ich warte schon seit Stunden auf dich
2 (*with pp: forming passives*): **to be killed** getötet werden; **the thief was nowhere to be seen** der Dieb war nirgendwo zu sehen
3 (*in tag questions*): **it was fun, wasn't it?** es hat Spaß gemacht, nicht wahr?
4 (*+to +infin*): **the house is to be sold** das Haus soll verkauft werden; **he's not to open it** er darf es nicht öffnen
♦ *vb +complement* 1 (*usu*) sein; **I'm tired** ich bin müde; **I'm hot/cold** mir ist heiß/kalt; **he's a doctor** er ist Arzt; **2 and 2 are 4** 2 und 2 ist *or* sind 4; **she's tall/pretty** sie ist groß/hübsch; **be careful/quiet** sei vorsichtig/ruhig
2 (*of health*): **how are you?** wie geht es dir?; **he's very ill** er ist sehr krank; **I'm fine now** jetzt geht es mir gut
3 (*of age*): **how old are you?** wie alt bist du?; **I'm sixteen (years old)** ich bin sechzehn (Jahre alt)
4 (*cost*): **how much was the meal?** was *or* wie viel hat das Essen gekostet?; **that'll be £5.75, please** das macht £5.75, bitte

♦ vi 1 (*exist, occur etc*) sein; **is there a God?** gibt es einen Gott?; **be that as it may** wie dem auch sei; **so be it** also gut
2 (*referring to place*) sein; **I won't be here tomorrow** iche werde morgen nicht hier sein
3 (*referring to movement*): **where have you been?** wo bist du gewesen?; **I've been in the garden** ich war im Garten
♦ impers vb 1 (*referring to time, distance, weather*) sein; **it's 5 o'clock** es ist 5 Uhr; **it's 10 km to the village** es sind 10 km bis zum Dorf; **it's too hot/cold** es ist zu heiß/kalt
2 (*emphatic*): **it's me** ich bins; **it's the postman** es ist der Briefträger

beach [biːtʃ] n Strand m ♦ vt (*ship*) auf den Strand setzen
beacon ['biːkən] n (*signal*) Leuchtfeuer nt; (*traffic ~*) Bake f
bead [biːd] n Perle f; (*drop*) Tropfen m
beak [biːk] n Schnabel m
beaker ['biːkəʳ] n Becher m
beam [biːm] n (*of wood*) Balken m; (*of light*) Strahl m; (*smile*) strahlende(s) Lächeln nt ♦ vi strahlen
bean [biːn] n Bohne f; (*also:* **baked ~s**) gebackene Bohnen pl; **~ sprouts** npl Sojasprossen pl
bear [bɛəʳ] (*pt* bore, *pp* borne) n Bär m ♦ vt (*weight, crops*) tragen; (*tolerate*) ertragen; (*young*) gebären ♦ vi: **to ~ right/left** sich rechts/links halten; **~ out** vt (*suspicions etc*) bestätigen; **~ up** vi sich halten
beard [bɪəd] n Bart m; **~ed** adj bärtig
bearer ['bɛərəʳ] n Träger m
bearing ['bɛərɪŋ] n (*posture*) Haltung f; (*relevance*) Relevanz f; (*relation*) Bedeutung f; (*TECH*) Kugellager nt; **~s** npl (*direction*) Orientierung f; (*also:* **ball ~s**) (Kugel)lager nt
beast [biːst] n Tier nt, Vieh nt; (*person*) Biest nt
beat [biːt] (*pt* beat, *pp* beaten) n (*stroke*) Schlag m; (*pulsation*) (Herz)schlag m; (*police round*) Runde f; Revier nt; (*MUS*) Takt m;

Beat m ♦ vt, vi schlagen; **to ~ it** abhauen; **off the ~en track** abgelegen; **~ off** vt abschlagen; **~ up** vt zusammenschlagen; **~en** pp of **beat**; **~ing** n Prügel pl
beautiful ['bjuːtɪful] adj schön; **~ly** adv ausgezeichnet
beauty ['bjuːtɪ] n Schönheit f; **~ salon** n Schönheitssalon m; **~ spot** n Schönheitsfleck m; (*BRIT: TOURISM*) (besonders) schöne(r) Ort m
beaver ['biːvəʳ] n Biber m
became [bɪ'keɪm] pt of **become**
because [bɪ'kɔz] conj weil ♦ prep: **~ of** wegen +gen, wegen +dat (*inf*)
beck [bek] n: **to be at the ~ and call of sb** nach jds Pfeife tanzen
beckon ['bekən] vt, vi: **to ~ to sb** jdm ein Zeichen geben
become [bɪ'kʌm] (*irreg: like* **come**) vi werden ♦ vt (*circumstances*) stehen +dat
becoming [bɪ'kʌmɪŋ] adj (*suitable*) schicklich; (*clothes*) kleidsam
bed [bed] n Bett nt; (*of river*) Flussbett nt; (*foundation*) Schicht f; (*in garden*) Beet nt; **to go to ~** zu Bett gehen; **~ and breakfast** n Übernachtung f mit Frühstück; **~clothes** npl Bettwäsche f; **~ding** n Bettzeug nt

Bed and Breakfast

🛈 **Bed and Breakfast** *bedeutet „Übernachtung mit Frühstück", wobei sich dies in Großbritannien nicht auf Hotels, sondern auf kleinere Pensionen, Privathäuser und Bauernhöfe bezieht, wo man wesentlich preisgünstiger übernachten kann als in Hotels. Oft wird für Bed and Breakfast, auch B & B genannt, durch ein entsprechendes Schild im Garten oder an der Einfahrt geworben.*

bedlam ['bedləm] n (*uproar*) tolle(s) Durcheinander nt
bed linen n Bettwäsche f
bedraggled [bɪ'drægld] adj ramponiert
bed: ~ridden adj bettlägerig; **~room** n Schlafzimmer nt; **~side** n: **at the ~side** am Bett; **~sit(ter)** (*BRIT*) n Einzimmerwohnung f

f, möblierte(s) Zimmer *nt*; **~spread** *n*
Tagesdecke *f*; **~time** *n* Schlafenszeit *f*
bee [biː] *n* Biene *f*
beech [biːtʃ] *n* Buche *f*
beef [biːf] *n* Rindfleisch *nt*; **roast ~** Roastbeef
nt; **~burger** *n* Hamburger *m*
beehive ['biːhaɪv] *n* Bienenstock *m*
beeline ['biːlaɪn] *n*: **to make a ~ for**
schnurstracks zugehen auf +*acc*
been [biːn] *pp of* **be**
beer [bɪəʳ] *n* Bier *nt*
beet [biːt] *n* (*vegetable*) Rübe *f*; (*US: also:* **red
~**) Rote Bete *f or* Rübe *f*
beetle ['biːtl] *n* Käfer *m*
beetroot ['biːtruːt] (*BRIT*) *n* Rote Bete *f*
before [bɪ'fɔːʳ] *prep* vor ♦ *conj* bevor ♦ *adv* (*of
time*) zuvor; früher; **the week ~** die Woche
zuvor *or* vorher; **I've done it ~** das hab ich
schon mal getan; **~ going** bevor er/sie *etc*
geht/ging; **~ she goes** bevor sie geht;
~hand *adv* im Voraus
beg [beg] *vt*, *vi* (*implore*) dringend bitten;
(*alms*) betteln
began [bɪ'gæn] *pt of* **begin**
beggar ['begəʳ] *n* Bettler(in) *m(f)*
begin [bɪ'gɪn] (*pt* **began**, *pp* **begun**) *vt*, *vi*
anfangen, beginnen; (*found*) gründen; **to ~
doing** *or* **to do sth** anfangen *or* beginnen,
etw zu tun; **to ~ with** zunächst (einmal);
~ner *n* Anfänger *m*; **~ning** *n* Anfang *m*
begun [bɪ'gʌn] *pp of* **begin**
behalf [bɪ'hɑːf] *n*: **on ~ of** im Namen +*gen*;
on my ~ für mich
behave [bɪ'heɪv] *vi* sich benehmen;
behaviour [bɪ'heɪvjəʳ] (*US* **behavior**) *n*
Benehmen *nt*
beheld [bɪ'held] *pt*, *pp of* **behold**
behind [bɪ'haɪnd] *prep* hinter ♦ *adv* (*late*) im
Rückstand; (*in the rear*) hinten ♦ *n* (*inf*)
Hinterteil *nt*; **~ the scenes** (*fig*) hinter den
Kulissen
behold [bɪ'həuld] (*irreg: like* **hold**) *vt*
erblicken
beige [beɪʒ] *adj* beige
Beijing ['beɪ'dʒɪŋ] *n* Peking *nt*
being ['biːɪŋ] *n* (*existence*) (Da)sein *nt*;
(*person*) Wesen *nt*; **to come into ~**

entstehen
Belarus [belə'rus] *n* Weißrussland *nt*
belated [bɪ'leɪtɪd] *adj* verspätet
belch [beltʃ] *vi* rülpsen ♦ *vt* (*smoke*)
ausspeien
belfry ['belfrɪ] *n* Glockenturm *m*
Belgian ['beldʒən] *adj* belgisch ♦ *n*
Belgier(in) *m(f)*
Belgium ['beldʒəm] *n* Belgien *nt*
belie [bɪ'laɪ] *vt* Lügen strafen +*acc*
belief [bɪ'liːf] *n* Glaube *m*; (*conviction*)
Überzeugung *f*; **~ in sb/sth** Glaube an
jdn/etw
believe [bɪ'liːv] *vt* glauben +*dat*; (*think*)
glauben, meinen, denken ♦ *vi* (*have faith*)
glauben; **to ~ in sth** an etw *acc* glauben;
~r *n* Gläubige(r) *f(m)*
belittle [bɪ'lɪtl] *vt* herabsetzen
bell [bel] *n* Glocke *f*
belligerent [bɪ'lɪdʒərənt] *adj* (*person*)
streitsüchtig; (*country*) Krieg führend
bellow ['beləu] *vt*, *vi* brüllen
bellows ['beləuz] *npl* (*TECH*) Gebläse *nt*; (*for
fire*) Blasebalg *m*
belly ['belɪ] *n* Bauch *m*
belong [bɪ'lɔŋ] *vi* gehören; **to ~ to sb** jdm
gehören; **to ~ to a club** *etc* einem Klub *etc*
angehören; **~ings** *npl* Habe *f*
beloved [bɪ'lʌvɪd] *adj* innig geliebt ♦ *n*
Geliebte(r) *f(m)*
below [bɪ'ləu] *prep* unter ♦ *adv* unten
belt [belt] *n* (*band*) Riemen *m*; (*round waist*)
Gürtel *m* ♦ *vt* (*fasten*) mit Riemen
befestigen; (*inf: beat*) schlagen; **~way** (*US*)
n (*AUT: ring road*) Umgehungsstraße *f*
bemused [bɪ'mjuːzd] *adj* verwirrt
bench [bentʃ] *n* (*seat*) Bank *f*; (*workshop*)
Werkbank *f*; (*judge's seat*) Richterbank *f*;
(*judges*) Richter *pl*
bend [bend] (*pt*, *pp* **bent**) *vt* (*curve*) biegen;
(*stoop*) beugen ♦ *vi* sich biegen; sich
beugen ♦ *n* Biegung *f*; (*BRIT: in road*) Kurve
f; **~ down** *or* **over** *vi* sich bücken
beneath [bɪ'niːθ] *prep* unter ♦ *adv* darunter
benefactor ['benɪfæktəʳ] *n* Wohltäter(in)
m(f)
beneficial [benɪ'fɪʃəl] *adj* vorteilhaft; (*to*

health) heilsam

benefit ['bɛnɪfɪt] n *(advantage)* Nutzen m
♦ vt fördern ♦ vi: **to ~ (from)** Nutzen ziehen
(aus)

Benelux ['bɛnɪlʌks] n Beneluxstaaten pl

benevolent [bɪ'nɛvələnt] adj wohlwollend

benign [bɪ'naɪn] adj *(person)* gütig; *(climate)*
mild

bent [bɛnt] pt, pp of **bend** ♦ n *(inclination)*
Neigung f ♦ adj *(inf: dishonest)* unehrlich; **to
be ~ on** versessen sein auf +acc

bequest [bɪ'kwɛst] n Vermächtnis nt

bereaved [bɪ'riːvd] npl: **the ~** die
Hinterbliebenen pl

beret ['bɛreɪ] n Baskenmütze f

Berlin [bəː'lɪn] n Berlin nt

berm [bəːm] *(US)* n *(AUT)* Seitenstreifen m

berry ['bɛrɪ] n Beere f

berserk [bə'səːk] adj: **to go ~** wild werden

berth [bəːθ] n *(for ship)* Ankerplatz m; *(in
ship)* Koje f; *(in train)* Bett nt ♦ vt am Kai
festmachen ♦ vi anlegen

beseech [bɪ'siːtʃ] *(pt, pp* **besought**) vt
anflehen

beset [bɪ'sɛt] *(pt, pp* **beset**) vt bedrängen

beside [bɪ'saɪd] prep neben, bei; *(except)*
außer; **to be ~ o.s. (with)** außer sich sein
(vor +dat); **that's ~ the point** das tut nichts
zur Sache

besides [bɪ'saɪdz] prep außer, neben ♦ adv
außerdem

besiege [bɪ'siːdʒ] vt *(MIL)* belagern;
(surround) umlagern, bedrängen

besought [bɪ'sɔːt] pt, pp of **beseech**

best [bɛst] adj beste(r, s) ♦ adv am besten;
the ~ part of *(quantity)* das meiste +gen; **at
~** höchstens; **to make the ~ of it** das Beste
daraus machen; **to do one's ~** sein Bestes
tun; **to the ~ of my knowledge** meines
Wissens; **to the ~ of my ability** so gut ich
kann; **for the ~** zum Besten; **~-before
date** n Mindesthaltbarkeitsdatum nt; **~
man** n Trauzeuge m

bestow [bɪ'stəʊ] vt verleihen

bet [bɛt] *(pt, pp* **bet** or **betted**) n Wette f ♦ vt,
vi wetten

betray [bɪ'treɪ] vt verraten

better ['bɛtər] adj, adv besser ♦ vt verbessern
♦ n: **to get the ~ of sb** jdn überwinden; **he
thought ~ of it** er hat sich eines Besseren
besonnen; **you had ~ leave** Sie gehen jetzt
wohl besser; **to get ~** *(MED)* gesund
werden; **~ off** adj *(richer)* wohlhabender

betting ['bɛtɪŋ] n Wetten nt; **~ shop** *(BRIT)* n
Wettbüro nt

between [bɪ'twiːn] prep zwischen; *(among)*
unter ♦ adv dazwischen

beverage ['bɛvərɪdʒ] n Getränk nt

bevy ['bɛvɪ] n Schar f

beware [bɪ'wɛər] vt, vi sich hüten vor +dat;
"~ of the dog" „Vorsicht, bissiger Hund!"

bewildered [bɪ'wɪldəd] adj verwirrt

beyond [bɪ'jɔnd] prep *(place)* jenseits +gen;
(time) über ... hinaus; *(out of reach)*
außerhalb +gen ♦ adv darüber hinaus; **~
doubt** ohne Zweifel; **~ repair** nicht mehr
zu reparieren

bias ['baɪəs] n *(slant)* Neigung f; *(prejudice)*
Vorurteil nt; **~(s)ed** adj voreingenommen

bib [bɪb] n Latz m

Bible ['baɪbl] n Bibel f

bicarbonate of soda [baɪ'kɑːbənɪt-] n
Natron nt

bicker ['bɪkər] vi zanken

bicycle ['baɪsɪkl] n Fahrrad nt

bid [bɪd] *(pt* **bade** *or* **bid**, *pp* **bid(den)**) n
(offer) Gebot nt; *(attempt)* Versuch m ♦ vt, vi
(offer) bieten; **to ~ farewell** Lebewohl
sagen; **~der** n *(person)* Steigerer m; **the
highest ~der** der Meistbietende; **~ding** n
(command) Geheiß nt

bide [baɪd] vt: **to ~ one's time** abwarten

bifocals [baɪ'fəʊklz] npl Bifokalbrille f

big [bɪg] adj groß; **~ dipper** [-'dɪpər] n
Achterbahn f; **~headed** ['bɪg'hɛdɪd] adj
eingebildet

bigot ['bɪgət] n Frömmler m; **~ed** adj bigott;
~ry n Bigotterie f

big top n Zirkuszelt nt

bike [baɪk] n Rad nt

bikini [bɪ'kiːnɪ] n Bikini m

bile [baɪl] n *(BIOL)* Galle f

bilingual [baɪ'lɪŋgwəl] adj zweisprachig

bill [bɪl] n *(account)* Rechnung f; *(POL)*

Gesetzentwurf m; (US: FIN) Geldschein m; **to fit** or **fill the ~** (fig) der/die/das Richtige sein; **"post no ~s"** „Plakate ankleben verboten"; **~board** ['bɪlbɔːd] n Reklameschild nt

billet ['bɪlɪt] n Quartier nt

billfold ['bɪlfəʊld] (US) n Geldscheintasche f

billiards ['bɪljədz] n Billard nt

billion ['bɪljən] n (BRIT) Billion f; (US) Milliarde f

bimbo ['bɪmbəʊ] (inf: pej) n Puppe f, Häschen nt

bin [bɪn] n Kasten m; (dustbin) (Abfall)eimer m

bind [baɪnd] (pt, pp **bound**) vt (tie) binden; (tie together) zusammenbinden; (oblige) verpflichten; **~ing** n (Buch)einband m ♦ adj verbindlich

binge [bɪndʒ] (inf) n Sauferei f

bingo ['bɪŋgəʊ] n Bingo nt

binoculars [bɪ'nɔkjʊləz] npl Fernglas nt

bio... [baɪəʊ] prefix: **~chemistry** n Biochemie f; **~degradable** adj biologisch abbaubar; **~graphy** n Biografie f; **~logical** [baɪə'lɔdʒɪkl] adj biologisch; **~logy** [baɪ'ɔlədʒɪ] n Biologie f

birch [bɜːtʃ] n Birke f

bird [bɜːd] n Vogel m; (BRIT: inf: girl) Mädchen nt; **~'s-eye view** n Vogelschau f; **~ watcher** n Vogelbeobachter(in) m(f); **~ watching** n Vogelbeobachten nt

Biro ['baɪərəʊ] ® n Kugelschreiber m

birth [bɜːθ] n Geburt f; **to give ~ to** zur Welt bringen; **~ certificate** n Geburtsurkunde f; **~ control** n Geburtenkontrolle f; **~day** n Geburtstag m; **~day card** n Geburtstagskarte f; **~place** n Geburtsort m; **~ rate** n Geburtenrate f

biscuit ['bɪskɪt] n Keks m

bisect [baɪ'sɛkt] vt halbieren

bishop ['bɪʃəp] n Bischof m

bit [bɪt] pt of **bite** ♦ n bisschen, Stückchen nt; (horse's) Gebiss nt; (COMPUT) Bit nt; **a ~ tired** etwas müde

bitch [bɪtʃ] n (dog) Hündin f; (unpleasant woman) Weibsstück nt

bite [baɪt] (pt **bit**, pp **bitten**) vt, vi beißen ♦ n

Biss m; (mouthful) Bissen m; **to ~ one's nails** Nägel kauen; **let's have a ~ to eat** lass uns etwas essen

bitten ['bɪtn] pp of **bite**

bitter ['bɪtər] adj bitter; (memory etc) schmerzlich; (person) verbittert ♦ n (BRIT: beer) dunkle(s) Bier nt; **~ness** n Bitterkeit f

blab [blæb] vi klatschen ♦ vt (also: ~ out) ausplaudern

black [blæk] adj schwarz; (night) finster ♦ vt schwärzen; (shoes) wichsen; (eye) blau schlagen; (BRIT: INDUSTRY) boykottieren; **to give sb a ~ eye** jdm ein blaues Auge schlagen; **in the ~** (bank account) in den schwarzen Zahlen; **~ and blue** adj grün und blau; **~berry** n Brombeere f; **~bird** n Amsel f; **~board** n (Wand)tafel f; **~ coffee** n schwarze(r) Kaffee m; **~currant** n schwarze Johannisbeere f; **~en** vt schwärzen; (fig) verunglimpfen; **B~ Forest** n Schwarzwald m; **~ ice** n Glatteis nt; **~leg** (BRIT) n Streikbrecher(in) m(f); **~list** n schwarze Liste f; **~mail** n Erpressung f ♦ vt erpressen; **~ market** n Schwarzmarkt m; **~out** n Verdunklung f; (MED): **to have a ~out** bewusstlos werden; **~ pudding** n ≈ Blutwurst f; **B~ Sea** n: **the B~ Sea** das Schwarze Meer; **~ sheep** n schwarze(s) Schaf nt; **~smith** n Schmied m; **~ spot** n (AUT) Gefahrenstelle f; (for unemployment etc) schwer betroffene(s) Gebiet nt

bladder ['blædər] n Blase f

blade [bleɪd] n (of weapon) Klinge f; (of grass) Halm m; (of oar) Ruderblatt nt

blame [bleɪm] n Tadel m, Schuld f ♦ vt Vorwürfe machen +dat; **to ~ sb for sth** jdm die Schuld an etw dat geben; **he is to ~** er ist daran schuld

bland [blænd] adj mild

blank [blæŋk] adj leer, unbeschrieben; (look) verdutzt; (verse) Blank- ♦ n (space) Lücke f; Zwischenraum m; (cartridge) Platzpatrone f; **~ cheque** n Blankoscheck m; (fig) Freibrief m

blanket ['blæŋkɪt] n (Woll)decke f

blare [bleər] vi (radio) plärren; (horn) tuten; (MUS) schmettern

blasé [ˈblɑːzeɪ] *adj* blasiert

blast [blɑːst] *n* Explosion *f*; (*of wind*) Windstoß *m* ♦ *vt* (*blow up*) sprengen; **~!** (*inf*) verflixt!; **~off** *n* (SPACE) (Raketen)abschuss *m*

blatant [ˈbleɪtənt] *adj* offenkundig

blaze [bleɪz] *n* (*fire*) lodernde(s) Feuer *nt* ♦ *vi* lodern ♦ *vt*: **to ~ a trail** Bahn brechen

blazer [ˈbleɪzəʳ] *n* Blazer *m*

bleach [bliːtʃ] *n* (*also*: **household ~**) Bleichmittel *nt* ♦ *vt* bleichen; **~ed** *adj* gebleicht

bleachers [ˈbliːtʃəz] (US) *npl* (SPORT) unüberdachte Tribüne *f*

bleak [bliːk] *adj* kahl, rau; (*future*) trostlos

bleary-eyed [ˈblɪərɪˈaɪd] *adj* triefäugig; (*on waking up*) mit verschlafenen Augen

bleat [bliːt] *vi* blöken; (*fig*: *complain*) meckern

bled [bled] *pt*, *pp of* **bleed**

bleed [bliːd] (*pt*, *pp* **bled**) *vi* bluten ♦ *vt* (*draw blood*) zur Ader lassen; **to ~ to death** verbluten

bleeper [ˈbliːpəʳ] *n* (*of doctor etc*) Funkrufempfänger *m*

blemish [ˈblemɪʃ] *n* Makel *m* ♦ *vt* verunstalten

blend [blend] *n* Mischung *f* ♦ *vt* mischen ♦ *vi* sich mischen; **~er** *n* Mixer *m*, Mixgerät *nt*

bless [bles] (*pt*, *pp* **blessed**) *vt* segnen; (*give thanks*) preisen; (*make happy*) glücklich machen; **~ you!** Gesundheit!; **~ing** *n* Segen *m*; (*at table*) Tischgebet *nt*; (*happiness*) Wohltat *f*; Segen *m*; (*good wish*) Glück *nt*

blew [bluː] *pt of* **blow**

blimey [ˈblaɪmɪ] (BRIT: *inf*) *excl* verflucht

blind [blaɪnd] *adj* blind; (*corner*) unübersichtlich ♦ *n* (*for window*) Rouleau *nt* ♦ *vt* blenden; **~ alley** *n* Sackgasse *f*; **~fold** *n* Augenbinde *f* ♦ *adj*, *adv* mit verbundenen Augen ♦ *vt*: **to ~fold sb** jdm die Augen verbinden; **~ly** *adv* blind; (*fig*) blindlings; **~ness** *n* Blindheit *f*; **~ spot** *n* (AUT) tote(r) Winkel *m*; (*fig*) schwache(r) Punkt *m*

blink [blɪŋk] *vi* blinzeln; **~ers** *npl* Scheuklappen *pl*

bliss [blɪs] *n* (Glück)seligkeit *f*

blister [ˈblɪstəʳ] *n* Blase *f* ♦ *vi* Blasen werfen

blitz [blɪts] *n* Luftkrieg *m*

blizzard [ˈblɪzəd] *n* Schneesturm *m*

bloated [ˈbləʊtɪd] *adj* aufgedunsen; (*inf*: *full*) nudelsatt

blob [blɒb] *n* Klümpchen *nt*

bloc [blɒk] *n* (POL) Block *m*

block [blɒk] *n* (*of wood*) Block *m*, Klotz *m*; (*of houses*) Häuserblock *m* ♦ *vt* (*block up*) [blɒˈkeɪd] *n* Blockade *f* ♦ *vt* blockieren; **~age** *n* Verstopfung *f*; **~buster** *n* Knüller *m*; **~ letters** *npl* Blockbuchstaben *pl*; **~ of flats** (BRIT) *n* Häuserblock *m*

bloke [bləʊk] (BRIT: *inf*) *n* Kerl *m*, Typ *m*

blond(e) [blɒnd] *adj* blond ♦ *n* Blondine *f*

blood [blʌd] *n* Blut *nt*; **~ donor** *n* Blutspender *m*; **~ group** *n* Blutgruppe *f*; **~ poisoning** *n* Blutvergiftung *f*; **~ pressure** *n* Blutdruck *m*; **~shed** *n* Blutvergießen *nt*; **~shot** *adj* blutunterlaufen; **~ sports** *npl* Jagdsport, Hahnenkampf *etc*; **~stained** *adj* blutbefleckt; **~stream** *n* Blut *nt*, Blutkreislauf *m*; **~ test** *n* Blutprobe *f*; **~thirsty** *adj* blutrünstig; **~ vessel** *n* Blutgefäß *nt*; **~y** *adj* blutig; (BRIT: *inf*) verdammt; **~y-minded** (BRIT: *inf*) *adj* stur

bloom [bluːm] *n* Blüte *f*; (*freshness*) Glanz *m* ♦ *vi* blühen

blossom [ˈblɒsəm] *n* Blüte *f* ♦ *vi* blühen

blot [blɒt] *n* Klecks *m* ♦ *vt* beklecksen; (*ink*) (ab)löschen; **~ out** *vt* auslöschen

blotchy [ˈblɒtʃɪ] *adj* fleckig

blotting paper [ˈblɒtɪŋ-] *n* Löschpapier *nt*

blouse [blaʊz] *n* Bluse *f*

blow [bləʊ] (*pt* **blew**, *pp* **blown**) *n* Schlag *m* ♦ *vt* blasen ♦ *vi* (*wind*) wehen; **to ~ one's nose** sich *dat* die Nase putzen; **~ away** *vt* wegblasen; **~ down** *vt* umwehen; **~ off** *vt* wegwehen ♦ *vi* wegfliegen; **~ out** *vi* ausgehen; **~ over** *vi* vorübergehen; **~ up** *vi* explodieren ♦ *vt* sprengen; **~-dry** *n*: **to have a ~-dry** sich föhnen lassen ♦ *vt* föhnen; **~lamp** (BRIT) *n* Lötlampe *f*; **~n** *pp of* **blow**; **~-out** *n* (AUT) geplatzte(r) Reifen *m*; **~torch** *n* = **blowlamp**

blue [bluː] *adj* blau; (*inf*: *unhappy*) niedergeschlagen; (*obscene*) pornografisch;

(*joke*) anzüglich ♦ *n*: **out of the ~** (*fig*) aus heiterem Himmel; **to have the ~s** traurig sein; ~**bell** *n* Glockenblume *f*; ~**bottle** *n* Schmeißfliege *f*; ~ **film** *n* Pornofilm *m*; ~**print** *n* (*fig*) Entwurf *m*

bluff [blʌf] *vi* bluffen, täuschen ♦ *n* (*deception*) Bluff *m*; **to call sb's ~** es darauf ankommen lassen

blunder ['blʌndəʳ] *n* grobe(r) Fehler *m*, Schnitzer *m* ♦ *vi* einen groben Fehler machen

blunt [blʌnt] *adj* (*knife*) stumpf; (*talk*) unverblümt ♦ *vt* abstumpfen

blur [blɜːʳ] *n* Fleck *m* ♦ *vt* verschwommen machen

blurb [blɜːb] *n* Waschzettel *m*

blush [blʌʃ] *vi* erröten

blustery ['blʌstəri] *adj* stürmisch

boar [bɔːʳ] *n* Keiler *m*, Eber *m*

board [bɔːd] *n* (*of wood*) Brett *nt*; (*of card*) Pappe *f*; (*committee*) Ausschuss *m*; (*of firm*) Aufsichtsrat *m*; (*SCH*) Direktorium *nt* ♦ *vt* (*train*) einsteigen in +*acc*; (*ship*) an Bord gehen +*gen*; **on ~** (*AVIAT, NAUT*) an Bord; **~ and lodging** Unterkunft *f* und Verpflegung; **full/half ~** (*BRIT*) Voll-/Halbpension *f*; **to go by the ~** (*fig*) flachfallen, über Bord gehen; **~ up** *vt* mit Brettern vernageln; ~**er** *n* Kostgänger *m*; (*SCH*) Internatsschüler(in) *m(f)*; **~ game** *n* Brettspiel *nt*; ~**ing card** *n* (*AVIAT, NAUT*) Bordkarte *f*; ~**ing house** *n* Pension *f*; ~**ing school** *n* Internat *nt*; ~**room** *n* Sitzungszimmer *nt*

boast [bəust] *vi* prahlen ♦ *vt* sich rühmen +*gen* ♦ *n* Großtuerei *f*, Prahlerei *f*; **to ~ about** *or* **of sth** mit etw prahlen

boat [bəut] *n* Boot *nt*; (*ship*) Schiff *nt*; ~**er** *n* (*hat*) Kreissäge *f*; ~**swain** *n* = **bosun**; ~ **train** *n* Zug *m* mit Fährenanschluss

bob [bɔb] *vi* sich auf und nieder bewegen; **~ up** *vi* auftauchen

bobbin ['bɔbɪn] *n* Spule *f*

bobby ['bɔbɪ] (*BRIT: inf*) *n* Bobby *m*

bobsleigh ['bɔbsleɪ] *n* Bob *m*

bode [bəud] *vi*: **to ~ well/ill** ein gutes/schlechtes Zeichen sein

bodily ['bɔdɪlɪ] *adj, adv* körperlich

body ['bɔdɪ] *n* Körper *m*; (*dead*) Leiche *f*; (*group*) Mannschaft *f*; (*AUT*) Karosserie *f*; (*trunk*) Rumpf *m*; ~ **building** *n* Bodybuilding *nt*; ~**guard** *n* Leibwache *f*; ~**work** *n* Karosserie *f*

bog [bɔg] *n* Sumpf *m* ♦ *vt*: **to get ~ged down** sich festfahren

boggle ['bɔgl] *vi* stutzen; **the mind ~s** es ist kaum auszumalen

bog-standard *adj* stinknormal (*inf*)

bogus ['bəugəs] *adj* unecht, Schein-

boil [bɔɪl] *vt, vi* kochen ♦ *n* (*MED*) Geschwür *nt*; **to come to the** (*BRIT*) **or a** (*US*) **~** zu kochen anfangen; **to ~ down to** (*fig*) hinauslaufen auf +*acc*; **~ over** *vi* überkochen; ~**ed egg** *n* (weich) gekochte(s) Ei *nt*; ~**ed potatoes** *npl* Salzkartoffeln *pl*; ~**er** *n* Boiler *m*; ~**er suit** (*BRIT*) *n* Arbeitsanzug *m*; ~**ing point** *n* Siedepunkt *m*

boisterous ['bɔɪstərəs] *adj* ungestüm

bold [bəuld] *adj* (*fearless*) unerschrocken; (*handwriting*) fest und klar

bollard ['bɔləd] *n* (*NAUT*) Poller *m*; (*BRIT: AUT*) Pfosten *m*

bolt [bəult] *n* Bolzen *m*; (*lock*) Riegel *m* ♦ *adv*: **~ upright** kerzengerade ♦ *vt* verriegeln; (*swallow*) verschlingen ♦ *vi* (*horse*) durchgehen

bomb [bɔm] *n* Bombe *f* ♦ *vt* bombardieren; ~**ard** [bɔm'bɑːd] *vt* bombardieren; ~**ardment** [bɔm'bɑːdmənt] *n* Beschießung *f*; **~ disposal** *n*: **~ disposal unit** Bombenräumkommando *nt*; ~**er** *n* Bomber *m*; (*terrorist*) Bombenattentäter(in) *m(f)*; ~**ing** *n* Bomben *pl*; ~**shell** *n* (*fig*) Bombe *f*

bona fide ['bəunə'faɪdɪ] *adj* echt

bond [bɔnd] *n* (*link*) Band *nt*; (*FIN*) Schuldverschreibung *f*

bondage ['bɔndɪdʒ] *n* Sklaverei *f*

bone [bəun] *n* Knochen *m*; (*of fish*) Gräte *f*; (*piece of ~*) Knochensplitter *m* ♦ *vt* die Knochen herausnehmen +*dat*; (*fish*) entgräten; **~ dry** *adj* (*inf*) knochentrocken; **~ idle** *adj* stinkfaul; **~ marrow** *n* (*ANAT*) Knochenmark *nt*

bonfire ['bɔnfaɪəʳ] *n* Feuer *nt* im Freien

bonnet ['bɒnɪt] *n* Haube *f*; (*for baby*) Häubchen *nt*; (BRIT: AUT) Motorhaube *f*

bonus ['bəʊnəs] *n* Bonus *m*; (*annual ~*) Prämie *f*

bony ['bəʊnɪ] *adj* knochig, knochendürr

boo [buː] *vt* auspfeifen

booby trap ['buːbɪ-] *n* Falle *f*

book [bʊk] *n* Buch *nt* ♦ *vt* (*ticket etc*) vorbestellen; (*person*) verwarnen; **~s** *npl* (COMM) Bücher *pl*; **~case** *n* Bücherregal *nt*, Bücherschrank *m*; **~ing office** (BRIT) *n* (RAIL) Fahrkartenschalter *m*; (THEAT) Vorverkaufsstelle *f*; **~-keeping** *n* Buchhaltung *f*; **~let** *n* Broschüre *f*; **~maker** *n* Buchmacher *m*; **~seller** *n* Buchhändler *m*; **~shelf** *n* Bücherbord *nt*; **~shop** ['bʊkʃɒp], **~store** *n* Buchhandlung *f*

boom [buːm] *n* (*noise*) Dröhnen *nt*; (*busy period*) Hochkonjunktur *f* ♦ *vi* dröhnen

boon [buːn] *n* Wohltat *f*, Segen *m*

boost [buːst] *n* Auftrieb *m*; (*fig*) Reklame *f* ♦ *vt* Auftrieb geben; **~er** *n* (MED) Wiederholungsimpfung *f*

boot [buːt] *n* Stiefel *m*; (BRIT: AUT) Kofferraum *m* ♦ *vt* (*kick*) einen Fußtritt geben; (COMPUT) laden; **to ~** (*in addition*) obendrein

booth [buːð] *n* (*at fair*) Bude *f*; (*telephone ~*) Zelle *f*; (*voting ~*) Kabine *f*

booze [buːz] (*inf*) *n* Alkohol *m*, Schnaps *m* ♦ *vi* saufen

border ['bɔːdə^r] *n* Grenze *f*; (*edge*) Kante *f*; (*in garden*) (Blumen)rabatte *f* ♦ *adj* Grenz-; **the B~s** *Grenzregion zwischen England und Schottland*; **~ on** *vt* grenzen an +acc; **~line** *n* Grenze *f*; **~line case** *n* Grenzfall *m*

bore [bɔː^r] *pt of* **bear** ♦ *vt* bohren; (*weary*) langweilen ♦ *n* (*person*) Langweiler *m*; (*thing*) langweilige Sache *f*; (*of gun*) Kaliber *nt*; **I am ~d** ich langweile mich; **~dom** *n* Langeweile *f*

boring ['bɔːrɪŋ] *adj* langweilig

born [bɔːn] *adj*: **to be ~** geboren werden

borne [bɔːn] *pp of* **bear**

borough ['bʌrə] *n* Stadt(gemeinde) *f*, Stadtbezirk *m*

borrow ['bɒrəʊ] *vt* borgen

Bosnia (and) Herzegovina ['bɒznɪə (ənd) hɜːtsəgəʊ'viːnə] *n* Bosnien und Herzegowina *nt*; **~n** *n* Bosnier(in) *m(f)* ♦ *adj* bosnisch

bosom ['bʊzəm] *n* Busen *m*

boss [bɒs] *n* Chef *m*, Boss *m* ♦ *vt*: **to ~ around** *or* **about** herumkommandieren; **~y** *adj* herrisch

bosun ['bəʊsn] *n* Bootsmann *m*

botany ['bɒtənɪ] *n* Botanik *f*

botch [bɒtʃ] *vt* (*also*: ~ **up**) verpfuschen

both [bəʊθ] *adj* beide(s) ♦ *pron* beide(s) ♦ *adv*: **~ X and Y** sowohl X wie *or* als auch Y; **~ (of) the books** beide Bücher; **~ of us went, we ~ went** wir gingen beide

bother ['bɒðə^r] *vt* (*pester*) quälen ♦ *vi* (*fuss*) sich aufregen ♦ *n* Mühe *f*, Umstand *m*; **to ~ doing sth** sich *dat* die Mühe machen, etw zu tun; **what a ~!** wie ärgerlich!

bottle ['bɒtl] *n* Flasche *f* ♦ *vt* (*in Flaschen*) abfüllen; **~ up** *vt* aufstauen; **~ bank** *n* Altglascontainer *m*; **~d beer** *n* Flaschenbier *nt*; **~d water** *n* in Flaschen abgefülltes Wasser; **~neck** *n* (*also fig*) Engpass *m*; **~ opener** *n* Flaschenöffner *m*

bottom ['bɒtəm] *n* Boden *m*; (*of person*) Hintern *m*; (*riverbed*) Flussbett *nt* ♦ *adj* unterste(r, s)

bough [baʊ] *n* Zweig *m*, Ast *m*

bought [bɔːt] *pt, pp of* **buy**

boulder ['bəʊldə^r] *n* Felsbrocken *m*

bounce [baʊns] *vi* (*person*) herumhüpfen; (*ball*) hochspringen; (*cheque*) platzen ♦ *vt* (*auf*)springen lassen ♦ *n* (*rebound*) Aufprall *m*; **~r** *n* Rausschmeißer *m*

bound [baʊnd] *pt, pp of* **bind** ♦ *n* Grenze *f*; (*leap*) Sprung *m* ♦ *vi* (*spring, leap*) (*auf*)springen ♦ *adj* (*obliged*) gebunden, verpflichtet; **out of ~s** Zutritt verboten; **to be ~ to do sth** verpflichtet sein, etw zu tun; **it's ~ to happen** es muss so kommen; **to be ~ for ...** nach ... fahren

boundary ['baʊndrɪ] *n* Grenze *f*

bouquet ['bʊkeɪ] *n* Strauß *m*; (*of wine*) Blume *f*

bourgeois ['bʊəʒwɑː] *adj* kleinbürgerlich, bourgeois ♦ *n* Spießbürger(in) *m(f)*

bout [baʊt] *n* (*of illness*) Anfall *m*; (*of contest*)

Kampf m

bow¹ [bəʊ] n (ribbon) Schleife f; (weapon, MUS) Bogen m

bow² [baʊ] n (with head, body) Verbeugung f; (of ship) Bug m ♦ vi sich verbeugen; (submit): **to ~ to** sich beugen +dat

bowels ['baʊəlz] npl (ANAT) Darm m

bowl [bəʊl] n (basin) Schüssel f; (of pipe) (Pfeifen)kopf m; (wooden ball) (Holz)kugel f ♦ vt, vi (die Kugel) rollen

bow-legged ['bəʊ'legɪd] adj o-beinig, O-beinig

bowler ['bəʊlə'] n Werfer m; (BRIT: also: ~ **hat**) Melone f

bowling ['bəʊlɪŋ] n Kegeln nt; ~ **alley** n Kegelbahn f; ~ **green** n Rasen m zum Bowlingspiel

bowls n (game) Bowlsspiel nt

bow tie [bəʊ-] n Fliege f

box [bɒks] n (also: **cardboard ~**) Schachtel f; (bigger) Kasten m; (THEAT) Loge f ♦ vt einpacken ♦ vi boxen; ~**er** n Boxer m; ~**er shorts** (BRIT) npl Boxershorts pl; ~**ing** n (SPORT) Boxen nt; B~**ing Day** (BRIT) n zweite(r) Weihnachtsfeiertag m; ~**ing gloves** npl Boxhandschuhe pl; ~**ing ring** n Boxring m; ~ **office** n (Theater)kasse f; ~**room** n Rumpelkammer f

---
Boxing Day

ⓘ **Boxing Day** (26.12.) ist ein Feiertag in Großbritannien. Wenn Weihnachten auf ein Wochenende fällt, wird der Feiertag am nächsten darauf folgenden Wochentag nachgeholt. Der Name geht auf einen alten Brauch zurück: früher erhielten Händler und Lieferanten an diesem Tag ein Geschenk, die so genannte Christmas Box.
---

boy [bɔɪ] n Junge m

boycott ['bɔɪkɒt] n Boykott m ♦ vt boykottieren

boyfriend ['bɔɪfrend] n Freund m

boyish ['bɔɪʃ] adj jungenhaft

B.R. n abbr = **British Rail**

bra [brɑː] n BH m

brace [breɪs] n (TECH) Stütze f; (MED)

Klammer f ♦ vt stützen; ~**s** npl (BRIT) Hosenträger pl; **to ~ o.s. for sth** (fig) sich auf etw acc gefasst machen

bracelet ['breɪslɪt] n Armband nt

bracing ['breɪsɪŋ] adj kräftigend

bracken ['brækən] n Farnkraut nt

bracket ['brækɪt] n Halter m, Klammer f; (in punctuation) Klammer f; (group) Gruppe f ♦ vt einklammern; (fig) in dieselbe Gruppe einordnen

brag [bræg] vi sich rühmen

braid [breɪd] n (hair) Flechte f; (trim) Borte f

Braille [breɪl] n Blindenschrift f

brain [breɪn] n (ANAT) Gehirn nt; (intellect) Intelligenz f, Verstand m; (person) kluge(r) Kopf m; ~**s** npl (intelligence) Verstand m; ~**child** n Erfindung f; ~**wash** vt eine Gehirnwäsche vornehmen bei; ~**wave** n Geistesblitz m; ~**y** adj gescheit

braise [breɪz] vt schmoren

brake [breɪk] n Bremse f ♦ vt, vi bremsen; ~ **fluid** n Bremsflüssigkeit f; ~ **light** n Bremslicht nt

bramble ['bræmbl] n Brombeere f

bran [bræn] n Kleie f; (food) Frühstücksflocken pl

branch [brɑːntʃ] n Ast m; (division) Zweig m ♦ vi (also: ~ **out**: road) sich verzweigen

brand [brænd] n (COMM) Marke f, Sorte f; (on cattle) Brandmal nt ♦ vt brandmarken; (COMM) ein Warenzeichen geben +dat

brandish ['brændɪʃ] vt (drohend) schwingen

brand-new ['brænd'njuː] adj funkelnagelneu

brandy ['brændɪ] n Weinbrand m, Kognak m

brash [bræʃ] adj unverschämt

brass [brɑːs] n Messing nt; **the ~** (MUS) das Blech; ~ **band** n Blaskapelle f

brassière ['bræsɪə'] n Büstenhalter m

brat [bræt] n Gör nt

bravado [brə'vɑːdəʊ] n Tollkühnheit f

brave [breɪv] adj tapfer ♦ vt die Stirn bieten +dat; ~**ry** n Tapferkeit f

brawl [brɔːl] n Rauferei f

brawn [brɔːn] n (ANAT) Muskeln pl; (strength) Muskelkraft f

bray [breɪ] vi schreien

brazen ['breɪzn] adj (shameless) unverschämt

♦ vt: **to ~ it out** sich mit Lügen und Betrügen durchsetzen

brazier ['breɪzɪə'] n (of workmen) offene(r) Kohlenofen m

Brazil [brə'zɪl] n Brasilien nt; ~**ian** adj brasilianisch ♦ n Brasilianer(in) m(f)

breach [briːtʃ] n (gap) Lücke f; (MIL) Durchbruch m; (of discipline) Verstoß m (gegen die Disziplin); (of faith) Vertrauensbruch m ♦ vt durchbrechen; ~ **of contract** Vertragsbruch m; ~ **of the peace** öffentliche Ruhestörung f

bread [bred] n Brot nt; ~ **and butter** Butterbrot nt; ~**bin** n Brotkasten m; ~ **box** (US) n Brotkasten m; ~**crumbs** npl Brotkrumen pl; (COOK) Paniermehl nt; ~**line** n: **to be on the ~line** sich gerade so durchschlagen

breadth [brɛtθ] n Breite f

breadwinner ['brɛdwɪnə'] n Ernährer m

break [breɪk] (pt **broke**, pp **broken**) vt (destroy) (ab- or zer)brechen; (promise) brechen, nicht einhalten ♦ vi (fall apart) auseinander brechen; (collapse) zusammenbrechen; (dawn) anbrechen ♦ n (gap) Lücke f; (chance) Chance f, Gelegenheit f; (fracture) Bruch m; (rest) Pause f; ~ **down** vt (figures, data) aufschlüsseln; (undermine) überwinden ♦ vi (car) eine Panne haben; (person) zusammenbrechen; ~ **even** vi die Kosten decken; ~ **free** vi sich losreißen; ~ **in** vt (horse) zureiten ♦ vi (burglar) einbrechen; ~ **into** vt fus (house) einbrechen in +acc; ~ **loose** vi sich losreißen; ~ **off** vi abbrechen; ~ **open** vt (door etc) aufbrechen; ~ **out** vi ausbrechen; **to ~ out in spots** Pickel bekommen; ~ **up** vi zerbrechen; (fig) sich zerstreuen; (BRIT: SCH) in die Ferien gehen ♦ vt brechen; ~**age** n Bruch m, Beschädigung f; ~**down** n (TECH) Panne f; (MED: also: **nervous ~down**) Zusammenbruch m; ~**down van** (BRIT) n Abschleppwagen m; ~**er** n Brecher m

breakfast ['brɛkfəst] n Frühstück nt

break: ~-**in** n Einbruch m; ~**ing** n: ~**ing and entering** (JUR) Einbruch m; ~**through**

n Durchbruch m; ~**water** n Wellenbrecher m

breast [brɛst] n Brust f; ~-**feed** (irreg: like **feed**) vt, vi stillen; ~-**stroke** n Brustschwimmen nt

breath [brɛθ] n Atem m; **out of ~** außer Atem; **under one's ~** flüsternd

Breathalyzer ['brɛθəlaɪzə'] ® n Röhrchen nt

breathe [briːð] vt, vi atmen; ~ **in** vt, vi einatmen; ~ **out** vt, vi ausatmen; ~**r** n Verschnaufpause f; **breathing** n Atmung f

breathless ['brɛθlɪs] adj atemlos

breathtaking ['brɛθteɪkɪŋ] adj atemberaubend

bred [brɛd] pt, pp of **breed**

breed [briːd] (pt, pp **bred**) vi sich vermehren ♦ vt züchten ♦ n (race) Rasse f, Zucht f; ~**ing** n Züchtung f; (upbringing) Erziehung f

breeze [briːz] n Brise f; **breezy** adj windig; (manner) munter

brevity ['brɛvɪtɪ] n Kürze f

brew [bruː] vt (beer) brauen ♦ vi (storm) sich zusammenziehen; ~**ery** n Brauerei f

bribe [braɪb] n Bestechungsgeld nt, Bestechungsgeschenk nt ♦ vt bestechen; ~**ry** ['braɪbərɪ] n Bestechung f

bric-a-brac ['brɪkəbræk] n Nippes pl

brick [brɪk] n Backstein m; ~**layer** n Maurer m; ~**works** n Ziegelei f

bridal ['braɪdl] adj Braut-

bride [braɪd] n Braut f; ~**groom** n Bräutigam m; ~**smaid** n Brautjungfer f

bridge [brɪdʒ] n Brücke f; (NAUT) Kommandobrücke f; (CARDS) Bridge nt; (ANAT) Nasenrücken m ♦ vt eine Brücke schlagen über +acc; (fig) überbrücken

bridle ['braɪdl] n Zaum m ♦ vt (fig) zügeln; (horse) aufzäumen; ~ **path** n Reitweg m

brief [briːf] adj kurz ♦ n (JUR) Akten pl ♦ vt instruieren; ~**s** npl (underwear) Schlüpfer m, Slip m; ~**case** n Aktentasche f; ~**ing** n (genaue) Anweisung f; ~**ly** adv kurz

brigadier [brɪgə'dɪə'] n Brigadegeneral m

bright [braɪt] adj hell; (cheerful) heiter; (idea) klug; ~**en (up)** ['braɪtn-] vt aufhellen; (person) aufheitern ♦ vi sich aufheitern

brilliance ['brɪljəns] n Glanz m; (of person)

Scharfsinn *m*

brilliant ['brɪljənt] *adj* glänzend

brim [brɪm] *n* Rand *m*

brine [braɪn] *n* Salzwasser *nt*

bring [brɪŋ] (*pt, pp* **brought**) *vt* bringen; ~ **about** *vt* zustande *or* zu Stande bringen; ~ **back** *vt* zurückbringen; ~ **down** *vt* (*price*) senken; ~ **forward** *vt* (*meeting*) vorverlegen; (*COMM*) übertragen; ~ **in** *vt* hereinbringen; (*harvest*) einbringen; ~ **off** *vt* davontragen; (*success*) erzielen; ~ **out** *vt* (*object*) herausbringen; ~ **round** *or* **to** *vt* wieder zu sich bringen; ~ **up** *vt* aufziehen; (*question*) zur Sprache bringen

brink [brɪŋk] *n* Rand *m*

brisk [brɪsk] *adj* lebhaft

bristle ['brɪsl] *n* Borste *f* ♦ *vi* sich sträuben; **bristling with** strotzend vor +*dat*

Britain ['brɪtən] *n* (*also*: **Great ~**) Großbritannien *nt*

British ['brɪtɪʃ] *adj* britisch ♦ *npl*: **the ~** die Briten *pl*; ~ **Isles** *npl*: **the ~ Isles** die Britischen Inseln *pl*; ~ **Rail** *n* die Britischen Eisenbahnen

Briton ['brɪtən] *n* Brite *m*, Britin *f*

Brittany ['brɪtənɪ] *n* die Bretagne

brittle ['brɪtl] *adj* spröde

broach [brəʊtʃ] *vt* (*subject*) anschneiden

broad [brɔːd] *adj* breit; (*hint*) deutlich; (*general*) allgemein; (*accent*) stark; **in ~ daylight** am helllichten Tag; ~**band** *n* Breitband *nt*; ~**cast** (*pt, pp* **broadcast**) *n* Rundfunkübertragung *f* ♦ *vt, vi* übertragen, senden; ~**en** *vt* erweitern ♦ *vi* sich erweitern; ~**ly** *adv* allgemein gesagt; ~**-minded** *adj* tolerant

broccoli ['brɒkəlɪ] *n* Brokkoli *pl*

brochure ['brəʊʃjʊəʳ] *n* Broschüre *f*

broil [brɔɪl] *vt* (*grill*) grillen

broke [brəʊk] *pt of* **break** ♦ *adj* (*inf*) pleite

broken ['brəʊkn] *pp of* **break** ♦ *adj*: ~ **leg** gebrochenes Bein; **in ~ English** in gebrochenem Englisch; ~**-hearted** *adj* untröstlich

broker ['brəʊkəʳ] *n* Makler *m*

brolly ['brɒlɪ] (*BRIT: inf*) *n* Schirm *m*

bronchitis [brɒŋ'kaɪtɪs] *n* Bronchitis *f*

bronze [brɒnz] *n* Bronze *f*

brooch [brəʊtʃ] *n* Brosche *f*

brood [bruːd] *n* Brut *f* ♦ *vi* brüten

brook [brʊk] *n* Bach *m*

broom [brʊm] *n* Besen *m*

Bros. *abbr* = **Brothers**

broth [brɒθ] *n* Suppe *f*, Fleischbrühe *f*

brothel ['brɒθl] *n* Bordell *nt*

brother ['brʌðəʳ] *n* Bruder *m*; ~**-in-law** *n* Schwager *m*

brought [brɔːt] *pt, pp of* **bring**

brow [braʊ] *n* (*eyebrow*) (Augen)braue *f*; (*forehead*) Stirn *f*; (*of hill*) Bergkuppe *f*

brown [braʊn] *adj* braun ♦ *n* Braun *nt* ♦ *vt* bräunen; ~ **bread** *n* Mischbrot *nt*; B~**ie** *n* Wichtel *m*; ~ **paper** *n* Packpapier *nt*

browse [braʊz] *vi* (*in books*) blättern; (*in shop*) schmökern, herumschauen; ~**r** *n* (*COMPUT*) Browser *m*

bruise [bruːz] *n* Bluterguss *m*, blaue(r) Fleck *m* ♦ *vt* einen blauen Fleck geben ♦ *vi* einen blauen Fleck bekommen

brunt [brʌnt] *n* volle Wucht *f*

brush [brʌʃ] *n* Bürste *f*; (*for sweeping*) Handbesen *m*; (*for painting*) Pinsel *m*; (*fight*) kurze(r) Kampf *m*; (*MIL*) Scharmützel *nt*; (*fig*) Auseinandersetzung *f* ♦ *vt* (*clean*) bürsten; (*sweep*) fegen; (*usu*: ~ *past*, ~ *against*) streifen; ~ **aside** *vt* abtun; ~ **up** *vt* (*knowledge*) auffrischen; ~**wood** *n* Gestrüpp *nt*

brusque [bruːsk] *adj* schroff

Brussels ['brʌslz] *n* Brüssel *nt*; ~ **sprout** *n* Rosenkohl *m*

brutal ['bruːtl] *adj* brutal

brute [bruːt] *n* (*person*) Scheusal *nt* ♦ *adj*: **by ~ force** mit roher Kraft

B.Sc. *n abbr* = **Bachelor of Science**

BSE *n abbr* (= *bovine spongiform encephalopathy*) BSE *f*

bubble ['bʌbl] *n* (Luft)blase *f* ♦ *vi* sprudeln; (*with joy*) übersprudeln; ~ **bath** *n* Schaumbad *nt*; ~ **gum** *n* Kaugummi *m or nt*

buck [bʌk] *n* Bock *m*; (*US: inf*) Dollar *m* ♦ *vi* bocken; **to pass the ~ (to sb)** die Verantwortung (auf jdn) abschieben; ~ **up** (*inf*) *vi* sich zusammenreißen

bucket ['bʌkɪt] n Eimer m

Buckingham Palace

i **Buckingham Palace** *ist die offizielle Londoner Residenz der britischen Monarchen und liegt am St James Park. Der Palast wurde 1703 für den Herzog von Buckingham erbaut, 1762 von George III. gekauft, zwischen 1821 und 1836 von John Nash umgebaut, und Anfang des 20. Jahrhunderts teilweise neu gestaltet. Teile des Buckingham Palace sind heute der Öffentlichkeit zugänglich.*

buckle ['bʌkl] n Schnalle f ♦ vt (an- or zusammen)schnallen ♦ vi (bend) sich verziehen

bud [bʌd] n Knospe f ♦ vi knospen, keimen

Buddhism ['budɪzəm] n Buddhismus m; **Buddhist** adj buddhistisch ♦ n Buddhist(in) m(f)

budding ['bʌdɪŋ] adj angehend

buddy ['bʌdɪ] n (inf) Kumpel m

budge [bʌdʒ] vt, vi (sich) von der Stelle rühren

budgerigar ['bʌdʒərɪgɑːʳ] n Wellensittich m

budget ['bʌdʒɪt] n Budget nt; (POL) Haushalt m ♦ vi: **to ~ for sth** etw einplanen

budgie ['bʌdʒɪ] n = **budgerigar**

buff [bʌf] adj (colour) lederfarben ♦ n (enthusiast) Fan m

buffalo ['bʌfələu] (pl ~ or ~es) n (BRIT) Büffel m; (US: bison) Bison m

buffer ['bʌfəʳ] n Puffer m; (COMPUT) Pufferspeicher m; ~ **zone** n Pufferzone f

buffet[1] ['bʌfɪt] n (blow) Schlag m ♦ vt (herum)stossen

buffet[2] ['bufei] (BRIT) n (bar) Imbissraum m, Erfrischungsraum m; (food) (kaltes) Büfett nt; ~ **car** (BRIT) n Speisewagen m

bug [bʌg] n (also fig) Wanze f ♦ vt verwanzen; **the room is bugged** das Zimmer ist verwanzt

bugle ['bjuːgl] n Jagdhorn nt; (MIL: MUS) Bügelhorn nt

build [bɪld] (pt, pp **built**) vt bauen ♦ n Körperbau m; ~ **up** vt aufbauen; ~**er** n

Bauunternehmer m; ~**ing** n Gebäude nt; ~**ing society** (BRIT) n Bausparkasse f

built [bɪlt] pt, pp of **build**; ~-**in** adj (cupboard) eingebaut; ~-**up area** n Wohngebiet nt

bulb [bʌlb] n (BOT) (Blumen)zwiebel f; (ELEC) Glühlampe f, Birne f

Bulgaria [bʌl'gɛərɪə] n Bulgarien nt; ~**n** adj bulgarisch ♦ n Bulgare m, Bulgarin f; (LING) Bulgarisch nt

bulge [bʌldʒ] n Wölbung f ♦ vi sich wölben

bulk [bʌlk] n Größe f, Masse f; (greater part) Großteil m; **in ~** (COMM) en gros; **the ~ of** der größte Teil +gen; ~**head** n Schott nt; ~**y** adj (sehr) umfangreich; (goods) sperrig

bull [bul] n Bulle m; (cattle) Stier m; ~**dog** n Bulldogge f

bulldozer ['buldəuzəʳ] n Planierraupe f

bullet ['bulɪt] n Kugel f

bulletin ['bulɪtɪn] n Bulletin nt, Bekanntmachung f

bulletproof ['bulɪtpruːf] adj kugelsicher

bullfight ['bulfaɪt] n Stierkampf m; ~**er** n Stierkämpfer m; ~**ing** n Stierkamp m

bullion ['buljən] n Barren m

bullock ['bulək] n Ochse m

bullring ['bulrɪŋ] n Stierkampfarena f

bull's-eye ['bulzaɪ] n Zentrum nt

bully ['bulɪ] n Raufbold m ♦ vt einschüchtern

bum [bʌm] n (inf: backside) Hintern m; (tramp) Landstreicher m

bumblebee ['bʌmblbiː] n Hummel f

bump [bʌmp] n (blow) Stoß m; (swelling) Beule f ♦ vt, vi stoßen, prallen; ~ **into** vt fus stoßen gegen ♦ vt (person) treffen; ~**er** n (AUT) Stoßstange f ♦ adj (edition) dick; (harvest) Rekord-

bumpy ['bʌmpɪ] adj holprig

bun [bʌn] n Korinthenbrötchen nt

bunch [bʌntʃ] n (of flowers) Strauß m; (of keys) Bund m; (of people) Haufen m; ~**es** npl (in hair) Zöpfe pl

bundle ['bʌndl] n Bündel nt ♦ vt (also: ~ **up**) bündeln

bungalow ['bʌŋgələu] n einstöckige(s) Haus nt, Bungalow m

bungle ['bʌŋgl] vt verpfuschen

bunion ['bʌnjən] n entzündete(r) Fußballen *m*

bunk [bʌŋk] *n* Schlafkoje *f*; ~ **beds** *npl* Etagenbett *nt*

bunker ['bʌŋkə*r*] *n* (*coal store*) Kohlenbunker *m*; (*GOLF*) Sandloch *nt*

bunny ['bʌnɪ] *n* (*also:* ~ **rabbit**) Häschen *nt*

bunting ['bʌntɪŋ] *n* Fahnentuch *nt*

buoy [bɔɪ] *n* Boje *f*; (*lifebuoy*) Rettungsboje *f*; ~**ant** *adj* (*floating*) schwimmend; (*fig*) heiter

burden ['bə:dn] *n* (*weight*) Ladung *f*, Last *f*; (*fig*) Bürde *f* ♦ *vt* belasten

bureau ['bjuərəu] (*pl* ~**x**) *n* (*BRIT: writing desk*) Sekretär *m*; (*US: chest of drawers*) Kommode *f*; (*for information etc*) Büro *nt*

bureaucracy [bjuə'rɔkrəsɪ] *n* Bürokratie *f*

bureaucrat ['bjuərəkræt] *n* Bürokrat(in) *m(f)*

bureaux ['bjuərəuz] *npl of* **bureau**

burglar ['bə:glə*r*] *n* Einbrecher *m*; ~ **alarm** *n* Einbruchssicherung *f*; ~**y** *n* Einbruch *m*

burial ['berɪəl] *n* Beerdigung *f*

burly ['bə:lɪ] *adj* stämmig

Burma ['bə:mə] *n* Birma *nt*

burn [bə:n] *n* (*pt, pp* **burned** *or* **burnt**) *vt* verbrennen ♦ *vi* brennen ♦ *n* Brandwunde *f*; ~ **down** *vt, vi* abbrennen; ~**er** *n* Brenner *m*; ~**ing** *adj* brennend; ~**t** [bə:nt] *pt, pp of* **burn**

burrow ['bʌrəu] *n* (*of fox*) Bau *m*; (*of rabbit*) Höhle *f* ♦ *vt* eingraben

bursar ['bə:sə*r*] *n* Kassenverwalter *m*, Quästor *m*; ~**y** (*BRIT*) *n* Stipendium *nt*

burst [bə:st] (*pt, pp* **burst**) *vt* zerbrechen ♦ *vi* platzen ♦ *n* Explosion *f*; (*outbreak*) Ausbruch *m*; (*in pipe*) Bruch(stelle *f*) *m*; **to ~ into flames** in Flammen aufgehen; **to ~ into tears** in Tränen ausbrechen; **to ~ out laughing** in Gelächter ausbrechen; ~ **into** *vt fus* (*room etc*) platzen in +*acc*; ~ **open** *vi* aufbrechen

bury ['berɪ] *vt* vergraben; (*in grave*) beerdigen

bus [bʌs] *n* (*Auto*)bus *m*, Omnibus *m*

bush [buʃ] *n* Busch *m*; **to beat about the ~** wie die Katze um den heißen Brei herumgehen; ~**y** ['buʃɪ] *adj* buschig

busily ['bɪzɪlɪ] *adv* geschäftig

business ['bɪznɪs] *n* Geschäft *nt*; (*concern*) Angelegenheit *f*; **it's none of your ~** es geht dich nichts an; **to mean ~** es ernst meinen; **to be away on ~** geschäftlich verreist sein; **it's my ~ to ...** es ist meine Sache, zu ...; ~**like** *adj* geschäftsmäßig; ~**man** (*irreg*) *n* Geschäftsmann *m*; ~ **trip** *n* Geschäftsreise *f*; ~**woman** (*irreg*) *n* Geschäftsfrau *f*

busker ['bʌskə*r*] (*BRIT*) *n* Straßenmusikant *m*

bus: ~ **shelter** *n* Wartehäuschen *nt*; ~ **station** *n* Busbahnhof *m*; ~ **stop** *n* Bushaltestelle *f*

bust [bʌst] *n* Büste *f* ♦ *adj* (*broken*) kaputt(gegangen); (*business*) pleite; **to go ~** Pleite machen

bustle ['bʌsl] *n* Getriebe *nt* ♦ *vi* hasten

bustling ['bʌslɪŋ] *adj* geschäftig

busy ['bɪzɪ] *adj* beschäftigt; (*road*) belebt ♦ *vt*: **to ~ o.s.** sich beschäftigen; ~**body** *n* Übereifrige(r) *mf*; ~ **signal** (*US*) *n* (*TEL*) Besetztzeichen *nt*

KEYWORD

but [bʌt] *conj* **1** (*yet*) aber; **not X but Y** nicht X sondern Y

2 (*however*): **I'd love to come, but I'm busy** ich würde gern kommen, bin aber beschäftigt

3 (*showing disagreement, surprise etc*): **but that's fantastic!** (aber) das ist ja fantastisch!

♦ *prep* (*apart from, except*): **nothing but trouble** nichts als Ärger; **no-one but him can do it** niemand außer ihn kann es machen; **but for you/your help** ohne dich/deine Hilfe; **anything but that** alles, nur das nicht

♦ *adv* (*just, only*): **she's but a child** sie ist noch ein Kind; **had I but known** wenn ich es nur gewusst hätte; **I can but try** ich kann es immerhin versuchen; **all but finished** so gut wie fertig

---

butcher ['butʃə*r*] *n* Metzger *m*; (*murderer*) Schlächter *m* ♦ *vt* schlachten; (*kill*) abschlachten; ~**'s (shop)** *n* Metzgerei *f*

butler ['bʌtlə*r*] *n* Butler *m*

butt [bʌt] n (*cask*) große(s) Fass nt; (*BRIT: fig: target*) Zielscheibe f; (*of gun*) Kolben m; (*of cigarette*) Stummel m ♦ vt (mit dem Kopf) stoßen; ~ **in** vi sich einmischen

butter ['bʌtə'] n Butter f ♦ vt buttern; ~ **bean** n Wachsbohne f; ~**cup** n Butterblume f

butterfly ['bʌtəflaɪ] n Schmetterling m; (*SWIMMING: also:* ~ **stroke**) Butterflystil m

buttocks ['bʌtəks] npl Gesäß nt

button ['bʌtn] n Knopf m ♦ vt, vi (*also:* ~ **up**) zuknöpfen

buttress ['bʌtrɪs] n Strebepfeiler m; Stützbogen m

buxom ['bʌksəm] adj drall

buy [baɪ] (*pt, pp* bought) vt kaufen ♦ n Kauf m; **to** ~ **sb a drink** jdm einen Drink spendieren; ~**er** n Käufer(in) m(f)

buzz [bʌz] n Summen nt ♦ vi summen; ~**er** ['bʌzə'] n Summer m; ~ **word** n Modewort nt

---
KEYWORD
---

by [baɪ] prep 1 (*referring to cause, agent*) of, durch; **killed by lightning** vom Blitz getötet; **a painting by Picasso** ein Gemälde von Picasso

2 (*referring to method, manner*): **by bus/ car/train** mit dem Bus/Auto/Zug; **to pay by cheque** per Scheck bezahlen; **by moonlight** bei Mondschein; **by saving hard, he ...** indem er eisern sparte, ... er ...

3 (*via, through*) über +acc; **he came in by the back door** er kam durch die Hintertür herein

4 (*close to, past*) bei, an +dat; **a holiday by the sea** ein Urlaub am Meer; **she rushed by me** sie eilte an mir vorbei

5 (*not later than*): **by 4 o'clock** bis 4 Uhr; **by this time tomorrow** morgen um diese Zeit; **by the time I got here it was too late** als ich hier ankam, war es zu spät

6 (*during*): **by day** bei Tag

7 (*amount*): **by the kilo/metre** kiloweise/ meterweise; **paid by the hour** stundenweise bezahlt

8 (*MATH, measure*): **to divide by 3** durch 3

teilen; **to multiply by 3** mit 3 malnehmen; **a room 3 metres by 4** ein Zimmer 3 mal 4 Meter; **it's broader by a metre** es ist (um) einem Meter breiter

9 (*according to*) nach; **it's all right by me** von mir aus gern

10: **(all) by oneself** etc ganz allein

11: **by the way** übrigens

♦ adv 1 see **go**; **pass** etc

2: **by and by** irgendwann; (*with past tenses*) nach einiger Zeit; **by and large** (*on the whole*) im Großen und Ganzen

bye(-bye) ['baɪ'baɪ] excl (auf) Wiedersehen

by(e)-law ['baɪlɔ:] n Verordnung f

by-election ['baɪlekʃən] (*BRIT*) n Nachwahl f

bygone ['baɪgɒn] adj vergangen ♦ n: **let** ~**s be** ~**s** lass(t) das Vergangene vergangen sein

bypass ['baɪpɑ:s] n Umgehungsstraße f ♦ vt umgehen

by-product ['baɪprɒdʌkt] n Nebenprodukt nt

bystander ['baɪstændə'] n Zuschauer m

byte [baɪt] n (*COMPUT*) Byte nt

byword ['baɪwə:d] n Inbegriff m

C, c

C [si:] n (*MUS*) C nt

C. abbr (= centigrade) C

C.A. abbr = **chartered accountant**

cab [kæb] n Taxi nt; (*of train*) Führerstand m; (*of truck*) Führersitz m

cabaret ['kæbəreɪ] n Kabarett nt

cabbage ['kæbɪdʒ] n Kohl(kopf) m

cabin ['kæbɪn] n Hütte f; (*NAUT*) Kajüte f; (*AVIAT*) Kabine f; ~ **crew** n (*AVIAT*) Flugbegleitpersonal nt; ~ **cruiser** n Motorjacht f

cabinet ['kæbɪnɪt] n Schrank m; (*for china*) Vitrine f; (*POL*) Kabinett nt; ~-**maker** n Kunsttischler m

cable ['keɪbl] n Drahtseil nt, Tau nt; (*TEL*) (Leitungs)kabel nt; (*telegram*) Kabel nt ♦ vt kabeln, telegrafieren; ~ **car** n Seilbahn f; ~ **television** n Kabelfernsehen nt cache [kæʃ] n geheime(s) (Waffen)lager nt; geheime(s) (Proviant)lager nt

cackle ['kækl] vi gackern

cacti ['kæktaɪ] npl of cactus

cactus ['kæktəs] (pl cacti) n Kaktus m, Kaktee f

caddie ['kædɪ] n (GOLF) Golfjunge m; caddy ['kædɪ] n = caddie

cadet [kə'det] n Kadett m

cadge [kædʒ] vt schmarotzen

Caesarean [sɪ'zɛərɪən] adj: ~ (section) Kaiserschnitt m

café ['kæfeɪ] n Café nt, Restaurant nt

cafeteria [kæfɪ'tɪərɪə] n Selbstbedienungsrestaurant nt

caffein(e) ['kæfiːn] n Koffein nt

cage [keɪdʒ] n Käfig m ♦ vt einsperren

cagey ['keɪdʒɪ] adj geheimnistuerisch, zurückhaltend

cagoule [kə'guːl] n Windhemd nt

Cairo ['kaɪərəu] n Kairo nt

cajole [kə'dʒəul] vt überreden

cake [keɪk] n Kuchen m; (of soap) Stück nt; ~d adj verkrustet

calamity [kə'læmɪtɪ] n Unglück nt, (Schicksals)schlag m

calcium ['kælsɪəm] n Kalzium nt

calculate ['kælkjuleɪt] vt berechnen, kalkulieren; calculating adj berechnend; calculation [kælkju'leɪʃən] n Berechnung f; calculator n Rechner m

calendar ['kæləndəʳ] n Kalender m; ~ month n Kalendermonat m

calf [kɑːf] (pl calves) n Kalb nt; (also: ~skin) Kalbsleder nt; (ANAT) Wade f

calibre ['kælɪbəʳ] (US caliber) n Kaliber nt

call [kɔːl] vt rufen; (name) nennen; (meeting) einberufen; (awaken) wecken; (TEL) anrufen ♦ vi (shout) rufen; (visit: also: ~ in, ~ round) vorbeikommen ♦ n (shout) Ruf m; (TEL) Anruf m; to be ~ed heißen; on ~ in Bereitschaft; ~ back vi (return) wiederkommen; (TEL) zurückrufen; ~ for vt fus (demand) erfordern, verlangen; (fetch) abholen; ~ off vt (cancel) absagen; ~ on vt fus (visit) besuchen; (turn to) bitten; ~ out vi rufen; ~ up vt (MIL) einberufen;

~box (BRIT) n Telefonzelle f; ~ centre n Telefoncenter nt, Callcenter nt; ~er n Besucher(in) m(f); (TEL) Anrufer m; ~ girl n Callgirl nt; ~-in (US) n (phone-in) Phone-in nt; ~ing n (vocation) Berufung f; ~ing card (US) n Visitenkarte f

callous ['kæləs] adj herzlos

calm [kɑːm] n Ruhe f; (NAUT) Flaute f ♦ vt beruhigen ♦ adj ruhig; (person) gelassen; ~ down vi sich beruhigen ♦ vt beruhigen

Calor gas ['kælə-] ® n Propangas nt

calorie ['kælərɪ] n Kalorie f

calves [kɑːvz] npl of calf

Cambodia [kæm'bəudɪə] n Kambodscha nt

camcorder ['kæmkɔːdəʳ] n Camcorder m

came [keɪm] pt of come

cameo ['kæmɪəu] n Kamee f

camera ['kæmərə] n Fotoapparat m; (CINE, TV) Kamera f; in ~ unter Ausschluss der Öffentlichkeit; ~man (irreg) n Kameramann m; ~phone n Fotohandy nt

camouflage ['kæməflɑːʒ] n Tarnung f ♦ vt tarnen

camp [kæmp] n Lager nt ♦ vi zelten, campen ♦ adj affektiert

campaign [kæm'peɪn] n Kampagne f; (MIL) Feldzug m ♦ vi (MIL) Krieg führen; (fig) werben, Propaganda machen; (POL) den Wahlkampf führen

camp: ~ bed ['kæmp'bed] (BRIT) n Campingbett nt; ~er n Camper(in) m(f); (vehicle) Campingwagen m; ~ing ['kæmpɪŋ] n: to go ~ing zelten, Camping machen; ~ing gas (US) n Campinggas nt; ~site ['kæmpsaɪt] n Campingplatz nt

campus ['kæmpəs] n Universitätsgelände nt, Campus m

can¹ [kæn] n Büchse f, Dose f; (for water) Kanne f ♦ vt konservieren, in Büchsen einmachen

---
KEYWORD
---

can² [kæn] (negative cannot, can't, conditional could) aux vb 1 (be able to, know how to) können; I can see you tomorrow, if you like ich könnte Sie morgen sehen, wenn Sie wollen; **I can swim** ich kann schwimmen; **can you speak German?** sprechen Sie Deutsch? **2** (*may*) können, dürfen; **could I have a word with you?** könnte ich Sie kurz sprechen?

Canada ['kænədə] *n* Kanada *nt*; **Canadian** [kə'neɪdɪən] *adj* kanadisch ♦ *n* Kanadier(in) *m(f)*

canal [kə'næl] *n* Kanal *m*

canapé ['kænəpeɪ] *n* Cocktail- *or* Appetithappen *m*

canary [kə'nɛərɪ] *n* Kanarienvogel *m*

cancel ['kænsəl] *vt* absagen; (*delete*) durchstreichen; (*train*) streichen; **~lation** [kænsə'leɪʃən] *n* Absage *f*; Streichung *f*

cancer ['kænsə'] *n* (*ASTROL: C~*) Krebs *m*

candid ['kændɪd] *adj* offen, ehrlich

candidate ['kændɪdeɪt] *n* Kandidat(in) *m(f)*

candle ['kændl] *n* Kerze *f*; **~light** *n* Kerzenlicht *nt*; **~stick** *n* (*also:* **~ holder**) Kerzenhalter *m*

candour ['kændə'] (*US* **candor**) *n* Offenheit *f*

candy ['kændɪ] *n* Kandis(zucker) *m*; (*US*) Bonbons *pl*; **~floss** (*BRIT*) *n* Zuckerwatte *f*

cane [keɪn] *n* (*BOT*) Rohr *nt*; (*stick*) Stock *m* ♦ *vt* (*BRIT: beat*) schlagen

canine ['keɪnaɪn] *adj* Hunde-

canister ['kænɪstə'] *n* Blechdose *f*

cannabis ['kænəbɪs] *n* Hanf *m*, Haschisch *nt*

canned [kænd] *adj* Büchsen-, eingemacht

cannon ['kænən] (*pl* **~** *or* **~s**) *n* Kanone *f*

cannot ['kænɔt] = **can not**

canny ['kænɪ] *adj* schlau

canoe [kə'nu:] *n* Kanu *nt*; **~ing** *n* Kanusport *m*, Kanufahren *nt*

canon ['kænən] *n* (*clergyman*) Domherr *m*; (*standard*) Grundsatz *m*

can-opener ['kænəʊpnə'] *n* Büchsenöffner *m*

canopy ['kænəpɪ] *n* Baldachin *m*

can't [kænt] = **can not**

cantankerous [kæn'tæŋkərəs] *adj* zänkisch, mürrisch

canteen [kæn'ti:n] *n* Kantine *f*; (*BRIT: of cutlery*) Besteckkasten *m*

canter ['kæntə'] *n* Kanter *m* ♦ *vi* in kurzem Galopp reiten

canvas ['kænvəs] *n* Segeltuch *nt*; (*sail*) Segel *nt*; (*for painting*) Leinwand *f*; **under ~** (*camping*) in Zelten

canvass ['kænvəs] *vi* um Stimmen werben; **~ing** *n* Wahlwerbung *f*

canyon ['kænjən] *n* Felsenschlucht *f*

cap [kæp] *n* Mütze *f*; (*of pen*) Kappe *f*; (*of bottle*) Deckel *m* ♦ *vt* (*surpass*) übertreffen; (*SPORT*) aufstellen; (*put limit on*) einen Höchstsatz festlegen für

capability [keɪpə'bɪlɪtɪ] *n* Fähigkeit *f*

capable ['keɪpəbl] *adj* fähig

capacity [kə'pæsɪtɪ] *n* Fassungsvermögen *nt*; (*ability*) Fähigkeit *f*; (*position*) Eigenschaft *f*

cape [keɪp] *n* (*garment*) Cape *nt*, Umhang *m*; (*GEOG*) Kap *nt*

caper ['keɪpə'] *n* (*COOK: usu:* **~s**) Kaper *f*; (*prank*) Kapriole *f*

capital ['kæpɪtl] *n* (*~ city*) Hauptstadt *f*; (*FIN*) Kapital *nt*; (*~ letter*) Großbuchstabe *m*; **~ gains tax** *n* Kapitalertragssteuer *f*; **~ism** *n* Kapitalismus *m*; **~ist** *adj* kapitalistisch ♦ *n* Kapitalist(in) *m(f)*; **~ize** *vi*: **to ~ize on** Kapital schlagen aus; **~ punishment** *n* Todesstrafe *f*

Capitol

i **Capitol** ist das Gebäude in Washington auf dem Capitol Hill, in dem der Kongress der USA zusammentritt. Die Bezeichnung wird in vielen amerikanischen Bundesstaaten auch für das Parlamentsgebäude des jeweiligen Staates verwendet.

Capricorn ['kæprɪkɔ:n] *n* Steinbock *m*

capsize [kæp'saɪz] *vt*, *vi* kentern

capsule ['kæpsju:l] *n* Kapsel *f*

captain ['kæptɪn] *n* Kapitän *m*; (*MIL*) Hauptmann *m* ♦ *vt* anführen

caption ['kæpʃən] *n* (*heading*) Überschrift *f*; (*to picture*) Unterschrift *f*

captivate ['kæptɪveɪt] *vt* fesseln

captive ['kæptɪv] *n* Gefangene(r) *f(m)* ♦ *adj* gefangen (gehalten); **captivity** [kæp'tɪvɪtɪ] *n* Gefangenschaft *f*

capture ['kæptʃə'] *vt* gefangen nehmen; (*place*) erobern; (*attention*) erregen ♦ *n* Gefangennahme *f*; (*data ~*) Erfassung *f*

car [kɑːʳ] *n* Auto *nt*, Wagen *m*; (*RAIL*) Wagen *m*

caramel ['kærəməl] *n* Karamelle *f*, Karamellbonbon *m or nt*; (*burnt sugar*) Karamell *m*

carat ['kærət] *n* Karat *nt*

caravan ['kærəvæn] *n* (*BRIT*) Wohnwagen *m*; (*in desert*) Karawane *f*; ~**ning** *n* Caravaning *nt*, Urlaub *m* im Wohnwagen; ~ **site** (*BRIT*) *n* Campingplatz *m* für Wohnwagen

carbohydrate [kɑːbəu'haɪdreɪt] *n* Kohlenhydrat *nt*

carbon ['kɑːbən] *n* Kohlenstoff *m*; ~ **copy** *n* Durchschlag *m*; ~ **dioxide** *n* Kohlendioxyd *nt*; ~ **monoxide** *n* Kohlenmonoxyd *nt*; ~ **paper** *n* Kohlepapier *nt*

car boot sale *n auf einem Parkplatz stattfindender Flohmarkt mit dem Kofferraum als Auslage*

carburettor [kɑːbju'retəʳ] (*US* **carburetor**) *n* Vergaser *m*

carcass ['kɑːkəs] *n* Kadaver *m*

card [kɑːd] *n* Karte *f*; ~**board** *n* Pappe *f*; ~ **game** *n* Kartenspiel *nt*

cardiac ['kɑːdiæk] *adj* Herz-

cardigan ['kɑːdɪgən] *n* Strickjacke *f*

cardinal ['kɑːdɪnl] *adj*: ~ **number** Kardinalzahl *f* ♦ *n* (*REL*) Kardinal *m*

card index *n* Kartei *f*; (*in library*) Katalog *m*

cardphone *n* Kartentelefon *nt*

care [kɛəʳ] *n* (*of teeth, car etc*) Pflege *f*; (*of children*) Fürsorge *f*; (~*fulness*) Sorgfalt *f*; (*worry*) Sorge *f* ♦ *vi*: **to ~ about** sich kümmern um; ~ **of** bei; **in sb's ~** in jds Obhut; **I don't ~** das ist mir egal; **I couldn't ~ less** es ist mir doch völlig egal; **to take ~** aufpassen; **to take ~ of** sorgen für; **to take ~ to do sth** sich bemühen, etw zu tun; ~ **for** *vt* sorgen für; (*like*) mögen

career [kə'rɪəʳ] *n* Karriere *f*, Laufbahn *f* ♦ *vi* (*also*: ~ **along**) rasen; ~ **woman** (*irreg*) *n* Karrierefrau *f*

care: ~**free** *adj* sorgenfrei; ~**ful** *adj*

sorgfältig; (be) ~ful! pass auf!; ~**fully** *adv* vorsichtig; (*methodically*) sorgfältig; ~**less** *adj* nachlässig; ~**lessness** *n* Nachlässigkeit *f*; ~**r** *n* (*MED*) Betreuer(in) *m(f)*

caress [kə'res] *n* Liebkosung *f* ♦ *vt* liebkosen

caretaker ['kɛəteɪkəʳ] *n* Hausmeister *m*

car ferry *n* Autofähre *f*

cargo ['kɑːgəu] (*pl* ~**es**) *n* Schiffsladung *f*

car hire *n* Autovermietung *f*

Caribbean [kærɪ'biːən] *n*: **the ~ (Sea)** die Karibik

caricature ['kærɪkətjuəʳ] *n* Karikatur *f*

caring ['kɛərɪŋ] *adj* (*society, organization*) sozial eingestellt; (*person*) liebevoll

carnage ['kɑːnɪdʒ] *n* Blutbad *nt*

carnation [kɑː'neɪʃən] *n* Nelke *f*

carnival ['kɑːnɪvl] *n* Karneval *m*, Fasching *m*; (*US: fun fair*) Kirmes *f*

carnivorous [kɑː'nɪvərəs] *adj* Fleisch fressend

carol ['kærəl] *n*: **(Christmas) ~** (Weihnachts)lied *nt*

carp [kɑːp] *n* (*fish*) Karpfen *m*

car park (*BRIT*) *n* Parkplatz *m*; (*covered*) Parkhaus *nt*

carpenter ['kɑːpɪntəʳ] *n* Zimmermann *m*; **carpentry** ['kɑːpɪntrɪ] *n* Zimmerei *f*

carpet ['kɑːpɪt] *n* Teppich *m* ♦ *vt* mit einem Teppich auslegen; ~ **bombing** *n* Flächenbombardierung *f*; ~ **slippers** *npl* Pantoffeln *pl*; ~ **sweeper** [kɑːpɪtswiːpəʳ] *n* Teppichkehrer *m*

car phone *n* (*TEL*) Autotelefon *nt*

car rental (*US*) *n* Autovermietung *f*

carriage ['kærɪdʒ] *n* Kutsche *f*; (*RAIL, of typewriter*) Wagen *m*; (*of goods*) Beförderung *f*; (*bearing*) Haltung *f*; ~ **return** *n* (*on typewriter*) Rücklauftaste *f*; ~**way** (*BRIT*) *n* (*part of road*) Fahrbahn *f*

carrier ['kærɪəʳ] *n* Träger(in) *m(f)*; (*COMM*) Spediteur *m*; ~ **bag** (*BRIT*) *n* Tragetasche *f*

carrot ['kærət] *n* Möhre *f*, Karotte *f*

carry ['kærɪ] *vt*, *vi* tragen; **to get carried away** (*fig*) sich nicht mehr bremsen können; ~ **on** *vi* (*continue*) weitermachen; (*inf: complain*) Theater machen; ~ **out** *vt* (*orders*) ausführen; (*investigation*) durchführen;~**cot** (BRIT) n Babytragetasche f; ~**on** (inf) n (fuss) Theater nt

cart [kɑːt] n Wagen m, Karren m ♦ vt schleppen

cartilage ['kɑːtɪlɪdʒ] n Knorpel m

carton ['kɑːtən] n Karton m; (of milk) Tüte f

cartoon [kɑː'tuːn] n (PRESS) Karikatur f; (comic strip) Comics pl; (CINE) (Zeichen)trickfilm m

cartridge ['kɑːtrɪdʒ] n Patrone f

carve [kɑːv] vt (wood) schnitzen; (stone) meißeln; (meat) (vor)schneiden;~ **up** vt aufschneiden; **carving** ['kɑːvɪŋ] n Schnitzerei f; **carving knife** n Tran(s)chiermesser nt

car wash n Autowäsche f

cascade [kæs'keɪd] n Wasserfall m ♦ vi kaskadenartig herabfallen

case [keɪs] n (box) Kasten m; (BRIT: also: **suitcase**) Koffer m; (JUR, matter) Fall m; **in ~** falls, im Falle; **in any ~** jedenfalls, auf jeden Fall

cash [kæʃ] n (Bar)geld nt ♦ vt einlösen; ~ **on delivery** per Nachnahme;~ **book** n Kassenbuch nt;~ **card** n Scheckkarte f; ~ **desk** (BRIT) n Kasse f;~ **dispenser** n Geldautomat m

cashew [kæ'ʃuː] n (also: ~ **nut**) Cashewnuss f

cash flow n Cashflow m

cashier [kæ'ʃɪəʳ] n Kassierer(in) m(f)

cashmere ['kæʃmɪəʳ] n Kaschmirwolle f

cash register n Registrierkasse f

casing ['keɪsɪŋ] n Gehäuse nt

casino [kə'siːnəu] n Kasino nt

casket ['kɑːskɪt] n Kästchen nt; (US: coffin) Sarg m

casserole ['kæsərəul] n Kasserolle f; (food) Auflauf m

cassette [kæ'set] n Kassette f; ~ **player** n Kassettengerät nt

cast [kɑːst] (pt, pp **cast**) vt werfen; (horns) verlieren; (metal) gießen; (THEAT) besetzen; (vote) abgeben ♦ n (THEAT) Besetzung f; (also: **plaster ~**) Gipsverband m; ~ **off** vi (NAUT) losmachen

castaway ['kɑːstəweɪ] n Schiffbrüchige(r) f(m)

caste [kɑːst] n Kaste f

caster sugar ['kɑːstə-] (BRIT) n Raffinade f

casting vote ['kɑːstɪŋ-] (BRIT) n entscheidende Stimme f

cast iron n Gusseisen nt

castle ['kɑːsl] n Burg f; Schloss nt; (CHESS) Turm m

castor ['kɑːstəʳ] n (wheel) Laufrolle f

castor oil n Rizinusöl nt

castrate [kæs'treɪt] vt kastrieren

casual ['kæʒjul] adj (attitude) nachlässig; (dress) leger; (meeting) zufällig; (work) Gelegenheits-;~**ly** adv (dress) zwanglos, leger; (remark) beiläufig

casualty ['kæʒjultɪ] n Verletzte(r) f(m); (dead) Tote(r) f(m); (also: ~ **department**) Unfallstation f

cat [kæt] n Katze f

catalogue ['kætəlɔg] (US **catalog**) n Katalog m ♦ vt katalogisieren

catalyst ['kætəlɪst] n Katalysator m

catalytic converter [kætə'lɪtɪk kən'vɜːtəʳ] n Katalysator m

catapult ['kætəpʌlt] n Schleuder f

cataract ['kætərækt] n (MED) graue(r) Star m

catarrh [kə'tɑːʳ] n Katarr(h) m

catastrophe [kə'tæstrəfɪ] n Katastrophe f

catch [kætʃ] (pt, pp **caught**) vt fangen; (arrest) fassen; (train) erreichen; (person: by surprise) ertappen; (also: ~ **up**) einholen ♦ vi (fire) in Gang kommen; (in branches etc) hängen bleiben ♦ n (fish etc) Fang m; (trick) Haken m; (of lock) Sperrhaken m; **to ~ an illness** sich dat eine Krankheit holen; **to ~ fire** Feuer fangen; ~ **on** vi (understand) begreifen; (grow popular) ankommen; ~ **up** vi (fig) aufholen;~**ing** ['kætʃɪŋ] adj ansteckend; ~**ment area** ['kætʃmənt-] (BRIT) n Einzugsgebiet nt; ~ **phrase** n Slogan m; ~**y** ['kætʃɪ] adj (tune) eingängig

categoric(al) [kætɪ'gɔrɪk(l)] adj kategorisch

category ['kætɪgərɪ] n Kategorie f

cater ['keɪtəʳ] vi versorgen; ~ **for** (BRIT) vt fus (party) ausrichten; (needs) eingestellt sein auf +acc; ~**er** n Lieferant(in) m(f) von Speisen und Getränken; ~**ing** n

Gastronomie f

caterpillar ['kætəpɪləʳ] n Raupe f; ~ **track** ® n Gleiskette f

cathedral [kə'θiːdrəl] n Kathedrale f, Dom m

Catholic ['kæθəlɪk] adj (REL) katholisch ♦ n Katholik(in) m(f); **c~** adj (tastes etc) vielseitig

CAT scan [kæt-] n Computertomografie f

Catseye ['kæts'aɪ] (BRIT: ®) n (AUT) Katzenauge nt

cattle ['kætl] npl Vieh nt

catty ['kætɪ] adj gehässig

caucus ['kɔːkəs] n (POL) Gremium nt; (US: meeting) Sitzung f

caught [kɔːt] pt, pp of **catch**

cauliflower ['kɔlɪflauəʳ] n Blumenkohl m

cause [kɔːz] n Ursache f; (purpose) Sache f ♦ vt verursachen

causeway ['kɔːzweɪ] n Damm m

caustic ['kɔːstɪk] adj ätzend; (fig) bissig

caution ['kɔːʃən] n Vorsicht f; (warning) Verwarnung f ♦ vt verwarnen; **cautious** ['kɔːʃəs] adj vorsichtig

cavalry ['kævəlrɪ] n Kavallerie f

cave [keɪv] n Höhle f; ~ **in** vi einstürzen; ~**man** (irreg) n Höhlenmensch m

cavern ['kævən] n Höhle f

caviar(e) ['kævɪɑːʳ] n Kaviar m

cavity ['kævɪtɪ] n Loch nt

cavort [kə'vɔːt] vi umherspringen

C.B. n abbr (= Citizens' Band (Radio)) CB

C.B.I. n abbr (= Confederation of British Industry) ≃ BDI m

cc n abbr = **carbon copy; cubic centimetres**

CCTV n abbr (= closed-circuit television) Videoüberwachung f

CD n abbr (= compact disc) CD f

CDI n abbr (= Compact Disk Interactive) CD-I f

CD player n CD-Spieler m

CD-ROM n abbr (= compact disc read-only memory) CD-Rom f

cease [siːs] vi aufhören ♦ vt beenden; ~**fire** n Feuereinstellung f; ~**less** adj unaufhörlich

cedar ['siːdəʳ] n Zeder f

ceiling ['siːlɪŋ] n Decke f; (fig) Höchstgrenze f

celebrate ['selɪbreɪt] vt, vi feiern; ~**d** adj gefeiert; **celebration** [selɪ'breɪʃən] n Feier f

celebrity [sɪ'lebrɪtɪ] n gefeierte Persönlichkeit f

celery ['selərɪ] n Sellerie m or f

celibacy ['selɪbəsɪ] n Zölibat nt or m

cell [sel] n Zelle f; (ELEC) Element nt

cellar ['seləʳ] n Keller m

cello ['tʃelou] n Cello nt

Cellophane ['seləfeɪn] ® n Cellophan nt ®

cellphone ['selfəun] n Funktelefon nt

cellular ['seljuləʳ] adj zellular

cellulose ['seljuləus] n Zellulose f

Celt [kelt, selt] n Kelte m, Keltin f; ~**ic** ['keltɪk, 'seltɪk] adj keltisch

cement [sə'ment] n Zement m ♦ vt zementieren; ~ **mixer** n Betonmischmaschine f

cemetery ['semɪtrɪ] n Friedhof m

censor ['sensəʳ] n Zensor m ♦ vt zensieren; ~**ship** n Zensur f

censure ['senʃəʳ] vt rügen

census ['sensəs] n Volkszählung f

cent [sent] n (coin) Cent m; see also **per cent**

centenary [sen'tiːnərɪ] n Jahrhundertfeier f

center ['sentəʳ] (US) n = **centre**

centigrade ['sentɪgreɪd] adj Celsius

centimetre ['sentɪmiːtəʳ] (US **centimeter**) n Zentimeter m

centipede ['sentɪpiːd] n Tausendfüßler m

central ['sentrəl] adj zentral; **C~ America** n Mittelamerika nt; ~ **heating** n Zentralheizung f; ~**ize** vt zentralisieren; ~ **reservation** (BRIT) n (AUT) Mittelstreifen m

centre ['sentəʳ] (US **center**) n Zentrum nt ♦ vt zentrieren; ~**-forward** n (SPORT) Mittelstürmer m; ~**-half** n (SPORT) Stopper m

century ['sentjurɪ] n Jahrhundert nt

ceramic [sɪ'ræmɪk] adj keramisch; ~**s** npl Keramiken pl

cereal ['siːrɪəl] n (grain) Getreide nt; (at breakfast) Getreideflocken pl

cerebral ['serɪbrəl] adj zerebral; (intellectual) geistig

ceremony ['serɪmənɪ] n Zeremonie f; **to**

stand on ~ förmlich sein

certain ['sɜːtən] *adj* sicher; (*particular*) gewiss; **for ~** ganz bestimmt; **~ly** *adv* sicher, bestimmt; **~ty** *n* Gewissheit *f*

certificate [sə'tɪfɪkɪt] *n* Bescheinigung *f*; (*SCH etc*) Zeugnis *nt*

certified mail ['sɜːtɪfaɪd-] (*US*) *n* Einschreiben *nt*

certified public accountant ['sɜːtɪfaɪd-] (*US*) *n* geprüfte(r) Buchhalter *m*

certify ['sɜːtɪfaɪ] *vt* bescheinigen

cervical ['sɜːvɪkl] *adj* (*smear, cancer*) Gebärmutterhals-

cervix ['sɜːvɪks] *n* Gebärmutterhals *m*

cf. *abbr* (= *compare*) vgl.

CFC *n abbr* (= *chlorofluorocarbon*) FCKW *m*

ch. *abbr* (= *chapter*) Kap.

chafe [tʃeɪf] *vt* scheuern

chaffinch ['tʃæfɪntʃ] *n* Buchfink *m*

chain [tʃeɪn] *n* Kette *f* ♦ *vt* (*also:* **~ up**) anketten; **~ reaction** *n* Kettenreaktion *f*; **~-smoke** *vi* kettenrauchen; **~ store** *n* Kettenladen *m*

chair [tʃeəʳ] *n* Stuhl *m*; (*armchair*) Sessel *m*; (*UNIV*) Lehrstuhl *m* ♦ *vt* (*meeting*) den Vorsitz führen bei; **~lift** *n* Sessellift *m*; **~man** (*irreg*) *n* Vorsitzende(r) *m*

chalet ['ʃæleɪ] *n* Chalet *nt*

chalk [tʃɔːk] *n* Kreide *f*

challenge ['tʃælɪndʒ] *n* Herausforderung *f* ♦ *vt* herausfordern; (*contest*) bestreiten; **challenging** *adj* (*tone*) herausfordernd; (*work*) anspruchsvoll

chamber ['tʃeɪmbəʳ] *n* Kammer *f*; **~ of commerce** Handelskammer *f*; **~maid** *n* Zimmermädchen *nt*; **~ music** *n* Kammermusik *f*

chamois ['ʃæmwɑː] *n* Gämse *f*

champagne [ʃæm'peɪn] *n* Champagner *m*, Sekt *m*

champion ['tʃæmpɪən] *n* (*SPORT*) Meister(in) *m(f)*; (*of cause*) Verfechter(in) *m(f)*; **~ship** *n* Meisterschaft *f*

chance [tʃɑːns] *n* (*luck*) Zufall *m*; (*possibility*) Möglichkeit *f*; (*opportunity*) Gelegenheit *f*, Chance *f*; (*risk*) Risiko *nt* ♦ *adj* zufällig ♦ *vt*: **to ~ it** es darauf ankommen lassen; **by ~**

zufällig; **to take a ~** ein Risiko eingehen

chancellor ['tʃɑːnsələʳ] *n* Kanzler *m*; **C~ of the Exchequer** (*BRIT*) *n* Schatzkanzler *m*

chandelier [ʃændə'lɪəʳ] *n* Kronleuchter *m*

change [tʃeɪndʒ] *vt* ändern; (*replace, COMM: money*) wechseln; (*exchange*) umtauschen; (*transform*) verwandeln ♦ *vi* sich ändern; (*~ trains*) umsteigen; (*~ clothes*) sich umziehen ♦ *n* Veränderung *f*; (*money returned*) Wechselgeld *nt*; (*coins*) Kleingeld *nt*; **to ~ one's mind** es sich *dat* anders überlegen; **to ~ into sth** (*be transformed*) sich in etw *acc* verwandeln; **for a ~** zur Abwechslung; **~able** *adj* (*weather*) wechselhaft; **~ machine** *n* Geldwechselautomat *m*; **~over** *n* Umstellung *f*

changing ['tʃeɪndʒɪŋ] *adj* veränderlich; **~ room** (*BRIT*) *n* Umkleideraum *m*

channel ['tʃænl] *n* (*stream*) Bachbett *nt*; (*NAUT*) Straße *f*; (*TV*) Kanal *m*; (*fig*) Weg *m* ♦ *vt* (*efforts*) lenken; **the (English) C~** der Ärmelkanal; **~-hopping** *n* (*TV*) ständiges Umschalten *n*; **C~ Islands** *npl*: **the C~ Islands** die Kanalinseln *pl*; **C~ Tunnel** *n*: **the C~ Tunnel** der Kanaltunnel

chant [tʃɑːnt] *n* Gesang *m*; (*of fans*) Sprechchor *m* ♦ *vt* intonieren

chaos ['keɪɒs] *n* Chaos *nt*

chap [tʃæp] (*inf*) *n* Kerl *m*

chapel ['tʃæpl] *n* Kapelle *f*

chaperon ['ʃæpərəʊn] *n* Anstandsdame *f*

chaplain ['tʃæplɪn] *n* Kaplan *m*

chapped [tʃæpt] *adj* (*skin, lips*) spröde

chapter ['tʃæptəʳ] *n* Kapitel *nt*

char [tʃɑːʳ] *vt* (*burn*) verkohlen

character ['kærɪktəʳ] *n* Charakter *m*, Wesen *nt*; (*in novel, film*) Figur *f*; **~istic** [kærɪktə'rɪstɪk] *adj*: **~istic (of sb/sth)** (für jdn/etw) charakteristisch ♦ *n* Kennzeichen *nt*; **~ize** *vt* charakterisieren, kennzeichnen

charade [ʃə'rɑːd] *n* Scharade *f*

charcoal ['tʃɑːkəʊl] *n* Holzkohle *f*

charge [tʃɑːdʒ] *n* (*cost*) Preis *m*; (*JUR*) Anklage *f*; (*explosive*) Ladung *f*; (*attack*) Angriff *m* ♦ *vt* (*gun, battery*) laden; (*price*) verlangen; (*JUR*) anklagen; (*MIL*) angreifen ♦ *vi* (*rush*) (an)stürmen; **bank ~s**

Bankgebühren *pl*; **free of ~** kostenlos; **to reverse the ~s** (*TEL*) ein R-Gespräch führen; **to be in ~ of** verantwortlich sein für; **to take ~** (die Verantwortung) übernehmen; **to ~ sth (up) to sb's account** jdm etw in Rechnung stellen; **~ card** *n* Kundenkarte *f*

charitable ['tʃærɪtəbl] *adj* wohltätig; (*lenient*) nachsichtig

charity ['tʃærɪtɪ] *n* (*institution*) Hilfswerk *nt*; (*attitude*) Nächstenliebe *f*

charm [tʃɑːm] *n* Charme *m*; (*spell*) Bann *m*; (*object*) Talisman *m* ♦ *vt* bezaubern; **~ing** *adj* reizend

chart [tʃɑːt] *n* Tabelle *f*; (*NAUT*) Seekarte *f* ♦ *vt* (*course*) abstecken

charter ['tʃɑːtəʳ] *vt* chartern ♦ *n* Schutzbrief *m*; **~ed accountant** *n* Wirtschaftsprüfer(in) *m(f)*; **~ flight** *n* Charterflug *m*

chase [tʃeɪs] *vt* jagen, verfolgen ♦ *n* Jagd *f*

chasm ['kæzəm] *n* Kluft *f*

chassis ['ʃæsɪ] *n* Fahrgestell *nt*

chat [tʃæt] *vi* (*also*: **have a ~**) plaudern ♦ *n* Plauderei *f*; **~ show** (*BRIT*) *n* Talkshow *f*

chatter ['tʃætəʳ] *vi* schwatzen; (*teeth*) klappern ♦ *n* Geschwätz *nt*; **~box** *n* Quasselstrippe *f*

chatty ['tʃætɪ] *adj* geschwätzig

chauffeur ['ʃəʊfəʳ] *n* Chauffeur *m*

chauvinist ['ʃəʊvɪnɪst] *n* (*male ~*) Chauvi *m* (*inf*)

cheap [tʃiːp] *adj, adv* billig; **~ day return** *n* Tagesrückfahrkarte *f* (*zu einem günstigeren Tarif*); **~ly** *adv* billig

cheat [tʃiːt] *vt, vi* betrügen; (*SCH*) mogeln ♦ *n* Betrüger(in) *m(f)*

check [tʃɛk] *vt* (*examine*) prüfen; (*make sure*) nachsehen; (*control*) kontrollieren; (*restrain*) zügeln; (*stop*) anhalten ♦ *n* (*examination, restraint*) Kontrolle *f*; (*bill*) Rechnung *f*; (*pattern*) Karo(muster) *nt*; (*US*) = **cheque** ♦ *adj* (*pattern, cloth*) kariert; **~ in** *vi* (*in hotel, airport*) einchecken ♦ *vt* (*luggage*) abfertigen lassen; **~ out** *vi* (*of hotel*) abreisen; **~ up** *vi* nachschauen; **~ up on** *vt* kontrollieren; **~ered** (*US*) *adj* =

chequered; **~ers** (*US*) *n* (*draughts*) Damespiel *nt*; **~-in (desk)** *n* Abfertigung *f*; **~ing account** (*US*) *n* (*current account*) Girokonto *nt*; **~mate** *n* Schachmatt *nt*; **~out** *n* Kasse *f*; **~point** *n* Kontrollpunkt *m*; **~ room** (*US*) *n* (*left-luggage office*) Gepäckaufbewahrung *f*; **~up** *n* (Nach)prüfung *f*; (*MED*) (ärztliche) Untersuchung *f*

cheek [tʃiːk] *n* Backe *f*; (*fig*) Frechheit *f*; **~bone** *n* Backenknochen *m*; **~y** *adj* frech

cheep [tʃiːp] *vi* piepsen

cheer [tʃɪəʳ] *n* (*usu pl*) Hurra- *or* Beifallsruf *m* ♦ *vt* zujubeln; (*encourage*) aufmuntern ♦ *vi* jauchzen; **~s!** Prost!; **~ up** *vi* bessere Laune bekommen ♦ *vt* aufmuntern; **~ up!** nun lach doch mal!; **~ful** *adj* fröhlich

cheerio [tʃɪərɪ'əʊ] (*BRIT*) *excl* tschüss!

cheese [tʃiːz] *n* Käse *m*; **~board** *n* (gemischte) Käseplatte *f*

cheetah ['tʃiːtə] *n* Gepard *m*

chef [ʃɛf] *n* Küchenchef *m*

chemical ['kɛmɪkl] *adj* chemisch ♦ *n* Chemikalie *f*

chemist ['kɛmɪst] *n* (*BRIT: pharmacist*) Apotheker *m*, Drogist *m*; (*scientist*) Chemiker *m*; **~ry** *n* Chemie *f*; **~'s (shop)** (*BRIT*) *n* Apotheke *f*; Drogerie *f*

cheque [tʃɛk] (*BRIT*) *n* Scheck *m*; **~book** *n* Scheckbuch *nt*; **~ card** *n* Scheckkarte *f*

chequered ['tʃɛkəd] *adj* (*fig*) bewegt

cherish ['tʃɛrɪʃ] *vt* (*person*) lieben; (*hope*) hegen

cherry ['tʃɛrɪ] *n* Kirsche *f*

chess [tʃɛs] *n* Schach *nt*; **~board** *n* Schachbrett *nt*; **~man** (*irreg*) *n* Schachfigur *f*

chest [tʃɛst] *n* (*ANAT*) Brust *f*; (*box*) Kiste *f*; **~ of drawers** Kommode *f*

chestnut ['tʃɛsnʌt] *n* Kastanie *f*

chew [tʃuː] *vt, vi* kauen; **~ing gum** *n* Kaugummi *m*

chic [ʃiːk] *adj* schick, elegant

chick [tʃɪk] *n* Küken *nt*; (*US: inf: girl*) Biene *f*

chicken ['tʃɪkɪn] *n* Huhn *nt*; (*food*) Hähnchen *nt*; **~ out** (*inf*) *vi* kneifen

chickenpox ['tʃɪkɪnpɔks] *n* Windpocken *pl*

chicory ['tʃɪkərɪ] n (in coffee) Zichorie f; (plant) Chicorée f, Schikoree f

chief [tʃiːf] n (of tribe) Häuptling m; (COMM) Chef m ♦ adj Haupt-; ~ **executive** n Geschäftsführer(in) m(f); **~ly** adv hauptsächlich

chilblain ['tʃɪlbleɪn] n Frostbeule f

child [tʃaɪld] (pl **~ren**) n Kind nt; **~birth** n Entbindung f; **~hood** n Kindheit f; **~ish** adj kindisch; **~like** adj kindlich; **~ minder** (BRIT) n Tagesmutter f; **~ren** ['tʃɪldrən] npl of **child**; **~ seat** n Kindersitz m

Chile ['tʃɪlɪ] n Chile nt; **~an** adj chilenisch

chill [tʃɪl] n Kühle f; (MED) Erkältung f ♦ vt (CULIN) kühlen

chilli ['tʃɪlɪ] n Peperoni pl; (meal, spice) Chili m

chilly ['tʃɪlɪ] adj kühl, frostig

chime [tʃaɪm] n Geläut nt ♦ vi ertönen

chimney ['tʃɪmnɪ] n Schornstein m; **~ sweep** n Schornsteinfeger(in) m(f)

chimpanzee [tʃɪmpæn'ziː] n Schimpanse m

chin [tʃɪn] n Kinn nt

China ['tʃaɪnə] n China nt

china ['tʃaɪnə] n Porzellan nt

Chinese [tʃaɪ'niːz] adj chinesisch ♦ n (inv) Chinese m, Chinesin f; (LING) Chinesisch nt

chink [tʃɪŋk] n (opening) Ritze f; (noise) Klirren nt

chip [tʃɪp] n (of wood etc) Splitter m; (in poker etc; US: crisp) Chip m ♦ vt absplittern; **~s** npl (BRIT: COOK) Pommes frites pl; **~ in** vi Zwischenbemerkungen machen

Chip shop

i **Chip shop**, auch fish-and-chip shop, ist die traditionelle britische Imbissbude, in der vor allem fritierte Fischfilets und Pommes frites, aber auch andere einfache Mahlzeiten angeboten werden. Früher wurde das Essen zum Mitnehmen in Zeitungspapier verpackt. Manche chip shops haben auch einen Essraum.

chiropodist [kɪ'rɔpədɪst] (BRIT) n Fußpfleger(in) m(f)

chirp [tʃəːp] vi zwitschern

chisel ['tʃɪzl] n Meißel m

chit [tʃɪt] n Notiz f

chivalrous ['ʃɪvəlrəs] adj ritterlich; **chivalry** ['ʃɪvəlrɪ] n Ritterlichkeit f

chives [tʃaɪvz] npl Schnittlauch m

chlorine ['klɔːriːn] n Chlor nt

chock-a-block ['tʃɔkə'blɔk] adj voll gepfropft

chock-full [tʃɔk'ful] adj voll gepfropft

chocolate ['tʃɔklɪt] n Schokolade f

choice [tʃɔɪs] n Wahl f; (of goods) Auswahl f ♦ adj Qualitäts-

choir ['kwaɪə'] n Chor m; **~boy** n Chorknabe m

choke [tʃəuk] vi ersticken ♦ vt erdrosseln; (block) (ab)drosseln ♦ n (AUT) Starterklappe f

cholera ['kɔlərə] n Cholera f

cholesterol [kə'lestərɔl] n Cholesterin nt

choose [tʃuːz] (pt **chose**, pp **chosen**) vt wählen; **choosy** ['tʃuːzɪ] adj wählerisch

chop [tʃɔp] vt (wood) spalten; (COOK: also: ~ up) (zer)hacken ♦ n Hieb m; (COOK) Kotelett nt; **~s** npl (jaws) Lefzen pl

chopper ['tʃɔpə'] n (helicopter) Hubschrauber m

choppy ['tʃɔpɪ] adj (sea) bewegt

chopsticks ['tʃɔpstɪks] npl (Ess)stäbchen pl

choral ['kɔːrəl] adj Chor-

chord [kɔːd] n Akkord m

chore [tʃɔː'] n Pflicht f; **~s** npl (housework) Hausarbeit f

choreographer [kɔrɪ'ɔgrəfə'] n Choreograf(in) m(f)

chorister ['kɔrɪstə'] n Chorsänger(in) m(f)

chortle ['tʃɔːtl] vi glucksen

chorus ['kɔːrəs] n Chor m; (in song) Refrain m

chose [tʃəuz] pt of **choose**

chosen ['tʃəuzn] pp of **choose**

chowder ['tʃaudə'] (US) n sämige Fischsuppe f

Christ [kraɪst] n Christus m

christen ['krɪsn] vt taufen; **~ing** n Taufe f

Christian ['krɪstɪən] adj christlich ♦ n Christ(in) m(f); **~ity** [krɪstɪ'ænɪtɪ] n Christentum nt; **~ name** n Vorname m

Christmas ['krɪsməs] n Weihnachten pl;
  Happy or **Merry** ~! frohe or fröhliche
  Weihnachten!; ~ **card** n Weihnachtskarte f;
  ~ **Day** n der erste Weihnachtstag; ~ **Eve** n
  Heiligabend m; ~ **tree** n Weihnachtsbaum
  m
chrome [krəum] n Verchromung f
chromium ['krəumɪəm] n Chrom nt
chronic ['krɒnɪk] adj chronisch
chronicle ['krɒnɪkl] n Chronik f
chronological [krɒnə'lɒdʒɪkl] adj
  chronologisch
chubby ['tʃʌbɪ] adj rundlich
chuck [tʃʌk] vt werfen; (BRIT: also: ~ **up**)
  hinwerfen; ~ **out** vt (person) rauswerfen;
  (old clothes etc) wegwerfen
chuckle ['tʃʌkl] vi in sich hineinlachen
chug [tʃʌg] vi tuckern
chunk [tʃʌŋk] n Klumpen m; (of food)
  Brocken m
church [tʃɜːtʃ] n Kirche f; ~**yard** n Kirchhof
  m
churn [tʃɜːn] n (for butter) Butterfass nt; (for
  milk) Milchkanne f; ~ **out** (inf) vt
  produzieren
chute [ʃuːt] n Rutsche f; (rubbish ~)
  Müllschlucker m
chutney ['tʃʌtnɪ] n Chutney nt
CIA (US) n abbr (= Central Intelligence Agency)
  CIA m
CID (BRIT) n abbr (= Criminal Investigation
  Department) ≈ Kripo f
cider ['saɪdər] n Apfelwein m
cigar [sɪ'gɑːr] n Zigarre f
cigarette [sɪgə'ret] n Zigarette f; ~ **case** n
  Zigarettenetui nt; ~ **end** n
  Zigarettenstummel m
Cinderella [sɪndə'relə] n Aschenbrödel nt
cinders ['sɪndəz] npl Asche f
cine camera ['sɪnɪ-] (BRIT) n Filmkamera f
cine film (BRIT) n Schmalfilm m
cinema ['sɪnəmə] n Kino nt
cinnamon ['sɪnəmən] n Zimt m
circle ['sɜːkl] n Kreis m; (in cinema etc) Rang
  m ♦ vi kreisen ♦ vt (surround) umgeben;
  (move round) kreisen um
circuit ['sɜːkɪt] n (track) Rennbahn f; (lap)

Runde f; (ELEC) Stromkreis m
circular ['sɜːkjulər] adj rund ♦ n
  Rundschreiben nt
circulate ['sɜːkjuleɪt] vi zirkulieren ♦ vt in
  Umlauf setzen; **circulation** [sɜːkju'leɪʃən] n
  (of blood) Kreislauf m; (of newspaper) Auflage
  f; (of money) Umlauf m
circumcise ['sɜːkəmsaɪz] vt beschneiden
circumference [sə'kʌmfərəns] n
  (Kreis)umfang m
circumspect ['sɜːkəmspekt] adj umsichtig
circumstances ['sɜːkəmstənsɪz] npl
  Umstände pl; (financial) Verhältnisse pl
circumvent [sɜːkəm'vent] vt umgehen
circus ['sɜːkəs] n Zirkus m
CIS n abbr (= Commonwealth of Independent
  States) GUS f
cistern ['sɪstən] n Zisterne f; (of W.C.)
  Spülkasten m
cite [saɪt] vt zitieren, anführen
citizen ['sɪtɪzn] n Bürger(in) m(f); ~**ship** n
  Staatsbürgerschaft f
citrus fruit ['sɪtrəs-] n Zitrusfrucht f
city ['sɪtɪ] n Großstadt f; **the C~** die City, das
  Finanzzentrum Londons
city technology college n ≈ Technische
  Fachschule f
civic ['sɪvɪk] adj (of town) städtisch; (of citizen)
  Bürger-; ~ **centre** (BRIT) n Stadtverwaltung
  f
civil ['sɪvɪl] adj bürgerlich; (not military) zivil;
  (polite) höflich; ~ **engineer** n Bauingenieur
  m; ~**ian** [sɪ'vɪlɪən] n Zivilperson f ♦ adj zivil,
  Zivil-
civilization [sɪvɪlaɪ'zeɪʃən] n Zivilisation f
civilized ['sɪvɪlaɪzd] adj zivilisiert
civil: ~ **law** n Zivilrecht nt; ~ **servant** n
  Staatsbeamte(r) m; **C~ Service** n
  Staatsdienst m; ~ **war** n Bürgerkrieg m
clad [klæd] adj: ~ **in** gehüllt in +acc
claim [kleɪm] vt beanspruchen; (have opinion)
  behaupten ♦ vi (for insurance) Ansprüche
  geltend machen ♦ n (demand) Forderung f;
  (right) Anspruch m; (pretension) Behauptung
  f; ~**ant** n Antragsteller(in) m(f)
clairvoyant [kleə'vɔɪənt] n Hellseher(in) m(f)
clam [klæm] n Venusmuschel f

clamber ['klæmbəʳ] *vi* kraxeln

clammy ['klæmɪ] *adj* klamm

clamour ['klæməʳ] *vi*: **to ~ for sth** nach etw verlangen

clamp [klæmp] *n* Schraubzwinge *f* ♦ *vt* einspannen; (*AUT: wheel*) krallen; **~ down on** *vt fus* Maßnahmen ergreifen gegen

clan [klæn] *n* Clan *m*

clandestine [klæn'dɛstɪn] *adj* geheim

clang [klæŋ] *vi* scheppern

clap [klæp] *vi* klatschen ♦ *vt* Beifall klatschen +*dat* ♦ *n* (*of hands*) Klatschen *nt*; (*of thunder*) Donnerschlag *m*; **~ping** *n* Klatschen *nt*

claret ['klærət] *n* rote(r) Bordeaux(wein) *m*

clarify ['klærɪfaɪ] *vt* klären, erklären

clarinet [klærɪ'nɛt] *n* Klarinette *f*

clarity ['klærɪtɪ] *n* Klarheit *f*

clash [klæʃ] *n* (*fig*) Konflikt *m* ♦ *vi* zusammenprallen; (*colours*) sich beißen; (*argue*) sich streiten

clasp [klɑːsp] *n* Griff *m*; (*on jewels, bag*) Verschluss *m* ♦ *vt* umklammern

class [klɑːs] *n* Klasse *f* ♦ *vt* einordnen; **~-conscious** *adj* klassenbewusst

classic ['klæsɪk] *n* Klassiker *m* ♦ *adj* klassisch; **~al** *adj* klassisch

classified ['klæsɪfaɪd] *adj* (*information*) Geheim-; **~ advertisement** *n* Kleinanzeige *f*

classify ['klæsɪfaɪ] *vt* klassifizieren

classmate ['klɑːsmeɪt] *n* Klassenkamerad(in) *m(f)*

classroom ['klɑːsrum] *n* Klassenzimmer *nt*

clatter ['klætəʳ] *vi* klappern; (*feet*) trappeln

clause [klɔːz] *n* (*JUR*) Klausel *f*; (*GRAM*) Satz *m*

claustrophobia [klɔːstrə'fəʊbɪə] *n* Platzangst *f*

claw [klɔː] *n* Kralle *f* ♦ *vt* (zer)kratzen

clay [kleɪ] *n* Lehm *m*; (*for pots*) Ton *m*

clean [kliːn] *adj* sauber ♦ *vt* putzen; (*clothes*) reinigen; **~ out** *vt* gründlich putzen; **~ up** *vt* aufräumen; **~-cut** *adj* (*person*) adrett; (*clear*) klar; **~er** *n* (*person*) Putzfrau *f*; **~er's** *n* (*also:* **dry ~er's**) Reinigung *f*; **~ing** *n* Putzen *nt*; (*clothes*) Reinigung *f*; **~liness** ['klɛnlɪnɪs] *n* Reinlichkeit *f*

cleanse [klɛnz] *vt* reinigen; **~r** *n* (*for face*) Reinigungsmilch *f*

clean-shaven ['kliːn'ʃeɪvn] *adj* glatt rasiert

cleansing department ['klɛnzɪŋ-] (*BRIT*) *n* Stadtreinigung *f*

clear [klɪəʳ] *adj* klar; (*road*) frei ♦ *vt* (*road etc*) freimachen; (*obstacle*) beseitigen; (*JUR: suspect*) freisprechen ♦ *vi* klar werden; (*fog*) sich lichten ♦ *adv*: **~ of** von ... entfernt; **to ~ the table** den Tisch abräumen; **~ up** *vt* aufräumen; (*solve*) aufklären; **~ance** ['klɪərəns] *n* (*removal*) Räumung *f*; (*free space*) Lichtung *f*; (*permission*) Freigabe *f*; **~-cut** *adj* (*case*) eindeutig; **~ing** *n* Lichtung *f*; **~ing bank** (*BRIT*) *n* Clearingbank *f*; **~ly** *adv* klar; (*obviously*) eindeutig; **~way** (*BRIT*) *n* (Straße *f* mit) Halteverbot *nt*

cleaver ['kliːvəʳ] *n* Hackbeil *f*

cleft [klɛft] *n* (*in rock*) Spalte *f*

clementine ['klɛməntaɪn] *n* (*fruit*) Klementine *f*

clench [klɛntʃ] *vt* (*teeth*) zusammenbeißen; (*fist*) ballen

clergy ['klɜːdʒɪ] *n* Geistliche(n) *pl*; **~man** (*irreg*) *n* Geistliche(r) *m*

clerical ['klɛrɪkl] *adj* (*office*) Schreib-, Büro-; (*REL*) geistlich

clerk [klɑːk, (*US*) klɜːrk] *n* (*in office*) Büroangestellte(r) *mf*; (*US: sales person*) Verkäufer(in) *m(f)*

clever ['klɛvəʳ] *adj* klug; (*crafty*) schlau

cliché ['kliːʃeɪ] *n* Klischee *nt*

click [klɪk] *vt* (*tongue*) schnalzen mit; (*heels*) zusammenklappen; **~ on** *vt* (*COMPUT*) anklicken

client ['klaɪənt] *n* Klient(in) *m(f)*; **~ele** [kliːɑ̃ːn'tɛl] *n* Kundschaft *f*

cliff [klɪf] *n* Klippe *f*

climate ['klaɪmɪt] *n* Klima *nt*

climax ['klaɪmæks] *n* Höhepunkt *m*

climb [klaɪm] *vt* besteigen ♦ *vi* steigen, klettern ♦ *n* Aufstieg *m*; **~-down** *n* Abstieg *m*; **~er** *n* Bergsteiger(in) *m(f)*; **~ing** *n* Bergsteigen *nt*

clinch [klɪntʃ] *vt* (*decide*) entscheiden; (*deal*) festmachen

cling [klɪŋ] (*pt, pp* **clung**) *vi* (*clothes*) eng anliegen; **to ~ to** sich festklammern an +*dat*

clinic ['klɪnɪk] *n* Klinik *f*; **~al** *adj* klinisch

clink [klɪŋk] vi klimpern

clip [klɪp] n Spange f; (also: **paper ~**) Klammer f ♦ vt (papers) heften; (hair, hedge) stutzen; ~**pers** npl (for hedge) Heckenschere f; (for hair) Haarschneidemaschine f; ~**ping** n Ausschnitt m

cloak [kləuk] n Umhang m ♦ vt hüllen; ~**room** n (for coats) Garderobe f; (BRIT: W.C.) Toilette f

clock [klɔk] n Uhr f; ~ **in** or **on** vi stempeln; ~ **off** or **out** vi stempeln; ~**wise** adv im Uhrzeigersinn; ~**work** n Uhrwerk nt ♦ adj zum Aufziehen

clog [klɔg] n Holzschuh m ♦ vt verstopfen

cloister ['klɔɪstər] n Kreuzgang m

clone [kləun] n Klon m ♦ vt klonen

close¹ [kləus] adj (near) in der Nähe; (friend, connection, print) eng; (relative) nahe; (result) knapp; (examination) eingehend; (weather) schwül; (room) stickig ♦ adv nahe, dicht; ~ **by** in der Nähe; ~ **at hand** in der Nähe; **to have a ~ shave** (fig) mit knapper Not davonkommen

close² [kləuz] vt (shut) schließen; (end) beenden ♦ vi (shop etc) schließen; (door etc) sich schließen ♦ n Ende nt; ~ **down** vi schließen; ~**d** adj (shop etc) geschlossen; ~**d shop** n Gewerkschaftszwang m

close-knit ['kləus'nɪt] adj eng zusammengewachsen

closely ['kləuslɪ] adv eng; (carefully) genau

closet ['klɔzɪt] n Schrank m

close-up ['kləusʌp] n Nahaufnahme f

closure ['kləuʒər] n Schließung f

clot [klɔt] n (of blood) Blutgerinnsel nt; (fool) Blödmann m ♦ vi gerinnen

cloth [klɔθ] n (material) Tuch nt; (rag) Lappen m

clothe [kləuð] vt kleiden

clothes [kləuðz] npl Kleider pl; ~ **brush** n Kleiderbürste f; ~ **line** n Wäscheleine f; ~ **peg**, ~ **pin** (US) n Wäscheklammer f

clothing ['kləuðɪŋ] n Kleidung f

clotted cream ['klɔtɪd-] (BRIT) n Sahne aus erhitzter Milch

cloud [klaud] n Wolke f; ~**burst** n

Wolkenbruch m; ~**y** adj bewölkt; (liquid) trüb

clout [klaut] vt hauen

clove [kləuv] n Gewürznelke f; ~ **of garlic** Knoblauchzehe f

clover ['kləuvər] n Klee m

clown [klaun] n Clown m ♦ vi (also: ~ **about**, ~ **around**) kaspern

cloying ['klɔɪɪŋ] adj (taste, smell) übersüß

club [klʌb] n (weapon) Knüppel m; (society) Klub m; (also: **golf ~**) Golfschläger m ♦ vt prügeln ♦ vi: **to ~ together** zusammenlegen; ~**s** npl (CARDS) Kreuz nt; ~ **car** (US) n (RAIL) Speisewagen m; ~ **class** n (AVIAT) Club-Klasse f; ~**house** n Klubhaus nt

cluck [klʌk] vi glucken

clue [kluː] n Anhaltspunkt m; (in crosswords) Frage f; **I haven't a ~** (ich hab) keine Ahnung

clump [klʌmp] n Gruppe f

clumsy ['klʌmzɪ] adj (person) unbeholfen; (shape) unförmig

clung [klʌŋ] pt, pp of **cling**

cluster ['klʌstər] n (of trees etc) Gruppe f ♦ vi sich drängen, sich scharen

clutch [klʌtʃ] n Griff m; (AUT) Kupplung f ♦ vt sich festklammern an +dat

clutter ['klʌtər] vt voll pfropfen; (desk) übersäen

CND n abbr = **Campaign for Nuclear Disarmament**

Co. abbr = **county**; **company**

c/o abbr (= care of) c/o

coach [kəutʃ] n (bus) Reisebus m; (horse-drawn) Kutsche f; (RAIL) (Personen)wagen m; (trainer) Trainer m ♦ vt (SCH) Nachhilfeunterricht geben +dat; (SPORT) trainieren; ~ **trip** n Busfahrt f

coal [kəul] n Kohle f; ~ **face** n Streb m

coalition [kəuə'lɪʃən] n Koalition f

coalman ['kəulmən] (irreg) n Kohlenhändler m

coal mine n Kohlenbergwerk nt

coarse [kɔːs] adj grob; (fig) ordinär

coast [kəust] n Küste f ♦ vi dahinrollen; (AUT) im Leerlauf fahren; ~**al** adj Küsten-;

~guard n Küstenwache f; ~line n Küste(nlinie) f

coat [kəut] n Mantel m; (on animals) Fell nt; (of paint) Schicht f ♦ vt überstreichen; ~hanger n Kleiderbügel m; ~ing n Überzug m; (of paint) Schicht f; ~ of arms n Wappen nt

coax [kəuks] vt beschwatzen

cob [kɔb] n see corn

cobbler ['kɔblə'] n Schuster m

cobbles ['kɔblz] npl Pflastersteine pl

cobweb ['kɔbwɛb] n Spinnennetz nt

cocaine [kə'keɪn] n Kokain nt

cock [kɔk] n Hahn m ♦ vt (gun) entsichern; ~erel n junge(r) Hahn m; ~eyed adj (fig) verrückt

cockle ['kɔkl] n Herzmuschel f

cockney ['kɔknɪ] n echte(r) Londoner m

cockpit ['kɔkpɪt] n (AVIAT) Pilotenkanzel f

cockroach ['kɔkrəutʃ] n Küchenschabe f

cocktail ['kɔkteɪl] n Cocktail m; ~ cabinet n Hausbar f; ~ party n Cocktailparty f

cocoa ['kəukəu] n Kakao m

coconut ['kəukənʌt] n Kokosnuss f

cocoon [kə'kuːn] n Kokon m

cod [kɔd] n Kabeljau m

C.O.D. abbr = cash on delivery

code [kəud] n Kode m; (JUR) Kodex m

cod-liver oil ['kɔdlɪvə-] n Lebertran m

coercion [kəu'əːʃən] n Zwang m

coffee ['kɔfɪ] n Kaffee m; ~ bar (BRIT) n Café nt; ~ bean n Kaffeebohne f; ~ break n Kaffeepause f; ~pot n Kaffeekanne f; ~ table n Couchtisch m

coffin ['kɔfɪn] n Sarg m

cog [kɔg] n (Rad)zahn m

cognac ['kɔnjæk] n Kognak m

coherent [kəu'hɪərənt] adj zusammenhängend; (person) verständlich

coil [kɔɪl] n Rolle f; (ELEC) Spule f; (contraceptive) Spirale f ♦ vt aufwickeln

coin [kɔɪn] n Münze f ♦ vt prägen; ~age ['kɔɪnɪdʒ] n (word) Prägung f; ~ box (BRIT) n Münzfernsprecher m

coincide [kəuɪn'saɪd] vi (happen together) zusammenfallen; (agree) übereinstimmen; ~nce [kəu'ɪnsɪdəns] n Zufall m

coinphone ['kɔɪnfəun] n Münzfernsprecher m

Coke [kəuk] ® n (drink) Coca-Cola ® f

coke [kəuk] n Koks m

colander ['kɔləndə'] n Durchschlag m

cold [kəuld] adj kalt ♦ n Kälte f; (MED) Erkältung f; I'm ~ mir ist kalt; to catch ~ sich erkälten; in ~ blood kaltblütig; to give sb the ~ shoulder jdm die kalte Schulter zeigen; ~ly adv kalt; ~-shoulder vt die kalte Schulter zeigen +dat; ~ sore n Erkältungsbläschen nt

coleslaw ['kəulslɔː] n Krautsalat m

colic ['kɔlɪk] n Kolik f

collaborate [kə'læbəreɪt] vi zusammenarbeiten

collapse [kə'læps] vi (people) zusammenbrechen; (things) einstürzen ♦ n Zusammenbruch m; Einsturz m; collapsible adj zusammenklappbar, Klapp-

collar ['kɔlə'] n Kragen m; ~bone n Schlüsselbein nt

collateral [kə'lætərl] n (zusätzliche) Sicherheit f

colleague ['kɔliːg] n Kollege m, Kollegin f

collect [kə'lɛkt] vt sammeln; (BRIT: call and pick up) abholen ♦ vi sich sammeln ♦ adv: to call ~ (US: TEL) ein R-Gespräch führen; ~ion [kə'lɛkʃən] n Sammlung f; (REL) Kollekte f; (of post) Leerung f; ~ive [kə'lɛktɪv] adj gemeinsam; (POL) kollektiv; ~or [kə'lɛktə'] n Sammler m; (tax ~or) (Steuer)einnehmer m

college ['kɔlɪdʒ] n (UNIV) College nt; (TECH) Fach-, Berufsschule f

collide [kə'laɪd] vi zusammenstoßen

collie ['kɔlɪ] n Collie m

colliery ['kɔlɪərɪ] (BRIT) n Zeche f

collision [kə'lɪʒən] n Zusammenstoß m

colloquial [kə'ləukwɪəl] adj umgangssprachlich

colon ['kəulən] n Doppelpunkt m; (MED) Dickdarm m

colonel ['kəːnl] n Oberst m

colonial [kə'ləunɪəl] adj Kolonial-

colonize ['kɔlənaɪz] vt kolonisieren

colony ['kɒlənɪ] n Kolonie f

colour ['kʌlə*] (US **color**) n Farbe f ♦ vt (also fig) färben ♦ vi sich verfärben; **~s** npl (of club) Fahne f; **~ bar** n Rassenschranke f; **~-blind** adj farbenblind; **~ed** adj farbig; **~ film** n Farbfilm m; **~ful** adj bunt; (personality) schillernd; **~ing** n (complexion) Gesichtsfarbe f; (substance) Farbstoff m; **~ scheme** n Farbgebung f; **~ television** n Farbfernsehen nt

colt [kəult] n Fohlen nt

column ['kɒləm] n Säule f; (MIL) Kolonne f; (of print) Spalte f; **~ist** ['kɒləmnɪst] n Kolumnist m

coma ['kəumə] n Koma nt

comb [kəum] n Kamm m ♦ vt kämmen; (search) durchkämmen

combat ['kɒmbæt] n Kampf m ♦ vt bekämpfen

combination [kɒmbɪ'neɪʃən] n Kombination f

combine [vb kəm'baɪn, n 'kɒmbaɪn] vt verbinden ♦ vi sich vereinigen ♦ n (COMM) Konzern m; **~ (harvester)** n Mähdrescher m

combustion [kəm'bʌstʃən] n Verbrennung f

come [kʌm] (pt **came**, pp **come**) vi kommen; **to ~ undone** aufgehen; **~ about** vi geschehen; **~ across** vt fus (find) stoßen auf +acc; **~ away** vi (person) weggehen; (handle etc) abgehen; **~ back** vi zurückkommen; **~ by** vt fus (find): **to ~ by sth** zu etw kommen; **~ down** vi (price) fallen; **~ forward** vi (volunteer) sich melden; **~ from** vt fus (result) kommen von; **where do you ~ from?** wo kommen Sie her?; **I ~ from London** ich komme aus London; **~ in** vi hereinkommen; (train) einfahren; **~ in for** vt fus abkriegen; **~ into** vt fus (inherit) erben; **~ off** vi (handle) abgehen; (succeed) klappen; **~ on** vi (progress) vorankommen; **~ on!** komm!; (hurry) beeil dich!; **~ out** vi herauskommen; **~ round** vi (MED) wieder zu sich kommen; **~ to** vi (MED) wieder zu sich kommen ♦ vt (bill) sich belaufen auf +acc; **~ up** vi hochkommen; (sun)

aufgehen; (problem) auftauchen; **~ up against** vt fus (resistance, difficulties) stoßen auf +acc; **~ upon** vt fus stoßen auf +acc; **~ up with** vt fus sich einfallen lassen +acc; **~ up with** vi sich einfallen lassen

comedian [kə'miːdɪən] n Komiker m; **comedienne** [kəmiːdɪ'ɛn] n Komikerin f

comedown ['kʌmdaun] n Abstieg m

comedy ['kɒmɪdɪ] n Komödie f

comet ['kɒmɪt] n Komet m

comeuppance [kʌm'ʌpəns] n: **to get one's ~** seine Quittung bekommen

comfort ['kʌmfət] n Komfort m; (consolation) Trost m ♦ vt trösten; **~able** adj bequem; **~ably** adv (sit etc) bequem; (live) angenehm; **~ station** (US) n öffentliche Toilette f

comic ['kɒmɪk] n Comic(heft) nt; (comedian) Komiker m ♦ adj (also: **~al**) komisch; **~ strip** n Comicstrip m

coming ['kʌmɪŋ] n Kommen nt; **~(s) and going(s)** n(pl) Kommen und Gehen nt

comma ['kɒmə] n Komma nt

command [kə'mɑːnd] n Befehl m; (control) Führung f; (MIL) Kommando nt; (mastery) Beherrschung f ♦ vt befehlen +dat; (MIL) kommandieren; (be able to get) verfügen über +acc; **~eer** [kɒmən'dɪə*] vt requirieren; **~er** n Kommandant m; **~ment** n (REL) Gebot nt

commando [kə'mɑːndəu] n Kommandotruppe nt; (person) Mitglied nt einer Kommandotruppe

commemorate [kə'mɛməreɪt] vt gedenken +gen

commence [kə'mɛns] vt, vi beginnen

commend [kə'mɛnd] vt (recommend) empfehlen; (praise) loben

commensurate [kə'mɛnsərɪt] adj: **~ with sth** einer Sache dat entsprechend

comment ['kɒmɛnt] n Bemerkung f ♦ vi: **to ~ (on)** sich äußern (zu); **~ary** n Kommentar m; **~ator** n Kommentator m; (TV) Reporter(in) m(f)

commerce ['kɒmɜːs] n Handel m

commercial [kə'mɜːʃəl] adj kommerziell, geschäftlich; (training) kaufmännisch ♦ n (TV) Fernsehwerbung f; **~ break** n

Werbespot *m*; ~**ize** *vt* kommerzialisieren

commiserate [kə'mɪzəreɪt] *vi*: **to ~ with** Mitleid haben mit

commission [kə'mɪʃən] *n* (*act*) Auftrag *m*; (*fee*) Provision *f*; (*body*) Kommission *f* ♦ *vt* beauftragen; (*MIL*) zum Offizier ernennen; (*work of art*) in Auftrag geben; **out of ~** außer Betrieb; **~er** *n* (*POLICE*) Polizeipräsident *m*

commit [kə'mɪt] *vt* (*crime*) begehen; (*entrust*) anvertrauen; **to ~ o.s.** sich festlegen; **~ment** *n* Verpflichtung *f*

committee [kə'mɪtɪ] *n* Ausschuss *m*

commodity [kə'mɒdɪtɪ] *n* Ware *f*

common ['kɒmən] *adj* (*cause*) gemeinsam; (*pej*) gewöhnlich; (*widespread*) üblich, häufig ♦ *n* Gemeindeland *nt*; **C~s** *npl* (*BRIT*): **the C~s** das Unterhaus; **~er** *n* Bürgerliche(r) *mf*; **~ law** *n* Gewohnheitsrecht *nt*; **~ly** *adv* gewöhnlich; **C~ Market** *n* Gemeinsame(r) Markt *m*; **~place** *adj* alltäglich; **~ room** *n* Gemeinschaftsraum *m*; **~ sense** *n* gesunde(r) Menschenverstand *m*; **C~wealth** *n*: **the C~wealth** das Commonwealth

commotion [kə'məʊʃən] *n* Aufsehen *nt*

communal ['kɒmjuːnl] *adj* Gemeinde-; Gemeinschafts-

commune [*n* 'kɒmjuːn, *vb* kə'mjuːn] *n* Kommune *f* ♦ *vi*: **to ~ with** sich mitteilen +*dat*

communicate [kə'mjuːnɪkeɪt] *vt* (*transmit*) übertragen ♦ *vi* (*be in touch*) in Verbindung stehen; (*make self understood*) sich verständigen; **communication** [kəmjuːnɪ'keɪʃən] *n* (*message*) Mitteilung *f*; (*making understood*) Kommunikation *f*; **communication cord** (*BRIT*) *n* Notbremse *f*

communion [kə'mjuːnɪən] *n* (*also*: **Holy C~**) Abendmahl *nt*, Kommunion *f*

communism ['kɒmjunɪzəm] *n* Kommunismus *m*; **communist** ['kɒmjunɪst] *n* Kommunist(in) *m(f)* ♦ *adj* kommunistisch

community [kə'mjuːnɪtɪ] *n* Gemeinschaft *f*; **~ centre** *n* Gemeinschaftszentrum *nt*; **~**

chest (*US*) *n* Wohltätigkeitsfonds *m*; **~ home** (*BRIT*) *n* Erziehungsheim *nt*

commutation ticket [kɒmjuː'teɪʃən-] (*US*) *n* Zeitkarte *f*

commute [kə'mjuːt] *vi* pendeln ♦ *vt* umwandeln; **~r** *n* Pendler *m*

compact [*adj* kəm'pækt, *n* 'kɒmpækt] *adj* kompakt ♦ *n* (*for make-up*) Puderdose *f*; **~ disc** *n* Compactdisc *f*, Compact Disc *f*; **~ disc player** *n* CD-Spieler *m*

companion [kəm'pænjən] *n* Begleiter(in) *m(f)*; **~ship** *n* Gesellschaft *f*

company ['kʌmpənɪ] *n* Gesellschaft *f*; (*COMM*) Firma *f*, Gesellschaft *f*; **to keep sb ~** jdm Gesellschaft leisten; **~ secretary** (*BRIT*) *n* ≈ Prokurist(in) *m(f)*

comparable ['kɒmpərəbl] *adj* vergleichbar

comparative [kəm'pærətɪv] *adj* (*relative*) relativ; **~ly** *adv* verhältnismäßig

compare [kəm'pɛəʳ] *vt* vergleichen ♦ *vi* sich vergleichen lassen; **comparison** [kəm'pærɪsn] *n* Vergleich *m*; **in comparison (with)** im Vergleich (mit *or* zu)

compartment [kəm'pɑːtmənt] *n* (*RAIL*) Abteil *nt*; (*in drawer*) Fach *nt*

compass ['kʌmpəs] *n* Kompass *m*; **~es** *npl* (*MATH etc*: *also*: **pair of ~es**) Zirkel *m*

compassion [kəm'pæʃən] *n* Mitleid *nt*; **~ate** *adj* mitfühlend

compatible [kəm'pætɪbl] *adj* vereinbar; (*COMPUT*) kompatibel

compel [kəm'pɛl] *vt* zwingen

compensate ['kɒmpənseɪt] *vt* entschädigen ♦ *vi*: **to ~ for** Ersatz leisten für; **compensation** [kɒmpən'seɪʃən] *n* Entschädigung *f*

compère ['kɒmpɛəʳ] *n* Conférencier *m*

compete [kəm'piːt] *vi* (*take part*) teilnehmen; (*vie with*) konkurrieren

competent ['kɒmpɪtənt] *adj* kompetent

competition [kɒmpɪ'tɪʃən] *n* (*contest*) Wettbewerb *m*; (*COMM, rivalry*) Konkurrenz *f*; **competitive** [kəm'pɛtɪtɪv] *adj* Konkurrenz-; (*COMM*) konkurrenzfähig; **competitor** [kəm'pɛtɪtəʳ] *n* (*COMM*) Konkurrent(in) *m(f)*; (*participant*) Teilnehmer(in) *m(f)* compile [kəm'paɪl] vt zusammenstellen

complacency [kəm'pleɪsnsɪ] n Selbstzufriedenheit f

complacent [kəm'pleɪsnt] adj selbstzufrieden

complain [kəm'pleɪn] vi sich beklagen; (formally) sich beschweren; ~t n Klage f; (formal ~t) Beschwerde f; (MED) Leiden nt

complement [n 'komplɪmənt, vb 'komplɪment] n Ergänzung f; (ship's crew etc) Bemannung f ♦ vt ergänzen; ~ary [komplɪ'mentərɪ] adj (sich) ergänzend

complete [kəm'pli:t] adj (full) vollkommen, ganz; (finished) fertig ♦ vt vervollständigen; (finish) beenden; (fill in: form) ausfüllen; ~ly adv ganz; completion [kəm'pli:ʃən] n Fertigstellung f; (of contract etc) Abschluss m

complex ['kompleks] adj kompliziert

complexion [kəm'plekʃən] n Gesichtsfarbe f; (fig) Aspekt m

complexity [kəm'pleksɪtɪ] n Kompliziertheit f

compliance [kəm'plaɪəns] n Fügsamkeit f, Einwilligung f; in ~ with sth einer Sache dat gemäß

complicate ['komplɪkeɪt] vt komplizieren; ~d adj kompliziert; complication [komplɪ'keɪʃən] n Komplikation f

compliment [n 'komplɪmənt, vb 'komplɪment] n Kompliment nt ♦ vt ein Kompliment machen +dat; ~s npl (greetings) Grüße pl; to pay sb a ~ jdm ein Kompliment machen; ~ary [komplɪ'mentərɪ] adj schmeichelhaft; (free) Frei-, Gratis-

comply [kəm'plaɪ] vi: to ~ with erfüllen +acc; entsprechen +dat

component [kəm'pəʊnənt] adj Teil- ♦ n Bestandteil m

compose [kəm'pəʊz] vt (music) komponieren; (poetry) verfassen; to ~ o.s. sich sammeln; (poetry) sich gefasst; ~r n Komponist(in) m(f); composition ['kompə'zɪʃən] n (MUS) Komposition f; (SCH) Aufsatz m; (structure) Zusammensetzung f, Aufbau m

composure [kəm'pəʊzər] n Fassung f

compound ['kompaund] n (CHEM) Verbindung f; (enclosure) Lager nt; (LING)

Kompositum nt ♦ adj zusammengesetzt; (fracture) kompliziert; ~ interest n Zinseszins m

comprehend [komprɪ'hend] vt begreifen; comprehension n Verständnis nt

comprehensive [komprɪ'hensɪv] adj umfassend ♦ n = comprehensive school; ~ insurance n Vollkasko nt; ~ school (BRIT) n Gesamtschule f

compress [vb kəm'pres, n 'kompres] vt komprimieren ♦ n (MED) Kompresse f

comprise [kəm'praɪz] vt (also: be ~d of) umfassen, bestehen aus

compromise ['komprəmaɪz] n Kompromiss m ♦ vt kompromittieren ♦ vi einen Kompromiss schließen

compulsion [kəm'pʌlʃən] n Zwang m; compulsive [kəm'pʌlsɪv] adj zwanghaft; compulsory [kəm'pʌlsərɪ] adj obligatorisch

computer [kəm'pju:tər] n Computer m, Rechner m; ~ game n Computerspiel nt; ~-generated adj computergeneriert; ~ize vt (information) computerisieren; (company, accounts) auf Computer umstellen; ~ programmer n Programmierer(in) m(f); ~ programming n Programmieren nt; ~ science n Informatik f; computing [kəm'pju:tɪŋ] n (science) Informatik f; (work) Computerei f

comrade ['komrɪd] n Kamerad m; (POL) Genosse m

con [kon] vt hereinlegen ♦ n Schwindel nt

concave ['konkeɪv] adj konkav

conceal [kən'si:l] vt (secret) verschweigen; (hide) verbergen

concede [kən'si:d] vt (grant) gewähren; (point) zugeben ♦ vi (admit defeat) nachgeben

conceit [kən'si:t] n Einbildung f; ~ed adj eingebildet

conceivable [kən'si:vəbl] adj vorstellbar

conceive [kən'si:v] vt (idea) ausdenken; (imagine) sich vorstellen; (baby) empfangen ♦ vi empfangen

concentrate ['konsəntreɪt] vi sich konzentrieren ♦ vt konzentrieren; to ~ on sth sich auf etw acc konzentrieren;

concentration [kɔnsən'treɪʃən] n
Konzentration f; **concentration camp** n
Konzentrationslager nt, KZ nt

concept ['kɔnsept] n Begriff m

conception [kən'sepʃən] n (idea) Vorstellung
f; (BIOL) Empfängnis f

concern [kən'sə:n] n (affair) Angelegenheit
f; (COMM) Unternehmen nt; (worry) Sorge f
♦ vt (interest) angehen; (be about) handeln
von; (have connection with) betreffen; **to be
~ed (about)** sich Sorgen machen (um);
~ing prep hinsichtlich +gen

concert ['kɔnsət] n Konzert nt

concerted [kən'sə:tɪd] adj gemeinsam

concert hall n Konzerthalle f

concertina [kɔnsə'ti:nə] n Handharmonika f

concerto [kən'tʃə:təu] n Konzert nt

concession [kən'seʃən] n (yielding)
Zugeständnis nt; **tax ~** Steuerkonzession f

conciliation [kənsɪlɪ'eɪʃən] n Versöhnung f;
(official) Schlichtung f

concise [kən'saɪs] adj präzis

conclude [kən'klu:d] vt (end) beenden;
(treaty) (ab)schließen; (decide) schließen,
folgern; **conclusion** [kən'klu:ʒən] n
(Ab)schluss m; (deduction) Schluss m;
conclusive [kən'klu:sɪv] adj schlüssig

concoct [kən'kɔkt] vt zusammenbrauen;
~ion [kən'kɔkʃən] n Gebräu nt

concourse ['kɔŋkɔ:s] n (Bahnhofs)halle f,
Vorplatz m

concrete ['kɔŋkri:t] n Beton m ♦ adj konkret

concur [kən'kə:r] vi übereinstimmen

concurrently [kən'kʌrntlɪ] adv gleichzeitig

concussion [kən'kʌʃən] n
(Gehirn)erschütterung f

condemn [kən'dem] vt (JUR) verurteilen;
(building) abbruchreif erklären

condensation [kɔndən'seɪʃən] n
Kondensation f

condense [kən'dens] vi (CHEM)
kondensieren ♦ vt (fig) zusammendrängen;
~d milk n Kondensmilch f

condescending [kɔndɪ'sendɪŋ] adj
herablassend

condition [kən'dɪʃən] n (state) Zustand m;
(presupposition) Bedingung f ♦ vt (hair etc)

behandeln; (accustom) gewöhnen; **~s** npl
(circumstances) Verhältnisse pl; **on ~ that ...**
unter der Bedingung, dass ...; **~al** adj
bedingt; **~er** n (for hair) Spülung f; (for
fabrics) Weichspüler m

condolences [kən'dəulənsɪz] npl Beileid nt

condom ['kɔndəm] n Kondom nt or m

condominium [kɔndə'mɪnɪəm] (US) n
Eigentumswohnung f; (block)
Eigentumsblock m

condone [kən'dəun] vt gutheißen

conducive [kən'dju:sɪv] adj: **~ to** dienlich
+dat

conduct [n 'kɔndʌkt, vb kən'dʌkt] n
(behaviour) Verhalten nt; (management)
Führung f ♦ vt führen; (MUS) dirigieren;
~ed tour n Führung f; **~or** [kən'dʌktər] n
(of orchestra) Dirigent m; (in bus, US: on
train) Schaffner m; (ELEC) Leiter m; **~ress**
[kən'dʌktrɪs] n (in bus) Schaffnerin f

cone [kəun] n (MATH) Kegel m; (for ice cream)
(Waffel)tüte f; (BOT) Tannenzapfen m

confectioner's (shop) [kən'fekʃənəz-] n
Konditorei f; **~y** [kən'fekʃənrɪ] n Süßigkeiten
pl

confederation [kənfedə'reɪʃən] n Bund m

confer [kən'fə:r] vt (degree) verleihen ♦ vi
(discuss) konferieren, verhandeln; **~ence**
['kɔnfərəns] n Konferenz f

confess [kən'fes] vt, vi gestehen; (ECCL)
beichten; **~ion** [kən'feʃən] n Geständnis nt;
(ECCL) Beichte f; **~ional** n Beichtstuhl m

confide [kən'faɪd] vi: **to ~ in** (sich)
anvertrauen +dat

confidence ['kɔnfɪdns] n Vertrauen nt;
(assurance) Selbstvertrauen nt; (secret)
Geheimnis nt; **in ~** (speak, write) vertraulich;
~ trick n Schwindel m

confident ['kɔnfɪdənt] adj (sure) überzeugt;
(self-assured) selbstsicher

confidential [kɔnfɪ'denʃəl] adj vertraulich

confine [kən'faɪn] vt (limit) beschränken;
(lock up) einsperren; **~d** adj (space) eng;
~ment n (in prison) Haft f; (MED)
Wochenbett nt; **~s** ['kɔnfaɪnz] npl Grenzen
pl

confirm [kən'fə:m] vt bestätigen; **~ation**

[konfə'meɪʃən] n Bestätigung f; (REL) Konfirmation f; **~ed** adj unverbesserlich; (bachelor) eingefleischt

confiscate ['konfɪskeɪt] vt beschlagnahmen

conflict [n 'konflɪkt, vb kən'flɪkt] n Konflikt m ♦ vi im Widerspruch stehen; **~ing** [kən'flɪktɪŋ] adj widersprüchlich

conform [kən'fɔːm] vi: **to ~ (to)** (things) entsprechen +dat; (people) sich anpassen +dat; (to rules) sich richten (nach)

confound [kən'faund] vt verblüffen; (confuse) durcheinander bringen

confront [kən'frʌnt] vt (enemy) entgegentreten +dat; (problems) sich stellen +dat; **to ~ sb with sth** jdn mit etw konfrontieren; **~ation** [konfrən'teɪʃən] n Konfrontation f

confuse [kən'fjuːz] vt verwirren; (sth with sth) verwechseln; **~d** adj verwirrt; **confusing** adj verwirrend; **confusion** [kən'fjuːʒən] n (perplexity) Verwirrung f; (mixing up) Verwechslung f; (tumult) Aufruhr m

congeal [kən'dʒiːl] vi (freeze) gefrieren; (clot) gerinnen

congested [kən'dʒestɪd] adj überfüllt

congestion [kən'dʒestʃən] n Stau m

conglomerate [kən'glɔmərɪt] n (COMM, GEOL) Konglomerat nt

conglomeration [kənglɔmə'reɪʃən] n Anhäufung f

congratulate [kən'grætjuleɪt] vt: **to ~ sb (on sth)** jdn (zu etw) beglückwünschen; **congratulations** [kəngrætju'leɪʃənz] npl Glückwünsche pl; **congratulations!** gratuliere!, herzlichen Glückwunsch!

congregate ['kɔŋgrɪgeɪt] vi sich versammeln; **congregation** [kɔŋgrɪ'geɪʃən] n Gemeinde f

congress ['kɔŋgres] n Kongress m; **C~man** (irreg: US) n Mitglied nt des amerikanischen Repräsentantenhauses

conifer ['kɔnɪfə'] n Nadelbaum m

conjunction [kən'dʒʌŋkʃən] n Verbindung f; (GRAM) Konjunktion f

conjunctivitis [kəndʒʌŋktɪ'vaɪtɪs] n Bindehautentzündung f

conjure ['kʌndʒə'] vi zaubern; **~ up** vt heraufbeschwören; **~r** n Zauberkünstler(in) m(f)

conk out [kɔŋk-] (inf) vi den Geist aufgeben

con man (irreg) n Schwindler m

connect [kə'nekt] vt verbinden; (ELEC) anschließen; **to be ~ed with** eine Beziehung haben zu; (be related to) verwandt sein mit; **~ion** [kə'nekʃən] n Verbindung f; (relation) Zusammenhang m; (ELEC, TEL, RAIL) Anschluss m

connive [kə'naɪv] vi: **to ~ at** stillschweigend dulden

connoisseur [kɔnɪ'səː'] n Kenner m

conquer ['kɔŋkə'] vt (feelings) überwinden; (enemy) besiegen; (country) erobern; **~or** n Eroberer m

conquest ['kɔŋkwest] n Eroberung f

cons [kɔnz] npl see **convenience**; **pro**

conscience ['kɔnʃəns] n Gewissen nt

conscientious [kɔnʃɪ'enʃəs] adj gewissenhaft

conscious ['kɔnʃəs] adj bewusst; (MED) bei Bewusstsein; **~ness** n Bewusstsein nt

conscript ['kɔnskrɪpt] n Wehrpflichtige(r) m; **~ion** [kən'skrɪpʃən] n Wehrpflicht f

consecutive [kən'sekjutɪv] adj aufeinander folgend

consensus [kən'sensəs] n allgemeine Übereinstimmung f

consent [kən'sent] n Zustimmung f ♦ vi zustimmen

consequence ['kɔnsɪkwəns] n (importance) Bedeutung f; (effect) Folge f

consequently ['kɔnsɪkwəntlɪ] adv folglich

conservation [kɔnsə'veɪʃən] n Erhaltung f; (nature ~) Umweltschutz m

conservative [kən'səːvətɪv] adj konservativ; **C~** (BRIT) adj konservativ ♦ n Konservative(r) mf

conservatory [kən'səːvətrɪ] n (room) Wintergarten m

conserve [kən'səːv] vt erhalten

consider [kən'sɪdə'] vt überlegen; (take into account) in Betracht ziehen; (regard as) halten für; **to ~ doing sth** daran denken, etw zu tun; **~able** [kən'sɪdərəbl] adj betrachtlich; **~ably** *adv* beträchtlich; **~ate** *adj* rücksichtsvoll; **~ation** [kənsɪdəˈreɪʃən] *n* Rücksicht(nahme) *f*; (*thought*) Erwägung *f*; **~ing** *prep* in Anbetracht *+gen*

consign [kənˈsaɪn] *vt* übergeben; **~ment** *n* Sendung *f*

consist [kənˈsɪst] *vi*: **to ~ of** bestehen aus

consistency [kənˈsɪstənsɪ] *n* (*of material*) Konsistenz *f*; (*of argument, person*) Konsequenz *f*

consistent [kənˈsɪstənt] *adj* (*person*) konsequent; (*argument*) folgerichtig

consolation [kɒnsəˈleɪʃən] *n* Trost *m*

console¹ [kənˈsəʊl] *vt* trösten

console² [ˈkɒnsəʊl] *n* Kontroll(pult) *nt*

consolidate [kənˈsɒlɪdeɪt] *vt* festigen

consommé [kənˈsɒmeɪ] *n* Fleischbrühe *f*

consonant [ˈkɒnsənənt] *n* Konsonant *m*, Mitlaut *m*

conspicuous [kənˈspɪkjʊəs] *adj* (*prominent*) auffällig; (*visible*) deutlich sichtbar

conspiracy [kənˈspɪrəsɪ] *n* Verschwörung *f*

conspire [kənˈspaɪəʳ] *vi* sich verschwören

constable [ˈkʌnstəbl] (*BRIT*) *n* Polizist(in) *m(f)*; **chief ~** Polizeipräsident *m*; **constabulary** [kənˈstæbjʊlərɪ] *n* Polizei *f*

constant [ˈkɒnstənt] *adj* (*continuous*) ständig; (*unchanging*) konstant; **~ly** *adv* ständig

constellation [kɒnstəˈleɪʃən] *n* Sternbild *nt*

consternation [kɒnstəˈneɪʃən] *n* Bestürzung *f*

constipated [ˈkɒnstɪpeɪtɪd] *adj* verstopft; **constipation** [kɒnstɪˈpeɪʃən] *n* Verstopfung *f*

constituency [kənˈstɪtjʊənsɪ] *n* Wahlkreis *m*

constituent [kənˈstɪtjʊənt] *n* (*person*) Wähler *m*; (*part*) Bestandteil *m*

constitute [ˈkɒnstɪtjuːt] *vt* (*make up*) bilden; (*amount to*) darstellen

constitution [kɒnstɪˈtjuːʃən] *n* Verfassung *f*; **~al** *adj* Verfassungs-

constraint [kənˈstreɪnt] *n* Zwang *m*; (*shyness*) Befangenheit *f*

construct [kənˈstrʌkt] *vt* bauen; **~ion** [kənˈstrʌkʃən] *n* Konstruktion *f*; (*building*) Bau *m*; **~ive** *adj* konstruktiv

construe [kənˈstruː] *vt* deuten

consul [ˈkɒnsl] *n* Konsul *m*; **~ate** *n* Konsulat *nt*

consult [kənˈsʌlt] *vt* um Rat fragen; (*doctor*) konsultieren; (*book*) nachschlagen in *+dat*; **~ant** *n* (*MED*) Facharzt *m*; (*other specialist*) Gutachter *m*; **~ation** [kɒnsəlˈteɪʃən] *n* Beratung *f*; (*MED*) Konsultation *f*; **~ing room** *n* Sprechzimmer *nt*

consume [kənˈsjuːm] *vt* verbrauchen; (*food*) konsumieren; **~r** *n* Verbraucher *m*; **~r goods** *npl* Konsumgüter *pl*; **~rism** *n* Konsum *m*; **~r society** *n* Konsumgesellschaft *f*

consumption [kənˈsʌmpʃən] *n* Verbrauch *m*; (*of food*) Konsum *m*

cont. *abbr* (= *continued*) Forts.

contact [ˈkɒntækt] *n* (*touch*) Berührung *f*; (*connection*) Verbindung *f*; (*person*) Kontakt *m* ♦ *vt* sich in Verbindung setzen mit; **~ lenses** *npl* Kontaktlinsen *pl*

contagious [kənˈteɪdʒəs] *adj* ansteckend

contain [kənˈteɪn] *vt* enthalten; **to ~ o.s.** sich zügeln; **~er** *n* Behälter *m*; (*transport*) Container *m*

contaminate [kənˈtæmɪneɪt] *vt* verunreinigen

cont'd *abbr* (= *continued*) Forts.

contemplate [ˈkɒntəmpleɪt] *vt* (*look at*) (nachdenklich) betrachten; (*think about*) überdenken; (*plan*) vorhaben

contemporary [kənˈtempərərɪ] *adj* zeitgenössisch ♦ *n* Zeitgenosse *m*

contempt [kənˈtempt] *n* Verachtung *f*; **~ of court** (*JUR*) Missachtung *f* des Gerichts; **~ible** *adj* verachtenswert; **~uous** *adj* verächtlich

contend [kənˈtend] *vt* (*argue*) behaupten ♦ *vi* kämpfen; **~er** *n* (*for post*) Bewerber(in) *m(f)*; (*SPORT*) Wettkämpfer(in) *m(f)*

content [*adj, vb* kənˈtent, *n* ˈkɒntent] *adj* zufrieden ♦ *vt* befriedigen ♦ *n* (*also:* **~s**) Inhalt *m*; **~ed** *adj* zufrieden

contention [kənˈtenʃən] *n* (*dispute*) Streit *m*; (*argument*) Behauptung *f*

contentment [kənˈtentmənt] *n* Zufriedenheit f

contest [n 'kɒntest, vb kən'test] n (Wett)kampf m ♦ vt (dispute) bestreiten; (JUR) anfechten; (POL) kandidieren in +dat; **~ant** [kən'testənt] n Bewerber(in) m(f)

context ['kɒntekst] n Zusammenhang m

continent ['kɒntɪnənt] n Kontinent m; **the C~** (BRIT) das europäische Festland; **~al** [kɒntɪ'nentl] adj kontinental; **~al breakfast** n kleines Frühstück nt; **~al quilt** (BRIT) n Federbett nt

contingency [kən'tɪndʒənsɪ] n Möglichkeit f

contingent [kən'tɪndʒənt] n Kontingent nt

continual [kən'tɪnjuəl] adj (endless) fortwährend; (repeated) immer wiederkehrend; **~ly** adv immer wieder

continuation [kəntɪnju'eɪʃən] n Fortsetzung f

continue [kən'tɪnjuː] vi (person) weitermachen; (thing) weitergehen ♦ vt fortsetzen

continuity [kɒntɪ'njuːɪtɪ] n Kontinuität f

continuous [kən'tɪnjuəs] adj ununterbrochen; **~ stationery** n Endlospapier nt

contort [kən'tɔːt] vt verdrehen; **~ion** [kən'tɔːʃən] n Verzerrung f

contour ['kɒntuə'] n Umriss m; (also: **~ line**) Höhenlinie f

contraband ['kɒntrəbænd] n Schmuggelware f

contraception [kɒntrə'sepʃən] n Empfängnisverhütung f

contraceptive [kɒntrə'septɪv] n empfängnisverhütende(s) Mittel nt ♦ adj empfängnisverhütend

contract [n 'kɒntrækt, vb kən'trækt] n Vertrag m ♦ vi (muscle, metal) sich zusammenziehen ♦ vt zusammenziehen; **to ~ to do sth** (COMM) sich vertraglich verpflichten, etw zu tun; **~ion** [kən'trækʃən] n (shortening) Verkürzung f; **~or** [kən'træktə'] n Unternehmer m

contradict [kɒntrə'dɪkt] vt widersprechen +dat; **~ion** [kɒntrə'dɪkʃən] n Widerspruch m

contraflow ['kɒntrəfləʊ] n (AUT) Gegenverkehr m

contraption [kən'træpʃən] (inf) n Apparat m

contrary¹ ['kɒntrərɪ] adj (opposite) entgegengesetzt ♦ n Gegenteil nt; **on the ~** im Gegenteil

contrary² [kən'treərɪ] adj (obstinate) widerspenstig

contrast [n 'kɒntrɑːst, vb kən'trɑːst] n Kontrast m ♦ vt entgegensetzen; **~ing** [kən'trɑːstɪŋ] adj Kontrast-

contravene [kɒntrə'viːn] vt verstoßen gegen

contribute [kən'trɪbjuːt] vt, vi: **to ~ to** beitragen zu; **contribution** [kɒntrɪ'bjuːʃən] n Beitrag m; **contributor** [kən'trɪbjutə'] n Beitragende(r) f(m)

contrive [kən'traɪv] vt ersinnen ♦ vi: **to ~ to do sth** es schaffen, etw zu tun

control [kən'trəʊl] vt (direct, test) kontrollieren ♦ n Kontrolle f; **~s** npl (of vehicle) Steuerung f; (of engine) Schalttafel f; **to be in ~ of** (business, office) leiten; (group of children) beaufsichtigen; **out of ~** außer Kontrolle; **under ~** unter Kontrolle; **~led substance** n verschreibungspflichtiges Medikament; **~ panel** n Schalttafel f; **~ room** n Kontrollraum m; **~ tower** n (AVIAT) Kontrollturm m

controversial [kɒntrə'vɜːʃl] adj umstritten; **controversy** ['kɒntrəvɜːsɪ] n Kontroverse f

conurbation [kɒnə'beɪʃən] n Ballungsgebiet nt

convalesce [kɒnvə'les] vi genesen; **convalescence** [kɒnvə'lesns] n Genesung f

convector [kən'vektə'] n Heizlüfter m

convene [kən'viːn] vt zusammenrufen ♦ vi sich versammeln

convenience [kən'viːnɪəns] n Annehmlichkeit f; **all modern ~s** or (BRIT) **mod cons** mit allem Komfort; **at your ~** wann es Ihnen passt

convenient [kən'viːnɪənt] adj günstig

convent ['kɒnvənt] n Kloster nt

convention [kən'venʃən] n Versammlung f; (custom) Konvention f; **~al** adj konventionell

convent school n Klosterschule f

converge [kən'vɜːdʒ] vi zusammenlaufen

conversant [kən'vɜːsnt] *adj*: **to be ~ with** bewandert sein in +*dat*

conversation [kɔnvə'seɪʃən] *n* Gespräch *nt*; **~al** *adj* Unterhaltungs-

converse [*n* 'kɔnvɜːs, *vb* kən'vɜːs] *n* Gegenteil *nt* ♦ *vi* sich unterhalten

conversion [kən'vɜːʃən] *n* Umwandlung *f*; (REL) Bekehrung *f*

convert [*vb* kən'vɜːt, *n* 'kɔnvɜːt] *vt* (*change*) umwandeln; (REL) bekehren ♦ *n* Bekehrte(r) *mf*; **~ible** *n* (AUT) Kabriolett *nt* ♦ *adj* umwandelbar; (FIN) konvertierbar

convex ['kɔnveks] *adj* konvex

convey [kən'veɪ] *vt* (*carry*) befördern; (*feelings*) vermitteln; **~or belt** *n* Fließband *nt*

convict [*vb* kən'vɪkt, *n* 'kɔnvɪkt] *vt* verurteilen ♦ *n* Häftling *m*; **~ion** [kən'vɪkʃən] *n* Verurteilung *f*; (*belief*) Überzeugung *f*

convince [kən'vɪns] *vt* überzeugen; **~d** *adj*: **~d that** überzeugt davon, dass; **convincing** *adj* überzeugend

convoluted ['kɔnvəluːtɪd] *adj* verwickelt; (*style*) gewunden

convoy ['kɔnvɔɪ] *n* (*of vehicles*) Kolonne *f*; (*protected*) Konvoi *m*

convulse [kən'vʌls] *vt* zusammenzucken lassen; **to be ~d with laughter** sich vor Lachen krümmen; **convulsion** [kən'vʌlʃən] *n* (*esp* MED) Zuckung *f*, Krampf *m*

coo [kuː] *vi* gurren

cook [kuk] *vt*, *vi* kochen ♦ *n* Koch *m*, Köchin *f*; **~ book** *n* Kochbuch *nt*; **~er** *n* Herd *m*; **~ery** *n* Kochkunst *f*; **~ery book** (BRIT) *n* = **cook book**; **~ie** (US) *n* Plätzchen *nt*; **~ing** *n* Kochen *nt*

cool [kuːl] *adj* kühl ♦ *vt*, *vi* (ab)kühlen; **~ down** *vt*, *vi* (*fig*) (sich) beruhigen; **~ness** *n* Kühle *f*; (*of temperature*) kühle(r) Kopf *m*

coop [kuːp] *n* Hühnerstall *m* ♦ *vt*: **~ up** (*fig*) einpferchen

cooperate [kəu'ɔpəreɪt] *vi* zusammenarbeiten; **cooperation** [kəuɔpə'reɪʃən] *n* Zusammenarbeit *f*

cooperative [kəu'ɔpərətɪv] *adj* hilfsbereit; (COMM) genossenschaftlich ♦ *n* (*of farmers*) Genossenschaft *f*; (~ *store*) Konsumladen *m*

coordinate [*vb* kəu'ɔːdɪneɪt, *n* kəu'ɔːdɪnɪt] *vt* koordinieren ♦ *n* (MATH) Koordinate *f*; **~s** *npl* (*clothes*) Kombinationen *pl*; **coordination** [kəuɔːdɪ'neɪʃən] *n* Koordination *f*

cop [kɔp] (*inf*) *n* Polyp *m*, Bulle *m*

cope [kəup] *vi*: **to ~ with** fertig werden mit

copious ['kəupɪəs] *adj* reichhaltig

copper ['kɔpə*] *n* (*metal*) Kupfer *nt*; (*inf*: *policeman*) Polyp *m*, Bulle *m*; **~s** *npl* (*money*) Kleingeld *nt*

copse [kɔps] *n* Unterholz *nt*

copy ['kɔpɪ] *n* (*imitation*) Kopie *f*; (*of book etc*) Exemplar *nt*; (*of newspaper*) Nummer *f* ♦ *vt* kopieren, abschreiben; **~right** *n* Copyright *nt*

coral ['kɔrəl] *n* Koralle *f*; **~ reef** *n* Korallenriff *nt*

cord [kɔːd] *n* Schnur *f*; (ELEC) Kabel *nt*

cordial ['kɔːdɪəl] *adj* herzlich ♦ *n* Fruchtsaft *m*

cordon ['kɔːdn] *n* Absperrkette *f*; **~ off** *vt* abriegeln

corduroy ['kɔːdərɔɪ] *n* Kord(samt) *m*

core [kɔː*] *n* Kern *m* ♦ *vt* entkernen

cork [kɔːk] *n* (*bark*) Korkrinde *f*; (*stopper*) Korken *m*; **~screw** *n* Korkenzieher *m*

corn [kɔːn] *n* (BRIT: *wheat*) Getreide *nt*, Korn *nt*; (US: *maize*) Mais *m*; (*on foot*) Hühnerauge *nt*; **~ on the cob** Maiskolben *m*

corned beef ['kɔːnd-] *n* Cornedbeef *nt*, Corned Beef *nt*

corner ['kɔːnə*] *n* Ecke *f*; (*on road*) Kurve *f* ♦ *vt* in die Enge treiben; (*market*) monopolisieren ♦ *vi* (AUT) in die Kurve gehen; **~stone** *n* Eckstein *m*

cornet ['kɔːnɪt] *n* (MUS) Kornett *nt*; (BRIT: *of ice cream*) Eistüte *f*

corn: **~flakes** ['kɔːnfleɪks] *npl* Cornflakes *pl* ®; **~flour** ['kɔːnflauə*] (BRIT) *n* Maizena *nt* ®; **~starch** ['kɔːnstɑːtʃ] (US) *n* Maizena *nt* ®

corny ['kɔːnɪ] *adj* (*joke*) blöd(e)

coronary ['kɔrənərɪ] *n* (*also:* **~ thrombosis**) Herzinfarkt *m*

coronation [kɔrəˈneɪʃən] n Krönung f

coroner [ˈkɔrənər] n Untersuchungsrichter m

corporal [ˈkɔːpərl] n Obergefreite(r) m ♦ adj: ~ punishment Prügelstrafe f

corporate [ˈkɔːpərɪt] adj gemeinschaftlich, korporativ

corporation [kɔːpəˈreɪʃən] n (of town) Gemeinde f; (COMM) Körperschaft f, Aktiengesellschaft f

corps [kɔːr] (pl ~) n (Armee)korps nt

corpse [kɔːps] n Leiche f

corral [kɔˈrɑːl] n Pferch m, Korral m

correct [kəˈrekt] adj (accurate) richtig; (proper) korrekt ♦ vt korrigieren; ~ion [kəˈrekʃən] n Berichtigung f

correlation [kɔrɪˈleɪʃən] n Wechselbeziehung f

correspond [kɔrɪsˈpɔnd] vi (agree) übereinstimmen; (exchange letters) korrespondieren; ~ence (similarity) Entsprechung f; (letters) Briefwechsel m, Korrespondenz f; ~ence course n Fernkurs m; ~ent n (PRESS) Berichterstatter m

corridor [ˈkɔrɪdɔːr] n Gang m

corroborate [kəˈrɔbəreɪt] vt bestätigen

corrode [kəˈrəud] vt zerfressen ♦ vi rosten

corrosion [kəˈrəuʒən] n Korrosion f

corrugated [ˈkɔrəgeɪtɪd] adj gewellt; ~ iron n Wellblech nt

corrupt [kəˈrʌpt] adj korrupt ♦ vt verderben; (bribe) bestechen; ~ion [kəˈrʌpʃən] n Verdorbenheit f; (bribery) Bestechung f

corset [ˈkɔːsɪt] n Korsett nt

Corsica [ˈkɔːsɪkə] n Korsika nt

cosmetics [kɔzˈmetɪks] npl Kosmetika pl

cosmic [ˈkɔzmɪk] adj kosmisch

cosmonaut [ˈkɔzmənɔːt] n Kosmonaut(in) m(f)

cosmopolitan [kɔzməˈpɔlɪtn] adj international; (city) Welt-

cosmos [ˈkɔzmɔs] n Kosmos m

cost [kɔst] (pt, pp cost) n Kosten pl, Preis m ♦ vt, vi kosten; ~s npl (JUR) Kosten pl; how much does it ~? wie viel kostet das?; at all ~s um jeden Preis

co-star [ˈkəustɑːr] n zweite(r) or weitere(r)

Hauptdarsteller(in) m(f)

cost: ~-effective adj rentabel; ~ly [ˈkɔstlɪ] adj kostspielig; ~-of-living [ˈkɔstəvˈlɪvɪŋ] adj (index) Lebenshaltungskosten-; ~ price (BRIT) n Selbstkostenpreis m

costume [ˈkɔstjuːm] n Kostüm nt; (fancy dress) Maskenkostüm m; (BRIT: also: swimming ~) Badeanzug m; ~ jewellery n Modeschmuck m

cosy [ˈkəuzɪ] (BRIT) adj behaglich; (atmosphere) gemütlich

cot [kɔt] n (BRIT: child's) Kinderbett(chen) nt; (US: camp bed) Feldbett nt

cottage [ˈkɔtɪdʒ] n kleine(s) Haus nt; ~ cheese n Hüttenkäse m; ~ industry n Heimindustrie f; ~ pie n Auflauf mit Hackfleisch und Kartoffelbrei

cotton [ˈkɔtn] n Baumwolle f; (thread) Garn nt; ~ on to (inf) vt kapieren; ~ candy (US) n Zuckerwatte f; ~ wool (BRIT) n Watte f

couch [kautʃ] n Couch f

couchette [kuːˈʃet] n (on train, boat) Liegewagenplatz m

cough [kɔf] vi husten ♦ n Husten m; ~ drop n Hustenbonbon m

could [kud] pt of can[2]

couldn't [ˈkudnt] = could not

council [ˈkaunsl] n (of town) Stadtrat m; ~ estate (BRIT) n Siedlung f des sozialen Wohnungsbaus; ~ house (BRIT) n Haus nt des sozialen Wohnungsbaus; ~lor [ˈkaunslər] n Stadtrat m/-rätin f

counsel [ˈkaunsl] n (barrister) Anwalt m; (advice) Rat(schlag) m ♦ vt beraten; ~lor [ˈkaunslər] n Berater m

count [kaunt] vt, vi zählen ♦ n (reckoning) Abrechnung f; (nobleman) Graf m; ~ on vt zählen auf +acc

countenance [ˈkauntɪnəns] n (old) Antlitz nt ♦ vt (tolerate) gutheißen

counter [ˈkauntər] n (in shop) Ladentisch m; (in café) Theke f; (in bank, post office) Schalter m ♦ vt entgegnen

counteract [ˈkauntərˈækt] vt entgegenwirken +dat

counterfeit [ˈkauntəfɪt] n Fälschung f ♦ vt fälschen ♦ adj gefälscht

counterfoil ['kauntəfɔɪl] *n* (Kontroll)abschnitt *m*

counterpart ['kauntəpɑːt] *n* (*object*) Gegenstück *nt*; (*person*) Gegenüber *nt*

counterproductive ['kauntəprə'dʌktɪv] *adj* destruktiv

countersign ['kauntəsaɪn] *vt* gegenzeichnen

countess ['kauntɪs] *n* Gräfin *f*

countless ['kauntlɪs] *adj* zahllos, unzählig

country ['kʌntrɪ] *n* Land *nt*; **~ dancing** (*BRIT*) *n* Volkstanz *m*; **~ house** *n* Landhaus *nt*; **~man** (*irreg*) *n* (*national*) Landsmann *m*; (*rural*) Bauer *m*; **~side** *n* Landschaft *f*

county ['kauntɪ] *n* Landkreis *m*; (*BRIT*) Grafschaft *f*

coup [kuː] (*pl* **~s**) *n* Coup *m*; (*also*: **~ d'état**) Staatsstreich *m*, Putsch *m*

couple ['kʌpl] *n* Paar *nt* ♦ *vt* koppeln; **a ~ of** ein paar

coupon ['kuːpɔn] *n* Gutschein *m*

coups [kuː] *npl of* **coup**

courage ['kʌrɪdʒ] *n* Mut *m*; **~ous** [kə'reɪdʒəs] *adj* mutig

courgette [kuə'ʒet] (*BRIT*) *n* Zucchini *f or pl*

courier ['kurɪə'] *n* (*for holiday*) Reiseleiter *m*; (*messenger*) Kurier *m*

course [kɔːs] *n* (*race*) Bahn *f*; (*of stream*) Lauf *m*; (*golf ~*) Platz *m*; (*NAUT, SCH*) Kurs *m*; (*in meal*) Gang *m*; **of ~** natürlich

court [kɔːt] *n* (*royal*) Hof *m*; (*JUR*) Gericht *nt* ♦ *vt* (*woman*) gehen mit; (*danger*) herausfordern; **to take to ~** vor Gericht bringen

courteous ['kəːtɪəs] *adj* höflich

courtesy ['kəːtəsɪ] *n* Höflichkeit *f*

courtesy bus, courtesy coach *n* gebührenfreier Bus *m*

court: ~ house (*US*) *n* Gerichtsgebäude *nt*; **~ier** ['kɔːtɪə'] *n* Höfling *m*; **~ martial** ['kɔːt'mɑːʃəl] (*pl* **~s martial**) *n* Kriegsgericht *nt* ♦ *vt* vor ein Kriegsgericht stellen; **~room** *n* Gerichtssaal *m*; **~s martial** *npl of* **court martial**; **~yard** ['kɔːtjɑːd] *n* Hof *m*

cousin ['kʌzn] *n* Cousin *m*, Vetter *m*; Kusine *f*

cove [kəuv] *n* kleine Bucht *f*

covenant ['kʌvənənt] *n* (*ECCL*) Bund *m*; (*JUR*) Verpflichtung *f*

cover ['kʌvə'] *vt* (*spread over*) bedecken; (*shield*) abschirmen; (*include*) sich erstrecken über +*acc*; (*protect*) decken; (*distance*) zurücklegen; (*report on*) berichten über +*acc* ♦ *n* (*lid*) Deckel *m*; (*for bed*) Decke *f*; (*MIL*) Bedeckung *f*; (*of book*) Einband *m*; (*of magazine*) Umschlag *m*; (*insurance*) Versicherung *f*; **to take ~** (*from rain*) sich unterstellen; (*MIL*) in Deckung gehen; **under ~** (*indoors*) drinnen; **under ~ of** im Schutze +*gen*; **under separate ~** (*COMM*) mit getrennter Post; **to ~ up for sb** jdn decken; **~age** *n* (*PRESS: reports*) Berichterstattung *f*; (*distribution*) Verbreitung *f*; **~ charge** *n* Bedienungsgeld *nt*; **~ing** *n* Bedeckung *f*; **~ing letter** (*US* **~ letter**) *n* Begleitbrief *m*; **~ note** *n* (*INSURANCE*) vorläufige(r) Versicherungsschein *m*

covert ['kʌvət] *adj* geheim

cover-up ['kʌvərʌp] *n* Vertuschung *f*

cow [kau] *n* Kuh *f* ♦ *vt* einschüchtern

coward ['kauəd] *n* Feigling *m*; **~ice** ['kauədɪs] *n* Feigheit *f*; **~ly** *adj* feige

cower ['kauə'] *vi* kauern

coy [kɔɪ] *adj* schüchtern

coyote [kɔɪ'əutɪ] *n* Präriewolf *m*

cozy ['kəuzɪ] (*US*) *adj* = **cosy**

CPA (*US*) *n abbr* = **certified public accountant**

crab [kræb] *n* Krebs *m*

crab apple *n* Holzapfel *m*

crack [kræk] *n* Riss *m*, Sprung *m*; (*noise*) Knall *m*; (*drug*) Crack *nt* ♦ *vt* (*break*) springen lassen; (*joke*) reißen; (*nut, safe*) knacken; (*whip*) knallen lassen ♦ *vi* springen ♦ *adj* erstklassig; Elite-; **~ down** *vi*: **to ~ down (on)** hart durchgreifen (bei); **~ up** *vi* (*fig*) zusammenbrechen

cracked [krækt] *adj* (*glass, plate, ice*) gesprungen; (*rib, bone*) gebrochen, angeknackst (*umg*); (*broken*) gebrochen; (*surface, walls*) rissig; (*inf: mad*) übergeschnappt

cracker ['krækə'] *n* (*firework*) Knallkörper *m*, Kracher *m*; (*biscuit*) Keks *m*; (*Christmas ~*)

Knallbonbon nt

crackle ['krækl] vi knistern; (fire) prasseln

cradle ['kreɪdl] n Wiege f

craft [krɑ:ft] n (skill) (Hand- or Kunst)fertigkeit f; (trade) Handwerk nt; (NAUT) Schiff nt; ~sman (irreg) n Handwerker m; ~smanship n (quality) handwerkliche Ausführung f; (ability) handwerkliche(s) Können nt

crafty ['krɑ:ftɪ] adj schlau

crag [kræg] n Klippe f

cram [kræm] vt voll stopfen ♦ vi (learn) pauken; **to ~ sth into sth** etw in etw acc stopfen

cramp [kræmp] n Krampf m ♦ vt (limit) einengen; (hinder) hemmen; ~ed adj (position) verkrampft; (space) eng

crampon ['kræmpən] n Steigeisen nt

cranberry ['krænbərɪ] n Preiselbeere f

crane [kreɪn] n (machine) Kran m; (bird) Kranich m

crank [kræŋk] n (lever) Kurbel f; (person) Spinner m; ~shaft n Kurbelwelle f

cranny ['krænɪ] n see **nook**

crash [kræʃ] n (noise) Krachen nt; (with cars) Zusammenstoß m; (with plane) Absturz m; (COMM) Zusammenbruch m ♦ vt (plane) abstürzen mit ♦ vi (cars) zusammenstoßen; (plane) abstürzen; (economy) zusammenbrechen; (noise) knallen; ~ course n Schnellkurs m; ~ helmet n Sturzhelm m; ~ landing n Bruchlandung f

crass [kræs] adj krass

crate [kreɪt] n (also fig) Kiste f

crater ['kreɪtər] n Krater m

cravat(e) [krə'væt] n Halstuch nt

crave [kreɪv] vt verlangen nach

crawl [krɔ:l] vi kriechen; (baby) krabbeln ♦ n Kriechen nt; (swim) Kraul nt

crayfish ['kreɪfɪʃ] n inv (freshwater) Krebs m; (saltwater) Languste f

crayon ['kreɪən] n Buntstift m

craze [kreɪz] n Fimmel m

crazy ['kreɪzɪ] adj verrückt

creak [kri:k] vi knarren

cream [kri:m] n (from milk) Rahm m, Sahne f; (polish, cosmetic) Creme f; (fig: people)

Elite f ♦ adj cremefarbig; ~ **cake** n Sahnetorte f; ~ **cheese** n Rahmquark m; ~**y** adj sahnig

crease [kri:s] n Falte f ♦ vt falten; (wrinkle) zerknittern ♦ vi (wrinkle up) knittern; ~**d** adj zerknittert, faltig

create [kri:'eɪt] vt erschaffen; (cause) verursachen; **creation** [kri:'eɪʃən] n Schöpfung f; **creative** adj kreativ; **creator** n Schöpfer m

creature ['kri:tʃər] n Geschöpf nt

crèche [kreʃ] n Krippe f

credence ['kri:dns] n: **to lend** or **give ~ to sth** etw dat Glauben schenken

credentials [krɪ'denʃlz] npl Beglaubigungsschreiben nt

credibility [kredɪ'bɪlɪtɪ] n Glaubwürdigkeit f

credible ['kredɪbl] adj (person) glaubwürdig; (story) glaubhaft

credit ['kredɪt] n (also COMM) Kredit m ♦ vt Glauben schenken +dat; (COMM) gutschreiben; ~**s** npl (of film) Mitwirkenden pl; ~**able** adj rühmlich; ~ **card** n Kreditkarte f; ~**or** n Gläubiger m

creed [kri:d] n Glaubensbekenntnis nt

creek [kri:k] n (inlet) kleine Bucht f; (US: river) kleine(r) Wasserlauf m

creep [kri:p] (pt, pp **crept**) vi kriechen; ~**er** n Kletterpflanze f; ~**y** adj (frightening) gruselig

cremate [krɪ'meɪt] vt einäschern; **cremation** [krɪ'meɪʃən] n Einäscherung f; **crematorium** [kremə'tɔ:rɪəm] n Krematorium n

crêpe [kreɪp] n Krepp m; ~ **bandage** (BRIT) n Elastikbinde f

crept [krept] pt, pp of **creep**

crescent ['kresnt] n (of moon) Halbmond m

cress [kres] n Kresse f

crest [krest] n (of cock) Kamm m; (of wave) Wellenkamm m; (coat of arms) Wappen nt

crestfallen ['krestfɔ:lən] adj niedergeschlagen

Crete [kri:t] n Kreta nt

crevice ['krevɪs] n Riss m

crew [kru:] n Besatzung f, Mannschaft f; ~-**cut** n Bürstenschnitt m; ~ **neck** n runde(r)

Ausschnitt m

crib [krɪb] n (bed) Krippe f ♦ vt (inf) spicken

crick [krɪk] n Muskelkrampf m

cricket ['krɪkɪt] n (insect) Grille f; (game) Kricket nt

crime [kraɪm] n Verbrechen nt

criminal ['krɪmɪnl] n Verbrecher m ♦ adj kriminell; (act) strafbar

crimson ['krɪmzn] adj leuchtend rot

cringe [krɪndʒ] vi sich ducken

crinkle ['krɪŋkl] vt zerknittern

cripple ['krɪpl] n Krüppel m ♦ vt lahm legen; (MED) verkrüppeln

crisis ['kraɪsɪs] (pl crises) n Krise f

crisp [krɪsp] adj knusprig; ~s (BRIT) npl Chips pl

crisscross ['krɪskrɔs] adj gekreuzt, Kreuz-

criteria [kraɪ'tɪərɪə] npl of criterion

criterion [kraɪ'tɪərɪən] (pl criteria) n Kriterium nt

critic ['krɪtɪk] n Kritiker(in) m(f); ~al adj kritisch; (ill) gefährlich; ~ally adv kritisch; (ill) gefährlich; ~ism ['krɪtɪsɪzəm] n Kritik f; ~ize ['krɪtɪsaɪz] vt kritisieren

croak [krəuk] vi krächzen; (frog) quaken

Croatia [krəu'eɪʃə] n Kroatien nt

crochet ['krəuʃeɪ] n Häkelei f

crockery ['krɔkərɪ] n Geschirr nt

crocodile ['krɔkədaɪl] n Krokodil nt

crocus ['krəukəs] n Krokus m

croft [krɔft] (BRIT) n kleine(s) Pachtgut nt

crony ['krəunɪ] (inf) n Kumpel m

crook [kruk] n (criminal) Gauner m; (stick) Hirtenstab m

crooked ['krukɪd] adj krumm

crop [krɔp] n (harvest) Ernte f; (riding ~) Reitpeitsche f ♦ vt ernten; ~ up vi passieren

croquet ['krəukeɪ] n Krocket nt

croquette [krə'ket] n Krokette f

cross [krɔs] n Kreuz nt ♦ vt (road) überqueren; (legs) übereinander legen; kreuzen ♦ adj (annoyed) böse; ~ out vt streichen; ~ over vi hinübergehen; ~bar n Querstange f; ~-country (race) n Geländelauf m; ~-examine vt ins Kreuzverhör nehmen; ~-eyed adj: to be

~-eyed schielen; ~fire n Kreuzfeuer nt; ~ing n (~roads) (Straßen)kreuzung f; (of ship) Überfahrt f; (for pedestrians) Fußgängerübergang m; ~ing guard (US) n Schülerlotse m; ~ purposes npl: to be at ~ purposes aneinander vorbeireden; ~-reference n Querverweis m; ~roads n Straßenkreuzung f; (fig) Scheideweg m; ~-section n Querschnitt m; ~-walk (US) n Fußgängerübergang m; ~wind n Seitenwind m; ~word (puzzle) n Kreuzworträtsel nt

crotch [krɔtʃ] n Zwickel m; (ANAT) Unterleib nt

crouch [krautʃ] vi hocken

crow [krəu] n (bird) Krähe f; (of cock) Krähen nt ♦ vi krähen

crowbar ['krəubɑ:] n Stemmeisen nt

crowd [kraud] n Menge f ♦ vt (fill) überfüllen ♦ vi drängen; ~ed adj überfüllt

crown [kraun] n Krone f; (of head, hat) Kopf m ♦ vt krönen; ~ jewels npl Kronjuwelen pl; ~ prince n Kronprinz m

crow's-feet ['krəuzfi:t] npl Krähenfüße pl

crucial ['kru:ʃl] adj entscheidend

crucifix ['kru:sɪfɪks] n Kruzifix nt; ~ion [kru:sɪ'fɪkʃən] n Kreuzigung f

crude [kru:d] adj (raw) roh; (humour, behaviour) grob; (basic) primitiv; ~ (oil) n Rohöl nt

cruel ['kruəl] adj grausam; ~ty n Grausamkeit f

cruise [kru:z] n Kreuzfahrt f ♦ vi kreuzen; ~r n (MIL) Kreuzer m

crumb [krʌm] n Krume f

crumble ['krʌmbl] vt, vi zerbröckeln; crumbly adj krümelig

crumpet ['krʌmpɪt] n Tee(pfann)kuchen m

crumple ['krʌmpl] vt zerknittern

crunch [krʌntʃ] n: the ~ (fig) der Knackpunkt m ♦ vt knirschen; ~y adj knusprig

crusade [kru:'seɪd] n Kreuzzug m

crush [krʌʃ] n Gedränge nt ♦ vt zerdrücken; (rebellion) unterdrücken

crust [krʌst] n Kruste f

crutch [krʌtʃ] n Krücke f

crux [krʌks] n springende(r) Punkt m

cry [kraɪ] vi (shout) schreien; (weep) weinen
♦ n (call) Schrei m; **~ off** vi (plötzlich)
absagen

crypt [krɪpt] n Krypta f

cryptic ['krɪptɪk] adj hintergründig

crystal ['krɪstl] n Kristall m; (glass) Kristallglas
nt; (mineral) Bergkristall m; **~-clear** adj
kristallklar

crystallize ['krɪstəlaɪz] vt, vi kristallisieren;
(fig) klären

CSA n abbr (= Child Support Agency) Amt zur
Regelung von Unterhaltszahlungen für
Kinder

CTC (BRIT) n abbr = **city technology college**

cub [kʌb] n Junge(s) nt; (also: **C~ scout**)
Wölfling m

Cuba ['kjuːbə] n Kuba nt; **~n** adj kubanisch
♦ n Kubaner(in) m(f)

cubbyhole ['kʌbɪhəʊl] n Eckchen nt

cube [kjuːb] n Würfel m ♦ vt (MATH) hoch
drei nehmen

cubic ['kjuːbɪk] adj würfelförmig; (centimetre
etc) Kubik-; **~ capacity** n
Fassungsvermögen nt

cubicle ['kjuːbɪkl] n Kabine f

cuckoo ['kukuː] n Kuckuck m; **~ clock** n
Kuckucksuhr f

cucumber ['kjuːkʌmbər] n Gurke f

cuddle ['kʌdl] vt, vi herzen, drücken (inf)

cue [kjuː] n (THEAT) Stichwort nt; (snooker ~)
Billardstock m

cuff [kʌf] n (BRIT: of shirt, coat etc)
Manschette f; Aufschlag m; (US) = **turn-up**;
off the ~ aus dem Handgelenk; **~link** n
Manschettenknopf m

cuisine [kwɪ'ziːn] n Kochkunst f, Küche f

cul-de-sac ['kʌldəsæk] n Sackgasse f

culinary ['kʌlɪnərɪ] adj Koch-

cull [kʌl] vt (select) auswählen

culminate ['kʌlmɪneɪt] vi gipfeln;
culmination [kʌlmɪ'neɪʃən] n Höhepunkt m

culottes [kjuː'lɒts] npl Hosenrock m

culpable ['kʌlpəbl] adj schuldig

culprit ['kʌlprɪt] n Täter m

cult [kʌlt] n Kult m

cultivate ['kʌltɪveɪt] vt (AGR) bebauen;
(mind) bilden; **cultivation** [kʌltɪ'veɪʃən] n

(AGR) Bebauung f; (of person) Bildung f

cultural ['kʌltʃərəl] adj kulturell, Kultur-

culture ['kʌltʃər] n Kultur f; **~d** adj gebildet

cumbersome ['kʌmbəsəm] adj (object)
sperrig

cumulative ['kjuːmjulətɪv] adj gehäuft

cunning ['kʌnɪŋ] n Verschlagenheit f ♦ adj
schlau

cup [kʌp] n Tasse f; (prize) Pokal m

cupboard ['kʌbəd] n Schrank m

cup tie (BRIT) n Pokalspiel nt

curate ['kjuərɪt] n (Catholic) Kurat m;
(Protestant) Vikar m

curator [kjuə'reɪtər] n Kustos m

curb [kəːb] vt zügeln ♦ n (on spending etc)
Einschränkung f; (US) Bordstein m

curdle ['kəːdl] vi gerinnen

cure [kjuər] n Heilmittel nt; (process)
Heilverfahren nt ♦ vt heilen

curfew ['kəːfjuː] n Ausgangssperre f;
Sperrstunde f

curio ['kjuərɪəʊ] n Kuriosität f

curiosity [kjuərɪ'ɒsɪtɪ] n Neugier f

curious ['kjuərɪəs] adj neugierig; (strange)
seltsam

curl [kəːl] n Locke f ♦ vt locken ♦ vi sich
locken; **~ up** vi sich zusammenrollen;
(person) sich ankuscheln; **~er** n
Lockenwickler m; **~y** ['kəːlɪ] adj lockig

currant ['kʌrnt] n Korinthe f

currency ['kʌrnsɪ] n Währung f; **to gain ~**
an Popularität gewinnen

current ['kʌrnt] n Strömung f ♦ adj
(expression) gängig, üblich; (issue) neueste;
~ account (BRIT) n Girokonto nt; **~ affairs**
npl Zeitgeschehen nt; **~ly** adv zurzeit

curricula [kə'rɪkjulə] npl of **curriculum**

curriculum [kə'rɪkjuləm] (pl **~s** or **curricula**)
n Lehrplan m; **~ vitae** [-'viːtaɪ] n Lebenslauf
m

curry ['kʌrɪ] n Currygericht nt ♦ vt: **to ~
favour with** sich einschmeicheln bei; **~
powder** n Curry(pulver) nt

curse [kəːs] vi (swear): **to ~ (at)** fluchen (auf
or über +acc) ♦ vt (insult) verwünschen ♦ n
Fluch m

cursor ['kəːsər] n (COMPUT) Cursor m

cursory ['kɜːsərɪ] adj flüchtig

curt [kɜːt] adj schroff

curtail [kɜːˈteɪl] vt abkürzen; (rights) einschränken

curtain ['kɜːtn] n Vorhang m

curts(e)y ['kɜːtsɪ] n Knicks m ♦ vi knicksen

curve [kɜːv] n Kurve f; (of body, vase etc) Rundung f ♦ vi sich biegen; (hips, breasts) sich runden; (road) einen Bogen machen

cushion ['kʊʃən] n Kissen nt ♦ vt dämpfen

custard ['kʌstəd] n Vanillesoße f

custodian [kʌsˈtəʊdɪən] n Kustos m, Verwalter(in) m(f)

custody ['kʌstədɪ] n Aufsicht f; (police ~) Haft f; **to take into ~** verhaften

custom ['kʌstəm] n (tradition) Brauch m; (COMM) Kundschaft f; **~ary** adj üblich

customer ['kʌstəmər] n Kunde m, Kundin f

customized ['kʌstəmaɪzd] adj (car etc) mit Spezialausrüstung

custom-made ['kʌstəm'meɪd] adj speziell angefertigt

customs ['kʌstəmz] npl Zoll m; **~ duty** n Zollabgabe f; **~ officer** n Zollbeamte(r) m, Zollbeamtin f

cut [kʌt] (pt, pp **cut**) vt schneiden; (wages) kürzen; (prices) heruntersetzen ♦ vi schneiden; (intersect) sich schneiden ♦ n Schnitt m; (wound) Schnittwunde f; (in income etc) Kürzung f; (share) Anteil m; **to ~ a tooth** zahnen; **~ down** vt (tree) fällen; (reduce) einschränken; **~ off** vt (also fig) abschneiden; (allowance) sperren; **~ out** vt (shape) ausschneiden; (delete) streichen; **~ up** vt (meat) aufschneiden; **~back** n Kürzung f

cute [kjuːt] adj niedlich

cuticle ['kjuːtɪkl] n Nagelhaut f

cutlery ['kʌtlərɪ] n Besteck nt

cutlet ['kʌtlɪt] n (pork) Kotelett nt; (veal) Schnitzel nt

cut: **~out** n (cardboard ~out) Ausschneidemodell nt; **~-price, ~-rate** (US) adj verbilligt; **~throat** n Verbrechertyp m ♦ adj mörderisch

cutting ['kʌtɪŋ] adj schneidend ♦ n (BRIT: PRESS) Ausschnitt m; (: RAIL) Durchstich m

CV n abbr = **curriculum vitae**

cwt abbr = **hundredweight(s)**

cyanide ['saɪənaɪd] n Zyankali nt

cybercafé ['saɪbəkæfeɪ] n Internet-Café nt

cyberspace ['saɪbəspeɪs] n Cyberspace m

cycle ['saɪkl] n Fahrrad nt; (series) Reihe f ♦ vi Rad fahren; **~ hire** n Fahrradverleih m; **~ lane, ~ path** n (Fahr)radweg m; **cycling** n Radfahren nt; **cyclist** n Radfahrer(in) m(f)

cyclone ['saɪkləʊn] n Zyklon m

cygnet ['sɪgnɪt] n junge(r) Schwan m

cylinder ['sɪlɪndər] n Zylinder m; (TECH) Walze f

cymbals ['sɪmblz] npl Becken nt

cynic ['sɪnɪk] n Zyniker(in) m(f); **~al** adj zynisch; **~ism** ['sɪnɪsɪzəm] n Zynismus m

cypress ['saɪprɪs] n Zypresse f

Cyprus ['saɪprəs] n Zypern nt

cyst [sɪst] n Zyste f

cystitis [sɪsˈtaɪtɪs] n Blasenentzündung f

czar [zɑːr] n Zar m

Czech [tʃɛk] adj tschechisch ♦ n Tscheche m, Tschechin f

Czechoslovakia [tʃɛkəsləˈvækɪə] (HIST) n die Tschechoslowakei; **~n** adj tschechoslowakisch ♦ n Tschechoslowake m, Tchechoslowakin f

D, d

D [diː] n (MUS) D nt

dab [dæb] vt (wound, paint) betupfen ♦ n (little bit) bisschen nt; (of paint) Tupfer m

dabble ['dæbl] vi: **to ~ in sth** in etw dat machen

dad [dæd] n Papa m, Vati m; **~dy** ['dædɪ] n Papa m, Vati m; **~dy-long-legs** n Weberknecht m

daffodil ['dæfədɪl] n Osterglocke f

daft [dɑːft] (inf) adj blöd(e), doof

dagger ['dægər] n Dolch m

daily ['deɪlɪ] adj täglich ♦ n (PRESS) Tageszeitung f; (BRIT: cleaner) Haushaltshilfe f ♦ adv täglich

dainty ['deɪntɪ] adj zierlich

dairy ['dɛərɪ] n (shop) Milchgeschäft nt; (on

farm) Molkerei f ♦ adj Milch-; ~ **farm** n Hof m mit Milchwirtschaft; ~ **produce** n Molkereiprodukte pl; ~ **products** npl Milchprodukte pl, Molkereiprodukte pl; ~ **store** (US) n Milchgeschäft nt

dais ['deɪs] n Podium nt

daisy ['deɪzɪ] n Gänseblümchen nt

dale [deɪl] n Tal nt

dam [dæm] n (Stau)damm m ♦ vt stauen

damage ['dæmɪdʒ] n Schaden m ♦ vt beschädigen; ~**s** npl (JUR) Schaden(s)ersatz m

damn [dæm] vt verdammen ♦ n (inf): **I don't give a** ~ das ist mir total egal ♦ adj (inf: also: ~**ed**) verdammt; ~ **it!** verflucht!; ~**ing** adj vernichtend

damp [dæmp] adj feucht ♦ n Feuchtigkeit f ♦ vt (also: ~**en**) befeuchten; (discourage) dämpfen

damson ['dæmzən] n Damaszenerpflaume f

dance [dɑːns] n Tanz m ♦ vi tanzen; ~ **hall** n Tanzlokal nt; ~**r** n Tänzer(in) m(f);

dancing ['dɑːnsɪŋ] n Tanzen nt

dandelion ['dændɪlaɪən] n Löwenzahn m

dandruff ['dændrəf] n (Kopf)schuppen pl

Dane [deɪn] n Däne m, Dänin f

danger ['deɪndʒəʳ] n Gefahr f; ~! (sign) Achtung!; **to be in** ~ **of doing sth** Gefahr laufen, etw zu tun; ~**ous** adj gefährlich

dangle ['dæŋgl] vi baumeln ♦ vt herabhängen lassen

Danish ['deɪnɪʃ] adj dänisch ♦ n Dänisch nt

dare [dɛəʳ] vt herausfordern ♦ vi: **to** ~ (**to**) **do sth** es wagen, etw zu tun; **I** ~ **say** ich würde sagen; **daring** ['dɛərɪŋ] adj (audacious) verwegen; (bold) wagemutig; (dress) gewagt ♦ n Mut m

dark [dɑːk] adj dunkel; (fig) düster, trübe; (deep colour) dunkel- ♦ n Dunkelheit f; **to be left in the** ~ **about** im Dunkeln sein über +acc; **after** ~ nach Anbruch der Dunkelheit; ~**en** vt, vi verdunkeln; ~ **glasses** npl Sonnenbrille f; ~**ness** n Finsternis nt; ~**room** n Dunkelkammer f

darling ['dɑːlɪŋ] n Liebling m ♦ adj lieb

darn [dɑːn] vt stopfen

dart [dɑːt] n (weapon) Pfeil m; (in sewing)

Abnäher m ♦ vi sausen; ~**s** n (game) Pfeilwerfen nt; ~**board** n Zielscheibe f

dash [dæʃ] n Sprung m; (mark) (Gedanken)strich m; (small amount) bisschen nt ♦ vt (hopes) zunichte machen ♦ vi stürzen; ~ **away** vi davonstürzen; ~ **off** vi davonstürzen

dashboard ['dæʃbɔːd] n Armaturenbrett nt

dashing ['dæʃɪŋ] adj schneidig

data ['deɪtə] npl Einzelheiten pl, Daten pl; ~**base** n Datenbank f; ~ **processing** n Datenverarbeitung f

date [deɪt] n Datum nt; (for meeting etc) Termin m; (with person) Verabredung f; (fruit) Dattel f ♦ vt (letter etc) datieren; (person) gehen mit; ~ **of birth** Geburtsdatum nt; **to** ~ bis heute; **out of** ~ überholt; **up to** ~ (clothes) modisch; (report) up-to-date; (with news) auf dem Laufenden; ~**d** adj altmodisch; ~ **rape** n Vergewaltigung f nach einem Rendezvous

daub [dɔːb] vt beschmieren; (paint) schmieren

daughter ['dɔːtəʳ] n Tochter f; ~**-in-law** n Schwiegertochter f

daunting ['dɔːntɪŋ] adj entmutigend

dawdle ['dɔːdl] vi trödeln

dawn [dɔːn] n Morgendämmerung f ♦ vi dämmern; (fig): **it** ~**ed on him that ...** es dämmerte ihm, dass ...

day [deɪ] n Tag m; **the** ~ **before/after** am Tag zuvor/danach; **the** ~ **after tomorrow** übermorgen; **the** ~ **before yesterday** vorgestern; **by** ~ am Tage; ~**break** n Tagesanbruch m; ~**dream** vi mit offenen Augen träumen; ~**light** n Tageslicht nt; ~ **return** (BRIT) n Tagesrückfahrkarte f; ~**time** n Tageszeit f; ~**-to-** adj alltäglich

daze [deɪz] vt betäuben ♦ n Betäubung f; **in a** ~ benommen

dazzle ['dæzl] vt blenden

DC abbr (= direct current) Gleichstrom m

D-day ['diːdeɪ] n (HIST) Tag der Invasion durch die Alliierten (6.6.44.); (fig) der Tag X

deacon ['diːkən] n Diakon m

dead [dɛd] adj tot; (without feeling) gefühllos ♦ adv ganz; (exactly) genau ♦ npl: **the** ~ die

Toten pl; **to shoot sb ~** jdn erschießen; **~ tired** todmüde; **to stop ~** abrupt stehen bleiben; **~en** vt (pain) abtöten; (sound) ersticken; **~ end** n Sackgasse f; **~ heat** n tote(s) Rennen nt; **~line** n Stichtag m; **~lock** n Stillstand m; **~ loss** (inf) n: **to be a ~ loss** ein hoffnungsloser Fall sein; **~ly** adj tödlich; **~pan** adj undurchdringlich; **D~ Sea** n: **the D~ Sea** das Tote Meer

deaf [def] adj taub; **~en** vt taub machen; **~ening** adj (noise) ohrenbetäubend; (noise) lautstark; **~-mute** n Taubstumme(r) mf; **~ness** n Taubheit f

deal [diːl] (pt, pp **dealt**) n Geschäft nt ♦ vt austeilen; (CARDS) geben; **a great ~ of** sehr viel; **~ in** vt fus handeln mit; **~ with** vt fus (person) behandeln; (subject) sich befassen mit; (problem) in Angriff nehmen; **~er** n (COMM) Händler m; (CARDS) Kartengeber m; **~ings** npl (FIN) Geschäfte pl; (relations) Beziehungen pl; **~t** [delt] pt, pp of **deal**

dean [diːn] n (Protestant) Superintendent m; (Catholic) Dechant m; (UNIV) Dekan m

dear [dɪəʳ] adj lieb; (expensive) teuer ♦ n Liebling m ♦ excl: **~ me!** du liebe Zeit!; **D~ Sir** Sehr geehrter Herr!; **D~ John** Lieber John!; **~ly** adv (love) herzlich; (pay) teuer

death [deθ] n Tod m; (statistic) Todesfall m; **~ certificate** n Totenschein m; **~ly** adj totenähnlich, Toten-; **~ penalty** n Todesstrafe f; **~ rate** n Sterblichkeitsziffer f

debar [dɪˈbɑːʳ] vt ausschließen

debase [dɪˈbeɪs] vt entwerten

debatable [dɪˈbeɪtəbl] adj anfechtbar

debate [dɪˈbeɪt] n Debatte f ♦ vt debattieren, diskutieren; (consider) überlegen

debilitating [dɪˈbɪlɪteɪtɪŋ] adj schwächend

debit [ˈdebɪt] n Schuldposten m ♦ vt belasten

debris [ˈdebriː] n Trümmer pl

debt [det] n Schuld f; **to be in ~** verschuldet sein; **~or** n Schuldner m

debunk [diːˈbʌŋk] vt entlarven

decade [ˈdekeɪd] n Jahrzehnt nt

decadence [ˈdekədəns] n Dekadenz f

decaff [ˈdiːkæf] (inf) n koffeinfreier Kaffee

decaffeinated [dɪˈkæfɪneɪtɪd] adj koffeinfrei

decanter [dɪˈkæntəʳ] n Karaffe f

decay [dɪˈkeɪ] n Verfall m; (tooth ~) Karies m ♦ vi verfallen; (teeth, meat etc) faulen; (leaves etc) verrotten

deceased [dɪˈsiːst] adj verstorben

deceit [dɪˈsiːt] n Betrug m; **~ful** adj falsch

deceive [dɪˈsiːv] vt täuschen

December [dɪˈsembəʳ] n Dezember m

decency [ˈdiːsənsɪ] n Anstand m

decent [ˈdiːsənt] adj (respectable) anständig; (pleasant) annehmbar

deception [dɪˈsepʃən] n Betrug m

deceptive [dɪˈseptɪv] adj irreführend

decibel [ˈdesɪbel] n Dezibel nt

decide [dɪˈsaɪd] vt entscheiden ♦ vi sich entscheiden; **to ~ on sth** etw beschließen; **~d** adj entschieden; **~dly** [dɪˈsaɪdɪdlɪ] adv entschieden

deciduous [dɪˈsɪdjuəs] adj Laub-

decimal [ˈdesɪməl] adj dezimal ♦ n Dezimalzahl f; **~ point** n Komma nt

decipher [dɪˈsaɪfəʳ] vt entziffern

decision [dɪˈsɪʒən] n Entscheidung f, Entschluss m

decisive [dɪˈsaɪsɪv] adj entscheidend; (person) entschlossen

deck [dek] n (NAUT) Deck nt; (of cards) Pack m; **~chair** n Liegestuhl m

declaration [dekləˈreɪʃən] n Erklärung f

declare [dɪˈkleəʳ] vt erklären; (CUSTOMS) verzollen

decline [dɪˈklaɪn] n (decay) Verfall m; (lessening) Rückgang m ♦ vt (invitation) ablehnen ♦ vi (say no) ablehnen; (of strength) nachlassen

decode [ˈdiːˈkəʊd] vt entschlüsseln; **~r** n (TV) Decoder m

decompose [diːkəmˈpəʊz] vi (sich) zersetzen

décor [ˈdeɪkɔːʳ] n Ausstattung f

decorate [ˈdekəreɪt] vt (room: paper) tapezieren; (: paint) streichen; (adorn) (aus)schmücken; (cake) verzieren; (honour) auszeichnen; **decoration** [dekəˈreɪʃən] n (of house) (Wand)dekoration f; (medal) Orden m; **decorator** [ˈdekəreɪtəʳ] n Maler m, Anstreicher m

decorum [dɪˈkɔːrəm] n Anstand m

decoy ['diːkɔɪ] n Lockvogel m

decrease [n 'diːkriːs, vb diːˈkriːs] n Abnahme f ♦ vt vermindern ♦ vi abnehmen

decree [dɪˈkriː] n Erlass m; ~ **nisi** n vorläufige(s) Scheidungsurteil nt

decrepit [dɪˈkrepɪt] adj hinfällig

dedicate ['dedɪkeɪt] vt widmen; ~d adj hingebungsvoll, engagiert; (COMPUT) dediziert; **dedication** [dedɪˈkeɪʃən] n (devotion) Ergebenheit f; (in book) Widmung f

deduce [dɪˈdjuːs] vt: **to ~ sth (from sth)** etw (aus etw) ableiten, etw (aus etw) schließen

deduct [dɪˈdʌkt] vt abziehen; ~ion [dɪˈdʌkʃən] n (of money) Abzug m; (conclusion) (Schluss)folgerung f

deed [diːd] n Tat f; (document) Urkunde f

deem [diːm] vt: **to ~ sb/sth (to be) sth** jdn/etw für etw halten

deep [diːp] adj tief ♦ adv: **the spectators stood 20 ~** die Zuschauer standen in 20 Reihen hintereinander; **to be 4m ~** 4 Meter tief sein; ~**en** vt vertiefen ♦ vi (darkness) tiefer werden; ~ **end** n: **the ~ end** (of swimming pool) das Tiefe; ~-**freeze** n Tiefkühlung f; ~-**fry** vt frittieren; ~**ly** adv tief; ~-**sea diving** n Tiefseetauchen nt; ~-**seated** adj tief sitzend

deer [dɪəʳ] n Reh nt; ~**skin** n Hirsch-/Rehleder nt

deface [dɪˈfeɪs] vt entstellen

defamation [defəˈmeɪʃən] n Verleumdung f

default [dɪˈfɔːlt] n Versäumnis nt; (COMPUT) Standardwert m ♦ vi versäumen; **by ~** durch Nichterscheinen

defeat [dɪˈfiːt] n Niederlage f ♦ vt schlagen; ~**ist** adj defätistisch ♦ n Defätist m

defect [n 'diːfekt, vb dɪˈfekt] n Fehler m ♦ vi überlaufen; ~**ive** [dɪˈfektɪv] adj fehlerhaft

defence [dɪˈfens] n Verteidigung f; ~**less** adj wehrlos

defend [dɪˈfend] vt verteidigen; ~**ant** n Angeklagte(r) m; ~**er** n Verteidiger m

defense [dɪˈfens] (US) n = **defence**

defensive [dɪˈfensɪv] adj defensiv ♦ n: **on the ~** in der Defensive

defer [dɪˈfɜːʳ] vt verschieben

deference ['defərəns] n Rücksichtnahme f

defiance [dɪˈfaɪəns] n Trotz m, Unnachgiebigkeit f; **in ~ of sth** einer Sache dat zum Trotz

defiant [dɪˈfaɪənt] adj trotzig, unnachgiebig

deficiency [dɪˈfɪʃənsɪ] n (lack) Mangel m; (weakness) Schwäche f

deficient [dɪˈfɪʃənt] adj mangelhaft

deficit ['defɪsɪt] n Defizit nt

defile [vb dɪˈfaɪl, n 'diːfaɪl] vt beschmutzen ♦ n Hohlweg m

define [dɪˈfaɪn] vt bestimmen; (explain) definieren

definite ['defɪnɪt] adj (fixed) definitiv; (clear) eindeutig; ~**ly** adv bestimmt

definition [defɪˈnɪʃən] n Definition f

deflate [diːˈfleɪt] vt die Luft ablassen aus

deflect [dɪˈflekt] vt ablenken

deformity [dɪˈfɔːmɪtɪ] n Missbildung f

defraud [dɪˈfrɔːd] vt betrügen

defrost [diːˈfrɔst] vt (fridge) abtauen; (food) auftauen; ~**er** (US) n (demister) Gebläse nt

deft [deft] adj geschickt

defunct [dɪˈfʌŋkt] adj verstorben

defuse [diːˈfjuːz] vt entschärfen

defy [dɪˈfaɪ] vt (disobey) sich widersetzen +dat; (orders, death) trotzen +dat; (challenge) herausfordern

degenerate [v dɪˈdʒenəreɪt, adj dɪˈdʒenərɪt] vi degenerieren ♦ adj degeneriert

degrading [dɪˈgreɪdɪŋ] adj erniedrigend

degree [dɪˈgriː] n Grad m; (UNIV) Universitätsabschluss m; **by ~s** allmählich; **to some ~** zu einem gewissen Grad

dehydrated [diːhaɪˈdreɪtɪd] adj (person) ausgetrocknet

de-ice ['diːˈaɪs] vt enteisen

deign [deɪn] vi sich herablassen

deity ['diːɪtɪ] n Gottheit f

dejected [dɪˈdʒektɪd] adj niedergeschlagen

delay [dɪˈleɪ] vt (hold back) aufschieben ♦ vi (linger) sich aufhalten ♦ n Aufschub m, Verzögerung f; (of train etc) Verspätung f; **to be ~ed** (train) Verspätung haben; **without ~** unverzüglich

delectable [dɪˈlektəbl] adj köstlich; (fig) reizend

delegate [*n* 'delɪgɪt, *vb* 'delɪgeɪt] *n* Delegierte(r) *mf* ♦ *vt* delegieren

delete [dɪ'liːt] *vt* (aus)streichen

deliberate [*adj* dɪ'lɪbərɪt, *vb* dɪ'lɪbəreɪt] *adj* (*intentional*) absichtlich; (*slow*) bedächtig ♦ *vi* (*consider*) überlegen; (*debate*) sich beraten; **~ly** *adv* absichtlich

delicacy ['delɪkəsɪ] *n* Zartheit *f*; (*weakness*) Anfälligkeit *f*; (*food*) Delikatesse *f*

delicate ['delɪkɪt] *adj* (*fine*) fein; (*fragile*) zart; (*situation*) heikel; (*MED*) empfindlich

delicatessen [delɪkə'tesn] *n* Feinkostgeschäft *nt*

delicious [dɪ'lɪʃəs] *adj* lecker

delight [dɪ'laɪt] *n* Wonne *f* ♦ *vt* entzücken; **to take ~ in sth** Freude an etw *dat* haben; **~ed** *adj*: **~ed (at** *or* **with sth)** entzückt (über +*acc* etw); **~ed to do sth** etw sehr gern tun; **~ful** *adj* entzückend, herrlich

delinquency [dɪ'lɪŋkwənsɪ] *n* Kriminalität *f*

delinquent [dɪ'lɪŋkwənt] *n* Straffällige(r) *mf* ♦ *adj* straffällig

delirious [dɪ'lɪrɪəs] *adj* im Fieberwahn

deliver [dɪ'lɪvə*] *vt* (*goods*) (ab)liefern; (*letter*) zustellen; (*speech*) halten; **~y** *n* (Ab)lieferung *f*; (*of letter*) Zustellung *f*; (*of speech*) Vortragsweise *f*; (*MED*) Entbindung *f*; **to take ~y of** in Empfang nehmen

delude [dɪ'luːd] *vt* täuschen

deluge ['deljuːdʒ] *n* Überschwemmung *f*; (*fig*) Flut *f* ♦ *vt* (*fig*) überfluten

delusion [dɪ'luːʒən] *n* (Selbst)täuschung *f*

de luxe [də'lʌks] *adj* Luxus-

delve [delv] *vi*: **to ~ into** sich vertiefen in +*acc*

demand [dɪ'mɑːnd] *vt* verlangen ♦ *n* (*request*) Verlangen *nt*; (*COMM*) Nachfrage *f*; **in ~** gefragt; **on ~** auf Verlangen; **~ing** *adj* anspruchsvoll

demean [dɪ'miːn] *vt*: **to ~ o.s.** sich erniedrigen

demeanour [dɪ'miːnə*] (*US* **demeanor**) *n* Benehmen *nt*

demented [dɪ'mentɪd] *adj* wahnsinnig

demister [diː'mɪstə*] *n* (*AUT*) Gebläse *nt*

demo ['deməu] (*inf*) *n abbr* (= **demonstration**) Demo *f*

democracy [dɪ'mɔkrəsɪ] *n* Demokratie *f*

democrat ['deməkræt] *n* Demokrat *m*; **democratic** [demə'krætɪk] *adj* demokratisch

demolish [dɪ'mɔlɪʃ] *vt* abreißen; (*fig*) vernichten

demolition [demə'lɪʃən] *n* Abbruch *m*

demon ['diːmən] *n* Dämon *m*

demonstrate ['demənstreɪt] *vt, vi* demonstrieren; **demonstration** [demən'streɪʃən] *n* Demonstration *f*; **demonstrator** ['demənstreɪtə*] *n* (*POL*) Demonstrant(in) *m(f)*

demote [dɪ'məut] *vt* degradieren

demure [dɪ'mjuə*] *adj* ernst

den [den] *n* (*of animal*) Höhle *f*; (*study*) Bude *f*

denatured alcohol [diː'neɪtʃəd-] (*US*) *n* ungenießbar gemachte(r) Alkohol *m*

denial [dɪ'naɪəl] *n* Leugnung *f*; **official ~** Dementi *nt*

denim ['denɪm] *adj* Denim-; **~s** *npl* Denimjeans *pl*

Denmark ['denmɑːk] *n* Dänemark *nt*

denomination [dɪnɔmɪ'neɪʃən] *n* (*ECCL*) Bekenntnis *nt*; (*type*) Klasse *f*; (*FIN*) Wert *m*

denote [dɪ'nəut] *vt* bedeuten

denounce [dɪ'nauns] *vt* brandmarken

dense [dens] *adj* dicht; (*stupid*) schwer von Begriff; **~ly** *adv* dicht; **density** ['densɪtɪ] *n* Dichte *f*; **single/double density disk** Diskette *f* mit einfacher/doppelter Dichte

dent [dent] *n* Delle *f* ♦ *vt* (*also:* **make a ~ in**) einbeulen

dental ['dentl] *adj* Zahn-; **~ surgeon** *n* = **dentist**

dentist ['dentɪst] *n* Zahnarzt(ärztin) *m(f)*

dentures ['dentʃəz] *npl* Gebiss *nt*

deny [dɪ'naɪ] *vt* leugnen; (*officially*) dementieren; (*help*) abschlagen

deodorant [diː'əudərənt] *n* Deodorant *nt*

depart [dɪ'pɑːt] *vi* abfahren; **to ~ from** (*fig: differ from*) abweichen von

department [dɪ'pɑːtmənt] *n* (*COMM*) Abteilung *f*; (*UNIV*) Seminar *nt*; (*POL*) Ministerium *nt*; **~ store** *n* Warenhaus *nt*

departure [dɪ'pɑːtʃə*] *n* (*of person*) Abreise *f*; (*of train*) Abfahrt *f*; (*of plane*) Abflug *m*; **new**

~ Neuerung f; ~ lounge n (at airport) Abflughalle f

depend [dɪ'pɛnd] vi: **to ~ on** abhängen von; (rely on) angewiesen sein auf +acc; **it ~s es** kommt darauf an; **~ing on the result ...** abhängend von Resultat ...;~**able** adj zuverlässig;~**ant** n Angehörige(r) f(m); ~**ence** n Abhängigkeit f;~**ent** adj abhängig ♦ n = **dependant**; ~**ent on** abhängig von

depict [dɪ'pɪkt] vt schildern

depleted [dɪ'pli:tɪd] adj aufgebraucht

deplorable [dɪ'plɔ:rəbl] adj bedauerlich

deploy [dɪ'plɔɪ] vt einsetzen

depopulation ['di:pɔpju'leɪʃən] n Entvölkerung f

deport [dɪ'pɔ:t] vt deportieren;~**ation** [di:pɔ:'teɪʃən] n Abschiebung f

deportment [dɪ'pɔ:tmənt] n Betragen nt

deposit [dɪ'pɔzɪt] n (in bank) Guthaben nt; (down payment) Anzahlung f; (security) Kaution f; (CHEM) Niederschlag m ♦ vt (in bank) deponieren; (put down) niederlegen; ~ **account** n Sparkonto nt

depot ['dɛpəʊ] n Depot nt

depraved [dɪ'preɪvd] adj verkommen

depreciate [dɪ'pri:ʃɪeɪt] vi im Wert sinken; **depreciation** [dɪpri:ʃɪ'eɪʃən] n Wertminderung f

depress [dɪ'prɛs] vt (press down) niederdrücken; (in mood) deprimieren;~**ed** adj deprimiert; ~**ion** [dɪ'prɛʃən] n (mood) Depression f; (in trade) Wirtschaftskrise f; (hollow) Vertiefung f; (MET) Tief(druckgebiet) nt

deprivation [dɛprɪ'veɪʃən] n Not f

deprive [dɪ'praɪv] vt: **to ~ sb of sth** jdn einer Sache gen berauben;~**d** adj (child) sozial benachteiligt; (area) unterentwickelt

depth [dɛpθ] n Tiefe f; **in the ~s of despair** in tiefster Verzweiflung

deputation [dɛpju'teɪʃən] n Abordnung f

deputize ['dɛpjutaɪz] vi: **to ~ (for sb)** (jdn) vertreten

deputy ['dɛpjutɪ] adj stellvertretend ♦ n (Stell)vertreter m;~ **head** (BRIT: SCOL) n Konrektor(in) m(f)

derail [dɪ'reɪl] vt: **to be ~ed** entgleisen; ~**ment** n Entgleisung f

deranged [dɪ'reɪndʒd] adj verrückt

derby ['də:rbɪ] (US) n Melone f

derelict ['dɛrɪlɪkt] adj verlassen

deride [dɪ'raɪd] vt auslachen

derisory [dɪ'raɪsərɪ] adj spöttisch

derivative [dɪ'rɪvətɪv] n Derivat nt ♦ adj abgeleitet

derive [dɪ'raɪv] vt (get) gewinnen; (deduce) ableiten ♦ vi (come from) abstammen

dermatitis [də:mə'taɪtɪs] n Hautentzündung f

derogatory [dɪ'rɔgətərɪ] adj geringschätzig

derrick ['dɛrɪk] n Drehkran m

descend [dɪ'sɛnd] vt, vi hinuntersteigen; **to ~ from** abstammen von;~**ant** n Nachkomme m; **descent** [dɪ'sɛnt] n (coming down) Abstieg m; (origin) Abstammung f

describe [dɪs'kraɪb] vt beschreiben

description [dɪs'krɪpʃən] n Beschreibung f; (sort) Art f

descriptive [dɪs'krɪptɪv] adj beschreibend; (word) anschaulich

desecrate ['dɛsɪkreɪt] vt schänden

desert [n 'dɛzət, vb dɪ'zə:t] n Wüste f ♦ vt verlassen; (temporarily) im Stich lassen ♦ vi (MIL) desertieren; ~**s** npl (what one deserves): **to get one's just ~s** seinen gerechten Lohn bekommen; ~**er** n Deserteur m;~**ion** [dɪ'zə:ʃən] n (of wife) Verlassen nt; (MIL) Fahnenflucht f;~ **island** n einsame Insel f

deserve [dɪ'zə:v] vt verdienen; **deserving** adj verdienstvoll

design [dɪ'zaɪn] n (plan) Entwurf m; (planning) Design nt ♦ vt entwerfen

designate [vb 'dɛzɪgneɪt, adj 'dɛzɪgnɪt] vt bestimmen ♦ adj designiert

designer [dɪ'zaɪnər] n Designer(in) m(f); (TECH) Konstrukteur(in) m(f); (fashion ~) Modeschöpfer(in) m(f)

desirable [dɪ'zaɪərəbl] adj wünschenswert

desire [dɪ'zaɪər] n Wunsch m, Verlangen nt ♦ vt (lust) begehren; (ask for) wollen

desk [dɛsk] n Schreibtisch m; (BRIT: in shop, restaurant) Kasse f;~**top publishing** n

Desktop-Publishing nt

desolate ['desəlɪt] *adj* öde; (*sad*) trostlos; **desolation** [desə'leɪʃən] *n* Trostlosigkeit *f*

despair [dɪs'peər] *n* Verzweiflung *f* ♦ *vi*: **to ~ (of)** verzweifeln (an +*dat*)

despatch [dɪs'pætʃ] *n*, *vt* = **dispatch**

desperate ['despərɪt] *adj* verzweifelt; **~ly** *adv* verzweifelt; **desperation** [despə'reɪʃən] *n* Verzweiflung *f*

despicable [dɪs'pɪkəbl] *adj* abscheulich

despise [dɪs'paɪz] *vt* verachten

despite [dɪs'paɪt] *prep* trotz +*gen*

despondent [dɪs'pɔndənt] *adj* mutlos

dessert [dɪ'zɜːt] *n* Nachtisch *m*; **~spoon** *n* Dessertlöffel *m*

destination [destɪ'neɪʃən] *n* (*of person*) (Reise)ziel *nt*; (*of goods*) Bestimmungsort *m*

destiny ['destɪnɪ] *n* Schicksal *nt*

destitute ['destɪtjuːt] *adj* Not leidend

destroy [dɪs'trɔɪ] *vt* zerstören; **~er** *n* (NAUT) Zerstörer *m*

destruction [dɪs'trʌkʃən] *n* Zerstörung *f*

destructive [dɪs'trʌktɪv] *adj* zerstörend

detach [dɪ'tætʃ] *vt* loslösen; **~able** *adj* abtrennbar; **~ed** *adj* (*attitude*) distanziert; (*house*) Einzel-; **~ment** *n* (*fig*) Abstand *m*; (MIL) Sonderkommando *nt*

detail ['diːteɪl] *n* Einzelheit *f*, Detail *nt* ♦ *vt* (*relate*) ausführlich berichten; (*appoint*) abkommandieren; **in ~** im Detail; **~ed** *adj* detailliert

detain [dɪ'teɪn] *vt* aufhalten; (*imprison*) in Haft halten

detect [dɪ'tekt] *vt* entdecken; **~ion** [dɪ'tekʃən] *n* Aufdeckung *f*; **~ive** *n* Detektiv *m*; **~ive story** *n* Kriminalgeschichte *f*, Krimi *m*

détente [der'tɑːnt] *n* Entspannung *f*

detention [dɪ'tenʃən] *n* Haft *f*; (SCH) Nachsitzen *nt*

deter [dɪ'tɜːr] *vt* abschrecken

detergent [dɪ'tɜːdʒənt] *n* Waschmittel *nt*

deteriorate [dɪ'tɪərɪəreɪt] *vi* sich verschlechtern; **deterioration** [dɪtɪərɪə'reɪʃən] *n* Verschlechterung *f*

determination [dɪtɜːmɪ'neɪʃən] *n* Entschlossenheit *f*

determine [dɪ'tɜːmɪn] *vt* bestimmen; **~d** *adj* entschlossen

deterrent [dɪ'terənt] *n* Abschreckungsmittel *nt*

detest [dɪ'test] *vt* verabscheuen

detonate ['detəneɪt] *vt* explodieren lassen ♦ *vi* detonieren

detour ['diːtuər] *n* Umweg *m*; (US: AUT: *diversion*) Umleitung *f* ♦ *vt* (US: AUT: *traffic*) umleiten

detract [dɪ'trækt] *vi*: **to ~ from** schmälern

detriment ['detrɪmənt] *n*: **to the ~ of** zum Schaden +*gen*; **~al** [detrɪ'mentl] *adj* schädlich

devaluation [diːvæljuːˈeɪʃən] *n* Abwertung *f*

devastate ['devəsteɪt] *vt* verwüsten; (*fig: shock*): **to be ~d by** niedergeschmettert sein von; **devastating** *adj* verheerend

develop [dɪ'veləp] *vt* entwickeln; (*resources*) erschließen ♦ *vi* sich entwickeln; **~ing country** *n* Entwicklungsland *nt*; **~ment** *n* Entwicklung *f*

deviate ['diːvɪeɪt] *vi* abweichen

device [dɪ'vaɪs] *n* Gerät *nt*

devil ['devl] *n* Teufel *m*

devious ['diːvɪəs] *adj* (*means*) krumm; (*person*) verschlagen

devise [dɪ'vaɪz] *vt* entwickeln

devoid [dɪ'vɔɪd] *adj*: **~ of** ohne

devolution [diːvə'luːʃən] *n* (POL) Dezentralisierung *f*

devote [dɪ'vəut] *vt*: **to ~ sth (to sth)** etw (einer Sache *dat*) widmen; **~d** *adj* ergeben; **~e** [devəu'tiː] *n* Anhänger(in) *m(f)*, Verehrer(in) *m(f)*; **devotion** [dɪ'vəuʃən] *n* (*piety*) Andacht *f*; (*loyalty*) Ergebenheit *f*, Hingabe *f*

devour [dɪ'vauər] *vt* verschlingen

devout [dɪ'vaut] *adj* andächtig

dew [djuː] *n* Tau *m*

dexterity [deks'terɪtɪ] *n* Geschicklichkeit *f*

DHSS (BRIT) *n abbr* = **Department of Health and Social Security**

diabetes [daɪə'biːtiːz] *n* Zuckerkrankheit *f*

diabetic [daɪə'betɪk] *adj* zuckerkrank; (*food*) Diabetiker- ♦ *n* Diabetiker *m*

diabolical [daɪə'bɔlɪkl] (*inf*) *adj* (*weather, behaviour*) saumäßig

diagnose [daɪəgˈnəʊz] vt diagnostizieren
diagnoses [daɪəgˈnəʊsiːz] npl of **diagnosis**
diagnosis [daɪəgˈnəʊsɪs] n Diagnose f
diagonal [daɪˈægənl] adj diagonal ♦ n Diagonale f
diagram [ˈdaɪəgræm] n Diagramm nt, Schaubild nt
dial [ˈdaɪəl] n (TEL) Wählscheibe f; (of clock) Zifferblatt nt ♦ vt wählen
dialect [ˈdaɪəlekt] n Dialekt m
dialling code [ˈdaɪəlɪŋ-] n Vorwahl f
dialling tone n Amtszeichen nt
dialogue [ˈdaɪəlɔg] n Dialog m
dial tone (US) n = **dialling tone**
diameter [daɪˈæmɪtəʳ] n Durchmesser m
diamond [ˈdaɪəmənd] n Diamant m; **~s** npl (CARDS) Karo nt
diaper [ˈdaɪəpəʳ] (US) n Windel f
diaphragm [ˈdaɪəfræm] n Zwerchfell nt
diarrhoea [daɪəˈriːə] (US **diarrhea**) n Durchfall m
diary [ˈdaɪərɪ] n Taschenkalender m; (account) Tagebuch nt
dice [daɪs] n Würfel pl ♦ vt in Würfel schneiden
dictate [dɪkˈteɪt] vt diktieren; **~s** [ˈdɪkteɪts] npl Gebote pl; **dictation** [dɪkˈteɪʃən] n Diktat nt
dictator [dɪkˈteɪtəʳ] n Diktator m; **~ship** [dɪkˈteɪtəʃɪp] n Diktatur f
dictionary [ˈdɪkʃənrɪ] n Wörterbuch nt
did [dɪd] pt of **do**
didn't [ˈdɪdnt] = **did not**
die [daɪ] vi sterben; **to be dying for sth** etw unbedingt haben wollen; **to be dying to do sth** darauf brennen, etw zu tun; **~ away** vi schwächer werden; **~ down** vi nachlassen; **~ out** vi aussterben
diesel [ˈdiːzl] n (car) Diesel m; **~ engine** n Dieselmotor m; **~ oil** n Dieselkraftstoff m
diet [ˈdaɪət] n Nahrung f; (special food) Diät f; (slimming) Abmagerungskur f ♦ vi (also: **be on a ~**) eine Abmagerungskur machen
differ [ˈdɪfəʳ] vi sich unterscheiden; (disagree) anderer Meinung sein; **~ence** n Unterschied m; **~ent** adj anders; (two things) verschieden; **~entiate** [dɪfəˈrenʃɪeɪt]

vt, vi unterscheiden; **~ently** adv anders; (from one another) unterschiedlich
difficult [ˈdɪfɪkəlt] adj schwierig; **~y** n Schwierigkeit f
diffident [ˈdɪfɪdənt] adj schüchtern
diffuse [adj dɪˈfjuːs, vb dɪˈfjuːz] adj langatmig ♦ vt verbreiten
dig [dɪg] (pt, pp **dug**) vt graben ♦ n (prod) Stoß m; (remark) Spitze f; (archaeological) Ausgrabung f; **~ in** vi (MIL) sich eingraben; **~ into** vt fus (savings) angreifen; **~ up** vt ausgraben; (fig) aufgabeln
digest [vb daɪˈdʒest, n ˈdaɪdʒest] vt verdauen ♦ n Auslese f; **~ion** [dɪˈdʒestʃən] n Verdauung f
digit [ˈdɪdʒɪt] n Ziffer f; (ANAT) Finger m; **~al** adj digital, Digital-; **~al camera** n Digitalkamera f; **~al TV** n Digitalfernsehen nt
dignified [ˈdɪgnɪfaɪd] adj würdevoll
dignity [ˈdɪgnɪtɪ] n Würde f
digress [daɪˈgres] vi abschweifen
digs [dɪgz] (BRIT: inf) npl Bude f
dilapidated [dɪˈlæpɪdeɪtɪd] adj baufällig
dilate [daɪˈleɪt] vt weiten ♦ vi sich weiten
dilemma [daɪˈlemə] n Dilemma nt
diligent [ˈdɪlɪdʒənt] adj fleißig
dilute [daɪˈluːt] vt verdünnen
dim [dɪm] adj trübe; (stupid) schwer von Begriff ♦ vt verdunkeln; **to ~ one's headlights** (esp US) abblenden
dime [daɪm] (US) n Zehncentstück nt
dimension [daɪˈmenʃən] n Dimension f
diminish [dɪˈmɪnɪʃ] vt, vi verringern
diminutive [dɪˈmɪnjutɪv] adj winzig ♦ n Verkleinerungsform f
dimmer [ˈdɪməʳ] (US) n (AUT) Abblendschalter m; **~s** npl Abblendlicht nt; (sidelights) Begrenzungsleuchten pl
dimple [ˈdɪmpl] n Grübchen nt
din [dɪn] n Getöse nt
dine [daɪn] vi speisen; **~r** n Tischgast m; (RAIL) Speisewagen m
dinghy [ˈdɪŋgɪ] n Dingi nt; **rubber ~** Schlauchboot nt
dingy [ˈdɪndʒɪ] adj armselig
dining car (BRIT) n Speisewagen m
dining room [ˈdaɪnɪŋ-] n Esszimmer nt; (in

hotel) Speisezimmer *nt*

dinner ['dɪnə^r] *n (lunch)* Mittagessen *nt;* *(evening)* Abendessen *nt; (public)* Festessen *nt;* **~ jacket** *n* Smoking *m;* **~ party** *n* Tischgesellschaft *f;* **~ time** *n* Tischzeit *f*

dinosaur ['daɪnəsɔː^r] *n* Dinosaurier *m*

dint [dɪnt] *n:* **by ~ of** durch

diocese ['daɪəsɪs] *n* Diözese *f*

dip [dɪp] *n (hollow)* Senkung *f; (bathe)* kurze(s) Baden *nt ♦ vt* eintauchen; *(BRIT: AUT)* abblenden *♦ vi (slope)* sich senken, abfallen

diploma [dɪ'pləʊmə] *n* Diplom *nt*

diplomacy [dɪ'pləʊməsɪ] *n* Diplomatie *f*

diplomat ['dɪpləmæt] *n* Diplomat(in) *m(f);* **~ic** [dɪplə'mætɪk] *adj* diplomatisch

dip stick *n* Ölmessstab *m*

dipswitch ['dɪpswɪtʃ] *(BRIT)* *n (AUT)* Abblendschalter *m*

dire [daɪə^r] *adj* schrecklich

direct [daɪ'rekt] *adj* direkt *♦ vt* leiten; *(film)* die Regie führen +*gen; (aim)* richten; *(order)* anweisen; **can you ~ me to ...?** können Sie mir sagen, wo ich zu ... komme?; **~ debit** *n (BRIT)* Einzugsauftrag *m; (transaction)* automatische Abbuchung *f*

direction [dɪ'rekʃən] *n* Richtung *f; (CINE)* Regie *f;* Leitung *f;* **~s** *npl (for use)* Gebrauchsanleitung *f; (orders)* Anweisungen *pl;* **sense of ~** Orientierungssinn *m*

directly [dɪ'rektlɪ] *adv* direkt; *(at once)* sofort

director [dɪ'rektə^r] *n* Direktor *m; (of film)* Regisseur *m*

directory [dɪ'rektərɪ] *n (TEL)* Telefonbuch *nt;* **~ enquiries, ~ assistance** *(US) n* (Fernsprech)auskunft *f*

dirt [dɜːt] *n* Schmutz *m,* Dreck *m;* **~-cheap** *adj* spottbillig; **~y** *adj* schmutzig *♦ vt* beschmutzen; **~y trick** *n* gemeine(r) Trick *m*

disability [dɪsə'bɪlɪtɪ] *n* Körperbehinderung *f*

disabled [dɪs'eɪbld] *adj* körperbehindert

disadvantage [dɪsəd'vɑːntɪdʒ] *n* Nachteil *m*

disagree [dɪsə'griː] *vi* nicht übereinstimmen; *(quarrel)* (sich) streiten; *(food):* **to ~ with sb** jdm nicht bekommen; **~able** *adj*

unangenehm; **~ment** *n (between persons)* Streit *m; (between things)* Widerspruch *m*

disallow ['dɪsə'laʊ] *vt* nicht zulassen

disappear [dɪsə'pɪə^r] *vi* verschwinden; **~ance** *n* Verschwinden *nt*

disappoint [dɪsə'pɔɪnt] *vt* enttäuschen; **~ed** *adj* enttäuscht; **~ment** *n* Enttäuschung *f*

disapproval [dɪsə'pruːvəl] *n* Missbilligung *f*

disapprove [dɪsə'pruːv] *vi:* **to ~ of** missbilligen

disarm [dɪs'ɑːm] *vt* entwaffnen; *(POL)* abrüsten; **~ament** *n* Abrüstung *f*

disarray [dɪsə'reɪ] *n:* **to be in ~** *(army)* in Auflösung (begriffen) sein; *(clothes)* in unordentlichen Zustand sein

disaster [dɪ'zɑːstə^r] *n* Katastrophe *f;* **disastrous** [dɪ'zɑːstrəs] *adj* verhängnisvoll

disband [dɪs'bænd] *vt* auflösen *♦ vi* auseinander gehen

disbelief ['dɪsbə'liːf] *n* Ungläubigkeit *f*

disc [dɪsk] *n* Scheibe *f; (record)* (Schall)platte *f; (COMPUT)* = **disk**

discard [dɪs'kɑːd] *vt* ablegen

discern [dɪ'sɜːn] *vt* erkennen; **~ing** *adj* scharfsinnig

discharge [*vb* dɪs'tʃɑːdʒ, *n* 'dɪstʃɑːdʒ] *vt (ship)* entladen; *(duties)* nachkommen +*dat; (dismiss)* entlassen; *(gun)* abschießen; *(JUR)* freisprechen *♦ n (of ship, ELEC)* Entladung *f; (dismissal)* Entlassung *f; (MED)* Ausfluss *m*

disciple [dɪ'saɪpl] *n* Jünger *m*

discipline ['dɪsɪplɪn] *n* Disziplin *f ♦ vt (train)* schulen; *(punish)* bestrafen

disc jockey *n* Diskjockey *m*

disclaim [dɪs'kleɪm] *vt* nicht anerkennen

disclose [dɪs'kləʊz] *vt* enthüllen; **disclosure** [dɪs'kləʊʒə^r] *n* Enthüllung *f*

disco ['dɪskəʊ] *n abbr* = **discotheque**

discoloured [dɪs'kʌləd] *(US* **discolored**) *adj* verfärbt

discomfort [dɪs'kʌmfət] *n* Unbehagen *nt*

disconcert [dɪskən'sɜːt] *vt* aus der Fassung bringen

disconnect [dɪskə'nekt] *vt* abtrennen

discontent [dɪskən'tent] *n* Unzufriedenheit *f;* **~ed** *adj* unzufrieden

discontinue [dɪskən'tɪnjuː] *vt* einstellen

discord ['dɪskɔːd] n Zwietracht f; (noise) Dissonanz f

discotheque ['dɪskəʊtɛk] n Diskothek f

discount [n 'dɪskaʊnt, vb dɪs'kaʊnt] n Rabatt m ♦ vt außer Acht lassen

discourage [dɪs'kʌrɪdʒ] vt entmutigen; (prevent) abraten

discourteous [dɪs'kəːtɪəs] adj unhöflich

discover [dɪs'kʌvəʳ] vt entdecken;~y n Entdeckung f

discredit [dɪs'krɛdɪt] vt in Verruf bringen

discreet [dɪs'kriːt] adj diskret

discrepancy [dɪs'krɛpənsɪ] n Diskrepanz f

discriminate [dɪs'krɪmɪneɪt] vi unterscheiden; **to ~ against** diskriminieren; **discriminating** adj anspruchsvoll; **discrimination** [dɪskrɪmɪ'neɪʃən] n Urteilsvermögen nt; (pej) Diskriminierung f

discuss [dɪs'kʌs] vt diskutieren, besprechen; ~ion [dɪs'kʌʃən] n Diskussion f, Besprechung f

disdain [dɪs'deɪn] n Verachtung f

disease [dɪ'ziːz] n Krankheit f

disembark [dɪsɪm'bɑːk] vi von Bord gehen

disenchanted ['dɪsɪn'tʃɑːntɪd] adj desillusioniert

disengage [dɪsɪn'geɪdʒ] vt (AUT) auskuppeln

disentangle [dɪsɪn'tæŋgl] vt entwirren

disfigure [dɪs'fɪgəʳ] vt entstellen

disgrace [dɪs'greɪs] n Schande f ♦ vt Schande bringen über +acc;~ful adj unerhört

disgruntled [dɪs'grʌntld] adj verärgert

disguise [dɪs'gaɪz] vt verkleiden; (feelings) verhehlen ♦ n Verkleidung f; **in ~** verkleidet, maskiert

disgust [dɪs'gʌst] n Abscheu f ♦ vt anwidern; ~ed adj angeekelt; (at sb's behaviour) empört;~ing adj widerlich

dish [dɪʃ] n Schüssel f; (food) Gericht nt; **to do** or **wash the ~es** abwaschen;~ **up** vt auftischen;~ **cloth** n Spüllappen m

dishearten [dɪs'hɑːtn] vt entmutigen

dishevelled [dɪ'ʃɛvəld] adj (hair) zerzaust; (clothing) ungepflegt

dishonest [dɪs'ɔnɪst] adj unehrlich

dishonour [dɪs'ɔnəʳ] (US **dishonor**) n Unehre f;~**able** adj unehrenhaft

dishtowel ['dɪʃtaʊəl] n Geschirrtuch nt

dishwasher ['dɪʃwɔʃəʳ] n Geschirrspülmaschine f

disillusion [dɪsɪ'luːʒən] vt enttäuschen, desillusionieren

disincentive [dɪsɪn'sɛntɪv] n Entmutigung f

disinfect [dɪsɪn'fɛkt] vt desinfizieren;~ant n Desinfektionsmittel nt

disintegrate [dɪs'ɪntɪgreɪt] vi sich auflösen

disinterested [dɪs'ɪntrəstɪd] adj uneigennützig; (inf) uninteressiert

disjointed [dɪs'dʒɔɪntɪd] adj unzusammenhängend

disk [dɪsk] n (COMPUT) Diskette f; **single/ double sided ~** einseitige/beidseitige Diskette;~ **drive** n Diskettenlaufwerk nt; ~**ette** [dɪs'kɛt] (US) n = **disk**

dislike [dɪs'laɪk] n Abneigung f ♦ vt nicht leiden können

dislocate ['dɪsləkeɪt] vt auskugeln

dislodge [dɪs'lɔdʒ] vt verschieben; (MIL) aus der Stellung werfen

disloyal [dɪs'lɔɪəl] adj treulos

dismal ['dɪzml] adj trostlos, trübe

dismantle [dɪs'mæntl] vt demontieren

dismay [dɪs'meɪ] n Bestürzung f ♦ vt bestürzen

dismiss [dɪs'mɪs] vt (employee) entlassen; (idea) von sich weisen; (send away) wegschicken; (JUR) abweisen;~al n Entlassung f

dismount [dɪs'maʊnt] vi absteigen

disobedience [dɪsə'biːdɪəns] n Ungehorsam m;**disobedient** [dɪsə'biːdɪənt] adj ungehorsam

disobey [dɪsə'beɪ] vt nicht gehorchen +dat

disorder [dɪs'ɔːdəʳ] n (confusion) Verwirrung f; (commotion) Aufruhr m; (MED) Erkrankung f

disorderly [dɪs'ɔːdəlɪ] adj (untidy) unordentlich; (unruly) ordnungswidrig

disorganized [dɪs'ɔːgənaɪzd] adj unordentlich

disorientated [dɪs'ɔːrɪənteɪtɪd] adj (person: after journey) verwirrt

disown [dɪs'əʊn] vt (child) verstoßen

disparaging [dɪs'pærɪdʒɪŋ] adj

geringschätzig

dispassionate [dɪsˈpæʃənət] *adj* objektiv

dispatch [dɪsˈpætʃ] *vt* (*goods*) abschicken, abfertigen ♦ *n* Absendung *f*; (*esp MIL*) Meldung *f*

dispel [dɪsˈpel] *vt* zerstreuen

dispensary [dɪsˈpensərɪ] *n* Apotheke *f*

dispense [dɪsˈpens] *vt* verteilen, austeilen; ~ **with** *vt fus* verzichten auf +*acc*; ~**r** *n* (*container*) Spender *m*; **dispensing** *adj*: **dispensing chemist** (*BRIT*) Apotheker *m*

dispersal [dɪsˈpəːsl] *n* Zerstreuung *f*

disperse [dɪsˈpəːs] *vt* zerstreuen ♦ *vi* sich verteilen

dispirited [dɪsˈpɪrɪtɪd] *adj* niedergeschlagen

displace [dɪsˈpleɪs] *vt* verschieben; ~**d person** *n* Verschleppte(r) *mf*

display [dɪsˈpleɪ] *n* (*of goods*) Auslage *f*; (*of feeling*) Zurschaustellung *f* ♦ *vt* zeigen; (*ostentatiously*) vorführen; (*goods*) ausstellen

displease [dɪsˈpliːz] *vt* missfallen +*dat*

displeasure [dɪsˈpleʒər] *n* Missfallen *nt*

disposable [dɪsˈpəuzəbl] *adj* Wegwerf-; ~ **nappy** *n* Papierwindel *f*

disposal [dɪsˈpəuzl] *n* (*of property*) Verkauf *m*; (*throwing away*) Beseitigung *f*; **to be at one's** ~ einem zur Verfügung stehen

dispose [dɪsˈpəuz] *vi*: **to** ~ **of** loswerden; ~**d** *adj* geneigt

disposition [dɪspəˈzɪʃən] *n* Wesen *nt*

disproportionate [dɪsprəˈpɔːʃənət] *adj* unverhältnismäßig

disprove [dɪsˈpruːv] *vt* widerlegen

dispute [dɪsˈpjuːt] *n* Streit *m*; (*also:* **industrial** ~) Arbeitskampf *m* ♦ *vt* bestreiten

disqualify [dɪsˈkwɔlɪfaɪ] *vt* disqualifizieren

disquiet [dɪsˈkwaɪət] *n* Unruhe *f*

disregard [dɪsrɪˈgɑːd] *vt* nicht (be)achten

disrepair [ˈdɪsrɪˈpeər] *n*: **to fall into** ~ verfallen

disreputable [dɪsˈrepjʊtəbl] *adj* verrufen

disrespectful [dɪsrɪˈspektful] *adj* respektlos

disrupt [dɪsˈrʌpt] *vt* stören; (*service*) unterbrechen; ~**ion** [dɪsˈrʌpʃən] *n* Störung *f*; Unterbrechung *f*

dissatisfaction [dɪssætɪsˈfækʃən] *n* Unzufriedenheit *f*; **dissatisfied** [dɪsˈsætɪsfaɪd] *adj* unzufrieden

dissect [dɪˈsekt] *vt* zerlegen, sezieren

dissent [dɪˈsent] *n* abweichende Meinung *f*

dissertation [dɪsəˈteɪʃən] *n* wissenschaftliche Arbeit *f*; (*Ph.D.*) Doktorarbeit *f*

disservice [dɪsˈsəːvɪs] *n*: **to do sb a** ~ jdm einen schlechten Dienst erweisen

dissident [ˈdɪsɪdnt] *adj* anders denkend ♦ *n* Dissident *m*

dissimilar [dɪˈsɪmɪlər] *adj*: ~ (**to sb/sth**) (jdm/etw) unähnlich

dissipate [ˈdɪsɪpeɪt] *vt* (*waste*) verschwenden; (*scatter*) zerstreuen

dissociate [dɪˈsəuʃɪeɪt] *vt* trennen

dissolve [dɪˈzɔlv] *vt* auflösen ♦ *vi* sich auflösen

dissuade [dɪˈsweɪd] *vt*: **to** ~ **sb from doing sth** jdn davon abbringen, etw zu tun

distance [ˈdɪstns] *n* Entfernung *f*; **in the** ~ in der Ferne; **distant** *adj* entfernt, fern; (*with time*) fern

distaste [dɪsˈteɪst] *n* Abneigung *f*; ~**ful** *adj* widerlich

distended [dɪsˈtendɪd] *adj* (*stomach*) aufgebläht

distil [dɪsˈtɪl] *vt* destillieren; ~**lery** *n* Brennerei *f*

distinct [dɪsˈtɪŋkt] *adj* (*separate*) getrennt; (*clear*) klar, deutlich; **as** ~ **from** im Unterschied zu; ~**ion** [dɪsˈtɪŋkʃən] *n* Unterscheidung *f*; (*eminence*) Auszeichnung *f*; ~**ive** *adj* bezeichnend

distinguish [dɪsˈtɪŋgwɪʃ] *vt* unterscheiden; ~**ed** *adj* (*eminent*) berühmt; ~**ing** *adj* bezeichnend

distort [dɪsˈtɔːt] *vt* verdrehen; (*misrepresent*) entstellen; ~**ion** [dɪsˈtɔːʃən] *n* Verzerrung *f*

distract [dɪsˈtrækt] *vt* ablenken; ~**ing** *adj* verwirrend; ~**ion** [dɪsˈtrækʃən] *n* (*distress*) Raserei *f*; (*diversion*) Zerstreuung *f*

distraught [dɪsˈtrɔːt] *adj* bestürzt

distress [dɪsˈtres] *n* Not *f*; (*suffering*) Qual *f* ♦ *vt* quälen; ~**ing** *adj* erschütternd; ~ **signal** *n* Notsignal *nt*

distribute [dɪsˈtrɪbjuːt] *vt* verteilen; **distribution** [dɪstrɪˈbjuːʃən] *n* Verteilung *f*;

distributor n Verteiler m

district ['dɪstrɪkt] n (of country) Kreis m; (of town) Bezirk m; ~ attorney (US) n Oberstaatsanwalt m; ~ nurse n Kreiskrankenschwester f

distrust [dɪs'trʌst] n Misstrauen nt ♦ vt misstrauen +dat

disturb [dɪs'tɜːb] vt stören; (agitate) erregen; ~ance n Störung f; ~ed adj beunruhigt; emotionally ~ed emotional gestört; ~ing adj beunruhigend

disuse [dɪs'juːs] n: to fall into ~ außer Gebrauch kommen; ~d [dɪs'juːzd] adj außer Gebrauch; (mine, railway line) stillgelegt

ditch [dɪtʃ] n Graben m ♦ vt (person) loswerden; (plan) fallen lassen

dither ['dɪðər] vi verdattert sein

ditto ['dɪtəʊ] adv dito, ebenfalls

divan [dɪ'væn] n Liegesofa nt

dive [daɪv] n (into water) Kopfsprung m; (AVIAT) Sturzflug m ♦ vi tauchen; ~r n Taucher m

diverge [daɪ'vɜːdʒ] vi auseinander gehen

diverse [daɪ'vɜːs] adj verschieden

diversion [daɪ'vɜːʃən] n Ablenkung f; (BRIT: AUT) Umleitung f

diversity [daɪ'vɜːsɪtɪ] n Vielfalt f

divert [daɪ'vɜːt] vt ablenken; (traffic) umleiten

divide [dɪ'vaɪd] vt teilen ♦ vi sich teilen; ~d highway (US) n Schnellstraße f

divine [dɪ'vaɪn] adj göttlich

diving ['daɪvɪŋ] n (SPORT) Turmspringen nt; (underwater ~) Tauchen nt; ~ board n Sprungbrett nt

divinity [dɪ'vɪnɪtɪ] n Gottheit f; (subject) Religion f

division [dɪ'vɪʒən] n Teilung f; (MIL) Division f; (part) Abteilung f; (in opinion) Uneinigkeit f; (BRIT: POL) Abstimmung f durch Hammelsprung f

divorce [dɪ'vɔːs] n (Ehe)scheidung f ♦ vt scheiden; ~d adj geschieden; ~e [dɪvɔː'siː] n Geschiedene(r) f(m)

divulge [daɪ'vʌldʒ] vt preisgeben

DIY (BRIT) n abbr = do-it-yourself

dizzy ['dɪzɪ] adj schwindlig

DJ n abbr = disc jockey

DNA fingerprinting n genetische Fingerabdrücke pl

KEYWORD

do [duː] (pt did, pp done) n (inf: party etc) Fete f
♦ aux vb 1 (in negative constructions and questions): I don't understand ich verstehe nicht; didn't you know? wusstest du das nicht?; what do you think? was meinen Sie?
2 (for emphasis, in polite phrases): she does seem rather tired sie scheint wirklich sehr müde zu sein; do sit down/help yourself setzen Sie sich doch hin/greifen Sie doch zu
3 (used to avoid repeating vb): she swims better than I do sie schwimmt besser als ich; she lives in Glasgow - so do I sie wohnt in Glasgow - ich auch
4 (in tag questions): you like him, don't you? du magst ihn doch, oder?
♦ vt 1 (carry out, perform etc) tun, machen; what are you doing tonight? was machst du heute Abend?; I've got nothing to do ich habe nichts zu tun; to do one's hair/nails sich die Haare/Nägel machen
2 (AUT etc) fahren
♦ vi 1 (act, behave): do as I do mach es wie ich
2 (get on, fare): he's doing well/badly at school er ist gut/schlecht in der Schule; how do you do? guten Tag
3 (be suitable) gehen; (be sufficient) reichen; to make do (with) auskommen mit
do away with vt (kill) umbringen; (abolish: law etc) abschaffen
do up vt (laces, dress, buttons) zumachen; (room, house) renovieren
do with vt (need) brauchen; (be connected) zu tun haben mit
do without vt, vi auskommen ohne

---

docile ['dəʊsaɪl] adj gefügig

dock [dɒk] n Dock nt; (JUR) Anklagebank f ♦ vi ins Dock gehen; ~er n Hafenarbeiter m; ~yard n Werft f

doctor ['dɔktə'] n Arzt m, Ärztin f; (UNIV) Doktor m ♦ vt (fig) fälschen; (drink etc) etw beimischen +dat; **D~ of Philosophy** n Doktor m der Philosophie

document ['dɔkjumənt] n Dokument nt; **~ary** [dɔkju'mɛntəri] n Dokumentarbericht m; (film) Dokumentarfilm m ♦ adj dokumentarisch; **~ation** [dɔkjumən'teɪʃən] n dokumentarische(r) Nachweis m

dodge [dɔdʒ] n Kniff m ♦ vt ausweichen +dat

dodgems ['dɔdʒəmz] (BRIT) npl Autoskooter m

doe [dəu] n (roe deer) Ricke f; (red deer) Hirschkuh f; (rabbit) Weibchen nt

does [dʌz] vb see **do**; **~n't** = **does not**

dog [dɔg] n Hund m; **~ collar** n Hundehalsband nt; (ECCL) Kragen m des Geistlichen; **~-eared** adj mit Eselsohren

dogged ['dɔgɪd] adj hartnäckig

dogsbody ['dɔgzbɔdɪ] n Mädchen nt für alles

doings ['duɪŋz] npl (activities) Treiben nt

do-it-yourself ['duːɪtjɔː'sɛlf] n Do-it-yourself nt

doldrums ['dɔldrəmz] npl: **to be in the ~** (business) Flaute haben; (person) deprimiert sein

dole [dəul] (BRIT) n Stempelgeld nt; **to be on the ~** stempeln gehen; **~ out** vt ausgeben, austeilen

doleful ['dəulful] adj traurig

doll [dɔl] n Puppe f ♦ vt: **to ~ o.s. up** sich aufdonnern

dollar ['dɔlə'] n Dollar m

dolphin ['dɔlfɪn] n Delfin m, Delphin m

dome [dəum] n Kuppel f

domestic [də'mɛstɪk] adj häuslich; (within country) Innen-, Binnen-; (animal) Haus-; **~ated** adj (person) häuslich; (animal) zahm

dominant ['dɔmɪnənt] adj vorherrschend

dominate ['dɔmɪneɪt] vt beherrschen

domineering [dɔmɪ'nɪərɪŋ] adj herrisch

dominion [də'mɪnɪən] n (rule) Regierungsgewalt f; (land) Staatsgebiet nt mit Selbstverwaltung

domino ['dɔmɪnəu] (pl **-es**) n Dominostein m; **~es** n (game) Domino(spiel) nt

don [dɔn] (BRIT) n akademische(r) Lehrer m

donate [də'neɪt] vt (blood, money) spenden; (lot of money) stiften; **donation** [də'neɪʃən] n Spende f

done [dʌn] pp of **do**

donkey ['dɔŋkɪ] n Esel m

donor ['dəunə'] n Spender m; **~ card** n Organspenderausweis m

don't [dəunt] = **do not**

doodle ['duːdl] vi kritzeln

doom [duːm] n böse(s) Geschick nt; (downfall) Verderben nt ♦ vt: **to be ~ed** zum Untergang verurteilt sein; **~sday** n der Jüngste Tag

door [dɔː'] n Tür f; **~bell** n Türklingel f; **~handle** n Türklinke f; **~man** (irreg) n Türsteher m; **~mat** n Fußmatte f; **~step** n Türstufe f; **~way** n Türöffnung f

dope [dəup] n (drug) Aufputschmittel nt ♦ vt (horse) dopen

dopey ['dəupɪ] (inf) adj bekloppt

dormant ['dɔːmənt] adj latent

dormitory ['dɔːmɪtrɪ] n Schlafsaal m

dormouse ['dɔːmaus] (pl **-mice**) n Haselmaus f

DOS [dɔs] n abbr (= disk operating system) DOS nt

dosage ['dəusɪdʒ] n Dosierung f

dose [dəus] n Dosis f

dosh [dɔʃ] (inf) n (money) Moos nt, Knete f

doss house ['dɔs-] (BRIT) n Bleibe f

dot [dɔt] n Punkt m; **~ted with** übersät mit; **on the ~** pünktlich

dote [dəut]: **to ~ on** vt fus vernarrt sein in +acc

dotted line ['dɔtɪd-] n punktierte Linie f

double ['dʌbl] adj, adv doppelt ♦ n Doppelgänger m ♦ vt verdoppeln ♦ vi sich verdoppeln; **~s** npl (TENNIS) Doppel nt; **on** or **at the ~** im Laufschritt; **~ bass** n Kontrabass m; **~ bed** n Doppelbett nt; **~ bend** (BRIT) n S-Kurve f; **~-breasted** adj zweireihig; **~-cross** vt hintergehen; **~-decker** n Doppeldecker m; **~ glazing** (BRIT) n Doppelverglasung f; **~ room** n Doppelzimmer nt

doubly ['dʌblɪ] adv doppelt

doubt [daut] n Zweifel m ♦ vt bezweifeln; **~ful** adj zweifelhaft; **~less** adv ohne Zweifel

dough [dəu] n Teig m; **~nut** n Berliner m

douse [dauz] vt (drench) mit Wasser begießen, durchtränken; (extinguish) ausmachen

dove [dʌv] n Taube f

dovetail ['dʌvteil] vi (plans) übereinstimmen

dowdy ['daudi] adj unmodern

down [daun] n (fluff) Flaum m; (hill) Hügel m ♦ adv unten; (motion) herunter; hinunter ♦ prep: **to go ~ the street** die Straße hinuntergehen ♦ vt niederschlagen; **~ with X!** nieder mit X!; **~-and-out** n Tramp m; **~-at-heel** adj schäbig; **~cast** adj niedergeschlagen; **~fall** n Sturz m; **~hearted** adj niedergeschlagen; **~hill** adv bergab; **~ payment** n Anzahlung f; **~pour** n Platzregen m; **~right** adj ausgesprochen; **~size** vi (ECON: company) sich verkleinern

---

Downing Street

ⓘ **Downing Street** ist die Straße in London, die von Whitehall zum St James Park führt und in der sich der offizielle Wohnsitz des Premierministers (Nr. 10) und des Finanzministers (Nr. 11) befindet. Im weiteren Sinne bezieht sich der Begriff Downing Street auf die britische Regierung.

Down's syndrome [daunz-] n (MED) Down-Syndrom nt

down: **~stairs** adv unten; (motion) nach unten; **~stream** adv flussabwärts; **~-to-earth** adj praktisch; **~town** adv in der Innenstadt; (motion) in die Innenstadt; **~under** (BRIT: inf) adv in/nach Australien/Neuseeland; **~ward** adj Abwärts-, nach unten ♦ adv abwärts, nach unten; **~wards** adv abwärts, nach unten

dowry ['dauri] n Mitgift f

doz. abbr (= dozen) Dtzd.

doze [dəuz] vi dösen; **~ off** vi einnicken

dozen ['dʌzn] n Dutzend nt; **a ~ books** ein Dutzend Bücher; **~s of** dutzende or

Dutzende von

Dr. abbr = **doctor; drive**

drab [dræb] adj düster, eintönig

draft [drɑːft] n Entwurf m; (FIN) Wechsel m; (US: MIL) Einberufung f ♦ vt skizzieren; see also **draught**

draftsman ['drɑːftsmən] (US: irreg) n = **draughtsman**

drag [dræg] vt schleppen; (river) mit einem Schleppnetz absuchen ♦ vi sich (dahin)schleppen ♦ n (bore) etwas Blödes; **in ~** als Tunte; **a man in ~** eine Tunte; **~ on** vi sich in die Länge ziehen; **~ and drop** vt (COMPUT) Drag & Drop nt

dragon ['drægn] n Drache m; **~fly** ['drægənflai] n Libelle f

drain [drein] n Abfluss m; (fig: burden) Belastung f ♦ vt ableiten; (exhaust) erschöpfen ♦ vi (of water) abfließen; **~age** n Kanalisation f; **~ing board** (US **~board**) n Ablaufbrett nt; **~pipe** n Abflussrohr nt

dram [dræm] n Schluck m

drama ['drɑːmə] n Drama nt; **~tic** [drə'mætik] adj dramatisch; **~tist** ['dræmətist] n Dramatiker m; **~tize** ['dræmətaiz] vt (events) dramatisieren; (for TV etc) bearbeiten

drank [dræŋk] pt of **drink**

drape [dreip] vt drapieren; **~s** (US) npl Vorhänge pl

drastic ['dræstik] adj drastisch

draught [drɑːft] (US **draft**) n Zug m; (NAUT) Tiefgang m; **~s** n Damespiel nt; **on ~** (beer) vom Fass; **~ beer** n Bier nt vom Fass; **~board** (BRIT) n Zeichenbrett nt

draughtsman ['drɑːftsmən] (irreg) n technische(r) Zeichner m

draw [drɔː] (pt drew, pp drew) vt ziehen; (crowd) anlocken; (picture) zeichnen; (money) abheben; (water) schöpfen ♦ vi (SPORT) unentschieden spielen ♦ n (SPORT) Unentschieden nt; (lottery) Ziehung f; **~ near** vi näher rücken; **~ out** vi (train) ausfahren; (lengthen) sich hinziehen; **~ up** vi (stop) halten ♦ vt (document) aufsetzen

drawback ['drɔːbæk] n Nachteil m

drawbridge ['drɔːbridʒ] n Zugbrücke f

drawer [drɔ:ʳ] *n* Schublade *f*

drawing ['drɔːɪŋ] *n* Zeichnung *f*; Zeichnen *nt*; **~ board** *n* Reißbrett *nt*; **~ pin** (*BRIT*) *n* Reißzwecke *f*; **~ room** *n* Salon *m*

drawl [drɔ:l] *n* schleppende Sprechweise *f*

drawn [drɔ:n] *pp of* **draw**

dread [dred] *n* Furcht *f* ♦ *vt* fürchten; **~ful** *adj* furchtbar

dream [dri:m] (*pt, pp* **dreamed** *or* **dreamt**) *n* Traum *m* ♦ *vt* träumen ♦ *vi:* **to ~ (about)** träumen (von); **~er** *n* Träumer *m*; **~t** [dremt] *pt, pp of* **dream**; **~y** *adj* verträumt

dreary ['drɪərɪ] *adj* trostlos, öde

dredge [dredʒ] *vt* ausbaggern

dregs [dregz] *npl* Bodensatz *m*; (*fig*) Abschaum *m*

drench [drentʃ] *vt* durchnässen

dress [dres] *n* Kleidung *f*; (*garment*) Kleid *nt* ♦ *vt* anziehen; (*MED*) verbinden; **to get ~ed** sich anziehen; **~ up** *vi* sich fein machen; **~ circle** (*BRIT*) *n* erste(r) Rang *m*; **~er** *n* (*furniture*) Anrichte *f*; **~ing** *n* (*MED*) Verband *m*; (*COOK*) Soße *f*; **~ing gown** (*BRIT*) *n* Morgenrock *m*; **~ing room** *n* (*THEAT*) Garderobe *f*; (*SPORT*) Umkleideraum *m*; **~ing table** *n* Toilettentisch *m*; **~maker** *n* Schneiderin *f*; **~ rehearsal** *n* Generalprobe *f*

drew [dru:] *pt of* **draw**

dribble ['drɪbl] *vi* sabbern ♦ *vt* (*ball*) dribbeln

dried [draɪd] *adj* getrocknet; (*fruit*) Dörr-, gedörrte(r, s); **~ milk** *n* Milchpulver *nt*

drier ['draɪəʳ] *n* = **dryer**

drift [drɪft] *n* Strömung *f*; (*snowdrift*) Schneewehe *f*; (*fig*) Richtung *f* ♦ *vi* sich treiben lassen; **~wood** *n* Treibholz *nt*

drill [drɪl] *n* Bohrer *m*; (*MIL*) Drill *m* ♦ *vt* bohren; (*MIL*) ausbilden ♦ *vi:* **to ~ (for)** bohren (nach)

drink [drɪŋk] (*pt* **drank**, *pp* **drunk**) *n* Getränk *nt*; (*spirits*) Drink *m* ♦ *vt, vi* trinken; **to have a ~** etwas trinken; **~er** *n* Trinker *m*; **~ing water** *n* Trinkwasser *nt*

drip [drɪp] *n* Tropfen *m* ♦ *vi* tropfen; **~-dry** *adj* bügelfrei; **~ping** *n* Bratenfett *nt*

drive [draɪv] (*pt* **drove**, *pp* **driven**) *n* Fahrt *f*; (*road*) Einfahrt *f*; (*campaign*) Aktion *f*; (*energy*) Schwung *m*; (*SPORT*) Schlag *m*;

(*also:* **disk ~**) Diskettenlaufwerk *nt* ♦ *vt* (*car*) fahren; (*animals, people, objects*) treiben; (*power*) antreiben ♦ *vi* fahren; **left-/right-hand ~** Links-/Rechtssteuerung *f*; **to ~ sb mad** jdn verrückt machen; **~-by shooting** *n* Schusswaffenangriff aus einem vorbeifahrenden Wagen

drivel ['drɪvl] *n* Faselei *f*

driven ['drɪvn] *pp of* **drive**

driver ['draɪvəʳ] *n* Fahrer *m*; **~'s license** (*US*) *n* Führerschein *m*

driveway ['draɪvweɪ] *n* Auffahrt *f*; (*longer*) Zufahrtsstraße *f*

driving ['draɪvɪŋ] *adj* (*rain*) stürmisch; **~ instructor** *n* Fahrlehrer *m*; **~ lesson** *n* Fahrstunde *f*; **~ licence** (*BRIT*) *n* Führerschein *m*; **~ school** *n* Fahrschule *f*; **~ test** *n* Fahrprüfung *f*

drizzle ['drɪzl] *n* Nieselregen *m* ♦ *vi* nieseln

droll [drəʊl] *adj* drollig

drone [drəʊn] *n* (*sound*) Brummen *nt*; (*bee*) Drohne *f*

drool [dru:l] *vi* sabbern

droop [dru:p] *vi* (*schlaff*) herabhängen

drop [drɒp] *n* (*of liquid*) Tropfen *m*; (*fall*) Fall *m* ♦ *vt* fallen lassen; (*lower*) senken; (*abandon*) fallen lassen ♦ *vi* (*fall*) herunterfallen; **~s** *npl* (*MED*) Tropfen *pl*; **~ off** *vi* (*sleep*) einschlafen ♦ *vt* (*passenger*) absetzen; **~ out** *vi* (*withdraw*) ausscheiden; **~-out** *n* Aussteiger *m*; **~per** *n* Pipette *f*; **~pings** *npl* Kot *m*

drought [draʊt] *n* Dürre *f*

drove [drəʊv] *pt of* **drive**

drown [draʊn] *vt* ertränken; (*sound*) übertönen ♦ *vi* ertrinken

drowsy ['draʊzɪ] *adj* schläfrig

drudgery ['drʌdʒərɪ] *n* Plackerei *f*

drug [drʌg] *n* (*MED*) Arznei *f*; (*narcotic*) Rauschgift *nt* ♦ *vt* betäuben; **~ addict** *n* Rauschgiftsüchtige(r) *f(m)*; **~gist** (*US*) *n* Drogist(in) *m(f)*; **~store** (*US*) *n* Drogerie *f*

drum [drʌm] *n* Trommel *f* ♦ *vi* trommeln; **~s** *npl* (*MUS*) Schlagzeug *nt*; **~mer** *n* Trommler *m*

drunk [drʌŋk] *pp of* **drink** ♦ *adj* betrunken ♦ *n* (*also:* **~ard**) Trinker(in) *m(f)*; **~en** *adj* betrunken

dry [draɪ] *adj* trocken ♦ *vt* (ab)trocknen ♦ *vi* trocknen; ~ **up** *vi* austrocknen ♦ *vt* (dishes) abtrocknen; ~ **cleaner's** *n* chemische Reinigung *f*; ~ **cleaning** *n* chemische Reinigung *f*; ~**er** *n* Trockner *m*; (US: spin-dryer) (Wäsche)schleuder *f*; ~ **goods store** (US) *n* Kurzwarengeschäft *nt*; ~**ness** *n* Trockenheit *f*; ~ **rot** *n* Hausschwamm *m*

DSS (BRIT) *n abbr* (= Department of Social Security) ≃ Sozialministerium *nt*

DTP *n abbr* (= desktop publishing) DTP *nt*

dual ['djuəl] *adj* doppelt; ~ **carriageway** (BRIT) *n* zweispurige Fahrbahn *f*; ~ **nationality** *n* doppelte Staatsangehörigkeit *f*; ~**-purpose** *adj* Mehrzweck-

dubbed [dʌbd] *adj* (film) synchronisiert

dubious ['djuːbɪəs] *adj* zweifelhaft

duchess ['dʌtʃɪs] *n* Herzogin *f*

duck [dʌk] *n* Ente *f* ♦ *vi* sich ducken; ~**ling** *n* Entchen *nt*

duct [dʌkt] *n* Röhre *f*

dud [dʌd] *n* Niete *f* ♦ *adj* (cheque) ungedeckt

due [djuː] *adj* fällig; (fitting) angemessen ♦ *n* Gebühr *f*; (right) Recht *nt* ♦ *adv* (south etc) genau; ~**s** *npl* (for club) Beitrag *m*; (NAUT) Gebühren *pl*; ~ **to** wegen +gen

duel ['djuəl] *n* Duell *nt*

duet [djuːˈet] *n* Duett *nt*

duffel ['dʌfl] *adj*: ~ **bag** Matchbeutel *m*, Matchsack *m*

dug [dʌg] *pt, pp of* **dig**

duke [djuːk] *n* Herzog *m*

dull [dʌl] *adj* (colour, weather) trübe; (stupid) schwer von Begriff; (boring) langweilig ♦ *vt* abstumpfen

duly ['djuːlɪ] *adv* ordnungsgemäß

dumb [dʌm] *adj* stumm; (inf: stupid) doof, blöde; ~**founded** [dʌmˈfaundɪd] *adj* verblüfft

dummy ['dʌmɪ] *n* Schneiderpuppe *f*; (substitute) Attrappe *f*; (BRIT: for baby) Schnuller *m* ♦ *adj* Schein-

dump [dʌmp] *n* Abfallhaufen *m*; (MIL) Stapelplatz *m*; (inf: place) Nest *nt* ♦ *vt* abladen, auskippen; ~**ing** *n* (COMM) Schleuderexport *m*; (of rubbish)

Schuttabladen *nt*

dumpling ['dʌmplɪŋ] *n* Kloß *m*, Knödel *m*

dumpy ['dʌmpɪ] *adj* pummelig

dunce [dʌns] *n* Dummkopf *m*

dune [djuːn] *n* Düne *f*

dung [dʌŋ] *n* Dünger *m*

dungarees [dʌŋgəˈriːz] *npl* Latzhose *f*

dungeon ['dʌndʒən] *n* Kerker *m*

dupe [djuːp] *n* Gefoppte(r) *m* ♦ *vt* hintergehen, anführen

duplex ['djuːpleks] (US) *n* zweistöckige Wohnung *f*

duplicate [*n* 'djuːplɪkət, *vb* 'djuːplɪkeɪt] *n* Duplikat *nt* ♦ *vt* verdoppeln; (make copies) kopieren; **in** ~ in doppelter Ausführung

duplicity [djuːˈplɪsɪtɪ] *n* Doppelspiel *nt*

durable ['djuərəbl] *adj* haltbar

duration [djuəˈreɪʃən] *n* Dauer *f*

duress [djuəˈres] *n*: **under** ~ unter Zwang

during ['djuərɪŋ] *prep* während +gen

dusk [dʌsk] *n* Abenddämmerung *f*

dust [dʌst] *n* Staub *m* ♦ *vt* abstauben; (sprinkle) bestäuben; ~**bin** (BRIT) *n* Mülleimer *m*; ~**er** *n* Staubtuch *nt*; ~ **jacket** *n* Schutzumschlag *m*; ~**man** (BRIT: irreg) *n* Müllmann *m*; ~**y** *adj* staubig

Dutch [dʌtʃ] *adj* holländisch, niederländisch ♦ *n* (LING) Holländisch *nt*, Niederländisch *nt*; **the** ~ *npl* (people) die Holländer *pl*, die Niederländer *pl*; **to go** ~ getrennte Kasse machen; ~**man/woman** (irreg) *n* Holländer(in) *m(f)*, Niederländer(in) *m(f)*

dutiful ['djuːtɪful] *adj* pflichtbewusst

duty ['djuːtɪ] *n* Pflicht *f*; (job) Aufgabe *f*; (tax) Einfuhrzoll *m*; **on** ~ im Dienst; ~ **chemist's** *n* Apotheke *f* im Bereitschaftsdienst; ~**-free** *adj* zollfrei

duvet ['duːveɪ] (BRIT) *n* Daunendecke *nt*

DVD *n abbr* (= digital video disc) DVD *f*

dwarf [dwɔːf] (pl **dwarves**) *n* Zwerg *m* ♦ *vt* überragen

dwell [dwel] (pt, pp **dwelt**) *vi* wohnen; ~ **on** *vt fus* verweilen bei; ~**ing** *n* Wohnung *f*

dwelt [dwelt] *pt, pp of* **dwell**

dwindle ['dwɪndl] *vi* schwinden

dye [daɪ] *n* Farbstoff *m* ♦ *vt* färben

dying ['daɪɪŋ] *adj* (person) sterbend;

(*moments*) letzt

dyke [daɪk] (*BRIT*) n (*channel*) Kanal m; (*barrier*) Deich m, Damm m

dynamic [daɪˈnæmɪk] adj dynamisch

dynamite [ˈdaɪnəmaɪt] n Dynamit nt

dyslexia [dɪsˈleksɪə] n Legasthenie f

E, e

E [iː] n (*MUS*) E nt

each [iːtʃ] adj jeder/jede/jedes ♦ pron (ein) jeder/(eine) jede/(ein) jedes; **~ other** einander, sich; **they have two books ~** sie haben je zwei Bücher

eager [ˈiːgəʳ] adj eifrig

eagle [ˈiːgl] n Adler m

ear [ɪəʳ] n Ohr nt; (*of corn*) Ähre f; **~ache** n Ohrenschmerzen pl; **~drum** n Trommelfell nt

earl [əːl] n Graf m

earlier [ˈəːlɪəʳ] adj, adv früher; **I can't come any ~** ich kann nicht früher or eher kommen

early [ˈəːlɪ] adj, adv früh; **~ retirement** n vorzeitige Pensionierung

earmark [ˈɪəmɑːk] vt vorsehen

earn [əːn] vt verdienen

earnest [ˈəːnɪst] adj ernst; **in ~** im Ernst

earnings [ˈəːnɪŋz] npl Verdienst m

ear: ~phones [ˈɪəfəʊnz] npl Kopfhörer pl; **~ring** [ˈɪərɪŋ] n Ohrring m; **~shot** [ˈɪəʃɔt] n Hörweite f

earth [əːθ] n Erde f; (*BRIT: ELEC*) Erdung f ♦ vt erden; **~enware** n Steingut nt; **~quake** n Erdbeben nt; **~y** adj roh

earwig [ˈɪəwɪg] n Ohrwurm m

ease [iːz] n (*simplicity*) Leichtigkeit f; (*social*) Ungezwungenheit f ♦ vt (*pain*) lindern; (*burden*) erleichtern; **at ~** ungezwungen; (*MIL*) rührt euch!; **~ off** or **up** vi nachlassen

easel [ˈiːzl] n Staffelei f

easily [ˈiːzɪlɪ] adv leicht

east [iːst] n Osten m ♦ adj östlich ♦ adv nach Osten

Easter [ˈiːstəʳ] n Ostern nt; **~ egg** n Osterei nt

east: ~erly adj östlich, Ost-; **~ern** adj östlich; **~ward(s)** adv ostwärts

easy [ˈiːzɪ] adj (*task*) einfach; (*life*) bequem; (*manner*) ungezwungen, natürlich ♦ adv leicht; **~ chair** n Sessel m; **~-going** adj gelassen; (*lax*) lässig

eat [iːt] (pt **ate**, pp **eaten**) vt essen; (*animals*) fressen; (*destroy*) (zer)fressen ♦ vi essen; fressen; **~ away** vt zerfressen; **~ into** vt fus zerfressen; **~en** pp of **eat**

eau de Cologne [ˈəʊdəkəˈləʊn] n Kölnischwasser nt

eaves [iːvz] npl Dachrand m

eavesdrop [ˈiːvzdrɔp] vi lauschen; **to ~ on sb** jdn belauschen

ebb [eb] n Ebbe f ♦ vi (fig: also: **~ away**) (ab)ebben

ebony [ˈebənɪ] n Ebenholz nt

EC n abbr (= European Community) EG f

ECB n abbr (= European Central Bank) EZB f

eccentric [ɪkˈsentrɪk] adj exzentrisch ♦ n Exzentriker(in) m(f)

ecclesiastical [ɪkliːzɪˈæstɪkl] adj kirchlich

echo [ˈekəʊ] (pl **~es**) n Echo nt ♦ vt zurückwerfen; (fig) nachbeten ♦ vi widerhallen

eclipse [ɪˈklɪps] n Finsternis f ♦ vt verfinstern

ecology [ɪˈkɔlədʒɪ] n Ökologie f

e-commerce [ˈiːkɔmɜːs] n Onlinehandel m

economic [iːkəˈnɔmɪk] adj wirtschaftlich; **~al** adj wirtschaftlich; (*person*) sparsam; **~ refugee** n Wirtschaftsflüchtling m; **~s** n Volkswirtschaft f

economist [ɪˈkɔnəmɪst] n Volkswirt(schaftler) m

economize [ɪˈkɔnəmaɪz] vi sparen

economy [ɪˈkɔnəmɪ] n (*thrift*) Sparsamkeit f; (*of country*) Wirtschaft f; **~ class** n Touristenklasse f

ecstasy [ˈekstəsɪ] n Ekstase f; (*drug*) Ecstasy nt; **ecstatic** [eksˈtætɪk] adj hingerissen

ECU [ˈeɪkjuː] n abbr (= European Currency Unit) ECU m

eczema [ˈeksɪmə] n Ekzem nt

edge [edʒ] n Rand m; (*of knife*) Schneide f ♦ vt (*SEWING*) einfassen; **on ~** (fig) = **edgy**;

to ~ away from langsam abrücken von; **~ways** *adv*: **he couldn't get a word in ~ways** er kam überhaupt nicht zu Wort

edgy ['ɛdʒɪ] *adj* nervös

edible ['ɛdɪbl] *adj* essbar

edict ['iːdɪkt] *n* Erlass *m*

edit ['ɛdɪt] *vt* redigieren; **~ion** [ɪ'dɪʃən] *n* Ausgabe *f*; **~or** *n* (*of newspaper*) Redakteur *m*; (*of book*) Lektor *m*; **~orial** [ɛdɪ'tɔːrɪəl] *adj* Redaktions- ♦ *n* Leitartikel *m*

educate ['ɛdjʊkeɪt] *vt* erziehen, (aus)bilden; **~d** *adj* gebildet; **education** [ɛdjʊ'keɪʃən] *n* (*teaching*) Unterricht *m*; (*system*) Schulwesen *nt*; (*schooling*) Erziehung *f*; Bildung *f*; **educational** *adj* pädagogisch

eel [iːl] *n* Aal *m*

eerie ['ɪərɪ] *adj* unheimlich

effect [ɪ'fɛkt] *n* Wirkung *f* ♦ *vt* bewirken; **~s** *npl* (*sound, visual*) Effekte *pl*; **in ~** im Endeffekt, in der Tat; **to take ~** (*law*) in Kraft treten; (*drug*) wirken; **~ive** *adj* wirksam, effektiv; **~ively** *adv* wirksam, effektiv

effeminate [ɪ'fɛmɪnɪt] *adj* weibisch

effervescent [ɛfə'vɛsnt] *adj* (*also fig*) sprudelnd

efficiency [ɪ'fɪʃənsɪ] *n* Leistungsfähigkeit *f*

efficient [ɪ'fɪʃənt] *adj* tüchtig; (*TECH*) leistungsfähig; (*method*) wirksam

effigy ['ɛfɪdʒɪ] *n* Abbild *nt*

effort ['ɛfət] *n* Anstrengung *f*; **~less** *adj* mühelos

effusive [ɪ'fjuːsɪv] *adj* überschwänglich

e.g. *adv abbr* (= *exempli gratia*) z. B.

egalitarian [ɪgælɪ'tɛərɪən] *adj* Gleichheits-, egalitär

egg [ɛg] *n* Ei *nt*; **~ on** *vt* anstacheln; **~cup** *n* Eierbecher *m*; **~plant** (*esp US*) *n* Aubergine *f*; **~shell** *n* Eierschale *f*

ego ['iːgəʊ] *n* Ich *nt*, Selbst *nt*; **~tism** ['ɛgəʊtɪzəm] *n* Ichbezogenheit *f*; **~tist** ['ɛgəʊtɪst] *n* Egozentriker *m*

Egypt ['iːdʒɪpt] *n* Ägypten *nt*; **~ian** [ɪ'dʒɪpʃən] *adj* ägyptisch ♦ *n* Ägypter(in) *m(f)*

eiderdown ['aɪdədaʊn] *n* Daunendecke *f*

eight [eɪt] *num* acht; **~een** *num* achtzehn; **~h** [eɪtθ] *adj* achte(r, s) ♦ *n* Achtel *nt*; **~y** *num* achtzig

Eire ['ɛərə] *n* Irland *nt*

either ['aɪðər] *conj*: **~ ... or** entweder ... oder ♦ *pron*: **~ of the two** eine(r, s) von beiden ♦ *adj*: **on ~ side** auf beiden Seiten ♦ *adv*: **I don't ~** ich auch nicht; **I don't want ~** ich will keins von beiden

eject [ɪ'dʒɛkt] *vt* ausstoßen, vertreiben

eke [iːk] *vt*: **to ~ out** strecken

elaborate [*adj* ɪ'læbərɪt, *vb* ɪ'læbəreɪt] *adj* sorgfältig ausgearbeitet, ausführlich ♦ *vt* sorgfältig ausarbeiten ♦ *vi* ausführlich darstellen

elapse [ɪ'læps] *vi* vergehen

elastic [ɪ'læstɪk] *n* Gummiband *nt* ♦ *adj* elastisch; **~ band** (*BRIT*) *n* Gummiband *nt*

elated [ɪ'leɪtɪd] *adj* froh

elation [ɪ'leɪʃən] *n* gehobene Stimmung *f*

elbow ['ɛlbəʊ] *n* Ellbogen *m*

elder ['ɛldər] *adj* älter ♦ *n* Ältere(r) *f(m)*; **~ly** *adj* ältere(r, s) ♦ *npl*: **the ~ly** die Älteren *pl*; **eldest** ['ɛldɪst] *adj* älteste(r, s) ♦ *n* Älteste(r) *f(m)*

elect [ɪ'lɛkt] *vt* wählen ♦ *adj* zukünftig; **~ion** [ɪ'lɛkʃən] *n* Wahl *f*; **~ioneering** [ɪlɛkʃə'nɪərɪŋ] *n* Wahlpropaganda *f*; **~or** *n* Wähler *m*; **~oral** *adj* Wahl-; **~orate** *n* Wähler *pl*, Wählerschaft *f*

electric [ɪ'lɛktrɪk] *adj* elektrisch, Elektro-; **~al** *adj* elektrisch; **~ blanket** *n* Heizdecke *f*; **~ chair** *n* elektrische(r) Stuhl *m*; **~ fire** *n* elektrische(r) Heizofen *m*

electrician [ɪlɛk'trɪʃən] *n* Elektriker *m*

electricity [ɪlɛk'trɪsɪtɪ] *n* Elektrizität *f*

electrify [ɪ'lɛktrɪfaɪ] *vt* elektrifizieren; (*fig*) elektrisieren

electrocute [ɪ'lɛktrəkjuːt] *vt* durch elektrischen Strom töten

electronic [ɪlɛk'trɒnɪk] *adj* elektronisch, Elektronen-; **~ mail** *n* E-Mail *f*; **~s** *n* Elektronik *f*

elegance ['ɛlɪgəns] *n* Eleganz *f*; **elegant** ['ɛlɪgənt] *adj* elegant

element ['ɛlɪmənt] *n* Element *nt*; **~ary** [ɛlɪ'mɛntərɪ] *adj* einfach; (*primary*) Grund-

elephant ['ɛlɪfənt] *n* Elefant *m*

elevate ['ɛlɪveɪt] *vt* emporheben; **elevation** [ɛlɪ'veɪʃən] *n* (*height*) Erhebung *f*; (*ARCHIT*)

(Quer)schnitt *m*; **elevator** (*US*) *n* Fahrstuhl *m*, Aufzug *m*

eleven [ɪ'lɛvn] *num* elf; ~**ses** (*BRIT*) *npl* ≈ zweite(s) Frühstück *nt*; ~**th** *adj* elfte(r, s)

elicit [ɪ'lɪsɪt] *vt* herausbekommen

eligible ['ɛlɪdʒəbl] *adj* wählbar; **to be ~ for a pension** pensionsberechtigt sein

eliminate [ɪ'lɪmɪneɪt] *vt* ausschalten

elite [er'liːt] *n* Elite *f*

elm [ɛlm] *n* Ulme *f*

elocution [ɛlə'kjuːʃən] *n* Sprecherziehung *f*

elongated ['iːlɔŋgeɪtɪd] *adj* verlängert

elope [ɪ'ləup] *vi* entlaufen

eloquence ['ɛləkwəns] *n* Beredsamkeit *f*; **eloquent** *adj* redegewandt

else [ɛls] *adv* sonst; **who ~?** wer sonst?; **somebody ~** jemand anders; **or ~** sonst; ~**where** *adv* anderswo, woanders

elude [ɪ'luːd] *vt* entgehen +*dat*

elusive [ɪ'luːsɪv] *adj* schwer fassbar

emaciated [ɪ'meɪsɪeɪtɪd] *adj* abgezehrt

e-mail ['iːmeɪl] *n abbr* (= *electronic mail*) E-Mail *f* ♦ *vti* mailen

emancipation [ɪmænsɪ'peɪʃən] *n* Emanzipation *f*; Freilassung *f*

embankment [ɪm'bæŋkmənt] *n* (*of river*) Uferböschung *f*; (*of road*) Straßendamm *m*

embargo [ɪm'baːgəu] (*pl* -**es**) *n* Embargo *nt*

embark [ɪm'baːk] *vi* sich einschiffen; ~ **on** *vt fus* unternehmen; ~**ation** [embaː'keɪʃən] *n* Einschiffung *f*

embarrass [ɪm'bærəs] *vt* in Verlegenheit bringen; ~**ed** *adj* verlegen; ~**ing** *adj* peinlich; ~**ment** *n* Verlegenheit *f*

embassy ['ɛmbəsɪ] *n* Botschaft *f*

embed [ɪm'bɛd] *vt* einbetten

embellish [ɪm'bɛlɪʃ] *vt* verschönern

embers ['ɛmbəz] *npl* Glut(asche) *f*

embezzle [ɪm'bɛzl] *vt* unterschlagen; ~**ment** *n* Unterschlagung *f*

embitter [ɪm'bɪtər] *vt* verbittern

embody [ɪm'bɔdɪ] *vt* (*ideas*) verkörpern; (*new features*) (in sich) vereinigen

embossed [ɪm'bɔst] *adj* geprägt

embrace [ɪm'breɪs] *vt* umarmen; (*include*) einschließen ♦ *vi* sich umarmen ♦ *n* Umarmung *f*

embroider [ɪm'brɔɪdər] *vt* (be)sticken; (*story*) ausschmücken; ~**y** *n* Stickerei *f*

emerald ['ɛmərəld] *n* Smaragd *m*

emerge [ɪ'məːdʒ] *vi* auftauchen; (*truth*) herauskommen; ~**nce** *n* Erscheinen *nt*

emergency [ɪ'məːdʒənsɪ] *n* Notfall *m*; ~ **cord** (*US*) *n* Notbremse *f*; ~ **exit** *n* Notausgang *m*; ~ **landing** *n* Notlandung *f*; ~ **services** *npl* Notdienste *pl*

emery board ['ɛmərɪ-] *n* Papiernagelfeile *f*

emigrant ['ɛmɪgrənt] *n* Auswanderer *m*

emigrate ['ɛmɪgreɪt] *vi* auswandern; **emigration** [emɪ'greɪʃən] *n* Auswanderung *f*

eminence ['ɛmɪnəns] *n* hohe(r) Rang *m*

eminent ['ɛmɪnənt] *adj* bedeutend

emission [ɪ'mɪʃən] *n* Ausströmen *nt*; ~**s** *npl* Emissionen *fpl*

emit [ɪ'mɪt] *vt* von sich *dat* geben

emotion [ɪ'məuʃən] *n* Emotion *f*, Gefühl *nt*; ~**al** *adj* (*person*) emotional; (*scene*) ergreifend

emotive [ɪ'məutɪv] *adj* gefühlsbetont

emperor ['ɛmpərər] *n* Kaiser *m*

emphases ['ɛmfəsiːz] *npl of* **emphasis**

emphasis ['ɛmfəsɪs] *n* (*LING*) Betonung *f*; (*fig*) Nachdruck *m*; **emphasize** ['ɛmfəsaɪz] *vt* betonen

emphatic [em'fætɪk] *adj* nachdrücklich; ~**ally** *adv* nachdrücklich

empire ['ɛmpaɪər] *n* Reich *nt*

empirical [em'pɪrɪkl] *adj* empirisch

employ [ɪm'plɔɪ] *vt* (*hire*) anstellen; (*use*) verwenden; ~**ee** [ɪmplɔɪ'iː] *n* Angestellte(r) *f(m)*; ~**er** *n* Arbeitgeber(in) *m(f)*; ~**ment** *n* Beschäftigung *f*; ~**ment agency** *n* Stellenvermittlung *f*

empower [ɪm'pauər] *vt*: **to ~ sb to do sth** jdn ermächtigen, etw zu tun

empress ['ɛmprɪs] *n* Kaiserin *f*

emptiness ['ɛmptɪnɪs] *n* Leere *f*

empty ['ɛmptɪ] *adj* leer ♦ *n* (*bottle*) Leergut *nt* ♦ *vt* (*contents*) leeren; (*container*) ausleeren ♦ *vi* (*water*) abfließen; (*river*) münden; (*house*) sich leeren; ~-**handed** *adj* mit leeren Händen

EMU ['iːmjuː] *n abbr* (= *economic and monetary union*) EWU *f*

emulate ['emjuleɪt] vt nacheifern +dat

emulsion [ɪ'mʌlʃən] n Emulsion f

enable [ɪ'neɪbl] vt: **to ~ sb to do sth** es jdm ermöglichen, etw zu tun

enact [ɪ'nækt] vt (law) erlassen; (play) aufführen; (role) spielen

enamel [ɪ'næməl] n Email nt; (of teeth) (Zahn)schmelz m

encased [ɪn'keɪst] adj: **~ in** (enclosed) eingeschlossen in +dat; (covered) verkleidet mit

enchant [ɪn'tʃɑːnt] vt bezaubern; **~ing** adj entzückend

encircle [ɪn'sɜːkl] vt umringen

encl. abbr (= enclosed) Anl.

enclose [ɪn'kləuz] vt einschließen; **to ~ sth (in** or **with a letter)** etw (einem Brief) beilegen; **~d** (in letter) beiliegend, anbei; **enclosure** [ɪn'kləuʒə*] n Einfriedung f; (in letter) Anlage f

encompass [ɪn'kʌmpəs] vt (include) umfassen

encore [ɒŋ'kɔːr] n Zugabe f

encounter [ɪn'kauntər] n Begegnung f; (MIL) Zusammenstoß m ♦ vt treffen; (resistance) stoßen auf +acc

encourage [ɪn'kʌrɪdʒ] vt ermutigen; **~ment** n Ermutigung f, Förderung f; **encouraging** adj ermutigend, viel versprechend

encroach [ɪn'krəutʃ] vi: **to ~ (up)on** eindringen in +acc; (time) in Anspruch nehmen

encrusted [ɪn'krʌstɪd] adj: **~ with** besetzt mit

encyclop(a)edia [ensaɪklə'piːdɪə] n Konversationslexikon nt

end [end] n Ende nt, Schluss m; (purpose) Zweck m ♦ vt (also: **bring to an ~, put an ~ to**) beenden ♦ vi zu Ende gehen; **in the ~** zum Schluss; **on ~** (object) hochkant; **to stand on ~** (hair) zu Berge stehen; **for hours on ~** stundenlang; **~ up** vi landen

endanger [ɪn'deɪndʒər] vt gefährden; **~ed species** n eine vom Aussterben bedrohte Art

endearing [ɪn'dɪərɪŋ] adj gewinnend

endeavour [ɪn'devər] (US **endeavor**) n Bestrebung f ♦ vi sich bemühen

ending ['endɪŋ] n Ende nt

endless ['endlɪs] adj endlos

endorse [ɪn'dɔːs] vt unterzeichnen; (approve) unterstützen; **~ment** n (AUT) Eintrag m

endow [ɪn'dau] vt: **to ~ sb with sth** jdm etw verleihen; (with money) jdm etw stiften

endurance [ɪn'djuərəns] n Ausdauer f

endure [ɪn'djuər] vt ertragen ♦ vi (last) (fort)dauern

enemy ['enəmi] n Feind m ♦ adj feindlich

energetic [enə'dʒetɪk] adj tatkräftig

energy ['enədʒɪ] n Energie f

enforce [ɪn'fɔːs] vt durchsetzen

engage [ɪn'geɪdʒ] vt (employ) einstellen; (in conversation) verwickeln; (TECH) einschalten ♦ vi (TECH) ineinander greifen; (clutch) fassen; **to ~ in** sich beteiligen an +dat; **~d** adj verlobt; (BRIT: TEL, toilet) besetzt; (: busy) beschäftigt; **to get ~d** sich verloben; **~d tone** (BRIT) n (TEL) Besetztzeichen nt; **~ment** n (appointment) Verabredung f; (to marry) Verlobung f; (MIL) Gefecht nt; **~ment ring** n Verlobungsring m; **engaging** adj gewinnend

engender [ɪn'dʒendər] vt hervorrufen

engine ['endʒɪn] n (AUT) Motor m; (RAIL) Lokomotive f; **~ driver** n Lok(omotiv)führer(in) m(f)

engineer [endʒɪ'nɪər] n Ingenieur m; (US: RAIL) Lok(omotiv)führer(in) m(f); **~ing** [endʒɪ'nɪərɪŋ] n Technik f

England ['ɪŋglənd] n England nt

English ['ɪŋglɪʃ] adj englisch ♦ n (LING) Englisch nt; **the ~** npl (people) die Engländer pl; **~ Channel** n: **the ~ Channel** der Ärmelkanal m; **~man / woman** (irreg) n Engländer(in) m(f)

engraving [ɪn'greɪvɪŋ] n Stich m

engrossed [ɪn'grəust] adj vertieft

engulf [ɪn'gʌlf] vt verschlingen

enhance [ɪn'hɑːns] vt steigern, heben

enigma [ɪ'nɪgmə] n Rätsel nt; **~tic** [enɪg'mætɪk] adj rätselhaft

enjoy [ɪn'dʒɔɪ] vt genießen; (privilege) besitzen; **to ~ o.s.** sich amüsieren; **~able**

adj erfreulich; **~ment** *n* Genuss *m*, Freude *f*

enlarge [ɪn'lɑːdʒ] *vt* erweitern; (*PHOT*) vergrößern ♦ *vi*: **to ~ on sth** etw weiter ausführen; **~ment** *n* Vergrößerung *f*

enlighten [ɪn'laɪtn] *vt* aufklären; **~ment** *n*: **the E~ment** (*HIST*) die Aufklärung

enlist [ɪn'lɪst] *vt* gewinnen ♦ *vi* (*MIL*) sich melden

enmity ['enmɪtɪ] *n* Feindschaft *f*

enormity [ɪ'nɔːmɪtɪ] *n* Ungeheuerlichkeit *f*

enormous [ɪ'nɔːməs] *adj* ungeheuer

enough [ɪ'nʌf] *adj, adv* genug; **funnily ~** komischerweise

enquire [ɪn'kwaɪəʳ] *vt, vi* = **inquire**

enrage [ɪn'reɪdʒ] *vt* wütend machen

enrich [ɪn'rɪtʃ] *vt* bereichern

enrol [ɪn'rəʊl] *vt* einschreiben ♦ *vi* (*register*) sich anmelden; **~ment** *n* (*for course*) Anmeldung *f*

en route [ɒn'ruːt] *adv* unterwegs

ensign ['ensaɪn, 'ensən] *n* (*NAUT*) Flagge *f*; (*MIL*) Fähnrich *m*

enslave [ɪn'sleɪv] *vt* versklaven

ensue [ɪn'sjuː] *vi* folgen, sich ergeben

en suite [ɒnswiːt] *adj*: **room with ~ bathroom** Zimmer *nt* mit eigenem Bad

ensure [ɪn'ʃʊəʳ] *vt* garantieren

entail [ɪn'teɪl] *vt* mit sich bringen

entangle [ɪn'tæŋgl] *vt* verwirren, verstricken; **~d** *adj*: **to become ~d (in)** (*in net, rope etc*) sich verfangen (in +*dat*)

enter ['entəʳ] *vt* eintreten in +*dat*, betreten; (*club*) beitreten +*dat*; (*in book*) eintragen ♦ *vi* hereinkommen, hineingehen; **~ for** *vt fus* sich beteiligen an +*dat*; **~ into** *vt fus* (*agreement*) eingehen; (*plans*) eine Rolle spielen bei; **~ (up)on** *vt fus* beginnen

enterprise ['entəpraɪz] *n* (*in person*) Initiative *f*; (*COMM*) Unternehmen *nt*; **enterprising** ['entəpraɪzɪŋ] *adj* unternehmungslustig

entertain [entə'teɪn] *vt* (*guest*) bewirten; (*amuse*) unterhalten; **~er** *n* Unterhaltungskünstler(in) *m(f)*; **~ing** *adj* unterhaltsam; **~ment** *n* Unterhaltung *f*

enthralled [ɪn'θrɔːld] *adj* gefesselt

enthusiasm [ɪn'θuːzɪæzəm] *n* Begeisterung *f*

enthusiast [ɪn'θuːzɪæst] *n* Enthusiast *m*; **~ic**

[ɪnθuːzɪ'æstɪk] *adj* begeistert

entice [ɪn'taɪs] *vt* verleiten, locken

entire [ɪn'taɪəʳ] *adj* ganz; **~ly** *adv* ganz, völlig; **~ty** [ɪn'taɪərətɪ] *n*: **in its ~ty** in seiner Gesamtheit

entitle [ɪn'taɪtl] *vt* (*allow*) berechtigen; (*name*) betiteln; **~d** *adj* (*book*) mit dem Titel; **to be ~d to sth** das Recht auf etw *acc* haben; **to be ~d to do sth** das Recht haben, etw zu tun

entity ['entɪtɪ] *n* Ding *nt*, Wesen *nt*

entourage [ɒntu'rɑːʒ] *n* Gefolge *nt*

entrails ['entreɪlz] *npl* Eingeweide *pl*

entrance [*n* 'entrns, *vb* ɪn'trɑːns] *n* Eingang *m*; (*entering*) Eintritt *m* ♦ *vt* hinreißen; **~ examination** *n* Aufnahmeprüfung *f*; **~ fee** *n* Eintrittsgeld *nt*; **~ ramp** (*US*) *n* (*AUT*) Einfahrt *f*

entrant ['entrnt] *n* (*for exam*) Kandidat *m*; (*in race*) Teilnehmer *m*

entreat [en'triːt] *vt* anflehen

entrenched [en'trentʃt] *adj* (*fig*) verwurzelt

entrepreneur ['ɒntrəprə'nɜːʳ] *n* Unternehmer(in) *m(f)*

entrust [ɪn'trʌst] *vt*: **to ~ sb with sth** *or* **sth to sb** jdm etw anvertrauen

entry ['entrɪ] *n* Eingang *m*; (*THEAT*) Auftritt *m*; (*in account*) Eintragung *f*; (*in dictionary*) Eintrag *m*; **"no ~"** „Eintritt verboten"; (*for cars*) „Einfahrt verboten"; **~ form** *n* Anmeldeformular *nt*; **~ phone** *n* Sprechanlage *f*

enumerate [ɪ'njuːməreɪt] *vt* aufzählen

enunciate [ɪ'nʌnsɪeɪt] *vt* aussprechen

envelop [ɪn'veləp] *vt* einhüllen

envelope ['envələʊp] *n* Umschlag *m*

enviable ['envɪəbl] *adj* beneidenswert

envious ['envɪəs] *adj* neidisch

environment [ɪn'vaɪərnmənt] *n* Umgebung *f*; (*ECOLOGY*) Umwelt *f*; **~al** [ɪnvaɪərn'mentl] *adj* Umwelt-; **~-friendly** *adj* umweltfreundlich

envisage [ɪn'vɪzɪdʒ] *vt* sich *dat* vorstellen

envoy ['envɔɪ] *n* Gesandte(r) *mf*

envy ['envɪ] *n* Neid *m* ♦ *vt*: **to ~ sb sth** jdn um etw beneiden

enzyme ['enzaɪm] *n* Enzym *nt*

epic ['epik] n Epos nt ♦ adj episch

epidemic [epi'demik] n Epidemie f

epilepsy ['epilepsi] n Epilepsie f; **epileptic** [epi'leptik] adj epileptisch ♦ n Epileptiker(in) m(f)

episode ['episəud] n (incident) Vorfall m; (story) Episode f

epitaph ['epitɑːf] n Grabinschrift f

epitomize [i'pitəmaiz] vt verkörpern

equable ['ekwəbl] adj ausgeglichen

equal ['iːkwl] adj gleich ♦ n Gleichgestellte(r) mf ♦ vt gleichkommen +dat; **~ to the task** der Aufgabe gewachsen; **equality** [iː'kwɔliti] n Gleichheit f; (equal rights) Gleichberechtigung f; **~ize** vt gleichmachen ♦ vi (SPORT) ausgleichen; **~izer** n (SPORT) Ausgleich(streffer) m; **~ly** adv gleich

equanimity [ekwə'nimiti] n Gleichmut m

equate [i'kweit] vt gleichsetzen

equation [i'kweiʃən] n Gleichung f

equator [i'kweitə] n Äquator m

equestrian [i'kwestriən] adj Reit-

equilibrium [iːkwi'libriəm] n Gleichgewicht nt

equinox ['iːkwinɔks] n Tagundnachtgleiche f

equip [i'kwip] vt ausrüsten; **to be well ~ped** gut ausgerüstet sein; **~ment** n Ausrüstung f; (TECH) Gerät nt

equitable ['ekwitəbl] adj gerecht, billig

equities ['ekwitiz] (BRIT) npl (FIN) Stammaktien pl

equivalent [i'kwivələnt] adj gleichwertig, entsprechend ♦ n Äquivalent nt; (in money) Gegenwert m; **~ to** gleichwertig +dat, entsprechend +dat

equivocal [i'kwivəkl] adj zweideutig

era ['iərə] n Epoche f, Ära f

eradicate [i'rædikeit] vt ausrotten

erase [i'reiz] vt ausradieren; (tape) löschen; **~r** n Radiergummi m

erect [i'rekt] adj aufrecht ♦ vt errichten; **~ion** [i'rekʃən] n Errichtung f; (ANAT) Erektion f

ERM n abbr (= Exchange Rate Mechanism) Wechselkursmechanismus m

erode [i'rəud] vt zerfressen; (land)

auswaschen

erotic [i'rɔtik] adj erotisch

err [əː] vi sich irren

errand ['erənd] n Besorgung f

erratic [i'rætik] adj unberechenbar

erroneous [i'rəuniəs] adj irrig

error ['erə] n Fehler m

erupt [i'rʌpt] vi ausbrechen; **~ion** [i'rʌpʃən] n Ausbruch m

escalate ['eskəleit] vi sich steigern

escalator ['eskəleitə] n Rolltreppe f

escape [is'keip] n Flucht f; (of gas) Entweichen nt ♦ vi entkommen; (prisoners) fliehen; (leak) entweichen ♦ vt entkommen +dat; **escapism** n Flucht f (vor der Wirklichkeit)

escort [n 'eskɔːt, vb is'kɔːt] n (person accompanying) Begleiter m; (guard) Eskorte f ♦ vt (lady) begleiten; (MIL) eskortieren

Eskimo ['eskiməu] n Eskimo(frau) m(f)

especially [is'peʃli] adv besonders

espionage ['espiənɑːʒ] n Spionage f

esplanade [esplə'neid] n Promenade f

Esquire [is'kwaiə] n: **J. Brown ~** Herrn J. Brown

essay ['esei] n Aufsatz m; (LITER) Essay m

essence ['esns] n (quality) Wesen nt; (extract) Essenz f

essential [i'senʃl] adj (necessary) unentbehrlich; (basic) wesentlich ♦ n Allernötigste(s) nt; **~ly** adv eigentlich

establish [is'tæbliʃ] vt (set up) gründen; (prove) nachweisen; **~ed** adj anerkannt; (belief, laws etc) herrschend; **~ment** n (setting up) Einrichtung f

estate [is'teit] n Gut nt; (BRIT: housing ~) Siedlung f; (will) Nachlass m; **~ agent** (BRIT) n Grundstücksmakler m; **~ car** (BRIT) n Kombiwagen m

esteem [is'tiːm] n Wertschätzung f

esthetic [is'θetik] (US) adj = **aesthetic**

estimate [n 'estimət, vb 'estimeit] n Schätzung f; (of price) (Kosten)voranschlag m ♦ vt schätzen; **estimation** [esti'meiʃən] n Einschätzung f; (esteem) Achtung f

estranged [is'treindʒd] adj entfremdet

estuary ['estjuəri] n Mündung f

etc abbr (= et cetera) usw.

etching ['etʃɪŋ] n Kupferstich m

eternal [ɪ'tɜːnl] adj ewig

eternity [ɪ'tɜːnɪtɪ] n Ewigkeit f

ether ['iːθəʳ] n Äther m

ethical ['eθɪkl] adj ethisch

ethics ['eθɪks] n Ethik f ♦ npl Moral f

Ethiopia [iːθɪ'əʊpɪə] n Äthiopien nt

ethnic ['eθnɪk] adj Volks-, ethnisch; ~ minority n ethnische Minderheit f

ethos ['iːθɒs] n Gesinnung f

e-ticket ['iːtɪkɪt] n E-Ticket nt

etiquette ['etɪket] n Etikette f

EU abbr (= European Union) EU f

euphemism ['juːfəmɪzəm] n Euphemismus m

euro ['jʊərəʊ] n (FIN) Euro m

Eurocheque ['jʊərəʊtʃek] n Euroscheck m

Euroland ['jʊərəʊlænd] n Eurozone f, Euroland nt

Europe ['jʊərəp] n Europa nt; ~an [jʊərə'piːən] adj europäisch ♦ n Europäer(in) m(f); ~an Community n: the ~an Community die Europäische Gemeinschaft

Euro-sceptic ['jʊərəʊskeptɪk] n Kritiker der Europäischen Gemeinschaft

evacuate [ɪ'vækjʊeɪt] vt (place) räumen; (people) evakuieren; evacuation [ɪvækjʊ'eɪʃən] n Räumung f; Evakuierung f

evade [ɪ'veɪd] vt (escape) entkommen +dat; (avoid) meiden; (duty) sich entziehen +dat

evaluate [ɪ'væljʊeɪt] vt bewerten; (information) auswerten

evaporate [ɪ'væpəreɪt] vi verdampfen ♦ vt verdampfen lassen; ~d milk n Kondensmilch f

evasion [ɪ'veɪʒən] n Umgehung f

evasive [ɪ'veɪsɪv] adj ausweichend

eve [iːv] n: on the ~ of am Vorabend +gen

even ['iːvn] adj eben; gleichmäßig; (score etc) unentschieden; (number) gerade ♦ adv: ~ you sogar du; to get ~ with sb jdm heimzahlen; ~ if selbst wenn; ~ so dennoch; ~ though obwohl; ~ more sogar noch mehr; ~ out vi sich ausgleichen

evening ['iːvnɪŋ] n Abend m; in the ~ abends, am Abend; ~ class n Abendschule f; ~ dress n (man's) Gesellschaftsanzug m;

(woman's) Abendkleid nt

event [ɪ'vent] n (happening) Ereignis nt; (SPORT) Disziplin f; in the ~ of im Falle +gen; ~ful adj ereignisreich

eventual [ɪ'ventʃʊəl] adj (final) schließlich; ~ity [ɪventʃʊ'ælɪtɪ] n Möglichkeit f; ~ly adv am Ende; (given time) schließlich

ever ['evəʳ] adv (always) immer; (at any time) je(mals) ♦ conj seit; ~ since seitdem; have you ~ seen it? haben Sie es je gesehen?; ~green n Immergrün nt; ~lasting adj immer während

every ['evrɪ] adj jede(r, s); ~ other/third day jeden zweiten/dritten Tag; ~ one of them alle; I have ~ confidence in him ich habe uneingeschränktes Vertrauen in ihn; we wish you ~ success wir wünschen Ihnen viel Erfolg; he's ~ bit as clever as his brother er ist genauso klug wie sein Bruder; ~ now and then ab und zu; ~body pron = everyone; ~day adj (daily) täglich; (commonplace) alltäglich, Alltags-; ~one pron jeder, alle pl; ~thing pron alles; ~where adv überall(hin); (wherever) wohin; ~where you go wohin du auch gehst

evict [ɪ'vɪkt] vt ausweisen; ~ion [ɪ'vɪkʃən] n Ausweisung f

evidence ['evɪdns] n (sign) Spur f; (proof) Beweis m; (testimony) Aussage f

evident ['evɪdnt] adj augenscheinlich; ~ly adv offensichtlich

evil ['iːvl] adj böse ♦ n Böse nt

evocative [ɪ'vɒkətɪv] adj: to be ~ of sth an etw acc erinnern

evoke [ɪ'vəʊk] vt hervorrufen

evolution [iːvə'luːʃən] n Entwicklung f; (of life) Evolution f

evolve [ɪ'vɒlv] vt entwickeln ♦ vi sich entwickeln

ewe [juː] n Mutterschaf nt

ex- [eks] prefix Ex-, Alt-, ehemalig

exacerbate [eks'æsəbeɪt] vt verschlimmern

exact [ɪg'zækt] adj genau ♦ vt (demand) verlangen; ~ing adj anspruchsvoll; ~ly adv genau

exaggerate [ɪg'zædʒəreɪt] vt, vi übertreiben; exaggeration [ɪgzædʒə'reɪʃən] n

Übertreibung f

exalted [ɪgˈzɔːltɪd] adj (position, style) hoch; (person) exaltiert

exam [ɪgˈzæm] n abbr (SCH) = **examination**

examination [ɪgzæmɪˈneɪʃən] n Untersuchung f; (SCH) Prüfung f, Examen nt; (customs) Kontrolle f

examine [ɪgˈzæmɪn] vt untersuchen; (SCH) prüfen; (consider) erwägen; ~**r** n Prüfer m

example [ɪgˈzɑːmpl] n Beispiel nt; **for ~** zum Beispiel

exasperate [ɪgˈzɑːspəreɪt] vt zur Verzweiflung bringen; **exasperating** adj ärgerlich, zum Verzweifeln bringend; **exasperation** [ɪgzɑːspəˈreɪʃən] n Verzweiflung f

excavate [ˈekskəveɪt] vt ausgraben; **excavation** [ekskəˈveɪʃən] n Ausgrabung f

exceed [ɪkˈsiːd] vt überschreiten; (hopes) übertreffen; ~**ingly** adv äußerst

excel [ɪkˈsel] vi sich auszeichnen; ~**lence** [ˈeksələns] n Vortrefflichkeit f; **E~lency** [ˈeksələnsɪ] n: **His E~lency** Seine Exzellenz f; ~**lent** [ˈeksələnt] adj ausgezeichnet

except [ɪkˈsept] prep (also: ~ **for, ~ing**) außer +dat ♦ vt ausnehmen; ~**ion** [ɪkˈsepʃən] n Ausnahme f; **to take ~ion to** Anstoß nehmen an +dat; ~**ional** [ɪkˈsepʃənl] adj außergewöhnlich

excerpt [ˈeksɜːpt] n Auszug m

excess [ɪkˈses] n Übermaß nt; **an ~ of** ein Übermaß an +dat; ~ **baggage** n Mehrgepäck nt; ~ **fare** n Nachlösegebühr f; ~**ive** adj übermäßig

exchange [ɪksˈtʃeɪndʒ] n Austausch m; (also: **telephone ~**) Zentrale f ♦ vt (goods) tauschen; (greetings) austauschen; (money, blows) wechseln; ~ **rate** n Wechselkurs m

Exchequer [ɪksˈtʃekəʳ] (BRIT) n: **the ~** das Schatzamt

excise [ˈeksaɪz] n Verbrauchssteuer f

excite [ɪkˈsaɪt] vt erregen; **to get ~d** sich aufregen; ~**ment** n Aufregung f; **exciting** adj spannend

exclaim [ɪksˈkleɪm] vi ausrufen

exclamation [ekskləˈmeɪʃən] n Ausruf m; ~ **mark** n Ausrufezeichen nt

exclude [ɪksˈkluːd] vt ausschließen

exclusion [ɪksˈkluːʒən] n Ausschluss m; ~ **zone** n Sperrzone f

exclusive [ɪksˈkluːsɪv] adj (select) exklusiv; (sole) ausschließlich, Allein-; ~ **of** exklusive +gen; ~**ly** adv nur, ausschließlich

excrement [ˈekskrəmənt] n Kot m

excruciating [ɪksˈkruːʃieɪtɪŋ] adj qualvoll

excursion [ɪksˈkɜːʃən] n Ausflug m

excusable [ɪksˈkjuːzəbl] adj entschuldbar

excuse [n ɪksˈkjuːs, vb ɪksˈkjuːz] n Entschuldigung f ♦ vt entschuldigen; ~ **me!** entschuldigen Sie!

ex-directory [ˈeksdɪˈrektərɪ] (BRIT) adj: **to be ~** nicht im Telefonbuch stehen

execute [ˈeksɪkjuːt] vt (carry out) ausführen; (kill) hinrichten; **execution** [eksɪˈkjuːʃən] n Ausführung f; (killing) Hinrichtung f; **executioner** [eksɪˈkjuːʃnəʳ] n Scharfrichter m

executive [ɪgˈzekjutɪv] n (COMM) Geschäftsführer m; (POL) Exekutive f ♦ adj Exekutiv-, ausführend

executor [ɪgˈzekjutəʳ] n Testamentsvollstrecker m

exemplary [ɪgˈzemplərɪ] adj musterhaft

exemplify [ɪgˈzemplɪfaɪ] vt veranschaulichen

exempt [ɪgˈzempt] adj befreit ♦ vt befreien; ~**ion** [ɪgˈzempʃən] n Befreiung f

exercise [ˈeksəsaɪz] n Übung f ♦ vt (power) ausüben; (muscle, patience) üben; (dog) ausführen ♦ vi Sport treiben; ~ **bike** n Heimtrainer m; ~ **book** n (Schul)heft nt

exert [ɪgˈzɜːt] vt (influence) ausüben; **to ~ o.s.** sich anstrengen; ~**ion** [ɪgˈzɜːʃən] n Anstrengung f

exhale [eksˈheɪl] vt, vi ausatmen

exhaust [ɪgˈzɔːst] n (fumes) Abgase pl; (pipe) Auspuffrohr nt ♦ vt erschöpfen; ~**ed** adj erschöpft; ~**ion** [ɪgˈzɔːstʃən] n Erschöpfung f; ~**ive** adj erschöpfend

exhibit [ɪgˈzɪbɪt] n (JUR) Beweisstück nt; (ART) Ausstellungsstück nt ♦ vt ausstellen; ~**ion** [eksɪˈbɪʃən] n (ART) Ausstellung f; (of temper etc) Zurschaustellung f; ~**ionist** [eksɪˈbɪʃənɪst] n Exhibitionist m

exhilarating [ɪgˈzɪləreɪtɪŋ] adj erhebend

ex-husband *n* Ehemann *m*

exile ['ɛksaɪl] *n* Exil *nt*; (*person*) Verbannte(r) *f(m)* ♦ *vt* verbannen

exist [ɪg'zɪst] *vi* existieren; **~ence** *n* Existenz *f*; **~ing** *adj* bestehend

exit ['ɛksɪt] *n* Ausgang *m*; (*THEAT*) Abgang *m* ♦ *vi* (*THEAT*) abtreten; (*COMPUT*) aus einem Programm herausgehen; **~ poll** *n bei Wahlen unmittelbar nach Verlassen der Wahllokale durchgeführte Umfrage*; **~ ramp** (*US*) *n* (*AUT*) Ausfahrt *f*

exodus ['ɛksədəs] *n* Auszug *m*

exonerate [ɪg'zɔnəreɪt] *vt* entlasten

exorbitant [ɪg'zɔ:bɪtnt] *adj* übermäßig; (*price*) Fantasie-

exotic [ɪg'zɔtɪk] *adj* exotisch

expand [ɪks'pænd] *vt* ausdehnen ♦ *vi* sich ausdehnen

expanse [ɪks'pæns] *n* Fläche *f*

expansion [ɪks'pænʃən] *n* Erweiterung *f*

expatriate [eks'pætrɪət] *n* Ausländer(in) *m(f)*

expect [ɪks'pɛkt] *vt* erwarten; (*suppose*) annehmen ♦ *vi*: **to be ~ing** ein Kind erwarten; **~ancy** *n* Erwartung *f*; **~ant mother** *n* werdende Mutter *f*; **~ation** [ɛkspɛk'teɪʃən] *n* Hoffnung *f*

expedient [ɪks'pi:dɪənt] *adj* zweckdienlich ♦ *n* (Hilfs)mittel *nt*

expedition [ɛkspə'dɪʃən] *n* Expedition *f*

expel [ɪks'pɛl] *vt* ausweisen; (*student*) (ver)weisen

expend [ɪks'pɛnd] *vt* (*effort*) aufwenden; **~iture** *n* Ausgaben *pl*

expense [ɪks'pɛns] *n* Kosten *pl*; **~s** *npl* (*COMM*) Spesen *pl*; **at the ~ of** auf Kosten von; **~ account** *n* Spesenkonto *nt*; **expensive** [ɪks'pɛnsɪv] *adj* teuer

experience [ɪks'pɪərɪəns] *n* (*incident*) Erlebnis *nt*; (*practice*) Erfahrung *f* ♦ *vt* erleben; **~d** *adj* erfahren

experiment [ɪks'pɛrɪmənt] *n* Versuch *m*, Experiment *nt* ♦ *vi* experimentieren; **~al** [ɪkspɛrɪ'mɛntl] *adj* experimentell

expert ['ɛkspə:t] *n* Fachmann *m*; (*official*) Sachverständige(r) *m* ♦ *adj* erfahren; **~ise** [ɛkspə:'ti:z] *n* Sachkenntnis *f*

expire [ɪks'paɪər] *vi* (*end*) ablaufen; (*ticket*) verfallen; (*die*) sterben; **expiry** *n* Ablauf *m*

explain [ɪks'pleɪn] *vt* erklären

explanation [ɛksplə'neɪʃən] *n* Erklärung *f*; **explanatory** [ɪks'plænətrɪ] *adj* erklärend

explicit [ɪks'plɪsɪt] *adj* ausdrücklich

explode [ɪks'pləʊd] *vi* explodieren ♦ *vt* (*bomb*) sprengen

exploit [*n* 'ɛksplɔɪt, *vb* ɪks'plɔɪt] *n* (Helden)tat *f* ♦ *vt* ausbeuten; **~ation** [ɛksplɔɪ'teɪʃən] *n* Ausbeutung *f*

exploration [ɛksplə'reɪʃən] *n* Erforschung *f*

exploratory [ɪks'plɔrətrɪ] *adj* Probe-

explore [ɪks'plɔ:r] *vt* (*travel*) erforschen; (*search*) untersuchen; **~r** *n* Erforscher(in) *m(f)*

explosion [ɪks'pləʊʒən] *n* Explosion *f*; (*fig*) Ausbruch *m*

explosive [ɪks'pləʊsɪv] *adj* explosiv, Spreng- ♦ *n* Sprengstoff *m*

export [*vb* eks'pɔ:t, *n* 'ɛkspɔ:t] *vt* exportieren ♦ *n* Export *m* ♦ *cpd* (*trade*) Export-; **~er** [eks'pɔ:tər] *n* Exporteur *m*

expose [ɪks'pəʊz] *vt* (*to danger etc*) aussetzen; (*impostor*) entlarven; **to ~ sb to sth** jdn einer Sache aussetzen; **~d** *adj* (*position*) exponiert; **exposure** [ɪks'pəʊʒər] *n* (*MED*) Unterkühlung *f*; (*PHOT*) Belichtung *f*; **exposure meter** *n* Belichtungsmesser *m*

express [ɪks'prɛs] *adj* ausdrücklich; (*speedy*) Express-, Eil- ♦ *n* (*RAIL*) Schnellzug *m* ♦ *adv* (*send*) per Express ♦ *vt* ausdrücken; **to ~ o.s.** sich ausdrücken; **~ion** [ɪks'prɛʃən] *n* Ausdruck *m*; **~ive** *adj* ausdrucksvoll; **~ly** *adv* ausdrücklich; **~way** (*US*) *n* (*urban motorway*) Schnellstraße *f*

expulsion [ɪks'pʌlʃən] *n* Ausweisung *f*

exquisite [eks'kwɪzɪt] *adj* erlesen

extend [ɪks'tɛnd] *vt* (*visit etc*) verlängern; (*building*) ausbauen; (*hand*) ausstrecken; (*welcome*) bieten ♦ *vi* (*land*) sich erstrecken

extension [ɪks'tɛnʃən] *n* Erweiterung *f*; (*of building*) Anbau *m*; (*TEL*) Apparat *m*

extensive [ɪks'tɛnsɪv] *adj* (*knowledge*) umfassend; (*use*) weitgehend, weit gehend

extent [ɪks'tɛnt] *n* Ausdehnung *f*; (*fig*) Ausmaß *nt*; **to a certain ~** bis zu einem

gewissen Grade; **to such an ~ that ...**
dermaßen, dass ...; **to what ~?** inwieweit?

extenuating [ɪksˈtenjueɪtɪŋ] *adj* mildernd

exterior [eksˈtɪərɪəʳ] *adj* äußere(r, s), Außen-
♦ *n* Äußere(s) *nt*

exterminate [ɪksˈtəːmɪneɪt] *vt* ausrotten

external [eksˈtəːnl] *adj* äußere(r, s), Außen-

extinct [ɪksˈtɪŋkt] *adj* ausgestorben; **~ion**
[ɪksˈtɪŋkʃən] *n* Aussterben *nt*

extinguish [ɪksˈtɪŋgwɪʃ] *vt* (aus)löschen

extort [ɪksˈtɔːt] *vt* erpressen; **~ion** [ɪksˈtɔːʃən]
n Erpressung *f*; **~ionate** [ɪksˈtɔːʃnɪt] *adj*
überhöht, erpresserisch

extra [ˈekstrə] *adj* zusätzlich ♦ *adv* besonders
♦ *n* (*for car etc*) Extra *nt*; (*charge*) Zuschlag
m; (*THEAT*) Statist *m* ♦ *prefix* außer...

extract [*v* ɪksˈtrækt, *n* ˈekstrækt] *vt*
(heraus)ziehen ♦ *n* (*from book etc*) Auszug
m; (*COOK*) Extrakt *m*

extracurricular [ˈekstrəkəˈrɪkjuləʳ] *adj*
außerhalb des Stundenplans

extradite [ˈekstrədaɪt] *vt* ausliefern

extramarital [ˈekstrəˈmærɪtl] *adj*
außerehelich

extramural [ˈekstrəˈmjuərl] *adj* (*course*)
Volkshochschul-

extraordinary [ɪksˈtrɔːdnrɪ] *adj*
außerordentlich; (*amazing*) erstaunlich

extravagance [ɪksˈtrævəgəns] *n*
Verschwendung *f*; (*lack of restraint*)
Zügellosigkeit *f*; (*an ~*) Extravaganz *f*

extravagant [ɪksˈtrævəgənt] *adj* extravagant

extreme [ɪksˈtriːm] *adj* (*edge*) äußerste(r, s),
hinterste(r, s); (*cold*) äußerste(r, s);
(*behaviour*) außergewöhnlich, übertrieben
♦ *n* Extrem *nt*; **~ly** *adv* äußerst, höchst;

extremist *n* Extremist(in) *m(f)*

extremity [ɪksˈtremɪtɪ] *n* (*end*) Spitze *f*,
äußerste(s) Ende *nt*; (*hardship*) bitterste Not
f; (*ANAT*) Hand *f*; Fuß *m*

extricate [ˈekstrɪkeɪt] *vt* losmachen, befreien

extrovert [ˈekstrəvəːt] *n* extrovertierte(r)
Mensch *m*

exuberant [ɪgˈzjuːbərnt] *adj* ausgelassen

exude [ɪgˈzjuːd] *vt* absondern

eye [aɪ] *n* Auge *nt*; (*of needle*) Öhr *nt* ♦ *vt*
betrachten; (*up and down*) mustern; **to**
keep an ~ on aufpassen auf *+acc*; **~ball** *n*
Augapfel *m*; **~bath** *n* Augenbad *nt*; **~brow**
n Augenbraue *f*; **~brow pencil** *n*
Augenbrauenstift *m*; **~drops** *npl*
Augentropfen *pl*; **~lash** *n* Augenwimper *f*;
~lid *n* Augenlid *nt*; **~liner** *n* Eyeliner *nt*; **~-**
opener *n*: **that was an ~-opener** das hat
mir/ihm *etc* die Augen geöffnet; **~shadow**
n Lidschatten *m*; **~sight** *n* Sehkraft *f*;
~sore *n* Schandfleck *m*; **~ witness** *n*
Augenzeuge *m*

F, f

F [ɛf] *n* (*MUS*) F *nt*

F. *abbr* (= *Fahrenheit*) F

fable [ˈfeɪbl] *n* Fabel *f*

fabric [ˈfæbrɪk] *n* Stoff *m*; (*fig*) Gefüge *nt*

fabrication [fæbrɪˈkeɪʃən] *n* Erfindung *f*

fabulous [ˈfæbjuləs] *adj* sagenhaft

face [feɪs] *n* Gesicht *nt*; (*surface*) Oberfläche
f; (*of clock*) Zifferblatt *nt* ♦ *vt* (*point towards*)
liegen nach; (*situation, difficulty*) sich stellen
+dat; **~ down** (*person*) mit dem Gesicht
nach unten; (*card*) mit der Vorderseite nach
unten; **to make** *or* **pull a ~** das Gesicht
verziehen; **in the ~ of** angesichts *+gen*; **on**
the ~ of it so, wie es aussieht; **~ to ~** Auge
in Auge; **to ~ up to sth** einer Sache *dat* ins
Auge sehen; **~ cloth** (*BRIT*) *n* Waschlappen
m; **~ cream** *n* Gesichtscreme *f*; **~ lift** *n*
Facelifting *nt*; **~ powder** *n* (Gesichts)puder
m

facet [ˈfæsɪt] *n* Aspekt *m*; (*of gem*) Facette *f*,
Fassette *f*

facetious [fəˈsiːʃəs] *adj* witzig

face value *n* Nennwert *m*; **to take sth at**
(its) ~ (*fig*) etw für bare Münze nehmen

facial [ˈfeɪʃl] *adj* Gesichts-

facile [ˈfæsaɪl] *adj* (*easy*) leicht

facilitate [fəˈsɪlɪteɪt] *vt* erleichtern

facilities [fəˈsɪlɪtɪz] *npl* Einrichtungen *pl*;
credit ~ Kreditmöglichkeiten *pl*

facing [ˈfeɪsɪŋ] *adj* zugekehrt ♦ *prep*
gegenüber

facsimile [fækˈsɪmɪlɪ] *n* Faksimile *nt*;

(machine) Telekopierer m

fact [fækt] n Tatsache f; **in ~** in der Tat

faction ['fækʃən] n Splittergruppe f

factor ['fæktə'] n Faktor m

factory ['fæktəri] n Fabrik f

factual ['fæktjuəl] adj sachlich

faculty ['fækəltɪ] n Fähigkeit f; *(UNIV)* Fakultät f; *(US: teaching staff)* Lehrpersonal nt

fad [fæd] n Tick m; *(fashion)* Masche f

fade [feɪd] vi *(lose colour)* verblassen; *(dim)* nachlassen; *(sound, memory)* schwächer werden; *(wilt)* verwelken

fag [fæg] *(inf)* n *(cigarette)* Kippe f

fail [feɪl] vt *(exam)* nicht bestehen; *(student)* durchfallen lassen; *(courage)* verlassen; *(memory)* im Stich lassen ♦ vi *(supplies)* zu Ende gehen; *(student)* durchfallen; *(eyesight)* nachlassen; *(light)* schwächer werden; *(crop)* fehlschlagen; *(remedy)* nicht wirken; **to ~ to do sth** *(neglect)* es unterlassen, etw zu tun; *(be unable)* es nicht schaffen, etw zu tun; **without ~** unbedingt; **~ing** n Schwäche f ♦ prep mangels +gen; **~ure** ['feɪljə'] n *(person)* Versager m; *(act)* Versagen nt; *(TECH)* Defekt m

faint [feɪnt] adj schwach ♦ n Ohnmacht f ♦ vi ohnmächtig werden

fair [feə'] adj *(just)* gerecht, fair; *(hair)* blond; *(skin)* hell; *(weather)* schön; *(not very good)* mittelmäßig; *(sizeable)* ansehnlich ♦ adv *(play)* fair ♦ n *(COMM)* Messe f; *(BRIT: funfair)* Jahrmarkt m; **~ly** adv *(honestly)* gerecht, fair; *(rather)* ziemlich; **~ness** n Fairness f

fairy ['feərɪ] n Fee f; **~ tale** n Märchen nt

faith [feɪθ] n Glaube m; *(trust)* Vertrauen nt; *(sect)* Bekenntnis nt; **~ful** adj treu; **~fully** adv treu; **yours ~fully** *(BRIT)* hochachtungsvoll

fake [feɪk] n *(thing)* Fälschung f; *(person)* Schwindler m ♦ adj vorgetäuscht ♦ vt fälschen

falcon ['fɔːlkən] n Falke m

fall [fɔːl] *(pt fell, pp fallen)* n Fall m, Sturz m; *(decrease)* Fallen nt; *(of snow)* (Schnee)fall m; *(US: autumn)* Herbst m ♦ vi *(also fig)* fallen; *(night)* hereinbrechen; **~s** npl *(waterfall)* Fälle pl; **to ~ flat** platt hinfallen;

(joke) nicht ankommen; **~ back** vi zurückweichen; **~ back on** vt fus zurückgreifen auf +acc; **~ behind** vi zurückbleiben; **~ down** vi *(person)* hinfallen; *(building)* einstürzen; **~ for** vt fus *(trick)* hereinfallen auf +acc; *(person)* sich verknallen in +acc; **~ in** vi *(roof)* einstürzen; **~ off** vi herunterfallen; *(diminish)* sich vermindern; **~ out** vi sich streiten; *(MIL)* wegtreten; **~ through** vi *(plan)* ins Wasser fallen

fallacy ['fæləsɪ] n Trugschluss m

fallen ['fɔːlən] pp of **fall**

fallible ['fæləbl] adj fehlbar

fallout ['fɔːlaut] n radioaktive(r) Niederschlag m; **~ shelter** n Atombunker m

fallow ['fæləu] adj brach(liegend)

false [fɔːls] adj falsch; *(artificial)* künstlich; **under ~ pretences** unter Vorspiegelung falscher Tatsachen; **~ alarm** n Fehlalarm m; **~ teeth** *(BRIT)* npl Gebiss nt

falter ['fɔːltə'] vi schwanken; *(in speech)* stocken

fame [feɪm] n Ruhm m

familiar [fə'mɪlɪə'] adj bekannt; *(intimate)* familiär; **to be ~ with** vertraut sein mit; **~ize** vt vertraut machen

family ['fæmɪlɪ] n Familie f; *(relations)* Verwandtschaft f; **~ business** n Familienunternehmen nt; **~ doctor** n Hausarzt m

famine ['fæmɪn] n Hungersnot f

famished ['fæmɪʃt] adj ausgehungert

famous ['feɪməs] adj berühmt

fan [fæn] n *(folding)* Fächer m; *(ELEC)* Ventilator m; *(admirer)* Fan m ♦ vt fächeln; **~ out** vi sich (fächerförmig) ausbreiten

fanatic [fə'nætɪk] n Fanatiker(in) m(f)

fan belt n Keilriemen m

fanciful ['fænsɪful] adj *(odd)* seltsam; *(imaginative)* fantasievoll

fancy ['fænsɪ] n *(liking)* Neigung f; *(imagination)* Einbildung f ♦ adj schick ♦ vt *(like)* gern haben; wollen; *(imagine)* sich einbilden; **he fancies her** er mag sie; **~ dress** n Maskenkostüm nt; **~-dress ball** n Maskenball m

fang [fæŋ] n Fangzahn m; (of snake) Giftzahn m

fantastic [fæn'tæstɪk] adj fantastisch

fantasy ['fæntəsɪ] n Fantasie f

far [fɑːr] adj weit ♦ adv weit entfernt; (very much) weitaus; **by ~** bei weitem; **so ~** so weit; bis jetzt; **go as ~ as the station** gehen Sie bis zum Bahnhof; **as ~ as I know** soweit or soviel ich weiß; **~away** weit entfernt

farce [fɑːs] n Farce f; **farcical** ['fɑːsɪkl] adj lächerlich

fare [fɛər] n Fahrpreis m; Fahrgeld nt; (food) Kost f; **half/full ~** halber/voller Fahrpreis m

Far East n: **the ~** der Ferne Osten

farewell [fɛə'wɛl] n Abschied(sgruß) m ♦ excl lebe wohl!

farm [fɑːm] n Bauernhof m, Farm f ♦ vt bewirtschaften; **~er** n Bauer m, Landwirt m; **~hand** n Landarbeiter m; **~house** n Bauernhaus nt; **~ing** n Landwirtschaft f; **~land** n Ackerland nt; **~yard** n Hof m

far-reaching ['fɑː'riːtʃɪŋ] adj (reform, effect) weitreichend, weit reichend

fart [fɑːt] (infl) n Furz m ♦ vi furzen

farther ['fɑːðər] adv weiter; **farthest** ['fɑːðɪst] adj fernste(r, s) ♦ adv am weitesten

fascinate ['fæsɪneɪt] vt faszinieren; **fascinating** adj faszinierend; **fascination** [fæsɪ'neɪʃən] n Faszination f

fascism ['fæʃɪzəm] n Faschismus m

fashion ['fæʃən] n (of clothes) Mode f; (manner) Art f (und Weise f) ♦ vt machen; **in ~** in Mode; **out of ~** unmodisch; **~able** adj (clothes) modisch; (place) elegant; **~ show** n Mode(n)schau f

fast [fɑːst] adj schnell; (firm) fest ♦ adv schnell; fest ♦ n Fasten nt ♦ vi fasten; **to be ~** (clock) vorgehen

fasten ['fɑːsn] vt (attach) befestigen; (with rope) zuschnüren; (seat belt) festmachen; (coat) zumachen ♦ vi sich schließen lassen; **~er** n Verschluss m; **~ing** n Verschluss m

fast food n Fastfood nt, Fast Food nt

fastidious [fæs'tɪdɪəs] adj wählerisch

fat [fæt] adj dick ♦ n Fett nt

fatal ['feɪtl] adj tödlich; (disastrous)

verhängnisvoll; **~ity** [fə'tælɪtɪ] n (road death etc) Todesopfer nt; **~ly** adv tödlich

fate [feɪt] n Schicksal nt; **~ful** adj (prophetic) schicksalsschwer; (important) schicksalhaft

father ['fɑːðər] n Vater m; (REL) Pater m; **~-in-law** n Schwiegervater m; **~ly** adj väterlich

fathom ['fæðəm] n Klafter m ♦ vt ausloten; (fig) ergründen

fatigue [fə'tiːg] n Ermüdung f

fatten ['fætn] vt dick machen; (animals) mästen ♦ vi dick werden

fatty ['fætɪ] adj fettig ♦ n (inf) Dickerchen nt

fatuous ['fætjuəs] adj albern, affig

faucet ['fɔːsɪt] (US) n Wasserhahn m

fault [fɔːlt] n (defect) Defekt m; (ELEC) Störung f; (blame) Schuld f; (GEOG) Verwerfung f; **it's your ~** du bist daran schuld; **to find ~ with (sth/sb)** etwas auszusetzen haben an (etw/jdm); **at ~** im Unrecht; **~less** adj tadellos; **~y** adj fehlerhaft, defekt

fauna ['fɔːnə] n Fauna f

favour ['feɪvər] (US **favor**) n (approval) Wohlwollen nt; (kindness) Gefallen m ♦ vt (prefer) vorziehen; **in ~ of** für; zugunsten or zu Gunsten +gen; **to find ~ with sb** bei jdm Anklang finden; **~able** ['feɪvrəbl] adj günstig; **~ite** ['feɪvrɪt] adj Lieblings- ♦ n (child) Liebling m; (SPORT) Favorit m

fawn [fɔːn] adj rehbraun ♦ n (animal) (Reh)kitz nt ♦ vi: **to ~ (up)on** (fig) katzbuckeln vor +dat

fax [fæks] n (document) Fax nt; (machine) Telefax nt ♦ vt: **to ~ sth to sb** jdm etw faxen

FBI (US) n abbr (= Federal Bureau of Investigation) FBI nt

fear [fɪər] n Furcht f ♦ vt fürchten; **~ful** adj (timid) furchtsam; (terrible) fürchterlich; **~less** adj furchtlos

feasible ['fiːzəbl] adj durchführbar

feast [fiːst] n Festmahl nt; (REL: also: **~ day**) Feiertag m ♦ vi: **to ~ (on)** sich gütlich tun (an +dat)

feat [fiːt] n Leistung f

feather ['fɛðər] n Feder f

feature ['fiːtʃər] n (Gesichts)zug m;

(*important part*) Grundzug m; (CINE, PRESS)
Feature nt ♦ vt darstellen; (*advertising etc*)
groß herausbringen ♦ vi vorkommen;
~**featuring** X mit X; ~ **film** n Spielfilm m
February ['februəri] n Februar m
fed [fed] pt, pp of **feed**
federal ['fedərəl] adj Bundes-
federation [fedə'reifən] n (*society*) Verband
m; (*of states*) Staatenbund m
fed up adj: **to be ~ with sth** etw satt
haben; **I'm ~** ich habe die Nase voll
fee [fi:] n Gebühr f
feeble ['fi:bl] adj (*person*) schwach; (*excuse*)
lahm
feed [fi:d] (*pt, pp* **fed**) n (*for animals*) Futter
nt ♦ vt füttern; (*support*) ernähren; (*data*)
eingeben; **to ~ on** fressen; ~**back** n
(*information*) Feed-back nt, Feedback nt;
~**ing bottle** (BRIT) n Flasche f
feel [fi:l] (*pt, pp* **felt**) n: **it has a soft ~** es
fühlt sich weich an ♦ vt (*sense*) fühlen;
(*touch*) anfassen; (*think*) meinen ♦ vi
(*person*) sich fühlen; (*thing*) sich anfühlen;
to get the ~ of sth sich an etw acc
gewöhnen; **I ~ cold** mir ist kalt; **I ~ like a
cup of tea** ich habe Lust auf eine Tasse
Tee; ~ **about** or **around** vi
herumsuchen; ~**er** n Fühler m; ~**ing** n
Gefühl nt; (*opinion*) Meinung f
feet [fi:t] npl of **foot**
feign [fein] vt vortäuschen
feline ['fi:lain] adj katzenartig
fell [fel] pt of **fall** ♦ vt (*tree*) fällen
fellow ['feləu] n (*man*) Kerl m; ~ **citizen** n
Mitbürger(in) m(f); ~ **countryman** (*irreg*) n
Landsmann m; ~ **men** npl Mitmenschen pl;
~**ship** n (*group*) Körperschaft f; (*friendliness*)
Kameradschaft f; (*scholarship*)
Forschungsstipendium nt; ~ **student** n
Kommilitone m, Kommilitonin f
felony ['feləni] n schwere(s) Verbrechen nt
felt [felt] pt, pp of **feel** ♦ n Filz m; ~**-tip pen**
n Filzstift m
female ['fi:meil] n (*of animals*) Weibchen nt
♦ adj weiblich
feminine ['feminin] adj (LING) weiblich;
(*qualities*) fraulich

feminist ['feminist] n Feminist(in) m(f)
fence [fens] n Zaun m ♦ vt (*also:* ~ **in**)
einzäunen ♦ vi fechten; **fencing** ['fensiŋ] n
Zaun m; (SPORT) Fechten nt
fend [fend] vi: **to ~ for o.s.** sich (allein)
durchschlagen; ~ **off** vt abwehren
fender ['fendə] n Kaminvorsetzer m; (US:
AUT) Kotflügel m
ferment [vb fə'ment, n 'fɜ:ment] vi (CHEM)
gären ♦ n (*unrest*) Unruhe f
fern [fɜ:n] n Farn m
ferocious [fə'rəufəs] adj wild, grausam
ferret ['ferit] n Frettchen nt ♦ vt: **to ~ out**
aufspüren
ferry ['feri] n Fähre f ♦ vt übersetzen
fertile ['fɜ:tail] adj fruchtbar
fertilize ['fɜ:tilaiz] vt (AGR) düngen; (BIOL)
befruchten; ~**r** n (Kunst)dünger m
fervent ['fɜ:vənt] adj (*admirer*) glühend;
(*hope*) innig
fervour ['fɜ:və] (US **fervor**) n Leidenschaft f
fester ['festə] vi eitern
festival ['festivəl] n (REL etc) Fest nt; (ART,
MUS) Festspiele pl
festive ['festiv] adj festlich; **the ~ season**
(*Christmas*) die Festzeit; **festivities**
[fes'tivitiz] npl Feierlichkeiten pl
festoon [fes'tu:n] vt: **to ~ with** schmücken
mit
fetch [fetf] vt holen; (*in sale*) einbringen
fetching ['fetfiŋ] adj reizend
fête [feit] n Fest nt
fetus ['fi:təs] (*esp US*) n = **foetus**
feud [fju:d] n Fehde f
feudal ['fju:dl] adj Feudal-
fever ['fi:və] n Fieber nt; ~**ish** adj (MED)
fiebrig; (*fig*) fieberhaft
few [fju:] adj wenig; **a ~** einige; ~**er** adj
weniger; ~**est** adj wenigste(r,s)
fiancé [fi'ɒ:ŋsei] n Verlobte(r) m; ~**e** n
Verlobte f
fib [fib] n Flunkerei f ♦ vi flunkern
fibre ['faibə] (US **fiber**) n Faser f; ~**glass** n
Glaswolle f
fickle ['fikl] adj unbeständig
fiction ['fikfən] n (*novels*) Romanliteratur f;
(*story*) Erdichtung f; ~**al** adj erfunden

fictitious [fɪk'tɪʃəs] *adj* erfunden, fingiert

fiddle ['fɪdl] *n* Geige *f*; (*trick*) Schwindelei *f*
♦ *vt* (*BRIT: accounts*) frisieren; ~ **with** *vt fus*
herumfummeln an +*dat*

fidelity [fɪ'delɪtɪ] *n* Treue *f*

fidget ['fɪdʒɪt] *vi* zappeln

field [fiːld] *n* Feld *nt*; (*range*) Gebiet *nt*; ~
marshal *n* Feldmarschall *m*; ~**work** *n*
Feldforschung *f*

fiend [fiːnd] *n* Teufel *m*

fierce [fɪəs] *adj* wild

fiery ['faɪərɪ] *adj* (*person*) hitzig

fifteen [fɪf'tiːn] *num* fünfzehn

fifth [fɪfθ] *adj* fünfte(r, s) ♦ *n* Fünftel *nt*

fifty ['fɪftɪ] *num* fünfzig; ~-**fifty** *adj*, *adv*
halbe-halbe, fifty-fifty (*inf*)

fig [fɪg] *n* Feige *f*

fight [faɪt] (*pt*, *pp* **fought**) *n* Kampf *m*; (*brawl*)
Schlägerei *f*; (*argument*) Streit *m* ♦ *vt*
kämpfen gegen; sich schlagen mit; (*fig*)
bekämpfen ♦ *vi* kämpfen; sich schlagen;
streiten; ~**er** *n* Kämpfer(in) *m(f)*; (*plane*)
Jagdflugzeug *nt*; ~**ing** *n* Kämpfen *nt*; (*war*)
Kampfhandlungen *pl*

figment ['fɪgmənt] *n*: ~ **of the imagination**
reine Einbildung *f*

figurative ['fɪgjurətɪv] *adj* bildlich

figure ['fɪgər] *n* (*of person*) Figur *f*; (*person*)
Gestalt *f*; (*number*) Ziffer *f* ♦ *vt* (*US: imagine*)
glauben ♦ *vi* (*appear*) erscheinen; ~ **out** *vt*
herausbekommen; ~**head** *n* (*NAUT*, *fig*)
Galionsfigur *f*; ~ **of speech** *n* Redensart *f*

file [faɪl] *n* (*tool*) Feile *f*; (*dossier*) Akte *f*;
(*folder*) Aktenordner *m*; (*COMPUT*) Datei *f*;
(*row*) Reihe *f* ♦ *vt* (*metal, nails*) feilen;
(*papers*) abheften; (*claim*) einreichen ♦ *vi*: **to**
~ **in/out** hintereinander hereinkommen/
hinausgehen; **to** ~ **past** vorbeimarschieren;
filing ['faɪlɪŋ] *n* Ablage *f*; **filing cabinet** *n*
Aktenschrank *m*

fill [fɪl] *vt* füllen; (*occupy*) ausfüllen; (*satisfy*)
sättigen ♦ *n*: **to eat one's** ~ sich richtig
satt essen; ~ **in** *vt* (*hole*) (auf)füllen; (*form*)
ausfüllen; ~ **up** *vt* (*container*) auffüllen;
(*form*) ausfüllen ♦ *vi* (*AUT*) tanken

fillet ['fɪlɪt] *n* Filet *nt*; ~ **steak** *n* Filetsteak *nt*

filling ['fɪlɪŋ] *n* (*COOK*) Füllung *f*; (*for tooth*)
(Zahn)plombe *f*; ~ **station** *n* Tankstelle *f*

film [fɪlm] *n* Film *m* ♦ *vt* (*scene*) filmen; ~
star *n* Filmstar *m*

filter ['fɪltər] *n* Filter *m* ♦ *vt* filtern; ~ **lane**
n (*BRIT*) Abbiegespur *f*; ~-**tipped** *adj* Filter-

filth [fɪlθ] *n* Dreck *m*; ~**y** *adj* dreckig;
(*weather*) scheußlich

fin [fɪn] *n* Flosse *f*

final ['faɪnl] *adj* letzte(r, s); End-; (*conclusive*)
endgültig ♦ *n* (*FOOTBALL etc*) Endspiel *nt*; ~**s**
npl (*UNIV*) Abschlussexamen *nt*; (*SPORT*)
Schlussrunde *f*

finale [fɪ'nɑːlɪ] *n* (*MUS*) Finale *nt*

final: ~**ist** *n* (*SPORT*) Schluss-
rundenteilnehmer *m*; ~**ize** *vt* endgültige
Form geben; abschließen; ~**ly** *adv*
(*lastly*) zuletzt; (*eventually*) endlich;
(*irrevocably*) endgültig

finance [faɪ'næns] *n* Finanzwesen *nt* ♦ *vt*
finanzieren; ~**s** *npl* (*funds*) Finanzen *pl*;
financial [faɪ'nænʃəl] *adj* Finanz-; finanziell

find [faɪnd] (*pt*, *pp* **found**) *vt* finden ♦ *n* Fund
m; **to** ~ **sb guilty** jdn für schuldig erklären;
~ **out** *vt* herausfinden; ~**ings** *npl* (*JUR*)
Ermittlungsergebnis *nt*; (*of report*) Befund *m*

fine [faɪn] *adj* fein; (*good*) gut; (*weather*)
schön ♦ *adv* (*well*) gut; (*small*) klein ♦ *n* (*JUR*)
Geldstrafe *f* ♦ *vt* (*JUR*) mit einer Geldstrafe
belegen; ~ **arts** *npl* schöne(n) Künste *pl*

finger ['fɪŋgər] *n* Finger *m* ♦ *vt* befühlen;
~**nail** *n* Fingernagel *m*; ~**print** *n*
Fingerabdruck *m*; ~**tip** *n* Fingerspitze *f*

finicky ['fɪnɪkɪ] *adj* pingelig

finish ['fɪnɪʃ] *n* Ende *nt*; (*SPORT*) Ziel *nt*; (*of
object*) Verarbeitung *f*; (*of paint*)
Oberflächenwirkung *f* ♦ *vt* beenden; (*book*)
zu Ende lesen ♦ *vi* aufhören; (*SPORT*) ans
Ziel kommen; **to be** ~**ed with sth** fertig
sein mit etw; **to** ~ **doing sth** mit etw fertig
werden; ~ **off** *vt* (*complete*) fertig machen;
(*kill*) den Gnadenstoß geben +*dat*; (*knock
out*) erledigen (*umg*); ~ **up** *vt* (*food*)
aufessen; (*drink*) austrinken ♦ *vi* (*end up*)
enden; ~**ing line** *n* Ziellinie *f*; ~**ing
school** *n* Mädchenpensionat *nt*

finite ['faɪnaɪt] *adj* endlich, begrenzt

Finland ['fɪnlənd] *n* Finnland *nt*

Finn [fɪn] *n* Finne *m*, Finnin *f*; **~ish** *adj* finnisch ♦ *n* (*LING*) Finnisch *nt*

fir [fəːʳ] *n* Tanne *f*

fire ['faɪəʳ] *n* Feuer *nt*; (*in house etc*) Brand *m* ♦ *vt* (*gun*) abfeuern; (*imagination*) entzünden; (*dismiss*) hinauswerfen ♦ *vi* (*AUT*) zünden; **to be on ~** brennen; **~ alarm** *n* Feueralarm *m*; **~arm** *n* Schusswaffe *f*; **~ brigade** (*BRIT*) *n* Feuerwehr *f*; **~ department** (*US*) *n* Feuerwehr *f*; **~ engine** *n* Feuerwehrauto *nt*; **~ escape** *n* Feuerleiter *f*; **~ extinguisher** *n* Löschgerät *nt*; **~man** (*irreg*) *n* Feuerwehrmann *m*; **~place** *n* Kamin *m*; **~side** *n* Kamin *m*; **~ station** *n* Feuerwehrwache *f*; **~wood** *n* Brennholz *nt*; **~works** *npl* Feuerwerk *nt*; **~ squad** *n* Exekutionskommando *nt*

firm [fəːm] *adj* fest ♦ *n* Firma *f*; **~ly** ['fəːmlɪ] *adv* (*grasp, speak*) fest; (*push, tug*) energisch; (*decide*) endgültig

first [fəːst] *adj* erste(r, s) ♦ *adv* zuerst; (*arrive*) als Erste(r); (*happen*) zum ersten Mal ♦ *n* (*person: in race*) Erste(r) *mf*; (*UNIV*) Eins *f*; (*AUT*) erste(r) Gang *m*; **at ~** zuerst; **~ of all** zuallererst; **~ aid** *n* erste Hilfe *f*; **~-aid kit** *n* Verbandskasten *m*; **~-class** *adj* erstklassig; (*travel*) erster Klasse; **~-hand** *adj* aus erster Hand; **~ lady** (*US*) *n* First Lady *f*; **~ly** *adv* erstens; **~ name** *n* Vorname *m*; **~-rate** *adj* erstklassig

fiscal ['fɪskl] *adj* Finanz-

fish [fɪʃ] *n inv* Fisch *m* ♦ *vi* fischen; angeln; **to go ~ing** angeln gehen; (*in sea*) fischen gehen; **~erman** (*irreg*) *n* Fischer *m*; **~ farm** *n* Fischzucht *f*; **~ fingers** (*BRIT*) *npl* Fischstäbchen *pl*; **~ing boat** *n* Fischerboot *nt*; **~ing line** *n* Angelschnur *f*; **~ing rod** *n* Angel(rute) *f*; **~ing tackle** *n* (*for sport*) Angelgeräte *pl*; **~monger's (shop)** *n* Fischhändler *m*; **~ slice** *n* Fischvorlegemesser *nt*; **~ sticks** (*US*) *npl* = **fish fingers**

fishy ['fɪʃɪ] (*inf*) *adj* (*suspicious*) faul

fission ['fɪʃən] *n* Spaltung *f*

fissure ['fɪʃəʳ] *n* Riss *m*

fist [fɪst] *n* Faust *f*

fit [fɪt] *adj* (*MED*) gesund; (*SPORT*) in Form, fit; (*suitable*) geeignet ♦ *vt* passen +*dat*; (*insert, attach*) einsetzen ♦ *vi* passen; (*in space, gap*) hineinpassen ♦ *n* (*of clothes*) Sitz *m*; (*MED, of anger*) Anfall *m*; (*of laughter*) Krampf *m*; **by ~s and starts** (*move*) ruckweise; (*work*) unregelmäßig; **~ in** *vi* hineinpassen; (*fig: person*) passen; **~ out** *vt* (*also:* **~ up**) ausstatten; **~ful** *adj* (*sleep*) unruhig; **~ment** *n* Einrichtungsgegenstand *m*; **~ness** *n* (*suitability*) Eignung *f*; (*MED*) Gesundheit *f*; (*SPORT*) Fitness *f*; **~ted carpet** *n* Teppichboden *m*; **~ted kitchen** *n* Einbauküche *f*; **~ter** *n* (*TECH*) Monteur *m*; **~ting** *adj* passend ♦ *n* (*of dress*) Anprobe *f*; (*piece of equipment*) (Ersatz)teil *nt*; **~tings** *npl* (*equipment*) Zubehör *nt*; **~ting room** *n* Anproberaum *m*

five [faɪv] *num* fünf; **~r** (*inf*) *n* (*BRIT*) Fünfpfundnote *f*; (*US*) Fünfdollarnote *f*

fix [fɪks] *vt* befestigen; (*settle*) festsetzen; (*repair*) reparieren ♦ *n*: **in a ~** in der Klemme; **~ up** *vt* (*meeting*) arrangieren; **to ~ sb up with sth** jdm etw *acc* verschaffen; **~ation** [fɪk'seɪʃən] *n* Fixierung *f*; **~ed** [fɪkst] *adj* fest; **~ture** ['fɪkstʃəʳ] *n* Installationsteil *nt*; (*SPORT*) Spiel *nt*

fizzy ['fɪzɪ] *adj* Sprudel-, sprudelnd

flabbergasted ['flæbəgɑːstɪd] (*inf*) *adj* platt

flabby ['flæbɪ] *adj* wabbelig

flag [flæg] *n* Fahne *f* ♦ *vi* (*strength*) nachlassen; (*spirit*) erlahmen; **~ down** *vt* anhalten; **~pole** ['flægpəul] *n* Fahnenstange *f*

flair [fleəʳ] *n* Talent *nt*

flak [flæk] *n* Flakfeuer *nt*

flake [fleɪk] *n* (*of snow*) Flocke *f*; (*of rust*) Schuppe *f* ♦ *vi* (*also:* **~ off**) abblättern

flamboyant [flæm'bɔɪənt] *adj* extravagant

flame [fleɪm] *n* Flamme *f*

flamingo [flə'mɪŋgəu] *n* Flamingo *m*

flammable ['flæməbl] *adj* brennbar

flan [flæn] (*BRIT*) *n* Obsttorte *f*

flank [flæŋk] *n* Flanke *f* ♦ *vt* flankieren

flannel ['flænl] *n* Flanell *m*; (*BRIT: also:* **face ~**) Waschlappen *m*; (:. *inf*) Geschwafel *nt*; **~s** *npl* (*trousers*) Flanellhose *f*

flap [flæp] n Klappe f; (inf: crisis) (helle) Aufregung f ♦ vt (wings) schlagen mit ♦ vi flattern

flare [flɛəʳ] n (signal) Leuchtsignal nt; (in skirt etc) Weite f; ~ **up** vi aufflammen; (fig) aufbrausen; (revolt) (plötzlich) ausbrechen

flash [flæʃ] n Blitz m; (also: **news ~**) Kurzmeldung f; (PHOT) Blitzlicht nt ♦ vt aufleuchten lassen ♦ vi aufleuchten; **in a ~** im Nu; ~ **by** or **past** vi vorbeirasen; ~**back** n Rückblende f; ~**bulb** n Blitzlichtbirne f; ~ **cube** n Blitzwürfel m; ~**light** n Blitzlicht nt

flashy ['flæʃɪ] (pej) adj knallig

flask [flɑːsk] n (CHEM) Kolben m; (also: **vacuum ~**) Thermosflasche f ®

flat [flæt] adj flach; (dull) matt; (MUS) erniedrigt; (beer) schal; (tyre) platt ♦ n (BRIT: rooms) Wohnung f; (MUS) b nt; (AUT) Platte(r) m; **to work ~ out** auf Hochtouren arbeiten; ~**ly** adv glatt; ~**-screen** adj (TV, COMPUT) mit flachem Bildschirm; ~**ten** vt (also: ~**ten out**) ebnen

flatter ['flætəʳ] vt schmeicheln +dat; ~**ing** adj schmeichelhaft; ~**y** n Schmeichelei f

flatulence ['flætjʊləns] n Blähungen pl

flaunt [flɔːnt] vt prunken mit

flavour ['fleɪvəʳ] (US **flavor**) n Geschmack m ♦ vt würzen; ~**ed** adj: **strawberry-~ed** mit Erdbeergeschmack; ~**ing** n Würze f

flaw [flɔː] n Fehler m; ~**less** adj einwandfrei

flax [flæks] n Flachs m; ~**en** adj flachsfarben

flea [fliː] n Floh m

fleck [flɛk] n (mark) Fleck m; (pattern) Tupfen m

fled [flɛd] pt, pp of **flee**

flee [fliː] (pt, pp **fled**) vi fliehen ♦ vt fliehen vor +dat; (country) fliehen aus

fleece [fliːs] n Vlies nt ♦ vt (inf) schröpfen

fleet [fliːt] n Flotte f

fleeting ['fliːtɪŋ] adj flüchtig

Flemish ['flɛmɪʃ] adj flämisch

flesh [flɛʃ] n Fleisch nt; ~ **wound** n Fleischwunde f

flew [fluː] pt of **fly**

flex [flɛks] n Kabel nt ♦ vt beugen; ~**ibility** [flɛksɪ'bɪlɪtɪ] n Biegsamkeit f; (fig) Flexibilität

f; ~**ible** adj biegsam; (plans) flexibel

flick [flɪk] n leichte(r) Schlag m ♦ vt leicht schlagen; ~ **through** vt fus durchblättern

flicker ['flɪkəʳ] n Flackern nt ♦ vi flackern

flier ['flaɪəʳ] n Flieger m

flight [flaɪt] n Flug m; (fleeing) Flucht f; (also: ~ **of steps**) Treppe f; **to take ~** die Flucht ergreifen; ~ **attendant** (US) n Steward(ess) m(f); ~ **deck** n Flugdeck nt

flimsy ['flɪmzɪ] adj (thin) hauchdünn; (excuse) fadenscheinig

flinch [flɪntʃ] vi: **to ~ (away from)** zurückschrecken (vor +dat)

fling [flɪŋ] (pt, pp **flung**) vt schleudern

flint [flɪnt] n Feuerstein m

flip [flɪp] vt werfen

flippant ['flɪpənt] adj schnippisch

flipper ['flɪpəʳ] n Flosse f

flirt [flɜːt] vi flirten ♦ n: **he/she is a ~** er/sie flirtet gern

flit [flɪt] vi flitzen

float [fləʊt] n (FISHING) Schwimmer m; (esp in procession) Plattformwagen m ♦ vi schwimmen; (in air) schweben ♦ vt (COMM) gründen; (currency) floaten

flock [flɒk] n (of sheep, REL) Herde f; (of birds) Schwarm m

flog [flɒg] vt prügeln; (inf: sell) verkaufen

flood [flʌd] n Überschwemmung f; (fig) Flut f ♦ vt überschwemmen; ~**ing** n Überschwemmung f; ~**light** n Flutlicht nt

floor [flɔːʳ] n (Fuß)boden m; (storey) Stock m ♦ vt (person) zu Boden schlagen; **ground ~** (BRIT) Erdgeschoss nt; **first ~** (BRIT) erste(r) Stock m; (US) Erdgeschoss nt; ~**board** n Diele f; ~ **show** n Kabarettvorstellung f

flop [flɒp] n Plumps m; (failure) Reinfall m ♦ vi (fail) durchfallen

floppy ['flɒpɪ] adj hängend; ~ (**disk**) n (COMPUT) Diskette f

flora ['flɔːrə] n Flora f

floral ['flɔːrl] adj Blumen-

florist ['flɒrɪst] n Blumenhändler(in) m(f); ~**'s (shop)** n Blumengeschäft nt

flotation [fləʊ'teɪʃən] n (FIN) Auflegung f

flounce [flaʊns] n Volant m

flounder ['flaʊndəʳ] vi (fig) ins Schleudern kommen ♦ n (ZOOL) Flunder f

flour ['flaʊə^r] n Mehl nt

flourish ['flʌrɪʃ] vi blühen; gedeihen ♦ n (waving) Schwingen nt; (of trumpets) Tusch m, Fanfare f

flout [flaʊt] vt missachten

flow [fləʊ] n Fließen nt; (of sea) Flut f ♦ vi fließen; ~ **chart** n Flussdiagramm nt

flower ['flaʊə^r] n Blume f ♦ vi blühen; ~ **bed** n Blumenbeet nt; ~**pot** n Blumentopf m; ~**y** adj (style) blumenreich

flown [fləʊn] pp of **fly**

flu [fluː] n Grippe f

fluctuate ['flʌktjʊeɪt] vi schwanken; **fluctuation** [flʌktjʊ'eɪʃən] n Schwankung f

fluency ['fluːənsɪ] n Flüssigkeit f

fluent ['fluːənt] adj fließend; ~**ly** adv fließend

fluff [flʌf] n Fussel f; ~**y** adj flaumig

fluid ['fluːɪd] n Flüssigkeit f ♦ adj flüssig; (fig: plans) veränderbar

fluke [fluːk] (inf) n Dusel m

flung [flʌŋ] pt, pp of **fling**

fluoride ['flʊəraɪd] n Fluorid nt; ~ **toothpaste** n Fluorzahnpasta f

flurry ['flʌrɪ] n (of snow) Gestöber nt; (of activity) Aufregung f

flush [flʌʃ] n Erröten nt; (excited) Glühen nt ♦ vt ausspülen ♦ vi erröten ♦ adj glatt; ~ **out** vt aufstöbern; ~**ed** adj rot

flustered ['flʌstəd] adj verwirrt

flute [fluːt] n Querflöte f

flutter ['flʌtə^r] n Flattern nt ♦ vi flattern

flux [flʌks] n: **in a state of ~** im Fluss

fly [flaɪ] (pt **flew**, pp **flown**) n (insect) Fliege f; (on trousers: also: **flies**) (Hosen)schlitz m ♦ vt fliegen ♦ vi fliegen; (flee) fliehen; (flag) wehen; ~ **away** or **off** vi (bird, insect) wegfliegen; ~-**drive** n: ~-**drive holiday** Fly & Drive-Urlaub m; ~**ing** n Fliegen nt ♦ adj: **with ~ing colours** mit fliegenden Fahnen; ~**ing start** gute(r) Start m; ~**ing visit** Stippvisite f; ~**ing saucer** n fliegende Untertasse f; ~**over** (BRIT) n Überführung f; ~**sheet** n (for tent) Regendach nt

foal [fəʊl] n Fohlen nt

foam [fəʊm] n Schaum m ♦ vi schäumen; ~ **rubber** n Schaumgummi m

fob [fɒb] vt: **to ~ sb off with sth** jdm etw

andrehen; (with promise) jdn mit etw abspeisen

focal ['fəʊkl] adj Brenn-; ~ **point** n (of room, activity) Mittelpunkt m

focus ['fəʊkəs] (pl ~**es**) n Brennpunkt m ♦ vt (attention) konzentrieren; (camera) scharf einstellen ♦ vi: **to ~ (on)** sich konzentrieren (auf +acc); **in ~** scharf eingestellt; **out of ~** unscharf

fodder ['fɒdə^r] n Futter nt

foe [fəʊ] n Feind m

foetus ['fiːtəs] (US **fetus**) n Fötus m

fog [fɒg] n Nebel m; ~**gy** adj neblig; ~ **lamp** (BRIT), ~ **light** (US) n (AUT) Nebelscheinwerfer m

foil [fɔɪl] vt vereiteln ♦ n (metal, also fig) Folie f; (FENCING) Florett nt

fold [fəʊld] n (bend, crease) Falte f; (AGR) Pferch m ♦ vt falten; ~ **up** vt (map etc) zusammenfalten ♦ vi (business) eingehen; ~**er** n Schnellhefter m; ~**ing** adj (chair etc) Klapp-

foliage ['fəʊlɪɪdʒ] n Laubwerk nt

folk [fəʊk] npl Leute pl ♦ adj Volks-; ~**s** npl (family) Leute pl; ~**lore** ['fəʊklɔː^r] n (study) Volkskunde f; (tradition) Folklore f; ~ **song** n Volkslied nt; (modern) Folksong m

follow ['fɒləʊ] vt folgen +dat; (fashion) mitmachen ♦ vi folgen; ~ **up** vt verfolgen; ~**er** n Anhänger(in) m(f); ~**ing** adj folgend ♦ n (people) Gefolgschaft f; ~-**on call** n weiteres Gespräch in einer Telefonzelle um Guthaben zu verbrauchen

folly ['fɒlɪ] n Torheit f

fond [fɒnd] adj: **to be ~ of** gern haben

fondle ['fɒndl] vt streicheln

font [fɒnt] n Taufbecken nt

food [fuːd] n Essen nt; (fodder) Futter nt; ~ **mixer** n Küchenmixer m; ~ **poisoning** n Lebensmittelvergiftung f; ~ **processor** n Küchenmaschine f; ~**stuffs** npl Lebensmittel pl

fool [fuːl] n Narr m, Närrin f ♦ vt (deceive) hereinlegen ♦ vi (also: ~ **around**) (herum)albern; ~**hardy** adj tollkühn; ~**ish** adj albern; ~**proof** adj idiotensicher

foot [fʊt] (pl **feet**) n Fuß m ♦ vt (bill)

bezahlen; **on ~** zu Fuß
footage ['futɪdʒ] n (CINE) Filmmaterial nt
football ['futbɔ:l] n Fußball m; (game: BRIT)
Fußball m; (: US) Football m; **~ player** n
(BRIT: also: **~er**) Fußballspieler m, Fußballer
m; (US) Footballer m

Football Pools

i Football Pools, *umgangssprachlich
auch* the pools *genannt, ist das in
Großbritannien sehr beliebte Fußballtoto,
bei dem auf die Ergebnisse der
samstäglichen Fußballspiele gewettet wird.
Teilnehmer schicken ihren ausgefüllten
Totoschein vor den Spielen an die
Totogesellschaft und vergleichen nach den
Spielen die Ergebnisse mit ihrem Schein. Die
Gewinne können sehr hoch sein und
gelegentlich Millionen von Pfund betragen.*

---

foot: ~brake n Fußbremse f; **~bridge** n
Fußgängerbrücke f; **~hills** npl Ausläufer pl;
~hold n Halt m; **~ing** n Halt m; (fig)
Verhältnis nt; **~lights** npl Rampenlicht nt;
~man (irreg) n Bedienstete(r) m; **~note** n
Fußnote f; **~path** n Fußweg m; **~print** n
Fußabdruck m; **~sore** adj fußkrank; **~step**
n Schritt m; **~wear** n Schuhzeug nt

KEYWORD

for [fɔ:ʳ] prep **1** für; **is this for me?** ist das für
mich?; **the train for London** der Zug nach
London; **he went for the paper** er ging die
Zeitung holen; **give it to me – what for?**
gib es mir – warum?
2 (because of) wegen; **for this reason** aus
diesem Grunde
3 (referring to distance): **there are
roadworks for 5 km** die Baustelle ist 5 km
lang; **we walked for miles** wir sind
meilenweit gegangen
4 (referring to time) seit; (: with future sense)
für; **he was away for 2 years** er war zwei
Jahre lang weg
5 (+infin clauses): **it is not for me to decide**
das kann ich nicht entscheiden; **for this to
be possible ...** damit dies möglich wird/

wurde ...
6 (in spite of) trotz +gen or (inf) dat ; **for all
his complaints** obwohl er sich ständig
beschwert
♦ conj denn

---

forage ['fɔrɪdʒ] n (Vieh)futter nt
foray ['fɔreɪ] n Raubzug m
forbad(e) [fə'bæd] pt of **forbid**
forbid [fə'bɪd] (pt **forbad(e)**, pp **forbidden**)
vt verbieten; **~ding** adj einschüchternd
force [fɔ:s] n Kraft f; (compulsion) Zwang m
♦ vt zwingen; (lock) aufbrechen; **the F~s**
npl (BRIT) die Streitkräfte; **in ~** (rule) gültig;
(group) in großer Stärke; **~d** adj (smile)
gezwungen; (landing) Not-; **~-feed** vt
zwangsernähren; **~ful** adj (speech) kraftvoll;
(personality) resolut
forceps ['fɔ:seps] npl Zange f
forcibly ['fɔ:səblɪ] adv zwangsweise
ford [fɔ:d] n Furt f ♦ vt durchwaten
fore [fɔ:ʳ] n: **to the ~** in den Vordergrund;
~arm ['fɔ:rɑ:m] n Unterarm m; **~boding**
[fɔ:'bəudɪŋ] n Vorahnung f; **~cast** ['fɔ:kɑ:st]
(irreg: like **cast**) n Vorhersage f ♦ vt
voraussagen; **~court** ['fɔ:kɔ:t] n (of garage)
Vorplatz m; **~fathers** ['fɔ:fɑ:ðəz] npl
Vorfahren pl; **~finger** ['fɔ:fɪŋgəʳ] n
Zeigefinger m; **~front** ['fɔ:frʌnt] n Spitze f
forego [fɔ:'gəu] (irreg: like **go**) vt verzichten
auf +acc
fore: ~gone ['fɔ:gɒn] adj: **it's a ~gone
conclusion** es steht von vornherein fest;
~ground ['fɔ:graund] n Vordergrund m;
~head ['fɔrɪd] n Stirn f
foreign ['fɔrɪn] adj Auslands-; (accent)
ausländisch; (trade) Außen-; (body) Fremd-;
~er n Ausländer(in) m(f); **~ exchange** n
Devisen pl; **F~ Office** (BRIT) n
Außenministerium nt; **F~ Secretary** (BRIT)
n Außenminister m
fore: ~leg n Vorderbein nt; **~man**
(irreg) n Vorarbeiter m; **~most** adj erste(r,
s) ♦ adv: **first and ~most** vor allem
forensic [fə'rɛnsɪk] adj gerichtsmedizinisch
fore ['fɔ:-]: **~runner** n Vorläufer m; **~see**
[fɔ:'si:] (irreg: like **see**) vt vorhersehen;

~seeable adj absehbar; **~shadow** [ˈfɔːˈʃædəu] vt andeuten; **~sight** [ˈfɔːsaɪt] n Voraussicht f

forest [ˈfɒrɪst] n Wald m

forestall [fɔːˈstɔːl] vt zuvorkommen +dat

forestry [ˈfɒrɪstrɪ] n Forstwirtschaft f

foretaste [ˈfɔːteɪst] n Vorgeschmack m

foretell [fɔːˈtel] (irreg: like **tell**) vt vorhersagen

forever [fəˈrevəʳ] adv für immer

foreword [ˈfɔːwəːd] n Vorwort nt

forfeit [ˈfɔːfɪt] n Einbuße f ♦ vt verwirken

forgave [fəˈgeɪv] pt of **forgive**

forge [fɔːdʒ] n Schmiede f ♦ vt fälschen; (iron) schmieden; **~ ahead** vi Fortschritte machen; **~d** adj gefälscht; **~d banknotes** Blüten (inf) pl; **~r** n Fälscher m; **~ry** n Fälschung f

forget [fəˈget] (pt **forgot**, pp **forgotten**) vt, vi vergessen; **~ful** adj vergesslich; **~-me-not** n Vergissmeinnicht nt

forgive [fəˈgɪv] (pt **forgave**, pp **forgiven**) vt verzeihen; **to ~ sb (for sth)** jdm (etw) verzeihen; **~ness** n Verzeihung f

forgot [fəˈgɒt] pt of **forget**; **~ten** pp of **forget**

fork [fɔːk] n Gabel f; (in road) Gabelung f ♦ vi (road) sich gabeln; **~ out** (inf) vt (pay) blechen; **~-lift truck** n Gabelstapler m

forlorn [fəˈlɔːn] adj (person) verlassen; (hope) vergeblich

form [fɔːm] n Form f; (type) Art f; (figure) Gestalt f; (SCH) Klasse f; (bench) (Schul)bank f; (document) Formular nt ♦ vt formen; (be part of) bilden

formal [ˈfɔːməl] adj formell; (occasion) offiziell; **~ly** adv (ceremoniously) formell; (officially) offiziell

format [ˈfɔːmæt] n Format nt ♦ vt (COMPUT) formatieren

formation [fɔːˈmeɪʃən] n Bildung f; (AVIAT) Formation f

formative [ˈfɔːmətɪv] adj (years) formend

former [ˈfɔːməʳ] adj früher; (opposite of latter) erstere(r, s); **~ly** adv früher

formidable [ˈfɔːmɪdəbl] adj furchtbar

formula [ˈfɔːmjulə] (pl **~e** or **~s**) n Formel f; **~e** [ˈfɔːmjuliː] npl of **formula**; **~te**

[ˈfɔːmjuleɪt] vt formulieren

fort [fɔːt] n Feste f, Fort nt

forte [ˈfɔːtɪ] n Stärke f, starke Seite f

forth [fɔːθ] adv: **and so ~** und so weiter; **~coming** adj kommend; (character) entgegenkommend; **~right** adj offen; **~with** adv umgehend

fortify [ˈfɔːtɪfaɪ] vt (ver)stärken; (protect) befestigen

fortitude [ˈfɔːtɪtjuːd] n Seelenstärke f

fortnight [ˈfɔːtnaɪt] n (BRIT) vierzehn Tage pl; **~ly** (BRIT) adj zweiwöchentlich ♦ adv alle vierzehn Tage

fortress [ˈfɔːtrɪs] n Festung f

fortunate [ˈfɔːtʃənɪt] adj glücklich; **~ly** adv glücklicherweise, zum Glück

fortune [ˈfɔːtʃən] n Glück nt; (money) Vermögen nt; **~-teller** n Wahrsager(in) m(f)

forty [ˈfɔːtɪ] num vierzig

forum [ˈfɔːrəm] n Forum nt

forward [ˈfɔːwəd] adj vordere(r, s); (movement) Vorwärts-; (person) vorlaut; (planning) Voraus- ♦ adv vorwärts ♦ n (SPORT) Stürmer m ♦ vt (send) schicken; (help) fördern; **~s** adv vorwärts

fossil [ˈfɒsl] n Fossil nt, Versteinerung f

foster [ˈfɒstəʳ] vt (talent) fördern; **~ child** n Pflegekind nt; **~ mother** n Pflegemutter f

fought [fɔːt] pt, pp of **fight**

foul [faul] adj schmutzig; (language) gemein; (weather) schlecht ♦ n (SPORT) Foul nt ♦ vt (mechanism) blockieren; (SPORT) foulen; **~ play** n (SPORT) Foulspiel nt; (LAW) Verbrechen nt

found [faund] pt, pp of **find** ♦ vt gründen; **~ation** [faunˈdeɪʃən] n (act) Gründung f; (fig) Fundament nt; (also: **~ation cream**) Grundierungscreme f; **~ations** npl (of house) Fundament nt; **~er** n Gründer(in) m(f) ♦ vi sinken

foundry [ˈfaundrɪ] n Gießerei f

fountain [ˈfauntɪn] n (Spring)brunnen m; **~ pen** n Füllfederhalter m

four [fɔːʳ] num vier; **on all ~s** auf allen vieren; **~-poster** n Himmelbett nt; **~some** n Quartett nt; **~teen** num vierzehn;

~**teenth** *adj* vierzehnte(r, s); ~**th** *adj*
vierte(r, s)

fowl [faul] *n* Huhn *nt*; (*food*) Geflügel *nt*

fox [fɒks] *n* Fuchs *m* ♦ *vt* täuschen

foyer ['fɔɪeɪ] *n* Foyer *nt*, Vorhalle *f*

fraction ['frækʃən] *n* (MATH) Bruch *m*; (*part*)
Bruchteil *m*

fracture ['fræktʃər] *n* (MED) Bruch *m* ♦ *vt*
brechen

fragile ['frædʒaɪl] *adj* zerbrechlich

fragment ['frægmənt] *n* Bruchstück *nt*; (*small
part*) Splitter *m*

fragrance ['freɪɡrəns] *n* Duft *m*; **fragrant**
['freɪɡrənt] *adj* duftend

frail [freɪl] *adj* schwach, gebrechlich

frame [freɪm] *n* Rahmen *m*; (*of spectacles:
also:* ~**s**) Gestell *nt*; (*body*) Gestalt *f* ♦ *vt*
einrahmen; **to ~ sb** (*inf: incriminate*) jdm
etwas anhängen; ~ **of mind** Verfassung *f*;
~**work** *n* Rahmen *m*; (*of society*) Gefüge *nt*

France [frɑːns] *n* Frankreich *nt*

franchise ['fræntʃaɪz] *n* (POL) (aktives)
Wahlrecht *nt*; (COMM) Lizenz *f*

frank [fræŋk] *adj* offen ♦ *vt* (*letter*) frankieren;
~**ly** *adv* offen gesagt

frantic ['fræntɪk] *adj* verzweifelt

fraternal [frə'tɜːnl] *adj* brüderlich

fraternity [frə'tɜːnɪtɪ] *n* (*club*) Vereinigung *f*;
(*spirit*) Brüderlichkeit *f*; (US: SCH)
Studentenverbindung *f*

fraternize ['frætənaɪz] *vi* fraternisieren

fraud [frɔːd] *n* (*trickery*) Betrug *m*; (*person*)
Schwindler(in) *m(f)*; ~**ulent** ['frɔːdjulənt] *adj*
betrügerisch

fraught [frɔːt] *adj*: ~ **with** voller +*gen*

fray [freɪ] *vt*, *vi* ausfransen; **tempers were
~ed** die Gemüter waren erhitzt

freak [friːk] *n* Monstrosität *f* ♦ *cpd* (*storm etc*)
anormal

freckle ['frekl] *n* Sommersprosse *f*

free [friː] *adj* frei; (*loose*) lose; (*liberal*)
freigebig ♦ *vt* (*set* ~) befreien; (*unblock*)
freimachen; ~ **(of charge)** gratis, umsonst;
for ~ gratis, umsonst; ~**dom** ['friːdəm] *n*
Freiheit *f*; **F~fone** ® *n*: **call F~fone 0800
...** rufen Sie gebührenfrei 0800 ... an; ~~
for-all *n* (*fight*) allgemeine(s)

Handgemenge *nt*; ~ **gift** *n* Geschenk *nt*; ~
kick *n* Freistoß *m*; ~**lance** *adj* frei; (*artist*)
freischaffend; ~**ly** *adv* frei; (*admit*) offen;
F~post ® *n* ≈ Gebühr zahlt Empfänger;
~~**range** *adj* (*hen*) Farmhof-; (*eggs*) Land-; ~
trade *n* Freihandel *m*; ~**way** (US) *n*
Autobahn *f*; ~**wheel** *vi* im Freilauf fahren;
~ **will** *n*: **of one's own ~ will** aus freien
Stücken

freeze [friːz] (*pt* **froze**, *pp* **frozen**) *vi*
gefrieren; (*feel cold*) frieren ♦ *vt* (*also fig*)
einfrieren ♦ *n* (*fig, FIN*) Stopp *m*; ~**r** *n*
Tiefkühltruhe *f*; (*in fridge*) Gefrierfach *nt*;

freezing *adj* eisig; (*freezing cold*) eiskalt;
freezing point *n* Gefrierpunkt *m*

freight [freɪt] *n* Fracht *f*; ~ **train** *n* Güterzug
m

French [frentʃ] *adj* französisch ♦ *n* (LING)
Französisch *nt*; **the** ~ *npl* (*people*) die
Franzosen *pl*; ~ **bean** *n* grüne Bohne *f*; ~
fried potatoes (BRIT) *npl* Pommes frites *pl*;
~ **fries** (US) *npl* Pommes frites *pl*; ~ **horn** *n*
(MUS) (Wald)horn *nt*; ~ **kiss** *n* Zungenkuss
m; ~ **loaf** *n* Baguette *f*; ~**man/woman**
(*irreg*) *n* Franzose *m*/Französin *f*; ~ **window**
n Verandatür *f*

frenzy ['frenzɪ] *n* Raserei *f*

frequency ['friːkwənsɪ] *n* Häufigkeit *f*; (PHYS)
Frequenz *f*

frequent [*adj* 'friːkwənt, *vb* frɪ'kwent] *adj*
häufig ♦ *vt* (*regelmäßig*) besuchen; ~**ly** *adv*
(*often*) häufig, oft

fresh [freʃ] *adj* frisch; ~**en** *vi* (*also:* ~**en up**)
(sich) auffrischen; (*person*) sich frisch
machen; ~**er** (*inf: BRIT*) *n* (UNIV)
Erstsemester *nt*; ~**ly** *adv* gerade; ~**man**
(*irreg*) (US) *n* = **fresher**; ~**ness** *n* Frische *f*;
~**water** *adj* (*fish*) Süßwasser-

fret [fret] *vi* sich *dat* Sorgen machen

friar ['fraɪər] *n* Klosterbruder *m*

friction ['frɪkʃən] *n* (*also fig*) Reibung *f*

Friday ['fraɪdɪ] *n* Freitag *m*

fridge [frɪdʒ] (BRIT) *n* Kühlschrank *m*

fried [fraɪd] *adj* gebraten

friend [frend] *n* Freund(in) *m(f)*; ~**ly** *adj*
freundlich; (*relations*) freundschaftlich; ~**ly
fire** *n* Beschuss *m* durch die eigene Seite;

~ship n Freundschaft f

frieze [friːz] n Fries m

frigate ['frɪgɪt] n Fregatte f

fright [fraɪt] n Schrecken m; to take ~ es mit der Angst zu tun bekommen; ~en vt erschrecken; to be ~ened Angst haben; ~ening adj schrecklich; ~ful (inf) adj furchtbar

frigid ['frɪdʒɪd] adj frigide

frill [frɪl] n Rüsche f

fringe [frɪndʒ] n Besatz m; (BRIT: of hair) Pony m; (fig) Peripherie f; ~ benefits npl zusätzliche Leistungen pl

Frisbee ['frɪzbɪ] ® n Frisbee ® nt

frisk [frɪsk] vt durchsuchen

frisky ['frɪskɪ] adj lebendig, ausgelassen

fritter ['frɪtə*] n: to ~ away vergeuden

frivolous ['frɪvələs] adj frivol

frizzy ['frɪzɪ] adj kraus

fro [frəu] adv see to

frock [frɒk] n Kleid nt

frog [frɒg] n Frosch m; ~man (irreg) n Froschmann m

frolic ['frɒlɪk] vi ausgelassen sein

┌─────────────┐
│ KEYWORD   │
└─────────────┘

from [frɒm] prep 1 (indicating starting place) of; (indicating origin from) aus +dat; a letter/ telephone call from my sister ein Brief/ Anruf von meiner Schwester; where do you come from? woher kommen Sie?; to drink from the bottle aus der Flasche trinken

2 (indicating time) von ... an; (: past) seit; from one o'clock to or until or till two von ein Uhr bis zwei; from January (on) ab Januar

3 (indicating distance) von ... (entfernt)

4 (indicating price, number etc) ab +dat; from £10 ab £10; there were from 20 to 30 people there es waren zwischen 20 und 30 Leute da

5 (indicating difference): he can't tell red from green er kann nicht zwischen Rot und Grün unterscheiden; to be different from sb/sth anders sein als jd/etw

6 (because of, based on): from what he says aus dem, was er sagt; weak from hunger schwach vor Hunger

front [frʌnt] n Vorderseite f; (of house) Fassade f; (promenade: also: sea ~) Strandpromenade f; (MIL, POL, MET) Front f; (fig: appearances) Fassade f ♦ adj (forward) vordere(r, s), Vorder-; (first) vorderste(r, s); in ~ vorne; in ~ of vor; ~age ['frʌntɪdʒ] n Vorderfront f; ~ door n Haustür f; ~ier ['frʌntɪə*] n Grenze f; ~ page n Titelseite f; ~ room n (BRIT) Wohnzimmer nt; ~-wheel drive n Vorderradantrieb m

frost [frɒst] n Frost m; ~bite n Erfrierung f; ~ed adj (glass) Milch-; ~y adj frostig

froth [frɒθ] n Schaum m

frown [fraun] n Stirnrunzeln nt ♦ vi die Stirn runzeln

froze [frəuz] pt of freeze

frozen ['frəuzn] pp of freeze

frugal ['fruːgl] adj sparsam, bescheiden

fruit [fruːt] n inv (as collective) Obst nt; (particular) Frucht f; ~ful adj fruchtbar; ~ion [fruːˈɪʃən] n: to come to ~ion in Erfüllung gehen; ~ juice n Fruchtsaft m; ~ machine n (BRIT) Spielautomat m; ~ salad n Obstsalat m

frustrate [frʌsˈtreɪt] vt vereiteln; ~d adj gehemmt; (PSYCH) frustriert

fry [fraɪ] (pt, pp fried) vt braten ♦ npl: small ~ kleine Fische pl; ~ing pan n Bratpfanne f

ft. abbr = foot; feet

fuddy-duddy ['fʌdɪdʌdɪ] n altmodische(r) Kauz m

fudge [fʌdʒ] n Fondant m

fuel ['fjuəl] n Treibstoff m; (for heating) Brennstoff m; (for lighter) Benzin nt; ~ oil n (diesel fuel) Heizöl nt; ~ tank n Tank m

fugitive ['fjuːdʒɪtɪv] n Flüchtling m

fulfil [fulˈfɪl] vt (duty) erfüllen; (promise) einhalten; ~ment n Erfüllung f

full [ful] adj (box, bottle, price) voll; (person: satisfied) satt; (member, power, employment) Voll-; (complete) vollständig, Voll-; (speed) höchste(r, s); (skirt) weit ♦ adv: ~ well sehr wohl; in ~ vollständig; a ~ two hours volle zwei Stunden; ~-length adj (lifesize) lebensgroß; a ~-length photograph eine Ganzaufnahme; ~ moon n Vollmond m; ~-scale adj (attack) General-; (drawing) in Originalgröße; ~ stop n Punkt m; ~-time adj (job) Ganztags- ♦ adv (work) ganztags ♦ n (SPORT) Spielschluss nt; ~y adv völlig; ~y fledged adj (also fig) flügge; ~y licensed adj (hotel, restaurant) mit voller Schankkonzession or -erlaubnis

fumble ['fʌmbl] vi: to ~ (with) herumfummeln (an +dat)

fume [fjuːm] vi qualmen; (fig) kochen (inf); ~s npl (of fuel, car) Abgase pl

fumigate ['fjuːmɪɡeɪt] vt ausräuchern

fun [fʌn] n (money) Spaß m; to make ~ of sich lustig machen über +acc

function ['fʌŋkʃən] n Funktion f; (occasion) Veranstaltung f ♦ vi funktionieren; ~al adj funktionell

fund [fʌnd] n (money) Geldmittel pl, Fonds m; (store) Vorrat m; ~s npl (resources) Mittel pl

fundamental [fʌndə'mentl] adj fundamental, grundlegend

funeral ['fjuːnərəl] n Beerdigung f; ~ parlour n Leichenhalle f; ~ service n Trauergottesdienst m

funfair ['fʌnfeər] (BRIT) n Jahrmarkt m

fungi ['fʌŋɡaɪ] npl of fungus

fungus ['fʌŋɡəs] n Pilz m

funnel ['fʌnl] n Trichter m; (NAUT) Schornstein m

funny ['fʌnɪ] adj komisch

fur [fɜːr] n Pelz m; ~ coat n Pelzmantel m

furious ['fjuərɪəs] adj wütend; (attempt) heftig

furlong ['fɜːlɔŋ] n = 201.17 m

furnace ['fɜːnɪs] n (Brenn)ofen m

furnish ['fɜːnɪʃ] vt einrichten; (supply) versehen; ~ings npl Einrichtung f

furniture ['fɜːnɪtʃər] n Möbel pl; piece of ~ Möbelstück m

furrow ['fʌrəu] n Furche f

furry ['fɜːrɪ] adj (tongue) pelzig; (animal) Pelz-

further ['fɜːðər] adj weitere(r, s) ♦ adv weiter ♦ vt fördern; ~ education n Weiterbildung

f; Erwachsenenbildung f; ~more adv ferner

furthest ['fɜːðɪst] superl of far

furtive ['fɜːtɪv] adj verstohlen

fury ['fjuərɪ] n Wut f, Zorn m

fuse [fjuːz] (US fuze) n (ELEC) Sicherung f; (of bomb) Zünder m ♦ vt verschmelzen ♦ vi (BRIT: ELEC) durchbrennen; ~ box n Sicherungskasten m

fuselage ['fjuːzəlɑːʒ] n Flugzeugrumpf m

fusion ['fjuːʒən] n Verschmelzung f

fuss [fʌs] n Theater nt; ~y adj kleinlich

futile ['fjuːtaɪl] adj zwecklos, sinnlos; futility [fjuː'tɪlɪtɪ] n Zwecklosigkeit f

future ['fjuːtʃər] adj zukünftig ♦ n Zukunft f; in (the) ~ in Zukunft

fuze [fjuːz] (US) = fuse

fuzzy ['fʌzɪ] adj (indistinct) verschwommen; (hair) kraus

G, g

G [dʒiː] n (MUS) G nt

G7 n abbr (= Group of Seven) G7 f

gabble ['ɡæbl] vi plappern

gable ['ɡeɪbl] n Giebel m

gadget ['ɡædʒɪt] n Vorrichtung f

Gaelic ['ɡeɪlɪk] adj gälisch ♦ n (LING) Gälisch nt

gaffe [ɡæf] n Fauxpas m

gag [ɡæɡ] n Knebel m; (THEAT) Gag m ♦ vt knebeln

gaiety ['ɡeɪɪtɪ] n Fröhlichkeit f

gain [ɡeɪn] vt (obtain) erhalten; (win) gewinnen ♦ vi (clock) vorgehen ♦ n Gewinn m; to ~ in sth an etw dat gewinnen; ~ on sth vt fus einholen

gait [ɡeɪt] n Gang m

gal. abbr = gallon

gala ['ɡɑːlə] n Fest nt

galaxy ['ɡæləksɪ] n Sternsystem nt

gale [ɡeɪl] n Sturm m

gallant ['ɡælənt] adj tapfer; (polite) galant

gallbladder [ɡɔːl-] n Gallenblase f

gallery ['ɡælərɪ] n (also: art ~) Galerie f

galley ['ɡælɪ] n (ship's kitchen) Kombüse f; (ship) Galeere f

gallon ['gælən] n Gallone f

gallop ['gæləp] n Galopp m ♦ vi galoppieren

gallows ['gæləuz] n Galgen m

gallstone ['gɔ:lstəun] n Gallenstein m

galore [gə'lɔ:r] adv in Hülle und Fülle

galvanize ['gælvənaiz] vt (metal) galvanisieren; (fig) elektrisieren

gambit ['gæmbit] n (fig): **opening ~** (einleitende(r)) Schachzug m

gamble ['gæmbl] vi (um Geld) spielen ♦ vt (risk) aufs Spiel setzen ♦ n Risiko nt; **~r** n Spieler(in) m(f); **gambling** n Glücksspiel nt

game [geim] n Spiel nt; (hunting) Wild nt ♦ adj: **~ (for)** bereit (zu); **~keeper** n Wildhüter m; **~s console** (COMPUT) Gameboy m ®, Konsole f

gammon ['gæmən] n geräucherte(r) Schinken m

gamut ['gæmət] n Tonskala f

gang [gæŋ] n (of criminals, youths) Bande f; (of workmen) Kolonne f ♦ vi: **to ~ up on sb** sich gegen jdn verschwören

gangrene ['gæŋgri:n] n Brand m

gangster ['gæŋstər] n Gangster m

gangway ['gæŋwei] n (NAUT) Laufplanke f; (aisle) Gang m

gaol [dʒeil] (BRIT) n, vt = **jail**

gap [gæp] n Lücke f

gape [geip] vi glotzen; **gaping** ['geipiŋ] adj (wound) klaffend; (hole) gähnend

garage ['gærɑ:ʒ] n Garage f; (for repair) (Auto)reparaturwerkstatt f; (for petrol) Tankstelle f

garbage ['gɑ:bidʒ] n Abfall m; **~ can** (US) n Mülltonne f

garbled ['gɑ:bld] adj (story) verdreht

garden ['gɑ:dn] n Garten m; **~s** npl (public park) Park m; (private) Gartenanlagen pl; **~er** n Gärtner(in) m(f); **~ing** n Gärtnern nt

gargle ['gɑ:gl] vi gurgeln

gargoyle ['gɑ:gɔil] n Wasserspeier m

garish ['gɛəriʃ] adj grell

garland ['gɑ:lənd] n Girlande f

garlic ['gɑ:lik] n Knoblauch m

garment ['gɑ:mənt] n Kleidungsstück nt

garnish ['gɑ:niʃ] vt (food) garnieren

garrison ['gærisn] n Garnison f

garter ['gɑ:tər] n Strumpfband nt; (US) Strumpfhalter m

gas [gæs] n Gas nt; (esp US: petrol) Benzin nt ♦ vt vergasen; **~ cooker** (BRIT) n Gasherd m; **~ cylinder** n Gasflasche f; **~ fire** n Gasofen m

gash [gæʃ] n klaffende Wunde f ♦ vt tief verwunden

gasket ['gæskit] n Dichtungsring m

gas mask n Gasmaske f

gas meter n Gaszähler m

gasoline ['gæsəli:n] (US) n Benzin nt

gasp [gɑ:sp] vi keuchen; (in surprise) tief Luft holen ♦ n Keuchen nt

gas: ~ ring n Gasring m; **~ station** (US) n Tankstelle f; **~ tap** n Gashahn m

gastric ['gæstrik] adj Magen-

gate [geit] n Tor nt; (barrier) Schranke f

gateau ['gætəu] (pl **~x**) n Torte f

gatecrash ['geitkræʃ] (BRIT) vt (party) platzen in +acc

gateway ['geitwei] n Toreingang m

gather ['gæðər] vt (people) versammeln; (things) sammeln; (understand) annehmen ♦ vi (assemble) sich versammeln; **to ~ speed** schneller werden; **to ~ (from)** schließen (aus); **~ing** n Versammlung f

gauche [gəuʃ] adj linkisch

gaudy ['gɔ:di] adj schreiend

gauge [geidʒ] n (instrument) Messgerät nt; (RAIL) Spurweite f; (dial) Anzeiger m; (measure) Maß nt ♦ vt (ab)messen; (fig) abschätzen

gaunt [gɔ:nt] adj hager

gauze [gɔ:z] n Gaze f

gave [geiv] pt of **give**

gay [gei] adj (homosexual) schwul; (lively) lustig

gaze [geiz] n Blick m ♦ vi starren; **to ~ at sth** etw dat anstarren

gazelle [gə'zɛl] n Gazelle f

gazumping [gə'zʌmpiŋ] (BRIT) n Hausverkauf an Höherbietenden trotz Zusage an anderen

GB n abbr = **Great Britain**

GCE (BRIT) n abbr = **General Certificate of Education**

GCSE (BRIT) n abbr = **General Certificate of Secondary Education**

gear [gɪər] n Getriebe nt; (equipment) Ausrüstung f; (AUT) Gang m ♦ vt (fig: adapt): **to be ~ed to** ausgerichtet sein auf +acc; **top ~** höchste(r) Gang m; **high ~** (US) höchste(r) Gang m; **low ~** niedrige(r) Gang m; **in ~** eingekuppelt; **~ box** n Getriebe(gehäuse) nt; **~ lever** n Schalthebel m; **~ shift** (US) n Schalthebel m

geese [giːs] npl of **goose**

gel [dʒɛl] n Gel nt

gelatin(e) ['dʒɛlətiːn] n Gelatine f

gem [dʒɛm] n Edelstein m; (fig) Juwel nt

Gemini ['dʒɛmɪnaɪ] n Zwillinge pl

gender ['dʒɛndər] n (GRAM) Geschlecht nt

gene [dʒiːn] n Gen nt

general ['dʒɛnərəl] n General m ♦ adj allgemein; **~ delivery** (US) n Ausgabe(schalter m) f postlagernder Sendungen; **~ election** n allgemeine Wahlen pl; **~ize** vi verallgemeinern; **~ knowledge** n Allgemeinwissen nt; **~ly** adv allgemein, im Allgemeinen; **~ practitioner** n praktische(r) Arzt m, praktische Ärztin f

generate ['dʒɛnəreɪt] vt erzeugen

generation [dʒɛnəˈreɪʃən] n Generation f; (act) Erzeugung f

generator ['dʒɛnəreɪtər] n Generator m

generosity [dʒɛnəˈrɔsɪtɪ] n Großzügigkeit f

generous ['dʒɛnərəs] adj großzügig

genetic [dʒɪˈnɛtɪk] adj genetisch; **~ally** adv genetisch; **~ally modified** genmanipuliert; **~ engineering** n Gentechnik f; **~ fingerprinting** [-ˈfɪŋɡəprɪntɪŋ] n genetische Fingerabdrücke pl

genetics [dʒɪˈnɛtɪks] n Genetik f

Geneva [dʒɪˈniːvə] n Genf nt

genial ['dʒiːnɪəl] adj freundlich, jovial

genitals ['dʒɛnɪtlz] npl Genitalien pl

genius ['dʒiːnɪəs] n Genie nt

genocide ['dʒɛnəʊsaɪd] n Völkermord m

gent [dʒɛnt] n abbr = **gentleman**

genteel [dʒɛnˈtiːl] adj (polite) wohlanständig; (affected) affektiert

gentle ['dʒɛntl] adj sanft, zart

gentleman ['dʒɛntlmən] (irreg) n Herr m;

(polite) Gentleman m

gentleness ['dʒɛntlnɪs] n Zartheit f, Milde f

gently ['dʒɛntlɪ] adv zart, sanft

gentry ['dʒɛntrɪ] n Landadel m

gents [dʒɛnts] n: **G~** (lavatory) Herren pl

genuine ['dʒɛnjʊɪn] adj echt

geographic(al) [dʒɪəˈɡræfɪk(l)] adj geografisch

geography [dʒɪˈɔɡrəfɪ] n Geografie f

geological [dʒɪəˈlɔdʒɪkl] adj geologisch

geology [dʒɪˈɔlədʒɪ] n Geologie f

geometric(al) [dʒɪəˈmɛtrɪk(l)] adj geometrisch

geometry [dʒɪˈɔmətrɪ] n Geometrie f

geranium [dʒɪˈreɪnɪəm] n Geranie f

geriatric [dʒɛrɪˈætrɪk] adj Alten- ♦ n Greis(in) m(f)

germ [dʒɜːm] n Keim m; (MED) Bazillus m

German ['dʒɜːmən] adj deutsch ♦ n Deutsche(r) f(m); (LING) Deutsch nt; **~ measles** n Röteln pl; **~y** n Deutschland nt

germination [dʒɜːmɪˈneɪʃən] n Keimen nt

gesticulate [dʒɛsˈtɪkjʊleɪt] vi gestikulieren

gesture ['dʒɛstjər] n Geste f

KEYWORD

get [gɛt] (pt, pp **got**, pp **gotten** (US)) vi 1 (become, be) werden; **to get old/tired** alt/müde werden; **to get married** heiraten
2 (go) (an)kommen, gehen
3 (begin): **to get to know sb** jdn kennen lernen; **let's get going** or **started!** fangen wir an!
4 (modal aux vb): **you've got to do it** du musst es tun
♦ vt 1: **to get sth done** (do) etw machen; (have done) etw machen lassen; **to get sth going** or **to go** etw in Gang bringen or bekommen; **to get sb to do sth** jdn dazu bringen, etw zu tun
2 (obtain: money, permission, results) erhalten; (find: job, flat) finden; (fetch: person, object) holen; **to get sth for sb** jdm etw besorgen; **get me Mr Jones, please** (TEL) verbinden Sie mich bitte mit Mr Jones
3 (receive: present, letter) bekommen, kriegen; (acquire: reputation etc) erwerben

4(*catch*) bekommen, kriegen; (*hit: target etc*) treffen, erwischen; **get him!** (*to dog*) fass!

5(*take, move*) bringen; **to get sth to sb** jdm etw bringen

6(*understand*) verstehen; (*hear*) mitbekommen; **I've got it!** ich habs!

7(*have, possess*): **to have got sth** etw haben

get about *vi* herumkommen; (*news*) sich verbreiten

get along *vi* (*people*) (gut) zurechtkommen; (*depart*) sich *acc* auf den Weg machen

get at *vt* (*facts*) herausbekommen; **to get at sb** (*nag*) an jdm herumnörgeln

get away *vi* (*leave*) sich *acc* davonmachen; (*escape*): **to get away from sth** von etw *dat* entkommen; **to get away with sth** mit etw davonkommen

get back *vi* (*return*) zurückkommen ♦ *vt* zurückbekommen

get by *vi* (*pass*) vorbeikommen; (*manage*) zurechtkommen

get down *vi* (her)untergehen ♦ *vt* (*depress*) fertig machen; **to get down to** in Angriff nehmen; (*find time to do*) kommen zu

get in *vi* (*train*) ankommen; (*arrive home*) heimkommen

get into *vt* (*enter*) hinein-/hereinkommen in +*acc*; (: *car, train etc*) einsteigen in +*acc*; (*clothes*) anziehen

get off *vi* (*from train etc*) aussteigen; (*from horse*) absteigen ♦ *vt* aussteigen aus; absteigen von

get on *vi* (*progress*) vorankommen; (*be friends*) auskommen; (*age*) alt werden; (*onto train etc*) einsteigen; (*onto horse*) aufsteigen ♦ *vt* einsteigen in +*acc*; auf etw *acc* aufsteigen

get out *vi* (*of house*) herauskommen; (*of vehicle*) aussteigen ♦ *vt* (*take out*) herausholen

get out of *vt* (*duty etc*) herumkommen um

get over *vt* (*illness*) sich *acc* erholen von;

(*surprise*) verkraften; (*news*) fassen; (*loss*) sich abfinden mit

get round *vt* herumkommen; (*fig: person*) herumkriegen

get through to *vt* (*TEL*) durchkommen zu

get together *vi* zusammenkommen

get up *vi* aufstehen ♦ *vt* hinaufbringen; (*go up*) hinaufgehen; (*organize*) auf die Beine stellen

get up to *vt* (*reach*) erreichen; (*prank etc*) anstellen

getaway ['getəweɪ] *n* Flucht *f*

get-up ['getʌp] (*inf*) *n* Aufzug *m*

geyser ['giːzə^r] *n* Geiser *m*; (*heater*) Durchlauferhitzer *m*

ghastly ['gɑːstlɪ] *adj* grässlich

gherkin ['gɜːkɪn] *n* Gewürzgurke *f*

ghetto ['getəu] *n* G(h)etto *nt*; ~ **blaster** *n* (große(r)) Radiorekorder *m*

ghost [gəust] *n* Gespenst *nt*

giant ['dʒaɪənt] *n* Riese *m* ♦ *adj* riesig, Riesen-

gibberish ['dʒɪbərɪʃ] *n* dumme(s) Geschwätz *nt*

gibe [dʒaɪb] *n* spöttische Bemerkung *f*

giblets ['dʒɪblɪts] *npl* Geflügelinnereien *pl*

giddiness ['gɪdɪnɪs] *n* Schwindelgefühl *nt*

giddy ['gɪdɪ] *adj* schwindlig

gift [gɪft] *n* Geschenk *nt*; (*ability*) Begabung *f*; ~**ed** *adj* begabt; ~ **shop** *n* Geschenkeladen *m*; ~ **token** *n*, ~ **voucher** *n* Geschenkgutschein *m*

gigantic [dʒaɪ'gæntɪk] *adj* riesenhaft

giggle ['gɪgl] *vi* kichern ♦ *n* Gekicher *nt*

gild [gɪld] *vt* vergolden

gill [dʒɪl] *n* (1/4 *pint*) Viertelpinte *f*

gills [gɪlz] *npl* (*of fish*) Kiemen *pl*

gilt [gɪlt] *n* Vergoldung *f* ♦ *adj* vergoldet; ~~-**edged** *adj* mündelsicher

gimmick ['gɪmɪk] *n* Gag *m*

gin [dʒɪn] *n* Gin *m*

ginger ['dʒɪndʒə^r] *n* Ingwer *m*; ~ **ale** *n* Ingwerbier *nt*; ~ **beer** *n* Ingwerbier *nt*; ~**bread** *n* Pfefferkuchen *m*; ~~-**haired** *adj* rothaarig

gingerly ['dʒɪndʒəlɪ] *adv* behutsam

gipsy ['dʒɪpsɪ] n Zigeuner(in) m(f)

giraffe [dʒɪ'rɑːf] n Giraffe f

girder ['gəːdə'] n Eisenträger m

girdle ['gəːdl] n Hüftgürtel m

girl [gəːl] n Mädchen nt; **an English ~** eine (junge) Engländerin; **~friend** n Freundin f; **~ish** adj mädchenhaft

giro ['dʒaɪrəʊ] n (bank ~) Giro nt; (post office ~) Postscheckverkehr m

girth [gəːθ] n (measure) Umfang m; (strap) Sattelgurt m

gist [dʒɪst] n Wesentliche(s) nt

give [gɪv] (pt **gave**, pp **given**) vt geben ♦ vi (break) nachgeben; **~ away** vt verschenken; (betray) verraten; **~ back** vt zurückgeben; **~ in** vi nachgeben ♦ vt (hand in) abgeben; **~ off** vt abgeben; **~ out** vt verteilen; (announce) bekannt geben; **~ up** vt, vi aufgeben; **to ~ o.s. up** sich stellen; (after siege) sich ergeben; **~ way** vi (BRIT: traffic) Vorfahrt lassen; (to feelings): **to ~ way to** nachgeben +dat

glacier ['glæsɪə'] n Gletscher m

glad [glæd] adj froh; **~ly** ['glædlɪ] adv gern(e)

glamorous ['glæmərəs] adj reizvoll

glamour ['glæmə'] n Glanz m

glance [glɑːns] n Blick m ♦ vi: **to ~ (at)** (hin)blicken (auf +acc); **~ off** vt fus (fly off) abprallen von; **glancing** ['glɑːnsɪŋ] adj (blow) Streif-

gland [glænd] n Drüse f

glare [glɛə'] n (light) grelle(s) Licht nt; (stare) wilde(r) Blick m ♦ vi grell scheinen; (angrily): **to ~ at** böse ansehen; **glaring** ['glɛərɪŋ] adj (injustice) schreiend; (mistake) krass

glass [glɑːs] n Glas nt; (mirror: also: **looking ~**) Spiegel m; **~es** npl (spectacles) Brille f; **~house** n Gewächshaus nt; **~ware** n Glaswaren pl; **~y** adj glasig

glaze [gleɪz] vt verglasen; (finish with a ~) glasieren ♦ n Glasur f; **~d** adj (eye) glasig; (pot) glasiert; **glazier** ['gleɪzɪə'] n Glaser m

gleam [gliːm] n Schimmer m ♦ vi schimmern

glean [gliːn] vt (fig) ausfindig machen

glen [glɛn] n Bergtal nt

glib [glɪb] adj oberflächlich

glide [glaɪd] vi gleiten; **~r** n (AVIAT) Segelflugzeug nt; **gliding** ['glaɪdɪŋ] n Segelfliegen nt

glimmer ['glɪmə'] n Schimmer m

glimpse [glɪmps] n flüchtige(r) Blick m ♦ vt flüchtig erblicken

glint [glɪnt] n Glitzern nt ♦ vi glitzern

glisten ['glɪsn] vi glänzen

glitter ['glɪtə'] vi funkeln ♦ n Funkeln nt

gloat [gləʊt] vi: **to ~ over** sich weiden an +dat

global ['gləʊbl] adj: **~ warming** globale(r) Temperaturanstieg m

globe [gləʊb] n Erdball m; (sphere) Globus m

gloom [gluːm] n (darkness) Dunkel nt; (depression) düstere Stimmung f; **~y** adj düster

glorify ['glɔːrɪfaɪ] vt verherrlichen

glorious ['glɔːrɪəs] adj glorreich

glory ['glɔːrɪ] n Ruhm m

gloss [glɔs] n (shine) Glanz m; **~ over** vt fus übertünchen

glossary ['glɔsərɪ] n Glossar nt

glossy ['glɔsɪ] adj (surface) glänzend

glove [glʌv] n Handschuh m; **~ compartment** n (AUT) Handschuhfach nt

glow [gləʊ] vi glühen ♦ n Glühen nt

glower ['glaʊə'] vi: **to ~ at** finster anblicken

glucose ['gluːkəʊs] n Traubenzucker m

glue [gluː] n Klebstoff m ♦ vt kleben

glum [glʌm] adj bedrückt

glut [glʌt] n Überfluss m

glutton ['glʌtn] n Vielfraß m; **a ~ for work** ein Arbeitstier nt

glycerin(e) ['glɪsəriːn] n Glyzerin nt

GM abbr = **genetically modified**

gnarled [nɑːld] adj knorrig

gnat [næt] n Stechmücke f

gnaw [nɔː] vt nagen an +dat

gnome [nəʊm] n Gnom m

go [gəʊ] (pt **went**, pp **gone**, pl **~es**) vi gehen; (travel) reisen, fahren; (depart: train) (ab)fahren; (be sold) verkauft werden; (work) gehen, funktionieren; (fit, suit) passen; (become) werden; (break etc) nachgeben ♦ n (energy) Schwung m;

(attempt) Versuch m; **he's ~ing to do it** er wird es tun; **to ~ for a walk** spazieren gehen; **to ~ dancing** tanzen gehen; **how did it ~?** wie wars?; **to ~ with** (be suitable) passen zu; **to have a ~ at sth** etw versuchen; **to be on the ~** auf Trab sein; **whose ~ is it?** wer ist dran?; **~ about** vi (rumour) umgehen ♦ vt fus: **how do I ~ about this?** wie packe ich das an?; **~ after** vt fus (pursue: person) nachgehen +dat; **~ ahead** vi (proceed) weitergehen; **~ along** vi dahingehen, dahinfahren ♦ vt entlanggehen, entlangfahren; **to ~ along with** (support) zustimmen +dat; **~ away** vi (depart) weggehen; **~ back** vi (return) zurückgehen; **~ back on** vt fus (promise) nicht halten; **~ by** vi (years, time) vergehen ♦ vt fus sich richten nach; **~ down** vi (sun) untergehen ♦ vt fus hinuntergehen, hinunterfahren; **~ for** vt fus (fetch) holen (gehen); (like) mögen; (attack) sich stürzen auf +acc; **~ in** vi hineingehen; **~ in for** vt fus (competition) teilnehmen an; **~ into** vt fus (enter) hineingehen in +acc; (study) sich befassen mit; **~ off** vi (depart) weggehen; (lights) ausgehen; (milk etc) sauer werden; (explode) losgehen ♦ vt fus (dislike) nicht mehr mögen; **~ on** vi (continue) weitergehen; (inf: complain) meckern; (lights) angehen; **to ~ on with sth** mit etw weitermachen; **~ out** vi (of fire, light) ausgehen; (of house) hinausgehen; **~ over** vi (ship) kentern ♦ vt fus (examine, check) durchgehen; **~ past** vi: **to ~ past sth** an etw dat vorbeigehen; **~ round** vi (visit): **to ~ round (to sb's)** (bei jdm) vorbeigehen; **~ through** vt fus (town etc) durchgehen, durchfahren; **~ up** vi (price) steigen; **~ with** vt fus (suit) zu etw passen; **~ without** vt fus sich behelfen ohne; (food) entbehren

goad [gəʊd] vt anstacheln

go-ahead ['gəʊəhed] adj zielstrebig; (progressive) fortschrittlich ♦ n grüne(s) Licht nt

goal [gəʊl] n Ziel nt; (SPORT) Tor nt; **~keeper** n Torwart m; **~ post** n

Torpfosten m

goat [gəʊt] n Ziege f

gobble ['gɒbl] vt (also: **~ down, ~ up**) hinunterschlingen

go-between ['gəʊbɪtwiːn] n Mittelsmann m

god [gɒd] n Gott m; **G~** n Gott m; **~child** n Patenkind nt; **~daughter** n Patentochter f; **~dess** n Göttin f; **~father** n Pate m; **~forsaken** adj gottverlassen; **~mother** n Patin f; **~send** n Geschenk nt des Himmels; **~son** n Patensohn m

goggles ['gɒglz] npl Schutzbrille f

going ['gəʊɪŋ] n (HORSE-RACING) Bahn f ♦ adj (rate) gängig; (concern) gut gehend; **it's hard ~** es ist schwierig

gold [gəʊld] n Gold nt ♦ adj golden; **~en** adj golden, Gold-; **~fish** n Goldfisch m; **~ mine** n Goldgrube f; **~-plated** adj vergoldet; **~smith** n Goldschmied(in) m(f)

golf [gɒlf] n Golf nt; **~ ball** n Golfball m; (on typewriter) Kugelkopf m; **~ club** n (society) Golfklub m; (stick) Golfschläger m; **~ course** n Golfplatz m; **~er** n Golfspieler(in) m(f)

gondola ['gɒndələ] n Gondel f

gone [gɒn] pp of **go**

gong [gɒŋ] n Gong m

good [gʊd] n (benefit) Wohl nt; (moral excellence) Güte f ♦ adj gut; **~s** npl (merchandise etc) Waren pl, Güter pl; **a ~ deal (of)** ziemlich viel; **a ~ many** ziemlich viele; **~ morning!** guten Morgen!; **~ afternoon!** guten Tag!; **~ evening!** guten Abend!; **~ night!** gute Nacht!; **would you be ~ enough to ...?** könnten Sie bitte ...?

goodbye [gʊd'baɪ] excl auf Wiedersehen!

good: **G~ Friday** n Karfreitag m; **~-looking** adj gut aussehend; **~-natured** adj gutmütig; (joke) harmlos; **~ness** n Güte f; (virtue) Tugend f; **~s train** n (BRIT) n Güterzug m; **~will** n (favour) Wohlwollen nt; (COMM) Firmenansehen nt

goose [guːs] (pl **geese**) n Gans f

gooseberry ['gʊzbərɪ] n Stachelbeere f

gooseflesh ['guːsfleʃ] n Gänsehaut f

goose pimples npl Gänsehaut f

gore [gɔːr] vt aufspießen ♦ n Blut nt

gorge [gɔːdʒ] n Schlucht f ♦ vt: **to ~ o.s.** (sich voll) fressen

gorgeous ['gɔːdʒəs] adj prächtig

gorilla [gə'rɪlə] n Gorilla m

gorse [gɔːs] n Stechginster m

gory ['gɔːrɪ] adj blutig

go-slow ['gəu'sləu] (BRIT) n Bummelstreik m

gospel ['gɔspl] n Evangelium nt

gossip ['gɔsɪp] n Klatsch m; (person) Klatschbase f ♦ vi klatschen

got [gɔt] pt, pp of **get**

gotten ['gɔtn] (US) pp of **get**

gout [gaut] n Gicht f

govern ['gʌvən] vt regieren; verwalten

governess ['gʌvənɪs] n Gouvernante f

government ['gʌvnmənt] n Regierung f

governor ['gʌvənə⁺] n Gouverneur m

gown [gaun] n Gewand nt; (UNIV) Robe f

G.P. n abbr = **general practitioner**

grab [græb] vt packen

grace [greɪs] n Anmut f; (blessing) Gnade f; (prayer) Tischgebet nt ♦ vt (adorn) zieren; (honour) auszeichnen; **5 days'** ~ 5 Tage Aufschub; **~ful** adj anmutig

gracious ['greɪʃəs] adj gnädig; (kind) freundlich

grade [greɪd] n Grad m; (slope) Gefälle nt ♦ vt (classify) einstufen; ~ **crossing** (US) n Bahnübergang m; ~ **school** (US) n Grundschule f

gradient ['greɪdɪənt] n Steigung f; Gefälle nt

gradual ['grædjuəl] adj allmählich; ~**ly** adv allmählich

graduate [n 'grædjuɪt, vb 'grædjueɪt] n: **to be a ~** das Staatsexamen haben ♦ vi das Staatsexamen machen; **graduation** [grædju'eɪʃən] n Abschlussfeier f

graffiti [grə'fiːtɪ] npl Graffiti pl

graft [grɑːft] n (hard work) Schufterei f; (MED) Verpflanzung f ♦ vt pfropfen; (fig) aufpfropfen; (MED) verpflanzen

grain [greɪn] n Korn nt; (in wood) Maserung f

gram [græm] n Gramm nt

grammar ['græmə⁺] n Grammatik f; ~ **school** (BRIT) n Gymnasium nt; **grammatical** [grə'mætɪkl] adj grammat(ikal)isch

gramme [græm] n = **gram**

granary ['grænərɪ] n Kornspeicher m

grand [grænd] adj großartig; ~**child** (pl ~**children**) n Enkelkind nt, Enkel(in) m(f); ~**dad** n Opa m; ~**daughter** n Enkelin f; ~**eur** ['grændjə⁺] n Erhabenheit f; ~**father** n Großvater m; ~**iose** ['grændɪəus] adj (imposing) großartig; (pompous) schwülstig; ~**ma** n Oma f; ~**mother** n Großmutter f; ~**pa** n = **granddad**; ~**parents** npl Großeltern pl; ~ **piano** n Flügel m; ~**son** n Enkel m; ~**stand** n Haupttribüne f

granite ['grænɪt] n Granit m

granny ['grænɪ] n Oma f

grant [grɑːnt] vt gewähren ♦ n Unterstützung f; (UNIV) Stipendium nt; **to take sth for ~ed** etw als selbstverständlich (an)nehmen

granulated sugar ['grænjuleɪtɪd-] n Zuckerraffinade f

granule ['grænjuːl] n Körnchen nt

grape [greɪp] n (Wein)traube f

grapefruit ['greɪpfruːt] n Pampelmuse f, Grapefruit f

graph [grɑːf] n Schaubild nt; ~**ic** ['græfɪk] adj (descriptive) anschaulich; (drawing) grafisch; ~**ics** npl Grafik f

grapple ['græpl] vi: **to ~ with** kämpfen mit

grasp [grɑːsp] vt ergreifen; (understand) begreifen ♦ n Griff m; (of subject) Beherrschung f; ~**ing** adj habgierig

grass [grɑːs] n Gras nt; ~**hopper** n Heuschrecke f; ~**land** n Weideland nt; ~**roots** adj an der Basis; ~ **snake** n Ringelnatter f

grate [greɪt] n Kamin m ♦ vi (sound) knirschen ♦ vt (cheese etc) reiben; **to ~ on the nerves** auf die Nerven gehen

grateful ['greɪtful] adj dankbar

grater ['greɪtə⁺] n Reibe f

gratify ['grætɪfaɪ] vt befriedigen; ~**ing** adj erfreulich

grating ['greɪtɪŋ] n (iron bars) Gitter nt ♦ adj (noise) knirschend

gratitude ['grætɪtjuːd] n Dankbarkeit f

gratuity [grə'tjuːɪtɪ] n Gratifikation f

grave [greɪv] n Grab nt ♦ adj (serious) ernst

gravel ['grævl] n Kies m
gravestone ['greɪvstəun] n Grabstein m
graveyard ['greɪvjɑːd] n Friedhof m
gravity ['grævɪtɪ] n Schwerkraft f;
(seriousness) Schwere f
gravy ['greɪvɪ] n (Braten)soße f
gray [greɪ] adj = grey
graze [greɪz] vi grasen ♦ vt (touch) streifen;
(MED) abschürfen ♦ n Abschürfung f
grease [griːs] n (fat) Fett nt; (lubricant)
Schmiere f ♦ vt (ab)schmieren; ~proof
(BRIT) adj (paper) Butterbrot-; greasy
['griːsɪ] adj fettig
great [greɪt] adj groß; (inf: good) prima; G~
Britain n Großbritannien nt; ~~
grandfather n Urgroßvater m; ~~
grandmother n Urgroßmutter f; ~ly adv
sehr
Greece [griːs] n Griechenland nt
greed [griːd] n (also: ~iness) Gier f;
(meanness) Geiz m; ~(iness) for Gier nach;
~y adj gierig
Greek [griːk] adj griechisch ♦ n Grieche m,
Griechin f; (LING) Griechisch nt
green [griːn] adj grün ♦ n (village ~)
Dorfwiese f; ~ belt n Grüngürtel m; ~
card n (AUT) grüne Versicherungskarte f;
~ery n Grün nt; grüne(s) Laub nt; ~gage
n Reneklode f, Reineclaude f; ~grocer
(BRIT) n Obst- und Gemüsehändler m;
~house n Gewächshaus nt; ~house
effect n Treibhauseffekt m; ~house gas n
Treibhausgas nt
Greenland ['griːnlənd] n Grönland nt
greet [griːt] vt grüßen; ~ing n Gruß m;
~ing(s) card n Glückwunschkarte f
gregarious [grə'geərɪəs] adj gesellig
grenade [grə'neɪd] n Granate f
grew [gruː] pt of grow
grey [greɪ] adj grau; ~-haired adj
grauhaarig; ~hound n Windhund m
grid [grɪd] n Gitter nt; (ELEC) Leitungsnetz nt;
(on map) Gitternetz nt
gridlock ['grɪdlɔk] n (AUT: traffic jam)
totale(r) Stau m; ~ed adj: to be ~ed (roads)
total verstopft sein; (talks etc) festgefahren
sein

grief [griːf] n Gram m, Kummer m
grievance ['griːvəns] n Beschwerde f
grieve [griːv] vi sich grämen ♦ vt betrüben
grievous ['griːvəs] adj: ~ bodily harm (JUR)
schwere Körperverletzung f
grill [grɪl] n Grill m ♦ vt (BRIT) grillen;
(question) in die Mangel nehmen
grille [grɪl] n (AUT) (Kühler)gitter nt
grim [grɪm] adj grimmig; (situation) düster
grimace [grɪ'meɪs] n Grimasse f ♦ vi
Grimassen schneiden
grime [graɪm] n Schmutz m; grimy ['graɪmɪ]
adj schmutzig
grin [grɪn] n Grinsen nt ♦ vi grinsen
grind [graɪnd] (pt, pp ground) vt mahlen;
(US: meat) durch den Fleischwolf drehen;
(sharpen) schleifen; (teeth) knirschen mit ♦ n
(bore) Plackerei f
grip [grɪp] n Griff m; (suitcase) Handkoffer m
♦ vt packen; ~ping adj (exciting) spannend
grisly ['grɪzlɪ] adj grässlich
gristle ['grɪsl] n Knorpel m
grit [grɪt] n Splitt m; (courage) Mut m ♦ vt
(teeth) zusammenbeißen; (road) (mit Splitt
be)streuen
groan [grəun] n Stöhnen nt ♦ vi stöhnen
grocer ['grəusər] n Lebensmittelhändler m;
~ies npl Lebensmittel pl; ~'s (shop) n
Lebensmittelgeschäft nt
groggy ['grɔgɪ] adj benommen
groin [grɔɪn] n Leistengegend f
groom [gruːm] n (also: bridegroom)
Bräutigam m; (for horses) Pferdeknecht m
♦ vt (horse) striegeln; (well-)ed gepflegt
groove [gruːv] n Rille f, Furche f
grope [grəup] vi tasten; ~ for vt fus suchen
nach
gross [grəus] adj (coarse) dick, plump; (bad)
grob, schwer; (COMM) brutto; ~ly adv
höchst
grotesque [grə'tɛsk] adj grotesk
grotto ['grɔtəu] n Grotte f
ground [graund] pt, pp of grind ♦ n Boden
m; (land) Grundbesitz m; (reason) Grund m;
(US: also: ~ wire) Endleitung f ♦ vi (run
ashore) stranden, auflaufen; ~s npl (dregs)
Bodensatz m; (around house)

(Garten)anlagen *pl*; **on the ~** am Boden; **to the ~** zu Boden; **to gain/lose ~** Boden gewinnen/verlieren; **~ cloth** (*US*) *n* = **groundsheet**; **~ing** *n* (*instruction*) Anfangsunterricht *m*; **~less** *adj* grundlos; **~sheet** (*BRIT*) *n* Zeltboden *m*; **~ staff** *n* Bodenpersonal *nt*; **~work** *n* Grundlage *f*

group [gruːp] *n* Gruppe *f* ♦ *vt* (*also:* ~ **together**) gruppieren ♦ *vi* sich gruppieren

grouse [graus] *n inv* (*bird*) schottische(s) Moorhuhn *nt*

grove [grəuv] *n* Gehölz *nt*, Hain *m*

grovel ['grɔvl] *vi* (*fig*) kriechen

grow [grəu] (*pt* **grew**, *pp* **grown**) *vi* wachsen; (*become*) werden ♦ *vt* (*raise*) anbauen; ~ **up** *vi* aufwachsen; **~er** *n* Züchter *m*; **~ing** *adj* zunehmend

growl [graul] *vi* knurren

grown [grəun] *pp of* **grow**; **~-up** *n* Erwachsene(r) *mf*

growth [grəuθ] *n* Wachstum *nt*; (*increase*) Zunahme *f*; (*of chest etc*) Wuchs *m*.

grub [grʌb] *n* Made *f*, Larve *f*; (*inf: food*) Futter *nt*; **~by** ['grʌbɪ] *adj* schmutzig

grudge [grʌdʒ] *n* Groll *m* ♦ *vt*: **to ~ sb sth** jdm etw missgönnen; **to bear sb a ~** einen Groll gegen jdn hegen

gruelling ['gruəlɪŋ] *adj* (*climb, race*) mörderisch

gruesome ['gruːsəm] *adj* grauenhaft

gruff [grʌf] *adj* barsch

grumble ['grʌmbl] *vi* murren

grumpy ['grʌmpɪ] *adj* verdrießlich

grunt [grʌnt] *vi* grunzen ♦ *n* Grunzen *nt*

G-string ['dʒiːstrɪŋ] *n* Minislip *m*

guarantee [gærən'tiː] *n* Garantie *f* ♦ *vt* garantieren

guard [gɑːd] *n* (*sentry*) Wache *f*; (*BRIT: RAIL*) Zugbegleiter *m* ♦ *vt* bewachen

guarded ['gɑːdɪd] *adj* vorsichtig

guardian ['gɑːdɪən] *n* Vormund *m*; (*keeper*) Hüter *m*

guard's van ['gɑːdz] (*BRIT*) *n* (*RAIL*) Dienstwagen *m*

guerrilla [gə'rɪlə] *n* Guerilla(kämpfer) *m*; ~ **warfare** *n* Guerillakrieg *m*

guess [gɛs] *vt*, *vi* (er)raten, schätzen ♦ *n* Vermutung *f*; **~work** *n* Raterei *f*

guest [gɛst] *n* Gast *m*; ~ **house** *n* Pension *f*; ~ **room** *n* Gastzimmer *nt*

guffaw [gʌ'fɔː] *vi* schallend lachen

guidance ['gaɪdəns] *n* (*control*) Leitung *f*; (*advice*) Beratung *f*

guide [gaɪd] *n* Führer *m*; (*also:* **girl ~**) Pfadfinderin *f* ♦ *vt* führen; **~book** *n* Reiseführer *m*; ~ **dog** *n* Blindenhund *m*; **~lines** *npl* Richtlinien *pl*

guild [gɪld] *n* (*HIST*) Gilde *f*

guillotine ['gɪlətiːn] *n* Guillotine *f*

guilt [gɪlt] *n* Schuld *f*; **~y** *adj* schuldig

guinea pig ['gɪnɪ-] *n* Meerschweinchen *nt*; (*fig*) Versuchskaninchen *nt*

guise [gaɪz] *n*: **in the ~ of** in der Form +*gen*

guitar [gɪ'tɑːr] *n* Gitarre *f*

gulf [gʌlf] *n* Golf *m*; (*fig*) Abgrund *m*

gull [gʌl] *n* Möwe *f*

gullet ['gʌlɪt] *n* Schlund *m*

gullible ['gʌlɪbl] *adj* leichtgläubig

gully ['gʌlɪ] *n* (Wasser)rinne *f*

gulp [gʌlp] *vt* (*also:* ~ **down**) hinunterschlucken ♦ *vi* (*gasp*) schlucken

gum [gʌm] *n* (*around teeth*) Zahnfleisch *nt*; (*glue*) Klebstoff *m*; (*also:* **chewing ~**) Kaugummi *m* ♦ *vt* gummieren; **~boots** (*BRIT*) *npl* Gummistiefel *pl*

gun [gʌn] *n* Schusswaffe *f*; **~boat** *n* Kanonenboot *nt*; **~fire** *n* Geschützfeuer *nt*; **~man** (*irreg*) *n* bewaffnete(r) Verbrecher *m*; **~point** *n*: **at ~point** mit Waffengewalt; **~powder** *n* Schießpulver *nt*; **~shot** *n* Schuss *m*

gurgle ['gəːgl] *vi* gluckern

gush [gʌʃ] *vi* (*rush out*) hervorströmen; (*fig*) schwärmen

gust [gʌst] *n* Windstoß *m*, Bö *f*

gusto ['gʌstəu] *n* Genuss *m*, Lust *f*

gut [gʌt] *n* (*ANAT*) Gedärme *pl*; (*string*) Darm *m*; **~s** *npl* (*fig*) Schneid *m*

gutter ['gʌtər] *n* Dachrinne *f*; (*in street*) Gosse *f*

guttural ['gʌtərl] *adj* guttural, Kehl-

guy [gaɪ] *n* (*also:* **~rope**) Halteseil *nt*; (*man*) Typ *m*, Kerl *m*

guzzle ['gʌzl] *vt, vi (drink)* saufen; *(eat)* fressen

gym [dʒɪm] *n (also:* **~nasium**) Turnhalle *f; (also:* **~nastics**) Turnen *nt*

gymnast ['dʒɪmnæst] *n* Turner(in) *m(f)*

gymnastics [dʒɪm'næstɪks] *n* Turnen *nt*, Gymnastik *f*

gym shoes *npl* Turnschuhe *pl*

gynaecologist [gaɪn'kɔlədʒɪst] *(US* **gynecologist**) *n* Frauenarzt(-ärztin) *m(f)*

gypsy ['dʒɪpsɪ] *n* = **gipsy**

gyrate [dʒaɪ'reɪt] *vi* kreisen

H, h

haberdashery [hæbə'dæʃərɪ] *(BRIT) n* Kurzwaren *pl*

habit ['hæbɪt] *n* (An)gewohnheit *f; (monk's)* Habit *nt or m*

habitable ['hæbɪtəbl] *adj* bewohnbar

habitat ['hæbɪtæt] *n* Lebensraum *m*

habitual [hə'bɪtjuəl] *adj* gewohnheitsmäßig; **~ly** *adv* gewöhnlich

hack [hæk] *vt* hacken ♦ *n* Hieb *m; (writer)* Schreiberling *m*

hacker ['hækər] *n (COMPUT)* Hacker *m*

hackneyed ['hæknɪd] *adj* abgedroschen

had [hæd] *pt, pp of* **have**

haddock ['hædək] *(pl* **~** *or* **~s**) *n* Schellfisch *m*

---

hadn't ['hædnt] = **had not**

haemorrhage ['hemərɪdʒ] *(US* **hemorrhage**) *n* Blutung *f*

haemorrhoids ['hemərɔɪdz] *(US* **hemorrhoids**) *npl* Hämorr(ho)iden *pl*

haggard ['hægəd] *adj* abgekämpft

haggle ['hægl] *vi* feilschen

Hague [heɪg] *n (GEOG)* **The ~** Den Haag *nt*

hail [heɪl] *n* Hagel *m* ♦ *vt* umjubeln ♦ *vi* hageln; **~stone** *n* Hagelkorn *nt*

hair [heər] *n* Haar *nt*, Haare *pl; (one ~)* Haar *nt*; **~brush** *n* Haarbürste *f*; **~cut** *n* Haarschnitt *m*; **to get a ~cut** sich *dat* die Haare schneiden lassen; **~do** *n* Frisur *f*; **~dresser** *n* Friseur *m*, Friseuse *f*; **~dresser's** *n* Friseursalon *m*; **~ dryer** *n* Trockenhaube *f; (hand-held)* Föhn *m*, Fön *m* ®; **~ gel** *n* Haargel *nt*; **~grip** *n* Klemme *f*; **~net** *n* Haarnetz *nt*; **~pin** *n* Haarnadel *f*; **~pin bend** *(US* **~pin curve**) *n* Haarnadelkurve *f*; **~-raising** *adj* haarsträubend; **~ removing cream** *n* Enthaarungscreme *nt*; **~ spray** *n* Haarspray *nt*; **~style** *n* Frisur *f*

hairy ['heərɪ] *adj* haarig

hake [heɪk] *n* Seehecht *m*

half [hɑːf] *(pl* **halves**) *n* Hälfte *f* ♦ *adj* halb ♦ *adv* halb, zur Hälfte; **~ an hour** eine halbe Stunde; **two and a ~** zweieinhalb; **to cut sth in ~** etw halbieren; **~ a dozen** ein halbes Dutzend, sechs; **~ board** *n* Halbpension *f*; **~-caste** *n* Mischling *m*; **~ fare** *n* halbe(r) Fahrpreis *m*; **~-hearted** *adj* lustlos; **~-hour** *n* halbe Stunde *f*; **~-price** *n:* **(at) ~-price** zum halben Preis; **~ term** *(BRIT) n (SCH)* Ferien *pl* in der Mitte des Trimesters; **~-time** *n* Halbzeit *f*; **~way** *adv* halbwegs, auf halbem Wege

halibut ['hælɪbət] *n inv* Heilbutt *m*

hall [hɔːl] *n* Saal *m; (entrance ~)* Hausflur *m; (building)* Halle *f*; **~ of residence** *(BRIT)* Studentenwohnheim *nt*

hallmark ['hɔːlmɑːk] *n* Stempel *m*

hallo [hə'ləu] *excl* = **hello**

Hallowe'en ['hæləu'iːn] *n* Tag *m* vor Allerheiligen

Guy Fawkes' Night

i **Guy Fawkes' Night**, *auch bonfire night genannt, erinnert an den Gunpowder Plot, einen Attentatsversuch auf James I. und sein Parlament am 5. November 1605. Einer der Verschwörer, Guy Fawkes, wurde auf frischer Tat ertappt, als er das Parlamentsgebäude in die Luft sprengen wollte. Vor der Guy Fawkes' Night basteln Kinder in Großbritannien eine Puppe des Guy Fawkes, mit der sie Geld für Feuerwerkskörper von Passanten erbetteln, und die dann am 5. November auf einem Lagerfeuer mit Feuerwerk verbrannt wird.*

Hallowe'en

ⓘ **Hallowe'en** ist der 31. Oktober, der Vorabend von Allerheiligen und nach altem Glauben der Abend, an dem man Geister und Hexen sehen kann. In Großbritannien und vor allem in den USA feiern die Kinder Hallowe'en, indem sie sich verkleiden und mit selbst gemachten Laternen aus Kürbissen von Tür zu Tür ziehen.

---

hallucination [həluːsɪ'neɪʃən] *n* Halluzination *f*

hallway ['hɔːlweɪ] *n* Korridor *m*

halo ['heɪləu] *n* Heiligenschein *m*

halt [hɔːlt] *n* Halt *m* ♦ *vt, vi* anhalten

halve [hɑːv] *vt* halbieren

halves [hɑːvz] *pl of* **half**

ham [hæm] *n* Schinken *m*

hamburger ['hæmbəːgəʳ] *n* Hamburger *m*

hamlet ['hæmlɪt] *n* Weiler *m*

hammer ['hæməʳ] *n* Hammer *m* ♦ *vt, vi* hämmern

hammock ['hæmək] *n* Hängematte *f*

hamper ['hæmpəʳ] *vt* (be)hindern ♦ *n* Picknickkorb *m*

hamster ['hæmstəʳ] *n* Hamster *m*

hand [hænd] *n* Hand *f*; (of clock) (Uhr)zeiger *m*; (worker) Arbeiter *m* ♦ *vt* (pass) geben; **to give sb a ~** jdm helfen; **at ~** nahe; **to ~** zur Hand; **in ~** (under control) unter Kontrolle; (being done) im Gange; (extra) übrig; **on ~** zur Verfügung; **on the one ~ ...,** **the other ~ ...** einerseits ..., andererseits ...; **~ in** *vt* abgeben; (forms) einreichen; **~ out** *vt* austeilen; **~ over** *vt* (deliver) übergeben; (surrender) abgeben; (: prisoner) ausliefern; **~bag** *n* Handtasche *f*; **~book** *n* Handbuch *nt*; **~brake** *n* Handbremse *f*; **~cuffs** *npl* Handschellen *pl*; **~ful** *n* Hand *f* voll; (inf: person) Plage *f*

handicap ['hændɪkæp] *n* Handikap *nt* ♦ *vt* benachteiligen; **mentally/physically ~ped** geistig/körperlich behindert

handicraft ['hændɪkrɑːft] *n* Kunsthandwerk *nt*

handiwork ['hændɪwəːk] *n* Arbeit *f*; (fig) Werk *nt*

handkerchief ['hæŋkətʃɪf] *n* Taschentuch *nt*

handle ['hændl] *n* (of door etc) Klinke *f*; (of cup etc) Henkel *m*; (for winding) Kurbel *f* ♦ *vt* (touch) anfassen; (deal with: things) sich befassen mit; (: people) umgehen mit; **~bar(s)** *n(pl)* Lenkstange *f*

hand: **~ luggage** *n* Handgepäck *nt*; **~made** *adj* handgefertigt; **~out** *n* (distribution) Verteilung *f*; (charity) Geldzuwendung *f*; (leaflet) Flugblatt *nt*; **~rail** *n* Geländer *nt*; (on ship) Reling *f*; **~set** *n* (TEL) Hörer *m*; **please replace the ~set** bitte legen Sie auf; **~shake** *n* Händedruck *f*

handsome ['hænsəm] *adj* gut aussehend

handwriting ['hændraɪtɪŋ] *n* Handschrift *f*

handy ['hændɪ] *adj* praktisch; (shops) leicht erreichbar; **~man** ['hændɪmæn] (irreg) *n* Bastler *m*

hang [hæŋ] (pt, pp **hung**) *vt* aufhängen; (pt, pp **hanged**: criminal) hängen ♦ *vi* hängen ♦ *n*: **to get the ~ of sth** (inf) den richtigen Dreh bei etw herauskriegen; **~ about, ~ around** *vi* sich herumtreiben; **~ on** *vi* (wait) warten; **~ up** *vi* (TEL) auflegen

hangar ['hæŋəʳ] *n* Hangar *m*

hanger ['hæŋəʳ] *n* Kleiderbügel *m*

hanger-on [hæŋər'ɔn] *n* Anhänger(in) *m(f)*

hang ['hæŋ-]: **~-gliding** *n* Drachenfliegen *nt*; **~over** *m* Kater *m*; **~up** *n* Komplex *m*

hanker ['hæŋkəʳ] *vi*: **to ~ for** *or* **after** sich sehnen nach

hankie ['hæŋkɪ] *n* abbr = **handkerchief**

hanky ['hæŋkɪ] *n* abbr = **handkerchief**

haphazard [hæp'hæzəd] *adj* zufällig

happen ['hæpən] *vi* sich ereignen, passieren; **as it ~s I'm going there today** zufällig(erweise) gehe ich heute (dort)hin; **~ing** *n* Ereignis *nt*

happily ['hæpɪlɪ] *adv* glücklich; (fortunately) glücklicherweise

happiness ['hæpɪnɪs] *n* Glück *nt*

happy ['hæpɪ] *adj* glücklich; **~ birthday!** alles Gute zum Geburtstag!; **~-go-lucky** *adj* sorglos; **~ hour** *n* Happy Hour *f*

harass [ˈhærəs] *vt* plagen; **~ment** *n*
Belästigung *f*

harbour [ˈhɑːbəʳ] (*US* **harbor**) *n* Hafen *m*
♦ *vt* (*hope etc*) hegen; (*criminal etc*)
Unterschlupf gewähren

hard [hɑːd] *adj* (*firm*) hart; (*difficult*) schwer;
(*harsh*) hart(herzig) ♦ *adv* (*work*) hart; (*try*)
sehr; (*push, hit*) fest; **no ~ feelings!** ich
nehme es dir nicht übel; **~ of hearing**
schwerhörig; **to be ~ done by** übel dran
sein; **~back** *n* kartonierte Ausgabe *f*; **~
cash** *n* Bargeld *nt*; **~ disk** *n* (*COMPUT*)
Festplatte *f*; **~en** *vt* erhärten; (*fig*) verhärten
♦ *vi* hart werden; (*fig*) sich verhärten; **~-
headed** *adj* nüchtern; **~ labour** *n*
Zwangsarbeit *f*

hardly [ˈhɑːdlɪ] *adv* kaum

hard: ~ship *n* Not *f*; **~ shoulder** (*BRIT*) *n*
(*AUT*) Seitenstreifen *m*; **~ up** *adj* knapp bei
Kasse; **~ware** *n* Eisenwaren *pl*; (*COMPUT*)
Hardware *f*; **~ware shop** *n*
Eisenwarenhandlung *f*; **~-wearing** *adj*
strapazierfähig; **~-working** *adj* fleißig

hardy [ˈhɑːdɪ] *adj* widerstandsfähig

hare [hɛəʳ] *n* Hase *m*; **~-brained** *adj*
schwachsinnig

harm [hɑːm] *n* Schaden *m* ♦ *vt* schaden
+*dat*; **out of ~'s way** in Sicherheit; **~ful** *adj*
schädlich; **~less** *adj* harmlos

harmonica [hɑːˈmɒnɪkə] *n* Mundharmonika
f

harmonious [hɑːˈməʊnɪəs] *adj* harmonisch

harmonize [ˈhɑːmənaɪz] *vt* abstimmen ♦ *vi*
harmonieren

harmony [ˈhɑːmənɪ] *n* Harmonie *f*

harness [ˈhɑːnɪs] *n* Geschirr *nt* ♦ *vt* (*horse*)
anschirren; (*fig*) nutzbar machen

harp [hɑːp] *n* Harfe *f* ♦ *vi*: **to ~ on about sth**
auf etw *dat* herumreiten

harpoon [hɑːˈpuːn] *n* Harpune *f*

harrowing [ˈhærəʊɪŋ] *adj* nervenaufreibend

harsh [hɑːʃ] *adj* (*rough*) rau; (*severe*) streng;
~ness *n* Härte *f*

harvest [ˈhɑːvɪst] *n* Ernte *f* ♦ *vt, vi* ernten

has [hæz] *vb see* **have**

hash [hæʃ] *vt* klein hacken ♦ *n* (*mess*)
Kuddelmuddel *m*

hashish [ˈhæʃɪʃ] *n* Haschisch *nt*

hasn't [ˈhæznt] = **has not**

hassle [ˈhæsl] (*inf*) *n* Theater *nt*

haste [heɪst] *n* Eile *f*; **~n** [ˈheɪsn] *vt*
beschleunigen ♦ *vi* eilen; **hasty** *adj* hastig;
(*rash*) vorschnell

hat [hæt] *n* Hut *m*

hatch [hætʃ] *n* (*NAUT: also:* **~way**) Luke *f*; (*in
house*) Durchreiche *f* ♦ *vi* (*young*)
ausschlüpfen ♦ *vt* (*brood*) ausbrüten; (*plot*)
aushecken; **~back** [ˈhætʃbæk] *n* (*AUT*) (Auto
nt mit) Heckklappe *f*

hatchet [ˈhætʃɪt] *n* Beil *nt*

hate [heɪt] *vt* hassen ♦ *n* Hass *m*; **~ful** *adj*
verhasst

hatred [ˈheɪtrɪd] *n* Hass *m*

haughty [ˈhɔːtɪ] *adj* hochnäsig, überheblich

haul [hɔːl] *vt* ziehen ♦ *n* (*catch*) Fang *m*;
~age *n* Spedition *f*; **~ier** (*US* **hauler**) *n*
Spediteur *m*

haunch [hɔːntʃ] *n* Lende *f*

haunt [hɔːnt] *vt* (*ghost*) spuken in +*dat*;
(*memory*) verfolgen; (*pub*) häufig besuchen
♦ *n* Lieblingsplatz *m*; **the castle is ~ed** in
dem Schloss spukt es

KEYWORD

---

have [hæv] (*pt, pp* **had**) *aux vb* **1** haben; (*esp
with vbs of motion*) sein; **to have arrived/
slept** angekommen sein/geschlafen haben;
to have been gewesen sein; **having eaten**
or **when he had eaten, he left** nachdem
er gegessen hatte, ging er
2 (*in tag questions*): **you've done it,
haven't you?** du hast es doch gemacht,
oder nicht?
3 (*in short answers and questions*): **you've
made a mistake – so I have/no I haven't**
du hast einen Fehler gemacht – ja,
stimmt/nein; **we haven't paid – yes we
have!** wir haben nicht bezahlt – doch; **I've
been there before, have you?** ich war
schon einmal da, du auch?
♦ *modal aux vb* (*be obliged*): **to have (got)
to do sth** etw tun müssen; **you haven't to
tell her** du darfst es ihr nicht erzählen
♦ *vt* **1** (*possess*) haben; **he has (got) blue**

eyes er hat blaue Augen; **I have (got) an idea** ich habe eine Idee
2 (*referring to meals etc*): **to have breakfast/a cigarette** frühstücken/eine Zigarette rauchen
3 (*receive, obtain etc*) haben; **may I have your address?** kann ich Ihre Adresse haben?; **to have a baby** ein Kind bekommen
4 (*maintain, allow*): **he will have it that he is right** er besteht darauf, dass er Recht hat; **I won't have it** das lasse ich mir nicht bieten
5: to have sth done etw machen lassen; **to have sb do sth** jdn etw machen lassen; **he soon had them all laughing** er brachte sie alle zum Lachen
6 (*experience, suffer*): **she had her bag stolen** man hat ihr die Tasche gestohlen; **he had his arm broken** er hat sich den Arm gebrochen
7 (*+noun: take, hold etc*): **to have a walk/rest** spazieren gehen/sich ausruhen; **to have a meeting/party** eine Besprechung/Party haben
have out *vt*: **to have it out with sb** (*settle problem*) etw mit jdm bereden

haven ['heɪvn] *n* Zufluchtsort *m*
haven't ['hævnt] = **have not**
havoc ['hævək] *n* Verwüstung *f*
hawk [hɔːk] *n* Habicht *m*
hay [heɪ] *n* Heu *nt*; **~ fever** *n* Heuschnupfen *m*; **~stack** *n* Heuschober *m*
haywire ['heɪwaɪər] (*inf*) *adj* durcheinander
hazard ['hæzəd] *n* Risiko *nt* ♦ *vt* aufs Spiel setzen; **~ous** *adj* gefährlich; **~ (warning) lights** *npl* (*AUT*) Warnblinklicht *nt*
haze [heɪz] *n* Dunst *m*
hazelnut ['heɪzlnʌt] *n* Haselnuss *f*
hazy ['heɪzɪ] *adj* (*misty*) dunstig; (*vague*) verschwommen
he [hiː] *pron* er
head [hɛd] *n* Kopf *m*; (*leader*) Leiter *m* ♦ *vt* (an)führen, leiten; (*ball*) köpfen; **~s (or tails)** Kopf (oder Zahl); **~ first** mit dem Kopf nach unten; **~ over heels** kopfüber;

~ for *vt fus* zugehen auf +*acc*; **~ache** *n* Kopfschmerzen *pl*; **~dress** *n* Kopfschmuck *m*; **~ing** *n* Überschrift *f*; **~lamp** (*BRIT*) *n* Scheinwerfer *m*; **~land** *n* Landspitze *f*; **~light** *n* Scheinwerfer *m*; **~line** *n* Schlagzeile *f*; **~long** *adv* kopfüber; **~master** *n* (*of primary school*) Rektor *m*; (*of secondary school*) Direktor *m*; **~mistress** *n* Rektorin *f*; Direktorin *f*; **~ office** *n* Zentrale *f*; **~-on** *adj* Frontal-; **~phones** *npl* Kopfhörer *pl*; **~quarters** *npl* Zentrale *f*; (*MIL*) Hauptquartier *nt*; **~rest** *n* Kopfstütze *f*; **~room** *n* (*of bridges etc*) lichte Höhe *f*; **~scarf** *n* Kopftuch *nt*; **~strong** *adj* eigenwillig; **~teacher** (*BRIT*) *n* Schulleiter(in) *m(f)*; (*of secondary school also*) Direktor(in) *m*; **~ waiter** *n* Oberkellner *m*; **~way** *n* Fortschritte *pl*; **~wind** *n* Gegenwind *m*; **~y** *adj* berauschend
heal [hiːl] *vt* heilen ♦ *vi* verheilen
health [hɛlθ] *n* Gesundheit *f*; **~ food** *n* Reformkost *f*; **H~ Service** (*BRIT*) *n*: **the H~ Service** das Gesundheitswesen; **~y** *adj* gesund
heap [hiːp] *n* Haufen *m* ♦ *vt* häufen
hear [hɪər] (*pt, pp* **heard**) *vt* hören; (*listen to*) anhören ♦ *vi* hören; **~d** [hɜːd] *pt, pp of* **hear**; **~ing** *n* Gehör *nt*; (*JUR*) Verhandlung *f*; **~ing aid** *n* Hörapparat *m*; **~say** *n* Hörensagen *nt*
hearse [hɜːs] *n* Leichenwagen *m*
heart [hɑːt] *n* Herz *nt*; **~s** *npl* (*CARDS*) Herz *nt*; **by ~** auswendig; **~ attack** *n* Herzanfall *m*; **~beat** *n* Herzschlag *m*; **~breaking** *adj* herzzerbrechend; **~broken** *adj* untröstlich; **~burn** *n* Sodbrennen *nt*; **~ failure** *n* Herzschlag *m*; **~felt** *adj* aufrichtig
hearth [hɑːθ] *n* Herd *m*
heartily ['hɑːtɪlɪ] *adv* herzlich; (*eat*) herzhaft
heartless ['hɑːtlɪs] *adj* herzlos
hearty ['hɑːtɪ] *adj* kräftig; (*friendly*) freundlich
heat [hiːt] *n* Hitze *f*; (*of food, water etc*) Wärme *f*; (*SPORT: also:* **qualifying ~**) Ausscheidungsrunde *f* ♦ *vt* (*house*) heizen; (*substance*) heiß machen, erhitzen; **~ up** *vi* warm werden ♦ *vt* aufwärmen; **~ed** *adj* erhitzt; (*fig*) hitzig; **~er** *n* (Heiz)ofen *m*

heath [hiːθ] (*BRIT*) *n* Heide *f*
heathen [ˈhiːðən] *n* Heide *m*/Heidin *f* ♦ *adj* heidnisch, Heiden-
heather [ˈhɛðəʳ] *n* Heidekraut *nt*
heat: ~**ing** *n* Heizung *f*; ~**-seeking** *adj* Wärme suchend; ~**stroke** *n* Hitzschlag *m*; ~ **wave** *n* Hitzewelle *f*
heave [hiːv] *vt* hochheben; (*sigh*) ausstoßen ♦ *vi* wogen; (*breast*) sich heben ♦ *n* Heben *nt*
heaven [ˈhɛvn] *n* Himmel *m*; ~**ly** *adj* himmlisch
heavily [ˈhɛvɪlɪ] *adv* schwer
heavy [ˈhɛvɪ] *adj* schwer; ~ **goods vehicle** *n* Lastkraftwagen *m*; ~**weight** *n* (*SPORT*) Schwergewicht *nt*
Hebrew [ˈhiːbruː] *adj* hebräisch ♦ *n* (*LING*) Hebräisch *nt*
Hebrides [ˈhɛbrɪdiːz] *npl* Hebriden *pl*
heckle [ˈhɛkl] *vt* unterbrechen
hectic [ˈhɛktɪk] *adj* hektisch
he'd [hiːd] = **he had; he would**
hedge [hɛdʒ] *n* Hecke *f* ♦ *vt* einzäunen ♦ *vi* (*fig*) ausweichen; **to ~ one's bets** sich absichern
hedgehog [ˈhɛdʒhɒɡ] *n* Igel *m*
heed [hiːd] *vt* (*also:* **take ~ of**) beachten ♦ *n* Beachtung *f*; ~**less** *adj* achtlos
heel [hiːl] *n* Ferse *f*; (*of shoe*) Absatz *m* ♦ *vt* mit Absätzen versehen
hefty [ˈhɛftɪ] *adj* (*person*) stämmig; (*portion*) reichlich
heifer [ˈhɛfəʳ] *n* Färse *f*
height [haɪt] *n* (*of person*) Größe *f*; (*of object*) Höhe *f*; ~**en** *vt* erhöhen
heir [ɛəʳ] *n* Erbe *m*; ~**ess** [ˈɛəres] *n* Erbin *f*; ~**loom** *n* Erbstück *nt*
held [hɛld] *pt*, *pp of* **hold**
helicopter [ˈhɛlɪkɒptəʳ] *n* Hubschrauber *m*
heliport [ˈhɛlɪpɔːt] *n* Hubschrauberlandeplatz *m*
hell [hɛl] *n* Hölle *f* ♦ *excl* verdammt!
he'll [hiːl] = **he will; he shall**
hellish [ˈhɛlɪʃ] *adj* höllisch, verteufelt
hello [həˈləu] *excl* hallo
helm [hɛlm] *n* Ruder *nt*, Steuer *nt*
helmet [ˈhɛlmɪt] *n* Helm *m*

help [hɛlp] *n* Hilfe *f* ♦ *vt* helfen +*dat*; **I can't ~ it** ich kann nichts dafür; ~ **yourself** bedienen Sie sich; ~**er** *n* Helfer *m*; ~**ful** *adj* hilfreich; ~**ing** *n* Portion *f*; ~**less** *adj* hilflos
hem [hɛm] *n* Saum *m* ♦ *vt* säumen; ~ **in** *vt* einengen
hemorrhage [ˈhɛmərɪdʒ] (*US*) *n* = **haemorrhage**
hemorrhoids [ˈhɛmərɔɪdz] (*US*) *npl* = **haemorrhoids**
hen [hɛn] *n* Henne *f*
hence [hɛns] *adv* von jetzt an; (*therefore*) daher; ~**forth** *adv* von nun an; (*from then on*) von da an
henchman [ˈhɛntʃmən] (*irreg*) *n* Gefolgsmann *m*
her [həːʳ] *pron* (*acc*) sie; (*dat*) ihr ♦ *adj* ihr; *see also* **me; my**
herald [ˈhɛrəld] *n* (Vor)bote *m* ♦ *vt* verkünden
heraldry [ˈhɛrəldrɪ] *n* Wappenkunde *f*
herb [həːb] *n* Kraut *nt*
herd [həːd] *n* Herde *f*
here [hɪəʳ] *adv* hier; (*to this place*) hierher; ~**after** [hɪərˈɑːftəʳ] *adv* hernach, künftig ♦ *n* Jenseits *nt*; ~**by** [hɪəˈbaɪ] *adv* hiermit
hereditary [hɪˈrɛdɪtrɪ] *adj* erblich
heredity [hɪˈrɛdɪtɪ] *n* Vererbung *f*
heritage [ˈhɛrɪtɪdʒ] *n* Erbe *nt*
hermit [ˈhəːmɪt] *n* Einsiedler *m*
hernia [ˈhəːnɪə] *n* Bruch *m*
hero [ˈhɪərəu] (*pl* ~**es**) *n* Held *m*; ~**ic** [hɪˈrəuɪk] *adj* heroisch
heroin [ˈhɛrəuɪn] *n* Heroin *nt*
heroine [ˈhɛrəuɪn] *n* Heldin *f*
heroism [ˈhɛrəuɪzəm] *n* Heldentum *nt*
heron [ˈhɛrən] *n* Reiher *m*
herring [ˈhɛrɪŋ] *n* Hering *m*
hers [həːz] *pron* ihre(r, s); *see also* **mine²**
herself [həːˈsɛlf] *pron* sich (selbst); (*emphatic*) selbst; *see also* **oneself**
he's [hiːz] = **he is; he has**
hesitant [ˈhɛzɪtənt] *adj* zögernd
hesitate [ˈhɛzɪteɪt] *vi* zögern; **hesitation** [hɛzɪˈteɪʃən] *n* Zögern *nt*
heterosexual [ˈhɛtərəuˈsɛksjuəl] *adj* heterosexuell ♦ *n* Heterosexuelle(r) *mf*

hew [hjuː] (*pt* **hewed**, *pp* **hewn**) *vt* hauen, hacken

hexagonal [hɛkˈsægənl] *adj* sechseckig

heyday [ˈheɪdeɪ] *n* Blüte *f*, Höhepunkt *m*

HGV *n abbr* = **heavy goods vehicle**

hi [haɪ] *excl* he, hallo

hibernate [ˈhaɪbəneɪt] *vi* Winterschlaf *m* halten; **hibernation** [haɪbəˈneɪʃən] *n* Winterschlaf *m*

hiccough [ˈhɪkʌp] *vi* den Schluckauf haben; **~s** *npl* Schluckauf *m*

hiccup [ˈhɪkʌp] = **hiccough**

hid [hɪd] *pt of* **hide**; **~den** [ˈhɪdn] *pp of* **hide**

hide [haɪd] (*pt* **hid**, *pp* **hidden**) *n* (*skin*) Haut *f*, Fell *nt* ♦ *vt* verstecken ♦ *vi* sich verstecken; **~-and-seek** *n* Versteckspiel *nt*; **~away** *n* Versteck *nt*

hideous [ˈhɪdɪəs] *adj* abscheulich

hiding [ˈhaɪdɪŋ] *n* (*beating*) Tracht *f* Prügel; **to be in ~** (*concealed*) sich versteckt halten; **~ place** *n* Versteck *nt*

hi-fi [ˈhaɪfaɪ] *n* Hi-Fi *nt* ♦ *adj* Hi-Fi-

high [haɪ] *adj* hoch; (*wind*) stark ♦ *adv* hoch; **it is 20m ~** es ist 20 Meter hoch; **~brow** *adj* (betont) intellektuell; **~chair** *n* Hochstuhl *m*; **~er education** *n* Hochschulbildung *f*; **~-handed** *adj* eigenmächtig; **~-heeled** *adj* hochhackig; **~ jump** *n* (*SPORT*) Hochsprung *m*; **H~lands** *npl*: **the H~lands** das schottische Hochland; **~light** *n* (*fig*) Höhepunkt *m* ♦ *vt* hervorheben; **~ly** *adv* höchst; **~ly strung** *adj* überempfindlich; **~ness** *n* Höhe *f*; **Her H~ness** Ihre Hoheit *f*; **~-pitched** *adj* hoch; **~-rise block** *n* Hochhaus *nt*; **~ school** (*US*) *n* Oberschule *f*; **~ season** (*BRIT*) *n* Hochsaison *f*; **~ street** (*BRIT*) *n* Hauptstraße *f*

highway [ˈhaɪweɪ] *n* Landstraße *f*; **H~ Code** (*BRIT*) *n* Straßenverkehrsordnung *f*

hijack [ˈhaɪdʒæk] *vt* entführen; **~er** *n* Entführer(in) *m(f)*

hike [haɪk] *vi* wandern ♦ *n* Wanderung *f*; **~r** *n* Wanderer *m*; **hiking** *n* Wandern *nt*

hilarious [hɪˈlɛərɪəs] *adj* lustig

hill [hɪl] *n* Berg *m*; **~side** *n* (Berg)hang *m*; **~ walking** *n* Bergwandern *nt*; **~y** *adj* hügelig

hilt [hɪlt] *n* Heft *nt*; **(up) to the ~** ganz und gar

him [hɪm] *pron* (*acc*) ihn; (*dat*) ihm; *see also* **me**; **~self** *pron* sich (selbst); (*emphatic*) selbst; *see also* **oneself**

hind [haɪnd] *adj* hinter, Hinter-

hinder [ˈhɪndər] *vt* (*stop*) hindern; (*delay*) behindern; **hindrance** *n* (*delay*) Behinderung *f*; (*obstacle*) Hindernis *nt*

hindsight [ˈhaɪndsaɪt] *n*: **with ~** im nachhinein

Hindu [ˈhɪnduː] *n* Hindu *m*

hinge [hɪndʒ] *n* Scharnier *nt*; (*on door*) Türangel *f* ♦ *vi* (*fig*): **to ~ on** abhängen von

hint [hɪnt] *n* Tipp *m*; (*trace*) Anflug *m* ♦ *vt*: **to ~ that** andeuten, dass ♦ *vi*: **to ~ at** andeuten

hip [hɪp] *n* Hüfte *f*

hippie [ˈhɪpɪ] *n* Hippie *m*

hippo [ˈhɪpəʊ] (*inf*) *n* Nilpferd *nt*

hippopotami [hɪpəˈpɒtəmaɪ] *npl of* **hippopotamus**

hippopotamus [hɪpəˈpɒtəməs] (*pl* **~es** *or* **hippopotami**) *n* Nilpferd *nt*

hire [ˈhaɪər] *vt* (*worker*) anstellen; (*BRIT*: *car*) mieten ♦ *n* Miete *f*; **for ~** (*taxi*) frei; **~(d) car** (*BRIT*) *n* Mietwagen *m*, Leihwagen *m*; **~ purchase** (*BRIT*) *n* Teilzahlungskauf *m*

his [hɪz] *adj* sein ♦ *pron* seine(r, s); *see also* **my**; **mine²**

hiss [hɪs] *vi* zischen ♦ *n* Zischen *nt*

historian [hɪˈstɔːrɪən] *n* Historiker *m*

historic [hɪˈstɒrɪk] *adj* historisch; **~al** *adj* historisch, geschichtlich

history [ˈhɪstərɪ] *n* Geschichte *f*

hit [hɪt] (*pt, pp* **hit**) *vt* schlagen; (*injure*) treffen ♦ *n* (*blow*) Schlag *m*; (*success*) Erfolg *m*; (*MUS*) Hit *m*; **to ~ it off with sb** prima mit jdm auskommen; **~-and-run driver** *n* jemand, der Fahrerflucht begeht

hitch [hɪtʃ] *vt* festbinden; (*also*: **~ up**) hochziehen ♦ *n* (*difficulty*) Haken *m*; **to ~ a lift** trampen; **~hike** *vi* trampen; **~hiker** *n* Tramper *m*; **~hiking** *n* Trampen *nt*

hi-tech [ˈhaɪˈtɛk] *adj* Hightech- ♦ *n* Spitzentechnologie *f*

hitherto [hɪðəˈtuː] *adv* bislang

hit man (inf) (irreg) n Killer m
HIV n abbr: **HIV-negative/-positive** HIV-negativ/-positiv
hive [haɪv] n Bienenkorb m
HMS abbr = **His/Her Majesty's Ship**
hoard [hɔːd] n Schatz m ♦ vt horten, hamstern
hoarding ['hɔːdɪŋ] n Bretterzaun m; (BRIT: for posters) Reklamewand f
hoarse [hɔːs] adj heiser, rau
hoax [həʊks] n Streich m
hob [hɒb] n Kochmulde f
hobble ['hɒbl] vi humpeln
hobby ['hɒbɪ] n Hobby nt
hobby-horse ['hɒbɪhɔːs] n (fig) Steckenpferd nt
hobo ['həʊbəʊ] (US) n Tippelbruder m
hockey ['hɒkɪ] n Hockey nt
hoe [həʊ] n Hacke f ♦ vt hacken
hog [hɒg] n Schlachtschwein m ♦ vt mit Beschlag belegen; **to go the whole ~** aufs Ganze gehen
hoist [hɔɪst] n Winde f ♦ vt hochziehen
hold [həʊld] (pt, pp **held**) vt halten; (contain) enthalten; (be able to contain) fassen; (breath) anhalten; (meeting) abhalten ♦ vi (withstand pressure) aushalten ♦ n (grasp) Halt m; (NAUT) Schiffsraum m; **~ the line!** (TEL) bleiben Sie am Apparat!; **to ~ one's own** sich behaupten; **~ back** vt zurückhalten; **~ down** vt niederhalten; (job) behalten; **~ off** vt (enemy) abwehren; **~ on** vi sich festhalten; (resist) durchhalten; (wait) warten; **~ on to** vt fus festhalten an +dat; (keep) behalten; **~ out** vt hinhalten ♦ vi aushalten; **~ up** vt (delay) aufhalten; (rob) überfallen; **~all** (BRIT) n Reisetasche f; **~er** n Behälter m; **~ing** n (share) (Aktien)anteil m; **~up** n (BRIT: in traffic) Stockung f; (robbery) Überfall m; (delay) Verzögerung f
hole [həʊl] n Loch nt; **~ in the wall** (inf) n (cash dispenser) Geldautomat m
holiday ['hɒlɪdeɪ] n (day) Feiertag m; freie(r) Tag m; (vacation) Urlaub m; (SCH) Ferien pl; **~-maker** (BRIT) n Urlauber(in) m(f); **~ resort** n Ferienort m

Holland ['hɒlənd] n Holland nt
hollow ['hɒləʊ] adj hohl; (fig) leer ♦ n Vertiefung f; **~ out** vt aushöhlen
holly ['hɒlɪ] n Stechpalme f
holocaust ['hɒləkɔːst] n Inferno nt
holster ['həʊlstə*] n Pistolenhalfter m
holy ['həʊlɪ] adj heilig; **H~ Ghost** or **Spirit** n: **the H~ Ghost** or **Spirit** der Heilige Geist
homage ['hɒmɪdʒ] n Huldigung f; **to pay ~ to** huldigen +dat
home [həʊm] n Zuhause nt; (institution) Heim nt, Anstalt f ♦ adj einheimisch; (POL) inner ♦ adv heim, nach Hause; **at ~** zu Hause; **~ address** n Heimatadresse f; **~coming** n Heimkehr f; **~land** n Heimat(land nt) f; **~less** adj obdachlos; **~ly** adj häuslich; (US: ugly) unscheinbar; **~made** adj selbst gemacht; **~ match** adj Heimspiel nt; **H~ Office** (BRIT) n Innenministerium nt; **~ page** n (COMPUT) Homepage f; **~ rule** n Selbstverwaltung f; **H~ Secretary** (BRIT) n Innenminister(in) m(f); **~sick** adj: **to be ~sick** Heimweh haben; **~ town** n Heimatstadt f; **~ward** adj (journey) Heim-; **~work** n Hausaufgaben pl
homicide ['hɒmɪsaɪd] (US) n Totschlag m
homoeopathic [həʊmɪə'pæθɪk] (US **homeopathic**) adj homöopathisch; **homoeopathy** [həʊmɪ'ɒpəθɪ] (US **homeopathy**) n Homöopathie f
homogeneous [hɒməʊ'dʒiːnɪəs] adj homogen
homosexual [hɒməʊ'sɛksjʊəl] adj homosexuell ♦ n Homosexuelle(r) mf
honest ['ɒnɪst] adj ehrlich; **~ly** adv ehrlich; **~y** n Ehrlichkeit f
honey ['hʌnɪ] n Honig m; **~comb** n Honigwabe f; **~moon** n Flitterwochen pl, Hochzeitsreise f; **~suckle** ['hʌnɪsʌkl] n Geißblatt nt
honk [hɒŋk] vi hupen
honor etc ['ɒnə*] (US) vt, n = **honour** etc
honorary ['ɒnərərɪ] adj Ehren-
honour ['ɒnə*] (US **honor**) vt ehren; (cheque) einlösen ♦ n Ehre f; **~able** adj ehrenwert; (intention) ehrenhaft; **~s degree** n (UNIV) akademischer Grad mit Prüfung im

Spezialfach

hood [hud] *n* Kapuze *f*; (*BRIT: AUT*) Verdeck *nt*; (*US: AUT*) Kühlerhaube *f*

hoof [hu:f] (*pl* **hooves**) *n* Huf *m*

hook [huk] *n* Haken *m* ♦ *vt* einhaken

hooligan ['hu:lɪɡən] *n* Rowdy *m*

hoop [hu:p] *n* Reifen *m*

hooray [hu:'reɪ] *excl* = **hurrah**

hoot [hu:t] *vi* (*AUT*) hupen; **~er** *n* (*NAUT*) Dampfpfeife *f*; (*BRIT: AUT*) (Auto)hupe *f*

Hoover ['hu:və'] (®); *BRIT*) *n* Staubsauger *m* ♦ *vt*: **to h~** staubsaugen, Staub saugen

hooves [hu:vz] *pl of* **hoof**

hop [hɔp] *vi* hüpfen, hopsen ♦ *n* (*jump*) Hopser *m*

hope [həup] *vt, vi* hoffen ♦ *n* Hoffnung *f*; **I ~ so/not** hoffentlich/hoffentlich nicht; **~ful** *adj* hoffnungsvoll; (*promising*) viel versprechend; **~fully** *adv* hoffentlich; **~less** *adj* hoffnungslos

hops [hɔps] *npl* Hopfen *m*

horizon [hə'raɪzn] *n* Horizont *m*; **~tal** [hɔrɪ'zɔntl] *adj* horizontal

hormone ['hɔ:məun] *n* Hormon *nt*

horn [hɔ:n] *n* Horn *nt*; (*AUT*) Hupe *f*

hornet ['hɔ:nɪt] *n* Hornisse *f*

horny ['hɔ:nɪ] *adj* schwielig; (*US: inf*) scharf

horoscope ['hɔrəskəup] *n* Horoskop *nt*

horrendous [hə'rendəs] *adj* (*crime*) abscheulich; (*error*) schrecklich

horrible ['hɔrɪbl] *adj* fürchterlich

horrid ['hɔrɪd] *adj* scheußlich

horrify ['hɔrɪfaɪ] *vt* entsetzen

horror ['hɔrə'] *n* Schrecken *m*; **~ film** *n* Horrorfilm *m*

hors d'oeuvre [ɔ:'də:vrə] *n* Vorspeise *f*

horse [hɔ:s] *n* Pferd *nt*; **~back** *n*: **on ~back** beritten; **~ chestnut** *n* Rosskastanie *f*; **~man/woman** (*irreg*) *n* Reiter(in) *m(f)*; **~power** *n* Pferdestärke *f*; **~-racing** *n* Pferderennen *nt*; **~radish** *n* Meerrettich *m*; **~shoe** *n* Hufeisen *nt*

horticulture ['hɔ:tɪkʌltʃə'] *n* Gartenbau *m*

hose [həuz] *n* (*also*: **~pipe**) Schlauch *m*

hosiery ['həuzɪərɪ] *n* Strumpfwaren *pl*

hospitable ['hɔspɪtəbl] *adj* gastfreundlich

hospital ['hɔspɪtl] *n* Krankenhaus *nt*

hospitality [hɔspɪ'tælɪtɪ] *n* Gastfreundschaft *f*

host [həust] *n* Gastgeber *m*; (*innkeeper*) (Gast)wirt *m*; (*large number*) Heerschar *f*; (*ECCL*) Hostie *f*

hostage ['hɔstɪdʒ] *n* Geisel *f*

hostel ['hɔstl] *n* Herberge *f*; (*also*: **youth ~**) Jugendherberge *f*

hostess ['həustɪs] *n* Gastgeberin *f*

hostile ['hɔstaɪl] *adj* feindlich; **hostility** [hɔ'stɪlɪtɪ] *n* Feindschaft *f*; **hostilities** *npl* (*fighting*) Feindseligkeiten *pl*

hot [hɔt] *adj* heiß; (*food, water*) warm; (*spiced*) scharf; **I'm ~** mir ist heiß; **~bed** *n* (*fig*) Nährboden *m*; **~ dog** *n* heiße(s) Würstchen *nt*

hotel [həu'tel] *n* Hotel *nt*; **~ier** [həu'telɪə'] *n* Hotelier *m*

hot: **~house** *n* Treibhaus *nt*; **~ line** *n* (*POL*) heiße(r) Draht *m*; **~ly** *adv* (*argue*) hitzig; **~plate** *n* Kochplatte *f*; **~pot** ['hɔtpɔt] (*BRIT*) *n* Fleischeintopf *m*; **~-water bottle** *n* Wärmflasche *f*

hound [haund] *n* Jagdhund *m* ♦ *vt* hetzen

hour ['auə'] *n* Stunde *f*; (*time of day*) (Tages)zeit *f*; **~ly** *adj, adv* stündlich

house [*n* haus, *vb* hauz] *n* Haus *nt* ♦ *vt* unterbringen; **on the ~** auf Kosten des Hauses; **~ arrest** *n* (*POL, MIL*) Hausarrest *m*; **~boat** *n* Hausboot *nt*; **~breaking** *n* Einbruch *m*; **~coat** *n* Morgenmantel *m*; **~hold** *n* Haushalt *m*; **~keeper** *n* Haushälterin *f*; **~keeping** *n* Haushaltung *f*; **~-warming party** *n* Einweihungsparty *f*; **~wife** (*irreg*) *n* Hausfrau *f*; **~work** *n* Hausarbeit *f*

housing ['hauzɪŋ] *n* (*act*) Unterbringung *f*; (*houses*) Wohnungen *pl*; (*POL*) Wohnungsbau *m*; (*covering*) Gehäuse *nt*; **~ estate** (*US* **~ development**) *n* (Wohn)siedlung *f*

hovel ['hɔvl] *n* elende Hütte *f*

hover ['hɔvə'] *vi* (*bird*) schweben; (*person*) herumstehen; **~craft** *n* Luftkissenfahrzeug *nt*

how [hau] *adv* wie; **~ are you?** wie geht es Ihnen?; **~ much milk?** wie viel Milch?; **~**

many people? wie viele Leute?

however [hau'ɛvəʳ] *adv* (but) (je)doch, aber; **~ you phrase it** wie Sie es auch ausdrücken

howl [haul] *n* Heulen *nt* ♦ *vi* heulen

H.P. *abbr* = **hire purchase**

h.p. *abbr* = **horsepower**

H.Q. *abbr* = **headquarters**

HTML *abbr* (= *hypertext markup language*) HTML

hub [hʌb] *n* Radnabe *f*

hubbub ['hʌbʌb] *n* Tumult *m*

hubcap ['hʌbkæp] *n* Radkappe *f*

huddle ['hʌdl] *vi:* **to ~ together** sich zusammendrängen

hue [hju:] *n* Färbung *f*; **~ and cry** *n* Zetergeschrei *nt*

huff [hʌf] *n:* **to go into a ~** einschnappen

hug [hʌg] *vt* umarmen ♦ *n* Umarmung *f*

huge [hju:dʒ] *adj* groß, riesig

hulk [hʌlk] *n* (ship) abgetakelte(s) Schiff *nt*; (person) Koloss *m*

hull [hʌl] *n* Schiffsrumpf *m*

hullo [hə'ləu] *excl* = **hello**

hum [hʌm] *vt, vi* summen

human ['hju:mən] *adj* menschlich ♦ *n* (also: **~ being**) Mensch *m*

humane [hju:'mein] *adj* human

humanitarian [hju:mænɪ'tɛəriən] *adj* humanitär

humanity [hju:'mænɪtɪ] *n* Menschheit *f*; (kindliness) Menschlichkeit *f*

humble ['hʌmbl] *adj* demütig; (modest) bescheiden ♦ *vt* demütigen

humbug ['hʌmbʌg] *n* Humbug *m*; (BRIT: sweet) Pfefferminzbonbon *nt*

humdrum ['hʌmdrʌm] *adj* stumpfsinnig

humid ['hju:mɪd] *adj* feucht; **~ity** [hju:'mɪdɪtɪ] *n* Feuchtigkeit *f*

humiliate [hju:'mɪlɪeɪt] *vt* demütigen; **humiliation** [hju:mɪlɪ'eɪʃən] *n* Demütigung *f*

humility [hju:'mɪlɪtɪ] *n* Demut *f*

humor ['hju:məʳ] (US) *n, vt* = **humour**

humorous ['hju:mərəs] *adj* humorvoll

humour ['hju:məʳ] (US **humor**) *n* (fun) Humor *m*; (mood) Stimmung *f* ♦ *vt* bei Stimmung halten

hump [hʌmp] *n* Buckel *m*

hunch [hʌntʃ] *n* Buckel *m*; (premonition) (Vor)ahnung *f*; **~back** *n* Bucklige(r) *mf*; **~ed** *adj* gekrümmt

hundred ['hʌndrəd] *num* hundert; **~weight** *n* Zentner *m* (BRIT = 50.8 kg; US = 45.3 kg)

hung [hʌŋ] *pt, pp* of **hang**

Hungarian [hʌŋ'gɛəriən] *adj* ungarisch ♦ *n* Ungar(in) *m(f)*; (LING) Ungarisch *nt*

Hungary ['hʌŋgəri] *n* Ungarn *nt*

hunger ['hʌŋgəʳ] *n* Hunger *m* ♦ *vi* hungern

hungry ['hʌŋgrɪ] *adj* hungrig; **to be ~** Hunger haben

hunk [hʌŋk] *n* (of bread) Stück *nt*

hunt [hʌnt] *vt, vi* jagen ♦ *n* Jagd *f*; **to ~ for** suchen; **~er** *n* Jäger *m*; **~ing** *n* Jagd *f*

hurdle ['hə:dl] *n* (also fig) Hürde *f*

hurl [hə:l] *vt* schleudern

hurrah [hu'rɑ:] *n* Hurra *nt*

hurray [hu'reɪ] *n* Hurra *nt*

hurricane ['hʌrɪkən] *n* Orkan *m*

hurried ['hʌrɪd] *adj* eilig; (hasty) übereilt; **~ly** *adv* übereilt, hastig

hurry ['hʌrɪ] *n* Eile *f* ♦ *vi* sich beeilen ♦ *vt* (an)treiben; (job) übereilen; **to be in a ~** es eilig haben; **~ up** *vi* sich beeilen ♦ *vt* (person) zur Eile antreiben; (work) vorantreiben

hurt [hə:t] (pt, pp **hurt**) *vt* wehtun +*dat*; (injure, fig) verletzen ♦ *vi* wehtun; **~ful** *adj* schädlich; (remark) verletzend

hurtle ['hə:tl] *vi* sausen

husband ['hʌzbənd] *n* (Ehe)mann *m*

hush [hʌʃ] *n* Stille *f* ♦ *vt* zur Ruhe bringen ♦ *excl* pst, still

husky ['hʌskɪ] *adj* (voice) rau ♦ *n* Eskimohund *m*

hustle ['hʌsl] *vt* (push) stoßen; (hurry) antreiben ♦ *n:* **~ and bustle** Geschäftigkeit *f*

hut [hʌt] *n* Hütte *f*

hutch [hʌtʃ] *n* (Kaninchen)stall *m*

hyacinth ['haɪəsɪnθ] *n* Hyazinthe *f*

hydrant ['haɪdrənt] *n* (also: **fire ~**) Hydrant *m*

hydraulic [haɪ'drɔ:lɪk] *adj* hydraulisch

hydroelectric ['haɪdrəʊɪ'lektrɪk] *adj* (energy) durch Wasserkraft erzeugt; **~ power station** *n* Wasserkraftwerk *nt*

hydrofoil ['haɪdrəfɔɪl] *n* Tragflügelboot *nt*

hydrogen ['haɪdrədʒən] *n* Wasserstoff *m*
hyena [haɪ'iːnə] *n* Hyäne *f*
hygiene ['haɪdʒiːn] *n* Hygiene *f*; **hygienic** [haɪ'dʒiːnɪk] *adj* hygienisch
hymn [hɪm] *n* Kirchenlied *nt*
hype [haɪp] (*inf*) *n* Publicity *f*
hypermarket ['haɪpəmɑːkɪt] (*BRIT*) *n* Hypermarket *m*
hypertext ['haɪpətɛkst] *n* (*COMPUT*) Hypertext *m*
hyphen ['haɪfn] *n* Bindestrich *m*
hypnosis [hɪp'nəʊsɪs] *n* Hypnose *f*
hypnotize ['hɪpnətaɪz] *vt* hypnotisieren
hypocrisy [hɪ'pɔkrɪsɪ] *n* Heuchelei *f*
hypocrite ['hɪpəkrɪt] *n* Heuchler *m*; **hypocritical** [hɪpə'krɪtɪkl] *adj* scheinheilig, heuchlerisch
hypothermia [haɪpə'θəːmɪə] *n* Unterkühlung *f*
hypotheses [haɪ'pɔθɪsiːz] *npl of* **hypothesis**
hypothesis [haɪ'pɔθɪsɪs] (*pl* **hypotheses**) *n* Hypothese *f*
hypothetic(al) [haɪpəʊ'θetɪk(l)] *adj* hypothetisch
hysterical [hɪ'sterɪkl] *adj* hysterisch
hysterics [hɪ'sterɪks] *npl* hysterische(r) Anfall *m*

I, i

I [aɪ] *pron* ich
ice [aɪs] *n* Eis *nt* ♦ *vt* (*COOK*) mit Zuckerguss überziehen ♦ *vi* (*also:* **~ up**) vereisen; **~ axe** *n* Eispickel *m*; **~berg** *n* Eisberg *m*; **~box** (*US*) *n* Kühlschrank *m*; **~ cream** *n* Eis *nt*; **~ cube** *n* Eiswürfel *m*; **~d** [aɪst] *adj* (*cake*) mit Zuckerguss überzogen, glasiert; (*tea, coffee*) Eis-; **~ hockey** *n* Eishockey *nt*
Iceland ['aɪslənd] *n* Island *nt*
ice: ~ lolly (*BRIT*) *n* Eis *nt* am Stiel; **~ rink** *n* (Kunst)eisbahn *f*; **~ skating** *n* Schlittschuhlaufen *nt*
icicle ['aɪsɪkl] *n* Eiszapfen *m*
icing ['aɪsɪŋ] *n* (*on cake*) Zuckerguss *m*; (*on window*) Vereisung *f*; **~ sugar** (*BRIT*) *n* Puderzucker *m*

icon ['aɪkɔn] *n* Ikone *f*; (*COMPUT*) Icon *nt*
icy ['aɪsɪ] *adj* (*slippery*) vereist; (*cold*) eisig
I'd [aɪd] = **I would**; **I had**
idea [aɪ'dɪə] *n* Idee *f*
ideal [aɪ'dɪəl] *n* Ideal *nt* ♦ *adj* ideal
identical [aɪ'dentɪkl] *adj* identisch; (*twins*) eineiig
identification [aɪdentɪfɪ'keɪʃən] *n* Identifizierung *f*; **means of ~** Ausweispapiere *pl*
identify [aɪ'dentɪfaɪ] *vt* identifizieren; (*regard as the same*) gleichsetzen
Identikit [aɪ'dentɪkɪt] ® *n*: **~ picture** Phantombild *nt*
identity [aɪ'dentɪtɪ] *n* Identität *f*; **~ card** *n* Personalausweis *m*
ideology [aɪdɪ'ɔlədʒɪ] *n* Ideologie *f*
idiom ['ɪdɪəm] *n* (*expression*) Redewendung *f*; (*dialect*) Idiom *nt*; **~atic** [ɪdɪə'mætɪk] *adj* idiomatisch
idiosyncrasy [ɪdɪəʊ'sɪŋkrəsɪ] *n* Eigenart *f*
idiot ['ɪdɪət] *n* Idiot(in) *m(f)*; **~ic** [ɪdɪ'ɔtɪk] *adj* idiotisch
idle ['aɪdl] *adj* (*doing nothing*) untätig; (*lazy*) faul; (*useless*) nutzlos; (*machine*) still(stehend); (*threat, talk*) leer ♦ *vi* (*machine*) leer laufen ♦ *vt*: **to ~ away the time** die Zeit vertrödeln; **~ness** *n* Müßiggang *m*; Faulheit *f*
idol ['aɪdl] *n* Idol *nt*; **~ize** *vt* vergöttern
i.e. *abbr* (= *id est*) d. h.

| KEYWORD |

if [ɪf] *conj* **1** wenn; (*in case also*) falls; **if I were you** wenn ich Sie wäre
2 (*although*): **(even) if** (selbst *or* auch) wenn
3 (*whether*) ob
4: **if so/not** wenn ja/nicht; **if only ...** wenn ... doch nur ...; **if only I could** wenn ich doch nur könnte; *see also* **as**

ignite [ɪg'naɪt] *vt* (an)zünden ♦ *vi* sich entzünden; **ignition** [ɪg'nɪʃən] *n* Zündung *f*; **to switch on/off the ignition** den Motor anlassen/abstellen; **ignition key** *n* (*AUT*) Zündschlüssel *m*

ignorance [ˈɪgnərəns] *n* Unwissenheit *f*

ignorant [ˈɪgnərənt] *adj* unwissend; **to be ~ of** nicht wissen

ignore [ɪgˈnɔːʳ] *vt* ignorieren

I'll [aɪl] = **I will; I shall**

ill [ɪl] *adj* krank ♦ *n* Übel *nt* ♦ *adv* schlecht; **~-advised** *adj* unklug; **~-at-ease** *adj* unbehaglich

illegal [ɪˈliːgl] *adj* illegal

illegible [ɪˈledʒɪbl] *adj* unleserlich

illegitimate [ɪlɪˈdʒɪtɪmət] *adj* unehelich

ill-fated [ɪlˈfeɪtɪd] *adj* unselig

ill feeling *n* Verstimmung *f*

illicit [ɪˈlɪsɪt] *adj* verboten

illiterate [ɪˈlɪtərət] *adj* ungebildet

ill-mannered [ɪlˈmænəd] *adj* ungehobelt

illness [ˈɪlnɪs] *n* Krankheit *f*

illogical [ɪˈlɒdʒɪkl] *adj* unlogisch

ill-treat [ɪlˈtriːt] *vt* misshandeln

illuminate [ɪˈluːmɪneɪt] *vt* beleuchten; **illumination** [ɪluːmɪˈneɪʃən] *n* Beleuchtung *f*; **illuminations** *pl* (*decorative lights*) festliche Beleuchtung *f*

illusion [ɪˈluːʒən] *n* Illusion *f*; **to be under the ~ that ...** sich *dat* einbilden, dass ...

illustrate [ˈɪləstreɪt] *vt* (*book*) illustrieren; (*explain*) veranschaulichen; **illustration** [ɪləˈstreɪʃən] *n* Illustration *f*; (*explanation*) Veranschaulichung *f*

illustrious [ɪˈlʌstrɪəs] *adj* berühmt

I'm [aɪm] = **I am**

image [ˈɪmɪdʒ] *n* Bild *nt*; (*public ~*) Image *nt*; **~ry** *n* Symbolik *f*

imaginary [ɪˈmædʒɪnərɪ] *adj* eingebildet; (*world*) Fantasie-

imagination [ɪmædʒɪˈneɪʃən] *n* Einbildung *f*; (*creative*) Fantasie *f*

imaginative [ɪˈmædʒɪnətɪv] *adj* fantasiereich, einfallsreich

imagine [ɪˈmædʒɪn] *vt* sich vorstellen; (*wrongly*) sich einbilden

imbalance [ɪmˈbæləns] *n* Unausgeglichenheit *f*

imbecile [ˈɪmbəsiːl] *n* Schwachsinnige(r) *mf*

imitate [ˈɪmɪteɪt] *vt* imitieren; **imitation** [ɪmɪˈteɪʃən] *n* Imitation *f*

immaculate [ɪˈmækjulət] *adj* makellos; (*dress*) tadellos; (*ECCL*) unbefleckt

immaterial [ɪməˈtɪərɪəl] *adj* unwesentlich; **it is ~ whether ...** es ist unwichtig, ob ...

immature [ɪməˈtjuəʳ] *adj* unreif

immediate [ɪˈmiːdɪət] *adj* (*instant*) sofortig; (*near*) unmittelbar; (*relatives*) nächste(r, s); (*needs*) dringlich; **~ly** *adv* sofort; **~ly next to** direkt neben

immense [ɪˈmens] *adj* unermesslich

immerse [ɪˈmɜːs] *vt* eintauchen; **to be ~d in** (*fig*) vertieft sein in +*acc*

immersion heater [ɪˈmɜːʃən-] (*BRIT*) *n* Boiler *m*

immigrant [ˈɪmɪgrənt] *n* Einwanderer *m*

immigrate [ˈɪmɪgreɪt] *vi* einwandern; **immigration** [ɪmɪˈgreɪʃən] *n* Einwanderung *f*

imminent [ˈɪmɪnənt] *adj* bevorstehend

immobile [ɪˈməubaɪl] *adj* unbeweglich; **immobilize** [ɪˈməubɪlaɪz] *vt* lähmen

immoral [ɪˈmɒrl] *adj* unmoralisch; **~ity** [ɪməˈrælɪtɪ] *n* Unsittlichkeit *f*

immortal [ɪˈmɔːtl] *adj* unsterblich

immune [ɪˈmjuːn] *adj* (*secure*) sicher; (*MED*) immun; **~ from** sicher vor +*dat*; **immunity** *n* (*MED, JUR*) Immunität *f*; (*fig*) Freiheit *f*; **immunize** [ˈɪmjunaɪz] *vt* immunisieren

impact [ˈɪmpækt] *n* Aufprall *m*; (*fig*) Wirkung *f*

impair [ɪmˈpeəʳ] *vt* beeinträchtigen

impart [ɪmˈpɑːt] *vt* mitteilen; (*knowledge*) vermitteln; (*exude*) abgeben

impartial [ɪmˈpɑːʃl] *adj* unparteiisch

impassable [ɪmˈpɑːsəbl] *adj* unpassierbar

impassive [ɪmˈpæsɪv] *adj* gelassen

impatience [ɪmˈpeɪʃəns] *n* Ungeduld *f*; **impatient** *adj* ungeduldig; **impatiently** *adv* ungeduldig

impeccable [ɪmˈpekəbl] *adj* tadellos

impede [ɪmˈpiːd] *vt* (be)hindern; **impediment** [ɪmˈpedɪmənt] *n* Hindernis *nt*; **speech impediment** Sprachfehler *m*

impending [ɪmˈpendɪŋ] *adj* bevorstehend

impenetrable [ɪmˈpenɪtrəbl] *adj* (*also fig*) undurchdringlich

imperative [ɪmˈperətɪv] *adj* (*necessary*) unbedingt erforderlich

imperceptible [ɪmpəˈsɛptɪbl] *adj* nicht wahrnehmbar

imperfect [ɪmˈpəːfɪkt] *adj* (*faulty*) fehlerhaft; **~ion** [ɪmpəˈfɛkʃən] *n* Unvollkommenheit *f*; (*fault*) Fehler *m*

imperial [ɪmˈpɪərɪəl] *adj* kaiserlich

impersonal [ɪmˈpəːsənl] *adj* unpersönlich

impersonate [ɪmˈpəːsəneɪt] *vt* sich ausgeben als; (*for fun*) imitieren

impertinent [ɪmˈpəːtɪnənt] *adj* unverschämt, frech

impervious [ɪmˈpəːvɪəs] *adj* (*fig*): **~ (to)** unempfänglich (für)

impetuous [ɪmˈpɛtjuəs] *adj* ungestüm

impetus [ˈɪmpətəs] *n* Triebkraft *f*; (*fig*) Auftrieb *m*

impinge [ɪmˈpɪndʒ]: **~ on** *vt* beeinträchtigen

implacable [ɪmˈplækəbl] *adj* unerbittlich

implement [*n* ˈɪmplɪmənt, *vb* ˈɪmplɪment] *n* Werkzeug *nt* ♦ *vt* ausführen

implicate [ˈɪmplɪkeɪt] *vt* verwickeln; **implication** [ɪmplɪˈkeɪʃən] *n* (*effect*) Auswirkung *f*; (*in crime*) Verwicklung *f*

implicit [ɪmˈplɪsɪt] *adj* (*suggested*) unausgesprochen; (*utter*) vorbehaltlos

implore [ɪmˈplɔː] *vt* anflehen

imply [ɪmˈplaɪ] *vt* (*hint*) andeuten; (*be evidence for*) schließen lassen auf *+acc*

impolite [ɪmpəˈlaɪt] *adj* unhöflich

import [*vb* ɪmˈpɔːt, *n* ˈɪmpɔːt] *vt* einführen ♦ *n* Einfuhr *f*; (*meaning*) Bedeutung *f*

importance [ɪmˈpɔːtns] *n* Bedeutung *f*

important [ɪmˈpɔːtənt] *adj* wichtig; **it's not ~** es ist unwichtig

importer [ɪmˈpɔːtə] *n* Importeur *m*

impose [ɪmˈpəuz] *vt*, *vi*: **to ~ (on)** auferlegen (*+dat*); (*penalty, sanctions*) verhängen (gegen); **to ~ (o.s.) on sb** sich jdm aufdrängen

imposing [ɪmˈpəuzɪŋ] *adj* eindrucksvoll

imposition [ɪmpəˈzɪʃən] *n* (*of burden, fine*) Auferlegung *f*; **to be an ~** (*on person*) eine Zumutung sein

impossible [ɪmˈpɔsɪbl] *adj* unmöglich

impostor [ɪmˈpɔstə] *n* Hochstapler *m*

impotent [ˈɪmpətnt] *adj* machtlos; (*sexually*) impotent

impound [ɪmˈpaund] *vt* beschlagnahmen

impoverished [ɪmˈpɔvərɪʃt] *adj* verarmt

impracticable [ɪmˈpræktɪkəbl] *adj* undurchführbar

impractical [ɪmˈpræktɪkl] *adj* unpraktisch

imprecise [ɪmprɪˈsaɪs] *adj* ungenau

impregnable [ɪmˈprɛgnəbl] *adj* (*castle*) uneinnehmbar

impregnate [ˈɪmprɛgneɪt] *vt* (*saturate*) sättigen; (*fertilize*) befruchten

impress [ɪmˈprɛs] *vt* (*influence*) beeindrucken; (*imprint*) (auf)drücken; **to ~ sth on sb** jdm etw einschärfen; **~ed** *adj* beeindruckt; **~ion** [ɪmˈprɛʃən] *n* Eindruck *m*; (*on wax, footprint*) Abdruck *m*; (*of book*) Auflage *f*; (*take-off*) Nachahmung *f*; **I was under the ~ion** ich hatte den Eindruck; **~ionable** *adj* leicht zu beeindrucken; **~ive** *adj* eindrucksvoll

imprint [ˈɪmprɪnt] *n* Abdruck *m*

imprison [ɪmˈprɪzn] *vt* ins Gefängnis schicken; **~ment** *n* Inhaftierung *f*

improbable [ɪmˈprɔbəbl] *adj* unwahrscheinlich

impromptu [ɪmˈprɔmptjuː] *adj*, *adv* aus dem Stegreif, improvisiert

improper [ɪmˈprɔpə] *adj* (*indecent*) unanständig; (*unsuitable*) unpassend

improve [ɪmˈpruːv] *vt* verbessern ♦ *vi* besser werden; **~ment** *n* (Ver)besserung *f*

improvise [ˈɪmprəvaɪz] *vt*, *vi* improvisieren

imprudent [ɪmˈpruːdnt] *adj* unklug

impudent [ˈɪmpjudnt] *adj* unverschämt

impulse [ˈɪmpʌls] *n* Impuls *m*; **to act on ~** spontan handeln; **impulsive** [ɪmˈpʌlsɪv] *adj* impulsiv

impure [ɪmˈpjuə] *adj* (*dirty*) verunreinigt; (*bad*) unsauber; **impurity** [ɪmˈpjuərɪtɪ] *n* Unreinheit *f*; (*TECH*) Verunreinigung *f*

KEYWORD

in [ɪn] *prep* **1** (*indicating place, position*) in *+dat*; (*with motion*) in *+acc*; **in here/there** hier/dort; **in London** in London; **in the United States** in den Vereinigten Staaten **2** (*indicating time: during*) in *+dat*; **in summer** im Sommer; **in 1988** (im Jahre)

1988; **in the afternoon** nachmittags, am Nachmittag
3 (*indicating time: in the space of*) innerhalb von; **I'll see you in 2 weeks** *or* **in 2 weeks' time** ich sehe Sie in 2 Wochen
4 (*indicating manner, circumstances, state etc*) in +*dat*; **in the sun/rain** in der Sonne/im Regen; **in English/French** auf Englisch/ Französisch; **in a loud/soft voice** mit lauter/leiser Stimme
5 (*with ratios, numbers*): **1 in 10** jeder Zehnte; **20 pence in the pound** 20 Pence pro Pfund; **they lined up in twos** sie stellten sich in Zweierreihe auf
6 (*referring to people, works*): **the disease is common in children** die Krankheit ist bei Kindern häufig; **in Dickens** bei Dickens; **we have a loyal friend in him** er ist uns ein treuer Freund
7 (*indicating profession etc*): **to be in teaching/the army** Lehrer(in)/beim Militär sein; **to be in publishing** im Verlagswesen arbeiten
8 (*with present participle*): **in saying this, I ...** wenn ich das sage, ... ich; **in accepting this view, he ...** weil er diese Meinung akzeptierte, ... er
♦ *adv*: **to be in** (*person: at home, work*) da sein; (*train, ship, plane*) angekommen sein; (*in fashion*) in sein; **to ask sb in** jdn hereinbitten; **to run/limp** *etc* **in** hereingerannt/gehumpelt *etc* kommen
♦ *n*: **the ins and outs** (*of proposal, situation etc*) die Feinheiten

---

in. *abbr* = **inch**
inability [ɪnəˈbɪlɪtɪ] *n* Unfähigkeit *f*
inaccessible [ɪnəkˈsesɪbl] *adj* unzugänglich
inaccurate [ɪnˈækjurət] *adj* ungenau; (*wrong*) unrichtig
inactivity [ɪnækˈtɪvɪtɪ] *n* Untätigkeit *f*
inadequate [ɪnˈædɪkwət] *adj* unzulänglich
inadvertently [ɪnədˈvəːtntlɪ] *adv* unabsichtlich
inadvisable [ɪnədˈvaɪzəbl] *adj* nicht ratsam
inane [ɪˈneɪn] *adj* dumm, albern
inanimate [ɪnˈænɪmət] *adj* leblos

inappropriate [ɪnəˈprəuprɪət] *adj* (*clothing*) ungeeignet; (*remark*) unangebracht
inarticulate [ɪnɑːˈtɪkjulət] *adj* unklar
inasmuch as [ɪnəzˈmʌtʃ-] *adv* da; (*in so far as*) so weit
inaudible [ɪnˈɔːdɪbl] *adj* unhörbar
inauguration [ɪnɔːgjuˈreɪʃən] *n* Eröffnung *f*; (feierliche) Amtseinführung *f*
inborn [ɪnˈbɔːn] *adj* angeboren
inbred [ɪnˈbred] *adj* angeboren
Inc. *abbr* = **incorporated**
incalculable [ɪnˈkælkjuləbl] *adj* (*consequences*) unabsehbar
incapable [ɪnˈkeɪpəbl] *adj*: **~ (of doing sth)** unfähig(, etw zu tun)
incapacitate [ɪnkəˈpæsɪteɪt] *vt* untauglich machen
incapacity [ɪnkəˈpæsɪtɪ] *n* Unfähigkeit *f*
incarcerate [ɪnˈkɑːsəreɪt] *vt* einkerkern
incarnation [ɪnkɑːˈneɪʃən] *n* (*ECCL*) Menschwerdung *f*; (*fig*) Inbegriff *m*
incendiary [ɪnˈsendɪərɪ] *adj* Brand-
incense [*n* ˈɪnsens, *vb* ɪnˈsens] *n* Weihrauch *m* ♦ *vt* erzürnen
incentive [ɪnˈsentɪv] *n* Anreiz *m*
incessant [ɪnˈsesnt] *adj* unaufhörlich
incest [ˈɪnsest] *n* Inzest *m*
inch [ɪntʃ] *n* Zoll *m* ♦ *vi*: **to ~ forward** sich Stückchen für Stückchen vorwärts bewegen; **to be within an ~ of** kurz davor sein; **he didn't give an ~** er gab keinen Zentimeter nach
incidence [ˈɪnsɪdns] *n* Auftreten *nt*; (*of crime*) Quote *f*
incident [ˈɪnsɪdnt] *n* Vorfall *m*; (*disturbance*) Zwischenfall *m*
incidental [ɪnsɪˈdentl] *adj* (*music*) Begleit-; (*unimportant*) nebensächlich; (*remark*) beiläufig; **~ly** *adv* übrigens
incinerator [ɪnˈsɪnəreɪtə] *n* Verbrennungsofen *m*
incision [ɪnˈsɪʒən] *n* Einschnitt *m*
incisive [ɪnˈsaɪsɪv] *adj* (*style*) treffend; (*person*) scharfsinnig
incite [ɪnˈsaɪt] *vt* anstacheln
inclination [ɪnklɪˈneɪʃən] *n* Neigung *f*
incline [*n* ˈɪnklaɪn, *vb* ɪnˈklaɪn] *n* Abhang *m*

♦ vt neigen; (fig) veranlassen ♦ vi sich neigen; **to be ~d to do sth** dazu neigen, etw zu tun

include [ɪnˈkluːd] vt einschließen; (on list, in group) aufnehmen; **including** prep: **including X** X inbegriffen; **inclusion** [ɪnˈkluːʒən] n Aufnahme f; **inclusive** [ɪnˈkluːsɪv] adj einschließlich; (COMM) inklusive; **inclusive of** einschließlich +gen

incoherent [ɪnkəʊˈhɪərənt] adj zusammenhanglos

income [ˈɪnkʌm] n Einkommen nt; (from business) Einkünfte pl; ~ **tax** n Lohnsteuer f; (of self-employed) Einkommensteuer f

incoming [ˈɪnkʌmɪŋ] adj: ~ **flight** eintreffende Maschine f

incomparable [ɪnˈkɒmpərəbl] adj unvergleichlich

incompatible [ɪnkəmˈpætɪbl] adj unvereinbar; (people) unverträglich

incompetence [ɪnˈkɒmpɪtns] n Unfähigkeit f; **incompetent** adj unfähig

incomplete [ɪnkəmˈpliːt] adj unvollständig

incomprehensible [ɪnkɒmprɪˈhensɪbl] adj unverständlich

inconceivable [ɪnkənˈsiːvəbl] adj unvorstellbar

incongruous [ɪnˈkɒŋgruəs] adj seltsam; (remark) unangebracht

inconsiderate [ɪnkənˈsɪdərət] adj rücksichtslos

inconsistency [ɪnkənˈsɪstənsɪ] n Widersprüchlichkeit f; (state) Unbeständigkeit f

inconsistent [ɪnkənˈsɪstnt] adj (action, speech) widersprüchlich; (person, work) unbeständig; ~ **with** nicht übereinstimmend mit

inconspicuous [ɪnkənˈspɪkjuəs] adj unauffällig

incontinent [ɪnˈkɒntɪnənt] adj (MED) nicht fähig, Stuhl und Harn zurückzuhalten

inconvenience [ɪnkənˈviːnjəns] n Unbequemlichkeit f; (trouble to others) Unannehmlichkeiten pl

inconvenient [ɪnkənˈviːnjənt] adj ungelegen; (journey) unbequem

incorporate [ɪnˈkɔːpəreɪt] vt (include) aufnehmen; (contain) enthalten; ~**d** adj: ~**d company** (US) eingetragene Aktiengesellschaft f

incorrect [ɪnkəˈrekt] adj unrichtig

incorrigible [ɪnˈkɒrɪdʒɪbl] adj unverbesserlich

incorruptible [ɪnkəˈrʌptɪbl] adj unzerstörbar; (person) unbestechlich

increase [n ˈɪnkriːs, vb ɪnˈkriːs] n Zunahme f; (pay ~) Gehaltserhöhung f; (in size) Vergrößerung f ♦ vt erhöhen; (wealth, rage) vermehren; (business) erweitern ♦ vi zunehmen; (prices) steigen; (in size) größer werden; (in number) sich vermehren; **increasing** adj (number) steigend; **increasingly** [ɪnˈkriːsɪŋlɪ] adv zunehmend

incredible [ɪnˈkredɪbl] adj unglaublich

incredulous [ɪnˈkredjuləs] adj ungläubig

increment [ˈɪnkrɪmənt] n Zulage f

incriminate [ɪnˈkrɪmɪneɪt] vt belasten

incubation [ɪnkjuˈbeɪʃən] n Ausbrüten nt

incubator [ˈɪnkjubeɪtə*] n Brutkasten m

incumbent [ɪnˈkʌmbənt] n ♦ adj: **it is ~ on him to ...** es obliegt ihm, ...

incur [ɪnˈkəː*] vt sich zuziehen; (debts) machen

incurable [ɪnˈkjuərəbl] adj unheilbar

indebted [ɪnˈdetɪd] adj (obliged): ~ **(to sb)** (jdm) verpflichtet

indecent [ɪnˈdiːsnt] adj unanständig; ~ **assault** (BRIT) n Notzucht f; ~ **exposure** n Exhibitionismus m

indecisive [ɪndɪˈsaɪsɪv] adj (battle) nicht entscheidend; (person) unentschlossen

indeed [ɪnˈdiːd] adv tatsächlich, in der Tat; **yes ~!** allerdings!

indefinite [ɪnˈdefɪnɪt] adj unbestimmt; ~**ly** adv auf unbestimmte Zeit; (wait) unbegrenzt lange

indelible [ɪnˈdelɪbl] adj unauslöschlich

indemnity [ɪnˈdemnɪtɪ] n (insurance) Versicherung f; (compensation) Entschädigung f

independence [ɪndɪˈpendns] n Unabhängigkeit f; **independent** adj unabhängig *i* **Independence Day** *(der 4. Juli) ist in den USA ein gesetzlicher Feiertag zum Gedenken an die Unabhängigkeitserklärung am 4. Juli 1776, mit der die 13 amerikanischen Kolonien ihre Freiheit und Unabhängigkeit von Großbritannien erklärten.*

indestructible [ɪndɪsˈtrʌktəbl] *adj* unzerstörbar

indeterminate [ɪndɪˈtəːmɪnɪt] *adj* unbestimmt

index [ˈɪndeks] (*pl* **-es** *or* **indices**) *n* Index *m*; ~ **card** *n* Karteikarte *f*; ~ **finger** *n* Zeigefinger *m*; **~-linked** (*US* **-ed**) *adj* (*salaries*) der Inflationsrate *dat* angeglichen; (*pensions*) dynamisch

India [ˈɪndɪə] *n* Indien *nt*; **~n** *adj* indisch ♦ *n* Inder(in) *m(f)*; **American ~n** Indianer(in) *m(f)*; **~n Ocean** *n*: **the ~n Ocean** der Indische Ozean

indicate [ˈɪndɪkeɪt] *vt* anzeigen; (*hint*) andeuten; **indication** [ɪndɪˈkeɪʃən] *n* Anzeichen *nt*; (*information*) Angabe *f*; **indicative** [ɪnˈdɪkətɪv] *adj*: **indicative of** bezeichnend für; **indicator** *n* (An)zeichen *nt*; (*AUT*) Richtungsanzeiger *m*

indict [ɪnˈdaɪt] *vt* anklagen; **~ment** *n* Anklage *f*

indifference [ɪnˈdɪfrəns] *n* Gleichgültigkeit *f*; Unwichtigkeit *f*; **indifferent** *adj* gleichgültig; (*mediocre*) mäßig

indigenous [ɪnˈdɪdʒɪnəs] *adj* einheimisch

indigestion [ɪndɪˈdʒestʃən] *n* Verdauungsstörung *f*

indignant [ɪnˈdɪɡnənt] *adj*: **to be ~ about sth** über etw *acc* empört sein

indignation [ɪndɪɡˈneɪʃən] *n* Entrüstung *f*

indignity [ɪnˈdɪɡnɪtɪ] *n* Demütigung *f*

indirect [ɪndɪˈrekt] *adj* indirekt

indiscreet [ɪndɪsˈkriːt] *adj* (*insensitive*) taktlos; (*telling secrets*) indiskret; **indiscretion** [ɪndɪsˈkreʃən] *n* Taktlosigkeit *f*; Indiskretion *f*

indiscriminate [ɪndɪsˈkrɪmɪnət] *adj* wahllos; kritiklos

indispensable [ɪndɪsˈpensəbl] *adj* unentbehrlich

indisposed [ɪndɪsˈpəuzd] *adj* unpässlich

indisputable [ɪndɪsˈpjuːtəbl] *adj* unbestreitbar; (*evidence*) unanfechtbar

indistinct [ɪndɪsˈtɪŋkt] *adj* undeutlich

individual [ɪndɪˈvɪdjuəl] *n* Individuum *nt* ♦ *adj* individuell; (*case*) Einzel-; (*of, for one person*) eigen, individuell; (*characteristic*) eigentümlich; **~ly** *adv* einzeln, individuell

indivisible [ɪndɪˈvɪzbl] *adj* unteilbar

indoctrinate [ɪnˈdɒktrɪneɪt] *vt* indoktrinieren

Indonesia [ɪndəˈniːzɪə] *n* Indonesien *nt*

indoor [ˈɪndɔː] *adj* Haus-; Zimmer-; Innen-; (*SPORT*) Hallen-; **~s** [ɪnˈdɔːz] *adv* drinnen, im Haus

induce [ɪnˈdjuːs] *vt* dazu bewegen; (*reaction*) herbeiführen

induction course [ɪnˈdʌkʃən-] (*BRIT*) *n* Einführungskurs *m*

indulge [ɪnˈdʌldʒ] *vt* (*give way*) nachgeben +*dat*; (*gratify*) frönen +*dat* ♦ *vi*: **to ~ (in)** frönen (+*dat*); **~nce** *n* Nachsicht *f*; (*enjoyment*) Genuss *m*; **~nt** *adj* nachsichtig; (*pej*) nachgiebig

industrial [ɪnˈdʌstrɪəl] *adj* Industrie-, industriell; (*dispute, injury*) Arbeits-; ~ **action** *n* Arbeitskampfmaßnahmen *pl*; ~ **estate** (*BRIT*) *n* Industriegebiet *nt*; **~ist** *n* Industrielle(r) *mf*; **~ize** *vt* industrialisieren; ~ **park** (*US*) *n* Industriegebiet *nt*

industrious [ɪnˈdʌstrɪəs] *adj* fleißig

industry [ˈɪndəstrɪ] *n* Industrie *f*; (*diligence*) Fleiß *m*

inebriated [ɪˈniːbrɪeɪtɪd] *adj* betrunken

inedible [ɪnˈedɪbl] *adj* ungenießbar

ineffective [ɪnɪˈfektɪv] *adj* unwirksam; (*person*) untauglich

ineffectual [ɪnɪˈfektjuəl] *adj* = **ineffective**

inefficiency [ɪnɪˈfɪʃənsɪ] *n* Ineffizienz *f*

inefficient [ɪnɪˈfɪʃənt] *adj* ineffizient; (*ineffective*) unwirksam

inept [ɪˈnept] *adj* (*remark*) unpassend; (*person*) ungeeignet

inequality [ɪnɪˈkwɒlɪtɪ] *n* Ungleichheit *f*

inert [ɪˈnəːt] *adj* träge; (*CHEM*) inaktiv;

(*motionless*) unbeweglich

inescapable [ɪnɪˈskeɪpəbl] *adj* unvermeidbar

inevitable [ɪnˈevɪtəbl] *adj* unvermeidlich; **inevitably** *adv* zwangsläufig

inexcusable [ɪnɪksˈkjuːzəbl] *adj* unverzeihlich

inexhaustible [ɪnɪgˈzɔːstɪbl] *adj* unerschöpflich

inexpensive [ɪnɪkˈspensɪv] *adj* preiswert

inexperience [ɪnɪkˈspɪərɪəns] *n* Unerfahrenheit *f*; **~d** *adj* unerfahren

inexplicable [ɪnɪkˈsplɪkəbl] *adj* unerklärlich

inextricably [ɪnɪkˈstrɪkəbl] *adv* untrennbar

infallible [ɪnˈfælɪbl] *adj* unfehlbar

infamous [ˈɪnfəməs] *adj* (*deed*) schändlich; (*person*) niederträchtig

infancy [ˈɪnfənsɪ] *n* frühe Kindheit *f*; (*fig*) Anfangsstadium *nt*

infant [ˈɪnfənt] *n* kleine(s) Kind *nt*, Säugling *m*; **~ile** [-aɪl] *adj* kindisch, infantil; **~ school** (*BRIT*) *n* Vorschule *f*

infatuated [ɪnˈfætjueɪtɪd] *adj* vernarrt; **to become ~ with** sich vernarren in +*acc*; **infatuation** [ɪnfætjuˈeɪʃən] *n*: **infatuation (with)** Vernarrtheit *f* (in +*acc*)

infect [ɪnˈfekt] *vt* anstecken (*also fig*); **~ed with** (*illness*) infiziert mit; **~ion** [ɪnˈfekʃən] *n* Infektion *f*; **~ious** [ɪnˈfekʃəs] *adj* ansteckend

infer [ɪnˈfɜːr] *vt* schließen

inferior [ɪnˈfɪərɪər] *adj* (*rank*) untergeordnet; (*quality*) minderwertig ♦ *n* Untergebene(r) *m*; **~ity** [ɪnfɪərɪˈɔrətɪ] *n* Minderwertigkeit *f*; (*in rank*) untergeordnete Stellung *f*; **~ity complex** *n* Minderwertigkeitskomplex *m*

infernal [ɪnˈfɜːnl] *adj* höllisch

infertile [ɪnˈfɜːtaɪl] *adj* unfruchtbar; **infertility** [ɪnfəˈtɪlɪtɪ] *n* Unfruchtbarkeit *f*

infested [ɪnˈfestɪd] *adj*: **to be ~ with** wimmeln von

infidelity [ɪnfɪˈdelɪtɪ] *n* Untreue *f*

infighting [ˈɪnfaɪtɪŋ] *n* Nahkampf *m*

infiltrate [ˈɪnfɪltreɪt] *vt* infiltrieren; (*spies*) einschleusen ♦ *vi* (*MIL, liquid*) einsickern; (*POL*): **to ~ (into)** unterwandern (+*acc*)

infinite [ˈɪnfɪnɪt] *adj* unendlich

infinitive [ɪnˈfɪnɪtɪv] *n* Infinitiv *m*

infinity [ɪnˈfɪnɪtɪ] *n* Unendlichkeit *f*

infirm [ɪnˈfɜːm] *adj* gebrechlich; **~ary** *n* Krankenhaus *nt*

inflamed [ɪnˈfleɪmd] *adj* entzündet

inflammable [ɪnˈflæməbl] (*BRIT*) *adj* feuergefährlich

inflammation [ɪnfləˈmeɪʃən] *n* Entzündung *f*

inflatable [ɪnˈfleɪtəbl] *adj* aufblasbar

inflate [ɪnˈfleɪt] *vt* aufblasen; (*tyre*) aufpumpen; (*prices*) hoch treiben; **inflation** [ɪnˈfleɪʃən] *n* Inflation *f*; **inflationary** [ɪnˈfleɪʃənərɪ] *adj* (*increase*) inflationistisch; (*situation*) inflationär

inflexible [ɪnˈfleksɪbl] *adj* (*person*) nicht flexibel; (*opinion*) starr; (*thing*) unbiegsam

inflict [ɪnˈflɪkt] *vt*: **to ~ sth on sb** jdm etw zufügen; (*wound*) jdm etw beibringen

influence [ˈɪnfluəns] *n* Einfluss *m* ♦ *vt* beeinflussen

influential [ɪnfluˈenʃl] *adj* einflussreich

influenza [ɪnfluˈenzə] *n* Grippe *f*

influx [ˈɪnflʌks] *n* (*of people*) Zustrom *m*; (*of ideas*) Eindringen *nt*

infomercial [ˈɪnfəuməːʃl] *n* Werbeinformationssendung *f*

inform [ɪnˈfɔːm] *vt* informieren ♦ *vi*: **to ~ on sb** jdn denunzieren; **to keep sb ~ed** jdn auf dem Laufenden halten

informal [ɪnˈfɔːml] *adj* zwanglos; **~ity** [ɪnfɔːˈmælɪtɪ] *n* Ungezwungenheit *f*

informant [ɪnˈfɔːmənt] *n* Informant(in) *m(f)*

information [ɪnfəˈmeɪʃən] *n* Auskunft *f*, Information *f*; **a piece of ~** eine Auskunft, eine Information; **~ desk** *n* Auskunftsschalter *m*; **~ office** *n* Informationsbüro *nt*

informative [ɪnˈfɔːmətɪv] *adj* informativ; (*person*) mitteilsam

informer [ɪnˈfɔːmər] *n* Denunziant(in) *m(f)*

infra-red [ɪnfrəˈred] *adj* infrarot

infrequent [ɪnˈfriːkwənt] *adj* selten

infringe [ɪnˈfrɪndʒ] *vt* (*law*) verstoßen gegen; **~ upon** *vt* verletzen; **~ment** *n* Verstoß *m*, Verletzung *f*

infuriating [ɪnˈfjuərɪeɪtɪŋ] *adj* ärgerlich

ingenuity [ɪndʒɪˈnjuːɪtɪ] *n* Genialität *f*

ingenuous [ɪnˈdʒenjuəs] *adj* aufrichtig; (*naive*) naiv

ingot ['ɪŋgət] *n* Barren *m*

ingrained [ɪn'greɪnd] *adj* tief sitzend

ingratiate [ɪn'greɪʃɪeɪt] *vt*: **to ~ o.s. with sb** sich bei jdm einschmeicheln

ingratitude [ɪn'grætɪtjuːd] *n* Undankbarkeit *f*

ingredient [ɪn'griːdɪənt] *n* Bestandteil *m*; (*COOK*) Zutat *f*

inhabit [ɪn'hæbɪt] *vt* bewohnen; **~ant** *n* Bewohner(in) *m(f)*; (*of island, town*) Einwohner(in) *m(f)*

inhale [ɪn'heɪl] *vt* einatmen; (*MED, cigarettes*) inhalieren

inherent [ɪn'hɪərənt] *adj*: **~ (in)** innewohnend (+*dat*)

inherit [ɪn'herɪt] *vt* erben; **~ance** *n* Erbe *nt*, Erbschaft *f*

inhibit [ɪn'hɪbɪt] *vt* hemmen; **to ~ sb from doing sth** jdn daran hindern, etw zu tun; **~ion** [ɪnhɪ'bɪʃən] *n* Hemmung *f*

inhospitable [ɪnhɔs'pɪtəbl] *adj* (*person*) ungastlich; (*country*) unwirtlich

inhuman [ɪn'hjuːmən] *adj* unmenschlich

initial [ɪ'nɪʃl] *adj* anfänglich, Anfangs- ♦ *n* Initiale *f* ♦ *vt* abzeichnen; (*POL*) paraphieren; **~ly** *adv* anfangs

initiate [ɪ'nɪʃɪeɪt] *vt* einführen; (*negotiations*) einleiten; **to ~ proceedings against sb** (*JUR*) gerichtliche Schritte gegen jdn einleiten; **initiation** [ɪnɪʃɪ'eɪʃən] *n* Einführung *f*; Einleitung *f*

initiative [ɪ'nɪʃətɪv] *n* Initiative *f*

inject [ɪn'dʒekt] *vt* einspritzen; (*fig*) einflößen; **~ion** [ɪn'dʒekʃən] *n* Spritze *f*

injunction [ɪn'dʒʌŋkʃən] *n* Verfügung *f*

injure ['ɪndʒəʳ] *vt* verletzen; **~d** *adj* (*person, arm*) verletzt; **injury** ['ɪndʒərɪ] *n* Verletzung *f*; **to play injury time** (*SPORT*) nachspielen

injustice [ɪn'dʒʌstɪs] *n* Ungerechtigkeit *f*

ink [ɪŋk] *n* Tinte *f*

inkling ['ɪŋklɪŋ] *n* (dunkle) Ahnung *f*

inlaid ['ɪnleɪd] *adj* eingelegt, Einlege-

inland [*adj* 'ɪnlənd, *adv* ɪn'lænd] *adj* Binnen-; (*domestic*) Inlands- ♦ *adv* landeinwärts; **~ revenue** (*BRIT*) *n* Fiskus *m*

in-laws ['ɪnlɔːz] *npl* (*parents-in-law*) Schwiegereltern *pl*; (*others*) angeheiratete Verwandte *pl*

inlet ['ɪnlet] *n* Einlass *m*; (*bay*) kleine Bucht *f*

inmate ['ɪnmeɪt] *n* Insasse *m*

inn [ɪn] *n* Gasthaus *nt*, Wirtshaus *nt*

innate [ɪ'neɪt] *adj* angeboren

inner ['ɪnəʳ] *adj* inner, Innen-; (*fig*) verborgen; **~ city** *n* Innenstadt *f*; **~ tube** *n* (*of tyre*) Schlauch *m*

innings ['ɪnɪŋz] *n* (*CRICKET*) Innenrunde *f*

innocence ['ɪnəsns] *n* Unschuld *f*; (*ignorance*) Unkenntnis *f*

innocent ['ɪnəsnt] *adj* unschuldig

innocuous [ɪ'nɔkjuəs] *adj* harmlos

innovation [ɪnəʊ'veɪʃən] *n* Neuerung *f*

innuendo [ɪnju'endəʊ] *n* (versteckte) Anspielung *f*

innumerable [ɪ'njuːmrəbl] *adj* unzählig

inoculation [ɪnɔkju'leɪʃən] *n* Impfung *f*

inopportune [ɪn'ɔpətjuːn] *adj* (*remark*) unangebracht; (*visit*) ungelegen

inordinately [ɪ'nɔːdɪnətlɪ] *adv* unmäßig

inpatient ['ɪnpeɪʃənt] *n* stationäre(r) Patient *m*/stationäre Patientin *f*

input ['ɪnput] *n* (*COMPUT*) Eingabe *f*; (*power ~*) Energiezufuhr *f*; (*of energy, work*) Aufwand *m*

inquest ['ɪnkwest] *n* gerichtliche Untersuchung *f*

inquire [ɪn'kwaɪəʳ] *vi* sich erkundigen ♦ *vt* (*price*) sich erkundigen nach; **~ into** *vt* untersuchen; **inquiry** [ɪn'kwaɪərɪ] *n* (*question*) Erkundigung *f*; (*investigation*) Untersuchung *f*; **inquiries** Auskunft *f*; **inquiry office** (*BRIT*) *n* Auskunft(sbüro *nt*) *f*

inquisitive [ɪn'kwɪzɪtɪv] *adj* neugierig

ins. *abbr* = **inches**

insane [ɪn'seɪn] *adj* wahnsinnig; (*MED*) geisteskrank; **insanity** [ɪn'sænɪtɪ] *n* Wahnsinn *m*

insatiable [ɪn'seɪʃəbl] *adj* unersättlich

inscribe [ɪn'skraɪb] *vt* eingravieren; **inscription** [ɪn'skrɪpʃən] *n* (*on stone*) Inschrift *f*; (*in book*) Widmung *f*

insect ['ɪnsekt] *n* Insekt *nt*; **~icide** [ɪn'sektɪsaɪd] *n* Insektenvertilgungsmittel *nt*; **~ repellent** *n* Insektenbekämpfungsmittel *nt*

insecure [ɪnsɪ'kjuəʳ] *adj* (*person*) unsicher;

(*thing*) nicht fest *or* sicher; **insecurity** [ɪnsɪˈkjʊərɪtɪ] *n* Unsicherheit *f*

insemination [ɪnsemɪˈneɪʃən] *n*: **artificial ~** künstliche Befruchtung *f*

insensible [ɪnˈsensɪbl] *adj* (*unconscious*) bewusstlos

insensitive [ɪnˈsensɪtɪv] *adj* (*to pain*) unempfindlich; (*unfeeling*) gefühllos

inseparable [ɪnˈseprəbl] *adj* (*people*) unzertrennlich; (*word*) untrennbar

insert [*vb* ɪnˈsɜːt, *n* ˈɪnsɜːt] *vt* einfügen; (*coin*) einwerfen; (*stick into*) hineinstecken; (*advertisement*) aufgeben ♦ *n* (*in book*) Einlage *f*; (*in magazine*) Beilage *f*; **~ion** [ɪnˈsɜːʃən] *n* Einfügung *f*; (*PRESS*) Inserat *nt*

in-service [ˈɪnˈsɜːvɪs] *adj* (*training*) berufsbegleitend

inshore [ˈɪnˈʃɔːʳ] *adj* Küsten- ♦ *adv* an der Küste

inside [ˈɪnˈsaɪd] *n* Innenseite *f*, Innere(s) *nt* ♦ *adj* innere(r, s), Innen- ♦ *adv* (*place*) innen; (*direction*) nach innen, hinein ♦ *prep* (*place*) in +*dat*; (*direction*) in +*acc* ... hinein; (*time*) innerhalb +*gen*; **~s** *npl* (*inf*) Eingeweide *nt*; **~ 10 minutes** unter 10 Minuten; **~ information** *n* interne Informationen *pl*; **~ lane** *n* (*AUT: in Britain*) linke Spur; **~ out** *adv* linksherum; (*know*) in- und auswendig

insider dealing, insider trading [ɪnˈsaɪdəʳ-] *n* (*STOCK EXCHANGE*) Insiderhandel *m*

insidious [ɪnˈsɪdɪəs] *adj* heimtückisch

insight [ˈɪnsaɪt] *n* Einsicht *f*; **~ into** Einblick *m* in +*acc*

insignificant [ɪnsɪgˈnɪfɪknt] *adj* unbedeutend

insincere [ɪnsɪnˈsɪəʳ] *adj* unaufrichtig

insinuate [ɪnˈsɪnjʊeɪt] *vt* (*hint*) andeuten

insipid [ɪnˈsɪpɪd] *adj* fad(e)

insist [ɪnˈsɪst] *vi*: **to ~ on** bestehen (auf +*acc*); **~ence** *n* Bestehen *nt*; **~ent** *adj* hartnäckig; (*urgent*) dringend

insole [ˈɪnsəʊl] *n* Einlegesohle *f*

insolence [ˈɪnsələns] *n* Frechheit *f*

insolent [ˈɪnsələnt] *adj* frech

insoluble [ɪnˈsɔljʊbl] *adj* unlösbar; (*CHEM*)

unlöslich

insolvent [ɪnˈsɔlvənt] *adj* zahlungsunfähig

insomnia [ɪnˈsɔmnɪə] *n* Schlaflosigkeit *f*

inspect [ɪnˈspekt] *vt* prüfen; (*officially*) inspizieren; **~ion** [ɪnˈspekʃən] *n* Inspektion *f*; **~or** *n* (*official*) Inspektor *m*; (*police*) Polizeikommissar *m*; (*BRIT: on buses, trains*) Kontrolleur *m*

inspiration [ɪnspəˈreɪʃən] *n* Inspiration *f*

inspire [ɪnˈspaɪəʳ] *vt* (*person*) inspirieren; **to ~ sth in sb** (*respect*) jdm etw einflößen; (*hope*) etw in jdm wecken

instability [ɪnstəˈbɪlɪtɪ] *n* Unbeständigkeit *f*, Labilität *f*

install [ɪnˈstɔːl] *vt* (*put in*) installieren; (*telephone*) anschließen; (*establish*) einsetzen; **~ation** [ɪnstəˈleɪʃən] *n* (*of person*) (Amts)einsetzung *f*; (*of machinery*) Installierung *f*; (*machines etc*) Anlage *f*

instalment [ɪnˈstɔːlmənt] (*US* **installment**) *n* Rate *f*; (*of story*) Fortsetzung *f*; **to pay in ~s** in Raten zahlen

instance [ˈɪnstəns] *n* Fall *m*; (*example*) Beispiel *nt*; **for ~** zum Beispiel; **in the first ~** zunächst

instant [ˈɪnstənt] *n* Augenblick *m* ♦ *adj* augenblicklich, sofortig; **~aneous** [ɪnstənˈteɪnɪəs] *adj* unmittelbar; **~ coffee** *n* Pulverkaffee *m*; **~ly** *adv* sofort

instead [ɪnˈsted] *adv* stattdessen; **~ of** *prep* anstatt +*gen*

instep [ˈɪnstep] *n* Spann *m*; (*of shoe*) Blatt *nt*

instil [ɪnˈstɪl] *vt* (*fig*): **to ~ sth in sb** jdm etw beibringen

instinct [ˈɪnstɪŋkt] *n* Instinkt *m*; **~ive** [ɪnˈstɪŋktɪv] *adj* instinktiv

institute [ˈɪnstɪtjuːt] *n* Institut *nt* ♦ *vt* einführen; (*search*) einleiten

institution [ɪnstɪˈtjuːʃən] *n* Institution *f*; (*home*) Anstalt *f*

instruct [ɪnˈstrʌkt] *vt* anweisen; (*officially*) instruieren; **~ion** [ɪnˈstrʌkʃən] *n* Unterricht *m*; **~ions** *npl* (*orders*) Anweisungen *pl*; (*for use*) Gebrauchsanweisung *f*; **~or** *n* Lehrer *m*

instrument [ˈɪnstrumənt] *n* Instrument *nt*; **~al** [ɪnstrʊˈmentl] *adj* (*MUS*) Instrumental-;

(*helpful*): **~al (in)** behilflich (bei); **~ panel** *n* Armaturenbrett *nt*

insubordinate [ɪnsəˈbɔːdənɪt] *adj* aufsässig, widersetzlich

insufferable [ɪnˈsʌfrəbl] *adj* unerträglich

insufficient [ɪnsəˈfɪʃənt] *adj* ungenügend

insular [ˈɪnsjuləʳ] *adj* (*fig*) engstirnig

insulate [ˈɪnsjuleɪt] *vt* (*ELEC*) isolieren; (*fig*): **to ~ (from)** abschirmen (vor +*dat*); **insulating tape** *n* Isolierband *nt*; **insulation** [ɪnsjuˈleɪʃən] *n* Isolierung *f*

insulin [ˈɪnsjulɪn] *n* Insulin *nt*

insult [*n* ˈɪnsʌlt, *vb* ɪnˈsʌlt] *n* Beleidigung *f* ♦ *vt* beleidigen

insurance [ɪnˈʃuərəns] *n* Versicherung *f*; **fire/life ~** Feuer-/Lebensversicherung; **~ agent** *n* Versicherungsvertreter *m*; **~ policy** *n* Versicherungspolice *f*

insure [ɪnˈʃuəʳ] *vt* versichern

intact [ɪnˈtækt] *adj* unversehrt

intake [ˈɪnteɪk] *n* (*place*) Einlassöffnung *f*; (*act*) Aufnahme *f*; (*BRIT: SCH*): **an ~ of 200 a year** ein Neuzugang von 200 im Jahr

intangible [ɪnˈtændʒɪbl] *adj* nicht greifbar

integral [ˈɪntɪɡrəl] *adj* (*essential*) wesentlich; (*complete*) vollständig; (*MATH*) Integral-

integrate [ˈɪntɪɡreɪt] *vt* integrieren ♦ *vi* sich integrieren

integrity [ɪnˈtɛɡrɪtɪ] *n* (*honesty*) Redlichkeit *f*, Integrität *f*

intellect [ˈɪntəlɛkt] *n* Intellekt *m*; **~ual** [ɪntəˈlɛktjuəl] *adj* geistig, intellektuell ♦ *n* Intellektuelle(r) *mf*

intelligence [ɪnˈtɛlɪdʒəns] *n* (*understanding*) Intelligenz *f*; (*news*) Information *f*; (*MIL*) Geheimdienst *m*; **~ service** *n* Nachrichtendienst *m*, Geheimdienst *m*

intelligent [ɪnˈtɛlɪdʒənt] *adj* intelligent; **~ly** *adv* klug; (*write, speak*) verständlich

intelligentsia [ɪntɛlɪˈdʒɛntsɪə] *n* Intelligenz *f*

intelligible [ɪnˈtɛlɪdʒɪbl] *adj* verständlich

intend [ɪnˈtɛnd] *vt* beabsichtigen; **that was ~ed for you** das war für dich gedacht

intense [ɪnˈtɛns] *adj* stark, intensiv; (*person*) ernsthaft; **~ly** *adv* äußerst; (*study*) intensiv

intensify [ɪnˈtɛnsɪfaɪ] *vt* verstärken, intensivieren

intensity [ɪnˈtɛnsɪtɪ] *n* Intensität *f*

intensive [ɪnˈtɛnsɪv] *adj* intensiv; **~ care unit** *n* Intensivstation *f*

intent [ɪnˈtɛnt] *n* Absicht *f* ♦ *adj*: **to be ~ on doing sth** fest entschlossen sein, etw zu tun; **to all ~s and purposes** praktisch

intention [ɪnˈtɛnʃən] *n* Absicht *f*; **~al** *adj* absichtlich

intently [ɪnˈtɛntlɪ] *adv* konzentriert

interact [ɪntərˈækt] *vi* aufeinander einwirken; **~ion** [ɪntərˈækʃən] *n* Wechselwirkung *f*; **~ive** *adj* (*COMPUT*) interaktiv

intercept [ɪntəˈsɛpt] *vt* abfangen

interchange [*n* ˈɪntətʃeɪndʒ, *vb* ɪntəˈtʃeɪndʒ] *n* (*exchange*) Austausch *m*; (*on roads*) Verkehrskreuz *nt* ♦ *vt* austauschen; **~able** [ɪntəˈtʃeɪndʒəbl] *adj* austauschbar

intercom [ˈɪntəkɔm] *n* (Gegen)sprechanlage *f*

intercourse [ˈɪntəkɔːs] *n* (*exchange*) Beziehungen *pl*; (*sexual*) Geschlechtsverkehr *m*

interest [ˈɪntrɪst] *n* Interesse *nt*; (*FIN*) Zinsen *pl*; (*COMM: share*) Anteil *m*; (*group*) Interessengruppe *f* ♦ *vt* interessieren; **~ed** *adj* (*having claims*) beteiligt; (*attentive*) interessiert; **to be ~ed in** sich interessieren für; **~ing** *adj* interessant; **~ rate** *n* Zinssatz *m*

interface [ˈɪntəfeɪs] *n* (*COMPUT*) Schnittstelle *f*, Interface *nt*

interfere [ɪntəˈfɪəʳ] *vi*: **to ~ (with)** (*meddle*) sich einmischen (in +*acc*); (*disrupt*) stören +*acc*; **~nce** [ɪntəˈfɪərəns] *n* Einmischung *f*; (*TV*) Störung *f*

interim [ˈɪntərɪm] *n*: **in the ~** inzwischen

interior [ɪnˈtɪərɪəʳ] *n* Innere(s) *nt* ♦ *adj* innere(r, s), Innen-; **~ designer** *n* Innenarchitekt(in) *m(f)*

interjection [ɪntəˈdʒɛkʃən] *n* Ausruf *m*

interlock [ɪntəˈlɔk] *vi* ineinander greifen

interlude [ˈɪntəluːd] *n* Pause *f*

intermediary [ɪntəˈmiːdɪərɪ] *n* Vermittler *m*

intermediate [ɪntəˈmiːdɪət] *adj* Zwischen-, Mittel-

interminable [ɪnˈtɜːmɪnəbl] *adj* endlos

intermission [ɪntəˈmɪʃən] *n* Pause *f*

intermittent [ɪntə'mɪtnt] *adj* periodisch, stoßweise

intern [*vb* ɪn'tɜːn, *n* 'ɪntɜːn] *vt* internieren ♦ *n* (*US*) Assistenzarzt *m*/-ärztin *f*

internal [ɪn'tɜːnl] *adj* (*inside*) innere(r, s); (*domestic*) Inlands-; **~ly** *adv* innen; (*MED*) innerlich; **"not to be taken ~ly"** „nur zur äußerlichen Anwendung"; **Internal Revenue Service** (*US*) *n* Finanzamt *nt*

international [ɪntə'næʃənl] *adj* international ♦ *n* (*SPORT*) Nationalspieler(in) *m(f)*; (: *match*) internationale(s) Spiel *nt*

Internet ['ɪntənet] *n*: **the ~** das Internet; **~ café** *n* Internet-Café *nt*

interplay ['ɪntəpleɪ] *n* Wechselspiel *nt*

interpret [ɪn'tɜːprɪt] *vt* (*explain*) auslegen, interpretieren; (*translate*) dolmetschen; **~er** *n* Dolmetscher(in) *m(f)*

interrelated [ɪntərɪ'leɪtɪd] *adj* untereinander zusammenhängend

interrogate [ɪn'terəɡeɪt] *vt* verhören; **interrogation** [ɪnterəʊ'ɡeɪʃən] *n* Verhör *nt*

interrupt [ɪntə'rʌpt] *vt* unterbrechen; **~ion** [ɪntə'rʌpʃən] *n* Unterbrechung *f*

intersect [ɪntə'sekt] *vt* (*durch*)schneiden ♦ *vi* sich schneiden; **~ion** [ɪntə'sekʃən] *n* (*of roads*) Kreuzung *f*; (*of lines*) Schnittpunkt *m*

intersperse [ɪntə'spɜːs] *vt*: **to ~ sth with sth** etw mit etw durchsetzen

intertwine [ɪntə'twaɪn] *vt* verflechten ♦ *vi* sich verflechten

interval ['ɪntəvl] *n* Abstand *m*; (*BRIT: THEAT, SPORT*) Pause *f*; **at ~s** in Abständen

intervene [ɪntə'viːn] *vi* dazwischenliegen; (*act*): **to ~ (in)** einschreiten (gegen); **intervention** [ɪntə'venʃən] *n* Eingreifen *nt*, Intervention *f*

interview ['ɪntəvjuː] *n* (*PRESS etc*) Interview *nt*; (*for job*) Vorstellungsgespräch *nt* ♦ *vt* interviewen; **~er** *n* Interviewer *m*

intestine [ɪn'testɪn] *n*: **large/small ~** Dick-/Dünndarm *m*

intimacy ['ɪntɪməsɪ] *n* Intimität *f*

intimate [*adj* 'ɪntɪmət, *vb* 'ɪntɪmeɪt] *adj* (*inmost*) innerste(r, s); (*knowledge*) eingehend; (*familiar*) vertraut; (*friends*) eng ♦ *vt* andeuten

intimidate [ɪn'tɪmɪdeɪt] *vt* einschüchtern

into ['ɪntu] *prep* (*motion*) in +*acc* ... hinein; **5 ~ 25** 25 durch 5

intolerable [ɪn'tɔlərəbl] *adj* unerträglich

intolerant [ɪn'tɔlərnt] *adj*: **~ of** unduldsam gegen(über)

intoxicate [ɪn'tɔksɪkeɪt] *vt* berauschen; **~d** *adj* betrunken; **intoxication** [ɪntɔksɪ'keɪʃən] *n* Rausch *m*

intractable [ɪn'træktəbl] *adj* schwer zu handhaben; (*problem*) schwer lösbar

intranet ['ɪntrənet] *n* Intranet *nt*

intransitive [ɪn'trænsɪtɪv] *adj* intransitiv

intravenous [ɪntrə'viːnəs] *adj* intravenös

in-tray ['ɪntreɪ] *n* Eingangskorb *m*

intrepid [ɪn'trepɪd] *adj* unerschrocken

intricate ['ɪntrɪkət] *adj* kompliziert

intrigue [ɪn'triːɡ] *n* Intrige *f* ♦ *vt* faszinieren ♦ *vi* intrigieren

intrinsic [ɪn'trɪnsɪk] *adj* innere(r, s); (*difference*) wesentlich

introduce [ɪntrə'djuːs] *vt* (*person*) vorstellen; (*sth new*) einführen; (*subject*) anschneiden; **to ~ sb to sb** jdm jdn vorstellen; **to ~ sb to sth** jdn in etw *acc* einführen; **introduction** [ɪntrə'dʌkʃən] *n* Einführung *f*; (*to book*) Einleitung *f*; **introductory** [ɪntrə'dʌktərɪ] *adj* Einführungs-, Vor-

introspective [ɪntrəʊ'spektɪv] *adj* nach innen gekehrt

introvert ['ɪntrəʊvɜːt] *n* Introvertierte(r) *mf* ♦ *adj* introvertiert

intrude [ɪn'truːd] *vi*: **to ~ (on sb/sth)** (jdn/etw) stören; **~r** *n* Eindringling *m*

intrusion [ɪn'truːʒən] *n* Störung *f*

intrusive [ɪn'truːsɪv] *adj* aufdringlich

intuition [ɪntjuː'ɪʃən] *n* Intuition *f*

inundate ['ɪnʌndeɪt] *vt* überschwemmen

invade [ɪn'veɪd] *vt* einfallen in +*acc*; **~r** *n* Eindringling *m*

invalid¹ ['ɪnvəlɪd] *n* (*disabled*) Invalide *m* ♦ *adj* (*ill*) krank; (*disabled*) invalide

invalid² [ɪn'vælɪd] *adj* (*not valid*) ungültig

invaluable [ɪn'væljuəbl] *adj* unschätzbar

invariable [ɪn'veərɪəbl] *adj* unveränderlich; **invariably** *adv* ausnahmslos

invent [ɪn'vent] *vt* erfinden; **~ion** [ɪn'venʃən]

n Erfindung *f*; **~ive** *adj* erfinderisch; **~or** *n* Erfinder *m*

inventory ['ɪnvəntrɪ] *n* Inventar *nt*

inverse [ɪn'vɜːs] *n* Umkehrung *f* ♦ *adj* umgekehrt

invert [ɪn'vɜːt] *vt* umdrehen; **~ed commas** (*BRIT*) *npl* Anführungsstriche *pl*

invest [ɪn'vest] *vt* investieren

investigate [ɪn'vestɪgeɪt] *vt* untersuchen; **investigation** [ɪnvestɪ'geɪʃən] *n* Untersuchung *f*; **investigator** [ɪn'vestɪgeɪtə'] *n* Untersuchungsbeamte(r) *m*

investiture [ɪn'vestɪtʃə'] *n* Amtseinsetzung *f*

investment [ɪn'vestmənt] *n* Investition *f*

investor [ɪn'vestə'] *n* (Geld)anleger *m*

invigilate [ɪn'vɪdʒɪleɪt] *vi* (*in exam*) Aufsicht führen ♦ *vt* Aufsicht führen bei

invigorating [ɪn'vɪgəreɪtɪŋ] *adj* stärkend

invincible [ɪn'vɪnsɪbl] *adj* unbesiegbar

invisible [ɪn'vɪzɪbl] *adj* unsichtbar

invitation [ɪnvɪ'teɪʃən] *n* Einladung *f*

invite [ɪn'vaɪt] *vt* einladen

invoice ['ɪnvɔɪs] *n* Rechnung *f* ♦ *vt* (*goods*): **to ~ sb for sth** jdm etw *acc* in Rechnung stellen

invoke [ɪn'vəuk] *vt* anrufen

involuntary [ɪn'vɔləntrɪ] *adj* unabsichtlich

involve [ɪn'vɔlv] *vt* (*entangle*) verwickeln; (*entail*) mit sich bringen; **~d** *adj* verwickelt; **~ment** *n* Verwicklung *f*

inward ['ɪnwəd] *adj* innere(r, s); (*curve*) Innen- ♦ *adv* nach innen; **~ly** *adv* im Innern; **~s** *adv* nach innen

I/O *abbr* (*COMPUT*) (= *input/output*) I/O

iodine ['aɪəudiːn] *n* Jod *nt*

ioniser ['aɪənaɪzə'] *n* Ionisator *m*

iota [aɪ'əutə] *n* (*fig*) bisschen *nt*

IOU *n abbr* (= *I owe you*) Schuldschein *m*

IQ *n abbr* (= *intelligence quotient*) IQ *m*

IRA *n abbr* (= *Irish Republican Army*) IRA *f*

Iran [ɪ'rɑːn] *n* Iran *m*; **~ian** [ɪ'reɪnɪən] *adj* iranisch ♦ *n* Iraner(in) *m(f)*; (*LING*) Iranisch *nt*

Iraq [ɪ'rɑːk] *n* Irak *m*; **~i** *adj* irakisch ♦ *n* Iraker(in) *m(f)*

irate [aɪ'reɪt] *adj* zornig

Ireland ['aɪələnd] *n* Irland *nt*

iris ['aɪrɪs] (*pl* **~es**) *n* Iris *f*

Irish ['aɪrɪʃ] *adj* irisch ♦ *npl*: **the ~** die Iren *pl*, die Irländer *pl*; **~man** (*irreg*) *n* Ire *m*, Irländer *m*; **~ Sea** *n*: **the ~ Sea** die Irische See *f*; **~woman** (*irreg*) *n* Irin *f*, Irländerin *f*

irksome ['ɜːksəm] *adj* lästig

iron ['aɪən] *n* Eisen *nt*; (*for ~ing*) Bügeleisen *nt* ♦ *adj* eisern ♦ *vt* bügeln; **~ out** *vt* (*also fig*) ausbügeln; **Iron Curtain** *n* (*HIST*) Eiserne(r) Vorhang *m*

ironic(al) [aɪ'rɒnɪk(l)] *adj* ironisch; (*coincidence etc*) witzig

iron: **~ing** *n* Bügeln *nt*; (*laundry*) Bügelwäsche *f*; **~ing board** *n* Bügelbrett *nt*; **~monger's (shop)** *n* Eisen- und Haushaltswarenhandlung *f*

irony ['aɪrənɪ] *n* Ironie *f*

irrational [ɪ'ræʃənl] *adj* irrational

irreconcilable [ɪrekən'saɪləbl] *adj* unvereinbar

irrefutable [ɪrɪ'fjuːtəbl] *adj* unwiderlegbar

irregular [ɪ'regjulə'] *adj* unregelmäßig; (*shape*) ungleich(mäßig); (*fig*) unüblich; (*: behaviour*) ungehörig

irrelevant [ɪ'reləvənt] *adj* belanglos, irrelevant

irreparable [ɪ'reprəbl] *adj* nicht wieder gutzumachen

irreplaceable [ɪrɪ'pleɪsəbl] *adj* unersetzlich

irresistible [ɪrɪ'zɪstɪbl] *adj* unwiderstehlich

irrespective [ɪrɪ'spektɪv]: **~ of** *prep* ungeachtet +*gen*

irresponsible [ɪrɪ'spɒnsɪbl] *adj* verantwortungslos

irreverent [ɪ'revərənt] *adj* respektlos

irrevocable [ɪ'revəkəbl] *adj* unwiderrufbar

irrigate ['ɪrɪgeɪt] *vt* bewässern

irritable ['ɪrɪtəbl] *adj* reizbar

irritate ['ɪrɪteɪt] *vt* irritieren, reizen (*also MED*); **irritating** *adj* ärgerlich, irritierend; **he is irritating** er kann einem auf die Nerven gehen; **irritation** [ɪrɪ'teɪʃən] *n* (*anger*) Ärger *m*; (*MED*) Reizung *f*

IRS *n abbr* = **Internal Revenue Service**

is [ɪz] *vb see* **be**

Islam ['ɪzlɑːm] *n* Islam *m*; **~ic** [ɪz'læmɪk] *adj* islamisch

island ['aɪlənd] n Insel f; **~er** n Inselbewohner(in) m(f)

isle [aɪl] n (kleine) Insel f

isn't ['ɪznt] = **is not**

isolate ['aɪsəleɪt] vt isolieren; **~d** adj isoliert; (case) Einzel-; **isolation** [aɪsə'leɪʃən] n Isolierung f

ISP n abbr (= Internet Service Provider) Internet-Anbieter m

Israel ['ɪzreɪl] n Israel nt; **~i** [ɪz'reɪlɪ] adj israelisch ♦ n Israeli mf

issue ['ɪʃuː] n (matter) Frage f; (outcome) Ausgang m; (of newspaper, shares) Ausgabe f; (offspring) Nachkommenschaft f ♦ vt ausgeben; (warrant) erlassen; (documents) ausstellen; (orders) erteilen; (books) herausgeben; (verdict) aussprechen; **to be at ~** zur Debatte stehen; **to take ~ with sb over sth** jdm in etw dat widersprechen

---

KEYWORD

it [ɪt] pron **1** (specific: subject) er/sie/es; (: direct object) ihn/sie/es; (: indirect object) ihm/ihr/ihm; **about/from/of/in/of it** darüber/davon/darin/davon
2 (impers) es; **it's raining** es regnet; **it's Friday tomorrow** morgen ist Freitag; **who is it? – it's me** wer ist da? – ich (bin's)

Italian [ɪ'tæljən] adj italienisch ♦ n Italiener(in) m(f); (LING) Italienisch nt

italic [ɪ'tælɪk] adj kursiv; **~s** npl Kursivschrift f

Italy ['ɪtəlɪ] n Italien nt

itch [ɪtʃ] n Juckreiz m; (fig) Lust f ♦ vi jucken; **to be ~ing to do sth** darauf brennen, etw zu tun; **~y** adj juckend

it'd ['ɪtd] = **it would; it had**

item ['aɪtəm] n Gegenstand m; (on list) Posten m; (in programme) Nummer f; (in agenda) (Programm)punkt m; (in newspaper) (Zeitungs)notiz f; **~ize** vt verzeichnen

itinerant [ɪ'tɪnərənt] adj umherreisend

itinerary [aɪ'tɪnərərɪ] n Reiseroute f

it'll ['ɪtl] = **it will; it shall**

its [ɪts] adj (masculine, neuter) sein; (feminine) ihr

it's [ɪts] = **it is; it has**

itself [ɪt'sɛlf] pron sich (selbst); (emphatic) selbst

ITV (BRIT) n abbr = **Independent Television**

I.U.D. n abbr (= intra-uterine device) Pessar nt

I've [aɪv] = **I have**

ivory ['aɪvərɪ] n Elfenbein nt

ivy ['aɪvɪ] n Efeu nt

J, j

jab [dʒæb] vt (hinein)stechen ♦ n Stich m, Stoß m; (inf) Spritze f

jack [dʒæk] n (AUT) (Wagen)heber m; (CARDS) Bube m; **~ up** vt aufbocken

jackal ['dʒækl] n (ZOOL) Schakal m

jackdaw ['dʒækdɔː] n Dohle f

jacket ['dʒækɪt] n Jacke f; (of book) Schutzumschlag m; (TECH) Ummantelung f; **~ potatoes** npl in der Schale gebackene Kartoffeln pl

jackknife ['dʒæknaɪf] vi (truck) sich zusammenschieben

jack plug n (ELEC) Buchsenstecker m

jackpot ['dʒækpɔt] n Haupttreffer m

jaded ['dʒeɪdɪd] adj ermattet

jagged ['dʒægɪd] adj zackig

jail [dʒeɪl] n Gefängnis nt ♦ vt einsperren; **~er** n Gefängniswärter m

jam [dʒæm] n Marmelade f; (also: **traffic ~**) (Verkehrs)stau m; (inf: trouble) Klemme f ♦ vt (wedge) einklemmen; (cram) hineinzwängen; (obstruct) blockieren ♦ vi sich verklemmen; **to ~ sth into sth** etw in etw acc hineinstopfen

Jamaica [dʒə'meɪkə] n Jamaika nt

jam jar n Marmeladenglas nt

jammed [dʒæmd] adj: **it's ~** es klemmt

jam-packed [dʒæm'pækt] adj überfüllt, proppenvoll

jangle ['dʒæŋgl] vt, vi klimpern

janitor ['dʒænɪtə*] n Hausmeister m

January ['dʒænjuərɪ] n Januar m

Japan [dʒə'pæn] n Japan nt; **~ese** [dʒæpə'niːz] adj japanisch ♦ n inv Japaner(in) m(f); (LING) Japanisch nt

jar [dʒɑː*] n Glas nt ♦ vi kreischen; (colours

etc) nicht harmonieren

jargon ['dʒɑːgən] *n* Fachsprache *f*, Jargon *m*

jaundice ['dʒɔːndɪs] *n* Gelbsucht *f*; ~**d** *adj* (*fig*) missgünstig

jaunt [dʒɔːnt] *n* Spritztour *f*

javelin ['dʒævlɪn] *n* Speer *m*

jaw [dʒɔː] *n* Kiefer *m*

jay [dʒeɪ] *n* (*ZOOL*) Eichelhäher *m*

jaywalker ['dʒeɪwɔːkəʳ] *n* unvorsichtige(r) Fußgänger *m*

jazz [dʒæz] *n* Jazz *m*; ~ **up** *vt* (*MUS*) verjazzen; (*enliven*) aufpolieren

jealous ['dʒeləs] *adj* (*envious*) missgünstig; (*husband*) eifersüchtig; ~**y** *n* Missgunst *f*; Eifersucht *f*

jeans [dʒiːnz] *npl* Jeans *pl*

Jeep [dʒiːp] ® *n* Jeep *m* ®

jeer [dʒɪəʳ] *vi*: to ~ **(at sb)** (über jdn) höhnisch lachen, (jdn) verspotten

Jehovah's Witness [dʒɪ'həʊvəz-] *n* Zeuge *m*/Zeugin *f* Jehovas

jelly ['dʒelɪ] *n* Gelee *nt*; (*dessert*) Grütze *f*; ~**fish** *n* Qualle *f*

jeopardize ['dʒepədaɪz] *vt* gefährden

jeopardy ['dʒepədɪ] *n*: to be in jeopardy in Gefahr sein

jerk [dʒəːk] *n* Ruck *m*; (*inf: idiot*) Trottel *m* ♦ *vt* ruckartig bewegen ♦ *vi* sich ruckartig bewegen

jerky ['dʒəːkɪ] *adj* (*movement*) ruckartig; (*ride*) rüttelnd

jersey ['dʒəːzɪ] *n* Pullover *m*

jest [dʒest] *n* Scherz *m* ♦ *vi* spaßen; **in ~** im Spaß

Jesus ['dʒiːzəs] *n* Jesus *m*

jet [dʒet] *n* (*stream: of water etc*) Strahl *m*; (*spout*) Düse *f*; (*AVIAT*) Düsenflugzeug *nt*; ~~**black** *adj* rabenschwarz; ~ **engine** *n* Düsenmotor *m*; ~ **lag** *n* Jetlag *m*

jettison ['dʒetɪsn] *vt* über Bord werfen

jetty ['dʒetɪ] *n* Landesteg *m*, Mole *f*

Jew [dʒuː] *n* Jude *m*

jewel ['dʒuːəl] *n* (*also fig*) Juwel *nt*; ~**ler** (*US* **jeweler**) *n* Juwelier *m*; ~**ler's (shop)** *n* Juwelier *m*; ~**lery** (*US* **jewelry**) *n* Schmuck *m*

Jewess ['dʒuːɪs] *n* Jüdin *f*

Jewish ['dʒuːɪʃ] *adj* jüdisch

jibe [dʒaɪb] *n* spöttische Bemerkung *f*

jiffy ['dʒɪfɪ] (*inf*) *n*: **in a ~** sofort

jigsaw ['dʒɪgsɔː] *n* (*also*: ~ **puzzle**) Puzzle(spiel) *nt*

jilt [dʒɪlt] *vt* den Laufpass geben +*dat*

jingle ['dʒɪŋgl] *n* (*advertisement*) Werbesong *m* ♦ *vi* klimpern; (*bells*) bimmeln ♦ *vt* klimpern mit; bimmeln lassen

jinx [dʒɪŋks] *n*: **there's a ~ on it** es ist verhext

jitters ['dʒɪtəz] (*inf*) *npl*: **to get the ~** einen Bammel kriegen

job [dʒɔb] *n* (*piece of work*) Arbeit *f*; (*position*) Stellung *f*; (*duty*) Aufgabe *f*; (*difficulty*) Mühe *f*; **it's a good ~ he ...** es ist ein Glück, dass er ...; **just the ~** genau das Richtige; **J~centre** (*BRIT*) *n* Arbeitsamt *nt*; ~**less** *adj* arbeitslos

jockey ['dʒɔkɪ] *n* Jockei *m*, Jockey *m* ♦ *vi*: to ~ **for position** sich in eine gute Position drängeln

jocular ['dʒɔkjʊləʳ] *adj* scherzhaft

jog [dʒɔg] *vt* (an)stoßen ♦ *vi* (*run*) joggen; to ~ **along** vor sich *acc* hinwursteln; (*work*) seinen Gang gehen; ~**ging** *n* Jogging *nt*

join [dʒɔɪn] *vt* (*club*) beitreten +*dat*; (*person*) sich anschließen +*dat*; (*fasten*): to ~ **(sth to sth)** (etw mit etw) verbinden ♦ *vi* (*unite*) sich vereinigen ♦ *n* Verbindungsstelle *f*, Naht *f*; ~ **in** *vt*, *vi*: to ~ **in (sth)** (bei etw) mitmachen; ~ **up** *vi* (*MIL*) zur Armee gehen

joiner ['dʒɔɪnəʳ] *n* Schreiner *m*; ~**y** *n* Schreinerei *f*

joint [dʒɔɪnt] *n* (*TECH*) Fuge *f*; (*of bones*) Gelenk *nt*; (*of meat*) Braten *m*; (*inf: place*) Lokal *nt* ♦ *adj* gemeinsam; ~ **account** *n* (*with bank etc*) gemeinsame(s) Konto *nt*; ~**ly** *adv* gemeinsam

joke [dʒəʊk] *n* Witz *m* ♦ *vi* Witze machen; **to play a ~ on sb** jdm einen Streich spielen

joker [dʒəʊkəʳ] *n* Witzbold *m*; (*CARDS*) Joker *m*

jolly ['dʒɔlɪ] *adj* lustig ♦ *adv* (*inf*) ganz schön

jolt [dʒəʊlt] *n* (*shock*) Schock *m*; (*jerk*) Stoß *m*

♦ vt (*push*) stoßen; (*shake*) durchschütteln; (*fig*) aufrütteln ♦ vi holpern

Jordan ['dʒɔːdən] n Jordanien nt

jostle ['dʒɔsl] vt anrempeln

jot [dʒɔt] n: **not one ~** kein Jota nt; **~ down** vt notieren; **~ter** (*BRIT*) n Notizblock m

journal ['dʒɜːnl] n (*diary*) Tagebuch nt; (*magazine*) Zeitschrift f; **~ism** n Journalismus m; **~ist** n Journalist(in) m(f)

journey ['dʒɜːnɪ] n Reise f

jovial ['dʒəʊvɪəl] adj jovial

joy [dʒɔɪ] n Freude f; **~ful** adj freudig; **~ous** adj freudig; **~ ride** n Schwarzfahrt f; **~rider** n Autodieb, der den Wagen nur für eine Spritztour stiehlt; **~stick** n Steuerknüppel m; (*COMPUT*) Joystick m

J.P. n abbr = **Justice of the Peace**

Jr abbr = **junior**

jubilant ['dʒuːbɪlnt] adj triumphierend

jubilee ['dʒuːbɪliː] n Jubiläum nt

judge [dʒʌdʒ] n Richter m; (*fig*) Kenner m ♦ vt (*JUR: person*) die Verhandlung führen über +acc; (*case*) verhandeln; (*assess*) beurteilen; (*estimate*) einschätzen; **~ment** n (*JUR*) Urteil nt; (*ECCL*) Gericht nt; (*ability*) Urteilsvermögen nt

judicial [dʒuː'dɪʃl] adj gerichtlich, Justiz-

judiciary [dʒuː'dɪʃɪərɪ] n Gerichtsbehörden pl; (*judges*) Richterstand m

judicious [dʒuː'dɪʃəs] adj weise

judo ['dʒuːdəu] n Judo nt

jug [dʒʌɡ] n Krug m

juggernaut ['dʒʌɡənɔːt] (*BRIT*) n (*huge truck*) Schwertransporter m

juggle ['dʒʌɡl] vt, vi jonglieren; **~r** n Jongleur m

Jugoslav etc ['juːɡəʊ'slɑːv] = **Yugoslav** etc

juice [dʒuːs] n Saft m; **juicy** ['dʒuːsɪ] adj (*also fig*) saftig

jukebox ['dʒuːkbɔks] n Musikautomat m

July [dʒuː'laɪ] n Juli m

jumble ['dʒʌmbl] n Durcheinander nt ♦ vt (*also: ~ up*) durcheinander werfen; (*facts*) durcheinander bringen

jumble sale (*BRIT*) n Basar m, Flohmarkt m

┌─────────────────┐
│ **Jumble sale** │
└─────────────────┘

i **Jumble sale** *ist ein Wohltätig-keitsbasar, meist in einer Aula oder einem Gemeindehaus abgehalten, bei dem alle möglichen Gebrauchtwaren (vor allem Kleidung, Spielzeug, Bücher, Geschirr und Möbel) verkauft werden. Der Erlös fließt entweder einer Wohltätigkeits-organisation zu oder wird für örtliche Zwecke verwendet, z.B. die Pfadfinder, die Grundschule, Reparatur der Kirche usw.*

---

jumbo (jet) ['dʒʌmbəu-] n Jumbo(jet) m

jump [dʒʌmp] vi springen; (*nervously*) zusammenzucken ♦ vt überspringen ♦ n Sprung m; **to ~ the queue** (*BRIT*) sich vordrängeln

jumper ['dʒʌmpə'] n (*BRIT: pullover*) Pullover m; (*US: dress*) Trägerkleid nt

jump leads *BRIT*, **jumper cables** *US* npl Überbrückungskabel nt

jumpy ['dʒʌmpɪ] adj nervös

Jun. abbr = **junior**

junction ['dʒʌŋkʃən] n (*BRIT: of roads*) (Straßen)kreuzung f; (*RAIL*) Knotenpunkt m

juncture ['dʒʌŋktʃə'] n: **at this ~** in diesem Augenblick

June [dʒuːn] n Juni m

jungle ['dʒʌŋɡl] n Dschungel m

junior ['dʒuːnɪə'] adj (*younger*) jünger; (*after name*) junior; (*SPORT*) Junioren-; (*lower position*) untergeordnet; (*for young people*) Junioren- ♦ n Jüngere(r) mf; **~ school** (*BRIT*) n Grundschule f

junk [dʒʌŋk] n (*rubbish*) Plunder m; (*ship*) Dschunke f; **~ bond** n (*COMM*) niedrig eingestuftes Wertpapier mit hohen Ertragschancen bei erhöhtem Risiko; **~ food** n Junk food nt; **~ mail** n Reklame, die unangefordert in den Briefkasten gesteckt wird; **~ shop** n Ramschladen m

Junr abbr = **junior**

jurisdiction [dʒuərɪs'dɪkʃən] n Gerichtsbarkeit f; (*range of authority*) Zuständigkeit(sbereich m) f

juror ['dʒuərər] n Geschworene(r) mf; (in competition) Preisrichter m

jury ['dʒuərɪ] n (court) Geschworene pl; (panel) Jury f

just [dʒʌst] adj gerecht ♦ adv (recently, now) gerade, eben; (barely) gerade noch; (exactly) genau, gerade; (only) nur, bloß; (a small distance) gleich; (absolutely) einfach; **~ as I arrived** gerade als ich ankam; **~ as nice** genauso nett; **~ as well** umso besser; **~ now** soeben, gerade; **~ try** versuch es mal; **she's ~ left** sie ist gerade or (so)eben gegangen; **he's ~ done it** er hat es gerade or (so)eben getan; **~ before** gerade or kurz bevor; **~ enough** gerade genug; **he ~ missed** er hat fast or beinahe getroffen

justice ['dʒʌstɪs] n (fairness) Gerechtigkeit f; **J~ of the Peace** n Friedensrichter m

justifiable [dʒʌstɪ'faɪəbl] adj berechtigt

justification [dʒʌstɪfɪ'keɪʃən] n Rechtfertigung f

justify ['dʒʌstɪfaɪ] vt rechtfertigen; (text) justieren

justly ['dʒʌstlɪ] adv (say) mit Recht; (condemn) gerecht

jut [dʒʌt] vi (also: **~ out**) herausragen, vorstehen

juvenile ['dʒuːvənaɪl] adj (young) jugendlich; (for the young) Jugend- ♦ n Jugendliche(r) mf

juxtapose ['dʒʌkstəpəʊz] vt nebeneinander stellen

K, k

K [keɪ] abbr (= one thousand) Tsd.; (= kilobyte) K

kangaroo [kæŋɡə'ruː] n Känguru nt

karate [kə'rɑːtɪ] n Karate nt

kebab [kə'bæb] n Kebab m

keel [kiːl] n Kiel m; **on an even ~** (fig) im Lot

keen [kiːn] adj begeistert; (wind, blade, intelligence) scharf; (sight, hearing) gut; **to be ~ to do** or **on doing sth** etw unbedingt tun wollen; **to be ~ on sth/sb** scharf auf

etw/jdn sein

keep [kiːp] (pt, pp **kept**) vt (retain) behalten; (have) haben; (animals, one's word) halten; (support) versorgen; (maintain in state) halten; (preserve) aufbewahren; (restrain) abhalten ♦ vi (continue in direction) sich halten; (food) sich halten; (remain: quiet etc) bleiben ♦ n Unterhalt m; (tower) Burgfried m; (inf): **for ~s** für immer; **to ~ sth to o.s.** etw für sich behalten; **it ~s happening** es passiert immer wieder; **~ back** vt fern halten; (information) verschweigen; **~ on** vi: **~ on doing sth** etw immer weiter tun; **~ out** vt nicht hereinlassen; **"~ out"** „Eintritt verboten!"; **~ up** vi Schritt halten ♦ vt aufrechterhalten; (continue) weitermachen; **to ~ up with** Schritt halten mit; **~er** n Wärter(in) m(f); (goalkeeper) Torhüter(in) m(f); **~-fit** n Keep-fit nt; **~ing** n (care) Obhut f; **in ~ing with** in Übereinstimmung mit; **~sake** n Andenken nt

keg [keɡ] n Fass nt

kennel ['kenl] n Hundehütte f; **~s** npl: **to put a dog in ~s** (for boarding) einen Hund in Pflege geben

Kenya ['kenjə] n Kenia nt; **~n** adj kenianisch ♦ n Kenianer(in) m(f)

kept [kept] pt, pp of **keep**

kerb [kɜːb] (BRIT) n Bordstein m

kernel ['kɜːnl] n Kern m

kerosene ['kerəsiːn] n Kerosin nt

kettle ['ketl] n Kessel m; **~drum** n Pauke f

key [kiː] n Schlüssel m; (of piano, typewriter) Taste f; (MUS) Tonart f ♦ vt (also: **~ in**) eingeben; (person) überdreht; **~hole** n Schlüsselloch nt; **~hole surgery** n minimal invasive Chirurgie f, Schlüssellochchirurgie f; **~note** n Grundton m; **~ ring** n Schlüsselring m

khaki ['kɑːkɪ] n K(h)aki nt ♦ adj k(h)aki(farben)

kick [kɪk] vt einen Fußtritt geben +dat, treten ♦ vi treten; (baby) strampeln; (horse) ausschlagen ♦ n (Fuß)tritt m; (thrill) Spaß m; **he does it for ~s** er macht das aus Jux;

~ **off** vi (*SPORT*) anstoßen; **~~off** n (*SPORT*) Anstoß m

kid [kɪd] n (*inf: child*) Kind nt; (*goat*) Zicklein nt; (*leather*) Glacéleder nt, Glaceeleder nt ♦ vi (*inf*) Witze machen

kidnap ['kɪdnæp] vt entführen; **~per** n Entführer m; **~ping** n Entführung f

kidney ['kɪdnɪ] n Niere f

kill [kɪl] vt töten, umbringen ♦ vi töten ♦ n (*hunting*) (Jagd)beute f; **~er** n Mörder(in) m(f); **~ing** n Mord m; **~joy** n Spaßverderber(in) m(f)

kiln [kɪln] n Brennofen m

kilo ['ki:ləu] n Kilo nt; **~byte** n (*COMPUT*) Kilobyte nt; **~gram(me)** n Kilogramm nt; **~metre** ['kɪləmi:tə'] (*US* **kilometer**) n Kilometer m; **~watt** n Kilowatt nt

kilt [kɪlt] n Schottenrock m

kind [kaɪnd] adj freundlich ♦ n Art f; **a ~ of** eine Art von; **(two) of a ~** (zwei) von der gleichen Art; **in ~** auf dieselbe Art; (*in goods*) in Naturalien

kindergarten ['kɪndəgɑ:tn] n Kindergarten m

kind-hearted [kaɪnd'hɑ:tɪd] adj gutherzig

kindle ['kɪndl] vt (*set on fire*) anzünden; (*rouse*) reizen, (er)wecken

kindly ['kaɪndlɪ] adj freundlich ♦ adv liebenswürdig(erweise); **would you ~ ...?** wären Sie so freundlich und ...?

kindness ['kaɪndnɪs] n Freundlichkeit f

kindred ['kɪndrɪd] adj: **~ spirit** Gleichgesinnte(r) mf

king [kɪŋ] n König m; **~dom** n Königreich nt

kingfisher ['kɪŋfɪʃə'] n Eisvogel m

king-size(d) ['kɪŋsaɪz(d)] adj (*cigarette*) Kingsize

kinky ['kɪŋkɪ] (*inf*) adj (*person, ideas*) verrückt; (*sexual*) abartig

kiosk ['ki:ɔsk] (*BRIT*) n (*TEL*) Telefonhäuschen nt

kipper ['kɪpə'] n Räucherhering m

kiss [kɪs] n Kuss m ♦ vt küssen ♦ vi: **they ~ed** sie küssten sich; **~ of life** (*BRIT*) n: **the ~ of life** Mund-zu-Mund-Beatmung f

kit [kɪt] n Ausrüstung f; (*tools*) Werkzeug nt

kitchen ['kɪtʃɪn] n Küche f; **~ sink** n Spülbecken nt

kite [kaɪt] n Drachen m

kitten ['kɪtn] n Kätzchen nt

kitty ['kɪtɪ] n (*money*) Kasse f

km abbr (= *kilometre*) km

knack [næk] n Dreh m, Trick m

knapsack ['næpsæk] n Rucksack m; (*MIL*) Tornister m

knead [ni:d] vt kneten

knee [ni:] n Knie nt; **~cap** n Kniescheibe f

kneel [ni:l] (*pt, pp* **knelt**) vi (*also:* **~ down**) knien

knelt [nɛlt] pt, pp of **kneel**

knew [nju:] pt of **know**

knickers ['nɪkəz] (*BRIT*) npl Schlüpfer m

knife [naɪf] (*pl* **knives**) n Messer nt ♦ vt erstechen

knight [naɪt] n Ritter m; (*chess*) Springer m; **~hood** n (*title*): **to get a ~hood** zum Ritter geschlagen werden

knit [nɪt] vt stricken ♦ vi stricken; (*bones*) zusammenwachsen; **~ting** n (*occupation*) Stricken nt; (*work*) Strickzeug nt; **~ting needle** n Stricknadel f; **~wear** n Strickwaren pl

knives [naɪvz] pl of **knife**

knob [nɔb] n Knauf m; (*on instrument*) Knopf m; (*BRIT: of butter etc*) kleine(s) Stück nt

knock [nɔk] vt schlagen; (*criticize*) heruntermachen ♦ vi: **to ~ at** or **on the door** an die Tür klopfen ♦ n Schlag m; (*on door*) Klopfen nt; **~ down** vt umwerfen; (*with car*) anfahren; **~ off** vt (*do quickly*) hinhauen; (*inf: steal*) klauen ♦ vi (*finish*) Feierabend machen; **~ out** vt ausschlagen; (*BOXING*) k. o. schlagen; **~ over** vt (*person, object*) umwerfen; (*with car*) anfahren; **~er** n (*on door*) Türklopfer m; **~out** n K.-o.-Schlag m; (*fig*) Sensation f

knot [nɔt] n Knoten m ♦ vt (ver)knoten

knotty ['nɔtɪ] adj (*fig*) kompliziert

know [nəu] (*pt* **knew**, *pp* **known**) vt, vi wissen; (*be able to*) können; (*be acquainted with*) kennen; (*recognize*) erkennen; **to ~ how to do sth** wissen, wie man etw macht, etw tun können; **to ~ about** or **of sth/sb** etw/jdn kennen; **~-all** n Alleswisser

m; **~-how** n Kenntnis f, Know-how nt;
~ing adj (look, smile) wissend; (intentionally) wissentlich
knowledge ['nɒlɪdʒ] n Wissen nt, Kenntnis f; **~able** adj informiert
known [nəʊn] pp of **know**
knuckle ['nʌkl] n Fingerknöchel m
K.O. n abbr = **knockout**
Koran [kɔ'rɑːn] n Koran m
Korea [kə'rɪə] n Korea nt
kosher ['kəʊʃər] adj koscher

L, l

L [ɛl] abbr (BRIT: AUT) (= learner) am Auto angebrachtes Kennzeichen für Fahrschüler; = **lake**; (= large) gr.; (= left) l.
l. abbr = **litre**
lab [læb] (inf) n Labor nt
label ['leɪbl] n Etikett nt ♦ vt etikettieren
labor etc ['leɪbər] (US) = **labour** etc
laboratory [lə'bɒrətəri] n Laboratorium nt
laborious [lə'bɔːrɪəs] adj mühsam
labour ['leɪbər] (US **labor**) n Arbeit f; (workmen) Arbeitskräfte pl; (MED) Wehen pl ♦ vi: **to ~ (at)** sich abmühen (mit) ♦ vt breittreten (inf); **in ~** (MED) in den Wehen; **L~** (BRIT: also: **the L~ party**) die Labour Party; **~ed** adj (movement) gequält; (style) schwerfällig; **~er** n Arbeiter m; **farm ~er** (Land)arbeiter m
lace [leɪs] n (fabric) Spitze f; (of shoe) Schnürsenkel m; (braid) Litze f ♦ vt (also: ~ **up**) (zu)schnüren
lack [læk] n Mangel m ♦ vt nicht haben; **sb ~s sth** jdm fehlt etw nom; **to be ~ing** fehlen; **sb is ~ing in sth** es fehlt jdm an etw dat; **for** or **through ~ of** aus Mangel an +dat
lacquer ['lækər] n Lack m
lad [læd] n Junge m
ladder ['lædər] n Leiter f; (BRIT: in tights) Laufmasche f ♦ vt (BRIT: tights) Laufmaschen bekommen in +dat
laden ['leɪdn] adj beladen, voll
ladle ['leɪdl] n Schöpfkelle f

lady ['leɪdɪ] n Dame f; (title) Lady f; **young ~** junge Dame; **the ladies' (room)** die Damentoilette; **~bird** (US **~bug**) n Marienkäfer m; **~like** adj damenhaft, vornehm; **~ship** n: **your L~ship** Ihre Ladyschaft
lag [læg] vi (also: ~ **behind**) zurückbleiben ♦ vt (pipes) verkleiden
lager ['lɑːgər] n helle(s) Bier nt
lagging ['lægɪŋ] n Isolierung f
lagoon [lə'guːn] n Lagune f
laid [leɪd] pt, pp of **lay**; ~ **back** (inf) adj cool
lain [leɪn] pp of **lie**
lair [leər] n Lager nt
lake [leɪk] n See m
lamb [læm] n Lamm nt; (meat) Lammfleisch nt; ~ **chop** n Lammkotelett nt; **~swool** n Lammwolle f
lame [leɪm] adj lahm; (excuse) faul
lament [lə'ment] n Klage f ♦ vt beklagen
laminated ['læmɪneɪtɪd] adj beschichtet
lamp [læmp] n Lampe f; (in street) Straßenlaterne f; **~post** n Laternenpfahl m; **~shade** n Lampenschirm m
lance [lɑːns] n Lanze f; ~ **corporal** (BRIT) n Obergefreite(r) m
land [lænd] n Land nt ♦ vi (from ship) an Land gehen; (AVIAT, end up) landen ♦ vt (obtain) kriegen; (passengers) absetzen; (goods) abladen; (troops, space probe) landen; **~fill site** ['lændfɪl-] n Mülldeponie f; **~ing** n Landung f; (on stairs) (Treppen)absatz m; **~ing gear** n Fahrgestell nt; **~ing stage** (BRIT) n Landesteg m; **~ing strip** n Landebahn f; **~lady** n (Haus)wirtin f; **~locked** adj landumschlossen, Binnen-; **~lord** n (of house) Hauswirt m, Besitzer m; (of pub) Gastwirt m; (of area) Grundbesitzer m; **~mark** n Wahrzeichen nt; (fig) Meilenstein m; **~owner** n Grundbesitzer m; **~scape** n Landschaft f; ~ **gardener** n Landschaftsgärtner(in) m(f); **~slide** n (GEOG) Erdrutsch m; (POL) überwältigende(r) Sieg m
lane [leɪn] n (in town) Gasse f; (in country) Weg m; (of motorway) Fahrbahn f, Spur f;

(*SPORT*) Bahn f; **"get in ~"** „bitte einordnen"

language ['læŋgwɪdʒ] n Sprache f; **bad ~** unanständige Ausdrücke pl; **~ laboratory** n Sprachlabor nt

languish ['læŋgwɪʃ] vi schmachten

lank [læŋk] adj dürr

lanky ['læŋkɪ] adj schlaksig

lantern ['læntən] n Laterne f

lap [læp] n Schoß m; (*SPORT*) Runde f ♦ vt (*also: ~ up*) auflecken ♦ vi (*water*) plätschern

lapel [lə'pel] n Revers nt or m

Lapland ['læplænd] n Lappland nt

lapse [læps] n (*moral*) Fehltritt m ♦ vi (*decline*) nachlassen; (*expire*) ablaufen; (*claims*) erlöschen; **to ~ into bad habits** sich schlechte Gewohnheiten angewöhnen

laptop (computer) ['læptɒp-] n Laptop(-Computer) m

lard [lɑːd] n Schweineschmalz nt

larder ['lɑːdə'] n Speisekammer f

large [lɑːdʒ] adj groß; **at ~** auf freiem Fuß; **~ly** adv zum größten Teil; **~-scale** adj groß angelegt, Groß-

lark [lɑːk] n (*bird*) Lerche f; (*joke*) Jux m; **~ about** (*inf*) vi herumalbern

laryngitis [lærɪn'dʒaɪtɪs] n Kehlkopfentzündung f

laser ['leɪzə'] n Laser m; **~ printer** n Laserdrucker m

lash [læʃ] n Peitschenhieb m; (*eyelash*) Wimper f ♦ vt (*rain*) schlagen gegen; (*whip*) peitschen; (*bind*) festbinden; **~ out** vi (*with fists*) um sich schlagen

lass [læs] n Mädchen nt

lasso [læ'suː] n Lasso nt

last [lɑːst] adj letzte(r, s) ♦ adv zuletzt; (*~ time*) das letzte Mal ♦ vi (*continue*) dauern; (*remain good*) sich halten; (*money*) ausreichen; **at ~** endlich; **~ night** gestern Abend; **~ week** letzte Woche; **~ but one** vorletzte(r, s); **~-ditch** adj (*attempt*) in letzter Minute; **~ing** adj dauerhaft; (*shame etc*) andauernd; **~ly** adv schließlich; **~-minute** adj in letzter Minute

latch [lætʃ] n Riegel m

late [leɪt] adj spät; (*dead*) verstorben ♦ adv spät; (*after proper time*) zu spät; **to be ~** zu spät kommen; **of ~** in letzter Zeit; **in ~ May** Ende Mai; **~comer** n Nachzügler(in) m(f); **~ly** adv in letzter Zeit; **later** ['leɪtə'] adj (*date*) später; (*version*) neuer ♦ adv später

lateral ['lætərəl] adj seitlich

latest ['leɪtɪst] adj (*fashion*) neueste(r, s) ♦ n (*news*) Neu(e)ste(s) nt; **at the ~** spätestens

lathe [leɪð] n Drehbank f

lather ['lɑːðə'] n (*Seifen*)schaum m ♦ vt einschäumen ♦ vi schäumen

Latin ['lætɪn] n Latein nt ♦ adj lateinisch; (*Roman*) römisch; **~ America** n Lateinamerika nt; **~ American** adj lateinamerikanisch

latitude ['lætɪtjuːd] n (*GEOG*) Breite f; (*freedom*) Spielraum m

latter ['lætə'] adj (*second of two*) letztere; (*coming at end*) letzte(r, s), später ♦ n: **the ~** der/die/das letztere, die letzteren; **~ly** adv in letzter Zeit

lattice ['lætɪs] n Gitter nt

laudable ['lɔːdəbl] adj löblich

laugh [lɑːf] n Lachen nt ♦ vi lachen; **~ at** vt lachen über +acc; **~ off** vt lachend abtun; **~able** adj lachhaft; **~ing stock** n Zielscheibe f des Spottes; **~ter** n Gelächter nt

launch [lɔːntʃ] n (*of ship*) Stapellauf m; (*of rocket*) Abschuss m; (*boat*) Barkasse f; (*of product*) Einführung f ♦ vt (*set afloat*) vom Stapel lassen; (*rocket*) (ab)schießen; (*product*) auf den Markt bringen; **~(ing) pad** n Abschussrampe f

launder ['lɔːndə'] vt waschen

Launderette [lɔːn'dret] (® *BRIT*) n Waschsalon m

Laundromat ['lɔːndrəmæt] (® *US*) n Waschsalon m

laundry ['lɔːndrɪ] n (*place*) Wäscherei f; (*clothes*) Wäsche f; **to do the ~** waschen

laureate ['lɔːrɪət] adj see **poet**

laurel ['lɒrl] n Lorbeer m

lava ['lɑːvə] n Lava f

lavatory ['lævətərɪ] n Toilette f

lavender ['lævəndər] n Lavendel m

lavish ['lævɪʃ] adj (extravagant)
verschwenderisch; (generous) großzügig
♦ vt (money): **to ~ sth on sth** etw auf etw
acc verschwenden; (attention, gifts): **to ~ sth
on sb** jdn mit etw überschütten

law [lɔː] n Gesetz nt; (system) Recht nt; (as
studies) Jura no acc nt; **~abiding** adj
gesetzestreu; **~ and order** n Recht und
Ordnung f; **~ court** n Gerichtshof m; **~ful**
adj gesetzlich; **~less** adj gesetzlos

lawn [lɔːn] n Rasen m; **~mower** n
Rasenmäher m; **~ tennis** n Rasentennis m

law: ~ school n Rechtsakademie f; **~suit** n
Prozess m; **~yer** n Rechtsanwalt m,
Rechtsanwältin f

lax [læks] adj (behaviour) nachlässig;
(standards) lax

laxative ['læksətɪv] n Abführmittel nt

lay [leɪ] (pt, pp **laid**) pt of **lie** ♦ adj Laien- ♦ vt
(place) legen; (table) decken; (egg) legen;
(trap) stellen; (money) wetten; **~ aside** vt
zurücklegen; **~ by** vt (set aside) beiseite
legen; **~ down** vt hinlegen; (rules)
vorschreiben; (arms) strecken; **to ~ down
the law** Vorschriften machen; **~ off** vt
(workers) (vorübergehend) entlassen; **~ on**
vt (water, gas) anschließen; (concert etc)
veranstalten; **~ out** vt (her)auslegen;
(money) ausgeben; (corpse) aufbahren; **~
up** vt (subj: illness) ans Bett fesseln; **~about**
n Faulenzer m; **~by** n (BRIT) n Parkbucht f;
(bigger) Rastplatz m

layer ['leɪər] n Schicht f

layman ['leɪmən] (irreg) n Laie m

layout ['leɪaut] n Anlage f; (ART) Lay-out nt,
Layout nt

laze [leɪz] vi faulenzen

laziness ['leɪzɪnɪs] n Faulheit f

lazy ['leɪzɪ] adj faul; (slow-moving) träge

lb. abbr = **pound** (weight)

lead¹ [led] n (chemical) Blei nt; (of pencil)
(Bleistift)mine f ♦ adj bleiern, Blei-

lead² [liːd] (pt, pp **led**) n (front position)
Führung f; (distance, time ahead) Vorsprung
f; (example) Vorbild nt; (clue) Tipp m; (of
police) Spur f; (THEAT) Hauptrolle f; (dog's)

Leine f ♦ vt (guide) führen; (group etc) leiten
♦ vi (be first) führen; (in the ~, SPORT, fig) in
Führung; **~ astray** vt irreführen; **~ away**
vt wegführen; (prisoner) abführen; **~ back**
vi zurückführen; **~ on** vt anführen; **~ on
to** vt (induce) dazu bringen; **~ to** vt (street)
(hin)führen nach; (result in) führen zu; **~
up to** vt (drive) führen zu; (speaker etc)
hinführen auf +acc

leaded petrol ['ledɪd-] n verbleites Benzin
nt

leaden ['ledn] adj (sky, sea) bleiern; (heavy:
footsteps) bleischwer

leader ['liːdər] n Führer m, Leiter m; (of
party) Vorsitzende(r) m; (PRESS) Leitartikel m;
~ship n (office) Leitung f; (quality)
Führerschaft f

lead-free ['ledfriː] adj (petrol) bleifrei

leading ['liːdɪŋ] adj führend; **~ lady** n
(THEAT) Hauptdarstellerin f; **~ light** n
(person) führende(r) Geist m

lead singer [liːd-] n Leadsänger(in) m(f)

leaf [liːf] (pl **leaves**) n Blatt nt ♦ vi: **to ~
through** durchblättern; **to turn over a new
~** einen neuen Anfang machen

leaflet ['liːflɪt] n (advertisement) Prospekt m;
(pamphlet) Flugblatt nt; (for information)
Merkblatt nt

league [liːg] n (union) Bund m; (SPORT) Liga
f; **to be in ~ with** unter einer Decke
stecken mit

leak [liːk] n undichte Stelle f; (in ship) Leck nt
♦ vt (liquid etc) durchlassen ♦ vi (pipe etc)
undicht sein; (liquid etc) auslaufen; **the
information was ~ed to the enemy** die
Information wurde dem Feind zugespielt; **~
out** vi (liquid etc) auslaufen; (information)
durchsickern; **~y** adj undicht

lean [liːn] (pt, pp **leaned** or **leant**) adj mager
♦ vi sich neigen ♦ vt (an)lehnen; **to ~
against sth** an etw dat angelehnt sein; sich
an etw acc anlehnen; **~ back** vi sich
zurücklehnen; **~ forward** vi sich
vorbeugen; **~ on** vt fus sich stützen auf
+acc; **~ out** vi sich hinauslehnen; **~ over**
vi sich hinüberbeugen; **~ing** n Neigung f
♦ adj schief; **~t** [lent] pt, pp of **lean**; **~-to** n

Anbau m

leap [liːp] (pt, pp **leaped** or **leapt**) n Sprung m ♦ vi springen; **~frog** n Bockspringen nt; **~t** [lɛpt] pt, pp of **leap**; **~ year** n Schaltjahr nt

learn [ləːn] (pt, pp **learned** or **learnt**) vt, vi lernen; (find out) erfahren; **to ~ how to do sth** etw (er)lernen; **~ed** [ˈləːnɪd] adj gelehrt; **~er** n Anfänger(in) m(f); (AUT: BRIT: also: **~er driver**) Fahrschüler(in) m(f); **~ing** n Gelehrsamkeit f; **~t** [ləːnt] pt, pp of **learn**

lease [liːs] n (of property) Mietvertrag m ♦ vt pachten

leash [liːʃ] n Leine f

least [liːst] adj geringste(r, s) ♦ adv am wenigsten ♦ n Mindeste(s) nt; **the ~ possible effort** möglichst geringer Aufwand; **at ~** zumindest; **not in the ~!** durchaus nicht!

leather [ˈlɛðəʳ] n Leder nt

leave [liːv] (pt, pp **left**) vt verlassen; (~ behind) zurücklassen; (forget) vergessen; (allow to remain) lassen; (after death) hinterlassen; (entrust): **to ~ sth to sb** jdm etw überlassen ♦ vi weggehen, wegfahren; (for journey) abreisen; (bus, train) abfahren ♦ n Erlaubnis f; (MIL) Urlaub m; **to be left** (remain) übrig bleiben; **there's some milk left over** es ist noch etwas Milch übrig; **on ~** auf Urlaub; **~ behind** vt (person, object) dalassen; (forget) liegen lassen, stehen lassen; **~ out** vt auslassen; **~ of absence** n Urlaub m

leaves [liːvz] pl of **leaf**

Lebanon [ˈlɛbənən] n Libanon m

lecherous [ˈlɛtʃərəs] adj lüstern

lecture [ˈlɛktʃəʳ] n Vortrag m; (UNIV) Vorlesung f ♦ vi einen Vortrag halten; (UNIV) lesen ♦ vt (scold) abkanzeln; **to give a ~ on sth** einen Vortrag über etw halten; **~r** [ˈlɛktʃərəʳ] n Vortragende(r) mf; (BRIT: UNIV) Dozent(in) m(f)

led [lɛd] pt, pp of **lead²**

ledge [lɛdʒ] n Leiste f; (window ~) Sims m or nt; (of mountain) (Fels)vorsprung m

ledger [ˈlɛdʒəʳ] n Hauptbuch nt

leech [liːtʃ] n Blutegel m

leek [liːk] n Lauch m

leer [lɪəʳ] vi: **to ~ (at sb)** (nach jdm) schielen

leeway [ˈliːweɪ] n (fig): **to have some ~** etwas Spielraum haben

left [lɛft] pt, pp of **leave** ♦ adj linke(r, s) ♦ n (side) linke Seite f ♦ adv links; **on the ~** links; **to the ~** nach links; **the L~** (POL) die Linke f; **~-hand** adj: **~-hand drive** mit Linkssteuerung; **~-handed** adj linkshändig; **~-hand side** n linke Seite f; **~-luggage locker** n Gepäckschließfach nt; **~-luggage (office)** (BRIT) n Gepäckaufbewahrung f; **~-overs** npl Reste pl; **~-wing** adj linke(r, s)

leg [lɛg] n Bein nt; (of meat) Keule f; (stage) Etappe f; **1st/2nd ~** (SPORT) 1./2. Etappe

legacy [ˈlɛgəsɪ] n Erbe nt, Erbschaft f

legal [ˈliːgl] adj gesetzlich; (allowed) legal; **~ holiday** (US) n gesetzliche(r) Feiertag m; **~ize** vt legalisieren; **~ly** adv gesetzlich; legal; **~ tender** n gesetzliche(s) Zahlungsmittel nt

legend [ˈlɛdʒənd] n Legende f; **~ary** adj legendär

leggings [ˈlɛgɪŋz] npl Leggings pl

legible [ˈlɛdʒəbl] adj leserlich

legislation [lɛdʒɪsˈleɪʃən] n Gesetzgebung f; **legislative** [ˈlɛdʒɪslətɪv] adj gesetzgebend; **legislature** [ˈlɛdʒɪslətʃəʳ] n Legislative f

legitimate [lɪˈdʒɪtɪmət] adj rechtmäßig, legitim; (child) ehelich

legroom [ˈlɛgruːm] n Platz m für die Beine

leisure [ˈlɛʒəʳ] n Freizeit f; **to be at ~** Zeit haben; **~ centre** n Freizeitzentrum nt; **~ly** adj gemächlich

lemon [ˈlɛmən] n Zitrone f; (colour) Zitronengelb nt; **~ade** [lɛməˈneɪd] n Limonade f; **~ tea** n Zitronentee m

lend [lɛnd] (pt, pp **lent**) vt leihen; **to ~ sb sth** jdm etw leihen; **~ing library** n Leihbibliothek f

length [lɛŋθ] n Länge f; (of road, pipe etc) Strecke f; (of material) Stück nt; **at ~** (lengthily) ausführlich; (at last) schließlich; **~en** vt verlängern ♦ vi länger werden; **~ways** adv längs; **~y** adj sehr lang, langatmig

lenient [ˈliːnɪənt] adj nachsichtig

lens [lɛnz] n Linse f; (PHOT) Objektiv nt

Lent [lɛnt] n Fastenzeit f

lent [lɛnt] pt, pp of **lend**

lentil ['lɛntɪl] n Linse f

Leo ['liːəu] n Löwe m

leotard ['liːətɑːd] n Trikot nt, Gymnastikanzug m

leper ['lɛpər] n Leprakranke(r) f(m)

leprosy ['lɛprəsɪ] n Lepra f

lesbian ['lɛzbɪən] adj lesbisch ♦ n Lesbierin f

less [lɛs] adj, adv weniger ♦ n weniger ♦ pron weniger; **~ than half** weniger als die Hälfte; **~ than ever** weniger denn je; **~ and ~** immer weniger; **the ~ he works** je weniger er arbeitet; **~en** ['lɛsn] vi abnehmen ♦ vt verringern, verkleinern; **~er** ['lɛsər] adj kleiner, geringer; **to a ~er extent** in geringerem Maße

lesson ['lɛsn] n (SCH) Stunde f; (unit of study) Lektion f; (fig) Lehre f; (ECCL) Lesung f; **a maths ~** eine Mathestunde

lest [lɛst] conj: **~ it happen** damit es nicht passiert

let [lɛt] (pt, pp **let**) vt lassen; (BRIT: lease) vermieten; **to ~ sb do sth** jdn etw tun lassen; **to ~ sb know sth** jdn etw wissen lassen; **~'s go!** gehen wir!; **~ him come** soll er doch kommen; **~ down** vt hinunterlassen; (disappoint) enttäuschen; **~ go** vi loslassen ♦ vt (things) loslassen; (person) gehen lassen; **~ in** vt hereinlassen; (water) durchlassen; **~ off** vt (gun) abfeuern; (steam) ablassen; (forgive) laufen lassen; **~ on** vi durchblicken lassen; (pretend) vorgeben; **~ out** vt herauslassen; (scream) fahren lassen; **~ up** vi nachlassen; (stop) aufhören

lethal ['liːθl] adj tödlich

lethargic [lɛ'θɑːdʒɪk] adj lethargisch

letter ['lɛtər] n Brief m; (of alphabet) Buchstabe m; **~ bomb** n Briefbombe f; **~box** (BRIT) n Briefkasten m; **~ing** n Beschriftung f; **~ of credit** n Akkreditiv m

lettuce ['lɛtɪs] n (Kopf)salat m

let-up ['lɛtʌp] (inf) n Nachlassen nt

leukaemia [luːˈkiːmɪə] (US **leukemia**) n Leukämie f

level ['lɛvl] adj (ground) eben; (at same height) auf gleicher Höhe; (equal) gleich gut; (head) kühl ♦ adv auf gleicher Höhe ♦ n (instrument) Wasserwaage f; (altitude) Höhe f; (flat place) ebene Fläche f; (position on scale) Niveau nt; (amount, degree) Grad m ♦ vt (ground) einebnen; **to draw ~ with** gleichziehen mit; **to be ~ with** auf einer Höhe sein mit; **A ~s** (BRIT) ≈ Abitur nt; **O ~s** (BRIT) ≈ mittlere Reife f; **on the ~** (fig: honest) ehrlich; **to ~ sth at sb** (blow) jdm etw versetzen; (remark) etw gegen jdn richten; **~ off** or **out** vi flach or eben werden; (fig) sich ausgleichen; (plane) horizontal fliegen ♦ vt (ground) planieren; (differences) ausgleichen; **~ crossing** (BRIT) n Bahnübergang m; **~-headed** adj vernünftig

lever ['liːvər] n Hebel m; (fig) Druckmittel nt ♦ vt (hoch)stemmen; **~age** n Hebelkraft f; (fig) Einfluss m

levy ['lɛvɪ] n (of taxes) Erhebung f; (tax) Abgaben pl; (MIL) Aushebung f ♦ vt erheben; (MIL) ausheben

lewd [luːd] adj unzüchtig, unanständig

liability [laɪə'bɪlətɪ] n (burden) Belastung f; (duty) Pflicht f; (debt) Verpflichtung f; (responsibility) Haftung f; (proneness) Anfälligkeit f

liable ['laɪəbl] adj (responsible) haftbar; (prone) anfällig; **to be ~ for sth** etw dat unterliegen; **it's ~ to happen** es kann leicht vorkommen

liaise [liːˈeɪz] vi: **to ~ (with sb)** (mit jdm) zusammenarbeiten; **liaison** n Verbindung f

liar ['laɪər] n Lügner m

libel ['laɪbl] n Verleumdung f ♦ vt verleumden

liberal ['lɪbərl] adj (generous) großzügig; (open-minded) aufgeschlossen; (POL) liberal

liberate ['lɪbəreɪt] vt befreien; **liberation** [lɪbəˈreɪʃən] n Befreiung f

liberty ['lɪbətɪ] n Freiheit f; (permission) Erlaubnis f; **to be at ~ to do sth** etw tun dürfen; **to take the ~ of doing sth** sich dat erlauben, etw zu tun

Libra ['liːbrə] n Waage f

librarian [laɪˈbrɛərɪən] n Bibliothekar(in) m(f)

library [ˈlaɪbrərɪ] n Bibliothek f; (lending ~) Bücherei f

Libya [ˈlɪbɪə] n Libyen nt; ~**n** adj libysch ♦ n Libyer(in) m(f)

lice [laɪs] npl of **louse**

licence [ˈlaɪsns] (US **license**) n (permit) Erlaubnis f; (also: **driving** ~, (US) **driver's** ~) Führerschein m

license [ˈlaɪsns] n (US) = **licence** ♦ vt genehmigen, konzessionieren; ~**d** adj (for alcohol) konzessioniert (für den Alkoholausschank); ~ **plate** (US) n (AUT) Nummernschild nt

lichen [ˈlaɪkən] n Flechte f

lick [lɪk] vt lecken ♦ n Lecken nt; **a** ~ **of paint** ein bisschen Farbe

licorice [ˈlɪkərɪs] (US) n = **liquorice**

lid [lɪd] n Deckel m; (eyelid) Lid nt

lie [laɪ] (pt **lay**, pp **lain**) vi (rest, be situated) liegen; (put o.s. in position) sich legen; (pt, pp **lied**: tell lies) lügen ♦ n Lüge f; **to** ~ **low** (fig) untertauchen; ~ **about** vi (things) herumliegen; (people) faulenzen; ~**down** (BRIT) n: **to have a** ~**down** ein Nickerchen machen; ~**in** (BRIT) n: **to have a** ~**in** sich ausschlafen

lieu [luː] n: **in** ~ **of** anstatt +gen

lieutenant [lefˈtɛnənt, (US) luːˈtɛnənt] n Leutnant m

life [laɪf] (pl **lives**) n Leben nt; ~ **assurance** (BRIT) n = **life insurance**; ~**belt** (BRIT) n Rettungsring m; ~**boat** n Rettungsboot nt; ~**guard** n Rettungsschwimmer m; ~ **insurance** n Lebensversicherung f; ~ **jacket** n Schwimmweste f; ~**less** adj (dead) leblos; (dull) langweilig; ~**like** adj lebenswahr, naturgetreu; ~**line** n Rettungsleine f; (fig) Rettungsanker m; ~**long** adj lebenslang; ~ **preserver** (US) n = **lifebelt**; ~**-saver** n Lebensretter(in) m(f); ~**-saving** adj lebensrettend, Rettungs-; ~ **sentence** n lebenslängliche Freiheitsstrafe f; ~ **span** n Lebensspanne f; ~**style** n Lebensstil m; ~ **support system** n (MED) Lebenserhaltungssystem nt; ~**time** n: **in his** ~**time** während er lebte; **once in a**

~**time** einmal im Leben

lift [lɪft] vt hochheben ♦ vi sich heben ♦ n (BRIT: elevator) Aufzug m, Lift m; **to give sb a** ~ jdn mitnehmen; ~**-off** n Abheben nt (vom Boden)

ligament [ˈlɪgəmənt] n Band nt

light [laɪt] (pt, pp **lighted** or **lit**) n Licht nt; (for cigarette etc): **have you got a** ~? haben Sie Feuer? ♦ vt beleuchten; (lamp) anmachen; (fire, cigarette) anzünden ♦ adj (bright) hell; (pale) hell-; (not heavy, easy) leicht; (punishment) milde; (touch) leicht; ~**s** npl (AUT) Beleuchtung f; ~ **up** vi (lamp) angehen; (face) aufleuchten ♦ vt (illuminate) beleuchten; (~s) anmachen; ~ **bulb** n Glühbirne f; ~**en** vi (brighten) hell werden; (~ning) blitzen ♦ vt (give ~ to) erhellen; (hair) aufhellen; (gloom) aufheitern; (make less heavy) leichter machen; (fig) erleichtern; ~**er** n Feuerzeug nt; ~**-headed** adj (thoughtless) leichtsinnig; (giddy) schwindlig; ~**-hearted** adj leichtherzig, fröhlich; ~**house** n Leuchtturm m; ~**ing** n Beleuchtung f; ~**ly** adv leicht; (irresponsibly) leichtfertig; **to get off** ~**ly** mit einem blauen Auge davonkommen; ~**ness** n (of weight) Leichtigkeit f; (of colour) Helle f

lightning [ˈlaɪtnɪŋ] n Blitz m; ~ **conductor** (US ~ **rod**) n Blitzableiter m

light: ~ **pen** n Lichtstift m; ~**weight** adj (suit) leicht; ~**weight** n (BOXING) Leichtgewichtler m; ~ **year** n Lichtjahr nt

like [laɪk] vt mögen, gern haben ♦ prep wie ♦ adj (similar) ähnlich; (equal) gleich ♦ n: **the** ~ dergleichen; **I would** or **I'd** ~ ich möchte gern; **would you** ~ **a coffee?** möchten Sie einen Kaffee?; **to be** or **look** ~ **sb/sth** jdm/etw ähneln; **that's just** ~ **him** das ist typisch für ihn; **do it** ~ **this** mach es so; **it is nothing** ~ **...** es ist nicht zu vergleichen mit ...; **what does it look** ~? wie sieht es aus?; **what does it sound** ~? wie hört es sich an?; **what does it taste** ~? wie schmeckt es?; **his** ~**s and dislikes** was er mag und was er nicht mag; ~**able** adj sympathisch

likelihood [ˈlaɪklɪhud] n Wahrscheinlichkeit f

likely ['laɪklɪ] *adj* wahrscheinlich; **he's ~ to leave** er geht möglicherweise; **not ~!** wohl kaum!

likeness ['laɪknɪs] *n* Ähnlichkeit *f*; *(portrait)* Bild *nt*

likewise ['laɪkwaɪz] *adv* ebenso

liking ['laɪkɪŋ] *n* Zuneigung *f*; *(taste)* Vorliebe *f*

lilac ['laɪlək] *n* Flieder *m* ♦ *adj (colour)* fliederfarben

lily ['lɪlɪ] *n* Lilie *f*; **~ of the valley** *n* Maiglöckchen *nt*

limb [lɪm] *n* Glied *nt*

limber up ['lɪmbər-] *vi* sich auflockern; *(fig)* sich vorbereiten

limbo ['lɪmbəu] *n*: **to be in ~** *(fig)* in der Schwebe sein

lime [laɪm] *n (tree)* Linde *f*; *(fruit)* Limone *f*; *(substance)* Kalk *m*

limelight ['laɪmlaɪt] *n*: **to be in the ~** *(fig)* im Rampenlicht stehen

limestone ['laɪmstəun] *n* Kalkstein *m*

limit ['lɪmɪt] *n* Grenze *f*; *(inf)* Höhe *f* ♦ *vt* begrenzen, einschränken; **~ation** [lɪmɪ'teɪʃən] *n* Einschränkung *f*; **~ed** *adj* beschränkt; **to be ~ed to** sich beschränken auf +*acc*; **~ed (liability) company** *(BRIT)* *n* Gesellschaft *f* mit beschränkter Haftung

limousine ['lɪməziːn] *n* Limousine *f*

limp [lɪmp] *n* Hinken *nt* ♦ *vi* hinken ♦ *adj* schlaff

limpet ['lɪmpɪt] *n (fig)* Klette *f*

line [laɪn] *n* Linie *f*; *(rope)* Leine *f*; *(on face)* Falte *f*; *(row)* Reihe *f*; *(of hills)* Kette *f*; *(US: queue)* Schlange *f*; *(of business)* Linie *f*, Gesellschaft *f*; *(RAIL)* Strecke *f*; *(TEL)* Leitung *f*; *(written)* Zeile *f*; *(direction)* Richtung *f*; *(fig: business)* Branche *f*; *(range of items)* Kollektion *f* ♦ *vt (coat)* füttern; *(border)* säumen; **~s** *npl (RAIL)* Gleise *pl*; **in ~ with** in Übereinstimmung mit; **~ up** *vi* sich aufstellen ♦ *vt* aufstellen; *(prepare)* sorgen für; *(support)* mobilisieren; *(surprise)* planen; **~ar** ['lɪnɪər] *adj* gerade; *(measure)* Längen-; **~d** *adj (face)* faltig; *(paper)* liniert

linen ['lɪnɪn] *n* Leinen *nt*; *(sheets etc)* Wäsche *f*

liner ['laɪnər] *n* Überseedampfer *m*

linesman ['laɪnzmən] *(irreg)* *n (SPORT)* Linienrichter *m*

line-up ['laɪnʌp] *n* Aufstellung *f*

linger ['lɪŋgər] *vi (remain long)* verweilen; *(taste)* (zurück)bleiben; *(delay)* zögern, verharren

lingerie ['lænʒəriː] *n* Damenunterwäsche *f*

lingering ['lɪŋgərɪŋ] *adj (doubt)* zurückbleibend; *(disease)* langwierig; *(taste)* nachhaltend; *(look)* lang

lingo ['lɪŋgəu] *(pl* **~es)** *(inf)* *n* Sprache *f*

linguist ['lɪŋgwɪst] *n* Sprachkundige(r) *mf*; *(UNIV)* Sprachwissenschaftler(in) *m(f)*; **~ic** [lɪŋ'gwɪstɪk] *adj* sprachlich; sprachwissenschaftlich; **~ics** *n* Sprachwissenschaft *f*, Linguistik *f*

lining ['laɪnɪŋ] *n* Futter *nt*

link [lɪŋk] *n* Glied *nt*; *(connection)* Verbindung *f* ♦ *vt* verbinden; **~s** *npl (GOLF)* Golfplatz *m*; **~ up** *vt* verbinden ♦ *vi* zusammenkommen; *(companies)* sich zusammenschließen; **~-up** *n (TEL)* Verbindung *f*; *(of spaceships)* Kopplung *f*

lino ['laɪnəu] *n* = **linoleum**

linoleum [lɪ'nəuliəm] *n* Linoleum *nt*

linseed oil ['lɪnsiːd-] *n* Leinöl *nt*

lion ['laɪən] *n* Löwe *m*; **~ess** *n* Löwin *f*

lip [lɪp] *n* Lippe *f*; *(of jug)* Schnabel *m*; **to pay ~ service (to)** ein Lippenbekenntnis ablegen (zu)

liposuction ['lɪpəusʌkʃən] *n* Fettabsaugen *nt*

lip: ~read *(irreg)* *vi* von den Lippen ablesen; **~ salve** *n* Lippenbalsam *m*; **~stick** *n* Lippenstift *m*

liqueur [lɪ'kjuər] *n* Likör *m*

liquid ['lɪkwɪd] *n* Flüssigkeit *f* ♦ *adj* flüssig

liquidate ['lɪkwɪdeɪt] *vt* liquidieren

liquidize ['lɪkwɪdaɪz] *vt (COOK)* (im Mixer) pürieren; **~r** ['lɪkwɪdaɪzə'] *n* Mixgerät *nt*

liquor ['lɪkər] *n* Alkohol *m*

liquorice ['lɪkərɪs] *(BRIT)* *n* Lakritze *f*

liquor store *(US)* *n* Spirituosengeschäft *nt*

Lisbon ['lɪzbən] *n* Lissabon *f*

lisp [lɪsp] *n* Lispeln *nt* ♦ *vt, vi* lispeln

list [lɪst] *n* Liste *f*, Verzeichnis *nt*; *(of ship)* Schlagseite *f* ♦ *vt (write down)* eine Liste machen von; (*verbally*) aufzählen ♦ *vi* (*ship*) Schlagseite haben

listen ['lɪsn] *vi* hören; **~ to** *vt* zuhören +*dat*; **~er** *n* (Zu)hörer(in) *m(f)*

listless ['lɪstlɪs] *adj* lustlos

lit [lɪt] *pt, pp of* **light**

liter ['liːtər] (*US*) *n* = **litre**

literacy ['lɪtərəsɪ] *n* Fähigkeit *f* zu lesen und zu schreiben

literal ['lɪtərəl] *adj* buchstäblich; (*translation*) wortwörtlich; **~ly** *adv* wörtlich; buchstäblich

literary ['lɪtərərɪ] *adj* literarisch

literate ['lɪtərət] *adj* des Lesens und Schreibens kundig

literature ['lɪtrɪtʃər] *n* Literatur *f*

litigation [lɪtɪ'geɪʃən] *n* Prozess *m*

litre ['liːtər] (*US* **liter**) *n* Liter *m*

litter ['lɪtər] *n* (*rubbish*) Abfall *m*; (*of animals*) Wurf *m* ♦ *vt* in Unordnung bringen; **to be ~ed with** übersät sein mit; **~ bin** (*BRIT*) *n* Abfalleimer *m*

little ['lɪtl] *adj* klein ♦ *adv, n* wenig; **a ~** ein bisschen; **~ by ~** nach und nach

live¹ [laɪv] *adj* lebendig; (*MIL*) scharf; (*ELEC*) geladen; (*broadcast*) live

live² [lɪv] *vi* leben; (*dwell*) wohnen ♦ *vt* (*life*) führen; **~ down** *vt*: **I'll never ~ it down** das wird man mir nie vergessen; **~ on** *vi* weiterleben ♦ *vt fus*: **to ~ on sth** von etw leben; **~ together** *vi* zusammenleben; (*share a flat*) zusammenwohnen; **~ up to** *vt* (*standards*) gerecht werden +*dat*; (*principles*) anstreben; (*hopes*) entsprechen +*dat*

livelihood ['laɪvlɪhʊd] *n* Lebensunterhalt *m*

lively ['laɪvlɪ] *adj* lebhaft, lebendig

liven up ['laɪvn-] *vt* beleben

liver ['lɪvər] *n* (*ANAT*) Leber *f*

lives [laɪvz] *pl of* **life**

livestock ['laɪvstɒk] *n* Vieh *nt*

livid ['lɪvɪd] *adj* bläulich; (*furious*) fuchsteufelswild

living ['lɪvɪŋ] *n* (Lebens)unterhalt *m* ♦ *adj* lebendig; (*language etc*) lebend; **to earn** *or* **make a ~** sich *dat* seinen Lebensunterhalt verdienen; **~ conditions** *npl*

Wohnverhältnisse *pl*; **~ room** *n* Wohnzimmer *nt*; **~ standards** *npl* Lebensstandard *m*; **~ wage** *n* ausreichender Lohn *m*

lizard ['lɪzəd] *n* Eidechse *f*

load [ləʊd] *n* (*burden*) Last *f*; (*amount*) Ladung *f* ♦ *vt* (*also*: **~ up**) (be)laden; (*COMPUT*) laden; (*camera*) Film einlegen in +*acc*; (*gun*) laden; **~ a of, ~s of** (*fig*) jede Menge; **~ed** *adj* beladen; (*dice*) präpariert; (*question*) Fang-; (*inf*: *rich*) steinreich; **~ing bay** *n* Ladeplatz *m*

loaf [ləʊf] (*pl* **loaves**) *n* Brot *nt* ♦ *vi* (*also*: **~ about, ~ around**) herumlungern, faulenzen

loan [ləʊn] *n* Leihgabe *f*; (*FIN*) Darlehen *nt* ♦ *vt* leihen; **on ~** geliehen

loath [ləʊθ] *adj*: **to be ~ to do sth** etw ungern tun

loathe [ləʊð] *vt* verabscheuen

loaves [ləʊvz] *pl of* **loaf**

lobby ['lɒbɪ] *n* Vorhalle *f*; (*POL*) Lobby *f* ♦ *vt* politisch beeinflussen (wollen)

lobster ['lɒbstər] *n* Hummer *m*

local ['ləʊkl] *adj* ortsansässig, Orts- ♦ *n* (*pub*) Stammwirtschaft *f*; **the ~s** *npl* (*people*) die Ortsansässigen *pl*; **~ anaesthetic** *n* (*MED*) örtliche Betäubung *f*; **~ authority** *n* städtische Behörden *pl*; **~ call** *n* (*TEL*) Ortsgespräch *nt*; **~ government** *n* Gemeinde-/Kreisverwaltung *f*; **~ity** [ləʊ'kælɪtɪ] *n* Ort *m*; **~ly** *adv* örtlich, am Ort

locate [ləʊ'keɪt] *vt* ausfindig machen; (*establish*) errichten; **location** [ləʊ'keɪʃən] *n* Platz *m*, Lage *f*; **on location** (*CINE*) auf Außenaufnahme

loch [lɒx] (*SCOTTISH*) *n* See *m*

lock [lɒk] *n* Schloss *nt*; (*NAUT*) Schleuse *f*; (*of hair*) Locke *f* ♦ *vt* (*fasten*) (ver)schließen ♦ *vi* (*door etc*) sich schließen (lassen); (*wheels*) blockieren; **~ up** *vt* (*criminal, mental patient*) einsperren; (*house*) abschließen

locker ['lɒkər] *n* Spind *m*

locket ['lɒkɪt] *n* Medaillon *nt*

lock ['lɒk-]: **~out** *n* Aussperrung *f*; **~smith** *n* Schlosser(in) *m(f)*; **~up** *n* (*jail*) Gefängnis *nt*; (*garage*) Garage *f*

locum ['ləʊkəm] *n* (*MED*) Vertreter(in) *m(f)*

lodge [lɔdʒ] n (*gatehouse*) Pförtnerhaus nt; (*freemasons'*) Loge f ♦ vi (*get stuck*) stecken (bleiben); (*in Untermiete*): **to ~ (with)** wohnen (bei) ♦ vt (*protest*) einreichen; **~r** n (Unter)mieter m; **lodgings** n (Miet)wohnung f

loft [lɔft] n (Dach)boden m

lofty ['lɔftɪ] adj hoch(ragend); (*proud*) hochmütig

log [lɔg] n Klotz m; (*book*) = **logbook**

logbook ['lɔgbuk] n Bordbuch nt; (*for lorry*) Fahrtenschreiber m; (AUT) Kraftfahrzeugbrief m

loggerheads ['lɔgəhɛdz] npl: **to be at ~** sich in den Haaren liegen

logic ['lɔdʒɪk] n Logik f; **~al** adj logisch

log in or **on** vi (COMPUT) einloggen

log off or **out** vi (COMPUT) ausloggen

logistics [lɔ'dʒɪstɪks] npl Logistik f

logo ['ləugəu] n Firmenzeichen nt

loin [lɔɪn] n Lende f

loiter ['lɔɪtə*] vi herumstehen

loll [lɔl] vi (*also*: **~ about**) sich rekeln or räkeln

lollipop ['lɔlɪpɔp] n (Dauer)lutscher m; **~ man/lady** (*irreg*, BRIT) n ≈ Schülerlotse m

---
Lollipop man/lady

i **Lollipop man/lady** *heißen in Großbritannien die Männer bzw. Frauen, die mit Hilfe eines runden Stopp-schildes den Verkehr anhalten, damit Schul-kinder die Straße überqueren können. Der Name bezieht sich auf die Form des Schildes, die an einen Lutscher erinnert.*

---

lolly ['lɔlɪ] (*inf*) n (*sweet*) Lutscher m

London ['lʌndən] n London nt; **~er** n Londoner(in) m(f)

lone [ləun] adj einsam

loneliness ['ləunlɪnɪs] n Einsamkeit f

lonely ['ləunlɪ] adj einsam

loner ['ləunə*] n Einzelgänger(in) m(f)

long [lɔŋ] adj lang; (*distance*) weit ♦ adv lange ♦ vi: **to ~ for** sich sehnen nach; **before ~** bald; **as ~ as** solange; **in the ~ run** auf die Dauer; **don't be ~!** beeil dich!;

how ~ is the street? wie lang ist die Straße?; **how ~ is the lesson?** wie lange dauert die Stunde?; **6 metres ~** 6 Meter lang; **6 months ~** 6 Monate lang; **all night ~** die ganze Nacht; **he no ~er comes** er kommt nicht mehr; **~ ago** vor langer Zeit; **~ before** lange vorher; **at ~ last** endlich; **~-distance** adj Fern-

longevity [lɔn'dʒevɪtɪ] n Langlebigkeit f

long: **~-haired** adj langhaarig; **~hand** n Langschrift f; **~ing** n Sehnsucht f ♦ adj sehnsüchtig

longitude ['lɔŋgɪtjuːd] n Längengrad m

long: **~ jump** n Weitsprung m; **~-life** adj (*batteries etc*) mit langer Lebensdauer; **~-lost** adj längst verloren geglaubt; **~-playing record** n Langspielplatte f; **~-range** adj Langstrecken-, Fern-; **~-sighted** adj weitsichtig; **~-standing** adj alt, seit langer Zeit bestehend; **~-suffering** adj schwer geprüft; **~-term** adj langfristig; **~ wave** n Langwelle f; **~-winded** adj langatmig

loo [luː] (BRIT: *inf*) n Klo nt

look [luk] vi schauen; (*seem*) aussehen; (*building etc*): **to ~ on to the sea** aufs Meer gehen ♦ n Blick m; **~s** npl (*appearance*) Aussehen nt; **~ after** vt (*care for*) sorgen für; (*watch*) aufpassen auf +acc; **~ at** vt ansehen; (*consider*) sich überlegen; **~ back** vi sich umsehen; (*fig*) zurückblicken; **~ down on** vt (*fig*) herabsehen auf +acc; **~ for** vt (*seek*) suchen; **~ forward to** vt sich freuen auf +acc; (*in letters*): **we ~ forward to hearing from you** wir hoffen, bald von Ihnen zu hören; **~ into** vt untersuchen; **~ on** vi zusehen; **~ out** vi hinaussehen; (*take care*) aufpassen; **~ out for** vt Ausschau halten nach; (*be careful*) Acht geben auf +acc; **~ round** vi sich umsehen; **~ to** vt (*take care of*) Acht geben auf +acc; (*rely on*) sich verlassen auf +acc; **~ up** vi aufblicken; (*improve*) sich bessern ♦ vt (*word*) nachschlagen; (*person*) besuchen; **~ up to** vt aufsehen zu; **~out** n (*watch*) Ausschau f; (*person*) Wachposten m; (*place*) Ausguck m; (*prospect*) Aussichten pl; **to be on the ~ out**

for sth nach etw Ausschau halten
loom [luːm] *n* Webstuhl *m* ♦ *vi* sich abzeichnen
loony ['luːni] (*inf*) *adj* Verrückte(r) *mf*
loop [luːp] *n* Schlaufe *f*; **~hole** *n* (*fig*) Hintertürchen *nt*
loose [luːs] *adj* lose, locker; (*free*) frei; (*inexact*) unpräzise ♦ *vt* lösen, losbinden; **~ change** *n* Kleingeld *nt*; **~ chippings** *npl* (*on road*) Rollsplit *m*; **~ end** *n*: **to be at a ~ end** (*BRIT*) *or* **at ~ ends** (*US*) nicht wissen, was man tun soll; **~ly** *adv* locker, lose; **~n** *vt* lockern, losmachen
loot [luːt] *n* Beute *f* ♦ *vt* plündern
lop off [lɒp-] *vt* abhacken
lopsided ['lɒp'saɪdɪd] *adj* schief
lord [lɔːd] *n* (*ruler*) Herr *m*; (*BRIT: title*) Lord *m*; **the L~** (*God*) der Herr; **the (House of) L~s** das Oberhaus; **~ship** *n*: **Your L~ship** Eure Lordschaft
lorry ['lɒri] (*BRIT*) *n* Lastwagen *m*; **~ driver** (*BRIT*) *n* Lastwagenfahrer(in) *m(f)*
lose [luːz] (*pt, pp* **lost**) *vt* verlieren; (*chance*) verpassen ♦ *vi* verlieren; **to ~ (time)** (*clock*) nachgehen; **~r** *n* Verlierer *m*
loss [lɒs] *n* Verlust *m*; **at a ~** (*COMM*) mit Verlust; (*unable*) außerstande, außer Stande
lost [lɒst] *pt, pp of* **lose** ♦ *adj* verloren; **~ property** (*US* ~ **and found**) *n* Fundsachen *pl*
lot [lɒt] *n* (*quantity*) Menge *f*; (*fate, at auction*) Los *nt*; (*inf: people, things*) Haufen *m*; **the ~** alles; (*people*) alle; **a ~ of** (*with sg*) viel; (*with pl*) viele; **~s of** massenhaft, viel(e); **I read a ~** ich lese viel; **to draw ~s for sth** etw verlosen
lotion ['ləʊʃən] *n* Lotion *f*
lottery ['lɒtəri] *n* Lotterie *f*
loud [laʊd] *adj* laut; (*showy*) schreiend ♦ *adv* laut; **~ly** *adv* laut; **~speaker** *n* Lautsprecher *m*
lounge [laʊndʒ] *n* (*in hotel*) Gesellschaftsraum *m*; (*in house*) Wohnzimmer *nt* ♦ *vi* sich herumlümmeln
louse [laʊs] *n* (*pl* **lice**) *n* Laus *f*
lousy ['laʊzi] *adj* (*fig*) miserabel
lout [laʊt] *n* Lümmel *m*

louvre ['luːvəʳ] (*US* **louver**) *adj* (*door, window*) Jalousie-
lovable ['lʌvəbl] *adj* liebenswert
love [lʌv] *n* Liebe *f*; (*person*) Liebling *m*; (*SPORT*) null ♦ *vt* (*person*) lieben; (*activity*) gerne mögen; **to be in ~ with sb** in jdn verliebt sein; **to make ~** sich lieben; **for the ~ of** aus Liebe zu; **"15 ~"** (*TENNIS*) „15 null"; **to ~ to do sth** etw (sehr) gerne tun; **~ affair** *n* (*Liebes*)verhältnis *nt*; **~ letter** *n* Liebesbrief *m*; **~ life** *n* Liebesleben *nt*
lovely ['lʌvli] *adj* schön
lover ['lʌvəʳ] *n* Liebhaber(in) *m(f)*
loving ['lʌvɪŋ] *adj* liebend, liebevoll
low [ləʊ] *adj* niedrig; (*rank*) niedere(r, s); (*level, note, neckline*) tief; (*intelligence, density*) gering; (*vulgar*) ordinär; (*not loud*) leise; (*depressed*) gedrückt ♦ *adv* (*not high*) niedrig; (*not loudly*) leise ♦ *n* (~ *point*) Tiefstand *m*; (*MET*) Tief *nt*; **to feel ~** sich mies fühlen; **to turn (down)** ~ leiser stellen; **~ alcohol** *adj* alkoholarm; **~-calorie** *adj* kalorienarm; **~-cut** *adj* (*dress*) tief ausgeschnitten; **~er** *vt* herunterlassen; (*eyes, gun*) senken; (*reduce*) herabsetzen, senken ♦ *vr*: **to ~er o.s. to** (*fig*) sich herablassen zu; **~er sixth** (*BRIT*) *n* (*SCOL*) ≈ zwölfte Klasse; **~-fat** *adj* fettarm, Mager-; **~lands** *npl* (*GEOG*) Flachland *nt*; **~ly** *adj* bescheiden; **~-lying** *adj* tief gelegen
loyal ['lɔɪəl] *adj* treu; **~ty** *n* Treue *f*; **~ty card** *n* Kundenkarte *f*
lozenge ['lɒzɪndʒ] *n* Pastille *f*
L-plates ['ɛlpleɪts] (*BRIT*) *npl* L-Schild *nt*

> **L-Plates**
>
> ***i*** Als **L-Plates** werden in Großbritannien die weißen Schilder mit einem roten „L" bezeichnet, die an jedem von einem Fahrschüler geführten Fahrzeug befestigt werden müssen. Fahrschüler bekommen einen vorläufigen Führerschein und dürfen damit unter Aufsicht eines erfahrenen Autofahrers auf allen Straßen außer Autobahnen fahren.

Ltd *abbr* (= *limited company*) GmbH
lubricant ['luːbrɪkənt] *n* Schmiermittel *nt*

lubricate ['lu:brɪkeɪt] vt schmieren
lucid ['lu:sɪd] adj klar; (sane) bei klarem
Verstand; (moment) licht
luck [lʌk] n Glück nt; **bad** or **hard** or **tough**
~**!** (so ein) Pech!; **good** ~**!** viel Glück!; ~**ily**
adv glücklicherweise, zum Glück; ~**y** adj
Glücks-; **to be** ~**y** Glück haben
lucrative ['lu:krətɪv] adj einträglich
ludicrous ['lu:dɪkrəs] adj grotesk
lug [lʌg] vt schleppen
luggage ['lʌgɪdʒ] n Gepäck nt; ~ **rack** n
Gepäcknetz nt
lukewarm ['lu:kwɔ:m] adj lauwarm;
(indifferent) lau
lull [lʌl] n Flaute f ♦ vt einlullen; (calm)
beruhigen
lullaby ['lʌləbaɪ] n Schlaflied nt
lumbago [lʌm'beɪgəu] n Hexenschuss m
lumber ['lʌmbər] n Plunder m; (wood) Holz
nt; ~**jack** n Holzfäller m
luminous ['lu:mɪnəs] adj Leucht-
lump [lʌmp] n Klumpen m; (MED)
Schwellung f; (in breast) Knoten m; (of
sugar) Stück nt ♦ vt (also: ~ **together**)
zusammentun; (judge together) in einen
Topf werfen; ~ **sum** n Pauschalsumme f;
~**y** adj klumpig
lunacy ['lu:nəsɪ] n Irrsinn m
lunar ['lu:nər] adj Mond-
lunatic ['lu:nətɪk] n Wahnsinnige(r) mf ♦ adj
wahnsinnig, irr
lunch [lʌntʃ] n Mittagessen nt; ~**eon**
['lʌntʃən] n Mittagessen nt; ~**eon meat** n
Frühstücksfleisch nt; ~**eon voucher** (BRIT)
n Essenmarke f; ~**time** n Mittagszeit f
lung [lʌŋ] n Lunge f
lunge [lʌndʒ] vi (also: ~ **forward**)
(los)stürzen; **to** ~ **at** sich stürzen auf +acc
lurch [lə:tʃ] vi taumeln; (NAUT) schlingern ♦ n
Ruck m; (NAUT) Schlingern nt; **to leave sb**
in the ~ jdn im Stich lassen
lure [luər] n Köder m; (fig) Lockung f ♦ vt
(ver)locken
lurid ['luərɪd] adj (shocking) grausig,
widerlich; (colour) grell
lurk [lə:k] vi lauern
luscious ['lʌʃəs] adj köstlich

lush [lʌʃ] adj satt; (vegetation) üppig
lust [lʌst] n Wollust f; (greed) Gier f ♦ vi: **to** ~
after gieren nach
lustre ['lʌstər] (US **luster**) n Glanz m
Luxembourg ['lʌksəmbə:g] n Luxemburg nt
luxuriant [lʌg'zjuərɪənt] adj üppig
luxurious [lʌg'zjuərɪəs] adj luxuriös, Luxus-
luxury ['lʌkʃərɪ] n Luxus m ♦ cpd Luxus-
lying ['laɪɪŋ] n Lügen nt ♦ adj verlogen
lynx [lɪŋks] n Luchs m
lyric ['lɪrɪk] n Lyrik f ♦ adj lyrisch; ~**s** pl (words
for song) (Lied)text m; ~**al** adj lyrisch,
gefühlvoll

M, m

m abbr = **metre**; **mile**; **million**
M.A. n abbr = **Master of Arts**
mac [mæk] (BRIT: inf) n Regenmantel m
macaroni [mækə'rəunɪ] n Makkaroni pl
machine [mə'ʃi:n] n Maschine f ♦ vt (dress
etc) mit der Maschine nähen; ~ **gun** n
Maschinengewehr nt; ~ **language** n
(COMPUT) Maschinensprache f; ~**ry** n
Maschinerie f
macho ['mætʃəu] adj macho
mackerel ['mækrɪl] n Makrele f
mackintosh ['mækɪntɔʃ] (BRIT) n
Regenmantel m
mad [mæd] adj verrückt; (dog) tollwütig;
(angry) wütend; ~ **about** (fond of) verrückt
nach, versessen auf +acc
madam ['mædəm] n gnädige Frau f
madden ['mædn] vt verrückt machen; (make
angry) ärgern
made [meɪd] pt, pp of **make**
made-to-measure ['meɪdtə'mɛʒər] (BRIT)
adj Maß-
mad [mæd-]: ~**ly** adv wahnsinnig; ~**man**
(irreg) n Verrückte(r) m, Irre(r) m; ~**ness** n
Wahnsinn m
magazine [mægə'zi:n] n Zeitschrift f; (in
gun) Magazin nt
maggot ['mægət] n Made f
magic ['mædʒɪk] n Zauberei f, Magie f; (fig)
Zauber m ♦ adj magisch, Zauber-; ~**al** adj

magisch; **~ian** [mə'dʒɪʃən] n Zauberer m

magistrate ['mædʒɪstreɪt] n (Friedens)richter m

magnanimous [mæg'nænɪməs] adj großmütig

magnet ['mægnɪt] n Magnet m; **~ic** [mæg'netɪk] adj magnetisch; **~ic tape** n Magnetband nt; **~ism** n Magnetismus m; (fig) Ausstrahlungskraft f

magnificent [mæg'nɪfɪsnt] adj großartig

magnify ['mægnɪfaɪ] vt vergrößern; **~ing glass** n Lupe f

magnitude ['mægnɪtjuːd] n (size) Größe f; (importance) Ausmaß nt

magpie ['mægpaɪ] n Elster f

mahogany [mə'hɒgənɪ] n Mahagoni nt ♦ cpd Mahagoni-

maid [meɪd] n Dienstmädchen nt; **old ~** alte Jungfer f

maiden ['meɪdn] n Maid f ♦ adj (flight, speech) Jungfern-; **~ name** n Mädchenname m

mail [meɪl] n Post f ♦ vt aufgeben; **~ box** (US) n Briefkasten m; **~ing list** n Anschreibeliste f; **~ order** n Bestellung f durch die Post; **~ order firm** n Versandhaus nt

maim [meɪm] vt verstümmeln

main [meɪn] adj hauptsächlich, Haupt- ♦ n (pipe) Hauptleitung f; **the ~s** npl (ELEC) das Stromnetz; **in the ~** im Großen und Ganzen; **~frame** n (COMPUT) Großrechner m; **~land** n Festland nt; **~ly** adv hauptsächlich; **~ road** n Hauptstraße f; **~stay** n (fig) Hauptstütze f; **~stream** n Hauptrichtung f

maintain [meɪn'teɪn] vt (machine, roads) instand or in Stand halten; (support) unterhalten; (keep up) aufrechterhalten; (claim) behaupten; (innocence) beteuern

maintenance ['meɪntənəns] n (TECH) Wartung f; (of family) Unterhalt m

maize [meɪz] n Mais m

majestic [mə'dʒestɪk] adj majestätisch

majesty ['mædʒɪstɪ] n Majestät f

major ['meɪdʒə*] n Major m ♦ adj (MUS) Dur; (more important) Haupt-; (bigger) größer

Majorca [mə'jɔːkə] n Mallorca nt

majority [mə'dʒɒrɪtɪ] n Mehrheit f; (JUR) Volljährigkeit f

make [meɪk] (pt, pp **made**) vt machen; (appoint) ernennen (zu); (cause to do sth) veranlassen; (reach) erreichen; (in time) schaffen; (earn) verdienen ♦ n Marke f; **to ~ sth happen** etw geschehen lassen; **to ~ it** es schaffen; **what time do you ~ it?** wie spät hast du es?; **to ~ do with** auskommen mit; **~ for** vi gehen/fahren nach; **~ out** vt (write out) ausstellen; (understand) verstehen; **~ up** vt machen; (face) schminken; (quarrel) beilegen; (story etc) erfinden ♦ vi sich versöhnen; **~ up for** vt wieder gutmachen; (COMM) vergüten; **~-believe** n Fantasie f; **~r** n (COMM) Hersteller m; **~shift** adj behelfsmäßig, Not-; **~-up** n Schminke f, Make-up nt; **~-up remover** n Make-up-Entferner m; **making** n: **in the making** im Entstehen; **to have the makings of** das Zeug haben zu

malaria [mə'lɛərɪə] n Malaria f

Malaysia [mə'leɪzɪə] n Malaysia nt

male [meɪl] n Mann m; (animal) Männchen nt ♦ adj männlich

malevolent [mə'levələnt] adj übel wollend

malfunction [mæl'fʌŋkʃən] n (MED) Funktionsstörung f; (of machine) Defekt m

malice ['mælɪs] n Bosheit f; **malicious** [mə'lɪʃəs] adj böswillig, gehässig

malign [mə'laɪn] vt verleumden ♦ adj böse

malignant [mə'lɪgnənt] adj bösartig

mall [mɔːl] n (also: **shopping ~**) Einkaufszentrum nt

malleable ['mælɪəbl] adj formbar

mallet ['mælɪt] n Holzhammer m

malnutrition [mælnjuː'trɪʃən] n Unterernährung f

malpractice [mæl'præktɪs] n Amtsvergehen nt

malt [mɔːlt] n Malz m

Malta ['mɔːltə] n Malta nt; **Maltese** [mɔːl'tiːz] adj inv maltesisch ♦ n inv Malteser(in) m(f)

maltreat [mæl'triːt] vt misshandeln

mammal ['mæml] n Säugetier nt

mammoth ['mæməθ] *n* Mammut *nt* ♦ *adj* Mammut-

man [mæn] (*pl* **men**) *n* Mann *m*; (*human race*) der Mensch, die Menschen *pl* ♦ *vt* bemannen; **an old ~** ein alter Mann, ein Greis *m*; **~ and wife** Mann und Frau

manage ['mænɪdʒ] *vi* zurechtkommen ♦ *vt* (*control*) führen, leiten; (*cope with*) fertig werden mit; **~able** *adj* (*person, animal*) fügsam; (*object*) handlich; **~ment** *n* (*control*) Führung *f*, Leitung *f*; (*directors*) Management *nt*; **~r** *n* Geschäftsführer *m*; **~ress** [mænɪdʒə'res] *n* Geschäftsführerin *f*; **~rial** [mænɪ'dʒɪərɪəl] *adj* (*post*) leitend; (*problem etc*) Management-; **managing** ['mænɪdʒɪŋ] *adj*: **managing director** Betriebsleiter *m*

mandarin ['mændərɪn] *n* (*fruit*) Mandarine *f*

mandatory ['mændətərɪ] *adj* obligatorisch

mane [meɪn] *n* Mähne *f*

maneuver [mə'nuːvər] (*US*) = **manoeuvre**

manfully ['mænfəlɪ] *adv* mannhaft

mangle ['mæŋɡl] *vt* verstümmeln ♦ *n* Mangel *f*

mango ['mæŋɡəʊ] (*pl* **~es**) *n* Mango(pflaume) *f*

mangy ['meɪndʒɪ] *adj* (*dog*) räudig

man ['mæn-]: **~handle** *vt* grob behandeln; **~hole** *n* (Straßen)schacht *m*; **~hood** *n* Mannesalter *nt*; (*~liness*) Männlichkeit *f*; **~-hour** *n* Arbeitsstunde *f*; **~hunt** *n* Fahndung *f*

mania ['meɪnɪə] *n* Manie *f*; **~c** ['meɪnɪæk] *n* Wahnsinnige(r) *mf*

manic ['mænɪk] *adj* (*behaviour, activity*) hektisch

manicure ['mænɪkjʊər] *n* Maniküre *f*; **~ set** *n* Necessaire *nt*, Nessessär *nt*

manifest ['mænɪfest] *vt* offenbaren ♦ *adj* offenkundig; **~ation** [mænɪfes'teɪʃən] *n* (*sign*) Anzeichen *nt*

manifesto [mænɪ'festəʊ] *n* Manifest *nt*

manipulate [mə'nɪpjʊleɪt] *vt* handhaben; (*fig*) manipulieren

man [mæn'-]: **~kind** *n* Menschheit *f*; **~ly** ['mænlɪ] *adj* männlich; mannhaft; **~-made** *adj* (*fibre*) künstlich

manner ['mænər] *n* Art *f*, Weise *f*; **~s** *npl* (*behaviour*) Manieren *pl*; **in a ~ of speaking** sozusagen; **~ism** *n* (*of person*) Angewohnheit *f*; (*of style*) Manieriertheit *f*

manoeuvre [mə'nuːvər] (*US* **maneuver**) *vt*, *vi* manövrieren ♦ *n* (*MIL*) Feldzug *m*; (*general*) Manöver *nt*, Schachzug *m*

manor ['mænər] *n* Landgut *nt*

manpower ['mænpaʊər] *n* Arbeitskräfte *pl*

mansion ['mænʃən] *n* Villa *f*

manslaughter ['mænslɔːtər] *n* Totschlag *m*

mantelpiece ['mæntlpiːs] *n* Kaminsims *m*

manual ['mænjʊəl] *adj* manuell, Hand- ♦ *n* Handbuch *nt*

manufacture [mænju'fæktʃər] *vt* herstellen ♦ *n* Herstellung *f*; **~r** *n* Hersteller *m*

manure [mə'njʊər] *n* Dünger *m*

manuscript ['mænjuskrɪpt] *n* Manuskript *nt*

Manx [mæŋks] *adj* der Insel Man

many ['menɪ] *adj, pron* viele; **a great ~** sehr viele; **~ a time** oft

map [mæp] *n* (Land)karte *f*; (*of town*) Stadtplan *m* ♦ *vt* eine Karte machen von; **~ out** *vt* (*fig*) ausarbeiten

maple ['meɪpl] *n* Ahorn *m*

mar [mɑːr] *vt* verderben

marathon ['mærəθən] *n* (*SPORT*) Marathonlauf *m*; (*fig*) Marathon *m*

marble ['mɑːbl] *n* Marmor *m*; (*for game*) Murmel *f*

March [mɑːtʃ] *n* März *m*

march [mɑːtʃ] *vi* marschieren ♦ *n* Marsch *m*

mare [mɛər] *n* Stute *f*

margarine [mɑːdʒə'riːn] *n* Margarine *f*

margin ['mɑːdʒɪn] *n* Rand *m*; (*extra amount*) Spielraum *m*; (*COMM*) Spanne *f*; **~al** *adj* (*note*) Rand-; (*difference etc*) geringfügig; **~al (seat)** *n* (*POL*) Wahlkreis, der nur mit knapper Mehrheit gehalten wird

marigold ['mærɪɡəʊld] *n* Ringelblume *f*

marijuana [mærɪ'wɑːnə] *n* Marihuana *nt*

marina [mə'riːnə] *n* Jachthafen *m*

marinate ['mærɪneɪt] *vt* marinieren

marine [mə'riːn] *adj* Meeres-, See- ♦ *n* (*MIL*) Marineinfanterist *m*

marital ['mærɪtl] *adj* ehelich, Ehe-; **~ status** *n* Familienstand *m*

maritime ['mærɪtaɪm] adj See-

mark [maːk] n (HIST: coin) Mark f; (spot) Fleck m; (scar) Kratzer m; (sign) Zeichen nt; (target) Ziel nt; (SCH) Note f ♦ vt (make ~ on) Flecken/Kratzer machen auf +acc; (indicate) markieren; (exam) korrigieren; **to ~ time** (also fig) auf der Stelle treten; **~ out** vt bestimmen; (area) abstecken; ~ed adj deutlich; ~er n (in book) (Lese)zeichen nt; (on road) Schild nt

market ['maːkɪt] n Markt m; (stock ~) Börse f ♦ vt (COMM: new product) auf den Markt bringen; (sell) vertreiben; **~ garden** (BRIT) n Handelsgärtnerei f; **~ing** n Marketing nt; **~ research** n Marktforschung f; **~ value** n Marktwert m

marksman ['maːksmən] (irreg) n Scharfschütze m

marmalade ['maːməleɪd] n Orangenmarmelade f

maroon [mə'ruːn] vt aussetzen ♦ adj (colour) kastanienbraun

marquee [maː'kiː] n große(s) Zelt nt

marriage ['mærɪdʒ] n Ehe f; (wedding) Heirat f; **~ bureau** n Heiratsinstitut nt; **~ certificate** n Heiratsurkunde f

married ['mærɪd] adj (person) verheiratet; (couple, life) Ehe-

marrow ['mærəʊ] n (Knochen)mark nt; (BOT) Kürbis m

marry ['mærɪ] vt (join) trauen; (take as husband, wife) heiraten ♦ vi (also: **get married**) heiraten

marsh [maːʃ] n Sumpf m

marshal ['maːʃl] n (US) Bezirkspolizeichef m ♦ vt (an)ordnen, arrangieren

marshy ['maːʃɪ] adj sumpfig

martial law ['maːʃl] n Kriegsrecht nt

martyr ['maːtə] n (also fig) Märtyrer(in) m(f) ♦ vt zum Märtyrer machen; **~dom** n Martyrium nt

marvel ['maːvl] n Wunder nt ♦ vi: **to ~ (at)** sich wundern (über +acc); **~lous** (US **marvelous**) adj wunderbar

Marxist ['maːksɪst] n Marxist(in) m(f)

marzipan ['maːzɪpæn] n Marzipan nt

mascara [mæs'kaːrə] n Wimperntusche f

mascot ['mæskət] n Maskottchen nt

masculine ['mæskjulɪn] adj männlich

mash [mæʃ] n Brei m; **~ed potatoes** npl Kartoffelbrei m or -püree nt

mask [maːsk] n (also fig) Maske f ♦ vt maskieren, verdecken

mason ['meɪsn] n (stonemason) Steinmetz m; (freemason) Freimaurer m; **~ry** n Mauerwerk nt

masquerade [mæskə'reɪd] n Maskerade f ♦ vi: **to ~ as** sich ausgeben als

mass [mæs] n Masse f; (greater part) Mehrheit f; (REL) Messe f ♦ vi sich sammeln; **the ~es** npl (people) die Masse(n) f(pl)

massacre ['mæsəkə] n Blutbad nt ♦ vt niedermetzeln, massakrieren

massage ['mæsaːʒ] n Massage f ♦ vt massieren

massive ['mæsɪv] adj gewaltig, massiv

mass media npl Massenmedien pl

mass production n Massenproduktion f

mast [maːst] n Mast m

master ['maːstə] n Herr m; (NAUT) Kapitän m; (teacher) Lehrer m; (artist) Meister m ♦ vt meistern; (language etc) beherrschen; **~ly** adj meisterhaft; **~mind** n Kapazität f ♦ vt geschickt lenken; **M~ of Arts** n Magister m der philosophischen Fakultät; **M~ of Science** n Magister m der naturwissenschaftlichen Fakultät; **~piece** n Meisterwerk nt; **~ plan** n kluge(r) Plan m; **~y** n Können nt

masturbate ['mæstəbeɪt] vi masturbieren, onanieren

mat [mæt] n Matte f; (for table) Untersetzer m ♦ adj = **matt**

match [mætʃ] n Streichholz nt; (sth corresponding) Pendant nt; (SPORT) Wettkampf m; (ball games) Spiel nt ♦ vt (be like, suit) passen zu; (equal) gleichkommen +dat ♦ vi zusammenpassen; **it's a good ~ (for)** es passt gut (zu); **~box** n Streichholzschachtel f; **~ing** adj passend

mate [meɪt] n (companion) Kamerad m; (spouse) Lebensgefährte m; (of animal) Weibchen nt/Männchen nt; (NAUT) Schiffsoffizier m ♦ vi (animals) sich paaren

♦ *vt* (*animals*) paaren

material [mə'tɪərɪəl] *n* Material *nt*; (*for book, cloth*) Stoff *m* ♦ *adj* (*important*) wesentlich; (*damage*) Sach-; (*comforts etc*) materiell; **~s** *npl* (*for building etc*) Materialien *pl*; **~istic** [mətɪərɪə'lɪstɪk] *adj* materialistisch; **~ize** *vi* sich verwirklichen, zustande *or* zu Stande kommen

maternal [mə'tɜːnl] *adj* mütterlich, Mutter-

maternity [mə'tɜːnɪtɪ] *adj* (*dress*) Umstands-; (*benefit*) Wochen-; **~ hospital** *n* Entbindungsheim *nt*

math [mæθ] (*US*) *n* = **maths**

mathematical [mæθə'mætɪkl] *adj* mathematisch; **mathematics** *n* Mathematik *f*; **maths** (*US* **math**) *n* Mathe *f*

matinée ['mætɪneɪ] *n* Matinee *f*

matrices ['meɪtrɪsiːz] *npl of* **matrix**

matriculation [mətrɪkju'leɪʃən] *n* Immatrikulation *f*

matrimonial [mætrɪ'məunɪəl] *adj* ehelich, Ehe-

matrimony ['mætrɪmənɪ] *n* Ehestand *m*

matrix ['meɪtrɪks] (*pl* **matrices**) *n* Matrize *f*; (*GEOL etc*) Matrix *f*

matron ['meɪtrən] *n* (*MED*) Oberin *f*; (*SCH*) Hausmutter *f*

matt [mæt] *adj* (*paint*) matt

matted ['mætɪd] *adj* verfilzt

matter ['mætə'] *n* (*substance*) Materie *f*; (*affair*) Angelegenheit *f* ♦ *vi* darauf ankommen; **no** *or* **how/what** egal wie/was; **what is the ~?** was ist los?; **as a ~ of course** selbstverständlich; **as a ~ of fact** eigentlich; **it doesn't ~** es macht nichts; **~-of-fact** *adj* sachlich, nüchtern

mattress ['mætrɪs] *n* Matratze *f*

mature [mə'tjuə'] *adj* reif ♦ *vi* reif werden; **maturity** [mə'tjuərɪtɪ] *n* Reife *f*

maul [mɔːl] *vt* übel zurichten

maxima ['mæksɪmə] *npl of* **maximum**

maximum ['mæksɪməm] (*pl* **maxima**) *adj* Höchst-, Maximal- ♦ *n* Maximum *nt*

May [meɪ] *n* Mai *m*

may [meɪ] (*conditional* **might**) *vi* (*be possible*) können; (*have permission*) dürfen; **he ~ come** er kommt vielleicht; **~be** ['meɪbiː]

adv vielleicht

May Day *n* der 1. Mai

mayhem ['meɪhɛm] *n* Chaos *nt*; (*US*) Körperverletzung *f*

mayonnaise [meɪə'neɪz] *n* Majonäse *f*, Mayonnaise *f*

mayor [meə'] *n* Bürgermeister *m*; **~ess** *n* Bürgermeisterin *f*; (*wife*) (die) Frau *f* Bürgermeister

maypole ['meɪpəul] *n* Maibaum *m*

maze [meɪz] *n* Irrgarten *m*; (*fig*) Wirrwarr *nt*

M.D. *abbr* = **Doctor of Medicine**

KEYWORD

---

me [miː] *pron* **1** (*direct*) mich; **it's me** ich bins

2 (*indirect*) mir; **give them to me** gib sie mir

3 (*after prep: +acc*) mich; (: *+dat*) mir; **with/without me** mit mir/ohne mich

---

meadow ['mɛdəu] *n* Wiese *f*

meagre ['miːgə'] (*US* **meager**) *adj* dürftig, spärlich

meal [miːl] *n* Essen *nt*, Mahlzeit *f*; (*grain*) Schrotmehl *nt*; **to have a ~** essen (gehen); **~time** *n* Essenszeit *f*

mean [miːn] (*pt, pp* **meant**) *adj* (*stingy*) geizig; (*spiteful*) gemein; (*average*) durchschnittlich, Durchschnitts- ♦ *vt* (*signify*) bedeuten; (*intend*) vorhaben, beabsichtigen ♦ *n* (*average*) Durchschnitt *m*; **~s** *npl* (*wherewithal*) Mittel *pl*; (*wealth*) Vermögen *nt*; **do you ~ me?** meinst du mich?; **do you ~ it?** meinst du das ernst?; **what do you ~?** was willst du damit sagen?; **to be ~t for sb/sth** für jdn/etw bestimmt sein; **by ~s of** durch; **by all ~s** selbstverständlich; **by no ~s** keineswegs

meander [mɪ'ændə'] *vi* sich schlängeln

meaning ['miːnɪŋ] *n* Bedeutung *f*; (*of life*) Sinn *m*; **~ful** *adj* bedeutungsvoll; (*life*) sinnvoll; **~less** *adj* sinnlos

meanness ['miːnnɪs] *n* (*stinginess*) Geiz *m*; (*spitefulness*) Gemeinheit *f*

meant [mɛnt] *pt, pp of* **mean**

meantime ['miːntaɪm] *adv* inzwischen

meanwhile ['miːnwaɪl] *adv* inzwischen

measles ['miːzlz] *n* Masern *pl*

measly ['miːzlɪ] (*inf*) *adj* poplig

measure ['mɛʒəʳ] *vt, vi* messen ♦ *n* Maß *nt*; (*step*) Maßnahme *f*; **~ments** *npl* Maße *pl*

meat [miːt] *n* Fleisch *nt*; **cold ~** Aufschnitt *m*; **~ ball** *n* Fleischkloß *m*; **~ pie** *n* Fleischpastete *f*; **~y** *adj* fleischig; (*fig*) gehaltvoll

Mecca ['mɛkə] *n* Mekka *nt* (*also fig*)

mechanic [mɪ'kænɪk] *n* Mechaniker *m*; **~al** *adj* mechanisch; **~s** *n* Mechanik *f* ♦ *npl* Technik *f*

mechanism ['mɛkənɪzəm] *n* Mechanismus *m*

mechanize ['mɛkənaɪz] *vt* mechanisieren

medal ['mɛdl] *n* Medaille *f*; (*decoration*) Orden *m*; **~list** (*US* **medalist**) *n* Medaillengewinner(in) *m(f)*

meddle ['mɛdl] *vi*: **to ~ (in)** sich einmischen (in +*acc*); **to ~ with sth** sich an etw *dat* zu schaffen machen

media ['miːdɪə] *npl* Medien *pl*

mediaeval [mɛdɪ'iːvl] *adj* = **medieval**

median ['miːdɪən] (*US*) *n* (*also*: ~ **strip**) Mittelstreifen *m*

mediate ['miːdɪeɪt] *vi* vermitteln; **mediator** *n* Vermittler *m*

Medicaid ['mɛdɪkeɪd] (®) (*US*) *n* medizinisches Versorgungsprogramm für sozial Schwache

medical ['mɛdɪkl] *adj* medizinisch; Medizin-; ärztlich ♦ *n* (ärztliche) Untersuchung *f*

Medicare ['mɛdɪkɛəʳ] (*US*) *n* staatliche Krankenversicherung besonders für Ältere

medicated ['mɛdɪkeɪtɪd] *adj* medizinisch

medication [mɛdɪ'keɪʃən] *n* (*drugs etc*) Medikamente *pl*

medicinal [mɛ'dɪsɪnl] *adj* medizinisch, Heil-

medicine ['mɛdsɪn] *n* Medizin *f*; (*drugs*) Arznei *f*

medieval [mɛdɪ'iːvl] *adj* mittelalterlich

mediocre [miːdɪ'əʊkəʳ] *adj* mittelmäßig

meditate ['mɛdɪteɪt] *vi* meditieren; **to ~ (on sth)** (über etw *acc*) nachdenken; **meditation** [mɛdɪ'teɪʃən] *n* Nachsinnen *nt*; Meditation *f*

Mediterranean [mɛdɪtə'reɪnɪən] *adj*

Mittelmeer-; (*person*) südländisch; **the ~ (Sea)** das Mittelmeer

medium ['miːdɪəm] *adj* mittlere(r, s), Mittel-, mittel- ♦ *n* Mitte *f*; (*means*) Mittel *nt*; (*person*) Medium *nt*; **happy ~** goldener Mittelweg *m*; **~-sized** *adj* mittelgroß; **~ wave** *n* Mittelwelle *f*

medley ['mɛdlɪ] *n* Gemisch *nt*

meek [miːk] *adj* sanft(mütig)

meet [miːt] (*pt, pp* **met**) *vt* (*encounter*) treffen, begegnen +*dat*; (*by arrangement*) sich treffen mit; (*difficulties*) stoßen auf +*acc*; (*get to know*) kennen lernen; (*fetch*) abholen; (*join*) zusammentreffen mit; (*satisfy*) entsprechen +*dat* ♦ *vi* sich treffen; (*become acquainted*) sich kennen lernen; **~ with** *vt* (*problems*) stoßen auf +*acc*; (*US: people*) zusammentreffen mit; **~ing** *n* Treffen *nt*; (*business ~ing*) Besprechung *f*; (*of committee*) Sitzung *f*; (*assembly*) Versammlung *f*

mega- ['mɛgə-] (*inf*) *prefix* Mega-; **~byte** *n* (*COMPUT*) Megabyte *nt*; **~phone** *n* Megafon *nt*, Megaphon *nt*

melancholy ['mɛlənkəlɪ] *adj* (*person*) melancholisch; (*sight, event*) traurig

mellow ['mɛləʊ] *adj* mild, weich; (*fruit*) reif; (*fig*) gesetzt ♦ *vi* reif werden

melodious [mɪ'ləʊdɪəs] *adj* wohlklingend

melody ['mɛlədɪ] *n* Melodie *f*

melon ['mɛlən] *n* Melone *f*

melt [mɛlt] *vi* schmelzen; (*anger*) verfliegen ♦ *vt* schmelzen; **~ away** *vi* dahinschmelzen; **~ down** *vt* einschmelzen; **~down** *n* (*in nuclear reactor*) Kernschmelze *f*; **~ing point** *n* Schmelzpunkt *m*; **~ing pot** *n* (*fig*) Schmelztiegel *m*

member ['mɛmbəʳ] *n* Mitglied *nt*; (*of tribe, species*) Angehörige(r) *f(m)*; (*ANAT*) Glied *nt*; **M~ of Parliament** (*BRIT*) *n* Parlamentsmitglied *nt*; **M~ of the European Parliament** (*BRIT*) *n* Mitglied *nt* des Europäischen Parlaments; **M~ of the Scottish Parliament** *n* Mitglied *nt* des schottischen Parlaments; **~ship** *n* Mitgliedschaft *f*; **to seek ~ship of** einen Antrag auf Mitgliedschaft stellen; **~ship**

card *n* Mitgliedskarte *f*

memento [mə'mentəu] *n* Andenken *nt*

memo ['meməu] *n* Mitteilung *f*

memoirs ['memwɑːz] *npl* Memoiren *pl*

memorable ['memərəbl] *adj* denkwürdig

memoranda [memə'rændə] *npl of* **memorandum**

memorandum [memə'rændəm] (*pl* **memoranda**) *n* Mitteilung *f*

memorial [mɪ'mɔːrɪəl] *n* Denkmal *nt* ♦ *adj* Gedenk-

memorize ['meməraɪz] *vt* sich einprägen

memory ['memərɪ] *n* Gedächtnis *nt*; (*of computer*) Speicher *m*; (*sth recalled*) Erinnerung *f*

men [men] *pl of* **man** ♦ *n* (*human race*) die Menschen *pl*

menace ['menɪs] *n* Drohung *f*; Gefahr *f* ♦ *vt* bedrohen; **menacing** *adj* drohend

menagerie [mɪ'nædʒərɪ] *n* Tierschau *f*

mend [mend] *vt* reparieren, flicken ♦ *vi* (ver)heilen ♦ *n* ausgebesserte Stelle *f*; **on the ~** auf dem Wege der Besserung; **~ing** *n* (*articles*) Flickarbeit *f*

menial ['miːnɪəl] *adj* niedrig

meningitis [menɪn'dʒaɪtɪs] *n* Hirnhautentzündung *f*, Meningitis *f*

menopause ['menəupɔːz] *n* Wechseljahre *pl*, Menopause *f*

menstruation [menstru'eɪʃən] *n* Menstruation *f*

mental ['mentl] *adj* geistig, Geistes-; (*arithmetic*) Kopf-; (*hospital*) Nerven-; (*cruelty*) seelisch; (*inf: abnormal*) verrückt; **~ity** [men'tælɪtɪ] *n* Mentalität *f*

menthol ['menθɒl] *n* Menthol *nt*

mention ['menʃən] *n* Erwähnung *f* ♦ *vt* erwähnen; **don't ~ it!** bitte (sehr), gern geschehen

mentor ['mentɔː] *n* Mentor *m*

menu ['menjuː] *n* Speisekarte *f*

MEP *n abbr* = **Member of the European Parliament**

mercenary ['mɜːsɪnərɪ] *adj* (*person*) geldgierig ♦ *n* Söldner *m*

merchandise ['mɜːtʃəndaɪz] *n* (Handels)ware *f*

merchant ['mɜːtʃənt] *n* Kaufmann *m*; **~ bank** (*BRIT*) *n* Handelsbank *f*; **~ navy** (*US* **~ marine**) *n* Handelsmarine *f*

merciful ['mɜːsɪful] *adj* gnädig

merciless ['mɜːsɪlɪs] *adj* erbarmungslos

mercury ['mɜːkjurɪ] *n* Quecksilber *nt*

mercy ['mɜːsɪ] *n* Erbarmen *nt*; Gnade *f*; **at the ~ of** ausgeliefert +*dat*

mere [mɪə'] *adj* bloß; **~ly** *adv* bloß

merge [mɜːdʒ] *vt* verbinden; (*COMM*) fusionieren ♦ *vi* verschmelzen; (*roads*) zusammenlaufen; (*COMM*) fusionieren; **~r** *n* (*COMM*) Fusion *f*

meringue [mə'ræŋ] *n* Baiser *nt*

merit ['merɪt] *n* Verdienst *nt*; (*advantage*) Vorzug *m* ♦ *vt* verdienen

mermaid ['mɜːmeɪd] *n* Wassernixe *f*

merry ['merɪ] *adj* fröhlich; **~-go-round** *n* Karussell *nt*

mesh [meʃ] *n* Masche *f*

mesmerize ['mezməraɪz] *vt* hypnotisieren; (*fig*) faszinieren

mess [mes] *n* Unordnung *f*; (*dirt*) Schmutz *m*; (*trouble*) Schwierigkeiten *pl*; (*MIL*) Messe *f*; **~ about** *or* **around** *vi* (*play the fool*) herumalbern; (*do nothing in particular*) herumgammeln; **~ about** *or* **around with** *vt fus* (*tinker with*) herummurksen an +*dat*; **~ up** *vt* verpfuschen; (*make untidy*) in Unordnung bringen

message ['mesɪdʒ] *n* Mitteilung *f*; **to get the ~** kapieren

messenger ['mesɪndʒə'] *n* Bote *m*

Messrs ['mesəz] *abbr* (*on letters*) die Herren

messy ['mesɪ] *adj* schmutzig; (*untidy*) unordentlich

met [met] *pt, pp of* **meet**

metabolism [me'tæbəlɪzəm] *n* Stoffwechsel *m*

metal ['metl] *n* Metall *nt*; **~lic** *adj* metallisch; (*made of ~*) aus Metall

metaphor ['metəfə'] *n* Metapher *f*

meteorology [miːtɪə'rɒlədʒɪ] *n* Meteorologie *f*

meter ['miːtə'] *n* Zähler *m*; (*US*) = **metre**

method ['meθəd] *n* Methode *f*; **~ical** [mɪ'θɒdɪkl] *adj* methodisch; **M~ist**

['mɛθədɪst] *adj* methodistisch ♦ *n*
Methodist(in) *m(f)*; **~ology** [mɛθə'ɒlədʒɪ] *n*
Methodik *f*

meths [mɛθs] (*BRIT*) *n(pl)* = **methylated spirit(s)**

methylated spirit(s) ['mɛθɪleɪtɪd-] (*BRIT*) *n*
(Brenn)spiritus *m*

meticulous [mɪ'tɪkjuləs] *adj* (über)genau

metre ['miːtər] (*US* **meter**) *n* Meter *m or nt*

metric ['mɛtrɪk] *adj* (*also:* **~al**) metrisch

metropolitan [mɛtrə'pɒlɪtn] *adj* der
Großstadt; **M~ Police** *n*: **the M~
Police** die Londoner Polizei

mettle ['mɛtl] *n* Mut *m*

mew [mjuː] *vi* (*cat*) miauen

mews [mjuːz] *n*: **~ cottage** ehemaliges
Kutscherhäuschen

Mexican ['mɛksɪkən] *adj* mexikanisch ♦ *n*
Mexikaner(in) *m(f)*

Mexico ['mɛksɪkəu] *n* Mexiko *nt*

miaow [miː'au] *vi* miauen

mice [maɪs] *pl of* **mouse**

micro ['maɪkrəu] *n* (*also:* **~computer**)
Mikrocomputer *m*; **~chip** *n* Mikrochip *m*;
~cosm ['maɪkrəukɒzəm] *n* Mikrokosmos *m*;
~phone *n* Mikrofon *nt*, Mikrophon *nt*;
~scope *n* Mikroskop *nt*; **~wave** *n* (*also:*
~wave oven) Mikrowelle(nherd *nt*) *f*

mid [mɪd] *adj*: **in ~ afternoon** am
Nachmittag; **in ~ air** in der Luft; **in ~ May**
Mitte Mai

midday [mɪd'deɪ] *n* Mittag *m*

middle ['mɪdl] *n* Mitte *f*; (*waist*) Taille *f* ♦ *adj*
mittlere(r, s), Mittel-; **in the ~ of** in
+*dat*; **~-aged** *adj* mittleren Alters; **M~
Ages** *npl*: **the M~ Ages** das Mittelalter;
~-class *adj* Mittelstands-; **M~ East** *n*: **the
M~ East** der Nahe Osten; **~man** (*irreg*) *n*
(*COMM*) Zwischenhändler *m*; **~ name** *n*
zweiter Vorname *m*; **~ weight** *n* (*BOXING*)
Mittelgewicht *nt*

middling ['mɪdlɪŋ] *adj* mittelmäßig

midge [mɪdʒ] *n* Mücke *f*

midget ['mɪdʒɪt] *n* Liliputaner(in) *m(f)*

midnight ['mɪdnaɪt] *n* Mitternacht *f*

midriff ['mɪdrɪf] *n* Taille *f*

midst [mɪdst] *n*: **in the ~ of** (*persons*) mitten

unter +*dat*; (*things*) mitten in +*dat*

mid [mɪd-]: **~summer** *n* Hochsommer *m*;
~way *adv* auf halbem Wege ♦ *adj* Mittel-;
~week *adv* in der Mitte der Woche

midwife ['mɪdwaɪf] (*irreg*) *n* Hebamme *f*; **~ry**
['mɪdwɪfərɪ] *n* Geburtshilfe *f*

midwinter [mɪd'wɪntər] *n* tiefste(r) Winter *m*

might [maɪt] *vi see* **may** ♦ *n* Macht *f*, Kraft *f*;
I ~ come ich komme vielleicht; **~y** *adj, adv*
mächtig

migraine ['miːgreɪn] *n* Migräne *f*

migrant ['maɪgrənt] *adj* Wander-; (*bird*) Zug-

migrate [maɪ'greɪt] *vi* (ab)wandern; (*birds*)
(fort)ziehen; **migration** [maɪ'greɪʃən] *n*
Wanderung *f*, Zug *m*

mike [maɪk] *n* = **microphone**

Milan [mɪ'læn] *n* Mailand *nt*

mild [maɪld] *adj* mild; (*medicine, interest*)
leicht; (*person*) sanft ♦ *n* (*beer*) leichtes
dunkles Bier

mildew ['mɪldjuː] *n* (*on plants*) Mehltau *m*;
(*on food*) Schimmel *m*

mildly ['maɪldlɪ] *adv* leicht; **to put it ~**
gelinde gesagt

mile [maɪl] *n* Meile *f*; **~age** *n* Meilenzahl *f*;
~ometer *n* = **milometer**; **~stone** *n* (*also
fig*) Meilenstein *m*

militant ['mɪlɪtnt] *adj* militant ♦ *n*
Militante(r) *mf*

military ['mɪlɪtərɪ] *adj* militärisch, Militär-,
Wehr-

militate ['mɪlɪteɪt] *vi*: **to ~ against**
entgegenwirken +*dat*

militia [mɪ'lɪʃə] *n* Miliz *f*

milk [mɪlk] *n* Milch *f* ♦ *vt* (*also fig*) melken; **~
chocolate** *n* Milchschokolade *f*; **~man**
(*irreg*) *n* Milchmann *m*; **~ shake** *n*
Milchmixgetränk *nt*; **~y** *adj* milchig; **M~y
Way** *n* Milchstraße *f*

mill [mɪl] *n* Mühle *f*; (*factory*) Fabrik *f* ♦ *vt*
mahlen ♦ *vi* umherlaufen

millennia [mɪ'lɛnɪə] *npl of* **millennium**

millennium [mɪ'lɛnɪəm] (*pl* **~s** *or* **millennia**)
n Jahrtausend *nt*; **~ bug** *n* (*COMPUT*)
Jahrtausendfehler *m*

miller ['mɪlər] *n* Müller *m*

milligram(me) ['mɪlɪgræm] *n* Milligramm *nt*

millimetre ['mɪlɪmiːtə^r] (*US* **millimeter**) *n*
Millimeter *m*

million ['mɪljən] *n* Million *f*; **a ~ times**
tausendmal; **~aire** [mɪljə'neə^r] *n*
Millionär(in) *m(f)*

millstone ['mɪlstəʊn] *n* Mühlstein *m*

milometer [maɪ'lɒmɪtə^r] *n* ≃ Kilometerzähler
m

mime [maɪm] *n* Pantomime *f* ♦ *vt, vi* mimen

mimic ['mɪmɪk] *n* Mimiker *m* ♦ *vt, vi*
nachahmen; **~ry** *n* Nachahmung *f*; (*BIOL*)
Mimikry *f*

min. *abbr* = **minutes**; **minimum**

mince [mɪns] *vt* (zer)hacken ♦ *n* (*meat*)
Hackfleisch *nt*; **~meat** *n* süße
Pastetenfüllung *f*; **~ pie** *n* gefüllte (süße)
Pastete *f*; **~r** *n* Fleischwolf *m*

mind [maɪnd] *n* Verstand *m*, Geist *m*;
(*opinion*) Meinung *f* ♦ *vt* aufpassen auf +*acc*;
(*object to*) etwas haben gegen; **on my ~** auf
dem Herzen; **to my ~** meiner Meinung
nach; **to be out of one's ~** wahnsinnig
sein; **to bear** *or* **keep in ~** bedenken; **to
change one's ~** es sich *dat* anders
überlegen; **to make up one's ~** sich
entschließen; **I don't ~** das macht mir
nichts aus; **~ you, ...** allerdings ...; **never
~!** macht nichts!; **"~ the step"** „Vorsicht
Stufe"; **~ your own business** kümmern Sie
sich um Ihre eigenen Angelegenheiten; **~er**
n Aufpasser(in) *m(f)*; **~ful** *adj*: **~ful of**
achtsam auf +*acc*; **~less** *adj* sinnlos

mine[1] [maɪn] *n* (*coalmine*) Bergwerk *nt*;
(*MIL*) Mine *f* ♦ *vt* abbauen; (*MIL*) verminen

mine[2] [maɪn] *pron* meine(r, s); **that book is
~** das Buch gehört mir; **a friend of ~** ein
Freund von mir

minefield ['maɪnfiːld] *n* Minenfeld *nt*

miner ['maɪnə^r] *n* Bergarbeiter *m*

mineral ['mɪnərəl] *adj* mineralisch, Mineral-
♦ *n* Mineral *nt*; **~s** *npl* (*BRIT*: *soft drinks*)
alkoholfreie Getränke *pl*; **~ water** *n*
Mineralwasser *nt*

minesweeper ['maɪnswiːpə^r] *n*
Minensuchboot *nt*

mingle ['mɪŋgl] *vi*: **to ~ (with)** sich mischen
(unter +*acc*)

miniature ['mɪnətʃə^r] *adj* Miniatur- ♦ *n*
Miniatur *f*

minibus ['mɪnɪbʌs] *n* Kleinbus *m*

Minidisc ['mɪnɪdɪsk] *n* Minidisc ® *f*

minimal ['mɪnɪml] *adj* minimal

minimize ['mɪnɪmaɪz] *vt* auf das
Mindestmaß beschränken

minimum ['mɪnɪməm] (*pl* **minima**) *n*
Minimum *nt* ♦ *adj* Mindest-

mining ['maɪnɪŋ] *n* Bergbau *m* ♦ *adj*
Bergbau-, Berg-

miniskirt ['mɪnɪskəːt] *n* Minirock *m*

minister ['mɪnɪstə^r] *n* (*BRIT*: *POL*) Minister *m*;
(*ECCL*) Pfarrer *m* ♦ *vi*: **to ~ to sb/sb's
needs** sich um jdn kümmern; **~ial**
[mɪnɪs'tɪərɪəl] *adj* ministeriell, Minister-

ministry ['mɪnɪstrɪ] *n* (*BRIT*: *POL*) Ministerium
nt; (*ECCL*: *office*) geistliche(s) Amt *nt*

mink [mɪŋk] *n* Nerz *m*

minnow ['mɪnəʊ] *n* Elritze *f*

minor ['maɪnə^r] *adj* kleiner; (*operation*) leicht;
(*problem, poet*) unbedeutend; (*MUS*) Moll
♦ *n* (*BRIT*: *under 18*) Minderjährige(r) *mf*

minority [maɪ'nɒrɪtɪ] *n* Minderheit *f*

mint [mɪnt] *n* Minze *f*; (*sweet*)
Pfefferminzbonbon *nt* ♦ *vt* (*coins*) prägen;
the (Royal (*BRIT*) *or* **US** (*US*)) **M~** die
Münzanstalt; **in ~ condition** in tadellosem
Zustand

minus ['maɪnəs] *n* Minuszeichen *nt*; (*amount*)
Minusbetrag *m* ♦ *prep* minus, weniger

minuscule ['mɪnəskjuːl] *adj* winzig

minute[1] [maɪ'njuːt] *adj* winzig; (*detailed*)
minutiös, minuziös

minute[2] ['mɪnɪt] *n* Minute *f*; (*moment*)
Augenblick *m*; **~s** *npl* (*of meeting etc*)
Protokoll *nt*

miracle ['mɪrəkl] *n* Wunder *nt*

miraculous [mɪ'rækjʊləs] *adj* wunderbar

mirage ['mɪrɑːʒ] *n* Fata Morgana *f*

mire ['maɪə^r] *n* Morast *m*

mirror ['mɪrə^r] *n* Spiegel *m* ♦ *vt*
(wider)spiegeln

mirth [məːθ] *n* Heiterkeit *f*

misadventure [mɪsəd'ventʃə^r] *n*
Missgeschick *nt*, Unfall *m*

misanthropist [mɪ'zænθrəpɪst] *n*

Menschenfeind *m*

misapprehension [ˈmɪsæprɪˈhɛnʃən] *n* Missverständnis *nt*

misbehave [mɪsbɪˈheɪv] *vi* sich schlecht benehmen

miscalculate [mɪsˈkælkjʊleɪt] *vt* falsch berechnen

miscarriage [ˈmɪskærɪdʒ] *n* (*MED*) Fehlgeburt *f*; **~ of justice** Fehlurteil *nt*

miscellaneous [mɪsɪˈleɪnɪəs] *adj* verschieden

mischief [ˈmɪstʃɪf] *n* Unfug *m*; **mischievous** [ˈmɪstʃɪvəs] *adj* (*person*) durchtrieben; (*glance*) verschmitzt; (*rumour*) bösartig

misconception [ˈmɪskənˈsɛpʃən] *n* fälschliche Annahme *f*

misconduct [mɪsˈkɒndʌkt] *n* Vergehen *nt*; **professional ~** Berufsvergehen *nt*

misconstrue [mɪskənˈstruː] *vt* missverstehen

misdemeanour [mɪsdɪˈmiːnər] (*US* **misdemeanor**) *n* Vergehen *nt*

miser [ˈmaɪzər] *n* Geizhals *m*

miserable [ˈmɪzərəbl] *adj* (*unhappy*) unglücklich; (*headache, weather*) fürchterlich; (*poor*) elend; (*contemptible*) erbärmlich

miserly [ˈmaɪzəlɪ] *adj* geizig

misery [ˈmɪzərɪ] *n* Elend *nt*, Qual *f*

misfire [mɪsˈfaɪər] *vi* (*gun*) versagen; (*engine*) fehlzünden; (*plan*) fehlgehen

misfit [ˈmɪsfɪt] *n* Außenseiter *m*

misfortune [mɪsˈfɔːtʃən] *n* Unglück *nt*

misgiving(s) [mɪsˈgɪvɪŋ(z)] *n(pl)* Bedenken *pl*

misguided [mɪsˈgaɪdɪd] *adj* fehlgeleitet; (*opinions*) irrig

mishandle [mɪsˈhændl] *vt* falsch handhaben

mishap [ˈmɪshæp] *n* Missgeschick *nt*

misinform [mɪsɪnˈfɔːm] *vt* falsch unterrichten

misinterpret [mɪsɪnˈtɜːprɪt] *vt* falsch auffassen

misjudge [mɪsˈdʒʌdʒ] *vt* falsch beurteilen

mislay [mɪsˈleɪ] (*irreg: like* **lay**) *vt* verlegen

mislead [mɪsˈliːd] (*irreg: like* **lead²**) *vt*

(*deceive*) irreführen; **~ing** *adj* irreführend

mismanage [mɪsˈmænɪdʒ] *vt* schlecht verwalten

misnomer [mɪsˈnəʊmər] *n* falsche Bezeichnung *f*

misplace [mɪsˈpleɪs] *vt* verlegen

misprint [ˈmɪsprɪnt] *n* Druckfehler *m*

Miss [mɪs] *n* Fräulein *nt*

miss [mɪs] *vt* (*fail to hit, catch*) verfehlen; (*not notice*) verpassen; (*be too late*) versäumen, verpassen; (*omit*) auslassen; (*regret the absence of*) vermissen ♦ *vi* fehlen ♦ *n* (*shot*) Fehlschuss *m*; (*failure*) Fehlschlag *m*; **I ~ you** du fehlst mir; **~ out** *vt* auslassen

misshapen [mɪsˈʃeɪpən] *adj* missgestaltet

missile [ˈmɪsaɪl] *n* Rakete *f*

missing [ˈmɪsɪŋ] *adj* (*person*) vermisst; (*thing*) fehlend; **to be ~** fehlen

mission [ˈmɪʃən] *n* (*work*) Auftrag *m*; (*people*) Delegation *f*; (*REL*) Mission *f*; **~ary** *n* Missionar(in) *m(f)*; **~ statement** *n* Kurzdarstellung *f* der Firmenphilosophie

misspell [ˈmɪsˈspɛl] (*irreg: like* **spell**) *vt* falsch schreiben

misspent [ˈmɪsˈspɛnt] *adj* (*youth*) vergeudet

mist [mɪst] *n* Dunst *m*, Nebel *m* ♦ *vi* (*also:* **~ over, ~ up**) sich trüben; (*BRIT: windows*) sich beschlagen

mistake [mɪsˈteɪk] (*irreg: like* **take**) *n* Fehler *m* ♦ *vt* (*misunderstand*) missverstehen; (*mix up*): **to ~ (sth for sth)** (etw mit etw) verwechseln; **to make a ~** einen Fehler machen; **by ~** aus Versehen; **to ~ A for B** A mit B verwechseln; **~n** *pp of* **mistake** ♦ *adj* (*idea*) falsch; **to be ~n** sich irren

mister [ˈmɪstər] *n* (*inf*) Herr *m*; *see* **Mr**

mistletoe [ˈmɪsltəʊ] *n* Mistel *f*

mistook [mɪsˈtʊk] *pt of* **mistake**

mistress [ˈmɪstrɪs] *n* (*teacher*) Lehrerin *f*; (*in house*) Herrin *f*; (*lover*) Geliebte *f*; *see* **Mrs**

mistrust [mɪsˈtrʌst] *vt* misstrauen +*dat*

misty [ˈmɪstɪ] *adj* neblig

misunderstand [mɪsʌndəˈstænd] (*irreg: like* **understand**) *vt, vi* missverstehen, falsch verstehen; **~ing** *n* Missverständnis *nt*; (*disagreement*) Meinungsverschiedenheit *f*

misuse [*n* mɪsˈjuːs, *vb* mɪsˈjuːz] *n* falsche(r)

Gebrauch *m* ♦ *vt* falsch gebrauchen

mitigate ['mɪtɪgeɪt] *vt* mildern

mitt(en) ['mɪt(n)] *n* Fausthandschuh *m*

mix [mɪks] *vt* (*blend*) (ver)mischen ♦ *vi* (*liquids*) sich (ver)mischen lassen; (*people: get on*) sich vertragen; (: *associate*) Kontakt haben ♦ *n* (~*ture*) Mischung *f*; **~ up** *vt* zusammenmischen; (*confuse*) verwechseln; **~ed** *adj* gemischt; **~ed-up** *adj* durcheinander; **~er** *n* (*for food*) Mixer *m*; **~ture** *n* Mischung *f*; **~-up** *n* Durcheinander *nt*

mm *abbr* (= *millimetre(s)*) mm

moan [məʊn] *n* Stöhnen *nt*; (*complaint*) Klage *f* ♦ *vi* stöhnen; (*complain*) maulen

moat [məʊt] *n* (Burg)graben *m*

mob [mɒb] *n* Mob *m*; (*the masses*) Pöbel *m* ♦ *vt* herfallen über +*acc*

mobile ['məʊbaɪl] *adj* beweglich; (*library etc*) fahrbar ♦ *n* (*decoration*) Mobile *nt*; **~ home** *n* Wohnwagen *m*; **~ phone** *n* (TEL) Mobiltelefon *nt*; **mobility** [məʊ'bɪlɪtɪ] *n* Beweglichkeit *f*; **mobilize** ['məʊbɪlaɪz] *vt* mobilisieren

mock [mɒk] *vt* verspotten; (*defy*) trotzen +*dat* ♦ *adj* Schein-; **~ery** *n* Spott *m*; (*person*) Gespött *nt*

mod [mɒd] *adj see* **convenience**

mode [məʊd] *n* (Art *f* und) Weise *f*

model ['mɒdl] *n* Modell *nt*; (*example*) Vorbild *nt*; (*in fashion*) Mannequin *nt* ♦ *adj* (*railway*) Modell-; (*perfect*) Muster-; vorbildlich ♦ *vt* (*make*) bilden; (*clothes*) vorführen ♦ *vi* als Mannequin arbeiten

modem ['məʊdɛm] *n* (COMPUT) Modem *nt*

moderate [*adj, n* 'mɒdərət, *vb* 'mɒdəreɪt] *adj* gemäßigt ♦ *n* (POL) Gemäßigte(r) *mf* ♦ *vi* sich mäßigen ♦ *vt* mäßigen; **moderation** [mɒdə'reɪʃən] *n* Mäßigung *f*; **in moderation** mit Maßen

modern ['mɒdən] *adj* modern; (*history, languages*) neuere(r, s); **~ize** *vt* modernisieren

modest ['mɒdɪst] *adj* bescheiden; **~y** *n* Bescheidenheit *f*

modicum ['mɒdɪkəm] *n* bisschen *nt*

modification [mɒdɪfɪ'keɪʃən] *n* (Ab)änderung *f*

modify ['mɒdɪfaɪ] *vt* abändern

module ['mɒdjuːl] *n* (*component*) (Bau)element *nt*; (SPACE) (Raum)kapsel *f*

mogul ['məʊgl] *n* (*fig*) Mogul *m*

mohair ['məʊheəʳ] *n* Mohär *m*, Mohair *m*

moist [mɔɪst] *adj* feucht; **~en** ['mɔɪsn] *vt* befeuchten; **~ure** ['mɔɪstʃəʳ] *n* Feuchtigkeit *f*; **~urizer** ['mɔɪstʃəraɪzəʳ] *n* Feuchtigkeitscreme *f*

molar ['məʊləʳ] *n* Backenzahn *m*

molasses [mə'læsɪz] *n* Melasse *f*

mold [məʊld] (US) = **mould**

mole [məʊl] *n* (*spot*) Leberfleck *m*; (*animal*) Maulwurf *m*; (*pier*) Mole *f*

molest [mə'lɛst] *vt* belästigen

mollycoddle ['mɒlɪkɒdl] *vt* verhätscheln

molt [məʊlt] (US) *vi* = **moult**

molten ['məʊltən] *adj* geschmolzen

mom [mɒm] (US) *n* = **mum**

moment ['məʊmənt] *n* Moment *m*, Augenblick *m*; (*importance*) Tragweite *f*; **at the** ~ im Augenblick; **~ary** *adj* kurz; **~ous** [məʊ'mɛntəs] *adj* folgenschwer

momentum [məʊ'mɛntəm] *n* Schwung *m*; **to gather** ~ in Fahrt kommen

mommy ['mɒmɪ] (US) *n* = **mummy**

Monaco ['mɒnəkəʊ] *n* Monaco *nt*

monarch ['mɒnək] *n* Herrscher(in) *m(f)*; **~y** *n* Monarchie *f*

monastery ['mɒnəstərɪ] *n* Kloster *nt*

monastic [mə'næstɪk] *adj* klösterlich, Kloster-

Monday ['mʌndɪ] *n* Montag *m*

monetary ['mʌnɪtərɪ] *adj* Geld-; (*of currency*) Währungs-

money ['mʌnɪ] *n* Geld *nt*; **to make** ~ Geld verdienen; **~ belt** *n* Geldgürtel *m*; **~lender** *n* Geldverleiher *m*; **~ order** *n* Postanweisung *f*; **~-spinner** (*inf*) *n* Verkaufsschlager *m*

mongol ['mɒŋgl] *n* (MED) mongoloide(s) Kind *nt* ♦ *adj* mongolisch; (MED) mongoloid

mongrel ['mʌŋgrəl] *n* Promenadenmischung *f*

monitor ['mɒnɪtəʳ] *n* (SCH) Klassenordner *m*; (*television* ~) Monitor *m* ♦ *vt* (*broadcasts*) abhören; (control) überwachen

monk [mʌŋk] n Mönch m

monkey ['mʌŋki] n Affe m; ~ **nut** (BRIT) n Erdnuss f; ~ **wrench** n (TECH) Engländer m, Franzose m

monochrome ['mɔnəkrəum] adj schwarzweiß, schwarzweiß

monopolize [mə'nɔpəlaiz] vt beherrschen

monopoly [mə'nɔpəli] n Monopol nt

monosyllable ['mɔnəsiləbl] n einsilbige(s) Wort nt

monotone ['mɔnətəun] n gleich bleibende(r) Ton(fall) m; **to speak in a ~** monoton sprechen; **monotonous** [mə'nɔtənəs] adj eintönig; **monotony** [mə'nɔtəni] n Eintönigkeit f, Monotonie f

monsoon [mɔn'su:n] n Monsun m

monster ['mɔnstəʳ] n Ungeheuer nt; (person) Scheusal nt

monstrosity [mɔn'strɔsiti] n Ungeheuerlichkeit f; (thing) Monstrosität f

monstrous ['mɔnstrəs] adj (shocking) grässlich, ungeheuerlich; (huge) riesig

month [mʌnθ] n Monat m; **~ly** adj monatlich, Monats- ♦ adv einmal im Monat ♦ n (magazine) Monatsschrift f

monument ['mɔnjumənt] n Denkmal nt; **~al** [mɔnju'mentl] adj (huge) gewaltig; (ignorance) ungeheuer

moo [mu:] vi muhen

mood [mu:d] n Stimmung f, Laune f; **to be in a good/bad ~** gute/schlechte Laune haben; **~y** adj launisch

moon [mu:n] n Mond m; **~light** n Mondlicht nt; **~lighting** n Schwarzarbeit f; **~lit** adj mondhell

moor [muəʳ] n Heide f, Hochmoor nt ♦ vt (ship) festmachen, verankern ♦ vi anlegen; **~ings** npl Liegeplatz m; **~land** ['muələnd] n Heidemoor nt

moose [mu:s] n Elch m

mop [mɔp] n Mopp m ♦ vt (auf)wischen; **~ up** vt aufwischen

mope [məup] vi Trübsal blasen

moped ['məupεd] n Moped nt

moral ['mɔrl] adj moralisch; (values) sittlich; (virtuous) tugendhaft ♦ n Moral f; **~s** npl

(ethics) Moral f

morale [mɔ'rɑ:l] n Moral f

morality [mə'ræliti] n Sittlichkeit f

morass [mə'ræs] n Sumpf m

morbid ['mɔ:bid] adj krankhaft; (jokes) makaber

| KEYWORD |

more [mɔ:ʳ] adj (greater in number etc) mehr; (additional) noch mehr; **do you want (some) more tea?** möchten Sie noch etwas Tee?; **I have no** or **I don't have any more money** ich habe kein Geld mehr

♦ pron (greater amount) mehr; (further or additional amount) noch mehr; **is there any more?** gibt es noch mehr?; (left over) ist noch etwas da?; **there's no more** es ist nichts mehr da

♦ adv mehr; **more dangerous/easily etc (than)** gefährlicher/einfacher etc (als); **more and more** immer mehr; **more and more excited** immer aufgeregter; **more or less** mehr oder weniger; **more than ever** mehr denn je; **more beautiful than ever** schöner denn je

moreover [mɔ:'rəuvəʳ] adv überdies

morgue [mɔ:g] n Leichenschauhaus nt

Mormon ['mɔ:mən] n Mormone m, Mormonin f

morning ['mɔ:niŋ] n Morgen m; **in the ~** am Morgen; **7 o'clock in the ~** 7 Uhr morgens; **~ sickness** n (Schwangerschafts)übelkeit f

Morocco [mə'rɔkəu] n Marokko nt

moron ['mɔ:rɔn] n Schwachsinnige(r) mf

morose [mə'rəus] adj mürrisch

morphine ['mɔ:fi:n] n Morphium nt

Morse [mɔ:s] n (also: ~ **code**) Morsealphabet nt

morsel ['mɔ:sl] n Bissen m

mortal ['mɔ:tl] adj sterblich; (deadly) tödlich; (very great) Todes- ♦ n (human being) Sterbliche(r) mf; **~ity** [mɔ:'tæliti] n Sterblichkeit f; (death rate) Sterblichkeitsziffer f

mortar ['mɔ:təʳ] n (for building) Mörtel m;

(MIL) Granatwerfer m

mortgage ['mɔːɡɪdʒ] n Hypothek f ♦ vt hypothekarisch belasten; ~ **company** *(US)* n ≃ Bausparkasse f

mortify ['mɔːtɪfaɪ] vt beschämen

mortuary ['mɔːtjuərɪ] n Leichenhalle f

mosaic [məu'zeɪɪk] n Mosaik nt

Moscow ['mɔskəu] n Moskau nt

Moslem ['mɔzləm] = **Muslim**

mosque [mɔsk] n Moschee f

mosquito [mɔs'kiːtəu] (pl ~**es**) n Moskito m

moss [mɔs] n Moos nt

most [məust] adj meiste(r, s) ♦ adv am meisten; *(very)* höchst ♦ n das meiste, der größte Teil; *(people)* die meisten; ~ **men** die meisten Männer; **at the (very)** ~ allerhöchstens; **to make the** ~ **of** das Beste machen aus; **a** ~ **interesting book** ein höchstinteressantes Buch; ~**ly** adv größtenteils

MOT *(BRIT)* n abbr (= Ministry of Transport): **the MOT (test)** ≃ der TÜV

motel [məu'tel] n Motel nt

moth [mɔθ] n Nachtfalter m; *(wool-eating)* Motte f; ~**ball** n Mottenkugel f

mother ['mʌðər] n Mutter f ♦ vt bemuttern; ~**hood** n Mutterschaft f; ~**-in-law** n Schwiegermutter f; ~**ly** adj mütterlich; ~-**of-pearl** n Perlmut nt; **M~'s Day** *(BRIT)* n Muttertag m; ~**-to-be** n werdende Mutter f; ~**tongue** n Muttersprache f

motion ['məuʃən] n Bewegung f; *(in meeting)* Antrag m ♦ vt, vi: **to** ~ **(to) sb** jdm winken, jdm zu verstehen geben; ~**less** adj regungslos; ~ **picture** n Film m

motivated ['məutɪveɪtɪd] adj motiviert

motivation [məutɪ'veɪʃən] n Motivierung f

motive ['məutɪv] n Motiv nt, Beweggrund m ♦ adj treibend

motley ['mɔtlɪ] adj bunt

motor ['məutər] n Motor m; *(BRIT: inf: vehicle)* Auto nt ♦ adj Motor-; ~**bike** n Motorrad nt; ~**boat** n Motorboot nt; ~**car** *(BRIT)* n Auto nt; ~**cycle** n Motorrad nt; ~**cyclist** n Motorradfahrer(in) m(f); ~**ing** *(BRIT)* n Autofahren nt ♦ adj Auto-; ~**ist** n Autofahrer(in) m(f); ~ **mechanic** n

Kraftfahrzeugmechaniker(in) m(f), Kfz-Mechaniker(in) m(f); ~ **racing** *(BRIT)* n Autorennen nt; ~ **vehicle** n Kraftfahrzeug nt; ~**way** *(BRIT)* n Autobahn f

mottled ['mɔtld] adj gesprenkelt

mould [məuld] *(US* **mold)** n Form f; *(mildew)* Schimmel m ♦ vt *(also fig)* formen; ~**y** adj schimmelig

moult [məult] *(US* **molt)** vi sich mausern

mound [maund] n (Erd)hügel m

mount [maunt] n *(liter: hill)* Berg m; *(horse)* Pferd nt; *(for jewel etc)* Fassung f ♦ vt *(horse)* steigen auf +acc; *(put in setting)* fassen; *(exhibition)* veranstalten; *(attack)* unternehmen ♦ vi *(also:* ~ **up)** sich häufen; *(on horse)* aufsitzen

mountain ['mauntɪn] n Berg m ♦ cpd Berg-; ~ **bike** n Mountainbike nt; ~**eer** n Bergsteiger(in) m(f); ~**eering** [mauntɪ'nɪərɪŋ] n Bergsteigen nt; ~**ous** adj bergig; ~ **rescue team** n Bergwacht f; ~**side** n Berg(ab)hang m

mourn [mɔːn] vt betrauern, beklagen ♦ vi: **to** ~ **(for sb)** (um jdn) trauern; ~**er** n Trauernde(r) mf; ~**ful** adj traurig; ~**ing** n *(grief)* Trauer f ♦ cpd *(dress)* Trauer-; **in** ~**ing** *(period etc)* in Trauer; *(dress)* in Trauerkleidung f

mouse [maus] *(pl* **mice)** n Maus f; ~**trap** n Mausefalle f; ~ **mat**, ~ **pad** n *(COMPUT)* Mousepad nt

mousse [muːs] n *(COOK)* Creme f; *(cosmetic)* Schaumfestiger m

moustache [məs'taːʃ] n Schnurrbart m

mousy ['mausɪ] adj *(colour)* mausgrau; *(person)* schüchtern

mouth [mauθ] n Mund m; *(opening)* Öffnung f; *(of river)* Mündung f; ~**ful** n Mund m voll; ~ **organ** n Mundharmonika f; ~**piece** n Mundstück nt; *(fig)* Sprachrohr nt; ~**wash** n Mundwasser nt; ~**watering** adj lecker, appetitlich

movable ['muːvəbl] adj beweglich

move [muːv] n (~ment) Bewegung f; *(in game)* Zug m; *(step)* Schritt m; *(of house)* Umzug m ♦ vt bewegen; *(people)* transportieren; *(in job)* versetzen;

(*emotionally*) bewegen ♦ *vi* sich bewegen; (*vehicle, ship*) fahren; (~ *house*) umziehen; **to get a ~ on** sich beeilen; **to ~ sb to do sth** jdn veranlassen, etw zu tun; **~ about** *or* **around** *vi* sich hin und her bewegen; (*travel*) unterwegs sein; **~ along** *vi* weitergehen; (*cars*) weiterfahren; **~ away** *vi* weggehen; **~ back** *vi* zurückgehen; (*to the rear*) zurückweichen; **~ forward** *vi* vorwärts gehen, sich vorwärts bewegen ♦ *vt* vorschieben; (*time*) vorverlegen; **~ in** *vi* (*to house*) einziehen; (*troops*) einrücken; **~ on** *vi* weitergehen ♦ *vt* weitergehen lassen; **~ out** *vi* (*of house*) ausziehen; (*troops*) abziehen; **~ over** *vi* zur Seite rücken; **~ up** *vi* aufsteigen; (*in job*) befördert werden ♦ *vt* nach oben bewegen; (*in job*) befördern; **~ment** ['muːvmənt] *n* Bewegung *f*

movie ['muːvɪ] *n* Film *m*; **to go to the ~s** ins Kino gehen; **~ camera** *n* Filmkamera *f*

moving ['muːvɪŋ] *adj* beweglich; (*touching*) ergreifend

mow [məu] (*pt* **mowed**, *pp* **mowed** *or* **mown**) *vt* mähen; **~ down** *vt* (*fig*) niedermähen; **~er** *n* (*lawnmower*) Rasenmäher *m*; **~n** *pp* of **mow**

MP *n abbr* = **Member of Parliament**

MP3 player *n* MP3-Spieler *m*

m.p.h. *abbr* = **miles per hour**

Mr ['mɪstər] (*US* **Mr.**) *n* Herr *m*

Mrs ['mɪsɪz] (*US* **Mrs.**) *n* Frau *f*

Ms [mɪz] (*US* **Ms.**) *n* (= *Miss or Mrs*) Frau *f*

M.Sc. *n abbr* = **Master of Science**

MSP *n abbr* (= *Member of the Scottish Parliament*) Mitglied *nt* des schottischen Parlaments

much [mʌtʃ] *adj* viel ♦ *adv* sehr; viel ♦ *n* viel, eine Menge; **how ~ is it?** wie viel kostet das?; **too ~** zu viel; **it's not ~** es ist nicht viel; **as ~ as** so sehr, so viel; **however ~ he tries** sosehr er es auch versucht

muck [mʌk] *n* Mist *m*; (*fig*) Schmutz *m*; **~ about** *or* **around** (*inf*) *vi*: **to ~ about** *or* **around (with sth)** (an etw *dat*) herumalbern; **~ up** *vt* (*inf: ruin*) vermasseln; (*dirty*) dreckig machen; **~y** *adj* (*dirty*) dreckig

mud [mʌd] *n* Schlamm *m*

muddle ['mʌdl] *n* Durcheinander *nt* ♦ *vt* (*also:* **~ up**) durcheinander bringen; **~ through** *vi* sich durchwursteln

mud ['mʌd-]: **~dy** *adj* schlammig; **~guard** *n* Schutzblech *nt*; **~-slinging** (*inf*) *n* Verleumdung *f*

muesli ['mjuːzlɪ] *n* Müsli *nt*

muffin ['mʌfɪn] *n* süße(s) Teilchen *nt*

muffle ['mʌfl] *vt* (*sound*) dämpfen; (*wrap up*) einhüllen; **~d** *adj* gedämpft; **~r** (*US*) *n* (*AUT*) Schalldämpfer *m*

mug [mʌg] *n* (*cup*) Becher *m*; (*inf: face*) Visage *f*; (: *fool*) Trottel *m* ♦ *vt* überfallen und ausrauben; **~ger** *n* Straßenräuber *m*; **~ging** *n* Überfall *m*

muggy ['mʌgɪ] *adj* (*weather*) schwül

mule [mjuːl] *n* Maulesel *m*

mull [mʌl]: **~ over** *vt* nachdenken über +*acc*

multicoloured ['mʌltɪkʌləd] (*US* **multicolored**) *adj* mehrfarbig

multi-level ['mʌltɪlevl] (*US*) *adj* = **multistorey**

multiple ['mʌltɪpl] *n* Vielfache(s) *nt* ♦ *adj* mehrfach; (*many*) mehrere; **~ sclerosis** *n* multiple Sklerose *f*

multiplex cinema ['mʌltɪpleks-] *n* Kinocenter *nt*

multiplication [mʌltɪplɪ'keɪʃən] *n* Multiplikation *f*; (*increase*) Vervielfachung *f*

multiply ['mʌltɪplaɪ] *vt*: **to ~ (by)** multiplizieren (mit) ♦ *vi* (*BIOL*) sich vermehren

multistorey ['mʌltɪ'stɔːrɪ] (*BRIT*) *adj* (*building, car park*) mehrstöckig

multitude ['mʌltɪtjuːd] *n* Menge *f*

mum [mʌm] *n* (*BRIT: inf*) Mutti *f* ♦ *adj*: **to keep ~ (about)** den Mund halten über +*acc*)

mumble ['mʌmbl] *vt*, *vi* murmeln ♦ *n* Gemurmel *nt*

mummy ['mʌmɪ] *n* (*dead body*) Mumie *f*; (*BRIT: inf*) Mami *f*

mumps [mʌmps] *n* Mumps *m*

munch [mʌntʃ] *vt*, *vi* mampfen

mundane [mʌn'deɪn] *adj* banal

municipal [mjuː'nɪsɪpl] *adj* städtisch, Stadt-

mural ['mjuərl] *n* Wandgemälde *nt*

murder ['mɜːdər] *n* Mord *m* ♦ *vt* ermorden; **~er** *n* Mörder *m*; **~ous** *adj* Mord-; (*fig*) mörderisch

murky ['mɜːkɪ] adj finster

murmur ['mɜːmər] n Murmeln nt; (of water, wind) Rauschen nt ♦ vt, vi murmeln

muscle ['mʌsl] n Muskel m; ~ **in** vi mitmischen; **muscular** ['mʌskjulər] adj Muskel-; (strong) muskulös

museum [mju:'zɪəm] n Museum nt

mushroom ['mʌʃrum] n Champignon m; Pilz m ♦ vi (fig) emporschießen

music ['mju:zɪk] n Musik f; (printed) Noten pl; ~**al** adj (sound) melodisch; (person) musikalisch ♦ n (show) Musical nt; ~**al instrument** n Musikinstrument nt; ~ **centre** n Stereoanlage f; ~ **hall** (BRIT) n Varietee nt, Varieté nt; ~**ian** [mju:'zɪʃən] n Musiker(in) m(f)

Muslim ['mʌzlɪm] adj moslemisch ♦ n Moslem m

muslin ['mʌzlɪn] n Musselin m

mussel ['mʌsl] n Miesmuschel f

must [mʌst] vb aux müssen; (in negation) dürfen ♦ n Muss nt; **the film is a ~** den Film muss man einfach gesehen haben

mustard ['mʌstəd] n Senf m

muster ['mʌstər] vt (MIL) antreten lassen; (courage) zusammennehmen

mustn't ['mʌsnt] = **must not**

musty ['mʌstɪ] adj muffig

mute [mju:t] adj stumm ♦ n (person) Stumme(r) mf; (MUS) Dämpfer m; ~**d** adj gedämpft

mutilate ['mju:tɪleɪt] vt verstümmeln

mutiny ['mju:tɪnɪ] n Meuterei f ♦ vi meutern

mutter ['mʌtər] vt, vi murmeln

mutton ['mʌtn] n Hammelfleisch nt

mutual ['mju:tʃuəl] adj gegenseitig; beiderseitig; ~**ly** adv gegenseitig; für beide Seiten

muzzle ['mʌzl] n (of animal) Schnauze f; (for animal) Maulkorb m; (of gun) Mündung f ♦ vt einen Maulkorb anlegen +dat

my [maɪ] adj mein; **this is ~ car** das ist mein Auto; **I've washed ~ hair** ich habe mir die Haare gewaschen

myself [maɪ'self] pron mich acc; mir dat; (emphatic) selbst; see also **oneself**

mysterious [mɪs'tɪərɪəs] adj geheimnisvoll

mystery ['mɪstərɪ] n (secret) Geheimnis nt; (sth difficult) Rätsel nt

mystify ['mɪstɪfaɪ] vt ein Rätsel nt sein +dat; verblüffen

mystique [mɪs'ti:k] n geheimnisvolle Natur f

myth [mɪθ] n Mythos m; (fig) Erfindung f; ~**ology** [mɪ'θɒlədʒɪ] n Mythologie f

N, n

n/a abbr (= not applicable) nicht zutreffend

nab [næb] (inf) vt schnappen

naff [næf] (BRIT: inf) adj blöd

nag [næg] n (horse) Gaul m; (person) Nörgler(in) m(f) ♦ vt, vi: **to ~ (at) sb** an jdm herumnörgeln; ~**ging** adj (doubt) nagend ♦ n Nörgelei f

nail [neɪl] n Nagel m ♦ vt nageln; **to ~ sb down to doing sth** jdn darauf festnageln, etw zu tun; ~**brush** n Nagelbürste f; ~**file** n Nagelfeile f; ~ **polish** n Nagellack m; ~ **polish remover** n Nagellackentferner m; ~ **scissors** npl Nagelschere f; ~ **varnish** (BRIT) n = **nail polish**

naïve [naɪ'i:v] adj naiv

naked ['neɪkɪd] adj nackt

name [neɪm] n Name m; (reputation) Ruf m ♦ vt nennen; (sth new) benennen; (appoint) ernennen; **by ~** mit Namen; **I know him only by ~** ich kenne ihn nur dem Namen nach; **what's your ~?** wie heißen Sie?; **in the ~ of** im Namen +gen; (for the sake of) um ~ ... willen; ~**less** adj namenlos; ~**ly** adv nämlich; ~**sake** n Namensvetter m

nanny ['nænɪ] n Kindermädchen nt

nap [næp] n (sleep) Nickerchen nt; (on cloth) Strich m ♦ vi: **to be caught ~ping** (fig) überrumpelt werden

nape [neɪp] n Nacken m

napkin ['næpkɪn] n (at table) Serviette f; (BRIT: for baby) Windel f

nappy ['næpɪ] (BRIT) n (for baby) Windel f; ~ **rash** n wunde Stellen pl

narcotic [nɑː'kɒtɪk] adj betäubend ♦ n Betäubungsmittel nt

narrative ['nærətɪv] n Erzählung f ♦ adj
erzählend

narrator [nə'reɪtə'] n Erzähler(in) m(f)

narrow ['nærəʊ] adj eng, schmal; (limited)
beschränkt ♦ vi sich verengen; **to have a ~
escape** mit knapper Not davonkommen;
to ~ sth down to sth etw auf etw acc
einschränken; **~ly** adv (miss) knapp;
(escape) mit knapper Not; **~-minded** adj
engstirnig

nasty ['nɑːstɪ] adj ekelhaft, fies; (business,
wound) schlimm

nation ['neɪʃən] n Nation f, Volk nt; **~al**
['næʃənl] adj national, National-, Landes-
♦ n Staatsangehörige(r) mf; **~al anthem**
(BRIT) n Nationalhymne f; **~al dress** n
Tracht f; **N~al Health Service** (BRIT) n
staatliche(r) Gesundheitsdienst m; **N~al
Insurance** (BRIT) n Sozialversicherung f;
~alism ['næʃnəlɪzəm] n Nationalismus m;
~alist ['næʃnəlɪst] n Nationalist(in) m(f)
♦ adj nationalistisch; **~ality** [næʃə'nælɪtɪ] n
Staatsangehörigkeit f; **~alize** ['næʃnəlaɪz] vt
verstaatlichen; **~ally** ['næʃnəlɪ] adv national,
auf Staatsebene; **~al park** (BRIT) n
Nationalpark m; **~wide** ['neɪʃənwaɪd] adj,
adv allgemein, landesweit

National Trust

ⓘ *Der* **National Trust** *ist ein 1895
gegründeter Natur- und
Denkmalschutzverband in Großbritannien,
der Gebäude und Gelände von besonderem
historischen oder ästhetischen Interesse
erhält und der Öffentlichkeit zugänglich
macht. Viele Gebäude im Besitz des
National Trust sind (z.T. gegen ein
Eintrittsgeld) zu besichtigen.*

native ['neɪtɪv] n (born in) Einheimische(r)
mf; (original inhabitant) Eingeborene(r) mf
♦ adj einheimisch; Eingeborenen-;
(belonging by birth) heimatlich, Heimat-;
(inborn) angeboren, natürlich; **a ~ of
Germany** ein gebürtiger Deutscher; **a ~
speaker of French** ein französischer
Muttersprachler; **N~ American** n

Indianer(in) m(f), Ureinwohner(in) m(f)
Amerikas; **~ language** n Muttersprache f

Nativity [nə'tɪvɪtɪ] n: **the ~** Christi Geburt no
art

NATO ['neɪtəʊ] n abbr (= North Atlantic Treaty
Organization) NATO f

natural ['nætʃrəl] adj natürlich; Natur-;
(inborn) (an)geboren; **~ gas** n Erdgas nt;
~ist n Naturkundler(in) m(f); **~ly** adv
natürlich

nature ['neɪtʃə'] n Natur f; **by ~** von Natur
(aus)

naught [nɔːt] n = **nought**

naughty ['nɔːtɪ] adj (child) unartig,
ungezogen; (action) ungehörig

nausea ['nɔːsɪə] n (sickness) Übelkeit f;
(disgust) Ekel m; **~te** ['nɔːsɪeɪt] vt anekeln

nautical ['nɔːtɪkl] adj nautisch; See-;
(expression) seemännisch

naval ['neɪvl] adj Marine-, Flotten-; **~
officer** n Marineoffizier m

nave [neɪv] n Kirchen(haupt)schiff nt

navel ['neɪvl] n Nabel m

navigate ['nævɪgeɪt] vi navigieren;
navigation [nævɪ'geɪʃən] n Navigation f;
navigator ['nævɪgeɪtə'] n Steuermann m;
(AVIAT) Navigator m; (AUT) Beifahrer(in) m(f)

navvy ['nævɪ] (BRIT) n Straßenarbeiter m

navy ['neɪvɪ] n (Kriegs)marine f ♦ adj (also: ~
blue) marineblau

Nazi ['nɑːtsɪ] n Nazi m

NB abbr (= nota bene) NB

near [nɪə'] adj nah ♦ adv in der Nähe ♦ prep
(also: ~ **to**: space) in der Nähe +gen;
(: time) um +acc ... herum ♦ vt sich nähern
+dat; **a ~ miss** knapp daneben; **~by** adj
nahe (gelegen) ♦ adv in der Nähe; **~ly** adv
fast; **I ~ly fell** ich wäre fast gefallen; **~side**
n (AUT) Beifahrerseite f ♦ adj auf der
Beifahrerseite; **~-sighted** adj kurzsichtig

neat [niːt] adj (tidy) ordentlich; (solution)
sauber; (pure) pur; **~ly** adv (tidily)
ordentlich

necessarily ['nesɪsrɪlɪ] adv unbedingt

necessary ['nesɪsrɪ] adj notwendig, nötig;
he did all that was ~ er erledigte alles, was
nötig war; **it is ~ to/that ...** man

muss ...

necessitate [nɪˈsesɪteɪt] *vt* erforderlich machen

necessity [nɪˈsesɪtɪ] *n* (*need*) Not *f*; (*compulsion*) Notwendigkeit *f*; **necessities** *npl* (*things needed*) das Notwendigste

neck [nek] *n* Hals *m* ♦ *vi* (*inf*) knutschen; **~ and ~** Kopf an Kopf; **~lace** [ˈneklɪs] *n* Halskette *f*; **~line** [ˈneklaɪn] *n* Ausschnitt *m*; **~tie** [ˈnektaɪ] *n* (*US*) Krawatte *f*

née [neɪ] *adj* geborene

need [niːd] *n* Bedürfnis *nt*; (*lack*) Mangel *m*; (*necessity*) Notwendigkeit *f*; (*poverty*) Not *f* ♦ *vt* brauchen; **I ~ to do it** ich muss es tun; **you don't ~ to go** du brauchst nicht zu gehen

needle [ˈniːdl] *n* Nadel *f* ♦ *vt* (*fig: inf*) ärgern

needless [ˈniːdlɪs] *adj* unnötig; **~ to say** natürlich

needlework [ˈniːdlwəːk] *n* Handarbeit *f*

needn't [ˈniːdnt] = **need not**

needy [ˈniːdɪ] *adj* bedürftig

negative [ˈnegətɪv] *n* (*PHOT*) Negativ *nt* ♦ *adj* negativ; (*answer*) abschlägig; **~ equity** *n Differenz zwischen gefallenem Wert und hypothekarischer Belastung eines Wohneigentums*

neglect [nɪˈglekt] *vt* vernachlässigen ♦ *n* Vernachlässigung *f*; **~ed** *adj* vernachlässigt

negligee [ˈneglɪʒeɪ] *n* Negligee *nt*, Negligé *nt*

negligence [ˈneglɪdʒəns] *n* Nachlässigkeit *f*

negligible [ˈneglɪdʒɪbl] *adj* unbedeutend, geringfügig

negotiable [nɪˈgəʊʃɪəbl] *adj* (*cheque*) übertragbar, einlösbar

negotiate [nɪˈgəʊʃɪeɪt] *vi* verhandeln ♦ *vt* (*treaty*) abschließen; (*difficulty*) überwinden; (*corner*) nehmen; **negotiation** [nɪgəʊʃɪˈeɪʃən] *n* Verhandlung *f*; **negotiator** *n* Unterhändler *m*

neigh [neɪ] *vi* wiehern

neighbour [ˈneɪbəʳ] (*US* **neighbor**) *n* Nachbar(in) *m(f)*; **~hood** *n* Nachbarschaft *f*; Umgebung *f*; **~ing** *adj* benachbart, angrenzend; **~ly** *adj* (*person, attitude*) nachbarlich

neither [ˈnaɪðəʳ] *adj, pron* keine(r, s) (von

beiden) ♦ *conj*: **he can't do it, and ~ can I** er kann es nicht und ich auch nicht ♦ *adv*: **~ good nor bad** weder gut noch schlecht; **~ story is true** keine der beiden Geschichten stimmt

neon [ˈniːɔn] *n* Neon *nt*; **~ light** *n* Neonlampe *f*

nephew [ˈnevjuː] *n* Neffe *m*

nerve [nɜːv] *n* Nerv *m*; (*courage*) Mut *m*; (*impudence*) Frechheit *f*; **to have a fit of ~s** in Panik geraten; **~-racking** *adj* nervenaufreibend

nervous [ˈnɜːvəs] *adj* (*of the nerves*) Nerven-; (*timid*) nervös, ängstlich; **~ breakdown** *n* Nervenzusammenbruch *m*; **~ness** *n* Nervosität *f*

nest [nest] *n* Nest *nt* ♦ *vi* nisten; **~ egg** *n* (*fig*) Notgroschen *m*

nestle [ˈnesl] *vi* sich kuscheln

Net [net] *n*: **the ~** das Internet

net [net] *n* Netz *nt* ♦ *adj* netto, Netto- ♦ *vt* netto einnehmen; **~ball** *n* Netzball *m*

Netherlands [ˈneðələndz] *npl*: **the ~** die Niederlande *pl*

nett [net] *adj* = **net**

netting [ˈnetɪŋ] *n* Netz(werk) *nt*

nettle [ˈnetl] *n* Nessel *f*

network [ˈnetwəːk] *n* Netz *nt*

neurotic [njuəˈrɔtɪk] *adj* neurotisch

neuter [ˈnjuːtəʳ] *adj* (*BIOL*) geschlechtslos; (*GRAM*) sächlich ♦ *vt* kastrieren

neutral [ˈnjuːtrəl] *adj* neutral ♦ *n* (*AUT*) Leerlauf *m*; **~ity** [njuːˈtrælɪtɪ] *n* Neutralität *f*; **~ize** *vt* (*fig*) ausgleichen

never [ˈnevəʳ] *adv* nie(mals); **I ~ went** ich bin gar nicht gegangen; **~ in my life** nie im Leben; **~-ending** *adj* endlos; **~theless** [nevəðəˈles] *adv* trotzdem, dennoch

new [njuː] *adj* neu; **N~ Age** *n* Newage-, New-Age-; **~born** *adj* neugeboren; **~comer** [ˈnjuːkʌməʳ] *n* Neuankömmling *m*; **~-fangled** (*pej*) *adj* neumodisch; **~-found** *adj* neu entdeckt; **~ly** *adv* frisch, neu; **~ly-weds** *npl* Frischvermählte *pl*; **~ moon** *n* Neumond *m*

news [njuːz] *n* Nachricht *f*; (*RAD, TV*) Nachrichten *pl*; **a piece of ~** eine

Nachricht; ~ **agency** *n*
Nachrichtenagentur *f*; ~**agent** (*BRIT*) *n*
Zeitungshändler *m*; ~**caster** *n*
Nachrichtensprecher(in) *m(f)*; ~ **flash** *n*
Kurzmeldung *f*; ~**letter** *n* Rundschreiben
nt; ~**paper** *n* Zeitung *f*; ~**print** *n*
Zeitungspapier *nt*; ~**reader** *n* =
newscaster; ~**reel** *n* Wochenschau *f*; ~
stand *n* Zeitungsstand *m*

newt [njuːt] *n* Wassermolch *m*

New Year *n* Neujahr *nt*; ~'**s Day** *n*
Neujahrstag *m*; ~'**s Eve** *n* Silvester(abend
m) *nt*

New Zealand [-'ziːlənd] *n* Neuseeland *nt*;
~**er** *n* Neuseeländer(in) *m(f)*

next [nɛkst] *adj* nächste(r, s) ♦ *adv* (*after*)
dann, darauf; (~ *time*) das nächste Mal; **the
~ day** am nächsten *or* folgenden Tag; ~
time das nächste Mal; ~ **year** nächstes
Jahr; ~ **door** *adv* nebenan ♦ *adj* (*neighbour,
flat*) von nebenan; ~ **of kin** *n* nächste(r)
Verwandte(r) *mf*; ~ **to** *prep* neben; ~ **to
nothing** so gut wie nichts

NHS *n abbr* = **National Health Service**

nib [nɪb] *n* Spitze *f*

nibble ['nɪbl] *vt* knabbern an +*dat*

nice [naɪs] *adj* (*person*) nett; (*thing*) schön;
(*subtle*) fein; ~**-looking** *adj* gut aussehend;
~**ly** *adv* gut, nett; ~**ties** ['naɪsɪtɪz] *npl*
Feinheiten *pl*

nick [nɪk] *n* Einkerbung *f* ♦ *vt* (*inf: steal*)
klauen; **in the ~ of time** gerade rechtzeitig

nickel ['nɪkl] *n* Nickel *nt*; (*US*) Nickel *m* (*5
cents*)

nickname ['nɪkneɪm] *n* Spitzname *m* ♦ *vt*
taufen

nicotine patch ['nɪkətiːn-] *n* Nikotinpflaster
nt

niece [niːs] *n* Nichte *f*

Nigeria [naɪ'dʒɪərɪə] *n* Nigeria *nt*

niggling ['nɪglɪŋ] *adj* pedantisch; (*doubt,
worry*) quälend

night [naɪt] *n* Nacht *f*; (*evening*) Abend *m*;
the ~ before last vorletzte Nacht; **at** *or* **by
~** (*before midnight*) abends; (*after midnight*)
nachts; ~**cap** *n* (*drink*) Schlummertrunk *m*;
~**club** *n* Nachtlokal *nt*; ~**dress** *n*

Nachthemd *nt*; ~**fall** *n* Einbruch *m* der
Nacht; ~ **gown** *n* = **nightdress**; ~**ie** (*inf*) *n*
Nachthemd *nt*

nightingale ['naɪtɪŋgeɪl] *n* Nachtigall *f*

night: ~**life** ['naɪtlaɪf] *n* Nachtleben *nt*; ~**ly**
['naɪtlɪ] *adj*, *adv* jeden Abend; jede Nacht;
~**mare** ['naɪtmɛər] *n* Albtraum *m*; ~ **porter**
n Nachtportier *m*; ~ **school** *n* Abendschule
f; ~ **shift** *n* Nachtschicht *f*; ~**time** *n* Nacht
f

nil [nɪl] *n* Null *f*

Nile [naɪl] *n*: **the ~** der Nil

nimble ['nɪmbl] *adj* beweglich

nine [naɪn] *num* neun; ~**teen** *num*
neunzehn; ~**ty** *num* neunzig

ninth [naɪnθ] *adj* neunte(r, s)

nip [nɪp] *vt* kneifen ♦ *n* Kneifen *nt*

nipple ['nɪpl] *n* Brustwarze *f*

nippy ['nɪpɪ] (*inf*) *adj* (*person*) flink; (*BRIT*: *car*)
flott; (: *cold*) frisch

nitrogen ['naɪtrədʒən] *n* Stickstoff *m*

KEYWORD

no [nəʊ] (*pl* **noes**) *adv* (*opposite of yes*) nein;
to answer no (*to question*) mit Nein
antworten; (*to request*) Nein *or* nein sagen;
no thank you nein, danke
♦ *adj* (*not any*) kein(e); **I have no money/
time** ich habe kein Geld/keine Zeit; "**no
smoking**" „Rauchen verboten"
♦ *n* Nein *nt*; (*no vote*) Neinstimme *f*

---

nobility [nəʊ'bɪlɪtɪ] *n* Adel *m*

noble ['nəʊbl] *adj* (*rank*) adlig; (*splendid*)
nobel, edel

nobody ['nəʊbədɪ] *pron* niemand, keiner

nocturnal [nɔk'tɜːnl] *adj* (*tour, visit*)
nächtlich; (*animal*) Nacht-

nod [nɔd] *vt* nicken ♦ *vt* nicken mit ♦ *n*
Nicken *nt*; ~ **off** *vi* einnicken

noise [nɔɪz] *n* (*sound*) Geräusch *nt*;
(*unpleasant, loud*) Lärm *m*; **noisy** ['nɔɪzɪ] *adj*
laut; (*crowd*) lärmend

nominal ['nɔmɪnl] *adj* nominell

nominate ['nɔmɪneɪt] *vt* (*suggest*)
vorschlagen; (*in election*) aufstellen;
(*appoint*) ernennen; **nomination**

[nɔmɪˈneɪʃən] n (*election*) Nominierung f; (*appointment*) Ernennung f; **nominee** [nɔmɪˈniː] n Kandidat(in) m(f)

non... [nɔn] *prefix* Nicht-, un-; **~-alcoholic** *adj* alkoholfrei

nonchalant [ˈnɔnʃələnt] *adj* lässig

non-committal [nɔnkəˈmɪtl] *adj* (*reserved*) zurückhaltend; (*uncommitted*) unverbindlich

nondescript [ˈnɔndɪskrɪpt] *adj* mittelmäßig

none [nʌn] *adj, pron* kein(e, er, es) ♦ *adv*: **he's ~ the worse for it** es hat ihm nicht geschadet; **~ of you** keiner von euch; **I've ~ left** ich habe keinen mehr

nonentity [nɔˈnɛntɪtɪ] n Null f (*inf*)

nonetheless [ˈnʌnðəˈlɛs] *adv* nichtsdestoweniger

non-existent [nɔnɪgˈzɪstənt] *adj* nicht vorhanden

non-fiction [nɔnˈfɪkʃən] n Sachbücher *pl*

nonplussed [nɔnˈplʌst] *adj* verdutzt

nonsense [ˈnɔnsəns] n Unsinn *m*

non: **~-smoker** n Nichtraucher(in) m(f); **~-smoking** *adj* Nichtraucher-; **~-stick** *adj* (*pan, surface*) Teflon- ®; **~-stop** *adj* Nonstop-, Non-Stop-

noodles [ˈnuːdlz] *npl* Nudeln *pl*

nook [nuk] n Winkel *m*; **~s and crannies** Ecken und Winkel

noon [nuːn] n (12 Uhr) Mittag *m*

no one [ˈnəʊwʌn] *pron* = **nobody**

noose [nuːs] n Schlinge f

nor [nɔː] *conj* = **neither** ♦ *adv see* **neither**

norm [nɔːm] n (*convention*) Norm f; (*rule, requirement*) Vorschrift f

normal [ˈnɔːməl] *adj* normal; **~ly** *adv* normal; (*usually*) normalerweise

Normandy [ˈnɔːməndɪ] n Normandie f

north [nɔːθ] n Norden *m* ♦ *adj* nördlich, Nord- ♦ *adv* nördlich, nach *or* im Norden; **N~ Africa** n Nordafrika *nt*; **N~ America** n Nordamerika *nt*; **~-east** n Nordosten *m*; **~erly** [ˈnɔːðəlɪ] *adj* nördlich; **~ern** [ˈnɔːðən] *adj* nördlich, Nord-; **N~ern Ireland** n Nordirland *nt*; **N~ Pole** n Nordpol *m*; **N~ Sea** n Nordsee f; **~ward(s)** [ˈnɔːθwəd(z)] *adv* nach Norden; **~-west** n Nordwesten *m*

Norway [ˈnɔːweɪ] n Norwegen *nt*

Norwegian [nɔːˈwiːdʒən] *adj* norwegisch ♦ n Norweger(in) m(f); (*LING*) Norwegisch *nt*

nose [nəʊz] n Nase f ♦ *vi*: **to ~ about** herumschnüffeln; **~bleed** n Nasenbluten *nt*; **~ dive** n Sturzflug *m*; **~y** *adj* = **nosy**

nostalgia [nɔsˈtældʒɪə] n Nostalgie f; **nostalgic** *adj* nostalgisch

nostril [ˈnɔstrɪl] n Nasenloch *nt*

nosy [ˈnəʊzɪ] (*inf*) *adj* neugierig

not [nɔt] *adv* nicht; **he is ~** *or* **isn't here** er ist nicht hier; **it's too late, isn't it?** es ist zu spät, oder *or* nicht wahr?; **~ yet/now** noch nicht/nicht jetzt; *see also* **all**; **only**

notably [ˈnəʊtəblɪ] *adv* (*especially*) besonders; (*noticeably*) bemerkenswert

notary [ˈnəʊtərɪ] n Notar(in) m(f)

notch [nɔtʃ] n Kerbe f, Einschnitt *m*

note [nəʊt] n (*MUS*) Note f, Ton *m*; (*short letter*) Nachricht f; (*POL*) Note f; (*comment, attention*) Notiz f; (*of lecture etc*) Aufzeichnung f; (*banknote*) Schein *m*; (*fame*) Ruf *m* ♦ *vt* (*observe*) bemerken; (*also:* **~ down**) notieren; **~book** n Notizbuch *nt*; **~d** *adj* bekannt; **~pad** n Notizblock *m*; **~paper** n Briefpapier *nt*

nothing [ˈnʌθɪŋ] n nichts; **~ new/much** nichts Neues/nicht viel; **for ~** umsonst

notice [ˈnəʊtɪs] n (*announcement*) Bekanntmachung f; (*warning*) Ankündigung f; (*dismissal*) Kündigung f ♦ *vt* bemerken; **to take ~ of** beachten; **at short ~** kurzfristig; **until further ~** bis auf weiteres; **to hand in one's ~** kündigen; **~able** *adj* merklich; **~ board** n Anschlagtafel f

notify [ˈnəʊtɪfaɪ] *vt* benachrichtigen

notion [ˈnəʊʃən] n Idee f

notorious [nəʊˈtɔːrɪəs] *adj* berüchtigt

notwithstanding [nɔtwɪθˈstændɪŋ] *adv* trotzdem; **~ this** ungeachtet dessen

nought [nɔːt] n Null f

noun [naʊn] n Substantiv *nt*

nourish [ˈnʌrɪʃ] *vt* nähren; **~ing** *adj* nahrhaft; **~ment** n Nahrung f

novel [ˈnɔvl] n Roman *m* ♦ *adj* neu(artig); **~ist** n Schriftsteller(in) m(f); **~ty** n Neuheit f

November [nəuˈvɛmbəʳ] n November m
novice [ˈnɔvɪs] n Neuling m
now [nau] adv jetzt; **right ~** jetzt, gerade; **by ~** inzwischen; **just ~** gerade; **~ and then**, **~ and again** ab und zu, manchmal; **from ~ on** von jetzt an; **~adays** adv heutzutage
nowhere [ˈnəuwɛəʳ] adv nirgends
nozzle [ˈnɔzl] n Düse f
nuclear [ˈnjuːklɪəʳ] adj (energy etc) Atom-, Kern-
nuclei [ˈnjuːklɪaɪ] npl of **nucleus**
nucleus [ˈnjuːklɪəs] n Kern m
nude [njuːd] adj nackt ♦ n (ART) Akt m; **in the ~** nackt
nudge [nʌdʒ] vt leicht anstoßen
nudist [ˈnjuːdɪst] n Nudist(in) m(f)
nudity [ˈnjuːdɪtɪ] n Nacktheit f
nuisance [ˈnjuːsns] n Ärgernis nt; **what a ~!** wie ärgerlich!
nuke [njuːk] (inf) n Kernkraftwerk nt ♦ vt atomar vernichten
null [nʌl] adj: **~ and void** null und nichtig
numb [nʌm] adj taub, gefühllos ♦ vt betäuben
number [ˈnʌmbəʳ] n Nummer f; (numeral also) Zahl f; (quantity) (An)zahl f ♦ vt nummerieren; (amount to) sein; **to be ~ed among** gezählt werden zu; **a ~ of** (several) einige; **they were ten in ~** sie waren zehn an der Zahl; **~ plate** (BRIT) n (AUT) Nummernschild nt
numeral [ˈnjuːmərəl] n Ziffer f
numerate [ˈnjuːmərɪt] adj rechenkundig
numerical [njuːˈmɛrɪkl] adj (order) zahlenmäßig
numerous [ˈnjuːmərəs] adj zahlreich
nun [nʌn] n Nonne f
nurse [nəːs] n Krankenschwester f; (for children) Kindermädchen nt ♦ vt (patient) pflegen; (doubt etc) hegen
nursery [ˈnəːsərɪ] n (for children) Kinderzimmer nt; (for plants) Gärtnerei f; (for trees) Baumschule f; **~ rhyme** n Kinderreim m; **~ school** n Kindergarten m; **~ slope** (BRIT) n (SKI) Idiotenhügel m (inf), Anfängerhügel m

nursing [ˈnəːsɪŋ] n (profession) Krankenpflege f; **~ home** n Privatklinik f
nurture [ˈnəːtʃəʳ] vt aufziehen
nut [nʌt] n Nuss f; (TECH) Schraubenmutter f; (inf) Verrückte(r) mf; **he's ~s** er ist verrückt; **~crackers** [ˈnʌtkrækəz] npl Nussknacker m
nutmeg [ˈnʌtmɛg] n Muskat(nuss f) m
nutrient [ˈnjuːtrɪənt] n Nährstoff m
nutrition [njuːˈtrɪʃən] n Nahrung f;
nutritious [njuːˈtrɪʃəs] adj nahrhaft
nutshell [ˈnʌtʃɛl] n Nussschale f; **in a ~** (fig) kurz gesagt
nutter [ˈnʌtəʳ] (BRIT: inf) n Spinner(in) m(f)
nylon [ˈnaɪlɔn] n Nylon nt ♦ adj Nylon-

O, o

oak [əuk] n Eiche f ♦ adj Eichen(holz)-
O.A.P. abbr = **old-age pensioner**
oar [ɔːʳ] n Ruder nt
oases [əuˈeɪsiːz] npl of **oasis**
oasis [əuˈeɪsɪs] n Oase f
oath [əuθ] n (statement) Eid m, Schwur m; (swearword) Fluch m
oatmeal [ˈəutmiːl] n Haferschrot m
oats [əuts] npl Hafer m
obedience [əˈbiːdɪəns] n Gehorsam m
obedient [əˈbiːdɪənt] adj gehorsam
obesity [əuˈbiːsɪtɪ] n Fettleibigkeit f
obey [əˈbeɪ] vt, vi: **to ~ (sb)** (jdm) gehorchen
obituary [əˈbɪtjuərɪ] n Nachruf m
object [n ˈɔbdʒɪkt, vb əbˈdʒɛkt] n (thing) Gegenstand m, Objekt nt; (purpose) Ziel nt ♦ vi dagegen sein; **expense is no ~** Ausgaben spielen keine Rolle; **I ~!** ich protestiere!; **to ~ to sth** Einwände gegen etw haben; (morally) Anstoß an etw acc nehmen; **to ~ that** einwenden, dass; **~ion** [əbˈdʒɛkʃən] n (reason against) Einwand m, Einspruch m; (dislike) Abneigung f; **I have no ~ion to ...** ich habe nichts gegen ... einzuwenden; **~ionable** [əbˈdʒɛkʃənəbl] adj nicht einwandfrei; (language) anstößig
objective [əbˈdʒɛktɪv] n Ziel nt ♦ adj objektiv
obligation [ɔblɪˈgeɪʃən] n Verpflichtung f; **without ~** unverbindlich; **obligatory**

[ə'blɪɡətərɪ] *adj* obligatorisch

oblige [ə'blaɪdʒ] *vt* (*compel*) zwingen; (*do a favour*) einen Gefallen tun +*dat*; **to be ~d to sb for sth** jdm für etw verbunden sein

obliging [ə'blaɪdʒɪŋ] *adj* entgegenkommend

oblique [ə'bliːk] *adj* schräg, schief ♦ *n* Schrägstrich *m*

obliterate [ə'blɪtəreɪt] *vt* auslöschen

oblivion [ə'blɪvɪən] *n* Vergessenheit *f*

oblivious [ə'blɪvɪəs] *adj* nicht bewusst

oblong ['ɒblɒŋ] *n* Rechteck *nt* ♦ *adj* länglich

obnoxious [əb'nɒkʃəs] *adj* widerlich

oboe ['əʊbəʊ] *n* Oboe *f*

obscene [əb'siːn] *adj* obszön; **obscenity** [əb'senɪtɪ] *n* Obszönität *f*; **obscenities** *npl* (*oaths*) Zoten *pl*

obscure [əb'skjuər] *adj* unklar; (*indistinct*) undeutlich; (*unknown*) unbekannt, obskur; (*dark*) düster ♦ *vt* verdunkeln; (*view*) verbergen; (*confuse*) verwirren; **obscurity** [əb'skjuərɪtɪ] *n* Unklarheit *f*; (*darkness*) Dunkelheit *f*

observance [əb'zɜːvəns] *n* Befolgung *f*

observant [əb'zɜːvənt] *adj* aufmerksam

observation [ɒbzə'veɪʃən] *n* (*noticing*) Beobachtung *f*; (*surveillance*) Überwachung *f*; (*remark*) Bemerkung *f*

observatory [əb'zɜːvətrɪ] *n* Sternwarte *f*, Observatorium *nt*

observe [əb'zɜːv] *vt* (*notice*) bemerken; (*watch*) beobachten; (*customs*) einhalten; **~r** *n* Beobachter(in) *m(f)*

obsess [əb'ses] *vt* verfolgen, quälen; **~ion** [əb'seʃən] *n* Besessenheit *f*, Wahn *m*; **~ive** *adj* krankhaft

obsolete ['ɒbsəliːt] *adj* überholt, veraltet

obstacle ['ɒbstəkl] *n* Hindernis *nt*; **~ race** *n* Hindernisrennen *nt*

obstetrics [ɒb'stetrɪks] *n* Geburtshilfe *f*

obstinate ['ɒbstɪnɪt] *adj* hartnäckig, stur

obstruct [əb'strʌkt] *vt* versperren; (*pipe*) verstopfen; (*hinder*) hemmen; **~ion** [əb'strʌkʃən] *n* Versperrung *f*; Verstopfung *f*; (*obstacle*) Hindernis *nt*

obtain [əb'teɪn] *vt* erhalten, bekommen; (*result*) erzielen

obtrusive [əb'truːsɪv] *adj* aufdringlich

obvious ['ɒbvɪəs] *adj* offenbar, offensichtlich; **~ly** *adv* offensichtlich

occasion [ə'keɪʒən] *n* Gelegenheit *f*; (*special event*) Ereignis *nt*; (*reason*) Anlass *m* ♦ *vt* veranlassen; **~al** *adj* gelegentlich; **~ally** *adv* gelegentlich

occupant ['ɒkjupənt] *n* Inhaber(in) *m(f)*; (*of house*) Bewohner(in) *m(f)*

occupation [ɒkju'peɪʃən] *n* (*employment*) Tätigkeit *f*, Beruf *m*; (*pastime*) Beschäftigung *f*; (*of country*) Besetzung *f*, Okkupation *f*; **~al hazard** *n* Berufsrisiko *nt*

occupier ['ɒkjupaɪər] *n* Bewohner(in) *m(f)*

occupy ['ɒkjupaɪ] *vt* (*take possession of*) besetzen; (*seat*) belegen; (*live in*) bewohnen; (*position, office*) bekleiden; (*position in sb's life*) einnehmen; (*time*) beanspruchen; **to ~ o.s. with sth** sich mit etw beschäftigen; **to ~ o.s. by doing sth** sich damit beschäftigen, etw zu tun

occur [ə'kɜːr] *vi* vorkommen; **to ~ to sb** jdm einfallen; **~rence** *n* (*event*) Ereignis *nt*; (*appearing*) Auftreten *nt*

ocean ['əʊʃən] *n* Ozean *m*, Meer *nt*; **~-going** *adj* Hochsee-

o'clock [ə'klɒk] *adv*: **it is 5 ~** es ist 5 Uhr

OCR *n abbr* = **optical character reader**

octagonal [ɒk'tægənl] *adj* achteckig

October [ɒk'təʊbər] *n* Oktober *m*

octopus ['ɒktəpəs] *n* Krake *f*; (*small*) Tintenfisch *m*

odd [ɒd] *adj* (*strange*) sonderbar; (*not even*) ungerade; (*sock etc*) einzeln; (*surplus*) übrig; **60-~** so um die 60; **at ~ times** ab und zu; **to be the ~ one out** (*person*) das fünfte Rad am Wagen sein; (*thing*) nicht dazugehören; **~ity** *n* (*strangeness*) Merkwürdigkeit *f*; (*queer person*) seltsame(r) Kauz *m*; (*thing*) Kuriosität *f*; **~-job man** (*irreg*) *n* Mädchen *nt* für alles; **~ jobs** *npl* gelegentlich anfallende Arbeiten; **~ly** *adv* seltsam; **~ments** *npl* Reste *pl*; **~s** *npl* Chancen *pl*; (*betting*) Gewinnchancen *pl*; **it makes no ~s** es spielt keine Rolle; **at ~s** uneinig; **~s and ends** *npl* Krimskrams *m*

odometer [ɒ'dɒmɪtər] (*esp US*) *n* Tacho(meter) *m*

odour ['əʊdə'] (*US* **odor**) *n* Geruch *m*

KEYWORD

of [ɒv, əv] *prep* **1** von +*dat*; *use of gen*; **the history of Germany** die Geschichte Deutschlands; **a friend of ours** ein Freund von uns; **a boy of 10** ein 10-jähriger Junge; **that was kind of you** das war sehr freundlich von Ihnen

2 (*expressing quantity, amount, dates etc*): **a kilo of flour** ein Kilo Mehl; **how much of this do you need?** wie viel brauchen Sie (davon)?; **there were 3 of them** (*people*) sie waren zu dritt; (*objects*) es gab 3 (davon); **a cup of tea/vase of flowers** eine Tasse Tee/Vase mit Blumen; **the 5th of July** der 5. Juli

3 (*from, out of*) aus; **a bridge made of wood** eine Holzbrücke, eine Brücke aus Holz

off [ɒf] *adj, adv* (*absent*) weg, fort; (*switch*) aus(geschaltet), ab(geschaltet); (*BRIT: food: bad*) schlecht; (*cancelled*) abgesagt ♦ *prep* von +*dat*; **to be ~** (*to leave*) gehen; **to be ~ sick** krank sein; **a day ~** ein freier Tag; **to have an ~ day** einen schlechten Tag haben; **he had his coat ~** er hatte seinen Mantel aus; **10% ~** (*COMM*) 10% Rabatt; **5 km ~ (the road)** 5 km (von der Straße) entfernt; **~ the coast** vor der Küste; **I'm ~ meat** (*no longer eat it*) ich esse kein Fleisch mehr; (*no longer like it*) ich mag kein Fleisch mehr; **on the ~ chance** auf gut Glück

offal ['ɒfl] *n* Innereien *pl*

off-colour ['ɒf'kʌlə'] *adj* nicht wohl

offence [ə'fɛns] (*US* **offense**) *n* (*crime*) Vergehen *nt*, Straftat *f*; (*insult*) Beleidigung *f*; **to take ~ at** gekränkt sein wegen

offend [ə'fɛnd] *vt* beleidigen; **~er** *n* Gesetzesübertreter *m*

offense [ə'fɛns] (*US*) *n* = **offence**

offensive [ə'fɛnsɪv] *adj* (*unpleasant*) übel, abstoßend; (*weapon*) Kampf-; (*remark*) verletzend ♦ *n* Angriff *m*

offer ['ɒfə'] *n* Angebot *f* ♦ *vt* anbieten; (*opinion*) äußern; (*resistance*) leisten; **on ~**

zum Verkauf angeboten; **~ing** *n* Gabe *f*

offhand [ɒf'hænd] *adj* lässig ♦ *adv* ohne weiteres

office ['ɒfɪs] *n* Büro *nt*; (*position*) Amt *nt*; **doctor's ~** (*US*) Praxis *f*; **to take ~** = sein Amt antreten; (*POL*) die Regierung übernehmen; **~ automation** *n* Büroautomatisierung *f*; **~ block** (*US* **~ building**) *n* Büro(hoch)haus *nt*; **~ hours** *npl* Dienstzeit *f*; (*US: MED*) Sprechstunde *f*

officer ['ɒfɪsə'] *n* (*MIL*) Offizier *m*; (*public ~*) Beamte(r) *m*

official [ə'fɪʃl] *adj* offiziell, amtlich ♦ *n* Beamte(r) *m*; **~dom** *n* Beamtentum *nt*

officiate [ə'fɪʃɪeɪt] *vi* amtieren

officious [ə'fɪʃəs] *adj* aufdringlich

offing ['ɒfɪŋ] *n*: **in the ~** in (Aus)sicht

Off-licence

> **Off-licence** *ist ein Geschäft (oder eine Theke in einer Gaststätte), wo man alkoholische Getränke kaufen kann, die aber anderswo konsumiert werden müssen. In solchen Geschäften, die oft von landesweiten Ketten betrieben werden, kann man auch andere Getränke, Süßigkeiten, Zigaretten und Knabbereien kaufen.*

off: ~-licence (*BRIT*) *n* (*shop*) Wein- und Spirituosenhandlung *f*; **~-line** *adj* (*COMPUT*) Offline- ♦ *adv* (*COMPUT*) offline; **~-peak** *adj* (*charges*) verbilligt; **~-putting** (*BRIT*) *adj* (*person, remark etc*) abstoßend; **~-road vehicle** *n* Geländefahrzeug *nt*; **~-season** *adj* außer Saison; **~set** (*irreg: like* **set**) *vt* ausgleichen ♦ *n* (*also:* **~set printing**) Offset(druck) *m*; **~shoot** *n* (*fig: of organization*) Zweig *m*; (*: of discussion etc*) Randergebnis *nt*; **~shore** *adv* in einiger Entfernung von der Küste ♦ *adj* küstennah, Küsten-; **~side** *adj* (*SPORT*) im Abseits ♦ *adv* abseits ♦ *n* (*AUT*) Fahrerseite *f*; **~spring** *n* Nachkommenschaft *f*; (*one*) Sprössling *m*; **~stage** *adv* hinter den Kulissen; **~-the-cuff** *adj* unvorbereitet, aus dem Stegreif; **~-the-peg** (*US* **~-the-rack**) *adv* von der Stange; **~-white** *adj* naturweiß

Oftel ['ɔftel] *n Überwachungsgremium zum Verbraucherschutz nach Privatisierung der Telekommunikationsindustrie*

often ['ɔfn] *adv* oft

Ofwat ['ɔfwɔt] *n Überwachungsgremium zum Verbraucherschutz nach Privatisierung der Wasserindustrie*

ogle ['əugl] *vt* liebäugeln mit

oil [ɔɪl] *n* Öl *nt ♦ vt* ölen; **~can** *n* Ölkännchen *nt;* **~field** *n* Ölfeld *nt;* **~ filter** *n* (*AUT*) Ölfilter *m;* **~-fired** *adj* Öl-; **~ painting** *n* Ölgemälde *nt;* **~ rig** *n* Ölplattform *f;* **~skins** *npl* Ölzeug *nt;* **~ slick** *n* Ölteppich *m;* **~ tanker** *n* (Öl)tanker *m;* **~ well** *n* Ölquelle *f;* **~y** *adj* ölig; (*dirty*) ölbeschmiert

ointment ['ɔɪntmənt] *n* Salbe *f*

O.K. ['əu'keɪ] *excl* in Ordnung, O. K., o. k. ♦ *adj* in Ordnung ♦ *vt* genehmigen

okay ['əu'keɪ] = **O.K.**

old [əuld] *adj* alt; **how ~ are you?** wie alt bist du?; **he's 10 years ~** er ist 10 Jahre alt; **~er brother** ältere(r) Bruder *m;* **~ age** *n* Alter *nt;* **~-age pensioner** (*BRIT*) *n* Rentner(in) *m(f);* **~-fashioned** *adj* altmodisch

olive ['ɔlɪv] *n* (*fruit*) Olive *f;* (*colour*) Olive *nt ♦ adj* Oliven-; (*coloured*) olivenfarbig; **~ oil** *n* Olivenöl *nt*

Olympic [əu'lɪmpɪk] *adj* olympisch; **the ~ Games, the ~s** die Olympischen Spiele

omelet(te) ['ɔmlɪt] *n* Omelett *nt*

omen ['əumən] *n* Omen *nt*

ominous ['ɔmɪnəs] *adj* bedrohlich

omission [əu'mɪʃən] *n* Auslassung *f;* (*neglect*) Versäumnis *nt*

omit [əu'mɪt] *vt* auslassen; (*fail to do*) versäumen

KEYWORD

on [ɔn] *prep* **1** (*indicating position*) auf +*dat;* (*with vb of motion*) auf +*acc;* (*on vertical surface, part of body*) an +*dat/acc;* **it's on the table** es ist auf dem Tisch; **she put the book on the table** sie legte das Buch auf den Tisch; **on the left** links

2 (*indicating means, method, condition etc*): **on foot** (*go, be*) zu Fuß; **on the train/plane** (*go*) mit dem Zug/Flugzeug; (*be*) im Zug/Flugzeug; **on the telephone/television** am Telefon/im Fernsehen; **to be on drugs** Drogen nehmen; **to be on holiday/business** im Urlaub/auf Geschäftsreise sein

3 (*referring to time*): **on Friday** (am) Freitag; **on Fridays** freitags; **on June 20th** am 20. Juni; **a week on Friday** Freitag in einer Woche; **on arrival he ...** als er ankam, ... er ...

4 (*about, concerning*) über +*acc*

♦ *adv* **1** (*referring to dress*) an; **she put her boots/hat on** sie zog ihre Stiefel an/setzte ihren Hut auf

2 (*further, continuously*) weiter; **to walk on** weitergehen

♦ *adj* **1** (*functioning, in operation: machine, TV, light*) an; (: *tap*) aufgedreht; (: *brakes*) angezogen; **is the meeting still on?** findet die Versammlung noch statt?; **there's a good film on** es läuft ein guter Film

2: that's not on! (*inf: of behaviour*) das liegt nicht drin!

---

once [wʌns] *adv* einmal ♦ *conj* wenn ... einmal; **~ he had left/it was done** nachdem er gegangen war/es fertig war; **at ~** sofort; (*at the same time*) gleichzeitig; **~ a week** einmal in der Woche; **~ more** noch einmal; **~ and for all** ein für alle Mal; **~ upon a time** es war einmal

oncoming ['ɔnkʌmɪŋ] *adj* (*traffic*) Gegen-, entgegenkommend

---

KEYWORD

one [wʌn] *num* eins; (*with noun, referring back to noun*) ein/eine/ein; **it is one (o'clock)** es ist eins, es ist ein Uhr; **one hundred and fifty** einhundertfünfzig

♦ *adj* **1** (*sole*) einzige(r, s); **the one book which** das einzige Buch, welches

2 (*same*) derselbe/dieselbe/dasselbe; **they came in the one car** sie kamen alle in dem einen Auto

3 (*indef*): **one day I discovered ...** eines Tages bemerkte ich ...

♦ *pron* **1** eine(r, s); **do you have a red one?** haben Sie einen roten/eine rote/ein rotes?; **this one** diese(r, s); **that one** der/die/das; **which one?** welche(r, s)?; **one by one** einzeln

2: one another einander; **do you two ever see one another?** seht ihr beide euch manchmal?

3 (*impers*) man; **one never knows** man kann nie wissen; **to cut one's finger** sich in den Finger schneiden

one: **~-armed bandit** *n* einarmiger Bandit *m*; **~-day excursion** (*US*) *n* (*day return*) Tagesrückfahrkarte *f*; **~-man** *adj* Einmann-; **~-man band** *n* Einmannkapelle *f*; (*fig*) Einmannbetrieb *m*; **~-off** (*BRIT: inf*) *n* Einzelfall *m*

oneself [wʌn'self] *pron* (*reflexive: after prep*) sich; (*~ personally*) sich selbst *or* selber; (*emphatic*) (sich) selbst; **to hurt ~** sich verletzen

one: **~-sided** *adj* (*argument*) einseitig; **~-to-~** *adj* (*relationship*) eins-zu-eins; **~-upmanship** *n* die Kunst, anderen um eine Nasenlänge voraus zu sein; **~-way** *adj* (*street*) Einbahn-

ongoing ['ɒngəʊɪŋ] *adj* momentan; (*progressing*) sich entwickelnd

onion ['ʌnjən] *n* Zwiebel *f*

on-line *adj* (*COMPUT*) Online-

onlooker ['ɒnlʊkəʳ] *n* Zuschauer(in) *m(f)*

only ['əʊnlɪ] *adv* nur, bloß ♦ *adj* einzige(r, s) ♦ *conj* nur, bloß; **an ~ child** ein Einzelkind *n*; **not ~ ... but also ...** nicht nur ..., sondern auch ...

onset ['ɒnset] *n* (*start*) Beginn *m*

onshore ['ɒnʃɔːr] *adj* (*wind*) See-

onslaught ['ɒnslɔːt] *n* Angriff *m*

onto ['ɒntʊ] *prep* = **on to**

onus ['əʊnəs] *n* Last *f*, Pflicht *f*

onward(s) ['ɒnwəd(z)] *adv* (*place*) voran, vorwärts; **from that day ~** von dem Tag an; **from today ~** ab heute

ooze [uːz] *vi* sickern

opaque [əʊ'peɪk] *adj* undurchsichtig

OPEC ['əʊpɛk] *n abbr* (= *Organization of Petroleum-Exporting Countries*) OPEC *f*

open ['əʊpn] *adj* offen; (*public*) öffentlich; (*mind*) aufgeschlossen ♦ *vt* öffnen, aufmachen; (*trial, motorway, account*) eröffnen ♦ *vi* (*begin*) anfangen; (*shop*) aufmachen; (*door, flower*) aufgehen; (*play*) Premiere haben; **in the ~ (air)** im Freien; **~ on to** *vt fus* sich öffnen auf +*acc*; **~ up** *vt* (*route*) erschließen; (*shop, prospects*) eröffnen ♦ *vi* öffnen; **~ing** *n* (*hole*) Öffnung *f*; (*beginning*) Anfang *m*; (*good chance*) Gelegenheit *f*; **~ing hours** *npl* Öffnungszeiten *pl*; **~ learning centre** *n* Weiterbildungseinrichtung auf Teilzeitbasis; **~ly** *adv* offen; (*publicly*) öffentlich; **~-minded** *adj* aufgeschlossen; **~-necked** *adj* offen; **~-plan** *adj* (*office*) Großraum-; (*flat etc*) offen angelegt

Open University

i **Open University** *ist eine 1969 in Großbritannien gegründete Fernuniversität für Spätstudierende. Der Unterricht findet durch Fernseh- und Radiosendungen statt, schriftliche Arbeiten werden mit der Post verschickt, und der Besuch von Sommerkursen ist Pflicht. Die Studenten müssen eine bestimmte Anzahl von Unterrichtseinheiten in einem bestimmten Zeitraum absolvieren und für die Verleihung eines akademischen Grades eine Mindestzahl von Scheinen machen.*

opera ['ɒpərə] *n* Oper *f*; **~ house** *n* Opernhaus *nt*

operate ['ɒpəreɪt] *vt* (*machine*) bedienen; (*brakes, light*) betätigen ♦ *vi* (*machine*) laufen, in Betrieb sein; (*person*) arbeiten; (*MED*): **to ~ on** operieren

operatic [ɒpə'rætɪk] *adj* Opern-

operating ['ɒpəreɪtɪŋ] *adj*: **~ table/theatre** Operationstisch *m*/-saal *m*

operation [ɒpə'reɪʃən] *n* (*working*) Betrieb *m*; (*MED*) Operation *f*; (*undertaking*) Unternehmen *nt*; (*MIL*) Einsatz *m*; **to be in ~** (*JUR*) in Kraft sein; (*machine*) in Betrieb sein; **to have an ~** (*MED*) operiert werden;

~al *adj* einsatzbereit

operative ['ɔpərətɪv] *adj* wirksam

operator ['ɔpəreɪtəʳ] *n* (*of machine*) Arbeiter *m*; (*TEL*) Telefonist(in) *m(f)*

opinion [ə'pɪnjən] *n* Meinung *f*; **in my ~** meiner Meinung nach; **~ated** *adj* starrsinnig; **~ poll** *n* Meinungsumfrage *f*

opponent [ə'pəunənt] *n* Gegner *m*

opportunity [ɔpə'tju:nɪtɪ] *n* Gelegenheit *f*, Möglichkeit *f*; **to take the ~ of doing sth** die Gelegenheit ergreifen, etw zu tun

oppose [ə'pəuz] *vt* entgegentreten +*dat*; (*argument, idea*) ablehnen; (*plan*) bekämpfen; **to be ~d to sth** gegen etw sein; **as ~d to** im Gegensatz zu; **opposing** *adj* gegnerisch; (*points of view*) entgegengesetzt

opposite ['ɔpəzɪt] *adj* (*house*) gegenüberliegend; (*direction*) entgegengesetzt ♦ *adv* gegenüber ♦ *prep* gegenüber ♦ *n* Gegenteil *nt*

opposition [ɔpə'zɪʃən] *n* (*resistance*) Widerstand *m*; (*POL*) Opposition *f*; (*contrast*) Gegensatz *m*

oppress [ə'pres] *vt* unterdrücken; (*heat etc*) bedrücken; **~ion** [ə'preʃən] *n* Unterdrückung *f*; **~ive** *adj* (*authority, law*) repressiv; (*burden, thought*) bedrückend; (*heat*) drückend

opt [ɔpt] *vi*: **to ~ for** sich entscheiden für; **to ~ to do sth** sich entscheiden, etw zu tun; **to ~ out of** sich drücken vor +*dat*

optical ['ɔptɪkl] *adj* optisch; **~ character reader** *n* optische(s) Lesegerät *nt*

optician [ɔp'tɪʃən] *n* Optiker *m*

optimist ['ɔptɪmɪst] *n* Optimist *m*; **~ic** [ɔptɪ'mɪstɪk] *adj* optimistisch

optimum ['ɔptɪməm] *adj* optimal

option ['ɔpʃən] *n* Wahl *f*; (*COMM*) Option *f*; **to keep one's ~s open** sich alle Möglichkeiten offen halten; **~al** *adj* freiwillig; (*subject*) wahlfrei; **~al extras** *npl* Extras auf Wunsch

or [ɔ:ʳ] *conj* oder; **he could not read ~ write** er konnte weder lesen noch schreiben; **~ else** sonst

oral ['ɔ:rəl] *adj* mündlich ♦ *n* (*exam*)

mündliche Prüfung *f*

orange ['ɔrɪndʒ] *n* (*fruit*) Apfelsine *f*, Orange *f*; (*colour*) Orange *nt* ♦ *adj* orange

orator ['ɔrətəʳ] *n* Redner(in) *m(f)*

orbit ['ɔ:bɪt] *n* Umlaufbahn *f*

orbital (motorway) ['ɔ:bɪtəl-] *n* Ringautobahn *f*

orchard ['ɔ:tʃəd] *n* Obstgarten *m*

orchestra ['ɔ:kɪstrə] *n* Orchester *nt*; (*US: seating*) Parkett *nt*; **~l** [ɔ:'kestrəl] *adj* Orchester-, orchestral

orchid ['ɔ:kɪd] *n* Orchidee *f*

ordain [ɔ:'deɪn] *vt* (*ECCL*) weihen

ordeal [ɔ:'di:l] *n* Qual *f*

order ['ɔ:dəʳ] *n* (*sequence*) Reihenfolge *f*; (*good arrangement*) Ordnung *f*; (*command*) Befehl *m*; (*JUR*) Anordnung *f*; (*peace*) Ordnung *f*; (*condition*) Zustand *m*; (*rank*) Klasse *f*; (*COMM*) Bestellung *f*; (*ECCL, honour*) Orden *m* ♦ *vt* (*also*: **put in ~**) ordnen; (*command*) befehlen; (*COMM*) bestellen; **in ~** in der Reihenfolge; **in (working) ~** in gutem Zustand; **in ~ to do sth** um etw zu tun; **on ~** (*COMM*) auf Bestellung; **to ~ sb to do sth** jdm befehlen, etw zu tun; **to ~ sth** (*command*) etw *acc* befehlen; **~ form** *n* Bestellschein *m*; **~ly** *n* (*MIL*) Sanitäter *m*; (*MED*) Pfleger *m* ♦ *adj* (*tidy*) ordentlich; (*well-behaved*) ruhig

ordinary ['ɔ:dnrɪ] *adj* gewöhnlich ♦ *n*: **out of the ~** außergewöhnlich

Ordnance Survey ['ɔ:dnəns-] (*BRIT*) *n* amtliche(r) Kartografiedienst *m*

ore [ɔ:ʳ] *n* Erz *nt*

organ ['ɔ:gən] *n* (*MUS*) Orgel *f*; (*BIOL, fig*) Organ *nt*

organic [ɔ:'gænɪk] *adj* (*food, farming etc*) biodynamisch

organization [ɔ:gənaɪ'zeɪʃən] *n* Organisation *f*; (*make-up*) Struktur *f*

organize ['ɔ:gənaɪz] *vt* organisieren; **~r** *n* Organisator *m*, Veranstalter *m*

orgasm ['ɔ:gæzəm] *n* Orgasmus *m*

orgy ['ɔ:dʒɪ] *n* Orgie *f*

Orient ['ɔ:rɪənt] *n* Orient *m*; **o~al** [ɔ:rɪ'entl] *adj* orientalisch

origin ['ɔrɪdʒɪn] *n* Ursprung *m*; (*of the world*)

Anfang m, Entstehung f; **~al** [ə'rɪdʒɪnl] adj
(first) ursprünglich; (painting) original; (idea)
originell ♦ n Original nt; **~ally** adv
ursprünglich; originell; **~ate** [ə'rɪdʒɪneɪt] vi
entstehen ♦ vt ins Leben rufen; **to ~ate
from** stammen aus

Orkney ['ɔːknɪ] npl (also: **the ~ Islands**) die
Orkneyinseln pl

ornament ['ɔːnəmənt] n Schmuck m; (on
mantelpiece) Nippesfigur f; **~al** [ɔːnə'mɛntl]
adj Zier-

ornate [ɔː'neɪt] adj reich verziert

orphan ['ɔːfn] n Waise f, Waisenkind nt ♦ vt:
to be ~ed Waise werden; **~age** n
Waisenhaus nt

orthodox ['ɔːθədɔks] adj orthodox; **~y** n
Orthodoxie f; (fig) Konventionalität f

orthopaedic [ɔːθə'piːdɪk] (US **orthopedic**)
adj orthopädisch

ostentatious [ɔstɛn'teɪʃəs] adj großtuerisch,
protzig

ostracize ['ɔstrəsaɪz] vt ausstoßen

ostrich ['ɔstrɪtʃ] n Strauß m

other ['ʌðə*] adj andere(r, s) ♦ pron andere(r,
s) ♦ adv: **~ than** anders als; **the ~ (one)**
der/die/das andere; **the ~ day** neulich; **~s**
(~ people) andere; **~wise** adv (in a different
way) anders; (or else) sonst

otter ['ɔtə*] n Otter m

ouch [autʃ] excl aua

ought [ɔːt] vb aux sollen; **I ~ to do it** ich
sollte es tun; **this ~ to have been
corrected** das hätte korrigiert werden
sollen

ounce [auns] n Unze f

our ['auə*] adj unser; see also **my**; **~s** pron
unsere(r, s); see also **mine²**; **~selves** pron
uns (selbst); (emphatic) (wir) selbst; see also
oneself

oust [aust] vt verdrängen

out [aut] adv hinaus/heraus; (not indoors)
draußen; (not alight) aus; (unconscious)
bewusstlos; (results) bekannt gegeben; **to
eat/go ~** auswärts essen/ausgehen; **~
there** da draußen; **he is ~** (absent) er ist
nicht da; **he was ~ in his calculations**
seine Berechnungen waren nicht richtig; **~**

loud laut; **~ of** aus; (away from) außerhalb
+gen; **to be ~ of milk** etc keine Milch etc
mehr haben; **~ of order** außer Betrieb; **~-
and-~** adj (liar, thief etc) ausgemacht;
~back n Hinterland nt; **~board (motor)** n
Außenbordmotor m; **~break** n Ausbruch
m; **~burst** n Ausbruch m; **~cast** n
Ausgestoßene(r) mf; **~come** n Ergebnis nt;
~crop n (of rock) Felsnase f; **~cry** n Protest
m; **~dated** adj überholt; **~do** (irreg: like
do) vt übertrumpfen; **~door** adj Außen-;
(SPORT) im Freien; **~doors** adv im Freien

outer ['autə*] adj äußere(r, s); **~ space** n
Weltraum m

outfit ['autfɪt] n Kleidung f

out: ~going (character) aufgeschlossen;
~goings (BRIT) npl Ausgaben pl; **~grow**
(irreg: like **grow**) vt (clothes) herauswachsen
aus; (habit) ablegen; **~house** n
Nebengebäude nt

outing ['autɪŋ] n Ausflug m

outlandish [aut'lændɪʃ] adj eigenartig

out: ~law n Geächtete(r) f(m) ♦ vt ächten;
(thing) verbieten; **~lay** n Auslage f; **~let** n
Auslass m, Abfluss m; (also: **retail ~let**)
Absatzmarkt m; (US: ELEC) Steckdose f; (for
emotions) Ventil nt

outline ['autlaɪn] n Umriss m

out: ~live vt überleben; **~look** n (also fig)
Aussicht f; (attitude) Einstellung f; **~lying**
adj entlegen; (district) Außen-; **~moded** adj
veraltet; **~number** vt zahlenmäßig
überlegen sein +dat; **~-of-date** adj
(passport) abgelaufen; (clothes etc)
altmodisch; (ideas etc) überholt; **~-of-the-
way** adj abgelegen; **~patient** n
ambulante(r) Patient m/ambulante
Patientin f; **~post** n (MIL, fig) Vorposten m;
~put n Leistung f, Produktion f; (COMPUT)
Ausgabe f

outrage ['autreɪdʒ] n (cruel deed)
Ausschreitung f; (indecency) Skandal m ♦ vt
(morals) verstoßen gegen; (person)
empören; **~ous** [aut'reɪdʒəs] adj unerhört

outreach worker [aut'riːtʃ-] n
Streetworker(in) m(f)

outright [adv aut'raɪt, adj 'autraɪt] adv (at

once) sofort; *(openly)* ohne Umschweife
♦ *adj (denial)* völlig; *(sale)* Total-; *(winner)*
unbestritten

outset ['autset] *n* Beginn *m*

outside [aut'said] *n* Außenseite *f* ♦ *adj*
äußere(r, s), Außen-; *(chance)* gering ♦ *adv*
außen ♦ *prep* außerhalb +*gen*; **at the ~** *(fig)*
maximal; *(time)* spätestens; **to go ~** nach
draußen gehen; **~ lane** *n (AUT)* äußere
Spur *f*; **~ line** *n (TEL)* Amtsanschluss *m*; **~r**
n Außenseiter(in) *m(f)*

out: ~size *adj* übergroß; **~skirts** *npl*
Stadtrand *m*; **~spoken** *adj* freimütig;
~standing *adj* hervorragend; *(debts etc)*
ausstehend; **~stay** *vt*: **to ~stay one's**
welcome länger bleiben als erwünscht;
~stretched *adj* ausgestreckt; **~strip** *vt*
übertreffen; **~ tray** *n* Ausgangskorb *m*

outward ['autwəd] *adj* äußere(r, s); *(journey)*
Hin-; *(freight)* ausgehend ♦ *adv* nach außen;
~ly *adv* äußerlich

outweigh [aut'wei] *vt (fig)* überwiegen

outwit [aut'wit] *vt* überlisten

oval ['əuvl] *adj* oval ♦ *n* Oval *nt*

┌─────────────────────────────────────┐
│ **Oval Office**   │
│   │
│ ⓘ **Oval Office**, *ein großer ovaler Raum im* │
│ *Weißen Haus, ist das private Büro des* │
│ *amerikanischen Präsidenten. Im weiteren* │
│ *Sinne bezieht sich dieser Begriff oft auf die* │
│ *Präsidentschaft selbst.*   │
└─────────────────────────────────────┘

ovary ['əuvəri] *n* Eierstock *m*

ovation [əu'veiʃən] *n* Beifallssturm *m*

oven ['ʌvn] *n* Backofen *m*; **~proof** *adj*
feuerfest

over ['əuvər] *adv (across)* hinüber/herüber;
(finished) vorbei; *(left)* übrig; *(again)* wieder,
noch einmal ♦ *prep* über ♦ *prefix (excessively)*
übermäßig; **~ here** hier(hin); **~ there**
dort(hin); **all ~** *(everywhere)* überall;
(finished) vorbei; **~ and ~** immer wieder; **~**
and above darüber hinaus; **to ask sb ~**
jdn einladen; **to bend ~** sich bücken

overall [*adj, n* 'əuvərɔːl, *adv* əuvər'ɔːl] *adj*
(situation) allgemein; *(length)* Gesamt- ♦ *n*
(BRIT) Kittel *m* ♦ *adv* insgesamt; **~s** *npl (for*

man) Overall *m*

over: ~awe *vt (frighten)* einschüchtern;
(make impression) überwältigen; **~balance**
vi Übergewicht bekommen; **~bearing** *adj*
aufdringlich; **~board** *adv* über Bord;
~book *vi* überbuchen

overcast ['əuvəkɑːst] *adj* bedeckt

overcharge [əuvə'tʃɑːdʒ] *vt*: **to ~ sb** von
jdm zu viel verlangen

overcoat ['əuvəkəut] *n* Mantel *m*

overcome [əuvə'kʌm] *(irreg: like* **come***) vt*
überwinden

over: ~crowded *adj* überfüllt; **~crowding**
n Überfüllung *f*; **~do** *(irreg: like* **do***) vt (cook*
too much) verkochen; *(exaggerate)*
übertreiben; **~done** *adj* übertrieben;
(COOK) verbraten, verkocht; **~dose** *n*
Überdosis *f*; **~draft** *n* (Konto)überziehung
f; **~drawn** *adj (account)* überzogen; **~due**
adj überfällig; **~estimate** *vt* überschätzen;
~excited *adj* überreizt; *(children)* aufgeregt

overflow [əuvə'fləu] *vi* überfließen ♦ *n*
(excess) Überschuss *m*; *(also:* **~ pipe***)*
Überlaufrohr *nt*

overgrown [əuvə'grəun] *adj (garden)*
verwildert

overhaul [*vb* əuvə'hɔːl, *n* 'əuvəhɔːl] *vt (car)*
überholen; *(plans)* überprüfen ♦ *n*
Überholung *f*

overhead [*adv* əuvə'hed, *adj, n* 'əuvəhed] *adv*
oben ♦ *adj* Hoch-; *(wire)* oberirdisch;
(lighting) Decken- ♦ *n (US)* = **overheads**; **~s**
npl (costs) allgemeine Unkosten *pl*; **~**
projector *n* Overheadprojektor *m*

over: ~hear *(irreg: like* **hear***) vt* (mit
an)hören; **~heat** *vi (engine)* heiß laufen;
~joyed *adj* überglücklich; **~kill** *n (fig)*
Rundumschlag *m*

overland ['əuvəlænd] *adj* Überland- ♦ *adv*
(travel) über Land

overlap [*vb* əuvə'læp, *n* 'əuvəlæp] *vi* sich
überschneiden; *(objects)* sich teilweise
decken ♦ *n* Überschneidung *f*

over: ~leaf *adv* umseitig; **~load** *vt*
überladen; **~look** *vt (view from above)*
überblicken; *(not notice)* übersehen;
(pardon) hinwegsehen über +*acc*

overnight [adv əuvə'naɪt, adj 'əuvənaɪt] adv über Nacht ♦ adj (journey) Nacht-; **~ stay** Übernachtung f; **to stay ~** übernachten

overpass ['əuvəpɑːs] n Überführung f

overpower [əuvə'pauəʳ] vt überwältigen

over-: ~rate vt überschätzen; **~ride** (irreg: like **ride**) vt (order, decision) aufheben; (objection) übergehen; **~riding** adj vorherrschend; **~rule** vt verwerfen; **~run** (irreg: like **run**) vt (country) einfallen in; (time limit) überziehen

overseas [əuvə'siːz] adv nach/in Übersee ♦ adj überseeisch, Übersee-

overseer ['əuvəsɪəʳ] n Aufseher m

overshadow [əuvə'ʃædəu] vt überschatten

overshoot [əuvə'ʃuːt] (irreg: like **shoot**) vt (runway) hinausschießen über +acc

oversight ['əuvəsaɪt] n (mistake) Versehen nt

over-: ~sleep (irreg: like **sleep**) vi verschlafen; **~spill** n (Bevölkerungs)überschuss m; **~state** vt übertreiben; **~step** vt: **to ~step the mark** zu weit gehen

overt [əu'vɜːt] adj offen(kundig)

overtake [əuvə'teɪk] (irreg: like **take**) vt, vi überholen

over-: ~throw (irreg: like **throw**) vt (POL) stürzen; **~time** n Überstunden pl; **~tone** n (fig) Note f

overture ['əuvətʃuəʳ] n Ouvertüre f

over-: ~turn vt, vi umkippen; **~weight** adj zu dick; **~whelm** vt überwältigen; **~work** n Überarbeitung f ♦ vt überlasten ♦ vi sich überarbeiten; **~wrought** adj überreizt

owe [əu] vt schulden; **to ~ sth to sb** (money) jdm etw schulden; (favour etc) jdm etw verdanken; **owing to** prep wegen +gen

owl [aul] n Eule f

own [əun] vt besitzen ♦ adj eigen; **a room of my ~** mein eigenes Zimmer; **to get one's ~ back** sich rächen; **on one's ~** allein; **~ up** vi: **to ~ up (to sth)** (etw) zugeben; **~er** n Besitzer(in) m(f); **~ership** n Besitz m

ox [ɔks] n (pl **~en**) n Ochse m

oxtail ['ɔksteɪl] n: **~ soup** Ochsenschwanzsuppe f

oxygen ['ɔksɪdʒən] n Sauerstoff m; **~ mask** n Sauerstoffmaske f; **~ tent** n Sauerstoffzelt nt

oyster ['ɔɪstəʳ] n Auster f

oz. abbr = **ounce(s)**

ozone ['əuzəun] n Ozon nt; **~-friendly** adj (aerosol) ohne Treibgas; (fridge) FCKW-frei; **~ hole** n Ozonloch nt; **~ layer** n Ozonschicht f

P, p

p abbr = **penny; pence**

pa [pɑː] (inf) n Papa m

P.A. n abbr = **personal assistant; public address system**

p.a. abbr = **per annum**

pace [peɪs] n Schritt m; (speed) Tempo nt ♦ vi schreiten; **to keep ~ with** Schritt halten mit; **~maker** n Schrittmacher m

pacific [pə'sɪfɪk] adj pazifisch ♦ n: **the P~ (Ocean)** der Pazifik

pacifist ['pæsɪfɪst] n Pazifist m

pacify ['pæsɪfaɪ] vt befrieden; (calm) beruhigen

pack [pæk] n (of goods) Packung f; (of hounds) Meute f; (of cards) Spiel nt; (gang) Bande f ♦ vt (case) packen; (clothes) einpacken ♦ vi packen; **to ~ sb off to ...** jdn nach ... schicken; **~ it in!** lass es gut sein!

package ['pækɪdʒ] n Paket nt; **~ tour** n Pauschalreise f

packed [pækt] adj abgepackt; **~ lunch** n Lunchpaket nt

packet ['pækɪt] n Päckchen nt

packing ['pækɪŋ] n (action) Packen nt; (material) Verpackung f; **~ case** n (Pack)kiste f

pact [pækt] n Pakt m, Vertrag m

pad [pæd] n (of paper) (Schreib)block m; (stuffing) Polster nt ♦ vt polstern; **~ding** n Polsterung f

paddle ['pædl] n Paddel nt; (US: SPORT) Schläger m ♦ vt (boat) paddeln ♦ vi (in sea) plan(t)schen; **~ steamer** n Raddampfer m

paddling pool ['pædlɪŋ-] (BRIT) n

Plan(t)schbecken *nt*

paddock ['pædək] *n* Koppel *f*

paddy field ['pædɪ-] *n* Reisfeld *nt*

padlock ['pædlɔk] *n* Vorhängeschloss *nt* ♦ *vt* verschließen

paediatrics [piːdɪ'ætrɪks] (*US* **pediatrics**) *n* Kinderheilkunde *f*

pagan ['peɪgən] *adj* heidnisch ♦ *n* Heide *m*, Heidin *f*

page [peɪdʒ] *n* Seite *f*; (*person*) Page *m* ♦ *vt* (*in hotel*) ausrufen lassen

pageant ['pædʒənt] *n* Festzug *m*; **~ry** *n* Gepränge *nt*

pager ['peɪdʒəʳ] *n* (*TEL*) Funkrufempfänger *m*, Piepser *m* (*inf*)

paging device ['peɪdʒɪŋ-] *n* (*TEL*) = **pager**

paid [peɪd] *pt, pp of* **pay** ♦ *adj* bezahlt; **to put ~ to** (*BRIT*) zunichte machen

pail [peɪl] *n* Eimer *m*

pain [peɪn] *n* Schmerz *m*; **to be in ~** Schmerzen haben; **on ~ of death** bei Todesstrafe; **to take ~s to do sth** sich *dat* Mühe geben, etw zu tun; **~ed** *adj* (*expression*) gequält; **~ful** *adj* (*physically*) schmerzhaft; (*embarrassing*) peinlich; (*difficult*) mühsam; **~fully** *adv* (*fig: very*) schrecklich; **~killer** *n* Schmerzmittel *nt*; **~less** *adj* schmerzlos; **~staking** ['zteɪkɪŋ] *adj* gewissenhaft

paint [peɪnt] *n* Farbe *f* ♦ *vt* anstreichen; (*picture*) malen; **to ~ the door blue** die Tür blau streichen; **~brush** *n* Pinsel *m*; **~er** *n* Maler *m*; **~ing** *n* Malerei *f*; (*picture*) Gemälde *nt*; **~work** *n* Anstrich *m*; (*of car*) Lack *m*

pair [peəʳ] *n* Paar *nt*; **~ of scissors** Schere *f*; **~ of trousers** Hose *f*

pajamas [pə'dʒɑːməz] (*US*) *npl* Schlafanzug *m*

Pakistan [pɑːkɪ'stɑːn] *n* Pakistan *nt*; **~i** *adj* pakistanisch ♦ *n* Pakistani *mf*

pal [pæl] (*inf*) *n* Kumpel *m*

palace ['pæləs] *n* Palast *m*, Schloss *nt*

palatable ['pælɪtəbl] *adj* schmackhaft

palate ['pælɪt] *n* Gaumen *m*

palatial [pə'leɪʃəl] *adj* palastartig

pale [peɪl] *adj* blass, bleich ♦ *n*: **to be**

beyond the ~ die Grenzen überschreiten

Palestine ['pælɪstaɪn] *n* Palästina *nt*; **Palestinian** [pælɪs'tɪnɪən] *adj* palästinensisch ♦ *n* Palästinenser(in) *m(f)*

palette ['pælɪt] *n* Palette *f*

paling ['peɪlɪŋ] *n* (*stake*) Zaunpfahl *m*; (*fence*) Lattenzaun *m*

pall [pɔːl] *vi* jeden Reiz verlieren, verblassen

pallet ['pælɪt] *n* (*for goods*) Palette *f*

pallid ['pælɪd] *adj* blass, bleich

pallor ['pæləʳ] *n* Blässe *f*

palm [pɑːm] *n* (*of hand*) Handfläche *f*; (*also:* **~ tree**) Palme *f* ♦ *vt*: **to ~ sth off on sb** jdm etw andrehen; **P~ Sunday** *n* Palmsonntag *m*

palpable ['pælpəbl] *adj* (*also fig*) greifbar

palpitation [pælpɪ'teɪʃən] *n* Herzklopfen *nt*

paltry ['pɔːltrɪ] *adj* armselig

pamper ['pæmpəʳ] *vt* verhätscheln

pamphlet ['pæmflət] *n* Broschüre *f*

pan [pæn] *n* Pfanne *f* ♦ *vi* (*CINE*) schwenken

panache [pə'næʃ] *n* Schwung *m*

pancake ['pænkeɪk] *n* Pfannkuchen *m*

pancreas ['pæŋkrɪəs] *n* Bauchspeicheldrüse *f*

panda ['pændə] *n* Panda *m*; **~ car** (*BRIT*) *n* (Funk)streifenwagen *m*

pandemonium [pændɪ'məʊnɪəm] *n* Hölle *f*; (*noise*) Höllenlärm *m*

pander ['pændəʳ] *vi*: **to ~ to** sich richten nach

pane [peɪn] *n* (Fenster)scheibe *f*

panel ['pænl] *n* (*of wood*) Tafel *f*; (*TV*) Diskussionsrunde *f*; **~ling** (*US* **paneling**) *n* Täfelung *f*

pang [pæŋ] *n*: **~s of hunger** quälende(r) Hunger *m*; **~s of conscience** Gewissensbisse *pl*

panic ['pænɪk] *n* Panik *f* ♦ *vi* in Panik geraten; **don't ~** (nur) keine Panik; **~ky** *adj* (*person*) überängstlich; **~-stricken** *adj* von panischem Schrecken erfasst; (*look*) panisch

pansy ['pænzɪ] *n* Stiefmütterchen *nt*; (*inf*) Schwule(r) *m*

pant [pænt] *vi* keuchen; (*dog*) hecheln

panther ['pænθəʳ] *n* Pant(h)er *m*

panties ['pæntɪz] npl (Damen)slip m
pantihose ['pæntɪhəʊz] (US) n Strumpfhose f
pantomime ['pæntəmaɪm] (BRIT) n Märchenkomödie f um Weihnachten

| Pantomime |

ⓘ **Pantomime** oder umgangssprachlich **panto** ist in Großbritannien ein zur Weihnachtszeit aufgeführtes Märchenspiel mit possenhaften Elementen, Musik, Standardrollen (ein als Frau verkleideter Mann, ein Junge, ein Bösewicht) und aktuellen Witzen. Publikumsbeteiligung wird gern gesehen (z.B. warnen die Kinder den Helden mit dem Ruf „He's behind you" vor einer drohenden Gefahr), und viele der Witze sprechen vor allem Erwachsene an, so dass pantomimes Unterhaltung für die ganze Familie bieten.

pantry ['pæntrɪ] n Vorratskammer f
pants [pænts] npl (BRIT: woman's) Schlüpfer m; (: man's) Unterhose f; (US: trousers) Hose f
papal ['peɪpəl] adj päpstlich
paper ['peɪpər] n Papier nt; (newspaper) Zeitung f; (essay) Referat nt ♦ adj Papier-, aus Papier ♦ vt (wall) tapezieren; ~s npl (identity ~s) Ausweis(papiere pl) m; ~back n Taschenbuch nt; ~ bag n Tüte f; ~ clip n Büroklammer f; ~ hankie n Tempotaschentuch nt ®; ~weight n Briefbeschwerer m; ~work n Schreibarbeit f
par [pɑːr] n (COMM) Nennwert m; (GOLF) Par nt; **on a ~ with** ebenbürtig +dat
parable ['pærəbl] n (REL) Gleichnis nt
parachute ['pærəʃuːt] n Fallschirm m ♦ vi (mit dem Fallschirm) abspringen
parade [pəˈreɪd] n Parade f ♦ vt aufmarschieren lassen; (fig) zur Schau stellen ♦ vi paradieren, vorbeimarschieren
paradise ['pærədaɪs] n Paradies nt
paradox ['pærədɔks] n Paradox nt; ~ically [pærəˈdɔksɪklɪ] adv paradoxerweise
paraffin ['pærəfɪn] (BRIT) n Paraffin nt

paragraph ['pærəgrɑːf] n Absatz m
parallel ['pærəlel] adj parallel ♦ n Parallele f
paralyse ['pærəlaɪz] (US **paralyze**) vt (MED) lähmen, paralysieren; (fig: organization, production etc) lahm legen; **~d** adj gelähmt; **paralysis** [pəˈrælɪsɪs] n Lähmung f
paralyze ['pærəlaɪz] (US) = **paralyse** vt
parameter [pəˈræmɪtər] n Parameter m; **~s** npl (framework, limits) Rahmen m
paramount ['pærəmaʊnt] adj höchste(r, s), oberste(r, s)
paranoid ['pærənɔɪd] adj (person) an Verfolgungswahn leidend, paranoid; (feeling) krankhaft
parapet ['pærəpɪt] n Brüstung f
paraphernalia [pærəfəˈneɪlɪə] n Zubehör nt, Utensilien pl
paraphrase ['pærəfreɪz] vt umschreiben
paraplegic [pærəˈpliːdʒɪk] n Querschnittsgelähmte(r) f(m)
parasite ['pærəsaɪt] n (also fig) Schmarotzer m, Parasit m
parasol ['pærəsɔl] n Sonnenschirm m
paratrooper ['pærətruːpər] n Fallschirmjäger m
parcel ['pɑːsl] n Paket nt ♦ vt (also: ~ up) einpacken
parch [pɑːtʃ] vt (aus)dörren; **~ed** adj ausgetrocknet; (person) am Verdursten
parchment ['pɑːtʃmənt] n Pergament nt
pardon ['pɑːdn] n Verzeihung f ♦ vt (JUR) begnadigen; **~ me!, I beg your ~!** verzeihen Sie bitte!; **~ me?** (US) wie bitte?; **(I beg your) ~?** wie bitte?
parent ['pɛərənt] n Elternteil m; **~s** npl (mother and father) Eltern pl; **~al** [pəˈrentl] adj elterlich, Eltern-
parentheses [pəˈrenθɪsiːz] npl of **parenthesis**
parenthesis [pəˈrenθɪsɪs] n Klammer f; (sentence) Parenthese f
Paris ['pærɪs] n Paris nt
parish ['pærɪʃ] n Gemeinde f
park [pɑːk] n Park m ♦ vt, vi parken
parking ['pɑːkɪŋ] n Parken nt; **"no ~"** „Parken verboten"; **~ lot** (US) n Parkplatz m; **~ meter** n Parkuhr f; **~ ticket** n

Strafzettel *m*

parlance ['pɑːləns] *n* Sprachgebrauch *m*

parliament ['pɑːləmənt] *n* Parlament *nt*;
~**ary** [pɑːlə'mentəri] *adj* parlamentarisch,
Parlaments-

parlour ['pɑːləʳ] (*US* **parlor**) *n* Salon *m*

parochial [pə'rəukɪəl] *adj* (*narrow-minded*)
eng(stirnig)

parole [pə'rəul] *n*: **on** ~ (*prisoner*) auf
Bewährung

parrot ['pærət] *n* Papagei *m*

parry ['pærɪ] *vt* parieren, abwehren

parsley ['pɑːslɪ] *n* Petersilie *f*

parsnip ['pɑːsnɪp] *n* Pastinake *f*

parson ['pɑːsn] *n* Pfarrer *m*

part [pɑːt] *n* (*piece*) Teil *m*; (*THEAT*) Rolle *f*; (*of
machine*) Teil *nt* ♦ *adv* = **partly**; ♦ *vt*
trennen; (*hair*) scheiteln ♦ *vi* (*people*) sich
trennen; **to take ~ in** teilnehmen an +*dat*;
to take sth in good ~ etw nicht übel
nehmen; **to take sb's** ~ sich auf jds Seite
acc stellen; **for my** ~ ich für meinen Teil;
for the most ~ meistens, größtenteils; **in** ~
exchange (*BRIT*) in Zahlung; ~ **with** *vt fus*
hergeben; (*renounce*) aufgeben; ~**ial** ['pɑːʃl]
adj (*incomplete*) teilweise; (*biased*) parteiisch;
to be ~**ial to** eine (besondere) Vorliebe
haben für

participant [pɑː'tɪsɪpənt] *n* Teilnehmer(in)
m(f)

participate [pɑː'tɪsɪpeɪt] *vi*: **to** ~ **(in)**
teilnehmen (an +*dat*); **participation**
[pɑːtɪsɪ'peɪʃən] *n* Teilnahme *f*; (*sharing*)
Beteiligung *f*

participle ['pɑːtɪsɪpl] *n* Partizip *nt*

particle ['pɑːtɪkl] *n* Teilchen *nt*

particular [pə'tɪkjuləʳ] *adj* bestimmt; (*exact*)
genau; (*fussy*) eigen; **in** ~ besonders; ~**ly**
adv besonders

particulars *npl* (*details*) Einzelheiten *pl*; (*of
person*) Personalien *pl*

parting ['pɑːtɪŋ] *n* (*separation*) Abschied *m*;
(*BRIT: of hair*) Scheitel *m* ♦ *adj* Abschieds-

partition [pɑː'tɪʃən] *n* (*wall*) Trennwand *f*;
(*division*) Teilung *f* ♦ *vt* aufteilen

partly ['pɑːtlɪ] *adv* zum Teil, teilweise

partner ['pɑːtnəʳ] *n* Partner *m* ♦ *vt* der

Partner sein von; ~**ship** *n* Partnerschaft *f*;
(*COMM*) Teilhaberschaft *f*

partridge ['pɑːtrɪdʒ] *n* Rebhuhn *nt*

part-time ['pɑːt'taɪm] *adj* Teilzeit- ♦ *adv*
stundenweise

party ['pɑːtɪ] *n* (*POL, JUR*) Partei *f*; (*group*)
Gesellschaft *f*; (*celebration*) Party *f* ♦ *adj*
(*dress*) Party-; (*politics*) Partei-; ~ **line** *n* (*TEL*)
Gemeinschaftsanschluss *m*

pass [pɑːs] *vt* (*on foot*) vorbeigehen an +*dat*;
(*driving*) vorbeifahren an +*dat*; (*surpass*)
übersteigen; (*hand on*) weitergeben;
(*approve*) genehmigen; (*time*) verbringen;
(*exam*) bestehen ♦ *vi* (*go by*) vorbeigehen,
vorbeifahren; (*years*) vergehen; (*be
successful*) bestehen ♦ *n* (*in mountains,
SPORT*) Pass *m*; (*permission*) Passierschein *m*;
(*in exam*): **to get a** ~ bestehen; **to** ~ **sth
through sth** etw durch etw führen; **to
make a** ~ **at sb** (*inf*) bei jdm
Annäherungsversuche machen; ~ **away** *vi*
(*euph*) verscheiden; ~ **by** *vi* vorbeigehen;
vorbeifahren; (*years*) vergehen; ~ **on** *vt*
weitergeben; ~ **out** *vi* (*faint*) ohnmächtig
werden; ~ **up** *vt* vorbeigehen lassen;
~**able** *adj* (*road*) passierbar; (*fairly good*)
passabel

passage ['pæsɪdʒ] *n* (*corridor*) Gang *m*; (*in
book*) (*Text*)stelle *f*; (*voyage*) Überfahrt *f*;
~**way** *n* Durchgang *m*

passbook ['pɑːsbuk] *n* Sparbuch *nt*

passenger ['pæsɪndʒəʳ] *n* Passagier *m*; (*on
bus*) Fahrgast *m*

passer-by [pɑːsə'baɪ] *n* Passant(in) *m(f)*

passing ['pɑːsɪŋ] *adj* (*car*) vorbeifahrend;
(*thought, affair*) momentan ♦ *n*: **in** ~
beiläufig; ~ **place** *n* (*AUT*) Ausweichstelle *f*

passion ['pæʃən] *n* Leidenschaft *f*; ~**ate** *adj*
leidenschaftlich

passive ['pæsɪv] *adj* passiv; (*LING*) passivisch;
~ **smoking** *n* Passivrauchen *nt*

Passover ['pɑːsəuvəʳ] *n* Passahfest *nt*

passport ['pɑːspɔːt] *n* (*Reise*)pass *m*; ~
control *n* Passkontrolle *f*; ~ **office** *n*
Passamt *nt*

password ['pɑːswɜːd] *n* Parole *f*, Kennwort
nt, Losung *f*

past [pɑːst] *prep* (*motion*) an +*dat* ... vorbei; (*position*) hinter +*dat*; (*later than*) nach ♦ *adj* (*years*) vergangen; (*president etc*) ehemalig ♦ *n* Vergangenheit *f*; **he's ~ forty** er ist über vierzig; **for the ~ few/3 days** in den letzten paar/3 Tagen; **to run ~** vorbeilaufen; **ten/quarter ~ eight** zehn/ Viertel nach acht

pasta ['pæstə] *n* Teigwaren *pl*

paste [peɪst] *n* (*fish ~ etc*) Paste *f*; (*glue*) Kleister *m* ♦ *vt* kleben

pasteurized ['pæstʃəraɪzd] *adj* pasteurisiert

pastime ['pɑːstaɪm] *n* Zeitvertreib *m*

pastor ['pɑːstə*r*] *n* Pfarrer *m*

pastry ['peɪstrɪ] *n* Blätterteig *m*; **pastries** *npl* (*tarts etc*) Stückchen *pl*

pasture ['pɑːstʃə*r*] *n* Weide *f*

pasty [*n* 'pæstɪ, *adj* 'peɪstɪ] *n* (Fleisch)pastete *f* ♦ *adj* blässlich, käsig

pat [pæt] *n* leichte(r) Schlag *m*, Klaps *m* ♦ *vt* tätscheln

patch [pætʃ] *n* Fleck *m* ♦ *vt* flicken; **(to go through) a bad ~** eine Pechsträhne (haben); **~ up** *vt* flicken; (*quarrel*) beilegen; **~ed** *adj* geflickt; **~y** *adj* (*irregular*) ungleichmäßig

pâté ['pæteɪ] *n* Pastete *f*

patent ['peɪtnt] *n* Patent *nt* ♦ *vt* patentieren lassen; (*by authorities*) patentieren ♦ *adj* offenkundig; **~ leather** *n* Lackleder *nt*

paternal [pə'tɜːnl] *adj* väterlich

paternity [pə'tɜːnɪtɪ] *n* Vaterschaft *f*

path [pɑːθ] *n* Pfad *m*; Weg *m*

pathetic [pə'θetɪk] *adj* (*very bad*) kläglich

pathological [pæθə'lɔdʒɪkl] *adj* pathologisch

pathology [pə'θɔlədʒɪ] *n* Pathologie *f*

pathos ['peɪθɔs] *n* Rührseligkeit *f*

pathway ['pɑːθweɪ] *n* Weg *m*

patience ['peɪʃns] *n* Geduld *f*; (*BRIT: CARDS*) Patience *f*

patient ['peɪʃnt] *n* Patient(in) *m(f)*, Kranke(r) *mf* ♦ *adj* geduldig

patio ['pætɪəu] *n* Terrasse *f*

patriotic [pætrɪ'ɔtɪk] *adj* patriotisch

patrol [pə'trəul] *n* Patrouille *f*; (*police*) Streife *f* ♦ *vt* patrouillieren in +*dat* ♦ *vi* (*police*) die Runde machen; (*MIL*) patrouillieren; **~ car** *n* Streifenwagen *m*; **~man** (*US*) (*irreg*) *n* (Streifen)polizist *m*

patron ['peɪtrən] *n* (*in shop*) (Stamm)kunde *m*; (*in hotel*) (Stamm)gast *m*; (*supporter*) Förderer *m*; **~ of the arts** Mäzen *m*; **~age** ['pætrənɪdʒ] *n* Schirmherrschaft *f*; **~ize** ['pætrənaɪz] *vt* (*support*) unterstützen; (*shop*) besuchen; (*treat condescendingly*) von oben herab behandeln; **~ saint** *n* Schutzpatron(in) *m(f)*

patter ['pætə*r*] *n* (*sound: of feet*) Trappeln *nt*; (: *of rain*) Prasseln *nt*; (*sales talk*) Gerede *nt* ♦ *vi* (*feet*) trappeln; (*rain*) prasseln

pattern ['pætən] *n* Muster *nt*; (*SEWING*) Schnittmuster *nt*; (*KNITTING*) Strickanleitung *f*

pauper ['pɔːpə*r*] *n* Arme(r) *mf*

pause [pɔːz] *n* Pause *f* ♦ *vi* innehalten

pave [peɪv] *vt* pflastern; **to ~ the way for** den Weg bahnen für

pavement ['peɪvmənt] (*BRIT*) *n* Bürgersteig *m*

pavilion [pə'vɪlɪən] *n* Pavillon *m*; (*SPORT*) Klubhaus *nt*

paving ['peɪvɪŋ] *n* Straßenpflaster *nt*; **~ stone** *n* Pflasterstein *m*

paw [pɔː] *n* Pfote *f*; (*of big cats*) Tatze *f*, Pranke *f* ♦ *vt* (*scrape*) scharren; (*handle*) betatschen

pawn [pɔːn] *n* Pfand *nt*; (*chess*) Bauer *m* ♦ *vt* verpfänden; **~broker** *n* Pfandleiher *m*; **~shop** *n* Pfandhaus *nt*

pay [peɪ] (*pt, pp* **paid**) *n* Bezahlung *f*, Lohn *m* ♦ *vt* bezahlen ♦ *vi* zahlen; (*be profitable*) sich bezahlt machen; **to ~ attention (to)** Acht geben (auf +*acc*); **to ~ sb a visit** jdn besuchen; **~ back** *vt* zurückzahlen; **~ for** *vt fus* bezahlen; **~ in** *vt* einzahlen; **~ off** *vt* abzahlen ♦ *vi* (*scheme, decision*) sich bezahlt machen; **~ up** *vi* bezahlen; **~able** *adj* zahlbar, fällig; **~ee** *n* Zahlungsempfänger *m*; **~ envelope** (*US*) *n* Lohntüte *f*; **~ment** *n* Bezahlung *f*; **advance ~ment** Vorauszahlung *f*; **monthly ~ment** monatliche Rate *f*; **~ packet** (*BRIT*) *n* Lohntüte *f*; **~phone** *n* Münzfernsprecher

m; ~**roll** *n* Lohnliste *f*; ~ **slip** *n* Lohn-/
Gehaltsstreifen *m*; ~ **television** *n*
Abonnenten-Fernsehen *nt*

PC *n abbr* = **personal computer**

p.c. *abbr* = **per cent**

pea [pi:] *n* Erbse *f*

peace [pi:s] *n* Friede(n) *m*; ~**able** *adj*
friedlich; ~**ful** *adj* friedlich, ruhig;
~**keeping** *adj* Friedens-

peach [pi:tʃ] *n* Pfirsich *m*

peacock ['pi:kɔk] *n* Pfau *m*

peak [pi:k] *n* Spitze *f*; (*of mountain*) Gipfel *m*;
(*fig*) Höhepunkt *m*; ~ **hours** *npl* (*traffic*)
Hauptverkehrszeit *f*; (*telephone, electricity*)
Hauptbelastungszeit *f*; ~ **period** *n* Stoßzeit
f, Hauptzeit *f*

peal [pi:l] *n* (Glocken)läuten *nt*; ~**s of
laughter** schallende(s) Gelächter *nt*

peanut ['pi:nʌt] *n* Erdnuss *f*; ~ **butter** *n*
Erdnussbutter *f*

pear [pɛəʳ] *n* Birne *f*

pearl [pɜ:l] *n* Perle *f*

peasant ['pɛznt] *n* Bauer *m*

peat [pi:t] *n* Torf *m*

pebble ['pɛbl] *n* Kiesel *m*

peck [pɛk] *vt, vi* picken ♦ *n* (*with beak*)
Schnabelhieb *m*; (*kiss*) flüchtige(r) Kuss *m*;
~**ing order** *n* Hackordnung *f*; ~**ish** (*BRIT*:
inf) *adj* ein bisschen hungrig

peculiar [pɪˈkju:lɪəʳ] *adj* (*odd*) seltsam; ~ **to**
charakteristisch für; ~**ity** [pɪkju:lɪˈærɪtɪ] *n*
(*singular quality*) Besonderheit *f*;
(*strangeness*) Eigenartigkeit *f*

pedal ['pɛdl] *n* Pedal *nt* ♦ *vt, vi* (*cycle*) fahren,
Rad fahren

pedantic [pɪˈdæntɪk] *adj* pedantisch

peddler ['pɛdləʳ] *n* Hausierer(in) *m(f)*; (*of
drugs*) Drogenhändler(in) *m(f)*

pedestal ['pɛdəstl] *n* Sockel *m*

pedestrian [pɪˈdɛstrɪən] *n* Fußgänger *m*
♦ *adj* Fußgänger-; (*humdrum*) langweilig; ~
crossing (*BRIT*) *n* Fußgängerüberweg *m*;
~**ized** *n* in eine Fußgängerzone
umgewandelt; ~ **precinct** (*BRIT*), ~ **zone**
(*US*) *n* Fußgängerzone *f*

pediatrics [pi:dɪˈætrɪks] (*US*) *n* = **paediatrics**

pedigree ['pɛdɪgri:] *n* Stammbaum *m* ♦ *cpd*

(*animal*) reinrassig, Zucht-

pee [pi:] (*inf*) *vi* pissen, pinkeln

peek [pi:k] *vi* gucken

peel [pi:l] *n* Schale *f* ♦ *vt* schälen ♦ *vi* (*paint
etc*) abblättern; (*skin*) sich schälen

peep [pi:p] *n* (*BRIT*: *look*) kurze(r) Blick *m*;
(*sound*) Piepsen *nt* ♦ *vi* (*BRIT*: *look*) gucken;
~ **out** *vi* herausgucken; ~**hole** *n* Guckloch
nt

peer [pɪəʳ] *vi* starren; (*peep*) gucken ♦ *n*
(*nobleman*) Peer *m*; (*equal*) Ebenbürtige(r)
m; ~**age** *n* Peerswürde *f*

peeved [pi:vd] *adj* (*person*) sauer

peg [pɛg] *n* (*stake*) Pflock *m*; (*BRIT*: *also*:
clothes ~) Wäscheklammer *f*

Pekinese [pi:kɪˈni:z] *n* (*dog*) Pekinese *m*

pelican ['pɛlɪkən] *n* Pelikan *m*; ~ **crossing**
(*BRIT*) *n* (*AUT*) Ampelüberweg *m*

pellet ['pɛlɪt] *n* Kügelchen *nt*

pelmet ['pɛlmɪt] *n* Blende *f*

pelt [pɛlt] *vt* bewerfen ♦ *vi* (*rain*) schütten
♦ *n* Pelz *m*, Fell *nt*

pelvis ['pɛlvɪs] *n* Becken *nt*

pen [pɛn] *n* (*fountain* ~) Federhalter *m*; (*ballpoint* ~) Kuli *m*; (*for sheep*) Pferch *m*

penal ['pi:nl] *adj* Straf-; ~**ize** *vt* (*punish*)
bestrafen; (*disadvantage*) benachteiligen

penalty ['pɛnltɪ] *n* Strafe *f*; (*FOOTBALL*)
Elfmeter *m*; ~ (**kick**) *n* Elfmeter *m*

penance ['pɛnəns] *n* Buße *f*

pence [pɛns] (*BRIT*) *npl of* **penny**

pencil ['pɛnsl] *n* Bleistift *m*; ~ **case** *n*
Federmäppchen *nt*; ~ **sharpener** *n*
Bleistiftspitzer *m*

pendant ['pɛndənt] *n* Anhänger *m*

pending ['pɛndɪŋ] *prep* bis (zu) ♦ *adj*
unentschieden, noch offen

pendulum ['pɛndjuləm] *n* Pendel *nt*

penetrate ['pɛnɪtreɪt] *vt* durchdringen;
(*enter into*) eindringen in +*acc*;
penetration [pɛnɪˈtreɪʃən] *n* Durchdringen
nt; Eindringen *nt*

penfriend ['pɛnfrɛnd] (*BRIT*) *n* Brieffreund(in)
m(f)

penguin ['pɛŋgwɪn] *n* Pinguin *m*

penicillin [pɛnɪˈsɪlɪn] *n* Penizillin *nt*

peninsula [pəˈnɪnsjulə] *n* Halbinsel *f*

penis ['pi:nɪs] n Penis m

penitentiary [penɪ'tenʃəri] (US) n Zuchthaus nt

penknife ['pennaɪf] n Federmesser nt

pen name n Pseudonym nt

penniless ['penɪlɪs] adj mittellos

penny ['penɪ] (pl **pennies** or (BRIT) **pence**) n Penny m; (US) Centstück nt

penpal ['penpæl] n Brieffreund(in) m(f)

pension ['penʃən] n Rente f; **~er** (BRIT) n Rentner(in) m(f); **~ fund** n Rentenfonds m; **~ plan** n Rentenversicherung f

pensive ['pensɪv] adj nachdenklich

Pentagon

> 🛈 **Pentagon** heißt das fünfeckige Gebäude in Arlington, Virginia, in dem das amerikanische Verteidigungsministerium untergebracht ist. Im weiteren Sinne bezieht sich dieses Wort auf die amerikanische Militärführung.

pentathlon [pen'tæθlən] n Fünfkampf m

Pentecost ['pentɪkɔst] n Pfingsten pl or nt

penthouse ['penthaʊs] n Dach-terrassenwohnung f

pent-up ['pentʌp] adj (feelings) angestaut

penultimate [pe'nʌltɪmət] adj vorletzte(r, s)

people ['pi:pl] n (nation) Volk nt ♦ npl (persons) Leute pl; (inhabitants) Bevölkerung f ♦ vt besiedeln; **several ~ came** mehrere Leute kamen; **~ say that ...** man sagt, dass ...

pepper ['pepər] n Pfeffer m; (vegetable) Paprika m ♦ vt (pelt) bombardieren; **~ mill** n Pfeffermühle f; **~mint** n (plant) Pfefferminze f; (sweet) Pfefferminz nt

pep talk [pep-] (inf) n Anstachelung f

per [pɜ:ʳ] prep pro; **~ day/person** pro Tag/Person; **~ annum** adv pro Jahr; **~ capita** adj (income) Pro-Kopf- ♦ adv pro Kopf

perceive [pə'si:v] vt (realize) wahrnehmen; (understand) verstehen

per cent n Prozent nt; **percentage** [pə'sentɪdʒ] n Prozentsatz m

perception [pə'sepʃən] n Wahrnehmung f; (insight) Einsicht f

perceptive [pə'septɪv] adj (person) aufmerksam; (analysis) tief gehend

perch [pɜ:tʃ] n Stange f; (fish) Flussbarsch m ♦ vi sitzen, hocken

percolator ['pɜ:kəleɪtər] n Kaffeemaschine f

percussion [pə'kʌʃən] n (MUS) Schlagzeug nt

perennial [pə'renɪəl] adj wiederkehrend; (everlasting) unvergänglich

perfect [adj, n 'pɜ:fɪkt, vb pə'fekt] adj vollkommen; (crime, solution) perfekt ♦ n (GRAM) Perfekt nt ♦ vt vervollkommnen; **~ion** n Vollkommenheit f; **~ly** adv vollkommen, perfekt; (quite) ganz, einfach

perforate ['pɜ:fəreɪt] vt durchlöchern; **perforation** [pɜ:fə'reɪʃən] n Perforieren nt; (line of holes) Perforation f

perform [pə'fɔ:m] vt (carry out) durch- or ausführen; (task) verrichten; (THEAT) spielen, geben ♦ vi (THEAT) auftreten; **~ance** n Durchführung f; (efficiency) Leistung f; (show) Vorstellung f; **~er** n Künstler(in) m(f)

perfume ['pɜ:fju:m] n Duft m; (lady's) Parfüm n

perhaps [pə'hæps] adv vielleicht

peril ['perɪl] n Gefahr f

perimeter [pə'rɪmɪtər] n Peripherie f; (of circle etc) Umfang m

period ['pɪərɪəd] n Periode f; (GRAM) Punkt m; (MED) Periode f ♦ adj (costume) historisch; **~ic** [pɪərɪ'ɔdɪk] adj periodisch; **~ical** [pɪərɪ'ɔdɪkl] n Zeitschrift f; **~ically** [pɪərɪ'ɔdɪklɪ] adv periodisch

peripheral [pə'rɪfərəl] adj Rand-, peripher ♦ n (COMPUT) Peripheriegerät nt

perish ['perɪʃ] vi umkommen; (fruit) verderben; **~able** adj leicht verderblich

perjury ['pɜ:dʒərɪ] n Meineid m

perk [pɜ:k] (inf) n (fringe benefit) Vergünstigung f; **~ up** vi munter werden; **~y** adj keck

perm [pɜ:m] n Dauerwelle f

permanent ['pɜ:mənənt] adj dauernd, ständig

permeate ['pɜ:mɪeɪt] vt, vi durchdringen

permissible [pə'mɪsɪbl] adj zulässig

permission [pə'mɪʃən] n Erlaubnis f

permissive [pə'mɪsɪv] *adj* nachgiebig; **the ~ society** die permissive Gesellschaft

permit [*n* 'pɜːmɪt, *vb* pə'mɪt] *n* Zulassung *f* ♦ *vt* erlauben, zulassen

perpendicular [pɜːpən'dɪkjʊləʳ] *adj* senkrecht

perpetrate ['pɜːpɪtreɪt] *vt* begehen

perpetual [pə'petjʊəl] *adj* dauernd, ständig

perpetuate [pə'petjʊeɪt] *vt* verewigen, bewahren

perplex [pə'pleks] *vt* verblüffen

persecute ['pɜːsɪkjuːt] *vt* verfolgen; **persecution** [pɜːsɪ'kjuːʃən] *n* Verfolgung *f*

perseverance [pɜːsɪ'vɪərns] *n* Ausdauer *f*

persevere [pɜːsɪ'vɪəʳ] *vi* durchhalten

Persian ['pɜːʃən] *adj* persisch ♦ *n* Perser(in) *m(f)*; **the (Persian) Gulf** der Persische Golf

persist [pə'sɪst] *vi* (*in belief etc*) bleiben; (*rain, smell*) andauern; (*continue*) nicht aufhören; **to ~ in** bleiben bei; **~ence** *n* Beharrlichkeit *f*; **~ent** *adj* beharrlich; (*unending*) ständig

person ['pɜːsn] *n* Person *f*; **in ~** persönlich; **~able** *adj* gut aussehend; **~al** *adj* persönlich; (*private*) privat; (*of body*) körperlich, Körper-; **~al assistant** *n* Assistent(in) *m(f)*; **~al column** *n* private Kleinanzeigen *pl*; **~al computer** *n* Personalcomputer *m*; **~ality** [pɜːsə'nælɪtɪ] *n* Persönlichkeit *f*; **~ally** *adv* persönlich; **~al organizer** *n* Terminplaner *m*, Zeitplaner *m*; (*electronic*) elektronisches Notizbuch *nt*; **~al stereo** *n* Walkman *m* ®; **~ify** [pɜː'sɔnɪfaɪ] *vt* verkörpern

personnel [pɜːsə'nel] *n* Personal *nt*

perspective [pə'spektɪv] *n* Perspektive *f*

Perspex ['pɜːspeks] ® *n* Acrylglas *nt*, Akrylglas *nt*

perspiration [pɜːspɪ'reɪʃən] *n* Transpiration *f*

perspire [pə'spaɪəʳ] *vi* transpirieren

persuade [pə'sweɪd] *vt* überreden; (*convince*) überzeugen

persuasion [pə'sweɪʒən] *n* Überredung *f*; Überzeugung *f*

persuasive [pə'sweɪsɪv] *adj* überzeugend

pert [pɜːt] *adj* keck

pertaining [pɜː'teɪnɪŋ]: **~ to** *prep* betreffend +*acc*

pertinent ['pɜːtɪnənt] *adj* relevant

perturb [pə'tɜːb] *vt* beunruhigen

pervade [pə'veɪd] *vt* erfüllen

perverse [pə'vɜːs] *adj* pervers; (*obstinate*) eigensinnig

pervert [*n* 'pɜːvɜːt, *vb* pə'vɜːt] *n* perverse(r) Mensch *m* ♦ *vt* verdrehen; (*morally*) verderben

pessimist ['pesɪmɪst] *n* Pessimist *m*; **~ic** *adj* pessimistisch

pest [pest] *n* (*insect*) Schädling *m*; (*fig: person*) Nervensäge *f*; (: *thing*) Plage *f*; **~er** ['pestəʳ] *vt* plagen; **~icide** ['pestɪsaɪd] *n* Insektenvertilgungsmittel *nt*

pet [pet] *n* (*animal*) Haustier *nt* ♦ *vt* liebkosen, streicheln

petal ['petl] *n* Blütenblatt *nt*

peter out ['piːtə-] *vi* allmählich zu Ende gehen

petite [pə'tiːt] *adj* zierlich

petition [pə'tɪʃən] *n* Bittschrift *f*

petrified ['petrɪfaɪd] *adj* versteinert; (*person*) starr (vor Schreck)

petrify ['petrɪfaɪ] *vt* versteinern; (*person*) erstarren lassen

petrol ['petrəl] (*BRIT*) *n* Benzin *nt*, Kraftstoff *m*; **two-/four-star ~** ≈ Normal-/ Superbenzin *nt*; **~ can** *n* Benzinkanister *m*

petroleum [pə'trəʊlɪəm] *n* Petroleum *nt*

petrol: ~ pump (*BRIT*) *n* (*in car*) Benzinpumpe *f*; (*at garage*) Zapfsäule *f*; **~ station** (*BRIT*) *n* Tankstelle *f*; **~ tank** (*BRIT*) *n* Benzintank *m*

petticoat ['petɪkəʊt] *n* Unterrock *m*

petty ['petɪ] *adj* (*unimportant*) unbedeutend; (*mean*) kleinlich; **~ cash** *n* Portokasse *f*; **~ officer** *n* Maat *m*

pew [pjuː] *n* Kirchenbank *f*

pewter ['pjuːtəʳ] *n* Zinn *nt*

phantom ['fæntəm] *n* Phantom *nt*

pharmacist ['fɑːməsɪst] *n* Pharmazeut *m*; (*druggist*) Apotheker *m*

pharmacy ['fɑːməsɪ] *n* Pharmazie *f*; (*shop*) Apotheke *f*

phase [feɪz] *n* Phase *f* ♦ *vt*: **to ~ sth in** etw allmählich einführen; **to ~ sth out** etw auslaufen lassen

Ph.D. *n abbr* = **Doctor of Philosophy**

pheasant ['fɛznt] *n* Fasan *m*

phenomena [fə'nɒmɪnə] *npl of*
phenomenon

phenomenon [fə'nɒmɪnən] *n* Phänomen *nt*

philanthropist [fɪ'lænθrəpɪst] *n* Philanthrop
m, Menschenfreund *m*

Philippines ['fɪlɪpi:nz] *npl*: **the ~** die
Philippinen *pl*

philosopher [fɪ'lɒsəfə*r*] *n* Philosoph *m*;
philosophical [fɪlə'sɒfɪkl] *adj*
philosophisch; **philosophy** [fɪ'lɒsəfɪ] *n*
Philosophie *f*

phlegm [flɛm] *n (MED)* Schleim *m*

phobia ['fəubjə] *n (irrational fear: of insects,
flying, water etc)* Phobie *f*

phone [fəun] *n* Telefon *nt* ♦ *vt, vi*
telefonieren, anrufen; **to be on the ~**
telefonieren; **~ back** *vt, vi* zurückrufen; **~
up** *vt, vi* anrufen; **~ bill** *n* Telefonrechnung
f; **~ book** *n* Telefonbuch *nt*; **~ booth** *n*
Telefonzelle *f*; **~ box** *n* Telefonzelle *f*; **~
call** *n* Telefonanruf *m*; **~card** *n (TEL)*
Telefonkarte *f*; **~-in** *n (RAD, TV)* Phone-in *nt*;
~ number *n* Telefonnummer *f*

phonetics [fə'nɛtɪks] *n* Phonetik *f*

phoney ['fəunɪ] *(inf) adj* unecht ♦ *n (person)*
Schwindler *m*; *(thing)* Fälschung *f*;
(banknote) Blüte *f*

phony ['fəunɪ] *adj, n* = **phoney**

photo ['fəutəu] *n* Foto *nt*; **~copier**
['fəutəukɒpɪə*r*] *n* Kopiergerät *nt*; **~copy**
['fəutəukɒpɪ] *n* Fotokopie *f* ♦ *vt* fotokopieren;
~genic [fəutəu'dʒɛnɪk] *adj* fotogen; **~graph**
n Fotografie *f*, Aufnahme *f* ♦ *vt* fotografieren; **~grapher** ['fəutəgræf] *n* Fotograf *m*;
~graphic [fəutə'græfɪk] *adj* fotografisch;
~graphy [fə'tɒgrəfɪ] *n* Fotografie *f*

phrase [freɪz] *n* Satz *m*; *(expression)*
Ausdruck *m* ♦ *vt* ausdrücken, formulieren; **~
book** *n* Sprachführer *m*

physical ['fɪzɪkl] *adj* physikalisch; *(bodily)*
körperlich, physisch; **~ education** *n*
Turnen *nt*; **~ly** *adv* physikalisch

physician [fɪ'zɪʃən] *n* Arzt *m*

physicist ['fɪzɪsɪst] *n* Physiker(in) *m(f)*

physics ['fɪzɪks] *n* Physik *f*

physiotherapist [fɪzɪəu'θɛrəpɪst] *n*
Physiotherapeut(in) *m(f)*

physiotherapy [fɪzɪəu'θɛrəpɪ] *n*
Heilgymnastik *f*, Physiotherapie *f*

physique [fɪ'zi:k] *n* Körperbau *m*

pianist ['pi:ənɪst] *n* Pianist(in) *m(f)*

piano [pɪ'ænəu] *n* Klavier *nt*

pick [pɪk] *n (tool)* Pickel *m*; *(choice)* Auswahl *f*
♦ *vt (fruit)* pflücken; *(choose)* aussuchen;
take your ~ such dir etwas aus; **to ~ sb's
pocket** jdn bestehlen; **~ on** *vt fus (person)*
herumhacken auf +*dat*; **~ out** *vt*
auswählen; **~ up** *vi (improve)* sich erholen
♦ *vt (lift up)* aufheben; *(learn)* (schnell)
mitbekommen; *(collect)* abholen; *(girl)* (sich
dat) anlachen; *(AUT: passenger)* mitnehmen;
(speed) gewinnen an +*dat*; **to ~ o.s. up**
aufstehen

picket ['pɪkɪt] *n (striker)* Streikposten *m* ♦ *vt
(factory)* (Streik)posten aufstellen vor +*dat*
♦ *vi* (Streik)posten stehen

pickle ['pɪkl] *n (salty mixture)* Pökel *m*; *(inf)*
Klemme *f* ♦ *vt (in Essig)* einlegen; einpökeln

pickpocket ['pɪkpɒkɪt] *n* Taschendieb *m*

pick-up ['pɪkʌp] *n (BRIT: on record player)*
Tonabnehmer *m*; *(small truck)* Lieferwagen
m

picnic ['pɪknɪk] *n* Picknick *nt* ♦ *vi* picknicken;
~ area *n* Rastplatz *m*

pictorial [pɪk'tɔ:rɪəl] *adj* in Bildern

picture ['pɪktʃə*r*] *n* Bild *nt* ♦ *vt (visualize)* sich
dat vorstellen; **the ~s** *npl (BRIT)* das Kino; **~
book** *n* Bilderbuch *nt*; **~ message** *n*
Bildnachricht *f*

picturesque [pɪktʃə'rɛsk] *adj* malerisch

pie [paɪ] *n (meat)* Pastete *f*; *(fruit)* Torte *f*

piece [pi:s] *n* Stück *nt* ♦ *vt*: **to ~ together**
zusammenstückeln; *(fig)* sich *dat*
zusammenreimen; **to take to ~s** in
Einzelteile zerlegen; **~meal** *adv* stückweise,
Stück für Stück; **~work** *n* Akkordarbeit *f*

pie chart *n* Kreisdiagramm *nt*

pier [pɪə*r*] *n* Pier *m*, Mole *f*

pierce [pɪəs] *vt* durchstechen, durchbohren
(also look); **~d** *adj* durchgestochen;
piercing ['pɪəsɪŋ] *adj (cry)* durchdringend

pig [pɪg] *n* Schwein *nt*

pigeon ['pɪdʒən] n Taube f; **~hole** n (compartment) Ablegefach nt

piggy bank ['pɪgɪ-] n Sparschwein nt

pig: **~headed** ['pɪg'hedɪd] adj dickköpfig; **~let** ['pɪglɪt] n Ferkel nt; **~skin** ['pɪgskɪn] n Schweinsleder nt; **~sty** ['pɪgstaɪ] n Schweinestall m; **~tail** ['pɪgteɪl] n Zopf m

pike [paɪk] n Pike f; (fish) Hecht m

pilchard ['pɪltʃəd] n Sardine f

pile [paɪl] n Haufen m; (of books, wood) Stapel m; (in ground) Pfahl m; (on carpet) Flausch m ♦ vt (also: ~ **up**) anhäufen ♦ vi (also: ~ **up**) sich anhäufen

piles [paɪlz] npl Hämorr(ho)iden pl

pile-up ['paɪlʌp] n (AUT) Massenzusammenstoß m

pilfering ['pɪlfərɪŋ] n Diebstahl m

pilgrim ['pɪlgrɪm] n Pilger(in) m(f); **~age** n Wallfahrt f

pill [pɪl] n Tablette f, Pille f; **the ~** die (Antibaby)pille

pillage ['pɪlɪdʒ] vt plündern

pillar ['pɪlə'] n Pfeiler m, Säule f (also fig); **~ box** (BRIT) n Briefkasten m

pillion ['pɪljən] n Soziussitz m

pillow ['pɪləʊ] n Kissen nt; **~case** n Kissenbezug m

pilot ['paɪlət] n Pilot m; (NAUT) Lotse m ♦ adj (scheme etc) Versuchs- ♦ vt führen; (ship) lotsen; **~ light** n Zündflamme f

pimp [pɪmp] n Zuhälter m

pimple ['pɪmpl] n Pickel m

PIN n abbr (= personal identification number) PIN f

pin [pɪn] n Nadel f; (for sewing) Stecknadel f; (TECH) Stift m, Bolzen m ♦ vt stecken; (keep in one position) pressen, drücken; **to ~ sth to sth** etw an etw acc heften; **to ~ sth on sb** (fig) jdm etw anhängen; **~s and needles** Kribbeln nt; **~ down** vt (fig: person): **to ~ sb down (to sth)** jdn (auf etw acc) festnageln

pinafore ['pɪnəfɔ:'] n Schürze f; **~ dress** n Kleiderrock m

pinball ['pɪnbɔ:l] n Flipper m

pincers ['pɪnsəz] npl Kneif- or Beißzange f; (MED) Pinzette f

pinch [pɪntʃ] n Zwicken nt, Kneifen nt; (of salt) Prise f ♦ vt zwicken, kneifen; (inf: steal) klauen ♦ vi (shoe) drücken; **at a ~** notfalls, zur Not

pincushion ['pɪnkʊʃən] n Nadelkissen nt

pine [paɪn] n (also: ~ **tree**) Kiefer f ♦ vi: **to ~ for** sich sehnen nach; **~ away** vi sich zu Tode sehnen

pineapple ['paɪnæpl] n Ananas f

ping [pɪŋ] n Klingeln nt; **~-pong** ® n Pingpong nt

pink [pɪŋk] adj rosa inv ♦ n Rosa nt; (BOT) Nelke f

pinnacle ['pɪnəkl] n Spitze f

PIN (number) n Geheimnummer f

pinpoint ['pɪnpɔɪnt] vt festlegen

pinstripe ['pɪnstraɪp] n Nadelstreifen m

pint [paɪnt] n Pint nt; (BRIT: inf: of beer) große(s) Bier nt

pioneer [paɪə'nɪə'] n Pionier m; (fig also) Bahnbrecher m

pious ['paɪəs] adj fromm

pip [pɪp] n Kern m; **the ~s** npl (BRIT: RAD) das Zeitzeichen

pipe [paɪp] n (smoking) Pfeife f; (tube) Rohr nt; (in house) (Rohr)leitung f ♦ vt (durch Rohre) leiten; (MUS) blasen; **~s** npl (also: **bagpipes**) Dudelsack m; **~ down** vi (be quiet) die Luft anhalten; **~ cleaner** n Pfeifenreiniger m; **~ dream** n Luftschloss nt; **~line** n (for oil) Pipeline f; **~r** n Pfeifer m; (bagpipes) Dudelsackbläser m

piping ['paɪpɪŋ] adv: **~ hot** siedend heiß

pique ['pi:k] n gekränkte(r) Stolz m

pirate ['paɪərət] n Pirat m, Seeräuber m; **~d** adj: **~d version** Raubkopie f; **~ radio** (BRIT) n Piratensender m

Pisces ['paɪsi:z] n Fische pl

piss [pɪs] (inf) vi pissen; **~ed** (inf) adj (drunk) voll

pistol ['pɪstl] n Pistole f

piston ['pɪstən] n Kolben m

pit [pɪt] n Grube f; (THEAT) Parterre nt; (orchestra ~) Orchestergraben m ♦ vt (mark with scars) zerfressen; (compare): **to ~ sb against sb** jdn an jdm messen; **the ~s** npl (MOTOR RACING) die Boxen pl

pitch [pɪtʃ] n Wurf m; (of trader) Stand m; (SPORT) (Spiel)feld nt; (MUS) Tonlage f; (substance) Pech nt ♦ vt werfen; (set up) aufschlagen ♦ vi (NAUT) rollen; **to ~ a tent** ein Zelt aufbauen; **~-black** adj pechschwarz; **~ed battle** n offene Schlacht f

piteous ['pɪtɪəs] adj kläglich, erbärmlich

pitfall ['pɪtfɔ:l] n (fig) Falle f

pith [pɪθ] n Mark nt

pithy ['pɪθɪ] adj prägnant

pitiful ['pɪtɪful] adj (deserving pity) bedauernswert; (contemptible) jämmerlich

pitiless ['pɪtɪlɪs] adj erbarmungslos

pittance ['pɪtns] n Hungerlohn m

pity ['pɪtɪ] n (sympathy) Mitleid nt ♦ vt Mitleid haben mit; **what a ~!** wie schade!

pivot ['pɪvət] n Drehpunkt m ♦ vi: **to ~ (on)** sich drehen (um)

pizza ['pi:tsə] n Pizza f

placard ['plækɑ:d] n Plakat nt, Anschlag m

placate [plə'keɪt] vt beschwichtigen

place [pleɪs] n Platz m; (spot) Stelle f; (town etc) Ort m ♦ vt setzen, stellen, legen; (order) aufgeben; (SPORT) platzieren; (identify) unterbringen; **to take ~** stattfinden; **out of ~** nicht am rechten Platz; (fig: remark) unangebracht; **in the first ~** erstens; **to change ~s with sb** mit jdm den Platz tauschen; **to be ~d third** (in race, exam) auf dem dritten Platz liegen

placid ['plæsɪd] adj gelassen, ruhig

plagiarism ['pleɪdʒjərɪzəm] n Plagiat nt

plague [pleɪg] n Pest f; (fig) Plage f ♦ vt plagen

plaice [pleɪs] n Scholle f

plaid [plæd] n Plaid nt

plain [pleɪn] adj (clear) klar, deutlich; (simple) einfach, schlicht; (not beautiful) alltäglich ♦ n Ebene f; **in ~ clothes** (police) in Zivil(kleidung); **~ chocolate** n Bitterschokolade f

plaintiff ['pleɪntɪf] n Kläger m

plaintive ['pleɪntɪv] adj wehleidig

plait [plæt] n Zopf m ♦ vt flechten

plan [plæn] n Plan m ♦ vt, vi planen; **according to ~** planmäßig; **to ~ to do sth**

vorhaben, etw zu tun

plane [pleɪn] n Ebene f; (AVIAT) Flugzeug nt; (tool) Hobel m; (tree) Platane f

planet ['plænɪt] n Planet m

plank [plæŋk] n Brett nt

planning ['plænɪŋ] n Planung f; **family ~** Familienplanung f; **~ permission** n Baugenehmigung f

plant [plɑ:nt] n Pflanze f; (TECH) (Maschinen)anlage f; (factory) Fabrik f, Werk nt ♦ vt pflanzen; (set firmly) stellen; **~ation** [plæn'teɪʃən] n Plantage f

plaque [plæk] n Gedenktafel f; (on teeth) (Zahn)belag m

plaster ['plɑ:stə] n Gips m; (in house) Verputz m; (BRIT: also: **sticking ~**) Pflaster nt; (for fracture: **~ of Paris**) Gipsverband m ♦ vt gipsen; (hole) zugipsen; (ceiling) verputzen; (fig: with pictures etc) bekleben, verkleben; **~ed** (inf) adj besoffen; **~er** n Gipser m

plastic ['plæstɪk] n Plastik nt or f ♦ adj (made of ~) Plastik-; (ART) plastisch, bildend; **~ bag** n Plastiktüte f

plasticine ['plæstɪsi:n] ® n Plastilin nt

plastic surgery n plastische Chirurgie f

plate [pleɪt] n Teller m; (gold/silver ~) vergoldete(s)/versilberte(s) Tafelgeschirr nt; (in book) (Bild)tafel f

plateau ['plætəʊ] (pl **~s** or **~x**) n (GEOG) Plateau nt, Hochebene f

plateaux ['plætəʊz] npl of **plateau**

plate glass n Tafelglas nt

platform ['plætfɔ:m] n (at meeting) Plattform f, Podium nt; (RAIL) Bahnsteig m; (POL) Parteiprogramm nt; **~ ticket** n Bahnsteigkarte f

platinum ['plætɪnəm] n Platin nt

platoon [plə'tu:n] n (MIL) Zug m

platter ['plætə] n Platte f

plausible ['plɔ:zɪbl] adj (theory, excuse, statement) plausibel; (person) überzeugend

play [pleɪ] n (also TECH) Spiel nt; (THEAT) (Theater)stück nt ♦ vt spielen; (another team) spielen gegen ♦ vi spielen; **to ~ safe** auf Nummer sicher or Sicher gehen; **~ down** vt herunterspielen; **~ up** vi (cause *trouble)* frech werden; *(bad leg etc)* wehtun ♦ *vt (person)* plagen; **to ~ up to sb** jdm flattieren; **~-acting** *n* Schauspielerei *f;* **~er** *n* Spieler(in) *m(f);* **~ful** *adj* spielerisch; **~ground** *n* Spielplatz *m;* **~group** *n* Kindergarten *m;* **~ing card** *n* Spielkarte *f;* **~ing field** *n* Sportplatz *m;* **~mate** *n* Spielkamerad *m;* **~-off** *n (SPORT)* Entscheidungsspiel *nt;* **~pen** *n* Laufstall *m;* **~school** *n =* **playgroup**; **~thing** *n* Spielzeug *nt;* **~time** *n* (kleine) Pause *f;* **~wright** ['pleɪraɪt] *n* Theaterschriftsteller *m*

plc *abbr (= public limited company)* AG

plea [pli:] *n* Bitte *f; (general appeal)* Appell *m; (JUR)* Plädoyer *nt;* **~ bargaining** *n (LAW) Aushandeln der Strafe zwischen Staatsanwaltschaft und Verteidigung*

plead [pli:d] *vt (poverty)* zur Entschuldigung anführen; *(JUR: sb's case)* vertreten ♦ *vi (beg)* dringend bitten; *(JUR)* plädieren; **to ~ with sb** jdn dringend bitten

pleasant ['plɛznt] *adj* angenehm; **~ries** *npl (polite remarks)* Nettigkeiten *pl*

please [pli:z] *vt, vi (be agreeable to)* gefallen *+dat;* **~!** bitte!; **~ yourself!** wie du willst!; **~d** *adj* zufrieden; *(glad):* **~d (about sth)** erfreut (über etw *acc*); **~d to meet you** angenehm; **pleasing** ['pli:zɪŋ] *adj* erfreulich

pleasure ['plɛʒə^r] *n* Freude *f* ♦ *cpd* Vergnügungs-; **"it's a ~"** „gern geschehen"

pleat [pli:t] *n* Falte *f*

plectrum ['plɛktrəm] *n* Plektron *nt*

pledge [plɛdʒ] *n* Pfand *nt; (promise)* Versprechen *nt* ♦ *vt* verpfänden; *(promise)* geloben, versprechen

plentiful ['plɛntɪful] *adj* reichlich

plenty ['plɛntɪ] *n* Fülle *f,* Überfluss *m;* **~ of** eine Menge, viel

pleurisy ['pluərɪsɪ] *n* Rippenfellentzündung *f*

pliable ['plaɪəbl] *adj* biegsam; *(person)* beeinflussbar

pliers ['plaɪəz] *npl* (Kneif)zange *f*

plight [plaɪt] *n* (Not)lage *f*

plimsolls ['plɪmsəlz] *(BRIT) npl* Turnschuhe *pl*

plinth [plɪnθ] *n* Sockel *m*

P.L.O. *n abbr (= Palestine Liberation Organization)* PLO *f*

plod [plɔd] *vi (work)* sich abplagen; *(walk)* trotten

plonk [plɔŋk] *n (BRIT: inf: wine)* billige(r) Wein *m* ♦ *vt:* **to ~ sth down** etw hinknallen

plot [plɔt] *n* Komplott *nt; (story)* Handlung *f; (of land)* Grundstück *nt* ♦ *vt* markieren; *(curve)* zeichnen; *(movements)* nachzeichnen ♦ *vi (plan secretly)* sich verschwören

plough [plau] *(US* **plow)** *n* Pflug *m* ♦ *vt* pflügen; **~ back** *vt (COMM)* wieder in das Geschäft stecken; **~ through** *vt fus (water)* durchpflügen; *(book)* sich kämpfen durch

plow [plau] *(US) =* **plough**

ploy [plɔɪ] *n* Masche *f*

pluck [plʌk] *vt (fruit)* pflücken; *(guitar)* zupfen; *(goose etc)* rupfen ♦ *n* Mut *m;* **to ~ up courage** all seinen Mut zusammennehmen

plug [plʌg] *n* Stöpsel *m; (ELEC)* Stecker *m; (inf: publicity)* Schleichwerbung *f; (AUT)* Zündkerze *f* ♦ *vt (zu)*stopfen; *(inf: advertise)* Reklame machen für; **~ in** *vt (ELEC)* anschließen

plum [plʌm] *n* Pflaume *f,* Zwetsch(g)e *f*

plumage ['plu:mɪdʒ] *n* Gefieder *nt*

plumber ['plʌmə^r] *n* Klempner *m,* Installateur *m;* **plumbing** ['plʌmɪŋ] *n (craft)* Installieren *nt; (fittings)* Leitungen *pl*

plummet ['plʌmɪt] *vi* (ab)stürzen

plump [plʌmp] *adj* rundlich, füllig ♦ *vt* plumpsen lassen; **to ~ for** *(inf: choose)* sich entscheiden für

plunder ['plʌndə^r] *n* Plünderung *f; (loot)* Beute *f* ♦ *vt* plündern

plunge [plʌndʒ] *n* Sturz *m* ♦ *vt* stoßen ♦ *vi* (sich) stürzen; **to take the ~** den Sprung wagen; **plunging** ['plʌndʒɪŋ] *adj (neckline)* offenherzig

plural ['pluərl] *n* Plural *m,* Mehrzahl *f*

plus [plʌs] *n (also: ~* **sign)** Plus(zeichen) *nt* ♦ *prep* plus, und; **ten/twenty ~** mehr als zehn/zwanzig

plush [plʌʃ] *adj (also:* **~y** *inf)* feudal

ply [plaɪ] *vt (trade)* (be)treiben; *(with questions)* zusetzen *+dat; (ship, taxi)* befahren ♦ *vi (ship, taxi)* verkehren ♦ *n:*

three-~ (*wool*) Dreifach-; **to ~ sb with drink** jdn zum Trinken animieren; **~wood** *n* Sperrholz *nt*

P.M. *n abbr* = **prime minister**

p.m. *adv abbr* (= *post meridiem*) nachmittags

pneumatic drill *n* Presslufthammer *m*

pneumonia [njuːˈməʊnɪə] *n* Lungenentzündung *f*

poach [pəʊtʃ] *vt* (COOK) pochieren; (*game*) stehlen ♦ *vi* (*steal*) wildern; **~ed** *adj* (*egg*) verloren; **~er** *n* Wilddieb *m*

P.O. Box *n abbr* = **Post Office Box**

pocket [ˈpɒkɪt] *n* Tasche *f*; (*of resistance*) (Widerstands)nest *nt* ♦ *vt* einstecken; **to be out of ~** (BRIT) draufzahlen; **~book** *n* Taschenbuch *nt*; **~ calculator** *n* Taschenrechner *m*; **~ knife** *n* Taschenmesser *nt*; **~ money** *n* Taschengeld *nt*

pod [pɒd] *n* Hülse *f*; (*of peas also*) Schote *f*

podgy [ˈpɒdʒɪ] *adj* pummelig

podiatrist [pɒˈdiːətrɪst] (US) *n* Fußpfleger(in) *m(f)*

poem [ˈpəʊɪm] *n* Gedicht *nt*

poet [ˈpəʊɪt] *n* Dichter *m*, Poet *m*; **~ic** [pəʊˈetɪk] *adj* poetisch, dichterisch; **~ laureate** *n* Hofdichter *m*; **~ry** *n* Poesie *f*; (*poems*) Gedichte *pl*

poignant [ˈpɔɪnjənt] *adj* (*touching*) ergreifend

point [pɔɪnt] *n* (*also in discussion, scoring*) Punkt *m*; (*spot*) Punkt *m*, Stelle *f*; (*sharpened tip*) Spitze *f*; (*moment*) (Zeit)punkt *m*; (*purpose*) Zweck *m*; (*idea*) Argument *nt*; (*decimal*) Dezimalstelle *f*; (*personal characteristic*) Seite *f* ♦ *vt* zeigen mit; (*gun*) richten ♦ *vi* zeigen; **~s** *npl* (RAIL) Weichen *pl*; **to be on the ~ of doing sth** drauf und dran sein, etw zu tun; **to make a ~ of** Wert darauf legen; **to get the ~** verstehen, worum es geht; **to come to the ~** zur Sache kommen; **there's no ~ (in doing sth)** es hat keinen Sinn(, etw zu tun); **~ out** *vt* hinweisen auf +*acc*; **~ to** *vt fus* zeigen auf +*acc*; **~-blank** *adv* (*at close range*) aus nächster Entfernung; (*bluntly*) unverblümt; **~ed** *adj* (*also fig*) spitz, scharf;

~edly *adv* (*fig*) spitz; **~er** *n* Zeigestock *m*; (*on dial*) Zeiger *m*; **~less** *adj* sinnlos; **~ of view** *n* Stand- or Gesichtspunkt *m*

poise [pɔɪz] *n* Haltung *f*; (*fig*) Gelassenheit *f*

poison [ˈpɔɪzn] *n* (*also fig*) Gift *nt* ♦ *vt* vergiften; **~ing** *n* Vergiftung *f*; **~ous** *adj* giftig, Gift-

poke [pəʊk] *vt* stoßen; (*put*) stecken; (*fire*) schüren; (*hole*) bohren; **~ about** *vi* herumstochern; (*nose around*) herumwühlen

poker [ˈpəʊkəˈ] *n* Schürhaken *m*; (CARDS) Poker *nt*

poky [ˈpəʊkɪ] *adj* eng

Poland [ˈpəʊlənd] *n* Polen *nt*

polar [ˈpəʊləˈ] *adj* Polar-, polar; **~ bear** *n* Eisbär *m*

Pole [pəʊl] *n* Pole *m*, Polin *f*

pole [pəʊl] *n* Stange *f*, Pfosten *m*; (*flagpole, telegraph ~*) Stange *f*, Mast *m*; (ELEC, GEOG) Pol *m*; (SPORT: *vaulting ~*) Stab *m*; (*ski ~*) Stock *m*; **~ bean** (US) *n* (*runner bean*) Stangenbohne *f*; **~ vault** *n* Stabhochsprung *m*

police [pəˈliːs] *n* Polizei *f* ♦ *vt* kontrollieren; **~ car** *n* Polizeiwagen *m*; **~man** (*irreg*) *n* Polizist *m*; **~ state** *n* Polizeistaat *m*; **~ station** *n* (Polizei)revier *nt*, Wache *f*; **~woman** (*irreg*) *n* Polizistin *f*

policy [ˈpɒlɪsɪ] *n* Politik *f*; (*insurance*) (Versicherungs)police *f*

polio [ˈpəʊlɪəʊ] *n* (*spinale*) Kinderlähmung *f*, Polio *f*

Polish [ˈpəʊlɪʃ] *adj* polnisch ♦ *n* (LING) Polnisch *nt*

polish [ˈpɒlɪʃ] *n* Politur *f*; (*for floor*) Wachs *nt*; (*for shoes*) Creme *f*; (*for nails*) Lack *m*; (*shine*) Glanz *m*; (*of furniture*) Politur *f*; (*fig*) Schliff *m* ♦ *vt* polieren; (*shoes*) putzen; (*fig*) den letzten Schliff geben +*dat*; **~ off** *vt* (*inf*: *food*) wegputzen; (: *drink*) hinunterschütten; **~ed** *adj* glänzend; (*manners*) verfeinert

polite [pəˈlaɪt] *adj* höflich; **~ly** *adv* höflich; **~ness** *n* Höflichkeit *f*

politic-: **~al** [pəˈlɪtɪkl] *adj* politisch; **~ally** [pəˈlɪtɪklɪ] *adv* politisch; **~ally correct**

politisch korrekt; **~ian** [pɔlɪ'tɪʃən] n Politiker m; **~s** npl Politik f

polka dot ['pɔlkə-] n Tupfen m

poll [pəʊl] n Abstimmung f; (in election) Wahl f; (votes cast) Wahlbeteiligung f; (opinion ~) Umfrage f ♦ vt (votes) erhalten

pollen ['pɔlən] n (BOT) Blütenstaub m, Pollen m

polling ['pəʊlɪŋ-]: **~ booth** (BRIT) n Wahlkabine f; **~ day** (BRIT) n Wahltag m; **~ station** (BRIT) n Wahllokal nt

pollute [pə'luːt] vt verschmutzen, verunreinigen; **~d** adj verschmutzt; **pollution** [pə'luːʃən] n Verschmutzung f

polo ['pəʊləʊ] n Polo nt; **~ neck** n (also: **~- necked sweater**) Rollkragen m; Rollkragenpullover m; **~ shirt** n Polohemd nt

polystyrene [pɔlɪ'staɪriːn] n Styropor nt

polytechnic [pɔlɪ'tɛknɪk] n technische Hochschule f

polythene ['pɔlɪθiːn] n Plastik nt; **~ bag** n Plastiktüte f

pomegranate ['pɔmɪɡrænɪt] n Granatapfel m

pompom ['pɔmpɔm] n Troddel f, Pompon m

pompous ['pɔmpəs] adj aufgeblasen; (language) geschwollen

pond [pɔnd] n Teich m, Weiher m

ponder ['pɔndər] vt nachdenken über +acc; **~ous** adj schwerfällig

pong [pɔŋ] (BRIT: inf) n Mief m

pontiff ['pɔntɪf] n Pontifex m

pontoon [pɔn'tuːn] n Ponton m; (CARDS) 17-und-4 nt

pony ['pəʊnɪ] n Pony nt; **~tail** n Pferdeschwanz m; **~ trekking** (BRIT) n Ponyreiten nt

poodle ['puːdl] n Pudel m

pool [puːl] n (swimming ~) Schwimmbad nt; (: private) Swimmingpool m; (of liquid, blood) Lache f; (fund) (gemeinsame) Kasse f; (billiards) Poolspiel nt ♦ vt (money etc) zusammenlegen; **(football) ~s** Toto nt

poor [puər] adj arm; (not good) schlecht ♦ npl: **the ~** die Armen pl; **~ in** (resources)

arm an +dat; **~ly** adv schlecht; (dressed) ärmlich ♦ adj schlecht

pop [pɔp] n Knall m; (music) Popmusik f; (drink) Limo(nade) f; (US: inf) Pa m ♦ vt (put) stecken; (balloon) platzen lassen ♦ vi knallen; **~ in** vi kurz vorbeigehen or vorbeikommen; **~ out** vi (person) kurz rausgehen; (thing) herausspringen; **~ up** vi auftauchen; **~corn** n Puffmais m

pope [pəʊp] n Papst m

poplar ['pɔplər] n Pappel f

poppy ['pɔpɪ] n Mohn m

Popsicle ['pɔpsɪkl] (®) US) n (ice lolly) Eis nt am Stiel

populace ['pɔpjʊləs] n Volk nt

popular ['pɔpjʊlər] adj beliebt, populär; (of the people) volkstümlich; (widespread) allgemein; **~ity** [pɔpjʊ'lærɪtɪ] n Beliebtheit f, Popularität f; **~ly** adv allgemein, überall

population [pɔpjʊ'leɪʃən] n Bevölkerung f; (of town) Einwohner pl

populous ['pɔpjʊləs] adj dicht besiedelt

porcelain ['pɔːslɪn] n Porzellan nt

porch [pɔːtʃ] n Vorbau m, Veranda f

porcupine ['pɔːkjʊpaɪn] n Stachelschwein nt

pore [pɔː] n Pore f ♦ vi: **to ~ over** brüten über +dat

pork [pɔːk] n Schweinefleisch nt

porn [pɔːn] n Porno m; **~ographic** [pɔːnə'ɡræfɪk] adj pornografisch; **~ography** [pɔː'nɔɡrəfɪ] n Pornografie f

porous ['pɔːrəs] adj porös; (skin) porig

porpoise ['pɔːpəs] n Tümmler m

porridge ['pɔrɪdʒ] n Haferbrei m

port [pɔːt] n Hafen m; (town) Hafenstadt f; (NAUT: left side) Backbord nt; (wine) Portwein m; **~ of call** Anlaufhafen m

portable ['pɔːtəbl] adj tragbar

porter ['pɔːtər] n Pförtner(in) m(f); (for luggage) (Gepäck)träger m

portfolio [pɔːt'fəʊlɪəʊ] n (case) Mappe f; (POL) Geschäftsbereich m; (FIN) Portefeuille nt; (of artist) Kollektion f

porthole ['pɔːthəʊl] n Bullauge nt

portion ['pɔːʃən] n Teil m, Stück nt; (of food) Portion f

portrait ['pɔːtreɪt] n Porträt nt

portray [pɔːˈtreɪ] *vt* darstellen; **~al** *n* Darstellung *f*

Portugal [ˈpɔːtjugl] *n* Portugal *nt*

Portuguese [pɔːtjuˈɡiːz] *adj* portugiesisch ♦ *n inv* Portugiese *m*, Portugiesin *f*; (*LING*) Portugiesisch *nt*

pose [pauz] *n* Stellung *f*, Pose *f*; (*affectation*) Pose *f* ♦ *vi* posieren ♦ *vt* stellen

posh [pɔʃ] (*inf*) *adj* (piek)fein

position [pəˈzɪʃən] *n* Stellung *f*; (*place*) Lage *f*; (*job*) Stelle *f*; (*attitude*) Standpunkt *m* ♦ *vt* aufstellen

positive [ˈpɔzɪtɪv] *adj* positiv; (*convinced*) sicher; (*definite*) eindeutig

posse [ˈpɔsɪ] (*US*) *n* Aufgebot *nt*

possess [pəˈzɛs] *vt* besitzen; **~ion** [pəˈzɛʃən] *n* Besitz *m*; **~ive** *adj* besitzergreifend, eigensüchtig

possibility [pɔsɪˈbɪlɪtɪ] *n* Möglichkeit *f*

possible [ˈpɔsɪbl] *adj* möglich; **as big as ~** so groß wie möglich, möglichst groß; **possibly** *adv* möglicherweise, vielleicht; **I cannot possibly come** ich kann unmöglich kommen

post [paust] *n* (*BRIT: letters, delivery*) Post *f*; (*pole*) Pfosten *m*, Pfahl *m*; (*place of duty*) Posten *m*; (*job*) Stelle *f* ♦ *vt* (*notice*) anschlagen; (*BRIT: letters*) aufgeben; (: *appoint*) versetzen; (*soldiers*) aufstellen; **~age** *n* Postgebühr *f*, Porto *nt*; **~al** *adj* Post-; **~al order** *n* Postanweisung *f*; **~box** (*BRIT*) *n* Briefkasten *m*; **~card** *n* Postkarte *f*; **~code** (*BRIT*) *n* Postleitzahl *f*

postdate [ˈpaustˈdeɪt] *vt* (*cheque*) nachdatieren

poster [ˈpaustər] *n* Plakat *nt*, Poster *nt*

poste restante [paustˈrestãːnt] *n* Aufbewahrungsstelle *f* für postlagernde Sendungen

posterior [pɔsˈtɪərɪər] (*inf*) *n* Hintern *m*

posterity [pɔsˈtɛrɪtɪ] *n* Nachwelt *f*

postgraduate [ˈpaustˈɡrædjuət] *n* Weiterstudierende(r) *mf*

posthumous [ˈpɔstjuməs] *adj* post(h)um

postman [ˈpaustmən] (*irreg*) *n* Briefträger *m*

postmark [ˈpaustmɑːk] *n* Poststempel *m*

post-mortem [paustˈmɔːtəm] *n* Autopsie *f*

post office *n* Postamt *nt*, Post *f*; (*organization*) Post *f*; **Post Office Box** *n* Postfach *nt*

postpone [pausˈpaun] *vt* verschieben

postscript [ˈpaustskrɪpt] *n* Postskript *nt*; (*to affair*) Nachspiel *nt*

posture [ˈpɔstʃər] *n* Haltung *f* ♦ *vi* posieren

postwar [ˈpaustˈwɔːr] *adj* Nachkriegs-

postwoman [ˈpaustwumən] (*irreg*) *n* Briefträgerin *f*

posy [ˈpauzɪ] *n* Blumenstrauß *m*

pot [pɔt] *n* Topf *m*; (*teapot*) Kanne *f*; (*inf: marijuana*) Hasch *m* ♦ *vt* (*plant*) eintopfen; **to go to ~** (*inf: work*) auf den Hund kommen

potato [pəˈteɪtau] (*pl* **~es**) *n* Kartoffel *f*; **~ peeler** *n* Kartoffelschäler *m*

potent [ˈpautnt] *adj* stark; (*argument*) zwingend

potential [pəˈtɛnʃl] *adj* potenziell, potentiell ♦ *n* Potenzial *nt*, Potential *nt*; **~ly** *adv* potenziell, potentiell

pothole [ˈpɔthaul] *n* (*in road*) Schlagloch *nt*; (*BRIT: underground*) Höhle *f*; **potholing** (*BRIT*) *n*: **to go potholing** Höhlen erforschen

potion [ˈpauʃən] *n* Trank *m*

potluck [pɔtˈlʌk] *n*: **to take ~ with sth** etw auf gut Glück nehmen

pot plant *n* Topfpflanze *f*

potter [ˈpɔtər] *n* Töpfer *m* ♦ *vi* herumhantieren; **~y** *n* Töpferwaren *pl*; (*place*) Töpferei *f*

potty [ˈpɔtɪ] *adj* (*inf: mad*) verrückt ♦ *n* Töpfchen *nt*

pouch [pautʃ] *n* Beutel *m*

pouf(fe) [puːf] *n* Sitzkissen *nt*

poultry [ˈpaultrɪ] *n* Geflügel *nt*

pounce [pauns] *vi* sich stürzen ♦ *n* Sprung *m*, Satz *m*; **to ~ on** sich stürzen auf +*acc*

pound [paund] *n* (*FIN, weight*) Pfund *nt*; (*for cars, animals*) Auslösestelle *f* ♦ *vt* (zer)stampfen ♦ *vi* klopfen, hämmern; **~ sterling** *n* Pfund Sterling *nt*

pour [pɔːr] *vt* gießen, schütten ♦ *vi* gießen; (*crowds etc*) strömen; **~ away** *vt* abgießen; **~ in** *vi* (*people*) hereinströmen; **~ off** *vt* abgießen; **~ out** *vi* (*people*) herausströmen

♦ vt (*drink*) einschenken; **~ing** adj: **~ing rain** strömende(r) Regen m

pout [paut] vi schmollen

poverty ['pɒvətɪ] n Armut f; **~-stricken** adj verarmt, sehr arm

powder ['paudər] n Pulver nt; (*cosmetic*) Puder m ♦ vt pulverisieren; **to ~ one's nose** sich dat die Nase pudern; **~ compact** n Puderdose f; **~ed milk** n Milchpulver nt; **~ room** n Damentoilette f; **~y** adj pulverig

power ['pauər] n (*also POL*) Macht f; (*ability*) Fähigkeit f; (*strength*) Stärke f; (*MATH*) Potenz f; (*ELEC*) Strom m ♦ vt betreiben, antreiben; **to be in ~** (*POL etc*) an der Macht sein; **~ cut** n Stromausfall m; **~ed** adj: **~ed by** betrieben mit; **~ failure** (*US*) n Stromausfall m; **~ful** adj (*person*) mächtig; (*engine, government*) stark; **~less** adj machtlos; **~ point** (*BRIT*) n elektrische(r) Anschluss m; **~ station** n Elektrizitätswerk nt; **~ struggle** n Machtkampf m

p.p. abbr (= *per procurationem*): **p.p. J. Smith i. A. J. Smith**

PR n abbr = **public relations**

practicable ['præktɪkəbl] adj durchführbar

practical ['præktɪkl] adj praktisch; **~ity** [præktɪ'kælɪtɪ] n (*of person*) praktische Veranlagung f; (*of situation etc*) Durchführbarkeit f; **~ joke** n Streich m; **~ly** adv praktisch

practice ['præktɪs] n Übung f; (*reality, also of doctor, lawyer*) Praxis f; (*custom*) Brauch m; (*in business*) Usus m ♦ vt, vi (*US*) = **practise**; **in ~** (*in reality*) in der Praxis; **out of ~** außer Übung; **practicing** (*US*) adj = **practising**

practise ['præktɪs] (*US* **practice**) vt üben; (*profession*) ausüben ♦ vi (sich) üben; (*doctor, lawyer*) praktizieren; **practising** (*US* **practicing**) adj praktizierend; (*Christian etc*) aktiv

practitioner [præk'tɪʃənər] n praktische(r) Arzt m, praktische Ärztin f

pragmatic [præg'mætɪk] adj pragmatisch

prairie ['prɛərɪ] n Prärie f, Steppe f

praise [preɪz] n Lob nt ♦ vt loben; **~worthy** adj lobenswert

pram [præm] (*BRIT*) n Kinderwagen m

prance [prɑːns] vi (*horse*) tänzeln; (*person*) stolzieren

prank [præŋk] n Streich m

prawn [prɔːn] n Garnele f; Krabbe f; **~ cocktail** n Krabbencocktail m

pray [preɪ] vi beten; **~er** [prɛər] n Gebet nt

preach [priːtʃ] vi predigen; **~er** n Prediger m

preamble [prɪ'æmbl] n Einleitung f

precarious [prɪ'kɛərɪəs] adj prekär, unsicher

precaution [prɪ'kɔːʃən] n (Vorsichts)maßnahme f

precede [prɪ'siːd] vi vorausgehen ♦ vt vorausgehen +dat; **~nce** ['presɪdəns] n Vorrang m; **~nt** ['presɪdənt] n Präzedenzfall m; **preceding** [prɪ'siːdɪŋ] adj vorhergehend

precinct ['priːsɪŋkt] n (*US: district*) Bezirk m; **~s** npl (*round building*) Gelände nt; (*area, environs*) Umgebung f; **pedestrian ~** Fußgängerzone f; **shopping ~** Geschäftsviertel nt

precious ['preʃəs] adj kostbar, wertvoll; (*affected*) pretiös, preziös, geziert

precipice ['presɪpɪs] n Abgrund m

precipitate [adj prɪ'sɪpɪtɪt, vb prɪ'sɪpɪteɪt] adj überstürzt, übereilt ♦ vt hinunterstürzen; (*events*) heraufbeschwören

precise [prɪ'saɪs] adj genau, präzis; **~ly** adv genau, präzis

precision [prɪ'sɪʒən] n Präzision f

preclude [prɪ'kluːd] vt ausschließen

precocious [prɪ'kəuʃəs] adj frühreif

preconceived [priːkən'siːvd] adj (*idea*) vorgefasst

precondition ['priːkən'dɪʃən] n Vorbedingung f, Voraussetzung f

precursor [priː'kɜːsər] n Vorläufer m

predator ['predətər] n Raubtier nt

predecessor ['priːdɪsesər] n Vorgänger m

predicament [prɪ'dɪkəmənt] n missliche Lage f

predict [prɪ'dɪkt] vt voraussagen; **~able** adj vorhersagbar; **~ion** [prɪ'dɪkʃən] n Voraussage f

predominantly [prɪ'dɒmɪnəntlɪ] adv

überwiegend, hauptsächlich
predominate [prɪ'dɔmɪneɪt] *vi*
vorherrschen; (*fig*) vorherrschen,
überwiegen
pre-eminent [priː'emɪnənt] *adj*
hervorragend, herausragend
pre-empt [priː'empt] *vt* (*action, decision*)
vorwegnehmen
preen [priːn] *vt* putzen; **to ~ o.s.** (*person*)
sich brüsten
prefab ['priːfæb] *n* Fertighaus *nt*
preface ['prefəs] *n* Vorwort *nt*
prefect ['priːfekt] *n* Präfekt *m*; (*SCH*)
Aufsichtsschüler(in) *m(f)*
prefer [prɪ'fɜːʳ] *vt* vorziehen, lieber mögen;
to ~ to do sth etw lieber tun; **~ably**
['prefrəblɪ] *adv* vorzugsweise, am liebsten;
~ence ['prefrəns] *n* Präferenz *f*, Vorzug *m*;
~ential [prefə'renʃəl] *adj* bevorzugt,
Vorzugs-
prefix ['priːfɪks] *n* Vorsilbe *f*, Präfix *nt*
pregnancy ['pregnənsɪ] *n* Schwangerschaft *f*
pregnant ['pregnənt] *adj* schwanger
prehistoric ['priːhɪs'tɔrɪk] *adj* prähistorisch,
vorgeschichtlich
prejudice ['predʒudɪs] *n* (*bias*)
Voreingenommenheit *f*; (*opinion*) Vorurteil
nt; (*harm*) Schaden *m* ♦ *vt* beeinträchtigen;
~d (*person*) voreingenommen
preliminary [prɪ'lɪmɪnərɪ] *adj* einleitend,
Vor-
prelude ['preljuːd] *n* Vorspiel *nt*; (*fig*) Auftakt
m
premarital ['priː'mærɪtl] *adj* vorehelich
premature ['premətʃuəʳ] *adj* vorzeitig,
verfrüht; (*birth*) Früh-
premeditated [priː'medɪteɪtɪd] *adj* geplant;
(*murder*) vorsätzlich
premenstrual syndrome [priː'menstruəl-]
n prämenstruelles Syndrom *nt*
premier ['premɪəʳ] *adj* erste(r, s) ♦ *n* Premier
m
première ['premɪeəʳ] *n* Premiere *f*;
Uraufführung *f*
Premier League [-liːg] *n* ≈ 1. Bundesliga
(*höchste Spielklasse im Fußball*)
premise ['premɪs] *n* Voraussetzung *f*,

Prämisse *f*; **~s** *npl* (*shop*) Räumlichkeiten *pl*;
(*grounds*) Gelände *nt*; **on the ~s** im Hause
premium ['priːmɪəm] *n* Prämie *f*; **to be at a
~** über pari stehen; **~ bond** (*BRIT*) *n*
Prämienanleihe *f*
premonition [premə'nɪʃən] *n* Vorahnung *f*
preoccupation [priːɔkju'peɪʃən] *n* Sorge *f*
preoccupied [priː'ɔkjupaɪd] *adj* (*look*)
geistesabwesend
prep [prep] *n* (*SCH*) Hausaufgabe *f*
prepaid [priː'peɪd] *adj* vorausbezahlt; (*letter*)
frankiert
preparation [prepə'reɪʃən] *n* Vorbereitung *f*
preparatory [prɪ'pærətərɪ] *adj*
Vor(bereitungs)-; **~ school** *n* (*BRIT*) *private
Vorbereitungsschule für die Public School*;
(*US*) *private Vorbereitungsschule für die
Hochschule*
prepare [prɪ'peəʳ] *vt* vorbereiten ♦ *vi* sich
vorbereiten; **to ~ for/prepare sth for**
sich/etw vorbereiten auf +*acc*; **to be ~d to
...** bereit sein zu ...
preponderance [prɪ'pɔndərns] *n*
Übergewicht *nt*
preposition [prepə'zɪʃən] *n* Präposition *f*,
Verhältniswort *nt*
preposterous [prɪ'pɔstərəs] *adj* absurd
prep school *n* = **preparatory school**
prerequisite [priː'rekwɪzɪt] *n* (*unerlässliche*)
Voraussetzung *f*
prerogative [prɪ'rɔgətɪv] *n* Vorrecht *nt*
Presbyterian [prezbɪ'tɪərɪən] *adj*
presbyterianisch ♦ *n* Presbyterier(in) *m(f)*
preschool ['priː'skuːl] *adj* Vorschul-
prescribe [prɪ'skraɪb] *vt* vorschreiben; (*MED*)
verschreiben
prescription [prɪ'skrɪpʃən] *n* (*MED*) Rezept *nt*
presence ['prezns] *n* Gegenwart *f*; **~ of
mind** Geistesgegenwart *f*
present [*adj, n* 'preznt, *vb* prɪ'zent] *adj* (*here*)
anwesend; (*current*) gegenwärtig ♦ *n*
Gegenwart *f*; (*gift*) Geschenk *nt* ♦ *vt*
vorlegen; (*introduce*) vorstellen; (*show*)
zeigen; (*give*): **to ~ sb with sth** jdm etw
überreichen; **at ~** im Augenblick; **to give
sb a ~** jdm ein Geschenk machen; **~able**
[prɪ'zentəbl] *adj* präsentabel; **~ation**

[prezn'teɪʃən] n Überreichung f; **~-day** adj heutig; **~er** [prɪ'zentə'] n (RAD, TV) Moderator(in) m(f); **~ly** adv bald; (at ~) im Augenblick

preservation [prezə'veɪʃən] n Erhaltung f

preservative [prɪ'zɜ:'vətɪv] n Konservierungsmittel nt

preserve [prɪ'zɜ:v] vt erhalten; (food) einmachen ♦ (jam) Eingemachte(s) nt; (reserve) Schutzgebiet nt

preside [prɪ'zaɪd] vi den Vorsitz haben

president ['prezɪdənt] n Präsident m; **~ial** [prezɪ'denʃl] adj Präsidenten-; (election) Präsidentschafts-; (system) Präsidial-

press [pres] n Presse f; (printing house) Druckerei f ♦ vt drücken; (iron) bügeln; (urge) (be)drängen ♦ vi (push) drücken; **to be ~ed for time** unter Zeitdruck stehen; **to ~ for sth** drängen auf etw acc; **~ on** vi vorwärts drängen; **~ agency** n Presseagentur f; **~ conference** n Pressekonferenz f; **~ed** adj (clothes) gebügelt; **~ing** adj dringend; **~ stud** (BRIT) n Druckknopf m; **~-up** (BRIT) n Liegestütz m

pressure ['preʃə'] n Druck m; **~ cooker** n Schnellkochtopf m; **~ gauge** n Druckmesser m

pressurized ['preʃəraɪzd] adj Druck-

prestige [pres'ti:ʒ] n Prestige nt; **prestigious** [pres'tɪdʒəs] adj Prestige-

presumably [prɪ'zju:məblɪ] adv vermutlich

presume [prɪ'zju:m] vt, vi annehmen; **to ~ to do sth** sich erlauben, etw zu tun; **presumption** [prɪ'zʌmpʃən] n Annahme f; **presumptuous** [prɪ'zʌmpʃəs] adj anmaßend

pretence [prɪ'tens] (US **pretense**) n Vorgabe f, Vortäuschung f; (false claim) Vorwand m

pretend [prɪ'tend] vt vorgeben, so tun als ob ... ♦ vi so tun; **to ~ to sth** Anspruch erheben auf etw acc

pretense [prɪ'tens] (US) n = **pretence**

pretension [prɪ'tenʃən] n Anspruch m; (impudent claim) Anmaßung f

pretentious [prɪ'tenʃəs] adj angeberisch

pretext ['pri:tekst] n Vorwand m

pretty ['prɪtɪ] adj hübsch ♦ adv (inf) ganz

schön

prevail [prɪ'veɪl] vi siegen; (custom) vorherrschen; **to ~ against** or **over** siegen über +acc; **to ~ (up)on sb to do sth** jdn dazu bewegen, etw zu tun; **~ing** adj vorherrschend

prevalent ['prevələnt] adj vorherrschend

prevent [prɪ'vent] vt (stop) verhindern, verhüten; **to ~ sb from doing sth** jdn (daran) hindern, etw zu tun; **~ative** n Vorbeugungsmittel nt; **~ion** [prɪ'venʃən] n Verhütung f; **~ive** adj vorbeugend, Schutz-

preview ['pri:vju:] n private Voraufführung f; (trailer) Vorschau f

previous ['pri:vɪəs] adj früher, vorherig; **~ly** adv früher

prewar [pri:'wɔ:'] adj Vorkriegs-

prey [preɪ] n Beute f; **~ on** vt fus Jagd machen auf +acc; **it was ~ing on his mind** es quälte sein Gewissen

price [praɪs] n Preis m; (value) Wert m ♦ vt (label) auszeichnen; **~less** adj (also fig) unbezahlbar; **~ list** n Preisliste f

prick [prɪk] n Stich m ♦ vt, vi stechen; **to ~ up one's ears** die Ohren spitzen

prickle ['prɪkl] n Stachel m, Dorn m

prickly ['prɪklɪ] adj stachelig; (fig: person) reizbar; **~ heat** n Hitzebläschen pl

pride [praɪd] n Stolz m; (arrogance) Hochmut m ♦ vt: **to ~ o.s. on sth** auf etw acc stolz sein

priest [pri:st] n Priester m; **~hood** n Priesteramt nt

prim [prɪm] adj prüde

primarily ['praɪmərɪlɪ] adv vorwiegend

primary ['praɪmərɪ] adj (main) Haupt-; (SCH) Grund-; **~ school** (BRIT) n Grundschule f

prime [praɪm] adj erste(r, s); (excellent) erstklassig ♦ vt vorbereiten; (gun) laden; **in the ~ of life** in der Blüte der Jahre; **~ minister** n Premierminister m, Ministerpräsident m; **~r** ['praɪmə'] n Fibel f

primeval [praɪ'mi:vl] adj vorzeitlich; (forests) Ur-

primitive ['prɪmɪtɪv] adj primitiv

primrose ['prɪmrəuz] n (gelbe) Primel f

primus (stove) ['praɪməs-] (® BRIT) n

Primuskocher m

prince [prɪns] n Prinz m; (ruler) Fürst m; **princess** [prɪn'ses] n Prinzessin f; Fürstin f

principal ['prɪnsɪpl] adj Haupt- ♦ n (SCH) (Schul)direktor m, Rektor m; (money) (Grund)kapital nt

principle ['prɪnsɪpl] n Grundsatz m, Prinzip nt; **in ~** im Prinzip; **on ~** aus Prinzip, prinzipiell

print [prɪnt] n Druck m; (made by feet, fingers) Abdruck m; (PHOT) Abzug m ♦ vt drucken; (name) in Druckbuchstaben schreiben; (PHOT) abziehen; **out of ~** vergriffen; **~ed matter** n Drucksache f; **~er** n Drucker m; **~ing** n Drucken nt; (of photos) Abziehen nt; **~out** n (COMPUT) Ausdruck m

prior ['praɪə*] adj früher ♦ n Prior m; **~ to sth** vor etw dat; **~ to going abroad, she had ...** bevor sie ins Ausland ging, hatte sie ...

priority [praɪ'ɔrɪtɪ] n Vorrang m; Priorität f

prise [praɪz] vt: **to ~ open** aufbrechen

prison ['prɪzn] n Gefängnis nt ♦ adj Gefängnis-; (system etc) Strafvollzugs-; **~er** n Gefangene(r) mf

pristine ['prɪstiːn] adj makellos

privacy ['prɪvəsɪ] n Ungestörtheit f, Ruhe f; Privatleben nt

private ['praɪvɪt] adj privat, Privat-; (secret) vertraulich, geheim ♦ n einfache(r) Soldat m; **"~"** (on envelope) „persönlich"; (on door) „Privat"; **in ~** privat, unter vier Augen; **~ enterprise** n Privatunternehmen nt; **~ eye** n Privatdetektiv m; **~ property** n Privatbesitz m; **~ school** n Privatschule f; **privatize** vt privatisieren

privet ['prɪvɪt] n Liguster m

privilege ['prɪvɪlɪdʒ] n Privileg nt; **~d** adj bevorzugt, privilegiert

privy ['prɪvɪ] adj geheim, privat; **P~ Council** n Geheime(r) Staatsrat m

prize [praɪz] n Preis m ♦ adj (example) erstklassig; (idiot) Voll- ♦ vt (hoch) schätzen; **~-giving** n Preisverteilung f; **~winner** n Preisträger(in) m(f)

pro [prəʊ] n (professional) Profi m; **the ~s and cons** das Für und Wider

probability [prɒbə'bɪlɪtɪ] n

Wahrscheinlichkeit f

probable ['prɒbəbl] adj wahrscheinlich; **probably** adv wahrscheinlich

probation [prə'beɪʃən] n Probe(zeit) f; (JUR) Bewährung f; **on ~** auf Probe; auf Bewährung

probe [prəʊb] n Sonde f; (enquiry) Untersuchung f ♦ vt, vi erforschen

problem ['prɒbləm] n Problem nt; **~atic** [prɒblə'mætɪk] adj problematisch

procedure [prə'siːdʒə*] n Verfahren nt

proceed [prə'siːd] vi (advance) vorrücken; (start) anfangen; (carry on) fortfahren; (set about) vorgehen; **~ings** npl Verfahren nt

proceeds ['prəʊsiːdz] npl Erlös m

process ['prəʊses] n Prozess m; (method) Verfahren nt ♦ vt bearbeiten; (food) verarbeiten; (film) entwickeln; **~ing** n (PHOT) Entwickeln nt

procession [prə'seʃən] n Prozession f, Umzug m; **funeral ~** Trauerprozession f

pro-choice [prəʊ'tʃɔɪs] adj (movement) Pro-Abtreibungs-; **~ campaigner** Abtreibungsbefürworter(in) m(f)

proclaim [prə'kleɪm] vt verkünden

procrastinate [prəʊ'kræstɪneɪt] vi zaudern

procure [prə'kjʊə*] vt beschaffen

prod [prɒd] vt stoßen ♦ n Stoß m

prodigal ['prɒdɪgl] adj: **~ (with or of)** verschwenderisch (mit)

prodigy ['prɒdɪdʒɪ] n Wunder nt

produce [n 'prɒdjuːs, vb prə'djuːs] n (AGR) (Boden)produkte pl, (Natur)erzeugnis nt ♦ vt herstellen, produzieren; (cause) hervorrufen; (farmer) erzeugen; (yield) liefern, bringen; (play) inszenieren; **~r** n Hersteller m, Produzent m (also CINE); Erzeuger m

product ['prɒdʌkt] n Produkt nt, Erzeugnis nt; **~ion** [prə'dʌkʃən] n Produktion f, Herstellung f; (thing) Erzeugnis nt, Produkt nt; (THEAT) Inszenierung f; **~ion line** n Fließband nt; **~ive** [prə'dʌktɪv] adj produktiv; (fertile) ertragreich, fruchtbar

productivity [prɒdʌk'tɪvɪtɪ] n Produktivität f

profane [prə'feɪn] adj weltlich, profan; (language etc) gotteslästerlich

profess [prə'fɛs] vt bekennen; (*show*) zeigen; (*claim to be*) vorgeben

profession [prə'fɛʃən] n Beruf m; (*declaration*) Bekenntnis nt; **~al** n Fachmann m; (*SPORT*) Berufsspieler(in) m(f) ♦ adj Berufs-; (*expert*) fachlich; (*player*) professionell; **~ally** adv beruflich, fachmännisch

professor [prə'fɛsə*] n Professor m

proficiency [prə'fɪʃənsɪ] n Können nt

proficient [prə'fɪʃənt] adj fähig

profile ['prəʊfaɪl] n Profil nt; (*fig: report*) Kurzbiografie f

profit ['prɔfɪt] n Gewinn m ♦ vi: **to ~ (by** or **from)** profitieren (von); **~ability** [prɔfɪtə'bɪlɪtɪ] n Rentabilität f; **~able** adj einträglich, rentabel; **~eering** [prɔfɪ'tɪərɪŋ] n Profitmacherei f

profound [prə'faʊnd] adj tief

profuse [prə'fjuːs] adj überreich; **~ly** [prə'fjuːslɪ] adv überschwänglich; (*sweat*) reichlich; **profusion** [prə'fjuːʒən] n: **profusion (of)** Überfülle f (von), Überfluss m (an +dat)

program ['prəʊɡræm] n (*COMPUT*) Programm nt ♦ vt (*machine*) programmieren; **~me** (*US* **program**) n Programm nt ♦ vt planen; (*computer*) programmieren; **~mer** (*US* **programer**) n Programmierer(in) m(f)

progress [n 'prəʊɡrɛs, vb prə'ɡrɛs] n Fortschritt m ♦ vi fortschreiten, weitergehen; **in ~** im Gang; **~ion** [prə'ɡrɛʃən] n Folge f; **~ive** [prə'ɡrɛsɪv] adj fortschrittlich, progressiv

prohibit [prə'hɪbɪt] vt verbieten; **to ~ sb from doing sth** jdm untersagen, etw zu tun; **~ion** [prəʊɪ'bɪʃən] n Verbot nt; (*US*) Alkoholverbot nt, Prohibition f; **~ive** adj unerschwinglich

project [n 'prɔdʒɛkt, vb prə'dʒɛkt] n Projekt nt ♦ vt vorausplanen; (*film etc*) projizieren; (*personality, voice*) zum Tragen bringen ♦ vi (*stick out*) hervorragen, (her)vorstehen

projectile [prə'dʒɛktaɪl] n Geschoss nt

projection [prə'dʒɛkʃən] n Projektion f; (*sth prominent*) Vorsprung m

projector [prə'dʒɛktə*] n Projektor m

proletariat [prəʊlɪ'tɛərɪət] n Proletariat nt

pro-life [prəʊ'laɪf] adj (*movement*) Anti-Abtreibungs-; **~ campaigner** Abtreibungsgegner(in) m(f)

prolific [prə'lɪfɪk] adj fruchtbar; (*author etc*) produktiv

prologue ['prəʊlɔɡ] n Prolog m; (*event*) Vorspiel nt

prolong [prə'lɔŋ] vt verlängern

prom [prɔm] n abbr = **promenade**; **promenade concert**

Prom

🛈 **Prom** (*promenade concert*) ist in Großbritannien ein Konzert, bei dem ein Teil der Zuhörer steht (ursprünglich spazieren ging). Die seit 1895 alljährlich stattfindenden Proms (seit 1941 immer in der Londoner Royal Albert Hall) zählen zu den bedeutendsten Musikereignissen in England. Der letzte Abend der Proms steht ganz im Zeichen des Patriotismus und gipfelt im Singen des Lieds „Land of Hope and Glory". In den USA und Kanada steht das Wort für **promenade**, ein Ball an einer **High School** oder einem **College**.

---

promenade [prɔmə'nɑːd] n Promenade f; **~ concert** n Promenadenkonzert nt

prominence ['prɔmɪnəns] n (große) Bedeutung f

prominent ['prɔmɪnənt] adj bedeutend; (*politician*) prominent; (*easily seen*) herausragend, auffallend

promiscuous [prə'mɪskjuəs] adj lose

promise ['prɔmɪs] n Versprechen nt; (*hope: ~ of sth*) Aussicht f auf etw acc ♦ vt, vi versprechen; **promising** adj viel versprechend

promontory ['prɔməntrɪ] n Vorsprung m

promote [prə'məʊt] vt befördern; (*help on*) fördern, unterstützen; **~r** n (*in entertainment, sport*) Veranstalter m; (*for charity etc*) Organisator m; **promotion** [prə'məʊʃən] n (*in rank*) Beförderung f; (*furtherance*) Förderung f; (*COMM*): **promotion (of)** Werbung f (für)

prompt [prɒmpt] *adj* prompt, schnell ♦ *adv* (*punctually*) genau ♦ *n* (COMPUT) Meldung *f* ♦ *vt* veranlassen; (THEAT) soufflieren +*dat*; **to ~ sb to do sth** jdn dazu veranlassen, etw zu tun; **~ly** *adv* sofort

prone [prəun] *adj* hingestreckt; **to be ~ to sth** zu etw neigen

prong [prɒŋ] *n* Zinke *f*

pronoun ['prəunaun] *n* Fürwort *nt*

pronounce [prə'nauns] *vt* aussprechen; (JUR) verkünden ♦ *vi*: **to ~ (on)** sich äußern (zu)

pronunciation [prənʌnsɪ'eɪʃən] *n* Aussprache *f*

proof [pruːf] *n* Beweis *m*; (PRINT) Korrekturfahne *f*; (*of alcohol*) Alkoholgehalt *m* ♦ *adj* sicher

prop [prɒp] *n* (*also fig*) Stütze *f*; (THEAT) Requisit *nt* ♦ *vt* (*also*: **~ up**) (ab)stützen

propaganda [prɒpə'gændə] *n* Propaganda *f*

propel [prə'pel] *vt* (an)treiben; **~ler** *n* Propeller *m*; **~ling pencil** (BRIT) *n* Drehbleistift *m*

propensity [prə'pensɪtɪ] *n* Tendenz *f*

proper ['prɒpə*r*] *adj* richtig; (*seemly*) schicklich; **~ly** *adv* richtig; **~ noun** *n* Eigenname *m*

property ['prɒpətɪ] *n* Eigentum *nt*; (*quality*) Eigenschaft *f*; (*land*) Grundbesitz *m*; **~ owner** *n* Grundbesitzer *m*

prophecy ['prɒfɪsɪ] *n* Prophezeiung *f*

prophesy ['prɒfɪsaɪ] *vt* prophezeien

prophet ['prɒfɪt] *n* Prophet *m*

proportion [prə'pɔːʃən] *n* Verhältnis *nt*; (*share*) Teil *m* ♦ *vt*: **to ~ (to)** abstimmen (auf +*acc*); **~al** *adj* proportional; **~ate** *adj* verhältnismäßig

proposal [prə'pəuzl] *n* Vorschlag *m*; (*of marriage*) Heiratsantrag *m*

propose [prə'pəuz] *vt* vorschlagen; (*toast*) ausbringen ♦ *vi* (*offer marriage*) einen Heiratsantrag machen; **to ~ to do sth** beabsichtigen, etw zu tun

proposition [prɒpə'zɪʃən] *n* Angebot *nt*; (*statement*) Satz *m*

proprietor [prə'praɪətə*r*] *n* Besitzer *m*, Eigentümer *m*

propriety [prə'praɪətɪ] *n* Anstand *m*

pro rata [prəu'rɑːtə] *adv* anteilmäßig

prose [prəuz] *n* Prosa *f*

prosecute ['prɒsɪkjuːt] *vt* (strafrechtlich) verfolgen; **prosecution** [prɒsɪ'kjuːʃən] *n* (JUR) strafrechtliche Verfolgung *f*; (*party*) Anklage *f*; **prosecutor** *n* Vertreter *m* der Anklage; **Public Prosecutor** Staatsanwalt *m*

prospect [*n* 'prɒspekt, *vb* prə'spekt] *n* Aussicht *f* ♦ *vt* auf Bodenschätze hin untersuchen ♦ *vi*: **to ~ (for)** suchen (nach); **~ing** ['prɒspektɪŋ] *n* (*for minerals*) Suche *f*; **~ive** [prə'spektɪv] *adj* (*son-in-law etc*) zukünftig; (*customer, candidate*) voraussichtlich

prospectus [prə'spektəs] *n* (Werbe)prospekt *m*

prosper ['prɒspə*r*] *vi* blühen, gedeihen; (*person*) erfolgreich sein; **~ity** [prɒ'sperɪtɪ] *n* Wohlstand *m*; **~ous** *adj* wohlhabend, reich

prostitute ['prɒstɪtjuːt] *n* Prostituierte *f*

prostrate ['prɒstreɪt] *adj* ausgestreckt (liegend)

protagonist [prə'tægənɪst] *n* Hauptperson *f*, Held *m*

protect [prə'tekt] *vt* (be)schützen; **~ed species** *n* geschützte Art; **~ion** [prə'tekʃən] *n* Schutz *m*; **~ive** *adj* Schutz-, (be)schützend

protégé ['prəutəʒeɪ] *n* Schützling *m*

protein ['prəutiːn] *n* Protein *nt*, Eiweiß *nt*

protest [*n* 'prəutest, *vb* prə'test] *n* Protest *m* ♦ *vi* protestieren ♦ *vt* (*affirm*) beteuern

Protestant ['prɒtɪstənt] *adj* protestantisch ♦ *n* Protestant(in) *m(f)*

protester [prə'testə*r*] *n* (*demonstrator*) Demonstrant(in) *m(f)*

protracted [prə'træktɪd] *adj* sich hinziehend

protrude [prə'truːd] *vi* (her)vorstehen

proud [praud] *adj*: **~ (of)** stolz (auf +*acc*)

prove [pruːv] *vt* beweisen ♦ *vi*: **to ~ (to be) correct** sich als richtig erweisen; **to ~ o.s.** sich bewähren

proverb ['prɒvəːb] *n* Sprichwort *nt*; **~ial** [prə'vəːbɪəl] *adj* sprichwörtlich

provide [prə'vaɪd] *vt* versehen; (*supply*) besorgen; **to ~ sb with sth** jdn mit etw versorgen; **~ for** *vt fus* sorgen für; (*emergency*) Vorkehrungen treffen für; **~d (that)** *conj* vorausgesetzt(, dass)

providing [prə'vaɪdɪŋ] *conj* vorausgesetzt(, dass)

province ['prɒvɪns] *n* Provinz *f*; (*division of work*) Bereich *m*; **provincial** [prə'vɪnʃəl] *adj* provinziell, Provinz-

provision [prə'vɪʒən] *n* Vorkehrung *f*; (*condition*) Bestimmung *f*; **~s** *npl* (*food*) Vorräte *pl*, Proviant *m*; **~al** *adj* provisorisch

proviso [prə'vaɪzəu] *n* Bedingung *f*

provocative [prə'vɒkətɪv] *adj* provozierend

provoke [prə'vəuk] *vt* provozieren; (*cause*) hervorrufen

prowess ['prauɪs] *n* überragende(s) Können *nt*

prowl [praul] *vi* herumstreichen; (*animal*) schleichen ♦ *n*: **on the ~** umherstreifend; **~er** *n* Herumtreiber(in) *m(f)*

proximity [prɒk'sɪmɪtɪ] *n* Nähe *f*

proxy ['prɒksɪ] *n* (Stell)vertreter *m*; (*authority, document*) Vollmacht *f*; **by ~** durch einen Stellvertreter

prudent ['pru:dnt] *adj* klug, umsichtig

prudish ['pru:dɪʃ] *adj* prüde

prune [pru:n] *n* Backpflaume *f* ♦ *vt* ausputzen; (*fig*) zurechtstutzen

pry [praɪ] *vi*: **to ~ (into)** seine Nase stecken (in +*acc*)

PS *n abbr* (= *postscript*) PS

pseudonym ['sju:dənɪm] *n* Pseudonym *nt*, Deckname *m*

psychiatric [saɪkɪ'ætrɪk] *adj* psychiatrisch

psychiatrist [saɪ'kaɪətrɪst] *n* Psychiater *m*

psychic ['saɪkɪk] *adj* (*also*: **~al**) übersinnlich; (*person*) paranormal begabt

psychoanalyse [saɪkəu'ænəlaɪz] (*US* **psychoanalyze**) *vt* psychoanalytisch behandeln; **psychoanalyst** [saɪkəu'ænəlɪst] *n* Psychoanalytiker(in) *m(f)*

psychological [saɪkə'lɒdʒɪkl] *adj* psychologisch; **psychologist** [saɪ'kɒlədʒɪst] *n* Psychologe *m*, Psychologin *f*; **psychology** [saɪ'kɒlədʒɪ] *n* Psychologie *f*

PTO *abbr* = **please turn over**

pub [pʌb] *n abbr* (= *public house*) Kneipe *f*

Pub

i **Pub** ist ein Gasthaus mit einer Lizenz zum Ausschank von alkoholischen Getränken. Ein Pub besteht meist aus verschiedenen gemütlichen (**lounge, snug**) oder einfacheren Räumen (**public bar**), in der oft auch Spiele wie Darts, Domino und Poolbillard zur Verfügung stehen. In Pubs werden vor allem mittags oft auch Mahlzeiten angeboten. Pubs sind normalerweise von 11 bis 23 Uhr geöffnet, aber manchmal nachmittags geschlossen.

---

pubic ['pju:bɪk] *adj* Scham-

public ['pʌblɪk] *adj* öffentlich ♦ *n* (*also*: **general ~**) Öffentlichkeit *f*; **in ~** in der Öffentlichkeit; **~ address system** *n* Lautsprecheranlage *f*

publican ['pʌblɪkən] *n* Wirt *m*

publication [pʌblɪ'keɪʃən] *n* Veröffentlichung *f*

public: **~ company** *n* Aktiengesellschaft *f*; **~ convenience** (*BRIT*) *n* öffentliche Toiletten *pl*; **~ holiday** *n* gesetzliche(r) Feiertag *m*; **~ house** (*BRIT*) *n* Lokal *nt*, Kneipe *f*

publicity [pʌb'lɪsɪtɪ] *n* Publicity *f*, Werbung *f*

publicize ['pʌblɪsaɪz] *vt* bekannt machen; (*advertise*) Publicity machen für

publicly ['pʌblɪklɪ] *adv* öffentlich

public: **~ opinion** *n* öffentliche Meinung *f*; **~ relations** *npl* Publicrelations *pl*, Public Relations *pl*; **~ school** *n* (*BRIT*) Privatschule *f*; (*US*) staatliche Schule *f*; **~-spirited** *adj* mit Gemeinschaftssinn; **~ transport** *n* öffentliche Verkehrsmittel *pl*

publish ['pʌblɪʃ] *vt* veröffentlichen; (*event*) bekannt geben; **~er** *n* Verleger *m*; **~ing** *n* (*business*) Verlagswesen *nt*

pub lunch *n* in Pubs servierter Imbiss

pucker ['pʌkər] *vt* (*face*) verziehen; (*lips*) kräuseln

pudding ['pudɪŋ] *n* (*BRIT*: *course*) Nachtisch *m*; Pudding *m*; **black ~** ≈ Blutwurst *f*

puddle ['pʌdl] *n* Pfütze *f*

puff [pʌf] *n* (*of wind etc*) Stoß *m*; (*cosmetic*)

Puderquaste *f* ♦ *vt* blasen, pusten; (*pipe*)
paffen ♦ *vi* keuchen, schnaufen; (*smoke*)
paffen; **to ~ out smoke** Rauch ausstoßen;
~ pastry (*US* **~ paste**) *n* Blätterteig *m*; **~y**
adj aufgedunsen

pull [pʊl] *n* Ruck *m*; (*influence*) Beziehung *f*
♦ *vt* ziehen; (*trigger*) abdrücken ♦ *vi* ziehen;
to ~ sb's leg jdn auf den Arm nehmen; **to
~ to pieces** in Stücke reißen; (*fig*)
verreißen; **to ~ one's punches** sich
zurückhalten; **to ~ one's weight** sich in die
Riemen legen; **to ~ o.s. together** sich
zusammenreißen; **~ apart** *vt* (*break*)
zerreißen; (*dismantle*) auseinander nehmen;
(*separate*) trennen; **~ down** *vt* (*house*)
abreißen; **~ in** *vi* hineinfahren; (*stop*)
anhalten; (*RAIL*) einfahren; **~ off** *vt* (*deal
etc*) abschließen; **~ out** *vi* (*car*)
herausfahren; (*fig: partner*) aussteigen ♦ *vt*
herausziehen; **~ over** *vi* (*AUT*) an die Seite
fahren; **~ through** *vi* durchkommen; **~
up** *vi* anhalten ♦ *vt* (*uproot*) herausreißen;
(*stop*) anhalten

pulley ['pʊlɪ] *n* Rolle *f*, Flaschenzug *m*
pullover ['pʊləʊvər] *n* Pullover *m*
pulp [pʌlp] *n* Brei *m*; (*of fruit*) Fruchtfleisch *nt*
pulpit ['pʊlpɪt] *n* Kanzel *f*
pulsate [pʌl'seɪt] *vi* pulsieren
pulse [pʌls] *n* Puls *m*; **~s** *npl* (*BOT*)
Hülsenfrüchte *pl*
pummel ['pʌml] *vt* mit den Fäusten
bearbeiten
pump [pʌmp] *n* Pumpe *f*; (*shoe*) leichter
(Tanz)schuh *m* ♦ *vt* pumpen; **~ up** *vt* (*tyre*)
aufpumpen
pumpkin ['pʌmpkɪn] *n* Kürbis *m*
pun [pʌn] *n* Wortspiel *nt*
punch [pʌntʃ] *n* (*tool*) Locher *m*; (*blow*)
(Faust)schlag *m*; (*drink*) Punsch *m*, Bowle *f*
♦ *vt* lochen; (*strike*) schlagen, boxen; **~ line**
n Pointe *f*; **~-up** (*BRIT: inf*) *n* Keilerei *f*
punctual ['pʌŋktjʊəl] *adj* pünktlich
punctuate ['pʌŋktjʊeɪt] *vt* mit Satzzeichen
versehen; (*fig*) unterbrechen; **punctuation**
[pʌŋktjʊ'eɪʃən] *n* Zeichensetzung *f*,
Interpunktion *f*
puncture ['pʌŋktʃər] *n* Loch *nt*; (*AUT*)

Reifenpanne *f* ♦ *vt* durchbohren
pundit ['pʌndɪt] *n* Gelehrte(r) *m*
pungent ['pʌndʒənt] *adj* scharf
punish ['pʌnɪʃ] *vt* bestrafen; (*in boxing etc*)
übel zurichten; **~ment** *n* Strafe *f*; (*action*)
Bestrafung *f*
punk [pʌŋk] *n* (*also: ~ rocker*) Punker(in)
m(f); (*also: ~ rock*) Punk *m*; (*US: inf:
hoodlum*) Ganove *m*
punt [pʌnt] *n* Stechkahn *m*
punter ['pʌntər] (*BRIT*) *n* (*better*) Wetter *m*
puny ['pjuːnɪ] *adj* kümmerlich
pup [pʌp] *n* = **puppy**
pupil ['pjuːpl] *n* Schüler(in) *m(f)*; (*in eye*)
Pupille *f*
puppet ['pʌpɪt] *n* Puppe *f*; Marionette *f*
puppy ['pʌpɪ] *n* junge(r) Hund *m*
purchase ['pəːtʃɪs] *n* Kauf *m*; (*grip*) Halt *m*
♦ *vt* kaufen, erwerben; **~r** *n* Käufer(in) *m(f)*
pure [pjʊər] *adj* (*also fig*) rein; **~ly** ['pjʊəlɪ]
adv rein
purgatory ['pəːgətərɪ] *n* Fegefeuer *nt*
purge [pəːdʒ] *n* (*also POL*) Säuberung *f* ♦ *vt*
reinigen; (*body*) entschlacken
purify ['pjʊərɪfaɪ] *vt* reinigen
purity ['pjʊərɪtɪ] *n* Reinheit *f*
purple ['pəːpl] *adj* violett; (*face*) dunkelrot
purport [pəː'pɔːt] *vi* vorgeben
purpose ['pəːpəs] *n* Zweck *m*, Ziel *nt*; (*of
person*) Absicht *f*; **on ~** absichtlich; **~ful** *adj*
zielbewusst, entschlossen
purr [pəː] *n* Schnurren *nt* ♦ *vi* schnurren
purse [pəːs] *n* Portemonnaie *nt*, Portmonee
nt, Geldbeutel *m* ♦ *vt* (*lips*)
zusammenpressen, schürzen
purser ['pəːsə] *n* Zahlmeister *m*
pursue [pə'sjuː] *vt* verfolgen; (*study*)
nachgehen +*dat*; **~r** *n* Verfolger *m*; **pursuit**
[pə'sjuːt] *n* Verfolgung *f*; (*occupation*)
Beschäftigung *f*
pus [pʌs] *n* Eiter *m*
push [pʊʃ] *n* Stoß *m*, Schub *m*; (*MIL*) Vorstoß
m ♦ *vt* stoßen, schieben; (*button*) drücken;
(*idea*) durchsetzen ♦ *vi* stoßen, schieben; **~
aside** *vt* beiseite schieben; **~ off** (*inf*) *vi*
abschieben; **~ on** *vi* weitermachen; **~
through** *vt* durchdrücken; (*policy*)

durchsetzen; ~ **up** *vt* (*total*) erhöhen; (*prices*) hoch treiben; ~**chair** (*BRIT*) *n* (Kinder)sportwagen *m*; ~**er** *n* (*drug dealer*) Pusher *m*; ~**over** (*inf*) *n* Kinderspiel *nt*; ~-**up** (*US*) *n* (*press-up*) Liegestütz *m*; ~**y** (*inf*) *adj* aufdringlich

puss [pus] *n* Mieze(katze) *f*; ~**y(cat)** *n* Mieze(katze) *f*

put [put] (*pt, pp* **put**) *vt* setzen, stellen, legen; (*express*) ausdrücken, sagen; (*write*) schreiben; ~ **about** *vi* (*turn back*) wenden ♦ *vt* (*spread*) verbreiten; ~ **across** *vt* (*explain*) erklären; ~ **away** *vt* (*store*) beiseite legen; ~ **back** *vt* zurückstellen *or* -legen; ~ **by** *vt* zurücklegen, sparen; ~ **down** *vt* hinstellen *or* -legen; (*rebellion*) niederschlagen; (*animal*) einschläfern; (*in writing*) niederschreiben; ~ **forward** *vt* (*idea*) vorbringen; (*clock*) vorstellen; ~ **in** *vt* (*application, complaint*) einreichen; ~ **off** *vt* verschieben; (*discourage*): **to ~ sb off sth** jdn von etw abbringen; ~ **on** *vt* (*clothes etc*) anziehen; (*light etc*) anschalten, anmachen; (*play etc*) aufführen; (*brake*) anziehen; ~ **out** *vt* (*hand etc*) (her)ausstrecken; (*news, rumour*) verbreiten; (*light etc*) ausschalten, ausmachen; ~ **through** (*TEL: person*) verbinden; (: *call*) durchstellen; ~ **up** *vt* (*tent*) aufstellen; (*building*) errichten; (*price*) erhöhen; (*person*) unterbringen; ~ **up with** *vt fus* sich abfinden mit

putrid [ˈpjuːtrɪd] *adj* faul

putt [pʌt] *vt* (*golf*) putten ♦ *n* (*golf*) Putten *nt*; ~**ing green** *n* kleine(r) Golfplatz *m* nur zum Putten

putty [ˈpʌtɪ] *n* Kitt *m*; (*fig*) Wachs *nt*

put-up [ˈputʌp] *adj*: ~ **job** abgekartete(s) Spiel *nt*

puzzle [ˈpʌzl] *n* Rätsel *nt*; (*toy*) Geduldspiel *nt* ♦ *vt* verwirren ♦ *vi* sich den Kopf zerbrechen; ~**d** *adj* verdutzt, verblüfft; **puzzling** *adj* rätselhaft, verwirrend

pyjamas [pəˈdʒɑːməz] (*BRIT*) *npl* Schlafanzug *m*, Pyjama *m*

pylon [ˈpaɪlən] *n* Mast *m*

pyramid [ˈpɪrəmɪd] *n* Pyramide *f*

Q, q

quack [kwæk] *n* Quaken *nt*; (*doctor*) Quacksalber *m* ♦ *vi* quaken

quad [kwɔd] *n abbr* = **quadrangle**; **quadruplet**

quadrangle [ˈkwɔdræŋgl] *n* (*court*) Hof *m*; (*MATH*) Viereck *nt*

quadruple [kwɔˈdruːpl] *adj* ♦ *vi* sich vervierfachen ♦ *vt* vervierfachen

quadruplets [kwɔˈdruːplɪts] *npl* Vierlinge *pl*

quagmire [ˈkwægmaɪəʳ] *n* Morast *m*

quail [kweɪl] *n* (*bird*) Wachtel *f* ♦ *vi* (*vor Angst*) zittern

quaint [kweɪnt] *adj* kurios; malerisch

quake [kweɪk] *vi* beben, zittern ♦ *n abbr* = **earthquake**

qualification [kwɔlɪfɪˈkeɪʃən] *n* Qualifikation *f*; (*sth which limits*) Einschränkung *f*

qualified [ˈkwɔlɪfaɪd] *adj* (*competent*) qualifiziert; (*limited*) bedingt

qualify [ˈkwɔlɪfaɪ] *vt* (*prepare*) befähigen; (*limit*) einschränken ♦ *vi* sich qualifizieren; **to ~ as a doctor/lawyer** sein medizinisches/juristisches Staatsexamen machen

quality [ˈkwɔlɪtɪ] *n* Qualität *f*; (*characteristic*) Eigenschaft *f*

Quality press
---

i **Quality press** bezeichnet die seriösen *Tages- und Wochenzeitungen, im Gegensatz zu den Massenblättern. Diese Zeitungen sind fast alle großformatig und wenden sich an den anspruchvolleren Leser, der voll informiert sein möchte und bereit ist, für die Zeitungslektüre viel Zeit aufzuwenden. Siehe auch* **tabloid press.**

---

quality time *n* intensiv genutzte Zeit

qualm [kwɑːm] *n* Bedenken *nt*

quandary [ˈkwɔndrɪ] *n*: **to be in a ~** in Verlegenheit sein

quantity [ˈkwɔntɪtɪ] *n* Menge *f*; ~ **surveyor**

n Baukostenkalkulator *m*

quarantine ['kworntiːn] *n* Quarantäne *f*

quarrel ['kwɔrl] *n* Streit *m* ♦ *vi* sich streiten; **~some** *adj* streitsüchtig

quarry ['kwɔrɪ] *n* Steinbruch *m*; (*animal*) Wild *nt*; (*fig*) Opfer *nt*

quarter ['kwɔːtər] *n* Viertel *nt*; (*of year*) Quartal *nt* ♦ *vt* (*divide*) vierteln; (*MIL*) einquartieren; **~s** *npl* (*esp MIL*) Quartier *nt*; **~ of an hour** Viertelstunde *f*; **~ final** *n* Viertelfinale *nt*; **~ly** *adj* vierteljährlich

quartet(te) [kwɔːˈtet] *n* Quartett *nt*

quartz [kwɔːts] *n* Quarz *m*

quash [kwɔʃ] *vt* (*verdict*) aufheben

quaver ['kweɪvər] *vi* (*tremble*) zittern

quay [kiː] *n* Kai *m*

queasy ['kwiːzɪ] *adj* übel

queen [kwiːn] *n* Königin *f*; **~ mother** *n* Königinmutter *f*

queer [kwɪər] *adj* seltsam ♦ *n* (*inf*: *homosexual*) Schwule(r) *m*

quell [kwel] *vt* unterdrücken

quench [kwentʃ] *vt* (*thirst*) löschen

querulous ['kwerʊləs] *adj* nörglerisch

query ['kwɪərɪ] *n* (*question*) (An)frage *f*; (*question mark*) Fragezeichen *n* ♦ *vt* in Zweifel ziehen, infrage *or* in Frage stellen

quest [kwest] *n* Suche *f*

question ['kwestʃən] *n* Frage *f* ♦ *vt* (*ask*) (be)fragen; (*suspect*) verhören; (*doubt*) infrage *or* in Frage stellen, bezweifeln; **beyond ~** ohne Frage; **out of the ~** ausgeschlossen; **~able** *adj* zweifelhaft; **~ mark** *n* Fragezeichen *nt*

questionnaire [kwestʃəˈneər] *n* Fragebogen *m*

queue [kjuː] (*BRIT*) *n* Schlange *f* ♦ *vi* (*also*: **~ up**) Schlange stehen

quibble ['kwɪbl] *vi* kleinlich sein

quick [kwɪk] *adj* schnell ♦ *n* (*of nail*) Nagelhaut *f*; **be ~!** mach schnell!; **cut to the ~** (*fig*) tief getroffen; **~en** *vt* (*hasten*) beschleunigen ♦ *vi* sich beschleunigen; **~ly** *adv* schnell; **~sand** *n* Treibsand *m*; **~-witted** *adj* schlagfertig

quid [kwɪd] (*BRIT*: *inf*) *n* Pfund *nt*

quiet ['kwaɪət] *adj* (*without noise*) leise; (*peaceful, calm*) still, ruhig ♦ *n* Stille *f*, Ruhe *f* ♦ *vt*, *vi* (*US*) = **quieten**; **keep ~!** sei still!; **~en** *vi* (*also*: **~en down**) ruhig werden ♦ *vt* beruhigen; **~ly** *adv* leise, ruhig; **~ness** *n* Ruhe *f*, Stille *f*

quilt [kwɪlt] *n* (*continental ~*) Steppdecke *f*

quin [kwɪn] *n abbr* = **quintuplet**

quintuplets [kwɪnˈtjuːplɪts] *npl* Fünflinge *pl*

quip [kwɪp] *n* witzige Bemerkung *f*

quirk [kwəːk] *n* (*oddity*) Eigenart *f*

quit [kwɪt] (*pt*, *pp* **quit** *or* **quitted**) *vt* verlassen ♦ *vi* aufhören

quite [kwaɪt] *adv* (*completely*) ganz, völlig; (*fairly*) ziemlich; **~ a few of them** ziemlich viele von ihnen; **~ (so)!** richtig!

quits [kwɪts] *adj* quitt; **let's call it ~** lassen wirs gut sein

quiver ['kwɪvər] *vi* zittern ♦ *n* (*for arrows*) Köcher *m*

quiz [kwɪz] *n* (*competition*) Quiz *nt* ♦ *vt* prüfen; **~zical** *adj* fragend

quota ['kwəʊtə] *n* Anteil *m*; (*COMM*) Quote *f*

quotation [kwəʊˈteɪʃən] *n* Zitat *nt*; (*price*) Kostenvoranschlag *m*; **~ marks** *npl* Anführungszeichen *pl*

quote [kwəʊt] *n* = **quotation** ♦ *vi* (*from book*) zitieren ♦ *vt* zitieren; (*price*) angeben

R, r

rabbi ['ræbaɪ] *n* Rabbiner *m*; (*title*) Rabbi *m*

rabbit ['ræbɪt] *n* Kaninchen *nt*; **~ hole** *n* Kaninchenbau *m*; **~ hutch** *n* Kaninchenstall *m*

rabble ['ræbl] *n* Pöbel *m*

rabies ['reɪbiːz] *n* Tollwut *f*

RAC (*BRIT*) *n abbr* = **Royal Automobile Club**

raccoon [rəˈkuːn] *n* Waschbär *m*

race [reɪs] *n* (*species*) Rasse *f*; (*competition*) Rennen *nt*; (*on foot*) Rennen *nt*, Wettlauf *m*; (*rush*) Hetze *f* ♦ *vt* um die Wette laufen mit; (*horses*) laufen lassen ♦ *vi* (*run*) rennen; (*in contest*) am Rennen teilnehmen; **~ car** (*US*) *n* = **racing car**; **~ car driver** (*US*) *n* = **racing driver**; **~course** *n* (*for horses*) Rennbahn *f*; **~horse** *n* Rennpferd *nt*; **~r** *n*

(*person*) Rennfahrer(in) *m(f)*; (*car*)
Rennwagen *m*; ~track *n* (*for cars etc*)
Rennstrecke *f*

racial ['reɪʃl] *adj* Rassen-

racing ['reɪsɪŋ] *n* Rennen *nt*; ~ car (*BRIT*) *n*
Rennwagen *m*; ~ driver (*BRIT*) *n*
Rennfahrer *m*

racism ['reɪsɪzəm] *n* Rassismus *m*; racist
['reɪsɪst] *n* Rassist *m* ♦ *adj* rassistisch

rack [ræk] *n* Ständer *m*, Gestell *nt* ♦ *vt*
plagen; **to go to ~ and ruin** verfallen; **to ~
one's brains** sich *dat* den Kopf zerbrechen

racket ['rækɪt] *n* (*din*) Krach *m*; (*scheme*)
(Schwindel)geschäft *nt*; (*TENNIS*)
(Tennis)schläger *m*

racquet ['rækɪt] *n* (Tennis)schläger *m*

racy ['reɪsɪ] *adj* gewagt; (*style*) spritzig

radar ['reɪdɑːʳ] *n* Radar *nt* or *m*

radial ['reɪdɪəl] *adj* (*also: US*: **~ply**) radial

radiant ['reɪdɪənt] *adj* strahlend; (*giving out
rays*) Strahlungs-

radiate ['reɪdɪeɪt] *vi* ausstrahlen; (*roads, lines*)
strahlenförmig wegführen ♦ *vt* ausstrahlen;

radiation [reɪdɪ'eɪʃən] *n* (Aus)strahlung *f*

radiator ['reɪdɪeɪtəʳ] *n* (*for heating*)
Heizkörper *m*; (*AUT*) Kühler *m*

radical ['rædɪkl] *adj* radikal

radii ['reɪdɪaɪ] *npl of* **radius**

radio ['reɪdɪəu] *n* Rundfunk *m*, Radio *nt*; (*set*)
Radio *nt*, Radioapparat *m*; **on the ~** im
Radio; ~active ['reɪdɪəu'æktɪv] *adj*
radioaktiv; ~ cassette *n* Radiorekorder *m*;
~-controlled *adj* ferngesteuert; ~logy
[reɪdɪ'ɔlədʒɪ] *n* Strahlenkunde *f*; ~ station *n*
Rundfunkstation *f*; ~therapy
['reɪdɪəu'θerəpɪ] *n* Röntgentherapie *f*

radish ['rædɪʃ] *n* (*big*) Rettich *m*; (*small*)
Radieschen *nt*

radius ['reɪdɪəs] *n* (*pl* **radii**) *n* Radius *m*; (*area*)
Umkreis *m*

RAF *n abbr* = **Royal Air Force**

raffle ['ræfl] *n* Verlosung *f*, Tombola *f* ♦ *vt*
verlosen

raft [rɑːft] *n* Floß *nt*

rafter ['rɑːftəʳ] *n* Dachsparren *m*

rag [ræg] *n* (*cloth*) Lumpen *m*, Lappen *m*;
(*inf: newspaper*) Käseblatt *nt*; (*UNIV: for

charity*) studentische Sammelaktion *f* ♦ *vt*
(*BRIT*) auf den Arm nehmen; ~**s** *npl* (*cloth*)
Lumpen *pl*; ~ **doll** *n* Flickenpuppe *f*

rage [reɪdʒ] *n* Wut *f*; (*fashion*) große Mode *f*
♦ *vi* wüten, toben

ragged ['rægɪd] *adj* (*edge*) gezackt; (*clothes*)
zerlumpt

raid [reɪd] *n* Überfall *m*; (*MIL*) Angriff *m*; (*by
police*) Razzia *f* ♦ *vt* überfallen

rail [reɪl] *n* (*also* RAIL) Schiene *f*; (*on stair*)
Geländer *nt*; (*of ship*) Reling *f*; ~**s** *npl* (RAIL)
Geleise *pl*; **by ~** per Bahn; ~ing(s) *n(pl)*
Geländer *nt*; ~road (*US*) *n* Eisenbahn *f*;
~way (*BRIT*) *n* Eisenbahn *f*; ~way line
(*BRIT*) *n* (Eisen)bahnlinie *f*; (*track*) Gleis *nt*;
~wayman (*irreg*; *BRIT*) *n* Eisenbahner *m*;
~way station (*BRIT*) *n* Bahnhof *m*

rain [reɪn] *n* Regen *m* ♦ *vt, vi* regnen; **in the
~** im Regen; **it's ~ing** es regnet; ~bow *n*
Regenbogen *m*; ~coat *n* Regenmantel *m*;
~drop *n* Regentropfen *m*; ~fall *n*
Niederschlag *m*; ~forest *n* Regenwald *m*;
~y *adj* (*region, season*) Regen-; (*day*)
regnerisch, verregnet

raise [reɪz] *n* (*esp US: increase*)
(Gehalts)erhöhung *f* ♦ *vt* (*lift*) (hoch)heben;
(*increase*) erhöhen; (*question*) aufwerfen;
(*doubts*) äußern; (*funds*) beschaffen; (*family*)
großziehen; (*livestock*) züchten; **to ~ one's
voice** die Stimme erheben

raisin ['reɪzn] *n* Rosine *f*

rake [reɪk] *n* Rechen *m*, Harke *f*; Wüstling *m*
♦ *vt* rechen, harken; (*search*) (durch)suchen

rally ['rælɪ] *n* (*POL etc*) Kundgebung *f*; (*AUT*)
Rallye *f* ♦ *vt* (*MIL*) sammeln ♦ *vi* Kräfte
sammeln; ~ round *vt fus* (sich) scharen
um; (*help*) zu Hilfe kommen +*dat* ♦ *vi* zu
Hilfe kommen

RAM [ræm] *n abbr* (= *random access memory*)
RAM *m*

Ramadan ['ræmədɑːn] *n* Ramadan *m*

ram [ræm] *n* Widder *m* ♦ *vt* (*hit*) rammen;
(*stuff*) (hinein)stopfen

ramble ['ræmbl] *n* Wanderung *f* ♦ *vi* (*talk*)
schwafeln; ~r *n* Wanderer *m*; rambling *adj*
(*speech*) weitschweifig; (*town*) ausgedehnt

ramp [ræmp] *n* Rampe *f*; **on/off ~** (*US*: AUT)

Ein-/Ausfahrt f

rampage [ræm'peɪdʒ] n: **to be on the ~** randalieren ♦ vi randalieren

rampant ['ræmpənt] adj wild wuchernd

rampart ['ræmpɑːt] n (Schutz)wall m

ram raid n Raubüberfall, bei dem eine Geschäftsfront mit einem Fahrzeug gerammt wird

ramshackle ['ræmʃækl] adj baufällig

ran [ræn] pt of **run**

ranch [rɑːntʃ] n Ranch f

rancid ['rænsɪd] adj ranzig

rancour ['ræŋkər] (US **rancor**) n Verbitterung f, Groll m

random ['rændəm] adj ziellos, wahllos ♦ n: **at ~** aufs Geratewohl; **~ access** n (COMPUT) wahlfreie(r) Zugriff m

randy ['rændɪ] (BRIT: inf) adj geil, scharf

rang [ræŋ] pt of **ring**

range [reɪndʒ] n Reihe f; (of mountains) Kette f; (COMM) Sortiment nt; (reach) (Reich)weite f; (of gun) Schussweite f; (for shooting practice) Schießplatz m; (stove) (großer) Herd m ♦ vt (set in row) anordnen, aufstellen; (roam) durchstreifen ♦ vi: **to ~ over** (wander) umherstreifen in +dat; (extend) sich erstrecken auf +acc; **a ~ of** (selection) eine (große) Auswahl an +dat; **prices ranging from £5 to £10** Preise, die sich zwischen £5 und £10 bewegen; **~r** ['reɪndʒər] n Förster m

rank [ræŋk] n (row) Reihe f; (BRIT: also: **taxi ~**) (Taxi)stand m; (MIL) Rang m; (social position) Stand m ♦ vi (have ~): **to ~ among** gehören zu +acc ♦ adj (strong-smelling) stinkend; (extreme) kraß; **the ~ and file** (fig) die breite Masse

rankle ['ræŋkl] vi nagen

ransack ['rænsæk] vt (plunder) plündern; (search) durchwühlen

ransom ['rænsəm] n Lösegeld nt; **to hold sb to ~** jdn gegen Lösegeld festhalten

rant [rænt] vi hochtrabend reden

rap [ræp] n Schlag m; (music) Rap m ♦ vt klopfen

rape [reɪp] n Vergewaltigung f; (BOT) Raps m ♦ vt vergewaltigen; **~(seed) oil** n Rapsöl nt

rapid ['ræpɪd] adj rasch, schnell; **~ity** [rə'pɪdɪtɪ] n Schnelligkeit f; **~s** npl Stromschnellen pl

rapist ['reɪpɪst] n Vergewaltiger m

rapport [ræ'pɔːr] n gute(s) Verhältnis nt

rapture ['ræptʃər] n Entzücken nt; **rapturous** ['ræptʃərəs] adj (applause) stürmisch; (expression) verzückt

rare [reər] adj selten, rar; (underdone) nicht durchgebraten; **~ly** ['reəlɪ] adv selten

raring ['reərɪŋ] adj: **to be ~ to go** (inf) es kaum erwarten können, bis es losgeht

rarity ['reərɪtɪ] n Seltenheit f

rascal ['rɑːskl] n Schuft m

rash [ræʃ] adj übereilt; (reckless) unbesonnen ♦ n (Haut)ausschlag m

rasher ['ræʃər] n Speckscheibe f

raspberry ['rɑːzbərɪ] n Himbeere f

rasping ['rɑːspɪŋ] adj (noise) kratzend; (voice) krächzend

rat [ræt] n (animal) Ratte f; (person) Halunke m

rate [reɪt] n (proportion) Rate f; (price) Tarif m; (speed) Tempo nt ♦ vt (ein)schätzen; **~s** npl (BRIT: tax) Grundsteuer f; **to ~ as** für etw halten; **~able value** (BRIT) n Einheitswert m (als Bemessungsgrundlage); **~payer** (BRIT) n Steuerzahler(in) m(f)

rather ['rɑːðər] adv (in preference) lieber, eher; (to some extent) ziemlich; **I would** or **I'd ~ go** ich würde lieber gehen; **it's ~ expensive** (quite) es ist ziemlich teuer; (too) es ist etwas zu teuer; **there's ~ a lot** es ist ziemlich viel

ratify ['rætɪfaɪ] vt (POL) ratifizieren

rating ['reɪtɪŋ] n Klasse f

ratio ['reɪʃɪəʊ] n Verhältnis nt; **in the ~ of 100 to 1** im Verhältnis 100 zu 1

ration ['ræʃən] n (usu pl) Ration f ♦ vt rationieren

rational ['ræʃənl] adj rational

rationale [ræʃə'nɑːl] n Grundprinzip nt

rationalize ['ræʃnəlaɪz] vt rationalisieren

rat race n Konkurrenzkampf m

rattle ['rætl] n (sound) Rasseln nt; (toy) Rassel f ♦ vi ratteln, klappern ♦ vt rasseln mit; **~snake** n Klapperschlange f

raucous ['rɔːkəs] *adj* heiser, rau

rave [reɪv] *vi* (*talk wildly*) fantasieren; (*rage*) toben ♦ *n* (*BRIT: inf: party*) Rave *m*, Fete *f*

raven ['reɪvən] *n* Rabe *m*

ravenous ['rævənəs] *adj* heißhungrig

ravine [rə'viːn] *n* Schlucht *f*

raving ['reɪvɪŋ] *adj*: ~ **lunatic** völlig Wahnsinnige(r) *mf*

ravishing ['rævɪʃɪŋ] *adj* atemberaubend

raw [rɔː] *adj* roh; (*tender*) wund (gerieben); (*inexperienced*) unerfahren; **to get a ~ deal** (*inf*) schlecht wegkommen; ~ **material** *n* Rohmaterial *nt*

ray [reɪ] *n* (*of light*) Strahl *m*; ~ **of hope** Hoffnungsschimmer *m*

raze [reɪz] *vt* (*also*: ~ **to the ground**) dem Erdboden gleichmachen

razor ['reɪzəʳ] *n* Rasierapparat *m*; ~ **blade** *n* Rasierklinge *f*

Rd *abbr* = **road**

RE (*BRIT: SCH*) *abbr* (= *religious education*) Religionsunterricht *m*

re [riː] *prep* (*COMM*) betreffs +*gen*

reach [riːtʃ] *n* Reichweite *f*; (*of river*) Strecke *f* ♦ *vt* (*arrive at*) erreichen; (*give*) reichen ♦ *vi* (*stretch*) sich erstrecken; **within ~** (*shops etc*) in erreichbarer Weite *or* Entfernung; **out of ~** außer Reichweite; **to ~ for** (*try to get*) langen nach; ~ **out** *vi* die Hand ausstrecken; **to ~ out for sth** nach etw greifen

react [riː'ækt] *vi* reagieren; ~**ion** [riː'ækʃən] *n* Reaktion *f*; ~**or** [riː'æktəʳ] *n* Reaktor *m*

read¹ [rɛd] *pt, pp of* **read²**

read² [riːd] (*pt, pp* **read**) *vt, vi* lesen; (*aloud*) vorlesen; ~ **out** *vi* vorlesen; ~**able** *adj* leserlich; (*worth ~ing*) lesenswert; ~**er** *n* (*person*) Leser(in) *m(f)*; ~**ership** *n* Leserschaft *f*

readily ['rɛdɪlɪ] *adv* (*willingly*) bereitwillig; (*easily*) prompt

readiness ['rɛdɪnɪs] *n* (*willingness*) Bereitwilligkeit *f*; (*being ready*) Bereitschaft *f*; **in ~** (*prepared*) bereit

reading ['riːdɪŋ] *n* Lesen *nt*

readjust [riːə'dʒʌst] *vt* neu einstellen ♦ *vi* (*person*): **to ~ to** sich wieder anpassen an

+*acc*

ready ['rɛdɪ] *adj* (*prepared, willing*) bereit ♦ *adv*: ~-**cooked** vorgekocht ♦ *n*: **at the ~** bereit; ~-**made** *adj* gebrauchsfertig, Fertig-; (*clothes*) Konfektions-; ~ **money** *n* Bargeld *nt*; ~ **reckoner** *n* Rechentabelle *f*; ~-**to-wear** *adj* Konfektions-

real [rɪəl] *adj* wirklich; (*actual*) eigentlich; (*not fake*) echt; **in ~ terms** effektiv; ~ **estate** *n* Grundbesitz *m*; ~**istic** [rɪə'lɪstɪk] *adj* realistisch

reality [riː'ælɪtɪ] *n* Wirklichkeit *f*, Realität *f*; **in ~** in Wirklichkeit

realization [rɪəlaɪ'zeɪʃən] *n* (*understanding*) Erkenntnis *f*; (*fulfilment*) Verwirklichung *f*

realize ['rɪəlaɪz] *vt* (*understand*) begreifen; (*make real*) verwirklichen; **I didn't ~ ...** ich wusste nicht, ...

really ['rɪəlɪ] *adv* wirklich; ~? (*indicating interest*) tatsächlich?; (*expressing surprise*) wirklich?

realm [rɛlm] *n* Reich *nt*

realtor ['rɪəltɔːʳ] *n* (*US*) *n* Grundstücks-makler(in) *m(f)*

reap [riːp] *vt* ernten

reappear [riːə'pɪəʳ] *vi* wieder erscheinen

rear [rɪəʳ] *adj* hintere(r, s), Rück- ♦ *n* Rückseite *f*; (*last part*) Schluss *m* ♦ *vt* (*bring up*) aufziehen ♦ *vi* (*horse*) sich aufbäumen; ~**guard** *n* Nachhut *f*

rearmament [riː'ɑːməmənt] *n* Wiederaufrüstung *f*

rearrange [riːə'reɪndʒ] *vt* umordnen

rear-view mirror ['rɪəvjuː-] *n* Rückspiegel *m*

reason ['riːzn] *n* (*cause*) Grund *m*; (*ability to think*) Verstand *m*; (*sensible thoughts*) Vernunft *f* ♦ *vi* (*think*) denken; (*use arguments*) argumentieren; **it stands to ~ that** es ist logisch, dass; **to ~ with sb** mit jdm diskutieren; ~**able** *adj* vernünftig; ~**ably** *adv* vernünftig; (*fairly*) ziemlich; ~**ed** *adj* (*argument*) durchdacht; ~**ing** *n* Urteilen *nt*; (*argumentation*) Beweisführung *f*

reassurance [riːə'ʃuərəns] *n* Beruhigung *f*; (*confirmation*) Bestätigung *f*; **reassure** [riːə'ʃuəʳ] *vt* beruhigen; **to reassure sb of**

sth jdm etw versichern

rebate ['riːbeɪt] n Rückzahlung f

rebel [n 'rɛbl, vb rɪ'bɛl] n Rebell m ♦ vi rebellieren; **~lion** [rɪ'bɛljən] n Rebellion f, Aufstand m; **~lious** [rɪ'bɛljəs] adj rebellisch

rebirth [riː'bɜːθ] n Wiedergeburt f

rebound [vb rɪ'baʊnd, n 'riːbaʊnd] vi zurückprallen ♦ n Rückprall m

rebuff [rɪ'bʌf] n Abfuhr f ♦ vt abblitzen lassen

rebuild [riː'bɪld] (irreg) vt wieder aufbauen; (fig) wieder herstellen

rebuke [rɪ'bjuːk] n Tadel m ♦ vt tadeln, rügen

rebut [rɪ'bʌt] vt widerlegen

recall [vb rɪ'kɔːl, n 'riːkɔl] vt (call back) zurückrufen; (remember) sich erinnern an +acc ♦ n Rückruf m

recap ['riːkæp] vt, vi wiederholen

rec'd abbr (= received) Eing.

recede [rɪ'siːd] vi zurückweichen; **receding** adj: **receding hairline** Stirnglatze f

receipt [rɪ'siːt] n (document) Quittung f; (receiving) Empfang m; **~s** npl (ECON) Einnahmen pl

receive [rɪ'siːv] vt erhalten; (visitors etc) empfangen; **~r** n (TEL) Hörer m

recent ['riːsnt] adj vor kurzem (geschehen), neuerlich; (modern) neu; **~ly** adv kürzlich, neulich

receptacle [rɪ'sɛptɪkl] n Behälter m

reception [rɪ'sɛpʃən] n Empfang m; **~ desk** n Empfang m; (in hotel) Rezeption f; **~ist** n (in hotel) Empfangschef m, Empfangsdame f; (MED) Sprechstundenhilfe f

receptive [rɪ'sɛptɪv] adj aufnahmebereit

recess [rɪ'sɛs] n (break) Ferien pl; (hollow) Nische f

recession [rɪ'sɛʃən] n Rezession f

recharge [riː'tʃɑːdʒ] vt (battery) aufladen

recipe ['rɛsɪpɪ] n Rezept nt

recipient [rɪ'sɪpɪənt] n Empfänger m

reciprocal [rɪ'sɪprəkl] adj gegenseitig; (mutual) wechselseitig

recital [rɪ'saɪtl] n Vortrag m

recite [rɪ'saɪt] vt vortragen, aufsagen

reckless ['rɛkləs] adj leichtsinnig; (driving)

fahrlässig

reckon ['rɛkən] vt (count) rechnen, berechnen, errechnen; (estimate) schätzen; (think): **I ~ that ...** ich nehme an, dass ...; **~ on** vt fus rechnen mit; **~ing** n (calculation) Rechnen nt

reclaim [rɪ'kleɪm] vt (expenses) zurückverlangen; (land): **to ~ (from sth)** (etw dat) gewinnen; **reclamation** [rɛklə'meɪʃən] n (of land) Gewinnung f

recline [rɪ'klaɪn] vi sich zurücklehnen; **reclining** adj Liege-

recluse [rɪ'kluːs] n Einsiedler m

recognition [rɛkəg'nɪʃən] n (recognizing) Erkennen nt; (acknowledgement) Anerkennung f; **transformed beyond ~** völlig verändert

recognizable ['rɛkəgnaɪzəbl] adj erkennbar

recognize ['rɛkəgnaɪz] vt erkennen; (POL, approve) anerkennen; **to ~ as** anerkennen als; **to ~ by** erkennen an +dat

recoil [rɪ'kɔɪl] vi (in horror) zurückschrecken; (rebound) zurückprallen; (person): **to ~ from doing sth** davor zurückschrecken, etw zu tun

recollect [rɛkə'lɛkt] vt sich erinnern an +acc; **~ion** [rɛkə'lɛkʃən] n Erinnerung f

recommend [rɛkə'mɛnd] vt empfehlen; **~ation** [rɛkəmən'deɪʃən] n Empfehlung f

recompense ['rɛkəmpɛns] n (compensation) Entschädigung f; (reward) Belohnung f ♦ vt entschädigen; belohnen

reconcile ['rɛkənsaɪl] vt (facts) vereinbaren; (people) versöhnen; **to ~ o.s. to sth** sich mit etw abfinden; **reconciliation** [rɛkənsɪlɪ'eɪʃən] n Versöhnung f

recondition [riːkən'dɪʃən] vt (machine) generalüberholen

reconnoitre [rɛkə'nɔɪtər] (US **reconnoiter**) vt erkunden ♦ vi aufklären

reconsider [riːkən'sɪdər] vt von neuem erwägen, noch einmal überdenken ♦ vi es noch einmal überdenken

reconstruct [riːkən'strʌkt] vt wieder aufbauen; (crime) rekonstruieren

record [n 'rɛkɔːd, vb rɪ'kɔːd] n Aufzeichnung f; (MUS) Schallplatte f; (best performance)

Rekord *m* ♦ *vt* aufzeichnen; *(music etc)* aufnehmen; **off the ~** vertraulichi, im Vertrauen; **in ~ time** in Rekordzeit; **~ card** *n (in file)* Karteikarte *f*; **~ed delivery** *(BRIT) (POST)* Einschreiben *nt*; **~er** *n (TECH)* Registriergerät *nt*; *(MUS)* Blockflöte *f*; **~ holder** *n (SPORT)* Rekordinhaber *m*; **~ing** *n (MUS)* Aufnahme *f*; **~ player** *n* Plattenspieler *m*

recount [rɪˈkaunt] *vt (tell)* berichten

re-count [ˈriːkaunt] *n* Nachzählung *f*

recoup [rɪˈkuːp] *vt:* **to ~ one's losses** seinen Verlust wieder gutmachen

recourse [rɪˈkɔːs] *n:* **to have ~ to** Zuflucht nehmen zu *or* bei

recover [rɪˈkʌvəʳ] *vt (get back)* zurückerhalten ♦ *vi* sich erholen

re-cover [riːˈkʌvəʳ] *vt (quilt etc)* neu überziehen

recovery [rɪˈkʌvərɪ] *n* Wiedererlangung *f*; *(of health)* Erholung *f*

recreate [riːkrɪˈeɪt] *vt* wieder herstellen

recreation [rekrɪˈeɪʃən] *n* Erholung *f*; **~al** *adj* Erholungs-; **~al drug** *n* Freizeitdroge *f*

recrimination [rɪkrɪmɪˈneɪʃən] *n* Gegenbeschuldigung *f*

recruit [rɪˈkruːt] *n* Rekrut *m* ♦ *vt* rekrutieren; **~ment** *n* Rekrutierung *f*

rectangle [ˈrektæŋɡl] *n* Rechteck *nt*; **rectangular** [rekˈtæŋɡjuləʳ] *adj* rechteckig, rechtwinklig

rectify [ˈrektɪfaɪ] *vt* berichtigen

rector [ˈrektəʳ] *n (REL)* Pfarrer *m*; *(SCH)* Direktor(in) *m(f)*; **~y** [ˈrektərɪ] *n* Pfarrhaus *nt*

recuperate [rɪˈkjuːpəreɪt] *vi* sich erholen

recur [rɪˈkɜːʳ] *vi* sich wiederholen; **~rence** *n* Wiederholung *f*; **~rent** *adj* wiederkehrend

recycle [riːˈsaɪkl] *vt* wieder verwerten, wieder aufbereiten; **recycling** *n* Recycling *nt*

red [red] *n* Rot *nt*; *(POL)* Rote(r) *m* ♦ *adj* rot; **in the ~** in den roten Zahlen; **~ carpet treatment** *n* Sonderbehandlung *f*, große(r) Bahnhof *m*; **R~ Cross** *n* Rote(s) Kreuz *nt*; **~currant** *n* rote Johannisbeere *f*; **~den** *vi* sich röten; *(blush)* erröten ♦ *vt* röten; **~dish** *adj* rötlich

redecorate [riːˈdekəreɪt] *vt* neu tapezieren, neu streichen

redeem [rɪˈdiːm] *vt (COMM)* einlösen; *(save)* retten; **~ing** *adj:* **~ing feature** *n* versöhnende(s) Moment *nt*

redeploy [riːdɪˈplɔɪ] *vt (resources)* umverteilen

red: ~-haired [redˈhɛəd] *adj* rothaarig; **~-handed** [redˈhændɪd] *adv:* **to be caught ~-handed** auf frischer Tat ertappt werden; **~head** [ˈredhɛd] *n* Rothaarige(r) *mf*; **~ herring** *n* Ablenkungsmanöver *nt*; **~-hot** [redˈhɔt] *adj* rot glühend

redirect [riːdaɪˈrekt] *vt* umleiten

red light *n:* **to go through a ~** *(AUT)* bei Rot über die Ampel fahren; **red-light district** *n* Strichviertel *nt*

redo [riːˈduː] *(irreg: like* **do***) vt* nochmals machen

redolent [ˈredələnt] *adj:* **~ of** *(fig)* erinnernd an +*acc*

redouble [riːˈdʌbl] *vt:* **to ~ one's efforts** seine Anstrengungen verdoppeln

redress [rɪˈdres] *vt* wieder gutmachen

red: R~ Sea *n:* **the R~ Sea** das Rote Meer; **~skin** [ˈredskɪn] *n* Rothaut *f*; **~ tape** *n* Bürokratismus *m*

reduce [rɪˈdjuːs] *vt (speed, temperature)* vermindern; *(photo)* verkleinern; **"~ speed now"** *(AUT)* ≃ „langsam"; **to ~ the price (to)** den Preis herabsetzen (auf +*acc*); **at a ~d price** zum ermäßigten Preis

reduction [rɪˈdʌkʃən] *n* Verminderung *f*; Verkleinerung *f*; Herabsetzung *f*; *(amount of money)* Nachlass *m*

redundancy [rɪˈdʌndənsɪ] *n* Überflüssigkeit *f*; *(of workers)* Entlassung *f*

redundant [rɪˈdʌndnt] *adj* überflüssig; *(workers)* ohne Arbeitsplatz; **to be made ~** arbeitslos werden

reed [riːd] *n* Schilf *nt*; *(MUS)* Rohrblatt *nt*

reef [riːf] *n* Riff *nt*

reek [riːk] *vi:* **to ~ (of)** stinken (nach)

reel [riːl] *n* Spule *f*, Rolle *f* ♦ *vt (also:* **~ in***)* wickeln, spulen ♦ *vi (stagger)* taumeln

ref [ref] *(inf) n abbr (=* **referee***)* Schiri *m*

refectory [rɪˈfektərɪ] *n (UNIV)* Mensa *f*; *(SCH)*

Speisesaal m; (ECCL) Refektorium nt

refer [rɪ'fɜːʳ] vt: **to ~ sb to sb/sth** jdn an jdn/etw verweisen ♦ vi: **to ~ to** (to book) nachschlagen in +dat; (mention) sich beziehen auf +acc

referee [refə'riː] n Schiedsrichter m; (BRIT: for job) Referenz f ♦ vt schiedsrichtern

reference ['refrəns] n (for job) Referenz f; (in book) Verweis m; (number, code) Aktenzeichen nt; (allusion): **~ (to)** Anspielung (auf +acc); **with ~ to** in Bezug auf +acc; **~ book** n Nachschlagewerk nt; **~ number** n Aktenzeichen nt

referenda [refə'rendə] npl of **referendum**

referendum [refə'rendəm] (pl **-da**) n Volksabstimmung f

refill [vb riː'fɪl, n 'riːfɪl] vt nachfüllen ♦ n (for pen) Ersatzmine f

refine [rɪ'faɪn] vt (purify) raffinieren; **~d** adj kultiviert; **~ment** n Kultiviertheit f; **~ry** n Raffinerie f

reflect [rɪ'flekt] vt (light) reflektieren; (fig) (wider)spiegeln ♦ vi (meditate): **to ~ (on)** nachdenken (über +acc); **it ~s badly/well on him** das stellt ihn in ein schlechtes/ gutes Licht; **~ion** [rɪ'flekʃən] n Reflexion f; (image) Spiegelbild nt; (thought) Überlegung f; **on ~ion** wenn man sich dat das recht überlegt

reflex ['riːfleks] adj Reflex- ♦ n Reflex m; **~ive** [rɪ'fleksɪv] adj reflexiv

reform [rɪ'fɔːm] n Reform f ♦ vt (person) bessern; **~atory** (US) n Besserungsanstalt f

refrain [rɪ'freɪn] vi: **to ~ from** unterlassen ♦ n Refrain m

refresh [rɪ'freʃ] vt erfrischen; **~er course** (BRIT) n Wiederholungskurs m; **~ing** adj erfrischend; **~ments** npl Erfrischungen pl

refrigeration [rɪfrɪdʒə'reɪʃən] n Kühlung f

refrigerator [rɪ'frɪdʒəreɪtəʳ] n Kühlschrank m

refuel [riː'fjuəl] vt, vi auftanken

refuge ['refjuːdʒ] n Zuflucht f; **to take ~ in** sich flüchten in +acc; **~e** [refju'dʒiː] n Flüchtling m

refund [n 'riːfʌnd, vb rɪ'fʌnd] n Rückvergütung f ♦ vt zurückerstatten

refurbish [riː'fɜːbɪʃ] vt aufpolieren

refusal [rɪ'fjuːzəl] n (Ver)weigerung f; **first ~** Vorkaufsrecht nt

refuse¹ [rɪ'fjuːz] vt abschlagen ♦ vi sich weigern

refuse² ['refjuːs] n Abfall m, Müll m; **~ collection** n Müllabfuhr f

refute [rɪ'fjuːt] vt widerlegen

regain [rɪ'geɪn] vt wiedergewinnen; (consciousness) wiedererlangen

regal ['riːgl] adj königlich

regalia [rɪ'geɪlɪə] npl Insignien pl

regard [rɪ'gɑːd] n Achtung f ♦ vt ansehen; **to send one's ~s to sb** jdn grüßen lassen; **"with kindest ~s"** „mit freundlichen Grüßen"; **~ing** or **as ~s** or **with ~ to** bezüglich +gen, in Bezug auf +acc; **~less** adj: **~less of** ohne Rücksicht auf +acc ♦ adv trotzdem

regenerate [rɪ'dʒenəreɪt] vt erneuern

régime [reɪ'ʒiːm] n Regime nt

regiment [n 'redʒɪmənt, vb 'redʒɪment] n Regiment nt ♦ vt (fig) reglementieren; **~al** [redʒɪ'mentl] adj Regiments-

region ['riːdʒən] n Region f; **in the ~ of** (fig) so um; **~al** adj örtlich, regional

register ['redʒɪstəʳ] n Register nt ♦ vt (list) registrieren; (emotion) zeigen; (write down) eintragen ♦ vi (at hotel) sich eintragen; (with police) sich melden; (make impression) wirken, ankommen; **~ed** (BRIT) adj (letter) Einschreibe-, eingeschrieben; **~ed trademark** n eingetragene(s) Warenzeichen nt

registrar ['redʒɪstrɑː] n Standesbeamte(r) m

registration [redʒɪs'treɪʃən] n (act) Registrierung f; (AUT: also: **~ number**) polizeiliche(s) Kennzeichen nt

registry ['redʒɪstrɪ] n Sekretariat nt; **~ office** (BRIT) n Standesamt nt; **to get married in a ~ office** standesamtlich heiraten

regret [rɪ'gret] n Bedauern nt ♦ vt bedauern; **~fully** adv mit Bedauern, ungern; **~table** adj bedauerlich

regroup [riː'gruːp] vt umgruppieren ♦ vi sich umgruppieren

regular ['regjuləʳ] adj regelmäßig; (usual) üblich; (inf) regelrecht ♦ n (client etc)

Stammkunde *m*; **~ity** [regju'lærɪtɪ] *n*
Regelmäßigkeit *f*; **~ly** *adv* regelmäßig
regulate ['regjuleɪt] *vt* regeln, regulieren;
regulation [regju'leɪʃən] *n* (*rule*) Vorschrift *f*;
(*control*) Regulierung *f*
rehabilitation ['ri:əbɪlɪ'teɪʃən] *n* (*of criminal*)
Resozialisierung *f*
rehearsal [rɪ'hɜːsəl] *n* Probe *f*
rehearse [rɪ'hɜːs] *vt* proben
reign [reɪn] *n* Herrschaft *f* ♦ *vi* herrschen
reimburse [riːɪm'bɜːs] *vt*: **to ~ sb for sth**
jdn für etw entschädigen, jdm etw
zurückzahlen
rein [reɪn] *n* Zügel *m*
reincarnation [riːɪnkɑː'neɪʃən] *n*
Wiedergeburt *f*
reindeer ['reɪndɪə'] *n* Ren *nt*
reinforce [riːɪn'fɔːs] *vt* verstärken; **~d**
concrete *n* Stahlbeton *m*; **~ment** *n*
Verstärkung *f*; **~ments** *npl* (*MIL*)
Verstärkungstruppen *pl*
reinstate [riːɪn'steɪt] *vt* wieder einsetzen
reissue [riː'ɪʃjuː] *vt* neu herausgeben
reiterate [riː'ɪtəreɪt] *vt* wiederholen
reject [*n* 'riːdʒekt, *vb* rɪ'dʒekt] *n* (*COMM*)
Ausschuss(artikel) *m* ♦ *vt* ablehnen; **~ion**
[rɪ'dʒekʃən] *n* Zurückweisung *f*
rejoice [rɪ'dʒɔɪs] *vi*: **to ~ at** *or* **over** sich
freuen über +*acc*
rejuvenate [rɪ'dʒuːvəneɪt] *vt* verjüngen
rekindle [riː'kɪndl] *vt* wieder anfachen
relapse [rɪ'læps] *n* Rückfall *m*
relate [rɪ'leɪt] *vt* (*tell*) erzählen; (*connect*)
verbinden ♦ *vi*: **to ~ to** zusammenhängen
mit; (*form relationship*) eine Beziehung
aufbauen zu; **~d** *adj*: **~d (to)** verwandt
(mit); **relating** *prep*: **relating to** bezüglich
+*gen*; **relation** [rɪ'leɪʃən] *n* Verwandte(r) *mf*;
(*connection*) Beziehung *f*; **relationship** *n*
Verhältnis *nt*, Beziehung *f*
relative ['relətɪv] *n* Verwandte(r) *mf* ♦ *adj*
relativ; **~ly** *adv* verhältnismäßig
relax [rɪ'læks] *vi* (*slacken*) sich lockern;
(*muscles, person*) sich entspannen ♦ *vt* (*ease*)
lockern, entspannen; **~ation** [riː'læk'seɪʃən] *n*
Entspannung *f*; **~ed** *adj* entspannt, locker;
~ing *adj* entspannend

relay [*n* 'riːleɪ, *vb* rɪ'leɪ] *n* (*SPORT*) Staffel *f* ♦ *vt*
(*message*) weiterleiten; (*RAD, TV*) übertragen
release [rɪ'liːs] *n* (*freedom*) Entlassung *f*;
(*TECH*) Auslöser *m* ♦ *vt* befreien; (*prisoner*)
entlassen; (*report, news*) verlautbaren,
bekannt geben
relegate ['reləgeɪt] *vt* (*SPORT*): **to be ~d**
absteigen
relent [rɪ'lent] *vi* nachgeben; **~less** *adj*
unnachgiebig
relevant ['reləvənt] *adj* wichtig, relevant; **~**
to relevant für
reliability [rɪlaɪə'bɪlɪtɪ] *n* Zuverlässigkeit *f*
reliable [rɪ'laɪəbl] *adj* zuverlässig; **reliably**
adv zuverlässig; **to be reliably informed**
that ... aus zuverlässiger Quelle wissen,
dass ...
reliance [rɪ'laɪəns] *n*: **~ (on)** Abhängigkeit *f*
(von)
relic ['relɪk] *n* (*from past*) Überbleibsel *nt*;
(*REL*) Reliquie *f*
relief [rɪ'liːf] *n* Erleichterung *f*; (*help*) Hilfe *f*;
(*person*) Ablösung *f*
relieve [rɪ'liːv] *vt* (*ease*) erleichtern; (*help*)
entlasten; (*person*) ablösen; **to ~ sb of sth**
jdm etw abnehmen; **to ~ o.s.** (*euph*) sich
erleichtern (*euph*); **~d** *adj* erleichtert
religion [rɪ'lɪdʒən] *n* Religion *f*; **religious**
[rɪ'lɪdʒəs] *adj* religiös
relinquish [rɪ'lɪŋkwɪʃ] *vt* aufgeben
relish ['relɪʃ] *n* Würze *f* ♦ *vt* genießen; **to ~**
doing gern tun
relocate [riːləu'keɪt] *vt* verlegen ♦ *vi*
umziehen
reluctance [rɪ'lʌktəns] *n* Widerstreben *nt*,
Abneigung *f*
reluctant [rɪ'lʌktənt] *adj* widerwillig; **~ly** *adv*
ungern
rely [rɪ'laɪ] *vt fus*: **to ~ on** sich verlassen auf
+*acc*
remain [rɪ'meɪn] *vi* (*be left*) übrig bleiben;
(*stay*) bleiben; **~der** *n* Rest *m*; **~ing** *adj*
übrig (geblieben); **~s** *npl* Überreste *pl*
remake ['riːmeɪk] *n* (*CINE*) Neuverfilmung *f*
remand [rɪ'mɑːnd] *n*: **on ~** in
Untersuchungshaft ♦ *vt*: **to ~ in custody** in
Untersuchungshaft schicken; **~ home**

(BRIT) n Untersuchungsgefängnis nt für Jugendliche

remark [rɪ'mɑːk] n Bemerkung f ♦ vt bemerken; **~able** adj bemerkenswert; **remarkably** adv außergewöhnlich

remarry [riː'mæri] vi sich wieder verheiraten

remedial [rɪ'miːdɪəl] adj Heil-; (teaching) Hilfsschul-

remedy ['remədi] n Mittel nt ♦ vt (pain) abhelfen +dat; (trouble) in Ordnung bringen

remember [rɪ'membər] vt sich erinnern an +acc; **remembrance** [rɪ'membrəns] n Erinnerung f; (official) Gedenken nt; **R~ Day** n ≈ Volkstrauertag m

---
Remembrance Day
---

i Remembrance Day **oder**
Remembrance Sunday *ist der britische Gedenktag für die Gefallenen der beiden Weltkriege und anderer Konflikte. Er fällt auf einen Sonntag vor oder nach dem 11. November (am 11. November 1918 endete der erste Weltkrieg) und wird mit einer Schweigeminute, Kranzniederlegungen an Kriegerdenkmälern und dem Tragen von Ansteckbadeln in Form einer Mohnblume begangen.*
---

remind [rɪ'maɪnd] vt: **to ~ sb to do sth** jdn daran erinnern, etw zu tun; **to ~ sb of sth** jdn an etw acc erinnern; **she ~s me of her mother** sie erinnert mich an ihre Mutter; **~er** n Mahnung f

reminisce [remɪ'nɪs] vi in Erinnerungen schwelgen; **~nt** [remɪ'nɪsnt] adj: **to be ~nt of sth** an etw acc erinnern

remiss [rɪ'mɪs] adj nachlässig

remission [rɪ'mɪʃən] n Nachlass m; (of debt, sentence) Erlass m

remit [rɪ'mɪt] vt (money): **to ~ (to)** überweisen (an +acc); **~tance** n Geldanweisung f

remnant ['remnənt] n Rest m; **~s** npl (COMM) Einzelstücke pl

remorse [rɪ'mɔːs] n Gewissensbisse pl; **~ful** adj reumütig; **~less** adj unbarmherzig

remote [rɪ'məut] adj abgelegen; (slight)

gering; **~ control** n Fernsteuerung f; **~ly** adv entfernt

remould ['riːməuld] (BRIT) n runderneuerte(r) Reifen m

removable [rɪ'muːvbl] adj entfernbar

removal [rɪ'muːvəl] n Beseitigung f; (of furniture) Umzug m; (from office) Entlassung f; **~ van** (BRIT) n Möbelwagen m

remove [rɪ'muːv] vt beseitigen, entfernen; **~rs** npl Möbelspedition f

remuneration [rɪmjuːnə'reɪʃən] n Vergütung f, Honorar nt

render ['rendər] vt machen; (translate) übersetzen; **~ing** n (MUS) Wiedergabe f

rendezvous ['rɒndɪvuː] n (meeting) Rendezvous nt; (place) Treffpunkt m ♦ vi sich treffen

renew [rɪ'njuː] vt erneuern; (contract, licence) verlängern; (replace) ersetzen; **~able** adj regenerierbar; **~al** n Erneuerung f; Verlängerung f

renounce [rɪ'nauns] vt (give up) verzichten auf +acc; (disown) verstoßen

renovate ['renəveɪt] vt renovieren; (building) restaurieren

renown [rɪ'naun] n Ruf m; **~ed** adj namhaft

rent [rent] n Miete f; (for land) Pacht f ♦ vt (hold as tenant) mieten; pachten; (let) vermieten; verpachten; (car etc) mieten; (firm) vermieten; **~al** n Miete f

renunciation [rɪnʌnsɪ'eɪʃən] n: **~ (of)** Verzicht m (auf +acc)

reorganize [riː'ɔːgənaɪz] vt umgestalten, reorganisieren

rep [rep] n abbr (COMM) = **representative**; (THEAT) = **repertory**

repair [rɪ'peər] n Reparatur f ♦ vt reparieren; (damage) wieder gutmachen; **in good/bad ~** in gutem/schlechtem Zustand; **~ kit** n Werkzeugkasten m

repartee [repɑː'tiː] n Witzeleien pl

repatriate [riː'pætrɪeɪt] vt in die Heimat zurückschicken

repay [riː'peɪ] (irreg) vt zurückzahlen; (reward) vergelten; **~ment** n Rückzahlung f; (fig) Vergeltung f

repeal [rɪ'piːl] vt aufheben

repeat [rɪ'piːt] n (RAD, TV) Wiederholung(ssendung) f ♦ vt wiederholen; ~**edly** adv wiederholt

repel [rɪ'pel] vt (drive back) zurückschlagen; (disgust) abstoßen; ~**lent** adj abstoßend ♦ n: **insect ~lent** Insektenmittel nt

repent [rɪ'pent] vt, vi: **to ~ (of)** bereuen; ~**ance** n Reue f

repercussion [riːpə'kʌʃən] n Auswirkung f; **to have ~s** ein Nachspiel haben

repertory ['repətərɪ] n Repertoire nt

repetition [repɪ'tɪʃən] n Wiederholung f

repetitive [rɪ'petɪtɪv] adj sich wiederholend

replace [rɪ'pleɪs] vt ersetzen; (put back) zurückstellen; ~**ment** n Ersatz m

replay ['riːpleɪ] n (of match) Wiederholungsspiel nt; (of tape, film) Wiederholung f

replenish [rɪ'plenɪʃ] vt ergänzen

replica ['replɪkə] n Kopie f

reply [rɪ'plaɪ] n Antwort f ♦ vi antworten; ~ **coupon** n Antwortschein m

report [rɪ'pɔːt] n Bericht m; (BRIT: SCH) Zeugnis nt ♦ vt (tell) berichten; (give information against) melden; (to police) anzeigen ♦ vi (make ~) Bericht erstatten; (present o.s.): **to ~ (to sb)** sich (bei jdm) melden; ~ **card** n (US, SCOTTISH) Zeugnis nt; ~**edly** adv wie verlautet; ~**er** n Reporter m

reprehensible [reprɪ'hensɪbl] adj tadelnswert

represent [reprɪ'zent] vt darstellen; (speak for) vertreten; ~**ation** [reprɪzen'teɪʃən] n Darstellung f; (being ~ed) Vertretung f; ~**ations** npl (protest) Vorhaltungen pl; ~**ative** n (person) Vertreter m; (US: POL) Abgeordnete(r) mf ♦ adj repräsentativ

repress [rɪ'pres] vt unterdrücken; ~**ion** [rɪ'preʃən] n Unterdrückung f

reprieve [rɪ'priːv] n (JUR) Begnadigung f; (fig) Gnadenfrist f ♦ vt (JUR) begnadigen

reprimand ['reprɪmɑːnd] n Verweis m ♦ vt einen Verweis erteilen +dat

reprint [n 'riːprɪnt, vb riː'prɪnt] n Neudruck m ♦ vt wieder abdrucken

reprisal [rɪ'praɪzl] n Vergeltung f

reproach [rɪ'prəutʃ] n Vorwurf m ♦ vt Vorwürfe machen +dat; **to ~ sb with sth** jdm etw vorwerfen; ~**ful** adj vorwurfsvoll

reproduce [riːprə'djuːs] vt reproduzieren ♦ vi (have offspring) sich vermehren; **reproduction** [riːprə'dʌkʃən] n (ART, PHOT) Reproduktion f; (breeding) Fortpflanzung f; **reproductive** [riːprə'dʌktɪv] adj reproduktiv; (breeding) Fortpflanzungs-

reprove [rɪ'pruːv] vt tadeln

reptile ['reptaɪl] n Reptil nt

republic [rɪ'pʌblɪk] n Republik f

repudiate [rɪ'pjuːdɪeɪt] vt zurückweisen

repugnant [rɪ'pʌgnənt] adj widerlich

repulse [rɪ'pʌls] vt (drive back) zurückschlagen; (reject) abweisen

repulsive [rɪ'pʌlsɪv] adj abstoßend

reputable ['repjutəbl] adj angesehen

reputation [repju'teɪʃən] n Ruf m

reputed [rɪ'pjuːtɪd] adj angeblich; ~**ly** [rɪ'pjuːtɪdlɪ] adv angeblich

request [rɪ'kwest] n Bitte f ♦ vt (thing) erbitten; **to ~ sth of or from sb** jdn um etw bitten; (formally) jdn um etw ersuchen; ~ **stop** n (BRIT) Bedarfshaltestelle f

require [rɪ'kwaɪə*] vt (need) brauchen; (demand) erfordern; ~**ment** n (condition) Anforderung f; (need) Bedarf m

requisite ['rekwɪzɪt] adj erforderlich

requisition [rekwɪ'zɪʃən] n Anforderung f ♦ vt beschlagnahmen

rescue ['reskjuː] n Rettung f ♦ vt retten; ~ **party** n Rettungsmannschaft f; ~**r** n Retter m

research [rɪ'səːtʃ] n Forschung f ♦ vi forschen ♦ vt erforschen; ~**er** n Forscher m

resemblance [rɪ'zembləns] n Ähnlichkeit f

resemble [rɪ'zembl] vt ähneln +dat

resent [rɪ'zent] vt übel nehmen; ~**ful** adj nachtragend, empfindlich; ~**ment** n Verstimmung f, Unwille m

reservation [rezə'veɪʃən] n (booking) Reservierung f; (THEAT) Vorbestellung f; (doubt) Vorbehalt m; (land) Reservat nt

reserve [rɪ'zəːv] n (store) Vorrat m, Reserve f; (manner) Zurückhaltung f; (game ~) Naturschutzgebiet nt; (SPORT)

Ersatzspieler(in) *m(f)* ♦ *vt* reservieren; (*judgement*) sich *dat* vorbehalten; **~s** *npl* (*MIL*) Reserve *f*; **in ~** in Reserve; **~d** *adj* reserviert

reshuffle [riːˈʃʌfl] *n* (*POL*): **cabinet ~** Kabinettsumbildung *f* ♦ *vt* (*POL*) umbilden

reside [rɪˈzaɪd] *vi* wohnen, ansässig sein

residence [ˈrezɪdəns] *n* (*house*) Wohnsitz *m*; (*living*) Aufenthalt *m*; **~ permit** (*BRIT*) *n* Aufenthaltserlaubnis *f*

resident [ˈrezɪdənt] *n* (*in house*) Bewohner *m*; (*in area*) Einwohner *m* ♦ *adj* wohnhaft, ansässig; **~ial** [rezɪˈdenʃəl] *adj* Wohn-

residue [ˈrezɪdjuː] *n* Rest *m*; (*CHEM*) Rückstand *m*; (*fig*) Bodensatz *m*

resign [rɪˈzaɪn] *vt* (*office*) aufgeben, zurücktreten von ♦ *vi* (*from office*) zurücktreten; (*employee*) kündigen; **to be ~ed to sth, to ~ o.s. to sth** sich mit etw abfinden; **~ation** [rezɪɡˈneɪʃən] *n* (*from job*) Kündigung *f*; (*POL*) Rücktritt *m*; (*submission*) Resignation *f*; **~ed** *adj* resigniert

resilience [rɪˈzɪlɪəns] *n* Spannkraft *f*; (*of person*) Unverwüstlichkeit *f*; **resilient** [rɪˈzɪlɪənt] *adj* unverwüstlich

resin [ˈrezɪn] *n* Harz *nt*

resist [rɪˈzɪst] *vt* widerstehen +*dat*; **~ance** *n* Widerstand *m*

resit [*vb* riːˈsɪt, *n* ˈriːsɪt] *vt* (*exam*) wiederholen ♦ *n* Wiederholung(sprüfung) *f*

resolute [ˈrezəluːt] *adj* entschlossen, resolut; **resolution** [rezəˈluːʃən] *n* (*firmness*) Entschlossenheit *f*; (*intention*) Vorsatz *m*; (*decision*) Beschluss *m*

resolve [rɪˈzɒlv] *n* Entschlossenheit *f* ♦ *vt* (*decide*) beschließen ♦ *vi* sich lösen; **~d** *adj* (*fest*) entschlossen

resonant [ˈrezənənt] *adj* voll

resort [rɪˈzɔːt] *n* (*holiday place*) Erholungsort *m*; (*help*) Zuflucht *f* ♦ *vi*: **to ~ to** Zuflucht nehmen zu; **as a last ~** als letzter Ausweg

resound [rɪˈzaʊnd] *vi*: **to ~ (with)** widerhallen (von); **~ing** *adj* nachhallend; (*success*) groß

resource [rɪˈsɔːs] *n* Findigkeit *f*; **~s** *npl* (*financial*) Geldmittel *pl*; (*natural*) Bodenschätze *pl*; **~ful** *adj* findig

respect [rɪsˈpekt] *n* Respekt *m* ♦ *vt* achten, respektieren; **~s** *npl* (*regards*) Grüße *pl*; **with ~ to** in Bezug auf +*acc*, hinsichtlich +*gen*; **in this ~** in dieser Hinsicht; **~able** *adj* anständig; (*not bad*) leidlich; **~ful** *adj* höflich

respective [rɪsˈpektɪv] *adj* jeweilig; **~ly** *adv* beziehungsweise

respiration [respɪˈreɪʃən] *n* Atmung *f*

respite [ˈrespaɪt] *n* Ruhepause *f*

resplendent [rɪsˈplendənt] *adj* strahlend

respond [rɪsˈpɒnd] *vi* antworten; (*react*): **to ~ (to)** reagieren (auf +*acc*); **response** [rɪsˈpɒns] *n* Antwort *f*; Reaktion *f*; (*to advert*) Resonanz *f*

responsibility [rɪspɒnsɪˈbɪlɪtɪ] *n* Verantwortung *f*

responsible [rɪsˈpɒnsɪbl] *adj* verantwortlich; (*reliable*) verantwortungsvoll

responsive [rɪsˈpɒnsɪv] *adj* empfänglich

rest [rest] *n* Ruhe *f*; (*break*) Pause *f*; (*remainder*) Rest *m* ♦ *vi* sich ausruhen; (*be supported*) (auf)liegen ♦ *vt* (*lean*): **to ~ sth on/against sth** etw gegen etw *acc* lehnen; **the ~ of them** die Übrigen; **it ~s with him to ...** es liegt bei ihm, zu ...

restaurant [ˈrestərɒŋ] *n* Restaurant *nt*; **~ car** (*BRIT*) *n* Speisewagen *m*

restful [ˈrestful] *adj* erholsam, ruhig

rest home *n* Erholungsheim *nt*

restive [ˈrestɪv] *adj* unruhig

restless [ˈrestlɪs] *adj* unruhig

restoration [restəˈreɪʃən] *n* Rückgabe *f*; (*of building etc*) Rückerstattung *f*

restore [rɪsˈtɔː] *vt* (*order*) wieder herstellen; (*customs*) wieder einführen; (*person to position*) wieder einsetzen; (*give back*) zurückgeben; (*style etc*) restaurieren

restrain [rɪsˈtreɪn] *vt* zurückhalten; (*curiosity etc*) beherrschen; (*person*): **to ~ sb from doing sth** jdn davon abhalten, etw zu tun; **~ed** *adj* (*style etc*) gedämpft, verhalten; **~t** *n* (*self-control*) Zurückhaltung *f*

restrict [rɪsˈtrɪkt] *vt* einschränken; **~ion** [rɪsˈtrɪkʃən] *n* Einschränkung *f*; **~ive** *adj* einschränkend

rest room (*US*) *n* Toilette *f*

restructure [riːˈstrʌktʃəʳ] vt umstrukturieren

result [rɪˈzʌlt] n Resultat nt, Folge f; (of exam, game) Ergebnis nt ♦ vi: **to ~ in sth** etw zur Folge haben; **as a ~ of** als Folge +gen

resume [rɪˈzjuːm] vt fortsetzen; (occupy again) wieder einnehmen ♦ vi (work etc) wieder beginnen

résumé [ˈreɪzjuːmeɪ] n Zusammenfassung f

resumption [rɪˈzʌmpʃən] n Wiederaufnahme f

resurgence [rɪˈsəːdʒəns] n Wiedererwachen nt

resurrection [rezəˈrekʃən] n Auferstehung f

resuscitate [rɪˈsʌsɪteɪt] vt wieder beleben; **resuscitation** [rɪsʌsɪˈteɪʃən] n Wiederbelebung f

retail [n, adj ˈriːteɪl, vb riːˈteɪl] n Einzelhandel m ♦ adj Einzelhandels- ♦ vt im Kleinen verkaufen ♦ vi im Einzelhandel kosten; **~er** [ˈriːteɪləʳ] n Einzelhändler m, Kleinhändler m; **~ price** n Ladenpreis m

retain [rɪˈteɪn] vt (keep) (zurück)behalten; **~er** n (fee) (Honorar)vorschuss m

retaliate [rɪˈtælɪeɪt] vi zum Vergeltungsschlag ausholen; **retaliation** [rɪtælɪˈeɪʃən] n Vergeltung f

retarded [rɪˈtɑːdɪd] adj zurückgeblieben

retch [retʃ] vi würgen

retentive [rɪˈtentɪv] adj (memory) gut

reticent [ˈretɪsnt] adj schweigsam

retina [ˈretɪnə] n Netzhaut f

retire [rɪˈtaɪəʳ] vi (from work) in den Ruhestand treten; (withdraw) sich zurückziehen; (go to bed) schlafen gehen; **~d** adj (person) pensioniert, im Ruhestand; **~ment** n Ruhestand m

retiring [rɪˈtaɪərɪŋ] adj zurückhaltend

retort [rɪˈtɔːt] n (reply) Erwiderung f ♦ vi (scharf) erwidern

retrace [riːˈtreɪs] vt zurückverfolgen; **to ~ one's steps** denselben Weg zurückgehen

retract [rɪˈtrækt] vt (statement) zurücknehmen; (claws) einziehen ♦ vi einen Rückzieher machen; **~able** adj (aerial) ausziehbar

retrain [riːˈtreɪn] vt umschulen

retread [ˈriːtred] n (tyre) Reifen m mit erneuerter Lauffläche

retreat [rɪˈtriːt] n Rückzug m; (place) Zufluchtsort m ♦ vi sich zurückziehen

retribution [retrɪˈbjuːʃən] n Strafe f

retrieval [rɪˈtriːvəl] n Wiedergewinnung f

retrieve [rɪˈtriːv] vt wiederbekommen; (rescue) retten; **~r** n Apportierhund m

retrograde [ˈretrəgreɪd] adj (step) Rück-; (policy) rückschrittlich

retrospect [ˈretrəspekt] n: **in ~** im Rückblick, rückblickend; **~ive** [retrəˈspektɪv] adj (action) rückwirkend; (look) rückblickend

return [rɪˈtəːn] n Rückkehr f; (profits) Ertrag m; (BRIT: rail ticket etc) Rückfahrkarte f; (: plane ticket) Rückflugkarte f ♦ adj (journey, match) Rück- ♦ vi zurückkehren, zurückkommen ♦ vt zurückgeben, zurücksenden; (pay back) zurückzahlen; (elect) wählen; (verdict) aussprechen; **~s** npl (COMM) Gewinn m; (receipts) Einkünfte pl; **in ~** dafür; **by ~ of post** postwendend; **many happy ~s!** herzlichen Glückwunsch zum Geburtstag!

reunion [riːˈjuːnɪən] n Wiedervereinigung f; (SCH etc) Treffen nt

reunite [riːjuːˈnaɪt] vt wieder vereinigen

reuse [riːˈjuːz] vt wieder verwenden, wieder verwerten

rev [rev] n abbr (AUT: = revolution) Drehzahl f

revamp [riːˈvæmp] vt aufpolieren

reveal [rɪˈviːl] vt enthüllen; **~ing** adj aufschlussreich

revel [ˈrevl] vi: **to ~ in sth/in doing sth** seine Freude an etw dat haben/daran haben, etw zu tun

revelation [revəˈleɪʃən] n Offenbarung f

revelry [ˈrevlrɪ] n Rummel m

revenge [rɪˈvendʒ] n Rache f; **to take ~ on** sich rächen an +dat

revenue [ˈrevənjuː] n Einnahmen pl

reverberate [rɪˈvəːbəreɪt] vi widerhallen

revere [rɪˈvɪəʳ] vt (ver)ehren; **~nce** [ˈrevərəns] n Ehrfurcht f

Reverend [ˈrevərənd] adj: **the ~ Robert Martin** ≃ Pfarrer Robert Martin

reversal [rɪˈvəːsl] n Umkehrung f

reverse [rɪˈvəːs] n Rückseite f; (AUT: gear)

Rückwärtsgang m ♦ adj (order, direction) entgegengesetzt ♦ vt umkehren ♦ vi (BRIT: AUT) rückwärts fahren; **~-charge call** (BRIT) n R-Gespräch nt; **reversing lights** npl (AUT) Rückfahrscheinwerfer pl

revert [rɪ'vəːt] vi: **to ~ to** zurückkehren zu; (to bad state) zurückfallen in +acc

review [rɪ'vjuː] n (of book) Rezension f; (magazine) Zeitschrift f ♦ vt Rückschau halten auf +acc; (MIL) mustern; (book) rezensieren; (reexamine) von neuem untersuchen; **~er** n (critic) Rezensent m

revise [rɪ'vaɪz] vt (book) überarbeiten; (reconsider) ändern, revidieren; **revision** [rɪ'vɪʒən] n Prüfung f; (COMM) Revision f; (SCH) Wiederholung f

revitalize [riː'vaɪtəlaɪz] vt neu beleben

revival [rɪ'vaɪvəl] n Wiederbelebung f; (REL) Erweckung f; (THEAT) Wiederaufnahme f

revive [rɪ'vaɪv] vt wieder beleben; (fig) wieder auffrischen ♦ vi wieder erwachen; (fig) wieder aufleben

revoke [rɪ'vəuk] vt aufheben

revolt [rɪ'vəult] n Aufstand m, Revolte f ♦ vi sich auflehnen ♦ vt entsetzen; **~ing** adj widerlich

revolution [revə'luːʃən] n (turn) Umdrehung f; (POL) Revolution f; **~ary** adj revolutionär ♦ n Revolutionär m; **~ize** vt revolutionieren

revolve [rɪ'vɔlv] vi kreisen; (on own axis) sich drehen

revolver [rɪ'vɔlvə*] n Revolver m

revolving door [rɪ'vɔlvɪŋ-] n Drehtür f

revulsion [rɪ'vʌlʃən] n Ekel m

reward [rɪ'wɔːd] n Belohnung f ♦ vt belohnen; **~ing** adj lohnend

rewind [riː'waɪnd] (irreg: like **wind**) vt (tape etc) zurückspulen

rewire [riː'waɪə*] vt (house) neu verkabeln

reword [riː'wəːd] vt anders formulieren

rewrite [riː'raɪt] (irreg: like **write**) vt umarbeiten, neu schreiben

rheumatism ['ruːmətɪzəm] n Rheumatismus m, Rheuma nt

Rhine [raɪn] n: **the ~** der Rhein

rhinoceros [raɪ'nɔsərəs] n Nashorn nt

Rhone [rəun] n: **the ~** die Rhone

rhubarb ['ruːbɑːb] n Rhabarber m

rhyme [raɪm] n Reim m

rhythm ['rɪðm] n Rhythmus m

rib [rɪb] n Rippe f ♦ vt (mock) hänseln, aufziehen

ribbon ['rɪbən] n Band nt; **in ~s** (torn) in Fetzen

rice [raɪs] n Reis m; **~ pudding** n Milchreis m

rich [rɪtʃ] adj reich; (food) reichhaltig ♦ npl: **the ~** die Reichen pl; **~es** npl Reichtum m; **~ly** adv reich; (deserve) völlig

rickets ['rɪkɪts] n Rachitis f

rickety ['rɪkɪtɪ] adj wack(e)lig

rickshaw ['rɪkʃɔː] n Rikscha f

ricochet ['rɪkəʃeɪ] n Abprallen nt; (shot) Querschläger m ♦ vi abprallen

rid [rɪd] (pt, pp **rid**) vt befreien; **to get ~ of** loswerden

riddle ['rɪdl] n Rätsel nt ♦ vt: **to be ~d with** völlig durchlöchert sein von

ride [raɪd] (pt **rode**, pp **ridden**) n (in vehicle) Fahrt f; (on horse) Ritt m ♦ vt (horse) reiten; (bicycle) fahren ♦ vi fahren, reiten; **to take sb for a ~** mit jdm eine Fahrt etc machen; (fig) jdn aufs Glatteis führen; **~r** n Reiter m

ridge [rɪdʒ] n Kamm m; (of roof) First m

ridicule ['rɪdɪkjuːl] n Spott m ♦ vt lächerlich machen

ridiculous [rɪ'dɪkjuləs] adj lächerlich

riding ['raɪdɪŋ] n Reiten nt; **~ school** n Reitschule f

rife [raɪf] adj weit verbreitet; **to be ~** grassieren; **to be ~ with** voll sein von

riffraff ['rɪfræf] n Pöbel m

rifle ['raɪfl] n Gewehr nt ♦ vt berauben; **~ range** n Schießstand m

rift [rɪft] n Spalte f; (fig) Bruch m

rig [rɪg] n (oil ~) Bohrinsel f ♦ vt (election etc) manipulieren; **~ out** (BRIT) vt ausstatten; **~ up** vt zusammenbasteln; **~ging** n Takelage f

right [raɪt] adj (correct, just) richtig, recht; (~ side) rechte(r, s) ♦ n Recht nt; (not left, POL) Rechte f ♦ adv (on the ~) rechts; (to the ~) nach rechts; (look, work) richtig, recht; (directly) gerade; (exactly) genau ♦ vt in

Ordnung bringen, korrigieren ♦ *excl* gut;
on the ~ rechts; **to be in the ~** im Recht
sein; **by ~s** von Rechts wegen; **to be ~**
Recht haben; **~ away** sofort; **~ now** in
diesem Augenblick, eben; **~ in the middle**
genau in der Mitte; ~ **angle** n rechte(r)
Winkel m; ~**eous** ['raɪtʃəs] *adj*
rechtschaffen; ~**ful** *adj* rechtmäßig; ~-
hand *adj*: ~**-hand drive** mit
Rechtssteuerung; ~**-handed** *adj*
rechtshändig; ~**-hand man** (*irreg*) n rechte
Hand f; ~**-hand side** n rechte Seite f; ~**ly**
adv mit Recht; ~ **of way** n Vorfahrt f; ~**-**
wing *adj* rechtsorientiert

rigid ['rɪdʒɪd] *adj* (*stiff*) starr, steif; (*strict*)
streng; ~**ity** [rɪ'dʒɪdɪtɪ] n Starrheit f; Strenge f

rigmarole ['rɪgmərəʊl] n Gewäsch nt

rigor ['rɪgə'] (*US*) n = **rigour**

rigorous ['rɪgərəs] *adj* streng

rigour ['rɪgə'] (*US* **rigor**) n Strenge f, Härte f

rile [raɪl] *vt* ärgern

rim [rɪm] n (*edge*) Rand m; (*of wheel*) Felge f

rind [raɪnd] n Rinde f

ring [rɪŋ] (*pt* **rang**, *pp* **rung**) n Ring m; (*of*
people) Kreis m; (*arena*) Manege f; (*of*
telephone) Klingeln nt ♦ *vt*, *vi* (*bell*) läuten;
(*BRIT*) anrufen; ~ **back** (*BRIT*) *vt*, *vi*
zurückrufen; ~ **off** (*BRIT*) *vi* aufhängen; ~
up (*BRIT*) *vt* anrufen; ~ **binder** n Ringbuch
nt; ~**ing** n Klingeln nt; (*of large bell*) Läuten
nt; (*in ears*) Klingen nt; ~**ing tone** n (*TEL*)
Rufzeichen nt

ringleader ['rɪŋliːdə'] n Anführer m,
Rädelsführer m

ringlets ['rɪŋlɪts] *npl* Ringellocken pl

ring road (*BRIT*) n Umgehungsstraße f

ringtone ['rɪŋtəʊn] n Klingelton m

rink [rɪŋk] n (*ice ~*) Eisbahn f

rinse [rɪns] n Spülen nt ♦ *vt* spülen

riot ['raɪət] n Aufruhr m ♦ *vi* randalieren; **to**
run ~ (*people*) randalieren; (*vegetation*)
wuchern; ~**er** n Aufrührer m; ~**ous** *adj*
aufrührerisch; (*noisy*) lärmend

rip [rɪp] n Schlitz m, Riss m ♦ *vt*, *vi*
(zer)reißen; ~**cord** n Reißleine f

ripe [raɪp] *adj* reif; ~**n** *vi* reifen ♦ *vt* reifen
lassen

rip-off ['rɪpɔf] (*inf*) n: **it's a ~~~!** das ist
Wucher!

ripple ['rɪpl] n kleine Welle f ♦ *vt* kräuseln
♦ *vi* sich kräuseln

rise [raɪz] (*pt* **rose**, *pp* **risen**) n (*slope*)
Steigung f; (*esp in wages*: *BRIT*) Erhöhung f;
(*growth*) Aufstieg m ♦ *vi* (*sun*) aufgehen;
(*smoke*) aufsteigen; (*mountain*) sich
erheben; (*ground*) ansteigen; (*prices*)
steigen; (*in revolt*) sich erheben; **to give ~**
to Anlass geben zu; **to ~ to the occasion**
sich der Lage gewachsen zeigen; ~**n** [rɪzn]
pp of **rise**; ~**r** n: **to be an early ~r**
ein(e) Frühaufsteher(in) m(f) sein; **rising**
['raɪzɪŋ] *adj* (*tide, prices*) steigend; (*sun,*
moon) aufgehend ♦ n (*uprising*) Aufstand m

risk [rɪsk] n Gefahr f, Risiko nt ♦ *vt* (*venture*)
wagen; (*chance loss of*) riskieren, aufs Spiel
setzen; **to take** *or* **run the ~ of doing sth**
das Risiko eingehen, etw zu tun; **at ~** in
Gefahr; **at one's own ~** auf eigene Gefahr;
~**y** *adj* riskant

risqué ['riːskeɪ] *adj* gewagt

rissole ['rɪsəʊl] n Fleischklößchen nt

rite [raɪt] n Ritus m; **last ~s** Letzte Ölung f

ritual ['rɪtjuəl] n Ritual nt ♦ *adj* ritual, Ritual-;
(*fig*) rituell

rival ['raɪvl] n Rivale m, Konkurrent m ♦ *adj*
rivalisierend ♦ *vt* rivalisieren mit; (*COMM*)
konkurrieren mit; ~**ry** n Rivalität f;
Konkurrenz f

river ['rɪvə'] n Fluss m, Strom m ♦ *cpd* (*port,*
traffic) Fluss-; **up/down ~** flussaufwärts/
-abwärts; ~**bank** n Flussufer nt; ~**bed** n
Flussbett nt

rivet ['rɪvɪt] n Niete f ♦ *vt* (*fasten*) (ver)nieten

Riviera [rɪvɪ'eərə] n: **the ~** die Riviera

road [rəʊd] n Straße f ♦ *cpd* Straßen-;
major/minor ~ Haupt-/Nebenstraße f; ~
accident n Verkehrsunfall m; ~**block** n
Straßensperre f; ~**hog** n Verkehrsrowdy m;
~ **map** n Straßenkarte f; ~ **rage** n
Aggressivität f im Straßenverkehr; ~ **safety**
n Verkehrssicherheit f; ~**side** n Straßenrand
m ♦ *adj* an der Landstraße (gelegen); ~
sign n Straßenschild nt; ~ **user** n
Verkehrsteilnehmer m; ~**way** n Fahrbahn f;

~ works npl Straßenbauarbeiten pl;
~worthy adj verkehrssicher

roam [rəum] vi (umher)streifen ♦ vt
durchstreifen

roar [rɔ:r] n Brüllen nt, Gebrüll nt ♦ vi
brüllen; **to ~ with laughter** vor Lachen
brüllen; **to do a ~ing trade** ein
Riesengeschäft machen

roast [rəust] n Braten m ♦ vt braten,
schmoren; **~ beef** n Roastbeef nt

rob [rɔb] vt bestehlen, berauben; (bank)
ausrauben; **to ~ sb of sth** jdm etw rauben;
~ber n Räuber m; **~bery** n Raub m

robe [rəub] n (dress) Gewand nt; (US)
Hauskleid nt; (judge's) Robe f

robin ['rɔbin] n Rotkehlchen nt

robot ['rəubɔt] n Roboter m

robust [rəu'bʌst] adj (person) robust;
(appetite, economy) gesund

rock [rɔk] n Felsen m; (BRIT: sweet)
Zuckerstange f ♦ vt, vi wiegen, schaukeln;
on the ~s (drink) mit Eis(würfeln);
(marriage) gescheitert; (ship) aufgelaufen; **~
and roll** n Rock and Roll m; **~-bottom** n
(fig) Tiefpunkt m; **~ery** n Steingarten m

rocket ['rɔkit] n Rakete f

rocking chair ['rɔkiŋ-] n Schaukelstuhl m

rocking horse n Schaukelpferd nt

rocky ['rɔki] adj felsig

rod [rɔd] n (bar) Stange f; (stick) Rute f

rode [rəud] pt of **ride**

rodent ['rəudnt] n Nagetier nt

roe [rəu] n (also: **~ deer**) Reh nt; (of fish:
also: **hard ~**) Rogen m; **soft ~** Milch f

rogue [rəug] n Schurke m

role [rəul] n Rolle f; **~ play** n Rollenspiel nt

roll [rəul] n Rolle f; (bread) Brötchen nt; (list)
(Namens)liste f; (of drum) Wirbel m ♦ vt
(turn) rollen, (herum)wälzen; (grass etc)
walzen ♦ vi (swing) schlingern; (sound)
rollen, grollen; **~ about** or **around** vi
herumkugeln; (ship) schlingern; (dog etc)
sich wälzen; **~ by** vi (time) verfließen; **~
over** vi sich (herum)drehen; **~ up** vi
(arrive) kommen, auftauchen ♦ vt (carpet)
aufrollen; **~ call** n Namensaufruf m; **~er** n
Rolle f, Walze f; (road ~er) Straßenwalze f;

R~erblade ® n Rollerblade m; **~er
coaster** n Achterbahn f; **~er skates** npl
Rollschuhe pl; **~-skating** n Rollschuhlaufen
nt

rolling ['rəuliŋ] adj (landscape) wellig; **~ pin**
n Nudel- or Wellholz nt; **~ stock** n
Wagenmaterial nt

ROM [rɔm] n abbr (= read only memory) ROM
m

Roman ['rəumən] adj römisch ♦ n Römer(in)
m(f); **~ Catholic** adj römisch-katholisch ♦ n
Katholik(in) m(f)

romance [rə'mæns] n Romanze f; (story)
(Liebes)roman m

Romania [rəu'meiniə] n = **Rumania**; **~n** n =
Rumanian

Roman numeral n römische Ziffer

romantic [rə'mæntik] adj romantisch; **~ism**
[rə'mæntisizəm] n Romantik f

Rome [rəum] n Rom nt

romp [rɔmp] n Tollen n ♦ vi (also: **~ about**)
herumtollen

rompers ['rɔmpəz] npl Spielanzug m

roof [ru:f] (pl **~s**) n Dach nt; (of mouth)
Gaumen m ♦ vt überdachen, überdecken;
~ing n Deckmaterial nt; **~ rack** n (AUT)
Dachgepäckträger m

rook [ruk] n (bird) Saatkrähe f; (chess) Turm m

room [ru:m] n Zimmer nt, Raum m; (space)
Platz m; (fig) Spielraum m; **~s** npl
(accommodation) Wohnung f; **"~s to let**
(BRIT) or **for rent** (US)"** „Zimmer zu
vermieten"; **single/double ~** Einzel-/
Doppelzimmer nt; **~ing house** (US) n
Mietshaus nt (mit möblierten Wohnungen);
~mate n Mitbewohner(in) m(f); **~ service**
n Zimmerbedienung f; **~y** adj geräumig

roost [ru:st] n Hühnerstange f ♦ vi auf der
Stange hocken

rooster ['ru:stər] n Hahn m

root [ru:t] n (also fig) Wurzel f ♦ vi wurzeln;
~ about vi (fig) herumwühlen; **~ for** vt
fus Stimmung machen für; **~ out** vt
ausjäten; (fig) ausrotten

rope [rəup] n Seil nt ♦ vt (tie) festschnüren;
to know the ~s sich auskennen; **to ~ sb
in** jdn gewinnen; **~ off** vt absperren;

~ ladder *n* Strickleiter *f*

rosary ['rəʊzərɪ] *n* Rosenkranz *m*

rose [rəʊz] *pt of* **rise** ♦ *n* Rose *f* ♦ *adj* Rosen-, rosenrot

rosé ['rəʊzeɪ] *n* Rosé *m*

rosebud ['rəʊzbʌd] *n* Rosenknospe *f*

rosebush ['rəʊzbʊʃ] *n* Rosenstock *m*

rosemary ['rəʊzmərɪ] *n* Rosmarin *m*

rosette [rəʊ'zɛt] *n* Rosette *f*

roster ['rɒstər] *n* Dienstplan *m*

rostrum ['rɒstrəm] *n* Rednerbühne *f*

rosy ['rəʊzɪ] *adj* rosig

rot [rɒt] *n* Fäulnis *f*; (*nonsense*) Quatsch *m* ♦ *vi* verfaulen ♦ *vt* verfaulen lassen

rota ['rəʊtə] *n* Dienstliste *f*

rotary ['rəʊtərɪ] *adj* rotierend

rotate [rəʊ'teɪt] *vt* rotieren lassen; (*take turns*) turnusmäßig wechseln ♦ *vi* rotieren;

rotating *adj* rotierend; **rotation** [rəʊ'teɪʃən] *n* Umdrehung *f*

rote [rəʊt] *n*: **by ~** auswendig

rotten ['rɒtn] *adj* faul; (*fig*) schlecht, gemein; **to feel ~** (*ill*) sich elend fühlen

rotund [rəʊ'tʌnd] *adj* rundlich

rouble ['ru:bl] (*US* **ruble**) *n* Rubel *m*

rough [rʌf] *adj* (*not smooth*) rau; (*path*) uneben; (*violent*) roh, grob; (*crossing*) stürmisch; (*without comforts*) hart, unbequem; (*unfinished, makeshift*) grob; (*approximate*) ungefähr ♦ *n* (*BRIT: person*) Rowdy *m*, Rohling *m*; (*GOLF*): **in the ~** im Rau ♦ *vt*: **to ~ it** primitiv leben; **to sleep ~** im Freien schlafen; **~age** *n* Ballaststoffe *pl*; **~-and-ready** *adj* provisorisch; (*work*) zusammengehauen; **~ copy** *n* Entwurf *m*; **~ draft** *n* Entwurf *m*; **~ly** *adv* grob; (*about*) ungefähr; **~ness** *n* Rauheit *f*; (*of manner*) Ungeschliffenheit *f*

roulette [ru:'lɛt] *n* Roulett(e) *nt*

Roumania [ru:'meɪnɪə] *n* = **Rumania**

round [raʊnd] *adj* rund; (*figures*) aufgerundet ♦ *adv* (*in a circle*) rundherum ♦ *prep* um ... herum ♦ *n* Runde *f*; (*of ammunition*) Magazin *nt* ♦ *vt* (*corner*) biegen um; **all ~** überall; **the long way ~** der Umweg; **all the year ~** das ganze Jahr über; **it's just ~ the corner** (*fig*) es ist gerade um die Ecke;

~ the clock rund um die Uhr; **to go ~ to sb's (house)** jdn besuchen; **to go ~ the back** hintenherum gehen; **enough to go ~** genug für alle; **to go the ~s** (*story*) die Runde machen; **a ~ of applause** ein Beifall *m*; **a ~ of drinks** eine Runde Drinks; **a ~ of sandwiches** ein Sandwich *nt or m*, ein belegtes Brot; **~ off** *vt* abrunden; **~ up** *vt* (*end*) abschließen; (*figures*) aufrunden; (*criminals*) hochnehmen; **~about** *n* (*BRIT: traffic*) Kreisverkehr *m*; (: *merry-go-~*) Karussell *nt* ♦ *adj* auf Umwegen; **~ers** *npl* (*game*) ≈ Schlagball *m*; **~ly** *adv* (*fig*) gründlich; **~-shouldered** *adj* mit abfallenden Schultern; **~ trip** *n* Rundreise *f*; **~up** *n* Zusammentreiben *nt*, Sammeln *nt*

rouse [raʊz] *vt* (*waken*) (auf)wecken; (*stir up*) erregen; **rousing** (*welcome*) stürmisch; (*speech*) zündend

route [ru:t] *n* Weg *m*, Route *f*; **~ map** (*BRIT*) *n* (*for journey*) Streckenkarte *f*

routine [ru:'ti:n] *n* Routine *f* ♦ *adj* Routine-

row[1] [rəʊ] *n* (*noise*) Lärm *m*; (*dispute*) Streit *m* ♦ *vi* sich streiten

row[2] [rəʊ] *n* (*line*) Reihe *f* ♦ *vt, vi* (*boat*) rudern; **in a ~** (*fig*) hintereinander; **~boat** ['rəʊbəʊt] (*US*) *n* Ruderboot *nt*

rowdy ['raʊdɪ] *adj* rüpelhaft ♦ *n* (*person*) Rowdy *m*

rowing ['rəʊɪŋ] *n* Rudern *nt*; (*SPORT*) Rudersport *m*; **~ boat** (*BRIT*) *n* Ruderboot *nt*

royal ['rɔɪəl] *adj* königlich, Königs-; **R~ Air Force** *n* Königliche Luftwaffe *f*; **~ty** ['rɔɪəltɪ] *n* (*family*) Königliche Familie *f*; (*for novel etc*) Tantieme *f*

rpm *abbr* (= *revs per minute*) U/min

R.S.V.P. *abbr* (= *répondez s'il vous plaît*) u. A. w. g.

Rt. Hon. (*BRIT*) *abbr* (= *Right Honourable*) Abgeordnete(r) *mf*

rub [rʌb] *n* (*with cloth*) Polieren *nt*; (*on person*) Reiben *nt* ♦ *vt* reiben; **to ~ sb up** (*BRIT*) *or* **to ~ sb** (*US*) **the wrong way** jdn aufreizen; **~ off** *vi* (*also fig*): **to ~ off (on)** abfärben (auf +*acc*); **~ out** *vt* herausreiben; (*with eraser*) ausradieren

rubber ['rʌbər] *n* Gummi *m*; (*BRIT*)

Radiergummi *m;* ~ **band** *n* Gummiband *nt;* ~ **plant** *n* Gummibaum *m*

rubbish ['rʌbɪʃ] *n (waste)* Abfall *m; (nonsense)* Blödsinn *m,* Quatsch *m;* ~ **bin** *(BRIT)* *n* Mülleimer *m;* ~ **dump** *n* Müllabladeplatz *m*

rubble ['rʌbl] *n* (Stein)schutt *m*

ruby ['ru:bɪ] *n* Rubin *m ♦ adj* rubinrot

rucksack ['rʌksæk] *n* Rucksack *m*

rudder ['rʌdəʳ] *n* Steuerruder *nt*

ruddy ['rʌdɪ] *adj (colour)* rötlich; *(inf: bloody)* verdammt

rude [ru:d] *adj* unverschämt; *(shock)* hart; *(awakening)* unsanft; *(unrefined, rough)* grob; ~**ness** *n* Unverschämtheit *f;* Grobheit *f*

rudiment ['ru:dɪmənt] *n* Grundlage *f*

rueful ['ru:ful] *adj* reuevoll

ruffian ['rʌfɪən] *n* Rohling *m*

ruffle ['rʌfl] *vt* kräuseln

rug [rʌg] *n* Brücke *f; (in bedroom)* Bettvorleger *m; (BRIT: for knees)* (Reise)decke *f*

rugby ['rʌgbɪ] *n (also:* ~ **football)** Rugby *nt*

rugged ['rʌgɪd] *adj (coastline)* zerklüftet; *(features)* markig

rugger ['rʌgəʳ] *(BRIT: inf)* *n* = **rugby**

ruin ['ru:ɪn] *n* Ruine *f; (downfall)* Ruin *m ♦ vt* ruinieren; ~**s** *npl (fig)* Trümmer *pl;* ~**ous** *adj* ruinierend

rule [ru:l] *n* Regel *f; (government)* Regierung *f; (for measuring)* Lineal *m ♦ vt (govern)* herrschen über +*acc,* regieren; *(decide)* anordnen, entscheiden; *(make lines on)* linieren *♦ vi* herrschen, regieren; entscheiden; **as a** ~ in der Regel; ~ **out** *vt* ausschließen; ~**d** *adj (paper)* liniert; ~**r** *n* Lineal *nt;* Herrscher *m;* **ruling** ['ru:lɪŋ] *adj (party)* Regierungs-; *(class)* herrschend *♦ n (JUR)* Entscheid *m*

rum [rʌm] *n* Rum *m*

Rumania [ru:'meɪnɪə] *n* Rumänien *nt;* ~**n** *adj* rumänisch *♦ n* Rumäne *m,* Rumänin *f; (LING)* Rumänisch *nt*

rumble ['rʌmbl] *n* Rumpeln *nt; (of thunder)* Grollen *nt ♦ vi* rumpeln; grollen

rummage ['rʌmɪdʒ] *vi* durchstöbern

rumour ['ru:məʳ] *(US* **rumor)** *n* Gerücht *nt*

♦ vt: **it is ~ed that** man sagt *or* man munkelt, dass

rump [rʌmp] *n* Hinterteil *nt;* ~ **steak** *n* Rumpsteak *nt*

rumpus ['rʌmpəs] *n* Spektakel *m*

run [rʌn] *(pt* **ran,** *pp* **run)** *n* Lauf *m; (in car)* (Spazier)fahrt *f; (series)* Serie *f,* Reihe *f; (ski* ~*)* (Ski)abfahrt *f; (in stocking)* Laufmasche *f ♦ vt (cause to* ~*)* laufen lassen; *(car, train, bus)* fahren; *(race, distance)* laufen, rennen; *(manage)* leiten; *(COMPUT)* laufen lassen; *(pass: hand, eye)* gleiten lassen *♦ vi* laufen; *(move quickly)* laufen, rennen; *(bus, train)* fahren; *(flow)* fließen, laufen; *(colours)* (ab)färben; **there was a** ~ **on** *(meat, tickets)* es gab einen Ansturm auf +*acc;* **on the** ~ auf der Flucht; **in the long** ~ auf die Dauer; **I'll** ~ **you to the station** ich fahre dich zum Bahnhof; **to** ~ **a risk** ein Risiko eingehen; ~ **about** *or* **around** *vi (children)* umherspringen; ~ **across** *vt fus (find)* stoßen auf +*acc;* ~ **away** *vi* weglaufen; ~ **down** *vi (clock)* ablaufen *♦ vt (production, factory)* allmählich auflösen; *(with car)* überfahren; *(talk against)* heruntermachen; **to be** ~ **down** erschöpft *or* abgespannt sein; ~ **in** *(BRIT)* *vt (car)* einfahren; ~ **into** *vt fus (meet: person)* zufällig treffen; *(trouble)* bekommen; *(collide with)* rennen gegen; fahren gegen; ~ **off** *vi* fortlaufen; ~ **out** *vi (person)* hinausrennen; *(liquid)* auslaufen; *(lease)* ablaufen; *(money)* ausgeben; **he ran out of money/petrol** ihm ging das Geld/ Benzin aus; ~ **over** *vt (in accident)* überfahren; ~ **through** *vt (instructions)* durchgehen; ~ **up** *vt (debt, bill)* machen; ~ **up against** *vt fus (difficulties)* stoßen auf +*acc;* ~**away** *adj (horse)* ausgebrochen; *(person)* flüchtig

rung [rʌŋ] *pp of* **ring** *♦ n* Sprosse *f*

runner ['rʌnəʳ] *n* Läufer(in) *m(f); (for sleigh)* Kufe *f;* ~ **bean** *(BRIT)* *n* Stangenbohne *f;* ~**up** *n* Zweite(r) *mf*

running ['rʌnɪŋ] *n (of business)* Leitung *f; (of machine)* Betrieb *m ♦ adj (water)* fließend; *(commentary)* laufend; **to be in/out of the** ~ **for sth** im/aus dem Rennen für etw sein;

3 days ~ 3 Tage lang *or* hintereinander; **~ costs** *npl (of car, machine)* Unterhaltungskosten *pl*

runny ['rʌnɪ] *adj* dünn; *(nose)* laufend

run-of-the-mill ['rʌnəvðə'mɪl] *adj* gewöhnlich, alltäglich

runt [rʌnt] *n (animal)* Kümmerer *m*

run-up ['rʌnʌp] *n:* **the ~~~ to** *(election etc)* die Endphase vor *+dat*

runway ['rʌnweɪ] *n* Startbahn *f*

rupture ['rʌptʃə'] *n (MED)* Bruch *m*

rural ['ruərl] *adj* ländlich, Land-

ruse [ruːz] *n* Kniff *m*, List *f*

rush [rʌʃ] *n* Eile *f*, Hetze *f*; *(FIN)* starke Nachfrage *f* ♦ *vt (carry along)* auf dem schnellsten Wege schaffen *or* transportieren; *(attack)* losstürmen auf *+acc* ♦ *vi (hurry)* eilen, stürzen; **don't ~ me** dräng mich nicht; **~ hour** *n* Hauptverkehrszeit *f*

rusk [rʌsk] *n* Zwieback *m*

Russia ['rʌʃə] *n* Russland *nt*; **~n** *adj* russisch ♦ *n* Russe *m*, Russin *f*; *(LING)* Russisch *nt*

rust [rʌst] *n* Rost *m* ♦ *vi* rosten

rustic ['rʌstɪk] *adj* bäuerlich, ländlich

rustle ['rʌsl] *vi* rauschen, rascheln ♦ *vt* rascheln lassen

rustproof ['rʌstpruːf] *adj* rostfrei

rusty ['rʌstɪ] *adj* rostig

rut [rʌt] *n (in track)* Radspur *f*; **to be in a ~** im Trott stecken

ruthless ['ruːθlɪs] *adj* rücksichtslos

rye [raɪ] *n* Roggen *m*; **~ bread** *n* Roggenbrot *nt*

S, s

sabbath ['sæbəθ] *n* Sabbat *m*

sabotage ['sæbətɑːʒ] *n* Sabotage *f* ♦ *vt* sabotieren

saccharin ['sækərɪn] *n* Sa(c)charin *nt*

sachet ['sæʃeɪ] *n (of shampoo etc)* Briefchen *nt*, Kissen *nt*

sack [sæk] *n* Sack *m* ♦ *vt (inf)* hinauswerfen; *(pillage)* plündern; **to get the ~** rausfliegen; **~ing** *n (material)* Sackleinen *nt*; *(inf)* Rausschmiss *m*

sacrament ['sækrəmənt] *n* Sakrament *nt*

sacred ['seɪkrɪd] *adj* heilig

sacrifice ['sækrɪfaɪs] *n* Opfer *nt* ♦ *vt (also fig)* opfern

sacrilege ['sækrɪlɪdʒ] *n* Schändung *f*

sad [sæd] *adj* traurig; **~den** *vt* traurig machen, betrüben

saddle ['sædl] *n* Sattel *m* ♦ *vt (burden)*: **to ~ sb with sth** jdm etw aufhalsen; **~bag** *n* Satteltasche *f*

sadistic [sə'dɪstɪk] *adj* sadistisch

sadly ['sædlɪ] *adv* traurig; *(unfortunately)* leider

sadness ['sædnɪs] *n* Traurigkeit *f*

s.a.e. *abbr (= stamped addressed envelope)* adressierte(r) Rückumschlag *m*

safe [seɪf] *adj (careful)* vorsichtig ♦ *n* Safe *m*; **~ and sound** gesund und wohl; **(just) to be on the ~ side** um ganz sicherzugehen; **~ from** *(attack)* sicher vor *+dat*; **~-conduct** *n* freie(s) Geleit *nt*; **~-deposit** *n (vault)* Tresorraum *m*; *(box)* Banksafe *m*; **~guard** *n* Sicherung *f* ♦ *vt* sichern, schützen; **~keeping** *n* sichere Verwahrung *f*; **~ly** *adv* sicher; *(arrive)* wohlbehalten; **~ sex** *n* geschützter Sex *m*

safety ['seɪftɪ] *n* Sicherheit *f*; **~ belt** *n* Sicherheitsgurt *m*; **~ pin** *n* Sicherheitsnadel *f*; **~ valve** *n* Sicherheitsventil *nt*

sag [sæg] *vi (durch)sacken*

sage [seɪdʒ] *n (herb)* Salbei *m*; *(person)* Weise(r) *mf*

Sagittarius [sædʒɪ'tɛərɪəs] *n* Schütze *m*

Sahara [sə'hɑːrə] *n:* **the ~ (Desert)** die (Wüste) Sahara

said [sɛd] *pt, pp of* **say**

sail [seɪl] *n* Segel *nt*; *(trip)* Fahrt *f* ♦ *vt* segeln ♦ *vi* segeln; *(begin voyage: person)* abfahren; *(: ship)* auslaufen; *(fig: cloud etc)* dahinsegeln; **to go for a ~** segeln gehen; **they ~ed into Copenhagen** sie liefen in Kopenhagen ein; **~ through** *vt fus, vi (fig)* (es) spielend schaffen; **~boat** *(US)* *n* Segelboot *nt*; **~ing** *n* Segeln *nt*; **~ing ship** *n* Segelschiff *nt*; **~or** *n* Matrose *m*, Seemann *m*

saint [seɪnt] *n* Heilige(r) *mf*; **~ly** *adj* heilig, fromm

sake [seɪk] *n*: **for the ~ of** um +*gen* willen

salad ['sæləd] *n* Salat *m*; **~ bowl** *n* Salatschüssel *f*; **~ cream** (BRIT) *n* Salatmayonnaise *f*, Salatmajonäse *f*; **~ dressing** *n* Salatsoße *f*

salary ['sæləri] *n* Gehalt *nt*

sale [seɪl] *n* Verkauf *m*; (*reduced prices*) Schlussverkauf *m*; **"for ~"** „zu verkaufen"; **on ~** zu verkaufen; **~room** *n* Verkaufsraum *m*; **~s assistant** *n* Verkäufer(in) *m(f)*; **~s clerk** (US) *n* Verkäufer(in) *m(f)*; **~sman** (*irreg*) *n* Verkäufer *m*; (*representative*) Vertreter *m*; **~s rep** *n* (COMM) Vertreter(in) *m(f)*; **~swoman** (*irreg*) *n* Verkäuferin *f*

salient ['seɪlɪənt] *adj* bemerkenswert

saliva [sə'laɪvə] *n* Speichel *m*

sallow ['sæləʊ] *adj* fahl; (*face*) bleich

salmon ['sæmən] *n* Lachs *m*

salon ['sælɒn] *n* Salon *m*

saloon [sə'luːn] *n* (BRIT: AUT) Limousine *f*; (*ship's lounge*) Salon *m*; **~ car** (BRIT) *n* Limousine *f*

salt [sɔːlt] *n* Salz *nt* ♦ *vt* (*cure*) einsalzen; (*flavour*) salzen; **~cellar** *n* Salzfass *nt*; **~water** *adj* Salzwasser-; **~y** *adj* salzig

salute [sə'luːt] *n* (MIL) Gruß *m*; (*with guns*) Salutschüsse *pl* ♦ *vt* (MIL) salutieren

salvage ['sælvɪdʒ] *n* (*from ship*) Bergung *f*; (*property*) Rettung *f* ♦ *vt* bergen; retten

salvation [sæl'veɪʃən] *n* Rettung *f*; **S~ Army** *n* Heilsarmee *f*

same [seɪm] *adj, pron* (*similar*) gleiche(r, s); (*identical*) derselbe/dieselbe/dasselbe; **the ~ book as** das gleiche Buch wie; **at the ~ time** zur gleichen Zeit, gleichzeitig; (*however*) zugleich, andererseits; **all** *or* **just the ~** trotzdem; **the ~ to you!** gleichfalls!; **to do the ~ (as sb)** das Gleiche tun (wie jd)

sample ['sɑːmpl] *n* Probe *f* ♦ *vt* probieren

sanctify ['sæŋktɪfaɪ] *vt* weihen

sanctimonious [sæŋktɪ'məʊnɪəs] *adj* scheinheilig

sanction ['sæŋkʃən] *n* Sanktion *f*

sanctity ['sæŋktɪtɪ] *n* Heiligkeit *f*; (*fig*) Unverletzlichkeit *f*

sanctuary ['sæŋktjʊərɪ] *n* (*for fugitive*) Asyl *nt*; (*refuge*) Zufluchtsort *m*; (*for animals*) Schutzgebiet *nt*

sand [sænd] *n* Sand *m* ♦ *vt* (*furniture*) schmirgeln

sandal ['sændl] *n* Sandale *f*

sand: ~box (US) *n* = **sandpit**; **~castle** *n* Sandburg *f*; **~ dune** *n* (Sand)düne *f*; **~paper** *n* Sandpapier *nt*; **~pit** *n* Sandkasten *m*; **~stone** *n* Sandstein *m*

sandwich ['sændwɪtʃ] *n* Sandwich *m or nt* ♦ *vt* (*also*: **~ in**) einklemmen; **cheese/ham ~** Käse-/Schinkenbrot; **~ed between** eingeklemmt zwischen; **~ board** *n* Reklametafel *f*; **~ course** (BRIT) *n* Theorie und Praxis abwechselnde(r) Ausbildungsgang *m*

sandy ['sændɪ] *adj* sandig; (*hair*) rotblond

sane [seɪn] *adj* geistig gesund *or* normal; (*sensible*) vernünftig, gescheit

sang [sæŋ] *pt of* **sing**

sanitary ['sænɪtərɪ] *adj* hygienisch; **~ towel** *n* (Monats)binde *f*

sanitation [sænɪ'teɪʃən] *n* sanitäre Einrichtungen *pl*; **~ department** (US) *n* Stadtreinigung *f*

sanity ['sænɪtɪ] *n* geistige Gesundheit *f*; (*sense*) Vernunft *f*

sank [sæŋk] *pt of* **sink**

Santa Claus [sæntə'klɔːz] *n* Nikolaus *m*, Weihnachtsmann *m*

sap [sæp] *n* (*of plants*) Saft *m* ♦ *vt* (*strength*) schwächen

sapling ['sæplɪŋ] *n* junge(r) Baum *m*

sapphire ['sæfaɪə*] *n* Saphir *m*

sarcasm ['sɑːkæzm] *n* Sarkasmus *m*

sarcastic [sɑː'kæstɪk] *adj* sarkastisch

sardine [sɑː'diːn] *n* Sardine *f*

Sardinia [sɑː'dɪnɪə] *n* Sardinien *nt*

sardonic [sɑː'dɒnɪk] *adj* zynisch

sash [sæʃ] *n* Schärpe *f*

sat [sæt] *pt, pp of* **sit**

Satan ['seɪtn] *n* Satan *m*

satchel ['sætʃl] *n* (*for school*) Schulmappe *f*

satellite ['sætəlaɪt] *n* Satellit *m*; **~ dish** *n* (TECH) Parabolantenne *f*, Satellitenantenne *f*; ~ **television** *n* Satellitenfernsehen *nt*

satisfaction [sætɪsˈfækʃən] *n* Befriedigung *f*, Genugtuung *f*; **satisfactory** [sætɪsˈfæktərɪ] *adj* zufrieden stellend, befriedigend; **satisfied** *adj* befriedigt

satisfy [ˈsætɪsfaɪ] *vt* befriedigen, zufrieden stellen; (*convince*) überzeugen; (*conditions*) erfüllen; **~ing** *adj* befriedigend; (*meal*) sättigend

saturate [ˈsætʃəreɪt] *vt* (durch)tränken

Saturday [ˈsætədɪ] *n* Samstag *m*, Sonnabend *m*

sauce [sɔːs] *n* Soße *f*, Sauce *f*; **~pan** *n* Kasserolle *f*

saucer [ˈsɔːsəʳ] *n* Untertasse *f*

saucy [ˈsɔːsɪ] *adj* frech, keck

Saudi [ˈsaʊdɪ]: ~ **Arabia** *n* Saudi-Arabien *nt*; ~ **(Arabian)** *adj* saudi-arabisch ♦ *n* Saudi-Araber(in) *m(f)*

sauna [ˈsɔːnə] *n* Sauna *f*

saunter [ˈsɔːntəʳ] *vi* schlendern

sausage [ˈsɒsɪdʒ] *n* Wurst *f*; ~ **roll** *n* Wurst *f* im Schlafrock, Wurstpastete *f*

sauté [ˈsəʊteɪ] *adj* Röst-

savage [ˈsævɪdʒ] *adj* wild ♦ *n* Wilde(r) *mf* ♦ *vt* (*animals*) zerfleischen

save [seɪv] *vt* retten; (*money, electricity etc*) sparen; (*strength etc*) aufsparen; (*COMPUT*) speichern ♦ *vi* (*also*: ~ **up**) sparen ♦ *n* (*SPORT*) (Ball)abwehr *f* ♦ *prep, conj* außer, ausgenommen

saving [ˈseɪvɪŋ] *adj*: **the** ~ **grace of** das Versöhnende an +*dat* ♦ *n* Sparen *nt*, Ersparnis *f*; **~s** *npl* (*money*) Ersparnisse *pl*; **~s account** *n* Sparkonto *nt*; **~s bank** *n* Sparkasse *f*

saviour [ˈseɪvjəʳ] (*US* **savior**) *n* (*REL*) Erlöser *m*

savour [ˈseɪvəʳ] (*US* **savor**) *vt* (*taste*) schmecken; (*fig*) genießen; **~y** *adj* pikant, würzig

saw [sɔː] (*pt* **sawed**, *pp* **sawed** *or* **sawn**) *pt* of **see** ♦ *n* (*tool*) Säge *f* ♦ *vt, vi* sägen; **~dust** *n* Sägemehl *nt*; **~mill** *n* Sägewerk *nt*; **~n** *pp* of **saw**; **~n-off shotgun** *n* Gewehr *nt* mit abgesägtem Lauf

sax [sæks] (*inf*) *n* Saxofon *nt*, Saxophon *nt*

saxophone [ˈsæksəfəʊn] *n* Saxofon *nt*, Saxophon *nt*

say [seɪ] (*pt, pp* **said**) *n*: **to have a/no** ~ **in sth** Mitspracherecht/kein Mitspracherecht bei etw haben ♦ *vt, vi* sagen; **let him have his** ~ lass ihn doch reden; **to** ~ **yes/no** Ja/Nein *or* ja/nein sagen; **that goes without ~ing** das versteht sich von selbst; **that is to** ~ das heißt; **~ing** *n* Sprichwort *nt*

scab [skæb] *n* Schorf *m*; (*pej*) Streikbrecher *m*

scaffold [ˈskæfəld] *n* (*for execution*) Schafott *nt*; **~ing** *n* (Bau)gerüst *nt*

scald [skɔːld] *n* Verbrühung *f* ♦ *vt* (*burn*) verbrühen

scale [skeɪl] *n* (*of fish*) Schuppe *f*; (*MUS*) Tonleiter *f*; (*on map, size*) Maßstab *m*; (*gradation*) Skala *f* ♦ *vt* (*climb*) erklimmen; **~s** *npl* (*balance*) Waage *f*; **on a large** ~ (*fig*) im Großen, in großem Umfang; ~ **of charges** Gebührenordnung *f*; ~ **down** *vt* verkleinern; ~ **model** *n* maßstabgetreue(s) Modell *nt*

scallop [ˈskɒləp] *n* Kammmuschel *f*

scalp [skælp] *n* Kopfhaut *f*

scamper [ˈskæmpəʳ] *vi*: **to** ~ **away** *or* **off** sich davonmachen

scampi [ˈskæmpɪ] *npl* Scampi *pl*

scan [skæn] *vt* (*examine*) genau prüfen; (*quickly*) überfliegen; (*horizon*) absuchen

scandal [ˈskændl] *n* Skandal *m*; (*piece of gossip*) Skandalgeschichte *f*

Scandinavia [skændɪˈneɪvɪə] *n* Skandinavien *nt*; **~n** *adj* skandinavisch ♦ *n* Skandinavier(in) *m(f)*

scant [skænt] *adj* knapp; **~ily** *adv* knapp, dürftig; **~y** *adj* knapp, unzureichend

scapegoat [ˈskeɪpgəʊt] *n* Sündenbock *m*

scar [skɑːʳ] *n* Narbe *f* ♦ *vt* durch Narben entstellen

scarce [skeəs] *adj* selten, rar; (*goods*) knapp; **~ly** *adv* kaum; **scarcity** *n* Mangel *m*

scare [skeəʳ] *n* Schrecken *m* ♦ *vt* erschrecken; **bomb** ~ Bombendrohung *f*; **to** ~ **sb stiff** jdn zu Tode erschrecken; **to be ~d** Angst haben; ~ **away** *vt* (*animal*) verscheuchen; ~ **off** *vt* = **scare away**;

~crow n Vogelscheuche f

scarf [skɑːf] (pl **scarves**) n Schal m; (headscarf) Kopftuch nt

scarlet ['skɑːlɪt] adj scharlachrot ♦ n Scharlachrot nt; **~ fever** n Scharlach m

scarves [skɑːvz] npl of **scarf**

scary ['skɛərɪ] (inf) adj schaurig

scathing ['skeɪðɪŋ] adj scharf, vernichtend

scatter ['skætə*] vt (sprinkle) (ver)streuen; (disperse) zerstreuen ♦ vi sich zerstreuen; **~brained** adj flatterhaft, schusselig

scavenger ['skævəndʒə*] n (animal) Aasfresser m

scenario [sɪ'nɑːrɪəu] n (THEAT, CINE) Szenarium nt; (fig) Szenario nt

scene [siːn] n (of happening) Ort m; (of play, incident) Szene f; (view) Anblick m; (argument) Szene f, Auftritt m; **~ry** ['siːnərɪ] n (THEAT) Bühnenbild nt; (landscape) Landschaft f

scenic ['siːnɪk] adj landschaftlich

scent [sɛnt] n Parfüm nt; (smell) Duft m ♦ vt parfümieren

sceptical ['skɛptɪkl] (US **skeptical**) adj skeptisch

schedule ['ʃɛdjuːl, (US) 'skɛdjuːl] n (list) Liste f; (plan) Programm nt; (of work) Zeitplan m ♦ vt planen; **on ~** pünktlich; **to be ahead of/behind ~** dem Zeitplan voraus/im Rückstand sein; **~d flight** n (not charter) Linienflug m

scheme [skiːm] n Schema nt; (dishonest) Intrige f; (plan of action) Plan m ♦ vi intrigieren ♦ vt planen; **scheming** ['skiːmɪŋ] adj intrigierend

scholar ['skɔlə*] n Gelehrte(r) m; (holding ~ship) Stipendiat m; **~ly** adj gelehrt; **~ship** n Gelehrsamkeit f; (grant) Stipendium nt

school [skuːl] n Schule f; (UNIV) Fakultät f ♦ vt schulen; **~ age** n schulpflichtige(s) Alter nt; **~book** n Schulbuch nt; **~boy** n Schüler m; **~children** npl Schüler pl, Schulkinder pl; **~days** npl (alte) Schulzeit f; **~girl** n Schülerin f; **~ing** n Schulung f, Ausbildung f; **~master** n Lehrer m; **~mistress** n Lehrerin f; **~teacher** n Lehrer(in) m(f)

sciatica [saɪ'ætɪkə] n Ischias m or nt

science ['saɪəns] n Wissenschaft f; (natural ~) Naturwissenschaft f; **~ fiction** n Sciencefiction f; **scientific** [saɪən'tɪfɪk] adj wissenschaftlich; (natural ~s) naturwissenschaftlich; **scientist** ['saɪəntɪst] n Wissenschaftler(in) m(f)

scintillating ['sɪntɪleɪtɪŋ] adj sprühend

scissors ['sɪzəz] npl Schere f; **a pair of ~** eine Schere

scoff [skɔf] vt (BRIT: inf: eat) fressen ♦ vi (mock): **to ~ (at)** spotten (über +acc)

scold [skəuld] vt schimpfen

scone [skɔn] n weiche(s) Teegebäck nt

scoop [skuːp] n Schaufel f; (news) sensationelle Erstmeldung f; **~ out** vt herausschaufeln; **~ up** vt aufschaufeln; (liquid) aufschöpfen

scooter ['skuːtə*] n Motorroller m; (child's) Roller m

scope [skəup] n Ausmaß nt; (opportunity) (Spiel)raum m

scorch [skɔːtʃ] n Brandstelle f ♦ vt versengen; **~ing** adj brennend

score [skɔː*] n (in game) Punktzahl f; (final ~) (Spiel)ergebnis nt; (MUS) Partitur f; (line) Kratzer m; (twenty) zwanzig, zwanzig Stück ♦ vt (goal) schießen; (points) machen; (mark) einritzen ♦ vi (keep record) Punkte zählen; **on that ~** in dieser Hinsicht; **what's the ~?** wie stehts?; **to ~ 6 out of 10** 6 von 10 Punkten erzielen; **~ out** vt ausstreichen; **~board** n Anschreibetafel f; **~r** n Torschütze m; (recorder) (Auf)schreiber m

scorn [skɔːn] n Verachtung f ♦ vt verhöhnen; **~ful** adj verächtlich

Scorpio ['skɔːpɪəu] n Skorpion m

Scot [skɔt] n Schotte m, Schottin f

Scotch [skɔtʃ] n Scotch m

scotch [skɔtʃ] vt (end) unterbinden

scot-free ['skɔt'friː] adv: **to get off ~~** (unpunished) ungeschoren davonkommen

Scotland ['skɔtlənd] n Schottland nt

Scots [skɔts] adj schottisch; **~man/woman** (irreg) n Schotte m/Schottin f

Scottish ['skɔtɪʃ] adj schottisch

scoundrel ['skaʊndrl] n Schuft m

scour ['skaʊəʳ] vt (search) absuchen; (clean) schrubben

scourge [skə:dʒ] n (whip) Geißel f; (plague) Qual f

scout [skaʊt] n (MIL) Späher m; (also: **boy ~**) Pfadfinder m; **~ around** vi: **to ~ around (for)** sich umsehen (nach)

scowl [skaʊl] n finstere(r) Blick m ♦ vi finster blicken

scrabble ['skræbl] vi (also: **~ around**: search) (herum)tasten; (claw): **to ~ (at)** kratzen (an +dat) ♦ n: **S~** ® Scrabble nt ®

scraggy ['skrægɪ] adj dürr, hager

scram [skræm] (inf) vi abhauen

scramble ['skræmbl] n (climb) Kletterei f; (struggle) Kampf m ♦ vi klettern; (fight) sich schlagen; **to ~ out/through** krabbeln aus/ durch; **to ~ for sth** sich um etw raufen; **~d eggs** npl Rührei nt

scrap [skræp] n (bit) Stückchen nt; (fight) Keilerei f; (also: **~ iron**) Schrott m ♦ vt verwerfen ♦ vi (fight) streiten, sich prügeln; **~s** npl (leftovers) Reste pl; (waste) Abfall m; **~book** n Einklebealbum nt; **~ dealer** n Schrotthändler(in) m(f)

scrape [skreɪp] n Kratzen nt; (trouble) Klemme f ♦ vt kratzen; (car) zerkratzen; (clean) abkratzen ♦ vi (make harsh noise) kratzen; **to ~ through** gerade noch durchkommen; **~r** n Kratzer m

scrap: **~ heap** n Schrotthaufen m; **on the ~ heap** (fig) beim alten Eisen; **~ iron** n Schrott m; **~ merchant** (BRIT) ® n Altwarenhändler(in) m(f); **~ paper** n Schmierpapier nt

scrappy ['skræpɪ] adj zusammengestoppelt

scratch [skrætʃ] n (wound) Kratzer m, Schramme f ♦ adj: **~ team** zusammengewürfelte Mannschaft ♦ vt kratzen; (car) zerkratzen ♦ vi (sich) kratzen; **to start from ~** ganz von vorne anfangen; **to be up to ~** den Anforderungen entsprechen

scrawl [skrɔ:l] n Gekritzel nt ♦ vt, vi kritzeln

scrawny ['skrɔ:nɪ] adj (person, neck) dürr

scream [skri:m] n Schrei m ♦ vi schreien

scree [skri:] n Geröll(halde f) nt

screech [skri:tʃ] n Schrei m ♦ vi kreischen

screen [skri:n] n (protective) Schutzschirm m; (CINE) Leinwand f; (TV) Bildschirm m ♦ vt (shelter) (be)schirmen; (film) zeigen, vorführen; **~ing** n (MED) Untersuchung f; **~play** n Drehbuch nt; **~ saver** n (COMPUT) Bildschirmschoner m

screw [skru:] n Schraube f ♦ vt (fasten) schrauben; (vulgar) bumsen; **~ up** vt (paper etc) zerknüllen; (inf: ruin) vermasseln (inf); **~driver** n Schraubenzieher m

scribble ['skrɪbl] n Gekritzel nt ♦ vt kritzeln

script [skrɪpt] n (handwriting) Handschrift f; (for film) Drehbuch nt; (THEAT) Manuskript nt, Text m

Scripture ['skrɪptʃəʳ] n Heilige Schrift f

scroll [skrəʊl] n Schriftrolle f

scrounge [skraʊndʒ] (inf) vt: **to ~ sth off** or **from sb** etw bei jdm abstauben ♦ n: **on the ~** beim Schnorren

scrub [skrʌb] n (clean) Schrubben nt; (in countryside) Gestrüpp nt ♦ vt (clean) schrubben

scruff [skrʌf] n: **by the ~ of the neck** am Genick

scruffy ['skrʌfɪ] adj unordentlich, vergammelt

scrum(mage) ['skrʌm(ɪdʒ)] n Getümmel nt

scruple ['skru:pl] n Skrupel m, Bedenken nt

scrupulous ['skru:pjʊləs] adj peinlich genau, gewissenhaft

scrutinize ['skru:tɪnaɪz] vt genau prüfen; **scrutiny** ['skru:tɪnɪ] n genaue Untersuchung f

scuff [skʌf] vt (shoes) abstoßen

scuffle ['skʌfl] n Handgemenge nt

sculptor ['skʌlptəʳ] n Bildhauer(in) m(f)

sculpture ['skʌlptʃəʳ] n (ART) Bildhauerei f; (statue) Skulptur f

scum [skʌm] n (also fig) Abschaum m

scurry ['skʌrɪ] vi huschen

scuttle ['skʌtl] n (also: **coal ~**) Kohleneimer m ♦ vt (ship) versenken ♦ vi (scamper): **to ~ away** or **off** sich davonmachen

scythe [saɪð] n Sense f

SDP (BRIT) n abbr = **Social Democratic**

Party

sea [siː] n Meer nt, See f; (fig) Meer nt ♦ adj Meeres-, See-; **by ~** (travel) auf dem Seeweg; **on the ~** (boat) auf dem Meer; (town) am Meer; **out to ~** aufs Meer hinaus; **out at ~** aufs Meer; **~board** n Küste f; **~food** n Meeresfrüchte pl; **~ front** n Strandpromenade f; **~going** adj seetüchtig, Hochsee-; **~gull** n Möwe f

seal [siːl] n (animal) Robbe f, Seehund m; (stamp, impression) Siegel nt ♦ vt versiegeln; **~ off** vt (place) abriegeln

sea level n Meeresspiegel m

sea lion n Seelöwe m

seam [siːm] n Saum m; (edges joining) Naht f; (of coal) Flöz nt

seaman [ˈsiːmən] (irreg) n Seemann m

seaplane [ˈsiːpleɪn] n Wasserflugzeug nt

seaport [ˈsiːpɔːt] n Seehafen m

search [sɜːtʃ] n (for person, thing) Suche f; (of drawer, pockets, house) Durchsuchung f ♦ vi suchen ♦ vt durchsuchen; **in ~ of** auf der Suche nach; **to ~ for** suchen nach; **~ through** vt durchsuchen; **~ engine** n (COMPUT) Suchmaschine f; **~ing** adj (look) forschend; **~light** n Scheinwerfer m; **~ party** n Suchmannschaft f; **~ warrant** n Durchsuchungsbefehl m

sea: ~shore [ˈsiːʃɔːr] n Meeresküste f; **~sick** [ˈsiːsɪk] adj seekrank; **~side** [ˈsiːsaɪd] n Küste f; **~side resort** n Badeort m

season [ˈsiːzn] n Jahreszeit f; (Christmas etc) Zeit f, Saison f ♦ vt (flavour) würzen; **~al** adj Saison-; **~ed** adj (fig) erfahren; **~ing** n Gewürz nt, Würze f; **~ ticket** n (RAIL) Zeitkarte f; (THEAT) Abonnement nt

seat [siːt] n Sitz m, Platz m; (in Parliament) Sitz m; (part of body) Gesäß nt; (of trousers) Hosenboden m ♦ vt (place) setzen; (have space for) Sitzplätze bieten für; **to be ~ed** sitzen; **~ belt** n Sicherheitsgurt m

sea: ~ water n Meerwasser nt; **~weed** [ˈsiːwiːd] n (See)tang m; **~worthy** [ˈsiːwɜːðɪ] adj seetüchtig

sec. abbr (= second(s)) Sek.

secluded [sɪˈkluːdɪd] adj abgelegen

seclusion [sɪˈkluːʒən] n Zurückgezogenheit f

second [ˈsɛkənd] adj zweite(r,s) ♦ adv (in ~ position) an zweiter Stelle ♦ n Sekunde f; (person) Zweite(r) mf; (COMM: imperfect) zweite Wahl f; (SPORT) Sekundant m; (AUT: also: ~ **gear**) zweite(r) Gang m; (BRIT: UNIV: degree) mittlere Note bei Abschlussprüfungen ♦ vt (support) unterstützen; **~ary** adj zweitrangig; **~ary school** n höhere Schule f, Mittelschule f; **~-class** adj zweiter Klasse; **~hand** adj aus zweiter Hand; (car etc) gebraucht; **~ hand** n (on clock) Sekundenzeiger m; **~ly** adv zweitens

secondment [sɪˈkɒndmənt] (BRIT) n Abordnung f

second-rate [ˈsɛkəndˈreɪt] adj mittelmäßig

second thoughts npl: **to have ~** es sich dat anders überlegen; **on ~** (BRIT) or **thought** (US) oder lieber (nicht)

secrecy [ˈsiːkrəsɪ] n Geheimhaltung f

secret [ˈsiːkrɪt] n Geheimnis nt ♦ adj geheim, Geheim-; **in ~** geheim

secretarial [sɛkrɪˈtɛərɪəl] adj Sekretärinnen-

secretary [ˈsɛkrətərɪ] n Sekretär(in) m(f); **S~ of State** (BRIT) n (POL): **S~ of State (for)** Minister(in) m(f) (für)

secretion [sɪˈkriːʃən] n Absonderung f

secretive [ˈsiːkrətɪv] adj geheimtuerisch

secretly [ˈsiːkrɪtlɪ] adv geheim

sectarian [sɛkˈtɛərɪən] adj (riots etc) Konfessions-, zwischen den Konfessionen

section [ˈsɛkʃən] n Teil m; (department) Abteilung f; (of document) Abschnitt m

sector [ˈsɛktər] n Sektor m

secular [ˈsɛkjulər] adj weltlich, profan

secure [sɪˈkjuər] adj (safe) sicher; (firmly fixed) fest ♦ vt (make firm) befestigen, sichern; (obtain) sichern; **security** [sɪˈkjuərɪtɪ] n Sicherheit f; (pledge) Pfand nt; (document) Wertpapier nt; (national security) Staatssicherheit f; **security guard** n Sicherheitsbeamte(r) m, Wächter m, Wache f

sedan [səˈdæn] (US) n (AUT) Limousine f

sedate [sɪˈdeɪt] adj gesetzt ♦ vt (MED) ein Beruhigungsmittel geben +dat; **sedation** [sɪˈdeɪʃən] n (MED) Einfluss m von Beruhigungsmitteln; **sedative** [ˈsɛdɪtɪv] n

Beruhigungsmittel *nt* ♦ *adj* beruhigend, einschläfernd

sediment ['sɛdɪmənt] *n* (Boden)satz *m*

seduce [sɪ'djuːs] *vt* verführen; **seductive** [sɪ'dʌktɪv] *adj* verführerisch

see [siː] (*pt* **saw**, *pp* **seen**) *vt* sehen; (*understand*) (ein)sehen, erkennen; (*visit*) besuchen ♦ *vi* (*be aware*) sehen; (*find out*) nachsehen ♦ *n* (*ECCL: R.C.*) Bistum *nt*; (: *Protestant*) Kirchenkreis *m*; **to ~ sb to the door** jdn hinausbegleiten; **to ~ that** (*ensure*) dafür sorgen, dass; **~ you soon!** bis bald!; **~ about** *vt fus* sich kümmern um; **~ off** *vt*: **to ~ sb off** jdn zum Zug *etc* begleiten; **~ through** *vt*: **to ~ sth through** etw durchfechten; **to ~ through sb/sth** jdn/etw durchschauen; **~ to** *vt fus*: **to ~ to it** dafür sorgen

seed [siːd] *n* Samen *m* ♦ *vt* (*TENNIS*) platzieren; **to go to ~** (*plant*) schießen; (*fig*) herunterkommen; **~ling** *n* Setzling *m*; **~y** *adj* (*café*) übel; (*person*) zweifelhaft

seeing ['siːɪŋ] *conj*: **~ (that)** da

seek [siːk] (*pt*, *pp* **sought**) *vt* suchen

seem [siːm] *vi* scheinen; **it ~s that ...** es scheint, dass ...; **~ingly** *adv* anscheinend

seen [siːn] *pp of* **see**

seep [siːp] *vi* sickern

seesaw ['siːsɔː] *n* Wippe *f*

seethe [siːð] *vi*: **to ~ with anger** vor Wut kochen

see-through ['siːθruː] *adj* (*dress etc*) durchsichtig

segment ['sɛgmənt] *n* Teil *m*; (*of circle*) Ausschnitt *m*

segregate ['sɛgrɪgeɪt] *vt* trennen

seize [siːz] *vt* (*grasp*) (er)greifen, packen; (*power*) ergreifen; (*take legally*) beschlagnahmen; **~ (up)on** *vt fus* sich stürzen auf +*acc*; **~ up** *vi* (*TECH*) sich festfressen; **seizure** ['siːʒəʳ] *n* (*illness*) Anfall *m*

seldom ['sɛldəm] *adv* selten

select [sɪ'lɛkt] *adj* ausgewählt ♦ *vt* auswählen; **~ion** [sɪ'lɛkʃən] *n* Auswahl *f*; **~ive** *adj* (*person*) wählerisch

self [sɛlf] (*pl* **selves**) *pron* selbst ♦ *n* Selbst

nt, Ich *nt*; **the ~** das Ich; **~-assured** *adj* selbstbewusst; **~-catering** (*BRIT*) *adj* für Selbstversorger; **~-centred** (*US* **self-centered**) *adj* egozentrisch; **~-coloured** (*US* **self-colored**) *adj* (*of one colour*) einfarbig, uni; **~-confidence** *n* Selbstvertrauen *nt*, Selbstbewusstsein *nt*; **~-conscious** *adj* gehemmt, befangen; **~-contained** *adj* (*complete*) (in sich) geschlossen; (*person*) verschlossen; (*BRIT: flat*) separat; **~-control** *n* Selbstbeherrschung *f*; **~-defence** (*US* **self-defense**) *n* Selbstverteidigung *f*; (*JUR*) Notwehr *f*; **~-discipline** *n* Selbstdisziplin *f*; **~-employed** *adj* frei(schaffend); **~-evident** *adj* offensichtlich; **~-governing** *adj* selbst verwaltet; **~-indulgent** *adj* zügellos; **~-interest** *n* Eigennutz *m*

selfish ['sɛlfɪʃ] *adj* egoistisch, selbstsüchtig; **~ness** *n* Egoismus *m*, Selbstsucht *f*

self: **~-lessly** *adv* selbstlos; **~-made** *adj*: **~-made man** Selfmademan *m*; **~-pity** *n* Selbstmitleid *nt*; **~-portrait** *n* Selbstbildnis *nt*; **~-possessed** *adj* selbstbeherrscht; **~-preservation** *n* Selbsterhaltung *f*; **~-reliant** *adj* unabhängig; **~-respect** *n* Selbstachtung *f*; **~-righteous** *adj* selbstgerecht; **~-sacrifice** *n* Selbstaufopferung *f*; **~-satisfied** *adj* selbstzufrieden; **~-service** *adj* Selbstbedienungs-; **~-sufficient** *adj* selbstgenügsam; **~-taught** *adj* selbst erlernt; **~-taught person** Autodidakt *m*

sell [sɛl] (*pt*, *pp* **sold**) *vt* verkaufen ♦ *vi* verkaufen; (*goods*) sich verkaufen; **to ~ at or for £10** für £10 verkaufen; **~ off** *vt* verkaufen; **~ out** *vi* alles verkaufen; **~-by date** *n* Verfalldatum *nt*; **~er** *n* Verkäufer *m*; **~ing price** *n* Verkaufspreis *m*

Sellotape ['sɛləuteɪp] (® *BRIT*) *n* Tesafilm *m* ®

sellout ['sɛlaut] *n* (*of tickets*): **it was a ~** es war ausverkauft

selves [sɛlvz] *npl of* **self**

semaphore ['sɛməfɔːʳ] *n* Winkzeichen *pl*

semblance ['sɛmblns] *n* Anschein *m*

semen ['siːmən] *n* Sperma *nt*

semester ['sɪ'mestər] (US) n Semester nt

semi ['semɪ] n = **semidetached house**; **~circle** n Halbkreis m; **~colon** n Semikolon nt; **~conductor** n Halbleiter m; **~detached house** (BRIT) n halbe(s) Doppelhaus nt; **~final** n Halbfinale nt

seminary ['semɪnərɪ] n (REL) Priesterseminar nt

semiskilled [semɪ'skɪld] adj angelernt

semi-skimmed [semɪ'skɪmd] adj (milk) teilentrahmt, Halbfett-

senate ['senɪt] n Senat m; **senator** n Senator m

send [send] (pt, pp **sent**) vt senden, schicken; (inf: inspire) hinreißen; **~ away** vt wegschicken; **~ away for** vt fus anfordern; **~ back** vt zurückschicken; **~ for** vt fus holen lassen; **~ off** vt (goods) abschicken; (BRIT: SPORT: player) vom Feld schicken; (invitation) aussenden; **~ up** vt hinaufsenden; (BRIT: parody) verulken; **~er** n Absender m; **~-off** n: **to give sb a good ~-off** jdn (ganz) groß verabschieden

senior ['sɪːnɪər] adj älter; (older) älter; (higher rank) Ober- ♦ n (older person) Ältere(r) mf; (higher ranking) Rangälteste(r) mf; **~ citizen** n ältere(r) Mitbürger(in) m(f); **~ity** [sɪːnɪ'ɔrɪtɪ] n (of age) höhere(s) Alter nt; (in rank) höhere(r) Dienstgrad m

sensation [sen'seɪʃən] n Gefühl nt; (excitement) Sensation f, Aufsehen nt; **~al** adj (wonderful) wunderbar; (result) sensationell; (headlines etc) reißerisch

sense [sens] n Sinn m; (understanding) Verstand m, Vernunft f; (feeling) Gefühl nt ♦ vt fühlen, spüren; **~ of humour** Humor m; **to make ~** Sinn ergeben; **~less** adj sinnlos; (unconscious) besinnungslos

sensibility [sensɪ'bɪlɪtɪ] n Empfindsamkeit f; (feeling hurt) Empfindlichkeit f; **sensibilities** npl (feelings) Zartgefühl nt

sensible ['sensɪbl] adj vernünftig

sensitive ['sensɪtɪv] adj: **~ (to)** empfindlich (gegen); **sensitivity** [sensɪ'tɪvɪtɪ] n Empfindlichkeit f; (artistic) Feingefühl nt; (tact) Feinfühligkeit f

sensual ['sensjʊəl] adj sinnlich

sensuous ['sensjʊəs] adj sinnlich

sent [sent] pt, pp of **send**

sentence ['sentns] n Satz m; (JUR) Strafe f; Urteil nt ♦ vt: **to ~ sb to death/to 5 years** jdn zum Tode/zu 5 Jahren verurteilen

sentiment ['sentɪmənt] n Gefühl nt; (thought) Gedanke m; **~al** [sentɪ'mentl] adj sentimental; (of feelings rather than reason) gefühlsmäßig

sentry ['sentrɪ] n (Schild)wache f

separate [adj 'seprɪt, vb 'sepəreɪt] adj getrennt, separat ♦ vt trennen ♦ vi sich trennen; **~ly** adv getrennt; **~s** npl (clothes) Röcke, Pullover etc; **separation** [sepə'reɪʃən] n Trennung f

September [sep'tembər] n September m

septic ['septɪk] adj vereitert, septisch; **~ tank** n Klärbehälter m

sequel ['siːkwl] n Folge f

sequence ['siːkwəns] n (Reihen)folge f

sequin ['siːkwɪn] n Paillette f

Serbia ['sɑːbɪə] n Serbien nt

serene [sɪ'riːn] adj heiter

sergeant ['sɑːdʒənt] n Feldwebel m; (POLICE) (Polizei)wachtmeister m

serial ['sɪərɪəl] n Fortsetzungsroman m; (TV) Fernsehserie f ♦ adj (number) (fort)laufend; **~ize** vt in Fortsetzungen veröffentlichen; in Fortsetzungen senden

series ['sɪərɪz] n inv Serie f, Reihe f

serious ['sɪərɪəs] adj ernst; (injury) schwer; **~ly** adv ernst(haft); (hurt) schwer; **~ness** n Ernst m, Ernsthaftigkeit f

sermon ['sɜːmən] n Predigt f

serrated [sɪ'reɪtɪd] adj gezackt

servant ['sɜːvənt] n Diener(in) m(f)

serve [sɜːv] vt dienen +dat; (guest, customer) bedienen; (food) servieren ♦ vi dienen, nützen; (at table) servieren; (TENNIS) geben, aufschlagen; **it ~s him right** das geschieht ihm recht; **that'll ~ as a table** das geht als Tisch; **to ~ a summons (on sb)** (jdn) vor Gericht laden; **~ out** or **up** vt (food) auftragen, servieren

service ['sɜːvɪs] n (help) Dienst m; (trains etc) Verbindung f; (hotel) Service m, Bedienung f; (set of dishes) Service nt; (REL)

Gottesdienst m; (car) Inspektion f; (for TVs etc) Kundendienst m; (TENNIS) Aufschlag m ♦ vt (AUT, TECH) warten, überholen; **the S~s** npl (armed forces) die Streitkräfte pl; **to be of ~ to sb** jdm einen großen Dienst erweisen; ~ **included/not included** Bedienung inbegriffen/nicht inbegriffen; ~**able** adj brauchbar; ~ **area** n (on motorway) Raststätte f; ~ **charge** (BRIT) n Bedienung f; ~**man** (irreg) n (soldier etc) Soldat m; ~ **station** n (Groß)tankstelle f

serviette [sɜ:vɪ'et] n Serviette f

servile ['sɜ:vaɪl] adj unterwürfig

session ['seʃən] n Sitzung f; (POL) Sitzungsperiode f; **to be in ~** tagen

set [set] (pt, pp **set**) n (collection of things) Satz m, Set nt; (RAD, TV) Apparat m; (TENNIS) Satz m; (group of people) Kreis m; (CINE) Szene f; (THEAT) Bühnenbild m ♦ adj festgelegt; (ready) bereit ♦ vt (place) setzen, stellen, legen; (arrange) (an)ordnen; (table) decken; (time, price) festsetzen; (alarm, watch, task) stellen; (jewels) (ein)fassen; (exam) ausarbeiten ♦ vi (sun) untergehen; (become hard) fest werden; (bone) zusammenwachsen; **to be ~ on doing sth** etw unbedingt tun wollen; **to ~ to music** vertonen; **to ~ on fire** anstecken; **to ~ free** freilassen; **to ~ sth going** etw in Gang bringen; **to ~ sail** losfahren; ~ **about** vt fus (task) anpacken; ~ **aside** vt beiseite legen; ~ **back** vt: **to ~ back (by)** zurückwerfen (um); ~ **off** vi aufbrechen ♦ vt (explode) sprengen; (alarm) losgehen lassen; (show up well) hervorheben; ~ **out** vi: **to ~ out to do sth** vorhaben, etw zu tun ♦ vt (arrange) anlegen, arrangieren; (state) darlegen; ~ **up** vt (organization) aufziehen; (record) aufstellen; (monument) erstellen; ~**back** n Rückschlag m; ~ **meal** n Menü nt; ~ **menu** n Tageskarte f

settee [se'ti:] n Sofa nt

setting ['setɪŋ] n Hintergrund m

settle ['setl] vt beruhigen; (pay) begleichen, bezahlen; (agree) regeln ♦ vi sich einleben; (come to rest) sich niederlassen; (sink) sich setzen; (calm down) sich beruhigen; **to ~ for**

sth sich mit etw zufrieden geben; **to ~ on** sth sich für etw entscheiden; **to ~ up with sb** mit jdm abrechnen; ~ **down** vi (feel at home) sich einleben; (calm down) sich beruhigen; ~ **in** vi sich eingewöhnen; ~**ment** n Regelung f; (payment) Begleichung f; (colony) Siedlung f; ~**r** n Siedler m

setup ['setʌp] n (situation) Lage f

seven ['sevn] num sieben; ~**teen** num siebzehn; ~**th** adj siebte(r, s) ♦ n Siebtel nt; ~**ty** num siebzig

sever ['sevər] vt abtrennen

several ['sevrəl] adj mehrere, verschiedene ♦ pron mehrere; ~ **of us** einige von uns

severance ['sevərəns] n: ~ **pay** Abfindung f

severe [sɪ'vɪər] adj (strict) streng; (serious) schwer; (climate) rauh; **severity** [sɪ'verɪtɪ] n Strenge f; Schwere f; Rauheit f

sew [səu] (pt **sewed**, pp **sewn**) vt, vi nähen; ~ **up** vt zunähen

sewage ['su:ɪdʒ] n Abwässer pl

sewer ['su:ər] n (Abwasser)kanal m

sewing ['səuɪŋ] n Näharbeit f; ~ **machine** n Nähmaschine f

sewn [səun] pp of **sew**

sex [seks] n Sex m; (gender) Geschlecht nt; **to have ~ with sb** mit jdm Geschlechtsverkehr haben; ~**ism** n Sexismus m; ~**ist** adj sexistisch ♦ n Sexist(in) m(f); ~**ual** ['seksjuəl] adj sexuell, geschlechtlich, Geschlechts-; ~**uality** [seksju'ælɪtɪ] n Sexualität f; ~**y** adj sexy

shabby ['ʃæbɪ] adj (also fig) schäbig

shack [ʃæk] n Hütte f

shackles ['ʃæklz] npl (also fig) Fesseln pl, Ketten pl

shade [ʃeɪd] n Schatten m; (for lamp) Lampenschirm m; (colour) Farbton m ♦ vt abschirmen; **in the ~** im Schatten; **a ~ smaller** ein bisschen kleiner

shadow ['ʃædəu] n Schatten m ♦ vt (follow) beschatten ♦ adj: ~ **cabinet** (BRIT: POL) Schattenkabinett nt; ~**y** adj schattig

shady ['ʃeɪdɪ] adj schattig; (fig) zwielichtig

shaft [ʃɑːft] n (of spear etc) Schaft m; (in mine) Schacht m; (TECH) Welle f; (of light)

Strahl m

shaggy ['ʃægɪ] adj struppig

shake [ʃeɪk] (pt **shook**, pp **shaken**) vt schütteln, rütteln; (shock) erschüttern ♦ vi (move) schwanken; (tremble) zittern, beben ♦ n (jerk) Schütteln nt, Rütteln nt; **to ~ hands with** die Hand geben +dat; **to ~ one's head** den Kopf schütteln; **~ off** vt abschütteln; **~ up** vt aufschütteln; (fig) aufrütteln; **~n** [ʃeɪkn] pp of **shake**; **shaky** ['ʃeɪkɪ] adj zittrig; (weak) unsicher

shall [ʃæl] vb aux: **I ~ go** ich werde gehen; **~ I open the door?** soll ich die Tür öffnen?; **I'll buy some cake, ~ I?** soll ich Kuchen kaufen?, ich kaufe Kuchen, oder?

shallow ['ʃæləʊ] adj seicht

sham [ʃæm] n Schein m ♦ adj unecht, falsch

shambles ['ʃæmblz] n Durcheinander nt

shame [ʃeɪm] n Scham f; (disgrace, pity) Schande f ♦ vt beschämen; **it is a ~ that** es ist schade, dass; **it is a ~ to do ...** es ist eine Schande, ... zu tun; **what a ~!** wie schade!; **~faced** adj beschämt; **~ful** adj schändlich; **~less** adj schamlos

shampoo [ʃæm'puː] n Shampoo(n) nt ♦ vt (hair) waschen; **~ and set** n Waschen nt und Legen

shamrock ['ʃæmrɒk] n Kleeblatt nt

shandy ['ʃændɪ] n Bier nt mit Limonade

shan't [ʃɑːnt] = **shall not**

shantytown ['ʃæntɪtaʊn] n Bidonville f

shape [ʃeɪp] n Form f ♦ vt formen, gestalten ♦ vi (also: **~ up**) sich entwickeln; **to take ~** Gestalt annehmen; **~d** suffix: **heart-~d** herzförmig; **~less** adj formlos; **~ly** adj wohlproportioniert

share [ʃɛəʳ] n (An)teil m; (FIN) Aktie f ♦ vt teilen; **to ~ out (among/between)** verteilen (unter/zwischen); **~holder** n Aktionär(in) m(f)

shark [ʃɑːk] n Hai(fisch) m; (swindler) Gauner m

sharp [ʃɑːp] adj scharf; (pin) spitz; (person) clever; (MUS) erhöht ♦ n Kreuz nt ♦ adv zu hoch; **nine o'clock ~** Punkt neun; **~en** vt schärfen; (pencil) spitzen; **~ener** n (also: **pencil ~ener**) Anspitzer m; **~-eyed** adj

scharfsichtig; **~ly** adv (turn, stop) plötzlich; (stand out, contrast) deutlich; (criticize, retort) scharf

shatter ['ʃætəʳ] vt zerschmettern; (fig) zerstören ♦ vi zerspringen

shave [ʃeɪv] n Rasur f ♦ vt rasieren ♦ vi sich rasieren; **to have a ~** sich rasieren (lassen); **~r** n (also: **electric ~r**) Rasierapparat m

shaving ['ʃeɪvɪŋ] n (action) Rasieren nt; **~s** npl (of wood etc) Späne pl; **~ brush** n Rasierpinsel m; **~ cream** n Rasiercreme f; **~ foam** n Rasierschaum m

shawl [ʃɔːl] n Schal m, Umhang m

she [ʃiː] pron sie ♦ adj weiblich

sheaf [ʃiːf] (pl **sheaves**) n Garbe f

shear [ʃɪəʳ] (pt **sheared**, pp **sheared** or **shorn**) vt scheren; **~ off** vi abbrechen; **~s** npl Heckenschere f

sheath [ʃiːθ] n Scheide f; (condom) Kondom m or nt

sheaves [ʃiːvz] npl of **sheaf**

shed [ʃed] (pt, pp **shed**) n Schuppen m; (for animals) Stall m ♦ vt (leaves etc) verlieren; (tears) vergießen

she'd [ʃiːd] = **she had**; **she would**

sheen [ʃiːn] n Glanz m

sheep [ʃiːp] n inv Schaf nt; **~dog** n Schäferhund m; **~ish** adj verlegen; **~skin** n Schaffell nt

sheer [ʃɪəʳ] adj bloß, rein; (steep) steil; (transparent) (hauch)dünn ♦ adv (directly) direkt

sheet [ʃiːt] n Betttuch nt, Bettlaken nt; (of paper) Blatt nt; (of metal etc) Platte f; (of ice) Fläche f

sheik(h) [ʃeɪk] n Scheich m

shelf [ʃelf] (pl **shelves**) n Bord nt, Regal nt

shell [ʃel] n Schale f; (seashell) Muschel f; (explosive) Granate f ♦ vt (peas) schälen; (fire on) beschießen

she'll [ʃiːl] = **she will**; **she shall**

shellfish ['ʃelfɪʃ] n Schalentier nt; (as food) Meeresfrüchte pl

shell suit n Ballonseidenanzug m

shelter ['ʃeltəʳ] n Schutz m; (air-raid ~) Bunker m ♦ vt schützen, bedecken; (refugees) aufnehmen ♦ vi sich unterstellen;

~ed adj (life) behütet; (spot) geschützt; ~
housing n (for old people) Altenwohnungen
pl; (for handicapped people)
Behindertenwohnungen pl
shelve [ʃɛlv] vt aufschieben ♦ vi abfallen
shelves [ʃɛlvz] npl of **shelf**
shepherd [ˈʃɛpəd] n Schäfer m ♦ vt treiben,
führen; ~'**s pie** n Auflauf aus Hackfleisch
und Kartoffelbrei
sheriff [ˈʃɛrɪf] n Sheriff m; (SCOTTISH)
Friedensrichter m
she's [ʃiːz] = **she is**; **she has**
Shetland [ˈʃɛtlənd] n (also: **the ~s, the ~
Isles**) die Shetlandinseln pl
shield [ʃiːld] n Schild m; (fig) Schirm m ♦ vt
(be)schirmen; (TECH) abschirmen
shift [ʃɪft] n Verschiebung f; (work) Schicht f
♦ vt (ver)rücken, verschieben; (arm)
wegnehmen ♦ vi sich verschieben; ~**less**
adj (person) träge; ~ **work** n Schichtarbeit
f; ~**y** adj verschlagen
shilly-shally [ˈʃɪlɪʃælɪ] vi zögern
shin [ʃɪn] n Schienbein nt
shine [ʃaɪn] (pt, pp **shone**) n Glanz m,
Schein m ♦ vt polieren ♦ vi scheinen; (fig)
glänzen; **to ~ a torch on sb** jdn (mit einer
Lampe) anleuchten
shingle [ˈʃɪŋgl] n Strandkies m; ~**s** npl (MED)
Gürtelrose f
shiny [ˈʃaɪnɪ] adj glänzend
ship [ʃɪp] n Schiff nt ♦ vt verschiffen;
~**building** n Schiffbau m; ~**ment** n
Schiffsladung f; ~**per** n Verschiffer m;
~**ping** n (act) Verschiffung f; (~s)
Schifffahrt f; ~**wreck** n Schiffbruch m;
(destroyed ~) Wrack nt ♦ vt: **to be
~wrecked** Schiffbruch erleiden; ~**yard** n
Werft f
shire [ˈʃaɪə] (BRIT) n Grafschaft f
shirk [ʃɜːk] vt ausweichen +dat
shirt [ʃɜːt] n (Ober)hemd nt; **in ~ sleeves** in
Hemdsärmeln
shit [ʃɪt] (inf!) excl Scheiße (!)
shiver [ˈʃɪvə] n Schauer m ♦ vi frösteln,
zittern
shoal [ʃəʊl] n (Fisch)schwarm m
shock [ʃɔk] n Erschütterung f; (mental)

Schock m; (ELEC) Schlag m ♦ vt erschüttern;
(offend) schockieren; ~ **absorber** n
Stoßdämpfer m; ~**ed** adj geschockt,
schockiert, erschüttert; ~**ing** adj unerhört
shod [ʃɔd] pt, pp of **shoe**
shoddy [ˈʃɔdɪ] adj schäbig
shoe [ʃuː] (pt, pp **shod**) n Schuh m; (of horse)
Hufeisen nt ♦ vt (horse) beschlagen;
~**brush** n Schuhbürste f; ~**horn** n
Schuhlöffel m; ~**lace** n Schnürsenkel m; ~
polish n Schuhcreme f; ~ **shop** n
Schuhgeschäft nt; ~**string** n (fig): **on a
~string** mit sehr wenig Geld
shone [ʃɔn] pt, pp of **shine**
shoo [ʃuː] excl sch; (to dog etc) pfui
shook [ʃʊk] pt of **shake**
shoot [ʃuːt] (pt, pp **shot**) n (branch)
Schössling m ♦ vt (gun) abfeuern; (goal,
arrow) schießen; (person) anschießen; (kill)
erschießen; (film) drehen ♦ vi (move quickly)
schießen; **to ~ (at)** schießen (auf +acc); ~
down vt abschießen; ~ **in** vi
hineinschießen; ~ **out** vi hinausschießen;
~ **up** vi (fig) aus dem Boden schießen;
~**ing** n Schießerei f; ~**ing star** n
Sternschnuppe f
shop [ʃɔp] n (esp BRIT) Geschäft nt, Laden m;
(workshop) Werkstatt f ♦ vi (also: **go ~ping**)
einkaufen gehen; ~ **assistant** (BRIT) n
Verkäufer(in) m(f); ~ **floor** (BRIT) n
Werkstatt f; ~**keeper** n Geschäftsinhaber
m; ~**lifting** n Ladendiebstahl m; ~**per** n
Käufer(in) m(f); ~**ping** n Einkaufen nt,
Einkauf m; ~**ping bag** n Einkaufstasche f;
~**ping centre** (US **shopping center**) n
Einkaufszentrum nt; ~**-soiled** adj
angeschmutzt; ~ **steward** (BRIT) n
(INDUSTRY) Betriebsrat m; ~ **window** n
Schaufenster nt
shore [ʃɔː] n Ufer nt; (of sea) Strand m ♦ vt:
to ~ up abstützen
shorn [ʃɔːn] pp of **shear**
short [ʃɔːt] adj kurz; (person) klein; (curt) kurz
angebunden; (measure) zu knapp ♦ n (also:
~ **film**) Kurzfilm m ♦ adv (suddenly) plötzlich
♦ vi (ELEC) einen Kurzschluss haben; ~**s** npl
(clothes) Shorts pl; **to be ~ of sth** nicht

genug von etw haben; **in ~** kurz gesagt; **~ of doing sth** ohne so weit zu gehen, etw zu tun; **everything ~ of ...** alles außer ...; **it is ~ for** das ist die Kurzform von; **to cut ~** abkürzen; **to fall ~ of sth** etw nicht erreichen; **to stop ~** plötzlich anhalten; **to stop ~ of** Halt machen vor; **~age** n Knappheit f, Mangel m; **~bread** n Mürbegebäck nt; **~-change** vt: **to ~-change sb** jdm zu wenig herausgeben; **~-circuit** n Kurzschluss m ♦ vi einen Kurzschluss haben ♦ vt kurzschließen; **~-coming** n Mangel m; **~-(crust) pastry** (BRIT) n Mürbeteig m; **~ cut** n Abkürzung f; **~en** vt (ab)kürzen; (clothes) kürzer machen; **~fall** n Defizit nt; **~hand** (BRIT) n Stenografie f; **~-hand typist** (BRIT) n Stenotypistin f; **~ list** (BRIT) n (for job) engere Wahl f; **~-lived** adj kurzlebig; **~ly** adv bald; **~ notice** n: **at ~ notice** kurzfristig; **~-sighted** (BRIT) adj (also fig) kurzsichtig; **~-staffed** adj: **to be ~-staffed** zu wenig Personal haben; **~-stay** n (car park) Kurzparken nt; **~ story** n Kurzgeschichte f; **~-tempered** adj leicht aufbrausend; **~-term** adj (effect) kurzfristig; **~ wave** n (RAD) Kurzwelle f

shot [ʃɒt] pt, pp of **shoot** ♦ n (from gun) Schuss m; (person) Schütze m; (try) Versuch m; (injection) Spritze f; (PHOT) Aufnahme f; **like a ~** wie der Blitz; **~gun** n Schrotflinte f

should [ʃʊd] vb aux: **I ~ go now** ich sollte jetzt gehen; **he ~ be there now** er sollte eigentlich schon da sein; **I ~ go if I were you** ich würde gehen, wenn ich du wäre; **I ~ like to** ich möchte gerne

shoulder [ˈʃəʊldəʳ] n Schulter f; (BRIT: of road) Seitenstreifen m ♦ vt (rifle) schultern; (fig) auf sich nehmen; **~ bag** n Umhängetasche f; **~ blade** n Schulterblatt nt; **~ strap** n (of dress etc) Träger m

shouldn't [ˈʃʊdnt] = **should not**

shout [ʃaʊt] n Schrei m; (call) Ruf m ♦ vt rufen ♦ vi schreien; **~ down** vt niederbrüllen; **~ing** n Geschrei nt

shove [ʃʌv] n Schubs m, Stoß m ♦ vt

schieben, stoßen, schubsen; (inf: put): **to ~ sth in(to) sth** etw in etw acc hineinschieben; **~ off** vi (NAUT) abstoßen; (fig: inf) abhauen

shovel [ˈʃʌvl] n Schaufel f ♦ vt schaufeln

show [ʃəʊ] (pt showed, pp shown) n (display) Schau f; (exhibition) Ausstellung f; (CINE, THEAT) Vorstellung f, Show f ♦ vt zeigen; (kindness) erweisen ♦ vi zu sehen sein; **to be on ~** (exhibits etc) ausgestellt sein; **to ~ sb in** jdn hereinführen; **to ~ sb out** jdn hinausbegleiten; **~ off** vi (pej) angeben ♦ vt (display) ausstellen; **~ up** vi (stand out) sich abheben; (arrive) erscheinen ♦ vt aufzeigen; (unmask) bloßstellen; **~ business** n Showbusiness nt; **~down** n Kraftprobe f

shower [ˈʃaʊəʳ] n Schauer m; (of stones) (Stein)hagel m; (~ bath) Dusche f ♦ vi duschen ♦ vt: **to ~ sb with sth** jdn mit etw überschütten; **~proof** adj Wasser abstoßend

showing [ˈʃəʊɪŋ] n Vorführung f

show jumping n Turnierreiten nt

shown [ʃəʊn] pp of **show**

show: **~-off** [ˈʃəʊɒf] n Angeber(in) m(f); **~piece** [ˈʃəʊpiːs] n Paradestück nt; **~room** [ˈʃəʊruːm] n Ausstellungsraum m

shrank [ʃræŋk] pt of **shrink**

shred [ʃred] n Fetzen m ♦ vt zerfetzen; (COOK) raspeln; **~der** n (COOK) Gemüseschneider m; (for documents) Reißwolf m

shrewd [ʃruːd] adj clever

shriek [ʃriːk] n Schrei m ♦ vt, vi kreischen, schreien

shrill [ʃrɪl] adj schrill

shrimp [ʃrɪmp] n Krabbe f, Garnele f

shrine [ʃraɪn] n Schrein m; (fig) Gedenkstätte f

shrink [ʃrɪŋk] (pt shrank, pp shrunk) vi schrumpfen, eingehen ♦ vt einschrumpfen lassen; **to ~ from doing sth** davor zurückschrecken, etw zu tun; **~age** n Schrumpfung f; **~-wrap** vt einschweißen

shrivel [ˈʃrɪvl] vt, vi (also: ~ up) schrumpfen, schrumpeln

shroud [ʃraud] n Leichentuch nt ♦ vt: **~ed in mystery** mit einem Geheimnis umgeben

Shrove Tuesday ['ʃrəuv-] n Fastnachtsdienstag m

shrub [ʃrʌb] n Busch m, Strauch m; **~bery** n Gebüsch nt

shrug [ʃrʌg] n Achselzucken nt ♦ vt, vi: **to ~ (one's shoulders)** die Achseln zucken; **~ off** vt auf die leichte Schulter nehmen

shrunk [ʃrʌŋk] pp of **shrink**

shudder ['ʃʌdər] n Schauder m ♦ vi schaudern

shuffle ['ʃʌfl] vt (cards) mischen; **to ~ (one's feet)** schlurfen

shun [ʃʌn] vt scheuen, (ver)meiden

shunt [ʃʌnt] vt rangieren

shut [ʃʌt] (pt, pp **shut**) vt schließen, zumachen ♦ vi sich schließen (lassen); **~ down** vt, vi schließen; **~ off** vt (supply) abdrehen; **~ up** vi (keep quiet) den Mund halten ♦ vt (close) zuschließen; **~ter** n Fensterladen m; (PHOT) Verschluss m

shuttle ['ʃʌtl] n (plane, train etc) Pendelflugzeug nt/-zug m etc; (also: **~ service**) Raumtransporter m; Pendelverkehr m; **~cock** ['ʃʌtlkɔk] n Federball m; **~ diplomacy** n Pendeldiplomatie f

shy [ʃai] adj schüchtern; **~ness** n Schüchternheit f

Siamese [saiə'miːz] adj: **~ cat** Siamkatze f

Siberia [sai'biəriə] n Sibirien nt

sibling ['sibliŋ] n Geschwister nt

Sicily ['sisili] n Sizilien nt

sick [sik] adj krank; (joke) makaber; **I feel ~** mir ist schlecht; **I was ~** ich habe gebrochen; **to be ~ of sb/sth** jdn/etw satt haben; **~ bay** n (Schiffs)lazarett nt; **~en** vt (disgust) krank machen ♦ vi krank werden; **~ening** adj (annoying) zum Weinen

sickle ['sikl] n Sichel f

sick: ~ leave n: **to be on ~ leave** krankgeschrieben sein; **~ly** adj kränklich, blass; (causing nausea) widerlich; **~ness** n Krankheit f; (vomiting) Übelkeit f, Erbrechen nt; **~ note** n Arbeitsunfähigkeits-bescheinigung f; **~ pay** n Krankengeld

nt

side [said] n Seite f ♦ adj (door, entrance) Seiten-, Neben- ♦ vi: **to ~ with sb** jds Partei ergreifen; **by the ~ of** neben; **~ by ~** nebeneinander; **on all ~s** von allen Seiten; **to take ~s (with)** Partei nehmen (für); **from all ~s** von allen Seiten; **~board** n Sideboard nt; **~boards** (BRIT) npl Koteletten pl; **~burns** npl Koteletten pl; **~car** n Beiwagen m; **~ drum** n (MUS) kleine Trommel; **~ effect** n Nebenwirkung f; **~light** n (AUT) Parkleuchte f; **~line** n (SPORT) Seitenlinie f; (fig: hobby) Nebenbeschäftigung f; **~long** adj Seiten-; **~ order** n Beilage f; **~saddle** adv im Damensattel; **~ show** n Nebenausstellung f; **~step** vt (fig) ausweichen; **~ street** n Seitenstraße f; **~track** vt (fig) ablenken; **~walk** n (US) Bürgersteig m; **~ways** adv seitwärts

siding ['saidiŋ] n Nebengleis nt

sidle ['saidl] vi: **to ~ up (to)** sich heranmachen (an +acc)

siege [siːdʒ] n Belagerung f

sieve [siv] n Sieb nt ♦ vt sieben

sift [sift] vt sieben; (fig) sichten

sigh [sai] n Seufzer m ♦ vi seufzen

sight [sait] n (power of seeing) Sehvermögen nt; (look) Blick m; (fact of seeing) Anblick m; (of gun) Visier nt ♦ vt sichten; **in ~** in Sicht; **out of ~** außer Sicht; **~seeing** n Besuch m von Sehenswürdigkeiten; **to go ~seeing** Sehenswürdigkeiten besichtigen

sign [sain] n Zeichen nt; (notice, road ~ etc) Schild nt ♦ vt unterschreiben; **to ~ sth over to sb** jdm etw überschreiben; **~ on** vi (as unemployed) sich (arbeitslos) melden ♦ vt (employee) anstellen; **~ up** vi (MIL) sich verpflichten ♦ vt verpflichten

signal ['signl] n Signal nt ♦ vt ein Zeichen geben +dat; **~man** (irreg) n (RAIL) Stellwerkswärter m

signature ['signətʃər] n Unterschrift f; **~ tune** n Erkennungsmelodie f

signet ring ['signət-] n Siegelring m

significance [sig'nifikəns] n Bedeutung f

significant [sig'nifikənt] adj (meaning sth)

bedeutsam; (*important*) bedeutend

signify ['sɪgnɪfaɪ] *vt* bedeuten; (*show*) andeuten, zu verstehen geben

sign language *n* Zeichensprache *f*, Fingersprache *f*

signpost ['saɪnpəʊst] *n* Wegweiser *m*

silence ['saɪləns] *n* Stille *f*; (*of person*) Schweigen *nt* ♦ *vt* zum Schweigen bringen; **~r** *n* (*on gun*) Schalldämpfer *m*; (*BRIT: AUT*) Auspufftopf *m*

silent ['saɪlənt] *adj* still; (*person*) schweigsam; **to remain ~** schweigen; **~ partner** *n* (*COMM*) stille(r) Teilhaber *m*

silicon chip ['sɪlɪkən-] *n* Siliciumchip *m*, Siliziumchip *m*

silk [sɪlk] *n* Seide *f* ♦ *adj* seiden, Seiden-; **~y** *adj* seidig

silly ['sɪlɪ] *adj* dumm, albern

silt [sɪlt] *n* Schlamm *m*, Schlick *m*

silver ['sɪlvəʳ] *n* Silber *nt* ♦ *adj* silbern, Silber-; **~ paper** (*BRIT*) *n* Silberpapier *nt*; **~-plated** *adj* versilbert; **~smith** *n* Silberschmied *m*; **~ware** *n* Silber *nt*; **~y** *adj* silbern

similar ['sɪmɪləʳ] *adj*: **~ (to)** ähnlich (+*dat*); **~ity** [sɪmɪˈlærɪtɪ] *n* Ähnlichkeit *f*; **~ly** *adv* in ähnlicher Weise

simmer ['sɪməʳ] *vi* sieden ♦ *vt* sieden lassen

simple ['sɪmpl] *adj* einfach; **~(-minded)** *adj* einfältig

simplicity [sɪmˈplɪsɪtɪ] *n* Einfachheit *f*; (*of person*) Einfältigkeit *f*

simplify ['sɪmplɪfaɪ] *vt* vereinfachen

simply ['sɪmplɪ] *adv* einfach

simulate ['sɪmjʊleɪt] *vt* simulieren

simultaneous [sɪməlˈteɪnɪəs] *adj* gleichzeitig

sin [sɪn] *n* Sünde *f* ♦ *vi* sündigen

since [sɪns] *adv* seither ♦ *prep* seit, seitdem ♦ *conj* (*time*) seit; (*because*) da, weil; **~ then** seitdem

sincere [sɪnˈsɪəʳ] *adj* aufrichtig; **~ly** *adv*: **yours ~ly** mit freundlichen Grüßen; **sincerity** [sɪnˈsɛrɪtɪ] *n* Aufrichtigkeit *f*

sinew ['sɪnjuː] *n* Sehne *f*

sinful ['sɪnfʊl] *adj* sündig, sündhaft

sing [sɪŋ] (*pt* **sang**, *pp* **sung**) *vt*, *vi* singen

Singapore [sɪŋgəˈpɔːʳ] *n* Singapur *nt*

singe [sɪndʒ] *vt* versengen

singer ['sɪŋəʳ] *n* Sänger(in) *m(f)*

singing ['sɪŋɪŋ] *n* Singen *nt*, Gesang *m*

single ['sɪŋgl] *adj* (*one only*) einzig; (*bed, room*) Einzel-, einzeln; (*unmarried*) ledig; (*BRIT: ticket*) einfach; (*having one part only*) einzeln ♦ *n* (*BRIT: also*: **~ ticket**) einfache Fahrkarte *f*; **in ~ file** hintereinander; **~ out** *vt* aussuchen, auswählen; **~ bed** *n* Einzelbett *nt*; **~-breasted** *adj* einreihig; **~-handed** *adj* allein; **~-minded** *adj* zielstrebig; **~ parent** *n* Alleinerziehende(r) *f(m)*; **~ room** *n* Einzelzimmer *nt*; **~s** *n* (*TENNIS*) Einzel *nt*; **~-track road** *n* einspurige Straße (mit Ausweichstellen);

singly *adv* einzeln, allein

singular ['sɪŋgjʊləʳ] *adj* (*odd*) merkwürdig, seltsam ♦ *n* (*GRAM*) Einzahl *f*, Singular *m*

sinister ['sɪnɪstəʳ] *adj* (*evil*) böse; (*ghostly*) unheimlich

sink [sɪŋk] (*pt* **sank**, *pp* **sunk**) *n* Spülbecken *nt* ♦ *vt* (*ship*) versenken ♦ *vi* sinken; **to ~ sth into** (*teeth, claws*) etw schlagen in +*acc*; **~ in** *vi* (*news etc*) eingehen

sinner ['sɪnəʳ] *n* Sünder(in) *m(f)*

sinus ['saɪnəs] *n* (*ANAT*) Sinus *m*

sip [sɪp] *n* Schlückchen *nt* ♦ *vt* nippen an +*dat*

siphon ['saɪfən] *n* Siphon(flasche *f*) *m*; **~ off** *vt* absaugen; (*fig*) abschöpfen

sir [səʳ] *n* (*respect*) Herr *m*; (*knight*) Sir *m*; **S~ John Smith** Sir John Smith; **yes ~** ja(wohl, mein Herr)

siren ['saɪərn] *n* Sirene *f*

sirloin ['səːlɔɪn] *n* Lendenstück *nt*

sissy ['sɪsɪ] (*inf*) *n* Waschlappen *m*

sister ['sɪstəʳ] *n* Schwester *f*; (*BRIT: nurse*) Oberschwester *f*; (*nun*) Ordensschwester *f*; **~-in-law** *n* Schwägerin *f*

sit [sɪt] (*pt*, *pp* **sat**) *vi* sitzen; (*hold session*) tagen ♦ *vt* (*exam*) machen; **~ down** *vi* sich hinsetzen; **~ in on** *vt fus* dabei sein bei; **~ up** *vi* (*after lying*) sich aufsetzen; (*straight*) sich gerade setzen; (*at night*) aufbleiben

sitcom ['sɪtkɔm] *n abbr* (= *situation comedy*) Situationskomödie *f*

site [saɪt] *n* Platz *m*; (*also*: **building ~**)

Baustelle *f* ♦ *vt* legen

sitting ['sɪtɪŋ] *n* (*meeting*) Sitzung *f*; ~ **room** *n* Wohnzimmer *nt*

situated ['sɪtjueɪtɪd] *adj*: **to be** ~ liegen

situation [sɪtjʊ'eɪʃən] *n* Situation *f*, Lage *f*; (*place*) Lage *f*; (*employment*) Stelle *f*; **"~s vacant"** (*BRIT*) „Stellenangebote" *pl*

six [sɪks] *num* sechs; ~**teen** *num* sechzehn; ~**th** *adj* sechste(r, s) ♦ *n* Sechstel *nt*; ~**ty** *num* sechzig

size [saɪz] *n* Größe *f*; (*of project*) Umfang *m*; ~ **up** *vt* (*assess*) abschätzen, einschätzen; ~**able** *adj* ziemlich groß, ansehnlich

sizzle ['sɪzl] *vi* zischen; (*COOK*) brutzeln

skate [skeɪt] *n* Schlittschuh *m*; (*fish: pl inv*) Rochen *m* ♦ *vi* Schlittschuh laufen; ~**board** *n* Skateboard *nt*; ~**boarding** *n* Skateboardfahren *nt*; ~**r** *n* Schlittschuhläufer(in) *m(f)*; **skating** ['skeɪtɪŋ] *n* Eislauf *m*; **to go skating** Eis laufen gehen; **skating rink** *n* Eisbahn *f*

skeleton ['skelɪtn] *n* Skelett *nt*; (*fig*) Gerüst *nt*; ~ **key** *n* Dietrich *m*; ~ **staff** *n* Notbesetzung *f*

skeptical ['skeptɪkl] (*US*) *adj* = **sceptical**

sketch [sketʃ] *n* Skizze *f*; (*THEAT*) Sketch *m* ♦ *vt* skizzieren; ~**book** *n* Skizzenbuch *nt*; ~**y** *adj* skizzenhaft

skewer ['skjuːəʳ] *n* Fleischspieß *m*

ski [skiː] *n* Ski *m*, Schi *m* ♦ *vi* Ski *or* Schi laufen; ~ **boot** *n* Skistiefel *m*

skid [skɪd] *n* (*AUT*) Schleudern *nt* ♦ *vi* rutschen; (*AUT*) schleudern

ski: ~**er** ['skiːəʳ] *n* Skiläufer(in) *m(f)*; ~**ing** ['skiːɪŋ] *n*: **to go ~ing** Ski laufen gehen; ~-**jump** *n* Sprungschanze *f* ♦ *vi* Ski springen

skilful ['skɪlful] *adj* geschickt

ski-lift *n* Skilift *m*

skill [skɪl] *n* Können *nt*; ~**ed** *adj* geschickt; (*worker*) Fach-, gelernt

skim [skɪm] *vt* (*liquid*) abschöpfen; (*glide over*) gleiten über +*acc* ♦ *vi*: ~ **through** (*book*) überfliegen; ~**med milk** *n* Magermilch *f*

skimp [skɪmp] *vt* (*do carelessly*) oberflächlich tun; ~**y** *adj* (*dress*) knapp

skin [skɪn] *n* Haut *f*; (*peel*) Schale *f* ♦ *vt* abhäuten; schälen; ~ **cancer** *n* Hautkrebs *m*; ~-**deep** *adj* oberflächlich; ~ **diving** *n* Schwimmtauchen *nt*; ~**head** *n* Skinhead *m*; ~**ny** *adj* dünn; ~**tight** *adj* (*dress etc*) hauteng

skip [skɪp] *n* Sprung *m* ♦ *vi* hüpfen; (*with rope*) Seil springen ♦ *vt* (*pass over*) übergehen

ski: ~ **pants** *npl* Skihosen *pl*; ~ **pass** *n* Skipass *nt*; ~ **pole** *n* Skistock *m*

skipper ['skɪpəʳ] *n* Kapitän *m* ♦ *vt* führen

skipping rope ['skɪpɪŋ-] (*BRIT*) *n* Hüpfseil *nt*

skirmish ['skɜːmɪʃ] *n* Scharmützel *nt*

skirt [skɜːt] *n* Rock *m* ♦ *vt* herumgehen um; (*fig*) umgehen; ~**ing board** (*BRIT*) *n* Fußleiste *f*

ski suit *n* Skianzug *m*

skit [skɪt] *n* Parodie *f*

ski tow *n* Schlepplift *m*

skittle ['skɪtl] *n* Kegel *m*; ~**s** *n* (*game*) Kegeln *nt*

skive [skaɪv] (*BRIT*: *inf*) *vi* schwänzen

skulk [skʌlk] *vi* sich herumdrücken

skull [skʌl] *n* Schädel *m*

skunk [skʌŋk] *n* Stinktier *nt*

sky [skaɪ] *n* Himmel *m*; ~**light** *n* Oberlicht *nt*; ~**scraper** *n* Wolkenkratzer *m*

slab [slæb] *n* (*of stone*) Platte *f*

slack [slæk] *adj* (*loose*) locker; (*business*) flau; (*careless*) nachlässig, lasch ♦ *vi* nachlässig sein ♦ *n*: **to take up the ~** straff ziehen; ~**s** *npl* (*trousers*) Hose(n) *pl f*; ~**en** *vi* (*also*: ~**en off**) locker werden; (: *slow down*) stocken, nachlassen ♦ *vt* (: *loosen*) lockern

slag [slæg] (*BRIT*) *vt*: ~ **off** (*criticize*) (he)runtermachen

slag heap [slæg-] *n* Halde *f*

slain [sleɪn] *pp* of **slay**

slam [slæm] *n* Knall *m* ♦ *vt* (*door*) zuschlagen; (*throw down*) knallen ♦ *vi* zuschlagen

slander ['slɑːndəʳ] *n* Verleumdung *f* ♦ *vt* verleumden

slang [slæŋ] *n* Slang *m*; (*jargon*) Jargon *m*

slant [slɑːnt] *n* Schräge *f*; (*fig*) Tendenz *f* ♦ *vt* schräg legen ♦ *vi* schräg liegen; ~**ed** *adj* schräg; ~**ing** *adj* schräg

slap [slæp] *n* Klaps *m* ♦ *vt* einen Klaps geben +*dat* ♦ *adv* (*directly*) geradewegs; **~dash** *adj* salopp; **~stick** *n* (*comedy*) Klamauk *m*; **~-up** (*BRIT*) *adj* (*meal*) erstklassig, prima

slash [slæʃ] *n* Schnittwunde *f* ♦ *vt* (auf)schlitzen

slat [slæt] *n* Leiste *f*

slate [sleɪt] *n* (*stone*) Schiefer *m*; (*roofing*) Dachziegel *m* ♦ *vt* (*criticize*) verreißen

slaughter ['slɔːtə'] *n* (*of animals*) Schlachten *nt*; (*of people*) Gemetzel *nt* ♦ *vt* schlachten; (*people*) niedermetzeln; **~house** *n* Schlachthof *m*

Slav [slɑːv] *adj* slawisch

slave [sleɪv] *n* Sklave *m*, Sklavin *f* ♦ *vi* schuften, sich schinden; **~ry** *n* Sklaverei *f*

slay [sleɪ] (*pt* **slew**, *pp* **slain**) *vt* ermorden

sleazy ['sliːzɪ] *adj* (*place*) schmierig

sledge [sledʒ] *n* Schlitten *m*

sledgehammer ['sledʒhæmə'] *n* Schmiedehammer *m*

sledging *n* Schlittenfahren *nt*

sleek [sliːk] *adj* glatt; (*shape*) rassig

sleep [sliːp] (*pt, pp* **slept**) *n* Schlaf *m* ♦ *vi* schlafen; **to go to ~** einschlafen; **~ in** *vi* ausschlafen; (*oversleep*) verschlafen; **~er** *n* (*person*) Schläfer *m*; (*BRIT: RAIL*) Schlafwagen *m*; (*: beam*) Schwelle *f*; **~ing bag** *n* Schlafsack *m*; **~ing car** *n* Schlafwagen *m*; **~ing partner** *n* = **silent partner**; **~ing pill** *n* Schlaftablette *f*; **~less** *adj* (*night*) schlaflos; **~walker** *n* Schlafwandler(in) *m(f)*; **~y** *adj* schläfrig

sleet [sliːt] *n* Schneeregen *m*

sleeve [sliːv] *n* Ärmel *m*; (*of record*) Umschlag *m*; **~less** *adj* ärmellos

sleigh [sleɪ] *n* Pferdeschlitten *m*

sleight [slaɪt] *n*: **~ of hand** Fingerfertigkeit *f*

slender ['slendə'] *adj* schlank; (*fig*) gering

slept [slept] *pt, pp* of **sleep**

slew [sluː] *vi* (*veer*) (herum)schwenken ♦ *pt* of **slay**

slice [slaɪs] *n* Scheibe *f* ♦ *vt* in Scheiben schneiden

slick [slɪk] *adj* (*clever*) raffiniert, aalglatt ♦ *n* Ölteppich *m*

slid [slɪd] *pt, pp* of **slide**

slide [slaɪd] (*pt, pp* **slid**) *n* Rutschbahn *f*; (*PHOT*) Dia(positiv) *nt*; (*BRIT: for hair*) (Haar)spange *f* ♦ *vt* schieben ♦ *vi* (*slip*) gleiten, rutschen; **sliding** ['slaɪdɪŋ] *adj* (*door*) Schiebe-; **sliding scale** *n* gleitende Skala *f*

slight [slaɪt] *adj* zierlich; (*trivial*) geringfügig; (*small*) gering ♦ *n* Kränkung *f* ♦ *vt* (*offend*) kränken; **not in the ~est** nicht im Geringsten; **~ly** *adv* etwas, ein bisschen

slim [slɪm] *adj* schlank; (*book*) dünn; (*chance*) gering ♦ *vi* eine Schlankheitskur machen

slime [slaɪm] *n* Schleim *m*

slimming ['slɪmɪŋ] *n* Schlankheitskur *f*

slimy ['slaɪmɪ] *adj* glitschig; (*dirty*) schlammig; (*person*) schmierig

sling [slɪŋ] (*pt, pp* **slung**) *n* Schlinge *f*; (*weapon*) Schleuder *f* ♦ *vt* schleudern

slip [slɪp] *n* (*mistake*) Flüchtigkeitsfehler *m*; (*petticoat*) Unterrock *m*; (*of paper*) Zettel *m* ♦ *vt* (*put*) stecken, schieben ♦ *vi* (*lose balance*) ausrutschen; (*move*) gleiten, rutschen; (*decline*) nachlassen; (*move smoothly*): **to ~ in/out** hinein-/hinausschlüpfen; **to give sb the ~** jdm entwischen; **~ of the tongue** Versprecher *m*; **it ~ped my mind** das ist mir entfallen; **to ~ sth on/off** etw über-/abstreifen; **~ away** *vi* sich wegstehlen; **~ in** *vt* hineingleiten lassen ♦ *vi* (*errors*) sich einschleichen; **~ped disc** *n* Bandscheibenschaden *m*

slipper ['slɪpə'] *n* Hausschuh *m*

slippery ['slɪpərɪ] *adj* glatt

slip: ~ road (*BRIT*) *n* Auffahrt *f*/Ausfahrt *f*; **~shod** *adj* schlampig; **~-up** *n* Panne *f*; **~way** *n* Auslaufbahn *f*

slit [slɪt] (*pt, pp* **slit**) *n* Schlitz *m* ♦ *vt* aufschlitzen

slither ['slɪðə'] *vi* schlittern; (*snake*) sich schlängeln

sliver ['slɪvə'] *n* (*of glass, wood*) Splitter *m*; (*of cheese*) Scheibchen *nt*

slob [slɔb] (*inf*) *n* Klotz *m*

slog [slɔg] *vi* (*work hard*) schuften ♦ *n*: **it was a ~** es war eine Plackerei

slogan ['sləʊgən] *n* Schlagwort *nt*; (*COMM*)

Werbespruch *m*

slop [slɔp] *vi* (*also:* **~ over**) überschwappen
♦ *vt* verschütten

slope [sləʊp] *n* Neigung *f*; (*of mountains*)
(Ab)hang *m* ♦ *vi*: **to ~ down** sich senken; **to
~ up** ansteigen; **sloping** ['sləʊpɪŋ] *adj*
schräg

sloppy ['slɔpɪ] *adj* schlampig

slot [slɔt] *n* Schlitz *m* ♦ *vt*: **to ~ sth in** etw
einlegen

sloth [sləʊθ] *n* (*laziness*) Faulheit *f*

slot machine *n* (*BRIT*) Automat *m*; (*for
gambling*) Spielautomat *m*

slouch [slaʊtʃ] *vi*: **to ~ about** (*laze*)
herumhängen (*inf*)

slovenly ['slʌvənlɪ] *adj* schlampig; (*speech*)
salopp

slow [sləʊ] *adj* langsam ♦ *adv* langsam; **to
be ~** (*clock*) nachgehen; (*stupid*)
begriffsstutzig sein; **"~"** (*road sign*)
„Langsam"; **in ~ motion** in Zeitlupe; **~
down** *vi* langsamer werden ♦ *vt*
verlangsamen; **~ up** *vi* sich verlangsamen,
sich verzögern ♦ *vt* aufhalten, langsamer
machen; **~ly** *adv* langsam

sludge [slʌdʒ] *n* Schlamm *m*

slug [slʌg] *n* Nacktschnecke *f*; (*inf: bullet*)
Kugel *f*

sluggish ['slʌgɪʃ] *adj* träge; (*COMM*)
schleppend

sluice [sluːs] *n* Schleuse *f*

slum [slʌm] *n* (*house*) Elendsquartier *nt*

slump [slʌmp] *n* Rückgang *m* ♦ *vi* fallen,
stürzen

slung [slʌŋ] *pt, pp of* **sling**

slur [sləːʳ] *n* Undeutlichkeit *f*; (*insult*)
Verleumdung *f*; **~red** [sləːd] *adj*
(*pronunciation*) undeutlich

slush [slʌʃ] *n* (*snow*) Schneematsch *m*; **~
fund** *n* Schmiergeldfonds *m*

slut [slʌt] *n* Schlampe *f*

sly [slaɪ] *adj* schlau

smack [smæk] *n* Klaps *m* ♦ *vt* einen Klaps
geben +*dat* ♦ *vi*: **to ~ of** riechen nach; **to ~
one's lips** schmatzen, sich *dat* die Lippen
lecken

small [smɔːl] *adj* klein; **in the ~ hours** in den

frühen Morgenstunden; **~ ads** (*BRIT*) *npl*
Kleinanzeigen *pl*; **~ change** *n* Kleingeld *nt*;
~holder (*BRIT*) *n* Kleinbauer *m*; **~pox** *n*
Pocken *pl*; **~ talk** *n* Geplauder *nt*

smart [smɑːt] *adj* (*fashionable*) elegant,
schick; (*neat*) adrett; (*clever*) clever; (*quick*)
scharf ♦ *vi* brennen, schmerzen; **~ card** *n*
Chipkarte *f*; **~en up** *vi* sich in Schale
werfen ♦ *vt* herausputzen

smash [smæʃ] *n* Zusammenstoß *m*; (*TENNIS*)
Schmetterball *m* ♦ *vt* (*break*) zerschmettern;
(*destroy*) vernichten ♦ *vi* (*break*) zersplittern,
zerspringen; **~ing** (*inf*) *adj* toll

smattering ['smætərɪŋ] *n* oberflächliche
Kenntnis *f*

smear [smɪəʳ] *n* Fleck *m* ♦ *vt* beschmieren

smell [smɛl] *n* (*pt, pp* **smelt** *or* **smelled**) *vt*
Geruch *m*; (*sense*) Geruchssinn *m* ♦ *vt*
riechen ♦ *vi*: **to ~ (of)** riechen (nach);
(*fragrantly*) duften (nach); **~y** *adj* übel
riechend

smile [smaɪl] *n* Lächeln *nt* ♦ *vi* lächeln

smiling ['smaɪlɪŋ] *adj* lächelnd

smirk [sməːk] *n* blöde(s) Grinsen *nt*

smock [smɔk] *n* Kittel *m*

smoke [sməʊk] *n* Rauch *m* ♦ *vt* rauchen;
(*food*) räuchern ♦ *vi* rauchen; **~d** *adj*
(*bacon*) geräuchert; (*glass*) Rauch-; **~r** *n*
Raucher(in) *m(f)*; (*RAIL*) Raucherabteil *nt*; **~
screen** *n* Rauchwand *f*

smoking ['sməʊkɪŋ] *n*: **"no ~"** „Rauchen
verboten"; **~ compartment** (*BRIT*), **~ car**
(*US*) *n* Raucherabteil *nt*

smoky ['sməʊkɪ] *adj* rauchig; (*room*)
verraucht; (*taste*) geräuchert

smolder ['sməʊldəʳ] (*US*) *vi* = **smoulder**

smooth [smuːð] *adj* glatt ♦ *vt* (*also:* **~ out**)
glätten, glatt streichen

smother ['smʌðəʳ] *vt* ersticken

smoulder ['sməʊldəʳ] (*US* **smolder**) *vi*
schwelen

smudge [smʌdʒ] *n* Schmutzfleck *m* ♦ *vt*
beschmieren

smug [smʌg] *adj* selbstgefällig

smuggle ['smʌgl] *vt* schmuggeln; **~r** *n*
Schmuggler *m*

smuggling ['smʌglɪŋ] *n* Schmuggel *m*

smutty ['smʌtɪ] *adj* schmutzig

snack [snæk] *n* Imbiss *m*; ~ **bar** *n* Imbissstube *f*

snag [snæg] *n* Haken *m*

snail [sneɪl] *n* Schnecke *f*

snake [sneɪk] *n* Schlange *f*

snap [snæp] *n* Schnappen *nt*; (*photograph*) Schnappschuss *m* ♦ *adj* (*decision*) schnell ♦ *vt* (*break*) zerbrechen; (*PHOT*) knipsen ♦ *vi* (*break*) brechen; (*speak*) anfauchen; **to ~ shut** zuschnappen; ~ **at** *vt fus* schnappen nach; ~ **off** *vt* (*break*) abbrechen; ~ **up** *vt* aufschnappen; ~**shot** *n* Schnappschuss *m*

snare [snɛəʳ] *n* Schlinge *f* ♦ *vt* mit einer Schlinge fangen

snarl [snɑːl] *n* Zähnefletschen *nt* ♦ *vi* (*dog*) knurren

snatch [snætʃ] *n* (*small amount*) Bruchteil *m* ♦ *vt* schnappen, packen

sneak [sniːk] *vi* schleichen ♦ *n* (*inf*) Petze(r) *mf*; ~**ers** ['sniːkəz] (*US*) *npl* Freizeitschuhe *pl*; ~**y** ['sniːkɪ] *adj* raffiniert

sneer [snɪəʳ] *n* Hohnlächeln *nt* ♦ *vi* spötteln

sneeze [sniːz] *n* Niesen *nt* ♦ *vi* niesen

sniff [snɪf] *n* Schnüffeln *nt* ♦ *vi* schnieben; (*smell*) schnüffeln ♦ *vt* schnuppern

snigger ['snɪgəʳ] *n* Kichern *nt* ♦ *vi* hämisch kichern

snip [snɪp] *n* Schnippel *m*, Schnipsel *m* ♦ *vt* schnippeln

sniper ['snaɪpəʳ] *n* Heckenschütze *m*

snippet ['snɪpɪt] *n* Schnipsel *m*; (*of conversation*) Fetzen *m*

snivelling ['snɪvlɪŋ] *adj* weinerlich

snob [snɔb] *n* Snob *m*

snooker ['snuːkəʳ] *n* Snooker *nt*

snoop [snuːp] *vi*: **to ~ about** herumschnüffeln

snooze [snuːz] *n* Nickerchen *nt* ♦ *vi* ein Nickerchen machen, dösen

snore [snɔːʳ] *vi* schnarchen ♦ *n* Schnarchen *nt*

snorkel ['snɔːkl] *n* Schnorchel *m*

snort [snɔːt] *n* Schnauben *nt* ♦ *vi* schnauben

snout [snaut] *n* Schnauze *f*

snow [snəu] *n* Schnee *m* ♦ *vi* schneien; ~**ball** *n* Schneeball *m* ♦ *vi* eskalieren; ~**bound** *adj* eingeschneit; ~**drift** *n* Schneewehe *f*; ~**drop** *n* Schneeglöckchen *nt*; ~**fall** *n* Schneefall *m*; ~**flake** *n* Schneeflocke *f*; ~**man** (*irreg*) *n* Schneemann *m*; ~**plough** (*US* **snowplow**) *n* Schneepflug *m*; ~ **shoe** *n* Schneeschuh *m*; ~**storm** *n* Schneesturm *m*

snub [snʌb] *vt* schroff abfertigen ♦ *n* Verweis *m*; ~**-nosed** *adj* stupsnasig

snuff [snʌf] *n* Schnupftabak *m*

snug [snʌg] *adj* gemütlich, behaglich

snuggle ['snʌgl] *vi*: **to ~ up to sb** sich an jdn kuscheln

---

KEYWORD

so [səu] *adv* **1** (*thus*) so; (*likewise*) auch; **so saying he walked away** indem er das sagte, ging er; **if so** wenn ja; **I didn't do it – you did so!** ich hab das nicht gemacht – hast du wohl!; **so do I, so am I** *etc* ich auch; **so it is!** tatsächlich!; **I hope/think so** hoffentlich/ich glaube schon; **so far** bis jetzt

2 (*in comparisons etc: to such a degree*) so; **so quickly/big (that)** so schnell/groß, dass; **I'm so glad to see you** ich freue mich so, dich zu sehen

3: **so many** so viele; **so much work** so viel Arbeit; **I love you so much** ich liebe dich so sehr

4 (*phrases*): **10 or so** etwa 10; **so long!** (*inf: goodbye*) tschüss!

♦ *conj* **1** (*expressing purpose*): **so as to** um ... zu; **so (that)** damit

2 (*expressing result*) also; **so I was right after all** ich hatte also doch Recht; **so you see ...** wie du siehst ...

---

soak [səuk] *vt* durchnässen; (*leave in liquid*) einweichen ♦ *vi* (ein)weichen; ~ **in** *vi* einsickern; ~ **up** *vt* aufsaugen; ~**ed** *adj* völlig durchnässt; ~**ing** *adj* klitschnass, patschnass

so-and-so ['səuənsəu] *n* (*somebody*) Soundso *m*

soap [səup] *n* Seife *f*; ~**flakes** *npl* Seifenflocken *pl*; ~ **opera** *n* Familienserie *f* *(im Fernsehen, Radio);* **~ powder** *n* Waschpulver *nt;* **~y** *adj* seifig, Seifen-

soar [sɔːʳ] *vi* aufsteigen; *(prices)* in die Höhe schnellen

sob [sɒb] *n* Schluchzen *nt* ♦ *vi* schluchzen

sober ['səubəʳ] *adj (also fig)* nüchtern; **~ up** *vi* nüchtern werden

so-called ['səu'kɔːld] *adj* so genannt

soccer ['sɒkəʳ] *n* Fußball *m*

sociable ['səuʃəbl] *adj* gesellig

social ['səuʃl] *adj* sozial; *(friendly, living with others)* gesellig ♦ *n* gesellige(r) Abend *m;* **~ club** *n* Verein *m (für Freizeitgestaltung);* **~ism** *n* Sozialismus *m;* **~ist** *n* Sozialist(in) *m(f)* ♦ *adj* sozialistisch; **~ize** *vi:* **to ~ize (with)** gesellschaftlich verkehren (mit); **~ly** *adv* gesellschaftlich, privat; **~ security** *n* Sozialversicherung *f;* **~ work** *n* Sozialarbeit *f;* **~ worker** *n* Sozialarbeiter(in) *m(f)*

society [sə'saɪətɪ] *n* Gesellschaft *f;* *(fashionable world)* die große Welt

sociology [səusɪ'ɒlədʒɪ] *n* Soziologie *f*

sock [sɒk] *n* Socke *f*

socket ['sɒkɪt] *n (ELEC)* Steckdose *f;* *(of eye)* Augenhöhle *f*

sod [sɒd] *n* Rasenstück *nt;* *(inf!)* Saukerl *m (!)*

soda ['səudə] *n* Soda *f;* *(also:* **~ water)** Soda(wasser) *nt;* *(US: also:* **~ pop)** Limonade *f*

sodden ['sɒdn] *adj* durchweicht

sodium ['səudɪəm] *n* Natrium *nt*

sofa ['səufə] *n* Sofa *nt*

soft [sɒft] *adj* weich; *(not loud)* leise; *(weak)* nachgiebig; **~ drink** *n* alkoholfreie(s) Getränk *nt;* **~en** ['sɒfn] *vt* weich machen; *(blow)* abschwächen, mildern ♦ *vi* weich werden; **~ly** *adv* sanft; leise; **~ness** *n* Weichheit *f;* *(fig)* Sanftheit *f*

software ['sɒftwɛəʳ] *n (COMPUT)* Software *f*

soggy ['sɒgɪ] *adj (ground)* sumpfig; *(bread)* aufgeweicht

soil [sɔɪl] *n* Erde *f* ♦ *vt* beschmutzen

solace ['sɒlɪs] *n* Trost *m*

solar ['səuləʳ] *adj* Sonnen-; **~ cell** *n* Solarzelle *f;* **~ energy** *n* Sonnenenergie *f;* **~ panel** *n* Sonnenkollektor *m;* **~ power** *n* Sonnenenergie *f*

sold [səuld] *pt, pp of* **sell**; **~ out** *(COMM)* ausverkauft

solder ['səuldəʳ] *vt* löten

soldier ['səuldʒəʳ] *n* Soldat *m*

sole [səul] *n* Sohle *f;* *(fish)* Seezunge *f* ♦ *adj* alleinig, Allein-; **~ly** *adv* ausschließlich

solemn ['sɒləm] *adj* feierlich

sole trader *n (COMM)* Einzelunternehmen *nt*

solicit [sə'lɪsɪt] *vt (request)* bitten um ♦ *vi (prostitute)* Kunden anwerben

solicitor [sə'lɪsɪtəʳ] *n* Rechtsanwalt *m/*-anwältin *f*

solid ['sɒlɪd] *adj (hard)* fest; *(of same material, not hollow)* massiv; *(without break)* voll, ganz; *(reliable, sensible)* solide ♦ *n* Festkörper *m;* **~arity** [sɒlɪ'dærɪtɪ] *n* Solidarität *f;* **~ify** [sə'lɪdɪfaɪ] *vi* fest werden

solitary ['sɒlɪtərɪ] *adj* einsam, einzeln; **~ confinement** *n* Einzelhaft *f*

solitude ['sɒlɪtjuːd] *n* Einsamkeit *f*

solo ['səuləu] *n* Solo *nt;* **~ist** *n* ['səuləuɪst] *n* Solist(in) *m(f)*

soluble ['sɒljubl] *adj (substance)* löslich; *(problem)* (auf)lösbar

solution [sə'luːʃən] *n (also fig)* Lösung *f;* *(of mystery)* Erklärung *f*

solve [sɒlv] *vt* (auf)lösen

solvent ['sɒlvənt] *adj (FIN)* zahlungsfähig ♦ *n (CHEM)* Lösungsmittel *nt*

sombre ['sɒmbəʳ] *(US* **somber)** *adj* düster

KEYWORD

---

some [sʌm] *adj* **1** *(a certain amount or number of)* einige; *(a few)* ein paar; *(with singular nouns)* etwas; **some tea/biscuits** etwas Tee/ein paar Plätzchen; **I've got some money, but not much** ich habe ein bisschen Geld, aber nicht viel

2 *(certain: in contrasts)* manche(r, s); **some people say that ...** manche Leute sagen, dass ...

3 *(unspecified)* irgendein(e); **some woman was asking for you** da hat eine Frau nach Ihnen gefragt; **some day** eines Tages; **some day next week** irgendwann nächste Woche

♦ *pron* **1** (*a certain number*) einige; **have you got some?** haben Sie welche?
2 (*a certain amount*) etwas; **I've read some of the book** ich habe das Buch teilweise gelesen
♦ *adv*: **some 10 people** etwa 10 Leute

somebody ['sʌmbədı] *pron* = **someone**
somehow ['sʌmhaʊ] *adv* (*in some way, for some reason*) irgendwie
someone ['sʌmwʌn] *pron* jemand; (*direct obj*) jemand(en); (*indirect obj*) jemandem
someplace ['sʌmpleɪs] (*US*) *adv* = **somewhere**
somersault ['sʌməsɔːlt] *n* Salto *m* ♦ *vi* einen Salto machen
something ['sʌmθɪŋ] *pron* etwas
sometime ['sʌmtaɪm] *adv* (*irgend)einmal
sometimes ['sʌmtaɪmz] *adv* manchmal
somewhat ['sʌmwɒt] *adv* etwas
somewhere ['sʌmwɛəʳ] *adv* irgendwo; (*to a place*) irgendwohin; **~ else** irgendwo anders
son [sʌn] *n* Sohn *m*
sonar ['səʊnɑːʳ] *n* Echolot *nt*
song [sɒŋ] *n* Lied *nt*
sonic boom ['sɒnɪk-] *n* Überschallknall *m*
son-in-law ['sʌnɪnlɔː] *n* Schwiegersohn *m*
soon [suːn] *adv* bald; **~ afterwards** kurz danach; **~er** *adv* (*time*) früher; (*for preference*) lieber; **~er or later** früher oder später
soot [sʊt] *n* Ruß *m*
soothe [suːð] *vt* (*person*) beruhigen; (*pain*) lindern
sophisticated [sə'fɪstɪkeɪtɪd] *adj* (*person*) kultiviert; (*machinery*) hoch entwickelt
sophomore ['sɒfəmɔːʳ] (*US*) *n* College-student *m* im 2. Jahr
soporific [sɒpə'rɪfɪk] *adj* einschläfernd
sopping ['sɒpɪŋ] *adj* patschnass
soppy ['sɒpɪ] (*inf*) *adj* schmalzig
soprano [sə'prɑːnəʊ] *n* Sopran *m*
sorcerer ['sɔːsərəʳ] *n* Hexenmeister *m*
sordid ['sɔːdɪd] *adj* erbärmlich
sore [sɔːʳ] *adj* schmerzend; (*point*) wund ♦ *n* Wunde *f*; **~ly** *adv* (*tempted*) stark, sehr

sorrow ['sɒrəʊ] *n* Kummer *m*, Leid *nt*; **~ful** *adj* sorgenvoll
sorry ['sɒrɪ] *adj* traurig, erbärmlich; **~!** Entschuldigung!; **to feel ~ for sb** jdn bemitleiden; **I feel ~ for him** er tut mir Leid; **~?** (*pardon*) wie bitte?
sort [sɔːt] *n* Art *f*, Sorte *f* ♦ *vt* (*also*: **~ out**: *papers*) sortieren; (: *problems*) sichten, in Ordnung bringen; **~ing office** *n* Sortierstelle *f*
SOS *n* SOS *nt*
so-so ['səʊsəʊ] *adv* so(so) lala
sought [sɔːt] *pt, pp of* **seek**
soul [səʊl] *n* Seele *f*; (*music*) Soul *m*; **~-destroying** *adj* trostlos; **~ful** *adj* seelenvoll
sound [saʊnd] *adj* (*healthy*) gesund; (*safe*) sicher; (*sensible*) vernünftig; (*theory*) stichhaltig; (*thorough*) tüchtig, gehörig ♦ *adv*: **to be ~ asleep** fest schlafen ♦ *n* (*noise*) Geräusch *nt*, Laut *m*; (*GEOG*) Sund *m* ♦ *vt* erschallen lassen; (*alarm*) (Alarm) schlagen ♦ *vi* (*make a ~*) schallen, tönen; (*seem*) klingen; **to ~ like** sich anhören wie; **~ out** *vt* erforschen; (*person*) auf den Zahn fühlen +*dat*; **~ barrier** *n* Schallmauer *f*; **~ bite** *n* (*RAD, TV*) prägnante(s) Zitat *nt*; **~ effects** *npl* Toneffekte *pl*; **~ly** *adv* (*sleep*) fest; (*beat*) tüchtig; **~proof** *adj* (*room*) schalldicht; **~ track** *n* Tonstreifen *m*; (*music*) Filmmusik *f*
soup [suːp] *n* Suppe *f*; **~ plate** *n* Suppenteller *m*; **~spoon** *n* Suppenlöffel *m*
sour ['saʊəʳ] *adj* (*also fig*) sauer; **it's ~ grapes** (*fig*) die Trauben hängen zu hoch
source [sɔːs] *n* (*also fig*) Quelle *f*
south [saʊθ] *n* Süden *m* ♦ *adj* Süd-, südlich ♦ *adv* nach Süden, südwärts; **S~ Africa** *n* Südafrika *nt*; **S~ African** *adj* südafrikanisch ♦ *n* Südafrikaner(in) *m(f)*; **S~ America** *n* Südamerika *nt*; **S~ American** *adj* südamerikanisch ♦ *n* Südamerikaner(in) *m(f)*; **~-east** *n* Südosten *m*; **~erly** ['sʌðəlɪ] *adj* südlich; **~ern** ['sʌðən] *adj* südlich, Süd-; **S~ Pole** *n* Südpol *m*; **S~ Wales** *n* Südwales *nt*; **~ward(s)** *adv* südwärts, nach Süden; **~-west** *n* Südwesten *m*
souvenir [suːvə'nɪəʳ] *n* Souvenir *nt*

sovereign ['sɔvrɪn] *n (ruler)* Herrscher(in) *m(f)* ♦ *adj (independent)* souverän

soviet ['səuvɪət] *adj* sowjetisch; **the S~ Union** die Sowjetunion

sow[1] [sau] *n (place)* Sau *f*

sow[2] [səu] *(pt* **sowed**, *pp* **sown)** *vt (also fig)* säen

soya ['sɔɪə] *(US* **soy)** *n:* **~ bean** Sojabohne *f*; **~ sauce** Sojasauce *f*

spa [spɑː] *n (place)* Kurort *m*

space [speɪs] *n* Platz *m*, Raum *m*; *(universe)* Weltraum *m*, All *nt*; *(length of time)* Abstand *m* ♦ *vt (also:* **~ out)** verteilen; **~craft** *n* Raumschiff *nt*; **~man** *(irreg) n* Raumfahrer *m*; **~ ship** *n* Raumschiff *nt*

spacing ['speɪsɪŋ] *n* Abstand *m*; *(also:* **~ out)** Verteilung *f*

spacious ['speɪʃəs] *adj* geräumig, weit

spade [speɪd] *n* Spaten *m*; **~s** *npl (CARDS)* Pik *nt*

Spain [speɪn] *n* Spanien *nt*

span [spæn] *n* Spanne *f*; *(of bridge etc)* Spannweite *f* ♦ *vt* überspannen

Spaniard ['spænjəd] *n* Spanier(in) *m(f)*

spaniel ['spænjəl] *n* Spaniel *m*

Spanish ['spænɪʃ] *adj* spanisch ♦ *n (LING)* Spanisch *nt*; **the ~** *npl (people)* die Spanier *pl*

spank [spæŋk] *vt* verhauen, versohlen

spanner ['spænə*r*] *(BRIT) n* Schraubenschlüssel *m*

spar [spɑː*r*] *n (NAUT)* Sparren *m* ♦ *vi (BOXING)* einen Sparring machen

spare [speə*r*] *adj* Ersatz- ♦ *n* = **spare part** ♦ *vt (lives, feelings)* verschonen; *(trouble)* ersparen; *(surplus)* übrig; **~ part** *n* Ersatzteil *nt*; **~ time** *n* Freizeit *f*; **~ wheel** *n (AUT)* Reservereifen *m*

sparing ['speərɪŋ] *adj:* **to be ~ with** geizen mit; **~ly** *adv* sparsam; *(eat, spend etc)* in Maßen

spark [spɑːk] *n* Funken *m*; **~(ing) plug** *n* Zündkerze *f*

sparkle ['spɑːkl] *n* Funkeln *nt*; *(gaiety)* Schwung *m* ♦ *vi* funkeln; **sparkling** *adj* funkelnd; *(wine)* Schaum-; *(mineral water)* mit Kohlensäure, spritzig; *(conversation)* geistreich

sparrow ['spærəu] *n* Spatz *m*

sparse [spɑːs] *adj* spärlich

spasm ['spæzəm] *n (MED)* Krampf *m*; *(fig)* Anfall *m*; **~odic** [spæz'mɔdɪk] *adj (fig)* sprunghaft

spastic ['spæstɪk] *(old) n* Spastiker(in) *m(f)* ♦ *adj* spastisch

spat [spæt] *pt, pp of* **spit**

spate [speɪt] *n (fig)* Flut *f*, Schwall *m*; **in ~** *(river)* angeschwollen

spatter ['spætə*r*] *vt* bespritzen, verspritzen

spatula ['spætjulə] *n* Spatel *m*

spawn [spɔːn] *vi* laichen ♦ *n* Laich *m*

speak [spiːk] *(pt* **spoke**, *pp* **spoken)** *vt* sprechen, reden; *(truth)* sagen; *(language)* sprechen ♦ *vi:* **to ~ (to)** sprechen *(mit or* zu); **to ~ to sb of** *or* **about sth** mit jdm über etw *acc* sprechen; **~ up!** sprich lauter!; **~er** *n* Sprecher(in) *m(f)*, Redner(in) *m(f)*; *(loudspeaker)* Lautsprecher *m*; *(POL):* **the S~er** der Vorsitzende des Parlaments *(BRIT)* or des Kongresses *(US)*

spear [spɪə*r*] *n* Speer *m* ♦ *vt* aufspießen; **~head** *n (attack etc)* anführen

spec [spɛk] *(inf) n:* **on ~** auf gut Glück

special ['spɛʃl] *adj* besondere(r, s); **~ist** *n (TECH)* Fachmann *m*; *(MED)* Facharzt *m*/ Fachärztin *f*; **~ity** [spɛʃɪ'ælɪtɪ] *n* Spezialität *f*; *(study)* Spezialgebiet *nt*; **~ize** *vi:* **to ~ize (in)** sich spezialisieren (auf +*acc*); **~ly** *adv* besonders; *(explicitly)* extra; **~ needs** *adj:* **~ needs children** behinderte Kinder *pl*; **~ty** *(esp US) n* = **speciality**

species ['spiːʃiːz] *n* Art *f*

specific [spə'sɪfɪk] *adj* spezifisch; **~ally** *adv* spezifisch

specification [spɛsɪfɪ'keɪʃən] *n* Angabe *f*; *(stipulation)* Bedingung *f*; **~s** *npl (TECH)* technische Daten *pl*

specify ['spɛsɪfaɪ] *vt* genau angeben

specimen ['spɛsɪmən] *n* Probe *f*

speck [spɛk] *n* Fleckchen *nt*

speckled ['spɛkld] *adj* gesprenkelt

specs [spɛks] *(inf) npl* Brille *f*

spectacle ['spɛktəkl] *n* Schauspiel *nt*; **~s** *npl (glasses)* Brille *f*

spectacular [spɛk'tækjuləʳ] *adj* sensationell; (*success etc*) spektakulär

spectator [spɛk'teɪtəʳ] *n* Zuschauer(in) *m(f)*

spectre ['spɛktəʳ] (*US* **specter**) *n* Geist *m*, Gespenst *nt*

speculate ['spɛkjuleɪt] *vi* spekulieren

speech [spi:tʃ] *n* Sprache *f*; (*address*) Rede *f*; (*way one speaks*) Sprechweise *f*; **~less** *adj* sprachlos

speed [spi:d] *n* Geschwindigkeit *f*; (*gear*) Gang *m* ♦ *vi* (*JUR*) (zu) schnell fahren; **at full** *or* **top ~** mit Höchstgeschwindigkeit; **~ up** *vt* beschleunigen ♦ *vi* schneller werden; schneller fahren; **~boat** *n* Schnellboot *nt*; **~ily** *adv* schleunigst; **~ing** *n* Geschwindigkeitsüberschreitung *f*; **~ limit** *n* Geschwindigkeitsbegrenzung *f*; **~ometer** [spɪ'dɔmɪtəʳ] *n* Tachometer *m*; **~way** *n* (*bike racing*) Motorradrennstrecke *f*; **~y** *adj* schnell

spell [spɛl] (*pt, pp* **spelt** (*BRIT*) *or* **spelled**) *n* (*magic*) Bann *m*; (*period of time*) (eine) Zeit lang ♦ *vt* buchstabieren; (*imply*) bedeuten; **to cast a ~ on sb** jdn verzaubern; **~bound** *adj* (wie) gebannt; **~ing** *n* Rechtschreibung *f*

spelt [spɛlt] (*BRIT*) *pt, pp of* **spell**

spend [spɛnd] (*pt, pp* **spent**) *vt* (*money*) ausgeben; (*time*) verbringen; **~thrift** *n* Verschwender(in) *m(f)*

spent [spɛnt] *pt, pp of* **spend**

sperm [spə:m] *n* (*BIOL*) Samenflüssigkeit *f*

spew [spju:] *vt* (er)brechen

sphere [sfɪəʳ] *n* (*globe*) Kugel *f*; (*fig*) Sphäre *f*, Gebiet *nt*; **spherical** ['sfɛrɪkl] *adj* kugelförmig

spice [spaɪs] *n* Gewürz *nt* ♦ *vt* würzen

spick-and-span ['spɪkən'spæn] *adj* blitzblank

spicy ['spaɪsɪ] *adj* (*food*) stark gewürzt; (*fig*) pikant

spider ['spaɪdəʳ] *n* Spinne *f*

spike [spaɪk] *n* Dorn *m*, Spitze *f*

spill [spɪl] (*pt, pp* **spilt** *or* **spilled**) *vt* verschütten ♦ *vi* sich ergießen; **~ over** *vi* überlaufen; (*fig*) sich ausbreiten

spilt [spɪlt] *pt, pp of* **spill**

spin [spɪn] (*pt, pp* **spun**) *n* (*trip in car*) Spazierfahrt *f*; (*AVIAT*) (Ab)trudeln *nt*; (*on ball*) Drall *m* ♦ *vt* (*thread*) spinnen; (*like top*) (herum)wirbeln ♦ *vi* sich drehen; **~ out** *vt* in die Länge ziehen

spinach ['spɪnɪtʃ] *n* Spinat *m*

spinal ['spaɪnl] *adj* Rückgrat-; **~ cord** *n* Rückenmark *nt*

spindly ['spɪndlɪ] *adj* spindeldürr

spin doctor *n* PR-Fachmann *m*, PR-Fachfrau *f*

spin-dryer [spɪn'draɪəʳ] (*BRIT*) *n* Wäscheschleuder *f*

spine [spaɪn] *n* Rückgrat *nt*; (*thorn*) Stachel *m*; **~less** *adj* (*also fig*) rückgratlos

spinning ['spɪnɪŋ] *n* Spinnen *nt*; **~ top** *n* Kreisel *m*; **~ wheel** *n* Spinnrad *nt*

spin-off ['spɪnɔf] *n* Nebenprodukt *nt*

spinster ['spɪnstəʳ] *n* unverheiratete Frau *f*; (*pej*) alte Jungfer *f*

spiral ['spaɪərəl] *n* Spirale *f* ♦ *adj* spiralförmig; (*movement etc*) in Spiralen ♦ *vi* sich (hoch)winden; **~ staircase** *n* Wendeltreppe *f*

spire ['spaɪəʳ] *n* Turm *m*

spirit ['spɪrɪt] *n* Geist *m*; (*humour, mood*) Stimmung *f*; (*courage*) Mut *m*; (*verve*) Elan *m*; (*alcohol*) Alkohol *m*; **~s** *npl* (*drink*) Spirituosen *pl*; **in good ~s** gut aufgelegt; **~ed** *adj* beherzt; **~ level** *n* Wasserwaage *f*

spiritual ['spɪrɪtjuəl] *adj* geistig, seelisch; (*REL*) geistlich ♦ *n* Spiritual *nt*

spit [spɪt] (*pt, pp* **spat**) *n* (*for roasting*) (Brat)spieß *m*; (*saliva*) Spucke *f* ♦ *vi* spucken; (*rain*) sprühen; (*make a sound*) zischen; (*cat*) fauchen

spite [spaɪt] *n* Gehässigkeit *f* ♦ *vt* kränken; **in ~ of** trotz; **~ful** *adj* gehässig

spittle ['spɪtl] *n* Speichel *m*, Spucke *f*

splash [splæʃ] *n* Spritzer *m*; (*of colour*) (Farb)fleck *m* ♦ *vt* bespritzen ♦ *vi* spritzen

spleen [spli:n] *n* (*ANAT*) Milz *f*

splendid ['splɛndɪd] *adj* glänzend

splendour ['splɛndəʳ] (*US* **splendor**) *n* Pracht *f*

splint [splɪnt] *n* Schiene *f*

splinter ['splɪntəʳ] *n* Splitter *m* ♦ *vi* (zer)splittern

split [splɪt] (*pt, pp* **split**) *n* Spalte *f*; (*fig*) Spaltung *f*; (*division*) Trennung *f* ♦ *vt* spalten *vi* ♦ *vt* (*divide*) reißen; **~ up** *vi* sich trennen

splutter ['splʌtə*r*] *vi* stottern

spoil [spɔɪl] (*pt, pp* **spoilt** *or* **spoiled**) *vt* (*ruin*) verderben; (*child*) verwöhnen; **~s** *npl* Beute *f*; **~sport** *n* Spielverderber *m*; **~t** *pt, pp of* **spoil**

spoke [spəuk] *pt of* **speak** ♦ *n* Speiche *f*; **~n** *pp of* **speak**

spokesman ['spəuksmən] (*irreg*) *n* Sprecher *m*; **spokeswoman** ['spəukswumən] (*irreg*) *n* Sprecherin *f*

sponge [spʌndʒ] *n* Schwamm *m* ♦ *vt* abwaschen ♦ *vi*: **to ~ on** auf Kosten +*gen* leben; **~ bag** (*BRIT*) *n* Kulturbeutel *m*; **~ cake** *n* Rührkuchen *m*

sponsor ['spɔnsə*r*] *n* Sponsor *m* ♦ *vt* fördern; **~ship** *n* Finanzierung *f*; (*public*) Schirmherrschaft *f*

spontaneous [spɔn'teɪnɪəs] *adj* spontan

spooky ['spu:kɪ] (*inf*) *adj* gespenstisch

spool [spu:l] *n* Spule *f*, Rolle *f*

spoon [spu:n] *n* Löffel *m*; **~-feed** (*irreg*) *vt* mit dem Löffel füttern; (*fig*) hochpäppeln; **~ful** *n* Löffel *m* (voll)

sport [spɔ:t] *n* Sport *m*; (*person*) feine(r) Kerl *m*; **~ing** *adj* (*fair*) sportlich, fair; **to give sb a ~ing chance** jdm eine faire Chance geben; **~ jacket** (*US*) *n* = **sports jacket**; **~s car** *n* Sportwagen *m*; **~s jacket** *n* Sportjackett *nt*; **~sman** (*irreg*) *n* Sportler *m*; **~smanship** *n* Sportlichkeit *f*; **~swear** *n* Sportkleidung *f*; **~swoman** (*irreg*) *n* Sportlerin *f*; **~y** *adj* sportlich

spot [spɔt] *n* Punkt *m*; (*dirty*) Fleck(en) *m*; (*place*) Stelle *f*; (*MED*) Pickel *m* ♦ *vt* erspähen; (*mistake*) bemerken; **on the ~** an Ort und Stelle; (*at once*) auf der Stelle; **~ check** *n* Stichprobe *f*; **~less** *adj* fleckenlos; **~light** *n* Scheinwerferlicht *nt*; (*lamp*) Scheinwerfer *m*; **~ted** *adj* gefleckt; **~ty** *adj* (*face*) pickelig

spouse [spaus] *n* Gatte *m*/Gattin *f*

spout [spaut] *n* (*of pot*) Tülle *f*; (*jet*) Wasserstrahl *m* ♦ *vi* speien

sprain [spreɪn] *n* Verrenkung *f* ♦ *vt* verrenken

sprang [spræŋ] *pt of* **spring**

sprawl [sprɔ:l] *vi* sich strecken

spray [spreɪ] *n* Spray *nt*; (*off sea*) Gischt *f*; (*of flowers*) Zweig *m* ♦ *vt* besprühen, sprayen

spread [spred] (*pt, pp* **spread**) *n* (*extent*) Verbreitung *f*; (*inf: meal*) Schmaus *m*; (*for bread*) Aufstrich *m* ♦ *vt* ausbreiten; (*scatter*) verbreiten; (*butter*) streichen ♦ *vi* sich ausbreiten; **~ out** *vi* (*move apart*) sich verteilen; **~-eagled** ['spred:ɪgld] *adj*: **to be ~-eagled** alle viere von sich strecken; **~sheet** *n* Tabellenkalkulation *f*

spree [spri:] *n* (*shopping*) Einkaufsbummel *m*; **to go on a ~** einen draufmachen

sprightly ['spraɪtlɪ] *adj* munter, lebhaft

spring [sprɪŋ] (*pt* **sprang**, *pp* **sprung**) *n* (*leap*) Sprung *m*; (*TECH*) Feder *f*; (*season*) Frühling *m*; (*water*) Quelle *f* ♦ *vi* (*leap*) springen; **~ up** *vi* (*problem*) auftauchen; **~board** *n* Sprungbrett *nt*; **~-clean** *n* (*also*: **~-cleaning**) Frühjahrsputz *m*; **~time** *n* Frühling *m*; **~y** *adj* federnd, elastisch

sprinkle ['sprɪŋkl] *vt* (*salt*) streuen; (*liquid*) sprenkeln; **to ~ water on, to ~ with water** mit Wasser besprengen; **~r** ['sprɪŋklə*r*] *n* (*for lawn*) Sprenger *m*; (*for fire fighting*) Sprinkler *m*

sprint [sprɪnt] *n* (*race*) Sprint *m* ♦ *vi* (*run fast*) rennen; (*SPORT*) sprinten; **~er** *n* Sprinter(in) *m(f)*

sprout [spraut] *vi* sprießen

sprouts [sprauts] *npl* (*also*: **Brussels ~**) Rosenkohl *m*

spruce [spru:s] *n* Fichte *f* ♦ *adj* schmuck, adrett

sprung [sprʌŋ] *pp of* **spring**

spry [spraɪ] *adj* flink, rege

spun [spʌn] *pt, pp of* **spin**

spur [spə:*r*] *n* Sporn *m*; (*fig*) Ansporn *m* ♦ *vt* (*also*: **~ on**: *fig*) anspornen; **on the ~ of the moment** spontan

spurious ['spjuərɪəs] *adj* falsch

spurn [spə:n] *vt* verschmähen

spurt [spə:t] *n* (*jet*) Strahl *m*; (*acceleration*) Spurt *m* ♦ *vi* (*liquid*) schießen

spy [spaɪ] n Spion(in) m(f) ♦ vi spionieren ♦ vt erspähen; **~ing** n Spionage f

sq. abbr = **square**

squabble ['skwɔbl] n Zank m ♦ vi sich zanken

squad [skwɔd] n (MIL) Abteilung f; (POLICE) Kommando nt

squadron ['skwɔdrn] n (cavalry) Schwadron f; (NAUT) Geschwader nt; (air force) Staffel f

squalid ['skwɔlɪd] adj verkommen

squall [skwɔːl] n Bö(e) f, Windstoß m

squalor ['skwɔlə*] n Verwahrlosung f

squander ['skwɔndə*] vt verschwenden

square [skwɛə*] n Quadrat nt; (open space) Platz m; (instrument) Winkel m; (inf: person) Spießer m ♦ adj viereckig; (inf: ideas, tastes) spießig ♦ vt (arrange) ausmachen; (MATH) ins Quadrat erheben ♦ vi (agree) übereinstimmen; **all ~** quitt; **a ~ meal** eine ordentliche Mahlzeit; **2 metres ~** 2 Meter im Quadrat; **1 ~ metre** 1 Quadratmeter; **~ly** adv fest, gerade

squash [skwɔʃ] n (BRIT: drink) Saft m; (game) Squash nt ♦ vt zerquetschen

squat [skwɔt] adj untersetzt ♦ vi hocken; **~ter** n Hausbesetzer m

squawk [skwɔːk] vi kreischen

squeak [skwiːk] vi quiek(s)en; (spring, door etc) quietschen

squeal [skwiːl] vi schrill schreien

squeamish ['skwiːmɪʃ] adj empfindlich

squeeze [skwiːz] vt pressen, drücken; (orange) auspressen; **~ out** vt ausquetschen

squelch [skweltʃ] vi platschen

squib [skwɪb] n Knallfrosch m

squid [skwɪd] n Tintenfisch m

squiggle ['skwɪgl] n Schnörkel m

squint [skwɪnt] vi schielen ♦ n: **to have a ~** schielen; **to ~ at sb/sth** nach jdm/etw schielen

squirm [skwɜːm] vi sich winden

squirrel ['skwɪrəl] n Eichhörnchen nt

squirt [skwɜːt] vt, vi spritzen

Sr abbr (= senior) sen.

St abbr (= saint) hl., St.; (= street) Str.

stab [stæb] n (blow) Stich m; (inf: try) Versuch m ♦ vt erstechen

stabilize ['steɪbəlaɪz] vt stabilisieren ♦ vi sich stabilisieren

stable ['steɪbl] adj stabil ♦ n Stall m

stack [stæk] n Stapel m ♦ vt stapeln

stadium ['steɪdɪəm] n Stadion nt

staff [stɑːf] n (stick, MIL) Stab m; (personnel) Personal nt; (BRIT: SCH) Lehrkräfte pl ♦ vt besetzen

stag [stæg] n Hirsch m

stage [steɪdʒ] n Bühne f; (of journey) Etappe f; (degree) Stufe f; (point) Stadium nt ♦ vt (put on) aufführen; (simulate) inszenieren; (demonstration) veranstalten; **in ~s** etappenweise; **~coach** n Postkutsche f; **~ door** n Bühneneingang m; **~ manager** n Intendant m

stagger ['stægə*] vi wanken, taumeln ♦ vt (amaze) verblüffen; (hours) staffeln; **~ing** adj unglaublich

stagnant ['stægnənt] adj stagnierend; (water) stehend; **stagnate** [stæg'neɪt] vi stagnieren

stag party n Männerabend m (vom Bräutigam vor der Hochzeit gegeben)

staid [steɪd] adj gesetzt

stain [steɪn] n Fleck m ♦ vt beflecken; **~ed glass window** buntes Glasfenster nt; **~less** adj (steel) rostfrei; **~ remover** n Fleckentferner m

stair [stɛə*] n (Treppen)stufe f; **~s** npl (flight of steps) Treppe f; **~case** n Treppenhaus nt, Treppe f; **~way** n Treppenaufgang m

stake [steɪk] n (post) Pfahl m; (money) Einsatz m ♦ vt (bet: money) setzen; **to be at ~** auf dem Spiel stehen

stale [steɪl] adj alt; (bread) altbacken

stalemate ['steɪlmeɪt] n (CHESS) Patt nt; (fig) Stillstand m

stalk [stɔːk] n Stängel m, Stiel m ♦ vt (game) jagen; **~ off** vi abstolzieren

stall [stɔːl] n (in stable) Stand m, Box f; (in market) (Verkaufs)stand m ♦ vt (AUT) abwürgen ♦ vi (AUT) stehen bleiben; (fig) Ausflüchte machen; **~s** npl (BRIT: THEAT) Parkett nt

stallion ['stæljən] n Zuchthengst m

stalwart ['stɔːlwət] *n* treue(r) Anhänger *m*

stamina ['stæmɪnə] *n* Durchhaltevermögen *nt*, Zähigkeit *f*

stammer ['stæmər] *n* Stottern *nt* ♦ *vt, vi* stottern, stammeln

stamp [stæmp] *n* Briefmarke *f*; (*for document*) Stempel *m* ♦ *vi* stampfen ♦ *vt* (*mark*) stempeln; (*mail*) frankieren; (*foot*) stampfen mit; ~ **album** *n* Briefmarkenalbum *nt*; ~ **collecting** *n* Briefmarkensammeln *nt*

stampede [stæm'piːd] *n* panische Flucht *f*

stance [stæns] *n* Haltung *f*

stand [stænd] (*pt, pp* **stood**) *n* (*for objects*) Gestell *nt*; (*seats*) Tribüne *f* ♦ *vi* stehen; (*rise*) aufstehen; (*decision*) feststehen ♦ *vt* setzen, stellen; (*endure*) aushalten; (*person*) ausstehen; (*nonsense*) dulden; **to make a ~** Widerstand leisten; **to ~ for parliament** (*BRIT*) für das Parlament kandidieren; ~ **by** *vi* (*be ready*) bereitstehen ♦ *vt fus* (*opinion*) treu bleiben +*dat*; ~ **down** *vi* (*withdraw*) zurücktreten; ~ **for** *vt fus* (*signify*) stehen für; (*permit, tolerate*) hinnehmen; ~ **in for** *vt fus* einspringen für; ~ **out** *vi* (*be prominent*) hervorstechen; ~ **up** *vi* (*rise*) aufstehen; ~ **up for** *vt fus* sich einsetzen für; ~ **up to** *vt fus*: **to ~ up to sth** einer Sache *dat* gewachsen sein; **to ~ up to sb** sich jdm gegenüber behaupten

standard ['stændəd] *n* (*measure*) Norm *f*; (*flag*) Fahne *f* ♦ *adj* (*size etc*) Normal-; ~**s** *npl* (*morals*) Maßstäbe *pl*; ~**ize** *vt* vereinheitlichen; ~ **lamp** (*BRIT*) *n* Stehlampe *f*; ~ **of living** *n* Lebensstandard *m*

stand: ~**-by** *n* Reserve *f*; **to be on ~-by** Bereitschaft sein; ~**-by ticket** *n* (*AVIAT*) Standbyticket *nt*; ~**-in** ['stændɪn] *n* Ersatz *m*

standing ['stændɪŋ] *adj* (*erect*) stehend; (*permanent*) ständig; (*invitation*) offen ♦ *n* (*duration*) Dauer *f*; (*reputation*) Ansehen *nt*; **of many years'** ~ langjährig; ~ **order** (*BRIT*) *n* (*at bank*) Dauerauftrag *m*; ~ **room** *n* Stehplatz *m*

stand: ~**-offish** [stænd'ɔfɪʃ] *adj* zurückhaltend, sehr reserviert; ~**point** ['stændpɔɪnt] *n* Standpunkt *m*; ~**still** ['stændstɪl] *n*: **to be at a ~still** stillstehen; **to come to a ~still** zum Stillstand kommen

stank [stæŋk] *pt of* **stink**

staple ['steɪpl] *n* (*in paper*) Heftklammer *f*; (*article*) Haupterzeugnis *nt* ♦ *adj* Grund-, Haupt- ♦ *vt* (*fest*)klammern; ~**r** *n* Heftmaschine *f*

star [staːr] *n* Stern *m*; (*person*) Star *m* ♦ *vi* die Hauptrolle spielen ♦ *vt*: ~**ring ...** in der Hauptrolle/den Hauptrollen ...

starboard ['staːbɔːd] *n* Steuerbord *nt*

starch [staːtʃ] *n* Stärke *f*

stardom ['staːdəm] *n* Berühmtheit *f*

stare [steər] *n* starre(r) Blick *m* ♦ *vi*: **to ~ at** starren auf +*acc*, anstarren

starfish ['staːfɪʃ] *n* Seestern *m*

stark [staːk] *adj* öde ♦ *adv*: ~ **naked** splitternackt

starling ['staːlɪŋ] *n* Star *m*

starry ['staːrɪ] *adj* Sternen-; ~**-eyed** *adj* (*innocent*) blauäugig

start [staːt] *n* Anfang *m*; (*SPORT*) Start *m*; (*lead*) Vorsprung *m* ♦ *vt* in Gang setzen; (*car*) anlassen ♦ *vi* anfangen; (*car*) anspringen; (*on journey*) aufbrechen; (*SPORT*) starten; (*with fright*) zusammenfahren; **to ~ doing** *or* **to do sth** anfangen, etw zu tun; ~ **off** *vi* anfangen; (*begin moving*) losgehen; losfahren; ~ **up** *vi* anfangen ♦ *vt* beginnen; (*car*) anlassen; (*engine*) starten; ~**er** *n* (*AUT*) Anlasser *m*; (*for race*) Starter *m*; (*BRIT: COOK*) Vorspeise *f*; ~**ing point** *n* Ausgangspunkt *m*

startle ['staːtl] *vt* erschrecken; **startling** *adj* erschreckend

starvation [staː'veɪʃən] *n* Verhungern *nt*

starve [staːv] *vi* verhungern ♦ *vt* verhungern lassen; **I'm starving** ich sterbe vor Hunger

state [steɪt] *n* (*condition*) Zustand *m*; (*POL*) Staat *m* ♦ *vt* erklären; (*facts*) angeben; **the S~s** (*USA*) die Staaten; **to be in a ~** durchdrehen; ~**ly** *adj* würdevoll; ~**ly home** *n* herrschaftliches Anwesen *nt*, Schloss *nt*; ~**ment** *n* Aussage *f*; (*POL*) Erklärung *f*; ~**sman** (*irreg*) *n* Staatsmann *m*

static ['stætɪk] *n* (*also*: ~ **electricity**) Reibungselektrizität *f*

station ['steɪʃən] n (*RAIL etc*) Bahnhof m; (*police station*) Wache f; (*in society*) Stand m ♦ vt stationieren

stationary ['steɪʃnərɪ] adj stillstehend; (*car*) parkend

stationer's n (*shop*) Schreibwarengeschäft nt; **~y** n Schreibwaren pl

station master n Bahnhofsvorsteher m

station wagon n Kombiwagen m

statistics [stə'tɪstɪks] n Statistik f

statue ['stætjuː] n Statue f

stature ['stætʃər] n Größe f

status ['steɪtəs] n Status m

statute ['stætjuːt] n Gesetz nt; **statutory** ['stætjutrɪ] adj gesetzlich

staunch [stɔːntʃ] adj standhaft

stay [steɪ] n Aufenthalt m ♦ vi bleiben; (*reside*) wohnen; **to ~ put** an Ort und Stelle bleiben; **to ~ the night** übernachten; **~ behind** vi zurückbleiben; **~ in** vi (*at home*) zu Hause bleiben; **~ on** vi (*continue*) länger bleiben; **~ out** vi (*of house*) wegbleiben; **~ up** vi (*at night*) aufbleiben; **~ing power** n Durchhaltevermögen nt

stead [sted] n: **in sb's ~** an jds Stelle dat; **to stand sb in good ~** jdm zugute kommen

steadfast ['stedfɑːst] adj standhaft, treu

steadily ['stedɪlɪ] adv stetig, regelmäßig

steady ['stedɪ] adj (*firm*) fest, stabil; (*regular*) gleichmäßig; (*reliable*) beständig; (*hand*) ruhig; (*job, boyfriend*) fest ♦ vt festigen; **to ~ o.s. on/against sth** sich stützen auf/gegen etw acc

steak [steɪk] n Steak nt; (*fish*) Filet nt

steal [stiːl] (*pt* **stole**, *pp* **stolen**) vt stehlen ♦ vi stehlen; (*go quietly*) sich stehlen

stealth [stelθ] n Heimlichkeit f; **~y** adj verstohlen, heimlich

steam [stiːm] n Dampf m ♦ vt (*COOK*) im Dampfbad erhitzen ♦ vi dampfen; **~ engine** n Dampfmaschine f; **~er** n Dampfer m; **~roller** n Dampfwalze f; **~ship** n = **steamer**; **~y** adj dampfig

steel [stiːl] n Stahl m ♦ adj Stahl-; (*fig*) stählern; **~works** n Stahlwerke pl

steep [stiːp] adj steil; (*price*) gepfeffert ♦ vt einweichen

steeple ['stiːpl] n Kirchturm m; **~chase** n Hindernisrennen nt

steer [stɪər] vt, vi steuern; (*car etc*) lenken; **~ing** n (*AUT*) Steuerung f; **~ing wheel** n Steuer- or Lenkrad nt

stem [stem] n Stiel m ♦ vt aufhalten; **~ from** vt fus abstammen von

stench [stentʃ] n Gestank m

stencil ['stensl] n Schablone f ♦ vt (auf)drucken

stenographer [ste'nɔgrəfər] (*US*) n Stenograf(in) m(f)

step [step] n Schritt m; (*stair*) Stufe f ♦ vi treten, schreiten; **~s** npl (*BRIT*) = **stepladder**; **to take ~s** Schritte unternehmen; **in/out of ~ (with)** im/nicht im Gleichklang (mit); **~ down** vi (*fig*) abtreten; **~ off** vt fus aussteigen aus; **~ up** vt steigern

stepbrother ['stepbrʌðər] n Stiefbruder m

stepdaughter ['stepdɔːtər] n Stieftochter f

stepfather ['stepfɑːðər] n Stiefvater m

stepladder ['steplædər] n Trittleiter f

stepmother ['stepmʌðər] n Stiefmutter f

stepping stone ['stepɪŋ-] n Stein m; (*fig*) Sprungbrett nt

stepsister ['stepsɪstər] n Stiefschwester f

stepson ['stepsʌn] n Stiefsohn m

stereo ['steriəu] n Stereoanlage f ♦ adj (*also:* **~phonic**) stereofonisch, stereophonisch

stereotype ['stɪərɪətaɪp] n (*fig*) Klischee nt ♦ vt stereotypieren; (*fig*) stereotyp machen

sterile ['sterail] adj steril; (*person*) unfruchtbar; **sterilize** vt sterilisieren

sterling ['stɜːlɪŋ] adj (*FIN*) Sterling-; (*character*) gediegen ♦ n (*ECON*) das Pfund Sterling; **a pound ~** ein Pfund Sterling

stern [stɜːn] adj streng ♦ n Heck nt, Achterschiff nt

stew [stjuː] n Eintopf m ♦ vt, vi schmoren

steward ['stjuːəd] n Steward m; **~ess** n Stewardess f

stick [stɪk] (*pt, pp* **stuck**) n Stock m; (*of chalk etc*) Stück nt ♦ vt (*stab*) stechen; (*fix*) stecken; (*put*) stellen; (*gum*) (an)kleben; (*inf: tolerate*) vertragen ♦ vi (*stop*) stecken bleiben; (*get stuck*) klemmen; (*hold fast*) kleben, haften; **~ out** *vi* (*project*) hervorstehen; **~ up** *vi* (*project*) in die Höhe stehen; **~ up for** *vt fus* (*defend*) eintreten für; **~er** *n* Aufkleber *m*; **~ing plaster** *n* Heftpflaster *nt*

stickler ['stɪklər] *n*: **~ (for)** Pedant *m* (in +*acc*)

stick-up ['stɪkʌp] (*inf*) *n* (Raub)überfall *m*

sticky ['stɪkɪ] *adj* klebrig; (*atmosphere*) stickig

stiff [stɪf] *adj* steif; (*difficult*) hart; (*paste*) dick; (*drink*) stark; **to have a ~ neck** einen steifen Hals haben; **~en** *vt* versteifen, (ver)stärken ♦ *vi* sich versteifen

stifle ['staɪfl] *vt* unterdrücken; **stifling** *adj* drückend

stigma ['stɪgmə] (*pl* BOT, MED, REL **~ta**; *fig* **~s**) *n* Stigma *nt*

stigmata [stɪg'mɑːtə] *npl of* **stigma**

stile [staɪl] *n* Steige *f*

stiletto [stɪ'letəu] (BRIT) *n* (*also:* **~ heel**) Pfennigabsatz *m*

still [stɪl] *adj* still ♦ *adv* (immer) noch; (*anyhow*) immerhin; **~born** *adj* tot geboren; **~ life** *n* Stillleben *nt*

stilt [stɪlt] *n* Stelze *f*

stilted ['stɪltɪd] *adj* gestelzt

stimulate ['stɪmjuleɪt] *vt* anregen, stimulieren

stimuli ['stɪmjulaɪ] *npl of* **stimulus**

stimulus ['stɪmjuləs] (*pl* **-li**) *n* Anregung *f*, Reiz *m*

sting [stɪŋ] (*pt, pp* **stung**) *n* Stich *m*; (*organ*) Stachel *m* ♦ *vi* stechen; (*on skin*) brennen ♦ *vt* stechen

stingy ['stɪndʒɪ] *adj* geizig, knauserig

stink [stɪŋk] (*pt* **stank**, *pp* **stunk**) *n* Gestank *m* ♦ *vi* stinken; **~ing** *adj* (*fig*) widerlich

stint [stɪnt] *n* (*period*) Betätigung *f*; **to do one's ~** seine Arbeit tun; (*share*) seinen Teil beitragen

stipulate ['stɪpjuleɪt] *vt* festsetzen

stir [stɜːr] *n* Bewegung *f*; (COOK) Rühren *nt*; (*sensation*) Aufsehen *nt* ♦ *vt* (um)rühren ♦ *vi* sich rühren; **~ up** *vt* (*mob*) aufhetzen; (*mixture*) umrühren; (*dust*) aufwirbeln

stirrup ['stɪrəp] *n* Steigbügel *m*

stitch [stɪtʃ] *n* (*with needle*) Stich *m*; (MED)

Faden *m*; (*of knitting*) Masche *f*; (*pain*) Stich *m* ♦ *vt* nähen

stoat [stəut] *n* Wiesel *nt*

stock [stɔk] *n* Vorrat *m*; (COMM) (Waren)lager *nt*; (*livestock*) Vieh *nt*; (COOK) Brühe *f*; (FIN) Grundkapital *nt* ♦ *adj* stets vorrätig; (*standard*) Normal- ♦ *vt* (*in shop*) führen; **~s** *npl* (FIN) Aktien *pl*; **in/out of ~** vorrätig/nicht vorrätig; **to take ~ of** Inventur machen von; (*fig*) Bilanz ziehen aus; **~s and shares** Effekten *pl*; **~ up** *vi*: **to ~ up (with)** Reserven anlegen (von); **~broker** ['stɔkbrəukər] *n* Börsenmakler *m*; **~cube** *n* Brühwürfel *m*; **~ exchange** *n* Börse *f*

stocking ['stɔkɪŋ] *n* Strumpf *m*

stock: **~ market** *n* Börse *f*; **~ phrase** *n* Standardsatz *m*; **~pile** *n* Vorrat *m* ♦ *vt* aufstapeln; **~taking** (BRIT) *n* (COMM) Inventur *f*, Bestandsaufnahme *f*

stocky ['stɔkɪ] *adj* untersetzt

stodgy ['stɔdʒɪ] *adj* pampig

stoke [stəuk] *vt* schüren

stole [stəul] *pt of* **steal** ♦ *n* Stola *f*

stolen ['stəuln] *pp of* **steal**

stomach ['stʌmək] *n* Bauch *m*, Magen *m* ♦ *vt* vertragen; **~-ache** *n* Magen- *or* Bauchschmerzen *pl*

stone [stəun] *n* Stein *m*; (BRIT: *weight*) *Gewichtseinheit = 6.35 kg* ♦ *vt* (*olive*) entkernen; (*kill*) steinigen; **~-cold** *adj* eiskalt; **~-deaf** *adj* stocktaub; **~work** *n* Mauerwerk *nt*; **stony** ['stəunɪ] *adj* steinig

stood [stud] *pt, pp of* **stand**

stool [stuːl] *n* Hocker *m*

stoop [stuːp] *vi* sich bücken

stop [stɔp] *n* Halt *m*; (*bus* **~**) Haltestelle *f*; (*punctuation*) Punkt *m* ♦ *vt* anhalten; (*bring to an end*) aufhören (mit), sein lassen ♦ *vi* aufhören; (*clock*) stehen bleiben; (*remain*) bleiben; **to ~ doing sth** aufhören, etw zu tun; **to ~ dead** innehalten; **~ off** *vi* kurz Halt machen; **~ up** *vt* (*hole*) zustopfen, verstopfen; **~gap** *n* Notlösung *f*; **~lights** *npl* (AUT) Bremslichter *pl*; **~over** *n* (*on journey*) Zwischenaufenthalt *m*; **~page** ['stɔpɪdʒ] *n* (An)halten *nt*; (*traffic*)

Verkehrsstockung f; (strike)
Arbeitseinstellung f; **~per** ['stɔpər] n
Propfen m, Stöpsel m; **~ press** n letzte
Meldung f; **~watch** ['stɔpwɔtʃ] n Stoppuhr f

storage ['stɔːrɪdʒ] n Lagerung f; **~ heater** n
(Nachtstrom)speicherofen m

store [stɔː] n Vorrat m; (place) Lager nt,
Warenhaus nt; (BRIT: large shop) Kaufhaus
nt; (US) Laden m ♦ vt lagern; **~s** npl
(supplies) Vorräte pl; **~ up** vt sich
eindecken mit; **~room** n Lagerraum m,
Vorratsraum m

storey ['stɔːrɪ] (US story) n Stock m

stork [stɔːk] n Storch m

storm [stɔːm] n (also fig) Sturm m ♦ vt, vi
stürmen; **~y** adj stürmisch

story ['stɔːrɪ] n Geschichte f; (lie) Märchen
nt; (US) = storey; **~book** n
Geschichtenbuch nt; **~teller** n
Geschichtenerzähler m

stout [staut] adj (bold) tapfer; (fat) beleibt
♦ n Starkbier nt; (also: **sweet ~**) ≈ Malzbier
nt

stove [stəuv] n (Koch)herd m; (for heating)
Ofen m

stow [stəu] vt verstauen; **~away** n blinde(r)
Passagier m

straddle ['strædl] vt (horse, fence) rittlings
sitzen auf +dat; (fig) überbrücken

straggle ['strægl] vi (people) nachhinken; **~r**
n Nachzügler m; **straggly** (hair) zottig

straight [streɪt] adj gerade; (honest) offen,
ehrlich; (drink) pur ♦ adv (direct) direkt,
geradewegs; **to put** or **get sth in** ~ etw in
Ordnung bringen; **~ away** sofort; **~ off**
sofort; **~en** vt (also: **~en out**) gerade
machen; (fig) klarstellen; **~-faced** adv ohne
die Miene zu verziehen ♦ adj: **to be ~-
faced** keine Miene verziehen; **~forward**
adj einfach, unkompliziert

strain [streɪn] n Belastung f; (streak, trace)
Zug m; (of music) Fetzen m ♦ vt
überanstrengen; (stretch) anspannen;
(muscle) zerren; (filter) (durch)seihen ♦ vi
sich anstrengen; **~ed** adj (laugh)
gezwungen; (relations) gespannt; **~er** n
Sieb nt

strait [streɪt] n Straße f, Meerenge f;
~jacket n Zwangsjacke f; **~-laced** adj
engherzig, streng

strand [strænd] n (of hair) Strähne f; (also fig)
Faden m

stranded ['strændɪd] adj (also fig) gestrandet

strange [streɪndʒ] adj fremd; (unusual)
seltsam; **~r** n Fremde(r) mf

strangle ['stræŋgl] vt erwürgen; **~hold** n
(fig) Umklammerung f

strap [stræp] n Riemen m; (on clothes) Träger
m ♦ vt (fasten) festschnallen

strapping ['stræpɪŋ] adj stramm

strata ['strɑːtə] npl of **stratum**

strategic [strə'tiːdʒɪk] adj strategisch

strategy ['strætɪdʒɪ] n (fig) Strategie f

stratum ['strɑːtəm] n (pl **-ta**) n Schicht f

straw [strɔː] n Stroh nt; (single stalk, drinking
~) Strohhalm m; **that's the last ~!** das ist
der Gipfel!

strawberry ['strɔːbərɪ] n Erdbeere f

stray [streɪ] adj (animal) verirrt ♦ vi
herumstreunen

streak [striːk] n Streifen m; (in character)
Einschlag m; (in hair) Strähne f ♦ vt streifen
♦ vi zucken; (move quickly) flitzen; **~ of bad
luck** Pechsträhne f; **~y** adj gestreift; (bacon)
durchwachsen

stream [striːm] n (brook) Bach m; (fig) Strom
m ♦ vt (SCH) in (Leistungs)gruppen einteilen
♦ vi strömen; **to ~ in/out** (people) hinein-/
hinausströmen

streamer ['striːmər] n (flag) Wimpel m; (of
paper) Luftschlange f

streamlined ['striːmlaɪnd] adj
stromlinienförmig; (effective) rationell

street [striːt] n Straße f ♦ adj Straßen-; **~car**
(US) n Straßenbahn f; **~ lamp** n
Straßenlaterne f; **~ plan** n Stadtplan m;
~wise (inf) adj: **to be ~wise** wissen, wo es
langgeht

strength [streŋθ] n (also fig) Stärke f; Kraft f;
~en vt (ver)stärken

strenuous ['strenjuəs] adj anstrengend

stress [stres] n Druck m; (mental) Stress m;
(GRAM) Betonung f ♦ vt betonen

stretch [stretʃ] n Strecke f ♦ vt ausdehnen,

strecken ♦ vi sich erstrecken; (*person*) sich strecken; **~ out** vi sich ausstrecken ♦ vt ausstrecken

stretcher ['stretʃər] n Tragbahre f

stretchy ['stretʃi] adj elastisch, dehnbar

strewn [struːn] adj: **~ with** übersät mit

stricken ['strɪkən] adj (*person*) ergriffen; (*city, country*) heimgesucht; **~ with** (*disease*) leidend unter +dat

strict [strɪkt] adj (*exact*) genau; (*severe*) streng; **~ly** adv streng, genau

stridden ['strɪdn] pp of **stride**

stride [straɪd] (*pt* strode, *pp* stridden) n lange(r) Schritt m ♦ vi schreiten

strident ['straɪdnt] adj schneidend, durchdringend

strife [straɪf] n Streit m

strike [straɪk] (*pt, pp* struck) n Streik m; (*attack*) Schlag m ♦ vt (*hit*) schlagen; (*collide*) stoßen gegen; (*come to mind*) einfallen +dat; (*stand out*) auffallen +dat; (*find*) finden ♦ vi (*stop work*) streiken; (*attack*) zuschlagen; (*clock*) schlagen; **on ~** (*workers*) im Streik; **to ~ a match** ein Streichholz anzünden; **~ down** vt (*lay low*) niederschlagen; **~ out** vt (*cross out*) ausstreichen; **~ up** vt (*music*) anstimmen; (*friendship*) schließen; **~r** n Streikende(r) mf; **striking** ['straɪkɪŋ] adj auffallend

string [strɪŋ] (*pt, pp* strung) n Schnur f; (*row*) Reihe f; (*MUS*) Saite f ♦ vt: **to ~ together** aneinander reihen ♦ vi: **to ~ out** (sich) verteilen; **the ~s** npl (*MUS*) die Streichinstrumente pl; **to pull ~s** (*fig*) Fäden ziehen; **~ bean** n grüne Bohne f; **~(ed) instrument** n (*MUS*) Saiteninstrument nt

stringent ['strɪndʒənt] adj streng

strip [strɪp] n Streifen m ♦ vt (*uncover*) abstreifen, abziehen; (*clothes*) ausziehen; (*TECH*) auseinander nehmen ♦ vi (*undress*) sich ausziehen; **~ cartoon** n Bildserie f

stripe [straɪp] n Streifen m; **~d** adj gestreift

strip lighting n Neonlicht nt

stripper ['strɪpər] n Stripteasetänzerin f

strip-search ['strɪpsɜːtʃ] n Leibesvisitation f (*bei der man sich ausziehen muss*) ♦ vt: **to be ~~~ed** sich ausziehen müssen und durchsucht werden

stripy ['straɪpɪ] adj gestreift

strive [straɪv] (*pt* strove, *pp* striven) vi: **to ~ (for)** streben (nach)

strode [strəud] pt of **stride**

stroke [strəuk] n Schlag m; (*SWIMMING, ROWING*) Stoß m; (*MED*) Schlaganfall m; (*caress*) Streicheln nt ♦ vt streicheln; **at a ~** mit einem Schlag

stroll [strəul] n Spaziergang m ♦ vi schlendern; **~er** (*US*) n (*pushchair*) Sportwagen m

strong [strɒŋ] adj stark; (*firm*) fest; **they are 50 ~** sie sind 50 Mann stark; **~box** n Kassette f; **~hold** n Hochburg f; **~ly** adv stark; **~room** n Tresor m

strove [strəuv] pt of **strive**

struck [strʌk] pt, pp of **strike**

structure ['strʌktʃər] n Struktur f, Aufbau m; (*building*) Bau m

struggle ['strʌgl] n Kampf m ♦ vi (*fight*) kämpfen

strum [strʌm] vt (*guitar*) klimpern auf +dat

strung [strʌŋ] pt, pp of **string**

strut [strʌt] n Strebe f, Stütze f ♦ vi stolzieren

stub [stʌb] n Stummel m; (*of cigarette*) Kippe f ♦ vt: **to ~ one's toe** sich dat den Zeh anstoßen; **~ out** vt ausdrücken

stubble ['stʌbl] n Stoppel f

stubborn ['stʌbən] adj hartnäckig

stuck [stʌk] pt, pp of **stick** ♦ adj (*jammed*) klemmend; **~-up** adj hochnäsig

stud [stʌd] n (*button*) Kragenknopf m; (*place*) Gestüt nt ♦ vt (*fig*): **~ded with** übersät mit

student ['stjuːdənt] n Student(in) m(f); (*US*) Student(in) m(f), Schüler(in) m(f) ♦ adj Studenten-; **~ driver** (*US*) n Fahrschüler(in) m(f)

studio ['stjuːdɪəu] n Studio nt; (*for artist*) Atelier nt; **~ apartment** (*US*) n Appartement nt; **~ flat** n Appartement nt

studious ['stjuːdɪəs] adj lernbegierig

study ['stʌdɪ] n Studium nt; (*investigation*) Studium nt, Untersuchung f; (*room*) Arbeitszimmer nt; (*essay etc*) Studie f ♦ vt studieren; (*face*) erforschen; (*evidence*) prüfen ♦ vi studieren

stuff [stʌf] n Stoff m; (inf) Zeug nt ♦ vt stopfen, füllen; (animal) ausstopfen; **~ing** n Füllung f; **~y** adj (room) schwül; (person) spießig

stumble ['stʌmbl] vi stolpern; **to ~ across** (fig) zufällig stoßen auf +acc

stumbling block ['stʌmblɪŋ-] n Hindernis nt

stump [stʌmp] n Stumpf m

stun [stʌn] vt betäuben; (shock) niederschmettern

stung [stʌŋ] pt, pp of **sting**

stunk [stʌŋk] pp of **stink**

stunned adj benommen, fassungslos

stunning ['stʌnɪŋ] adj betäubend; (news) überwältigend, umwerfend

stunt [stʌnt] n Kunststück nt, Trick m

stunted ['stʌntɪd] adj verkümmert

stuntman ['stʌntmæn] (irreg) n Stuntman m

stupefy ['stju:pɪfaɪ] vt betäuben; (by news) bestürzen

stupendous [stju:'pendəs] adj erstaunlich, enorm

stupid ['stju:pɪd] adj dumm; **~ity** [stju:'pɪdɪtɪ] n Dummheit f

stupor ['stju:pə*] n Betäubung f

sturdy ['stɜ:dɪ] adj kräftig, robust

stutter ['stʌtə*] n Stottern nt ♦ vi stottern

sty [staɪ] n Schweinestall m

stye [staɪ] n Gerstenkorn nt

style [staɪl] n Stil m; (fashion) Mode f; **stylish** ['staɪlɪʃ] adj modisch; **stylist** ['staɪlɪst] n (hair stylist) Friseur m, Friseuse f

stylus ['staɪləs] n (Grammofon)nadel f

suave [swɑ:v] adj zuvorkommend

sub... [sʌb] prefix Unter...; **~conscious** adj unterbewusst ♦ n: **the ~conscious** das Unterbewusste; **~contract** vt (vertraglich) untervermitteln; **~divide** vt unterteilen; **~dued** adj (lighting) gedämpft; (person) still

subject [n, adj 'sʌbdʒɪkt, vb səb'dʒekt] n (of kingdom) Untertan m; (citizen) Staatsangehörige(r) mf; (topic) Thema nt; (SCH) Fach nt; (GRAM) Subjekt nt ♦ adj: **to be ~ to** unterworfen sein +dat; (exposed) ausgesetzt sein +dat ♦ vt (subdue) unterwerfen; (expose) aussetzen; **~ive** [səb'dʒektɪv] adj subjektiv; **~ matter** n Thema nt

sublet [sʌb'let] (irreg: like **let**) vt untervermieten

sublime [sə'blaɪm] adj erhaben

submachine gun ['sʌbmə'ʃi:n-] n Maschinenpistole f

submarine [sʌbmə'ri:n] n Unterseeboot nt, U-Boot nt

submerge [səb'mɜ:dʒ] vt untertauchen; (flood) überschwemmen ♦ vi untertauchen

submission [səb'mɪʃən] n (obedience) Gehorsam m; (claim) Behauptung f; (of plan) Unterbreitung f; **submissive** [səb'mɪsɪv] adj demütig, unterwürfig (pej)

submit [səb'mɪt] vt behaupten; (plan) unterbreiten ♦ vi sich ergeben

subnormal [sʌb'nɔ:ml] adj minderbegabt

subordinate [sə'bɔ:dɪnət] adj untergeordnet ♦ n Untergebene(r) mf

subpoena [sə'pi:nə] n Vorladung f ♦ vt vorladen

subscribe [səb'skraɪb] vi: **to ~ to** (view etc) unterstützen; (newspaper) abonnieren; **~r** n (to periodical) Abonnent m; (TEL) Telefonteilnehmer m

subscription [səb'skrɪpʃən] n Abonnement nt; (money subscribed) (Mitglieds)beitrag m

subsequent ['sʌbsɪkwənt] adj folgend, später; **~ly** adv später

subside [səb'saɪd] vi sich senken; **~nce** [səb'saɪdns] n Senkung f

subsidiarity [səbsɪdɪ'ærɪtɪ] n (POL) Subsidiarität f

subsidiary [səb'sɪdɪərɪ] adj Neben- ♦ n Tochtergesellschaft f

subsidize ['sʌbsɪdaɪz] vt subventionieren

subsidy ['sʌbsɪdɪ] n Subvention f

subsistence [səb'sɪstəns] n Unterhalt m

substance ['sʌbstəns] n Substanz f

substantial [səb'stænʃl] adj (strong) fest, kräftig; (important) wesentlich; **~ly** adv erheblich

substantiate [səb'stænʃɪeɪt] vt begründen, belegen

substitute ['sʌbstɪtju:t] n Ersatz m ♦ vt ersetzen; **substitution** [sʌbstɪ'tju:ʃən] n

Ersetzung f

subterfuge ['sʌbtəfju:dʒ] n Vorwand m; (*trick*) Trick m

subterranean [sʌbtə'reɪnɪən] adj unterirdisch

subtitle ['sʌbtaɪtl] n Untertitel m; ~d adj untertitelt, mit Untertiteln versehen

subtle ['sʌtl] adj fein; ~ty n Feinheit f

subtotal [sʌb'təʊtl] n Zwischensumme f

subtract [səb'trækt] vt abziehen; ~ion [səb'trækʃən] n Abziehen nt, Subtraktion f

suburb ['sʌbə:b] n Vorort m; **the ~s** die Außenbezirke pl; ~an [sə'bə:bən] adj Vorort(s)-; ~ia [sə'bə:bɪə] n Vorstadt f

subversive [səb'və:sɪv] adj subversiv

subway ['sʌbweɪ] n (US) U-Bahn f; (BRIT) Unterführung f

succeed [sək'si:d] vi (*person*) erfolgreich sein, Erfolg haben; (*plan etc also*) gelingen ♦ vt (nach)folgen +dat; **he ~ed in doing it** es gelang ihm, es zu tun; ~ing adj (nach)folgend

success [sək'ses] n Erfolg m; ~ful adj erfolgreich; **to be ~ful (in doing sth)** Erfolg haben (bei etw); ~fully adv erfolgreich

succession [sək'seʃən] n (Aufeinander)folge f; (*to throne*) Nachfolge f

successive [sək'sesɪv] adj aufeinander folgend

successor [sək'sesəʳ] n Nachfolger(in) m(f)

succinct [sək'sɪŋkt] adj knapp

succulent ['sʌkjulənt] adj saftig

succumb [sə'kʌm] vi: **to ~ (to)** erliegen (+dat); (*yield*) nachgeben (+dat)

such [sʌtʃ] adj solche(r, s); ~ **a book** so ein Buch; ~ **books** solche Bücher; ~ **courage** so ein Mut; ~ **a long trip** so eine lange Reise; ~ **a lot of** so viel(e); ~ **as** wie; **a noise ~ as** to so ein derartiger Lärm, dass; **as** ~ an sich; ~~**and**~~ **a time** die und die Zeit

suck [sʌk] vt saugen; (*lollipop etc*) lutschen

sucker ['sʌkəʳ] (*inf*) n Idiot m

suction ['sʌkʃən] n Saugkraft f

sudden ['sʌdn] adj plötzlich; **all of a** ~ auf einmal; ~ly adv plötzlich

suds [sʌdz] npl Seifenlauge f; (*lather*) Seifenschaum m

sue [su:] vt verklagen

suede [sweɪd] n Wildleder nt

Suez ['su:ɪz] n: **the** ~ **Canal** der Suezkanal

suffer ['sʌfəʳ] vt (er)leiden ♦ vi leiden; ~er n Leidende(r) mf; ~ing n Leiden nt

suffice [sə'faɪs] vi genügen

sufficient [sə'fɪʃənt] adj ausreichend; ~ly adv ausreichend

suffix ['sʌfɪks] n Nachsilbe f

suffocate ['sʌfəkeɪt] vt, vi ersticken

suffrage ['sʌfrɪdʒ] n Wahlrecht nt

sugar ['ʃugəʳ] n Zucker m ♦ vt zuckern; ~ **beet** n Zuckerrübe f; ~ **cane** n Zuckerrohr nt; ~y adj süß

suggest [sə'dʒest] vt vorschlagen; (*show*) schließen lassen auf +acc; ~ion [sə'dʒestʃən] n Vorschlag m; ~ive adj anregend; (*indecent*) zweideutig

suicide ['suɪsaɪd] n Selbstmord m; **to commit** ~ Selbstmord begehen ~ **bomber** n Selbstmordattentäter(in) m(f)

suit [su:t] n Anzug m; (*CARDS*) Farbe f ♦ vt passen +dat; (*clothes*) stehen +dat; **well ~ed** (*well matched*) gut zusammenpassend; ~**able** adj geeignet, passend; ~**ably** adv passend, angemessen

suitcase ['su:tkeɪs] n (Hand)koffer m

suite [swi:t] n (*of rooms*) Zimmerflucht f; (*of furniture*) Einrichtung f; (*MUS*) Suite f

suitor ['su:təʳ] n (*JUR*) Kläger(in) m(f)

sulfur ['sʌlfəʳ] (US) n = **sulphur**

sulk [sʌlk] vi schmollen; ~y adj schmollend

sullen ['sʌlən] adj mürrisch

sulphur ['sʌlfəʳ] (US **sulfur**) n Schwefel m

sultana [sʌl'tɑ:nə] n (*fruit*) Sultanine f

sultry ['sʌltrɪ] adj schwül

sum [sʌm] n Summe f; (*money*) Betrag m, Summe f; (*arithmetic*) Rechenaufgabe f; ~ **up** vt, vi zusammenfassen

summarize ['sʌməraɪz] vt kurz zusammenfassen

summary ['sʌmərɪ] n Zusammenfassung f ♦ adj (*justice*) kurzerhand erteilt

summer ['sʌməʳ] n Sommer m ♦ adj Sommer-; ~**house** n (*in garden*) Gartenhaus nt; ~**time** n Sommerzeit f

summit ['sʌmɪt] n Gipfel m; ~

(conference) n Gipfelkonferenz f

summon ['sʌmən] vt herbeirufen; (JUR)
vorladen; (gather up) aufbringen; **~s** (JUR)
Vorladung f ♦ vt vorladen

sump [sʌmp] (BRIT) n (AUT) Ölwanne f

sumptuous ['sʌmptjuəs] adj prächtig

sun [sʌn] n Sonne f; **~bathe** vi sich sonnen;
~block n Sonnenschutzcreme f; **~burn** n
Sonnenbrand m; **~burnt** adj
sonnenverbrannt, sonnengebräunt; **to be
~burnt** (painfully) einen Sonnenbrand
haben

Sunday ['sʌndɪ] n Sonntag m; **~ school** n
Sonntagsschule f

sundial ['sʌndaɪəl] n Sonnenuhr f

sundown ['sʌndaun] n Sonnenuntergang m

sundries ['sʌndrɪz] npl (miscellaneous items)
Verschiedene(s) nt

sundry ['sʌndrɪ] adj verschieden; **all and ~**
alle

sunflower ['sʌnflauə'] n Sonnenblume f

sung [sʌŋ] pp of **sing**

sunglasses ['sʌnglɑːsɪz] npl Sonnenbrille f

sunk [sʌŋk] pp of **sink**

sun: ~light ['sʌnlaɪt] n Sonnenlicht nt; **~lit**
['sʌnlɪt] adj sonnenbeschienen; **~ny** ['sʌnɪ]
adj sonnig; **~rise** n Sonnenaufgang m; **~
roof** n (AUT) Schiebedach nt; **~screen**
['sʌnskriːn] n Sonnenschutzcreme f; **~set**
['sʌnsɛt] n Sonnenuntergang m; **~shade**
['sʌnʃeɪd] n Sonnenschirm m; **~shine**
['sʌnʃaɪn] n Sonnenschein m; **~stroke**
['sʌnstrəuk] n Hitzschlag m; **~tan** ['sʌntæn] n
(Sonnen)bräune f; **~tan oil** n Sonnenöl nt

super ['suːpə'] (inf) adj prima, klasse

superannuation [suːpərænju'eɪʃən] n
Pension f

superb [suː'pəːb] adj ausgezeichnet,
hervorragend

supercilious [suːpə'sɪlɪəs] adj herablassend

superficial [suːpə'fɪʃəl] adj oberflächlich

superfluous [suː'pəːfluəs] adj überflüssig

superhuman [suːpə'hjuːmən] adj (effort)
übermenschlich

superimpose ['suːpərɪm'pəuz] vt
übereinander legen

superintendent [suːpərɪn'tɛndənt] n

Polizeichef m

superior [suː'pɪərɪə'] adj überlegen; (better)
besser ♦ n Vorgesetzte(r) mf; **~ity**
[supɪərɪ'ɔrɪtɪ] n Überlegenheit f

superlative [suː'pəːlətɪv] adj überragend

super: ~man ['suːpəmæn] (irreg) n
Übermensch m; **~market** ['suːpəmɑːkɪt] n
Supermarkt m; **~natural** [suːpə'nætʃərəl] adj
übernatürlich; **~power** ['suːpəpauə'] n
Weltmacht f

supersede [suːpə'siːd] vt ersetzen

supersonic ['suːpə'sɔnɪk] adj Überschall-

superstition [suːpə'stɪʃən] n Aberglaube m;
superstitious [suːpə'stɪʃəs] adj
abergläubisch

supervise ['suːpəvaɪz] vt beaufsichtigen,
kontrollieren; **supervision** [suːpə'vɪʒən] n
Aufsicht f; **supervisor** ['suːpəvaɪzə'] n
Aufsichtsperson f; **supervisory**
['suːpəvaɪzərɪ] adj Aufsichts-

supper ['sʌpə'] n Abendessen nt

supplant [sə'plɑːnt] vt (person, thing)
ersetzen

supple ['sʌpl] adj geschmeidig

supplement [n 'sʌplɪmənt, vb sʌplɪ'mɛnt] n
Ergänzung f; (in book) Nachtrag m ♦ vt
ergänzen; **~ary** [sʌplɪ'mɛntərɪ] adj
ergänzend; **~ary benefit** (BRIT: old) n ≃
Sozialhilfe f

supplier [sə'plaɪə'] n Lieferant m

supplies [sə'plaɪz] npl (food) Vorräte pl; (MIL)
Nachschub m

supply [sə'plaɪ] vt liefern ♦ n Vorrat m; (~ing)
Lieferung f; see also **supplies**; **~ teacher**
(BRIT) n Vertretung f

support [sə'pɔːt] n Unterstützung f; (TECH)
Stütze f ♦ vt (hold up) stützen, tragen;
(provide for) ernähren; (be in favour of)
unterstützen; **~er** n Anhänger(in) m(f)

suppose [sə'pəuz] vt, vi annehmen; **to be
~d to do sth** etw tun sollen; **~dly**
[sə'pəuzɪdlɪ] adv angeblich; **supposing** conj
angenommen; **supposition** [sʌpə'zɪʃən] n
Voraussetzung f

suppress [sə'prɛs] vt unterdrücken

supremacy [suː'prɛməsɪ] n Vorherrschaft f,
Oberhoheit f

supreme [suˈpriːm] *adj* oberste(r, s), höchste(r, s)

surcharge [ˈsɜːtʃɑːdʒ] *n* Zuschlag *m*

sure [ʃʊəʳ] *adj* sicher, gewiss; **~!** (*of course*) klar!; **to make ~ of sth/that** sich einer Sache *gen* vergewissern/vergewissern, dass; **~ enough** (*with past*) tatsächlich; (*with future*) ganz bestimmt; **~-footed** *adj* sicher (auf den Füßen); **~ly** *adv* (*certainly*) sicherlich, gewiss; **~ly it's wrong** das ist doch wohl falsch

surety [ˈʃʊərətɪ] *n* Sicherheit *f*

surf [sɜːf] *n* Brandung *f*

surface [ˈsɜːfɪs] *n* Oberfläche *f* ♦ *vt* (*roadway*) teeren ♦ *vi* auftauchen; **~ mail** *n* gewöhnliche Post *f*

surfboard [ˈsɜːfbɔːd] *n* Surfbrett *nt*

surfeit [ˈsɜːfɪt] *n* Übermaß *nt*

surfing [ˈsɜːfɪŋ] *n* Surfen *nt*

surge [sɜːdʒ] *n* Woge *f* ♦ *vi* wogen

surgeon [ˈsɜːdʒən] *n* Chirurg(in) *m(f)*

surgery [ˈsɜːdʒərɪ] *n* (*BRIT: place*) Praxis *f*; (: *time*) Sprechstunde *f*; (*treatment*) Operation *f*; **to undergo ~** operiert werden; **~ hours** (*BRIT*) *npl* Sprechstunden *pl*

surgical [ˈsɜːdʒɪkl] *adj* chirurgisch; **~ spirit** (*BRIT*) *n* Wundbenzin *nt*

surly [ˈsɜːlɪ] *adj* verdrießlich, grob

surmount [sɜːˈmaʊnt] *vt* überwinden

surname [ˈsɜːneɪm] *n* Zuname *m*

surpass [sɜːˈpɑːs] *vt* übertreffen

surplus [ˈsɜːpləs] *n* Überschuss *m* ♦ *adj* überschüssig, Über(schuss)-

surprise [səˈpraɪz] *n* Überraschung *f* ♦ *vt* überraschen; **~d** *adj* überrascht; **surprising** *adj* überraschend; **surprisingly** *adv* überraschend(erweise)

surrender [səˈrɛndəʳ] *n* Kapitulation *f* ♦ *vi* sich ergeben

surreptitious [sʌrəpˈtɪʃəs] *adj* heimlich; (*look also*) verstohlen

surrogate [ˈsʌrəgɪt] *n* Ersatz *m*; **~ mother** *n* Leihmutter *f*

surround [səˈraʊnd] *vt* umgeben; **~ing** *adj* (*countryside*) umliegend; **~ings** *npl* Umgebung *f*; (*environment*) Umwelt *f*

surveillance [sɜːˈveɪləns] *n* Überwachung *f*

survey [*n* ˈsɜːveɪ, *vb* sɜːˈveɪ] *n* Übersicht *f* ♦ *vt* überblicken; (*land*) vermessen; **~or** [səˈveɪəʳ] *n* Land(ver)messer(in) *m(f)*

survival [səˈvaɪvl] *n* Überleben *nt*

survive [səˈvaɪv] *vt*, *vi* überleben; **survivor** [səˈvaɪvəʳ] *n* Überlebende(r) *mf*

susceptible [səˈsɛptəbl] *adj*: **~ (to)** empfindlich (gegen); (*charms etc*) empfänglich (für)

suspect [*n* ˈsʌspɛkt, *vb* səsˈpɛkt] *n* Verdächtige(r) *mf* ♦ *adj* verdächtig ♦ *vt* verdächtigen; (*think*) vermuten

suspend [səsˈpɛnd] *vt* verschieben; (*from work*) suspendieren; (*hang up*) aufhängen; (*SPORT*) sperren; **~ed sentence** *n* (*JUR*) zur Bewährung ausgesetzte Strafe; **~er belt** *n* Strumpf(halter)gürtel *m*; **~ers** *npl* (*BRIT*) Strumpfhalter *m*; (*US*) Hosenträger *m*

suspense [səsˈpɛns] *n* Spannung *f*

suspension [səsˈpɛnʃən] *n* (*from work*) Suspendierung *f*; (*SPORT*) Sperrung *f*; (*AUT*) Federung *f*; **~ bridge** *n* Hängebrücke *f*

suspicion [səsˈpɪʃən] *n* Misstrauen *nt*; Verdacht *m*; **suspicious** [səsˈpɪʃəs] *adj* misstrauisch; (*causing ~*) verdächtig

sustain [səsˈteɪn] *vt* (*maintain*) aufrechterhalten; (*confirm*) bestätigen; (*injury*) davontragen; **~able** *adj* (*development, growth etc*) aufrechtzuerhalten; **~ed** *adj* (*effort*) anhaltend

sustenance [ˈsʌstɪnəns] *n* Nahrung *f*

swab [swɔb] *n* (*MED*) Tupfer *m*

swagger [ˈswægəʳ] *vi* stolzieren

swallow [ˈswɔləʊ] *n* (*bird*) Schwalbe *f*; (*of food etc*) Schluck *m* ♦ *vt* (ver)schlucken; **~ up** *vt* verschlingen

swam [swæm] *pt of* **swim**

swamp [swɔmp] *n* Sumpf *m* ♦ *vt* überschwemmen

swan [swɔn] *n* Schwan *m*

swap [swɔp] *n* Tausch *m* ♦ *vt*: **to ~ sth (for sth)** etw (gegen etw) tauschen *or* eintauschen

swarm [swɔːm] *n* Schwarm *m* ♦ *vi*: **to ~** *or* **be ~ing with** wimmeln von

swarthy ['swɔːðɪ] adj dunkel, braun
swastika ['swɒstɪkə] n Hakenkreuz nt
swat [swɒt] vt totschlagen
sway [sweɪ] vi schwanken; (branches) schaukeln, sich wiegen ♦ vt schwenken; (influence) beeinflussen
swear [sweə^r] (pt **swore**, pp **sworn**) vi (promise) schwören; (curse) fluchen; **to ~ to sth** schwören auf etw acc;**~word** n Fluch m
sweat [swet] n Schweiß m ♦ vi schwitzen
sweater ['swetə^r] n Pullover m
sweatshirt ['swetʃəːt] n Sweatshirt nt
sweaty ['swetɪ] adj verschwitzt
Swede [swiːd] n Schwede m, Schwedin f
swede [swiːd] (BRIT) n Steckrübe f
Sweden ['swiːdn] n Schweden nt
Swedish ['swiːdɪʃ] adj schwedisch ♦ n (LING) Schwedisch nt
sweep [swiːp] (pt, pp **swept**) n (chimney ~) Schornsteinfeger m ♦ vt fegen, kehren;**~ away** vt wegfegen;**~ past** vi vorbeisausen;**~ up** vt zusammenkehren;**~ing** adj (gesture) schwungvoll; (statement) verallgemeinernd
sweet [swiːt] n (course) Nachtisch m; (candy) Bonbon m ♦ adj süß;**~corn** n Zuckermais m;**~en** vt süßen; (fig) versüßen;**~heart** n Liebste(r) mf;**~ness** n Süße f;**~ pea** n Gartenwicke f
swell [swel] (pt **swelled**, pp **swollen** or **swelled**) n Seegang m ♦ adj (inf) todschick ♦ vt (numbers) vermehren ♦ vi (also: ~ **up**) (an)schwellen;**~ing** n Schwellung f
sweltering ['sweltərɪŋ] adj drückend
swept [swept] pt, pp of **sweep**
swerve [swəːv] vt, vi ausscheren
swift [swɪft] n Mauersegler m ♦ adj geschwind, schnell, rasch;**~ly** adv geschwind, schnell, rasch
swig [swɪg] n Zug m
swill [swɪl] n (for pigs) Schweinefutter nt ♦ vt spülen
swim [swɪm] (pt **swam**, pp **swum**) n: **to go for a ~** schwimmen gehen ♦ vi schwimmen ♦ vt (cross) (durch)schwimmen;**~mer** n Schwimmer(in) m(f);**~ming** n

Schwimmen nt;**~ming cap** n Badehaube f, Badekappe f;**~ming costume** (BRIT) n Badeanzug m;**~ming pool** n Schwimmbecken nt; (private) Swimmingpool m;**~ming trunks** npl Badehose f;**~suit** n Badeanzug m
swindle [swɪndl] n Schwindel m, Betrug m ♦ vt betrügen
swine [swaɪn] n (also fig) Schwein nt
swing [swɪŋ] (pt, pp **swung**) n (child's) Schaukel f; (movement) Schwung m ♦ vt schwingen ♦ vi schwingen, schaukeln; (turn quickly) schwenken; **in full ~** in vollem Gange;**~ bridge** n Drehbrücke f;**~ door** (BRIT) n Schwingtür f
swingeing ['swɪndʒɪŋ] (BRIT) adj hart; (taxation, cuts) extrem
swinging door ['swɪŋɪŋ-] (US) n Schwingtür f
swipe [swaɪp] n Hieb m ♦ vt (inf: hit) hart schlagen; (: steal) klauen
swirl [swəːl] vi wirbeln
swish [swɪʃ] adj (inf: smart) schick ♦ vi zischen; (grass, skirts) rascheln
Swiss [swɪs] adj Schweizer, schweizerisch ♦ n Schweizer(in) m(f); **the ~** npl (people) die Schweizer pl
switch [swɪtʃ] n (ELEC) Schalter m; (change) Wechsel m ♦ vt (ELEC) schalten; (change) wechseln ♦ vi wechseln;**~ off** vt ab- or ausschalten;**~ on** vt an- or einschalten;**~board** n Zentrale f; (board) Schaltbrett nt
Switzerland ['swɪtsələnd] n die Schweiz
swivel ['swɪvl] vt (also: ~ **round**) drehen ♦ vi (also: ~ **round**) sich drehen
swollen ['swəulən] pp of **swell**
swoon [swuːn] vi (old) in Ohnmacht fallen
swoop [swuːp] n Sturzflug m; (esp by police) Razzia f ♦ vi (also: ~ **down**) stürzen
swop [swɒp] = **swap**
sword [sɔːd] n Schwert nt;**~fish** n Schwertfisch m
swore [swɔː^r] pt of **swear**
sworn [swɔːn] pp of **swear**
swot [swɒt] vt, vi pauken
swum [swʌm] pp of **swim**
swung [swʌŋ] pt, pp of **swing**

sycamore ['sɪkəmɔːʳ] *n* (US) Platane *f*; (BRIT) Bergahorn *m*
syllable ['sɪləbl] *n* Silbe *f*
syllabus ['sɪləbəs] *n* Lehrplan *m*
symbol ['sɪmbl] *n* Symbol *nt*; **~ic(al)** [sɪm'bɔlɪk(l)] *adj* symbolisch
symmetry ['sɪmɪtrɪ] *n* Symmetrie *f*
sympathetic [sɪmpə'θetɪk] *adj* mitfühlend
sympathize ['sɪmpəθaɪz] *vi* mitfühlen; **~r** *n* (POL) Sympathisant(in) *m(f)*
sympathy ['sɪmpəθɪ] *n* Mitleid *nt*, Mitgefühl *nt*; (condolence) Beileid *nt*; **with our deepest ~** mit tief empfundenem Beileid
symphony ['sɪmfənɪ] *n* Sinfonie *f*
symptom ['sɪmptəm] *n* Symptom *nt*; **~atic** [sɪmptə'mætɪk] *adj* (fig): **~atic of** bezeichnend für
synagogue ['sɪnəgɔg] *n* Synagoge *f*
synchronize ['sɪŋkrənaɪz] *vt* synchronisieren
syndicate ['sɪndɪkɪt] *n* Konsortium *nt*
synonym ['sɪnənɪm] *n* Synonym *nt*; **~ous** [sɪ'nɔnɪməs] *adj* gleichbedeutend
synopsis [sɪ'nɔpsɪs] *n* Zusammenfassung *f*
synthetic [sɪn'θetɪk] *adj* synthetisch; **~s** *npl* (man-made fabrics) Synthetik *f*
syphon ['saɪfən] = **siphon**
Syria ['sɪrɪə] *n* Syrien *nt*
syringe [sɪ'rɪndʒ] *n* Spritze *f*
syrup ['sɪrəp] *n* Sirup *m*; (of sugar) Melasse *f*
system ['sɪstəm] *n* System *nt*; **~atic** [sɪstə'mætɪk] *adj* systematisch; **~ disk** *n* (COMPUT) Systemdiskette *f*; **~s analyst** *n* Systemanalytiker(in) *m(f)*

T, t

ta [tɑː] (BRIT: inf) *excl* danke!
tab [tæb] *n* Aufhänger *m*; (name ~) Schild *nt*; **to keep ~s on** (fig) genau im Auge behalten
tabby ['tæbɪ] *n* (also: **~ cat**) getigerte Katze *f*
table ['teɪbl] *n* Tisch *m*; (list) Tabelle *f* ♦ *vt* (PARL: propose) vorlegen, einbringen; **to lay** or **set the ~** den Tisch decken; **~cloth** *n* Tischtuch *nt*; **~ d'hôte** [tɑːbl'dəut] *n* Tagesmenü *nt*; **~ lamp** *n* Tischlampe *f*;

~mat *n* Untersatz *m*; **~ of contents** *n* Inhaltsverzeichnis *nt*; **~spoon** *n* Esslöffel *m*; **~spoonful** *n* Esslöffel *m* (voll)
tablet ['tæblɪt] *n* (MED) Tablette *f*
table tennis *n* Tischtennis *nt*
table wine *n* Tafelwein *m*
tabloid ['tæblɔɪd] *n* Zeitung *f* in kleinem Format; (pej) Boulevardzeitung *f*

---

tabloid press

ⓘ *Der Ausdruck* **tabloid press** *bezieht sich auf kleinformatige Zeitungen (ca 30 x 40cm); sie sind in Großbritannien fast ausschließlich Massenblätter. Im Gegensatz zur* **quality press** *verwenden diese Massenblätter viele Fotos und einen knappen, oft reißerischen Stil. Sie kommen den Lesern entgegen, die mehr Wert auf Unterhaltung legen.*

---

tabulate ['tæbjuleɪt] *vt* tabellarisch ordnen
tacit ['tæsɪt] *adj* stillschweigend
taciturn ['tæsɪtəːn] *adj* wortkarg
tack [tæk] *n* (small nail) Stift *m*; (US: thumbtack) Reißzwecke *f*; (stitch) Heftstich *m*; (NAUT) Lavieren *nt*; (course) Kurs *m* ♦ *vt* (nail) nageln; (stitch) heften ♦ *vi* aufkreuzen
tackle ['tækl] *n* (for lifting) Flaschenzug *m*; (NAUT) Takelage *f*; (SPORT) Tackling *nt* ♦ *vt* (deal with) anpacken, in Angriff nehmen; (person) festhalten; (player) angehen
tacky ['tækɪ] *adj* klebrig
tact [tækt] *n* Takt *m*; **~ful** *adj* taktvoll
tactical ['tæktɪkl] *adj* taktisch
tactics ['tæktɪks] *npl* Taktik *f*
tactless ['tæktlɪs] *adj* taktlos
tadpole ['tædpəul] *n* Kaulquappe *f*
taffy ['tæfɪ] *n* (US) Sahnebonbon *nt*
tag [tæg] *n* (label) Schild *nt*, Anhänger *m*; (maker's name) Etikett *nt*; **~ along** *vi* mitkommen
tail [teɪl] *n* Schwanz *m*; (of list) Schluss *m* ♦ *vt* folgen +dat; **~ away** or **off** *vi* abfallen, schwinden; **~back** (BRIT) *n* (AUT) (Rück)stau *m*; **~ coat** *n* Frack *m*; **~ end** *n* Schluss *m*, Ende *m*; **~gate** *n* (AUT) Heckklappe *f*
tailor ['teɪləʳ] *n* Schneider *m*; **~ing** *n*

Schneidern nt; **~-made** adj
maßgeschneidert; (fig): **~-made for sb** jdm
wie auf den Leib geschnitten
tailwind ['teɪlwɪnd] n Rückenwind m
tainted ['teɪntɪd] adj verdorben
take [teɪk] (pt **took**, pp **taken**) vt nehmen;
(trip, exam, PHOT) machen; (capture: person)
fassen; (: town; also COMM, FIN) einnehmen;
(carry to a place) bringen; (get for o.s.) sich
dat nehmen; (gain, obtain) bekommen; (put
up with) hinnehmen; (respond to)
aufnehmen; (interpret) auffassen; (assume)
annehmen; (contain) Platz haben für;
(GRAM) stehen mit; **to ~ sth from sb** jdm
etw wegnehmen; **to ~ sth from sth** (MATH:
subtract) etw von etw abziehen; (extract,
quotation) etw einer Sache dat entnehmen;
~ after vt fus ähnlich sein +dat; **~ apart**
vt auseinander nehmen; **~ away** vt
(remove) wegnehmen; (carry off)
wegbringen; **~ back** vt (return)
zurückbringen; (retract) zurücknehmen; **~
down** vt (pull down) abreißen; (write down)
aufschreiben; **~ in** vt (deceive) hereinlegen;
(understand) begreifen; (include)
einschließen; **~ off** vi (plane) starten ♦ vt
(remove) wegnehmen; (clothing) ausziehen;
(imitate) nachmachen; **~ on** vt (undertake)
übernehmen; (engage) einstellen;
(opponent) antreten gegen; **~ out** vt (girl,
dog) ausführen; (extract) herausnehmen;
(insurance) abschließen; (licence) sich dat
geben lassen; (book) ausleihen; (remove)
entfernen; **to ~ sth out of sth** (drawer,
pocket etc) etw aus etw herausnehmen; **~
over** vt übernehmen ♦ vi: **to ~ over from
sb** jdn ablösen; **~ to** vt fus (like) mögen;
(adopt as practice) sich dat angewöhnen; **~
up** vt (raise) aufnehmen; (dress etc) kürzer
machen; (occupy) in Anspruch nehmen;
(engage in) sich befassen mit; **~away** adj
zum Mitnehmen; **~-home pay** n
Nettolohn m; **~n** pp of **take**; **~off** n (AVIAT)
Start m; (imitation) Nachahmung f; **~out**
(US) adj = **takeaway**; **~over** n (COMM)
Übernahme f; **takings** ['teɪkɪŋz] npl (COMM)
Einnahmen pl

talc [tælk] n (also: **~um powder**)
Talkumpuder m
tale [teɪl] n Geschichte f, Erzählung f; **to tell
~s** (fig: lie) Geschichten erfinden
talent ['tælnt] n Talent nt; **~ed** adj begabt
talk [tɔːk] n (conversation) Gespräch nt;
(rumour) Gerede nt; (speech) Vortrag m ♦ vi
sprechen, reden; **~s** npl (POL etc) Gespräche
pl; **to ~ about** sprechen von +dat oder über
+acc; **to ~ sb into doing sth** jdn
überreden, etw zu tun; **to ~ sb out of
doing sth** jdm ausreden, etw zu tun; **to ~
shop** fachsimpeln; **~ over** vt besprechen;
~ative adj gesprächig
tall [tɔːl] adj groß; (building) hoch; **to be 1 m
80 ~** 1,80 m groß sein; **~boy** (BRIT) n
Kommode f; **~ story** n übertriebene
Geschichte f
tally ['tælɪ] n Abrechnung f ♦ vi
übereinstimmen
talon ['tælən] n Kralle f
tame [teɪm] adj zahm; (fig) fade
tamper ['tæmpər] vi: **to ~ with**
herumpfuschen an +dat
tampon ['tæmpɔn] n Tampon m
tan [tæn] n (Sonnen)bräune f; (colour)
Gelbbraun nt ♦ adj (colour) (gelb)braun ♦ vi
bräunen ♦ vi braun werden
tang [tæŋ] n Schärfe f
tangent ['tændʒənt] n Tangente f; **to go off
at a ~** (fig) vom Thema abkommen
tangerine [tændʒə'riːn] n Mandarine f
tangible ['tændʒəbl] adj greifbar
tangle ['tæŋgl] n Durcheinander nt; (trouble)
Schwierigkeiten pl; **to get in(to) a ~** sich
verheddern
tank [tæŋk] n (container) Tank m, Behälter m;
(MIL) Panzer m; **~er** ['tæŋkər] n (ship) Tanker
m; (vehicle) Tankwagen m
tanned [tænd] adj gebräunt
tantalizing ['tæntəlaɪzɪŋ] adj verlockend;
(annoying) quälend
tantamount ['tæntəmaunt] adj: **~ to**
gleichbedeutend mit
tantrum ['tæntrəm] n Wutanfall m
tap [tæp] n Hahn m; (gentle blow) Klopfen nt
♦ vt (strike) klopfen; (supply) anzapfen;

(*telephone*) abhören; **on ~** (*fig: resources*) zur Hand; **~-dancing** n Steppen nt

tape [teɪp] n Band nt; (*magnetic*) (Ton)band nt; (*adhesive*) Klebstreifen m ♦ vt (*record*) aufnehmen; **~ deck** n Tapedeck nt; **~ measure** n Maßband nt

taper ['teɪpə*r] vi spitz zulaufen

tape recorder n Tonbandgerät nt

tapestry ['tæpɪstrɪ] n Wandteppich m

tar [tɑː] n Teer m

target ['tɑːgɪt] n Ziel nt; (*board*) Zielscheibe f

tariff ['tærɪf] n (*duty paid*) Zoll m; (*list*) Tarif m

tarmac ['tɑːmæk] n (AVIAT) Rollfeld nt

tarnish ['tɑːnɪʃ] vt matt machen; (*fig*) beflecken

tarpaulin [tɑːˈpɔːlɪn] n Plane f

tarragon ['tærəgən] n Estragon m

tart [tɑːt] n (Obst)torte f; (*inf*) Nutte f ♦ adj scharf; **~ up** (*inf*) vt aufmachen; (*person*) auftakeln

tartan ['tɑːtn] n Schottenkaro nt ♦ adj mit Schottenkaro

tartar ['tɑːtə*r] n Zahnstein m

tartar(e) sauce ['tɑːtə-] n Remoulade f

task [tɑːsk] n Aufgabe f; **to take sb to ~** sich dat jdn vornehmen; **~ force** n Sondertrupp m

tassel ['tæsl] n Quaste f

taste [teɪst] n Geschmack m; (*sense*) Geschmackssinn m; (*small quantity*) Kostprobe f; (*liking*) Vorliebe f ♦ vt schmecken; (*try*) probieren ♦ vi schmecken; **can I have a ~ of this wine?** kann ich diesen Wein probieren?; **to have a ~ for sth** etw mögen; **in good/bad ~** geschmackvoll/geschmacklos; **you can ~ the garlic (in it)** man kann den Knoblauch herausschmecken; **to ~ of sth** nach einer Sache schmecken; **~ful** adj geschmackvoll; **~less** adj (*insipid*) fade; (*in bad ~*) geschmacklos; **tasty** ['teɪstɪ] adj schmackhaft

tattered ['tætəd] adj = **in tatters**

tatters ['tætəz] npl: **in ~** in Fetzen

tattoo [təˈtuː] n (MIL) Zapfenstreich m; (*on skin*) Tätowierung f ♦ vt tätowieren

tatty ['tætɪ] (BRIT: *inf*) adj schäbig

taught [tɔːt] pt, pp of **teach**

taunt [tɔːnt] n höhnische Bemerkung f ♦ vt verhöhnen

Taurus ['tɔːrəs] n Stier m

taut [tɔːt] adj straff

tawdry ['tɔːdrɪ] adj (bunt und) billig

tax [tæks] n Steuer f ♦ vt besteuern; (*strain*) strapazieren; (*strength*) angreifen; **~able** adj (*income*) steuerpflichtig; **~ation** [tækˈseɪʃən] n Besteuerung f; **~ avoidance** n Steuerumgehung f; **~ disc** (BRIT) n (AUT) Kraftfahrzeugsteuerplakette f; **~ evasion** n Steuerhinterziehung f; **~-free** adj steuerfrei

taxi ['tæksɪ] n Taxi nt ♦ vi (*plane*) rollen; **~ driver** n Taxifahrer m; **~ rank** (BRIT) n Taxistand m; **~ stand** n Taxistand m

tax: ~payer n Steuerzahler m; **~ relief** n Steuerermäßigung f; **~ return** n Steuererklärung f

TB n abbr (= tuberculosis) Tb f, Tbc f

tea [tiː] n Tee m; (*meal*) (frühes) Abendessen nt; **high ~** (BRIT) Abendessen nt; **~ bag** n Teebeutel m; **~ break** (BRIT) n Teepause f

teach [tiːtʃ] (pt, pp **taught**) vt lehren; (SCH) lehren, unterrichten; (*show*): **to ~ sb sth** jdm etw beibringen ♦ vi lehren, unterrichten; **~er** n Lehrer(in) m(f); **~er's pet** n Lehrers Liebling m; **~ing** n (~er's work) Unterricht m; (*doctrine*) Lehre f

tea: ~ cloth n Geschirrtuch nt; **~ cosy** n Teewärmer m; **~cup** n Teetasse f; **~ leaves** npl Teeblätter pl

team [tiːm] n (*workers*) Team nt; (SPORT) Mannschaft f; (*animals*) Gespann nt; **~work** n Gemeinschaftsarbeit f, Teamarbeit f

teapot ['tiːpɒt] n Teekanne f

tear[1] [tɛə*r] (pt **tore**, pp **torn**) n Riss m ♦ vt zerreißen; (*muscle*) zerren ♦ vi (zer)reißen; (*rush*) rasen; **~ along** vi (*rush*) entlangrasen; **~ up** vt (*sheet of paper etc*) zerreißen

tear[2] [tɪə*r] n Träne f; **~ful** ['tɪəful] adj weinend; (*voice*) weinerlich; **~ gas** ['tɪəgæs] n Tränengas nt

tearoom ['tiːruːm] n Teestube f

tease [tiːz] n Hänsler m ♦ vt necken

tea set n Teeservice nt

teaspoon ['ti:spu:n] n Teelöffel m

teat [ti:t] n Brustwarze f; (of animal) Zitze f; (of bottle) Sauger m

tea time n (in the afternoon) Teestunde f; (mealtime) Abendessen nt

tea towel n Geschirrtuch nt

technical ['teknɪkl] adj technisch; (knowledge, terms) Fach-; **~ity** [teknɪ'kælɪtɪ] n technische Einzelheit f; (JUR) Formsache f; **~ly** adv technisch; (speak) spezialisiert; (fig) genau genommen

technician [tek'nɪʃən] n Techniker m

technique [tek'ni:k] n Technik f

techno ['teknəʊ] n Techno m

technological [teknə'lɒdʒɪkl] adj technologisch

technology [tek'nɒlədʒɪ] n Technologie f

teddy (bear) ['tedɪ-] n Teddybär m

tedious ['ti:dɪəs] adj langweilig, ermüdend

tee [ti:] n (GOLF: object) Tee nt

teem [ti:m] vi (swarm): **to ~ (with)** wimmeln (von); **it is ~ing (with rain)** es gießt in Strömen

teenage ['ti:neɪdʒ] adj (fashions etc) Teenager-, jugendlich; **~r** n Teenager m, Jugendliche(r) mf

teens [ti:nz] npl Teenageralter nt

tee-shirt ['ti:ʃə:t] n T-Shirt nt

teeter ['ti:təʳ] vi schwanken

teeth [ti:θ] npl of **tooth**

teethe [ti:ð] vi zahnen; **teething ring** n Beißring m; **teething troubles** npl (fig) Kinderkrankheiten pl

teetotal ['ti:'təʊtl] adj abstinent

tele-: **~communications** npl Fernmeldewesen nt; **~conferencing** n Telefon- or Videokonferenz f; **~gram** n Telegramm nt; **~graph** n Telegraf m; **~graph pole** n Telegrafenmast m

telephone ['telɪfəʊn] n Telefon nt, Fernsprecher m ♦ vt anrufen; (message) telefonisch mitteilen; **to be on the ~** (talking) telefonieren; (possessing phone) Telefon haben; **~ booth** n Telefonzelle f; **~ box** (BRIT) n Telefonzelle f; **~ call** n Telefongespräch nt, Anruf m; **~ directory** n Telefonbuch nt; **~ number** n Telefonnummer f; **telephonist** [tə'lefənɪst] (BRIT) n Telefonist(in) m(f)

telephoto lens ['telɪ'fəʊtəʊ-] n Teleobjektiv nt

telesales ['telɪseɪlz] n Telefonverkauf m

telescope ['telɪskəʊp] n Teleskop nt, Fernrohr nt ♦ vt ineinander schieben

televise ['telɪvaɪz] vt durch das Fernsehen übertragen

television ['telɪvɪʒən] n Fernsehen nt; **on ~** im Fernsehen; **~ (set)** n Fernsehapparat m, Fernseher m

teleworking ['telɪwɜːkɪŋ] n Telearbeit f

telex ['teleks] n Telex nt ♦ vt per Telex schicken

tell [tel] (pt, pp **told**) vt (story) erzählen; (secret) ausplaudern; (say, make known) sagen; (distinguish) erkennen; (be sure) wissen ♦ vi (talk) sprechen; (be sure) wissen; (divulge) es verraten; (have effect) sich auswirken; **to ~ sb to do sth** jdm sagen, dass er etw tun soll; **to ~ sb sth** or **sth to sb** jdm etw sagen; **to ~ sb by sth** jdn an etw dat erkennen; **to ~ sth from** etw unterscheiden von; **to ~ of sth** von etw sprechen; **~ off** vt: **to ~ sb off** jdn ausschimpfen

teller ['teləʳ] n Kassenbeamte(r) mf

telling ['telɪŋ] adj verräterisch; (blow) hart

telltale ['telteɪl] adj verräterisch

telly ['telɪ] (BRIT: inf) n abbr (= television) TV nt

temp [temp] n abbr (= temporary) Aushilfssekretärin f

temper ['tempəʳ] n (disposition) Temperament nt; (anger) Zorn m ♦ vt (tone down) mildern; (metal) härten; **to be in a (bad) ~** wütend sein; **to lose one's ~** die Beherrschung verlieren

temperament ['tempərəmənt] n Temperament nt; **~al** [temprə'mentl] adj (moody) launisch

temperate ['temprət] adj gemäßigt

temperature ['temprətʃəʳ] n Temperatur f; (MED: high ~) Fieber nt; **to have** or **run a ~** Fieber haben

template ['templɪt] n Schablone f

temple ['templ] n Tempel m; (ANAT) Schläfe *f*

temporal ['tɛmpərl] *adj* (*of time*) zeitlich; (*worldly*) irdisch, weltlich

temporarily ['tɛmpərərɪlɪ] *adv* zeitweilig, vorübergehend

temporary ['tɛmpərərɪ] *adj* vorläufig; (*road, building*) provisorisch

tempt [tɛmpt] *vt* (*persuade*) verleiten; (*attract*) reizen, (ver)locken; **to ~ sb into doing sth** jdn dazu verleiten, etw zu tun; **~ation** [tɛmp'teɪʃən] *n* Versuchung *f*; **~ing** *adj* (*person*) verführerisch; (*object, situation*) verlockend

ten [tɛn] *num* zehn

tenable ['tɛnəbl] *adj* haltbar

tenacious [tə'neɪʃəs] *adj* zäh, hartnäckig

tenacity [tə'næsɪtɪ] *n* Zähigkeit *f*, Hartnäckigkeit *f*

tenancy ['tɛnənsɪ] *n* Mietverhältnis *nt*

tenant ['tɛnənt] *n* Mieter *m*; (*of larger property*) Pächter *m*

tend [tɛnd] *vt* (*look after*) sich kümmern um ♦ *vi*: **to ~ to do sth** etw gewöhnlich tun

tendency ['tɛndənsɪ] *n* Tendenz *f*; (*of person*) Tendenz *f*, Neigung *f*

tender ['tɛndə*] *adj* zart; (*loving*) zärtlich ♦ *n* (*COMM: offer*) Kostenanschlag *m* ♦ *vt* (an)bieten; (*resignation*) einreichen; **~ness** *n* Zartheit *f*; (*being loving*) Zärtlichkeit *f*

tendon ['tɛndən] *n* Sehne *f*

tenement ['tɛnəmənt] *n* Mietshaus *nt*

tennis ['tɛnɪs] *n* Tennis *nt*; **~ ball** *n* Tennisball *m*; **~ court** *n* Tennisplatz *m*; **~ player** *n* Tennisspieler(in) *m(f)*; **~ racket** *n* Tennisschläger *m*; **~ shoes** *npl* Tennisschuhe *pl*

tenor ['tɛnə*] *n* Tenor *m*

tenpin bowling ['tɛnpɪn-] *n* Bowling *nt*

tense [tɛns] *adj* angespannt ♦ *n* Zeitform *f*

tension ['tɛnʃən] *n* Spannung *f*

tent [tɛnt] *n* Zelt *nt*

tentacle ['tɛntəkl] *n* Fühler *m*; (*of sea animals*) Fangarm *m*

tentative ['tɛntətɪv] *adj* (*movement*) unsicher; (*offer*) Probe-; (*arrangement*) vorläufig; (*suggestion*) unverbindlich; **~ly** *adv* versuchsweise; (*try, move*) vorsichtig

tenterhooks ['tɛntəhuks] *npl*: **to be on ~** auf die Folter gespannt sein

tenth [tɛnθ] *adj* zehnte(r, s)

tent peg *n* Hering *m*

tent pole *n* Zeltstange *f*

tenuous ['tɛnjuəs] *adj* schwach

tenure ['tɛnjuə*] *n* (*of land*) Besitz *m*; (*of office*) Amtszeit *f*

tepid ['tɛpɪd] *adj* lauwarm

term [tə:m] *n* (*period of time*) Zeit(raum *m*) *f*; (*limit*) Frist *f*; (*SCH*) Quartal *nt*; (*UNIV*) Trimester *nt*; (*expression*) Ausdruck *m* ♦ *vt* (be)nennen; **~s** *npl* (*conditions*) Bedingungen *pl*; **in the short/long ~** kurze/lange Sicht; **to be on good ~s with sb** gut mit jdm auskommen; **to come to ~s with** (*person*) sich einigen mit; (*problem*) sich abfinden mit

terminal ['tə:mɪnl] *n* (*BRIT: also:* **coach ~**) Endstation *f*; (*AVIAT*) Terminal *m*; (*COMPUT*) Terminal *nt* or *m* ♦ *adj* Schluss-; (*MED*) unheilbar; **~ly** *adj* (*MED*): **~ly ill** unheilbar krank

terminate ['tə:mɪneɪt] *vt* beenden ♦ *vi* enden, aufhören

termini ['tə:mɪnaɪ] *npl of* **terminus**

terminus ['tə:mɪnəs] (*pl* **termini**) *n* Endstation *f*

terrace ['tɛrəs] *n* (*BRIT: row of houses*) Häuserreihe *f*; (*in garden etc*) Terrasse *f*; **the ~s** *npl* (*BRIT: SPORT*) die Ränge; **~d** *adj* (*garden*) terrassenförmig angelegt; (*house*) Reihen-

terrain [tɛ'reɪn] *n* Gelände *nt*

terrible ['tɛrɪbl] *adj* schrecklich, entsetzlich, fürchterlich; **terribly** *adv* fürchterlich

terrier ['tɛrɪə*] *n* Terrier *m*

terrific [tə'rɪfɪk] *adj* unwahrscheinlich; **~!** klasse!

terrified *adj*: **to be ~ of sth** vor etw schreckliche Angst haben

terrify ['tɛrɪfaɪ] *vt* erschrecken

territorial [tɛrɪ'tɔ:rɪəl] *adj* Gebiets-, territorial

territory ['tɛrɪtərɪ] *n* Gebiet *nt*

terror ['tɛrə*] *n* Schrecken *m*

terrorism ['tɛrərɪzəm] *n* Terrorismus *m*; **~ist** *n* Terrorist(in) *m(f)*; **~ize** *vt* terrorisieren

terse [tɜːs] *adj* knapp, kurz, bündig

test [tɛst] *n* Probe *f*; (*examination*) Prüfung *f*; (*PSYCH, TECH*) Test *m* ♦ *vt* prüfen; (*PSYCH*) testen

testicle ['tɛstɪkl] *n* (*ANAT*) Hoden *m*

testify ['tɛstɪfaɪ] *vi* aussagen; **to ~ to sth** etw bezeugen

testimony ['tɛstɪmənɪ] *n* (*JUR*) Zeugenaussage *f*; (*fig*) Zeugnis *nt*

test match *n* (*SPORT*) Länderkampf *m*

test tube *n* Reagenzglas *nt*

tether ['tɛðəʳ] *vt* anbinden ♦ *n*: **at the end of one's ~** völlig am Ende

text [tɛkst] *n* Text *m*; (*of document*) Wortlaut *m*; (*text message*) SMS-Nachricht *f*; ♦ *vti* eine SMS schicken; **ich schicke dir eine SMS** I'll send you a text; **~book** *n* Lehrbuch *nt*

textiles ['tɛkstaɪlz] *npl* Textilien *pl*

texture ['tɛkstʃəʳ] *n* Beschaffenheit *f*

Thai [taɪ] *adj* thailändisch ♦ *n* Thailänder(in) *m(f)*; **~land** *n* Thailand *nt*

Thames [tɛmz] *n*: **the ~** die Themse

than [ðæn, ðən] *prep* (*in comparisons*) als

thank [θæŋk] *vt* danken +*dat*; **you've him to ~ for your success** Sie haben Ihren Erfolg ihm zu verdanken; **~ you (very much)** danke (vielmals), danke schön; **~ful** *adj* dankbar; **~less** *adj* undankbar; **~s** *npl* Dank *m* ♦ *excl* danke!; **~s to** dank +*gen*; **T~sgiving (Day)** (*US*) *n* Thanksgiving Day *m*

Thanksgiving (Day)

🛈 **Thanksgiving (Day)** *ist ein Feiertag in den USA, der auf den vierten Donnerstag im November fällt. Er soll daran erinnern, wie die Pilgerväter die gute Ernte im Jahre 1621 feierten. In Kanada gibt es einen ähnlichen Erntedanktag (der aber nichts mit dem Pilgervätern zu tun hat) am zweiten Montag im Oktober.*

KEYWORD

that [ðæt, ðət] *adj* (*demonstrative: pl those*) der/die/das; jene(r, s); **that one** das da

♦ *pron* **1** (*demonstrative: pl those*) das; **who's/what's that?** wer ist da/was ist das?; **is that you?** bist du das?; **that's what he said** genau das hat er gesagt; **what happened after that?** was passierte danach?; **that is** das heißt

2 (*relative: subj*) der/die/das, die; (: *direct obj*) den/die/das, die; (: *indirect obj*) dem/der/dem, denen; **all (that) I have** alles, was ich habe

3 (*relative: of time*): **the day (that)** an dem Tag, als; **the winter (that) he came** in dem Winter, in dem er kam

♦ *conj* dass; **he thought that I was ill** er dachte, dass ich krank sei, er dachte, ich sei krank

♦ *adv* (*demonstrative*) so; **I can't work that much** ich kann nicht so viel arbeiten

---

thatched [θætʃt] *adj* strohgedeckt; (*cottage*) mit Strohdach

thaw [θɔː] *n* Tauwetter *nt* ♦ *vi* tauen; (*frozen foods, fig: people*) auftauen ♦ *vt* (auf)tauen lassen

KEYWORD

the [ðiː, ðə] *def art* **1** der/die/das; **to play the piano/violin** Klavier/Geige spielen; **I'm going to the butcher's/the cinema** ich gehe zum Fleischer/ins Kino; **Elizabeth the First** Elisabeth die Erste

2 (+*adj to form noun*) das, die; **the rich and the poor** die Reichen und die Armen

3 (*in comparisons*): **the more he works the more he earns** je mehr er arbeitet, desto mehr verdient er

---

theatre ['θɪətəʳ] (*US* **theater**) *n* Theater *nt*; (*for lectures etc*) Saal *m*; (*MED*) Operationssaal *m*; **~goer** *n* Theaterbesucher(in) *m(f)*; **theatrical** [θɪ'ætrɪkl] *adj* Theater-; (*career*) Schauspieler-; (*showy*) theatralisch

theft [θɛft] *n* Diebstahl *m*

their [ðɛəʳ] *adj* ihr; *see also* **my**; **~s** *pron* ihre(r, s); *see also* **mine²**

them [ðɛm, ðəm] *pron* (*acc*) sie; (*dat*) ihnen; *see also* **me**

theme [θiːm] *n* Thema *nt*; (*MUS*) Motiv *nt*; ~ **park** *n* (thematisch gestalteter) Freizeitpark *m*; ~ **song** *n* Titelmusik *f*

themselves [ðəmˈsɛlvz] *pl pron* (*reflexive*) sich (selbst); (*emphatic*) selbst; *see also* **oneself**

then [ðɛn] *adv* (*at that time*) damals; (*next*) dann ♦ *conj* also, folglich; (*furthermore*) ferner ♦ *adj* damalig; **from ~ on** von da an; **by ~** bis dahin; **the ~ president** der damalige Präsident

theology [θɪˈɔlədʒɪ] *n* Theologie *f*

theoretical [θɪəˈrɛtɪkl] *adj* theoretisch; ~**ly** *adv* theoretisch

theory [ˈθɪərɪ] *n* Theorie *f*

therapist [ˈθɛrəpɪst] *n* Therapeut(in) *m(f)*

therapy [ˈθɛrəpɪ] *n* Therapie *f*

KEYWORD
---

there [ðɛər] *adv* **1**: **there is, there are** es or da ist/sind; (*there exists/exist also*) es gibt; **there are 3 of them** (*people, things*) es gibt 3 davon; **there has been an accident** da war ein Unfall
2 (*place*) da, dort; (*direction*) dahin, dorthin; **put it in/on there** leg es dahinein/dorthinauf
3: **there, there** (*esp to child*) na, na

there: ~**abouts** [ˈðɛərəˈbauts] *adv* (*place*) dort in der Nähe, dort irgendwo; (*amount*): **20 or ~abouts** ungefähr 20; ~**after** [ðɛərˈɑːftər] *adv* danach; ~**by** [ˈðɛəbaɪ] *adv* dadurch, damit

therefore [ˈðɛəfɔːr] *adv* deshalb, daher

there's [ˈðɛəz] = **there is; there has**

thermometer [θəˈmɔmɪtər] *n* Thermometer *nt*

Thermos [ˈθəːməs] ® *n* Thermosflasche *f*

thesaurus [θɪˈsɔːrəs] *n* Synonymwörterbuch *nt*

these [ðiːz] *pron, adj* (*pl*) diese

theses [ˈθiːsiːz] *npl of* **thesis**

thesis [ˈθiːsɪs] (*pl* **theses**) *n* (*for discussion*) These *f*; (*UNIV*) Dissertation *f*, Doktorarbeit *f*

they [ðeɪ] *pl pron* sie; (*people in general*) man; ~ **say that ...** (*it is said that*) es wird gesagt, dass; ~**'d** = **they had; they would**; ~= **they shall; they will**; ~= **they are**; ~= **they have**

thick [θɪk] *adj* dick; (*forest*) dicht; (*liquid*) dickflüssig; (*slow, stupid*) dumm, schwer von Begriff ♦ *n*: **in the ~ of** mitten in +*dat*; **it's 20 cm ~** es ist 20 cm dick *or* stark; ~**en** *vi* (*fog*) dichter werden ♦ *vt* (*sauce etc*) verdicken; ~**ness** *n* Dicke *f*; Dichte *f*; Dickflüssigkeit *f*; ~**set** *adj* untersetzt; ~**skinned** *adj* dickhäutig

thief [θiːf] (*pl* **thieves**) *n* Dieb(in) *m(f)*

thieves [θiːvz] *npl of* **thief**

thieving [ˈθiːvɪŋ] *n* Stehlen *nt* ♦ *adj* diebisch

thigh [θaɪ] *n* Oberschenkel *m*

thimble [ˈθɪmbl] *n* Fingerhut *m*

thin [θɪn] *adj* dünn; (*person*) dünn, mager; (*excuse*) schwach ♦ *vt*: **to ~ (down)** (*sauce, paint*) dünnen

thing [θɪŋ] *n* Ding *nt*; (*affair*) Sache *f*; **my ~s** meine Sachen *pl*; **the best ~ would be to ...** das Beste wäre, ...; **how are ~s?** wie gehts?

think [θɪŋk] (*pt, pp* **thought**) *vt, vi* denken; **what did you ~ of them?** was halten Sie von ihnen?; **to ~ about sth/sb** nachdenken über etw/jdn; **I'll ~ about it** ich überlege es mir; **to ~ of doing sth** vorhaben *or* beabsichtigen, etw zu tun; **I ~ so/not** ich glaube (schon)/glaube nicht; **to ~ well of sb** viel von jdm halten; ~ **over** *vt* überdenken; ~ **up** *vt* sich *dat* ausdenken

think tank *n* Expertengruppe *f*

thinly [ˈθɪnlɪ] *adv* dünn; (*disguised*) kaum

third [θəːd] *adj* dritte(r, s) ♦ *n* (*person*) Dritte(r) *mf*; (*part*) Drittel *nt*; ~**ly** *adv* drittens; ~ **party insurance** (*BRIT*) *n* Haftpflichtversicherung *f*; ~**rate** *adj* minderwertig; **T~ World** *n*: **the T~ World** die Dritte Welt *f*

thirst [θəːst] *n* (*also fig*) Durst *m*; ~**y** *adj* (*person*) durstig; (*work*) durstig machend; **to be ~y** Durst haben

thirteen [θəːˈtiːn] *num* dreizehn

thirty [ˈθəːtɪ] *num* dreißig

KEYWORD

this [ðɪs] adj (demonstrative: pl these) diese(r, s); **this evening** heute Abend; **this one** diese(r, s) (da)
♦ pron (demonstrative: pl these) dies, das; **who/what is this?** wer/was ist das?; **this is where I live** hier wohne ich; **this is what he said** das hat er gesagt; **this is Mr Brown** dies ist Mr Brown; (on telephone) hier ist Mr Brown
♦ adv (demonstrative): **this high/long** etc so groß/lang etc

thistle ['θɪsl] n Distel f
thorn [θɔːn] n Dorn m; **~y** adj dornig; (problem) schwierig
thorough ['θʌrə] adj gründlich; **~bred** n Vollblut nt ♦ adj reinrassig, Vollblut-; **~fare** n Straße f; **"no ~fare"** „Durchfahrt verboten"; **~ly** adv gründlich; (extremely) äußerst
those [ðəuz] pl pron die (da), jene ♦ adj die, jene
though [ðəu] conj obwohl ♦ adv trotzdem
thought [θɔːt] pt, pp of **think** ♦ n (idea) Gedanke m; (thinking) Denken nt; (thinking) Denkvermögen nt; **~ful** adj (thinking) gedankenvoll, nachdenklich; (kind) rücksichtsvoll, aufmerksam; **~less** adj gedankenlos, unbesonnen; (unkind) rücksichtslos
thousand ['θauzənd] num tausend; **two ~** zweitausend; **~s of** tausende or Tausende (von); **~th** adj tausendste(r, s)
thrash [θræʃ] vt verdreschen; (fig) (vernichtend) schlagen; **~ about** vi um sich schlagen; **~ out** vt ausdiskutieren
thread [θred] n Faden m, Garn nt; (TECH) Gewinde nt; (in story) Faden m ♦ vt (needle) einfädeln; **~bare** adj fadenscheinig
threat [θret] n Drohung f; (danger) Gefahr f; **~en** vt bedrohen ♦ vi drohen; **to ~en sb with sth** jdm etw androhen
three [θriː] num drei; **~-dimensional** adj dreidimensional; **~-piece suite** n dreiteilige Polstergarnitur f; **~-wheeler** n

Dreiradwagen m
thresh [θreʃ] vt, vi dreschen
threshold ['θreʃhəuld] n Schwelle f
threw [θruː] pt of **throw**
thrift [θrɪft] n Sparsamkeit f; **~y** adj sparsam
thrill [θrɪl] n Reiz m, Erregung f ♦ vt begeistern, packen; **to be ~ed with** (gift etc) sich unheimlich freuen über +acc; **~er** n Krimi m; **~ing** adj spannend; (news) aufregend
thrive [θraɪv] (pt thrived, pp thrived) vi: **to ~ (on)** gedeihen (bei); **thriving** ['θraɪvɪŋ] adj blühend
throat [θrəut] n Hals m, Kehle f; **to have a sore ~** Halsschmerzen haben
throb [θrɒb] vi klopfen, pochen
throes [θrəuz] npl: **in the ~ of** mitten in +dat
throne [θrəun] n Thron m; **on the ~** auf dem Thron
throng ['θrɒŋ] n (Menschen)schar f ♦ vt sich drängen in +dat
throttle ['θrɒtl] n Gashebel m ♦ vt erdrosseln
through [θruː] prep durch; (time) während +gen; (because of) aus, durch ♦ adv durch ♦ adj (ticket, train) durchgehend; (finished) fertig; **to put sb ~ (to)** jdn verbinden (mit); **to be ~** (TEL) eine Verbindung haben; (have finished) fertig sein; **no ~ way** (BRIT) Sackgasse f; **~out** [θruː'aut] prep (place) überall in +dat; (time) während +gen ♦ adv überall; die ganze Zeit
throw [θrəu] (pt threw, pp thrown) n Wurf m ♦ vt werfen; **to ~ a party** eine Party geben; **~ away** vt wegwerfen; (waste) verschenken; (money) verschwenden; **~ off** vt abwerfen; (pursuer) abschütteln; **~ out** vt hinauswerfen; (rubbish) wegwerfen; (plan) verwerfen; **~ up** vt, vi (vomit) speien; **~away** adj Wegwerf-; **~in** n Einwurf m; **~n** pp of **throw**
thru [θruː] (US) = **through**
thrush [θrʌʃ] n Drossel f
thrust [θrʌst] (pt, pp thrust) vt, vi (push) stoßen
thud [θʌd] n dumpfe(r) (Auf)schlag m
thug [θʌg] n Schlägertyp m

thumb [θʌm] n Daumen m ♦ vt (book) durchblättern; **to ~ a lift** per Anhalter fahren (wollen); **~tack** (US) n Reißwecke f

thump [θʌmp] n (blow) Schlag m; (noise) Bums m ♦ vi hämmern, pochen ♦ vt schlagen auf +acc

thunder ['θʌndə'] n Donner m ♦ vi donnern; (train etc): **to ~ past** vorbeidonnern ♦ vt brüllen; **~bolt** n Blitz m; **~clap** n Donnerschlag m; **~storm** n Gewitter nt, Unwetter nt; **~y** adj gewitterschwül

Thursday ['θə:zdɪ] n Donnerstag m

thus [ðʌs] adv (in this way) so; (therefore) somit, also, folglich

thwart [θwɔ:t] vt vereiteln, durchkreuzen; (person) hindern

thyme [taɪm] n Thymian m

thyroid ['θaɪrɔɪd] n Schilddrüse f

tiara [tɪ'ɑ:rə] n Diadem nt

tic [tɪk] n Tick m

tick [tɪk] n (sound) Ticken nt; (mark) Häkchen nt ♦ vi ticken ♦ vt abhaken; **in a ~** (BRIT: inf) sofort; **~ off** vt abhaken; (person) ausschimpfen; **~ over** vi (engine) im Leerlauf laufen; (fig) auf Sparflamme laufen

ticket ['tɪkɪt] n (for travel) Fahrkarte f; (for entrance) (Eintritts)karte f; (price ~) Preisschild nt; (luggage ~) (Gepäck)schein m; (raffle ~) Los nt; (parking ~) Strafzettel m; (in car park) Parkschein m; **~ collector** n Fahrkartenkontrolleur m; **~ inspector** n Fahrkartenkontrolleur m; **~ office** n (THEAT etc) Kasse f; (RAIL etc) Fahrkartenschalter m

tickle ['tɪkl] n Kitzeln nt ♦ vt kitzeln; (amuse) amüsieren; **ticklish** ['tɪklɪʃ] adj (also fig) kitzlig

tidal ['taɪdl] adj Flut-, Tide-; **~ wave** n Flutwelle f

tidbit ['tɪdbɪt] (US) n Leckerbissen m

tiddlywinks ['tɪdlɪwɪŋks] n Floh(hüpf)spiel nt

tide [taɪd] n Gezeiten pl; **high/low ~** Flut f/ Ebbe f

tidy ['taɪdɪ] adj ordentlich ♦ vt aufräumen, in Ordnung bringen

tie [taɪ] n (BRIT: neck) Krawatte f, Schlips m; (sth connecting) Band nt; (SPORT)

Unentschieden nt ♦ vt (fasten, restrict) binden ♦ vi (SPORT) unentschieden spielen; (in competition) punktgleich sein; **to ~ in a bow** zur Schleife binden; **to ~ a knot in sth** einen Knoten in etw acc machen; **~ down** vt festbinden; **to ~ sb down to** jdn binden an +acc; **~ up** vt (dog) anbinden; (parcel) verschnüren; (boat) festmachen; (person) fesseln; **to be ~d up** (busy) beschäftigt sein

tier [tɪə'] n Rang m; (of cake) Etage f

tiff [tɪf] n Krach m

tiger ['taɪgə'] n Tiger m

tight [taɪt] adj (close) eng, knapp; (schedule) gedrängt; (firm) fest; (control) streng; (stretched) stramm, (an)gespannt; (inf: drunk) blau, stramm ♦ adv (squeeze) fest; **~en** vt anziehen, anspannen; (restrictions) verschärfen ♦ vi sich spannen; **~-fisted** adj knauserig; **~ly** adv eng; fest; (stretched) straff; **~-rope** n Seil nt; **~s** npl (esp BRIT) Strumpfhose f

tile [taɪl] n (on roof) Dachziegel m; (on wall or floor) Fliese f; **~d** adj (roof) gedeckt, Ziegel-; (floor, wall) mit Fliesen belegt

till [tɪl] n Kasse f ♦ vt bestellen ♦ prep, conj = **until**

tiller ['tɪlə'] n Ruderpinne f

tilt [tɪlt] vt kippen, neigen ♦ vi sich neigen

timber ['tɪmbə'] n (wood) Holz nt

time [taɪm] n Zeit f; (occasion) Mal nt; (rhythm) Takt m ♦ vt zur rechten Zeit tun, zeitlich einrichten; (SPORT) stoppen; **in 2 weeks'** ~ in 2 Wochen; **a long ~** lange; **for the ~ being** vorläufig; **4 at a ~** zu jeweils 4; **from ~ to ~** gelegentlich; **to have a good ~** sich amüsieren; **in ~** (soon enough) rechtzeitig; (after some ~) mit der Zeit; (MUS) im Takt; **in no ~** im Handumdrehen; **any ~** jederzeit; **on ~** pünktlich, rechtzeitig; **five ~s 5** fünfmal 5; **what ~ is it?** wie viel Uhr ist es?, wie spät ist es?; **at ~s** manchmal; **~ bomb** n Zeitbombe f; **~less** adj (beauty) zeitlos; **~ limit** n Frist f; **~ly** adj rechtzeitig; günstig; **~ off** n freie Zeit f; **~r** n (timer switch: in kitchen) Schaltuhr f; **~ scale** n Zeitspanne f; **~-share** adj Timesharing-; **~ switch**

(BRIT) n Zeitschalter m; **~table** n Fahrplan m; (SCH) Stundenplan m; **~ zone** n Zeitzone f

timid ['tɪmɪd] adj ängstlich, schüchtern

timing ['taɪmɪŋ] n Wahl f des richtigen Zeitpunkts, Timing nt

timpani ['tɪmpənɪ] npl Kesselpauken pl

tin [tɪn] n (metal) Blech nt; (BRIT: can) Büchse f, Dose f; **~foil** n Stanniolpapier nt

tinge [tɪndʒ] n (colour) Färbung f; (fig) Anflug m ♦ vt färben; **~d with** mit einer Spur von

tingle ['tɪŋgl] n Prickeln nt ♦ vi prickeln

tinker ['tɪŋkər] n Kesselflicker m; **~ with** vt fus herumpfuschen an +dat

tinkle ['tɪŋkl] vi klingeln

tinned [tɪnd] (BRIT) adj (food) Dosen-, Büchsen-

tin opener [-əʊpnər] (BRIT) n Dosen- or Büchsenöffner m

tinsel ['tɪnsl] n Rauschgold nt

tint [tɪnt] n Farbton m; (slight colour) Anflug m; (hair) Tönung f; **~ed** adj getönt

tiny ['taɪnɪ] adj winzig

tip [tɪp] n (pointed end) Spitze f; (money) Trinkgeld nt; (hint) Wink m, Tipp m ♦ vt (slant) kippen; (hat) antippen; (~ over) umkippen; (waiter) ein Trinkgeld geben +dat; **~-off** n Hinweis m, Tipp m; **~ped** (BRIT) adj (cigarette) Filter-

tipsy ['tɪpsɪ] adj beschwipst

tiptoe ['tɪptəʊ] n: **on ~** auf Zehenspitzen

tiptop ['tɪp'tɔp] adj: **in ~ condition** tipptopp, erstklassig

tire ['taɪər] n (US) = tyre ♦ vt, vi ermüden, müde machen/werden; **~d** adj müde; **to be ~d of sth** etw satt haben; **~less** adj unermüdlich; **~some** adj lästig

tiring ['taɪərɪŋ] adj ermüdend

tissue ['tɪʃuː] n Gewebe nt; (paper handkerchief) Papiertaschentuch nt; **~ paper** n Seidenpapier nt

tit [tɪt] n (bird) Meise f; **~ for tat** wie du mir, so ich dir

titbit ['tɪtbɪt] (US tidbit) n Leckerbissen m

titillate ['tɪtɪleɪt] vt kitzeln

title ['taɪtl] n Titel m; **~ deed** n Eigentumsurkunde f; **~ role** n Hauptrolle f

titter ['tɪtər] vi kichern

titular ['tɪtjʊlər] adj (in name only) nominell

TM abbr (= trademark) Wz

KEYWORD

to [tuː, tə] prep **1** (direction) zu, nach; **I go to France/school** ich gehe nach Frankreich/zur Schule; **to the left** nach links

2 (as far as) bis

3 (with expressions of time): **a quarter to 5** Viertel vor 5

4 (for, of) für; **secretary to the director** Sekretärin des Direktors

5 (expressing indirect object): **to give sth to sb** jdm etw geben; **to talk to sb** mit jdm sprechen; **I sold it to a friend** ich habe es einem Freund verkauft

6 (in relation to) zu; **30 miles to the gallon** 30 Meilen pro Gallone

7 (purpose, result) zu; **to my surprise** zu meiner Überraschung

♦ with vb **1** (infin): **to go/eat** gehen/essen; **to want to do sth** etw tun wollen; **to try/start to do sth** versuchen/anfangen, etw zu tun; **he has a lot to lose** er hat viel zu verlieren

2 (with vb omitted): **I don't want to** ich will (es) nicht

3 (purpose, result) um; **I did it to help you** ich tat es, um dir zu helfen

4 (after adj etc): **ready to use** gebrauchsfertig; **too old/young to ...** zu alt/jung, um ... zu ...

♦ adv: **push/pull the door to** die Tür zuschieben/zuziehen

---

toad [təʊd] n Kröte f; **~stool** n Giftpilz m

toast [təʊst] n (bread) Toast m; (drinking) Trinkspruch m ♦ vt trinken auf +acc; (bread) toasten; (warm) wärmen; **~er** n Toaster m

tobacco [tə'bækəʊ] n Tabak m; **~nist** [tə'bækənɪst] n Tabakhändler m; **~nist's (shop)** n Tabakladen m

toboggan [tə'bɔgən] n (Rodel)schlitten m; **~ing** n Rodeln nt

today [tə'deɪ] adv heute; (at the present time) heutzutage

toddler ['tɒdləʳ] n Kleinkind nt

toddy ['tɒdɪ] n (Whisky)grog m

to-do [tə'duː] n Theater nt

toe [təʊ] n Zehe f; (of sock, shoe) Spitze f
♦ vt: **to ~ the line** (fig) sich einfügen; **~nail** n Zehennagel m

toffee ['tɒfɪ] n Sahnebonbon nt; **~ apple** (BRIT) n kandierte(r) Apfel m

together [tə'geðəʳ] adv zusammen; (at the same time) gleichzeitig; **~ with** zusammen mit; gleichzeitig mit

toil [tɔɪl] n harte Arbeit f, Plackerei f ♦ vi sich abmühen, sich plagen

toilet ['tɔɪlət] n Toilette f ♦ cpd Toiletten-; **~ bag** n Waschbeutel m; **~ paper** n Toilettenpapier nt; **~ries** ['tɔɪlətrɪz] npl Toilettenartikel pl; **~ roll** n Rolle f Toilettenpapier; **~ water** n Toilettenwasser nt

token ['təʊkən] n Zeichen nt; (gift ~) Gutschein m; **book/record ~** (BRIT) Bücher-/Plattengutschein m

Tokyo ['təʊkjəʊ] n Tokio nt

told [təʊld] pt, pp of **tell**

tolerable ['tɒlərəbl] adj (bearable) erträglich; (fairly good) leidlich

tolerant ['tɒlərnt] adj: **be ~ (of)** vertragen +acc

tolerate ['tɒləreɪt] vt dulden; (noise) ertragen

toll [təʊl] n Gebühr f ♦ vi (bell) läuten

tomato [tə'mɑːtəʊ] (pl **~es**) n Tomate f

tomb [tuːm] n Grab(mal) nt

tomboy ['tɒmbɔɪ] n Wildfang m

tombstone ['tuːmstəʊn] n Grabstein m

tomcat ['tɒmkæt] n Kater m

tomorrow [tə'mɒrəʊ] n Morgen nt ♦ adv morgen; **the day after ~** übermorgen; **~ morning** morgen früh; **a week ~** morgen in einer Woche

ton [tʌn] n Tonne f (BRIT = 1016kg; US = 907kg); **~s of** (inf) eine Unmenge von

tone [təʊn] n Ton m; **~ down** vt (criticism, demands) mäßigen; (colours) abtonen; **~ up** vt in Form bringen; **~-deaf** adj ohne musikalisches Gehör

tongs [tɒŋz] npl Zange f; (curling ~) Lockenstab m

tongue [tʌŋ] n Zunge f; (language) Sprache f; **with ~ in cheek** scherzhaft; **~-tied** adj stumm, sprachlos; **~ twister** n Zungenbrecher m

tonic ['tɒnɪk] n (drink) Tonic nt; (MED) Stärkungsmittel nt

tonight [tə'naɪt] adv heute Abend

tonsil ['tɒnsl] n Mandel f; **~litis** [tɒnsɪ'laɪtɪs] n Mandelentzündung f

too [tuː] adv zu; (also) auch; **~ bad!** Pech!; **~ many** zu viele

took [tʊk] pt of **take**

tool [tuːl] n (also fig) Werkzeug nt; **~box** n Werkzeugkasten m

toot [tuːt] n Hupen nt ♦ vi tuten; (AUT) hupen

tooth [tuːθ] (pl **teeth**) n Zahn m; **~ache** n Zahnschmerzen pl, Zahnweh nt; **~brush** n Zahnbürste f; **~paste** n Zahnpasta f; **~pick** n Zahnstocher m

top [tɒp] n Spitze f; (of mountain) Gipfel m; (of tree) Wipfel m; (toy) Kreisel m; (~ gear) vierte(r)/fünfte(r) Gang m ♦ adj oberste(r, s) ♦ vt (list) an erster Stelle stehen auf +dat; **on ~ of** oben auf +dat; **from ~ to bottom** von oben bis unten; **~ off** (US) vt auffüllen; **~ up** vt auffüllen; **~ floor** n oberste(s) Stockwerk nt; **~ hat** n Zylinder m; **~-heavy** adj kopflastig

topic ['tɒpɪk] n Thema nt, Gesprächsgegenstand m; **~al** adj aktuell

top: ~less ['tɒplɪs] adj (bather etc) oben ohne; **~-level** ['tɒplevl] adj auf höchster Ebene; **~most** ['tɒpməʊst] adj oberste(r, s)

topple ['tɒpl] vt, vi stürzen, kippen

top-secret ['tɒp'siːkrɪt] adj streng geheim

topsy-turvy ['tɒpsɪ'tɜːvɪ] adv durcheinander ♦ adj auf den Kopf gestellt

torch [tɔːtʃ] n (BRIT: ELEC) Taschenlampe f; (with flame) Fackel f

tore [tɔːʳ] pt of **tear**[1]

torment [n 'tɔːment, vb tɔː'ment] n Qual f ♦ vt (distress) quälen

torn [tɔːn] pp of **tear**[1] ♦ adj hin- und hergerissen

torrent ['tɒrnt] n Sturzbach m; **~ial** [tɒ'renʃl] adj wolkenbruchartig

torrid ['tɒrɪd] *adj* heiß

tortoise ['tɔ:təs] *n* Schildkröte *f*; **~shell** ['tɔ:təʃel] *n* Schildpatt *m*

torture ['tɔ:tʃə'] *n* Folter *f* ♦ *vt* foltern

Tory ['tɔ:rɪ] (*BRIT*) *n* (*POL*) Tory *m* ♦ *adj* Tory-, konservativ

toss [tɒs] *vt* schleudern; **to ~ a coin** *or* **to ~ up for sth** etw mit einer Münze entscheiden; **to ~ and turn** (*in bed*) sich hin und her werfen

tot [tɒt] *n* (*small quantity*) bisschen *nt*; (*small child*) Knirps *m*

total ['təutl] *n* Gesamtheit *f*; (*money*) Endsumme *f* ♦ *adj* Gesamt-, total ♦ *vt* (*add up*) zusammenzählen; (*amount to*) sich belaufen auf

totalitarian [təutælɪ'tɛərɪən] *adj* totalitär

totally ['təutəlɪ] *adv* total

totter ['tɒtə'] *vi* wanken, schwanken

touch [tʌtʃ] *n* Berührung *f*; (*sense of feeling*) Tastsinn *m* ♦ *vt* (*feel*) berühren; (*come against*) leicht anstoßen; (*emotionally*) rühren; **a ~ of** (*fig*) eine Spur von; **to get in ~ with sb** mit jdm in Verbindung setzen; **to lose ~** (*friends*) Kontakt verlieren; **~ on** *vt fus* (*topic*) berühren, erwähnen; **~ up** *vt* (*paint*) auffrischen; **~-and-go** *adj* riskant, knapp; **~down** *n* Landen *nt*, Niedergehen *nt*; **~ed** *adj* (*moved*) gerührt; **~ing** *adj* rührend; **~line** *n* Seitenlinie *f*; **~-sensitive screen** *n* (*COMPUT*) berührungsempfindlicher Bildschirm *m*; **~y** *adj* empfindlich, reizbar

tough [tʌf] *adj* zäh; (*difficult*) schwierig ♦ *n* Schläger(typ) *m*; **~en** *vt* zäh machen; (*make strong*) abhärten

toupee ['tu:peɪ] *n* Toupet *nt*

tour ['tuə'] *n* Tour *f* ♦ *vi* umherreisen; (*THEAT*) auf Tour sein; **auf Tour gehen**; **~ guide** *n* Reiseleiter(in) *m(f)*

tourism ['tuərɪzm] *n* Fremdenverkehr *m*, Tourismus *m*

tourist ['tuərɪst] *n* Tourist(in) *m(f)* ♦ *cpd* (*class*) Touristen-; **~ office** *n* Verkehrsamt *nt*

tournament ['tuənəmənt] *n* Turnier *nt*

tousled ['tauzld] *adj* zerzaust

tout [taut] *vi*: **to ~ for** auf Kundenfang gehen für ♦ *n*: **ticket ~** Kundenschlepper(in) *m(f)*

tow [təu] *vt* (ab)schleppen; **on** (*BRIT*) *or* **in** (*US*) **~** (*AUT*) im Schlepp

toward(s) [tə'wɔ:d(z)] *prep* (*with time*) gegen; (*in direction of*) nach

towel ['tauəl] *n* Handtuch *nt*; **~ling** *n* (*fabric*) Frottee *nt or m*; **~ rack** (*US*) *n* Handtuchstange *f*; **~ rail** *n* Handtuchstange *f*

tower ['tauə'] *n* Turm *m*; **~ block** (*BRIT*) *n* Hochhaus *nt*; **~ing** *adj* hochragend

town [taun] *n* Stadt *f*; **to go to ~** (*fig*) sich ins Zeug legen; **~ centre** *n* Stadtzentrum *nt*; **~ clerk** *n* Stadtdirektor *m*; **~ council** *n* Stadtrat *m*; **~ hall** *n* Rathaus *nt*; **~ plan** *n* Stadtplan *m*; **~ planning** *n* Stadtplanung *f*

towrope ['təurəup] *n* Abschlepptau *nt*

tow truck (*US*) *n* Abschleppwagen *m*

toxic ['tɒksɪk] *adj* giftig, Gift-

toy [tɔɪ] *n* Spielzeug *nt*; **~ with** *vt fus* spielen mit; **~shop** *n* Spielwarengeschäft *nt*

trace [treɪs] *n* Spur *f* ♦ *vt* (*follow a course*) nachspüren +*dat*; (*find out*) aufspüren; (*copy*) durchpausen; **tracing paper** *n* Pauspapier *nt*

track [træk] *n* (*mark*) Spur *f*; (*path*) Weg *m*; (*racetrack*) Rennbahn *f*; (*RAIL*) Gleis *nt* ♦ *vt* verfolgen; **to keep ~ of sb** jdn im Auge behalten; **~ down** *vt* aufspüren; **~suit** *n* Trainingsanzug *m*

tract [trækt] *n* (*of land*) Gebiet *nt*

traction ['trækʃən] *n* (*power*) Zugkraft *f*; (*AUT*: *grip*) Bodenhaftung *f*; (*MED*): **in ~** im Streckverband

tractor ['træktə'] *n* Traktor *m*

trade [treɪd] *n* (*commerce*) Handel *m*; (*business*) Geschäft *nt*, Gewerbe *nt*; (*people*) Geschäftsleute *pl*; (*skilled manual work*) Handwerk *nt* ♦ *vi*: **to ~ (in)** handeln (mit) ♦ *vt* tauschen; **~ in** *vt* in Zahlung geben; **~ fair** *n* Messe *nt*; **~-in price** *n* Preis, zu dem etw in Zahlung genommen wird; **~mark** *n* Warenzeichen *nt*; **~ name** *n* Handelsbezeichnung *f*; **~r** *n* Händler *m*; **~sman** (*irreg*) *n* (*shopkeeper*) Geschäftsmann *m*; (*workman*) Handwerker

m; (*delivery man*) Lieferant m; ~ **union** n
Gewerkschaft f; ~ **unionist** n
Gewerkschaftler(in) m(f)

trading ['treɪdɪŋ] n Handel m; ~ **estate**
(*BRIT*) n Industriegelände nt

tradition [trə'dɪʃən] n Tradition f; ~**al** adj
traditionell, herkömmlich

traffic ['træfɪk] n Verkehr m; (*esp in drugs*): ~
(in) Handel m (mit) ♦ vi: **to ~ in** (*esp drugs*)
handeln mit; ~ **calming** n
Verkehrsberuhigung f; ~ **circle** (*US*) n
Kreisverkehr m; ~ **jam** n Verkehrsstauung f;
~ **lights** npl Verkehrsampel f; ~ **warden** n
≈ Verkehrspolizist m (*ohne amtliche
Befugnisse*), Politesse f (*ohne amtliche
Befugnisse*)

tragedy ['trædʒədɪ] n Tragödie f

tragic ['trædʒɪk] adj tragisch

trail [treɪl] n (*track*) Spur f; (*of smoke*)
Rauchfahne f; (*of dust*) Staubwolke f; (*road*)
Pfad m, Weg m ♦ vt (*animal*) verfolgen;
(*person*) folgen +dat; (*drag*) schleppen ♦ vi
(*hang loosely*) schleifen; (*plants*) sich ranken;
(*be behind*) hinterherhinken; (*SPORT*) weit
zurückliegen; (*walk*) zuckeln; ~ **behind** vi
zurückbleiben; ~**er** n Anhänger m; (*US:
caravan*) Wohnwagen m; (*for film*) Vorschau
f; ~**er truck** (*US*) n Sattelschlepper m

train [treɪn] n Zug m; (*of dress*) Schleppe f;
(*series*) Folge f ♦ vt (*teach: person*) ausbilden;
(: *animal*) abrichten; (: *mind*) schulen;
(*SPORT*) trainieren; (*aim*) richten ♦ vi
(*exercise*) trainieren; (*study*) ausgebildet
werden; ~ **of thought** Gedankengang m; **to
~ sth on** (*aim*) etw richten auf +acc; ~**ed**
adj (*eye*) geschult; (*person, voice*)
ausgebildet; ~**ee** n Lehrling m;
Praktikant(in) m(f); ~**er** n (*SPORT*) Trainer m;
Ausbilder m; ~**ers** npl Turnschuhe pl; ~**ing**
n (*for occupation*) Ausbildung f; (*SPORT*)
Training nt; **in ~ing** im Training; ~**ing
college** n pädagogische Hochschule f,
Lehrerseminar nt; ~**ing shoes** npl
Turnschuhe pl

traipse [treɪps] vi latschen

trait [treɪt] n Zug m, Merkmal nt

traitor ['treɪtə'] n Verräter m

trajectory [trə'dʒɛktərɪ] n Flugbahn f

tram [træm] (*BRIT*) n (*also:* ~**car**)
Straßenbahn f

tramp [træmp] n Landstreicher m ♦ vi
(*trudge*) stampfen, stapfen

trample ['træmpl] vt (*nieder*)trampeln ♦ vi
(*herum*)trampeln; **to ~ (underfoot)**
herumtrampeln auf +dat

trampoline ['træmpəliːn] n Trampolin m

tranquil ['træŋkwɪl] adj ruhig, friedlich; ~**lity**
[træŋ'kwɪlɪtɪ] (*US* **tranquility**) n Ruhe f;
~**lizer** (*US* **tranquilizer**) n
Beruhigungsmittel nt

transact [træn'zækt] vt abwickeln; ~**ion**
[træn'zækʃən] n Abwicklung f; (*piece of
business*) Geschäft nt, Transaktion f

transcend [træn'send] vt übersteigen

transcription [træn'skrɪpʃən] n Transkription
f; (*product*) Abschrift f

transfer [n 'trænsfə', vb træns'fə:'] n (~**ring**)
Übertragung f; (*of business*) Umzug m;
(*being* ~**red**) Versetzung f; (*design*)
Abziehbild nt; (*SPORT*) Transfer m ♦ vt
(*business*) verlegen; (*person*) versetzen;
(*prisoner*) überführen; (*drawing*) übertragen;
(*money*) überweisen; **to ~ the charges**
(*BRIT: TEL*) ein R-Gespräch führen; ~ **desk** n
(*AVIAT*) Transitschalter m

transform [træns'fɔ:m] vt umwandeln;
~**ation** [trænsfə'meɪʃən] n Umwandlung f,
Verwandlung f

transfusion [træns'fju:ʒən] n
Blutübertragung f, Transfusion f

transient ['trænzɪənt] adj kurz(lebig)

transistor [træn'zɪstə'] n (*ELEC*) Transistor m;
(*RAD*) Transistorradio nt

transit ['trænzɪt] n: **in ~** unterwegs

transition [træn'zɪʃən] n Übergang m; ~**al**
adj Übergangs-

transit lounge n Warteraum m

translate [trænz'leɪt] vt, vi übersetzen;
translation [trænz'leɪʃən] n Übersetzung f;
translator [trænz'leɪtə'] n Übersetzer(in)
m(f)

transmission [trænz'mɪʃən] n (*of
information*) Übermittlung f; (*ELEC, MED, TV*)
Übertragung f; (*AUT*) Getriebe nt

transmit [trænz'mɪt] vt (message) übermitteln; (ELEC, MED, TV) übertragen; **~ter** n Sender m

transparency [træns'pɛərnsɪ] n Durchsichtigkeit f; (BRIT: PHOT) Dia(positiv) nt

transparent [træns'pærnt] adj durchsichtig; (fig) offenkundig

transpire [træns'paɪər] vi (turn out) sich herausstellen; (happen) passieren

transplant [vb træns'plɑːnt, n 'trænsplɑːnt] vt umpflanzen; (MED, also fig: person) verpflanzen ♦ n (MED) Transplantation f; (organ) Transplantat nt

transport [n 'trænspɔːt, vb træns'pɔːt] Transport m, Beförderung f ♦ vt befördern; transportieren; **means of ~** Transportmittel nt; **~ation** ['trænspɔː'teɪʃən] n Transport m, Beförderung f; (means) Beförderungsmittel nt; (cost) Transportkosten pl; **~ café** (BRIT) n Fernfahrerlokal nt

trap [træp] n Falle f; (carriage) zweirädrige(r) Einspänner m; (inf: mouth) Klappe f ♦ vt fangen; (person) in eine Falle locken; **~door** n Falltür f

trappings ['træpɪŋz] npl Aufmachung f

trash [træʃ] n (rubbish) Plunder m; (nonsense) Mist m; **~ can** (US) n Mülleimer m; **~y** (inf) adj minderwertig, wertlos; (novel) Schund-

traumatic [trɔː'mætɪk] adj traumatisch

travel ['trævl] n Reisen nt ♦ vi reisen ♦ vt (distance) zurücklegen; (country) bereisen; **~s** npl (journeys) Reisen pl; **~ agency** n Reisebüro nt; **~ agent** n Reisebürokaufmann(-frau) m(f); **~ler** (US **traveler**) n Reisende(r) mf; (salesman) Handlungsreisende(r) m; **~ler's cheque** (US **traveler's check**) n Reisescheck m; **~ling** (US **traveling**) n Reisen nt; **~sick** adj reisekrank; **~ sickness** n Reisekrankheit f

trawler ['trɔːlər] n (NAUT, FISHING) Fischdampfer m, Trawler m

tray [treɪ] n (tea ~) Tablett nt; (for mail) Ablage f

treacherous ['tretʃərəs] adj verräterisch; (road) tückisch

treachery ['tretʃərɪ] n Verrat m

treacle ['triːkl] n Sirup m, Melasse f

tread [tred] (pt **trod**, pp **trodden**) n Schritt m, Tritt m; (of stair) Stufe f; (on tyre) Profil nt ♦ vi treten; **~ on** vt fus treten auf +acc

treason ['triːzn] n Verrat m

treasure ['treʒər] n Schatz m ♦ vt schätzen

treasurer ['treʒərər] n Kassenverwalter m, Schatzmeister m

treasury ['treʒərɪ] n (POL) Finanzministerium nt

treat [triːt] n besondere Freude f ♦ vt (deal with) behandeln; **to ~ sb to sth** jdm etw spendieren

treatise ['triːtɪz] n Abhandlung f

treatment ['triːtmənt] n Behandlung f

treaty ['triːtɪ] n Vertrag m

treble ['trebl] adj dreifach ♦ vt verdreifachen; **~ clef** n Violinschlüssel m

tree [triː] n Baum m; **~ trunk** n Baumstamm m

trek [trek] n Treck m, Zug m; (inf) anstrengende(r) Weg m ♦ vi trecken

trellis ['trelɪs] n Gitter nt; (for gardening) Spalier nt

tremble ['trembl] vi zittern; (ground) beben

tremendous [trɪ'mendəs] adj gewaltig, kolossal; (inf: good) prima

tremor ['tremər] n Zittern nt; (of earth) Beben nt

trench [trentʃ] n Graben m; (MIL) Schützengraben m

trend [trend] n Tendenz f; **~y** (inf) adj modisch

trepidation [trepɪ'deɪʃən] n Beklommenheit f

trespass ['trespəs] vi: **to ~ on** widerrechtlich betreten; **"no ~ing"** „Betreten verboten"

trestle ['tresl] n Bock m; **~ table** n Klapptisch m

trial ['traɪəl] n (JUR) Prozess m; (test) Versuch m, Probe f; (hardship) Prüfung f; **by ~ and error** durch Ausprobieren; **~ period** n Probezeit f

triangle ['traɪæŋgl] n Dreieck nt; (MUS) Triangel f; **triangular** [traɪ'æŋgjulər] adj dreieckig

tribal ['traɪbl] adj Stammes-

tribe [traɪb] n Stamm m; **~sman** (irreg) n

Stammesangehörige(r) *m*

tribulation [trɪbjuˈleɪʃən] *n* Not *f*, Mühsal *f*

tribunal [traɪˈbjuːnl] *n* Gericht *nt*; (*inquiry*) Untersuchungsausschuss *m*

tributary [ˈtrɪbjutərɪ] *n* Nebenfluss *m*

tribute [ˈtrɪbjuːt] *n* (*admiration*) Zeichen *nt* der Hochachtung; **to pay ~ to sb/sth** jdm/einer Sache Tribut zollen

trick [trɪk] *n* Trick *m*; (*CARDS*) Stich *m* ♦ *vt* überlisten, beschwindeln; **to play a ~ on sb** jdm einen Streich spielen; **that should do the ~** daß müsste eigentlich klappen; **~ery** *n* Tricks *pl*

trickle [ˈtrɪkl] *n* Tröpfeln *nt*; (*small river*) Rinnsal *nt* ♦ *vi* tröpfeln; (*seep*) sickern

tricky [ˈtrɪkɪ] *adj* (*problem*) schwierig; (*situation*) kitzlig

tricycle [ˈtraɪsɪkl] *n* Dreirad *nt*

trifle [ˈtraɪfl] *n* Kleinigkeit *f*; (*COOK*) Trifle *m* ♦ *adv*: **a ~ ...** ein bisschen ...; **trifling** *adj* geringfügig

trigger [ˈtrɪgər] *n* Drücker *m*; **~ off** *vt* auslösen

trim [trɪm] *adj* gepflegt; (*figure*) schlank ♦ *n* (*gute*) Verfassung *f*; (*embellishment, on car*) Verzierung *f* ♦ *vt* (*clip*) schneiden; (*trees*) stutzen; (*decorate*) besetzen; (*sails*) trimmen; **~mings** *npl* (*decorations*) Verzierung *f*, Verzierungen *pl*; (*extras*) Zubehör *nt*

Trinity [ˈtrɪnɪtɪ] *n*: **the ~** die Dreieinigkeit *f*

trinket [ˈtrɪŋkɪt] *n* kleine(s) Schmuckstück *nt*

trip [trɪp] *n* (*kurze*) Reise *f*; (*outing*) Ausflug *m*; (*stumble*) Stolpern *nt* ♦ *vi* (*stumble*) stolpern; **on a ~** auf Reisen; **~ up** *vi* stolpern; (*fig*) stolpern, einen Fehler machen ♦ *vt* zu Fall bringen; (*fig*) hereinlegen

tripe [traɪp] *n* (*food*) Kutteln *pl*; (*rubbish*) Mist *m*

triple [ˈtrɪpl] *adj* dreifach

triplets [ˈtrɪplɪts] *npl* Drillinge *pl*

triplicate [ˈtrɪplɪkət] *n*: **in ~** in dreifacher Ausfertigung

tripod [ˈtraɪpɔd] *n* (*PHOT*) Stativ *nt*

trite [traɪt] *adj* banal

triumph [ˈtraɪʌmf] *n* Triumph *m* ♦ *vi*: **to ~**

(over) triumphieren (über +*acc*); **~ant** [traɪˈʌmfənt] *adj* triumphierend

trivia [ˈtrɪvɪə] *npl* Trivialitäten *pl*

trivial [ˈtrɪvɪəl] *adj* gering(fügig), trivial

trod [trɔd] *pt of* **tread**; **~den** *pp of* **tread**

trolley [ˈtrɔlɪ] *n* Handwagen *m*; (*in shop*) Einkaufswagen *m*; (*for luggage*) Kofferkuli *m*; (*table*) Teewagen *m*; **~ bus** *n* Oberleitungsbus *m*, Obus *m*

trombone [trɔmˈbəun] *n* Posaune *f*

troop [truːp] *n* Schar *f*; (*MIL*) Trupp *m*; **~s** *npl* (*MIL*) Truppen *pl*; **~ in/out** *vi* hinein-/hinausströmen; **~ing the colour** *n* (*ceremony*) Fahnenparade *f*

trophy [ˈtrəufɪ] *n* Trophäe *f*

tropic [ˈtrɔpɪk] *n* Wendekreis *m*; **~al** *adj* tropisch

trot [trɔt] *n* Trott *m* ♦ *vi* trotten; **on the ~** (*BRIT: fig: inf*) in einer Tour

trouble [ˈtrʌbl] *n* (*problems*) Ärger *m*; (*worry*) Sorge *f*; (*in country, industry*) Unruhen *pl*; (*effort*) Mühe *f*; (*MED*): **stomach ~** Magenbeschwerden *pl* ♦ *vt* (*disturb*) stören; **~s** *npl* (*POL etc*) Unruhen *pl*; **to ~ to do sth** sich bemühen, etw zu tun; **to be in ~** Probleme *or* Ärger haben; **to go to the ~ of doing sth** sich die Mühe machen, etw zu tun; **what's the ~?** was ist los?; (*to sick person*) wo fehlts?; **~d** *adj* (*person*) beunruhigt; (*country*) geplagt; **~-free** *adj* sorglos; **~maker** *n* Unruhestifter *m*; **~shooter** *n* Vermittler *m*; **~some** *adj* lästig, unangenehm; (*child*) schwierig

trough [trɔf] *n* Trog *m*; (*channel*) Rinne *f*, Kanal *m*; (*MET*) Tief *nt*

trousers [ˈtrauzəz] *npl* Hose *f*

trout [traut] *n* Forelle *f*

trowel [ˈtrauəl] *n* Kelle *f*

truant [ˈtruənt] *n*: **to play ~** (*BRIT*) (die Schule) schwänzen

truce [truːs] *n* Waffenstillstand *m*

truck [trʌk] *n* Lastwagen *m*; (*RAIL*) offene(r) Güterwagen *m*; **~ driver** *n* Lastwagenfahrer *m*; **~ farm** (*US*) *n* Gemüsegärtnerei *f*

trudge [trʌdʒ] *vi* sich (mühselig) dahinschleppen

true [truː] *adj* (*exact*) wahr; (*genuine*) echt; (*friend*) treu

truffle ['trʌfl] *n* Trüffel *f or m*

truly ['truːlɪ] *adv* wirklich; **yours ~** Ihr sehr ergebener

trump [trʌmp] *n* (*CARDS*) Trumpf *m*

trumpet ['trʌmpɪt] *n* Trompete *f*

truncheon ['trʌntʃən] *n* Gummiknüppel *m*

trundle ['trʌndl] *vt* schieben ♦ *vi*: **to ~ along** entlangrollen

trunk [trʌŋk] *n* (*of tree*) (Baum)stamm *m*; (*ANAT*) Rumpf *m*; (*box*) Truhe *f*, Überseekoffer *m*; (*of elephant*) Rüssel *m*; (*US: AUT*) Kofferraum *m*; **~s** *npl* (*also:* **swimming ~s**) Badehose *f*

truss [trʌs] *vt* (*also:* **~ up**) fesseln

trust [trʌst] *n* (*confidence*) Vertrauen *nt*; (*for land etc*) Treuhandvermögen *nt* ♦ *vt* (*rely on*) vertrauen +*dat*, sich verlassen auf +*acc*; (*hope*) hoffen; (*entrust*): **to ~ sth to sb** jdm etw anvertrauen; **~ed** *adj* treu; **~ee** [trʌs'tiː] *n* Vermögensverwalter *m*; **~ful** *adj* vertrauensvoll; **~ing** *adj* vertrauensvoll; **~worthy** *adj* vertrauenswürdig; (*account*) glaubwürdig

truth [truːθ] *n* Wahrheit *f*; **~ful** *adj* ehrlich

try [traɪ] *n* Versuch *m* ♦ *vt* (*attempt*) versuchen; (*test*) (aus)probieren; (*JUR: person*) unter Anklage stellen; (: *case*) verhandeln; (*courage, patience*) auf die Probe stellen ♦ *vi* (*make effort*) versuchen, sich bemühen; **to have a ~** es versuchen; **to ~ to do sth** versuchen, etw zu tun; **~ on** *vt* (*dress*) anprobieren; (*hat*) aufprobieren; **~ out** *vt* ausprobieren; **~ing** *adj* schwierig

T-shirt ['tiːʃəːt] *n* T-Shirt *nt*

T-square ['tiːskweəʳ] *n* Reißschiene *f*

tub [tʌb] *n* Wanne *f*, Kübel *m*; (*for margarine etc*) Becher *m*

tubby ['tʌbɪ] *adj* rundlich

tube [tjuːb] *n* Röhre *f*, Rohr *nt*; (*for toothpaste etc*) Tube *f*; (*underground*) U-Bahn *f*; (*AUT*) Schlauch *m*

tuberculosis [tjubəːkju'ləusɪs] *n* Tuberkulose *f*

tube station *n* (*in London*) U-Bahnstation *f*;

tubing ['tjuːbɪŋ] *n* Schlauch *m*; **tubular** ['tjuːbjuləʳ] *adj* röhrenförmig

TUC (*BRIT*) *n abbr* = **Trades Union Congress**

tuck [tʌk] *n* (*fold*) Falte *f*, Einschlag *m* ♦ *vt* (*put*) stecken; (*gather*) fälteln, einschlagen; **~ away** *vt* wegstecken; **~ in** *vt* hineinstecken; (*blanket etc*) feststecken; (*person*) zudecken ♦ *vi* (*eat*) hineinhauen, zulangen; **~ up** *vt* (*child*) warm zudecken; **~ shop** *n* Süßwarenladen *m*

Tuesday ['tjuːzdɪ] *n* Dienstag *m*

tuft [tʌft] *n* Büschel *nt*

tug [tʌg] *n* (*jerk*) Zerren *nt*, Ruck *m*; (*NAUT*) Schleppdampfer *m* ♦ *vt, vi* zerren, ziehen; (*boat*) schleppen; **~ of war** *n* Tauziehen *nt*

tuition [tjuː'ɪʃən] *n* (*BRIT*) Unterricht *m*; (: *private ~*) Privatunterricht *m*; (*US: school fees*) Schulgeld *nt*

tulip ['tjuːlɪp] *n* Tulpe *f*

tumble ['tʌmbl] *n* (*fall*) Sturz *m* ♦ *vi* fallen, stürzen; **~ to** *vt fus* kapieren; **~down** *adj* baufällig; **~ dryer** (*BRIT*) *n* Trockner *m*; **~r** ['tʌmbləʳ] *n* (*glass*) Trinkglas *nt*

tummy ['tʌmɪ] (*inf*) *n* Bauch *m*; **~ upset** *n* Magenverstimmung *f*

tumour ['tjuːməʳ] (*US* **tumor**) *n* Geschwulst *f*, Tumor *m*

tumultuous [tjuː'mʌltjuəs] *adj* (*welcome, applause etc*) stürmisch

tuna ['tjuːnə] *n* T(h)unfisch *m*

tune [tjuːn] *n* Melodie *f* ♦ *vt* (*MUS*) stimmen; (*AUT*) richtig einstellen; **to sing in ~/out of ~** richtig/falsch singen; **to be out of ~ with** nicht harmonieren mit; **~ in** *vi* einschalten; **~ up** *vi* (*MUS*) stimmen; **~ful** *adj* melodisch; **~r** *n* (*RAD*) Tuner *m*; (*person*) (Instrumenten)stimmer *m*; **piano ~r** *n* Klavierstimmer(in) *m(f)*

tunic ['tjuːnɪk] *n* Waffenrock *m*; (*loose garment*) lange Bluse *f*

tuning ['tjuːnɪŋ] *n* (*RAD, AUT*) Einstellen *nt*; (*MUS*) Stimmen *nt*; **~ fork** *n* Stimmgabel *f*

Tunisia [tjuː'nɪzɪə] *n* Tunesien *nt*

tunnel ['tʌnl] *n* Tunnel *m*, Unterführung *f* ♦ *vi* einen Tunnel anlegen

turbulent ['təːbjulənt] *adj* stürmisch

tureen [təˈriːn] n Terrine f
turf [təːf] n Rasen m; (piece) Sode f ♦ vt mit Grassoden belegen; ~ **out** (inf) vt rauswerfen
turgid [ˈtəːdʒɪd] adj geschwollen
Turk [təːk] n Türke m, Türkin f
Turkey [ˈtəːkɪ] n Türkei f
turkey [ˈtəːkɪ] n Puter m, Truthahn m
Turkish [ˈtəːkɪʃ] adj türkisch ♦ n (LING) Türkisch nt
turmoil [ˈtəːmɔɪl] n Aufruhr m, Tumult m
turn [təːn] n (rotation) (Um)drehung f; (performance) Programm(nummer f; (MED) Schock m ♦ vt (rotate) drehen; (change position of) umdrehen, wenden; (page) umblättern; (transform): **to ~ sth into sth** etw in etw acc verwandeln; (direct) zuwenden ♦ vi (rotate) sich drehen; (change direction: in car) abbiegen; (: wind) drehen; (~ round) umdrehen, wenden; (become) werden; (leaves) sich verfärben; (milk) sauer werden; (weather) umschlagen; **to do sb a good ~** jdm etwas Gutes tun; **it's your ~** du bist dran or an der Reihe; **in ~, by ~s** abwechselnd; **to take ~s** sich abwechseln; **it gave me quite a ~** das hat mich schön erschreckt; **"no left ~"** (AUT) „Linksabbiegen verboten"; ~ **away** vi sich abwenden; ~ **back** vt umdrehen; (person) zurückschicken; (clock) zurückstellen ♦ vi umkehren; ~ **down** vt (refuse) ablehnen; (fold down) umschlagen; ~ **in** vi (go to bed) ins Bett gehen ♦ vt (fold inwards) einwärts biegen; ~ **off** vi abbiegen ♦ vt ausschalten; (tap) zudrehen; (machine, electricity) abstellen; ~ **on** vt (light) anschalten, einschalten; (tap) aufdrehen; (machine) anstellen; ~ **out** vi (prove to be) sich erweisen; (people) sich entwickeln ♦ vt (light) ausschalten; (gas) abstellen; (produce) produzieren; **how did the cake ~ out?** wie ist der Kuchen geworden?; ~ **over** vi (person) sich umdrehen ♦ vt (object) umdrehen, wenden; (page) umblättern; ~ **round** vi (person, vehicle) sich herumdrehen; (rotate) sich drehen; ~ **up** vi auftauchen ♦ vt (collar) hochklappen,

hochstellen; (nose) rümpfen; (increase: radio) lauter stellen; (: heat) höher drehen; ~**ing** n (in road) Abzweigung f; ~**ing point** n Wendepunkt m
turnip [ˈtəːnɪp] n Steckrübe f
turnout [ˈtəːnaut] n (Besucher)zahl f
turnover [ˈtəːnəuvəʳ] n Umsatz m; (of staff) Wechsel m
turnpike [ˈtəːnpaɪk] (US) n gebührenpflichtige Straße f
turn: ~**stile** [ˈtəːnstaɪl] n Drehkreuz nt; ~**table** [ˈtəːnteɪbl] n (of record player) Plattenteller m; (RAIL) Drehscheibe f; ~-**up** [ˈtəːnʌp] (BRIT) n (on trousers) Aufschlag m
turpentine [ˈtəːpəntaɪn] n Terpentin nt
turquoise [ˈtəːkwɔɪz] n (gem) Türkis m; (colour) Türkis nt ♦ adj türkisfarben
turret [ˈtʌrɪt] n Turm m
turtle [ˈtəːtl] n Schildkröte f; ~ **neck (sweater)** n Pullover m mit Schildkrötkragen
tusk [tʌsk] n Stoßzahn m
tussle [ˈtʌsl] n Balgerei f
tutor [ˈtjuːtəʳ] n (teacher) Privatlehrer m; (college instructor) Tutor m; ~**ial** [tjuːˈtɔːrɪəl] n (UNIV) Kolloquium nt, Seminarübung f
tuxedo [tʌkˈsiːdəu] (US) n Smoking m
TV [tiːˈviː] n abbr (= television) TV nt
twang [twæŋ] n scharfe(r) Ton m; (of voice) Näseln nt
tweezers [ˈtwiːzəz] npl Pinzette f
twelfth [twelfθ] adj zwölfte(r, s)
twelve [twelv] num zwölf; **at ~ o'clock** (midday) um 12 Uhr; (midnight) um null Uhr
twentieth [ˈtwentɪɪθ] adj zwanzigste(r, s)
twenty [ˈtwentɪ] num zwanzig
twice [twaɪs] adv zweimal; ~ **as much** doppelt so viel
twiddle [ˈtwɪdl] vt, vi: **to ~ (with) sth** an etw dat herumdrehen; **to ~ one's thumbs** (fig) Däumchen drehen
twig [twɪg] n dünne(r) Zweig m ♦ vt (inf) kapieren, merken
twilight [ˈtwaɪlaɪt] n Zwielicht nt
twin [twɪn] n Zwilling m ♦ adj Zwillings-; (very similar) Doppel- ♦ vt (towns) zu

Partnerstädten machen;**~-bedded room**
n Zimmer nt mit zwei Einzelbetten;**~ beds**
npl zwei (gleiche) Einzelbetten pl

twine [twaɪn] n Bindfaden m ♦ vi (plants)
sich ranken

twinge [twɪndʒ] n stechende(r) Schmerz m,
Stechen nt

twinkle ['twɪŋkl] n Funkeln nt, Blitzen nt ♦ vi
funkeln

twinned adj: **to be ~ with** die Partnerstadt
von ... sein

twirl [twɜːl] n Wirbel m ♦ vt, vi
(herum)wirbeln

twist [twɪst] n (~ing) Drehung f; (bend) Kurve
f ♦ vt (turn) drehen; (make crooked)
verbiegen; (distort) verdrehen ♦ vi (wind)
sich drehen; (curve) sich winden

twit [twɪt] (inf) n Idiot m

twitch [twɪtʃ] n Zucken nt ♦ vi zucken

two [tuː] num zwei; **to put ~ and ~ together**
seine Schlüsse ziehen;**~-door** adj
zweitürig;**~-faced** adj falsch;**~fold** adj,
adv zweifach, doppelt; **to increase ~fold**
verdoppeln;**~-piece** adj zweiteilig;**~-
piece (suit)** n Zweiteiler m;**~-piece
(swimsuit)** n zweiteilige(r) Badeanzug m;
~-seater n (plane, car) Zweisitzer m;
~some n Paar nt;**~-way** adj (traffic)
Gegen-

tycoon [taɪˈkuːn] n: **(business) ~**
(Industrie)magnat m

type [taɪp] n Typ m, Art f; (PRINT) Type f ♦ vt,
vi Maschine schreiben, tippen;**~-cast** adj
(THEAT, TV) auf eine Rolle festgelegt;**~-face**
n Schrift f;**~-script** n
maschinegeschriebene(r) Text m;**~-writer**
n Schreibmaschine f;**~-written** adj
maschinegeschrieben

typhoid ['taɪfɔɪd] n Typhus m

typical ['tɪpɪkl] adj: **~ (of)** typisch (für)

typify ['tɪpɪfaɪ] vt typisch sein für

typing ['taɪpɪŋ] n Maschineschreiben nt

typist ['taɪpɪst] n Maschinenschreiber(in)
m(f), Tippse f (inf)

tyrant ['taɪərnt] n Tyrann m

tyre ['taɪə'] (US **tire**) n Reifen m;**~ pressure**
n Reifendruck m

U, u

U-bend ['juːbend] n (in pipe) U-Bogen m

udder ['ʌdə'] n Euter nt

UFO ['juːfəu] n abbr (= unidentified flying
object) UFO nt

ugh [ə:h] excl hu

ugliness ['ʌglɪnɪs] n Hässlichkeit f

ugly ['ʌglɪ] adj hässlich; (bad) böse, schlimm

UHT abbr (= ultra heat treated): **UHT milk**
H-Milch f

UK n abbr = **United Kingdom**

ulcer ['ʌlsə'] n Geschwür nt

Ulster ['ʌlstə'] n Ulster nt

ulterior [ʌlˈtɪərɪə'] adj: **~ motive**
Hintergedanke m

ultimate ['ʌltɪmət] adj äußerste(r, s),
allerletzte(r, s);**~ly** adv schließlich, letzten
Endes

ultrasound ['ʌltrəsaund] n (MED) Ultraschall
m

umbilical cord [ʌmˈbɪlɪkl-] n Nabelschnur f

umbrella [ʌmˈbrelə] n Schirm m

umpire ['ʌmpaɪə'] n Schiedsrichter m ♦ vt, vi
schiedsrichtern

umpteenth [ʌmpˈtiːnθ] (inf) adj zig; **for the
~ time** zum x-ten Mal

UN n abbr = **United Nations**

unable [ʌnˈeɪbl] adj: **to be ~ to do sth** etw
nicht tun können

unacceptable [ʌnəkˈseptəbl] adj
unannehmbar, nicht akzeptabel

unaccompanied [ʌnəˈkʌmpənɪd] adj ohne
Begleitung

unaccountably [ʌnəˈkauntəblɪ] adv
unerklärlich

unaccustomed [ʌnəˈkʌstəmd] adj nicht
gewöhnt; (unusual) ungewohnt; **~ to** nicht
gewöhnt an +acc

unanimous [juːˈnænɪməs] adj einmütig;
(vote) einstimmig;**~ly** adv einmütig;
einstimmig

unarmed [ʌnˈɑːmd] adj unbewaffnet

unashamed [ʌnəˈʃeɪmd] adj schamlos

unassuming [ʌnəˈsjuːmɪŋ] adj bescheiden

unattached [ʌnəˈtætʃt] *adj* ungebunden

unattended [ʌnəˈtɛndɪd] *adj* (*person*) unbeaufsichtigt; (*thing*) unbewacht

unauthorized [ʌnˈɔːθəraɪzd] *adj* unbefugt

unavoidable [ʌnəˈvɔɪdəbl] *adj* unvermeidlich

unaware [ʌnəˈwɛəˈ] *adj*: **to be ~ of sth** sich *dat* einer Sache *gen* nicht bewusst sein; **~s** *adv* unversehens

unbalanced [ʌnˈbælənst] *adj* unausgeglichen; (*mentally*) gestört

unbearable [ʌnˈbɛərəbl] *adj* unerträglich

unbeatable [ʌnˈbiːtəbl] *adj* unschlagbar

unbeknown(st) [ʌnbɪˈnəun(st)] *adv*: **~ to me** ohne mein Wissen

unbelievable [ʌnbɪˈliːvəbl] *adj* unglaublich

unbend [ʌnˈbɛnd] (*irreg: like* **bend**) *vt* gerade biegen ♦ *vi* aus sich herausgehen

unbias(s)ed [ʌnˈbaɪəst] *adj* unparteiisch

unborn [ʌnˈbɔːn] *adj* ungeboren

unbreakable [ʌnˈbreɪkəbl] *adj* unzerbrechlich

unbridled [ʌnˈbraɪdld] *adj* ungezügelt

unbroken [ʌnˈbrəukən] *adj* (*period*) ununterbrochen; (*spirit*) ungebrochen; (*record*) unübertroffen

unburden [ʌnˈbəːdn] *vt*: **to ~ o.s.** (jdm) sein Herz ausschütten

unbutton [ʌnˈbʌtn] *vt* aufknöpfen

uncalled-for [ʌnˈkɔːldfɔːˈ] *adj* unnötig

uncanny [ʌnˈkænɪ] *adj* unheimlich

unceasing [ʌnˈsiːsɪŋ] *adj* unaufhörlich

unceremonious [ʌnsɛrɪˈməunɪəs] *adj* (*abrupt, rude*) brüsk; (*exit, departure*) überstürzt

uncertain [ʌnˈsəːtn] *adj* unsicher; (*doubtful*) ungewiss; (*unreliable*) unbeständig; (*vague*) undeutlich, vag(e); **~ty** *n* Ungewissheit *f*

unchanged [ʌnˈtʃeɪndʒd] *adj* unverändert

unchecked [ʌnˈtʃɛkt] *adj* ungeprüft; (*not stopped: advance*) ungehindert

uncivilized [ʌnˈsɪvɪlaɪzd] *adj* unzivilisiert

uncle [ˈʌŋkl] *n* Onkel *m*

uncomfortable [ʌnˈkʌmfətəbl] *adj* unbequem, ungemütlich

uncommon [ʌnˈkɔmən] *adj* ungewöhnlich; (*outstanding*) außergewöhnlich

uncompromising [ʌnˈkɔmprəmaɪzɪŋ] *adj* kompromisslos, unnachgiebig

unconcerned [ʌnkənˈsəːnd] *adj* unbekümmert; (*indifferent*) gleichgültig

unconditional [ʌnkənˈdɪʃənl] *adj* bedingungslos

unconscious [ʌnˈkɔnʃəs] *adj* (MED) bewusstlos; (*not meant*) unbeabsichtigt ♦ *n*: **the ~** das Unbewusste; **~ly** *adv* unbewusst

uncontrollable [ʌnkənˈtrəuləbl] *adj* unkontrollierbar, unbändig

unconventional [ʌnkənˈvɛnʃənl] *adj* unkonventionell

uncouth [ʌnˈkuːθ] *adj* grob

uncover [ʌnˈkʌvəˈ] *vt* aufdecken

undecided [ʌndɪˈsaɪdɪd] *adj* unschlüssig

undeniable [ʌndɪˈnaɪəbl] *adj* unleugbar

under [ˈʌndəˈ] *prep* unter ♦ *adv* darunter; **~ there** da drunter; **~ repair** in Reparatur

underage [ʌndərˈeɪdʒ] *adj* minderjährig

undercarriage [ˈʌndəkærɪdʒ] (BRIT) *n* (AVIAT) Fahrgestell *nt*

undercharge [ʌndəˈtʃɑːdʒ] *vt*: **to ~ sb** jdm zu wenig berechnen

undercoat [ˈʌndəkəut] *n* (*paint*) Grundierung *f*

undercover [ʌndəˈkʌvəˈ] *adj* Geheim-

undercurrent [ˈʌndəkʌrnt] *n* Unterströmung *f*

undercut [ʌndəˈkʌt] (*irreg: like* **cut**) *vt* unterbieten

underdeveloped [ˈʌndədɪˈvɛləpt] *adj* Entwicklungs-, unterentwickelt

underdog [ˈʌndədɔg] *n* Unterlegene(r) *mf*

underdone [ʌndəˈdʌn] *adj* (COOK) nicht gar, nicht durchgebraten

underestimate [ˈʌndərˈɛstɪmeɪt] *vt* unterschätzen

underexposed [ˈʌndərɪksˈpəuzd] *adj* unterbelichtet

underfoot [ʌndəˈfut] *adv* am Boden

undergo [ʌndəˈgəu] (*irreg: like* **go**) *vt* (*experience*) durchmachen; (*test, operation*) sich unterziehen +*dat*

undergraduate [ʌndəˈgrædjuət] *n* Student(in) *m(f)*

underground [ˈʌndəgraund] *n* U-Bahn *f*

♦ *adj* Untergrund-
undergrowth ['ʌndəgrəʊθ] *n* Gestrüpp *nt*, Unterholz *nt*
underhand(ed) [ʌndə'hænd(ɪd)] *adj* hinterhältig
underlie [ʌndə'laɪ] (*irreg: like* lie) *vt* zugrunde *or* zu Grunde liegen +*dat*
underline [ʌndə'laɪn] *vt* unterstreichen; (*emphasize*) betonen
underling ['ʌndəlɪŋ] *n* Handlanger *m*
undermine [ʌndə'maɪn] *vt* untergraben
underneath [ʌndə'niːθ] *adv* darunter ♦ *prep* unter
underpaid [ʌndə'peɪd] *adj* unterbezahlt
underpants ['ʌndəpænts] *npl* Unterhose *f*
underpass ['ʌndəpɑːs] (*BRIT*) *n* Unterführung *f*
underprivileged [ʌndə'prɪvɪlɪdʒd] *adj* benachteiligt, unterprivilegiert
underrate [ʌndə'reɪt] *vt* unterschätzen
undershirt ['ʌndəʃɜːt] (*US*) *n* Unterhemd *nt*
undershorts ['ʌndəʃɔːts] (*US*) *npl* Unterhose *f*
underside ['ʌndəsaɪd] *n* Unterseite *f*
underskirt ['ʌndəskɜːt] (*BRIT*) *n* Unterrock *m*
understand [ʌndə'stænd] (*irreg: like* stand) *vt, vi* verstehen; **I ~ that ...** ich habe gehört, dass ...; **am I to ~ that ...?** soll das (etwa) heißen, dass ...?; **what do you ~ by that?** was verstehen Sie darunter?; **it is understood that ...** es wurde vereinbart, dass ...; **to make o.s. understood** sich verständlich machen; **is that understood?** ist das klar?; **~able** *adj* verständlich; **~ing** *n* Verständnis *nt* ♦ *adj* verständnisvoll
understatement ['ʌndəsteɪtmənt] *n* (*quality*) Untertreibung *f*; **that's an ~!** das ist untertrieben!
understood [ʌndə'stʊd] *pt, pp of* **understand** ♦ *adj* klar; (*implied*) angenommen
understudy ['ʌndəstʌdɪ] *n* Ersatz(schau)spieler(in) *m(f)*
undertake [ʌndə'teɪk] (*irreg: like* take) *vt* unternehmen ♦ *vi*: **to ~ to do sth** sich verpflichten, etw zu tun
undertaker ['ʌndəteɪkə*r*] *n* Leichenbestat-

ter *m*
undertaking ['ʌndəteɪkɪŋ] *n* (*enterprise*) Unternehmen *nt*; (*promise*) Verpflichtung *f*
undertone ['ʌndətəʊn] *n*: **in an ~** mit gedämpfter Stimme
underwater ['ʌndə'wɔːtə*r*] *adv* unter Wasser ♦ *adj* Unterwasser-
underwear ['ʌndəweə*r*] *n* Unterwäsche *f*
underworld ['ʌndəwɜːld] *n* (*of crime*) Unterwelt *f*
underwriter ['ʌndəraɪtə*r*] *n* Assekurant *m*
undesirable [ʌndɪ'zaɪərəbl] *adj* unerwünscht
undies ['ʌndɪz] (*inf*) *npl* (Damen)unterwäsche *f*
undisputed ['ʌndɪs'pjuːtɪd] *adj* unbestritten
undo [ʌn'duː] (*irreg: like* do) *vt* (*unfasten*) öffnen, aufmachen; (*work*) zunichte machen; **~ing** *n* Verderben *nt*
undoubted [ʌn'daʊtɪd] *adj* unbezweifelt; **~ly** *adv* zweifellos, ohne Zweifel
undress [ʌn'dres] *vt* ausziehen ♦ *vi* sich ausziehen
undue [ʌn'djuː] *adj* übermäßig
undulating ['ʌndjʊleɪtɪŋ] *adj* wellenförmig; (*country*) wellig
unduly [ʌn'djuːlɪ] *adv* übermäßig
unearth [ʌn'ɜːθ] *vt* (*dig up*) ausgraben; (*discover*) ans Licht bringen
unearthly [ʌn'ɜːθlɪ] *adj* (*hour*) nachtschlafen
uneasy [ʌn'iːzɪ] *adj* (*worried*) unruhig; (*feeling*) ungut
uneconomic(al) ['ʌniːkə'nɔmɪk(l)] *adj* unwirtschaftlich
uneducated [ʌn'edjʊkeɪtɪd] *adj* ungebildet
unemployed [ʌnɪm'plɔɪd] *adj* arbeitslos ♦ *npl*: **the ~** die Arbeitslosen *pl*
unemployment [ʌnɪm'plɔɪmənt] *n* Arbeitslosigkeit *f*
unending [ʌn'endɪŋ] *adj* endlos
unerring [ʌn'ɜːrɪŋ] *adj* unfehlbar
uneven [ʌn'iːvn] *adj* (*surface*) uneben; (*quality*) ungleichmäßig
unexpected [ʌnɪks'pektɪd] *adj* unerwartet; **~ly** *adv* unerwartet
unfailing [ʌn'feɪlɪŋ] *adj* nie versagend
unfair [ʌn'feə*r*] *adj* ungerecht, unfair
unfaithful [ʌn'feɪθful] *adj* untreu

unfamiliar [ʌnfə'mɪliəʳ] *adj* ungewohnt; (*person, subject*) unbekannt; **to be ~ with** nicht kennen +*acc*, nicht vertraut sein mit

unfashionable [ʌn'fæʃnəbl] *adj* unmodern; (*area etc*) nicht in Mode

unfasten [ʌn'fɑ:sn] *vt* öffnen, aufmachen

unfavourable [ʌn'feɪvrəbl] (*US* **unfavorable**) *adj* ungünstig

unfeeling [ʌn'fi:lɪŋ] *adj* gefühllos, kalt

unfinished [ʌn'fɪnɪʃt] *adj* unvollendet

unfit [ʌn'fɪt] *adj* ungeeignet; (*in bad health*) nicht fit; **~ for sth** zu or für etw ungeeignet

unfold [ʌn'fəʊld] *vt* entfalten; (*paper*) auseinander falten ♦ *vi* (*develop*) sich entfalten

unforeseen [ʌnfɔː'siːn] *adj* unvorhergesehen

unforgettable [ʌnfə'getəbl] *adj* unvergesslich

unforgivable [ʌnfə'gɪvəbl] *adj* unverzeihlich

unfortunate [ʌn'fɔːtʃənət] *adj* unglücklich, bedauerlich; **~ly** *adv* leider

unfounded [ʌn'faʊndɪd] *adj* unbegründet

unfriendly [ʌn'frendlɪ] *adj* unfreundlich

ungainly [ʌn'geɪnlɪ] *adj* linkisch

ungodly [ʌn'gɒdlɪ] *adj* (*hour*) nachtschlafend; (*row*) heillos

ungrateful [ʌn'greɪtful] *adj* undankbar

unhappiness [ʌn'hæpɪnɪs] *n* Unglück *nt*, Unglückseligkeit *f*

unhappy [ʌn'hæpɪ] *adj* unglücklich; **~ with** (*arrangements etc*) unzufrieden mit

unharmed [ʌn'hɑːmd] *adj* wohlbehalten, unversehrt

UNHCR *n abbr* (= *United Nations High Commission for Refugees*) *Flüchtlingshochkommissariat der Vereinten Nationen*

unhealthy [ʌn'helθɪ] *adj* ungesund

unheard-of [ʌn'hɜːdɒv] *adj* unerhört

unhurt [ʌn'hɜːt] *adj* unverletzt

unidentified [ʌnaɪ'dentɪfaɪd] *adj* unbekannt, nicht identifiziert

uniform ['juːnɪfɔːm] *n* Uniform *f* ♦ *adj* einheitlich; **~ity** [juːnɪ'fɔːmɪtɪ] *n* Einheitlichkeit *f*

unify ['juːnɪfaɪ] *vt* vereinigen

unilateral [juːnɪ'lætərəl] *adj* einseitig

uninhabited [ʌnɪn'hæbɪtɪd] *adj* unbewohnt

unintentional [ʌnɪn'tenʃənəl] *adj* unabsichtlich

union ['juːnjən] *n* (*uniting*) Vereinigung *f*; (*alliance*) Bund *m*, Union *f*; (*trade ~*) Gewerkschaft *f*; **U~ Jack** *n* Union Jack *m*

unique [juː'niːk] *adj* einzig(artig)

UNISON ['juːnɪsn] *n* Gewerkschaft der Angestellten im öffentlichen Dienst

unison ['juːnɪsn] *n* Einstimmigkeit *f*; **in ~** einstimmig

unit ['juːnɪt] *n* Einheit *f*; **kitchen ~** Küchenelement *nt*

unite [juː'naɪt] *vt* vereinigen ♦ *vi* sich vereinigen; **~d** *adj* vereinigt; (*together*) vereint; **U~d Kingdom** *n* Vereinigte(s) Königreich *nt*; **U~d Nations (Organization)** *n* Vereinte Nationen *pl*; **U~d States (of America)** *n* Vereinigte Staaten *pl* (von Amerika)

unit trust (*BRIT*) *n* Treuhandgesellschaft *f*

unity ['juːnɪtɪ] *n* Einheit *f*; (*agreement*) Einigkeit *f*

universal [juːnɪ'vɜːsl] *adj* allgemein

universe ['juːnɪvɜːs] *n* (Welt)all *nt*

university [juːnɪ'vɜːsɪtɪ] *n* Universität *f*

unjust [ʌn'dʒʌst] *adj* ungerecht

unkempt [ʌn'kempt] *adj* ungepflegt

unkind [ʌn'kaɪnd] *adj* unfreundlich

unknown [ʌn'nəʊn] *adj*: **~ (to sb)** (jdm) unbekannt

unlawful [ʌn'lɔːful] *adj* illegal

unleaded ['ʌn'ledɪd] *adj* bleifrei, unverbleit; **I use ~** ich fahre bleifrei

unleash [ʌn'liːʃ] *vt* entfesseln

unless [ʌn'les] *conj* wenn nicht, es sei denn; **~ he comes** es sei denn, er kommt; **~ otherwise stated** sofern nicht anders angegeben

unlike [ʌn'laɪk] *adj* unähnlich ♦ *prep* im Gegensatz zu

unlikely [ʌn'laɪklɪ] *adj* (*not likely*) unwahrscheinlich; (*unexpected: combination etc*) merkwürdig

unlimited [ʌn'lɪmɪtɪd] *adj* unbegrenzt

unlisted ['ʌn'lɪstɪd] (*US*) *adj* nicht im

Telefonbuch stehend

unload [ʌn'ləud] vt entladen

unlock [ʌn'lɔk] vt aufschließen

unlucky [ʌn'lʌkɪ] adj unglücklich; (person) unglückselig; **to be ~** Pech haben

unmarried [ʌn'mærɪd] adj unverheiratet, ledig

unmask [ʌn'mɑːsk] vt entlarven

unmistakable [ʌnmɪs'teɪkəbl] adj unverkennbar

unmitigated [ʌn'mɪtɪgeɪtɪd] adj ungemildert, ganz

unnatural [ʌn'nætʃrəl] adj unnatürlich

unnecessary [ʌn'nɛsəsərɪ] adj unnötig

unnoticed [ʌn'nəutɪst] adj: **to go ~** unbemerkt bleiben

UNO ['juːnəu] n abbr = **United Nations Organization**

unobtainable [ʌnəb'teɪnəbl] adj: **this number is ~** kein Anschluss unter dieser Nummer

unobtrusive [ʌnəb'truːsɪv] adj unauffällig

unofficial [ʌnə'fɪʃl] adj inoffiziell

unpack [ʌn'pæk] vt, vi auspacken

unparalleled [ʌn'pærəleld] adj beispiellos

unpleasant [ʌn'plɛznt] adj unangenehm

unplug [ʌn'plʌg] vt den Stecker herausziehen von

unpopular [ʌn'pɔpjulər] adj (person) unbeliebt; (decision etc) unpopulär

unprecedented [ʌn'prɛsɪdentɪd] adj beispiellos

unpredictable [ʌnprɪ'dɪktəbl] adj unvorhersehbar; (weather, person) unberechenbar

unprofessional [ʌnprə'fɛʃənl] adj unprofessionell

UNPROFOR n abbr (= United Nations Protection Force) UNPROFOR f

unqualified [ʌn'kwɔlɪfaɪd] adj (success) uneingeschränkt, voll; (person) unqualifiziert

unquestionably [ʌn'kwɛstʃənəblɪ] adv fraglos

unravel [ʌn'rævl] vt (disentangle) ausfasern, entwirren; (solve) lösen

unreal [ʌn'rɪəl] adj unwirklich

unrealistic ['ʌnrɪə'lɪstɪk] adj unrealistisch

unreasonable [ʌn'riːznəbl] adj unvernünftig; (demand) übertrieben

unrelated [ʌnrɪ'leɪtɪd] adj ohne Beziehung; (family) nicht verwandt

unrelenting [ʌnrɪ'lɛntɪŋ] adj unerbittlich

unreliable [ʌnrɪ'laɪəbl] adj unzuverlässig

unremitting [ʌnrɪ'mɪtɪŋ] adj (efforts, attempts) unermüdlich

unreservedly [ʌnrɪ'zəːvɪdlɪ] adv offen; (believe, trust) uneingeschränkt; (cry) rückhaltlos

unrest [ʌn'rɛst] n (discontent) Unruhe f; (fighting) Unruhen pl

unroll [ʌn'rəul] vt aufrollen

unruly [ʌn'ruːlɪ] adj (child) undiszipliniert; schwer lenkbar

unsafe [ʌn'seɪf] adj nicht sicher

unsaid [ʌn'sɛd] adj: **to leave sth ~** etw ungesagt lassen

unsatisfactory ['ʌnsætɪs'fæktərɪ] adj unbefriedigend; unzulänglich

unsavoury [ʌn'seɪvərɪ] (US **unsavory**) adj (fig) widerwärtig

unscathed [ʌn'skeɪðd] adj unversehrt

unscrew [ʌn'skruː] vt aufschrauben

unscrupulous [ʌn'skruːpjuləs] adj skrupellos

unsettled [ʌn'sɛtld] adj (person) rastlos; (weather) wechselhaft

unshaven [ʌn'ʃeɪvn] adj unrasiert

unsightly [ʌn'saɪtlɪ] adj unansehnlich

unskilled [ʌn'skɪld] adj ungelernt

unspeakable [ʌn'spiːkəbl] adj (joy) unsagbar; (crime) scheußlich

unstable [ʌn'steɪbl] adj instabil; (mentally) labil

unsteady [ʌn'stɛdɪ] adj unsicher

unstuck [ʌn'stʌk] adj: **to come ~** sich lösen; (fig) ins Wasser fallen

unsuccessful [ʌnsək'sɛsful] adj erfolglos

unsuitable [ʌn'suːtəbl] adj unpassend

unsure [ʌn'ʃuər] adj unsicher; **to be ~ of o.s.** unsicher sein

unsuspecting [ʌnsəs'pɛktɪŋ] adj nichts ahnend

unsympathetic ['ʌnsɪmpə'θɛtɪk] adj gefühllos; (response) abweisend; (unlikeable) unsympathisch

untapped [ʌn'tæpt] *adj* (*resources*) ungenützt

unthinkable [ʌn'θɪŋkəbl] *adj* unvorstellbar

untidy [ʌn'taɪdɪ] *adj* unordentlich

untie [ʌn'taɪ] *vt* aufschnüren

until [ən'tɪl] *prep, conj* bis; ~ **he comes** bis er kommt; ~ **then** bis dann; ~ **now** bis jetzt

untimely [ʌn'taɪmlɪ] *adj* (*death*) vorzeitig

untold [ʌn'təʊld] *adj* unermesslich

untoward [ʌntə'wɔːd] *adj* widrig

untranslatable [ʌntrænz'leɪtəbl] *adj* unübersetzbar

unused [ʌn'juːzd] *adj* unbenutzt

unusual [ʌn'juːʒʊəl] *adj* ungewöhnlich

unveil [ʌn'veɪl] *vt* enthüllen

unwanted [ʌn'wɒntɪd] *adj* unerwünscht

unwavering [ʌn'weɪvərɪŋ] *adj* standhaft, unerschütterlich

unwelcome [ʌn'wɛlkəm] *adj* (*at a bad time*) unwillkommen; (*unpleasant*) unerfreulich

unwell [ʌn'wɛl] *adj*: **to feel** *or* **be** ~ sich nicht wohl fühlen

unwieldy [ʌn'wiːldɪ] *adj* sperrig

unwilling [ʌn'wɪlɪŋ] *adj*: **to be** ~ **to do sth** nicht bereit sein, etw zu tun; ~**ly** *adv* widerwillig

unwind [ʌn'waɪnd] (*irreg: like* wind[2]) *vt* abwickeln ♦ *vi* (*relax*) sich entspannen

unwise [ʌn'waɪz] *adj* unklug

unwitting [ʌn'wɪtɪŋ] *adj* unwissentlich

unworkable [ʌn'wəːkəbl] *adj* (*plan*) undurchführbar

unworthy [ʌn'wəːðɪ] *adj* (*person*): ~ **(of sth)** (einer Sache *gen*) nicht wert

unwrap [ʌn'ræp] *vt* auspacken

unwritten [ʌn'rɪtn] *adj* ungeschrieben

KEYWORD

up [ʌp] *prep*: **to be up sth** oben auf etw *dat* sein; **to go up sth** (auf) etw *acc* hinaufgehen; **go up that road** gehen Sie die Straße hinauf

♦ *adv* **1** (*upwards, higher*) oben; **put it up a bit higher** stell es etwas weiter nach oben; **up there** da oben, dort oben; **up above** hoch oben

2: **to be up** (*out of bed*) auf sein; (*prices, level*) gestiegen sein; (*building, tent*) stehen

3: **up to** (*as far as*) bis; **up to now** bis jetzt

4: **to be up to** (*depending on*): **it's up to you** das hängt von dir ab; (*equal to*): **he's not up to it** (*job, task etc*) er ist dem nicht gewachsen; (*inf: be doing: showing disapproval, suspicion*): **what is he up to?** was führt er im Schilde?; **it's not up to me to decide** die Entscheidung liegt nicht bei mir; **his work is not up to the required standard** seine Arbeit entspricht nicht dem geforderten Niveau

♦ *n*: **ups and downs** (*in life, career*) Höhen und Tiefen *pl*

---

up-and-coming [ʌpənd'kʌmɪŋ] *adj* aufstrebend

upbringing ['ʌpbrɪŋɪŋ] *n* Erziehung *f*

update [ʌp'deɪt] *vt* auf den neuesten Stand bringen

upgrade [ʌp'greɪd] *vt* höher einstufen

upheaval [ʌp'hiːvl] *n* Umbruch *m*

uphill ['ʌp'hɪl] *adj* ansteigend; (*fig*) mühsam ♦ *adv*: **to go** ~ bergauf gehen/fahren

uphold [ʌp'həʊld] (*irreg: like* hold) *vt* unterstützen

upholstery [ʌp'həʊlstərɪ] *n* Polster *nt*; Polsterung *f*

upkeep ['ʌpkiːp] *n* Instandhaltung *f*

upon [ə'pɒn] *prep* auf

upper ['ʌpəʳ] *n* (*on shoe*) Oberleder *nt* ♦ *adj* obere(r, s), höhere(r, s); **to have the** ~ **hand** die Oberhand haben; ~**-class** *adj* vornehm; ~**most** *adj* oberste(r, s), höchste(r, s); **what was** ~**most in my mind** was mich in erster Linie beschäftigte; ~**sixth** (*BRIT: SCOL*) *n* Abschlussklasse *f*

upright ['ʌpraɪt] *adj* aufrecht

uprising ['ʌpraɪzɪŋ] *n* Aufstand *m*

uproar ['ʌprɔːʳ] *n* Aufruhr *m*

uproot [ʌp'ruːt] *vt* ausreißen

upset [*n* 'ʌpset, *vb, adj* ʌp'set] (*irreg: like* set) *n* Aufregung *f* ♦ *vt* (*overturn*) umwerfen; (*disturb*) aufregen, bestürzen; (*plans*) durcheinander bringen ♦ *adj* (*person*) aufgeregt; (*stomach*) verdorben

upshot [ˈʌpʃɔt] n (End)ergebnis nt

upside-down [ˈʌpsaɪd-] adv verkehrt herum

upstairs [ʌpˈstɛəz] adv oben; (go) nach oben ♦ adj (room) obere(r, s), Ober- ♦ n obere(s) Stockwerk nt

upstart [ˈʌpstɑːt] n Emporkömmling m

upstream [ʌpˈstriːm] adv stromaufwärts

uptake [ˈʌpteɪk] n: **to be quick on the ~** schnell begreifen; **to be slow on the ~** schwer von Begriff sein

uptight [ʌpˈtaɪt] (inf) adj (nervous) nervös; (inhibited) verklemmt

up-to-date [ˈʌptəˈdeɪt] adj (clothes) modisch, modern; (information) neueste(r, s)

upturn [ˈʌptəːn] n Aufschwung m

upward [ˈʌpwəd] adj nach oben gerichtet; **~(s)** adv aufwärts

uranium [juəˈreɪnɪəm] n Uran nt

urban [ˈəːbən] adj städtisch, Stadt-; ~ **clearway** n Stadtautobahn f

urchin [ˈəːtʃɪn] n (boy) Schlingel m; (sea ~) Seeigel m

urge [əːdʒ] n Drang m ♦ vt: **to ~ sb to do sth** jdn (dazu) drängen, etw zu tun

urgency [ˈəːdʒənsɪ] n Dringlichkeit f

urgent [ˈəːdʒənt] adj dringend

urinal [ˈjuərɪnl] n (public) Pissoir nt

urinate [ˈjuərɪneɪt] vi urinieren

urine [ˈjuərɪn] n Urin m, Harn m

urn [əːn] n Urne f; (tea ~) Teemaschine f

US n abbr = **United States**

us [ʌs] pron uns; see also **me**

USA n abbr = **United States of America**

usage [ˈjuːzɪdʒ] n Gebrauch m; (esp LING) Sprachgebrauch m

use [n juːs, vb juːz] n (employment) Gebrauch m; (point) Zweck m ♦ vt gebrauchen; **in ~** in Gebrauch; **out of ~** außer Gebrauch; **to be of ~** nützlich sein; **it's no ~** es hat keinen Zweck; **what's the ~?** was solls?; **~d to** (accustomed to) gewöhnt an +acc; **she ~d to live here** (formerly) sie hat früher mal hier gewohnt; **~ up** vt aufbrauchen, verbrauchen; **~d** adj (car) Gebraucht-; **~ful** adj nützlich; **~fulness** n Nützlichkeit f; **~less** adj nutzlos, unnütz; **~r** n Benutzer m; **~r-friendly** adj (computer)

benutzerfreundlich

usher [ˈʌʃər] n Platzanweiser m; **~ette** [ʌʃəˈrɛt] n Platzanweiserin f

usual [ˈjuːʒuəl] adj gewöhnlich, üblich; **as ~** wie üblich; **~ly** adv gewöhnlich

usurp [juːˈzəːp] vt an sich reißen

utensil [juːˈtɛnsl] n Gerät nt; **kitchen ~s** Küchengeräte pl

uterus [ˈjuːtərəs] n Gebärmutter f

utilitarian [juːtɪlɪˈtɛərɪən] adj Nützlichkeits-

utility [juːˈtɪlɪtɪ] n (usefulness) Nützlichkeit f; (also: **public ~**) öffentliche(r) Versorgungsbetrieb m; **~ room** n Hauswirtschaftsraum m

utilize [ˈjuːtɪlaɪz] vt benützen

utmost [ˈʌtməust] adj äußerste(r, s) ♦ n: **to do one's ~** sein Möglichstes tun

utter [ˈʌtər] adj äußerste(r, s), höchste(r, s), völlig ♦ vt äußern, aussprechen; **~ance** n Äußerung f; **~ly** adv äußerst, absolut, völlig

U-turn [ˈjuːˈtəːn] n (AUT) Kehrtwendung f

V, v

v. abbr = **verse**; **versus**; **volt**; (= vide) see

vacancy [ˈveɪkənsɪ] n (BRIT: job) offene Stelle f; (room) freie(s) Zimmer nt; **"no vacancies"** „belegt"

vacant [ˈveɪkənt] adj leer; (unoccupied) frei; (house) leer stehend, unbewohnt; (stupid) (gedanken)leer; ~ **lot** (US) n unbebaute(s) Grundstück nt

vacate [vəˈkeɪt] vt (seat) frei machen; (room) räumen

vacation [vəˈkeɪʃən] n Ferien pl, Urlaub m; **~ist** (US) n Ferienreisende(r) f(m)

vaccinate [ˈvæksɪneɪt] vt impfen

vaccine [ˈvæksiːn] n Impfstoff m

vacuum [ˈvækjum] n Vakuum nt; ~ **bottle** (US) n Thermosflasche f; ~ **cleaner** n Staubsauger m; ~ **flask** (BRIT) n Thermosflasche f; **~-packed** adj vakuumversiegelt

vagina [vəˈdʒaɪnə] n Scheide f

vague [veɪg] adj vag(e); (absent-minded) geistesabwesend; **~ly** adv unbestimmt, vag(e)

vain [veɪn] *adj* eitel; (*attempt*) vergeblich; **in ~** vergebens, umsonst

valentine ['væləntaɪn] *n* (*also:* **~ card**) Valentinsgruß *m*; **V~'s Day** *n* Valentinstag *m*

valet ['vælɪt] *n* Kammerdiener *m*

valiant ['væliənt] *adj* tapfer

valid ['vælɪd] *adj* gültig; (*argument*) stichhaltig; (*objection*) berechtigt; **~ity** [vəˈlɪdɪtɪ] *n* Gültigkeit *f*

valley ['vælɪ] *n* Tal *nt*

valour ['vælər] (*US* **valor**) *n* Tapferkeit *f*

valuable ['væljuəbl] *adj* wertvoll; (*time*) kostbar; **~s** *npl* Wertsachen *pl*

valuation [vælju'eɪʃən] *n* (*FIN*) Schätzung *f*; Beurteilung *f*

value ['vælju:] *n* Wert *m*; (*usefulness*) Nutzen *m* ♦ *vt* (*prize*) (hoch) schätzen, werthalten; (*estimate*) schätzen; **~ added tax** (*BRIT*) *n* Mehrwertsteuer *f*; **~d** *adj* (hoch) geschätzt

valve [vælv] *n* Ventil *nt*; (*BIOL*) Klappe *f*; (*RAD*) Röhre *f*

van [væn] *n* Lieferwagen *m*; (*BRIT: RAIL*) Waggon *m*

vandal ['vændl] *n* Rowdy *m*; **~ism** *n* mutwillige Beschädigung *f*; **~ize** *vt* mutwillig beschädigen

vanguard ['vænɡɑːd] *n* (*fig*) Spitze *f*

vanilla [vəˈnɪlə] *n* Vanille *f*; **~ ice cream** *n* Vanilleeis *nt*

vanish ['vænɪʃ] *vi* verschwinden

vanity ['vænɪtɪ] *n* Eitelkeit *f*; **~ case** *n* Schminkkoffer *m*

vantage ['vɑːntɪdʒ] *n*: **~ point** gute(r) Aussichtspunkt *m*

vapour ['veɪpər] (*US* **vapor**) *n* (*mist*) Dunst *m*; (*gas*) Dampf *m*

variable ['vɛərɪəbl] *adj* wechselhaft, veränderlich; (*speed, height*) regulierbar

variance ['vɛərɪəns] *n*: **to be at ~ (with)** nicht übereinstimmen (mit)

variation [vɛərɪ'eɪʃən] *n* Variation *f*; (*in prices etc*) Schwankung *f*

varicose ['værɪkəʊs] *adj*: **~ veins** Krampfadern *pl*

varied ['vɛərɪd] *adj* unterschiedlich; (*life*)

abwechslungsreich

variety [vəˈraɪətɪ] *n* (*difference*) Abwechslung *f*; (*varied collection*) Vielfalt *f*; (*COMM*) Auswahl *f*; (*sort*) Sorte *f*, Art *f*; **~ show** *n* Varietee *nt*, Varieté *nt*

various ['vɛərɪəs] *adj* verschieden; (*several*) mehrere

varnish ['vɑːnɪʃ] *n* Lack *m*; (*on pottery*) Glasur *f* ♦ *vt* lackieren

vary ['vɛərɪ] *vt* (*alter*) verändern; (*give variety to*) abwechslungsreicher gestalten ♦ *vi* sich (ver)ändern; (*prices*) schwanken; (*weather*) unterschiedlich sein

vase [vɑːz] *n* Vase *f*

Vaseline ['væsɪliːn] ® *n* Vaseline *f*

vast [vɑːst] *adj* weit, groß, riesig

VAT [væt] *n abbr* (= *value added tax*) MwSt *f*

vat [væt] *n* große(s) Fass *nt*

vault [vɔːlt] *n* (*of roof*) Gewölbe *nt*; (*tomb*) Gruft *f*; (*in bank*) Tresorraum *m*; (*leap*) Sprung *m* ♦ *vt* (*also:* **~ over**) überspringen

vaunted ['vɔːntɪd] *adj*: **much-~** viel gerühmt

VCR *n abbr* = **video cassette recorder**

VD *n abbr* = **venereal disease**

VDU *n abbr* = **visual display unit**

veal [viːl] *n* Kalbfleisch *nt*

veer [vɪər] *vi* sich drehen; (*of car*) ausscheren

vegan ['viːɡən] *n* Vegan *m*, radikale(r) Vegetarier(in) *m(f)*

vegeburger ['vɛdʒɪbɜːɡər] *n* vegetarische Frikadelle *f*

vegetable ['vɛdʒtəbl] *n* Gemüse *nt* ♦ *adj* Gemüse-; **~s** *npl* (*CULIN*) Gemüse *nt*

vegetarian [vɛdʒɪ'tɛərɪən] *n* Vegetarier(in) *m(f)* ♦ *adj* vegetarisch

vegetate ['vɛdʒɪteɪt] *vi* (dahin)vegetieren

veggieburger ['vɛdʒɪbɜːɡər] *n* = **vegeburger**

vehement ['viːmənt] *adj* heftig

vehicle ['viːɪkl] *n* Fahrzeug *nt*; (*fig*) Mittel *nt*

veil [veɪl] *n* (*also fig*) Schleier *m* ♦ *vt* verschleiern

vein [veɪn] *n* Ader *f*; (*mood*) Stimmung *f*

velocity [vɪ'lɒsɪtɪ] *n* Geschwindigkeit *f*

velvet ['vɛlvɪt] *n* Samt *m* ♦ *adj* Samt-

vendetta [vɛn'dɛtə] *n* Fehde *f*; (*in family*)

Blutrache f
vending machine ['vendɪŋ-] n Automat m
vendor ['vendəʳ] n Verkäufer m
veneer [və'nɪəʳ] n Furnier(holz) nt; (fig) äußere(r) Anstrich m
venereal disease [vɪ'nɪərɪəl-] n Geschlechtskrankheit f
Venetian blind [vɪ'ni:ʃən-] n Jalousie f
vengeance ['vendʒəns] n Rache f; **with a ~** gewaltig
venison ['venɪsn] n Reh(fleisch) nt
venom ['venəm] n Gift nt
vent [vent] n Öffnung f; (in coat) Schlitz m; (fig) Ventil nt ♦ vt (emotion) abreagieren
ventilate ['ventɪleɪt] vt belüften; **ventilator** ['ventɪleɪtəʳ] n Ventilator m
ventriloquist [ven'trɪləkwɪst] n Bauchredner m
venture ['ventʃəʳ] n Unternehmung f, Projekt nt ♦ vt wagen; (life) aufs Spiel setzen ♦ vi sich wagen
venue ['venju:] n Schauplatz m
verb [və:b] n Zeitwort nt, Verb nt; **~al** adj (spoken) mündlich; (translation) wörtlich; **~ally** adv mündlich
verbatim [və:'beɪtɪm] adv Wort für Wort ♦ adj wortwörtlich
verbose [və:'bəus] adj wortreich
verdict ['və:dɪkt] n Urteil nt
verge [və:dʒ] n (BRIT) Rand m ♦ vi: **to ~ on** grenzen an +acc; **"soft ~s"** (BRIT: AUT) „Seitenstreifen nicht befahrbar"; **on the ~ of doing sth** im Begriff, etw zu tun
verify ['verɪfaɪ] vt (über)prüfen; (confirm) bestätigen; (theory) beweisen
veritable ['verɪtəbl] adj wirklich, echt
vermin ['və:mɪn] npl Ungeziefer nt
vermouth ['və:məθ] n Wermut m
versatile ['və:sətaɪl] adj vielseitig
verse [və:s] n (poetry) Poesie f, (stanza) Strophe f; (of Bible) Vers m; **in ~** in Versform
version ['və:ʃən] n Version f; (of car) Modell nt
versus ['və:səs] prep gegen
vertebrate ['və:tɪbrɪt] adj Wirbel-
vertical ['və:tɪkl] adj senkrecht

vertigo ['və:tɪgəu] n Schwindel m
very ['verɪ] adv sehr ♦ adj (extreme) äußerste(r, s); **the ~ book which** genau das Buch, welches; **the ~ last ...** der/die/das allerletzte ...; **at the ~ least** allerwenigstens; **~ much** sehr
vessel ['vesl] n (ship) Schiff nt; (container) Gefäß nt
vest [vest] n (BRIT) Unterhemd nt; (US: waistcoat) Weste f
vested interests ['vestɪd-] npl finanzielle Beteiligung f; (people) finanziell Beteiligte pl; (fig) persönliche(s) Interesse nt
vestige ['vestɪdʒ] n Spur f
vestry ['vestrɪ] n Sakristei f
vet [vet] n abbr (= veterinary surgeon) Tierarzt m/-ärztin f
veteran ['vetərn] n Veteran(in) m(f)
veterinarian [vetrɪ'neərɪən] (US) n Tierarzt m/-ärztin f
veterinary ['vetrɪnərɪ] adj Veterinär-; **~ surgeon** (BRIT) n Tierarzt m/-ärztin f
veto ['vi:təu] (pl **~es**) n Veto nt ♦ vt sein Veto einlegen gegen
vex [veks] vt ärgern; **~ed** adj verärgert; **~ed question** umstrittene Frage f
VHF abbr (= very high frequency) UKW f
via ['vaɪə] prep über +acc
viable ['vaɪəbl] adj (plan) durchführbar; (company) rentabel
vibrant ['vaɪbrnt] adj (lively) lebhaft; (bright) leuchtend; (full of emotion: voice) bebend
vibrate [vaɪ'breɪt] vi zittern, beben; (machine, string) vibrieren; **vibration** [vaɪ'breɪʃən] n Schwingung f; (of machine) Vibrieren nt
vicar ['vɪkəʳ] n Pfarrer m; **~age** n Pfarrhaus nt
vice [vaɪs] n (evil) Laster nt; (TECH) Schraubstock m
vice-chairman [vaɪs'tʃeəmən] n stellvertretende(r) Vorsitzende(r) m
vice-president [vaɪs'prezɪdənt] n Vizepräsident m
vice squad n ≈ Sittenpolizei f
vice versa ['vaɪsɪ'və:sə] adv umgekehrt
vicinity [vɪ'sɪnɪtɪ] n Umgebung f; (closeness) Nähe f

vicious ['vɪʃəs] *adj* gemein, böse; **~ circle** *n* Teufelskreis *m*

victim ['vɪktɪm] *n* Opfer *nt*

victor ['vɪktəʳ] *n* Sieger *m*

Victorian [vɪk'tɔːrɪən] *adj* viktorianisch; *(fig)* (sitten)streng

victorious [vɪk'tɔːrɪəs] *adj* siegreich

victory ['vɪktərɪ] *n* Sieg *m*

video ['vɪdɪəʊ] *adj* Fernseh-, Bild- ♦ *n* (~ *film*) Video *nt*; *(also:* **~ cassette**) Videokassette *f*; *(also:* **~ cassette recorder**) Videorekorder *m*; **~ tape** *n* Videoband *nt*; **~ wall** *n* Videowand *m*

vie [vaɪ] *vi* wetteifern

Vienna [vɪ'enə] *n* Wien *nt*

Vietnam ['vjet'næm] *n* Vietnam *nt*; **~ese** *adj* vietnamesisch ♦ *n inv (person)* Vietnamese *m*, Vietnamesin *f*

view [vjuː] *n (sight)* Sicht *f*, Blick *m*; *(scene)* Aussicht *f*; *(opinion)* Ansicht *f*; *(intention)* Absicht *f* ♦ *vt (situation)* betrachten; *(house)* besichtigen; **to have sth in ~** etw beabsichtigen; **on ~** ausgestellt; **in ~ of** wegen +*gen*, angesichts +*gen*; **~er** *n (PHOT: small projector)* Gucki *m*; *(TV)* Fernsehzuschauer(in) *m(f)*; **~finder** *n* Sucher *m*; **~point** *n* Standpunkt *m*

vigil ['vɪdʒɪl] *n* (Nacht)wache *f*; **~ant** *adj* wachsam

vigorous ['vɪgərəs] *adj* kräftig; *(protest)* energisch, heftig

vile [vaɪl] *adj (mean)* gemein; *(foul)* abscheulich

villa ['vɪlə] *n* Villa *f*

village ['vɪlɪdʒ] *n* Dorf *nt*; **~r** *n* Dorfbewohner(in) *m(f)*

villain ['vɪlən] *n* Schurke *m*

vindicate ['vɪndɪkeɪt] *vt* rechtfertigen

vindictive [vɪn'dɪktɪv] *adj* nachtragend, rachsüchtig

vine [vaɪn] *n* Rebstock *m*, Rebe *f*

vinegar ['vɪnɪgəʳ] *n* Essig *m*

vineyard ['vɪnjɑːd] *n* Weinberg *m*

vintage ['vɪntɪdʒ] *n (of wine)* Jahrgang *m*; **~ car** *n* Oldtimer *m (zwischen 1919 und 1930 gebaut)*; **~ wine** *n* edle(r) Wein *m*

viola [vɪ'əʊlə] *n* Bratsche *f*

violate ['vaɪəleɪt] *vt (law)* übertreten; *(rights, rule, neutrality)* verletzen; *(sanctity, woman)* schänden; **violation** [vaɪə'leɪʃən] *n* Übertretung *f*; Verletzung *f*

violence ['vaɪələns] *n (force)* Heftigkeit *f*; *(brutality)* Gewalttätigkeit *f*

violent ['vaɪələnt] *adj (strong)* heftig; *(brutal)* gewalttätig, brutal; *(contrast)* krass; *(death)* gewaltsam

violet ['vaɪələt] *n* Veilchen *nt* ♦ *adj* veilchenblau, violett

violin [vaɪə'lɪn] *n* Geige *f*, Violine *f*; **~ist** *n* Geiger(in) *m(f)*

VIP *n abbr* (= *very important person*) VIP *m*

virgin ['vɜːdʒɪn] *n* Jungfrau *f* ♦ *adj* jungfräulich, unberührt; **~ity** [vɜː'dʒɪnɪtɪ] *n* Unschuld *f*

Virgo ['vɜːgəʊ] *n* Jungfrau *f*

virile ['vɪraɪl] *adj* männlich; **virility** [vɪ'rɪlɪtɪ] *n* Männlichkeit *f*

virtually ['vɜːtjʊəlɪ] *adv* praktisch, fast

virtual reality ['vɜːtjʊəl-] *n (COMPUT)* virtuelle Realität *f*

virtue ['vɜːtjuː] *n (moral goodness)* Tugend *f*; *(good quality)* Vorteil *m*, Vorzug *m*; **by ~ of** aufgrund *or* auf Grund +*gen*

virtuous ['vɜːtjʊəs] *adj* tugendhaft

virulent ['vɪrʊlənt] *adj (poisonous)* bösartig; *(bitter)* scharf, geharnischt

virus ['vaɪərəs] *n (also COMPUT)* Virus *m*

visa ['viːzə] *n* Visum *nt*

vis-à-vis [viːzə'viː] *prep* gegenüber

viscous ['vɪskəs] *adj* zähflüssig

visibility [vɪzɪ'bɪlɪtɪ] *n (MET)* Sicht(weite) *f*

visible ['vɪzəbl] *adj* sichtbar; **visibly** *adv* sichtlich

vision ['vɪʒən] *n (ability)* Sehvermögen *nt*; *(foresight)* Weitblick *m*; *(in dream, image)* Vision *f*

visit ['vɪzɪt] *n* Besuch *m* ♦ *vt* besuchen; *(town, country)* fahren nach; **~ing hours** *npl (in hospital etc)* Besuchszeiten *pl*; **~or** *n (in house)* Besucher(in) *m(f)*; *(in hotel)* Gast *m*; **~or centre** *n* Touristeninformation *f*

visor ['vaɪzəʳ] *n* Visier *nt*; *(on cap)* Schirm *m*; *(AUT)* Blende *f*

vista ['vɪstə] *n* Aussicht *f*

visual ['vɪzjuəl] *adj* Seh-, visuell; ~ **aid** *n* Anschauungsmaterial *nt*; ~ **display unit** *n* Bildschirm(gerät *nt*) *m*; **~ize** *vt* sich +*dat* vorstellen; **~ly-impaired** *adj* sehbehindert

vital ['vaɪtl] *adj* (*important*) unerlässlich; (*necessary for life*) Lebens-, lebenswichtig; (*lively*) vital; **~ity** [vaɪ'tælɪtɪ] *n* Vitalität *f*; **~ly** *adv*: **~ly important** äußerst wichtig; ~ **statistics** *npl* (*fig*) Maße *pl*

vitamin ['vɪtəmɪn] *n* Vitamin *nt*

vivacious [vɪ'veɪʃəs] *adj* lebhaft

vivid ['vɪvɪd] *adj* (*graphic*) lebendig; (*memory*) lebhaft; (*bright*) leuchtend; **~ly** *adv* lebendig; lebhaft; leuchtend

V-neck ['viːnɛk] *n* V-Ausschnitt *m*

vocabulary [vəu'kæbjulərɪ] *n* Wortschatz *m*, Vokabular *nt*

vocal ['vəukl] *adj* Vokal-, Gesang-; (*fig*) lautstark; ~ **cords** *npl* Stimmbänder *pl*

vocation [vəu'keɪʃən] *n* (*calling*) Berufung *f*; **~al** *adj* Berufs-

vociferous [və'sɪfərəs] *adj* lautstark

vodka ['vɒdkə] *n* Wodka *m*

vogue [vəug] *n* Mode *f*

voice [vɔɪs] *n* Stimme *f*; (*fig*) Mitspracherecht *nt* ♦ *vt* äußern; ~ **mail** *n* (*TEL*) Voicemail *f*

void [vɔɪd] *n* Leere *f* ♦ *adj* (*invalid*) nichtig, ungültig; (*empty*): ~ **of** ohne, bar +*gen*; *see* **null**

volatile ['vɒlətaɪl] *adj* (*gas*) flüchtig; (*person*) impulsiv; (*situation*) brisant

volcano [vɒl'keɪnəu] *n* Vulkan *m*

volition [və'lɪʃən] *n* Wille *m*; **of one's own** ~ aus freiem Willen

volley ['vɒlɪ] *n* (*of guns*) Salve *f*; (*of stones*) Hagel *m*; (*tennis*) Flugball *m*; **~ball** *n* Volleyball *m*

volt [vəult] *n* Volt *nt*; **~age** *n* Spannung *f*

volume ['vɒljuːm] *n* (*book*) Band *m*; (*size*) Umfang *m*; (*space*) Rauminhalt *m*; (*of sound*) Lautstärke *f*

voluntarily ['vɒləntrɪlɪ] *adv* freiwillig

voluntary ['vɒləntərɪ] *adj* freiwillig

volunteer [vɒlən'tɪəʳ] *n* Freiwillige(r) *mf* ♦ *vi* sich freiwillig melden; **to** ~ **to do sth** sich anbieten, etw zu tun

vomit ['vɒmɪt] *n* Erbrochene(s) *nt* ♦ *vt* spucken ♦ *vi* sich übergeben

vote [vəut] *n* Stimme *f*; (*ballot*) Abstimmung *f*; (*result*) Abstimmungsergebnis *nt*; (*franchise*) Wahlrecht *nt* ♦ *vt, vi* wählen; ~ **of thanks** *n* Dankesworte *pl*; **~r** *n* Wähler(in) *m(f)*; **voting** ['vəutɪŋ] *n* Wahl *f*

voucher ['vautʃəʳ] *n* Gutschein *m*

vouch for [vautʃ-] *vt* bürgen für

vow [vau] *n* Versprechen *nt*; (*REL*) Gelübde *nt* ♦ *vt* geloben

vowel ['vauəl] *n* Vokal *m*

voyage ['vɔɪdʒ] *n* Reise *f*

vulgar ['vʌlgəʳ] *adj* (*rude*) vulgär; **~ity** [vʌl'gærɪtɪ] *n* Vulgarität *f*

vulnerable ['vʌlnərəbl] *adj* (*easily injured*) verwundbar; (*sensitive*) verletzlich

vulture ['vʌltʃəʳ] *n* Geier *m*

W, w

wad [wɒd] *n* (*bundle*) Bündel *nt*; (*of paper*) Stoß *m*; (*of money*) Packen *m*

waddle ['wɒdl] *vi* watscheln

wade [weɪd] *vi*: **to ~ through** waten durch

wafer ['weɪfəʳ] *n* Waffel *f*; (*REL*) Hostie *f*; (*COMPUT*) Wafer *f*

waffle ['wɒfl] *n* Waffel *f*; (*inf: empty talk*) Geschwafel *nt* ♦ *vi* schwafeln

waft [wɒft] *vt, vi* wehen

wag [wæg] *vt* (*tail*) wedeln mit ♦ *vi* wedeln

wage [weɪdʒ] *n* (*also: ~s*) (Arbeits)lohn *m* ♦ *vt*: **to ~ war** Krieg führen; ~ **earner** *n* Lohnempfänger(in) *m(f)*; ~ **packet** *n* Lohntüte *f*

wager ['weɪdʒəʳ] *n* Wette *f* ♦ *vt, vi* wetten

waggle ['wægl] *vt, vi* wackeln

wag(g)on ['wægən] *n* (*horse-drawn*) Fuhrwerk *nt*; (*US: AUT*) Wagen *m*; (*BRIT: RAIL*) Wag(g)on *m*

wail [weɪl] *n* Wehgeschrei *nt* ♦ *vi* wehklagen, jammern

waist [weɪst] *n* Taille *f*; **~coat** (*BRIT*) *n* Weste *f*; **~line** *n* Taille *f*

wait [weɪt] *n* Wartezeit *f* ♦ *vi* warten; **to lie in** ~ **for sb** jdm auflauern; **I can't ~ to see**

him ich kanns kaum erwarten ihn zu sehen; **"no ~ing"** (*BRIT: AUT*) „Halteverbot"; **~ behind** *vi* zurückbleiben; **~ for** *vt fus* warten auf +*acc*; **~ on** *vt fus* bedienen; **~er** *n* Kellner *m*; **~ing list** *n* Warteliste *f*; **~ing room** *n* (*MED*) Wartezimmer *nt*; (*RAIL*) Wartesaal *m*; **~ress** *n* Kellnerin *f*

waive [weɪv] *vt* verzichten auf +*acc*

wake [weɪk] (*pt* **woke, waked,** *pp* **woken**) *vt* wecken ♦ *vi* (*also:* **~ up**) aufwachen ♦ *n* (*NAUT*) Kielwasser *nt*; (*for dead*) Totenwache *f*; **to ~ up to** (*fig*) sich bewusst werden +*gen*

waken [weɪk] *vt* aufwecken

Wales [weɪlz] *n* Wales *nt*

walk [wɔːk] *n* Spaziergang *m*; (*gait*) Gang *m*; (*route*) Weg *m* ♦ *vi* gehen; (*stroll*) spazieren gehen; (*longer*) wandern; **~s of life** Sphären *pl*; **a 10-minute ~** 10 Minuten zu Fuß; **to ~ out on sb** (*inf*) jdn sitzen lassen; **~er** *n* Spaziergänger *m*; (*hiker*) Wanderer *m*; **~ie-talkie** [wɔːkɪ'tɔːkɪ] *n* tragbare(s) Sprechfunkgerät *nt*; **~ing** *n* Gehen *nt*; (*hiking*) Wandern *nt* ♦ *adj* Wander-; **~ing shoes** *npl* Wanderschuhe *pl*; **~ing stick** *n* Spazierstock *m*; **W~man** [wɔːkmæn] ® *n* Walkman *m* ®; **~out** *n* Streik *m*; **~over** (*inf*) *n* leichte(r) Sieg *m*; **~way** *n* Fußweg *m*

wall [wɔːl] *n* (*inside*) Wand *f*; (*outside*) Mauer *f*; **~ed** *adj* von Mauern umgeben

wallet [wɒlɪt] *n* Brieftasche *f*

wallflower [wɔːlflauər] *n* Goldlack *m*; **to be a ~** (*fig*) ein Mauerblümchen sein

wallop [wɒləp] (*inf*) *vt* schlagen, verprügeln

wallow [wɒləu] *vi* sich wälzen

wallpaper [wɔːlpeɪpər] *n* Tapete *f*

walnut [wɔːlnʌt] *n* Walnuss *f*

walrus [wɔːlrəs] *n* Walross *n*

waltz [wɔːlts] *n* Walzer *m* ♦ *vi* Walzer tanzen

wan [wɒn] *adj* bleich

wand [wɒnd] *n* (*also:* **magic ~**) Zauberstab *m*

wander [wɒndər] *vi* (*roam*) (herum)wandern; (*fig*) abschweifen

wane [weɪn] *vi* abnehmen; (*fig*) schwinden

wangle [wæŋgl] (*BRIT: inf*) *vt*: **to ~ sth** etw richtig hindrehen

want [wɒnt] *n* (*lack*) Mangel *m* ♦ *vt* (*need*)

brauchen; (*desire*) wollen; (*lack*) nicht haben; **~s** *npl* (*needs*) Bedürfnisse *pl*; **for ~ of** aus Mangel an +*dat*; mangels +*gen*; **to ~ to do sth** etw tun wollen; **to ~ sb to do sth** wollen, dass jd etw tut; **~ed** *adj* (*criminal etc*) gesucht; **"cook ~ed"** (*in adverts*) „Koch/Köchin gesucht"; **~ing** *adj*: **to be found ~ing** sich als unzulänglich erweisen

wanton [wɒntn] *adj* mutwillig, zügellos

war [wɔː] *n* Krieg *m*; **to make ~** Krieg führen

ward [wɔːd] *n* (*in hospital*) Station *f*; (*of city*) Bezirk *m*; (*child*) Mündel *nt*; **~ off** *vt* abwenden, abwehren

warden [wɔːdn] *n* (*guard*) Wächter *m*, Aufseher *m*; (*BRIT: in youth hostel*) Herbergsvater *m*; (*UNIV*) Heimleiter *m*; (*BRIT: also:* **traffic ~**) ≃ Verkehrspolizist *m*, ≃ Politesse *f*

warder [wɔːdər] (*BRIT*) *n* Gefängniswärter *m*

wardrobe [wɔːdrəub] *n* Kleiderschrank *m*; (*clothes*) Garderobe *f*

warehouse [wɛəhaus] *n* Lagerhaus *nt*

wares [wɛəz] *npl* Ware *f*

warfare [wɔːfɛər] *n* Krieg *m*; Kriegsführung *f*

warhead [wɔːhed] *n* Sprengkopf *m*

warily [wɛərɪlɪ] *adv* vorsichtig

warlike [wɔːlaɪk] *adj* kriegerisch

warm [wɔːm] *adj* warm; (*welcome*) herzlich ♦ *vt, vi* wärmen; **I'm ~** mir ist warm; **it's ~** es ist warm; **~ up** *vt* aufwärmen ♦ *vi* warm werden; **~-hearted** *adj* warmherzig; **~ly** *adv* warm; herzlich; **~th** *n* Wärme *f*; Herzlichkeit *f*

warn [wɔːn] *vt*: **to ~ (of** *or* **against)** warnen (vor +*dat*); **~ing** *n* Warnung *f*; **without ~ing** unerwartet; **~ing light** *n* Warnlicht *nt*; **~ing triangle** *n* (*AUT*) Warndreieck *nt*

warp [wɔːp] *vt* verziehen; **~ed** *adj* wellig; (*fig*) pervers

warrant [wɒrnt] *n* (*for arrest*) Haftbefehl *m*

warranty [wɒrəntɪ] *n* Garantie *f*

warren [wɒrən] *n* Labyrinth *nt*

Warsaw [wɔːsɔː] *n* Warschau *nt*

warship [wɔːʃɪp] *n* Kriegsschiff *nt*

wart [wɔːt] *n* Warze *f*

wartime ['wɔ:taɪm] *n* Krieg *m*

wary ['weərɪ] *adj* misstrauisch

was [wɒz] *pt of* be

wash [wɒʃ] *n* Wäsche *f* ♦ *vt* waschen; *(dishes)* abwaschen ♦ *vi* sich waschen; *(do ~ing)* waschen; **to have a ~** sich waschen; **~ away** *vt* abwaschen, wegspülen; **~ off** *vt* abwaschen; **~ up** *vi (BRIT)* spülen; *(US)* sich waschen; **~able** *adj* waschbar; **~basin** *n* Waschbecken *nt*; **~ bowl** *(US) n* Waschbecken *nt*; **~ cloth** *(US) n (face cloth)* Waschlappen *m*; **~er** *n (TECH)* Dichtungsring *m; (machine)* Waschmaschine *f*; **~ing** *n* Wäsche *f*; **~ing machine** *n* Waschmaschine *f*; **~ing powder** *(BRIT) n* Waschpulver *nt*; **~ing-up** *n* Abwasch *m*; **~ing-up liquid** *n* Spülmittel *nt*; **~-out** *(inf) n (event)* Reinfall *m; (person)* Niete *f*; **~room** *n* Waschraum *m*

wasn't ['wɒznt] = **was not**

wasp [wɒsp] *n* Wespe *f*

wastage ['weɪstɪdʒ] *n* Verlust *m*; **natural ~** Verschleiß *m*

waste [weɪst] *n (wasting)* Verschwendung *f; (what is ~d)* Abfall *m* ♦ *adj (useless)* überschüssig, Abfall- ♦ *vt (object)* verschwenden; *(time, life)* vergeuden ♦ *vi:* **to ~ away** *vi* verfallen, verkümmern; **~s** *npl (land)* Einöde *f*; **~ disposal unit** *(BRIT) n* Müllschlucker *m*; **~ful** *adj* verschwenderisch; *(process)* aufwändig, aufwendig; **~ ground** *(BRIT) n* unbebaute(s) Grundstück *nt*; **~land** *n* Ödland *nt*; **~paper basket** *n* Papierkorb *m*; **~ pipe** *n* Abflussrohr *nt*

watch [wɒtʃ] *n* Wache *f; (for time)* Uhr *f* ♦ *vt* ansehen; *(observe)* beobachten; *(be careful of)* aufpassen auf +*acc; (guard)* bewachen ♦ *vi* zusehen; **to be on the ~ (for sth)** (auf etw *acc*) aufpassen; **to ~ TV** fernsehen; **to ~ sb doing sth** jdm bei etw zuschauen; **~ out** *vi* Ausschau halten; *(be careful)* aufpassen; **~ out!** pass auf!; **~dog** *n* Wachhund *m; (fig)* Wächter *m*; **~ful** *adj* wachsam; **~maker** *n* Uhrmacher *m*; **~man** *(irreg) n (also:* **night ~man***)* (Nacht)wächter *m*; **~ strap** *n* Uhrarmband *nt*

water ['wɔ:tər] *n* Wasser *nt* ♦ *vt* (be)gießen; *(river)* bewässern; *(horses)* tränken ♦ *vi (eye)* tränen; **~s** *npl (of sea, river etc)* Gewässer *nt*; **~ down** *vt* verwässern; **~ closet** *(BRIT) n* (Wasser)klosett *nt*; **~colour** *(US)* **~color***) n (painting)* Aquarell *nt; (paint)* Wasserfarbe *f*; **~cress** *n* (Brunnen)kresse *f*; **~fall** *n* Wasserfall *m*; **~ heater** *n* Heißwassergerät *nt*; **~ing can** *n* Gießkanne *f*; **~ level** *n* Wasserstand *m*; **~lily** *n* Seerose *f*; **~line** *n* Wasserlinie *f*; **~logged** *adj (ground)* voll Wasser; **~ main** *n* Haupt(wasser)leitung *f*; **~mark** *n* Wasserzeichen *nt; (on wall)* Wasserstandsmarke *f*; **~melon** *n* Wassermelone *f*; **~ polo** *n* Wasserball(spiel) *nt*; **~proof** *adj* wasserdicht; **~shed** *n* Wasserscheide *f*; **~-skiing** *n* Wasserskilaufen *nt*; **~ tank** *n* Wassertank *m*; **~tight** *adj* wasserdicht; **~way** *n* Wasserweg *m*; **~works** *npl* Wasserwerk *nt*; **~y** *adj* wäss(e)rig

watt [wɒt] *n* Watt *nt*

wave [weɪv] *n* Welle *f; (with hand)* Winken *nt* ♦ *vt (move to and fro)* schwenken; *(hand, flag)* winken mit ♦ *vi (person)* winken; *(flag)* wehen; **~length** *n (also fig)* Wellenlänge *f*

waver ['weɪvər] *vi* schwanken

wavy ['weɪvɪ] *adj* wellig

wax [wæks] *n* Wachs *nt; (sealing ~)* Siegellack *m; (in ear)* Ohrenschmalz *nt* ♦ *vt (floor)* (ein)wachsen ♦ *vi (moon)* zunehmen; **~works** *npl* Wachsfigurenkabinett *nt*

way [weɪ] *n* Weg *m; (method)* Art und Weise *f; (direction)* Richtung *f; (habit)* Gewohnheit *f; (distance)* Entfernung *f; (condition)* Zustand *m*; **which ~? - this ~** welche Richtung? - hier entlang; **on the ~** *(en route)* unterwegs; **to be in the ~** im Weg sein; **to go out of one's ~ to do sth** sich besonders anstrengen, um etw zu tun; **to lose one's ~** sich verirren; **"give ~"** *(BRIT: AUT)* „Vorfahrt achten!"; **in a ~** in gewisser Weise; **by the ~** übrigens; **in some ~s** in gewisser Hinsicht; **"~ in"** *(BRIT)* „Eingang"; **"~ out"** *(BRIT)* „Ausgang"

waylay [weɪ'leɪ] *(irreg: like* lay*) vt* auflauern

+*dat*

wayward ['weɪwəd] *adj* eigensinnig

W.C. (*BRIT*) *n* WC *nt*

we [wiː] *pl pron* wir

weak [wiːk] *adj* schwach; **~en** *vt* schwächen ♦ *vi* schwächer werden; **~ling** *n* Schwächling *m*; **~ness** *n* Schwäche *f*

wealth [welθ] *n* Reichtum *m*; (*abundance*) Fülle *f*; **~y** *adj* reich

wean [wiːn] *vt* entwöhnen

weapon ['wepən] *n* Waffe *f*

wear [weəᵈ] (*pt* **wore**, *pp* **worn**) *n* (*clothing*): **sports/baby** ~ Sport-/Babykleidung *f*; (*use*) Verschleiß *m* ♦ *vt* (*have on*) tragen; (*smile etc*) haben; (*use*) abnutzen ♦ *vi* (*last*) halten; (*become old*) (sich) verschleißen; **evening** ~ Abendkleidung *f*; **~ and tear** Verschleiß *m*; **~ away** *vt* verbrauchen ♦ *vi* schwinden; **~ down** *vt* (*people*) zermürben; **~ off** *vi* sich verlieren; **~ out** *vt* verschleißen; (*person*) erschöpfen

weary ['wɪərɪ] *adj* müde ♦ *vt* ermüden ♦ *vi* überdrüssig werden

weasel ['wiːzl] *n* Wiesel *nt*

weather ['weðəᵈ] *n* Wetter *nt* ♦ *vt* verwittern lassen; (*resist*) überstehen; **under the** ~ (*fig: ill*) angeschlagen (*inf*); **~-beaten** *adj* verwittert; **~cock** *n* Wetterhahn *m*; **~ forecast** *n* Wettervorhersage *f*; **~ vane** *n* Wetterfahne *f*

weave [wiːv] (*pt* **wove**, *pp* **woven**) *vt* weben; **~r** *n* Weber(in) *m(f)*; **weaving** *n* (*craft*) Webkunst *f*

Web [web] *n*: **the** ~ das Web

web *n* Netz *nt*; (*membrane*) Schwimmhaut *f*; **~ site** *n* (*COMPUT*) Website *f*, Webseite *f*

wed [wed] (*pt*, *pp* **wedded**) *vt* heiraten ♦ *n*: **the newly-~s** *npl* die Frischvermählten *pl*

we'd [wiːd] = **we had**; **we would**

wedding ['wedɪŋ] *n* Hochzeit *f*; **silver/ golden ~ anniversary** Silberhochzeit *f*/ goldene Hochzeit *f*; **~ day** *n* Hochzeitstag *m*; **~ dress** *n* Hochzeitskleid *nt*; **~ ring** *n* Trauring *m*, Ehering *m*

wedge [wedʒ] *n* Keil *m*; (*of cheese etc*) Stück *nt* ♦ *vt* (*fasten*) festklemmen; (*pack tightly*) einkeilen

Wednesday ['wednzdɪ] *n* Mittwoch *m*

wee [wiː] (*SCOTTISH*) *adj* klein, winzig

weed [wiːd] *n* Unkraut *nt* ♦ *vt* jäten; **~-killer** *n* Unkrautvertilgungsmittel *nt*

weedy ['wiːdɪ] *adj* (*person*) schmächtig

week [wiːk] *n* Woche *f*; **a ~ today/on Friday** heute/Freitag in einer Woche; **~day** *n* Wochentag *m*; **~end** *n* Wochenende *nt*; **~ly** *adj* wöchentlich; (*wages, magazine*) Wochen- ♦ *adv* wöchentlich

weep [wiːp] (*pt*, *pp* **wept**) *vi* weinen; **~ing willow** *n* Trauerweide *f*

weigh [weɪ] *vt*, *vi* wiegen; **to ~ anchor** den Anker lichten; **~ down** *vt* niederdrücken; **~ up** *vt* abschätzen

weight [weɪt] *n* Gewicht *nt*; **to lose/put on ~** abnehmen/zunehmen; **~ing** *n* (*allowance*) Zulage *f*; **~-lifter** *n* Gewichtheber *m*; **~-lifting** *n* Gewichtheben *nt*; **~y** *adj* (*heavy*) gewichtig; (*important*) schwerwiegend, schwer wiegend

weir [wɪəᵈ] *n* (Stau)wehr *nt*

weird [wɪəd] *adj* seltsam

welcome ['welkəm] *n* Willkommen *nt*, Empfang *m* ♦ *vt* begrüßen; **thank you - you're ~!** danke - nichts zu danken

welder ['weldəᵈ] *n* (*person*) Schweißer(in) *m(f)*

welding ['weldɪŋ] *n* Schweißen *nt*

welfare ['welfeəᵈ] *n* Wohl *nt*; (*social*) Fürsorge *f*; **~ state** *n* Wohlfahrtsstaat *m*; **~ work** *n* Fürsorge *f*

well [wel] *n* Brunnen *m*; (*oil* ~) Quelle *f* ♦ *adj* (*in good health*) gesund ♦ *adv* gut ♦ *excl* nun!, na schön!; **I'm** ~ es geht mir gut; **get ~ soon!** gute Besserung!; **as** ~ auch; **as ~ as** sowohl als auch; **~ done!** gut gemacht!; **to do ~** (*person*) gut zurechtkommen; (*business*) gut gehen; **~ up** *vi* emporsteigen; (*fig*) aufsteigen

we'll [wiːl] = **we will**; **we shall**

well: **~-behaved** ['welbɪ'heɪvd] *adj* wohlerzogen; **~-being** ['wel'biːɪŋ] *n* Wohl *nt*; **~-built** ['wel'bɪlt] *adj* kräftig gebaut; **~-deserved** ['weldɪ'zɜːvd] *adj* wohlverdient; **~-dressed** ['wel'drest] *adj* gut gekleidet; **~-heeled** ['wel'hiːld] (*inf*) *adj* (*wealthy*) gut gepolstert

wellingtons ['wɛlɪŋtənz] *npl* (*also:*
wellington boots) Gummistiefel *pl*

well: **~-known** ['wɛl'nəun] *adj* bekannt; **~-
mannered** ['wɛl'mænəd] *adj* wohlerzogen;
~-meaning ['wɛl'miːnɪŋ] *adj* (*person*)
wohlmeinend; (*action*) gut gemeint; **~-off**
['wɛl'ɔf] *adj* gut situiert; **~-read** ['wɛl'rɛd] *adj*
(sehr) belesen; **~-to-do** ['wɛltə'duː] *adj*
wohlhabend; **~-wisher** ['wɛlwɪʃər] *n*
Gönner *m*

Welsh [wɛlʃ] *adj* walisisch ♦ *n* (*LING*)
Walisisch *nt*; **the ~** *npl* (*people*) die Waliser
pl; **~ Assembly** *n* walisische Versammlung
f; **~man/woman** (*irreg*) *n* Waliser(in) *m(f)*

went [wɛnt] *pt of* **go**

wept [wɛpt] *pt, pp of* **weep**

were [wəːr] *pt pl of* **be**

we're [wɪər] = **we are**

weren't [wəːnt] = **were not**

west [wɛst] *n* Westen *m* ♦ *adj* West-, westlich
♦ *adv* westwärts, nach Westen; **the W~** der
Westen; **W~ Country** (*BRIT*) *n*: **the W~
Country** der Südwesten Englands; **~erly**
adj westlich; **~ern** *adj* westlich, West- ♦ *n*
(*CINE*) Western *m*; **W~ Indian** *adj*
westindisch ♦ *n* Westindier(in) *m(f)*; **W~
Indies** *npl* Westindische Inseln *pl*;
~ward(s) *adv* westwärts

wet [wɛt] *adj* nass; **to get ~** nass werden; **"~
paint"** „frisch gestrichen"; **~ blanket** *n*
(*fig*) Triefel *m*; **~ suit** *n* Taucheranzug *m*

we've [wiːv] = **we have**

whack [wæk] *n* Schlag *m* ♦ *vt* schlagen

whale [weɪl] *n* Wal *m*

wharf [wɔːf] *n* Kai *m*

wharves [wɔːvz] *npl of* **wharf**

what [wɔt] *adj* **1** (*in questions*) welche(r, s),
was für ein(e); **what size is it?** welche
Größe ist das?

2 (*in exclamations*) was für ein(e); **what a
mess!** was für ein Durcheinander!

♦ *pron* (*interrogative/relative*) was; **what are
you doing?** was machst du gerade?; **what
are you talking about?** wovon reden Sie?;

what is it called? wie heißt das?; **what
about ...?** wie wärs mit ...?; **I saw what
you did** ich habe gesehen, was du
gemacht hast

♦ *excl* (*disbelieving*) wie, was; **what, no
coffee!** wie, kein Kaffee?; **I've crashed the
car - what!** ich hatte einen Autounfall -
was!

whatever [wɔt'ɛvər] *adj*: **~ book** welches
Buch auch immer ♦ *pron*: **do ~ is
necessary** tu, was (immer auch) nötig ist;
~ happens egal, was passiert; **nothing ~**
überhaupt *or* absolut gar nichts; **do ~ you
want** tu, was (immer) du (auch) möchtest;
no reason ~ *or* **whatsoever** überhaupt *or*
absolut kein Grund

whatsoever [wɔtsəu'ɛvər] *adj see* **whatever**

wheat [wiːt] *n* Weizen *m*

wheedle ['wiːdl] *vt*: **to ~ sb into doing sth**
jdn dazu überreden, etw zu tun; **to ~ sth
out of sb** jdm etw abluchsen

wheel [wiːl] *n* Rad *nt*; (*steering ~*) Lenkrad
nt; (*disc*) Scheibe *f* ♦ *vt* schieben; **~barrow**
n Schubkarren *m*; **~chair** *n* Rollstuhl *m*; **~
clamp** *n* (*AUT*) Parkkralle *f*

wheeze [wiːz] *vi* keuchen

when [wɛn] *adv* wann

♦ *conj* **1** (*at, during, after the time that*)
wenn; (*in past*) als; **she was reading when
I came in** sie las, als ich hereinkam; **be
careful when you cross the road** seien Sie
vorsichtig, wenn Sie über die Straße gehen

2 (*on, at which*) als; **on the day when I met
him** an dem Tag, an dem ich ihn traf

3 (*whereas*) wo ... doch

whenever [wɛn'ɛvər] *adv* wann (auch)
immer; (*every time that*) jedes Mal wenn
♦ *conj* (*any time*) wenn

where [weər] *adv* (*place*) wo; (*direction*)
wohin; **~ from** woher; **this is ~ ...** hier ...;
~abouts ['weərəbauts] *adv* wo ♦ *n*
Aufenthaltsort *m*; **nobody knows his
~abouts** niemand weiß, wo er ist; **~as**

[wɛəˈæz] *conj* während, wo ... doch; **~by** *pron* woran, wodurch, womit, wovon; **~upon** *conj* worauf, wonach; (*at beginning of sentence*) daraufhin; **~ver** [wɛərˈɛvəʳ] *adv* wo (immer)

wherewithal [ˈwɛəwɪðɔːl] *n* nötige (Geld)mittel *pl*

whet [wɛt] *vt* (*appetite*) anregen

whether [ˈwɛðəʳ] *conj* ob; **I don't know ~ to accept or not** ich weiß nicht, ob ich es annehmen soll oder nicht; **~ you go or not** ob du gehst oder nicht; **it's doubtful/unclear ~ ...** es ist zweifelhaft/nicht klar, ob ...

KEYWORD

which [wɪtʃ] *adj* **1** (*interrogative: direct, indirect*) welche(r, s); **which one?** welche(r, s)?

2: in which case in diesem Fall; **by which time** zu dieser Zeit

♦ *pron* **1** (*interrogative*) welche(r, s); (*of people also*) wer

2 (*relative*) der/die/das; (*referring to people*) was; **the apple which you ate/which is on the table** der Apfel, den du gegessen hast/der auf dem Tisch liegt; **he said he saw her, which is true** er sagte, er habe sie gesehen, was auch stimmt

whichever [wɪtʃˈɛvəʳ] *adj* welche(r, s) auch immer; (*no matter which*) ganz gleich welche(r, s); **~ book you take** welches Buch du auch nimmst; **~ car you prefer** egal welches Auto du vorziehst

whiff [wɪf] *n* Hauch *m*

while [waɪl] *n* Weile *f* ♦ *conj* während; **for a ~** eine Zeit lang; **~ away** *vt* (*time*) sich *dat* vertreiben

whim [wɪm] *n* Laune *f*

whimper [ˈwɪmpəʳ] *n* Wimmern *nt* ♦ *vi* wimmern

whimsical [ˈwɪmzɪkəl] *adj* launisch

whine [waɪn] *n* Gewinsel *nt*, Gejammer *nt* ♦ *vi* heulen, winseln

whip [wɪp] *n* Peitsche *f*; (*POL*) Fraktionsführer *m* ♦ *vt* (*beat*) peitschen; (*snatch*) reißen;

~ped cream *n* Schlagsahne *f*

whip-round [ˈwɪpraund] (*BRIT: inf*) *n* Geldsammlung *f*

whirl [wəːl] *n* Wirbel *m* ♦ *vt, vi* (herum)wirbeln; **~pool** *n* Wirbel *m*; **~wind** *n* Wirbelwind *m*

whirr [wəːʳ] *vi* schwirren, surren

whisk [wɪsk] *n* Schneebesen *m* ♦ *vt* (*cream etc*) schlagen; **to ~ sb away** *or* **off** mit jdm davon sausen

whisker [ˈwɪskəʳ] *n*: **~s** (*of animal*) Barthaare *pl*; (*of man*) Backenbart *m*

whisky [ˈwɪskɪ] (*US, IRISH* **whiskey**) *n* Whisky *m*

whisper [ˈwɪspəʳ] *n* Flüstern *nt* ♦ *vt, vi* flüstern

whistle [ˈwɪsl] *n* Pfiff *m*; (*instrument*) Pfeife *f* ♦ *vt, vi* pfeifen

white [waɪt] *n* Weiß *nt*; (*of egg*) Eiweiß *nt* ♦ *adj* weiß; **~ coffee** (*BRIT*) *n* Kaffee *m* mit Milch; **~-collar worker** *n* Angestellte(r) *m*; **~ elephant** *n* (*fig*) Fehlinvestition *f*; **~ lie** *n* Notlüge *f*; **~ paper** *n* (*POL*) Weißbuch *nt*; **~wash** *n* (*paint*) Tünche *f*; (*fig*) Ehrenrettung *f* ♦ *vt* weißen, tünchen; (*fig*) rein waschen

whiting [ˈwaɪtɪŋ] *n* Weißfisch *m*

Whitsun [ˈwɪtsn] *n* Pfingsten *nt*

whittle [ˈwɪtl] *vt*: **to ~ away** *or* **down** stutzen, verringern

whizz [wɪz] *vi*: **to ~ past** *or* **by** vorbeizischen, vorbeischwirren; **~ kid** (*inf*) *n* Kanone *f*

KEYWORD

who [huː] *pron* **1** (*interrogative*) wer; (*acc*) wen; (*dat*) wem; **who is it?, who's there?** wer ist da?

2 (*relative*) der/die/das; **the woman/man who spoke to me** die Frau/der Mann, die/der mit mir sprach

whodu(n)nit [huːˈdʌnɪt] (*inf*) *n* Krimi *m*

whoever [huːˈɛvəʳ] *pron* wer/wen/wem auch immer; (*no matter who*) ganz gleich wer/wen/wem

whole [həul] *adj* ganz ♦ *n* Ganze(s) *nt*; **the ~ of the town** die ganze Stadt; **on the ~** im

Großen und Ganzen; **as a ~** im Großen und Ganzen; **~food(s)** ['həulfuːd(z)] *n(pl)* Vollwertkost *f*; **~hearted** [həul'hɑːtɪd] *adj* rückhaltlos; **~heartedly** *adv* von ganzem Herzen; **~meal** *adj* (*bread, flour*) Vollkorn-; **~sale** *n* Großhandel *m* ♦ *adj* (*trade*) Großhandels-; (*destruction*) Massen-; **~saler** *n* Großhändler *m*; **~some** *adj* bekömmlich, gesund; **~wheat** *adj* = **wholemeal**

wholly ['həulɪ] *adv* ganz, völlig

KEYWORD

whom [huːm] *pron* **1** (*interrogative: acc*) wen; (: *dat*) wem; **whom did you see?** wen haben Sie gesehen?; **to whom did you give it?** wem haben Sie es gegeben?
2 (*relative: acc*) den/die/das; (: *dat*) dem/der/dem; **the man whom I saw/to whom I spoke** der Mann, den ich sah/mit dem ich sprach

whooping cough ['huːpɪŋ-] *n* Keuchhusten *m*
whore [hɔːʳ] *n* Hure *f*
whose [huːz] *adj* (*possessive: interrogative*) wessen; (: *relative*) dessen; (*after f and pl*) deren ♦ *pron* wessen; **~ book is this?, ~ is this book?** wessen Buch ist dies?; **~ is this?** wem gehört das?

KEYWORD

why [waɪ] *adv* warum, weshalb
♦ *conj* warum, weshalb; **that's not why I'm here** ich bin nicht deswegen hier; **that's the reason why** deshalb
♦ *excl* (*expressing surprise, shock*) na so was; (*explaining*) also dann; **why, it's you!** na so was, du bist es!

wick [wɪk] *n* Docht *m*
wicked ['wɪkɪd] *adj* böse
wicker ['wɪkəʳ] *n* (*also:* **~work**) Korbgeflecht *nt*
wicket ['wɪkɪt] *n* Tor *nt*, Dreistab *m*
wide [waɪd] *adj* breit; (*plain*) weit; (*in firing*) daneben ♦ *adv:* **to open ~** weit öffnen; **to shoot ~** danebenschießen; **~-angle lens** *n*

Weitwinkelobjektiv *nt*; **~-awake** *adj* hellwach; **~ly** *adv* weit; (*known*) allgemein; **~n** *vt* erweitern; **~ open** *adj* weit geöffnet; **~spread** *adj* weitverbreitet, weit verbreitet

widow ['wɪdəu] *n* Witwe *f*; **~ed** *adj* verwitwet; **~er** *n* Witwer *m*
width [wɪdθ] *n* Breite *f*, Weite *f*
wield [wiːld] *vt* schwingen, handhaben
wife [waɪf] (*pl* **wives**) *n* (Ehe)frau *f*, Gattin *f*
wig [wɪg] *n* Perücke *f*
wiggle ['wɪgl] *n* Wackeln *nt* ♦ *vt* wackeln mit
♦ *vi* wackeln
wild [waɪld] *adj* wild; (*violent*) heftig; (*plan, idea*) verrückt; **~erness** ['wɪldənɪs] *n* Wildnis *f*, Wüste *f*; **~-goose chase** *n* (*fig*) fruchtlose(s) Unternehmen *nt*; **~life** *n* Tierwelt *f*; **~ly** *adv* wild, ungestüm; (*exaggerated*) irrsinnig; **~s** *npl:* **the ~s** die Wildnis *f*
wilful ['wɪlful] (*US* **willful**) *adj* (*intended*) vorsätzlich; (*obstinate*) eigensinnig

KEYWORD

will [wɪl] *aux vb* **1** (*forms future tense*) werden; **I will finish it tomorrow** ich mache es morgen zu Ende
2 (*in conjectures, predictions*): **he will** *or* **he'll be there by now** er dürfte jetzt da sein; **that will be the postman** das wird der Postbote sein
3 (*in commands, requests, offers*): **will you be quiet!** sei endlich still!; **will you help me?** hilfst du mir?; **will you have a cup of tea?** trinken Sie eine Tasse Tee?; **I won't put up with it!** das lasse ich mir nicht gefallen!
♦ *vt* wollen
♦ *n* Wille *m*; (*JUR*) Testament *nt*

willing ['wɪlɪŋ] *adj* gewillt, bereit; **~ly** *adv* bereitwillig, gern; **~ness** *n* (Bereit)willigkeit *f*
willow ['wɪləu] *n* Weide *f*
willpower ['wɪl'pauəʳ] *n* Willenskraft *f*
willy-nilly ['wɪlɪ'nɪlɪ] *adv* einfach so
wilt [wɪlt] *vi* (ver)welken
wily ['waɪlɪ] *adj* gerissen
win [wɪn] (*pt, pp* **won**) *n* Sieg *m* ♦ *vt, vi*

gewinnen; **to ~ sb over** *or* **round** jdn gewinnen, jdn dazu bringen

wince [wɪns] *vi* zusammenzucken

winch [wɪntʃ] *n* Winde *f*

wind¹ [wɪnd] *n* Wind *m*; (*MED*) Blähungen *pl*

wind² [waɪnd] (*pt, pp* **wound**) *vt* (*rope*) winden; (*bandage*) wickeln ♦ *vi* (*turn*) sich winden; **~ up** *vt* (*clock*) aufziehen; (*debate*) (ab)schließen

windfall ['wɪndfɔ:l] *n* unverhoffte(r) Glücksfall *m*

winding ['waɪndɪŋ] *adj* (*road*) gewunden

wind instrument ['wɪnd-] *n* Blasinstrument *nt*

windmill ['wɪndmɪl] *n* Windmühle *f*

window ['wɪndəu] *n* Fenster *nt*; **~ box** *n* Blumenkasten *m*; **~ cleaner** *n* Fensterputzer *m*; **~ envelope** *n* Fensterbriefumschlag *m*; **~ ledge** *n* Fenstersims *m*; **~ pane** *n* Fensterscheibe *f*; **~-shopping** *n* Schaufensterbummel *m*; **to go ~-shopping** einen Schaufensterbummel machen; **~sill** *n* Fensterbank *f*

wind: **~pipe** *n* Luftröhre *f*; **~ power** *n* Windenergie *f*; **~screen** (*BRIT*) *n* Windschutzscheibe *f*; **~screen washer** *n* Scheibenwaschanlage *f*; **~screen wiper** *n* Scheibenwischer *m*; **~shield** (*US*) *n* = **windscreen;** **~swept** *adj* vom Wind gepeitscht; (*person*) zerzaust; **~y** *adj* windig

wine [waɪn] *n* Wein *m*; **~ bar** *n* Weinlokal *nt*; **~ cellar** *n* Weinkeller *m*; **~ glass** *n* Weinglas *nt*; **~ list** *n* Weinkarte *f*; **~ merchant** *n* Weinhändler *m*; **~ tasting** *n* Weinprobe *f*; **~ waiter** *n* Weinkellner *m*

wing [wɪŋ] *n* Flügel *m*; (*MIL*) Gruppe *f*; **~s** *npl* (*THEAT*) Seitenkulisse *f*; **~er** *n* (*SPORT*) Flügelstürmer *m*

wink [wɪŋk] *n* Zwinkern *nt* ♦ *vi* zwinkern, blinzeln

winner ['wɪnəʳ] *n* Gewinner *m*; (*SPORT*) Sieger *m*

winning ['wɪnɪŋ] *adj* (*team*) siegreich, Sieger-; (*goal*) entscheidend; **~ post** *n* Ziel *nt*; **~s** *npl* Gewinn *m*

winter ['wɪntəʳ] *n* Winter *m* ♦ *adj* (*clothes*) Winter- ♦ *vi* überwintern; **~ sports** *npl*

Wintersport *m*; **wintry** ['wɪntrɪ] *adj* Winter-, winterlich

wipe [waɪp] *n*: **to give sth a ~** etw (ab)wischen ♦ *vt* wischen; **~ off** *vt* abwischen; **~ out** *vt* (*debt*) löschen; (*destroy*) auslöschen; **~ up** *vt* aufwischen

wire ['waɪəʳ] *n* Draht *m*; (*telegram*) Telegramm *nt* ♦ *vt* telegrafieren; **to ~ sb** jdm telegrafieren; **~less** ['waɪəlɪs] (*BRIT*) *n* Radio(apparat *m*) *nt*

wiring ['waɪərɪŋ] *n* elektrische Leitungen *pl*

wiry ['waɪərɪ] *adj* drahtig

wisdom ['wɪzdəm] *n* Weisheit *f*; (*of decision*) Klugheit *f*; **~ tooth** *n* Weisheitszahn *m*

wise [waɪz] *adj* klug, weise ♦ *suffix*: **timewise** zeitlich gesehen

wisecrack ['waɪzkræk] *n* Witzelei *f*

wish [wɪʃ] *n* Wunsch *m* ♦ *vt* wünschen; **best ~es** (*on birthday etc*) alles Gute; **with best ~es** herzliche Grüße; **to ~ sb goodbye** jdn verabschieden; **he ~ed me well** er wünschte mir Glück; **to ~ to do sth** etw tun wollen; **~ for** *vt fus* sich *dat* wünschen; **~ful thinking** *n* Wunschdenken *nt*

wishy-washy ['wɪʃɪ'wɒʃɪ] (*inf*) *adj* (*ideas, argument*) verschwommen

wisp [wɪsp] *n* (*Haar*)strähne *f*; (*of smoke*) Wölkchen *nt*

wistful ['wɪstful] *adj* sehnsüchtig

wit [wɪt] *n* (*also:* **~s**) Verstand *m no pl*; (*amusing ideas*) Witz *m*; (*person*) Witzbold *m*

witch [wɪtʃ] *n* Hexe *f*; **~craft** *n* Hexerei *f*

KEYWORD

with [wɪð, wɪθ] *prep* **1** (*accompanying, in the company of*) mit; **we stayed with friends** wir übernachteten bei Freunden; **I'll be with you in a minute** einen Augenblick, ich bin sofort da; **I'm not with you** (*I don't understand*) das verstehe ich nicht; **to be with it** (*inf:* up-to-date) auf dem Laufenden sein; (*: alert*) (voll) da sein (*inf*)
2 (*descriptive, indicating manner etc*) mit; **the man with the grey hat** der Mann mit dem grauen Hut; **red with anger** rot vor Wut

withdraw [wɪθ'drɔ:] (*irreg: like* **draw**) *vt*

zurückziehen; (*money*) abheben; (*remark*) zurücknehmen ♦ *vi* sich zurückziehen; **~al** *n* Zurückziehung *f*; Abheben *nt*; Zurücknahme *f*; **~n** *adj* (*person*) verschlossen

wither ['wɪðər] *vi* (ver)welken

withhold [wɪθ'həʊld] (*irreg: like* hold) *vt*: to ~ **sth (from sb)** (jdm) etw vorenthalten

within [wɪð'ɪn] *prep* innerhalb +*gen* ♦ *adv* innen; ~ **sight of** in Sichtweite von; ~ **the week** innerhalb dieser Woche; ~ **a mile of** weniger als eine Meile von

without [wɪð'aʊt] *prep* ohne; ~ **sleeping** *etc* ohne zu schlafen *etc*

withstand [wɪθ'stænd] (*irreg: like* stand) *vt* widerstehen +*dat*

witness ['wɪtnɪs] *n* Zeuge *m*, Zeugin *f* ♦ *vt* (*see*) sehen, miterleben; (*document*) beglaubigen; ~ **box** *n* Zeugenstand *m*; ~ **stand** (*US*) *n* Zeugenstand *m*

witticism ['wɪtɪsɪzəm] *n* witzige Bemerkung *f*

witty ['wɪtɪ] *adj* witzig, geistreich

wives [waɪvz] *pl of* **wife**

wk *abbr* = **week**

wobble ['wɒbl] *vi* wackeln

woe [wəʊ] *n* Kummer *m*

woke [wəʊk] *pt of* **wake**

woken ['wəʊkn] *pp of* **wake**

wolf [wʊlf] (*pl* wolves) *n* Wolf *m*

woman ['wʊmən] (*pl* women) *n* Frau *f*; ~ **doctor** *n* Ärztin *f*; **~ly** *adj* weiblich

womb [wuːm] *n* Gebärmutter *f*

women ['wɪmɪn] *npl of* **woman**; **~'s lib** (*inf*) *n* Frauenrechtsbewegung *f*

won [wʌn] *pt, pp of* **win**

wonder ['wʌndər] *n* (*marvel*) Wunder *nt*; (*surprise*) Staunen *nt*, Verwunderung *f* ♦ *vi* sich wundern ♦ *vt*: **I ~ whether ...** ich frage mich, ob ...; **it's no ~ that** es ist kein Wunder, dass; **to ~ at** sich wundern über +*acc*; **to ~ about** sich Gedanken machen über +*acc*; **~ful** *adj* wunderbar, herrlich

won't [wəʊnt] = **will not**

woo [wuː] *vt* (*audience etc*) umwerben

wood [wʊd] *n* Holz *nt*; (*forest*) Wald *m*; ~ **carving** *n* Holzschnitzerei *f*; **~ed** *adj* bewaldet; **~en** *adj* (*also fig*) hölzern;

~pecker *n* Specht *m*; **~wind** *n* Blasinstrumente *pl*; **~work** *n* Holzwerk *nt*; (*craft*) Holzarbeiten *pl*; **~worm** *n* Holzwurm *m*

wool [wʊl] *n* Wolle *f*; **to pull the ~ over sb's eyes** (*fig*) jdm Sand in die Augen streuen; **~len** (*US* woolen) *adj* Woll-; **~lens** *npl* Wollsachen *pl*; **~ly** (*US* wooly) *adj* wollig; (*fig*) schwammig

word [wəːd] *n* Wort *nt*; (*news*) Bescheid *m* ♦ *vt* formulieren; **in other ~s** anders gesagt; **to break/keep one's ~** sein Wort brechen/halten; **~ing** *n* Wortlaut *m*; ~ **processing** *n* Textverarbeitung *f*; ~ **processor** *n* Textverarbeitung *f*

wore [wɔːʳ] *pt of* **wear**

work [wəːk] *n* Arbeit *f*; (*ART, LITER*) Werk *nt* ♦ *vi* arbeiten; (*machine*) funktionieren; (*medicine*) wirken; (*succeed*) klappen; **~s** *n sg* (*BRIT: factory*) Fabrik *f*, Werk *nt* ♦ *npl* (*of watch*) Werk *nt*; **to be out of ~** arbeitslos sein; **in ~ing order** in betriebsfähigem Zustand; ~ **loose** *vi* sich lockern; ~ **on** *vi* weiterarbeiten ♦ *vt fus* arbeiten an +*dat*; (*influence*) bearbeiten; ~ **out** *vi* (*sum*) aufgehen; (*plan*) klappen ♦ *vt* (*problem*) lösen; (*plan*) ausarbeiten; **it ~s out at £100** das gibt *or* macht £100; ~ **up** *vt*: **to get ~ed up** sich aufregen; **~able** *adj* (*soil*) bearbeitbar; (*plan*) ausführbar; **~aholic** [wəːkə'hɒlɪk] *n* Arbeitssüchtige(r) *f(m)*; **~er** *n* Arbeiter(in) *m(f)*; ~ **experience** *n* Praktikum *nt*; **~force** *n* Arbeiterschaft *f*; **~ing class** *n* Arbeiterklasse *f*; **~ing-class** *adj* Arbeiter-; **~ing-class** *adj* Arbeiter-; **~man** (*irreg*) *n* Arbeiter *m*; **~manship** *n* Arbeit *f*, Ausführung *f*; **~sheet** *n* Arbeitsblatt *nt*; **~shop** *n* Werkstatt *f*; ~ **station** *n* Arbeitsplatz *m*; **~-to-rule** (*BRIT*) *n* Dienst *m* nach Vorschrift

world [wəːld] *n* Welt *f*; **to think the ~ of sb** große Stücke auf jdn halten; **~ly** *adj* weltlich, irdisch; **~-wide** *adj* weltweit

World-Wide Web ['wəːld'waɪd-] *n* World Wide Web *nt*

worm [wəːm] *n* Wurm *m*

worn [wɔːn] *pp of* **wear** ♦ *adj* (*clothes*) abgetragen; **~-out** *adj* (*object*) abgenutzt;

(*person*) völlig erschöpft

worried ['wʌrɪd] *adj* besorgt, beunruhigt

worry ['wʌrɪ] *n* Sorge *f* ♦ *vt* beunruhigen ♦ *vi* (*feel uneasy*) sich sorgen, sich *dat* Gedanken machen; **~ing** *adj* beunruhigend

worse [wəːs] *adj* schlechter, schlimmer ♦ *adv* schlimmer, ärger ♦ *n* Schlimmere(s) *nt*, Schlechtere(s) *nt*; **a change for the ~** eine Verschlechterung; **~n** *vt* verschlimmern ♦ *vi* sich verschlechtern; **~ off** *adj* (*fig*) schlechter dran

worship ['wəːʃɪp] *n* Verehrung *f* ♦ *vt* anbeten; **Your W~** (*BRIT: to mayor*) Herr/ Frau Bürgermeister; (: *to judge*) Euer Ehren

worst [wəːst] *adj* schlimmste(r, s), schlechteste(r, s) ♦ *adv* am schlimmsten, am ärgsten ♦ *n* Schlimmste(s) *nt*, Ärgste(s) *nt*; **at ~** schlimmstenfalls

worth [wəːθ] *n* Wert *m* ♦ *adj* wert; **it's ~ it** es lohnt sich; **to be ~ one's while (to do sth)** die Mühe wert sein(, etw zu tun); **~less** *adj* wertlos; (*person*) nichtsnutzig; **~while** *adj* lohnend, der Mühe wert; **~y** *adj* wert, würdig

<u>*KEYWORD*</u>

would [wʊd] *aux vb* **1** (*conditional tense*): **if you asked him he would do it** wenn du ihn fragtest, würde er es tun; **if you had asked him he would have done it** wenn du ihn gefragt hättest, hätte er es getan

2 (*in offers, invitations, requests*): **would you like a biscuit?** möchten Sie ein Plätzchen?; **would you ask him to come in?** würden Sie ihn bitte hineinbitten?

3 (*in indirect speech*): **I said I would do it** ich sagte, ich würde es tun

4 (*emphatic*): **it WOULD have to snow today!** es musste ja ausgerechnet heute schneien!

5 (*insistence*): **she wouldn't behave** sie wollte sich partout nicht anständig benehmen

6 (*conjecture*): **it would have been midnight** es mag ungefähr Mitternacht gewesen sein; **it would seem so** es sieht wohl so aus

7 (*indicating habit*): **he would go there on Mondays** er ging jeden Montag dorthin

would-be ['wʊdbiː] (*pej*) *adj* Möchtegern-

wouldn't ['wʊdnt] = **would not**

wound[1] [wuːnd] *n* (*also fig*) Wunde *f* ♦ *vt* verwunden, verletzen (*also fig*)

wound[2] [waʊnd] *pt, pp of* **wind**[2]

wove [wəʊv] *pt of* **weave**; **~n** *pp of* **weave**

wrangle ['ræŋgl] *n* Streit *m* ♦ *vi* sich zanken

wrap [ræp] *vt* einwickeln; **~ up** *vt* einwickeln; (*deal*) abschließen; **~per** *n* Umschlag *m*, Schutzhülle *f*; **~ping paper** *n* Einwickelpapier *nt*

wrath [rɔθ] *n* Zorn *m*

wreak [riːk] *vt* (*havoc*) anrichten; (*vengeance*) üben

wreath [riːθ] *n* Kranz *m*

wreck [rɛk] *n* (*ship*) Wrack *nt*; (*sth ruined*) Ruine *f* ♦ *vt* zerstören; **~age** *n* Trümmer *pl*

wren [rɛn] *n* Zaunkönig *m*

wrench [rɛntʃ] *n* (*spanner*) Schraubenschlüssel *m*; (*twist*) Ruck *m* ♦ *vt* reißen, zerren; **to ~ sth from sb** jdm etw entreißen *or* entwinden

wrestle ['rɛsl] *vi*: **to ~ (with sb)** (mit jdm) ringen; **~r** *n* Ringer(in) *m(f)*; **wrestling** *n* Ringen *nt*

wretched ['rɛtʃɪd] *adj* (*inf*) verflixt

wriggle ['rɪgl] *n* Schlängeln *nt* ♦ *vi* sich winden

wring [rɪŋ] (*pt, pp* **wrung**) *vt* wringen

wrinkle ['rɪŋkl] *n* Falte *f*, Runzel *f* ♦ *vt* runzeln ♦ *vi* sich runzeln; (*material*) knittern; **~d** *adj* faltig, schrumpelig

wrist [rɪst] *n* Handgelenk *nt*; **~watch** *n* Armbanduhr *f*

writ [rɪt] *n* gerichtliche(r) Befehl *m*

write [raɪt] (*pt* **wrote**, *pp* **written**) *vt, vi* schreiben; **~ down** *vt* aufschreiben; **~ off** *vt* (*dismiss*) abschreiben; **~ out** *vt* (*essay*) abschreiben; (*cheque*) ausstellen; **~ up** *vt* schreiben; **~-off** *n*: **it is a ~-off** das kann man abschreiben; **~r** *n* Schriftsteller *m*

writhe [raɪð] *vi* sich winden

writing ['raɪtɪŋ] *n* (*act*) Schreiben *nt*; (*handwriting*) (Hand)schrift *f*; **in ~** schriftlich;

~ **paper** n Schreibpapier nt

written ['rɪtn] pp of **write**

wrong [rɒŋ] adj (incorrect) falsch; (morally) unrecht ♦ n Unrecht nt ♦ vt Unrecht tun +dat; **he was ~ in doing that** es war nicht recht von ihm, das zu tun; **you are ~ about that, you've got it ~** da hast du Unrecht; **to be in the ~** im Unrecht sein; **what's ~ with your leg?** was ist mit deinem Bein los?; **to go ~** (plan) schief gehen; (person) einen Fehler machen; ~**ful** adj unrechtmäßig; ~**ly** adv falsch; (accuse) zu Unrecht

wrong number n (TEL): **you've got the ~** Sie sind falsch verbunden

wrote [rəʊt] pt of **write**

wrought [rɔːt] adj: ~ **iron** Schmiedeeisen nt

wrung [rʌŋ] pt, pp of **wring**

wry [raɪ] adj ironisch

wt. abbr = **weight**

WWW n abbr (= World Wide Web): **the ~** das WWW.

X, x

Xmas ['eksməs] n abbr = **Christmas**

X-ray ['eksreɪ] n Röntgenaufnahme f ♦ vt röntgen; ~~**s** npl Röntgenstrahlen pl

xylophone ['zaɪləfəʊn] n Xylofon nt, Xylophon nt

Y, y

yacht [jɒt] n Jacht f; ~**ing** n (Sport)segeln nt; ~**sman** (irreg) n Sportsegler m

Yank [jæŋk] (inf) n Ami m

yap [jæp] vi (dog) kläffen

yard [jɑːd] n Hof m; (measure) (englische) Elle f, Yard nt (0,91 m); ~**stick** n (fig) Maßstab m

yarn [jɑːn] n (thread) Garn nt; (story) (Seemanns)garn nt

yawn [jɔːn] n Gähnen nt ♦ vi gähnen; ~**ing** adj (gap) gähnend

yd. abbr = **yard(s)**

yeah [jeə] (inf) adv ja

year [jɪəʳ] n Jahr nt; **to be 8 ~s old** acht Jahre alt sein; **an eight-year-old child** ein achtjähriges Kind; ~**ly** adj, adv jährlich

yearn [jɜːn] vi: **to ~ (for)** sich sehnen (nach); ~**ing** n Verlangen nt, Sehnsucht f

yeast [jiːst] n Hefe f

yell [jel] n gellende(r) Schrei m ♦ vi laut schreien

yellow ['jeləʊ] adj gelb ♦ n Gelb nt

yelp [jelp] n Gekläff nt ♦ vi kläffen

yes [jes] adv ja ♦ n Ja nt, Jawort nt; **to say ~** Ja or ja sagen; **to answer ~** mit Ja antworten

yesterday ['jestədɪ] adv gestern ♦ n Gestern nt; ~ **morning/evening** gestern den ganzen Tag; **the day before ~** vorgestern

yet [jet] adv noch; (in question) schon; (up to now) bis jetzt ♦ conj doch, dennoch; **it is not finished ~** es ist noch nicht fertig; **the best ~** das bisher Beste; **as ~** bis jetzt; (in past) bis dahin

yew [juː] n Eibe f

yield [jiːld] n Ertrag m ♦ vt (result, crop) hervorbringen; (interest, profit) abwerfen; (concede) abtreten ♦ vi nachgeben; (MIL) sich ergeben; **"~"** (US: AUT) „Vorfahrt gewähren"

YMCA n abbr (= Young Men's Christian Association) CVJM m

yob [jɒb] (BRIT: inf) n Halbstarke(r) f(m)

yoga ['jəʊɡə] n Joga m

yog(h)urt ['jəʊɡət] n Jog(h)urt m

yoke [jəʊk] n (also fig) Joch nt

yolk [jəʊk] n Eidotter m, Eigelb nt

KEYWORD
---

you [juː] pron **1** (subj, in comparisons: familiar form: sg) du; (: pl) ihr; (in letters also) du, ihr; (: polite form) Sie; **you Germans** ihr Deutschen; **she's younger than you** sie ist jünger als du/Sie

2 (direct object, after prep +acc: familiar form: sg) dich; (: pl) euch; (in letters also) dich, euch; (: polite form) Sie; **I know you** ich kenne dich/euch/Sie

3 (*indirect object, after prep +dat: familiar form: sg*) dir; (: *pl*) euch; (*in letters also*) dir, euch; (: *polite form*) Ihnen; **I gave it to you** ich gab es dir/euch/Ihnen
4 (*impers: one: subj*) man; (: *direct object*) einen; (: *indirect object*) einem; **fresh air does you good** frische Luft tut gut

you'd [juːd] = **you had**; **you would**
you'll [juːl] = **you will**; **you shall**
young [jʌŋ] *adj* jung ♦ *npl:* **the ~** die Jungen *pl*; **~ster** *n* Junge *m*, junge(r) Bursche *m*, junge(s) Mädchen *nt*
your [jɔːʳ] *adj* (*familiar: sg*) dein; (: *pl*) euer, eure *pl*; (*polite*) Ihr; *see also* **my**
you're [juəʳ] = **you are**
yours [jɔːz] *pron* (*familiar: sg*) deine(r, s); (: *pl*) eure(r, s); (*polite*) Ihre(r, s); *see also* **mine²**
yourself [jɔːˈself] *pron* (*emphatic*) selbst; (*familiar: sg: acc*) dich (selbst); (: *dat*) dir (selbst); (: *pl*) euch (selbst); (*polite*) sich (selbst); *see also* **oneself**; **yourselves** *pl pron* (*reflexive: familiar*) euch; (: *polite*) sich; (*emphatic*) selbst; *see also* **oneself**
youth [juːθ] *n* Jugend *f*; (*young man*) junge(r) Mann *m*; **~s** *npl* (*young people*) Jugendliche *pl*; **~ club** *n* Jugendzentrum *nt*; **~ful** *adj* jugendlich; **~ hostel** *n* Jugendherberge *f*
you've [juːv] = **you have**
YTS (*BRIT*) *n abbr* (= *Youth Training Scheme*) staatliches Förderprogramm für arbeitslose Jugendliche
Yugoslav [ˈjuːgəʊslɑːv] *adj* jugoslawisch ♦ *n* Jugoslawe *m*, Jugoslawin *f*; **~ia**

[juːgəʊˈslɑːvɪə] *n* Jugoslawien *nt*
yuppie [ˈjʌpɪ] (*inf*) *n* Yuppie *m* ♦ *adj* yuppiehaft, Yuppie-
YWCA *n abbr* (= *Young Women's Christian Association*) CVJF *m*

Z, z

zany [ˈzeɪnɪ] *adj* (*ideas, sense of humour*) verrückt
zap [zæp] *vt* (*COMPUT*) löschen
zeal [ziːl] *n* Eifer *m*; **~ous** [ˈzeləs] *adj* eifrig
zebra [ˈziːbrə] *n* Zebra *nt*; **~ crossing** (*BRIT*) *n* Zebrastreifen *m*
zero [ˈzɪərəʊ] *n* Null *f*; (*on scale*) Nullpunkt *m*
zest [zest] *n* Begeisterung *f*
zigzag [ˈzɪgzæg] *n* Zickzack *m*
Zimbabwe [zɪmˈbɑːbwɪ] *n* Zimbabwe *nt*
Zimmer frame [ˈzɪmə-] *n* Laufgestell *nt*
zip [zɪp] *n* Reißverschluss *m* ♦ *vt* (*also:* **~ up**) den Reißverschluss zumachen +*gen*
zip code (*US*) *n* Postleitzahl *f*
zipper [ˈzɪpəʳ] (*US*) *n* Reißverschluss *m*
zit [zɪt] (*inf*) *n* Pickel *m*
zodiac [ˈzəʊdɪæk] *n* Tierkreis *m*
zombie [ˈzɒmbɪ] *n:* **like a ~** (*fig*) wie im Tran
zone [zəʊn] *n* (*also MIL*) Zone *f*, Gebiet *nt*; (*in town*) Bezirk *m*
zoo [zuː] *n* Zoo *m*
zoology [zuːˈɒlədʒɪ] *n* Zoologie *f*
zoom [zuːm] *vi:* **to ~ past** vorbeisausen; **~ lens** *n* Zoomobjektiv *nt*
zucchini [zuːˈkiːnɪ] (*US*) *npl* Zucchini *pl*

GERMAN IRREGULAR VERBS

*with 'sein'

infinitive	present indicative (2nd, 3rd sg)	imperfect	past participle
aufschrecken*	schrickst auf, schrickt auf	schrak *or* schreckte auf	aufgeschreckt
ausbedingen	bedingst aus, bedingt aus	bedang *or* bedingte aus	ausbedungen
backen	bäckst, bäckt	backte *or* buk	gebacken
befehlen	befiehlst, befiehlt	befahl	befohlen
beginnen	beginnst, beginnt	begann	begonnen
beißen	beißt, beißt	biss	gebissen
bergen	birgst, birgt	barg	geborgen
bersten*	birst, birst	barst	geborsten
bescheißen*	bescheißt, bescheißt	beschiss	beschissen
bewegen	bewegst, bewegt	bewog	bewogen
biegen	biegst, biegt	bog	gebogen
bieten	bietest, bietet	bot	geboten
binden	bindest, bindet	band	gebunden
bitten	bittest, bittet	bat	gebeten
blasen	bläst, bläst	blies	geblasen
bleiben*	bleibst, bleibt	blieb	geblieben
braten	brätst, brät	briet	gebraten
brechen*	brichst, bricht	brach	gebrochen
brennen	brennst, brennt	brannte	gebrannt
bringen	bringst, bringt	brachte	gebracht
denken	denkst, denkt	dachte	gedacht
dreschen	drisch(e)st, drischt	drosch	gedroschen
dringen*	dringst, dringt	drang	gedrungen
dürfen	darfst, darf	durfte	gedurft
empfehlen	empfiehlst, empfiehlt	empfahl	empfohlen
erbleichen*	erbleichst, erbleicht	erbleichte	erblichen
erlöschen*	erlischt, erlischt	erlosch	erloschen
erschrecken*	erschrickst, erschrickt	erschrak	erschrocken
essen	isst, isst	aß	gegessen
fahren*	fährst, fährt	fuhr	gefahren
fallen*	fällst, fällt	fiel	gefallen

infinitive	present indicative (2nd, 3rd sg)	imperfect	past participle
fangen	fängst, fängt	fing	gefangen
fechten	fichtst, ficht	focht	gefochten
finden	findest, findet	fand	gefunden
flechten	flichtst, flicht	flocht	geflochten
fliegen*	fliegst, fliegt	flog	geflogen
fliehen*	fliehst, flieht	floh	geflohen
fließen*	fließt, fließt	floss	geflossen
fressen	frisst, frisst	fraß	gefressen
frieren	frierst, friert	fror	gefroren
gären*	gärst, gärt	gor	gegoren
gebären	gebierst, gebiert	gebar	geboren
geben	gibst, gibt	gab	gegeben
gedeihen*	gedeihst, gedeiht	gedieh	gediehen
gehen*	gehst, geht	ging	gegangen
gelingen*	——, gelingt	gelang	gelungen
gelten	giltst, gilt	galt	gegolten
genesen*	gene(se)st, genest	genas	genesen
genießen	genießt, genießt	genoss	genossen
geraten*	gerätst, gerät	geriet	geraten
geschehen*	——, geschieht	geschah	geschehen
gewinnen	gewinnst, gewinnt	gewann	gewonnen
gießen	gießt, gießt	goss	gegossen
gleichen	gleichst, gleicht	glich	geglichen
gleiten*	gleitest, gleitet	glitt	geglitten
glimmen	glimmst, glimmt	glomm	geglommen
graben	gräbst, gräbt	grub	gegraben
greifen	greifst, greift	griff	gegriffen
haben	hast, hat	hatte	gehabt
halten	hältst, hält	hielt	gehalten
hängen	hängst, hängt	hing	gehangen
hauen	haust, haut	haute	gehauen
heben	hebst, hebt	hob	gehoben
heißen	heißt, heißt	hieß	geheißen
helfen	hilfst, hilft	half	geholfen
kennen	kennst, kennt	kannte	gekannt
klimmen*	klimmst, klimmt	klomm	geklommen
klingen	klingst, klingt	klang	geklungen
kneifen	kneifst, kneift	kniff	gekniffen
kommen*	kommst, kommt	kam	gekommen
können	kannst, kann	konnte	gekonnt
kriechen*	kriechst, kriecht	kroch	gekrochen
laden	lädst, lädt	lud	geladen
lassen	lässt, lässt	ließ	gelassen
laufen*	läufst, läuft	lief	gelaufen
leiden	leidest, leidet	litt	gelitten

infinitive	present indicative (2nd, 3rd sg)	imperfect	past participle
leihen	leihst, leiht	lieh	geliehen
lesen	liest, liest	las	gelesen
liegen*	liegst, liegt	lag	gelegen
lügen	lügst, lügt	log	gelogen
mahlen	mahlst, mahlt	mahlte	gemahlen
meiden	meidest, meidet	mied	gemieden
melken	melkst, melkt	melkte	gemolken
messen	misst, misst	maß	gemessen
misslingen*	——, misslingt	misslang	misslungen
mögen	magst, mag	mochte	gemocht
müssen	musst, muss	musste	gemusst
nehmen	nimmst, nimmt	nahm	genommen
nennen	nennst, nennt	nannte	genannt
pfeifen	pfeifst, pfeift	pfiff	gepfiffen
preisen	preist, preist	pries	gepriesen
quellen*	quillst, quillt	quoll	gequollen
raten	rätst, rät	riet	geraten
reiben	reibst, reibt	rieb	gerieben
reißen*	reißt, reißt	riss	gerissen
reiten*	reitest, reitet	ritt	geritten
rennen*	rennst, rennt	rannte	gerannt
riechen	riechst, riecht	roch	gerochen
ringen	ringst, ringt	rang	gerungen
rinnen*	rinnst, rinnt	rann	geronnen
rufen	rufst, ruft	rief	gerufen
salzen	salzt, salzt	salzte	gesalzen
saufen	säufst, säuft	soff	gesoffen
saugen	saugst, saugt	sog	gesogen
schaffen	schaffst, schafft	schuf	geschaffen
scheiden	scheidest, scheidet	schied	geschieden
scheinen	scheinst, scheint	schien	geschienen
schelten	schiltst, schilt	schalt	gescholten
scheren	scherst, schert	schor	geschoren
schieben	schiebst, schiebt	schob	geschoben
schießen	schießt, schießt	schoss	geschossen
schinden	schindest, schindet	schindete	geschunden
schlafen	schläfst, schläft	schlief	geschlafen
schlagen	schlägst, schlägt	schlug	geschlagen
schleichen*	schleichst, schleicht	schlich	geschlichen
schleifen	schleifst, schleift	schliff	geschliffen
schließen	schließt, schließt	schloss	geschlossen
schlingen	schlingst, schlingt	schlang	geschlungen

infinitive	present indicative (2nd, 3rd sg)	imperfect	past participle
schmeißen	schmeißt, schmeißt	schmiss	geschmissen
schmelzen*	schmilzt, schmilzt	schmolz	geschmolzen
schneiden	schneidest, schneidet	schnitt	geschnitten
schreiben	schreibst, schreibt	schrieb	geschrieben
schreien	schreist, schreit	schrie	geschrie(e)n
schreiten	schreitest, schreitet	schritt	geschritten
schweigen	schweigst, schweigt	schwieg	geschwiegen
schwellen*	schwillst, schwillt	schwoll	geschwollen
schwimmen*	schwimmst, schwimmt	schwamm	geschwommen
schwinden*	schwindest, schwindet	schwand	geschwunden
schwingen	schwingst, schwingt	schwang	geschwungen
schwören	schwörst, schwört	schwor	geschworen
sehen	siehst, sieht	sah	gesehen
sein*	bist, ist	war	gewesen
senden	sendest, sendet	sandte	gesandt
singen	singst, singt	sang	gesungen
sinken*	sinkst, sinkt	sank	gesunken
sinnen	sinnst, sinnt	sann	gesonnen
sitzen*	sitzt, sitzt	saß	gesessen
sollen	sollst, soll	sollte	gesollt
speien	speist, speit	spie	gespie(e)n
spinnen	spinnst, spinnt	spann	gesponnen
sprechen	sprichst, spricht	sprach	gesprochen
sprießen*	sprießt, sprießt	spross	gesprossen
springen*	springst, springt	sprang	gesprungen
stechen	stichst, sticht	stach	gestochen
stecken	steckst, steckt	steckte or stak	gesteckt
stehen	stehst, steht	stand	gestanden
stehlen	stiehlst, stiehlt	stahl	gestohlen
steigen*	steigst, steigt	stieg	gestiegen
sterben*	stirbst, stirbt	starb	gestorben
stinken	stinkst, stinkt	stank	gestunken
stoßen	stößt, stößt	stieß	gestoßen
streichen	streichst, streicht	strich	gestrichen
streiten*	streitest, streitet	stritt	gestritten
tragen	trägst, trägt	trug	getragen
treffen	triffst, trifft	traf	getroffen
treiben*	treibst, treibt	trieb	getrieben

infinitive	present indicative (2nd, 3rd sg)	imperfect	past participle
treten*	trittst, tritt	trat	getreten
trinken	trinkst, trinkt	trank	getrunken
trügen	trügst, trügt	trog	getrogen
tun	tust, tut	tat	getan
verderben	verdirbst, verdirbt	verdarb	verdorben
verdrießen	verdrießt, verdrießt	verdross	verdrossen
vergessen	vergisst, vergisst	vergaß	vergessen
verlieren	verlierst, verliert	verlor	verloren
verschleißen	verschleißt, verschleißt	verschliss	verschlissen
wachsen*	wächst, wächst	wuchs	gewachsen
weben	webst, webt	webte or wob	gewoben
wägen	wägst, wägt	wog	gewogen
waschen	wäschst, wäscht	wusch	gewaschen
weichen*	weichst, weicht	wich	gewichen
weisen	weist, weist	wies	gewiesen
wenden	wendest, wendet	wandte	gewandt
werben	wirbst, wirbt	warb	geworben
werden*	wirst, wird	wurde	geworden
werfen	wirfst, wirft	warf	geworfen
wiegen	wiegst, wiegt	wog	gewogen
winden	windest, windet	wand	gewunden
wissen	weißt, weiß	wusste	gewusst
wollen	willst, will	wollte	gewollt
wringen	wringst, wringt	wrang	gewrungen
zeihen	zeihst, zeiht	zieh	geziehen
ziehen*	ziehst, zieht	zog	gezogen
zwingen	zwingst, zwingt	zwang	gezwungen

GERMAN SPELLING CHANGES

In July 1996, all German-speaking countries signed a declaration concerning the reform of German spelling, with the result that the new spelling rules are now taught in all schools. To ensure that you have the most up-to-date information at your fingertips, the following list contains the old and new spellings of all German headwords and translations in this dictionary which are affected by the reform.

ALT/OLD	NEU/NEW	ALT/OLD	NEU/NEW
abend	**Abend**	aufsein	**auf sein**
Abfluß	**Abfluss**	aufwendig	**aufwendig**
Abflußrohr	**Abflussrohr**		*or* **aufwändig**
Abschluß	**Abschluss**	auseinanderbrechen	**auseinander brechen**
Abschlußexamen	**Abschlussexamen**	auseinanderbringen	**auseinander bringen**
Abschlußfeier	**Abschlussfeier**	auseinanderfallen	**auseinander fallen**
Abschlußklasse	**Abschlussklasse**	auseinanderfalten	**auseinander falten**
Abschlußprüfung	**Abschlussprüfung**	auseinandergehen	**auseinander gehen**
Abschuß	**Abschuss**	auseinanderhalten	**auseinander halten**
Abschußrampe	**Abschussrampe**	auseinandernehmen	**auseinander nehmen**
Abszeß	**Abszess**	auseinandersetzen	**auseinander setzen**
achtgeben	**Acht geben**	Ausfluß	**Ausfluss**
Adreßbuch	**Adressbuch**	Ausguß	**Ausguss**
Alleinerziehende(r)	**Alleinerziehende(r)**	Auslaß	**Auslass**
	or **allein Erziehende(r)**	Ausschluß	**Ausschluss**
alleinstehend	**allein stehend**	Ausschuß	**Ausschuss**
allgemeingültig	**allgemein gültig**	Ausschuß(artikel)	**Ausschuss(artikel)**
allzuoft	**allzu oft**	aussein	**aus sein**
allzuviel	**allzu viel**	außerstande	**außer Stande**
Alptraum	**Alptraum**	Autobiographie	**Autobiographie**
	or **Albtraum**		*or* **Autobiografie**
Amboß	**Amboss**	Baß	**Bass**
Amtsanschluß	**Amtsanschluss**	Baßstimme	**Bassstimme**
(Amts)mißbrauch	**(Amts)missbrauch**		*or* **Bass-Stimme**
andersdenkend	**anders denkend**	Ballettänzer(in)	**Balletttänzer(in)**
aneinandergeraten	**aneinander geraten**		*or* **Ballett-Tänzer(in)**
aneinanderreihen	**aneinander reihen**	beeinflußbar	**beeinflussbar**
Anlaß	**Anlass**	beiseitelegen	**beiseite legen**
anläßlich	**anlässlich**	bekanntgeben	**bekannt geben**
Anschluß	**Anschluss**	bekanntmachen	**bekannt machen**
Anschlußflug	**Anschlussflug**	Beschluß	**Beschluss**
As	**Ass**	Beschuß	**Beschuss**
aufeinanderfolgen	**aufeinander folgen**	bessergehen	**besser gehen**
aufeinanderfolgend	**aufeinander folgend**	Bettuch	**Betttuch**
aufeinanderlegen	**aufeinander legen**		*or* **Bett-Tuch**
aufeinanderprallen	**aufeinander prallen**	(Bevölkerungs)überschuß	
Aufschluß	**Aufschluss**		**(Bevölkerungs)überschuss**
aufschlußreich	**aufschlussreich**	bewußt	**bewusst**
aufsehenerregend	**Aufsehen erregend**	bewußtlos	**bewusstlos**

ALT/OLD	NEU/NEW	ALT/OLD	NEU/NEW
Bewußtlosigkeit	**Bewusstlosigkeit**	durchnummerieren	**durchnummerieren**
Bewußtsein	**Bewusstsein**	ehrfurchtgebietend	**Ehrfurcht gebietend**
bezug	**Bezug**	Einfluß	**Einfluss**
Bibliographie	**Bibliographie**	Einflußbereich	**Einflussbereich**
	or **Bibliografie**	einflußreich	**einflussreich**
Biographie	**Biographie**	einigemal	**einige Mal**
	or **Biografie**	einiggehen	**einig gehen**
Biß	**Biss**	Einlaß	**Einlass**
biß	**biss**	ekelerregend	**Ekel erregend**
bißchen	**bisschen**	Elsaß	**Elsass**
blaß	**blass**	Engpaß	**Engpass**
bläßlich	**blässlich**	Entschluß	**Entschluss**
bleibenlassen	**bleiben lassen**	entschlußfreudig	**entschlussfreudig**
Bluterguß	**Bluterguss**	Entschlußkraft	**Entschlusskraft**
Boß	**Boss**	epochemachend	**Epoche machend**
braungebrannt	**braun gebrannt**	Erdgeschoß	**Erdgeschoss**
breitmachen	**breit machen**	Erdnuß	**Erdnuss**
Brennessel	**Brennnessel**	Erdnußbutter	**Erdnussbutter**
	or **Brenn-Nessel**	erfolgversprechend	**Erfolg versprechend**
Büroschluß	**Büroschluss**	Erguß	**Erguss**
Butterfaß	**Butterfass**	Erlaß	**Erlass**
Cashewnuß	**Cashewnuss**	ernstgemeint	**ernst gemeint**
Chicorée	**Chicorée**	erstemal	**erste Mal**
	or **Schikoree**	Eß–	**Ess–**
Choreograph(in)	**Choreograph(in)**	erstenmal	**ersten Mal**
	or **Choreograf(in)**	eßbar	**essbar**
Computertomographie	**Computertomographie**	Eßbesteck	**Essbesteck**
	or **Computertomografie**	Eßecke	**Essecke**
dabeisein	**dabei sein**	Eßgeschirr	**Essgeschirr**
dafürkönnen	**dafür können**	Eßkastanie	**Esskastanie**
dahinterkommen	**dahinter kommen**	Eßlöffel	**Esslöffel**
darauffolgend	**darauf folgend**	Eßlöffel(voll)	**Esslöffel (voll)**
dasein	**da sein**	(Eß)stäbchen	**(Ess)stäbchen**
daß	**dass**		*or* **(Ess–)Stäbchen**
Dekolleté	**Dekolleté**	Eßtisch	**Esstisch**
	or **Dekolletee**	Eßwaren	**Esswaren**
Delphin	**Delphin**	Eßzimmer	**Esszimmer**
	or **Delfin**	Expreß	**Express**
dessenungeachtet	**dessen ungeachtet**	Expreß–	**Express–**
dichtbevölkert	**dicht bevölkert**	Expreßgut	**Expressgut**
diensthabend	**Dienst habend**	Expreßzug	**Expresszug**
differential	**differential**	Exzeß	**Exzess**
	or **differenzial**	Facette	**Facette**
Differentialrechnung	**Differentialrechnung**		*or* **Fassette**
	or **Differenzialrechnung**	Fährenanschluß	**Fährenanschluss**
Diktaphon	**Diktaphon**	Fairneß	**Fairness**
	or **Diktafon**	fallenlassen	**fallen lassen**
dreiviertel	**drei Viertel**	Faß	**Fass**
durcheinanderbringen	**durcheinander bringen**	faßbar	**fassbar**
durcheinanderreden	**durcheinander reden**	Fehlschuß	**Fehlschuss**
durcheinanderwerfen	**durcheinander werfen**	fernhalten	**fern halten**

ALT/OLD	NEU/NEW	ALT/OLD	NEU/NEW
fertigbringen	fertig bringen	gewiß	gewiss
fertigmachen	fertig machen	Gewißheit	Gewissheit
fertigstellen	fertig stellen	gewußt	gewusst
fertigwerden	fertig werden	glattrasiert	glatt rasiert
festangestellt	fest angestellt	glattstreichen	glatt streichen
Fitneß	Fitness	gleichbleibend	gleich bleibend
fleischfressend	Fleisch fressend	gleichgesinnt	gleich gesinnt
floß	floss	Glimmstengel	Glimmstängel
Fluß	Fluss	Grammophon	Grammophon
Fluß–	Fluss–		or Grammofon
flußabwärts	flussabwärts	(Grammophon)nadel	(Grammophon)nadel
Flußbarsch	Flussbarsch		or (Grammofon)nadel
Flußbett	Flussbett	Graphiker(in)	Graphiker(in)
Flußdiagramm	Flussdiagramm		or Grafiker(in)
flüssigmachen	flüssig machen	graphisch	graphisch
Flußufer	Flussufer		or grafisch
Fön ®	Fön	gräßlich	grässlich
	or Föhn ®	Greuel	Gräuel
fönen	föhnen	Greueltat	Gräueltat
Fönfrisur	Föhnfrisur	greulich	gräulich
Friedensschluß	Friedensschluss	Grundriß	Grundriss
Frischvermählte	frisch Vermählte	Guß	Guss
Frischvermählten	frisch Vermählten	Gußeisen	Gusseisen
frißt	frisst	gutaussehend	gut aussehend
fritieren	frittieren	gutgehen	gut gehen
Gebiß	Gebiss	gutgehend	gut gehend
Gebührenerlaß	Gebührenerlass	gutgemeint	gut gemeint
gefangen(gehalten)	gefangen (gehalten)	guttun	gut tun
gefangenhalten	gefangen halten	haftenbleiben	haften bleiben
gefangennehmen	gefangen nehmen	halboffen	halb offen
gefaßt	gefasst	haltmachen	Halt machen
geheimhalten	geheim halten	Hämorrhoiden	Hämorrhoiden
gehenlassen	gehen lassen		or Hämorriden
Gemeinschaftsanschluß		Handvoll	Hand voll
	Gemeinschaftsanschluss	hängenbleiben	hängen bleiben
Gemse	Gämse	hängenlassen	hängen lassen
gemußt	gemusst	hartgekocht	hart gekocht
genaugenommen	genau genommen	Haselnuß	Haselnuss
Genuß	Genuss	Haß	Hass
genüßlich	genüsslich	häßlich	hässlich
Genußmittel	Genussmittel	Häßlichkeit	Hässlichkeit
Geograph	Geograph	haushalten	haushalten
	or Geograf		or Haus halten
Geographie	Geographie	heiligsprechen	heilig sprechen
	or Geografie	Hexenschuß	Hexenschuss
geographisch	geographisch	hierbehalten	hier behalten
	or geografisch	hierbleiben	hier bleiben
geringachten	gering achten	hierlassen	hier lassen
Geschäftsschluß	Geschäftsschluss	hierzulande	hierzulande
Geschoß	Geschoss		or hier zu Lande
gewinnbringend	Gewinn bringend	hochachten	hoch achten

ALT/OLD	NEU/NEW	ALT/OLD	NEU/NEW
hochbegabt	hoch begabt	kompromißlos	kompromisslos
hochdotiert	hoch dotiert	Kompromißlösung	Kompromisslösung
hochentwickelt	hoch entwickelt	Kongreß	Kongress
(hoch)geschätzt	(hoch) geschätzt	Kongreßzentrum	Kongresszentrum
(hoch)schätzen	(hoch) schätzen	Kontrabaß	Kontrabass
(Honorar)vorschuß	(Honorar)vorschuss	kraß	krass
Imbiß	Imbiss	Kreppapier	Krepppapier
Imbißhalle	Imbisshalle		or Krepp-Papier
Imbißraum	Imbissraum	kriegführend	Krieg führend
Imbißstube	Imbissstube	krummnehmen	krumm nehmen
	or Imbiss-Stube	Kurzbiographie	Kurzbiographie
immerwährend	immer während		or Kurzbiografie
imstande	imstande	kurzhalten	kurz halten
	or im Stande	Kurzschluß	Kurzschluss
ineinandergreifen	ineinander greifen	Kuß	Kuss
ineinanderschieben	ineinander schieben	Ladenschluß	Ladenschluss
Intercity-Expreßzug	Intercity-Expresszug	Laufpaß	Laufpass
ißt	isst	leerlaufen	leer laufen
Jahresabschluß	Jahresabschluss	leerstehend	leer stehend
jedesmal	jedes Mal	leichtfallen	leicht fallen
Joghurt	Joghurt	leichtmachen	leicht machen
	or Jogurt	Lenkradschloß	Lenkradschloss
kahlgeschoren	kahl geschoren	letztemal	letzte Mal
kaltbleiben	kalt bleiben	liebgewinnen	lieb gewinnen
Kammuschel	Kammmuschel	liebhaben	lieb haben
	or Kamm-Muschel	liegenbleiben	liegen bleiben
Känguruh	Känguru	liegenlassen	liegen lassen
Karamel	Karamell	Litfaßsäule	Litfasssäule
Karamelbonbon	Karamellbonbon		or Litfass-Säule
Katarrh	Katarrh	Lithographie	Lithographie
	or Katarr		or Lithografie
Kellergeschoß	Kellergeschoss	Luftschloß	Luftschloss
kennenlernen	kennen lernen	maschineschreiben	Maschine schreiben
keß	kess	maßhalten	Maß halten
klarsehen	klar sehen	Megaphon	Megaphon
klarwerden	klar werden		or Megafon
klassenbewußt	klassenbewusst	Meldeschluß	Meldeschluss
Klassenbewußtsein	Klassenbewusstsein	meßbar	messbar
klatschnaß	klatschnass	Meßbecher	Messbecher
kleinhacken	klein hacken	Meßgerät	Messgerät
kleinschneiden	klein schneiden	Mikrophon	Mikrophon
klitschnaß	klitschnass		or Mikrofon
knapphalten	knapp halten	Miß-	Miss-
Kokosnuß	Kokosnuss	mißachten	missachten
Koloß	Koloss	Mißachtung	Missachtung
Kombinationsschloß	Kombinationsschloss	Mißbehagen	Missbehagen
Kommuniqué	Kommuniqué	Mißbildung	Missbildung
	or Kommunikee	mißbilligen	missbilligen
Kompaß	Kompass	Mißbilligung	Missbilligung
Kompromiß	Kompromiss	Mißbrauch	Missbrauch
kompromißbereit	kompromissbereit	mißbrauchen	missbrauchen

ALT/OLD	NEU/NEW	ALT/OLD	NEU/NEW
Mißerfolg	Misserfolg	Nebenanschluß	Nebenanschluss
Mißfallen	Missfallen	nebeneinanderlegen	nebeneinander legen
mißfallen	missfallen	nebeneinanderstellen	nebeneinander stellen
Mißgeburt	Missgeburt	Nebenfluß	Nebenfluss
Mißgeschick	Missgeschick	Necessaire	Necessaire
mißgestaltet	missgestaltet		or Nessessär
mißglücken	missglücken	Negligé	Negligé
mißgönnen	missgönnen		or Negligee
Mißgriff	Missgriff	Netzanschluß	Netzanschluss
Mißgunst	Missgunst	neuentdeckt	neu entdeckt
mißgünstig	missgünstig	nichtsahnend	nichts ahnend
mißhandeln	misshandeln	nichtssagend	nichts sagend
Mißhandlung	Misshandlung	Nonstop–	Nonstop–
Mißklang	Missklang		or Non–Stop–
Mißkredit	Misskredit	notleidend	Not leidend
mißlich	misslich	numerieren	nummerieren
mißlingen	misslingen	Nuß	Nuss
mißlungen	misslungen	Nußbaum	Nussbaum
Mißmut	Missmut	Nußknacker	Nussknacker
mißmutig	missmutig	Nußschale	Nussschale
mißraten	missraten		or Nuss–Schale
Mißstand	Missstand	obenerwähnt	oben erwähnt
	or Miss–Stand	obengenannt	oben genannt
Mißtrauen	Misstrauen	Obergeschoß	Obergeschoss
mißtrauen	misstrauen	offenbleiben	offen bleiben
Mißtrauensantrag	Misstrauensantrag	offenhalten	offen halten
Mißtrauensvotum	Misstrauensvotum	offenlassen	offen lassen
mißtrauisch	misstrauisch	offenstehen	offen stehen
Mißverhältnis	Missverhältnis	Ölmeßstab	Ölmessstab
Mißverständnis	Missverständnis		or Ölmess–Stab
mißverstehen	missverstehen	Orthographie	Orthographie
Mißwirtschaft	Misswirtschaft		or Orthografie
mittag	Mittag	orthographisch	orthographisch
Mop	Mopp		or orthografisch
Muß	Muss	paarmal	paar Mal
mußte	musste	Panther	Panther
nachhinein	Nachhinein		or Panter
Nachlaß	Nachlass	Paragraph	Paragraph
nahegehen	nahe gehen		or Paragraf
nahekommen	nahe kommen	Paranuß	Paranuss
nahelegen	nahe legen	Parlamentsbeschluß	Parlamentsbeschluss
naheliegen	nahe liegen	Paß	Pass
naheliegend	nahe liegend	Paß–	Pass–
näherkommen	näher kommen	Paßamt	Passamt
näherrücken	näher rücken	Paßbild	Passbild
nahestehen	nahe stehen	Paßkontrolle	Passkontrolle
nahestehend	nahe stehend	Paßstelle	Passstelle
nahetreten	nahe treten		or Pass–Stelle
naß	nass	Paßstraße	Passstraße
naßkalt	nasskalt		or Pass–Straße
Naßrasur	Nassrasur	patschnaß	patschnass

ALT/OLD	NEU/NEW	ALT/OLD	NEU/NEW
pflichtbewußt	pflichtbewusst	rotglühend	rot glühend
Phantasie	Phantasie	Rückschluß	Rückschluss
	or Fantasie	Rußland	Russland
Phantasie–	Phantasie–	Safe(r) Sex	Safe(r) Sex
	or Fantasie–		or Safe(r)–sex
phantasielos	phantasielos	Salzfaß	Salzfass
	or fantasielos	sauberhalten	sauber halten
phantasiereich	phantasiereich	Saxophon	Saxophon
	or fantasiereich		or Saxofon
phantasieren	phantasieren	Schattenriß	Schattenriss
	or fantasieren	schiefgehen	schief gehen
phantasievoll	phantasievoll	Schiffahrt	Schifffahrt
	or fantasievoll		or Schiff–Fahrt
phantastisch	phantastisch	Schiffahrtslinie	Schifffahrtslinie
	or fantastisch	Schlangenbiß	Schlangenbiss
platschnaß	platschnass	schlechtgehen	schlecht gehen
plazieren	platzieren	schlechtmachen	schlecht machen
Pornographie	Pornographie	Schlegel	Schlägel
	or Pornografie	Schloß	Schloss
pornographisch	pornographisch	schloß	schloss
	or pornografisch	Schluß	Schluss
Portemonnaie	Portemonnaie	Schluß–	Schluss–
	or Portmonee	(Schluß)folgerung	(Schluss)folgerung
Potential	Potential	Schlußlicht	Schlusslicht
	or Potenzial	Schlußrunde	Schlussrunde
potentiell	potentiell	Schlußrundenteilnehmer	
	or potenziell		Schlussrundenteilnehmer
preisbewußt	preisbewusst	Schlußstrich	Schlussstrich
Preßluft	Pressluft		or Schluss–Strich
Preßluftbohrer	Pressluftbohrer	Schlußverkauf	Schlussverkauf
Preßlufthammer	Presslufthammer	Schmiß	Schmiss
Prozeß	Prozess	Schnappschloß	Schnappschloss
Prüfungsausschuß	Prüfungsausschuss	Schnappschuß	Schnappschuss
radfahren	Rad fahren	Schnellimbiß	Schnellimbiss
(Raketen)abschuß	(Raketen)abschuss	schneuzen	schnäuzen
Rassenhaß	Rassenhass	schoß	schoss
rauh	rau	Schößling	Schössling
Rauhreif	Raureif	Schrittempo	Schritttempo
Raumschiffahrt	Raumschifffahrt		or Schritt–Tempo
	or Raumschiff–Fahrt	Schuß	Schuss
Rausschmiß	Rausschmiss	Schußbereich	Schussbereich
Rechnungsabschluß	Rechnungsabschluss	Schußlinie	Schusslinie
reinwaschen	rein waschen	Schußverletzung	Schussverletzung
Reisepaß	Reisepass	Schußwaffe	Schusswaffe
Reißverschluß	Reißverschluss	Schußweite	Schussweite
richtigstellen	richtig stellen	schwererziehbar	schwer erziehbar
Riß	Riss	schwerfallen	schwer fallen
Rolladen	Rollladen	schwermachen	schwer machen
	or Roll–Laden	schwernehmen	schwer nehmen
Roß	Ross	schwertun	schwer tun
Roßkastanie	Rosskastanie	schwerverdaulich	schwer verdaulich

619

ALT/OLD	NEU/NEW	ALT/OLD	NEU/NEW
schwerverletzt	schwer verletzt		or telegrafieren
Seismograph	Seismograph	Thunfisch	Thunfisch
	or Seismograf		or Tunfisch
selbständig	selbständig	tiefausgeschnitten	tief ausgeschnitten
	or selbstständig	tiefgehend	tief gehend
Selbständigkeit	Selbständigkeit	tiefgekühlt	tief gekühlt
	or Selbstständigkeit	tiefgreifend	tief greifend
selbstbewußt	selbstbewusst	tiefschürfend	tief schürfend
Selbstbewußtsein	Selbstbewusstsein	Tip	Tipp
selbstgemacht	selbst gemacht	topographisch	topographisch
selbstverständlich	selbst verständlich		or topografisch
selbstverwaltet	selbst verwaltet	totenblaß	totenblass
seßhaft	sesshaft	totgeboren	tot geboren
Showbusineß	Showbusiness	Trugschluß	Trugschluss
Sicherheitsschloß	Sicherheitsschloss	tschüs	tschüs
sitzenbleiben	sitzen bleiben		or tschüss
sitzenlassen	sitzen lassen	übelgelaunt	übel gelaunt
Skipaß	Skipass	übelnehmen	übel nehmen
sogenannt	so genannt	übelriechend	übel riechend
Sommerschlußverkauf		übelwollend	übel wollend
	Sommerschlussverkauf	Überdruß	Überdruss
sonstjemand	sonst jemand	übereinanderlegen	übereinander legen
sonstwo	sonst wo	Überfluß	Überfluss
sonstwoher	sonst woher	Überschuß	Überschuss
sonstwohin	sonst wohin	überschwenglich	überschwänglich
Spannbettuch	Spannbetttuch	übrigbleiben	übrig bleiben
	or Spannbett–Tuch	übriggeblieben	übrig geblieben
spazierenfahren	spazieren fahren	übriglassen	übrig lassen
spazierengehen	spazieren gehen	Umriß	Umriss
Sprößling	Sprössling	unbewußt	unbewusst
steckenbleiben	stecken bleiben	Unbewußte	Unbewusste
steckenlassen	stecken lassen	unerläßlich	unerlässlich
stehenbleiben	stehen bleiben	unermeßlich	unermesslich
stehenlassen	stehen lassen	unfaßbar	unfassbar
Stengel	Stängel	ungewiß	ungewiss
Stenographie	Stenographie	Ungewißheit	Ungewissheit
	or Stenografie	unmißverständlich	unmissverständlich
stenographieren	stenographieren	unpäßlich	unpässlich
	or stenografieren	unselbständig	unselbständig
Stenograph(in)	Stenograph(in)		or unselbstständig
	or Stenograf(in)	unterbewußt	unterbewusst
stereophonisch	stereophonisch	Unterbewußte	Unterbewusste
	or stereofonisch	Unterbewußtsein	Unterbewusstsein
Stewardeß	Stewardess	Untergeschoß	Untergeschoss
Stilleben	Stillleben	Untersuchungsausschuß	
	or Still–Leben		Untersuchungsausschuss
stillegen	stilllegen	unvergeßlich	unvergesslich
Streifschuß	Streifschuss	Varieté	Varieté
strenggenommen	streng genommen		or Varietee
Streß	Stress	verantwortungsbewußt	
telegraphieren	telegraphieren		verantwortungsbewusst

ALT/OLD	NEU/NEW	ALT/OLD	NEU/NEW
Verdruß	Verdruss	wiedergutzumachen	wieder gutzumachen
vergeßlich	vergesslich	wiederherstellen	wieder herstellen
Vergeßlichkeit	Vergesslichkeit	wiedersehen	wieder sehen
Vergißmeinnicht	Vergissmeinnicht	wiedervereinigen	wieder vereinigen
vergißt	vergisst	wiederverwenden	wieder verwenden
verhaßt	verhasst	wiederverwerten	wieder verwerten
Verlaß	Verlass	wieviel	wie viel
verläßlich	verlässlich	Wißbegier(de)	Wissbegier(de)
verlorengehen	verloren gehen	wißbegierig	wissbegierig
vermißt	vermisst	wohltun	wohl tun
Verschluß	Verschluss	wußte	wusste
vertrauenerweckend	Vertrauen erweckend	Xylophon	Xylophon
vielsagend	viel sagend		or Xylofon
vielversprechend	viel versprechend	Zahlenschloß	Zahlenschloss
(voll)fressen	(voll) fressen	zeitlang	Zeit lang
vollgepfropft	voll gepfropft	zielbewußt	zielbewusst
vollpfropfen	voll pfropfen	Zuckerguß	Zuckerguss
vollstopfen	voll stopfen	zufriedengeben	zufrieden geben
volltanken	voll tanken	zufriedenstellen	zufrieden stellen
vorgefaßt	vorgefasst	zufriedenstellend	zufrieden stellend
Vorhängeschloß	Vorhängeschloss	zugrunde	zugrunde
vorhinein	Vorhinein		or zu Grunde
vorliebnehmen	vorlieb nehmen	zugunsten	zugunsten
Vorschuß	Vorschuss		or zu Gunsten
vorwärtsbewegen	vorwärts bewegen	zuleide	zuleide
vorwärtsdrängen	vorwärts drängen		or zu Leide
vorwärtsgehen	vorwärts gehen	zumute	zumute
vorwärtskommen	vorwärts kommen		or zu Mute
Waggon	Waggon	Zündschloß	Zündschloss
	or Wagon	Zungenkuß	Zungenkuss
Walnuß	Walnuss	zunutze	zunutze
Walroß	Walross		or zu Nutze
wasserabstoßend	Wasser abstoßend	Zusammenschluß	Zusammenschluss
wäßrig	wässrig	zuschulden	zuschulden
Weißrußland	Weißrussland		or zu Schulden
weitblickend	weitblickend	Zuschuß	Zuschuss
	or weit blickend	zustande	zustande
weitreichend	weitreichend		or zu Stande
	or weit reichend	zustande bringen	zustande bringen
weitverbreitet	weitverbreitet		or zu Stande bringen
	or weit verbreitet	zustande kommen	zustande kommen
wiederaufbauen	wieder aufbauen		or zu Stande kommen
wiederaufbereiten	wieder aufbereiten	zutage	zutage
wiederaufnehmen	wieder aufnehmen		or zu Tage
wiederbeleben	wieder beleben	zuviel	zu viel
wiedereinsetzen	wieder einsetzen	zuwege	zuwege
wiedererkennen	wieder erkennen		or zu Wege
wiedererwachen	wieder erwachen	zuwenig	zu wenig
wiedergutmachen	wieder gutmachen		